Bankruptcy and Article 9

2024 Statutory Supplement

Bankruptcy and Article 9

2024 Statutory Supplement

Elizabeth Warren
Leo Gottlieb Professor of Law Emeritus
Harvard Law School

Robert M. Lawless
Max L. Rowe Professor of Law
University of Illinois

To contact Customer Service, e-mail customer.service@aspenpublishing.com,
call 1-800-950-5259, or mail correspondence to:

Aspen Publishing
Attn: Order Department
1 Wall Street
Burlington, MA 01803

Printed in the United States of America.

1 2 3 4 5 6 7 8 9 0

ISBN 979-8-8920-7666-1

About Aspen Publishing

Aspen Publishing is a leading provider of educational content and digital learning solutions to law schools in the U.S. and around the world. Aspen provides best-in-class solutions for legal education through authoritative textbooks, written by renowned authors, and breakthrough products such as Connected eBooks, Connected Quizzing, and PracticePerfect.

The Aspen Casebook Series (famously known among law faculty and students as the "red and black" casebooks) encompasses hundreds of highly regarded textbooks in more than eighty disciplines, from large enrollment courses, such as Torts and Contracts, to emerging electives, such as Sustainability and the Law of Policing. Study aids such as the *Examples & Explanations* and the *Emanuel Law Outlines* series, both highly popular collections, help law students master complex subject matter.

Major products, programs, and initiatives include:

- **Connected eBooks** are enhanced digital textbooks and study aids that come with a suite of online content and learning tools designed to maximize student success. Designed in collaboration with hundreds of faculty and students, the Connected eBook is a significant leap forward in the legal education learning tools available to students.

- **Connected Quizzing** is an easy-to-use formative assessment tool that tests law students' understanding and provides timely feedback to improve learning outcomes. Delivered through CasebookConnect.com, the learning platform already used by students to access their Aspen casebooks, Connected Quizzing is simple to implement and integrates seamlessly with law school course curricula.

- **PracticePerfect** is a visually engaging, interactive study aid to explain commonly encountered legal doctrines through easy-to-understand animated videos, illustrative examples, and numerous practice questions. Developed by a team of experts, PracticePerfect is the ideal study companion for today's law students.

- The **Aspen Learning Library** enables law schools to provide their students with access to the most popular study aids on the market across all of their courses. Available through an annual subscription, the online library consists of study aids in e-book, audio, and video formats with full text search, note-taking, and highlighting capabilities.

- Aspen's **Digital Bookshelf** is an institutional-level online education bookshelf, consolidating everything students and professors need to ensure success. This program ensures that every student has access to affordable course materials from day one.

- **Leading Edge** is a community centered on thinking differently about legal education and putting those thoughts into actionable strategies. At the core of the program is the Leading Edge Conference, an annual gathering of legal education thought leaders looking to pool ideas and identify promising directions of exploration.

Summary of Contents

Contents *ix*
Preface *xxvii*

STATE LAWS:

UCC Article 1—General Provisions 1

UCC Article 2—Sales 25

UCC Article 8—Investment Securities 35

UCC Article 9—Secured Transactions 49

UCC Article 12—Controllable Electronic Records 329

UCC Article A—Transitional Provisions for Uniform Commercial Code Amendments (2022) 351

Uniform Fraudulent Transfer Act 361

Uniform Voidable Transactions Act 367

Uniform Motor Vehicle Certificate of Title and Anti-Theft Act 373

FEDERAL LAWS:

Title 11—Bankruptcy 381

Federal Rules of Bankruptcy Procedure 555

Title 18—Crimes and Criminal Procedure 571

Title 28—Judiciary and Judicial Procedure 575

Fair Debt Collection Practices Act 587

Title 26—Federal Tax Lien Act 597

Contents

Preface *xxvii*

STATE LAWS:

UCC ARTICLE 1—GENERAL PROVISIONS **1**

Part 1. General Provisions **1**

§ 1-101. Short Titles 1
§ 1-102. Scope of Article 1
§ 1-103. Construction of [Uniform Commercial Code] to Promote Its Purposes and Policies; Applicability of Supplemental Principles of Law 1
§ 1-104. Construction Against Implied Repeal 3
§ 1-105. Severability 3
§ 1-106. Use of Singular and Plural; Gender 4
§ 1-107. Section Captions 4
§ 1-108. Relation to Electronic Signatures in Global and National Commerce Act 4

Part 2. General Definitions and Principles of Interpretation **4**

§ 1-201. General Definitions 4
§ 1-202. Notice; Knowledge 13
§ 1-203. Lease Distinguished from Security Interest 14
§ 1-204. Value 16
§ 1-205. Reasonable Time; Seasonableness 17
§ 1-206. Presumptions 17

Part 3. Territorial Applicability and General Rules **18**

§ 1-301. Territorial Applicability; Parties' Power to Choose Applicable Law 18
§ 1-302. Variation by Agreement 19
§ 1-303. Course of Performance, Course of Dealing, and Usage of Trade 20
§ 1-304. Obligation of Good Faith 21
§ 1-305. Remedies to Be Liberally Administered 22
§ 1-306. Waiver or Renunciation of Claim or Right After Breach 22
§ 1-307. Prima Facie Evidence by Third-Party Documents 22
§ 1-308. Performance or Acceptance Under Reservation of Rights 23
§ 1-309. Option to Accelerate at Will 23
§ 1-310. Subordinated Obligations 23

UCC ARTICLE 2—SALES **25**

Part 1. Short Title, General Construction, and Subject Matter **25**

§ 2-102. Scope; Certain Security and Other Transactions Excluded from This Article 25
§ 2-103. Definitions and Index of Definitions 27
§ 2-104. Definitions: "Merchant"; "Between Merchants"; "Financing Agency" 28

Part 4. Title, Creditors, and Good Faith Purchasers 29

§ 2-403. Power to Transfer; Good Faith Purchase of Goods; "Entrusting" 29

Part 5. Performance 30

§ 2-501. Insurable Interest in Goods; Manner of Identification of Goods 30
§ 2-502. Buyer's Right to Goods on Seller's Repudiation, Failure to Deliver, or Insolvency 32

Part 7. Remedies 32

§ 2-702. Seller's Remedies on Discovery of Buyer's Insolvency 32
§ 2-716. Buyer's Right to Specific Performance or Replevin 33

UCC ARTICLE 8—INVESTMENT SECURITIES 35

Part 1. Short Title and General Matters 35

§ 8-102. Definitions 35
§ 8-106. Control 42

Part 3. Transfer of Certificated and Uncertificated Securities 46

§ 8-301. Delivery 46

UCC ARTICLE 9—SECURED TRANSACTIONS 49

Part 1. General Provisions 62

[SUBPART 1. SHORT TITLE, DEFINITIONS, AND GENERAL CONCEPTS] 62

§ 9-101. Short Title 62
§ 9-102. Definitions and Index of Definitions 71
§ 9-103. Purchase-Money Security Interest; Application of Payments; Burden of Establishing 94
§ 9-104. Control of Deposit Account 97
§ 9-105. Control of Electronic Copy of Record Evidencing Chattel Paper 98
§ 9-105A. Control of Electronic Money 101
§ 9-106. Control of Investment Property 102
§ 9-107. Control of Letter-of-Credit Right 102
§ 9-107A. Control of Controllable Electronic Record, Controllable Account, or Controllable Payment Intangible 103
§ 9-107B. No Requirement to Acknowledge or Confirm; No Duties 104
§ 9-108. Sufficiency of Description 104

[SUBPART 2. APPLICABILITY OF ARTICLE] 106

§ 9-109. Scope 106
§ 9-110. Security Interests Arising Under Article 2 or 2A 111

Part 2. Effectiveness of Security Agreement; Attachment of Security Interest; Rights of Parties to Security Agreement **112**

[SUBPART 1. EFFECTIVENESS AND ATTACHMENT] 112

§ 9-201. General Effectiveness of Security Agreement 112
§ 9-202. Title to Collateral Immaterial 112
§ 9-203. Attachment and Enforceability of Security Interest; Proceeds; Supporting Obligations; Formal Requisites 113
§ 9-204. After-Acquired Property; Future Advances 116
§ 9-205. Use or Disposition of Collateral Permissible 117
§ 9-206. Security Interest Arising in Purchase or Delivery of Financial Asset 118

[SUBPART 2. RIGHTS AND DUTIES] 119

§ 9-207. Rights and Duties of Secured Party Having Possession or Control of Collateral 119
§ 9-208. Additional Duties of Secured Party Having Control of Collateral 122
§ 9-209. Duties of Secured Party If Account Debtor Has Been Notified of Assignment 123
§ 9-210. Request for Accounting; Request Regarding List of Collateral or Statement of Account 124

Part 3. Perfection and Priority **125**

[SUBPART 1. LAW GOVERNING PERFECTION AND PRIORITY] 125

§ 9-301. Law Governing Perfection and Priority of Security Interests 125
§ 9-302. Law Governing Perfection and Priority of Agricultural Liens 128
§ 9-303. Law Governing Perfection and Priority of Security Interests in Goods Covered by a Certificate of Title 129
§ 9-304. Law Governing Perfection and Priority of Security Interests in Deposit Accounts 130
§ 9-305. Law Governing Perfection and Priority of Security Interests in Investment Property 131
§ 9-306. Law Governing Perfection and Priority of Security Interests in Letter-of-Credit Rights 134
§ 9-306A. Law Governing Perfection and Priority of Security Interests in Chattel Paper 135
§ 9-306B. Law Governing Perfection and Priority of Security Interests in Controllable Accounts, Controllable Electronic Records, and Controllable Payment Intangibles 136
§ 9-307. Location of Debtor 137

[SUBPART 2. PERFECTION] 140

§ 9-308. When Security Interest or Agricultural Lien Is Perfected; Continuity of Perfection 140
§ 9-309. Security Interest Perfected upon Attachment 142
§ 9-310. When Filing Required to Perfect Security Interest or Agricultural Lien; Security Interests and Agricultural Liens to Which Filing Provisions Do Not Apply 144
§ 9-311. Perfection of Security Interests in Property Subject to Certain Statutes, Regulations, and Treaties 145
§ 9-312. Perfection of Security Interests in Chattel Paper, Controllable Accounts, Controllable Electronic Records, Controllable Payment Intangibles, Deposit Accounts, Documents, Goods Covered by Documents, Instruments, Investment Property, Letter-of-Credit Rights, and Money; Perfection by Permissive Filing; Temporary Perfection Without Filing or Transfer of Possession 148
§ 9-313. When Possession by or Delivery to Secured Party Perfects Security Interest Without Filing 151
§ 9-314. Perfection by Control 154
§ 9-314A. Perfection by Possession and Control of Chattel Paper 156

§ 9-315. Secured Party's Rights on Disposition of Collateral and in Proceeds 157
§ 9-316. Continued Perfection of Security Interest Following Change in Governing Law 160

[SUBPART 3. PRIORITY] 165

§ 9-317. Interests That Take Priority Over or Take Free of Security Interest or Agricultural Lien 165
§ 9-318. No Interest Retained in Right to Payment That Is Sold; Rights and Title of Seller of Account or Chattel Paper with Respect to Creditors and Purchasers 168
§ 9-319. Rights and Title of Consignee with Respect to Creditors and Purchasers 169
§ 9-320. Buyer of Goods 170
§ 9-321. Licensee of General Intangible and Lessee of Goods in Ordinary Course of Business 172
§ 9-322. Priorities among Conflicting Security Interests in and Agricultural Liens on Same Collateral 173
§ 9-323. Future Advances 178
§ 9-324. Priority of Purchase-Money Security Interests 180
§ 9-325. Priority of Security Interests in Transferred Collateral 185
§ 9-326. Priority of Security Interests Created by New Debtor 186
§ 9-326A. Priority of Security Interest in Controllable Account, Controllable Electronic Record, and Controllable Payment Intangible 188
§ 9-327. Priority of Security Interests in Deposit Account 189
§ 9-328. Priority of Security Interests in Investment Property 190
§ 9-329. Priority of Security Interests in Letter-of-Credit Right 194
§ 9-330. Priority of Purchaser of Chattel Paper or Instrument 196
§ 9-331. Priority of Rights of Purchasers of Controllable Accounts, Controllable Electronic Records, Controllable Payment Intangibles, Documents, Instruments, and Securities under Other Articles; Priority of Interests in Financial Assets and Security Entitlements and Protection Against Assertion of Claim Under Articles 8 and 12 201
§ 9-332. Transfer of Money; Transfer of Funds from Deposit Account 202
§ 9-333. Priority of Certain Liens Arising by Operation of Law 205
§ 9-334. Priority of Security Interests in Fixtures and Crops 205
§ 9-335. Accessions 209
§ 9-336. Commingled Goods 210
§ 9-337. Priority of Security Interests in Goods Covered by Certificate of Title 212
§ 9-338. Priority of Security Interest or Agricultural Lien Perfected by Filed Financing Statement Providing Certain Incorrect Information 212
§ 9-339. Priority Subject to Subordination 213

[SUBPART 4. RIGHTS OF BANK] 213

§ 9-340. Effectiveness of Right of Recoupment or Set-Off Against Deposit Account 213
§ 9-341. Bank's Rights and Duties with Respect to Deposit Account 214
§ 9-342. Bank's Right to Refuse to Enter into or Disclose Existence of Control Agreement 214

Part 4. Rights of Third Parties **215**

§ 9-401. Alienability of Debtor's Rights 215
§ 9-402. Secured Party Not Obligated on Contract of Debtor or in Tort 216
§ 9-403. Agreement Not to Assert Defenses Against Assignee 216
§ 9-404. Rights Acquired by Assignee; Claims and Defenses Against Assignee 218
§ 9-405. Modification of Assigned Contract 219

§ 9-406. Discharge of Account Debtor; Notification of Assignment; Identification and Proof of Assignment; Restrictions on Assignment of Accounts, Chattel Paper, Payment Intangibles, and Promissory Notes Ineffective 220
§ 9-407. Restrictions on Creation or Enforcement of Security Interest in Leasehold Interest or in Lessor's Residual Interest 224
§ 9-408. Restrictions on Assignment of Promissory Notes, Health-Care-Insurance Receivables, and Certain General Intangibles Ineffective 225
§ 9-409. Restrictions on Assignment of Letter-of-Credit Rights Ineffective 229

Part 5. Filing **230**

[SUBPART 1. FILING OFFICE; CONTENTS AND EFFECTIVENESS OF FINANCING STATEMENT] 230

§ 9-501. Filing Office 230
§ 9-502. Contents of Financing Statement; Record of Mortgage as Financing Statement; Time of Filing Financing Statement 231
§ 9-503. Name of Debtor and Secured Party 233
§ 9-504. Indication of Collateral 238
§ 9-505. Filing and Compliance with Other Statutes and Treaties for Consignments, Leases, Other Bailments, and Other Transactions 239
§ 9-506. Effect of Errors or Omissions 240
§ 9-507. Effect of Certain Events on Effectiveness of Financing Statement 241
§ 9-508. Effectiveness of Financing Statement If New Debtor Becomes Bound by Security Agreement 242
§ 9-509. Persons Entitled to File a Record 244
§ 9-510. Effectiveness of Filed Record 246
§ 9-511. Secured Party of Record 246
§ 9-512. Amendment of Financing Statement 247
§ 9-513. Termination Statement 249
§ 9-514. Assignment of Powers of Secured Party of Record 251
§ 9-515. Duration and Effectiveness of Financing Statement; Effect of Lapsed Financing Statement 251
§ 9-516. What Constitutes Filing; Effectiveness of Filing 253
§ 9-517. Effect of Indexing Errors 255
§ 9-518. Claim Concerning Inaccurate or Wrongfully Filed Record 255

[SUBPART 2. DUTIES AND OPERATION OF FILING OFFICE] 257

§ 9-519. Numbering, Maintaining, and Indexing Records; Communicating Information Provided in Records 257
§ 9-520. Acceptance and Refusal to Accept Record 259
§ 9-521. Uniform Form of Written Financing Statement and Amendment 260
§ 9-522. Maintenance and Destruction of Records 265
§ 9-523. Information from Filing Office; Sale or License of Records 266
§ 9-524. Delay by Filing Office 268
§ 9-525. Fees 268
§ 9-526. Filing-Office Rules 269
§ 9-527. Duty to Report 270

Part 6. Default **270**

[SUBPART 1. DEFAULT AND ENFORCEMENT OF SECURITY INTEREST] 270

§ 9-601. Rights after Default; Judicial Enforcement; Consignor or Buyer of Accounts, Chattel Paper, Payment Intangibles, or Promissory Notes 270
§ 9-602. Waiver and Variance of Rights and Duties 272
§ 9-603. Agreement on Standards Concerning Rights and Duties 273
§ 9-604. Procedure If Security Agreement Covers Real Property or Fixtures 273
§ 9-605. Unknown Debtor or Secondary Obligor 274
§ 9-606. Time of Default for Agricultural Lien 276
§ 9-607. Collection and Enforcement by Secured Party 276
§ 9-608. Application of Proceeds of Collection or Enforcement; Liability for Deficiency and Rights to Surplus 278
§ 9-609. Secured Party's Right to Take Possession After Default 280
§ 9-610. Disposition of Collateral After Default 281
§ 9-611. Notification Before Disposition of Collateral 285
§ 9-612. Timeliness of Notification Before Disposition of Collateral 287
§ 9-613. Contents and Form of Notification Before Disposition of Collateral: General 287
§ 9-614. Contents and Form of Notification Before Disposition of Collateral: Consumer-Goods Transaction 289
§ 9-615. Application of Proceeds of Disposition; Liability for Deficiency and Rights to Surplus 291
§ 9-616. Explanation of Calculation of Surplus or Deficiency 294
§ 9-617. Rights of Transferee of Collateral 296
§ 9-618. Rights and Duties of Certain Secondary Obligors 296
§ 9-619. Transfer of Record or Legal Title 298
§ 9-620. Acceptance of Collateral in Full or Partial Satisfaction of Obligation; Compulsory Disposition of Collateral 298
§ 9-621. Notification of Proposal to Accept Collateral 302
§ 9-622. Effect of Acceptance of Collateral 302
§ 9-623. Right to Redeem Collateral 303
§ 9-624. Waiver 304

[SUBPART 2. NONCOMPLIANCE WITH ARTICLE] 304

§ 9-625. Remedies for Secured Party's Failure to Comply with Article 304
§ 9-626. Action in Which Deficiency or Surplus Is in Issue 306
§ 9-627. Determination of Whether Conduct Was Commercially Reasonable 308
§ 9-628. Nonliability and Limitation on Liability of Secured Party; Liability of Secondary Obligor 309

Part 7. Transition **310**

§ 9-701. Effective Date 310
§ 9-702. Savings Clause 310
§ 9-703. Security Interest Perfected Before Effective Date 311
§ 9-704. Security Interest Unperfected Before Effective Date 312
§ 9-705. Effectiveness of Action Taken Before Effective Date 313
§ 9-706. When Initial Financing Statement Suffices to Continue Effectiveness of Financing Statement 315
§ 9-707. Amendment of Pre-Effective-Date Financing Statement 317

§ 9-708. Persons Entitled to File Initial Financing Statement or Continuation Statement 319
§ 9-709. Priority 319

Part 8. Transition Provisions for 2010 Amendments **321**

§ 9-801. Effective Date 321
§ 9-802. Savings Clause 321
§ 9-803. Security Interest Perfected Before Effective Date 322
§ 9-804. Security Interest Unperfected Before Effective Date 322
§ 9-805. Effectiveness of Action Taken Before Effective Date 322
§ 9-806. When Initial Financing Statement Suffices to Continue Effectiveness of Financing Statement 323
§ 9-807. Amendment of Pre-Effective-Date Financing Statement 323
§ 9-808. Person Entitled to File Initial Financing Statement or Continuation Statement 324
§ 9-809. Priority 324

Appendix **324**

Appendix I—Conforming Amendments to Other Articles [Omitted.] 324

Appendix II—Model Provisions for Production-Money Priority 324

UCC ARTICLE 12—CONTROLLABLE ELECTRONIC RECORDS **329**

PREFATORY NOTE TO ARTICLE 12 **329**

§ 12-101. Title 332
§ 12-102. Definitions 333
§ 12-103. Relation to Article 9 and Consumer Laws 334
§ 12-104. Rights in Controllable Account, Controllable Electronic Record, and Controllable Payment Intangible 334
§ 12-105. Control of Controllable Electronic Record 338
§ 12-106. Discharge of Account Debtor on Controllable Account or Controllable Payment Intangible 344
§ 12-107. Governing Law 346

UCC ARTICLE A—TRANSITIONAL PROVISIONS FOR UNIFORM COMMERCIAL CODE AMENDMENTS (2022) **351**

Part 1—General Provisions and Definitions **352**

§ A-101. Short Title 352
§ A-102. Definitions 352

Part 2—General Transitional Provision **352**

§ A-201. Saving Clause 352

Part 3—Transitional Provisions for Articles 9 and 12 **353**

§ A-301. Saving Clause 353
§ A-302. Security Interest Perfected Before Effective Date 353

§ A-303. Security Interest Unperfected Before Effective Date 355
§ A-304. Effectiveness of Actions Taken Before Effective Date 356
§ A-305. Priority 357
§ A-306. Priority of Claims When Priority Rules of Article 9 Do Not Apply 358

Part 4—Effective Date **360**

§ A-401. Effective Date 360

UNIFORM FRAUDULENT TRANSFER ACT **361**

§ 1. Definitions 361
§ 2. Insolvency 362
§ 3. Value 362
§ 4. Transfers Fraudulent as to Present and Future Creditors 362
§ 5. Transfers Fraudulent as to Present Creditors 363
§ 6. When Transfer Is Made or Obligation Is Incurred 363
§ 7. Remedies of Creditors 363
§ 8. Defenses, Liability, and Protection of Transferee 364
§ 9. Extinguishment of [Claim for Relief] [Cause of Action] 364
§ 10. Supplementary Provisions 364
§ 11. Uniformity of Application and Construction 365
§ 12. Short Title 365
§ 13. Repeal 365

UNIFORM VOIDABLE TRANSACTIONS ACT **367**

§ 1. Definitions 367
§ 2. Insolvency 368
§ 3. Value 368
§ 4. Transfer or Obligation Voidable as to Present or Future Creditor 369
§ 5. Transfer or Obligation Voidable as to Present Creditor 369
§ 6. When Transfer Is Made or Obligation Is Incurred 369
§ 7. Remedies of Creditor 370
§ 8. Defenses, Liability, and Protection of Transferee or Obligee 370
§ 9. Extinguishment of Claim for Relief 371
§ 10. Governing Law 371
§ 11. Application to Series Organization 371
§ 12. Supplementary Provisions 372
§ 13. Uniformity of Application and Construction 372
§ 14. Relation to Electronic Signature in Global and National Commerce Act 372
§ 15. Short Title 372
§ 16. Repeals; Conforming Amendments 372

UNIFORM MOTOR VEHICLE CERTIFICATE OF TITLE AND ANTI-THEFT ACT **373**

Part 1. Definitions and Exclusions **373**

§ 1. Definitions 373
§ 2. Exclusions 374
§ 3. Excepted Liens and Security Interests; Buyer from Manufacturer or Dealer 374

Part 2. Certificates of Title 374

§ 4. Certificate of Title Required 374
§ 5. Optional Certificates of Title 374
§ 6. Application for First Certificate of Title 374
§ 7. Examination of Records 375
§ 8. Issuance and Records 375
§ 9. Contents and Effect 375
§ 10. Delivery 376
§ 11. Registration Without Certificate of Title; Bond 376
§ 12. Refusing Certificate of Title 376
§ 13. Lost, Stolen, or Mutilated Certificates 376
§ 14. Transfer 376
§ 15. Transfer to or from Dealer; Records 377
§ 16. Transfer by Operation of Law 377
§ 17. Fees; Registration Cards; License Plates 377
§ 18. When Department to Issue New Certificate 378
§ 19. Scrapping, Dismantling, or Destroying Vehicle 378
§ 20. Perfection of Security Interests 378
§ 21. Security Interest 379
§ 22. Assignment by Lienholder 379
§ 23. Release of Security Interest 379
§ 24. Duty of Lienholder 379
§ 25. Exclusiveness of Procedure 379
§ 26. Suspension or Revocation of Certificates 380
§ 27. Fees 380
§ 28. Powers of Department 380
§ 29. Hearings 380
§ 30. Court Review 380

FEDERAL LAWS:

TITLE 11—BANKRUPTCY 381

Chapter 1. General Provisions 381

§ 101. Definitions 381
§ 102. Rules of Construction 394
§ 103. Applicability of Chapters 394
§ 104. Adjustment of Dollar Amounts 395
§ 105. Power of Court 395
§ 106. Waiver of Sovereign Immunity 395
§ 107. Public Access to Papers 396
§ 108. Extension of Time 396
§ 109. Who May Be a Debtor 397
§ 110. Penalty for Persons Who Negligently or Fraudulently Prepare Bankruptcy Petitions 399
§ 111. Nonprofit Budget and Credit Counseling Agencies; Financial Management Instructional Courses 401
§ 112. Prohibition on Disclosure of Name of Minor Children 403

Chapter 3. Case Administration **403**

SUBCHAPTER I—COMMENCEMENT OF A CASE 403

§ 301. Voluntary Cases 404
§ 302. Joint Cases 404
§ 303. Involuntary Cases 404
§ 305. Abstention 405
§ 306. Limited Appearance 405
§ 307. United States Trustee 406
§ 308. Debtor Reporting Requirements 406

SUBCHAPTER II—OFFICERS 406

§ 321. Eligibility to Serve as Trustee 406
§ 322. Qualification of Trustee 406
§ 323. Role and Capacity of Trustee 407
§ 324. Removal of Trustee or Examiner 407
§ 325. Effect of Vacancy 407
§ 326. Limitation on Compensation of Trustee 407
§ 327. Employment of Professional Persons 407
§ 328. Limitation on Compensation of Professional Persons 408
§ 329. Debtor's Transactions with Attorneys 408
§ 330. Compensation of Officers 408
§ 331. Interim Compensation 410
§ 332. Consumer Privacy Ombudsman 410
§ 333. Appointment of Patient Care Ombudsman 410

SUBCHAPTER III—ADMINISTRATION 411

§ 341. Meetings of Creditors and Equity Security Holders 411
§ 342. Notice 411
§ 343. Examination of the Debtor 412
§ 344. Self-Incrimination; Immunity 413
§ 345. Money of Estates 413
§ 346. Special Provisions Related to the Treatment of State and Local Taxes 413
§ 347. Unclaimed Property 414
§ 348. Effect of Conversion 414
§ 349. Effect of Dismissal 415
§ 350. Closing and Reopening Cases 416
§ 351. Disposal of Patient Records 416

SUBCHAPTER IV—ADMINISTRATIVE POWERS 416

§ 361. Adequate Protection 416
§ 362. Automatic Stay 416
§ 363. Use, Sale, or Lease of Property 426
§ 364. Obtaining Credit 428
§ 365. Executory Contracts and Unexpired Leases 429
§ 366. Utility Service 434

Chapter 5. Creditors, the Debtor, and the Estate **435**

SUBCHAPTER I—CREDITORS AND CLAIMS 435

§ 501. Filing of Proofs of Claims or Interests 435
§ 502. Allowance of Claims or Interests 435
§ 503. Allowance of Administrative Expenses 437
§ 504. Sharing of Compensation 439
§ 505. Determination of Tax Liability 439
§ 506. Determination of Secured Status 440
§ 507. Priorities 441
§ 508. Effect of Distribution Other Than Under This Title 443
§ 509. Claims of Codebtors 443
§ 510. Subordination 443
§ 511. Rate of Interest on Tax Claims 444

SUBCHAPTER II—DEBTOR'S DUTIES AND BENEFITS 444

§ 521. Debtor's Duties 444
§ 522. Exemptions 447
§ 523. Exceptions to Discharge 453
§ 524. Effect of Discharge 456
§ 525. Protection Against Discriminatory Treatment 465
§ 526. Restrictions on Debt Relief Agencies 466
§ 527. Disclosures 467
§ 528. Requirements for Debt Relief Agencies 469

SUBCHAPTER III—THE ESTATE 469

§ 541. Property of the Estate 470
§ 542. Turnover of Property to the Estate 472
§ 543. Turnover of Property by a Custodian 473
§ 544. Trustee as Lien Creditor and as Successor to Certain Creditors and Purchasers 473
§ 545. Statutory Liens 474
§ 546. Limitations on Avoiding Powers 474
§ 547. Preferences 476
§ 548. Fraudulent Transfers and Obligations 478
§ 549. Postpetition Transactions 479
§ 550. Liability of Transferee of Avoided Transfer 480
§ 551. Automatic Preservation of Avoided Transfer 481
§ 552. Postpetition Effect of Security Interest 481
§ 553. Setoff 481
§ 554. Abandonment of Property of the Estate 482
§ 555. Contractual Right to Liquidate, Terminate, or Accelerate a Securities Contract 482
§ 556. Contractual Right to Liquidate, Terminate, or Accelerate a Commodities Contract or Forward Contract 482
§ 557. Expedited Determination of Interests in, and Abandonment or Other Disposition of Grain Assets 482
§ 558. Defenses of the Estate 484
§ 559. Contractual Right to Liquidate, Terminate, or Accelerate a Repurchase Agreement 484
§ 560. Contractual Right to Liquidate, Terminate, or Accelerate a Swap Agreement 484

§ 561. Contractual Right to Terminate, Liquidate, Accelerate, or Offset Under a Master Netting Agreement and Across Contracts; Proceedings Under Chapter 15 485
§ 562. Timing of Damage Measurement in Connection with Swap Agreements, Securities Contracts, Forward Contracts, Commodity Contracts, Repurchase Agreements, and Master Netting Agreements 486

Chapter 7. Liquidation **486**

SUBCHAPTER I—OFFICERS AND ADMINISTRATION 486

§ 701. Interim Trustee 486
§ 702. Election of Trustee 486
§ 703. Successor Trustee 487
§ 704. Duties of Trustee 487
§ 705. Creditors' Committee 489
§ 706. Conversion 489
§ 707. Dismissal of a Case or Conversion to a Case under Chapter 11 or 13 489

SUBCHAPTER II—COLLECTION, LIQUIDATION, AND DISTRIBUTION OF THE ESTATE 493

§ 721. Authorization to Operate Business 493
§ 722. Redemption 493
§ 723. Rights of Partnership Trustee Against General Partners 494
§ 724. Treatment of Certain Liens 494
§ 725. Disposition of Certain Property 495
§ 726. Distribution of Property of the Estate 495
§ 727. Discharge 496

Chapter 9. Adjustment of Debts of a Municipality **498**

SUBCHAPTER I—GENERAL PROVISIONS 498

§ 901. Applicability of Other Sections of This Title 498
§ 902. Definitions for This Chapter 498
§ 903. Reservation of State Power to Control Municipalities 498
§ 904. Limitation on Jurisdiction and Powers of Court 499

SUBCHAPTER II—ADMINISTRATION 499

§ 921. Petition and Proceedings Relating to Petition 499
§ 922. Automatic Stay of Enforcement of Claims Against the Debtor 499
§ 923. Notice 500
§ 924. List of Creditors 500
§ 925. Effect of List of Claims 500
§ 926. Avoiding Powers 500
§ 927. Limitation on Recourse 500
§ 928. Post petition Effect of Security Interest 500
§ 929. Municipal Leases 500
§ 930. Dismissal 500

SUBCHAPTER III—THE PLAN 500

§ 941. Filing of Plan 500
§ 942. Modification of Plan 501
§ 943. Confirmation 501
§ 944. Effect of Confirmation 501
§ 945. Continuing Jurisdiction and Closing of the Case 501
§ 946. Effect of Exchange of Securities Before the Date of the Filing of the Petition. 501

Chapter 11. Reorganization **501**

SUBCHAPTER I—OFFICERS AND ADMINISTRATION 501

§ 1101. Definitions for This Chapter 502
§ 1102. Creditors' and Equity Security Holders' Committees 502
§ 1103. Powers and Duties of Committees 502
§ 1104. Appointment of Trustee or Examiner 503
§ 1105. Termination of Trustee's Appointment 504
§ 1106. Duties of Trustee and Examiner 504
§ 1107. Rights, Powers, and Duties of Debtor in Possession 505
§ 1108. Authorization to Operate Business 505
§ 1109. Right to Be Heard 505
§ 1110. Aircraft Equipment and Vessels 505
§ 1111. Claims and Interests 506
§ 1112. Conversion or Dismissal 507
§ 1113. Rejection of Collective Bargaining Agreements 508
§ 1114. Payment of Insurance Benefits to Retired Employees 509
§ 1115. Property of the Estate 511
§ 1116. Duties of Trustee or Debtor in Possession in Small Business Cases 512

SUBCHAPTER II—THE PLAN 512

§ 1121. Who May File a Plan 512
§ 1122. Classification of Claims or Interests 513
§ 1123. Contents of Plan 513
§ 1124. Impairment of Claims or Interests 514
§ 1125. Postpetition Disclosure and Solicitation 514
§ 1126. Acceptance of Plan 515
§ 1127. Modification of Plan 516
§ 1128. Confirmation Hearing 517
§ 1129. Confirmation of Plan 517

SUBCHAPTER III—POSTCONFIRMATION MATTERS 519

§ 1141. Effect of Confirmation 519
§ 1142. Implementation of Plan 520
§ 1143. Distribution 521
§ 1144. Revocation of an Order of Confirmation 521
§ 1145. Exemption from Securities Laws 521
§ 1146. Special Tax Provisions 522

SUBCHAPTER IV—RAILROAD REORGANIZATION 522

§ 1161. Inapplicability of Other Sections 522
§ 1162. Definition 522
§ 1163. Appointment of Trustee 522
§ 1164. Right to Be Heard 522
§ 1165. Protection of the Public Interest 523
§ 1166. Effect of Subtitle IV of Title 49 and of Federal, State, or Local Regulations 523
§ 1167. Collective Bargaining Agreements 523
§ 1168. Rolling Stock Equipment 523
§ 1169. Effect of Rejection of Lease of Railroad Line 524
§ 1170. Abandonment of Railroad Line 524
§ 1171. Priority Claims 525
§ 1172. Contents of Plan 525
§ 1173. Confirmation of Plan 525
§ 1174. Liquidation 525

SUBCHAPTER V—SMALL BUSINESS DEBTOR REORGANIZATION 526

§ 1181. Inapplicability of Other Sections 526
§ 1182. Definitions 526
§ 1183. Trustee 526
§ 1184. Rights and Powers of a Debtor in Possession 527
§ 1185. Removal of Debtor in Possession 527
§ 1186. Property of the Estate 527
§ 1187. Duties and Reporting Requirements of Debtors 527
§ 1188. Status Conference 528
§ 1189. Filing of the Plan 528
§ 1190. Contents of Plan 528
§ 1191. Confirmation of Plan 528
§ 1192. Discharge 529
§ 1193. Modification of Plan 529
§ 1194. Payments 529
§ 1195. Transactions with Professionals 530

Chapter 12. Adjustment of Debts of a Family Farmer or Fisherman with Regular Income 530

SUBCHAPTER I—OFFICERS, ADMINISTRATION, AND THE ESTATE 530

§ 1201. Stay of Action Against Codebtor 530
§ 1202. Trustee 530
§ 1203. Rights and Powers of Debtor 531
§ 1204. Removal of Debtor as Debtor in Possession 531
§ 1205. Adequate Protection 531
§ 1206. Sales Free of Interests 532
§ 1207. Property of the Estate 532
§ 1208. Conversion or Dismissal 532

SUBCHAPTER II—THE PLAN 532

§ 1221. Filing of Plan 533
§ 1222. Contents of Plan 533

§ 1223. Modification of Plan Before Confirmation 534
§ 1224. Confirmation Hearing 534
§ 1225. Confirmation of Plan 534
§ 1226. Payments 535
§ 1227. Effect of Confirmation 535
§ 1228. Discharge 535
§ 1229. Modification of Plan After Confirmation 536
§ 1230. Revocation of an Order of Confirmation 536
§ 1231. Special Tax Provisions 536

Chapter 13. Adjustment of Debts of an Individual with Regular Income 537

SUBCHAPTER I—OFFICERS, ADMINISTRATION, AND THE ESTATE 537

§ 1301. Stay of Action Against Codebtor 537
§ 1302. Trustee 537
§ 1303. Rights and Powers of Debtor 538
§ 1304. Debtor Engaged in Business 538
§ 1305. Filing and Allowance of Postpetition Claims 538
§ 1306. Property of the Estate 539
§ 1307. Conversion or Dismissal 539
§ 1308. Filing of Prepetition Tax Returns 539

SUBCHAPTER II—THE PLAN 540

§ 1321. Filing of Plan 540
§ 1322. Contents of Plan 540
§ 1323. Modification of Plan Before Confirmation 542
§ 1324. Confirmation Hearing 542
§ 1325. Confirmation of Plan 542
§ 1326. Payments 544
§ 1327. Effect of Confirmation 545
§ 1328. Discharge 545
§ 1329. Modification of Plan After Confirmation 546
§ 1330. Revocation of an Order of Confirmation 546

Chapter 15. Ancillary and Other Cross-Border Cases 547
§ 1501. Purpose and Scope of Application 547

SUBCHAPTER I—GENERAL PROVISIONS 547

§ 1502. Definitions 547
§ 1503. International Obligations of the United States 548
§ 1504. Commencement of Ancillary Case 548
§ 1505. Authorization to Act in a Foreign Country 548
§ 1506. Public Policy Exception 548
§ 1507. Additional Assistance 548
§ 1508. Interpretation 548

SUBCHAPTER II—ACCESS OF FOREIGN REPRESENTATIVES AND CREDITORS TO THE COURT 548

§ 1509. Right of Direct Access 548
§ 1510. Limited Jurisdiction 549
§ 1511. Commencement of Case Under Section 301, 302, or 303 549
§ 1512. Participation of a Foreign Representative in a Case Under This Title 549
§ 1513. Access of Foreign Creditors to a Case Under This Title 549
§ 1514. Notification to Foreign Creditors Concerning a Case Under This Title 549

SUBCHAPTER III—RECOGNITION OF A FOREIGN PROCEEDING AND RELIEF 550

§ 1515. Application for Recognition 550
§ 1516. Presumptions Concerning Recognition 550
§ 1517. Order Granting Recognition 550
§ 1518. Subsequent Information 551
§ 1519. Relief That May Be Granted upon Filing Petition for Recognition 551
§ 1520. Effects of Recognition of a Foreign Main Proceeding 551
§ 1521. Relief That May Be Granted upon Recognition 551
§ 1522. Protection of Creditors and Other Interested Persons 552
§ 1523. Actions to Avoid Acts Detrimental to Creditors 552
§ 1524. Intervention by a Foreign Representative 552

SUBCHAPTER IV—COOPERATION WITH FOREIGN COURTS AND FOREIGN REPRESENTATIVES 553

§ 1525. Cooperation and Direct Communication Between the Court and Foreign Courts or Foreign Representatives 553
§ 1526. Cooperation and Direct Communication Between the Trustee and Foreign Courts or Foreign Representatives 553
§ 1527. Forms of Cooperation 553

SUBCHAPTER V—CONCURRENT PROCEEDINGS 553

§ 1528. Commencement of a Case Under This Title After Recognition of a Foreign Main Proceeding 553
§ 1529. Coordination of a Case Under This Title and a Foreign Proceeding 553
§ 1530. Coordination of More Than 1 Foreign Proceeding 554
§ 1531. Presumption of Insolvency Based on Recognition of a Foreign Main Proceeding 554
§ 1532. Rule of Payment in Concurrent Proceedings 554

FEDERAL RULES OF BANKRUPTCY PROCEDURE 555

Rule 1015. Consolidation or Joint Administration of Cases Pending in Same Court 555
Rule 2002. Notices to Creditors, Equity Security Holders, Administrators in Foreign Proceedings, Persons Against Whom Provisional Relief is Sought in Ancillary and Other Cross-Border Cases, United States, and United States Trustee 555
Rule 2003. Meeting of Creditors or Equity Security Holders 559
Rule 2004. Examination 561
Rule 2014. Employment of Professional Persons 561
Rule 2016. Compensation for Services Rendered and Reimbursement of Expenses 561
Rule 2017. Examination of Debtor's Transactions with Debtor's Attorney 562

Rule 2019. Disclosure Regarding Creditors and Equity Security Holders in Chapter 9 and Chapter 11 Cases 562
Rule 3014. Election Under §1111(b) by Secured Creditor in Chapter 9 Municipality or Chapter 11 Reorganization Case 563
Rule 4001. Relief from Automatic Stay; Prohibiting or Conditioning the Use, Sale, or Lease of Property; Use of Cash Collateral; Obtaining Credit; Agreements 564
Rule 4005. Burden of Proof in Objecting to Discharge 566
Rule 4007. Determination of Dischargeability of a Debt 567
Rule 7001. Scope of Rules of Part VII 567
Rule 8002. Time for Filing Notice of Appeal 567
Rule 8007. Stay Pending Appeal; Bonds; Suspension of Proceedings 569
Rule 9014. Contested Matters 569
Rule 9029. Local Bankruptcy Rules; Procedure When There is No Controlling Law 570

TITLE 18—CRIMES AND CRIMINAL PROCEDURE 571

Chapter 9—Bankruptcy 571
§ 151. Definition 571
§ 152. Concealment of Assets; False Oaths and Claims; Bribery 571
§ 156. Knowing Disregard of Bankruptcy Law or Rule 572
§ 157. Bankruptcy Fraud 572
§ 158. Designation of United States Attorneys and Agents of the Federal Bureau of Investigation to Address Abusive Reaffirmations of Debt and Materially Fraudulent Statements in Bankruptcy Schedules 572

Chapter 203—Arrest and Commitment 572
§ 3057. Bankruptcy Investigations 572

Chapter 213—Limitations 573
§ 3284. Concealment of Bankrupt's Assets 573

TITLE 28—JUDICIARY AND JUDICIAL PROCEDURE 575

PART I—ORGANIZATION OF COURTS 575

Chapter 6—Bankruptcy Judges 575
§ 151. Designation of Bankruptcy Courts 575
§ 152. Appointment of Bankruptcy Judges 575
§ 157. Procedures 576
§ 158. Appeals 577
§ 159. Bankruptcy Statistics 578

PART II—DEPARTMENT OF JUSTICE **579**

Chapter 39—United States Trustees 579
§ 581. United States Trustees 579
§ 586. Duties; Supervision by Attorney General 580
§ 589b. Bankruptcy Data 583

PART III—COURT OFFICERS AND EMPLOYEES 584

Chapter 57—General Provisions Applicable to Court Officers and Employees **584**
§ 959. Trustees and Receivers Suable; Management; State Laws 584

PART IV—JURISDICTION AND VENUE 584

Chapter 85—District Courts; Jurisdiction **584**
§ 1334. Bankruptcy Cases and Proceedings 584

Chapter 87—District Courts; Venue **585**
§ 1408. Venue of Cases Under Title 11 585
§ 1409. Venue of Proceedings Arising Under Title 11 or Arising in or Related to Cases Under Title 11 585
§ 1410. Venue of Cases Ancillary to Foreign Proceedings 585
§ 1411. Jury Trials 586
§ 1412. Change of Venue 586

Chapter 89—District Courts; Removal of Cases from State Courts **586**
§ 1452. Removal of Claims Related to Bankruptcy Cases 586

FAIR DEBT COLLECTION PRACTICES ACT **587**

§ 801. Short Title 587
§ 802. Congressional Findings and Declaration of Purpose 587
§ 803. Definitions 587
§ 804. Acquisition of Location Information 588
§ 805. Communication in Connection with Debt Collection 588
§ 806. Harassment or Abuse 589
§ 807. False or Misleading Representations 589
§ 808. Unfair Practices 590
§ 809. Validation of Debts 591
§ 810. Multiple Debts 591
§ 811. Legal Actions by Debt Collectors 591
§ 812. Furnishing Certain Deceptive Forms 592
§ 813. Civil Liability 592
§ 814. Administrative Enforcement 592
§ 815. Reports to Congress by the Bureau; Views of Other Federal Agencies 593
§ 816. Relation to State Laws 594
§ 817. Exemption for State Regulation 594
§ 818. Exception for Certain Bad Check Enforcement Programs Operated by Private Entities 594
§ 819. Effective Date 595

TITLE 26—FEDERAL TAX LIEN ACT **597**

§ 6321. Lien for Taxes 597
§ 6322. Period of Lien 597
§ 6323. Validity and Priority Against Certain Persons 597

Preface

In the course of a career, the number of state and federal statutes that a serious practitioner of commercial law would likely consult must surely reach into the hundreds. Not many practitioners would try to carry such statutes around, either in books or in their heads. But a few statutes are used over and over. Together, those few form the core of two basic subjects in commercial law, secured transactions and bankruptcy. Those core statutes are reproduced here.

Part 1 is state law. The Uniform Commercial Code (UCC) forms the backbone of the statutes. In July 2022, the ULC and ALI enacted a new Article 12 to address "controllable electronic records," along with a new Article A containing transitional provisions. The 2022 amendments made other changes throughout Article 9. As of this writing, sixteen states and the District of Columbia have adopted the 2022 amendments, and they have been introduced in twelve other states. This supplement contains the UCC's official text and comments and thus includes the 2022 amendments. The current versions of Articles 1, 9, 12, and A also are reproduced in full with comments. Selected provisions of UCC Articles 2 and 8 are included, along with the Uniform Motor Vehicle Certificate of Title Act, and the Uniform Fraudulent Transfer Act. The latter has been renamed the Uniform Voidable Transaction Act and amended in minor respects. We include both the old and new Acts.

Part 2 is federal law. The Bankruptcy Code, as of April 1, 2024, is reproduced in full. In 2022, the Bankruptcy Threshold Adjustment and Technical Corrections Act changed the threshold for filing under Subchapter V of Chapter 11 to $7,500,000 and the Chapter 13 threshold to $2,750,000 (§ 109) for both secured and unsecured debt. Those changes will sunset on June 21, 2024, unless Congress extends them.

Bankruptcy Code § 104 provides for administrative readjustment of certain dollar figures at three-year intervals beginning in 1998. In this supplement we have inserted the current dollar amounts, effective April 1, 2022. Those amounts will change again on April 1, 2025. Technically, the official version of the Bankruptcy Code lists the original amounts, but looking up the numbers is an unnecessary hurdle for the reader. In addition to the Bankruptcy Code and related provisions, this supplement also includes the Fair Debt Collection Practices Act and the Federal Tax Lien Act.

This statutory supplement has evolved over time, incorporating the suggestions of several teachers and students. In their years at Harvard, Katherine Porter, Class of 2001, Peter Eyre, Class of 2005, Ryan Spear, Class of 2007, Maura Klugman, Class of 2008, Danielle D'Onfro, Class of 2011, and Sarah Levin, Class of 2014, have each provided important assistance in the preparation of the manuscript. In their years at UCLA School of Law, Gautam Viadyanathan, Class of 2015, Samuel Landau, Class of 2016, Scott Yousey, Class of 2019, Phillip Shaverdian, Class of 2019, Elise Aliotti, Class of 2020, Claire Hoffman, Class of 2021, and Diana Yen, Class of 2022, have done the same. Now we have the help of students from the University of Illinois, including Alec Klimowicz, Class of 2024, and Oluwakemi Adeyemi, JSD candidate. We are grateful for all the help.

ELIZABETH WARREN
LEO GOTTLIEB PROFESSOR OF LAW EMERITUS
HARVARD LAW SCHOOL

ROBERT M. LAWLESS
MAX L. ROWE PROFESSOR OF LAW
UNIVERSITY OF ILLINOIS

April 2024

UNIFORM COMMERCIAL CODE

Article 1—General Provisions

PART 1. GENERAL PROVISIONS

Section
1-101. Short Titles
1-102. Scope of Article
1-103. Construction of [Uniform Commercial Code] to Promote Its Purposes and Policies; Applicability of Supplemental Principles of Law
1-104. Construction Against Implied Repeal
1-105. Severability
1-106. Use of Singular and Plural; Gender
1-107. Section Captions
1-108. Relation to Electronic Signatures in Global and National Commerce Act

PART 2. GENERAL DEFINITIONS AND PRINCIPLES OF INTERPRETATION
1-201. General Definitions
1-202. Notice; Knowledge
1-203. Lease Distinguished from Security Interest
1-204. Value
1-205. Reasonable Time; Seasonableness
1-206. Presumptions

PART 3. TERRITORIAL APPLICABILITY AND GENERAL RULES
1-301. Territorial Applicability; Parties' Power to Choose Applicable Law
1-302. Variation by Agreement
1-303. Course of Performance, Course of Dealing, and Usage of Trade
1-304. Obligation of Good Faith
1-305. Remedies to Be Liberally Administered
1-306. Waiver or Renunciation of Claim or Right After Breach
1-307. Prima Facie Evidence by Third-Party Documents
1-308. Performance or Acceptance Under Reservation of Rights
1-309. Option to Accelerate at Will
1-310. Subordinated Obligations

PART 1. GENERAL PROVISIONS

§ 1-101. Short Titles.

(a) This [Act] may be cited as the Uniform Commercial Code.

(b) This article may be cited as Uniform Commercial Code—General Provisions.

Official Comment

Source: Former Section 1-101.

Changes from Former Law: Subsection (b) is new. It is added in order to make the structure of Article 1 parallel with that of the other articles of the Uniform Commercial Code.

1. Each other article of the Uniform Commercial Code may also be cited by its own short title. See Sections 2-101, 2A-101, 3-101, 4-101, 4A-101, 5-101, 6-101, 7-101, 8-101, 9-101, 12-101, and A-101.

§ 1-102. Scope of Article.

This article applies to a transaction to the extent that it is governed by another article of [the Uniform Commercial Code].

Preliminary Comment

Source: New.

1. This section is intended to resolve confusion that has occasionally arisen as to the applicability of the substantive rules in this article. This section makes clear what has always been the case—the rules in Article 1 apply to transactions to the extent that those transactions are governed by one of the other articles of the Uniform Commercial Code. See also Comment 1 to Section 1-301.

§ 1-103. Construction of [Uniform Commercial Code] to Promote Its Purposes and Policies; Applicability of Supplemental Principles of Law.

(a) [The Uniform Commercial Code] must be liberally construed and applied to promote its underlying purposes and policies, which are:

(1) to simplify, clarify, and modernize the law governing commercial transactions;

(2) to permit the continued expansion of commercial practices through custom, usage, and agreement of the parties; and

(3) to make uniform the law among the various jurisdictions.

(b) Unless displaced by the particular provisions of [the Uniform Commercial Code], the principles of law and equity, including the law merchant and the law relative to capacity to contract, principal and agent, estoppel, fraud, misrepresentation, duress, coercion, mistake, bankruptcy, and other validating or invalidating cause supplement its provisions.

Official Comment

Source: Former Section 1-102(1)-(2); Former Section 1-103.

Changes from Former Law: This section is derived from subsections (1) and (2) of former Section 1-102 and from former Section 1-103. Subsection (a) of this section combines subsections (1) and (2) of former Section 1-102. Except for changing the form of reference to the Uniform Commercial Code and minor stylistic changes, its language is the same as subsections (1) and (2) of former Section 1-102. Except for changing the form of reference to the Uniform Commercial Code and minor stylistic changes, subsection (b) of this section is identical to former Section 1-103. The provisions have been combined in this section to reflect the interrelationship between them.

1. The Uniform Commercial Code is drawn to provide flexibility so that, since it is intended to be a semi-permanent and infrequently-amended piece of legislation, it will provide its own machinery for expansion of commercial practices. It is intended to make it possible for the law embodied in the Uniform Commercial Code to be applied by the courts in the light of unforeseen and new circumstances and practices. The proper construction of the Uniform Commercial Code requires, of course, that its interpretation and application be limited to its reason.

Even prior to the enactment of the Uniform Commercial Code, courts were careful to keep broad acts from being hampered in their effects by later acts of limited scope. See *Pacific Wool Growers v. Draper & Co.*, 158 Or. 1, 73 P.2d 1391 (1937), and compare Section 1-104. The courts have often recognized that the policies embodied in an act are applicable in reason to subject-matter that was not expressly included in the language of the act, *Commercial Nat. Bank of New Orleans v. Canal-Louisiana Bank & Trust Co.*, 239 U.S. 520, 36 S.Ct. 194, 60 L. Ed. 417 (1916) (bona fide purchase policy of Uniform Warehouse Receipts Act extended to case not covered but of equivalent nature), and did the same where reason and policy so required, even where the subject-matter had been intentionally excluded from the act in general. *Agar v. Orda*, 264 N.Y. 248, 190 N.E. 479 (1934) (Uniform Sales Act change in seller's remedies applied to contract for sale of choses in action even though the general coverage of that Act was intentionally limited to goods "other than things in action.") They implemented a statutory policy with liberal and useful remedies not provided in the statutory text. They disregarded a statutory limitation of remedy where the reason of the limitation did not apply. *Fiterman v. J. N. Johnson & Co.*, 156 Minn. 201, 194 N.W. 399 (1923) (requirement of return of the goods as a condition to rescission for breach of warranty; also, partial rescission allowed). Nothing in the Uniform Commercial Code stands in the way of the continuance of such action by the courts.

The Uniform Commercial Code should be construed in accordance with its underlying purposes and policies. The text of each section should be read in the light of the purpose and policy of the rule or principle in question, as also of the Uniform Commercial Code as a whole, and the application of the language should be construed narrowly or broadly, as the case may be, in conformity with the purposes and policies involved.

2. Applicability of supplemental principles of law. Subsection (b) states the basic relationship of the Uniform Commercial Code to supplemental bodies of law. The Uniform Commercial Code was drafted against the backdrop of existing bodies of law, including the common law and equity, and relies on those bodies of law to supplement its provisions in many important ways. At the same time, the Uniform Commercial Code is the primary source of commercial law rules in areas that it governs, and its rules represent choices made by its drafters and the enacting legislatures about the appropriate policies to be furthered in the transactions it covers. Therefore, while principles of common law and equity may *supplement* provisions of the Uniform Commercial Code, they may not be used to *supplant* its provisions, or the purposes and policies those provisions reflect, unless a specific provision of the Uniform Commercial Code provides otherwise. In the absence of such a provision, the Uniform Commercial Code preempts principles of common law and equity that are inconsistent with either its provisions or its purposes and policies.

The language of subsection (b) is intended to reflect both the concept of supplementation and the concept of preemption. Some courts, however, had difficulty in applying the identical language of former Section 1-103 to determine when other law appropriately may be applied to supplement the Uniform Commercial Code, and when that law has been displaced by the Code. Some decisions applied other law in situations in which that application, while not inconsistent with the text of any particular provision of the Uniform Commercial Code, clearly was inconsistent with the underlying purposes and policies reflected in the relevant provisions of the Code. See, e.g., *Sheerbonnet, Ltd. v. American Express Bank, Ltd.*, 951 F. Supp. 403 (S.D.N.Y. 1995). In part, this difficulty arose from Comment 1 to former Section 1-103, which stated that "this section indicates the continued applicability to commercial contracts of all supplemental bodies of law except insofar as they are explicitly displaced by this Act." The "explicitly displaced" language of that Comment did not accurately reflect the proper scope of Uniform Commercial Code preemption, which extends to displacement of other law that is inconsistent with the purposes and policies of the Uniform Commercial Code, as well as with its text.

The supplemental principles of law and equity to which subsection (b) refers may evolve over time to take into account developments in technology. These developments may include, for example, developing case law on contract formation in an electronic environment and the use of automated transactions and arrangements that are sometimes referred to as "electronic agents" (which may or may not actually reflect or create agency relationships under the applicable law of agency). See generally Uniform Electronic Transactions Act (UETA); Restatement (Third) of Agency § 1.04, Reporter's Note to Comment *e* (2006) (discussing the relationship between "electronic agents" and the law of principal and agent). The supplementation recognized by subsection (b) should reflect this evolution.

3. Application of subsection (b) to statutes. The primary focus of Section 1-103 is on the relationship between the Uniform Commercial Code and principles of common law and equity as developed by the courts. State law, however, increasingly is statutory. Not only are there a growing number of state statutes addressing specific issues that come within the scope of the Uniform Commercial Code, but in some States many general principles of common law and equity have been codified. When the other law relating to a matter within the scope of the Uniform Commercial Code is a statute, the principles of subsection (b) remain relevant to the court's analysis of the relationship between that statute and the Uniform Commercial Code, but other principles of statutory interpretation that specifically address the interrelationship between statutes will be relevant as well. In some situations, the principles of subsection (b) still will be determinative. For example, the mere fact that an equitable principle is stated in statutory form rather than in judicial decisions should not change the court's analysis of whether the principle can be used to supplement the Uniform Commercial Code—under subsection (b), equitable principles may supplement provisions of the Uniform Commercial Code only if they are consistent with the purposes and policies of the Uniform Commercial Code as well as its text. In other situations, however, other interpretive principles addressing the interrelationship between statutes may lead the court to conclude that the other statute is controlling, even though it conflicts with the Uniform Commercial Code. This, for example, would be the result in a situation where the other statute was specifically intended to provide additional protection to a class of individuals engaging in transactions covered by the Uniform Commercial Code.

4. Listing not exclusive. The list of sources of supplemental law in subsection (b) is intended to be merely illustrative of the other law that may supplement the Uniform Commercial Code, and is not exclusive. No listing could be exhaustive. Further, the fact that a particular section of the Uniform Commercial Code makes express reference to other law is not intended to suggest the negation of the general application of the principles of subsection (b). Note also that the word "bankruptcy" in subsection (b), continuing the use of that word from former Section 1-103, should be understood not as a specific reference to federal bankruptcy law but, rather as a reference to general principles of insolvency, whether under federal or state law.

§ 1-104. Construction Against Implied Repeal.

[The Uniform Commercial Code] being a general act intended as a unified coverage of its subject matter, no part of it shall be deemed to be impliedly repealed by subsequent legislation if such construction can reasonably be avoided.

Official Comment

Source: Former Section 1-104.

Changes from Former Law: Except for changing the form of reference to the Uniform Commercial Code, this section is identical to former Section 1-104.

1. This section embodies the policy that an act that bears evidence of carefully considered permanent regulative intention should not lightly be regarded as impliedly repealed by subsequent legislation. The Uniform Commercial Code, carefully integrated and intended as a uniform codification of permanent character covering an entire "field" of law, is to be regarded as particularly resistant to implied repeal.

§ 1-105. Severability.

If any provision or clause of [the Uniform Commercial Code] or its application to any person or circumstance is held invalid, the invalidity does not affect other provisions or applications of [the Uniform Commercial Code] which can be given effect without the invalid provision or application, and to this end the provisions of [the Uniform Commercial Code] are severable.

Official Comment

Source: Former Section 1-108.

Changes from Former Law: Except for changing the form of reference to the Uniform Commercial Code, this section is identical to former Section 1-108.

1. This is the model severability section recommended by the National Conference of Commissioners on Uniform State Laws for inclusion in all acts of extensive scope.

§ 1-106. Use of Singular and Plural; Gender.

In [the Uniform Commercial Code], unless the statutory context otherwise requires:

(1) words in the singular number include the plural, and those in the plural include the singular; and

(2) words of any gender also refer to any other gender.

Official Comment

Source: Former Section 1-102(5). See also 1 U.S.C. Section 1.

Changes from Former Law: Other than minor stylistic changes, this section is identical to former Section 1-102(5).

1. This section makes it clear that the use of singular or plural in the text of the Uniform Commercial Code is generally only a matter of drafting style—singular words may be applied in the plural, and plural words may be applied in the singular. Only when it is clear from the statutory context that the use of the singular or plural does not include the other is this rule inapplicable. See, e.g., Section 9-322.

§ 1-107. Section Captions.

Section captions are part of [the Uniform Commercial Code].

Official Comment

Source: Former Section 1-109.

Changes from Former Law: None.

1. Section captions are a part of the text of the Uniform Commercial Code, and not mere surplusage. This is not the case, however, with respect to subsection headings appearing in Articles 9, 12, and A (Transitional Provisions). See Section 9-101, Comment 3 ("subsection headings are not a part of the official text itself and have not been approved by the sponsors."); Section 12-101, Comment; Section A-101, Comment.

§ 1-108. Relation to Electronic Signatures in Global and National Commerce Act.

This [Act] modifies, limits, and supersedes the federal Electronic Signatures in Global and National Commerce Act (15 U.S.C. Section 7001 et seq.) but does not modify, limit, or supersede Section 101(c) of that act (15 U.S.C. Section 7001(c)) or authorize electronic delivery of any of the notices described in Section 103(b) of that act (15 U.S.C. Section 103(b)).

Official Comment

Source: New.

1. The federal Electronic Signatures in Global and National Commerce Act, 15 U.S.C. Section 7001 et seq., became effective in 2000. Section 102(a) of that Act provides that a State statute may modify, limit, or supersede the provisions of section 101 of that Act with respect to state law if such statute, *inter alia*, specifies the alternative procedures or requirements for the use or acceptance (or both) of electronic records or electronic signatures to establish the legal effect, validity, or enforceability of contracts or other records, and (i) such alternative procedures or requirements are consistent with Titles I and II of that Act; (ii) such alternative procedures or requirements do not require, or accord greater legal status or effect to, the implementation or application of a specific technology or technical specification for performing the functions of creating, storing, generating, receiving, communicating, or authenticating electronic records or electronic signatures; and (iii) if enacted or adopted after the date of the enactment of that Act, makes specific reference to that Act. Article 1 fulfills the first two of those three criteria; this Section fulfills the third criterion listed above.

2. As stated in this section, however, Article 1 does not modify, limit, or supersede Section 101(c) of the Electronic Signatures in Global and National Commerce Act (requiring affirmative consent from a consumer to electronic delivery of transactional disclosures that are required by state law to be in writing); nor does it authorize electronic delivery of any of the notices described in Section 103(b) of that Act.

PART 2. GENERAL DEFINITIONS AND PRINCIPLES OF INTERPRETATION

§ 1-201. General Definitions.

(a) Unless the context otherwise requires, words or phrases defined in this section, or in the additional definitions contained in other articles of [the Uniform Commercial Code] that apply to particular articles or parts thereof, have the meanings stated.

(b) Subject to definitions contained in other articles of [the Uniform Commercial Code] that apply to particular articles or parts thereof:

(1) "Action", in the sense of a judicial proceeding, includes recoupment, counterclaim, set-off, suit in equity, and any other proceeding in which rights are determined.

(2) "Aggrieved party" means a party entitled to pursue a remedy.

(3) "Agreement", as distinguished from "contract", means the bargain of the parties in fact, as found in their language or inferred from other circumstances, including course of performance, course of dealing, or usage of trade as provided in Section 1-303.

(4) "Bank" means a person engaged in the business of banking and includes a savings bank, savings and loan association, credit union, and trust company.

(5) "Bearer" means a person in possession of a negotiable instrument, document of title, or certificated security that is payable to bearer or indorsed in blank.

(6) "Bill of lading" means a document evidencing the receipt of goods for shipment issued by a person engaged in the business of transporting or forwarding goods.

(7) "Branch" includes a separately incorporated foreign branch of a bank.

(8) "Burden of establishing" a fact means the burden of persuading the trier of fact that the existence of the fact is more probable than its nonexistence.

(9) "Buyer in ordinary course of business" means a person that buys goods in good faith, without knowledge that the sale violates the rights of another person in the goods, and in the ordinary course from a person, other than a pawnbroker, in the business of selling goods of that kind. A person buys goods in the ordinary course if the sale to the person comports with the usual or customary practices in the kind of business in which the seller is engaged or with the seller's own usual or customary practices. A person that sells oil, gas, or other minerals at the wellhead or minehead is a person in the business of selling goods of that kind. A buyer in ordinary course of business may buy for cash, by exchange of other property, or on secured or unsecured credit, and may acquire goods or documents of title under a preexisting contract for sale. Only a buyer that takes possession of the goods or has a right to recover the goods from the seller under Article 2 may be a buyer in ordinary course of business. "Buyer in ordinary course of business" does not include a person that acquires goods in a transfer in bulk or as security for or in total or partial satisfaction of a money debt.

(10) "Conspicuous", with reference to a term, means so written, displayed, or presented that, based on the totality of the circumstances, a reasonable person against which it is to operate ought to have noticed it. Whether a term is "conspicuous" or not is a decision for the court.

(11) "Consumer" means an individual who enters into a transaction primarily for personal, family, or household purposes.

(12) "Contract", as distinguished from "agreement", means the total legal obligation that results from the parties' agreement as determined by [the Uniform Commercial Code] as supplemented by any other applicable laws.

(13) "Creditor" includes a general creditor, a secured creditor, a lien creditor, and any representative of creditors, including an assignee for the benefit of creditors, a trustee in bankruptcy, a receiver in equity, and an executor or administrator of an insolvent debtor's or assignor's estate.

(14) "Defendant" includes a person in the position of defendant in a counterclaim, cross-claim, or third-party claim.

(15) "Delivery", with respect to an electronic document of title, means voluntary transfer of control and, with respect to an instrument, a tangible document of title, or an authoritative tangible copy of a record evidencing chattel paper, means voluntary transfer of possession.

(16) "Document of title" includes bill of lading, dock warrant, dock receipt, warehouse receipt or order for the delivery of goods, and also any other document which in the regular course of business or financing is treated as adequately evidencing that the person in possession of it is entitled to receive, hold, and dispose of the document and the goods it covers. To be a document of title, a document must purport to be issued by or addressed to a bailee and purport to cover goods in the bailee's possession which

are either identified or are fungible portions of an identified mass.

(16A) "Electronic" means relating to technology having electrical, digital, magnetic, wireless, optical, electromagnetic, or similar capabilities.

(17) "Fault" means a default, breach, or wrongful act or omission.

(18) "Fungible goods" means:

(A) goods of which any unit, by nature or usage of trade, is the equivalent of any other like unit; or

(B) goods that by agreement are treated as equivalent.

(19) "Genuine" means free of forgery or counterfeiting.

(20) "Good faith," except as otherwise provided in Article 5, means honesty in fact and the observance of reasonable commercial standards of fair dealing.

(21) "Holder" means:

(A) the person in possession of a negotiable instrument that is payable either to bearer or to an identified person that is the person in possession; or

(B) the person in possession of a negotiable tangible document of title if the goods are deliverable either to bearer or to the order of the person in possession; or

(C) the person in control, other than pursuant to Section 7-106(g), of a negotiable electronic document of title.

(22) "Insolvency proceeding" includes an assignment for the benefit of creditors or other proceeding intended to liquidate or rehabilitate the estate of the person involved.

(23) "Insolvent" means:

(A) having generally ceased to pay debts in the ordinary course of business other than as a result of bona fide dispute;

(B) being unable to pay debts as they become due; or

(C) being insolvent within the meaning of federal bankruptcy law.

(24) "Money" means a medium of exchange that is currently authorized or adopted by a domestic or foreign government. The term includes a monetary unit of account established by an intergovernmental organization, or pursuant to an agreement between two or more countries. The term does not include an electronic record that is a medium of exchange recorded and transferable in a system that existed and operated for the medium of exchange before the medium of exchange was authorized or adopted by the government.

(25) "Organization" means a person other than an individual.

(26) "Party", as distinguished from "third party", means a person that has engaged in a transaction or made an agreement subject to [the Uniform Commercial Code].

(27) "Person" means an individual, corporation, business trust, estate, trust, partnership, limited liability company, association, joint venture, government, governmental subdivision, agency, or instrumentality, or any other legal or commercial entity. The term includes a protected series, however denominated, of an entity if the protected series is established under law other than [the Uniform Commercial Code] that limits, or limits if conditions specified under the law are satisfied, the ability of a creditor of the entity or of any other protected series of the entity to satisfy a claim from assets of the protected series.

(28) "Present value" means the amount as of a date certain of one or more sums payable in the future, discounted to the date certain by use of either an interest rate specified by the parties if that rate is not manifestly unreasonable at the time the transaction is entered into or, if an interest rate is not so specified, a commercially reasonable rate that takes into account the facts and circumstances at the time the transaction is entered into.

(29) "Purchase" means taking by sale, lease, discount, negotiation, mortgage, pledge, lien, security interest, issue or reissue, gift, or any other voluntary transaction creating an interest in property.

(30) "Purchaser" means a person that takes by purchase.

(31) "Record" means information that is inscribed on a tangible medium or that is stored in an electronic or other medium and is retrievable in perceivable form.

(32) "Remedy" means any remedial right to which an aggrieved party is entitled with or without resort to a tribunal.

(33) "Representative" means a person empowered to act for another, including an

agent, an officer of a corporation or association, and a trustee, executor, or administrator of an estate.

(34) "Right" includes remedy.

(35) "Security interest" means an interest in personal property or fixtures which secures payment or performance of an obligation. "Security interest" includes any interest of a consignor and a buyer of accounts, chattel paper, a payment intangible, or a promissory note in a transaction that is subject to Article 9. "Security interest" does not include the special property interest of a buyer of goods on identification of those goods to a contract for sale under Section 2-401, but a buyer may also acquire a "security interest" by complying with Article 9. Except as otherwise provided in Section 2-505, the right of a seller or lessor of goods under Article 2 or 2A to retain or acquire possession of the goods is not a "security interest", but a seller or lessor may also acquire a "security interest" by complying with Article 9. The retention or reservation of title by a seller of goods notwithstanding shipment or delivery to the buyer under Section 2-401 is limited in effect to a reservation of a "security interest." Whether a transaction in the form of a lease creates a "security interest" is determined pursuant to Section 1-203.

(36) "Send", in connection with a record, or notification, means:

(A) to deposit in the mail, deliver for transmission, or transmit by any other usual means of communication, with postage or cost of transmission provided for, addressed to any address reasonable under the circumstances; or

(B) to cause the record or notification to be received within the time it would have been received if properly sent under subparagraph (A).

(37) "Sign" means, with present intent to authenticate or adopt a record:

(A) execute or adopt a tangible symbol; or

(B) attach to or logically associate with the record an electronic symbol, sound, or process.

"Signed", "signing", and "signature" have corresponding meanings.

(38) "State" means a State of the United States, the District of Columbia, Puerto Rico, the United States Virgin Islands, or any territory or insular possession subject to the jurisdiction of the United States.

(39) "Surety" includes a guarantor or other secondary obligor.

(40) "Term" means a portion of an agreement that relates to a particular matter.

(41) "Unauthorized signature" means a signature made without actual, implied, or apparent authority. The term includes a forgery.

(42) "Warehouse receipt" means a receipt issued by a person engaged in the business of storing goods for hire.

(43) "Writing" includes printing, typewriting, or any other intentional reduction to tangible form. "Written" has a corresponding meaning.

Legislative Note: *A state should review and amend any statute or regulation that relies on or refers to the definition of "money" in subsection (b)(24) to account for the amendment to that definition.*

A *state should enact the amendment to subsection (b)(27) whether the state has enacted the Uniform Protect Series Act (2017) or otherwise recognizes a protected series under its law. Because the amendment applies only under the enacting state's Uniform Commercial Code, inclusion of the amendment does not require the enacting state to recognize a limit on liability of a protected series organized under the law of another jurisdiction or a limit on liability of the entity that established the protected series. The amendment clarifies the status of a protected series as a "person" under the choice-of-law and substantive law rules of the enacting state's Uniform Commercial Code.*

Official Comment

Source: Former Section 1-201.

Changes from Former Law: In order to make it clear that all definitions in the Uniform Commercial Code (not just those appearing in Article 1, as stated in former Section 1-201, but also those appearing in other Articles) do not apply if the context otherwise requires, a new subsection (a) to that effect has been added, and the definitions now appear in subsection (b). The reference in subsection (a) to the "context" is intended to refer to the context in which the defined term is used in the Uniform Commercial Code. In other words, the definition applies whenever the defined term is used unless the context in which the defined term is used in the statute indicates that the term was not used in its defined sense. Consider, for example, Sections 3-103(a)(9) (defining "promise," in relevant part, as "a written undertaking to pay money signed by the person undertaking to pay") and 3-303(a)(1) (indicating that an instrument is issued or transferred for value if "the instrument is issued or transferred for a promise of performance, to the extent that the promise has been performed"). It is clear from the statutory context of the use of the word "promise" in Section 3-303(a)(1) that the term was not used in the sense of its definition in Section 3-103(a)(9). Thus, the Section 3-103(a)(9) definition should not be used to give meaning to the word "promise" in Section 3-303(a).

Some definitions in former Section 1-201 have been reformulated as substantive provisions and have been moved to other sections. See Sections 1-202 (explicating concepts of notice and knowledge formerly addressed in Sections 1-201(25)-(27)), 1-204 (determining when a person gives value for rights, replacing the definition of "value" in former Section 1-201(44)), and 1-206 (addressing the meaning of presumptions, replacing the definitions of "presumption" and "presumed" in former Section 1-201(31)). Similarly, the portion of the definition of "security interest" in former Section 1-201(37) which explained the difference between a security interest and a lease has been relocated to Section 1-203.

Two definitions in former Section 1-201 have been deleted. The definition of "honor" in former Section 1-201(21) has been moved to Section 2-103(1)(b), inasmuch as the definition only applies to the use of the word in Article 2. The definition of "telegram" in former Section 1-201(41) has been deleted because that word no longer appears in the definition of "conspicuous."

Other than minor stylistic changes and renumbering, the remaining definitions in this section are as in former Article 1 except as noted below.

1. "Action." Unchanged from former Section 1-201, which was derived from similar definitions in Section 191, Uniform Negotiable Instruments Law; Section 76, Uniform Sales Act; Section 58, Uniform Warehouse Receipts Act; Section 53, Uniform Bills of Lading Act.

2. "Aggrieved party." Unchanged from former Section 1-201.

3. "Agreement." Derived from former Section 1-201. As used in the Uniform Commercial Code the word is intended to include full recognition of usage of trade, course of dealing, course of performance and the surrounding circumstances as effective parts thereof, and of any agreement permitted under the provisions of the Uniform Commercial Code to displace a stated rule of law. Whether an agreement has legal consequences is determined by applicable provisions of the Uniform Commercial Code and, to the extent provided in Section 1-103, by the law of contracts. Concerning developments in technology, including, for example, contract formation in electronic environments, automated transactions, and electronic agents, see Section 1-103, Comment 2.

4. "Bank." Derived from Section 4A-104.

5. "Bearer." Unchanged from former Section 1-201, which was derived from Section 191, Uniform Negotiable Instruments Law.

6. "Bill of Lading." Derived from former Section 1-201. The reference to, and definition of, an "airbill" has been deleted as no longer necessary.

7. "Branch." Unchanged from former Section 1-201.

8. "Burden of establishing a fact." Unchanged from former Section 1-201.

9. "Buyer in ordinary course of business." Except for minor stylistic changes, identical to former Section 1-201 (as amended in conjunction with the 1999 revisions to Article 9). The major significance of the phrase lies in Section 2-403 and in the Article on Secured Transactions (Article 9).

The first sentence of paragraph (9) makes clear that a buyer from a pawnbroker cannot be a buyer in ordinary course of business. The second sentence explains what it means to buy "in the ordinary course." The penultimate sentence prevents a buyer that does not have the right to possession as against the seller from being a buyer in ordinary course of business. Concerning when a buyer obtains possessory rights, see Sections 2-502 and 2-716. However, the penultimate sentence is not intended to affect a buyer's status as a buyer in ordinary course of business in cases (such as a "drop shipment") involving delivery by the seller to a person buying from the buyer or a donee from the buyer. The requirement relates to whether as against the seller the buyer or one taking through the buyer has possessory rights.

10. "Conspicuous." Derived from former Section 1-201(10). This definition states the general standard that to be conspicuous a term ought to be noticed by a reasonable person against which the term is to operate. Whether a term is conspicuous is an issue for the court. Whether the appearance and presentation of a particular term satisfy this standard is determined by reference to the totality of the circumstances and requires a case-by-case analysis.

Historically, contract terms were presented in writing, making the use of standards that relate to the size and appearance of type relevant to the determination of conspicuousness. Today terms in a record are frequently communicated electronically. New technologies have created opportunities for terms to be displayed or presented in novel ways, such as by the use of pop-up windows, text balloons, dynamically expanding or dynamically magnifying text, and non-visual elements such as vibrations, to name a few.

The definition has been revised in the Uniform Commercial Code Amendments (2022) (2022 Amendments) by deleting the statutory examples relating to the appearance of type and instead indicating in these comments a broader universe of factors that are applicable to both written and electronic presentations. This approach is intended to be both more protective of consumers and more useful to drafters by providing more clarity and flexibility in the methods that may be used to call attention to a term.

The attributes of a reasonable person against which a term is to operate can vary depending upon the nature of the transaction and the market in which the transaction occurs. For example, assume that a merchant of goods wishes to enter into a transaction for the sale or lease of goods which does not include an implied warranty of merchantability or fitness for particular purpose. Depending on the particular transaction, the person against which the term excluding implied warranties is to operate may be a large business buyer or lessee, a small business, or a consumer. Similarly, the determination of whether a term is conspicuous may, depending on the context, yield a different conclusion when the term is used in a standard form agreement than when terms of the agreement are the subject of negotiation or discussion.

Terms presented in an online record raise issues that differ in some respects from the issues associated with presenting the same terms in a writing. For example, how a term appears depends to some extent on the equipment and settings used by the person presented with the term.

The test of whether a term is conspicuous remains constant notwithstanding the different contexts referenced above. A term is conspicuous if its appearance and presentation are such that it ought to be noticed by a reasonable person against which the term is to operate. If the term is in a standard form intended for use in many agreements, the determination of whether the term is conspicuous may be made with reference to typical likely parties to the agreements, taking into account all aspects of the transaction, the range of likely equipment and settings used by such parties, and the education, sophistication, disabilities, and other attributes of such parties. If the term is not in a standard form, the determination of whether it is conspicuous should be made with reference to a reasonable person in the position of the actual person against which it is to operate.

Factors relevant to whether a term is conspicuous include, but are not limited to, the following:

(i) The use of headings and text that contrast with the surrounding text. For example, a term is likely to be conspicuous if it is introduced by a heading in uppercase letters equal to or greater in size than the surrounding text. Similarly, a term is likely to be conspicuous if set out in language in the body of a record or display in larger type than the surrounding text, or in contrasting type, font, or color to the surrounding text of the same size, or set off from surrounding text of the same size by symbols or other marks that call attention to the language. However, even with those characteristics, for a term to be conspicuous the overall statutory test must always be met. For example, even if in bold, uppercase letters, a term might not be conspicuous if placed among other terms also in bold, uppercase letters so there is no contrast with the surrounding text or if the application of other factors causes the term not to be provided such that a reasonable person against which it is to operate ought to have noticed it.

(ii) The placement of the term in the record. A term appearing at, or hyperlinked from, text at the beginning of a record, or near the place where the person against which the term is to operate must signify assent, is more likely to be conspicuous than a term in the middle of a lengthy record absent the use of a method reasonably designed to draw the person's attention to the term in middle of the record (for example, by providing separate reasonable notice of the term before presenting the record containing the term to the person for assent or forcing the person to stop on a screen highlighting the term during the presentation of the record for assent).

(iii) If terms are available only through the use of a hyperlink, in addition to the placement of the hyperlink as described above, factors to be considered include whether there is language drawing attention to the hyperlink and describing its function, and the size and color of the text used for the hyperlink and any related language.

(iv) The language of the heading, if any. A misleading heading – such as the heading "Warranty" for a paragraph that contains a disclaimer of warranties – might cause a reasonable person to fail to notice the language that would disclaim warranties, so that the term would not be conspicuous.

(v) The effort needed to access the term. The process and flow of the display and presentation is also relevant. For example, a term accessible only by triggering multiple hyperlinks is less likely to be conspicuous than a term accessible from a single hyperlink.

(vi) Whether the person against which the term is to operate must separately assent to or acknowledge the term. Obtaining separate assent or acknowledgment of a term is generally sufficient to make the term conspicuous.

As noted above, the evolution of technology has led to an evolution in the ways in which terms in an electronic record are displayed or presented. A term displayed or presented in a novel way utilizing emerging technologies is, of course, conspicuous if the effect of the display or presentation is that a reasonable person against which the term is to operate ought to have noticed it.

This definition deals only with requirements that a term be conspicuous (or noted conspicuously) that are stated in particular provisions of the Uniform Commercial Code. Other protective doctrines designed to assure that assent is meaningful that are found in law outside the UCC may also apply. See Section 1-103(b).

11. "Consumer." Derived from Section 9-102(a)(25).

12. "Contract." Except for minor stylistic changes, identical to former Section 1-201.

13. "Creditor." Unchanged from former Section 1-201.

14. "Defendant." Except for minor stylistic changes, identical to former Section 1-201, which was derived from Section 76, Uniform Sales Act.

15. "Delivery." Derived from former Section 1-201. The reference to certificated securities in a pre-2022 version was deleted in light of the more specific treatment of the matter in Section 8-301. The definition also was revised to accommodate electronic documents of title. Control of an electronic document of title is defined in Article 7 (Section 7-106). Another revision in the 2022 Amendments conformed the reference to chattel paper to the revised definition of that term and the revised methods of perfection. See Sections 9-102(a)(11) (defining "chattel paper"); 9-314 (perfection by possession and control of chattel paper).

16. "Document of title." Unchanged from former Section 1-201, which was derived from Section 76, Uniform Sales Act. By making it explicit that the obligation or designation of a third party as "bailee" is essential to a document of title, this definition clearly rejects any such result as obtained in *Hixson v. Ward*, 254 Ill. App. 505 (1929), which treated a conditional sales contract as a document of title. Also the definition is left open so that new types of documents may be included. It is unforeseeable what documents may one day serve the essential purpose now filled by warehouse receipts and bills of lading. Truck transport has already opened up problems which do not fit the patterns of practice resting upon the assumption that a draft can move through banking channels faster than the goods themselves can reach their destination. There lie ahead air transport and such probabilities as teletype transmission of what may some day be regarded commercially as "Documents of Title." The definition is stated in terms of the function of the documents with the intention that any document which gains commercial recognition as accomplishing the desired result shall be included within its scope. Fungible goods are adequately identified within the language of the definition by identification of the mass of which they are a part.

Dock warrants were within the Sales Act definition of document of title apparently for the purpose of recognizing a valid tender by means of such paper. In current commercial practice a dock warrant or receipt is a kind of interim certificate issued by steamship companies upon delivery of the goods at the dock, entitling a designated person to have issued to him at the company's office a bill of lading. The receipt itself is invariably nonnegotiable in form although it may indicate that a negotiable bill is to be forthcoming. Such a document is not within the general compass of the definition, although trade usage may in some cases entitle such paper to be treated as a document of title. If the dock receipt actually represents a storage obligation undertaken by the shipping company, then it is a warehouse receipt within this section regardless of the name given to the instrument.

The goods must be "described," but the description may be by marks or labels and may be qualified in such a way as to disclaim personal knowledge of the issuer regarding contents or condition. However, baggage and parcel checks and similar "tokens" of storage which identify stored goods only as those received in exchange for the token are not covered by this Article.

The definition is broad enough to include an airway bill.

A document of title may be either tangible or electronic. Paper documents of title are "tangible documents of title." Electronic documents of title are documents that are stored in an electronic medium instead of in tangible form. "Electronic" is defined in paragraph 16A. As to reissuing a document of title in an alternative medium, see Article 7, Section 7-105. Control for electronic documents of title is defined in Article 7 (Section 7-106).

16A. "Electronic." The basic nature of most modern technologies and the need for a recognized, single term warrants the use of "electronic" as the defined term, even though not all technologies listed may be technically "electronic" in nature. The definition is intended to be applied broadly as new technologies develop. The term must be construed broadly in light of developing technologies in order to validate commercial transactions regardless of the medium used by the parties to document them. See generally Uniform Electronic Transactions Act, Section 2, Comment 4.

17. "Fault." Derived from former Section 1-201. "Default" has been added to the list of events constituting fault.

18. "Fungible goods." Derived from former Section 1-201. References to securities have been deleted because Article 8 no longer uses the term "fungible" to describe securities. Accordingly, this provision now defines the concept only in the context of goods.

19. "Genuine." Unchanged from former Section 1-201.

20. "Good faith." Former Section 1-201(19) defined "good faith" simply as honesty in fact; the definition contained no element of commercial reasonableness. Initially, that definition applied throughout the Code with only one exception. Former Section 2-103(1)(b) provided that in that article " 'good faith' in the case of a merchant means honesty in fact and the observance of reasonable commercial standards of fair dealing in the trade." This alternative definition was limited in applicability though because it applied only to transactions within the scope of Article 2 and it applied only to merchants.

Over time, however, amendments to the Uniform Commercial Code brought the Article 2 merchant concept of good faith (subjective honesty and objective commercial standards of fair dealing) into other Articles. First, Article 2A explicitly incorporated the Article 2 standard. Then, other Articles broadened the applicability of that standard by adopting it for all parties rather than just for merchants. Finally, Articles 2 and 2A were amended to apply the standard to non-merchants as well as merchants. All of these definitions are comprised of two elements—honesty in fact *and* the observance of reasonable commercial standards of fair dealing. Only revised Article 5 continued to define "good faith" solely in terms of subjective honesty, and Article 6 (in the few states that have not chosen to delete the Article) is without a definition of "good faith." (It should be noted, though, that, while revised Article 6 did not define good faith, Comment 2 to revised Section 6-102 states that "this Article adopts the definition of 'good faith' in Article 1 in all cases, even when the buyer is a merchant.")

Thus, the definition of "good faith" in this section merely confirms what has been the case for a number of years as Articles of the UCC have been amended or revised—the obligation of "good faith," applicable in each Article, is to be interpreted in the context of all Articles except for Article 5 as including both the subjective element of honesty in fact and the objective element of the observance of reasonable commercial standards of fair dealing. As a result, both the subjective and objective elements are part of the standard of "good faith," whether that obligation is specifically referenced in another Article of the Code (other than Article 5) or is provided by this Article.

Of course, as noted in the statutory text, the definition of "good faith" in this section does not apply when the narrower definition of "good faith" in revised Article 5 is applicable.

As noted above, the definition of "good faith" in this section requires not only honesty in fact but also "observance of reasonable commercial standards of fair dealing." Although "fair dealing" is a broad term that must be defined in context, it is clear that it is concerned with the fairness of conduct rather than the care with which an act is performed. This is an entirely different concept than whether a party exercised ordinary care in conducting a transaction. Both concepts are to be determined in the light of reasonable commercial standards, but those standards in each case are directed to different aspects of commercial conduct. See, e.g., Sections 3-103(a)(9) and 4-104(c) and Comment 4 to Section 3-103.

21. "Holder." The definition has been reorganized for clarity and amended to provide for electronic negotiable documents of title. The definition excludes persons who have control of an electronic document of title pursuant to Section 7-106(g) through the acknowledgment by a person in control. This ensures that an issuer of a document can ascertain who is entitled to delivery from the document itself or from the system in which the document is recorded, without any obligation to look behind the document or the system to ascertain the identity of an undisclosed principal.

22. "Insolvency proceedings." Unchanged from former Section 1-201.

23. "Insolvent." Derived from former Section 1-201. The three tests of insolvency—"generally ceased to pay debts in the ordinary course of business other than as a result of a bona fide dispute as to them," "unable to pay debts as they become due," and "insolvent within the meaning of the federal bankruptcy law"—are expressly set up as alternative tests and must be approached from a commercial standpoint.

24. "Money." The definition of "money" applies to the term only as used in the Uniform Commercial Code. The definition does not determine whether an asset constitutes "money" for other purposes. Only something currently authorized or adopted as a medium of exchange by a government can be money. As further elaborated in the second sentence of the definition, adoption by a government may occur through establishment by an intergovernmental organization or pursuant to an agreement between governments. Coins and pager currency previously, but not currently, authorized or adopted as a medium of exchange by a government, and currently owned and traded only for their numismatic or historical value, are not money.

An electronic medium of exchange established pursuant to a country's law and that is recorded and transferable in a system that did not exist and did not operate for that medium of exchange before the electronic medium of exchange was authorized or adopted by the country's government also constitutes money. This is so even if ownership is established or maintained through a system not operated by the government. In contrast, an existing medium of exchange created or distributed by one or more private persons is not money solely because the government of one or more countries later authorizes or adopts the pre-existing medium of exchange.

Although the term "money" is used in several articles, the definition is particularly significant under Article 9. Under the pre-2022 version of this definition, money was generally understood to include only tangible coins, bills, notes, and the like, although the statutory text did not explicitly so limit the term. This worked well under Article 9, which provided that the only method of perfecting a security interest in money as original collateral was by taking possession of it. See pre-2022 Section 9-312(b)(3). The 2022 revised definition of money in Section 1-201(b)(24) is broader and includes both "tangible money" and "electronic money" (new defined types of collateral under the 2022 revisions to Article 9). As under the pre-2022 Article

9, a security interest in tangible money as original collateral may be perfected only by possession. Section 9-312(b)(3). A security interest in electronic money as original collateral may be perfected only by control. Section 9-102(a)(31A) (defining "electronic money"); 9-312(b)(4) (perfection by control for electronic money). Note that the definition of "money" in Section 9-102(a)(54A) is narrower in two respects than the definition in this section—the Article 9 definition excludes deposit accounts and money in electronic form that cannot be subjected to control under Section 9-105A. See Section 9-102(a)(54A).

Examples: The following examples illustrate the definition of "money."

> **Example 1:** Nation A enacts legislation authorizing or adopting an existing cryptocurrency (spitcoin), created on a private blockchain, as a medium of exchange. Because spitcoin was recorded and transferable in a system that existed and operated for that cryptocurrency before the electronic record was authorized or adopted by Nation A, spitcoin does not become "money" under this definition as a result of Nation A's legislation.
>
> **Example 2**: Nation B creates a new cryptocurrency (beebuck) and authorizes or adopts it as a medium of exchange. Beebuck is "money." Beebuck is not recorded and transferable in a system that existed and operated for that cryptocurrency before the electronic record was authorized or adopted by Nation B.
>
> **Example 3:** Nation C enacts legislation authorizing or adopting as a medium of exchange beebuck, the cryptocurrency previously adopted by Nation B in Example 2. Although beebuck is recorded and transferable in a system that existed and operated for beebuck before it was authorized or adopted by Nation C, beebuck was already money when authorized or adopted by Nation C. Consequently, beebuck is "money." Nation C's action had no relevance or effect on the characterization of beebuck as money.

25. "Organization." The former definition of this word has been replaced with the standard definition used in acts prepared by the National Conference of Commissioners on Uniform State Laws. A protected series formed under the Uniform Protected Series Act (2017) is a "person." See PEB Commentary No. 23, dated February 24, 2021. The Commentary is available at https://www.ali.org/peb-ucc.

26. "Party." Substantively identical to former Section 1-201. Mention of a party includes, of course, a person acting through an agent. However, where an agent comes into opposition or contrast to the principal, particular account is taken of that situation.

27. "Person." A previous definition of this term was replaced with the standard language used in acts prepared by the National Conference of Commissioners on Uniform State Laws. This definition recognizes the wide range of subjects that can enjoy legal rights and possess legal duties, including the catchall residual category of "any other legal or commercial entity." See, e.g., John Chipman Gray, The Nature and Sources of the Law 27 (Roland Gray rev., 2d ed., The MacMillan Co. 1931) ("a 'person' is a subject of legal rights and duties"). For additional authorities, see PEB Commentary No. 23, n.5. The reference to a "public corporation" in the pre-2022 text of the definition has been deleted as unnecessary and duplicative of other examples in the definition of entities that are persons.

The second sentence of the definition provides needed clarity as to the status of a protected series for purposes of the Uniform Commercial Code. See PEB Commentary No. 23. Several states have enacted statutes that provide for protected series within a limited liability company or other unincorporated organization. These statutes afford rights and impose duties upon a protected series and generally empower a protected series to conduct its own activities under its own name. The types of protected series that are included as persons under the definition include, but are not limited to, those established under the Uniform Protected Series Act.

Providing that a protected series is a "person" for purposes of the enacting state's Uniform Commercial Code will expressly permit a protected series, whether created under the law of the enacting state or of another jurisdiction, to be a "seller" or a "buyer" under Article 2, a "lessor" or a "lessee" under Article 2A, or an "organization." It also permits a protected series to be a "debtor" under Article 9, and, if the law under which the protected series is organized requires a public filing for the protected series to be recognized under that law, a "registered organization" under Article 9.

A protected series formed under the Uniform Protected Series Act (2017) is a "person." See PEB Commentary No. 23, dated February 24, 2021. The Commentary is available at https://www.ali.ord/peb-ucc.

28. "Present value." This definition was formerly contained within the definition of "security interest" in former Section 1-201(37).

29. "Purchase." Derived from former Section 1-201. The form of definition has been changed from "includes" to "means."

30. "Purchaser." Unchanged from former Section 1-201.

31. "Record." Derived from Section 9-102(a)(69).

32. "Remedy." Unchanged from former Section 1-201. The purpose is to make it clear that both remedy and right (as defined) include those remedial rights of "self help" which are among the most important bodies of rights under the Uniform Commercial Code, remedial rights being those to which an aggrieved party may resort on its own.

33. "Representative." Concerning developments in technology, including, for example, contract formation in electronic environments, automated transactions, and electronic agents, see Section 1-103, Comment 2.

34. "Right." Except for minor stylistic changes, identical to former Section 1-201.

35. "Security interest." The definition is the first paragraph of the definition of "security interest" in former Section 1-201, with minor stylistic changes. The remaining portion of that definition has been moved to Section 1-203. Note that, because of the scope of Article 9, the term includes the interest of certain outright buyers of certain kinds of property.

36. "Send." The definition of "send" adopts pre-2022 Section 9-102(a)(75). The explicit statement in the previous text of this definition on the appropriateness of sending to an agreed-upon address or to an "address reasonable under the circumstances" was limited to "the case of an instrument." The definition no longer includes that limitation relating to an instrument. Moreover, it is common for parties to rely on their agreement as to appropriate addresses for purposes of notifications and communications. Nothing in the definition or in the Uniform Commercial Code limits the effectiveness of sending a record or notification to an address that has been agreed upon by affected persons. See generally Sections 1-103 and 1-302.

37. "Sign." The definition of "sign" adopted in the 2022 Amendments is broad—it encompasses the authentication or adoption of all records, not just writings. The definition replaces the definition of "signed" in pre-2022 texts of this Article. This definition also makes it clear that, as the terms "sign," "signed," and "signature" are used in the Uniform Commercial Code, a complete signature is not necessary. A symbol may be printed, stamped, or written on, or electronically attached or associated with, a record. It may be by initials or by thumbprint or by electronic symbol, sound, or process. It may be on any part of a writing or other record and in appropriate cases may be found in a billhead or letterhead. No catalog of possible situations can be complete and the court must use common sense and commercial experience in passing upon these matters. The question always is whether the symbol, sound, or process was executed or adopted by the party with present intention to authenticate or adopt the record.

A "writing," which necessarily is in tangible form, must exist at the time it is signed and must be signed by the execution or adoption of a tangible symbol to qualify as a signed writing. A writing adopted only by use of an electronic symbol, sound, or process would not be a signed writing until and unless it results in a tangible symbol being on or affixed to the writing. Moreover, if an electronic record is electronically signed and subsequently printed in tangible form, the resulting writing would not constitute a signed writing unless and until some action is taken with "present intent to authenticate or adopt" the writing.

Concerning developments in technology, including, for example, contract formation in electronic environments, automated transactions, and electronic agents, see also Section 1-103, Comment 2.

38. "State." This is the standard definition of the term used in acts prepared by the National Conference of Commissioners on Uniform State Laws.

39. "Surety." This definition makes it clear that "surety" includes all secondary obligors, not just those whose obligation refers to the person obligated as a surety. As to the nature of secondary obligations generally, see Restatement (Third), Suretyship and Guaranty Section 1 (1996).

40. "Term." Unchanged from former Section 1-201.

41. "Unauthorized signature." Unchanged from former Section 1-201.

42. "Warehouse receipt." Unchanged from former Section 1-201, which was derived from Section 76(1), Uniform Sales Act; Section 1, Uniform Warehouse Receipts Act. Receipts issued by a field warehouse are included, provided the warehouseman and the depositor of the goods are different persons.

43. "Written" or **"writing."** Several amendments to the Uniform Commercial Code over the years have replaced the terms "written" and "writing" with the term "record," defined in paragraph (31) and also in some other Articles. Pursuant to the 2022 Amendments, additional references to the terms "writing," "writings," and "written" have been replaced by "record." For example, the 2022 revisions to Articles 2 and 2A made these changes in provisions where an affected party may be assumed to have assented to the use of a record that is not a writing. Where references to those terms remain in Articles 2 and 2A, the use by parties of a record other than a writing may be given effect for purposes of those Articles under law other than the Uniform Commercial Code, such as the Electronic Signatures in Global and National Commerce Act, 15 U.S.C. Section 7001 et seq., and the Uniform Electronic Transactions Act. See Sections 2-207, Comment 8; 2A-102, Comment (g).

§ 1-202. Notice; Knowledge.

(a) Subject to subsection (f), a person has "notice" of a fact if the person:

(1) has actual knowledge of it;

(2) has received a notice or notification of it; or

(3) from all the facts and circumstances known to the person at the time in question, has reason to know that it exists.

(b) "Knowledge" means actual knowledge. "Knows" has a corresponding meaning.

(c) "Discover", "learn", or words of similar import refer to knowledge rather than to reason to know.

(d) A person "notifies" or "gives" a notice or notification to another person by taking such steps as may be reasonably required to inform the other person in ordinary course, whether or not the other person actually comes to know of it.

(e) Subject to subsection (f), a person "receives" a notice or notification when:

(1) it comes to that person's attention; or

(2) it is duly delivered in a form reasonable under the circumstances at the place of business through which the contract was made or at another location held out by that person as the place for receipt of such communications.

(f) Notice, knowledge, or a notice or notification received by an organization is effective for a particular transaction from the time it is brought to the attention of the individual conducting that transaction and, in any event, from the time it would have been brought to the individual's attention if the organization had exercised due diligence. An organization exercises due diligence if it maintains reasonable routines for communicating significant information to the person conducting the transaction and there is reasonable compliance with the routines. Due diligence does not require an individual acting for the organization to communicate information unless the communication is part of the individual's regular duties or the individual has reason to know of the transaction and that the transaction would be materially affected by the information.

Official Comment

Source: Derived from former Section 1-201(25)-(27).

Changes from Former Law: These provisions are substantive rather than purely definitional. Accordingly, they have been relocated from Section 1-201 to this section. The reference to the "forgotten notice" doctrine has been deleted.

1. Under subsection (a), a person has notice of a fact when, *inter alia*, the person has received a notification of the fact in question.

2. As provided in subsection (d), the word "notifies" is used when the essential fact is the proper dispatch of the notice, not its receipt. Compare "Send." When the essential fact is the other party's receipt of the notice, that is stated. Subsection (e) states when a notification is received.

3. Subsection (f) makes clear that notice, knowledge, or a notification, although "received," for instance, by a clerk in Department A of an organization, is effective for a transaction conducted in Department B only from the time when it was or should have been communicated to the individual conducting that transaction.

§ 1-203. Lease Distinguished from Security Interest.

(a) Whether a transaction in the form of a lease creates a lease or security interest is determined by the facts of each case.

(b) A transaction in the form of a lease creates a security interest if the consideration that the lessee is to pay the lessor for the right to possession and use of the goods is an obligation for the term of the lease and is not subject to termination by the lessee, and:

(1) the original term of the lease is equal to or greater than the remaining economic life of the goods;

(2) the lessee is bound to renew the lease for the remaining economic life of the goods or is bound to become the owner of the goods;

(3) the lessee has an option to renew the lease for the remaining economic life of the goods for no additional consideration or for nominal additional consideration upon compliance with the lease agreement; or

(4) the lessee has an option to become the owner of the goods for no additional consideration or for nominal additional consideration upon compliance with the lease agreement.

(c) A transaction in the form of a lease does not create a security interest merely because:

(1) the present value of the consideration the lessee is obligated to pay the lessor for the right to possession and use of the goods is substantially equal to or is greater than the fair market value of the goods at the time the lease is entered into;

(2) the lessee assumes risk of loss of the goods;

(3) the lessee agrees to pay, with respect to the goods, taxes, insurance, filing, recording, or registration fees, or service or maintenance costs;

(4) the lessee has an option to renew the lease or to become the owner of the goods;

(5) the lessee has an option to renew the lease for a fixed rent that is equal to or greater than the reasonably predictable fair market rent for the use of the goods for the term of the renewal at the time the option is to be performed; or

(6) the lessee has an option to become the owner of the goods for a fixed price that is equal to or greater than the reasonably predictable fair market value of the goods at the time the option is to be performed.

(d) Additional consideration is nominal if it is less than the lessee's reasonably predictable cost of performing under the lease agreement if the option is not exercised. Additional consideration is not nominal if:

(1) when the option to renew the lease is granted to the lessee, the rent is stated to be the fair market rent for the use of the goods for the term of the renewal determined at the time the option is to be performed; or

(2) when the option to become the owner of the goods is granted to the lessee, the price is stated to be the fair market value of the goods determined at the time the option is to be performed.

(e) The "remaining economic life of the goods" and "reasonably predictable" fair market rent, fair market value, or cost of performing under the lease agreement must be determined with reference to the facts and circumstances at the time the transaction is entered into.

Official Comment

Source: Former Section 1-201(37).

Changes from Former Law: This section is substantively identical to those portions of former Section 1-201(37) that distinguished "true" leases from security interests, except that the definition of "present value" formerly embedded in Section 1-201(37) has been placed in Section 1-201(28).

1. An interest in personal property or fixtures which secures payment or performance of an obligation is a "security interest." See Section 1-201(37). Security interests are sometimes created by transactions in the form of leases. Because it can be difficult to distinguish leases that create security interests from those that do not, this section provides rules that govern the determination of whether a transaction in the form of a lease creates a security interest.

2. One of the reasons it was decided to codify the law with respect to leases was to resolve an issue that created considerable confusion in the courts: what is a lease? The confusion existed, in part, due to the last two sentences of the definition of security interest in the 1978 Official Text of the Act, Section 1-201(37). The confusion was compounded by the rather considerable change in the federal, state and local tax laws and accounting rules as they relate to leases of goods. The answer is important because the definition of lease determines not only the rights and remedies of the parties to the lease but also those of third parties. If a transaction creates a lease and not a security interest, the lessee's interest in the goods is limited to its leasehold estate; the residual interest in the goods belongs to the lessor. This has significant implications to the lessee's creditors. "On common law theory, the lessor, since he has not parted with title, is entitled to full protection against the lessee's creditors and trustee in bankruptcy...." 1 G. Gilmore, *Security Interests in Personal Property*, Section 3.6, at 76 (1965).

Under pre-UCC chattel security law there was generally no requirement that the lessor file the lease, a financing statement, or the like, to enforce the lease agreement against the lessee or any third party; the Article on Secured Transactions (Article 9) did not change the common law in that respect. Coogan, Leasing and the Uniform Commercial Code, in *Equipment Leasing—Leveraged Leasing* 681, 700 n.25, 729 n.80 (2d ed. 1980). The Article on Leases (Article 2A) did not change the law in that respect, except for leases of fixtures. Section 2A-309. An examination of the common law will not provide an adequate answer to the question of what is a lease. The definition of security interest in Section 1-201(37) of the 1978 Official Text of the Act provided that the Article on Secured Transactions (Article 9) governs security interests disguised as leases, i.e., leases intended as security; however, the definition became vague and outmoded.

Lease is defined in Article 2A as a transfer of the right to possession and use of goods for a term, in return for consideration. Section 2A-103(1)(j). The definition continues by stating that the retention or creation of a security interest is not a lease. Thus, the task of sharpening the line between true leases and security interests disguised as leases continues to be a function of this Article.

This section begins where Section 1-201(b)(35) leaves off. It draws a sharper line between leases and security interests disguised as leases to create greater certainty in commercial transactions.

Prior to enactment of the rules now codified in this section, the 1978 Official Text of Section 1-201(37) provided that whether a lease was intended as security (i.e., a security interest disguised as a lease) was to be determined from the facts of each case; however, (a) the inclusion of an option to purchase did not itself make the lease one intended for security, and (b) an agreement that upon compliance with the terms of the lease the lessee would become, or had the option to become, the owner of the property for no additional consideration, or for a nominal consideration, did make the lease one intended for security.

Reference to the intent of the parties to create a lease or security interest led to unfortunate results. In discovering intent, courts relied upon factors that were thought to be more consistent with sales or loans than leases. Most of these criteria, however, were as applicable to true leases as to security interests. Examples include the typical net lease provisions, a purported lessor's lack of storage facilities or its character as a financing party rather than a dealer in goods. Accordingly, this section contains no reference to the parties' intent.

Subsections (a) and (b) were originally taken from Section 1(2) of the Uniform Conditional Sales Act (act withdrawn 1943), modified to reflect current leasing practice. Thus, reference to the case law prior to the incorporation of those concepts in this article will provide a useful source of precedent. Gilmore, *Security Law, Formalism and Article 9*, 47 Neb. L. Rev. 659, 671 (1968). Whether a transaction creates a lease or a security interest continues to be determined by the facts of each case. Subsection (b) further provides that a transaction creates a security interest if the lessee has an obligation to continue paying consideration for the term of the lease, if the obligation is not terminable by the lessee (thus correcting early statutory gloss, e.g., *In re Royer's Bakery, Inc.*, 1 U.C.C. Rep. Serv. (Callaghan) 342 (Bankr. E.D. Pa. 1963)) and if one of four additional tests is met. The first of these four tests, subparagraph (1), is that the original lease term is equal to or greater than the remaining economic life of the goods. The second of these tests, subparagraph (2), is that the lessee is either bound to renew the lease for the remaining economic life of the goods or to become the owner of the goods. *In re Gehrke Enters.*, 1 Bankr. 647, 651-52 (Bankr. W.D. Wis. 1979). The third of these tests, subparagraph (3), is whether the lessee has an option to renew the lease for the remaining economic life of the goods for no additional consideration or for nominal additional consideration, which is defined later in this section. *In re Celeryvale Transp.*, 44 Bankr. 1007, 1014-15 (Bankr. E.D. Tenn. 1984). The fourth of these tests, subparagraph (4), is whether the lessee has an option to become the owner of the goods for no additional consideration or for nominal additional consideration. All of these tests focus on economics, not the intent of the parties. *In re Berge*, 32 Bankr. 370, 371-73 (Bankr. W.D. Wis. 1983).

The focus on economics is reinforced by subsection (c). It states that a transaction does not create a security interest merely because the transaction has certain characteristics listed therein. Subparagraph (1) has no statutory derivative; it states that a full payout lease does not *per se* create a security interest. *Rushton v. Shea*, 419 F. Supp. 1349, 1365 (D. Del. 1976). Subparagraphs (2) and (3) provide the same regarding the provisions of the typical net lease. Compare *All-States Leasing Co. v. Ochs*, 42 Or. App. 319, 600 P.2d 899 (Ct. App. 1979), with *In re Tillery*, 571 F.2d 1361 (5th Cir. 1978). Subparagraph (4) restates and expands the provisions of the 1978 Official Text of Section 1-201(37) to make clear that the option can be to buy or renew. Subparagraphs (5) and (6) treat fixed price options and provide that fair market value must be determined at the time the transaction is entered into. Compare *Arnold Mach. Co. v. Balls*, 624 P.2d 678 (Utah 1981), with *Aoki v. Shepherd Mach. Co.*, 665 F.2d 941 (9th Cir. 1982).

The relationship of subsection (b) to subsection (c) deserves to be explored. The fixed price purchase option provides a useful example. A fixed price purchase option in a lease does not of itself create a security interest. This is particularly true if the fixed price is equal to or greater than the reasonably predictable fair market value of the goods at the time the option is to be performed. A security interest is created only if the option price is nominal and the conditions stated in the introduction to the second paragraph of this subsection are met. There is a set of purchase options whose fixed price is less than fair market value but greater than nominal that must be determined on the facts of each case to ascertain whether the transaction in which the option is included creates a lease or a security interest.

It was possible to provide for various other permutations and combinations with respect to options to purchase and renew. For example, this section could have stated a rule to govern the facts of *In re Marhoefer Packing Co.*, 674 F.2d 1139 (7th Cir. 1982). This was not done because it would unnecessarily complicate the definition. Further development of this rule is left to the courts.

Subsections (d) and (e) provide definitions and rules of construction.

§ 1-204. Value.

Except as otherwise provided in Articles 3, 4, 5, [6], and 12, a person gives value for rights if the person acquires them:

(1) in return for a binding commitment to extend credit or for the extension of immediately available credit, whether or not drawn upon and whether or not a charge-back is provided for in the event of difficulties in collection;

(2) as security for, or in total or partial satisfaction of, a preexisting claim;

(3) by accepting delivery under a preexisting contract for purchase; or

(4) in return for any consideration sufficient to support a simple contract.

Official Comment

Source: Former Section 1-201(44).

Changes from Former Law: Unchanged from former Section 1-201, which was derived from Sections 25, 26, 27, 191, Uniform Negotiable Instruments Law; Section 76, Uniform Sales Act; Section 53, Uniform Bills of Lading Act; Section 58, Uniform Warehouse Receipts Act; Section 22(1), Uniform Stock Transfer Act; Section 1, Uniform Trust Receipts Act. These provisions are substantive rather than purely definitional. Accordingly, they have been relocated from former Section 1-201 to this section.

1. Historically, most Uniform Acts in the commercial law field have carried definitions of "value." Those definitions provided that value was any consideration sufficient to support a simple contract, including the taking of property in satisfaction of or as security for a pre-existing claim. Subsections (1), (2), and (4) in substance continue the definitions of "value" in the earlier acts. Subsection (3) makes explicit that "value" is also given in a third situation: where a buyer by taking delivery under a pre-existing contract converts a contingent into a fixed obligation.

This definition is not applicable to Articles 3 and 4, but the express inclusion of immediately available credit as value follows the separate definitions in those Articles. See Sections 4-208, 4-209, 3-303. A bank or other financing agency which in good faith makes advances against property held as collateral becomes a bona fide purchaser of that property even though provision may be made for charge-back in case of trouble. Checking credit is "immediately available" within the meaning of this section if the bank would be subject to an action for slander of credit in case checks drawn against the credit were dishonored, and when a charge-back is not discretionary with the bank, but may only be made when difficulties in collection arise in connection with the specific transaction involved. Article 12 adopts the substance of the Article 3 definition. See Section 12-102(a)(4).

§ 1-205. Reasonable Time; Seasonableness.

(a) Whether a time for taking an action required by [the Uniform Commercial Code] is reasonable depends on the nature, purpose, and circumstances of the action.

(b) An action is taken seasonably if it is taken at or within the time agreed or, if no time is agreed, at or within a reasonable time.

Official Comment

Source: Former Section 1-204(2)-(3).

Changes from Former Law: This section is derived from subsections (2) and (3) of former Section 1-204. Subsection (1) of that section is now incorporated in Section 1-302(b).

1. Subsection (a) makes it clear that requirements that actions be taken within a "reasonable" time are to be applied in the transactional context of the particular action.

2. Under subsection (b), the agreement that fixes the time need not be part of the main agreement, but may occur separately. Notice also that under the definition of "agreement" (Section 1-201) the circumstances of the transaction, including course of dealing or usages of trade or course of performance may be material. On the question what is a reasonable time these matters will often be important.

§ 1-206. Presumptions.

Whenever [the Uniform Commercial Code] creates a "presumption" with respect to a fact, or provides that a fact is "presumed," the trier of fact must find the existence of the fact unless and until evidence is introduced that supports a finding of its nonexistence.

Legislative Note: Former Section 1-206, a Statute of Frauds for sales of "kinds of personal property not otherwise covered," has been deleted. The other articles of the Uniform Commercial Code make individual determinations as to requirements for memorializing transactions within their scope, so that the primary effect of former Section 1-206 was to impose a writing requirement on sales transactions not otherwise governed by the UCC. Deletion of former Section 1-206 does not constitute a recommendation to legislatures as to whether such sales transactions should be covered by a Statute of Frauds; rather, it reflects a determination that there is no need for uniform commercial law to resolve that issue.

Official Comment

Source: Former Section 1-201(31).

Changes from Former Law: None, other than stylistic changes.

1. Several sections of the Uniform Commercial Code state that there is a "presumption" as to a certain fact, or that the fact is "presumed." This section, derived from the definition appearing in former Section 1-201(31), indicates the effect of those provisions on the proof process.

PART 3. TERRITORIAL APPLICABILITY AND GENERAL RULES

§ 1-301. Territorial Applicability; Parties' Power to Choose Applicable Law.

(a) Except as otherwise provided in this section, when a transaction bears a reasonable relation to this state and also to another state or nation the parties may agree that the law either of this state or of such other state or nation shall govern their rights and duties.

(b) In the absence of an agreement effective under subsection (a), and except as provided in subsection (c), [the Uniform Commercial Code] applies to transactions bearing an appropriate relation to this state.

(c) If one of the following provisions of [the Uniform Commercial Code] specifies the applicable law, that provision governs and a contrary agreement is effective only to the extent permitted by the law so specified:

(1) Section 2-402;
(2) Sections 2A-105 and 2A-106;
(3) Section 4-102;
(4) Section 4A-507;
(5) Section 5-116;
[(6) Section 6-103;]
(7) Section 8-110;
(8) Sections 9-301 through 9-307;
(9) Section 12-107.

Official Comment

Source: Former Section 1-105.

Changes from former law: This section is substantively identical to former Section 1-105. Changes in language are stylistic only.

1. Subsection (a) states affirmatively the right of the parties to a multi-state transaction or a transaction involving foreign trade to choose their own law. That right is subject to the firm rules stated in the sections listed in subsection (c), and is limited to jurisdictions to which the transaction bears a "reasonable relation." In general, the test of "reasonable relation" is similar to that laid down by the Supreme Court in *Seeman v. Philadelphia Warehouse Co.*, 274 U.S. 403, 47 S. Ct. 626, 71 L. Ed. 1123 (1927). Ordinarily the law chosen must be that of a jurisdiction where a significant enough portion of the making or performance of the contract is to occur or occurs. But an agreement as to choice of law may sometimes take effect as a shorthand expression of the intent of the parties as to matters governed by their agreement, even though the transaction has no significant contact with the jurisdiction chosen.

2. Where there is no agreement as to the governing law, the Act is applicable to any transaction having an "appropriate" relation to any state which enacts it. Of course, the Act applies to any transaction which takes place in its entirety in a state which has enacted the Act. But the mere fact that suit is brought in a state does not make it appropriate to apply the substantive law of that state. Cases where a relation to the enacting state is not "appropriate" include, for example, those where the parties have clearly contracted on the basis of some other law, as where the law of the place of contracting and the law of the place of contemplated performance are the same and are contrary to the law under the Code.

3. Where a transaction has significant contacts with a state which has enacted the Act and also with other jurisdictions, the question what relation is "appropriate" is left to judicial decision. In deciding that question, the court is not strictly bound by precedents established in other contexts. Thus a conflict-of-laws decision refusing to apply a purely local statute or rule of law to a particular multi-state transaction may not be valid precedent for refusal to apply the Code in an analogous situation. Application of the Code in such circumstances may be justified by its comprehensiveness, by the policy of uniformity, and by the fact that it is in large part a reformulation and restatement of the law merchant and of the understanding of a business community which transcends state and even national boundaries. Compare *Global Commerce Corp. v. Clark-Babbitt Industries, Inc.*, 239 F.2d 716, 719 (2d Cir. 1956). In particular, where a transaction is governed in large part by the Code, application of another law to some detail of performance because of an accident of geography may violate the commercial understanding of the parties.

4. Subsection (c) spells out essential limitations on the parties' right to choose the applicable law. Especially in Article 9 parties taking a security interest or asked to extend credit which may be subject to a security interest must have sure ways to find out whether and where to file and where to look for possible existing filings.

5. Sections 9-301 through 9-307 should be consulted as to the rules for perfection of security interests and agricultural liens and the effect of perfection and nonperfection and priority. In transactions to which the Hague Securities Convention applies, the requirements for foreclosure and the like, the characterization of a transfer as being outright or by way of security, and certain other issues will generally be governed by the law specified in the account agreement. See PEB Commentary No. 19.

6. This section is subject to Section 1-102, which states the scope of Article 1. As that section indicates, the rules of Article 1, including this section, apply to a transaction to the extent that transaction is governed by one of the other Articles of the Uniform Commercial Code.

[Ed. Note. This text represents the editors' resolution of some minor ambiguities in the adoption of this Comment.]

§ 1-302. Variation by Agreement.

(a) Except as otherwise provided in subsection (b) or elsewhere in [the Uniform Commercial Code], the effect of provisions of [the Uniform Commercial Code] may be varied by agreement.

(b) The obligations of good faith, diligence, reasonableness, and care prescribed by [the Uniform Commercial Code] may not be disclaimed by agreement. The parties, by agreement, may determine the standards by which the performance of those obligations is to be measured if those standards are not manifestly unreasonable. Whenever [the Uniform Commercial Code] requires an action to be taken within a reasonable time, a time that is not manifestly unreasonable may be fixed by agreement.

(c) The presence in certain provisions of [the Uniform Commercial Code] of the phrase "unless otherwise agreed", or words of similar import, does not imply that the effect of other provisions may not be varied by agreement under this section.

Official Comment

Source: Former Sections 1-102(3)-(4) and 1-204(1).

Changes: This section combines the rules from subsections (3) and (4) of former Section 1-102 and subsection (1) of former Section 1-204. No substantive changes are made.

1. Subsection (a) states affirmatively at the outset that freedom of contract is a principle of the Uniform Commercial Code: "the effect" of its provisions may be varied by "agreement." The meaning of the statute itself must be found in its text, including its definitions, and in appropriate extrinsic aids; it cannot be varied by agreement. But the Uniform Commercial Code seeks to avoid the type of interference with evolutionary growth found in pre-Code cases such as *Manhattan Co. v. Morgan*, 242 N.Y. 38, 150 N.E. 594 (1926). Thus, private parties cannot make an instrument negotiable within the meaning of Article 3 except as provided in Section 3-104; nor can they change the meaning of such terms as "bona fide purchaser," "holder in due course," or "due negotiation," as used in the Uniform Commercial Code. But an agreement can change the legal consequences that would otherwise flow from the provisions of the Uniform Commercial Code. "Agreement" here includes the effect given to course of dealing, usage of trade and course of performance by Sections 1-201 and 1-303; the effect of an agreement on the rights of third parties is left to specific provisions of the Uniform Commercial Code and to supplementary principles applicable under Section 1-103. The rights of third parties under Section 9-317 when a security interest is unperfected, for example, cannot be destroyed by a clause in the security agreement.

This principle of freedom of contract is subject to specific exceptions found elsewhere in the Uniform Commercial Code and to the general exception stated here. The specific exceptions vary in explicitness: the statute of frauds found in Section 2-201, for example, does not explicitly preclude oral waiver of the requirement of a writing, but a fair reading denies enforcement to such a waiver as part of the "contract" made unenforceable; Section 9-602, on the other hand, is a quite explicit limitation on freedom of contract. Under the exception for "the obligations of good faith, diligence, reasonableness and care prescribed by [the Uniform Commercial Code]," provisions of the Uniform Commercial Code prescribing such obligations are not to be disclaimed. However, the section also recognizes the prevailing practice of having agreements set forth standards by which due diligence is measured and explicitly provides that, in the absence of a showing that the standards manifestly are unreasonable, the agreement controls. In this connection, Section 1-303 incorporating into the agreement prior course of dealing and usages of trade is of particular importance.

Subsection (b) also recognizes that nothing is stronger evidence of a reasonable time than the fixing of such time by a fair agreement between the parties. However, provision is made for disregarding a clause which whether by inadvertence or overreaching fixes a time so unreasonable that it amounts to eliminating all remedy under the contract. The parties are not required to fix the most reasonable time but may fix any time which is not obviously unfair as judged by the time of contracting.

2. An agreement that varies the effect of provisions of the Uniform Commercial Code may do so by stating the rules that will govern in lieu of the provisions varied. Alternatively, the parties may vary the effect of such provisions by stating that their relationship will be governed by recognized bodies of rules or principles applicable to commercial transactions. Such bodies of rules or principles may include, for example, those that are promulgated by intergovernmental authorities such as UNCITRAL or Unidroit (see, e.g., Unidroit Principles of International Commercial Contracts), or non-legal codes such as trade codes.

3. Subsection (c) is intended to make it clear that, as a matter of drafting, phrases such as "unless otherwise agreed" have been used to avoid controversy as to whether the subject matter of a particular section does or does not fall within the exceptions to subsection (b), but absence of such words contains no negative implication since under subsection (b) the general and residual rule is that the effect of all provisions of the Uniform Commercial Code may be varied by agreement.

§ 1-303. Course of Performance, Course of Dealing, and Usage of Trade.

(a) A "course of performance" is a sequence of conduct between the parties to a particular transaction that exists if:

(1) the agreement of the parties with respect to the transaction involves repeated occasions for performance by a party; and

(2) the other party, with knowledge of the nature of the performance and opportunity for objection to it, accepts the performance or acquiesces in it without objection.

(b) A "course of dealing" is a sequence of conduct concerning previous transactions between the parties to a particular transaction that is fairly to be regarded as establishing a common basis of understanding for interpreting their expressions and other conduct.

(c) A "usage of trade" is any practice or method of dealing having such regularity of observance in a place, vocation, or trade as to justify an expectation that it will be observed with respect to the transaction in question. The existence and scope of such a usage must be proved as facts. If it is established that such a usage is embodied in a trade code or similar record, the interpretation of the record is a question of law.

(d) A course of performance or course of dealing between the parties or usage of trade in the vocation or trade in which they are engaged or of which they are or should be aware is relevant in ascertaining the meaning of the parties' agreement, may give particular meaning to specific terms of the agreement, and may supplement or qualify the terms of the agreement. A usage of trade applicable in the place in which part of the performance under the agreement is to occur may be so utilized as to that part of the performance.

(e) Except as otherwise provided in subsection (f), the express terms of an agreement and any applicable course of performance, course of dealing, or usage of trade must be construed whenever reasonable as consistent with each other. If such a construction is unreasonable:

(1) express terms prevail over course of performance, course of dealing, and usage of trade;

(2) course of performance prevails over course of dealing and usage of trade; and

(3) course of dealing prevails over usage of trade.

(f) Subject to Section 2-209, a course of performance is relevant to show a waiver or modification of any term inconsistent with the course of performance.

(g) Evidence of a relevant usage of trade offered by one party is not admissible unless that party has given the other party notice that the court finds sufficient to prevent unfair surprise to the other party.

Official Comment

Source: Former Sections 1-205, 2-208, and Section 2A-207.

Changes from Former Law: This section integrates the "course of performance" concept from Articles 2 and 2A into the principles of former Section 1-205, which deals with course of dealing and usage of trade. In so doing, the section slightly modifies the articulation of the course of performance rules to fit more comfortably with the approach and structure of former Section 1-205. There are also slight modifications to be more consistent with the definition of "agreement" in former Section 1-201(3). It should be noted that a course of performance that might otherwise establish a defense to the obligation of a party to a negotiable instrument is not available as a defense against a holder in due course who took the instrument without notice of that course of performance.

1. The Uniform Commercial Code rejects both the "lay-dictionary" and the "conveyancer's" reading of a commercial agreement. Instead the meaning of the agreement of the parties is to be determined by the language used by them and by their action, read and interpreted in the light of commercial practices and other surrounding circumstances. The measure and background for interpretation are set by the commercial context, which may explain and supplement even the language of a formal or final writing.

2. "Course of dealing," as defined in subsection (b), is restricted, literally, to a sequence of conduct between the parties previous to the agreement. A sequence of conduct after or under the agreement, however, is a "course of performance." "Course of dealing" may enter the agreement either by explicit provisions of the agreement or by tacit recognition.

3. The Uniform Commercial Code deals with "usage of trade" as a factor in reaching the commercial meaning of the agreement that the parties have made. The language used is to be interpreted as meaning what it may fairly be expected to mean to parties involved in the particular commercial transaction in a given locality or in a given vocation or trade. By adopting in this context the term "usage of trade," the Uniform Commercial Code expresses its intent to reject those cases which see evidence of "custom" as representing an effort to displace or negate "established rules of law." A distinction is to be drawn between mandatory rules of law such as the Statute of Frauds provisions of Article 2 on Sales whose very office is to control and restrict the actions of the parties, and which cannot be abrogated by agreement, or by a usage of trade, and those rules of law (such as those in Part 3 of Article 2 on Sales) which fill in points which the parties have not considered and in fact agreed upon. The latter rules hold "unless otherwise agreed" but yield to the contrary agreement of the parties. Part of the agreement of the parties to which such rules yield is to be sought for in the usages of trade which furnish the background and give particular meaning to the language used, and are the framework of common understanding controlling any general rules of law which hold only when there is no such understanding.

4. A usage of trade under subsection (c) must have the "regularity of observance" specified. The ancient English tests for "custom" are abandoned in this connection. Therefore, it is not required that a usage of trade be "ancient or immemorial," "universal," or the like. Under the requirement of subsection (c) full recognition is thus available for new usages and for usages currently observed by the great majority of decent dealers, even though dissidents ready to cut corners do not agree. There is room also for proper recognition of usage agreed upon by merchants in trade codes.

5. The policies of the Uniform Commercial Code controlling explicit unconscionable contracts and clauses (Sections 1-304, 2-302) apply to implicit clauses that rest on usage of trade and carry forward the policy underlying the ancient requirement that a custom or usage must be "reasonable." However, the emphasis is shifted. The very fact of commercial acceptance makes out a *prima facie* case that the usage is reasonable, and the burden is no longer on the usage to establish itself as being reasonable. But the anciently established policing of usage by the courts is continued to the extent necessary to cope with the situation arising if an unconscionable or dishonest practice should become standard.

6. Subsection (d), giving the prescribed effect to usages of which the parties "are or should be aware," reinforces the provision of subsection (c) requiring not universality but only the described "regularity of observance" of the practice or method. This subsection also reinforces the point of subsection (c) that such usages may be either general to trade or particular to a special branch of trade.

7. Although the definition of "agreement" in Section 1-201 includes the elements of course of performance, course of dealing, and usage of trade, the fact that express reference is made in some sections to those elements is not to be construed as carrying a contrary intent or implication elsewhere. Compare Section 1-302(c).

8. In cases of a well established line of usage varying from the general rules of the Uniform Commercial Code where the precise amount of the variation has not been worked out into a single standard, the party relying on the usage is entitled, in any event, to the minimum variation demonstrated. The whole is not to be disregarded because no particular line of detail has been established. In case a dominant pattern has been fairly evidenced, the party relying on the usage is entitled under this section to go to the trier of fact on the question of whether such dominant pattern has been incorporated into the agreement.

9. Subsection (g) is intended to insure that this Act's liberal recognition of the needs of commerce in regard to usage of trade shall not be made into an instrument of abuse.

§ 1-304. Obligation of Good Faith.

Every contract or duty within [the Uniform Commercial Code] imposes an obligation of good faith in its performance and enforcement.

Official Comment

Source: Former Section 1-203.

Changes from Former Law: Except for changing the form of reference to the Uniform Commercial Code, this section is identical to former Section 1-203.

1. This section sets forth a basic principle running throughout the Uniform Commercial Code. The principle is that in commercial transactions good faith is required in the performance and enforcement of all agreements or duties. While this duty is explicitly stated in some provisions of the Uniform Commercial Code, the applicability of the duty is broader than merely these situations and applies generally, as stated in this section, to the performance or enforcement of every contract or duty within this Act. It is further implemented by Section 1-303 on course of dealing, course of performance, and usage of trade. This section does not support an independent cause of action for failure to perform or enforce in good faith. Rather, this section means that a failure to perform or enforce, in good faith, a specific duty or obligation under the contract, constitutes a breach of that contract or makes unavailable, under the particular circumstances, a remedial right or power. This distinction makes it clear that the doctrine of good faith merely directs a court towards interpreting contracts within the commercial context in which they are created, performed, and enforced, and does not create a separate duty of fairness and reasonableness which can be independently breached.

2. "Performance and enforcement" of contracts and duties within the Uniform Commercial Code include the exercise of rights created by the Uniform Commercial Code.

§ 1-305. Remedies to Be Liberally Administered.

(a) The remedies provided by [the Uniform Commercial Code] must be liberally administered to the end that the aggrieved party may be put in as good a position as if the other party had fully performed but neither consequential or special damages nor penal damages may be had except as specifically provided in [the Uniform Commercial Code] or by other rule of law.

(b) Any right or obligation declared by [the Uniform Commercial Code] is enforceable by action unless the provision declaring it specifies a different and limited effect.

Official Comment

Source: Former Section 1-106.

Changes from Former Law: Other than changes in the form of reference to the Uniform Commercial Code, this section is identical to former Section 1-106.

1. Subsection (a) is intended to effect three propositions. The first is to negate the possibility of unduly narrow or technical interpretation of remedial provisions by providing that the remedies in the Uniform Commercial Code are to be liberally administered to the end stated in this section. The second is to make it clear that compensatory damages are limited to compensation. They do not include consequential or special damages, or penal damages; and the Uniform Commercial Code elsewhere makes it clear that damages must be minimized. Cf. Sections 1-304, 2-706(1), and 2-712(2). The third purpose of subsection (a) is to reject any doctrine that damages must be calculable with mathematical accuracy. Compensatory damages are often at best approximate: they have to be proved with whatever definiteness and accuracy the facts permit, but no more. Cf. Section 2-204(3).

2. Under subsection (b), any right or obligation described in the Uniform Commercial Code is enforceable by action, even though no remedy may be expressly provided other than in this section, unless a particular provision specifies a different and limited effect. Whether specific performance or other equitable relief is available in a particular case is determined not by this section but by specific provisions and by supplementary principles. Cf. Sections 1-103, 2-716, 9-625.

3. "Consequential" or "special" damages and "penal" damages are not defined in the Uniform Commercial Code; rather, these terms are used in the sense in which they are used outside the Uniform Commercial Code.

§ 1-306. Waiver or Renunciation of Claim or Right After Breach.

A claim or right arising out of an alleged breach may be discharged in whole or in part without consideration by agreement of the aggrieved party in a signed record.

Official Comment

Source: Former Section 1-107.

Changes from Former Law: Former Section 1-107, requiring the "delivery" of a "written waiver or renunciation" merged the separate concepts of the aggrieved party's agreement to forego rights and the manifestation of that agreement. This section separates those concepts, and explicitly requires agreement of the aggrieved party.

1. This section makes consideration unnecessary to the effective renunciation or waiver of rights or claims arising out of an alleged breach of a contract where the agreement effecting such renunciation is memorialized in a record signed by the aggrieved party. Its provisions, however, must be read in conjunction with the section imposing an obligation of good faith. (Section 1-304.)

2. Consistent with the revised definition of "sign" in Section 1-201, the cognate term "signed" replaces the reference to "authenticated" in the pre-2022 text of this section.

§ 1-307. Prima Facie Evidence by Third-Party Documents.

A document in due form purporting to be a bill of lading, policy or certificate of insurance, official weigher's or inspector's certificate, consular invoice, or any other document authorized or required by the contract to be issued by a third party is prima facie evidence of its own authenticity and genuineness and of the facts stated in the document by the third party.

Official Comment

Source: Former Section 1-202.

Changes from Former Law: Except for minor stylistic changes, this Section is identical to former Section 1-202.

1. This section supplies judicial recognition for documents that are relied upon as trustworthy by commercial parties.

2. This section is concerned only with documents that have been given a preferred status by the parties themselves who have required their procurement in the agreement, and for this reason the applicability of the section is limited to actions arising out of the contract that authorized or required the document. The list of documents is intended to be illustrative and not exclusive.

3. The provisions of this section go no further than establishing the documents in question as prima facie evidence and leave to the court the ultimate determination of the facts where the accuracy or authenticity of the documents is questioned. In this connection the section calls for a commercially reasonable interpretation.

4. Documents governed by this section need not be writings if records in another medium are generally relied upon in the context.

§ 1-308. Performance or Acceptance Under Reservation of Rights.

(a) A party that with explicit reservation of rights performs or promises performance or assents to performance in a manner demanded or offered by the other party does not thereby prejudice the rights reserved. Such words as "without prejudice," "under protest," or the like are sufficient.

(b) Subsection (a) does not apply to an accord and satisfaction.

Official Comment

Source: Former Section 1-207.

Changes from Former Law: This section is identical to former Section 1-207.

1. This section provides machinery for the continuation of performance along the lines contemplated by the contract despite a pending dispute, by adopting the mercantile device of going ahead with delivery, acceptance, or payment "without prejudice," "under protest," "under reserve," "with reservation of all our rights," and the like. All of these phrases completely reserve all rights within the meaning of this section. The section therefore contemplates that limited as well as general reservations and acceptance by a party may be made "subject to satisfaction of our purchaser," "subject to acceptance by our customers," or the like.

2. This section does not add any new requirement of language of reservation where not already required by law, but merely provides a specific measure on which a party can rely as that party makes or concurs in any interim adjustment in the course of performance. It does not affect or impair the provisions of this Act such as those under which the buyer's remedies for defect survive acceptance without being expressly claimed if notice of the defects is given within a reasonable time. Nor does it disturb the policy of those cases which restrict the effect of a waiver of a defect to reasonable limits under the circumstances, even though no such reservation is expressed.

The section is not addressed to the creation or loss of remedies in the ordinary course of performance but rather to a method of procedure where one party is claiming as of right something which the other believes to be unwarranted.

3. Subsection (b) states that this section does not apply to an accord and satisfaction. Section 3-311 governs if an accord and satisfaction is attempted by tender of a negotiable instrument as stated in that section. If Section 3-311 does not apply, the issue of whether an accord and satisfaction has been effected is determined by the law of contract. Whether or not Section 3-311 applies, this section has no application to an accord and satisfaction.

§ 1-309. Option to Accelerate at Will.

A term providing that one party or that party's successor in interest may accelerate payment or performance or require collateral or additional collateral "at will" or when the party "deems itself insecure," or words of similar import, means that the party has power to do so only if that party in good faith believes that the prospect of payment or performance is impaired. The burden of establishing lack of good faith is on the party against which the power has been exercised.

Official Comment

Source: Former Section 1-208.

Changes from Former Law: Except for minor stylistic changes, this section is identical to former Section 1-208.

1. The common use of acceleration clauses in many transactions governed by the Uniform Commercial Code, including sales of goods on credit, notes payable at a definite time, and secured transactions, raises an issue as to the effect to be given to a clause that seemingly grants the power to accelerate at the whim and caprice of one party. This section is intended to make clear that despite language that might be so construed and which further might be held to make the agreement void as against public policy or to make the contract illusory or too indefinite for enforcement, the option is to be exercised only in the good faith belief that the prospect of payment or performance is impaired.

Obviously this section has no application to demand instruments or obligations whose very nature permits call at any time with or without reason. This section applies only to an obligation of payment or performance which in the first instance is due at a future date.

§ 1-310. Subordinated Obligations.

An obligation may be issued as subordinated to performance of another obligation of the person obligated, or a creditor may subordinate its right to performance of an obligation by agreement with either the person obligated or another creditor of the person obligated. Subordination does not create a security interest as against either the common debtor or a subordinated creditor.

Official Comment

Source: Former Section 1-209.

Changes from Former Law: This section is substantively identical to former Section 1-209. The language in that section stating that it "shall be construed as declaring the law as it existed prior to the enactment of this section and not as modifying it" has been deleted.

1. Billions of dollars of subordinated debt are held by the public and by institutional investors. Commonly, the subordinated debt is subordinated on issue or acquisition and is evidenced by an investment security or by a negotiable or non-negotiable note. Debt is also sometimes subordinated after it arises, either by agreement between the subordinating creditor and the debtor, by agreement between two creditors of the same debtor, or by agreement of all three parties. The subordinated creditor may be a stockholder or other "insider" interested in the common debtor; the subordinated debt may consist of accounts or other rights to payment not evidenced by any instrument. All such cases are included in the terms "subordinated obligation," "subordination," and "subordinated creditor."

2. Subordination agreements are enforceable between the parties as contracts; and in the bankruptcy of the common debtor dividends otherwise payable to the subordinated creditor are turned over to the superior creditor. This "turn-over" practice has on occasion been explained in terms of "equitable lien," "equitable assignment," or "constructive trust," but whatever the label the practice is essentially an equitable remedy and does not mean that there is a transaction "that creates a security interest in personal property... by contract" or a "sale of accounts, chattel paper, payment intangibles, or promissory notes" within the meaning of Section 9-109. On the other hand, nothing in this section prevents one creditor from assigning his rights to another creditor of the same debtor in such a way as to create a security interest within Article 9, where the parties so intend.

3. The enforcement of subordination agreements is largely left to supplementary principles under Section 1-103. If the subordinated debt is evidenced by a certificated security, Section 8-202(a) authorizes enforcement against purchasers on terms stated or referred to on the security certificate. If the fact of subordination is noted on a negotiable instrument, a holder under Sections 3-302 and 3-306 is subject to the term because notice precludes him from taking free of the subordination. Sections 3-302(3)(a), 3-306, and 8-317 severely limit the rights of levying creditors of a subordinated creditor in such cases.

UNIFORM COMMERCIAL CODE

Article 2—Sales

PART 1. SHORT TITLE, GENERAL CONSTRUCTION, AND SUBJECT MATTER

Section

2-102. Scope; Certain Security and Other Transactions Excluded from This Article

2-103. Definitions and Index of Definitions

2-104. Definitions: "Merchant"; "Between Merchants"; "Financing Agency"

PART 4. TITLE, CREDITORS, AND GOOD FAITH PURCHASERS

2-403. Power to Transfer; Good Faith Purchase of Goods; "Entrusting"

PART 5. PERFORMANCE

2-501. Insurable Interest in Goods; Manner of Identification of Goods

2-502. Buyer's Right to Goods on Seller's Repudiation, Failure to Deliver, or Insolvency

PART 7. REMEDIES

2-702. Seller's Remedies on Discovery of Buyer's Insolvency

2-716. Buyer's Right to Specific Performance or Replevin

PART 1. SHORT TITLE, GENERAL CONSTRUCTION, AND SUBJECT MATTER

§ 2-102. Scope; Certain Security and Other Transactions Excluded from This Article.

(1) Unless the context otherwise requires, and except as provided in subsection (3), this Article applies to transactions in goods and, in the case of a hybrid transaction, it applies to the extent provided in subsection (2).

(2) In a hybrid transaction:

(a) If the sale-of-goods aspects do not predominate, only the provisions of this Article which relate primarily to the sale-of-goods aspects of the transaction apply, and the provisions that relate primarily to the transaction as a whole do not apply.

(b) If the sale-of-goods aspects predominate, this Article applies to the transaction but does not preclude application in appropriate circumstances of other law to aspects of the transaction which do not relate to the sale of goods.

(3) This Article does not:

(a) apply to a transaction that, even though in the form of an unconditional contract to sell or present sale, operates only to create a security interest; or

(b) impair or repeal a statute regulating sales to consumers, farmers, or other specific classes of buyers.

Official Comment

Prior Uniform Statutory Provision: Section 75, Uniform Sales Act.

Changes: Section 75 has been rephrased.

Purposes:

1. Subsection (3) makes it clear that this Article does not govern aspects of a transaction that, although in the form of a sale or contract to sell, create a security interest. See Sections 1-201(b)(35); 9-109(a)(1). Of course, this Article does apply to any sales aspects of such a transaction.

2. Many ordinary transactions involve both a sale of goods and the provision of services, a lease of other goods, or a sale, lease, or license of property other than goods. In its original formulation, Article 2 provided no guidance on whether or to what extent the Article applied to such a hybrid transaction, although by defining a "sale" as "the passing of title [to goods] from the seller to the buyer for a price," Section 1-206 arguably regarded such transactions as sales. This section was substantially revised to address hybrid transactions pursuant to the Uniform Commercial Code Amendments (2022) (2022 Amendments). See Section 2-106(5) (defining "hybrid transaction").

In dealing with the issue of whether and to what extent, under the pre-2022 version of this section, Article 2 applied to hybrid transactions, most courts used some version of a "predominant purpose" test. Under those tests, Article 2 applied either in full or not at all, depending on whether the hybrid transaction, at its inception, was predominantly about the goods. In some cases, courts looked instead to the "gravamen of the claim," applying Article 2 to issues relating to the goods and applying other law to issues relating to other aspects of the transaction. Still other courts used what was sometimes referred to as the "bifurcation approach," under which Article 2 applied to the sale-of-goods aspect of a hybrid transaction and other law applied to the other aspects of the transaction. The bifurcation approach was similar to the gravamen of the claim, but instead of applying all of Article 2 to some, but not all, types of claims relating to a hybrid transaction, it distinguished the provisions in Article 2 that deal with the goods from those that deal with the transaction as a whole, and applied only the former in a hybrid transaction.

Subsection (2) codifies aspects of the predominant purpose test and the bifurcation approach, establishing a two-tiered test. If the sale-of-goods aspects of a hybrid transaction predominate, then Article 2 applies. If the other aspects of the hybrid transaction predominate, then the provisions of Article 2 which relate primarily to the sale of goods, as opposed to those that relate to the transaction as a whole, apply. This approach has the benefit, for example, of ensuring that a person acquiring ownership of goods in a transaction in which the sale-of-goods aspects do not predominate is a buyer that benefits from the warranty provisions of this Article and may have a right to recover the goods from the seller and thereby may qualify as a buyer in ordinary course of business under Section 1-201(b)(9).

3. It is important to note that, in contrast to the frequent reference (under prior case law in many states) to the predominant purpose of a hybrid transaction, subsection (2) focuses on which aspect of the transaction predominates without requiring a finding of the "purpose" of either or both parties (although that purpose, when evident, may be a relevant factor in deciding which aspect predominates). The determination of which aspect of a hybrid transaction predominates is left to the court, which should evaluate each transaction on a case-by-case basis without the necessity of applying any particular formula. Factors that may be relevant to that determination include, but are not limited to, the language of the agreement, the portion of the total price that is attributable to the sale of goods (as to which an agreed-upon allocation will ordinarily be binding on the parties), the purposes of the parties in entering into the transaction (when that is ascertainable), and the nature of the businesses of the parties (such as whether the seller is in the business of selling goods of that kind). Because the definition of "goods" expressly includes "specially manufactured goods," services involved in manufacturing goods are normally attributable to the sale-of-goods aspects of the transaction. Services in designing specially manufactured goods, however, would not normally be attributable to the sale-of-goods aspects of the transaction.

4. If the sale-of-goods aspects of a hybrid transaction predominate, then this Article applies to the transaction. However, the application of this Article to a hybrid transaction does not preclude the application of principles of law and equity to supplement the provisions of this Article, see Section 1-103(b), nor does it preclude, in appropriate circumstances, the application of other law to the non-sale-of-goods aspects of the transaction. Whether it is appropriate to apply such other law will depend in part on what purposes the other law is designed to achieve and whether application of the other law would be likely to interfere with the application of this Article.

Example 1. Owner hires Contractor to replace the roof on a structure. As part of the transaction, Contractor promises to remove the existing shingles and install new shingles, which Contractor is providing. The transaction is a hybrid transaction because it involves the passing of title to the new shingles and the provision of services. If the sale-of-goods aspects of the transaction predominate, this Article applies to the transaction.

Example 2. Same facts as in Example 1. Even if the sale-of-goods aspects of the transaction predominate, other law might apply to the services aspects of the transaction. For example, if applicable law regulates the provision of roofing services, such as by requiring the roofer to be licensed, requiring specified disclosures, requiring or implying a warranty with respect to the quality of services, or giving the property owner a brief period of time to cancel the contract, such other law might apply.

Example 3. In a single transaction, Seller agrees to sell a warehouse full of goods to Buyer. The transaction includes the goods contained in the warehouse, the warehouse itself, and the real property on which the warehouse is situated. Assume the goods aspects of the transaction predominate. The application of this Article to the transaction does not preclude the application of real property law to the real-property aspects of the transaction. Accordingly, whether the sale of the real property complies with the applicable requirements of real property law is determined by law other than this Article. Other law will also determine whether consummation of the sale of the real property is a condition to the parties' obligations to buy and sell the goods.

5. If the sale-of-goods aspects of a hybrid transaction do not predominate, under subsection (3), the provisions of this Article relating primarily to the sale of goods, as opposed to the transaction as a whole, apply. These provisions include those relating to warranties under Sections 2-212, 2-313, 2-314, 2-315, 2-316, 2-317,

2-318; tender of delivery and risk of loss under Sections 2-503, 2-504, 2-509, 2-510; acceptance, rejection, and cure under Sections 2-508, 2-601, 2-602, 2-603, 2-604, 2-605, 2-606; and remedies for non-delivery of the goods or for tender of nonconforming goods under Sections 2-711, 7-712, 7-713, 2-714, 2-715, 2-716. In contrast, the provisions of this Article dealing with the transaction as a whole do not apply. These provisions include those relating to: the requirement of a signed record, Section 2-201; contract formation, Sections 2-204 through 2-207; and whether consideration is needed to modify the agreement, Section 2-209.

Example 4. Owner sends a purchase order to Contractor offering to enter into a contract with Contractor to replace the roof on a structure. The proposed transaction involves Contractor removing the existing shingles and installing new shingles, which Contractor is to provide. Contractor responds with a confirmation purporting to accept but containing additional and different terms. The transaction is a hybrid transaction because it involves the passing of title to the new shingles and the provision of services. If the sale-of-goods aspects of the transaction do not predominate, this Article does not apply to determine whether a contract was formed. That issue is governed by other law.

Example 5. Under the facts of Example 1, assume that the sale-of-goods aspects of the transaction do not predominate. The agreement provides that the job will be completed by December 31. Due to unforeseen circumstances affecting the availability of supplies and labor, the job is not completed by the agreed-upon deadline. Whether Contractor's failure to perform on time is excused is determined by general contract law, rather than by this Article (Section 2-615).

Example 6. Under the facts of Example 1, assume that the sale-of-goods aspects of the transaction do not predominate. A dispute between the parties arises and during litigation one party seeks to admit evidence of usage of trade to supplement or explain the parties' written agreement. If the proffered evidence relates to the sale-of-goods aspects of the transaction, the parol evidence rule in this Article, Section 2-202 applies. If the proffered evidence relates to the other aspects of the transaction or to the transaction as a whole, other law will govern the admissibility of the evidence.

Example 7. Restaurateur hires Remodeler to remodel Restaurateur's kitchen. The transaction requires Remodeler to supply a new oven meeting detailed specifications, but the services aspects of the transaction predominate. The oven supplied does not meet a minor aspect of those specifications (but does substantially satisfy the specifications as a whole). Whether Restaurateur may reject the oven (or must retain it subject to price adjustment), whether Restaurateur has a right to cover by purchasing a substitute oven, and the measure of Restaurateur's damages for the oven's nonconformity to the specifications are determined by this Article.

Example 8. Restaurateur hires Remodeler to remodel Restaurateur's kitchen by a specified completion date. The transaction requires Remodeler to supply a new oven, but the services aspects of the transaction predominate. Remodeler breaches by failing to complete the project by the specified date. The measure of Restaurateur's damages for Remodeler's failure to timely complete the project is not determined by this Article.

6. The rules of subsections (1) and (2) are essentially gap fillers that apply when the parties' agreement is silent on what legal rules govern the different aspects of their transaction. In general, parties are free to preclude the application of this Article to the aspects of their transaction that are not about the sale of goods.

Example 9. Robotics Manufacturer contracts to design, build, and sell customized robotics to Car Maker. The transaction includes a sale of goods and the provision of services and is therefore a hybrid transaction. Assume that the sale-of-goods aspects predominate. The parties may, in their agreement, provide that Article 2 does not govern the services aspects of the transaction.

As Example 9 illustrates, parties may agree that Article 2 will not govern non-goods aspects of a hybrid transaction, even though the sale-of-goods aspects predominate. But, when sale-of-goods aspects predominate, the parties cannot agree that Article 2 does not govern matters that relate to the transaction as a whole, such as contract formation and enforceability. For example, in a situation such as Example 9, if the requirements of the Section 2-201 statute of frauds are not satisfied, it would make little sense to hold that the services aspects of the transaction are enforceable when the provision of services is clearly dependent on the existence of the sale-of- goods aspects. Of course, even when this article applies, its provisions may be varied by agreement to the extent provided in section 1-302.

§ 2-103. Definitions and Index of Definitions.

(1) In this Article unless the context otherwise requires

(a) "Buyer" means a person who buys or contracts to buy goods.

(b) [Reserved]

(c) "Receipt" of goods means taking physical possession of them.

(d) "Seller" means a person who sells or contracts to sell goods.

(2) Other definitions applying to this Article or to specified Parts thereof, and the sections in which they appear are:

"Acceptance". Section 2-606.
"Banker's credit". Section 2-325.
"Between merchants". Section 2-104.
"Cancellation". Section 2-106(4).
"Commercial unit". Section 2-105.
"Confirmed credit". Section 2-325.
"Conforming to contract". Section 2-106.
"Contract for sale". Section 2-106.
"Cover". Section 2-712.
"Entrusting". Section 2-403.
"Financing agency". Section 2-104.
"Future goods". Section 2-105.
"Goods". Section 2-105.
"Identification". Section 2-501.
"Installment contract". Section 2-612.
"Letter of Credit". Section 2-325.
"Lot". Section 2-105.
"Merchant". Section 2-104.
"Overseas". Section 2-323.
"Person in position of seller". Section 2-707.
"Present sale". Section 2-106.
"Sale". Section 2-106.
"Sale on approval". Section 2-326.
"Sale or return". Section 2-326.
"Termination". Section 2-106.

(3) The following definitions in other Articles apply to this Article:

"Check". Section 3-104.
"Consignee". Section 7-102.
"Consignor". Section 7-102.
"Consumer goods". Section 9-102.
"Dishonor". Section 3-502.
"Draft". Section 3-104.

(4) In addition Article 1 contains general definitions and principles of construction and interpretation applicable throughout this Article.

As amended in 1994, 1999, and 2001.

Official Comment

Prior Uniform Statutory Provision: Subsection (1): Section 76, Uniform Sales Act.

Changes: The definitions of "buyer" and "seller" have been slightly rephrased, the reference in Section 76 of the prior Act to "any legal successor in interest of such person" being omitted. The definition of "receipt" is new.

Purposes of Changes and New Matter:

1. The phrase "any legal successor in interest of such person" has been eliminated since Section 2-210 of this Article, which limits some types of delegation of performance on assignment of a sales contract, makes it clear that not every such successor can be safely included in the definition. In every ordinary case, however, such successors are as of course included.

2. "Receipt" must be distinguished from delivery particularly in regard to the problems arising out of shipment of goods, whether or not the contract calls for making delivery by way of documents of title, since the seller may frequently fulfill his obligations to "deliver" even though the buyer may never "receive" the goods. Delivery with respect to documents of title is defined in Article 1 and requires transfer of physical delivery. Otherwise the many divergent incidents of delivery are handled incident by incident.

§ 2-104. Definitions: "Merchant"; "Between Merchants"; "Financing Agency".

(1) "Merchant" means a person who deals in goods of the kind or otherwise by his occupation holds himself out as having knowledge or skill peculiar to the practices or goods involved in the transaction or to whom such knowledge or skill may be attributed by his employment of an agent or broker or other intermediary who by his occupation holds himself out as having such knowledge or skill.

(2) "Financing agency" means a bank, finance company or other person who in the ordinary course of business makes advances against goods or documents of title or who by arrangement with either the seller or the buyer intervenes in ordinary course to make or collect payment due or claimed under the contract for sale, as by purchasing or paying the seller's draft or making advances against it or by merely taking it for collection whether or not documents of title accompany the draft. "Financing agency" includes also a bank or other person who similarly intervenes between persons who are in the position of seller and buyer in respect to the goods (Section 2-707).

(3) "Between merchants" means in any transaction with respect to which both parties are chargeable with the knowledge or skill of merchants.

Official Comment

Prior Uniform Statutory Provision: None. But see Sections 15(2), (5), 16(c), 45(2) and 71, Uniform Sales Act, and Sections 35 and 37, Uniform Bills of Lading

Act for examples of the policy expressly provided for in this Article.

Purposes:

1. This Article assumes that transactions between professionals in a given field require special and clear rules which may not apply to a casual or inexperienced seller or buyer. It thus adopts a policy of expressly stating rules applicable "between merchants" and "as against a merchant", wherever they are needed instead of making them depend upon the circumstances of each case as in the statutes cited above. This section lays the foundation of this policy by defining those who are to be regarded as professionals or "merchants" and by stating when a transaction is deemed to be "between merchants".

2. The term "merchant" as defined here roots in the "law merchant" concept of a professional in business. The professional status under the definition may be based upon specialized knowledge as to the goods, specialized knowledge as to business practices, or specialized knowledge as to both and which kind of specialized knowledge may be sufficient to establish the merchant status is indicated by the nature of the provisions.

The special provisions as to merchants appear only in this Article and they are of three kinds. Sections 2-201(2), 2-205, 2-207 and 2-209 dealing with the statute of frauds, firm offers, confirmatory memoranda and modification rest on normal business practices which are or ought to be typical of and familiar to any person in business. For purposes of these sections almost every person in business would, therefore, be deemed to be a "merchant" under the language "who... by his occupation holds himself out as having knowledge or skill peculiar to the practices... involved in the transaction..." since the practices involved in the transaction are non-specialized business practices such as answering mail. In this type of provision, banks or even universities, for example, well may be "merchants." But even these sections only apply to a merchant in his mercantile capacity; a lawyer or bank president buying fishing tackle for his own use is not a merchant.

On the other hand, in Section 2-314 on the warranty of merchantability, such warranty is implied only "if the seller is a merchant with respect to goods of that kind." Obviously this qualification restricts the implied warranty to a much smaller group than everyone who is engaged in business and requires a professional status as to particular kinds of goods. The exception in Section 2-402(2) for retention of possession by a merchant-seller falls in the same class; as does Section 2-403(2) on entrusting of possession to a merchant "who deals in goods of that kind".

A third group of sections includes 2-103(1)(b), which provides that in the case of a merchant "good faith" includes observance of reasonable commercial standards of fair dealing in the trade; 2-327(1)(c), 2-603 and 2-605, dealing with responsibilities of merchant buyers to follow seller's instructions, etc.; 2-509 on risk of loss, and 2-609 on adequate assurance of performance. This group of sections applies to persons who are merchants under either the "practices" or the "goods" aspect of the definition of merchant.

3. The "or to whom such knowledge or skill may be attributed by his employment of an agent or broker..." clause of the definition of merchant means that even persons such as universities, for example, can come within the definition of merchant if they have regular purchasing departments or business personnel who are familiar with business practices and who are equipped to take any action required.

PART 4. TITLE, CREDITORS, AND GOOD FAITH PURCHASERS

§ 2-403. Power to Transfer; Good Faith Purchase of Goods; "Entrusting".

(1) A purchaser of goods acquires all title which his transferor had or had power to transfer except that a purchaser of a limited interest acquires rights only to the extent of the interest purchased. A person with voidable title has power to transfer a good title to a good faith purchaser for value. When goods have been delivered under a transaction of purchase the purchaser has such power even though

(a) the transferor was deceived as to the identity of the purchaser, or

(b) the delivery was in exchange for a check which is later dishonored, or

(c) it was agreed that the transaction was to be a "cash sale", or

(d) the delivery was procured through fraud punishable as larcenous under the criminal law.

(2) Any entrusting of possession of goods to a merchant who deals in goods of that kind gives him power to transfer all rights of the entruster to a buyer in ordinary course of business.

(3) "Entrusting" includes any delivery and any acquiescence in retention of possession regardless of any condition expressed between the parties to the delivery or acquiescence and regardless of whether the procurement of the entrusting or the possessor's disposition of the goods have been such as to be larcenous under the criminal law.

[*Note: If a state adopts the repealer of Article 6 — Bulk Transfers (Alternative A), subsec. (4) should read as follows:*]

(4) The rights of other purchasers of goods and of lien creditors are governed by the Articles on Secured Transactions (Article 9) and Documents of Title (Article 7).

[Note: If a state adopts Revised Article 6 — Bulk Sales (Alternative B), subsec. (4) should read as follows:]

(4) The rights of other purchasers of goods and of lien creditors are governed by the Articles on Secured Transactions (Article 9), Bulk Sales (Article 6) and Documents of Title (Article 7).

As amended in 1988.

For material relating to the changes made in text in 1988, see section 3 of Alternative A (Repealer of Article 6 — Bulk Transfers) and Conforming Amendment to Section 2-403 following end of Alternative B (Revised Article 6 — Bulk Sales).

Official Comment

Prior Uniform Statutory Provision: Sections 20(4), 23, 24, 25, Uniform Sales Act; Section 9, especially 9(2), Uniform Trust Receipts Act; Section 9, Uniform Conditional Sales Act.

Changes: Consolidated and rewritten.

Purposes of Changes: To gather together a series of prior uniform statutory provisions and the case-law thereunder and to state a unified and simplified policy on good faith purchase of goods.

1. The basic policy of our law allowing transfer of such title as the transferor has is generally continued and expanded under subsection (1). In this respect the provisions of the section are applicable to a person taking by any form of "purchase" as defined by this Act. Moreover the policy of this Act expressly providing for the application of supplementary general principles of law to sales transactions wherever appropriate joins with the present section to continue unimpaired all rights acquired under the law of agency or of apparent agency or ownership or other estoppel, whether based on statutory provisions or on case law principles. The section also leaves unimpaired the powers given to selling factors under the earlier Factors Acts. In addition subsection (1) provides specifically for the protection of the good faith purchaser for value in a number of specific situations which have been troublesome under prior law.

On the other hand, the contract of purchase is of course limited by its own terms as in a case of pledge for a limited amount or of sale of a fractional interest in goods.

2. The many particular situations in which a buyer in ordinary course of business from a dealer has been protected against reservation of property or other hidden interest are gathered by subsections (2)-(4) into a single principle protecting persons who buy in ordinary course out of inventory. Consignors have no reason to complain, nor have lenders who hold a security interest in the inventory, since the very purpose of goods in inventory is to be turned into cash by sale.

The principle is extended in subsection (3) to fit with the abolition of the old law of "cash sale" by subsection (1)(c). It is also freed from any technicalities depending on the extended law of larceny; such extension of the concept of theft to include trick, particular types of fraud, and the like is for the purpose of helping conviction of the offender; it has no proper application to the long-standing policy of civil protection of buyers from persons guilty of such trick or fraud. Finally, the policy is extended, in the interest of simplicity and sense, to any entrusting by a bailor; this is in consonance with the explicit provisions of Section 7-205 on the powers of a warehouseman who is also in the business of buying and selling fungible goods of the kind he warehouses. As to entrusting by a secured party, subsection (2) is limited by the more specific provisions of Section 9-307(1), which deny protection to a person buying farm products from a person engaged in farming operations.

3. The definition of "buyer in ordinary course of business" (Section 1-201) applies here and preserves the essence of the healthy limitations engrafted by the case-law on the older statutes. The older loose concept of good faith and wide definition of value combined to create apparent good faith purchasers in many situations in which the result outraged common sense; the court's solution was to protect the original title especially by use of "cash sale" or of over-technical construction of the enabling clauses of the statutes. But such rulings then turned into limitations on the proper protection of buyers in the ordinary market. Section 1-201(b)(9) cuts down the category of buyer in ordinary course in such fashion as to take care of the results of the cases, but with no price either in confusion or in injustice to proper dealings in the normal market.

4. Except as provided in subsection (1), the rights of purchasers other than buyers in ordinary course are left to the Articles on Secured Transactions, Documents of Title, and Bulk Sales.

PART 5. PERFORMANCE

§2-501. Insurable Interest In Goods; Manner of Identification of Goods.

(1) The buyer obtains a special property and an insurable interest in goods by identification of existing goods as goods to which the contract refers even if the goods so identified are nonconforming and the buyer has an option to return or reject them. Such identification may be made at any time and in any manner explicitly agreed to by the parties. In the absence of explicit agreement, identification occurs:

(a) when the contract is made if it is for the sale of goods already existing and identified;

(b) if the contract is for the sale of future goods other than those described in paragraph (c), when goods are shipped, marked, or otherwise designated by the seller as goods to which the contract refers;

(c) when the crops are planted or otherwise become growing crops or the young are conceived if the contract is for the sale of unborn young to be born within 12 months after contracting or for the sale of crops to be harvested within 12 months or the next normal harvest season after contracting, whichever is longer.

(2) The seller retains an insurable interest in goods so long as title to or any security interest in the goods remains in the seller. If the identification is by the seller alone, the seller may until default or insolvency or notification to the buyer that the identification is final substitute other goods for those identified.

(3) Nothing in this section impairs any insurable interest recognized under any other statute or rule of law.

Official Comment

Prior Uniform Statutory Provision: See Sections 17 and 19, Uniform Sales Act.

Purposes:

1. The present section deals with the manner of identifying goods to the contract so that an insurable interest in the buyer and the rights set forth in the next section will accrue. Generally speaking, identification may be made in any manner "explicitly agreed to" by the parties. The rules of paragraphs (a), (b) and (c) apply only in the absence of such "explicit agreement."

2. In the ordinary case identification of particular existing goods as goods to which the contract refers is unambiguous and may occur in one of many ways. It is possible, however, for the identification to be tentative or contingent. In view of the limited effect given to identification by this Article, the general policy is to resolve all doubts in favor of identification.

3. The provision of this section as to "explicit agreement" clarifies the present confusion in the law of sales which has arisen from the fact that under prior uniform legislation all rules of presumption with reference to the passing of title or to appropriation (which in turn depended upon identification) were regarded as subject to the contrary intention of the parties or of the party appropriating. Such uncertainty is reduced to a minimum under this section by requiring "explicit agreement" of the parties before the rules of paragraphs (a), (b), and (c) are displaced—as they would be by a term giving the buyer power to select the goods. An "explicit" agreement, however, need not necessarily be found in the terms used in the particular transaction. Thus, where a usage of the trade has previously been made explicit by reduction to a standard set of "rules and regulations" currently incorporated by reference into the contracts of the parties, a relevant provision of those "rules and regulations" is "explicit" within the meaning of this section.

4. In view of the limited function of identification there is no requirement in this section that the goods be in deliverable state or that all of the seller's duties with respect to the processing of the goods be completed in order that identification occur. For example, despite identification the risk of loss remains on the seller under the risk of loss provisions until completion of his duties as to the goods and all of his remedies remain dependent upon his not defaulting under the contract.

5. Undivided shares in an identified fungible bulk, such as grain in an elevator or oil in a storage tank, can be sold. The mere making of the contract with reference to an undivided share in an identified fungible bulk is enough under subsection (a) to effect an identification if there is no explicit agreement otherwise. The seller's duty, however, to segregate and deliver according to the contract is not affected by such an identification but is controlled by other provisions of this Article.

6. Identification of crops under paragraph (c) is made upon planting only if they are to be harvested within the year or within the next normal harvest season. The phrase "next normal harvest season" fairly includes nursery stock raised for normally quick "harvest," but plainly excludes a "timber" crop to which the concept of a harvest "season" is inapplicable.

Paragraph (c) is also applicable to a crop of wool or the young of animals to be born within twelve months after contracting. The product of a lumbering, mining or fishing operation, though seasonal, is not within the concept of "growing." Identification under a contract for all or part of the output of such an operation can be effected early in the operation.

Cross References:

Point 1: Section 2-502.

Point 4: Sections 2-509, 2-510, and 2-703.

Point 5: Sections 2-103, 2-105, 2-308, 2-503, and 2-509.

Point 6: Sections 2-103, 2-107(1), and 2-402.

Definitional Cross References:

"Agreement." Section 1-201.

"Contract." Section 1-201.

"Contract for sale." Section 2-106.

"Future goods." Section 2-105.

"Goods." Section 2-105.

"Notification." Section 1-201.

"Party." Section 1-201.

"Sale." Section 2-106.

"Security interest." Section 1-201.

"Seller." Section 2-103.

§ 2-502. Buyer's Right to Goods on Seller's Repudiation, Failure to Deliver, or Insolvency.

(1) Subject to subsections (2) and (3) and even though the goods have not been shipped a buyer who has paid a part or all of the price of goods in which he has a special property under the provisions of the immediately preceding section may on making and keeping good a tender of any unpaid portion of their price recover them from the seller if:

(a) in the case of goods bought for personal, family, or household purposes, the seller repudiates or fails to deliver as required by the contract; or

(b) in all cases, the seller becomes insolvent within ten days after receipt of the first installment on their price.

(2) The buyer's right to recover the goods under subsection (1)(a) vests upon acquisition of a special property, even if the seller had not then repudiated or failed to deliver.

(3) If the identification creating his special property has been made by the buyer he acquires the right to recover the goods only if they conform to the contract for sale.

Official Comment

Prior Uniform Statutory Provision: Compare Sections 17, 18 and 19, Uniform Sales Act.

Purposes:

1. This section gives an additional right to the buyer as a result of identification of the goods to the contract in the manner provided in Section 2-501. The buyer is given a right to recover the goods, conditioned upon making and keeping good a tender of any unpaid portion of the price, in two limited circumstances. First, the buyer may recover goods bought for personal, family, or household purposes if the seller repudiates the contract or fails to deliver the goods. Second, in any case, the buyer may recover the goods if the seller becomes insolvent within 10 days after the seller receives the first installment on their price. The buyer's right to recover the goods under this section is an exception to the usual rule, under which the disappointed buyer must resort to an action to recover damages.

2. The question of whether the buyer also acquires a security interest in identified goods and has rights to the goods when insolvency takes place after the ten-day period provided in this section depends upon compliance with the provisions of the Article on Secured Transactions (Article 9).

3. Under subsection (2), the buyer's right to recover consumer goods under subsection (1)(a) vests upon acquisition of a special property, which occurs upon identification of the goods to the contract. See Section 2-501. Inasmuch as a secured party normally acquires no greater rights in its collateral that its debtor had or had power to convey, see Section 2-403(1) (first sentence), a buyer who acquires a right to recover under this section will take free of a security interest created by the seller if it attaches to the goods after the goods have been identified to the contract. The buyer will take free, even if the buyer does not buy in ordinary course and even if the security interest is perfected. Of course, to the extent that the buyer pays the price after the security interest attaches, the payments will constitute proceeds of the security interest.

4. Subsection (3) is included to preclude the possibility of unjust enrichment, which would exist if the buyer were permitted to recover goods even though they were greatly superior in quality or quantity to that called for by the contract for sale.

Cross References:

Point 1: Sections 1-201 and 2-702.

Point 2: Article 9.

Definitional Cross References:

"Buyer". Section 2-103.

"Conform". Section 2-106.

"Contract for sale". Section 2-106.

"Goods". Section 2-105.

"Insolvent". Section 1-201.

"Rights". Section 1-201.

"Seller". Section 2-103.

PART 7. REMEDIES

§ 2-702. Seller's Remedies on Discovery of Buyer's Insolvency.

(1) Where the seller discovers the buyer to be insolvent he may refuse delivery except for cash including payment for all goods theretofore delivered under the contract, and stop delivery under this Article (Section 2-705).

(2) Where the seller discovers that the buyer has received goods on credit while insolvent he may reclaim the goods upon demand made within ten days after the receipt, but if misrepresentation of solvency has been made to the particular seller in writing within three months before delivery the ten day limitation does not apply. Except as provided in this subsection the seller may not base a right to reclaim goods on the buyer's fraudulent or innocent misrepresentation of solvency or of intent to pay.

(3) The seller's right to reclaim under subsection (2) is subject to the rights of a buyer in ordinary course or other good faith purchaser under this

Article (Section 2-403). Successful reclamation of goods excludes all other remedies with respect to them.

As amended in 1966.

Official Comment

Prior Uniform Statutory Provision: Subsection (1)—Sections 53(1)(b), 54(1)(c) and 57, Uniform Sales Act; Subsection (2)—none; Subsection (3)—Section 76(3), Uniform Sales Act.

Changes: Rewritten, the protection given to a seller who has sold on credit and has delivered goods to the buyer immediately preceding his insolvency being extended.

Purposes of Changes and New Matter: To make it clear that:

1. The seller's right to withhold the goods or to stop delivery except for cash when he discovers the buyer's insolvency is made explicit in subsection (1) regardless of the passage of title, and the concept of stoppage has been extended to include goods in the possession of any bailee who has not yet attorned to the buyer.

2. Subsection (2) takes as its base line the proposition that any receipt of goods on credit by an insolvent buyer amounts to a tacit business misrepresentation of solvency and therefore is fraudulent as against the particular seller. This Article makes discovery of the buyer's insolvency and demand within a ten day period a condition of the right to reclaim goods on this ground. The ten day limitation period operates from the time of receipt of the goods.

An exception to this time limitation is made when a written misrepresentation of solvency has been made to the particular seller within three months prior to the delivery. To fall within the exception the statement of solvency must be in writing, addressed to the particular seller and dated within three months of the delivery.

3. Because the right of the seller to reclaim goods under this section constitutes preferential treatment as against the buyer's other creditors, subsection (3) provides that such reclamation bars all his other remedies as to the goods involved. As amended 1966.

4. As to the use of a record other than a writing and communications that are not written, see Section 2-207, Comment 8.

§ 2-716. Buyer's Right to Specific Performance or Replevin.

(1) Specific performance may be decreed where the goods are unique or in other proper circumstances.

(2) The decree for specific performance may include such terms and conditions as to payment of the price, damages, or other relief as the court may deem just.

(3) The buyer has a right of replevin for goods identified to the contract if after reasonable effort he is unable to effect cover for such goods or the circumstances reasonably indicate that such effort will be unavailing or if the goods have been shipped under reservation and satisfaction of the security interest in them has been made or tendered. In the case of goods bought for personal, family, or household purposes, the buyer's right of replevin vests upon acquisition of a special property, even if the seller had not then repudiated or failed to deliver.

Official Comment

Prior Uniform Statutory Provision: Section 68, Uniform Sales Act.

Changes: Rephrased.

Purposes of Changes: To make it clear that:

1. The present section continues in general prior policy as to specific performance and injunction against breach. However, without intending to impair in any way the exercise of the court's sound discretion in the matter, this Article seeks to further a more liberal attitude than some courts have shown in connection with the specific performance of contracts of sale.

2. In view of this Article's emphasis on the commercial feasibility of replacement, a new concept of what are "unique" goods is introduced under this section. Specific performance is no longer limited to goods which are already specific or ascertained at the time of contracting. The test of uniqueness under this section must be made in terms of the total situation which characterizes the contract. Output and requirements contracts involving a particular or peculiarly available source or market present today the typical commercial specific performance situation, as contrasted with contracts for the sale of heirlooms or priceless works of art which were usually involved in the older cases. However, uniqueness is not the sole basis of the remedy under this section for the relief may also be granted "in other proper circumstances" and inability to cover is strong evidence of "other proper circumstances".

3. The legal remedy of replevin is given the buyer in cases in which cover is reasonably unavailable and goods have been identified to the contract. This is in addition to the buyer's right to recover identified goods under Section 2-502. For consumer goods, the buyer's right to replevin vests upon the buyer's acquisition of a special property, which occurs upon identification of the goods to the contract. See Section 2-501. Inasmuch as a secured party normally acquires no greater rights in its collateral than its debtor had or had power to convey, see Section 2-403(1) (first sentence), a buyer who acquires a right of replevin under subsection (3) will take free of a security interest created by the seller if it attaches to the goods after the goods have been identified to the contract. The buyer will take free, even if the buyer does not buy in ordinary course and even if the security interest is perfected. Of course, to the extent that the buyer pays the price after the security interest attaches, the payments will constitute proceeds of the security interest.

4. This section is intended to give the buyer rights to the goods comparable to the seller's rights to the price.

5. If a negotiable document of title is outstanding, the buyer's right of replevin relates of course to the document not directly to the goods. See Article 7, especially Section 7-602.

Cross References:

Point 3: Section 2-502.

Point 4: Section 2-709.

Point 5: Article 7.

Definitional Cross References:

"Buyer". Section 2-103.

"Goods". Section 1-201.

"Rights". Section 1-201.

UNIFORM COMMERCIAL CODE

Article 8—Investment Securities

PART 1. SHORT TITLE AND GENERAL MATTERS

Section
8-102. Definitions
8-106. Control

PART 3. TRANSFER OF CERTIFICATED AND UNCERTIFICATED SECURITIES

8-301. Delivery

PART 1. SHORT TITLE AND GENERAL MATTERS

§ 8-102. Definitions.

(a) In this Article:

(1) "Adverse claim" means a claim that a claimant has a property interest in a financial asset and that it is a violation of the rights of the claimant for another person to hold, transfer, or deal with the financial asset.

(2) "Bearer form," as applied to a certificated security, means a form in which the security is payable to the bearer of the security certificate according to its terms but not by reason of an indorsement.

(3) "Broker" means a person defined as a broker or dealer under the federal securities laws but without excluding a bank acting in that capacity.

(4) "Certificated security" means a security that is represented by a certificate.

(5) "Clearing corporation" means:

(i) a person that is registered as a "clearing agency" under the federal securities laws;

(ii) a federal reserve bank; or

(iii) any other person that provides clearance or settlement services with respect to financial assets that would require it to register as a clearing agency under the federal securities laws but for an exclusion or exemption from the registration requirement, if its activities as a clearing corporation, including promulgation of rules, are subject to regulation by a federal or state governmental authority.

(6) "Communicate" means to:

(i) send a signed record; or

(ii) transmit information by any mechanism agreed upon by the persons transmitting and receiving the information.

(7) "Entitlement holder" means a person identified in the records of a securities intermediary as the person having a security entitlement against the securities intermediary. If a person acquires a security entitlement by virtue of Section 8-501(b)(2) or (3), that person is the entitlement holder.

(8) "Entitlement order" means a notification communicated to a securities intermediary directing transfer or redemption of a financial asset to which the entitlement holder has a security entitlement.

(9) "Financial asset," except as otherwise provided in Section 8-103, means:

(i) a security;

(ii) an obligation of a person or a share, participation, or other interest in a person or in property or an enterprise of a person, which is, or is of a type, dealt in or traded on financial markets, or which is recognized in any area in which it is issued or dealt in as a medium for investment; or

(iii) any property that is held by a securities intermediary for another person in a securities account if the securities intermediary has expressly agreed with the other person that the property is to be treated as a financial asset under this Article.

As context requires, the term means either the interest itself or the means by which a person's claim to it is evidenced, including a certificated or uncertificated security, a security certificate, or a security entitlement.

(10) [Reserved]

(11) "Indorsement" means a signature that alone or accompanied by other words is made

on a security certificate in registered form or on a separate document for the purpose of assigning, transferring, or redeeming the security or granting a power to assign, transfer, or redeem it.

(12) "Instruction" means a notification communicated to the issuer of an uncertificated security which directs that the transfer of the security be registered or that the security be redeemed.

(13) "Registered form," as applied to a certificated security, means a form in which:

(i) the security certificate specifies a person entitled to the security; and

(ii) a transfer of the security may be registered upon books maintained for that purpose by or on behalf of the issuer, or the security certificate so states.

(14) "Securities intermediary" means:

(i) a clearing corporation; or

(ii) a person, including a bank or broker, that in the ordinary course of its business maintains securities accounts for others and is acting in that capacity.

(15) "Security," except as otherwise provided in Section 8-103, means an obligation of an issuer or a share, participation, or other interest in an issuer or in property or an enterprise of an issuer:

(i) which is represented by a security certificate in bearer or registered form, or the transfer of which may be registered upon books maintained for that purpose by or on behalf of the issuer;

(ii) which is one of a class or series or by its terms is divisible into a class or series of shares, participations, interests, or obligations; and

(iii) which:

(A) is, or is of a type, dealt in or traded on securities exchanges or securities markets; or

(B) is a medium for investment and by its terms expressly provides that it is a security governed by this Article.

(16) "Security certificate" means a certificate representing a security.

(17) "Security entitlement" means the rights and property interest of an entitlement holder with respect to a financial asset specified in Part 5.

(18) "Uncertificated security" means a security that is not represented by a certificate.

(b) The following definitions in this Article and other Articles apply to this Article:

Appropriate person. Section 8-107
Control. Section 8-106
Controllable account. Section 9-102
Controllable electronic record. Section 12-102
Controllable payment intangible. Section 9-102
Delivery. Section 8-301
Investment company security. Section 8-103
Issuer. Section 8-201
Overissue. Section 8-210
Protected purchaser. Section 8-303
Securities account. Section 8-501

(c) In addition, Article 1 contains general definitions and principles of construction and interpretation applicable throughout this Article.

(d) The characterization of a person, business, or transaction for purposes of this Article does not determine the characterization of the person, business, or transaction for purposes of any other law, regulation, or rule.

Official Comment

1. "Adverse claim." The definition of the term "adverse claim" has two components. First, the term refers only to property interests. Second, the term means not merely that a person has a property interest in a financial asset but that it is a violation of the claimant's property interest for the other person to hold or transfer the security or other financial asset.

The term adverse claim is not, of course, limited to ownership rights, but extends to other property interests established by other law. A security interest, for example, would be an adverse claim with respect to a transferee from the debtor since any effort by the secured party to enforce the security interest against the property would be an interference with the transferee's interest.

The definition of adverse claim in the prior version of Article 8 might have been read to suggest that any wrongful action concerning a security, even a simple breach of contract, gave rise to an adverse claim. Insofar as such cases as *Fallon v. Wall Street Clearing Corp.*, 586 N.Y.S.2d 953, 182 A.D.2d 245 (1992) and *Pentech Intl. v. Wall St. Clearing Co.*, 983 F.2d 441 (2d Cir. 1993) were based on that view, they are rejected by the new definition which explicitly limits the term adverse claim to property interests. Suppose, for example, that

A contracts to sell or deliver securities to B, but fails to do so and instead sells or pledges the securities to C. B, the promisee, has an action against A for breach of contract, but absent unusual circumstances the action for breach would not give rise to a property interest in the securities. Accordingly, B does not have an adverse claim. An adverse claim might, however, be based upon principles of equitable remedies that give rise to property claims. It would, for example, cover a right established by other law to rescind a transaction in which securities were transferred. Suppose, for example, that A holds securities and is induced by B's fraud to transfer them to B. Under the law of contract or restitution, A may have a right to rescind the transfer, which gives A a property claim to the securities. If so, A has an adverse claim to the securities in B's hands. By contrast, if B had committed no fraud, but had merely committed a breach of contract in connection with the transfer from A to B, A may have only a right to damages for breach, not a right to rescind. In that case, A would not have an adverse claim to the securities in B's hands.

2. "Bearer form." The definition of "bearer form" has remained substantially unchanged since the early drafts of the original version of Article 8. The requirement that the certificate be payable to bearer by its terms rather than by an indorsement has the effect of preventing instruments governed by other law, such as chattel paper or Article 3 negotiable instruments, from being inadvertently swept into the Article 8 definition of security merely by virtue of blank indorsements. Although the other elements of the definition of security in Section 8-102(a)(14) probably suffice for that purpose in any event, the language used in the prior version of Article 8 has been retained.

3. "Broker." Broker is defined by reference to the definitions of broker and dealer in the federal securities laws. The only difference is that banks, which are excluded from the federal securities law definition, are included in the Article 8 definition when they perform functions that would bring them within the federal securities law definition if it did not have the clause excluding banks. The definition covers both those who act as agents ("brokers" in securities parlance) and those who act as principals ("dealers" in securities parlance). Since the definition refers to persons "defined" as brokers or dealers under the federal securities law, rather than to persons required to "register" as brokers or dealers under the federal securities law, it covers not only registered brokers and dealers but also those exempt from the registration requirement, such as purely intrastate brokers. The only substantive rules that turn on the defined term broker are one provision of the section on warranties, Section 8-108(i), and the special perfection rule in Article 9 for security interests granted by brokers, Section 9-115(4)(c).

4. "Certificated security." The term "certificated security" means a security that is represented by a security certificate.

5. "Clearing corporation." The definition of clearing corporation limits its application to entities that are subject to a rigorous regulatory framework. Accordingly, the definition includes only federal reserve banks, persons who are registered as "clearing agencies" under the federal securities laws (which impose a comprehensive system of regulation of the activities and rules of clearing agencies), and other entities subject to a comparable system of regulatory oversight.

6. "Communicate." The term "communicate" assures that the Article 8 rules will be sufficiently flexible to adapt to changes in information technology. Sending a signed writing always suffices as a communication, but the parties can agree that a different means of transmitting information is to be used. Agreement is defined in Section 1-201(**b**)(3) as "the bargain of the parties in fact as found in their language or by implication from other circumstances including course of dealing or usage of trade or course of performance." Thus, use of an information transmission method might be found to be authorized by agreement, even though the parties have not explicitly so specified in a formal agreement. The term communicate is used in Sections 8-102(a)(7) (definition of entitlement order), 8-102(a)(11) (definition of instruction), and 8-403 (demand that issuer not register transfer). Also in furtherance of medium neutrality, pursuant to the Uniform Commercial Code Amendments (2022) (2022 Amendments) the reference in paragraph (6)(i) to a "signed writing" has been changed to refer to a "signed record."

7. "Entitlement holder." This term designates those who hold financial assets through intermediaries in the indirect holding system. Because many of the rules of Part 5 impose duties on securities intermediaries in favor of entitlement holders, the definition of entitlement holder is, in most cases, limited to the person specifically designated as such on the records of the intermediary. The last sentence of the definition covers the relatively unusual cases where a person may acquire a security entitlement under Section 8-501 even though the person may not be specifically designated as an entitlement holder on the records of the securities intermediary.

A person may have an interest in a security entitlement, and may even have the right to give entitlement orders to the securities intermediary with respect to it, even though the person is not the entitlement holder. For example, a person who holds securities through a securities account in its own name may have given discretionary trading authority to another person, such as an investment adviser. Similarly, the control provisions in Section 8-106 and the related provisions in Article 9 are designed to facilitate transactions in which a person who holds securities through a securities account uses them as collateral in an arrangement where the securities intermediary has agreed that if the secured party so directs the intermediary will dispose of the positions. In such arrangements, the debtor remains the entitlement holder but has agreed that the secured party can initiate entitlement orders. Moreover, an entitlement holder may be acting for another person as a nominee, agent, trustee, or in another capacity. Unless the entitlement holder is itself acting as a securities intermediary for the other person, in which case the other person would be an entitlement holder with respect to the securities entitlement, the relationship between an entitlement holder and another person for whose benefit the entitlement holder holds a securities entitlement is governed by other law.

8. "Entitlement order." This term is defined as a notification communicated to a securities intermediary directing transfer or redemption of the financial asset to which an entitlement holder has a security entitlement. The term is used in the rules for the indirect holding system in a fashion analogous to the use of the terms "indorsement" and "instruction" in the rules for the direct holding system. If a person directly holds a certificated security in registered form and wishes to transfer it, the means of transfer is an indorsement. If a person directly holds an uncertificated security and wishes to transfer it, the means of transfer is an instruction. If a person holds a security entitlement, the means of disposition is an entitlement order. An entitlement order includes a direction under Section 8-508 to the securities intermediary to transfer a financial asset to the account of the entitlement holder at another financial intermediary or to cause the financial asset to be transferred to the entitlement holder in the direct holding system (e.g., the delivery of a securities certificate registered in the name of the former entitlement holder). As noted in Comment 7, an entitlement order need not be initiated by the entitlement holder in order to be effective, so long as the entitlement holder has authorized the other party to initiate entitlement orders. See Section 8-107(b).

9. "Financial asset." The definition of "financial asset," in conjunction with the definition of "securities account" in Section 8-501, sets the scope of the indirect holding system rules of Part 5 of Revised Article 8. The Part 5 rules apply not only to securities held through intermediaries, but also to other financial assets held through intermediaries. The term financial asset is defined to include not only securities but also a broader category of obligations, shares, participations, and interests.

Having separate definitions of security and financial asset makes it possible to separate the question of the proper scope of the traditional Article 8 rules from the question of the proper scope of the new indirect holding system rules. Some forms of financial assets should be covered by the indirect holding system rules of Part 5, but not by the rules of Parts 2, 3, and 4. The term financial asset is used to cover such property. Because the term security entitlement is defined in terms of financial assets rather than securities, the rules concerning security entitlements set out in Part 5 of Article 8 and in Revised Article 9 apply to the broader class of financial assets.

The fact that something does or could fall within the definition of financial asset does not, without more, trigger Article 8 coverage. The indirect holding system rules of Revised Article 8 apply only if the financial asset is in fact held in a securities account, so that the interest of the person who holds the financial asset through the securities account is a security entitlement. Thus, questions of the scope of the indirect holding system rules cannot be framed as "Is such-and-such a 'financial asset' under Article 8?" Rather, one must analyze whether the relationship between an institution and a person on whose behalf the institution holds an asset falls within the scope of the term securities account as defined in Section 8-501. That question turns in large measure on whether it makes sense to apply the Part 5 rules to the relationship.

The term financial asset is used to refer both to the underlying asset and the particular means by which ownership of that asset is evidenced. Thus, with respect to a certificated security, the term financial asset may, as context requires, refer either to the interest or obligation of the issuer or to the security certificate representing that interest or obligation. Similarly, if a person holds a security or other financial asset through a securities account, the term financial asset may, as context requires, refer either to the underlying asset or to the person's security entitlement.

It is not necessary for all of the Part 5 rules to be relevant to a particular financial asset for the relevant property to qualify as a "financial asset" credited to a securities account. Many of the duties set forth in Part 5 will often be relevant to a digital asset such as a "controllable electronic record" (Section 12-102), or a "controllable account" or "controllable payment intangible" (Section 9-102) evidenced by a controllable electronic record, treated as a financial asset credited to a securities account. These duties include the duty to exercise rights as directed by the entitlement holder, comply with the entitlement holder's entitlement orders, and change the position to another form of holding.

If the parties agree to treat a digital asset as a financial asset under Article 8 and the digital asset is in fact held in a securities account for an entitlement holder, the rules applicable to controllable electronic records under Article 12 would not apply to the entitlement holder's security entitlement related to the financial asset. If the financial asset itself is a controllable electronic record, however, then the rules in Article 12 could apply to the securities intermediary's rights with respect to the controllable electronic record if the intermediary holds the asset directly.

10. "Good faith." Section 1-203 provides that "Every contract or duty within [the Uniform Commercial Code] imposes an obligation of good faith in its performance or enforcement." Section 1-201(b)(20) defines "good faith" as "honesty in fact and the observance of reasonable commercial standards of fair dealing." The reference to commercial standards makes clear that assessments of conduct are to be made in light of the commercial setting. The substantive rules of Article 8 have been drafted to take account of the commercial circumstances of the securities holding and processing system. For example, Section 8-115 provides that a securities intermediary acting on an effective entitlement order, or a broker or other agent acting as a conduit in a securities transaction, is not liable to an adverse claimant, unless the claimant obtained legal process or the intermediary acted in collusion with the wrongdoer. This and other similar provisions, see Sections 8-404 and 8-503(e), do not depend on notice of adverse claims, because it would impair rather than advance the interest of investors in having a sound and efficient securities clearance and settlement system to require intermediaries to investigate the propriety of the transactions they are processing. The good faith obligation does not supplant the standards of conduct established in provisions of this kind.

In Revised Article 8, the definition of good faith is not germane to the question whether a purchaser takes free from adverse claims. The rules on such questions as whether a purchaser who takes in suspicious circumstances is disqualified from protected purchaser status are treated not as an aspect of good faith but directly in the rules of Section 8-105 on notice of adverse claims.

11. "Indorsement" is defined as a signature made on a security certificate or separate document for purposes of transferring or redeeming the security. The definition is adapted from the language of Section 8-308(1) of the prior version and from the definition of indorsement in the Negotiable Instruments Article, see Section 3-204(a). The definition of indorsement does not include the requirement that the signature be made by an appropriate person or be authorized. Those questions are treated in the separate substantive provision on whether the indorsement is effective, rather than in the definition of indorsement. See Section 8-107.

12. "Instruction" is defined as a notification communicated to the issuer of an uncertificated security directing that transfer be registered or that the security be redeemed. Instructions are the analog for uncertificated securities of indorsements of certificated securities.

13. "Registered form." The definition of "registered form" is substantially the same as in the prior version of Article 8. Like the definition of bearer form, it serves primarily to distinguish Article 8 securities from instruments governed by other law, such as Article 3. Contrary to the holding in *Highland Capital Management LP v. Schneider,* 8 N.Y.3d 406 (2007), the registrability requirement in the definition of "registered form," and its parallel in the definition of "security," are satisfied only if books are maintained by or on behalf of the issuer for the purpose of registration of transfer, including the determination rights under Section 8-207(a) (or if, in the case of a certificated security, the security certificate so states). It is not sufficient that the issuer records ownership, or records transfers thereof, for other purposes. Nor is it sufficient that the issuer, while in fact maintaining books for the purpose of registration of transfer, could do so, for such is always the case.

14. "Securities intermediary." A "securities intermediary" is a person that in the ordinary course of its business maintains securities accounts for others and is acting in that capacity. The most common examples of securities intermediaries would be clearing corporations holding securities for their participants, banks acting as securities custodians, and brokers holding securities on behalf of their customers. However, a person need not be such an entity in order to be a securities intermediary. Because a "securities account" is an account to which a financial asset is or may be credited under Section 8-501(a) and the definition of "financial asset" is not limited to securities, a person may be a "securities intermediary" even if that person does not credit "securities" (as defined in Article 8) to the account. Rather, the securities accounts that a securities intermediary maintains may consist exclusively of financial assets described in Section 8-102(a)(9)(ii) and (iii). For example, a cryptocurrency exchange that holds only cryptocurrencies (and not securities) for customers might be a securities intermediary. Clearing corporations are listed separately as a category of securities intermediary in subparagraph (i) even though in most circumstances they would fall within the general definition in subparagraph (ii). The reason is to simplify the analysis of arrangements such as the NSCC-DTC system in which NSCC performs the comparison, clearance, and netting function, while DTC acts as the depository. Because NSCC is a registered clearing agency under the federal securities laws, it is a clearing corporation and hence a securities intermediary under Article 8, regardless of whether it is at any particular time or in any particular aspect of its operations holding securities on behalf of its participants.

The terms securities intermediary and broker have different meanings. Broker means a person engaged in the business of buying and selling securities, as agent for others or as principal. Securities intermediary means a person maintaining securities accounts for others. A stockbroker, in the colloquial sense, may or may not be acting as a securities intermediary.

The definition of securities intermediary includes the requirement that the person in question "in the ordinary course of its business maintain securities accounts for others." This "ordinary course" requirement does not have a fixed quantitative requirement and is determined by the facts of each case. Thus, a person need not necessarily satisfy a specified threshold of activity or necessarily have a minimum number of customers. Law other than the UCC may determine who may legally engage in such a business.

The definition of securities intermediary includes the requirement that the person in question is "acting in the capacity" of maintaining securities accounts for others. This is to take account of the fact that a particular entity, such as a bank, may act in many different capacities in securities transactions. A bank may act as a transfer agent for issuers, as a securities custodian for institutional investors and private investors, as a dealer in government securities, as a lender taking securities as collateral, and as a provider of general payment and collection services that might be used in connection with securities transactions. A bank that maintains securities accounts for its customers would be a securities intermediary with respect to those accounts; but if it takes a pledge of securities from a borrower to secure a loan, it is not thereby acting as a securities intermediary with respect to the pledged securities, since it holds them for its own account rather than for a customer. In other circumstances, those two functions might be combined. For example, if the bank is a government securities dealer it may maintain securities accounts for customers and also provide the customers with margin credit to purchase or carry the securities, in much the same way that brokers provide margin loans to their customers.

15. "Security." The definition of "security" has three components. First, there is the subparagraph (i) test that the interest or obligation be fully transferable, in the sense that the issuer either maintains transfer books or the obligation or interest is represented by a certificate in bearer or registered form. Second, there is the subparagraph (ii) test that the interest or obligation be divisible, that is, one of a class or series, as distinguished from individual obligations of the sort governed by ordinary contract law or by Article 3. Third, there is the subparagraph (iii) functional test, which generally turns on whether the interest or obligation is, or is of a type, dealt in or traded on securities markets or securities exchanges. There is, however, an "opt-in" provision in subparagraph (iii) which permits the issuer of any interest or obligation that is "a medium of investment" to specify that it is a security governed by Article 8.

The divisibility test of subparagraph (ii) applies to the security — that is, the underlying intangible interest — not the means by which that interest is evidenced. Thus, securities issued in book-entry only form meet the divisibility test because the underlying intangible interest is divisible via the mechanism of the indirect holding system. This is so even though the clearing corporation is the only eligible direct holder of the security.

The third component, the functional test in subparagraph (iii), provides flexibility while ensuring that the Article 8 rules do not apply to interests or obligations in circumstances so unconnected with the securities markets that parties are unlikely to have thought of the possibility that Article 8 might apply. Subparagraph (iii)(A) covers interests or obligations that either are dealt in or traded on securities exchanges or securities markets or are of a type dealt in or traded on securities exchanges or securities markets. The "is dealt in or traded on" phrase eliminates problems in the characterization of new forms of securities which are to be traded in the markets, even though no similar type has previously been dealt in or traded in the markets. Subparagraph (iii)(B) covers the broader category of media for investment, but it applies only if the terms of the interest or obligation specify that it is an Article 8 security. This opt-in provision allows for deliberate expansion of the scope of Article 8.

Section 8-103 contains additional rules on the treatment of particular interests as securities or financial assets.

16. "Security certificate." The term "security" refers to the underlying asset, e.g., 1000 shares of common stock of Acme, Inc. The term "security certificate" refers to the paper certificates that have traditionally been used to embody the underlying intangible interest.

17. "Security entitlement" means the rights and property interest of a person who holds securities or other financial assets through a securities intermediary. A security entitlement is both a package of personal rights against the securities intermediary and an interest in the property held by the securities intermediary. A security entitlement is not, however, a specific property interest in any financial asset held by the securities intermediary or by the clearing corporation through which the securities intermediary holds the financial asset. See Sections 8-104(c) and 8-503. The formal definition of security entitlement set out in subsection (a)(17) of this section is a cross-reference to the rules of Part 5. In a sense, then, the entirety of Part 5 is the definition of security entitlement. The Part 5 rules specify the rights and property interest that comprise a security entitlement. Rights and obligations relating to a security entitlement are enforceable by action. See Section 1-305(b) and PEB Commentary No. 25, dated August 12, 2022. The Commentary is available at https://www.ali.org/peb-ucc.

18. "Uncertificated security." The term "uncertificated security" means a security that is not represented by a security certificate—i.e., a paper certificate. This is so even if, for example, the organic documents relating to the security refer to it as being "certificated" or refer to the electronic record evidencing the security as an "electronic certificate." For uncertificated securities, there is no need to draw any distinction between the underlying asset and the means by which a direct holder's interest in that asset is evidenced. Compare "certificated security" and "security certificate."

As discussed above in Comment 9, a controllable electronic record may be a "financial asset." However, a controllable electronic record is not itself a "security," defined in part in Section 8-102(a)(15) as "an obligation of an issuer or a share, participation, or other interest in an issuer or in property or an enterprise of an issuer." It also is not "a share or similar equity interest," an "investment company security," or "an interest in a partnership or limited liability company." See Section 8-103(a), (b), and (c). Of course, a controllable electronic record might be involved in the issuance and distribution of something that is a security for other, non-Article 8 purposes, including the federal securities laws. For example, a controllable electronic record (perhaps labeled as a "token" or "coin") might provide a mechanism for facilitating investments in such securities. As Section 8-102(d) makes clear, however, characterization under Article 8 does not determine characterization for other purposes. The converse is also true—characterization for other purposes does not determine characterization under Article 8.

Although not itself an Article 8 security, a controllable electronic record might play a role in the facilitating transactions in Article 8 securities. The following examples address situations in which controllable electronic records may have such a role as well as situations in which investment property is not involved.

Example 1 (corporate shares: Article 8 uncertificated securities; token as instruction). A Delaware corporation (D Corp) issues shares of stock and maintains books and records evidencing the registered ownership of the shares. Because the shares are not represented by security certificates, they are uncertificated securities. Pursuant to the applicable law and the organic documentation of D Corp, D Corp creates, or causes to be created, controllable electronic records (CERs)—"tokens"—to facilitate transfers of the shares. Also pursuant to that law and documentation, the transfer of control of a token on the platform on which the token is recorded constitutes an instruction to D Corp, as issuer, for the transfer of registration of the share(s) represented by the token to the transferee of control. Following receipt of the instruction upon transfer of control of a token, D Corp transfers registration of the share(s) on its books and records. See Sections 8-102(a)(12) (defining "instruction"); 8-401 (duty of issuer to register transfer). Although Article 12 governs the tokens (as CERs) and the transfer of control thereof, other law, including Delaware corporate law and Delaware Article 8 (and Article 9 of the relevant jurisdiction, if applicable) governs rights in the uncertificated securities and the transfer of registration. See Sections 8-110(a); 12-104(f).

Example 2 (LLC membership interest: Article 8 uncertificated securities; token as instruction). A Delaware limited liability company (LLC) issues membership interests that are dealt in or traded on securities exchanges or in securities markets and which by their terms are securities governed by Article 8. See Section 8-103(c). LLC maintains books and records evidencing the registered ownership of the interests. Because the interests are not represented by security certificates, they are uncertificated securities. Pursuant to the applicable law and the organic documentation of LLC, LLC creates, or causes to be created, controllable electronic records (CERs)—"tokens"—to facilitate transfers of the interests. Also pursuant to that law and documentation, the transfer of control of a token on the platform on which the token is recorded constitutes an instruction to LLC, as issuer, for the transfer of registration of the interest(s) represented by the token to the transferee of control. Following receipt of the instruction upon transfer of control of a token, LLC transfers registration of the interest(s) on its books and records. See Sections 8-102(a)(12) (defining "instruction"); 8-401 (duty of issuer to register transfer). Although Article 12 governs the tokens (as CERs) and the transfer of control thereof, other law, including Delaware LLC law and Delaware Article 8 (and Article 9 of the relevant jurisdiction, if applicable), governs rights in the uncertificated securities and the transfer of registration. See Sections 8-110(a); 12-104(f).

Example 3 (LLC membership interests not covered by Article 8; interests are general intangibles). A Delaware limited liability company issues membership interests that are not securities governed by UCC Article 8 and, consequently, are not investment property. See Section 8-103(c). Instead, the membership interests are general intangibles. LLC maintains books and records evidencing ownership of the interests. Pursuant to the applicable law and the organic documentation of LLC, LLC creates, or causes to be created, controllable electronic records (CERs)—"tokens"—to facilitate transfers of the interests. Also pursuant to that law and documentation, the transfer of control of a token on the platform on which the token is recorded constitutes a request to LLC, as issuer, for the transfer of the interest(s) related to the token. Following receipt of the request upon transfer of control of a token, LLC transfers the interest(s) on its books and records. Although Article 12 governs the tokens (as CERs) and the transfer of control, other law (including Article 9 or the relevant jurisdiction, if applicable, but not Article 8) governs rights in the interests (general intangibles). See Section 12-104(f).

Examples 1 and 2 posit that controllable electronic records function as instructions to the issuers. For an analogous example in another context, see Section 4A-104, Comment 3 ("An instruction to pay might be a component of a computer program or a transaction protocol intended to execute automatically under specified circumstances."). The central point is that the roles of the controllable electronic records must comply with the organic corporate and LLC laws and documentation as well as the Article 8 regime for uncertificated securities. Although controllable electronic records might be structured to functionally "represent" the underlying uncertificated securities, Article 8 makes no provision for such a "representation" for uncertificated securities (unlike the role of security certificates for certificated securities). Whether it would be possible and feasible to expand the structure contemplated in Examples 1 and 2 so that transfer of control of a controllable electronic record would, ipso facto, constitute a transfer of registration on the issuer's books and records would depend on the terms of and compliance with both the underlying organic laws and documentation for the uncertificated securities, the requirements of Article 8, and, where applicable, other law.

If the securities issued by D Corp or LLC in Examples 1 and 2 were payment obligations of the issuers that met the definition of "security" in Section 8-102(a)(15)—i.e., debt securities— the same analysis discussed in those examples as to the applicability and scope of Articles 8 and 12 would apply. However, if the debt obligations were not Article 8 securities (as in Example 3) but were obligations of account debtors on controllable accounts or controllable payment intangibles, then the relevant provisions of Articles 9 and 12, and not those of Article 8, would apply. See, e.g., Sections 9-107A; 9-306B; 9-314; 12-104(a), (b), and (e) and Comments 6 – 10; Article 12, Prefatory Note 4.

Definitional Cross References:

"Agreement". Section 1-201(b)(3).
"Bank". Section 1-201(b)(4).
"Person". Section 1-201(b)(27).
"Send". Section 1-201(b)(36).
"Signed". Section 1-201(b)(37).
"Writing". Section 1-201(b)(43).

§ 8-106. Control.

(a) A purchaser has "control" of a certificated security in bearer form if the certificated security is delivered to the purchaser.

(b) A purchaser has "control" of a certificated security in registered form if the certificated security is delivered to the purchaser, and:

(1) the certificate is indorsed to the purchaser or in blank by an effective indorsement; or

(2) the certificate is registered in the name of the purchaser, upon original issue or registration of transfer by the issuer.

(c) A purchaser has "control" of an uncertificated security if:

(1) the uncertificated security is delivered to the purchaser; or

(2) the issuer has agreed that it will comply with instructions originated by the purchaser without further consent by the registered owner.

(d) A purchaser has "control" of a security entitlement if:

(1) the purchaser becomes the entitlement holder;

(2) the securities intermediary has agreed that it will comply with entitlement orders originated by the purchaser without further consent by the entitlement holder; or

(3) another person, other than the transferor to the purchaser of an interest in the security entitlement:

(A) has control of the security entitlement and acknowledges that it has control on behalf of the purchaser; or

(B) obtains control of the security entitlement after having acknowledged that it will obtain control of the security entitlement on behalf of the purchaser.

(e) If an interest in a security entitlement is granted by the entitlement holder to the entitlement holder's own securities intermediary, the securities intermediary has control.

(f) A purchaser who has satisfied the requirements of subsection (c) or (d) has control, even if the registered owner in the case of subsection (c) or the entitlement holder in the case of subsection (d) retains the right to make substitutions for the uncertificated security or security entitlement, to originate instructions or entitlement orders to the issuer or securities intermediary, or otherwise to deal with the uncertificated security or security entitlement.

(g) An issuer or a securities intermediary may not enter into an agreement of the kind described in subsection (c)(2) or (d)(2) without the consent of the registered owner or entitlement holder, but an issuer or a securities intermediary is not required to enter into such an agreement even though the registered owner or entitlement holder so directs. An issuer or securities intermediary that has entered into such an agreement is not required to confirm the existence of the agreement to another party unless requested to do so by the registered owner or entitlement holder.

(h) A person that has control under this section is not required to acknowledge that it has control on behalf of a purchaser.

(i) If a person acknowledges that it has or will obtain control on behalf of a purchaser, unless the person otherwise agrees or law other than this Article or Article 9 otherwise provides, the person does not owe any duty to the purchaser and is not required to confirm the acknowledgment to any other person.

Official Comment

1. The concept of "control" plays a key role in various provisions dealing with the rights of purchasers, including secured parties. See Sections 8-303 (protected purchasers); 8-503(e) (purchasers from securities intermediaries); 8-510 (purchasers of security entitlements from entitlement holders); 9-203(b)(3)(D) (attachment of security interests); 9-314 (perfection of security interests); 9-328 (priorities among conflicting security interests).

Obtaining "control" means that the purchaser has taken whatever steps are necessary, given the manner in which the securities or other financial assets are held, to place itself in a position where it can have the securities or other financial assets sold, without further action by the owner, registered owner, entitlement holder, transferor, or other person with an interest in the securities or other financial assets.

2. Subsection (a) provides that a purchaser obtains "control" with respect to a certificated security in bearer form by taking "delivery," as defined in Section 8-301. Subsection (b) provides that a purchaser obtains "control" with respect to a certificated security in registered form by taking "delivery," as defined in Section 8-301, provided that the security certificate has been indorsed to the purchaser or in blank. Section 8-301 provides that delivery of a certificated security occurs when the purchaser obtains possession of the security certificate, or when an agent for the purchaser (other than a securities intermediary) either acquires possession or acknowledges that the agent holds for the purchaser.

3. Subsection (c) specifies the means by which a purchaser can obtain control over uncertificated securities which the transferor holds directly. Two mechanisms are possible.

Under subsection (c)(1), securities can be "delivered" to a purchaser. Section 8-301(b) provides that "delivery" of an uncertificated security occurs when the purchaser becomes the registered holder. So far as the issuer is concerned, the purchaser would then be entitled to exercise all rights of ownership. See Section 8-207. As between the parties to a purchase transaction, however, the rights of the purchaser are determined by their contract. Cf. Section 9-202. Arrangements covered by this paragraph are analogous to arrangements in which bearer certificates are delivered to a secured party—so far as the issuer or any other parties are concerned, the secured party appears to be the outright owner, although it is in fact holding as collateral property that belongs to the debtor.

Under subsection (c)(2), a purchaser has control if the issuer has agreed to act on the instructions of the purchaser, even though the owner remains listed as the registered owner. The issuer, of course, would be acting wrongfully against the registered owner if it entered into such an agreement without the consent of the registered owner. Subsection (g) makes this point explicit. The subsection (c)(2) provision makes it possible for issuers to offer a service akin to the registered pledge device of the 1978 version of Article 8, without mandating that all issuers offer that service.

4. Subsection (d) specifies the means by which a purchaser can obtain control of a security entitlement. Three mechanisms are possible, analogous to those provided in subsection (c) for uncertificated securities. Under subsection (d)(1), a purchaser has control if it is the entitlement holder. This subsection would apply whether the purchaser holds through the same intermediary that the debtor used, or has the securities position transferred to its own intermediary. Subsection (d)(2) provides that a purchaser has control if the securities intermediary has agreed to act on entitlement orders originated by the purchaser if no further consent by the entitlement holder is required. Under subsection (d)(2), control may be achieved even though the original entitlement holder remains as the entitlement holder. Finally, a purchaser may obtain control under subsection (d)(3) if another person has control and the person acknowledges that it has control on the purchaser's behalf. In general, control under subsection (d)(3) parallels the delivery of certificated securities and uncertificated securities under Section 8-301. See the discussion of subsection (d)(3) in Comment 4A, below.

Subsection (d) specifies only the minimum requirements that such an arrangement must meet to confer "control" of a security entitlement; the details of the arrangement can be specified by agreement. The arrangement might cover all of the positions in a particular account or subaccount, or only specified positions. There is no requirement that the control party's right to give entitlement orders be exclusive. The arrangement might provide, for example, that only the control party can give entitlement orders, that either the entitlement holder or the control party can give entitlement orders, that more than one person has unilateral control, or that two or more persons share control. The essential factor is whether a person may originate entitlement orders without further consent of the entitlement holder. See subsection (f).

The following examples illustrate the application of subsection (d):

Example 1: Debtor grants Alpha Bank a security interest in a security entitlement that includes 1000 shares of XYZ Co. stock that Debtor holds through an account with Able & Co. Alpha Bank also has an account with Able. Debtor instructs Able to transfer the shares to Alpha Bank, and Able does so by crediting the shares to Alpha's account. Alpha has control of the 1000 shares under subsection (d)(1). Although Debtor may have become the beneficial owner of the new securities entitlement, as between Debtor and Alpha, Able has agreed to act on Alpha's entitlement orders because, as between Able and Alpha, Alpha has become the entitlement holder. See Section 8-506.

Example 2: Debtor grants Alpha Bank a security interest in a security entitlement that includes 1000 shares of XYZ Co. stock that Debtor holds through an account with Able & Co. Alpha does not have an account with Able. Alpha uses Beta Bank as its securities custodian. Debtor instructs Able to transfer the shares to Beta Bank, for the account of Alpha, and Able does so. Alpha has control of the 1000 shares under subsection (d)(1). As in Example 1, although Debtor may have become the beneficial owner of the new securities entitlement, as between Debtor and Alpha, Beta has agreed to act on Alpha's entitlement orders because, as between Beta and Alpha, Alpha has become the entitlement holder.

Example 3: Debtor grants Alpha Bank a security interest in a security entitlement that includes 1000 shares of XYZ Co. stock that Debtor holds through an account with Able & Co. Debtor, Able, and Alpha enter into an agreement under which Debtor will continue to receive dividends and distributions, and will continue to have the right to direct dispositions, but Alpha also has the right to direct dispositions. Alpha has control of the 1000 shares under subsection (d)(2).

Example 4: Able & Co., a securities dealer, grants Alpha Bank a security interest in a security entitlement that includes 1000 shares of XYZ Co. stock that Able holds through an account with Clearing Corporation. Able causes Clearing Corporation to transfer the shares into Alpha's account at Clearing Corporation. As in Example 1, Alpha has control of the 1000 shares under subsection (d)(1).

Example 5: Able & Co., a securities dealer, grants Alpha Bank a security interest in a security entitlement that includes 1000 shares of XYZ Co. stock that Able holds through an account with Clearing Corporation. Alpha does not have an account with Clearing Corporation. It holds its securities through Beta Bank, which does have an account with Clearing Corporation. Able causes Clearing Corporation to transfer the shares into Beta's account at Clearing Corporation. Beta credits the position to Alpha's account with Beta. As in Example 2, Alpha has control of the 1000 shares under subsection (d)(1).

Example 6: Able & Co., a securities dealer, grants Alpha Bank a security interest in a security entitlement that includes 1000 shares of XYZ Co. stock that Able holds through an account with Clearing Corporation. Able causes Clearing Corporation to transfer the shares into a pledge account, pursuant to an agreement under which Able will continue to receive dividends, distributions, and the like, but Alpha has the right to direct dispositions. As in Example 3, Alpha has control of the 1000 shares under subsection (d)(2).

Example 7: Able & Co., a securities dealer, grants Alpha Bank a security interest in a security entitlement that includes 1000 shares of XYZ Co. stock that Able holds through an account with Clearing Corporation. Able, Alpha, and Clearing Corporation enter into an agreement under which Clearing Corporation will act on instructions from Alpha with respect to the XYZ Co. stock carried in Able's account, but Able will continue to receive dividends, distributions, and the like, and will also have the right to direct dispositions. As in Example 3, Alpha has control of the 1000 shares under subsection (d)(2).

Example 8: Able & Co., a securities dealer, holds a wide range of securities through its account at Clearing Corporation. Able enters into an arrangement with Alpha Bank pursuant to which Alpha provides financing to Able secured by securities identified as the collateral on lists provided by Able to Alpha on a daily or other periodic basis. Able, Alpha, and Clearing Corporation enter into an agreement under which Clearing Corporation agrees that if at any time Alpha directs Clearing Corporation to do so, Clearing Corporation will transfer any securities from Able's account at Alpha's instructions. Because Clearing Corporation has agreed to act on Alpha's instructions with respect to any securities carried in Able's account, at the moment that Alpha's security interest attaches to securities listed by Able, Alpha obtains control of those securities under subsection (d)(2). There is no requirement that Clearing Corporation be informed of which securities Able has pledged to Alpha.

Example 9: Debtor grants Alpha Bank a security interest in a security entitlement that includes 1000 shares of XYZ Co. stock that Debtor holds through an account with Able & Co. Beta Bank agrees with Alpha to act as Alpha's collateral agent with respect to the security entitlement. Debtor, Able, and Beta enter into an agreement under which Debtor will continue to receive dividends and distributions, and will continue to have the right to direct dispositions, but Beta also has the right to direct dispositions. Because Able has agreed that it will comply with entitlement orders originated by Beta without further consent by Debtor, Beta has control of the security entitlement (see Example 3). Because Beta has acknowledged that it has control on behalf of Alpha, Alpha also has control under subsection (d)(3). It is not necessary for Able to enter into an agreement directly with Alpha or for Able to be aware of Beta's relationship with Alpha.

4A. Pursuant to the 2022 Amendments, subsection (d)(3) was revised to conform the provision for control through another person to the corresponding provisions for control of other types of assets. See Section 12-105, Comment 8; see also Sections 7-106(g) (control of electronic document of title); 9-104(a)(4) (control of deposit account); 9-105(g) (control of authoritative electronic copy of a record evidencing chattel paper); 9-105A(e) (control of electronic money). Control based on an acknowledgment under subsection (d)(3) by another person having control continues only while the other person retains control. This result necessarily follows because such control derives solely from the other person's continued control. Under subsection (d)(3), for an acknowledgment to be effective to confer control, it must be made by a person "other than the transferor of an interest in the security entitlement." See Section 12-105, Comment 9 (discussing the rationale for this requirement). Subsections (h) and (i) derive from Section 9- 313(f) and (g). Subsection (h) makes clear that a person that has control under this section has no duty to acknowledge that it has or will obtain control on behalf of a purchaser. Arrangements for a person to acknowledge that it has or will obtain control on behalf of another person are not standardized. Accordingly, subsection (i) leaves to the agreement of the parties and to any other applicable law (other than this Article or Article 9) any duties of a person that does acknowledge that it has or will obtain control on behalf of a purchaser and provides that a person making an acknowledgment is not required to confirm the acknowledgment to any other person.

5. For a purchaser to have "control" under subsection (c)(2) or (d)(2), it is essential that the issuer or securities intermediary, as the case may be, actually be a party to the agreement. If a debtor gives a secured party a power of attorney authorizing the secured party to act in the name of the debtor, but the issuer or securities intermediary does not specifically agree to this arrangement, the secured party does not have "control" within the meaning of subsection (c)(2) or (d)(2) because the issuer or securities intermediary is not a party to the agreement. The secured party does not have control under subsection (c)(1) or (d)(1) because, although the power of attorney might give the secured party authority to act on the debtor's behalf as an agent, the secured party has not actually become the registered owner or entitlement holder.

6. Subsection (e) provides that if an interest in a security entitlement is granted by an entitlement holder to the securities intermediary through which the security entitlement is maintained, the securities intermediary has control. A common transaction covered by this provision is a margin loan from a broker to its customer.

7. The term "control" is used in a particular defined sense. The requirements for obtaining control are set out in this section. The concept is not to be interpreted by reference to similar concepts in other bodies of law. In particular, the requirements for "possession" derived from the common law of pledge are not to be used as a basis for interpreting subsection (c)(2) or (d)(2). Those provisions are designed to supplant the concepts of "constructive possession" and the like. A principal purpose of the "control" concept is to eliminate the uncertainty and confusion that results from attempting to apply common law possession concepts to modern securities holding practices.

The key to the control concept is that the purchaser has the ability to have the securities sold or transferred without further action by the transferor. There is no requirement that the powers held by the purchaser be exclusive. For example, in a secured lending arrangement, if the secured party wishes, it can allow the debtor to retain the right to make substitutions, to direct the disposition of the uncertificated security or security entitlement, or otherwise to give instructions or entitlement orders. (As explained in Section 8-102, Comment 8, an entitlement order includes a direction under Section 8-508 to the securities intermediary to transfer a financial asset to the account of the entitlement holder at another financial intermediary or to cause the financial asset to be transferred to the entitlement holder in the direct holding system (e.g., by delivery of a securities certificate registered in the name of the former entitlement holder).) Subsection (f) is included to make clear the general point stated in subsections (c) and (d) that the test of control is whether the purchaser has obtained the requisite power, not whether the debtor has retained other powers. There is no implication that retention by the debtor of powers other than those mentioned in subsection (f) is inconsistent with the purchaser having control. Nor is there a requirement that the purchaser's powers be unconditional, provided that further consent of the entitlement holder is not a condition.

Example 10: Debtor grants to Alpha Bank and to Beta Bank a security interest in a security entitlement that includes 1000 shares of XYZ Co. stock that Debtor holds through an account with Able & Co. By agreement among the parties, Alpha's security interest is senior and Beta's is junior. Able agrees to act on the entitlement orders of either Alpha or Beta. Alpha and Beta each has control under subsection (d)(2). Moreover, Beta has control notwithstanding a term of Able's agreement to the effect that Able's obligation to act on Beta's entitlement orders is conditioned on Alpha's consent. The crucial distinction is that Able's agreement to act on Beta's entitlement orders is not conditioned on Debtor's further consent.

Example 11: Debtor grants to Alpha Bank a security interest in a security entitlement that includes 1000 shares of XYZ Co. stock that Debtor holds through an account with Able & Co. Able agrees to act on the entitlement orders of Alpha, but Alpha's right to give entitlement orders to the securities intermediary is conditioned on the Debtor's default. Alternatively, Alpha's right to give entitlement orders is conditioned upon Alpha's statement to Able that Debtor is in default. Because Able's agreement to act on Alpha's entitlement orders is not conditioned on Debtor's further consent, Alpha has control of the securities entitlement under either alternative.

In many situations, it will be better practice for both the securities intermediary and the purchaser to insist that any conditions relating in any way to the entitlement holder be effective only as between the purchaser and the entitlement holder. That practice would avoid the risk that the securities intermediary could be caught between conflicting assertions of the entitlement holder and the purchaser as to whether the conditions in fact have been met. Nonetheless, the existence of unfulfilled conditions effective against the intermediary would not preclude the purchaser from having control.

PART 3. TRANSFER OF CERTIFICATED AND UNCERTIFICATED SECURITIES

§ 8-301. Delivery.

(a) Delivery of a certificated security to a purchaser occurs when:

(1) the purchaser acquires possession of the security certificate;

(2) another person, other than a securities intermediary, either acquires possession of the security certificate on behalf of the purchaser or, having previously acquired possession of the certificate, acknowledges that it holds for the purchaser; or

(3) a securities intermediary acting on behalf of the purchaser acquires possession of the security certificate, only if the certificate is in registered form and has been specially indorsed to the purchaser by an effective indorsement.

(b) Delivery of an uncertificated security to a purchaser occurs when:

(1) the issuer registers the purchaser as the registered owner, upon original issue or registration of transfer; or

(2) another person, other than a securities intermediary, either becomes the registered owner of the uncertificated security on behalf of the purchaser or, having previously become the registered owner, acknowledges that it holds for the purchaser.

Official Comment

1. This section specifies the requirements for "delivery" of securities. Delivery is used in Article 8 to describe the formal steps necessary for a purchaser to acquire a direct interest in a security under this Article. The concept of delivery refers to the implementation of a transaction, not the legal categorization of the transaction which is consummated by delivery. Issuance and transfer are different kinds of transaction, though both may be implemented by delivery. Sale and pledge are different kinds of transfers, but both may be implemented by delivery.

2. Subsection (a) defines delivery with respect to certificated securities. Paragraph (1) deals with simple cases where purchasers themselves acquire physical possession of certificates. Paragraphs (2) and (3) of subsection (a) specify the circumstances in which delivery to a purchaser can occur although the certificate is in the possession of a person other than the purchaser. Paragraph (2) contains the general rule that a purchaser can take delivery through another person, so long as the other person is actually acting on behalf of the purchaser or acknowledges that it is holding on behalf of the purchaser. Paragraph (2) does not apply to acquisition of possession by a securities intermediary, because a person who holds securities through a securities account acquires a security entitlement, rather than having a direct interest. See Section 8-501. Subsection (a)(3) specifies the limited circumstances in which delivery of security certificates to a securities intermediary is treated as a delivery to the customer.

3. Subsection (b) defines delivery with respect to uncertificated securities. Use of the term "delivery" with respect to uncertificated securities, does, at least on first hearing, seem a bit solecistic. The word "delivery" is, however, routinely used in the securities business in a broader sense than manual tradition. For example, settlement by entries on the books of a clearing corporation is commonly called "delivery," as in the expression "delivery versus payment." The diction of this section has the advantage of using the same term for uncertificated securities as for certificated securities, for which delivery is conventional usage. Paragraph (1) of subsection (b) provides that delivery occurs when the purchaser becomes the registered owner of an uncertificated security, either upon original issue or registration of transfer. Paragraph (2) provides for delivery of an uncertificated security through a third person, in a fashion analogous to subsection (a)(2).

Definitional Cross References

"Certificated security". Section 8-102(a)(4).
"Effective". Section 8-107.
"Issuer". Section 8-201.
"Purchaser". Sections 1-201(33) & 8-116.
"Registered form". Section 8-102(a)(13).
"Securities intermediary". Section 8-102(a)(14).
"Security certificate". Section 8-102(a)(16).
"Special indorsement". Section 8-304(a).
"Uncertificated security". Section 8-102(a)(18).

UNIFORM COMMERCIAL CODE

Article 9—Secured Transactions

PART 1. GENERAL PROVISIONS

[SUBPART 1. SHORT TITLE, DEFINITIONS, AND GENERAL CONCEPTS]

Section

9-101. Short Title
9-102. Definitions and Index of Definitions
9-103. Purchase-Money Security Interest; Application of Payments; Burden of Establishing
9-104. Control of Deposit Account
9-105. Control of Electronic Copy of Record Evidencing Chattel Paper
9-105A. Control of Electronic Money
9-106. Control of Investment Property
9-107. Control of Letter-of-Credit Right
9-107A. Control of Controllable Electronic Record, Controllable Account, or Controllable Payment Intangible
9-107B. No Requirement to Acknowledge or Confirm; No Duties
9-108. Sufficiency of Description

[SUBPART 2. APPLICABILITY OF ARTICLE]

9-109. Scope
9-110. Security Interests Arising Under Article 2 or 2A

PART 2. EFFECTIVENESS OF SECURITY AGREEMENT; ATTACHMENT OF SECURITY INTEREST; RIGHTS OF PARTIES TO SECURITY AGREEMENT

[SUBPART 1. EFFECTIVENESS AND ATTACHMENT]

9-201. General Effectiveness of Security Agreement
9-202. Title to Collateral Immaterial
9-203. Attachment and Enforceability of Security Interest; Proceeds; Supporting Obligations; Formal Requisites
9-204. After-Acquired Property; Future Advances
9-205. Use or Disposition of Collateral Permissible
9-206. Security Interest Arising in Purchase or Delivery of Financial Asset

[SUBPART 2. RIGHTS AND DUTIES]

9-207. Rights and Duties of Secured Party Having Possession or Control of Collateral
9-208. Additional Duties of Secured Party Having Control of Collateral
9-209. Duties of Secured Party If Account Debtor Has Been Notified of Assignment
9-210. Request for Accounting; Request Regarding List of Collateral or Statement of Account

PART 3. PERFECTION AND PRIORITY

[SUBPART 1. LAW GOVERNING PERFECTION AND PRIORITY]

9-301. Law Governing Perfection and Priority of Security Interests
9-302. Law Governing Perfection and Priority of Agricultural Liens
9-303. Law Governing Perfection and Priority of Security Interests in Goods Covered by a Certificate of Title
9-304. Law Governing Perfection and Priority of Security Interests in Deposit Accounts
9-305. Law Governing Perfection and Priority of Security Interests in Investment Property
9-306. Law Governing Perfection and Priority of Security Interests in Letter-of-Credit Rights
9-306A. Law Governing Perfection and Priority of Security Interests in Chattel Paper

9-306B. Law Governing Perfection and Priority of Security Interests in Controllable Accounts, Controllable Electronic Records, and Controllable Payment Intangibles
9-307. Location of Debtor

[SUBPART 2. PERFECTION]

9-308. When Security Interest or Agricultural Lien Is Perfected; Continuity of Perfection
9-309. Security Interest Perfected upon Attachment
9-310. When Filing Required to Perfect Security Interest or Agricultural Lien; Security Interests and Agricultural Liens to Which Filing Provisions Do Not Apply
9-311. Perfection of Security Interests in Property Subject to Certain Statutes, Regulations, and Treaties
9-312. Perfection of Security Interests in Chattel Paper, Controllable Accounts, Controllable Electronic Records, Controllable Payment Intangibles, Deposit Accounts, Documents, Goods Covered by Documents, Instruments, Investment Property, Letter-of-Credit Rights, and Money; Perfection by Permissive Filing; Temporary Perfection Without Filing or Transfer of Possession
9-313. When Possession by or Delivery to Secured Party Perfects Security Interest Without Filing
9-314. Perfection by Control
9-314A. Perfection by Possession and Control of Chattel Paper
9-315. Secured Party's Rights on Disposition of Collateral and in Proceeds
9-316. Continued Perfection of Security Interest Following Change in Governing Law

[SUBPART 3. PRIORITY]

9-317. Interests That Take Priority Over or Take Free of Security Interest or Agricultural Lien
9-318. No Interest Retained in Right to Payment That Is Sold; Rights and Title of Seller of Account or Chattel Paper with Respect to Creditors and Purchasers
9-319. Rights and Title of Consignee with Respect to Creditors and Purchasers
9-320. Buyer of Goods
9-321. Licensee of General Intangible and Lessee of Goods in Ordinary Course of Business
9-322. Priorities among Conflicting Security Interests in and Agricultural Liens on Same Collateral
9-323. Future Advances
9-324. Priority of Purchase-Money Security Interests
9-325. Priority of Security Interests in Transferred Collateral
9-326. Priority of Security Interests Created by New Debtor
9-326A. Priority of Security Interest in Controllable Account, Controllable Electronic Record, and Controllable Payment Intangible
9-327. Priority of Security Interests in Deposit Account
9-328. Priority of Security Interests in Investment Property
9-329. Priority of Security Interests in Letter-of-Credit Right
9-330. Priority of Purchaser of Chattel Paper or Instrument
9-331. Priority of Rights of Purchasers of Controllable Accounts, Controllable Electronic Records, Controllable Payment Intangibles, Documents, Instruments, and Securities Under Other Articles; Priority of Interests in Financial Assets and Security Entitlements and Protection Against Assert of Claim Under Articles 8 and 12
9-332. Transfer of Money; Transfer of Funds from Deposit Account
9-333. Priority of Certain Liens Arising by Operation of Law
9-334. Priority of Security Interests in Fixtures and Crops
9-335. Accessions
9-336. Commingled Goods
9-337. Priority of Security Interests in Goods Covered by Certificate of Title
9-338. Priority of Security Interest or Agricultural Lien Perfected by Filed Financing Statement Providing Certain Incorrect Information

9-339. Priority Subject to Subordination

[SUBPART 4. RIGHTS OF BANK]

9-340. Effectiveness of Right of Recoupment or Set-Off Against Deposit Account
9-341. Bank's Rights and Duties with Respect to Deposit Account
9-342. Bank's Right to Refuse to Enter into or Disclose Existence of Control Agreement

PART 4. RIGHTS OF THIRD PARTIES

9-401. Alienability of Debtor's Rights
9-402. Secured Party Not Obligated on Contract of Debtor or in Tort
9-403. Agreement Not to Assert Defenses Against Assignee
9-404. Rights Acquired by Assignee; Claims and Defenses Against Assignee
9-405. Modification of Assigned Contract
9-406. Discharge of Account Debtor; Notification of Assignment; Identification and Proof of Assignment; Restrictions on Assignment of Accounts, Chattel Paper, Payment Intangibles, and Promissory Notes Ineffective
9-407. Restrictions on Creation or Enforcement of Security Interest in Leasehold Interest or in Lessor's Residual Interest
9-408. Restrictions on Assignment of Promissory Notes, Health-Care-Insurance Receivables, and Certain General Intangibles Ineffective
9-409. Restrictions on Assignment of Letter-of-Credit Rights Ineffective

PART 5. FILING

[SUBPART 1. FILING OFFICE; CONTENTS AND EFFECTIVENESS OF FINANCING STATEMENT]

9-501. Filing Office
9-502. Contents of Financing Statement; Record of Mortgage As Financing Statement; Time of Filing Financing Statement
9-503. Name of Debtor and Secured Party
9-504. Indication of Collateral
9-505. Filing and Compliance with Other Statutes and Treaties for Consignments, Leases, Other Bailments, and Other Transactions
9-506. Effect of Errors or Omissions
9-507. Effect of Certain Events on Effectiveness of Financing Statement
9-508. Effectiveness of Financing Statement If New Debtor Becomes Bound by Security Agreement
9-509. Persons Entitled to File a Record
9-510. Effectiveness of Filed Record
9-511. Secured Party of Record
9-512. Amendment of Financing Statement
9-513. Termination Statement
9-514. Assignment of Powers of Secured Party of Record
9-515. Duration and Effectiveness of Financing Statement; Effect of Lapsed Financing Statement
9-516. What Constitutes Filing; Effectiveness of Filing
9-517. Effect of Indexing Errors
9-518. Claim Concerning Inaccurate or Wrongfully Filed Record

[SUBPART 2. DUTIES AND OPERATION OF FILING OFFICE]

9-519. Numbering, Maintaining, and Indexing Records; Communicating Information Provided in Records
9-520. Acceptance and Refusal to Accept Record
9-521. Uniform Form of Written Financing Statement and Amendment
9-522. Maintenance and Destruction of Records
9-523. Information from Filing Office; Sale or License of Records
9-524. Delay by Filing Office
9-525. Fees
9-526. Filing-Office Rules
9-527. Duty to Report

PART 6. DEFAULT

[SUBPART 1. DEFAULT AND ENFORCEMENT OF SECURITY INTEREST]

9-601. Rights After Default; Judicial Enforcement; Consignor or Buyer of Accounts, Chattel Paper, Payment Intangibles, or Promissory Notes

9-602. Waiver and Variance of Rights and Duties
9-603. Agreement on Standards Concerning Rights and Duties
9-604. Procedure If Security Agreement Covers Real Property or Fixtures
9-605. Unknown Debtor or Secondary Obligor
9-606. Time of Default for Agricultural Lien
9-607. Collection and Enforcement by Secured Party
9-608. Application of Proceeds of Collection or Enforcement; Liability for Deficiency and Rights to Surplus
9-609. Secured Party's Right to Take Possession after Default
9-610. Disposition of Collateral After Default
9-611. Notification Before Disposition of Collateral
9-612. Timeliness of Notification Before Disposition of Collateral
9-613. Contents and Form of Notification Before Disposition of Collateral: General
9-614. Contents and Form of Notification Before Disposition of Collateral: Consumer-Goods Transaction
9-615. Application of Proceeds of Disposition; Liability for Deficiency and Rights to Surplus
9-616. Explanation of Calculation of Surplus or Deficiency
9-617. Rights of Transferee of Collateral
9-618. Rights and Duties of Certain Secondary Obligors
9-619. Transfer of Record or Legal Title
9-620. Acceptance of Collateral in Full or Partial Satisfaction of Obligation; Compulsory Disposition of Collateral
9-621. Notification of Proposal to Accept Collateral
9-622. Effect of Acceptance of Collateral
9-623. Right to Redeem Collateral
9-624. Waiver

[SUBPART 2. NONCOMPLIANCE WITH ARTICLE]

9-625. Remedies for Secured Party's Failure to Comply with Article
9-626. Action in Which Deficiency or Surplus Is in Issue
9-627. Determination of Whether Conduct Was Commercially Reasonable
9-628. Nonliability and Limitation on Liability of Secured Party; Liability of Secondary Obligor

PART 7. TRANSITION

9-701. Effective Date
9-702. Savings Clause
9-703. Security Interest Perfected Before Effective Date
9-704. Security Interest Unperfected Before Effective Date
9-705. Effectiveness of Action Taken Before Effective Date
9-706. When Initial Financing Statement Suffices to Continue Effectiveness of Financing Statement
9-707. Amendment of Pre-Effective-Date Financing Statement
9-708. Persons Entitled to File Initial Financing Statement or Continuation Statement
9-709. Priority

PART 8. TRANSITION PROVISIONS FOR 2010 AMENDMENTS

9-801. Effective Date. This [Act] takes effect on July 1, 2013
9-802. Savings Clause
9-803. Security Interest Perfected Before Effective Date
9-804. Security Interest Unperfected Before Effective Date
9-805. Effectiveness of Action Taken Before Effective Date
9-806. When Initial Financing Statement Suffices to Continue Effectiveness of Financing Statement
9-807. Amendment of Pre-Effective-Date Financing Statement
9-808. Person Entitled to File Initial Financing Statement or Continuation Statement
9-809. Priority

APPENDIX

Appendix I — Conforming Amendments to Other Articles [omitted]
Appendix II — Model Provisions for Production-Money Priority
Table of Dispositions
Table of Sources

Collateral Index

GOODS

GOODS, GENERALLY

Section	
9-102(a)(44)	Definition
9-103	Purchase-Money Security Interests
9-110	Security Interests Arising under Article 2 or 2A
9-205(a)(1)(A)	Use, Commingling, or Disposition of Returned or Repossessed Goods by Debtor Permissible
9-301(3)	Law Governing Perfection and Priority of Security Interests
9-310(b)(4,5)	Filing Not Necessary for Certain Goods Perfected Under 9-312
9-312(c,d)	Perfection of Goods in Possession of Bailee Covered by Document
9-312(f)	Temporary Perfection of Goods Made Available to Debtor
9-313(a)	Perfection by Possession or Delivery
9-313(c)	Goods in Possession of Person Other Than Debtor
9-315(b)(1)	When Commingled Proceeds Identifiable
9-317(b,c)	Rights of Buyer That Receives Delivery
9-319	Rights and Title of Consignee
9-320	Rights of Buyer
9-321(c)	Rights of Lessee in Ordinary Course of Business
9 323(d,e)	Future Advances, Buyer of Goods
9-323(f,g)	Future Advances, Lessee of Goods
9-324(a)	Priority of Purchase-Money Security Interests
9-330(c)(2)	Chattel Paper Purchaser's Priority in Proceeds
9-333	Priority of Possessory Lien
9-336	Security Interest in Commingled Goods
9-338(2)	Priority of Security Interest Perfected by Filing Providing Certain Incorrect Information
9-407	Restrictions on Security Interest in Leasehold Interest or in Lessor's Residual Interest
9-505(a)	Use of Terms Other Than "Debtor" and "Secured Party"
9-513(c)(3)	Termination Statement Requirements

GOODS, CONSUMER GOODS000

9-102(a)(23)	Definition
9-108(e)(2)	Description by Type Insufficient in a Consumer Transaction
9-204(b)(1)	After-Acquired Property Clause Not Effective
9-207(b)(4)(C)	Secured Party in Possession
9-309(1)	Perfection of Purchase-Money Security Interest in Consumer Goods
9-320(b)	Rights of Buyer of Consumer Goods
9-334(e)(2)(C)	Priority of Security Interests in Fixtures That Are Readily Removable Replacements of Domestic Appliances That Are Consumer Goods
9-513(a)	Termination Statement Requirements
9-620(a)(3)	Acceptance of Consumer Goods in Satisfaction of Obligation
9-620(e)	Mandatory Disposition of Consumer Goods by a Secured Party
9-625(c)(2)	Remedies for Secured Party's Failure to Comply with Article
9-628(c)	Limitation on Liability of Secured Party

GOODS, EQUIPMENT

9-102(a)(33)	Definition
9-334(e)(2)(B)	Priority of Security Interests in Fixtures That Are Certain Types of Readily Removable Equipment
9-609(a)(2)	After Default Secured Party May Render Equipment Unusable

GOODS, FARM PRODUCTS

9-102(a)(34)	Definition
9-302	Law Governing Perfection and Priority of Agricultural Liens on Farm Products
9-320(a)	Subsection Excludes a Person Buying Farm Products from a Person Engaged in Farming Operations
9-324(d)	Priority of Purchase-Money Security Interest in Livestock That Are Farm Products

GOODS, INVENTORY

9-102(a)(48) Definition
9-103(b)(2) Purchase-Money Security Interest in Inventory
9-103(d) Consignor's Inventory Purchase-Money Security Interest
9-311(d) Section Does Not Apply to Certain Inventory
9-324(b) Priority of Purchase-Money Security Interest in Inventory
9-324(c) Priority of Holders of Conflicting Purchase-Money Security Interests in Inventory
9-330(a) Priority of Purchaser of Chattel Paper Claimed As Proceeds of Inventory
9-330(e) Holder of a Purchase-Money Security Interest in Inventory Gives New Value

GOODS, AS-EXTRACTED COLLATERAL

9-102(a)(6)(A) Definition
9-301(4) Law Governing Perfection and Priority
9-501(a)(1)(A) Filing Office
9-502(b,c) Financing Statement Requirements
9-519(d,e) Indexing Requirements for Financing Statements
9-525(e) Fee Requirements for Record of a Mortgage Which Is Effective As a Financing Statement Covering As-Extracted Collateral

GOODS, MANUFACTURED HOMES

9-102(a)(53) Definition
9-334(e)(4) Priority of a Security Interest Created in a Manufactured Home in a Manufactured-Home Transaction
9-515(b) Duration and Effectiveness of Financing Statement
9-525(b)(2) Fees Requirements for Financing Statement Filed in Connection with a Manufactured-Home Transaction

GOODS, EMBEDDED SOFTWARE

9-102(a)(44) Definition

GOODS, ACCESSIONS

9-102(a)(1) Definition
9-335 Security Interests in Accessions

GOODS COVERED BY A CERTIFICATE OF TITLE

9-102(a)(10) Definition of Certificate of Title
9-303 Law Governing Perfection and Priority of Security Interests in Goods Covered by a Certificate of Title
9-311(a)(2,3) Perfection of Security Interests in Goods Covered by a Certificate of Title
9-313(b) When Possession by a Secured Party Perfects Security Interest Without Filing
9-316(d,e) Continued Perfection Following Change in Governing Law
9-337 Priority of Security Interests in Goods Covered by a Certificate of Title
9-619(b)(3) Effect of Transfer Statement

GOODS, FIXTURES

9-102(a)(41) Definition
9-301(3)(A) Law Governing Perfection by Fixture Filing
9-334 Priority of Security Interests in Fixtures
9-501(a)(1)(B) Filing Office When Financing Statement Filed As a Fixture Filing
9-501(a)(2) Filing Office When Financing Statement Not Filed As a Fixture Filing
9-501(b) Filing Office for Security Interest in Fixtures of a Transmitting Utility
9-502(b) Financing Statement Requirements
9-502(c) Record of Mortgage As Financing Statement Requirements
9-514(c) Assignment of Record of Mortgage As Financing Statement
9-515(g) Duration and Effectiveness of Record of Mortgage As Financing Statement
9-519(d,e) Indexing Requirements for Financing Statements
9-525(e) Fee Requirements for Record of Mortgage Filed As a Fixture Filing
9-604(b,c) Enforcement Procedures

ACCOUNTS

ACCOUNTS, GENERALLY

9-102(a)(2) Definition

9-109(a)(3) Sale of Accounts Within Scope of Article
9-109(d)(4,5,7) Certain Sales and Assignments of Accounts Not Within Scope of Article
9-202 Title to Collateral Immaterial
9-204(c) Accounts Sold in Connection with Future Advances
9-207(d) Rights of Buyer of Accounts
9-209(c) Section Does Not Apply to an Assignment Constituting the Sale of an Account
9-210(b) Subsection Does Not Apply to a Buyer of Accounts
9-309(2) Certain Assignment of Accounts Perfect upon Attachment
9-317(d) Certain Buyers of Accounts Take Free of a Security Interest
9-318 Retained Interest and Rights of Sellers and Buyers of Accounts
9-322(c)(2)(C) Priority of Certain Types of Proceeds
9-323(c) Subsections (a) and (b) Do Not Apply to a Security Interest Held by a Secured Party That Is a Buyer of Accounts
9-406 Discharge of an Account Debtor on an Account
9-513(c)(2) Termination Statement Requirements
9-601(g) No Duties Imposed by Part 6 on Buyers of Accounts Except As Otherwise Provided in 9-607(c)
9-608(b) No Surplus or Deficiency of Proceeds of Collection or Enforcement in Sales of Accounts
9-615(e) No Surplus or Deficiency of Proceeds of Disposition in Sales of Accounts

ACCOUNTS, AS-EXTRACTED COLLATERAL

9-102(a)(6)(B) Definition
9-301(4) Law Governing Perfection and Priority of Security Interests
9-501(a)(1)(A) Filing Office
9-502(b,c) Requirements for Financing Statements
9-519(d,e) Indexing Requirements for Financing Statements
9-525(e) Fee Requirements for Record of a Mortgage Which Is Effective As a Financing Statement Covering As-Extracted Collateral

ACCOUNTS, CONTROLLABLE

9-102(a)(27A) Definition
12-104 Rights in Controllable Accounts
12-105 Control of Controllable Electronic Record Evidencing Controllable Account
12-106 Discharge of Account Debtor on Controllable Account
12-107(b) Governing Law of Controllable Electronic Record that Evidences Controllable Account
9-107A(b) Control of Controllable Account
9-203(b)(3)(D) Enforceability of Security Interest in Controllable Account
9-207(c) Rights and Duties when Secured Party is in Control
9-306B Law Governing Perfection and Priority of Security Interests
9-310(b)(8) Filing of a Financing Statement Not Necessary to Perfect a Security Interest in Controllable Accounts if Secured Party has Control9-312(a) Perfection by Filing Permitted
9-314(a) Security Interest in Controllable Accounts may be Perfected by Control
9-316(f) Continued Perfection of Security Interest Following Change in Jurisdiction
9-317(i) Certain Buyers of Controllable Accounts Take Free of a Security Interest
9-326A Priority of Security Interest in Controllable Accounts
9-331 Priority of Rights of Purchasers of Controllable Accounts Under Other Articles
9-406(l) Subsections (a), (b), (c), and (g) of Section do not Apply to a Controllable Account
9-601(b) Rights of Secured Party are Provided in 9-207(c)
9-605(b) Secured Party Owes a Duty to Unknown Debtors or Secondary Obligors in Certain Circumstances
9-628(f) Limitations on Secured Party's Liability does not Apply to Controllable Accounts in Certain Circumstances

ACCOUNTS, HEALTH-CARE-INSURANCE RECEIVABLES

9-102(a)(46) Definition
9-109(d)(8) Article Applies to Assignment by or to a Health-Care Provider of a Health-Care-Insurance Receivable

9-309(5) Security Interest Created by Assignment of a Health-Care-Insurance Receivable to the Provider of the Health-Care Goods or Services Perfects upon Attachment
9-404(e) Section Does Not Apply to Assignment of Health-Care-Insurance Receivables
9-405(d) Section Does Not Apply to Assignment of Health-Care-Insurance Receivables
9-406(i) Section Does Not Apply to Assignment of Health-Care-Insurance Receivables
9-408 Restrictions on Assignment of Health-Care-Insurance Receivables Ineffective

CHATTEL PAPER

9-102(a)(11) Definition
9-105 Control of Electronic Copy of Record Evidencing Chattel Paper
9-107B No Requirement to Acknowledge or Confirm Control
9-109(a)(3) Sale of Chattel Paper Within Scope of Article
9-109(d)(4,5) Certain Sales and Assignments of Chattel Paper Not Within Scope of Article
9-202 Title to Collateral Immaterial
9-203(b)(3)(E) Enforceability of Security Interest in Chattel Paper
9-204(c) Chattel Paper Sold in Connection with Future Advances
9-207(a) Duty of Care When Secured Party in Possession of Chattel Paper
9-207(d) Rights of Buyer of Chattel Paper
9-208(b)(3) Duties of Secured Party Having Control of Authoritative Electronic Copy of a Record Evidencing Chattel Paper after Receiving Demand from Debtor
9-209(c) Section Does Not Apply to an Assignment Constituting the Sale of Chattel Paper
9-210(b) Subsection Does Not Apply to a Buyer of Chattel Paper
9-306A Law Governing Perfection and Priority of Security Interests in Chattel Paper
9-310(b)(8.1) Filing of a Financing Statement Not Necessary to Perfect a Security Interest in Chattel Paper in Certain Circumstances
9-312(a) Perfection by Filing Permitted
9-314A Perfection by Possession and Control of Chattel Paper
9-316(f) Continued Perfection of Security Interest Following Change in Jurisdiction
9-317(f) Certain Buyers of Chattel Paper Take Free of a Security Interest
9-318 Retained Interest and Rights of Sellers and Buyers of Chattel Paper
9-322(d,e) Conflicting Perfected Security Interests in Proceeds of Chattel Paper
9-323(c) Subsections (a) and (b) Do Not Apply to a Security Interest Held by a Secured Party That Is a Buyer of Chattel Paper
9-324(b) Priority of Conflicting Security Interest in Chattel Paper Constituting Proceeds of Inventory
9-330 Priority of Purchaser of Chattel Paper
9-338(2) Priority of Security Interest Perfected by Filing Providing Certain Incorrect Information
9-406 Discharge of an Account Debtor on Chattel Paper
9-513(c)(2) Termination Statement Requirements
9-601(g) No Duties Imposed by Part 6 on Buyers of Chattel Paper Except as Otherwise Provided in 9-607(c)
9-608(b) No Surplus or Deficiency of Proceeds of Collection or Enforcement in Sales of Chattel Paper
9-615(e) No Surplus or Deficiency of Proceeds of Disposition in Sales of Chattel Paper

COMMERCIAL TORT CLAIMS

9-102(a)(13) Definition
9-108(e)(1) Description Only by Type of Collateral Insufficient
9-204(b)(2) Security Interest Under a Term Constituting an After-Acquired Property Clause Does Not Attach to a Commercial Tort Claim

DEPOSIT ACCOUNTS

9-102(a)(29) Definition
9-104 Control of Deposit Accounts
9-107B No Requirement to Acknowledge or Confirm Control

9-109(d)(10)(A) Section 9-340 Applies with Respect to Effectiveness of Right of Recoupment or Set-Off Against Deposit Accounts
9-109(d)(13) Limits of Applicability of Article to an Assignment of a Deposit Account in a Consumer Transaction9-203(b)(3)(D) Enforceability of Security Interests in Deposit Accounts
9-207(c) Rights and Duties when Secured Party is in Control
9-208(b)(1,2) Duties of Secured Party Having Control of Deposit Account After Receiving Demand from Debtor
9-304 Law Governing Perfection and Priority of Security Interests in Deposit Accounts
9-310(b)(8) Filing Not Necessary to Perfect a Security Interest in a Deposit Account Perfected by Control under 9-314
9-312 Perfection of Security Interests in Deposit Accounts
9-314(a,b) Perfection by Control of Security Interests in Deposit Accounts
9-316(f) Continued Perfection of Security Interest Following Change in Jurisdiction of Bank
9-322(d) Priority of Conflicting Perfected Security Interests in Proceeds of Deposit Accounts
9-327 Priority of Security Interests in Deposit Account
9-332(b) Transferee of Funds from a Deposit Account
9-340 Effectiveness of Right of Recoupment or Set-Off Against Deposit Account
9-341 Bank's Rights and Duties with Respect to Deposit Account
9-601(b) Rights of Secured Party are Provided in 9-207(c)
9-607(a)(4,5) Collection and Enforcement by Secured Party

DOCUMENTS

DOCUMENTS, GENERALLY

9-102(a)(30) Definition9-310(b)(5) Filing Not Necessary to Perfect a Security Interest in Documents under Certain Circumstances9-312 Perfection of Security Interests in Documents
9-317(b) Certain Buyers of Documents Take Free of a Security Interest9-338(2) Priority of Security Interest Perfected by Filing Providing Certain Incorrect Information
9-601(a)(2) Rights of Secured Party After Default

DOCUMENTS, ELECTRONIC

7-106 Control of Electronic Documents of Title
9-208(b)(6) Duties of Secured Party Having Control of an Authoritative Electronic Copy of an Electronic Document after Receiving Demand from Debtor
9-310(b)(8) Filing Not Necessary to Perfect a Security Interest in Electronic Documents under Certain Circumstances
9-317(g) Certain Buyers of Electronic Documents Take Free of a Security Interest

DOCUMENTS, NEGOTIABLE

9-301(3) Law Governing Perfection and Priority of Security Interest in Negotiable Documents
9-312(a,c,e,f) Perfection of Security Interests in Negotiable Documents
9-313(a) Security Interests in Negotiable Documents May Be Perfected by Possession
9-322(d,e) Priority of Conflicting Perfected Security Interests in Proceeds of Negotiable Documents
9-331(a) Rights of Holder to Which a Negotiable Document of Title Has Been Duly Negotiated Not Limited by Article

GENERAL INTANGIBLES

GENERAL INTANGIBLES, GENERALLY

9-102(a)(42) Definition
9-317(d) Certain Licensees and Buyers of General Intangibles Take Free of a Security Interest
9-321(a,b) Rights of Licensees in Ordinary Course of Business
9-408 Restrictions on Assignment of Certain General Intangibles Ineffective

GENERAL INTANGIBLES, CONTROLLABLE ELECTRONIC RECORDS

12-102(a)(1)	Definition
12-104	Rights in Controllable Electronic Records
12-105	Control of Controllable Electronic Records
12-107	Governing Law of Controllable Electronic Records
9-107A(a)	Section 12-105 Governs Control of Controllable Electronic Records
9-203(b)(3)(D)	Enforceability of Security Interest in Controllable Electronic Records
9-207(c)	Rights and Duties when Secured Party is in Control
9-208(b)(8)	Duties of Secured Party Having Control of Controllable Electronic Record after Receiving Demand from Debtor
9-306B	Law Governing Perfection and Priority of Security Interests
9-310(b)(8)	Filing of a Financing Statement Not Necessary to Perfect a Security Interest in Controllable Electronic Records if Secured Party has Control
9-312(a)	Perfection by Filing Permitted
9-314(a)	Security Interest in Controllable Electronic Records may be Perfected by Control
9-316(f)	Continued Perfection of Security Interest Following Change in Jurisdiction
9-317(h)	Certain Buyers of Controllable Electronic Records Take Free of a Security Interest
9-326A	Priority of Security Interest in Controllable Electronic Records
9-331	Priority of Rights of Purchasers of Controllable Electronic Records Under Other Articles
9-601(b)	Rights of Secured Party are Provided in 9-207(c)
9-605(b)	Secured Party Owes a Duty to Unknown Debtors or Secondary Obligors in Certain Circumstances
9-628(f)	Limitations on Secured Party's Liability does not Apply to Controllable Electronic Records in Certain Circumstances

GENERAL INTANGIBLES, PAYMENT INTANGIBLES

9-102(a)(61)	Definition
9-109(a)(3)	Sales of Payment Intangibles with Scope of Article
9-109(d)(4,5,7)	Certain Sales and Assignments of Payment Intangibles Not Within Scope of Article
9-202	Title to Collateral Immaterial
9-204(c)	Payment Intangibles Sold in Connection with Future Advances
9-207(d)	Rights of Buyers of Payment Intangibles
9-209(c)	Section Does Not Apply to an Assignment Constituting the Sale of a Payment Intangible
9-210(b)	Subsection Does Not Apply to a Buyer of Payment Intangibles
9-309(2,3)	Certain Assignments and Sales of Payment Intangibles Perfect upon Attachment
9-318(a)	Retained Interest of Sellers of Payment Intangibles
9-323(c)	Subsections (a) and (b) Do Not Apply to a Security Interest Held by a Secured Party That Is a Buyer of Payment Intangibles
9-406	Discharge of an Account Debtor on Payment Intangibles
9-408(b)	Subsection (a) Applies to a Security Interest in a Payment Intangible Only If the Security Interest Arises Out of a Sale of the Payment Intangible
9-505	Filing and Compliance with Other Statutes and Treaties for Buyers of Payment Intangibles
9-601(g)	No Duties Imposed by Part 6 on Buyers of Payment Intangibles Except as Otherwise Provided in 9-607(c)
9-608(b)	No Surplus or Deficiency of Proceeds of Collection or Enforcement in Sales of Payment Intangibles
9-615(e)	No Surplus or Deficiency of Proceeds of Disposition in Sales of Payment Intangibles

GENERAL INTANGIBLES, CONTROLLABLE PAYMENT INTANGIBLES

9-102(a)(27B)	Definition

12-104	Rights in Controllable Payment Intangibles
12-105	Control of Controllable Electronic Record Evidencing Controllable Payment Intangible
12-106	Discharge of Account Debtor on Controllable Payment Intangible
12-107	Governing Law of Controllable Electronic Record Evidencing Controllable Payment Intangible
9-107A(b)	Control of Controllable Payment Intangible
9-207(c)	Rights and Duties when Secured Party is in Control
9-306B	Law Governing Perfection and Priority of Security Interests
9-310(b)(8)	Filing of a Financing Statement Not Necessary to Perfect a Security Interest in Controllable Payment Intangibles in Certain Circumstances
9-312(a)	Perfection by Filing Permitted
9-314(a)	Security Interest in Controllable Payment Intangibles may be Perfected by Control
9-316(f)	Continued Perfection of Security Interest Following Change in Jurisdiction
9-317(i)	Certain Buyers of Controllable Payment Intangibles Take Free of a Security Interest
9-326A	Priority of Security Interest in Controllable Payment Intangible
9-331	Priority of Rights of Purchasers of Controllable Payment Intangibles Under Other Articles
9-406(l)	Subsections (a), (b), (c), and (g) of Section do not Apply to a Controllable Payment Intangible
9-601(b)	Rights of Secured Party are Provided in 9-207(c)
9-605(b)	Secured Party Owes a Duty to Unknown Debtors or Secondary Obligors in Certain Circumstances
9-628(f)	Limitations on Secured Party's Liability do not Apply to Controllable Payment Intangibles in Certain Circumstances

GENERAL INTANGIBLES, SOFTWARE

9-102(a)(76)	Definition
9-103(a)(1)	Purchase-Money Collateral Can Be Software
9-103(b)(3)	Purchase-Money Security Interest in Software
9-103(c)	Purchase-Money Security Interest in Software Used in Goods
9-324(f)	Priority of Purchase-Money Security Interest in Software

INSTRUMENTS

INSTRUMENTS, GENERALLY

9-102(a)(47)	Definition
9-207(a)	Duty of Care When Secured Party in Possession of an Instrument
9-301(3)	Law Governing Perfection and Priority of Security Interests in Instruments
9-310(b)(5)	Filing Not Necessary to Perfect a Security Interest in Instruments Under Certain Circumstances
9-312(a)	Perfection by Filing
9-312(e,g)	Temporary Perfection of Security Interests in Instruments
9-313(a)	Security Interest in Instrument May Be Perfected by Possession
9-317(b)	Certain Buyers of Instruments Take Free of a Security Interest
9-322(d,e)	Conflicting Perfected Security Interests in Proceeds of Instruments
9-324(b)	Priority of Conflicting Security Interest in Instruments Constituting Proceeds of Inventory
9-330(d,f)	Priority of Purchaser of an Instrument
9-331	Priority of Rights of Purchasers of Instruments Under Other Articles
9-338(2)	Priority of Security Interest Perfected by Filing Providing Certain Incorrect Information
9-403(b)(4)	Agreement Not to Assert Claim or Defense in Recoupment of Type That May Be Asserted Against Person Entitled to Enforce Negotiable Instrument under 3-305(a)

INSTRUMENTS, PROMISSORY NOTES

9-102(a)(65)	Definition
9-109(a)(3)	Sale of Promissory Notes with Scope of Article
9-109(d)(4,5,7)	Certain Sales and Assignments of Promissory Notes Not Within Scope of Article
9-202	Title to Collateral Immaterial
9-204(c)	Promissory Notes Sold in Connection with Future Advances

9-207(d)	Rights of Buyers of Promissory Notes
9-210(b)	Subsection Does Not Apply to Buyers of Promissory Notes
9-309(4)	Security Interest Perfected upon Attachment
9-318(a)	Retained Interest of Sellers of Promissory Notes
9-323(c)	Subsections (a) and (b) Do Not Apply to a Security Interest Held by a Secured Party That Is a Buyer of Promissory Notes
9-406(d,e)	Terms Restricting Assignment Generally Ineffective
9-408	Restrictions on Assignment of Promissory Notes Ineffective
9-505	Filing and Compliance with Other Statutes and Treaties for Buyers of Promissory Notes
9-601(g)	No Duties Imposed by Part 6 on Buyers of Promissory Notes Except as Otherwise Provided in 9-607(c) and 9-608(b)
9-608(b)	No Surplus or Deficiency of Proceeds of Collection or Enforcement in Sales of Promissory Notes
9-615(e)	No Surplus or Deficiency of Proceeds of Disposition in Sales of Promissory Notes

INVESTMENT PROPERTY

INVESTMENT PROPERTY, GENERALLY

9-102(a)(49)	Definition
9-106	Control of Investment Property
9-203(b)(3)(D)	Enforceability of Security Interests in Investment Property
9-203(c)	Subsection (b) Is Subject to 9-206 on Security Interests in Investment Property
9-206	Security Interest Arising in Purchase or Delivery of Financial Asset
9-207(c)	Rights and Duties when Secured Party is in Control
9-305	Law Governing Perfection and Priority of Security Interests in Investment Property
9-309(10)	Security Interest in Investment Property Created by a Broker or Securities Intermediary Perfects upon Attachment
9-310(b)(8)	Filing Not Necessary to Perfect a Security Interest in Investment Property under Certain Circumstances
9-312(a)	Perfection by Filing
9-314(a,c)	Perfection by Control
9-316(f)	Continued Perfection of Security Interest Following Change in Jurisdiction
9-317(d)	Certain Buyers of Investment Property Take Free of a Security Interest
9-322(d,e)	Conflicting Perfected Security Interests in Proceeds of Investment Property
9-328	Priority of Security Interests in Investment Property
9-601(b)	Rights of Secured Party are Provided in 9-207(c)

INVESTMENT PROPERTY, CERTIFICATED SECURITIES

8-102	Definition
9-106(a)	Control of Certificated Securities
9-203(b)(3)(C)	Enforceability of Security Interests in Certificated Securities
9-206(c)	Security Interest in Payment Against Delivery Transaction
9-305(a)(1)	Law Governing Perfection and Priority of Security Interests in Certificated Securities
9-310(b)(5,7)	Filing Not Necessary to Perfect a Security Interest in Certificated Securities Under Certain Circumstances
9-312(e,g)	Temporary Perfection of Certificated Securities
9-313(a,e)	Perfection by Delivery
9-314(c)(2)(A)	Perfection by Control
9-328(2)(A)	Priority of Security Interests in Securities
9-328(5)	Priority of Security Interests in Certificated Securities
9-331	Priority of Rights of Purchasers of Securities Under Other Articles

INVESTMENT PROPERTY, UNCERTIFICATED SECURITIES

8-102	Definition
9-106(a)	Control of Uncertificated Securities
9-305(a)(2)	Law Governing Perfection and Priority of Security Interests in Certificated Securities
9-314(c)(2)(B)	Perfection by Control
9-328(2)(A)	Priority of Security Interests in Securities
9-331	Priority of Rights of Purchasers of Securities Under Other Articles

INVESTMENT PROPERTY, SECURITY ENTITLEMENTS

8-102	Definition
9-106(a,c)	Control of Security Entitlements
9-108(d,e)	Sufficiency of Description
9-203(h)	Attachment of a Security Entitlement Carried in a Securities Account
9-206(a)	Security Interest When Person Buys Through a Securities Intermediary
9-208(b)(4)	Duties of Secured Party Having Control of Security Entitlement After Receiving Demand from Debtor
9-305(a)(3)	Law Governing Perfection and Priority of Security Interests in Security Entitlements
9-308(f)	Perfection of a Security Interest in a Security Entitlement Carried in a Securities Account
9-314(c)(2)(C)	Perfection by Control
9-328(2)(B)	Priority of Security Interest in Security Entitlement Carried in a Securities Account
9-328(3)	Priority of Security Interest Held by a Securities Intermediary in a Security Entitlement
9-331	Priority of Interests in Security Entitlements Under Article 8

INVESTMENT PROPERTY, SECURITIES ACCOUNTS

8-501	Definition
9-106(c)	Control of Security Accounts
9-108(d)	Sufficiency of Description
9-108(e)(2)	Description Only by Type of a Security Entitlement in a Consumer Transaction Insufficient
9-203(h)	Attachment of a Security Entitlement Carried in a Securities Account
9-206(a)(2)	Security Interest When Person Buys Through a Securities Intermediary
9-305(a)(3)	Law Governing Perfection and Priority of Security Interests in Securities Accounts
9-308(f)	Perfection of a Security Interest in a Security Entitlement Carried in a Securities Account
9-328(2)(B)	Priority of Security Interest in Security Entitlement Carried in a Securities Account
9-328(3)	Priority of Security Interest Held by a Securities Intermediary in a Securities Account

INVESTMENT PROPERTY, COMMODITY CONTRACTS

9-102(a)(15)	Definition
9-106(b,c)	Control of Commodity Contracts
9-108(d)(2)	Sufficiency of Description
9-203(i)	Attachment of Commodity Contracts Carried in a Commodity Account
9-208(b)(4)	Duties of Secured Party Having Control of Commodity Contract after Receiving Demand from Debtor
9-305(a)(4)	Law Governing Perfection and Priority of Security Interests in Commodity Contracts
9-305(c)(3)	When Perfection Governed by Law of Jurisdiction Where Debtor Located
9-308(g)	Perfection of a Security Interest in a Commodity Contract Carried in a Commodity Account
9-309(11)	Security Interest in Commodity Contract Created by a Commodity Intermediary Perfects upon Attachment
9-328(2)(C)	Priority of Commodity Contract Carried with a Commodity Intermediary
9-328(4)	Priority of Security Interest Held by a Commodity Intermediary in a Commodity Contract

LETTER-OF-CREDIT RIGHTS

9-102(a)(51)	Definition
9-107	Control of Letter-of-Credit Right
9-109(c)(4)	Article Does Not Apply Under Certain Circumstances
9-203(b)(3)(D)	Enforceability of Security Interests in Letter-of-Credit Rights
9-207(c)	Rights and Duties when Secured Party is in Control
9-208(b)(5)	Duties of Secured Party Having Control of a Letter-of-Credit Right after Receiving Demand from Debtor
9-306	Law Governing Perfection and Priority of Security Interests in Letter-of-Credit Rights
9-310(b)(8)	Filing Not Necessary to Perfect a Security Interest in Letter-of-Credit Rights Under Certain Circumstances

9-312(b)(2)	Perfection of Security Interests in Letter-of-Credit Rights
9-314(a,b)	Perfection by Control
9-316(f)	Continued Perfection of Security Interest Following Change in Jurisdiction
9-322(d,e)	Conflicting Perfected Security Interests in Proceeds of Letter-of-Credit Rights
9-329	Priority of Security Interests in Letter-of-Credit Rights
9-409	Restrictions on Assignment of Letter-of-Credit Rights Ineffective
9-601(b)	Rights of Secured Party are Provided in 9-207(c)

MONEY

MONEY, GENERALLY

9-102(a)(54A)	Definition

MONEY, TANGIBLE

9-102(a)(79A)	Definition
9-301(3)	Law Governing Perfection and Priority of Security Interests
9-312(b)(3)	Security Interest in Tangible Money can Only be Perfected by Possession
9-313(a)	Secured Party May Perfect a Security Interest in Tangible Money by Taking Possession
9-332(a)	Transferee of Tangible Money

MONEY, ELECTRONIC

9-102(a)(31A)	Definition
9-105A	Control of Electronic Money
9-107B	No Requirement to Acknowledge or Confirm Control
9-203(b)(3)(D)	Enforceability of Security Interests in Electronic Money
9-207(c)	Rights and Duties when Secured Party is in Control
9-208(b)(7)	Duties of Secured Party Having Control of Electronic Money after Receiving Demand from Debtor
9-312(b)(4)	Security Interest in Electronic Money May be Perfected Only by Control
9-314(a)	Security Interest in Electric Money May be Perfected by Control
9-317(d)	Buyer Cannot Take Free of Security Interest in Electronic Money by Giving Value Without Knowledge of the Security Interest Before it is Perfected
9-332(c)	Transferee of Electronic Money
9-601(b)	Rights of Secured Party are Provided in 9-207(c)

PART 1. GENERAL PROVISIONS

[Subpart 1. Short Title, Definitions, and General Concepts]

§ 9-101. Short Title.

This article may be cited as Uniform Commercial Code—Secured Transactions.

Official Comment

1. Source, Background, and History. In 1990, the Permanent Editorial Board for the UCC with the support of its sponsors, The American Law Institute and the National Conference of Commissioners on Uniform State Laws, established a committee to study Uniform Commercial Code (UCC) Article 9. The study committee issued its report as of December 1, 1992, recommending the creation of a drafting committee for the revision of Article 9 and also recommending numerous specific changes to Article 9. Organized in 1993, a drafting committee met fifteen times from 1993 to 1998. Extensive revisions of this Article were approved by its sponsors in 1998 (1998 Revisions). The Article was conformed to revised Article 1 in 2001 and to amendments to Article 7 in 2003. The sponsors approved amendments to selected sections of this Article in 2010.

The 1998 Revisions superseded former Article 9 (pre-1998 Article 9) and, as did their predecessor, provided a comprehensive scheme for the regulation of security interests in personal property and fixtures. For the most part the 1998 Article 9 followed the general approach and retains much of the terminology of pre-1998 Article 9. Comment 3 describes the material changes made by the 1998 Revisions. Pre-1998 Article 9 superseded the wide variety of pre- UCC security devices. Unlike the Comments to pre-1998 Article 9, however, these Comments dwell very little on the pre-UCC state of the law. For that reason, the Comments to pre-1998 Article 9 will remain of substantial historical value and interest. They also will remain useful in understanding the background and general conceptual approach of this Article.

Article 9 was again extensively revised in 2022 (2022 Article 9 Revisions) pursuant to the Uniform Commercial Code Amendments (2022) (2022 Amendments). In particular, the 2022 Article 9 Revisions conform and adapt Article 9 to Article 12, covering controllable electronic records and rights to payment that are tethered to controllable electronic records—controllable accounts and controllable payment intangibles. For a brief summary of the 2022 Article 9 Revisions, see Comment 4, below.

Except as noted in Comments 3 and 4 below, the 1998 Article 9 remains substantially unchanged following the 2022 Article 9 Revisions.

Note also that citations to "Bankruptcy Code Section" in these Comments are to Title 11 of the United States Code as in effect on July 1, 2022.

2. 1998 Revisions: Reorganization and Renumbering; Captions; Style. The 1998 Revisions embraced a substantial reorganization of former Article 9 and renumbering of most sections of Article 9, including a new Part 4 dealing with several aspects of third-party rights and duties that are unrelated to perfection and priority. Some of these were covered by Part 3 of pre-1998 Article 9. Also added was Part 5, dealing with filing (formerly covered by pre-1998 Part 4), and Part 6, dealing with default and enforcement (formerly covered by pre-1998 Part 5. The 1998 Revisions also include headings for the subsections as an aid to readers. Unlike section captions, which are part of the UCC, see Section 1-107, subsection headings are not a part of the official text itself and have not been approved by the sponsors.

3. Summary of 1998 Revisions. Following is a brief summary of some of the more significant features of the 1998 Revisions of Article 9.

a. Scope of Article 9. The 1998 Revisions expanded the scope of Article 9 in several respects.

Deposit accounts. Section 9-109 includes within this Article's scope deposit accounts as original collateral, except in consumer transactions. Pre-1998 Article 9 dealt with deposit accounts only as proceeds of other collateral.

Sales of payment intangibles and promissory notes. Section 9-109 also includes within the scope of this Article most sales of "payment intangibles" (defined in Section 9-102 as general intangibles under which an account debtor's principal obligation is monetary) and "promissory notes" (also defined in Section 9-102). Pre-1998 Article 9 included sales of accounts and chattel paper, but not sales of payment intangibles or promissory notes. In its inclusion of sales of payment intangibles and promissory notes, this Article continues the drafting convention found in pre-1998 Article 9; the sale of accounts, chattel paper, payment intangibles, or promissory notes creates a "security interest." The definition of "account" in Section 9-102 also was expanded to include various rights to payment that were general intangibles under pre-1998 Article 9.

Health-care-insurance receivables. Section 9-109 narrows Article 9's exclusion of transfers of interests in insurance policies by carving out of the exclusion "health-care-insurance receivables" (defined in Section 9-102). A health-care-insurance receivable is included within the definition of "account" in Section 9-102.

Nonpossessory statutory agricultural liens. Section 9-109 also brings nonpossessory statutory agricultural liens within the scope of Article 9.

Consignments. Section 9-109 added "true" consignments—bailments for the purpose of sale by the bailee to the scope of Article 9, with certain exceptions. See Section 9-102 (defining "consignment"). Under the pre-1998 UCC, many consignments were subject to Article 9's filing requirements by operation of pre-1998 Section 2-326.

Supporting obligations and property securing rights to payment. The 1998 Revisions also addressed explicitly (i) obligations, such as guaranties and letters of credit, that support payment or performance of collateral such as accounts, chattel paper, and payment intangibles, and (ii) any property (including real property) that secures a right to payment or performance that is subject to an Article 9 security interest. See Sections 9-203, 9-308.

Commercial tort claims. Section 9-109 expands the scope of Article 9 to include the assignment of commercial tort claims by narrowing the exclusion of tort claims generally. However, Article 9 continues to exclude tort claims for bodily injury and other non-business tort claims of a natural person. See Section 9-102 (defining "commercial tort claim").

Transfers by States and governmental units of States. Section 9-109 narrows the exclusion of transfers by States and their governmental units by excluding only transfers covered by another statute (other than a statute generally applicable to security interests) to the extent the statute governs the creation, perfection, priority, or enforcement of security interests.

Nonassignable general intangibles, promissory notes, health-care-insurance receivables, and letter-of-credit rights. The 1998 Revisions enabled a security interest to attach to letter-of-credit rights, health-care-insurance receivables, promissory notes, and general intangibles, including contracts, permits, licenses, and franchises, notwithstanding a contractual or statutory prohibition against or limitation on assignment. The revised Article explicitly protects third parties against any adverse effect of the creation or attempted enforcement of the security interest. See Sections 9-408, 9-409.

Subject to Sections 9-408 and 9-409 and two other exceptions (Sections 9-406, concerning accounts, chattel paper, and payment intangibles, and 9-407, concerning interests in leased goods), Section 9-401 establishes a baseline rule that the inclusion of transactions and collateral within the scope of Article 9 has no effect on non-Article 9 law dealing with the alienability or inalienability of property. For example, if a commercial tort claim is nonassignable under other applicable law, the fact that a security interest in the claim is within the scope of Article 9 does not override the other applicable law's effective prohibition of assignment.

b. Duties of Secured Party. The 1998 Revisions provided for expanded duties of secured parties.

Release of control. Section 9-208 imposes upon a secured party having control of a deposit account, investment property, or a letter-of-credit right the duty to release control when there is no secured obligation and no commitment to give value. Section 9-209 contains analogous provisions when an account debtor has been notified to pay a secured party.

Information. Section 9-210 expands a secured party's duties to provide the debtor with information concerning collateral and the obligations that it secures.

Default and enforcement. Part 6 also includes some additional duties of secured parties in connection with default and enforcement. See, e.g., Section 9-616 (duty to explain calculation of deficiency or surplus in a consumer-goods transaction).

c. Choice of Law. The choice-of-law rules included in the 1998 Revisions for the law governing perfection, the effect of perfection or nonperfection, and priority are found in Part 3, Subpart 1 (Sections 9-301 through 9-307). See also Section 9-316.

Where to file: Location of debtor. The 1998 Revisions changed the choice-of-law rule governing perfection (i.e., where to file) for most collateral to the law of the jurisdiction where the debtor is located. See Section 9-301. Under pre-1998 Article 9, the jurisdiction of the debtor's location governed only perfection and priority of a security interest in accounts, general intangibles, mobile goods, and, for purposes of perfection by filing, chattel paper and investment property.

Determining debtor's location. As a baseline rule, Section 9-307 follows pre-1998 Section 9-103, under which the location of the debtor is the debtor's place of business (or chief executive office, if the debtor has more than one place of business). Section 9-307 contains three major exceptions. First, a "registered organization," such as a corporation or limited liability company, is located in the State under whose law the debtor is organized, e.g., a corporate debtor's State of incorporation. Second, an individual debtor is located at his or her principal residence. Third, there are special rules for determining the location of the United States and registered organizations organized under the law of the United States.

Location of non-U.S. debtors. If, applying the foregoing rules, a debtor is located in a jurisdiction whose law does not require public notice as a condition of perfection of a nonpossessory security interest, the entity is deemed located in the District of Columbia. See Section 9-307. Thus, to the extent that this Article applies to non-U.S. debtors, perfection could be accomplished in many cases by a domestic filing.

Priority. For tangible collateral such as goods and instruments, Section 9-301 provides that the law applicable to priority and the effect of perfection or nonperfection will remain the law of the jurisdiction where the collateral is located, as under pre-1998 Section 9-103 (but without the confusing "last event" test). For intangible collateral, such as accounts, the applicable law for priority is that of the jurisdiction in which the debtor is located.

Possessory security interests; agricultural liens. Perfection, the effect of perfection or nonperfection, and priority of a possessory security interest or an agricultural lien are governed by the law of the jurisdiction where the collateral subject to the security interest or lien is located. See Sections 9-301, 9-302.

Goods covered by certificates of title; deposit accounts; letter-of-credit rights; investment property. The 1998 Revisions to Article 9 included several refinements to the treatment of choice-of-law matters for goods covered by certificates of title. See Section 9-303. The revision also provided special choice-of-law rules, similar to those for investment property under current Articles 8 and 9, for deposit accounts (Section 9-304), investment property (Section 9-305), and letter-of-credit rights (Section 9-306).

Change in applicable law. Section 9-316 addresses perfection following a change in applicable law.

d. Perfection. The 1998 revised rules governing perfection of security interests and agricultural liens are found in Part 3, Subpart 2 (Sections 9-308 through 9-316).

Deposit accounts; letter-of-credit rights. With certain exceptions, the 1998 Revisions provided that a security interest in a deposit account or a letter-of-credit right may be perfected only by the secured party's acquiring "control" of the deposit account or letter-of-credit right. See Sections 9-312, 9-314. Under Section 9-104, a secured party has "control" of a deposit account when, with the consent of the debtor, the secured party obtains the depositary bank's agreement to act on the secured party's instructions (including when the secured party becomes the account holder) or when the secured party is itself the depositary bank. The control requirements are patterned on Section 8-106, which specifies the requirements for control of investment property. Under Section 9-107, "control" of a letter-of-credit right occurs when the issuer or nominated person consents to an assignment of proceeds under Section 5-114.

Electronic chattel paper and tangible chattel paper definitions deleted in 2022 Article 9 Revisions. Section 9-102 of the 1998 Revisions included new defined terms: "electronic chattel" and "tangible chattel paper." However, the 2022 Article 9 Revisions deleted those terms and modified the definition of "chattel paper" and the rules for chattel paper evidenced by electronic records, as discussed in Comment 4 and Section 9-102, Comment 5.b.

Investment property. The 1998 Revisions left the perfection requirements for "investment property" (defined in Section 9-102), including perfection by control under Section 9-106, substantially unchanged. However, a new provision in Section 9-314 is designed to ensure that a secured party retains control in "repledge" transactions that are typical in the securities markets.

Instruments and commercial tort claims. The 1998 Revisions expanded the types of collateral in which a security interest may be perfected by filing to include instruments. See Section 9-312. Under the revised Article security interests in commercial tort claims also are perfected by filing. See Sections 9-308, 9-310.

Sales of payment intangibles and promissory notes. Although pre-1998 Article 9 covered the outright sale of accounts and chattel paper, under the revised Article sales of most other types of receivables also are financing transactions to which Article 9 should apply. Accordingly, Section 9-102 expanded the definition of "account" to include many types of receivables (including "health-care-insurance receivables," defined in Section 9-102) that pre-1998 Article 9 classified as "general intangibles." It thereby subjects to Article 9's filing system sales of more types of receivables than did pre-1998 Article 9. Certain sales of payment intangibles—primarily bank loan participation transactions—should not be subject to the Article 9 filing rules. These transactions are placed in a residual category of collateral, "payment intangibles" (general intangibles under which the account debtor's principal obligation is monetary), the sale of which is exempt from the filing requirements of Article 9. See Sections 9-102, 9-109, 9-309 (perfection upon attachment). The perfection rules for sales of promissory notes are the same as those for sales of payment intangibles.

Possessory security interests. Several provisions of 1998 Article 9 address aspects of security interests involving a secured party or a third party who is in possession of collateral. In particular, Section 9-313 resolves a number of uncertainties under pre-1998 Section 9-305. It provides that a security interest in collateral in the possession of a third party is perfected when the third party acknowledges in an a signed record that it holds for the secured party's benefit. Section 9-313 also provides that a third party need not so acknowledge and that its acknowledgment does not impose any duties on it, unless it otherwise agrees. A special rule in Section 9-313 provides that if a secured party already is in possession of collateral, its security interest remains perfected by possession if it delivers the collateral to a third party and the collateral is accompanied by instructions to hold it for the secured party or to redeliver it to the secured party. Section 9-313 also clarifies the limited circumstances under which a security interest in goods covered by a certificate of title may be perfected by the secured party's taking possession.

Automatic perfection. The 1998 Revisions added Section 9-309, which lists various types of security interests as to which no public-notice step is required for perfection (e.g., purchase-money security interests in consumer goods other than automobiles). This automatic perfection also extends to a transfer of a health-care-insurance receivable to a health-care provider. Those transfers normally will be made by natural persons who receive health-care services; there is little value in requiring filing for perfection in that context. Automatic perfection also applies to security interests created by sales of payment intangibles and promissory notes. Section 9-308 provides that a perfected security interest in collateral supported by a "supporting obligation" (such as an account supported by a guaranty) also is a perfected security interest in the supporting obligation, and that a perfected security interest in an obligation secured by a security interest or lien on property (e.g., a real-property mortgage) also is a perfected security interest in the security interest or lien.

e. Priority; Special Rules for Banks and Deposit Accounts. The rules governing priority of security interests and agricultural liens under the 1998 Revisions are found in Part 3, Subpart 3 (Sections 9-317 through 9-342). The revised Article includes several new priority rules and some special rules relating to banks and deposit accounts (Sections 9-340 through 9-342).

Purchase-money security interests: General; consumer-goods transactions; inventory. Section 9-103 substantially rewrites the definition of purchase-money security interest (PMSI) (although the term is not formally "defined"). The substantive changes, however, apply only to non-consumer-goods transactions. (Consumer transactions and consumer-goods transactions are discussed below in Comment 4.j.) For non-consumer-goods transactions, Section 9-103 makes clear that a security interest in collateral may be (to some extent) both a PMSI as well as a non-PMSI, in accord with the "dual status" rule applied by some courts under pre-1998 Article 9 (thereby rejecting the "transformation" rule). The revised definition provides an even broader conception of a PMSI in inventory, yielding a result that accords with private agreements entered into in response to the uncertainty under pre-1998 Article 9. It also treats consignments as purchase-money security interests in inventory. Section 9-324 clarifies the PMSI priority rules, but for the most part without material change in substance. Section 9-324 also clarifies the priority rules for competing PMSIs in the same collateral.

Purchase-money security interests in livestock; agricultural liens. Section 9-324 provides a special PMSI priority, similar to the inventory PMSI priority rule, for livestock. Section 9-322 (the baseline first-to-file-or-perfect priority rule) also recognizes special non-Article 9 priority rules for agricultural liens, which can override the baseline first-in-time rule.

Purchase-money security interests in software. Section 9-324 contains a new priority rule for a software purchase-money security interest. (Section 9-102 includes a definition of "software.") Under Section 9-103, a software PMSI includes a PMSI in software that is used in goods that are also subject to a PMSI.

Investment property. The 1998 priority rules for investment property are substantially similar to the priority rules found in pre-1998 Section 9-115, which was added in conjunction with the 1994 revisions to

UCC Article 8. Under Section 9-328, if a secured party has control of investment property (Sections 8-106, 9-106), its security interest is senior to a security interest perfected in another manner (e.g., by filing). Also under Section 9-328, security interests perfected by control generally rank according to the time that control is obtained or, in the case of a security entitlement or a commodity contract carried in a commodity account, the time when the control arrangement is entered into. That was a change from pre-1998 Section 9-115, under which the security interests ranked equally. However, as between a securities intermediary's security interest in a security entitlement that it maintains for the debtor and a security interest held by another secured party, the securities intermediary's security interest is senior.

Deposit accounts. The 1998 priority rules applicable to deposit accounts are found in Section 9-327 and are patterned on and similar to those for investment property in pre-1998 Section 9-115 and Section 9-328. Under Section 9-327, if a secured party has control of a deposit account, its security interest is senior to a security interest perfected in another manner (i.e., as cash proceeds). Also under Section 9-327, security interests perfected by control rank according to the time that control is obtained, but as between a depositary bank's security interest and one held by another secured party, the depositary bank's security interest is senior. A corresponding rule in Section 9-340 makes a depositary bank's right of set-off generally senior to a security interest held by another secured party. However, if the other secured party becomes the depositary bank's customer with respect to the deposit account, then its security interest is senior to the depositary bank's security interest and right of set-off. Sections 9-327, 9-340.

Letter-of-credit rights. The 1998 priority rules for security interests in letter-of-credit rights are set out in Section 9-329. They are somewhat analogous to those for deposit accounts. A security interest perfected by control has priority over one perfected in another manner (i.e., as a supporting obligation for the collateral in which a security interest is perfected). Security interests in a letter-of-credit right perfected by control rank according to the time that control is obtained. However, the rights of a transferee beneficiary or a nominated person are independent and superior to the extent provided in Section 5-114. See Section 9-109(c)(4).

Chattel paper and instruments. Section 9-330 is the 1998 successor to pre-1998 Section 9-308. As under pre-1998 Section 9-308, under the 1998 Revisions differing priority rules apply to purchasers of chattel paper who give new value and take possession (or, in the case of electronic chattel paper, obtain control) of the collateral—depending on whether a conflicting security interest in the collateral is claimed merely as proceeds. The principal change related to the role of knowledge and the effect of an indication of a previous assignment of the collateral. 1998 Section 9-330 also afforded priority to purchasers of instruments who take possession in good faith and without knowledge that the purchase violates the rights of the competing secured party. In addition, to qualify for priority, purchasers of chattel paper, but not of instruments, must purchase in the ordinary course of business. The 2022 Article 9 Revisions eliminated the defined terms "electronic chattel paper" and "tangible chattel paper," revised the definition of "chattel paper" in Section 9-102 and modified the Section 9-330 priority rule accordingly. See Comment 4.b. and Section 9-102, Comment 5.b.

Proceeds. 1998 Section 9-322 contains new priority rules that clarify when a special priority of a security interest in collateral continues or does not continue with respect to proceeds of the collateral. Other 1998 refinements to the priority rules for proceeds are included in Sections 9-324 (purchase-money security interest priority) and 9-330 (priority of certain purchasers of chattel paper and instruments).

Miscellaneous priority provisions. The 1998 Revisions to Article 9 also included (i) clarifications of selected good-faith-purchase and similar issues (Sections 9-317, 9-331); (ii) new priority rules to deal with the "double debtor" problem arising when a debtor creates a security interest in collateral acquired by the debtor subject to a security interest created by another person (Section 9-325); (iii) new priority rules to deal with the problems created when a change in corporate structure or the like results in a new entity that has become bound by the original debtor's after-acquired property agreement (Section 9-326); (iv) a provision enabling most transferees of funds from a deposit account or money to take free of a security interest (Section 9-332); (v) substantially rewritten and refined priority rules dealing with accessions and commingled goods (Sections 9-335, 9-336); (vi) revised priority rules for security interests in goods covered by a certificate of title (Section 9-337); and (vii) provisions designed to ensure that security interests in deposit accounts will not extend to most transferees of funds on deposit or payees from deposit accounts and will not otherwise "clog" the payments system (Sections 9-341, 9-342).

Model provisions relating to production-money security interests. Appendix II to the 1998 Revisions contained model definitions and priority rules relating to "production-money security interests" held by secured parties who give new value used in the production of crops. Because no consensus emerged on the wisdom of these provisions during the drafting process, the sponsors made no recommendation on whether these model provisions should be enacted.

f. Proceeds. Revised Section 9-102 provides an expanded definition of "proceeds" of collateral, which includes additional rights and property that arise out of collateral, such as distributions on account of collateral and claims arising out of the loss or nonconformity of, defects in, or damage to collateral. The revised definition of "proceeds" also includes collections on account of "supporting obligations," such as guarantees.

g. Part 4: Additional Provisions Relating to Third-Party Rights. The 1998 Revisions added a new Part 4 that includes several provisions relating to the relationships between certain third parties and the parties to secured transactions. Part 4 contains new Sections 9-401 (replacing pre-1998 Section 9-311) (alienability of debtor's rights), 9-402 (replacing pre-1998 Section 9-317) (secured party not obligated on debtor's contracts), 9-403 (replacing pre-1998 Section 9-206) (agreement not to assert defenses against assignee), 9-404, 9-405, and 9-406 (replacing pre-1998 Section 9-318) (rights acquired by assignee, modification of assigned contract, discharge of account debtor, restrictions on assignment of account, chattel paper, promissory note, or payment intangible ineffective), 9-407 (replacing some provisions of pre-1998 Section 2A-303) (restrictions on creation or enforcement of security interest in leasehold interest or lessor's residual interest ineffective). New Part 4 also added new Sections 9-408 (restrictions on assignment of promissory notes, health-care-insurance receivables ineffective, and certain general intangibles ineffective) and 9-409 (restrictions on assignment of letter-of-credit rights ineffective). See Comment 3.a.

h. Filing. New Part 5 (replacing pre-1998 Part 4) of Article 9 was substantially rewritten to simplify the statutory text and to deal with numerous problems of interpretation and implementation that have arisen over the years.

Medium-neutrality. Part 5 is "medium-neutral"; that is, it makes clear that parties may file and otherwise communicate with a filing office by means of records communicated and stored in media other than on paper.

Identity of person who files a record; authorization. Part 5 also is largely indifferent as to the person who effects a filing. Instead, it addresses whose authorization is necessary for a person to file a record with a filing office. The filing scheme does not contemplate that the identity of a "filer" will be a part of the searchable records. This approach is consistent with, and a necessary aspect of, eliminating signatures or other evidence of authorization from the system (except to the extent that filing offices may choose to employ authentication procedures in connection with electronic communications). As long as the appropriate person authorizes the filing, or, in the case of a termination statement, the debtor is entitled to the termination, it is largely insignificant whether the secured party or another person files any given record.

Section 9-509 collects in one place most of the rules that determine when a record may be filed. In general, the debtor's authorization is required for the filing of an initial financing statement or an amendment that adds collateral. With one further exception, a secured party of record's authorization is required for the filing of other amendments. The exception arises if a secured party has failed to provide a termination statement that is required because there is no outstanding secured obligation or commitment to give value. In that situation, a debtor is authorized to file a termination statement indicating that it has been filed by the debtor.

Financing statement formal requisites. The formal requisites for a financing statement under the 1998 Revisions are set out in Section 9-502. A financing statement must provide the name of the debtor and the secured party and an indication of the collateral that it covers. Sections 9-503 and 9-506 address the sufficiency of a name provided on a financing statement and clarify when a debtor's name is correct and when an incorrect name is insufficient. Section 9-504 addresses the indication of collateral covered. Under Section 9-504, a super-generic description (e.g., "all assets" or "all personal property") in a financing statement is a sufficient indication of the collateral. (Note, however, that a super-generic description is inadequate for purposes of a security agreement. See Sections 9-108, 9-203.) To facilitate electronic filing, this Article does not require that the debtor's signature or other authorization appear on a financing statement. Instead, it prohibits the filing of unauthorized financing statements and imposes liability upon those who violate the prohibition. See Sections 9-509, 9-626.

Filing-office operations. The 1998 Part 5 introduced several provisions governing filing operations. First, it prohibits the filing office from rejecting an initial financing statement or other record for a reason other than one of the few that are specified. See Sections 9-520, 9-516. Second, the filing office is obliged to link all subsequent records (e.g., assignments, continuation statements, etc.) to the initial financing statement to which they relate. See Section 9-519. Third, the filing office may delete a financing statement and related records from the files no earlier than one year after lapse (lapse normally is five years after the filing date), and then only if a continuation statement has not been filed. See Sections 9-515, 9-519, 9-522. Thus, a financing statement and related records would be discovered by a search of the files even after the filing of a termination statement. This approach helps eliminate filing-office discretion and also eases problems associated with multiple secured parties and multiple partial assignments. Fourth, Part 5 mandates performance standards for filing offices. See Sections 9-519, 9-520, 9-523. Fifth, it provides for the promulgation of filing-office rules to deal with details best left out of the statute and requires the filing office to submit periodic reports. See Sections 9-526, 9-527.

Defaulting or missing secured parties and fraudulent filings. In some areas of the country, serious problems had arisen from fraudulent financing statements filed against public officials and other persons. The 1998 Article addressed the fraud problem by providing the opportunity for a debtor to file a termination statement when a secured party wrongfully refuses or fails to provide a termination statement. See Section 9-509. This opportunity also addresses the problem of secured parties that simply disappear through mergers or liquidations. In addition, Section 9-518 provides a statutory method by which a debtor who believes that a filed record is inaccurate or was wrongfully filed may indicate that fact in the files, albeit without affecting the efficacy, if any, of the challenged record.

Extended period of effectiveness for certain financing statements. Section 9-515 contains an exception to the usual rule that financing statements are effective for five years unless a continuation statement is filed to continue the effectiveness for another five years. Under that section, an initial financing statement filed in connection with a "public-finance transaction" or a "manufactured-home transaction" (terms defined in Section 9-102) is effective for 30 years.

National form of financing statement and related forms. Section 9-521 provides for uniform, national written forms of financing statements and related written records that must be accepted by a filing office that accepts written records.

i. Default and Enforcement. Part 6 of the 1998 Revisions to Article 9 extensively revised and replaced pre-1998 Part 5. Provisions relating to enforcement of consumer-goods transactions and consumer transactions are discussed in Comment 4.j.

Debtor, secondary obligor; waiver. Section 9-602 clarifies the identity of persons who have rights and persons to whom a secured party owes specified duties under Part 6. Under that section, the rights and duties are enjoyed by and run to the "debtor," defined in Section 9-102 to mean any person with a non-lien property interest in collateral, and to any "obligor." However, with one exception (Section 9-616, as it relates to a consumer obligor), the rights and duties concerned affect non-debtor obligors only if they are "secondary obligors." "Secondary obligor" is defined in Section 9-102 to include one who is secondarily obligated on the secured obligation, e.g., a guarantor, or one who has a right of recourse against the debtor or another obligor with respect to an obligation secured by collateral. However, under Sections 9-605 and 9-628, the secured party is relieved from any duties and liabilities to any person unless the secured party knows that the person is a debtor or obligor. (The 2022 Article 9 Revisions have modified Sections 9-605 and 9-628. See 2022 Section 9-605, Comments 2 and 3.) Resolving an issue on which courts disagreed under pre-1998 Article 9, this revised Article 9 generally prohibits waiver by a secondary obligor of its rights and a secured party's duties under Part 6. See Section 9-602. However, Section 9-624 permits a secondary obligor or debtor to waive the right to notification of disposition of collateral and, in a non-consumer transaction, the right to redeem collateral, if the secondary obligor or debtor agrees to do so after default.

Rights of collection and enforcement of collateral. Section 9-607 explains in greater detail than pre-1998 Section 9-502 the rights of a secured party who seeks to collect or enforce collateral, including accounts, chattel paper, and payment intangibles. It also sets forth the enforcement rights of a depositary bank holding a security interest in a deposit account maintained with the depositary bank. Section 9-607 relates solely to the rights of a secured party vis-à-vis a debtor with respect to collections and enforcement. It does not affect the rights or duties of third parties, such as account debtors on collateral, which are addressed elsewhere (e.g., new Section 9-406). Section 9-608 clarifies the manner in which proceeds of collection or enforcement are to be applied.

Disposition of collateral: Warranties of title. Section 9-610 imposes on a secured party who disposes of collateral the warranties of title, quiet possession, and the like that are otherwise applicable under other law. It also provides rules for the exclusion or modification of those warranties.

Disposition of collateral: Notification, application of proceeds, surplus and deficiency, other effects. Section 9-611 requires a secured party to give notification of a disposition of collateral to other secured parties and lienholders who have filed financing statements against the debtor covering the collateral. (That duty was eliminated by the 1972 revisions to Article 9.) However, that section relieves the secured party from that duty when the secured party undertakes a search of the records and a report of the results is unreasonably delayed. Section 9-613, which applies only to non-consumer transactions, specifies the contents of a sufficient notification of disposition and provides that a notification sent 10 days or more before the earliest time for disposition is sent within a reasonable time. Section 9-615 addresses the application of proceeds of disposition, the entitlement of a debtor to any surplus, and the liability of an obligor for any deficiency. Section 9-619 clarifies the effects of a disposition by a secured party, including the rights of transferees of the collateral.

Rights and duties of secondary obligor. Section 9-618 provides that a secondary obligor obtains the rights and assumes the duties of a secured party if the secondary obligor receives an assignment of a secured obligation, agrees to assume the secured party's rights and duties upon a transfer to it of collateral, or becomes subrogated to the rights of the secured party with respect to the collateral. The assumption, transfer, or subrogation is not a disposition of collateral under Section 9-610, but it does relieve the former secured party of further duties. Pre-1998 Section 9-504(5) did not address whether a secured party was relieved of its duties in this situation.

Transfer of record or legal title. Section 9-619 contains a new provision making clear that a transfer of record or legal title to a secured party is not of itself a disposition under Part 6. This rule applies regardless of the circumstances under which the transfer of title occurs.

Strict foreclosure. Section 9-620, unlike pre-1998 Section 9-505, permits a secured party to accept collateral in partial satisfaction, as well as full satisfaction, of the obligations secured. This right of strict foreclosure extends to intangible as well as tangible property. Section 9-622 clarifies the effects of an acceptance of collateral on the rights of junior claimants. It rejects the approach taken by some courts—deeming a secured party to have constructively retained collateral in satisfaction of the secured obligations—in the case of a secured party's unreasonable delay in the disposition of collateral. Instead, unreasonable delay is relevant when determining whether a disposition under Section 9-610 is commercially reasonable.

Effect of noncompliance: "Rebuttable presumption" test. Section 9-626 adopts the "rebuttable presumption" test for the failure of a secured party to proceed in accordance with certain provisions of Part 6. (As discussed in Comment 4.j., the test does not necessarily apply to consumer transactions.) Under this approach, the deficiency claim of a noncomplying secured party is calculated by crediting the obligor with the greater of the actual net proceeds of a disposition and the amount of net proceeds that would have been realized if the disposition had been conducted in accordance with Part 6 (e.g., in a commercially reasonable manner). For non-consumer transactions, Section 9-626 rejects the "absolute bar" test that some courts have imposed; that approach bars a noncomplying secured party from recovering any deficiency, regardless of the loss (if any) the debtor suffered as a consequence of the noncompliance.

"Low-price" dispositions: Calculation of deficiency and surplus. Section 9-615(f) addresses the problem of procedurally regular dispositions that fetch a low price. Subsection (f) provides a special method for calculating a deficiency if the proceeds of a disposition of collateral to a secured party, a person related to the secured party, or a secondary obligor are "significantly below the range of proceeds that a complying disposition to a person other than the secured party, a person related to the secured party, or a secondary obligor would have brought." ("Person related to" is defined in Section 9-102.) In these situations there is reason to suspect that there may be inadequate incentives to obtain a better price. Consequently, instead of calculating a deficiency (or surplus) based on the actual net proceeds, the deficiency (or surplus) would be calculated based on the proceeds that would have been received in a disposition to a person other than the secured party, a person related to the secured party, or a secondary obligor.

j. Consumer Goods, Consumer-Goods Transactions, and Consumer Transactions. The 1998 Revisions (including the accompanying conforming revisions (see Appendix I)) included several special rules for "consumer goods," "consumer transactions," and "consumer-goods transactions." Each term is defined in Section 9-102.

(i) Revised Sections 2-502 and 2-716 provide a buyer of consumer goods with enhanced rights to possession of the goods, thereby accelerating and enhancing the opportunity to achieve "buyer in ordinary course of business" status under Section 1-201.

(ii) Section 9-103(e) (allocation of payments for determining extent of purchase-money status), (f) (purchase-money status not affected by cross-collateralization, refinancing, restructuring, or the like), and (g) (secured party has burden of establishing extent of purchase-money status) do not apply to consumer-goods transactions. Section 9-103 also provides that the limitation of those provisions to transactions other than consumer-goods transactions leaves to the courts the proper rules for consumer-goods transactions and prohibits the courts from drawing inferences from that limitation.

(iii) Section 9-108 provides that in a consumer transaction a description of consumer goods, a security entitlement, securities account, or commodity account "only by [UCC-defined] type of collateral" is not a sufficient collateral description in a security agreement.

(iv) Sections 9-403 and 9-404 make effective the Federal Trade Commission's anti-holder-in-due-course rule (when applicable), 16 C.F.R. Part 433, even in the absence of the required legend.

(v) The 10-day safe-harbor for notification of a disposition provided by Section 9-612 does not apply in a consumer transaction.

(vi) Section 9-613 (contents and form of notice of disposition) does not apply to a consumer-goods transaction.

(vii) Section 9-614 contains special requirements for the contents of a notification of disposition and a safe-harbor, "plain English" form of notification, for consumer-goods transactions.

(viii) Section 9-616 requires a secured party in a consumer-goods transaction to provide a debtor with a notification of how it calculated a deficiency at the time it first undertakes to collect a deficiency.

(ix) Section 9-620 prohibits partial strict foreclosure with respect to consumer goods collateral and, unless the debtor agrees to waive the requirement in a signed record after default, in certain cases requires the secured party to dispose of consumer goods collateral which has been repossessed.

(x) Section 9-626 ("rebuttable presumption" rule) does not apply to a consumer transaction. Section 9-626 also provides that its limitation to transactions other than consumer transactions leaves to the courts the proper rules for consumer transactions and prohibits the courts from drawing inferences from that limitation.

k. Good Faith. The 1998 Revisions added in Section 9-102 a new definition of "good faith" that included not only "honesty in fact" but also "the observance of reasonable commercial standards of fair dealing." That definition was deleted by the conforming amendments to the 2001 revision of Article 1 as unnecessary, given the revised definition in Section 1-201(b)(20).

l. [Reserved.]

m. Conforming and Related Amendments to Other UCC Articles. Appendix I to the 1998 Revisions contained several proposed revisions to the provisions and Comments of other UCC articles. For the most part those revisions are explained in the Comments to the 1998 Revisions.

Article 1. Revised Section 1-201 provides revisions to the definitions of "buyer in ordinary course of business," "purchaser," and "security interest."

Articles 2 and 2A. Sections 2-210, 2-326, 2-502, 2-716, 2A-303, and 2A-307 are revised to address the intersection between Articles 2 and 2A and Article 9.

Article 5. New Section 5-118 is patterned on Section 4-210. It provides for a security interest in documents presented under a letter of credit in favor of the issuer and a nominated person on the letter of credit.

Article 8. Revisions to Section 8-106, which deals with "control" of securities and security entitlements, conform it to Section 8-302, which deals with "delivery." Revisions to Section 8-110, which deals with a "securities intermediary's jurisdiction," conform it to the revised treatment of a "commodity intermediary's jurisdiction" in Section 9-305. Sections 8-301 and 8-302 are revised for clarification. Section 8-510 is revised to conform it to the revised priority rules of Section 9-328. Several Comments in Article 8 also are revised.

4. Summary of 2022 Article 9 Revisions. Following is a brief summary of some of the more significant revisions that are included in the 2022 Article 9 Revisions. The 2022 amendments to Article 9 are extensive. Many of the amendments are necessary to conform Article 9 to new Article 12, which (along with its Comments) should be read along with the Article 9 amendments and Comments. Other material amendments include those relating to chattel paper and money, among other matters.

a. Article 12-Related Revisions. Article 12-related amendments to Article 9 include the addition of two new kinds of collateral under Article 9: controllable account (a subset of account) and controllable payment intangible (a subset of payment intangible, which is a subset of general intangible). A controllable account or controllable payment intangible is created when the account or payment intangible is evidenced by a controllable electronic record (defined in Section 12-102(a)(1), and a subset of general intangible), which results if the account debtor obligated on the account or payment intangible has agreed to pay the person in control of the controllable electronic record. Perfection of a security interest in a controllable electronic record, controllable account, or controllable payment intangible may be by control or by filing a financing statement. Control of a controllable electronic record is determined under Section 12-105. Control of a controllable account or controllable payment intangible is achieved by obtaining control of the controllable electronic record that evidences the account or payment intangible. Section 9- 107A(b). A security interest in a controllable account, controllable electronic record, or controllable payment intangible which is perfected by control has priority over a security interest held by a secured party that does not have control. Section 9-326A.

As is the case for secured parties protected by take-free rules under other articles, the rights of a secured party that takes free of competing property interests under Section 12-104(e) or that is protected from certain actions under Section 12-104(g), as a qualifying purchaser of a controllable account, controllable electronic record, or controllable payment intangible, are respected under Article 9. Section 9-331.

The law of the controllable electronic record's jurisdiction under Section 12-107 governs perfection by control and priority of a security interest in a controllable account, controllable electronic record, or controllable payment intangible. Section 9-306B(a). The law of the jurisdiction in which a debtor is located governs perfection by filing (but not priority) for such collateral. Section 9-306B(b).

The 2022 Article 9 Revisions also contains several other Article 12-related conforming amendments to Article 9.

b. Chattel Paper-Related Amendments. These amendments primarily address two issues that have arisen under the pre-2022 Article 9 with respect to transactions in chattel paper.

First, the definition of "chattel paper" created uncertainty in "bundled" or "hybrid" transactions in which monetary obligations exist not only under a lease of goods but also with respect to other property and services relating to the leased goods. Frequently, the value of the non-goods aspect of a transaction is substantially greater than the value of the lessee's rights under the lease of goods. Uncertainty existed among those who finance chattel paper and other rights to payment as to whether these transactions give rise to chattel paper. The revisions resolve this issue by treating only those transactions whose predominant purpose was to give the obligor (lessee) the right to possession and use of the goods as giving rise to "chattel paper." Some similar issues arise in connection with chattel paper that includes a security interest securing specific goods. See Section 9-102, Comment 5.b.

Second, the pre-2022 statutory distinction between "tangible chattel paper" and "electronic chattel paper" caused practical problems. As to tangible chattel paper (i.e., evidenced by writings), problems arose in the case of multiple originals of writings and situations in which separate writings covered different components of chattel paper. Official comments issued in connection with the 1998 Revisions addressed, but did not entirely resolve, these issues. As to electronic chattel paper, the safe harbor for control was based on a "single authoritative copy" of the chattel paper. Moreover, in some situations tangible chattel paper is converted to electronic form and electronic chattel paper is converted to tangible form. Additional uncertainty existed when one or more records comprised one or more authoritative tangible copies of the records that evidenced the right to payment and rights in related property and one or more authoritative electronic copies of those records also existed.

The 2022 Article 9 Revisions provide a single rule, under Ih a security Interest In chattel paper can be perfected by taking possession of the authoritative tangible copies, if any, and obtaining control of the electronic authoritative copies, if any. This single rule addresses cases where some records evidencing chattel paper are electronic and some are tangible or where a record in one medium is replaced by a record in another.

The 2022 Article 9 Revisions also define chattel paper more accurately, as the right to payment of a monetary obligation that is secured by a security interest in specific goods or owed under a lease of specific goods, if the right to payment and interest in the goods are evidenced by a record.

Finally, the 2022 Article 9 Revisions provide a new choice-of-law rule for perfection and priority of security interests in chattel paper that is evidenced by authoritative electronic copies of records or by such electronic copies and authoritative tangible copies. For such chattel paper, Section 9-306A provides that perfection by control and possession of authoritative copies and priority are governed by the law of the "chattel paper's jurisdiction," based loosely on Sections 8-110 and 9-305. For chattel paper evidenced only by authoritative tangible copies, Section 9- 306A(d) provides that perfection by possession and priority are governed by the law of the location of the authoritative tangible copies. Perfection by filing continues to be governed by the law of the location of the debtor for all chattel paper.

c. Money-Related Amendments.

Section 1-201(b)(24) defines "money" as including "a medium of exchange currently authorized or adopted by a domestic or foreign government. . . ." There is no way of knowing how money in an intangible form might develop, but there are indications that some countries might authorize or adopt intangible tokens as a medium of exchange and others might authorize or adopt deposit accounts with a central bank as money. (These tokens or accounts sometimes are referred to as central bank digital currency or CBDC.) For many purposes, there is no need for the UCC to distinguish among types of money. For Article 9 purposes, however, distinctions must be drawn. Only tangible money is susceptible of perfection by possession. And the steps needed for perfection by control with respect to intangible tokens, such as controllable electronic records, will not work for deposit accounts with a central bank, and vice versa. For this reason, the revisions provide an Article 9 definition of "money" that is narrower than the Article 1 definition. The Article 9 definition expressly excludes deposit accounts (but not CBDC that is a token). Thus, "electronic money," defined in Section 9-102 as "money in an electronic form," would not include deposit accounts. The Article 9 definition of "money" also excludes money in an electronic form that cannot be subjected to control under Section 9-105A.

The Article 9 provisions governing "deposit accounts" would remain suitable for accounts with a central bank, even if a government has adopted these accounts as money. The revisions leave Article 9's treatment of deposit accounts largely unchanged. Under the revisions, a security interest in electronic money as original collateral can be perfected only by control. The requirements for obtaining control of electronic money under Section 9-105A are essentially the same as those for obtaining control of a controllable electronic record under Article 12.

The 2022 Article 9 Revisions also make changes to Section 9-332, the take-free rules for transferees of money, including the addition of a new rule applicable to electronic money, and transferees of funds from deposit accounts.

d. Transitional Rules. Article A to the 2022 Amendments provides important transitional rules. These rules are designed to protect the expectations of parties to transactions entered into before the effective date of a state's enactment of the revisions. They also provide for an adequate period of time for parties to pre-effective date transactions to make adjustments so as to preserve certain pre-effective date priorities.

§ 9-102. Definitions and Index of Definitions.

(a) [Article 9 definitions.] In this article:

(1) "Accession" means goods that are physically united with other goods in such a manner that the identity of the original goods is not lost.

(2) "Account", except as used in "account for", "account statement", "account to", "commodity account" in paragraph (14), "customer's account", "deposit account" in paragraph (29), "on account of", and "statement of account", means a right to payment of a monetary obligation, whether or not earned by performance, (i) for property that has been or is to be sold, leased, licensed, assigned, or otherwise disposed of, (ii) for services rendered or to be rendered, (iii) for a policy of insurance issued or to be issued, (iv) for a secondary obligation

incurred or to be incurred, (v) for energy provided or to be provided, (vi) for the use or hire of a vessel under a charter or other contract, (vii) arising out of the use of a credit or charge card or information contained on or for use with the card, or (viii) as winnings in a lottery or other game of chance operated or sponsored by a State, governmental unit of a State, or person licensed or authorized to operate the game by a State or governmental unit of a State. The term includes controllable accounts and health-care-insurance receivables. The term does not include (i) chattel paper, (ii) commercial tort claims, (iii) deposit accounts, (iv) investment property, (v) letter-of-credit rights or letters of credit, (vi) rights to payment for money or funds advanced or sold, other than rights arising out of the use of a credit or charge card or information contained on or for use with the card, or (vii) rights to payment evidenced by an instrument.

(3) "Account debtor" means a person obligated on an account, chattel paper, or general intangible. The term does not include persons obligated to pay a negotiable instrument, even if the negotiable instrument evidences chattel paper.

(4) "Accounting", except as used in "accounting for", means a record:

(A) signed by a secured party;

(B) indicating the aggregate unpaid secured obligations as of a date not more than 35 days earlier or 35 days later than the date of the record; and

(C) identifying the components of the obligations in reasonable detail.

(5) "Agricultural lien" means an interest in farm products:

(A) which secures payment or performance of an obligation for:

(i) goods or services furnished in connection with a debtor's farming operation; or

(ii) rent on real property leased by a debtor in connection with its farming operation;

(B) which is created by statute in favor of a person that:

(i) in the ordinary course of its business furnished goods or services to a debtor in connection with a debtor's farming operation; or

(ii) leased real property to a debtor in connection with the debtor's farming operation; and

(C) whose effectiveness does not depend on the person's possession of the personal property.

(6) "As-extracted collateral" means:

(A) oil, gas, or other minerals that are subject to a security interest that:

(i) is created by a debtor having an interest in the minerals before extraction; and

(ii) attaches to the minerals as extracted; or

(B) accounts arising out of the sale at the wellhead or minehead of oil, gas, or other minerals in which the debtor had an interest before extraction.

(7) [Reserved.]

(7A) "Assignee", except as used in "assignee for benefit of creditors", means a person (i) in whose favor a security interest that secures an obligation is created or provided for under a security agreement, whether or not the obligation is outstanding or (ii) to which an account, chattel paper, payment intangible, or promissory note has been sold. The term includes a person to which a security interest has been transferred by a secured party.

(7B) "Assignor" means a person that (i) under a security agreement creates or provides for a security interest that secures an obligation or (ii) sells an account, chattel paper, payment intangible, or promissory note. The term includes a secured party that has transferred a security interest to another person.

(8) "Bank" means an organization that is engaged in the business of banking. The term includes savings banks, savings and loan associations, credit unions, and trust companies.

(9) "Cash proceeds" means proceeds that are money, checks, deposit accounts, or the like.

(10) "Certificate of title" means a certificate of title with respect to which a statute provides for the security interest in question to be indicated on the certificate as a condition or result of the security interest's obtaining priority over the rights of a lien creditor with respect to the collateral. The term includes another record maintained as an alternative to a certificate of title by the governmental unit that issues

certificates of title if a statute permits the security interest in question to be indicated on the record as a condition or result of the security interest's obtaining priority over the rights of a lien creditor with respect to the collateral.

(11) "Chattel paper" means:

(A) a right to payment of a monetary obligation secured by specific goods, if the right to payment and security agreement are evidenced by a record; or

(B) a right to payment of a monetary obligation owed by a lessee under a lease agreement with respect to specific goods and a monetary obligation owed by the lessee in connection with the transaction giving rise to the lease, if:

(i) the right to payment and lease agreement are evidenced by a record; and

(ii) the predominant purpose of the transaction giving rise to the lease was to give the lessee the right to possession and use of the goods.

The term does not include a right to payment arising out of a charter or other contract involving the use or hire of a vessel or a right to payment arising out of the use of a credit or charge card or information contained on or for use with the card.

(12) "Collateral" means the property subject to a security interest or agricultural lien. The term includes:

(A) proceeds to which a security interest attaches;

(B) accounts, chattel paper, payment intangibles, and promissory notes that have been sold; and

(C) goods that are the subject of a consignment.

(13) "Commercial tort claim" means a claim arising in tort with respect to which:

(A) the claimant is an organization; or

(B) the claimant is an individual and the claim:

(i) arose in the course of the claimant's business or profession; and

(ii) does not include damages arising out of personal injury to or the death of an individual.

(14) "Commodity account" means an account maintained by a commodity intermediary in which a commodity contract is carried for a commodity customer.

(15) "Commodity contract" means a commodity futures contract, an option on a commodity futures contract, a commodity option, or another contract if the contract or option is:

(A) traded on or subject to the rules of a board of trade that has been designated as a contract market for such a contract pursuant to federal commodities laws; or

(B) traded on a foreign commodity board of trade, exchange, or market, and is carried on the books of a commodity intermediary for a commodity customer.

(16) "Commodity customer" means a person for which a commodity intermediary carries a commodity contract on its books.

(17) "Commodity intermediary" means a person that:

(A) is registered as a futures commission merchant under federal commodities law; or

(B) in the ordinary course of its business provides clearance or settlement services for a board of trade that has been designated as a contract market pursuant to federal commodities law.

(18) "Communicate" means:

(A) to send a written or other tangible record;

(B) to transmit a record by any means agreed upon by the persons sending and receiving the record; or

(C) in the case of transmission of a record to or by a filing office, to transmit a record by any means prescribed by filing-office rule.

(19) "Consignee" means a merchant to which goods are delivered in a consignment.

(20) "Consignment" means a transaction, regardless of its form, in which a person delivers goods to a merchant for the purpose of sale and:

(A) the merchant:

(i) deals in goods of that kind under a name other than the name of the person making delivery;

(ii) is not an auctioneer; and

(iii) is not generally known by its creditors to be substantially engaged in selling the goods of others;

(B) with respect to each delivery, the aggregate value of the goods is $1,000 or more at the time of delivery;

(C) the goods are not consumer goods immediately before delivery; and

(D) the transaction does not create a security interest that secures an obligation.

(21) "Consignor" means a person that delivers goods to a consignee in a consignment.

(22) "Consumer debtor" means a debtor in a consumer transaction.

(23) "Consumer goods" means goods that are used or bought for use primarily for personal, family, or household purposes.

(24) "Consumer-goods transaction" means a consumer transaction in which:

(A) an individual incurs an obligation primarily for personal, family, or household purposes; and

(B) a security interest in consumer goods secures the obligation.

(25) "Consumer obligor" means an obligor who is an individual and who incurred the obligation as part of a transaction entered into primarily for personal, family, or household purposes.

(26) "Consumer transaction" means a transaction in which (i) an individual incurs an obligation primarily for personal, family, or household purposes, (ii) a security interest secures the obligation, and (iii) the collateral is held or acquired primarily for personal, family, or household purposes. The term includes consumer-goods transactions.

(27) "Continuation statement" means an amendment of a financing statement which:

(A) identifies, by its file number, the initial financing statement to which it relates; and

(B) indicates that it is a continuation statement for, or that it is filed to continue the effectiveness of, the identified financing statement.

(27A) "Controllable account" means an account evidenced by a controllable electronic record that provides that the account debtor undertakes to pay the person that has control under Section 12-105 of the controllable electronic record.

(27B) "Controllable payment intangible" means a payment intangible evidenced by a controllable electronic record that provides that the account debtor undertakes to pay the person that has control under Section 12-105 of the controllable electronic record.

(28) "Debtor" means:

(A) a person having an interest, other than a security interest or other lien, in the collateral, whether or not the person is an obligor;

(B) a seller of accounts, chattel paper, payment intangibles, or promissory notes; or

(C) a consignee.

(29) "Deposit account" means a demand, time, savings, passbook, or similar account maintained with a bank. The term does not include investment property or accounts evidenced by an instrument.

(30) "Document" means a document of title or a receipt of the type described in Section 7-201(b).

(31) [Reserved.]

(31A) "Electronic money" means money in an electronic form.

(32) "Encumbrance" means a right, other than an ownership interest, in real property. The term includes mortgages and other liens on real property.

(33) "Equipment" means goods other than inventory, farm products, or consumer goods.

(34) "Farm products" means goods, other than standing timber, with respect to which the debtor is engaged in a farming operation and which are:

(A) crops grown, growing, or to be grown, including:

(i) crops produced on trees, vines, and bushes; and

(ii) aquatic goods produced in aquacultural operations;

(B) livestock, born or unborn, including aquatic goods produced in aquacultural operations;

(C) supplies used or produced in a farming operation; or

(D) products of crops or livestock in their unmanufactured states.

(35) "Farming operation" means raising, cultivating, propagating, fattening, grazing, or any other farming, livestock, or aquacultural operation.

(36) "File number" means the number assigned to an initial financing statement pursuant to Section 9-519(a).

(37) "Filing office" means an office designated in Section 9-501 as the place to file a financing statement.

(38) "Filing-office rule" means a rule adopted pursuant to Section 9-526.

(39) "Financing statement" means a record or records composed of an initial financing statement and any filed record relating to the initial financing statement.

(40) "Fixture filing" means the filing of a financing statement covering goods that are or are to become fixtures and satisfying Section 9-502(a) and (b). The term includes the filing of a financing statement covering goods of a transmitting utility which are or are to become fixtures.

(41) "Fixtures" means goods that have become so related to particular real property that an interest in them arises under real property law.

(42) "General intangible" means any personal property, including things in action, other than accounts, chattel paper, commercial tort claims, deposit accounts, documents, goods, instruments, investment property, letter-of-credit rights, letters of credit, money, and oil, gas, or other minerals before extraction. The term includes controllable electronic records, payment intangibles and software.

(43) [Reserved] ["Good faith" means honesty in fact and the observance of reasonably commercial standards of fair dealing.]

(44) "Goods" means all things that are movable when a security interest attaches. The term includes (i) fixtures, (ii) standing timber that is to be cut and removed under a conveyance or contract for sale, (iii) the unborn young of animals, (iv) crops grown, growing, or to be grown, even if the crops are produced on trees, vines, or bushes, and (v) manufactured homes. The term also includes a computer program embedded in goods and any supporting information provided in connection with a transaction relating to the program if (i) the program is associated with the goods in such a manner that it customarily is considered part of the goods, or (ii) by becoming the owner of the goods, a person acquires a right to use the program in connection with the goods. The term does not include a computer program embedded in goods that consist solely of the medium in which the program is embedded. The term also does not include accounts, chattel paper, commercial tort claims, deposit accounts, documents, general intangibles, instruments, investment property, letter-of-credit rights, letters of credit, money, or oil, gas, or other minerals before extraction.

(45) "Governmental unit" means a subdivision, agency, department, county, parish, municipality, or other unit of the government of the United States, a State, or a foreign country. The term includes an organization having a separate corporate existence if the organization is eligible to issue debt on which interest is exempt from income taxation under the laws of the United States.

(46) "Health-care-insurance receivable" means an interest in or claim under a policy of insurance which is a right to payment of a monetary obligation for health-care goods or services provided or to be provided.

(47) "Instrument" means a negotiable instrument or any other writing that evidences a right to the payment of a monetary obligation, is not itself a security agreement or lease, and is of a type that in ordinary course of business is transferred by delivery with any necessary indorsement or assignment. The term does not include (i) investment property, (ii) letters of credit, (iii) writings that evidence a right to payment arising out of the use of a credit or charge card or information contained on or for use with the card, or (iv) writings that evidence chattel paper.

(48) "Inventory" means goods, other than farm products, which:

(A) are leased by a person as lessor;

(B) are held by a person for sale or lease or to be furnished under a contract of service;

(C) are furnished by a person under a contract of service; or

(D) consist of raw materials, work in process, or materials used or consumed in a business.

(49) "Investment property" means a security, whether certificated or uncertificated, security entitlement, securities account, commodity contract, or commodity account.

(50) "Jurisdiction of organization", with respect to a registered organization, means the jurisdiction under whose law the organization is formed or organized.

(51) "Letter-of-credit right" means a right to payment or performance under a letter of credit, whether or not the beneficiary has demanded or is at the time entitled to demand payment or performance. The term does not include the

right of a beneficiary to demand payment or performance under a letter of credit.

(52) "Lien creditor" means:

(A) a creditor that has acquired a lien on the property involved by attachment, levy, or the like;

(B) an assignee for benefit of creditors from the time of assignment;

(C) a trustee in bankruptcy from the date of the filing of the petition; or

(D) a receiver in equity from the time of appointment.

(53) "Manufactured home" means a structure, transportable in one or more sections, which, in the traveling mode, is eight body feet or more in width or 40 body feet or more in length, or, when erected on site, is 320 or more square feet, and which is built on a permanent chassis and designed to be used as a dwelling with or without a permanent foundation when connected to the required utilities, and includes the plumbing, heating, air-conditioning, and electrical systems contained therein. The term includes any structure that meets all of the requirements of this paragraph except the size requirements and with respect to which the manufacturer voluntarily files a certification required by the United States Secretary of Housing and Urban Development and complies with the standards established under Title 42 of the United States Code.

(54) "Manufactured-home transaction" means a secured transaction:

(A) that creates a purchase-money security interest in a manufactured home, other than a manufactured home held as inventory; or

(B) in which a manufactured home, other than a manufactured home held as inventory, is the primary collateral.

(54A) "Money" has the meaning in Section 1-201(b)(24), but does not include (i) a deposit account or (ii) money in an electronic form that cannot be subjected to control under Section 9-105A.

(55) "Mortgage" means a consensual interest in real property, including fixtures, which secures payment or performance of an obligation.

(56) "New debtor" means a person that becomes bound as debtor under Section 9-203(d) by a security agreement previously entered into by another person.

(57) "New value" means (i) money, (ii) money's worth in property, services, or new credit, or (iii) release by a transferee of an interest in property previously transferred to the transferee. The term does not include an obligation substituted for another obligation.

(58) "Noncash proceeds" means proceeds other than cash proceeds.

(59) "Obligor" means a person that, with respect to an obligation secured by a security interest in or an agricultural lien on the collateral, (i) owes payment or other performance of the obligation, (ii) has provided property other than the collateral to secure payment or other performance of the obligation, or (iii) is otherwise accountable in whole or in part for payment or other performance of the obligation. The term does not include issuers or nominated persons under a letter of credit.

(60) "Original debtor", except as used in Section 9-310(c), means a person that, as debtor, entered into a security agreement to which a new debtor has become bound under Section 9-203(d).

(61) "Payment intangible" means a general intangible under which the account debtor's principal obligation is a monetary obligation. The term includes a controllable payment intangible.

(62) "Person related to", with respect to an individual, means:

(A) the spouse of the individual;

(B) a brother, brother-in-law, sister, or sister-in-law of the individual;

(C) an ancestor or lineal descendant of the individual or the individual's spouse; or

(D) any other relative, by blood or marriage, of the individual or the individual's spouse who shares the same home with the individual.

(63) "Person related to", with respect to an organization, means:

(A) a person directly or indirectly controlling, controlled by, or under common control with the organization;

(B) an officer or director of, or a person performing similar functions with respect to, the organization;

(C) an officer or director of, or a person performing similar functions with respect to, a person described in subparagraph (A);

(D) the spouse of an individual described in subparagraph (A), (B), or (C); or

(E) an individual who is related by blood or marriage to an individual described in subparagraph (A), (B), (C), or (D) and shares the same home with the individual.

(64) "Proceeds", except as used in Section 9-609(b), means the following property:

(A) whatever is acquired upon the sale, lease, license, exchange, or other disposition of collateral;

(B) whatever is collected on, or distributed on account of, collateral;

(C) rights arising out of collateral;

(D) to the extent of the value of collateral, claims arising out of the loss, nonconformity, or interference with the use of, defects or infringement of rights in, or damage to, the collateral; or

(E) to the extent of the value of collateral and to the extent payable to the debtor or the secured party, insurance payable by reason of the loss or nonconformity of, defects or infringement of rights in, or damage to, the collateral.

(65) "Promissory note" means an instrument that evidences a promise to pay a monetary obligation, does not evidence an order to pay, and does not contain an acknowledgment by a bank that the bank has received for deposit a sum of money or funds.

(66) "Proposal" means a record signed by a secured party which includes the terms on which the secured party is willing to accept collateral in full or partial satisfaction of the obligation it secures pursuant to Sections 9-620, 9-621, and 9-622.

(67) "Public-finance transaction" means a secured transaction in connection with which:

(A) debt securities are issued;

(B) all or a portion of the securities issued have an initial stated maturity of at least 20 years; and

(C) the debtor, obligor, secured party, account debtor or other person obligated on collateral, assignor or assignee of a secured obligation, or assignor or assignee of a security interest is a State or a governmental unit of a State.

(68) "Public organic record" means a record that is available to the public for inspection and that is:

(A) a record consisting of the record initially filed with or issued by a State or the United States to form or organize an organization and any record filed with or issued by the State or the United States which amends or restates the initial record;

(B) an organic record of a business trust consisting of the record initially filed with a State and any record filed with the State which amends or restates the initial record, if a statute of the State governing business trusts requires that the record be filed with the State; or

(C) a record consisting of legislation enacted by the legislature of a State or the Congress of the United States which forms or organizes an organization, any record amending the legislation, and any record filed with or issued by the State or the United States which amends or restates the name of the organization.

(69) "Pursuant to commitment", with respect to an advance made or other value given by a secured party, means pursuant to the secured party's obligation, whether or not a subsequent event of default or other event not within the secured party's control has relieved or may relieve the secured party from its obligation.

(70) "Record", except as used in "for record", "of record", "record or legal title", and "record owner", means information that is inscribed on a tangible medium or which is stored in an electronic or other medium and is retrievable in perceivable form.

(71) "Registered organization" means an organization formed or organized solely under the law of a single State or the United States by the filing of a public organic record with, the issuance of a public organic record by, or the enactment of legislation by the State or the United States. The term includes a business trust that is formed or organized under the law of a single State if a statute of the State governing business trusts requires that the business trust's organic record be filed with the State.

(72) "Secondary obligor" means an obligor to the extent that:

(A) the obligor's obligation is secondary; or

(B) the obligor has a right of recourse with respect to an obligation secured by collateral against the debtor, another obligor, or property of either.

(73) "Secured party" means:

(A) a person in whose favor a security interest is created or provided for under a security agreement, whether or not any obligation to be secured is outstanding;

(B) a person that holds an agricultural lien;

(C) a consignor;

(D) a person to which accounts, chattel paper, payment intangibles, or promissory notes have been sold;

(E) a trustee, indenture trustee, agent, collateral agent, or other representative in whose favor a security interest or agricultural lien is created or provided for; or

(F) a person that holds a security interest arising under Section 2-401, 2-505, 2-711(3), 2A-508(5), 4-210, or 5-118.

(74) "Security agreement" means an agreement that creates or provides for a security interest.

(75) [Reserved.]

(76) "Software" means a computer program and any supporting information provided in connection with a transaction relating to the program. The term does not include a computer program that is included in the definition of goods.

(77) "State" means a State of the United States, the District of Columbia, Puerto Rico, the United States Virgin Islands, or any territory or insular possession subject to the jurisdiction of the United States.

(78) "Supporting obligation" means a letter-of-credit right or secondary obligation that supports the payment or performance of an account, chattel paper, a document, a general intangible, an instrument, or investment property.

(79) [Reserved.]

(79A) "Tangible money" means money in a tangible form.

(80) "Termination statement" means an amendment of a financing statement which:

(A) identifies, by its file number, the initial financing statement to which it relates; and

(B) indicates either that it is a termination statement or that the identified financing statement is no longer effective.

(81) "Transmitting utility" means a person primarily engaged in the business of:

(A) operating a railroad, subway, street railway, or trolley bus;

(B) transmitting communications electrically, electromagnetically, or by light;

(C) transmitting goods by pipeline or sewer; or

(D) transmitting or producing and transmitting electricity, steam, gas, or water.

(b) [Definitions in other articles.] "Control" as provided in Section 7-106 and the following definitions in other articles apply to this Article:

"Applicant" Section 5-102
"Beneficiary" Section 5-102
"Broker" Section 8-102
"Certificated security" Section 8-102
"Check" Section 3-104
"Clearing corporation" Section 8-102
"Contract for sale" Section 2-106
"Controllable electronic record." Section 12-102
"Customer" Section 4-104
"Entitlement holder" Section 8-102
"Financial asset" Section 8-102
"Holder in due course" Section 3-302
"Issuer" (with respect to a letter of credit or letter-of-credit right) Section 5-102
"Issuer" (with respect to a security) Section 8-201
"Issuer" (with respect to documents of title) Section 7-102
"Lease" Section 2A-103
"Lease agreement" Section 2A-103
"Lease contract" Section 2A-103
"Leasehold interest" Section 2A-103
"Lessee" Section 2A-103
"Lessee in ordinary course of business" Section 2A-103
"Lessor" Section 2A-103
"Lessor's residual interest" Section 2A-103
"Letter of credit" Section 5-102
"Merchant" Section 2-104
"Negotiable instrument" Section 3-104
"Nominated person" Section 5-102
"Note" Section 3-104
"Proceeds of a letter of credit" Section 5-114
"Protected purchaser" Section 8-303
"Prove" Section 3-103
"Qualifying purchaser" Section 12-102
"Sale" Section 2-106
"Securities account" Section 8-501
"Securities intermediary" Section 8-102

"Security"	Section 8-102
"Security certificate"	Section 8-102
"Security entitlement"	Section 8-102
"Uncertificated security"	Section 8-102

(c) [Article 1 definitions and principles.] Article 1 contains general definitions and principles of construction and interpretation applicable throughout this article.

Legislative Note: *Replicate the formatting of the tabulated material in subsection (a)(11) exactly to ensure that the meaning of the material is preserved.*

The Definition of "good faith" in subsection (a) (43) was deleted from subsection (a) pursuant to a conforming amendment accompanying the 2001 amendments of Article 1. However, any jurisdiction that has not adopted the revised definition of "good faith" in Section 1-201(b)(20) should retain the definition of "good faith" in subsection (a)(43).

Official Comment

1. Source. All terms that are defined in Article 9 and used in more than one section are consolidated in this section. Note that the definition of "security interest" is found in Section 1-201, not in this Article. Many of the definitions in this section derive from those in pre-1998 Section 9-105. Other definition were added by the 1998 Revisions or modified or added by the 2022 Article 9 Revisions.

2. Parties to Secured Transactions.

a. "Debtor"; "Obligor"; "Secondary Obligor." Determining whether a person was a "debtor" under pre-1998 Section 9-105(1)(d) required a close examination of the context in which the term was used. To reduce the need for this examination, the 1998 Revisions redefined "debtor" and added new defined terms, "secondary obligor" and "obligor." In the context of Part 6 (default and enforcement), these definitions distinguish among three classes of persons: (i) those persons who may have a stake in the proper enforcement of a security interest by virtue of their non-lien property interest (typically, an ownership interest) in the collateral, (ii) those persons who may have a stake in the proper enforcement of the security interest because of their obligation to pay the secured debt, and (iii) those persons who have an obligation to pay the secured debt but have no stake in the proper enforcement of the security interest. Persons in the first class are debtors. Persons in the second class are secondary obligors if any portion of the obligation is secondary or if the obligor has a right of recourse against the debtor or another obligor with respect to an obligation secured by collateral. One must consult the law of suretyship to determine whether an obligation is secondary. The Restatement (3d), Suretyship and Guaranty Restatement (3d), Suretyship and Guaranty 1 (1996), contains a useful explanation of the concept. Obligors in the third class are neither debtors nor secondary obligors. With one exception (Section 9-616, as it relates to a consumer obligor), the rights and duties provided by Part 6 affect non-debtor obligors only if they are "secondary obligors."

By including in the definition of "debtor" all persons with a property interest (other than a security interest in or other lien on collateral), the definition includes transferees of collateral, whether or not the secured party knows of the transfer or the transferee's identity. Exculpatory provisions in Part 6 protect the secured party in that circumstance. See Sections 9-605 and 9-628. The definition renders unnecessary pre-1998 Section 9-112, which governed situations in which collateral was not owned by the debtor. The definition also includes a "consignee," as defined in this section, as well as a seller of accounts, chattel paper, payment intangibles, or promissory notes.

Secured parties and other lienholders are excluded from the definition of "debtor" because the interests of those parties normally derive from and encumber a debtor's interest. However, if in a separate secured transaction a secured party grants, as debtor, a security interest in its own interest (i.e., its security interest and any obligation that it secures), the secured party is a debtor in that transaction. This typically occurs when a secured party with a security interest in specific goods assigns chattel paper.

Consider the following examples:

Example 1: Behnfeldt borrows money and grants a security interest in her Miata to secure the debt. Behnfeldt is a debtor and an obligor.

Example 2: Behnfeldt borrows money and grants a security interest in her Miata to secure the debt. Bruno co-signs a negotiable note as maker. As before, Behnfeldt is the debtor and an obligor. As an accommodation party (see Section 3-419), Bruno is a secondary obligor. Bruno has this status even if the note states that her obligation is a primary obligation and that she waives all suretyship defenses.

Example 3: Behnfeldt borrows money on an unsecured basis. Bruno co-signs the note and grants a security interest in her Honda to secure her obligation. Inasmuch as Behnfeldt does not have a property interest in the Honda, Behnfeldt is not a debtor. Having granted the security interest, Bruno is the debtor. Because Behnfeldt is a principal obligor, she is not a secondary obligor. Whatever the outcome of enforcement of the security interest against the Honda or Bruno's secondary obligation, Bruno will look to Behnfeldt for her losses. The enforcement will not affect Behnfeldt's aggregate obligations.

When the principal obligor (borrower) and the secondary obligor (surety) each has granted a security interest in different collateral, the status of each is determined by the collateral involved.

Example 4: Behnfeldt borrows money and grants a security interest in her Miata to secure the debt. Bruno co-signs the note and grants a security interest in her Honda to secure her obligation. When the secured party enforces the security interest in Behnfeldt's Miata, Behnfeldt is the debtor, and Bruno is a secondary obligor. When the secured party enforces the security interest in the Honda, Bruno is the "debtor." As in Example 3, Behnfeldt is an obligor, but not a secondary obligor.

If a security interest is granted by a protected series of a limited liability company formed under the Uniform Protected Series Act (2017), the debtor is the protected series. See PEB Commentary No. 23. The 2022 definition of "person" in Section 1-201(b)(27) includes a protected series.

b. "Secured Party." The secured party is the person in whose favor the security interest has been created, as determined by reference to the security agreement. This definition controls, among other things, which person has the duties and potential liability that Part 6 imposes upon a secured party. The definition of "secured party" also includes a "consignor," a person to which accounts, chattel paper, payment intangibles, or promissory notes have been sold, and the holder of an agricultural lien.

The definition of "secured party" clarifies the status of various types of representatives. Consider, for example, a multi-bank facility under which Bank A, Bank B, and Bank C are lenders and Bank A serves as the collateral agent. If the security interest is granted to the banks, then they are the secured parties. If the security interest is granted to Bank A as collateral agent, then Bank A is the secured party.

b.1 "Assignee"; "Assignor." Instead of referring to a "debtor," "secured party," and "security interest," all of which are defined terms, several provisions of Article 9, including Part 4, refer to the "assignment" or the "transfer" of property interests and some refer to an "assignor," "assignee," or "assigned contract." None of those terms are defined in the UCC. Some courts have read the undefined terms in an unduly narrow way. In 2020, the Permanent Editorial Board for the UCC issued a Commentary clarifying the meanings of these terms and amended the official comments accordingly. PEB Commentary No. 21. This Article generally follows common usage by using the terms "assignment" and "assign" to refer to transfers of rights to payment, claims, and liens and other security interests. It generally uses the term "transfer" to refer to other transfers of interests in property. Except when used in connection with a letter-of-credit transaction (see Section 9-107, Comment 4), no significance should be placed on the use of one term or the other. Depending on the substance of the transaction, each term as used in this Article refers to the assignment or transfer of an outright ownership interest or to the assignment or transfer of a limited interest, such as a security interest, or both.

The 2022 Article 9 Revisions added new definitions of "assignee" and "assignor." Paragraph 7A defines "assignee" as a person in whose favor a security interest securing an obligation is created or to which an account, chattel paper, a payment intangible, or a promissory note has been sold. Paragraph 7B defines "assignor" as creating a security interest securing an obligation or that sells an account, chattel paper, a payment intangible, or a promissory note. These definitions incorporate the essence of the 2020 PEB Commentary into the statutory text. The definitions also specify that an "assignor" includes a secured party that transfers a security interest to another person and an "assignee" includes a person to which a security interest has been transferred by a secured party. By their terms, the defined terms "assignee" and "assignor" contemplate assignments in particular contexts. However, several references in this article to "assigned," "assignment" and "assignee" include transfers in broader contexts than those addressed in the defined terms. See, e.g., subsection (a)(2) ("assigned," in definition of "account") and (a)(47) ("assignment," in definition of "instrument") and Sections 9-109, 9-408, 9-409, and 9-519.

Absent a contrary agreement, an assignee obtains the rights and powers of an assignor as against an account debtor on assigned collateral (e.g., under Section 9-406) and as between the assignee and the assignor (debtor) (e.g., under Section 9-607). See also Restatement (Second) of Contracts § 317(1) (1981) (emphasis added):

> An assignment of a right is a manifestation of the assignor's intention to transfer it *by virtue of which* the assignor's right to performance by the obligor is extinguished in whole or in part and *the assignee acquires a right to such performance.*

Several provisions of this Article and its official comments also refer to the "transfer" of property interests. Although that term and its cognates are not defined, depending on the context it may include an "assignment." Moreover, a transfer of property is not limited to transactions of "purchase" and may include the transfer of a limited interest. See also Section 9- 332, Comment 2A.

c. Other Parties. A "consumer obligor" is defined as the obligor in a consumer transaction. Definitions of "new debtor" and "original debtor" are used in the special rules found in Sections 9-326 and 9-508.

3. Definitions Relating to Creation of a Security Interest.

a. "Collateral." As under pre-1998 Section 9-105, "collateral" is the property subject to a security interest and includes accounts, chattel paper, payment intangibles, and promissory notes that have been sold. The 1998 Revisions expanded the term to include proceeds subject to a security interest and also broadened the scope of the Article to include as collateral property subject to an agricultural lien as well as payment intangibles and promissory notes that have been sold.

b. "Security Agreement." The definition of "security agreement" is substantially the same as under pre-1998 Section 9-105—an agreement that creates or provides for a security interest. However, the term frequently was used colloquially in pre-1998 Article 9 to refer to the document or writing that contained a debtor's security agreement. The 1998 Article 9 eliminated that usage, reserving the term for the more precise meaning specified in the definition.

Whether an agreement creates a security interest depends not on whether the parties intend that the law characterize the transaction as a security interest but rather on whether the transaction falls within the definition of "security interest" in Section 1-201. Thus, an agreement that the parties characterize as a "lease" of goods may be a "security agreement," notwithstanding the parties' stated intention that the law treat the transaction as a lease and not as a secured transaction. See Section 1-203.

4. Goods-Related Definitions.

a. "Goods"; "Consumer Goods"; "Equipment"; "Farm Products"; "Farming Operation"; "Inventory." The definition of "goods" is substantially the same as the definition in pre-1998 Section 9-105. This Article also retains the four mutually-exclusive "types" of collateral that consist of goods: "consumer goods," "equipment," "farm products," and "inventory." The revisions are primarily for clarification.

The classes of goods are mutually exclusive. For example, the same property cannot simultaneously be both equipment and inventory. In borderline cases—a physician's car or a farmer's truck that might be either consumer goods or equipment—the principal use to which the property is put is determinative. Goods can fall into different classes at different times. For example, a radio may be inventory in the hands of a dealer and consumer goods in the hands of a consumer. As under pre-1998 Article 9, goods are "equipment" if they do not fall into another category.

The definition of "consumer goods" follows pre-1998 Section 9-109. The classification turns on whether the debtor uses or bought the goods for use "primarily for personal, family, or household purposes."

Goods are inventory if they are leased by a lessor or held by a person for sale or lease. The revised definition of "inventory" makes clear that the term includes goods leased by the debtor to others as well as goods held for lease. (The same result should have obtained under the pre-1998 definition.) Goods to be furnished or furnished under a service contract, raw materials, and work in process also are inventory. Implicit in the definition is the criterion that the sales or leases are or will be in the ordinary course of business. For example, machinery used in manufacturing is equipment, not inventory, even though it is the policy of the debtor to sell machinery when it becomes obsolete or worn. Inventory also includes goods that are consumed in a business (e.g., fuel used in operations). In general, goods used in a business are equipment if they are fixed assets or have, as identifiable units, a relatively long period of use, but are inventory, even though not held for sale or lease, if they are used up or consumed in a short period of time in producing a product or providing a service.

Goods are "farm products" if the debtor is engaged in farming operations with respect to the goods. Animals in a herd of livestock are covered whether the debtor acquires them by purchase or as a result of natural increase. Products of crops or livestock remain farm products as long as they have not been subjected to a manufacturing process. The terms "crops" and "livestock" are not defined. The new definition of "farming operations" is for clarification only.

Crops, livestock, and their products cease to be "farm products" when the debtor ceases to be engaged in farming operations with respect to them. If, for example, they come into the possession of a marketing agency for sale or distribution or of a manufacturer or processor as raw materials, they become inventory. Products of crops or livestock, even though they remain in the possession of a person engaged in farming operations, lose their status as farm products if they are subjected to a manufacturing process. What is and what is not a manufacturing process is not specified in this Article. At one end of the spectrum, some processes are so closely connected with farming—such as pasteurizing milk or boiling sap to produce maple syrup or sugar—that they would not constitute manufacturing. On the other hand an extensive canning operation would be manufacturing. Once farm products have been subjected to a manufacturing process, they normally become inventory.

The revised definition of "farm products" clarifies the distinction between crops and standing timber and makes clear that aquatic goods produced in aquacultural operations may be either crops or livestock. Although aquatic goods that are vegetable in nature often would be crops and those that are animal would be livestock, this Article leaves the courts free to classify the goods on a case-by-case basis. See Section 9-324, Comment 11.

The definitions of "goods" and "software" are also mutually exclusive. Computer programs usually constitute "software", and, as such, are not "goods" as this Article uses the terms. However, under the circumstances specified in the definition of "goods," computer programs embedded in goods are part of the "goods" and are not "software".

b. "Accession"; "Manufactured Home"; "Manufactured-Home Transaction." Other specialized definitions of goods include "accession" (see the special priority and enforcement rules in Section 9-335), and "manufactured home" (see Section 9-515, permitting a financing statement in a "manufactured-home transaction" to be effective for 30 years). The definition of "manufactured home" borrows from the federal Manufactured Housing Act, 42 U.S.C. §§ 5401 et seq., and is intended to have the same meaning.

c. "As-Extracted Collateral." Under this Article, oil, gas, and other minerals that have not been extracted from the ground are treated as real property, to which this Article does not apply. Upon extraction, minerals become personal property (goods) and eligible to be collateral under this Article. See the definition of "goods," which excludes "oil, gas, and other minerals before extraction." To take account of financing practices reflecting the shift from real to personal property, this Article contains special rules for perfecting security interests in minerals which attach upon extraction and in accounts resulting from the sale of minerals at the wellhead or minehead. See, e.g., Sections 9-301(4) (law governing perfection and priority); 9-501 (place of filing), 9-502 (contents of financing statement), 9-519 (indexing of records). The term "as-extracted collateral," added by the 1998 Revisions, refers to the minerals and related accounts to which the special rules apply. The term "at the wellhead" encompasses arrangements based on a sale of the product (goods) at the moment that it issues from the ground and is measured, without technical distinctions as to whether title passes at the "Christmas tree" of a well, the far side of a gathering tank, or at some other point. The term "at . . . the minehead" is comparable.

The following examples explain the operation of these provisions.

> **Example 5:** Debtor owns an interest in oil that is to be extracted. To secure Debtor's obligations to Lender, Debtor enters into a signed agreement granting Lender an interest in the oil. Although Lender may acquire an interest in the oil under real-property law, Lender does not acquire a security interest under this Article until the oil becomes personal property, i.e., until is extracted and becomes "goods" to which this Article applies. Because Debtor had an interest in the oil before extraction and Lender's security interest attached to the oil as extracted, the oil is "as-extracted collateral."

> **Example 6:** Debtor owns an interest in oil that is to be extracted and contracts to sell the oil to Buyer at the wellhead. In a signed agreement, Debtor agrees to sell to Lender the right to payment from Buyer. This right to payment is an account that constitutes "as-extracted collateral." If Lender then resells the account to Financer, Financer acquires a security interest. However, inasmuch as the debtor-seller in that transaction, Lender, had no interest in the oil before extraction, Financer's collateral (the account it owns) is not "as-extracted collateral."

> **Example 7:** Under the facts of Example 6, before extraction, Buyer grants a security interest in the oil to Bank. Although Bank's security interest attaches when the oil is extracted, Bank's security interest is not in "as-extracted collateral," inasmuch as its debtor, Buyer, did not have an interest in the oil before extraction.

5. Receivables-Related Definitions.

a. "Account"; "Health-Care-Insurance Receivable"; "As-Extracted Collateral." The definition of "account" has been expanded and reformulated. It is no longer limited to rights to payment relating to goods or services. Many categories of rights to payment that were classified as general intangibles under pre-1998 Article 9 are accounts under this Article. Thus, if they are sold, a financing statement must be filed to perfect the buyer's interest in them. As used in the definition of "account," a right to payment "arising out of the use of a credit or charge card or information contained on or for use with the card" is the right of a card issuer to payment from its cardholder. A credit-card or charge-card transaction may give rise to other rights to payments; however, those other rights do not "arise out of the use" of the card or information contained on or for use with the card. Among the types of property that are expressly excluded from the definition of account is "a right to payment for money or funds advanced or sold." As used in the exclusion from the definition of "account," "funds" is a broader concept than money (although the term is not defined). For example, when a bank-lender credits a borrower's deposit account for the amount of a loan, the bank's advance of funds is not a transaction giving rise to an account. The 2022 Article 9 Revisions amended the definition of "money" in Section 1- 201(b)(24) and added a new, more narrow, definition of "money" in Section 9-102(a)(54A). See Comment 12A.

The definition of "health-care-insurance receivable" is new. It is a subset of the definition of "account." However, the rules generally applicable to account debtors on accounts do not apply to insurers obligated on health-care-insurance receivables. See Sections 9-404(e), 9-405(d), 9-406(i).

Note that certain accounts also are "as-extracted collateral." See Comment 4.c., Examples 6 and 7.

The 2022 Article 9 Revisions amended the definition of "account" to reflect the 2022 revised definition of "chattel paper," discussed in Comment 5.b. The revised definition of "account" also includes some additional exceptions that accommodate the use of the term "account" in other provisions. These new exceptions were implicit in the former definition. Moreover, the exceptions for the defined terms "commodity account" and "deposit account" implicitly apply to all uses of those terms in this Article.

b. "Chattel Paper." "Chattel paper" consists of a monetary obligation that is either secured by specific goods or arises in connection with a lease of specific goods, in each case if the obligation and security interest or lease is evidenced by a record. The monetary obligation itself need not be related to the goods. For example, a loan secured by specific goods and evidenced by one or more records creates chattel paper regardless of the purpose of the loan.

Rights to payment arising out of charters of vessels or the use of credit or charge cards are expressly excluded from the definition of chattel paper; they are accounts. The term "charter" as used in this section includes bareboat charters, time charters, successive voyage charters, contracts of affreightment, contracts of carriage, and all other arrangements for the use of vessels.

What distinguishes chattel paper from other rights to payment is the fact that creditor has an interest in specific goods to enforce the right to payment. For example, the fact that a secured party also has an interest in other property does not prevent the right to payment from being chattel paper, provided that the specific goods are the primary collateral.

> **Example 8.** To secure a loan, Borrower grants Lender a security interest in a specified item of equipment and a deposit account. The loan and the security interest are evidenced by one or more records. The right to payment is chattel paper, assuming the equipment is the primary collateral.

In Example 8, the inclusion of some incidental collateral, such as a deposit account, does not prevent characterization of the right to payment as chattel paper. Another typical example would be the inclusion of after-acquired replacement parts to be installed on the specific goods. On the other hand, to be chattel paper, a right to payment must be accompanied by a security interest in specific goods or a lease of specific goods. A right to payment secured by a security interest in rotating collateral is not chattel paper.

> **Example 9.** To secure a loan, Borrower grants Lender a security interest in all of Borrower's existing and after-acquired inventory. The loan and the security interest are evidenced by one or more records. The right to payment is not chattel paper.

> **Example 10.** To secure a loan, Borrower grants Lender a security interest in a specifically described item of equipment, which is not the primary collateral, and also in all of Borrower's existing and after-acquired equipment. The loan and the security interest are evidenced by one or more records. The right to payment is not chattel paper.

Example 9 is the easy case because no "specific goods" are identified. As to Example 10, it is true that the monetary obligation is secured by "specific goods" and the definition of chattel paper does not specify that the obligation must be secured only by specific goods. However, if the right to payment in Example 10 were to be characterized as chattel paper, it would be possible to convert virtually any monetary obligation evidenced by records and secured by any collateral into chattel paper merely by including as collateral a specific item of goods (whether inventory, equipment, consumer goods, or farm products). The special rules for chattel paper contemplate that specific goods are the primary collateral, even if some incidental property also might be included. If additional goods or other property are included and the specific goods are not the primary collateral, then classification as chattel paper would not be appropriate. Of course, there may be close cases. In those situations, parties should take appropriate precautions.

A right to payment arising from a lease of specific goods gives rise to chattel paper only if the predominant purpose of the transaction is to provide the lessee the right to possession and use of the goods. Therefore, under paragraph (11)(B)(ii), when a lease of specific goods is combined with an obligation to provide or right to receive other property or services, the resulting right to payment will be chattel paper only if the goods aspect of the transaction predominates.

> **Example 11.** Customer and Car Dealer enter into a transaction, evidenced by one or more records, pursuant to which, in exchange for a payment of $2,000 per month: (i) Customer is entitled to possession of a specific vehicle for 36 months; (ii) Car Dealer will provide round-the-clock monitoring of the vehicle's location and condition, and alert authorities to provide road-side assistance in the event of a malfunction or accident; and (iii) Car Dealer will, from time to time, remotely update the vehicle's operating system. The value of the right to possess and use the vehicle is significantly greater than the value of the monitoring service and updates. Because

the goods aspect of the transaction predominates, under paragraph (11)(B)(ii) Customer's monetary obligation, including the portion attributable to Car Dealer's obligation to provide monitoring and updates, constitutes chattel paper.

Example 12. Customer and Cableco enter into a transaction, evidenced by one or more records, pursuant to which, in exchange for a payment of $200 per month, Cableco will provide Customer with specified television programming and a device needed to access the programming (a "lease" of the device). If the components of the transaction were priced separately, the price for the programming would be substantially more than the price for possession and use of the device. Because the goods aspect of this transaction does not predominate, under paragraph (11)(B)(ii) Customer's monetary obligation does not constitute chattel paper.

The 2022 revision to the definition of chattel paper omits the references to "software used in the goods" and a "license of software used in the goods" as superfluous, inasmuch as there is no reason to single out software. Other types of property may secure an obligation or be included in a transaction involving a lease, as discussed above. See also Sections 2-102 (scope of Article 2); 2-106(5) (defining "hybrid transaction"); 2A-102 (scope of Article 2A); 2A-103(aa) (definition of "hybrid lease"). These references were omitted from the definition of chattel paper for clarification and did not result in any change in the scope of the definition.

The 2022 revision to the definition of "chattel paper" also changed the language from "a record or records that evidence a monetary obligation" to "a right to payment of a monetary obligation... evidenced by a record." This semantic change was for clarification purposes only; it does not imply a change in meaning. Chattel paper is and has always been a right to payment of a monetary obligation. Because the revised definition is based on the obligation, rather than the record, the definition no longer includes the following statement, which was included in the previous definition: "If a transaction is evidenced by records that include an instrument or series of instruments, the group of records taken together constitutes chattel paper." The omission of that statement also does not imply a change in meaning, except that writings evidencing chattel paper are excluded from the definition of "instrument" under Section 9-102(a)(47). Although the definition refers to "a record," chattel paper can be evidenced by one or more records because, under Section 1-106, unless the statutory context otherwise requires, words in the singular number include the plural.

Finally, the revised definition of "chattel paper" and the approach to perfection of a security interest by possession and control under Section 9-314A have eliminated the need to have separate definitions of "electronic chattel paper" and "tangible chattel paper" in Section 9-102. Consequently, those definitions have been deleted.

c. "Instrument"; "Promissory Note." The definition of "instrument" includes a negotiable instrument. As under pre-1998 Section 9-105, it also includes any other right to payment of a monetary obligation that is evidenced by a writing of a type that in ordinary course of business is transferred by delivery (and, if necessary, an indorsement or assignment). The 2022 revised definition of "instrument" explicitly excludes a writing that evidences a right to payment that is chattel paper. This revision clarifies and makes explicit the understanding before the revision that an obligation on an instrument that evidences chattel paper is to be treated (e.g., under Section 9-330) as an obligation on chattel paper and not on an instrument. With that exception, the fact that an instrument is secured by a security interest or encumbrance on property does not change the character of the instrument as such or convert the combination of the instrument and collateral into a separate classification of personal property. The definition also makes clear that rights to payment arising out of credit-card transactions are not instruments. The definition of "promissory note" added in the 1998 Revisions, was necessitated by the inclusion of sales of promissory notes within the scope of Article 9. It explicitly excludes obligations arising out of "orders" to pay (e.g., checks) as opposed to "promises" to pay. See Section 3-104. Under the 2022 Article 9 Revisions, Sections 9-406(d) and 9-408(g) adopt a modified meaning of "promissory note" as that term is used in Sections 9-406(d) and Sections 9-408(a) through (d). See Comment 5.h.; see also Sections 9-406, Comment 5; 9-408, Comment 11.

d. "General Intangible"; "Payment Intangible." "General intangible" is the residual category of personal property, including things in action, that is not included in the other defined types of collateral. Examples are various categories of intellectual property and the right to payment of a loan of funds that is not evidenced by chattel paper or an instrument. As used in the definition of "general intangible," "things in action" includes rights that arise under a license of intellectual property, including the right to exploit the intellectual property without liability for infringement. The definition was revised in 1998 to exclude commercial tort claims, deposit accounts, and letter-of-credit rights. Each of the three is a separate type of collateral. One important consequence of this exclusion is that tortfeasors (commercial tort claims), banks (deposit accounts), and persons obligated on letters of credit (letter-of-credit rights) are not "account debtors" having the rights and obligations set forth in Sections 9-404, 9-405, and 9-406. In particular, tortfeasors, banks, and persons obligated on letters of credit are not obligated to pay an assignee (secured party) upon receipt of the notification described in

Section 9-404(a). See Comment 5.h. Another important consequence relates to the adequacy of the description in the security agreement. See Section 9-108.

"Payment intangible" is a subset of the definition of "general intangible." The sale of a payment intangible is subject to this Article. See Section 9-109(a)(3). Virtually any intangible right could give rise to a right to payment of money once one hypothesizes, for example, that the account debtor is in breach of its obligation. The term "payment intangible," however, embraces only those general intangibles "under which the account debtor's principal obligation is a monetary obligation." (Emphasis added.) A debtor's right to payment from another person of amounts received by the other person on the debtor's behalf, including the right of a merchant in a credit-card, debit-card, prepaid-card, or other payment-card transaction to payment of amounts received by its bank from the card system in settlement of the transaction, is a "payment intangible." (In contrast, the right of a credit-card issuer to payment arising out of the use of a credit card is an "account.") If a bank is the obligor on a monetary obligation not evidenced by an instrument or chattel paper, the obligation or the right to payment of the obligation may be a deposit account, an account, a payment intangible, or another type of collateral depending on the facts and circumstances. Of course, the classification of a monetary obligation or a right to payment of the obligation for purposes of this Article would not necessarily affect the application of laws regulating, for example, banking, securities, commodities, money transmission, and taxation.

In classifying intangible collateral, a court should begin by identifying the particular rights that have been assigned. The account debtor (promisor) under a particular contract may owe several types of monetary obligations as well as other, nonmonetary obligations. If the promisee's right to payment of money is assigned separately, the right is an account or payment intangible, depending on how the account debtor's obligation arose. When all the promisee's rights are assigned together, an account, a payment intangible, and a general intangible all may be involved, depending on the nature of the rights.

A right to the payment of money is frequently buttressed by ancillary rights, such as rights arising from covenants in a purchase agreement, note, or mortgage requiring insurance on the collateral or forbidding removal of the collateral, rights arising from covenants to preserve the creditworthiness of the promisor, and the lessor's rights with respect to leased goods that arise upon the lessee's default (see Section 2A-523). This Article does not treat these ancillary rights separately from the rights to payment to which they relate. For example, attachment and perfection of an assignment of a right to payment of a monetary obligation, whether it be an account or payment intangible, also carries these ancillary rights. Thus, an assignment of the lessor's right to payment under a lease also transfers the lessor's rights with respect to the leased goods under Section 2A-523. If, taken together, the lessor's rights to payment and with respect to the leased goods are evidenced by chattel paper, then, contrary to *In re Commercial Money Center, Inc.*, 350 B.R. 465 (Bankr. App. 9th Cir. 2006), an assignment of the lessor's right to payment constitutes an assignment of the chattel paper. Although an agreement excluding the lessor's rights with respect to the leased goods from an assignment of the lessor's right to payment may be effective between the parties, the agreement does not affect the characterization of the collateral to the prejudice of creditors of, and purchasers from, the assignor.

Every "payment intangible" is also a "general intangible." Likewise, "software" is a "general intangible" for purposes of this Article. See Comment 25. Accordingly, except as otherwise provided, statutory provisions applicable to general intangibles apply to payment intangibles and software.

d.1 "Controllable Account"; "Controllable Payment Intangible." Article 9 affords special treatment for security interests in controllable accounts and controllable payment intangibles, i.e., those accounts and payment intangibles that are evidenced by a controllable electronic record and as to which the account debtor (obligor) undertakes to pay the person having control of the controllable electronic record. Of course, a person would be an account debtor only if it were actually obligated on the account or payment intangible evidenced by the controllable electronic record. Although the definitions refer to a controllable electronic record that "provides" for an account debtor's undertaking, an account debtor's promise to pay normally would arise and be evidenced apart from the controllable electronic record itself. However, the definitions contemplate that a controllable electronic record evidencing an account or payment intangible (or an associated record) would indicate in some fashion an account debtor's obligation and that the controllable electronic record evidences the account or payment intangible. If a bank is the obligor on a monetary obligation payable to the person in control of a controllable electronic record, the obligation or the right to payment of the obligation may be a deposit account, a controllable account, a controllable payment intangible, or another type of collateral depending on the facts and circumstances. The classification of a monetary obligation or a right to payment of the obligation for purposes of this Article would not necessarily affect the application of laws regulating, for example, banking, securities, commodities, money transmission, and taxation.

An undertaking to pay the "person that has control" means an undertaking to pay the person that has control at the time payment is made. However, an undertaking to pay Smith, even though Smith happens to have control of the relevant controllable electronic record at the time the undertaking was made, is not an undertaking to pay the person that has control.

The special treatment for controllable accounts and controllable payment intangibles includes the following:

- Perfection of a security interest in a controllable account or controllable payment intangible can be achieved by filing a financing statement or by obtaining control of the controllable electronic record that evidences the controllable account or controllable payment intangible. Sections 9-312(a); 9-314(a); 9-107A(b).
- A security interest in a controllable electronic record, controllable account, or controllable payment intangible that is perfected by control has priority over a conflicting security interest that is perfected by another method. Section 9-326A.
- The benefit of the take-free and no-action rules for qualifying purchasers (including secured parties) of controllable electronic records also extends to qualifying purchasers of controllable accounts and controllable payment intangibles, whether or not the qualifying purchaser also purchases the related controllable electronic record. See Section 12-104(a) and Comments 5 through 8.

e. "Letter-of-Credit Right." The term "letter-of-credit right" embraces the rights to payment and performance under a letter of credit (defined in Section 5-102). However, it does not include a beneficiary's right to demand payment or performance. Transfer of those rights to a transferee beneficiary is governed by Article 5. See Sections 9-107, Comment 4, and 9-329, Comments 3 and 4.

f. "Supporting Obligation." This new term covers the most common types of credit enhancements—suretyship obligations (including guarantees) and letter-of-credit rights that support one of the types of collateral specified in the definition. As explained in Comment 2.a., suretyship law determines whether an obligation is "secondary" for purposes of this definition. Section 9-109 generally excludes from this Article transfers of interests in insurance policies. However, the regulation of a secondary obligation as an insurance product does not necessarily mean that it is a "policy of insurance" for purposes of the exclusion in Section 9-109. Thus, this Article may cover a secondary obligation (as a supporting obligation), even if the obligation is issued by a regulated insurance company and the obligation is subject to regulation as an "insurance" product.

This Article contains rules explicitly governing attachment, perfection, and priority of security interests in supporting obligations. See Sections 9-203, 9-308, 9-310, and 9-322. These provisions reflect the principle that a supporting obligation is an incident of the collateral it supports.

Collections of or other distributions under a supporting obligation are "proceeds" of the supported collateral as well as "proceeds" of the supporting obligation itself. See Section 9-102 (defining "proceeds") and Comment 13.b. As such, the collections and distributions are subject to the priority rules applicable to proceeds generally. See Section 9-322. However, under the special rule governing security interests in a letter-of-credit right, a secured party's failure to obtain control (Section 9-107) of a letter-of-credit right supporting collateral may leave its security interest exposed to a priming interest of a party who does take control. See Section 9-329 (security interest in a letter-of-credit right perfected by control has priority over a conflicting security interest).

g. "Commercial Tort Claim." A tort claim may serve as original collateral under this Article only if it is a "commercial tort claim." See Section 9-109(d). Although security interests in commercial tort claims are within its scope, this Article does not override other applicable law restricting the assignability of a tort claim. See Section 9-401. A security interest in a tort claim also may exist under this Article if the claim is proceeds of other collateral. See Section 9-204(b.1) and Comment 4A.

h. "Account Debtor." An "account debtor" is a person obligated on an account, chattel paper, or general intangible. The account debtor's obligation often is a monetary obligation; however, this is not always the case. For example, if a franchisee uses its rights under a franchise agreement (a general intangible) as collateral, then the franchisor is an "account debtor." As a general matter, Article 3, and not Article 9, governs obligations on negotiable instruments. Accordingly, the definition of "account debtor" excludes obligors on negotiable instruments constituting part of chattel paper. The principal effect of this change from the definition in pre-1998 Article 9 is that the rules in Sections 9-403, 9-404, 9-405, and 9-406, dealing with the rights of an assignee and duties of an account debtor, do not apply to an assignment of chattel paper in which the obligation to pay is evidenced by a negotiable instrument. (Section 9-406(d), however, does apply to a negotiable instrument that is a "promissory note", as that term is used in the 2022 revisions of subsection (d). See Comment 5.c.) Rather, the rights of an assignee of a negotiable instrument are governed by Article 3. Similarly, the duties of an obligor on a nonnegotiable instrument are governed by non-Article 9 law unless the nonnegotiable instrument is a part of chattel paper, in which case the obligor is an account debtor.

The definition of "account debtor" was revised in 2022 to add the modifier "negotiable" to the second reference to "instrument," making it clear that an obligor on a negotiable instrument is not an account debtor.

This amendment (which is intended to clarify and not to change the meaning of the definition) is useful because the definition of "instrument" has been revised to exclude writings that evidence chattel paper. However, the definition of "negotiable instrument" in Section 1-201 continues to apply under Article 9. See Section 9- 102(a)(47) and (b); Comment 5.c. Of course, a record or records evidencing chattel paper must evidence either a security agreement or lease agreement in addition to a right to payment of a monetary obligation.

i. Receivables Under Government Entitlement Programs. This Article does not contain a defined term that encompasses specifically rights to payment or performance under the many and varied government entitlement programs. Depending on the nature of a right under a program, it could be an account, a payment intangible, a general intangible other than a payment intangible, or another type of collateral. The right also might be proceeds of collateral (e.g., crops).

6. Investment-Property-Related Definitions: "Commodity Account"; "Commodity Contract"; "Commodity Customer"; "Commodity Intermediary"; "Investment Property." These definitions are substantially the same as the corresponding definitions in pre-1998 Section 9-115. "Investment property" includes securities, both certificated and uncertificated, securities accounts, security entitlements, commodity accounts, and commodity contracts. The term investment property includes a "securities account" in order to facilitate transactions in which a debtor wishes to create a security interest in all of the investment positions held through a particular account rather than in particular positions carried in the account. Pre-1998 Section 9-115 was added in conjunction with Revised Article 8 and contained a variety of rules applicable to security interests in investment property. The 1998 Revisions relocated these rules to the appropriate sections of Article 9. See, e.g., Sections 9-203 (attachment), 9-314 (perfection by control), 9-328 (priority).

The terms "security," "security entitlement," and related terms are defined in Section 8-102, and the term "securities account" is defined in Section 8-501. The terms "commodity account," "commodity contract," "commodity customer," and "commodity intermediary" are defined in this section. Commodity contracts are not "securities" or "financial assets" under Article 8. See Section 8-103(f). Thus, the relationship between commodity intermediaries and commodity customers is not governed by the indirect-holding-system rules of Part 5 of Article 8. For securities, Article 9 contains rules on security interests, and Article 8 contains rules on the rights of transferees, including secured parties, on such matters as the rights of a transferee if the transfer was itself wrongful and gives rise to an adverse claim. For commodity contracts, Article 9 establishes rules on security interests, but questions relating to commodity contracts of the sort dealt with in Article 8 for securities are left to other law.

The indirect-holding-system rules of Article 8 are sufficiently flexible to be applied to new developments in the securities and financial markets, where that is appropriate. Accordingly, the definition of "commodity contract" is narrowly drafted to ensure that it does not operate as an obstacle to the application of the Article 8 indirect-holding-system rules to new products. The term "commodity contract" covers those contracts that are traded on or subject to the rules of a designated contract market and foreign commodity contracts that are carried on the books of American commodity intermediaries. The effect of this definition is that the category of commodity contracts that are excluded from Article 8 but governed by Article 9 is essentially the same as the category of contracts that fall within the exclusive regulatory jurisdiction of the federal Commodity Futures Trading Commission.

Commodity contracts are different from securities or other financial assets. A person who enters into a commodity futures contract is not buying an asset having a certain value and holding it in anticipation of increase in value. Rather the person is entering into a contract to buy or sell a commodity at set price for delivery at a future time. That contract may become advantageous or disadvantageous as the price of the commodity fluctuates during the term of the contract. The rules of the commodity exchanges require that the contracts be marked to market on a daily basis; that is, the customer pays or receives any increment attributable to that day's price change. Because commodity customers may incur obligations on their contracts, they are required to provide collateral at the outset, known as "original margin," and may be required to provide additional amounts, known as "variation margin," during the term of the contract.

The most likely setting in which a person would want to take a security interest in a commodity contract is where a lender who is advancing funds to finance an inventory of a physical commodity requires the borrower to enter into a commodity contract as a hedge against the risk of decline in the value of the commodity. The lender will want to take a security interest in both the commodity itself and the hedging commodity contract. Typically, such arrangements are structured as security interests in the entire commodity account in which the borrower carries the hedging contracts, rather than in individual contracts.

One important effect of including commodity contracts and commodity accounts in Article 9 is to provide a clearer legal structure for the analysis of the rights of commodity clearing organizations against their participants and futures commission merchants against their customers. The rules and agreements of commodity clearing organizations generally provide that the clearing organization has the right to liquidate any participant's positions in order to satisfy obligations of the participant to the clearing corporation. Similarly, agreements between futures commission merchants and their customers generally provide that the futures commission merchant has the right to liquidate a customer's positions in order to satisfy obligations of the customer to the futures commission merchant.

The main property that a commodity intermediary holds as collateral for the obligations that the commodity customer may incur under its commodity contracts is not other commodity contracts carried by the customer but the other property that the customer has posted as margin. Typically, this property will be securities. The commodity intermediary's security interest in such securities is governed by the rules of this Article on security interests in securities, not the rules on security interests in commodity contracts or commodity accounts.

Although there are significant analytic and regulatory differences between commodities and securities, the development of commodity contracts on financial products in the past few decades has resulted in a system in which the commodity markets and securities markets are closely linked. The rules on security interests in commodity contracts and commodity accounts provide a structure that may be essential in times of stress in the financial markets. Suppose, for example that a firm has a position in a securities market that is hedged by a position in a commodity market, so that payments that the firm is obligated to make with respect to the securities position will be covered by the receipt of funds from the commodity position. Depending upon the settlement cycles of the different markets, it is possible that the firm could find itself in a position where it is obligated to make the payment with respect to the securities position before it receives the matching funds from the commodity position. If cross-margining arrangements have not been developed between the two markets, the firm may need to borrow funds temporarily to make the earlier payment. The rules on security interests in investment property would facilitate the use of positions in one market as collateral for loans needed to cover obligations in the other market.

7. Consumer-Related Definitions: "Consumer Debtor"; "Consumer Goods"; "Consumer-Goods Transaction"; "Consumer Obligor"; "Consumer Transaction." The definition of "consumer goods" (discussed above) is substantially the same as the definition in pre-1998 Section 9-109. The 1998 Revisions added the definitions of "consumer debtor," "consumer obligor," "consumer-goods transaction," and "consumer transaction" in connection with various 1998 and pre-1998 consumer-related provisions and to designate certain provisions that are inapplicable in consumer transactions.

"Consumer-goods transaction" is a subset of "consumer transaction." Under each definition, both the obligation secured and the collateral must have a personal, family, or household purpose. However, "mixed" business and personal transactions also may be characterized as a consumer-goods transaction or consumer transaction. Subparagraph (A) of the definition of consumer-goods transactions and clause (i) of the definition of consumer transaction are primary purposes tests. Under these tests, it is necessary to determine the primary purpose of the obligation or obligations secured. Subparagraph (B) and clause (iii) of these definitions are satisfied if any of the collateral is consumer goods, in the case of a consumer-goods transaction, or "is held or acquired primarily for personal, family, or household purposes," in the case of a consumer transaction. The fact that some of the obligations secured or some of the collateral for the obligation does not satisfy the tests (e.g., some of the collateral is acquired for a business purpose) does not prevent a transaction from being a "consumer transaction" or "consumer-goods transaction."

8. Filing-Related Definitions: "Continuation Statement"; "File Number"; "Filing Office"; "Filing-Office Rule"; "Financing Statement"; "Fixture Filing"; "Manufactured-Home Transaction"; "New Debtor"; "Original Debtor"; "Public-Finance Transaction"; "Termination Statement"; "Transmitting Utility." These definitions are used exclusively or primarily in the filing-related provisions in Part 5. Most are self-explanatory and are discussed in the Comments to Part 5. A financing statement filed in a manufactured-home transaction or a public-finance transaction may remain effective for 30 years instead of the 5 years applicable to other financing statements. See Section 9-515(b). The definitions relating to medium neutrality also are significant for the filing provisions. See Comment 9.

The definition of "transmitting utility" embraces the business of transmitting communications generally to take account of new and future types of communications technology. The term designates a special class of debtors for whom separate filing rules are provided in Part 5, thereby obviating the many local fixture filings that would be necessary under the rules of Section 9-501 for a far-flung public-utility debtor. A transmitting utility will not necessarily be regulated by or operating as such in a jurisdiction where fixtures are located. For example, a utility might own transmission lines in a jurisdiction, although the utility generates no power and has no customers in the jurisdiction. Of course, the definition applies only for purposes of this Article and not for purposes of any other law, regulation, or rule.

9. Definitions Relating to Medium Neutrality.

a. "Record." In general the term "record" replaces the term "writing" and "written." A "record" includes information that is in intangible form (e.g., electronically stored) as well as tangible form (e.g., written on paper). Section 9-102(a)(70). Given the rapid development and commercial adoption of modern communication and storage technologies, requirements that documents or communications be "written," "in writing," or otherwise in tangible form do not necessarily reflect or aid commercial practices.

A "record" need not be permanent or indestructible, but the term does not include any oral or other communication that is not stored or preserved by any means. The information must be stored on paper or in some other medium. Information that has not been retained other than through human memory does not qualify as a record. Examples of current technologies commercially used to communicate or store information include, but are not limited to, magnetic media, optical discs, digital voice messaging systems, electronic mail, audio tapes, and photographic media, as well as paper. "Record" is an inclusive term that includes all of these methods of storing or communicating information. Any "writing" is a record. A record may be signed. See Comment 9.b. A record may be created without the knowledge or intent of a particular person.

Like the terms "written" or "in writing," the term "record" does not establish the purposes, permitted uses, or legal effect that a record may have under any particular provision of law. Whatever is filed in the Article 9 filing system, including financing statements, continuation statements, and termination statements, whether transmitted in tangible or intangible form, would fall within the definition. However, in some instances, statutes or filing-office rules may require that a paper record be filed. In such cases, even if this Article permits the filing of an electronic record, compliance with those statutes or rules is necessary. Similarly, a filer must comply with a statute or rule that requires a particular type of encoding or formatting for an electronic record.

This Article sometimes uses the terms "for record," "of record," "record or legal title," and "record owner." Some of these are terms traditionally used in real-property law. The definition of "record" in this Article now explicitly excepts these usages from the defined term. Also, this Article refers to a record that is filed or recorded in real-property recording systems to record a mortgage as a "record of a mortgage." This usage recognizes that the defined term "mortgage" means an interest in real property; it does not mean the record that evidences, or is filed or recorded with respect to, the mortgage.

b. "Sign"; "Communicate"; "Send." The defined term "authenticate" has been deleted in the 2022 Article 9 Revisions. That term and "authenticated" were generally used in Article 9 instead of "sign" and "signed." However, the 2022 revised definition of "sign" in Section 1-201, encompasses authentication of all records, not just writings. Accordingly, "sign" and "signed" are now used in Article 9. (References to signing of, e.g., an agreement, demand, or notification mean, of course, signing of a record containing an agreement, demand, or notification.) The terms "communicate" and "send" also contemplate the possibility of communication by nonwritten media. These definitions include the act of transmitting both tangible and intangible records. The 2022 Amendments deleted the definition of "send" in this section and added a corresponding definition to Section 1-201, replacing the pre-2022 definition in that section.

10. Scope-Related Definitions.

a. Expanded Scope of Article: "Agricultural Lien"; "Consignment"; "Payment Intangible"; "Promissory Note." These definitions reflect the expanded scope of 1998 Article 9, as provided in Section 9-109(a).

b. Reduced Scope of Exclusions: "Governmental Unit"; "Health-Care-Insurance Receivable"; "Commercial Tort Claims." These definitions reflect the reduced scope of the 1998 exclusions, provided in Section 9-109(c) and (d), of transfers by governmental debtors and assignments of interests in insurance policies and commercial tort claims.

11. Choice-of-Law-Related Definitions: "Certificate of Title"; "Governmental Unit"; "Jurisdiction of Organization"; "Public Organic Record"; "Registered Organization"; "State." These definitions reflect the changes in the law governing perfection and priority of security interests and agricultural liens provided in Part 3, Subpart 1 of the 1998 Revisions.

Statutes often require applicants for a certificate of title to identify all security interests on the application and require the issuing agency to indicate the identified security interests on the certificate. Some of these statutes provide that priority over the rights of a lien creditor (i.e., perfection of a security interest) in goods covered by the certificate occurs upon indication of the security interest on the certificate; that is, they provide for the indication of the security interest on the certificate as a "condition" of perfection. Other statutes contemplate that perfection is achieved upon the occurrence of another act, e.g., delivery of the application to the issuing agency, that "results" in the indication of the security interest on the certificate. A certificate governed by either type of statute can qualify as a "certificate of title" under this Article. The statute providing for the indication of a security interest need not expressly state the connection between the indication and perfection. For example, a certificate issued pursuant to a statute that requires applicants to identify security interests, requires the issuing agency to indicate the identified security interests on the certificate, but is silent concerning the legal consequences of the indication would be a "certificate of title" if, under a judicial interpretation of the statute, perfection of a security interest is a legal consequence of the indication. Likewise, a certificate would be a "certificate of title" if another statute provides, expressly or as interpreted, the requisite connection between the indication and perfection.

The first sentence of the definition of "certificate of title" includes certificates consisting of tangible records, of electronic records, and of combinations of tangible and electronic records.

In many States, a certificate of title covering goods that are encumbered by a security interest is delivered to the secured party by the issuing authority. To eliminate the need for the issuance of a paper certificate under these circumstances, several States have revised their certificate-of-title statutes to permit or require a State agency to maintain an electronic record that evidences ownership of the goods and in which a security interest in the goods may be noted. The second sentence of the definition provides that such a record is a "certificate of title" if it is in fact maintained as an alternative to the issuance of a paper certificate of title, regardless of whether the certificate-of-title statute provides that the record is a certificate of title and even if the statute does not expressly state that the record is maintained instead of issuing a paper certificate.

Not every organization that may provide information about itself in the public records is a "registered organization." For example, a general partnership is not a "registered organization," even if it files a statement of partnership authority under Section 303 of the Uniform Partnership Act (1994) or an assumed name ("dba") certificate. This is because such a partnership is not formed or organized by the filing of a record with, or the issuance of a record by, a State or the United States. Likewise, a limited liability partnership, which is a form of general partnership under the Uniform Partnership Act (1997), is not a "registered organization" even if it has filed a record that is a statement of qualification under Section 1-001 of the Uniform Partnership Act (1997). The filing of the record does not form or organize the partnership. The filing only provides the partners in the general partnership with a limited liability shield and evidences that the general partnership has limited liability partnership status. See PEB Commentary No. 17. As discussed in PEB Commentary No. 17, the same conclusion would apply to a limited liability partnership formed under the law of state that has not adopted the Uniform Partnership Act (1997) but has adopted for limited liability partnerships similar legislation having the material attributes of that Act. Also as discussed in PEB Commentary No. 17, the same conclusion would apply whether before or after giving effect to the 2010 amendments to this Article. In contrast, corporations, limited liability companies, and limited partnerships ordinarily are "registered organizations."

Not every record concerning a registered organization that is filed with, or issued by, a State or the United States is a "public organic record." For example, a certificate of good standing issued with respect to a corporation or a published index of domestic corporations would not be a "public organic record" because its issuance or publication does not form or organize the corporations named.

When collateral is held in a trust, one must look to non-UCC law to determine whether the trust is a "registered organization." Non-UCC law typically distinguishes between statutory trusts and common-law trusts. A statutory trust is formed by the filing of a record, commonly referred to as a certificate of trust, in a public office pursuant to a statute. See, e.g., Uniform Statutory Trust Entity Act § 201 (2009); Delaware Statutory Trust Act, Del. Code Ann. tit. 12, § 3-801 et seq. A statutory trust is a juridical entity, separate from its trustee and beneficial owners, that may sue and be sued, own property, and transact business in its own name. Inasmuch as a statutory trust is a "legal or commercial entity," it qualifies as a "person other than an individual," and therefore as an "organization," under Section 1-201. A statutory trust that is formed by the filing of a record in a public office is a "registered organization," and the filed record is a "public organic record" of the statutory trust, if the filed record is available to the public for inspection. (The requirement that a record be "available to the public for inspection" is satisfied if a copy of the relevant record is available for public inspection.)

Unlike a statutory trust, a common-law trust—whether its purpose is donative or commercial—arises from private action without the filing of a record in a public office. See Uniform Trust Code § 401 (2000); Restatement (Third) of Trusts § 10 (2003). Moreover, under traditional law, a common-law trust is not itself a juridical entity and therefore must sue and be sued, own property, and transact business in the name of the trustee acting in the capacity of trustee. A common-law trust that is a "business trust," i.e., that has a business or commercial purpose, is an "organization" under Section 1-201. However, such a trust would not be a "registered organization" if, as is typically the case, the filing of a public record is not needed to form it.

In some states, however, the trustee of a common-law trust that has a commercial or business purpose is required by statute to file a record in a public office following the trust's formation. See, e.g., Mass. Gen. Laws Ch. 182, § 2; Fla. Stat. Ann. § 609.02. A business trust that is required to file its organic record in a public office is a "registered organization" under the second sentence of the definition if the filed record is available to the public for inspection. Any organic record required to be filed, and filed, with respect to a common-law business trust after the trust is formed is a "public organic record" of the trust. Some statutes require a trust or other organization to file, after formation or organization, a record other than an organic record. See, e.g., N.Y. Gen Assn's Law § 18 (requiring associations doing business within New York to file a certificate designating the secretary of state as an agent upon whom process may be served). This requirement does not render the organization a "registered organization" under the second sentence of the definition, and the record is not a "public organic record."

12. Deposit-Account-Related Definitions: "Deposit Account"; "Bank." The 1998 revised definition of "deposit account" incorporates the definition of "bank," which is new. The new definition derives from the definitions of "bank" in Sections 4-105(1) and 4A-105(a)(2), which focus on whether the organization is "engaged in the business of banking."

Deposit accounts evidenced by Article 9 "instruments" are excluded from the term "deposit account." In contrast, pre-1998 Section 9-105 excluded from the former definition "an account evidenced by a certificate of deposit." The revised definition clarifies the proper treatment of nonnegotiable or uncertificated certificates of deposit. Under the definition, an uncertificated certificate of deposit would be a deposit account (assuming there is no writing evidencing the bank's obligation to pay) whereas a nonnegotiable certificate of deposit would be a deposit account only if it is not an "instrument" as defined in this section (a question that turns on whether the nonnegotiable certificate of deposit is "of a type that in ordinary course of business is transferred by delivery with any necessary indorsement or assignment").

A deposit account evidenced by an instrument is subject to the rules applicable to instruments generally. As a consequence, a security interest in such an instrument cannot be perfected by "control" (see Section 9-104), and the special priority rules applicable to deposit accounts (see Sections 9-327 and 9-340) do not apply. If a bank is the obligor on a monetary obligation not evidenced by an instrument or chattel paper, the obligation or the right to payment of the obligation may be a deposit account, an account, a payment intangible, or another type of collateral depending on the facts and circumstances. Of course, the classification of a monetary obligation or a right to payment of the obligation for purposes of this Article would not necessarily affect the application of laws regulating, for example, banking, securities, commodities, money transmission, and taxation.

The term "deposit account" does not include "investment property," such as securities and security entitlements. Thus, the term also does not include shares in a money-market mutual fund, even if the shares are redeemable by check.

12A. Money-Related Definitions and Terms: "Money"; "Electronic Money"; "Tangible Money"; "Funds"; "Monetary Obligation." The Article 9 definition of "money" in subsection (a)(54A), added by the 2022 Article 9 Revisions, is a subset of the definition of "money" as defined in Section 1-201(b)(24). It follows that cryptocurrencies, such as bitcoin, that are not "money" as defined in Section 1-201 because they were in existence and used before adoption by a government, also are not Article 9 money. An obligation to pay in such cryptocurrencies would not be an account, chattel paper, or a payment intangible or an obligation on an instrument because the obligation would not be a "monetary obligation" or an obligation to pay money. One purpose of the Article 9 definition is to ensure that even if some deposit accounts were to become "money" as defined in Article 1, the provisions relating to perfection and priority for security interests in deposit accounts, and not those for money, will apply to that collateral. Some countries may authorize or adopt deposit accounts with a central bank as a form of "money." See Section 9-101, Comment 4.c. However, the Article 9 provisions governing "deposit accounts" would remain suitable for such accounts with a central bank, even if a government has adopted these accounts as money. The 2022 Article 9 Revisions leave Article 9's treatment of deposit accounts largely unchanged. However, for purposes of Article 9 and in the interest of clarity, the definition of "money" in Section 9-102(a)(31A) excludes deposit accounts. Under this definition, deposit accounts would not be money for Article 9 purposes even if they were to become money under the Article 1 definition. Another purpose of the Article 9 definition of "money" is to exclude from that definition money (as defined in Section 1- 201(b)(24)) in an electronic form that cannot be subjected to control under Section 9-105A. Such property would be a general intangible, governed by the perfection and priority rules for that type of collateral.

Some countries may authorize or adopt intangible tokens as a medium of exchange that would be "money" as defined in both Article 1 and Article 9. See Section 9-101, Comment 4.c. Such intangible tokens would be "electronic money," as defined in Section 9-102(a)(31A). A security interest in electronic money as original collateral can be perfected only by control. Sections 9-312(b)(4); 9-314; 9-105A. The requirements for obtaining control of electronic money are essentially the same as those for obtaining control of a controllable electronic record under Article 12. Sections 9-105A; 12-105. The definition of "tangible money" in Section 9- 102(a)(79A) uses the word "tangible" with its normal meaning (as something that has physical or corporeal existence, such as goods).

"Monetary obligation" as used in the Uniform Commercial Code (including in Article 9) is not a defined term. The term contemplates an obligation to pay "money" as defined in Section 1-201(b)(24). Consequently, for example, a right to payment of money in an electronic form that cannot be subjected to control, excluded from the Article 9 definition of "money" in subsection (a)(54A), would be a monetary obligation. It follows that such a right to payment could be an account, chattel paper, a payment intangible, or an instrument—including a negotiable instrument, which is defined to include a promise to pay "money" as the term is defined in Section 1-201. See Section 3-104(a) (defining "negotiable instrument"). Also, the term "funds" (like "monetary obligation," an undefined term), as used in the Uniform Commercial Code includes a right to payment of money as defined in Section 1-201(b)(24). As mentioned above, because cryptocurrencies such as bitcoin are not "money" as defined in Section 1-201 (unless they were not in existence and used before adoption by a government), a cryptocurrency or an obligation to pay in cryptocurrency would not be a "monetary obligation" or "funds."

13. Proceeds-Related Definitions: "Cash Proceeds"; "Noncash Proceeds"; "Proceeds." The revised definition of "proceeds" expanded the definition beyond that contained in pre-1998 Section 9-306 and resolves ambiguities in the former definition.

a. Distributions on Account of Collateral. The phrase "whatever is collected on, or distributed on account of, collateral," in subparagraph (B), is broad enough to cover cash or stock dividends distributed on account of securities or other investment property that is original collateral. Compare pre-1998 Section 9-306 ("Any payments or distributions made with respect to investment property collateral are proceeds."). This section rejects the holding of *Hastie v. FDIC,* 2 F.3d 1042 (10th Cir. 1993) (postpetition cash dividends on stock subject to a prepetition pledge are not "proceeds" under Bankruptcy Code Section 552(b)), to the extent the holding relies on the Article 9 definition of "proceeds."

b. Distributions on Account of Supporting Obligations. Under subparagraph (B), collections on and distributions on account of collateral consisting of various credit-support arrangements ("supporting obligations," as defined in Section 9-102) also are proceeds. Consequently, they are afforded treatment identical to proceeds collected from or distributed by the obligor on the underlying (supported) right to payment or other collateral. Proceeds of supporting obligations also are proceeds of the underlying rights to payment or other collateral.

c. Proceeds of Proceeds. The definition of "proceeds" no longer provides that proceeds of proceeds are themselves proceeds. That idea is expressed in the revised definition of "collateral" in Section 9-102. No change in meaning is intended.

d. Proceeds Received by Person Who Did Not Create Security Interest. When collateral is sold subject to a security interest and the buyer then resells the collateral, a question arose under pre-1998 Article 9 concerning whether the "debtor" had "received" what the buyer received on resale and, therefore, whether those receipts were "proceeds" under pre-1998 Section 9-306(2). This Article contains no requirement that property be "received" by the debtor for the property to qualify as proceeds. It is necessary only that the property be traceable, directly or indirectly, to the original collateral.

e. Cash Proceeds and Noncash Proceeds. The definition of "cash proceeds" is substantially the same as the corresponding definition in pre-1998 Section 9-306. The phrase "and the like" covers property that is functionally equivalent to "money, checks, or deposit accounts," such as some money-market accounts that are securities or part of securities entitlements. Proceeds other than cash proceeds are noncash proceeds.

f. Forks and Airdrops for Controllable Electronic Records. Sometimes there occurs a change in the software (code) of a system (sometimes referred to as a "protocol" or "platform") in which a controllable electronic record is recorded. When such a change occurs in a blockchain platform, the blockchain may remain intact, no new blockchain may result, and the change sometimes is colloquially referred to as a "soft fork." If, instead, such a change results in a new, separate blockchain that exists alongside the original blockchain and a new controllable electronic record is created, the change is sometimes referred to as a "hard fork." But the terms "fork," "soft fork," and "hard fork" are ambiguous and not used consistently. Even in a hard fork situation the pre-fork controllable electronic record typically would remain intact (although its value might be affected). A person in control of the original record may not automatically obtain control of a new record. Additional steps may be required for the person in control of the original record to obtain control of the new record.

Depending on the nature and structure of the fork, a new controllable electronic record arising under a hard fork may be property "distributed on account of" the original record or "rights arising out of" the original record, thereby constituting proceeds of the original record under subparagraph (B) or (C), or both, of the definition of "proceeds." If the new record is identifiable "proceeds," then the rules on attachment, perfection, priority under Sections 9- 203(f), 9-315, and 9-322 would apply. If a security interest in the original record is perfected by control, the creation of the new record in connection with a hard fork typically results in the secured party obtaining control (or having the opportunity to obtain control) of the new record. If that is not the case and perfection of the security interest in the original record is only by control, however, then perfection would continue in the new record only until the 21st day after the security interest attaches to the new record, unless one of the exceptions under subsection (d) applies. Section 9-315(c), (d). For this reason, a secured party may wish also to perfect its security interest by filing so that the perfection would continue thereafter in any proceeds under Section 9-315(d)(1). A secured party that does so may, to ensure the priority of its perfected security interest, also wish to consider obtaining a release or subordination from any earlier filed secured party whose financing statement covers the same type of property. Even if that is achieved, a security interest in the record that is perfected by control (even if control is later obtained) would have priority over a security interest perfected only by filing. Section 9-326A.

New controllable electronic records also may be provided to persons in control of existing records by way of an "airdrop" that does not involve a fork in an existing blockchain. Depending on the circumstances, these new records may or may not be proceeds of the existing, original record.

If the original record were a financial asset credited to a securities account, the new record might become proceeds of a security entitlement for the reasons described above. Concerning the duties, if any, of a securities intermediary with respect to such a distribution, see Section 8-505, Comment 4.

This discussion focuses on forks and airdrops related to controllable electronic records in the context of blockchain technology, the prevailing relevant technology in 2022. In determining whether property may be proceeds of collateral in the contexts of other and future technologies, the principles and policies reflected in this discussion should be considered.

14. Consignment-Related Definitions: "Consignee"; "Consignment"; "Consignor." The definition of "consignment," added by the 1998, excludes, in subparagraphs (B) and (C), transactions for which filing would be inappropriate or of insufficient benefit to justify the costs. A consignment excluded from the application of this Article by one of those subparagraphs may still be a true consignment; however, it is governed by non-Article 9 law. The definition also excludes, in subparagraph (D), what have been called "consignments intended for security." These "consignments" are not bailments but secured transactions. Accordingly, all of Article 9 applies to them. See Sections 1-201(b)(35), 9-109(a)(1). The "consignor" is the person who delivers goods to the "consignee" in a consignment.

The definition of "consignment" requires that the goods be delivered "to a merchant for the purpose of sale." If the goods are delivered for another purpose as well, such as milling or processing, the transaction is a consignment nonetheless because a purpose of the delivery is "sale." On the other hand, if a merchant-processor-bailee will not be selling the goods itself but will be delivering to buyers to which the owner-bailor agreed to sell the goods, the transaction would not be a consignment.

Under clause (iii) of subparagraph (A), a transaction is not an Article 9 "consignment" if the consignee is "generally known by its creditors to be substantially engaged in selling the goods of others." Clause (iii) does not apply solely because a particular competing claimant knows that the goods are held on consignment. See PEB Commentary No. 20.

15. "Accounting." This definition describes the record and information that a debtor is entitled to request under Section 9-210. Consistent with the revised definition of "sign" in Section 1-201, the cognate term "signed" replaces the reference to "authenticated" in the pre- 2022 text of this definition.

16. "Document." The definition of "document" incorporates both tangible and electronic documents of title. See Section 1-201(b)(16) and Comment 16.

Legislative Note: *Former Article 1 defined document of title in Section 1-201(15) and accompanying Comment 15. Revised Article 1 defines document of title in Section 1-201(b)(16) and accompanying Comment 16. Cross references should be adapted depending upon which version of Article 1 is in force in the jurisdiction.*

17. "Encumbrance"; "Mortgage." The definitions of "encumbrance" and "mortgage" are unchanged in substance from the corresponding definitions in pre-1998 Section 9-105. They are used primarily in the special real-property-related priority and other provisions relating to crops, fixtures, and accessions.

18. "Fixtures." This definition is unchanged in substance from the corresponding definition in pre-1998 Section 9-313. See Section 9-334 (priority of security interests in fixtures and crops).

19. "Good Faith." The definition of "good faith" added by the 1998 Revisions, which incorporated the concept of "reasonable commercial standards of fair dealing," was deleted by the conforming amendments to the 2001 revision of Article 1. The definition is unnecessary given the revised definition in Section 1-201(b)(20).

20. "Lien Creditor." This definition is unchanged in substance from the corresponding definition in pre-1998 Section 9-301.

21. "New Value." The 1998 Revisions deleted pre-1998 Section 9-108. Its broad formulation of new value, which embraced the taking of after-acquired collateral for a pre-existing claim, was unnecessary, counterintuitive, and ineffective for its original purpose of sheltering after-acquired collateral from attack as a voidable preference in bankruptcy. The new definition of "new value" derives from Bankruptcy Code Section 547(a). The term is used with respect to temporary perfection of security interests in instruments, certificated securities, or negotiable documents under Section 9-312(e) and with respect to chattel paper priority in Section 9-330.

22. "Person Related To." Section 9-615 provides a special method for calculating a deficiency or surplus when "the secured party, a person related to the secured party, or a secondary obligor" acquires the collateral at a foreclosure disposition. Separate definitions of the term are provided with respect to an individual secured party and with respect to a secured party that is an organization. The definitions are patterned on the corresponding definition in Section 1.301(32) of the Uniform Consumer Credit Code (1974).

23. "Proposal." This definition describes a record that is sufficient to propose to retain collateral in full or partial satisfaction of a secured obligation. See Sections 9-620, 9-621, 9-622. Consistent with the revised definition of "sign" in Section 1-201, the 2022 revision of the definition adopts the cognate term "signed" to replace the term "authenticated" used in the pre- 2022 text.

24. "Pursuant to Commitment." This definition is unchanged in substance from the corresponding definition in pre-1998 Section 9-105. It is used in connection with special priority rules applicable to future advances. See Section 9-323.

25. "Software." The definition of "software" is used in connection with the priority rules applicable to purchase-money security interests. See Sections 9-103, 9-324. Software, like a payment intangible, is a type of general intangible for purposes of this Article. See Comment 4.a., above, regarding the distinction between "goods" and "software."

§ 9-103. Purchase-Money Security Interest; Application of Payments; Burden of Establishing.

(a) [Definitions.] In this section:

(1) "purchase-money collateral" means goods or software that secures a purchase-money obligation incurred with respect to that collateral; and

(2) "purchase-money obligation" means an obligation of an obligor incurred as all or part of the price of the collateral or for value given to enable the debtor to acquire rights in or the use of the collateral if the value is in fact so used.

(b) [Purchase-money security interest in goods.] A security interest in goods is a purchase-money security interest:

(1) to the extent that the goods are purchase-money collateral with respect to that security interest;

(2) if the security interest is in inventory that is or was purchase-money collateral, also to the extent that the security interest secures a purchase-money obligation incurred with respect to other inventory in which the secured party holds or held a purchase-money security interest; and

(3) also to the extent that the security interest secures a purchase-money obligation incurred with respect to software in which the secured party holds or held a purchase-money security interest.

(c) [Purchase-money security interest in software.] A security interest in software is a purchase-money security interest to the extent that the security interest also secures a purchase-money obligation incurred with respect to goods in which the secured party holds or held a purchase-money security interest if:

(1) the debtor acquired its interest in the software in an integrated transaction in which it acquired an interest in the goods; and

(2) the debtor acquired its interest in the software for the principal purpose of using the software in the goods.

(d) [Consignor's inventory purchase-money security interest.] The security interest of a consignor in goods that are the subject of a consignment is a purchase-money security interest in inventory.

(e) [Application of payment in non-consumer-goods transaction.] In a transaction other than a consumer-goods transaction, if the extent to which a security interest is a purchase-money security interest depends on the application of a payment to a particular obligation, the payment must be applied:

(1) in accordance with any reasonable method of application to which the parties agree;

(2) in the absence of the parties' agreement to a reasonable method, in accordance with any intention of the obligor manifested at or before the time of payment; or

(3) in the absence of an agreement to a reasonable method and a timely manifestation of the obligor's intention, in the following order:

(A) to obligations that are not secured; and

(B) if more than one obligation is secured, to obligations secured by purchase-money security interests in the order in which those obligations were incurred.

(f) [No loss of status of purchase-money security interest in non-consumer-goods transaction.] In a transaction other than a consumer-goods transaction, a purchase-money security interest does not lose its status as such, even if:

(1) the purchase-money collateral also secures an obligation that is not a purchase-money obligation;

(2) collateral that is not purchase-money collateral also secures the purchase-money obligation; or

(3) the purchase-money obligation has been renewed, refinanced, consolidated, or restructured.

(g) [Burden of proof in non-consumer-goods transaction.] In a transaction other than a consumer-goods transaction, a secured party claiming a purchase-money security interest has the burden of establishing the extent to which the security interest is a purchase-money security interest.

(h) [Non-consumer-goods transactions; no inference.] The limitation of the rules in subsections (e), (f), and (g) to transactions other than consumer-goods transactions is intended to leave to the court the determination of the proper rules in consumer-goods transactions. The court may not infer from that limitation the nature of the proper rule in consumer-goods transactions and may continue to apply established approaches.

Definitional Cross References:

Agreement	Section 1-201(b)(3)
Burden of establishing	Section 1-201(b)(8)
Collateral	Section 9-102(a)(12)
Consignment	Section 9-102(a)(20)
Consignor	Section 9-102(a)(21)
Consumer-goods transaction	Section 9-102(a)(24)
Debtor	Section 9-102(a)(28)
Goods	Section 9-102(a)(44)
Inventory	Section 9-102(a)(48)
Obligor	Section 9-102(a)(59)
Right	Section 1-201(b)(34)
Secured party	Section 9-102(a)(73)
Security interest	Section 1-201(b)(35)
Software	Section 9-102(a)(76)
Value	Section 1-204

Comment References: 9-109 C6

Official Comment

1. Source. Former Section 9-107.

2. Scope of This Section. Under Section 9-309(1), a purchase-money security interest in consumer goods is perfected when it attaches. Sections 9-317 and 9-324 provide special priority rules for purchase-money security interests in a variety of contexts. This section explains when a security interest enjoys purchase-money status.

3. "Purchase-Money Collateral"; "Purchase-Money Obligation"; "Purchase-Money Security Interest." Subsection (a) defines "purchase-money collateral" and "purchase-money obligation." These terms are essential to the description of what constitutes a purchase-money security interest under subsection (b). As used in subsection (a)(2), the definition of "purchase-money obligation," the "price" of collateral or the "value given to enable" includes obligations for expenses incurred in connection with acquiring rights in the collateral, sales taxes, duties, finance charges, interest, freight charges, costs of storage in transit, demurrage, administrative charges, expenses of collection and enforcement, attorney's fees, and other similar obligations.

The concept of "purchase-money security interest" requires a close nexus between the acquisition of collateral and the secured obligation. Thus, a security interest does not qualify as a purchase-money security interest if a debtor acquires property on unsecured credit and subsequently creates the security interest to secure the purchase price.

4. Cross-Collateralization of Purchase-Money Security Interests in Inventory. Subsection (b)(2) deals with the problem of cross-collateralized purchase-money security interests in inventory. Consider a simple example:

> **Example:** Seller (S) sells an item of inventory (Item-1) to Debtor (D), retaining a security interest in Item-1 to secure Item-1's price and all other obligations, existing and future, of D to S. S then sells another item of inventory to D (Item-2), again retaining a security interest in Item-2 to secure Item-2's price as well as all other obligations of D to S. D then pays to S Item-1's price. D then sells Item-2 to a buyer in ordinary course of business, who takes Item-2 free of S's security interest.
>
> Under subsection (b)(2), S's security interest in *Item-1* securing *Item-2's unpaid* price would be a purchase-money security interest. This is so because S has a purchase-money security interest in Item-1, Item-1 secures the price of (a "purchase-money obligation incurred with respect to") Item-2 ("other inventory"), and Item-2 itself was subject to a purchase-money security interest. Note that, to the extent Item-1 secures the price of Item-2, S's security interest in Item-1 would not be a purchase-money security interest under subsection (b)(1). The security interest in Item-1 is a purchase-money security interest under subsection (b)(1) only to the extent that Item-1 is "purchase-money collateral," i.e., only to the extent that Item-1 "secures a purchase-money obligation incurred with respect to that collateral" (i.e., Item-1). See subsection (a)(1).

5. Purchase-Money Security Interests in Goods and Software. Subsections (b) and (c) limit purchase-money security interests to security interests in goods, including fixtures, and software. Otherwise, no change in meaning from former Section 9-107 is intended. The second sentence of former Section 9-115(5)(f) made the purchase-money priority rule (former Section 9-312(4)) inapplicable to investment property. This section's limitation makes that provision unnecessary.

Subsection (c) describes the limited circumstances under which a security interest in goods may be accompanied by a purchase-money security interest in software. The software must be acquired by the debtor in a transaction integrated with the transaction in which the debtor acquired the goods, and the debtor must acquire the software for the principal purpose of using the software in the goods. "Software" is defined in Section 9-102.

6. Consignments. Under former Section 9-114, the priority of the consignor's interest is similar to that of a purchase-money security interest. Subsection (d) achieves this result more directly, by defining the interest of a "consignor," defined in Section 9-102, to be a purchase-money security interest in inventory for purposes of this Article. This drafting convention obviates any need to set forth special priority rules applicable to the interest of a consignor. Rather, the priority of the consignor's interest as against the rights of lien creditors of the consignee, competing secured parties, and purchasers of the goods from the consignee can be determined by reference to the priority rules generally applicable to inventory, such as Sections 9-317, 9-320, 9-322, and 9-324. For other purposes, including the rights and duties of the consignor and consignee as between themselves, the consignor would remain the owner of goods under a bailment arrangement with the consignee. See Section 9-319.

7. Provisions Applicable Only to Non-Consumer-Goods Transactions.

a. "Dual-Status" Rule. For transactions other than consumer-goods transactions, this Article approves what some cases have called the "dual-status" rule, under which a security interest may be a purchase-money security interest to some extent and a non-purchase-money security interest to some extent. (Concerning consumer-goods transactions, see subsection (h) and Comment 8.) Some courts have found this rule to be explicit or implicit in the words "to the extent," found in former Section 9-107 and continued in subsections (b)(1) and (b)(2). The rule is made explicit in subsection (e). For non-consumer-goods transactions, this Article rejects the "transformation" rule adopted by some cases, under which any cross-collateralization, refinancing, or the like destroys the purchase-money status entirely.

Consider, for example, what happens when a $10,000 loan secured by a purchase-money security interest is refinanced by the original lender, and, as part of the transaction, the debtor borrows an additional $2,000 secured by the collateral. Subsection (f) resolves any doubt that the security interest remains a purchase-money security interest. Under subsection (b), however, it enjoys purchase-money status only to the extent of $10,000.

b. Allocation of Payments. Continuing with the example, if the debtor makes a $1,000 payment on the $12,000 obligation, then one must determine the extent to which the security interest remains a purchase-money security interest—$9,000 or $10,000. Subsection (e)(1) expresses the overriding principle, applicable in cases other than consumer-goods transactions, for determining the extent to which a security interest is a purchase-money security interest under these circumstances: freedom of contract, as limited by principle of reasonableness. An unconscionable method of application, for example, is not a reasonable one and so would not be given effect under subsection (e)(1). In the absence of agreement, subsection (e)(2) permits the obligor to determine how payments should be allocated. If the obligor fails to manifest its intention, obligations that are not secured will be paid first. (As used in this Article, the concept of "obligations that are not secured" means obligations for which the debtor has not created a security interest. This concept is different from and should not be confused with the concept of an "unsecured claim" as it appears in Bankruptcy Code Section 506(a).) The obligor may prefer this approach, because unsecured debt is likely to carry a higher interest rate than secured debt. A creditor who would prefer to be secured rather than unsecured also would prefer this approach.

After the unsecured debt is paid, payments are to be applied first toward the obligations secured by purchase-money security interests. In the event that there is more than one such obligation, payments first received are to be applied to obligations first incurred. See subsection (e)(3). Once these obligations are paid, there are no purchase-money security interests and no additional allocation rules are needed.

Subsection (f) buttresses the dual-status rule by making it clear that (in a transaction other than a consumer-goods transaction) cross-collateralization and renewals, refinancings, and restructurings do not cause a purchase-money security interest to lose its status as such. The statutory terms "renewed," "refinanced," and "restructured" are not defined. Whether the terms encompass a particular transaction depends upon whether, under the particular facts, the purchase-money character of the security interest fairly can be said to survive. Each term contemplates that an identifiable portion of the purchase-money obligation could be traced to the new obligation resulting from a renewal, refinancing, or restructuring.

c. Burden of Proof. As is the case when the extent of a security interest is in issue, under subsection (g) the secured party claiming a purchase-money security interest in a transaction other than a consumer-goods transaction has the burden of establishing whether the security interest retains its purchase-money status. This is so whether the determination is to be made following a renewal, refinancing, or restructuring or otherwise.

8. Consumer-Goods Transactions; Characterization Under Other Law. Under subsection (h), the limitation of subsections (e), (f), and (g) to transactions other than consumer-goods transactions leaves to the court the determination of the proper rules in consumer-goods transactions. Subsection (h) also instructs the court not to draw any inference from this limitation as to the proper rules for consumer-goods transactions and leaves the court free to continue to apply established approaches to those transactions.

This section addresses only whether a security interest is a "purchase-money security interest" under this Article, primarily for purposes of perfection and priority. See, e.g., Sections 9-317, 9-324. In particular, its adoption of the dual-status rule, allocation of payments rules, and burden of proof standards for non-consumer-goods transactions is not intended to affect or influence characterizations under other statutes. Whether a security interest is a "purchase-money security interest" under other law is determined by that law. For example, decisions under Bankruptcy Code Section 522(f) have applied both the dual-status and the transformation rules. The Bankruptcy Code does not expressly adopt the state law definition of "purchase-money security interest." Where federal law does not defer to this Article, this Article does not, and could not, determine a question of federal law.

§ 9-104. Control of Deposit Account.

(a) [Requirements for control.] A secured party has control of a deposit account if:

(1) the secured party is the bank with which the deposit account is maintained;

(2) the debtor, secured party, and bank have agreed in a signed record that the bank will comply with instructions originated by the secured party directing disposition of the funds in the deposit account without further consent by the debtor; or

(3) the secured party becomes the bank's customer with respect to the deposit account; or

(4) another person, other than the debtor:

(A) has control of the deposit account and acknowledges that it has control on behalf of the secured party; or

(B) obtains control of the deposit account after having acknowledged that it will obtain control of the deposit account on behalf of the secured party.

(b) [Debtor's right to direct disposition.] A secured party that has satisfied subsection (a) has control, even if the debtor retains the right to direct the disposition of funds from the deposit account.

Definitional Cross References:

Account	Section 9-102(a)(2)
Bank	Section 9-102(a)(8)
Customer	Section 4-104(a)(5)
Debtor	Section 9-102(a)(28)
Deposit account	Section 9-102(a)(29)
Person	Section 1-201(b)(27)
Record	Section 9-102(a)(70)
Secured party	Section 9-102(a)(73)
Sign	Section 1-201(b)(37)

Comment References: 9-105 C4

Official Comment

1. Source. Derived Section 8-106.

2. Why "Control" Matters. This section explains the concept of "control" of a deposit account. "Control" under this section may serve two functions. First, "control . . . pursuant to the debtor's agreement" may substitute for a signed security agreement as an element of attachment. See Section 9-203(b)(3)(D). Second, when a deposit account is taken as original collateral, the only method of perfection is obtaining control under this section. See Section 9-312(b)(1).

3. Requirements for "Control: In General." This section derives from Section 8-106 of Revised Article 8, which defines "control" of securities and certain other investment property. Under subsection (a)(1), the bank with which the deposit account is maintained has control. The effect of this provision is to afford the bank automatic perfection. No other form of public notice is necessary; all actual and potential creditors of the debtor are always on notice that the bank with which the debtor's deposit account is maintained may assert a claim against the deposit account.

> **Example**: D maintains a deposit account with Bank A. To secure a loan from Banks X, Y, and Z, D creates a security interest in the deposit account in favor of Bank A, as agent for Banks X, Y, and Z. Because Bank A is a "secured party" as defined in Section 9-102, the security interest is perfected by control under subsection (a)(1).

Under subsection (a)(2), a secured party may obtain control by obtaining the bank's signed agreement that it will comply with the secured party's instructions without further consent by the debtor. The analogous provision in Section 8-106 does not require that the agreement be signed. An agreement to comply with the secured party's instructions suffices for "control" of a deposit account under this section even if the bank's agreement is subject to specified conditions, e.g., that the secured party's instructions are accompanied by a certification that the debtor is in default. (Of course, if the condition is the debtor's further consent, the statute explicitly provides that the agreement would not confer control.) See Section 8-106, Comment 7.

Under subsection (a)(3), a secured party may obtain control by becoming the bank's "customer," as defined in Section 4-104. As the customer, the secured party would enjoy the right (but not necessarily the exclusive right) to withdraw funds from, or close, the deposit account. See Sections 4-401(a), 4-403(a).

As is the case with possession under Section 9-313, in determining whether a particular person has control under subsection (a), the principles of agency apply. See Section 1-103 and Restatement (3d), Agency § 8.12, Comment *b*.

Although the arrangements giving rise to control may themselves prevent, or may enable the secured party at its discretion to prevent, the debtor from reaching the funds on deposit, subsection (b) makes clear that the debtor's ability to reach the funds is not inconsistent with "control."

Perfection by control is not available for bank accounts evidenced by an instrument (e.g., certain certificates of deposit), which by definition are "instruments" and not "deposit accounts." See Section 9-102 (defining "deposit account" and "instrument").

4. Control on behalf of another person. Subsection (a)(4) provides for a secured party to obtain control of a deposit account by virtue of the acknowledgment by another person, other than the debtor, in control of the deposit account. It generally follows revisions to the corresponding provisions for control of electronic documents of title (Section 7-106(g)), control of a security entitlement (8-106(d)), control of an electronic copy of a record evidencing chattel paper (Section 9-105(g)), control of electronic money (Section 9-105A(e)), and control of controllable electronic records (Section 12-105(e)). For a brief discussion, see Section 12-105, Comments 8 and 9.

An acknowledgment by a person in control under subsection (a)(4) would not impose any duties on the bank with which the deposit account is maintained. Indeed, the bank may have no knowledge or involvement whatsoever with a control person's acknowledgment under that subsection. On the other hand, subsection (a)(4) should not be construed to permit the bank with which the deposit account is maintained to short-circuit subsection (a)(2), which provides for control through a control agreement among the debtor, the bank, and the control person. However, it would be possible for the bank, acting in a capacity other than as the depositary bank (for example, as a secured party) to acknowledge that it has control on behalf of another purchaser under subsection (a)(4).

Section 9-107B(a) makes clear that a person that has control under this section has no duty to acknowledge that it has or will obtain control on behalf of another person. Arrangements for a person to acknowledge that it has or will obtain control on behalf of another person are not standardized. Accordingly, Section 9-107B(b) leaves to the agreement of the parties and to any other applicable law any duties of a person that does acknowledge that it has or will obtain control on behalf of another person and provides that a person making an acknowledgment is not required to confirm the acknowledgment to another person.

§ 9-105. Control of Electronic Copy of Record Evidencing Chattel Paper.

(a) [General rule: control of electronic copy of record evidencing chattel paper.] A purchaser has control of an authoritative electronic copy of a record evidencing chattel paper if a system employed for evidencing the assignment of interests in the chattel paper reliably establishes the purchaser as the person to which the authoritative electronic copy was assigned.

(b) [Single authoritative copy.] A system satisfies subsection (a) if the record or records evidencing the chattel paper are created, stored, and assigned in a manner that:

(1) a single authoritative copy of the record or records exists which is unique, identifiable, and, except as otherwise provided in paragraphs (4), (5), and (6), unalterable;

(2) the authoritative copy identifies the purchaser as the assignee of the record or records;

(3) the authoritative copy is communicated to and maintained by the purchaser or its designated custodian;

(4) copies or amendments that add or change an identified assignee of the authoritative copy can be made only with the consent of the purchaser;

(5) each copy of the authoritative copy and any copy of a copy is readily identifiable as a copy that is not the authoritative copy; and

(6) any amendment of the authoritative copy is readily identifiable as authorized or unauthorized.

(c) [One or more authoritative copies.] A system satisfies subsection (a), and a purchaser has control of an authoritative electronic copy of a record evidencing chattel paper, if the electronic copy, a record attached to or logically associated with the electronic copy, or a system in which the electronic copy is recorded:

(1) enables the purchaser readily to identify each electronic copy as either an authoritative copy or a nonauthoritative copy;

(2) enables the purchaser readily to identify itself in any way, including by name, identifying number, cryptographic key, office, or account number, as the assignee of the authoritative electronic copy; and

(3) gives the purchaser exclusive power, subject to subsection (d), to:

(A) prevent others from adding or changing an identified assignee of the authoritative electronic copy; and

(B) transfer control of the authoritative electronic copy.

(d) [Meaning of exclusive.] Subject to subsection (e), a power is exclusive under subsection (c)(3)(A) and (B) even if:

(1) the authoritative electronic copy, a record attached to or logically associated with the authoritative electronic copy, or a system in which the authoritative electronic copy is recorded limits the use of the authoritative electronic copy or has a protocol programmed to cause a change, including a transfer or loss of control; or

(2) the power is shared with another person.

(e) [When power not shared with another person.] A power of a purchaser is not shared with another person under subsection (d)(2) and the purchaser's power is not exclusive if:

(1) the purchaser can exercise the power only if the power also is exercised by the other person; and

(2) the other person:

(A) can exercise the power without exercise of the power by the purchaser; or

(B) is the transferor to the purchaser of an interest in the chattel paper.

(f) [Presumption of exclusivity of certain powers.] If a purchaser has the powers specified in subsection (c)(3)(A) and (B), the powers are presumed to be exclusive.

(g) [Obtaining control through another person.] A purchaser has control of an authoritative electronic copy of a record evidencing chattel paper if another person, other than the transferor to the purchaser of an interest in the chattel paper:

(1) has control of the authoritative electronic copy and acknowledges that it has control on behalf of the purchaser; or

(2) obtains control of the authoritative electronic copy after having acknowledged that it will obtain control of the electronic copy on behalf of the purchaser.

Definitional Cross References:

Account	Section 9-102(a)(2)
Assignee	Section 9-102(a)(7A)
Chattel paper	Section 9-102(a)(11)
Communicate	Section 9-102(a)(18)
Electronic	Section 1-201(b)(16A)
Person	Section 1-201(b)(27)
Purchaser	Section 1-201(b)(30)
Record	Section 9-102(a)(70)
Secured party	Section 9-102(a)(73)

Official Comment

1. **The Functions of Control.** A secured party can perfect a security interest in chattel paper by filing. See Section 9-312(a). Alternatively, a secured party can perfect a security interest in chattel paper by taking possession of all authoritative tangible copies of the record evidencing the chattel paper and obtaining control of all authoritative electronic copies of the record evidencing chattel paper. Section 9-314A. Possession and control also are conditions for achieving priority under Section 9-330(a), (b), and (c). A secured party's possession or control of chattel paper also may substitute for a signed security agreement for purposes of attachment under Section 9-203. Subsection (e) provides that in certain circumstances a power is not shared within the meaning of subsection (d)(2), the relaxation of the exclusivity requirement provided by subsection (d)(2) does not apply, and, consequently, a purchaser's power is not exclusive.

2. **Conditions for Obtaining Control: In General.** This section provides the requirements for obtaining control of chattel paper. As explained in the comment to the definition of "chattel paper," the definitions of "electronic chattel paper" and "tangible chattel paper" have been deleted as unnecessary. See Section 9-102, Comment 5.b.

Subsections (a) and (b) are substantially unchanged under the 2022 Article 9 Revisions. Subsection (a), which derives from Section 16 of the Uniform Electronic Transactions Act, sets forth the general test for control. (The amendments to subsection (a) primarily reflect the changes to the definition of chattel paper in Section 9-102.) Subsections (b) and (c) set forth safe harbor tests that, if satisfied, establish control under the general test in subsection (a). It is important to note that compliance with the conditions for control in subsection (c) would satisfy the conditions provided in subsection (b). However, subsection (b) has been retained out of an abundance of caution and to provide assurances of the continuing viability of pre-2022 systems for control of chattel paper evidenced by electronic records.

3. **Development of Control Systems and Application of Subsection (b).** This Article leaves to the marketplace the development of systems and procedures, through a combination of suitable technologies and business practices, for dealing with control of chattel paper in a commercial context. As under UETA and under the general standard for control under subsection (a), for control under subsection (b), as supplemented by subsection (g), a system must be shown to reliably

establish that the secured party is the assignee of the chattel paper. Reliability is a high standard and encompasses the general principle of identifiability of an assignee of an authoritative copy as found in subsection (b), but without setting forth specific guidelines as to how compliance with this principle must be achieved. Under subsection (b), at any point in time, a party should be able to identify the single authoritative copy of the record or records evidencing the chattel paper which is unique and identifiable as the authoritative copy. This does not mean that once created the authoritative copy need be static and never moved or copied from its original location. To the extent that backup systems exist which result in multiple copies, the key to this idea is that at any point in time, the one authoritative copy needs to be unique and identifiable. However, the standards applied to determine whether a party is in control of chattel paper should not be more stringent than the pre-2022 standards applied to determine whether a party is in possession of tangible chattel paper. For example, just as a secured party does not lose possession of tangible chattel paper merely by virtue of the possibility that a person acting on its behalf could wrongfully redeliver the chattel paper to the debtor, so control of chattel paper evidenced by an electronic copy of a record or records would not be defeated by the possibility that the secured party's control could be subverted by the wrongful conduct of a person (such as a custodian) acting on its behalf.

4. Subsection (c) Safe Harbor: In General. The subsection (c) "safe harbor" generally follows Section 12-105 for control of controllable electronic records. See generally Section 12-105 and Comments. It differs from subsection (b), which (as explained above) is based on a "single authoritative copy" of an electronic record or records. Subsection (b) would be inapplicable when the relevant record is maintained on a blockchain or another distributed ledger. The utility of distributed ledger technology depends on there being multiple authoritative copies of a record. However, as with subsection (b), control under subsection (c) also meets the high standard of reliability under subsection (a) as to the identifiability of an assignee of authoritative copies. The conditions for "control" in subsection (c) are meant to reflect the functions that possession serves with respect to writings, but in a more accurate and technologically flexible way than does the definition in subsection (b).

Subsection (c), as supplemented by subsections (d) through (g), sets forth the requirements for a purchaser to have "control of an authoritative electronic copy of a record evidencing chattel paper." However, for purposes of perfection of a security interest in the chattel paper under Section 9-314A and qualification for nontemporal priority under Section 9- 330, the purchaser must obtain control of each authoritative electronic copy (i.e., all of the copies) of a record evidencing the chattel paper and take possession of each tangible copy (if any) of the record evidencing the chattel paper.

5. Control of Electronic Copy of Record Evidencing Chattel Paper under Subsection (c). Under subsection (c), to obtain control of an electronic copy of a record evidencing chattel paper a purchaser must be able to identify each electronic copy as authoritative or nonauthoritative and identify itself as the assignee of the authoritative copy. As to the means of identification, see Section 12-105, Comment 7. In addition, the purchaser must have the exclusive power to prevent others from adding or changing an identified assignee and to transfer control of the authoritative copy. However, once it is established that a person has received those powers, subsection (f) provides a presumption of exclusivity. Consequently, a person asserting control need not prove exclusivity in order to make out a prima facie case. Application of the presumption will be governed also by Section 1-206 (effects of a presumption under the UCC) and applicable non-UCC law (including rules of procedure and evidence). See generally Section 12-105, Comment 5. Subsection (d) contains two qualifications of the term "exclusive" as used in subsection (c)(3). A power can be "exclusive" under subsection (c)(3) even if one or both of these qualifications apply.

Subsection (e) provides that a purchaser does not share an exclusive power with another person if the purchaser can exercise the power only with the other person's cooperation (subsection (e)(1)) but the other person either (i) can exercise the power without the purchaser's cooperation (subsection (e)(2)(A)) or (ii) is the transferor to the purchaser of an interest in the chattel paper (subsection (e)(2)(B)). It follows that a purchaser to which subsection (e) applies does not have control based on its exclusive powers (although it might have control through another person under subsection (g), discussed below, or if another person having control is acting as the person's agent). As to the rationale for disqualifying a purchaser (which includes a secured party in a secured transaction) from sharing powers with a transferor to the purchaser, as provided in subsection (e)(2)(B), and from the benefit of shared control under subsection (d)(2), and for examples of the operation of subsection (e) (in the context of the similar provision in Section 12- 105), see Section 12-105, Comments 5 and 9.

6. Control Through Another Person. Subsection (g) provides for a purchaser to obtain control of an electronic copy by virtue of the acknowledgment by another person in control of the electronic copy. It follows revisions to the corresponding provisions for control of electronic documents of title (Section 7-106(g)), control of a security entitlement (Section 8- 106(d)(3)), control of deposit accounts (Section 9-104(a)(4)), control of electronic money (Section 9-105A(e)), and control of controllable electronic records (Section 12-105(e)). For a brief discussion, see Section 12-105, Comment 8. For an acknowledgment by another person to be effective to confer control on a purchaser under subsection (g), the other person making the acknowledgment must be one "other than the transferor to the purchaser of an interest in the chattel paper." The rationale for this limitation is discussed in Section 12-105, Comment 9.

Section 9-107B(a) makes clear that a person that has control under this section has no duty to acknowledge that it has or will obtain control on behalf of another person. Arrangements for a person to acknowledge that it has or will obtain control on behalf of another person are not standardized. Accordingly, Section 9-107B(b) leaves to the agreement of the parties and to any other applicable law any duties of a person that does acknowledge that it has or will obtain control on behalf of another person and provides that a person making an acknowledgment is not required to confirm the acknowledgment to another person. For example, subsection (g) would apply to give control to a person, Alpha, when another person, Beta, has control of each authoritative electronic copy of a record evidencing chattel paper and acknowledges that it has control on behalf of Alpha. However, under Section 9-107B(a), Beta is not required to so acknowledge. And under Section 9-107B(b), even if Beta does so acknowledge, Beta owes no duty to Alpha unless Beta agrees or other law so provides and Beta is not required to confirm its acknowledgment to any other person.

7. References to "Secured Party" Changed to "Purchaser." References to a "secured party" in the pre-2022 text of this section have been changed to refer to a "purchaser." This change aligns the text with the priority rules of Section 9-330(a), (b), and (c).

§ 9-105A. Control of Electronic Money.

(a) [General rule: control of electronic money.] A person has control of electronic money if:

(1) the electronic money, a record attached to or logically associated with the electronic money, or a system in which the electronic money is recorded gives the person:

(A) power to avail itself of substantially all the benefit from the electronic money; and

(B) exclusive power, subject to subsection (b), to:

(i) prevent others from availing themselves of substantially all the benefit from the electronic money; and

(ii) transfer control of the electronic money to another person or cause another person to obtain control of other electronic money as a result of the transfer of the electronic money; and

(2) the electronic money, a record attached to or logically associated with the electronic money, or a system in which the electronic money is recorded enables the person readily to identify itself in any way, including by name, identifying number, cryptographic key, office, or account number, as having the powers under paragraph (1).

(b) [Meaning of exclusive.] Subject to subsection (c), a power is exclusive under subsection (a)(1)(B)(i) and (ii) even if:

(1) the electronic a record attached to or logically associated with the electronic money, or a system in which the electronic money is recorded limits the use of the electronic money or has a protocol programmed to cause a change, including a transfer or loss of control; or

(2) the power is shared with another person.

(c) [When power not shared with another person.] A power of a person is not shared with another person under subsection (b)(2) and the person's power is not exclusive if:

(1) the person can exercise the power only if the power also is exercised by the other person; and

(2) the other person:

(A) can exercise the power without exercise of the power by the person; or

(B) is the transferor to the person of an interest in the electronic money.

(d) [Presumption of exclusivity of certain powers.] If a person has the powers specified in subsection (a)(1)(B)(i) and (ii), the powers are presumed to be exclusive.

(e) [Control through another person.] A person has control of electronic money if another person, other than the transferor to the person of an interest in the electronic money:

(1) has control of the electronic money and acknowledges that it has control on behalf of the person; or

(2) obtains control of the electronic money after having acknowledged that it will obtain control of the electronic money on behalf of the person.

Definitional Cross References:

Account	Section 9-102(a)(2)
Electronic	Section 1-201(b)(16A)
Electronic money	Section 9-102(a)(31A)
Money	Section 9-102(a)(54A)

Person	Section 1-201(b)(27)
Record	Section 9-102(a)(70)

Official Comment

1. "Control of Electronic Money: In General. A security interest in electronic money as original collateral may be perfected only by control pursuant to this section. Section 9- 312(b)(4). These requirements for obtaining control generally track those in Section 12-105 for controllable electronic records. See generally Section 12-105, Comments.

2. Control on Behalf of Another Person. Subsection (e) provides for a person to obtain control of electronic money by virtue of the acknowledgment by another person in control of the electronic money. It follows revisions to the corresponding provisions for control of electronic documents of title (Section 7-106(g)), control of a security entitlement (Section 8- 106(d)(3)), control of deposit accounts (Section 9-104(a)(4)), control of an electronic copy of a record evidencing chattel paper (Section 9-105(g)), and control of controllable electronic records (Section 12-105(e)). For a brief discussion, see Section 12-105, Comment 8.

Section 9-107B(a) makes clear that a person that has control under this section has no duty to acknowledge that it has or will obtain control on behalf of another person. Arrangements for a person to acknowledge that it has or will obtain control on behalf of another person are not standardized. Accordingly, Section 9-107B(b) leaves to the agreement of the parties and to any other applicable law any duties of a person that does acknowledge that it has or will obtain control on behalf of another person and provides that a person making an acknowledgment is not required to confirm the acknowledgment to another person.

§ 9-106. Control of Investment Property.

(a) [Control under Section 8-106.] A person has control of a certificated security, uncertificated security, or security entitlement as provided in Section 8-106.

(b) [Control of commodity contract.] A secured party has control of a commodity contract if:

(1) the secured party is the commodity intermediary with which the commodity contract is carried; or

(2) the commodity customer, secured party, and commodity intermediary have agreed that the commodity intermediary will apply any value distributed on account of the commodity contract as directed by the secured party without further consent by the commodity customer.

(c) [Effect of control of securities account or commodity account.] A secured party having control of all security entitlements or commodity contracts carried in a securities account or commodity account has control over the securities account or commodity account.

Definitional Cross References:

Certificated security	Section 8-102(a)(4)
Commodity account	Section 9-102(a)(14)
Commodity contract	Section 9-102(a)(15)
Commodity customer	Section 9-102(a)(16)
Commodity intermediary	Section 9-102(a)(17)
Control	Section 8-106
Investment property	Section 9-102(a)(49)
Person	Section 1-201(b)(27)
Secured party	Section 9-102(a)(73)
Securities account	Section 8-501(a)
Security entitlement	Section 8-102(a)(17)
Uncertificated security	Section 8-102(a)(18)
Value	Section 1-204

Comment References: 9-105 C4

Official Comment

1. Source. Former Section 9-115(e).

2. "Control" Under Article 8. For an explanation of "control" of securities and certain other investment property, see Section 8-106, Comments 4 and 7.

3. "Control" of Commodity Contracts. This section, as did former Section 9-115(1)(e), contains provisions relating to control of commodity contracts which are analogous to those in Section 8-106 for other types of investment property.

4. Securities Accounts and Commodity Accounts. For drafting convenience, control with respect to a securities account or commodity account is defined in terms of obtaining control over the security entitlements or commodity contracts. Of course, an agreement that provides that (without further consent of the debtor) the securities intermediary or commodity intermediary will honor instructions from the secured party concerning a securities account or commodity account described as such is sufficient. Such an agreement necessarily implies that the intermediary will honor instructions concerning all security entitlements or commodity contracts carried in the account and thus affords the secured party control of all the security entitlements or commodity contracts.

§ 9-107. Control of Letter-of-Credit Right.

A secured party has control of a letter-of-credit right to the extent of any right to payment or performance by the issuer or any nominated person if the issuer or nominated person has consented to an assignment of proceeds of the letter of credit under Section 5-114(c) or otherwise applicable law or practice.

Definitional Cross References:

Issuer (letter of credit/ letter-of-credit right)	Section 5-102(a)(9)
Letter of credit	Section 5-102(a)(10)
Letter-of-credit right	Section 9-102(a)(51)
Nominated person	Section 5-102(a)(11)
Proceeds	Section 9-102(a)(64)
Secured party	Section 9-102(a)(73)

Comment References: 9-105 C4

Official Comment

1. Source. New.

2. "Control" of Letter-of-Credit Right. Whether a secured party has control of a letter-of-credit right may determine the secured party's priority as against competing secured parties. See Section 9-329. This section provides that a secured party acquires control of a letter-of-credit right by receiving an assignment if the secured party obtains the consent of the issuer or any nominated person, such as a confirmer or negotiating bank, under Section 5-114 or other applicable law or practice. Because both issuers and nominated persons may give or be obligated to give value under a letter of credit, this section contemplates that a secured party obtains control of a letter-of-credit right with respect to the issuer or a particular nominated person only to the extent that the issuer or that nominated person consents to the assignment. For example, if a secured party obtains control to the extent of an issuer's obligation but fails to obtain the consent of a nominated person, the secured party does not have control to the extent that the nominated person gives value. In many cases the person or persons who will give value under a letter of credit will be clear from its terms. In other cases, prudence may suggest obtaining consent from more than one person. The details of the consenting issuer's or nominated person's duties to pay or otherwise render performance to the secured party are left to the agreement of the parties.

3. "Proceeds of a Letter of Credit." Section 5-114 follows traditional banking terminology by referring to a letter of credit beneficiary's assignment of its right to receive payment thereunder as an assignment of the "proceeds of a letter of credit." However, as the seller of goods can assign its right to receive payment (an "account") before it has been earned by delivering the goods to the buyer, so the beneficiary of a letter of credit can assign its contingent right to payment before the letter of credit has been honored. See Section 5-114(b). If the assignment creates a security interest, the security interest can be perfected at the time it is created. An assignment of, including the creation of a security interest in, a letter-of-credit right is an assignment of a present interest.

4. "Transfer" vs. "Assignment." Letter-of-credit law and practice distinguish the "transfer" of a letter of credit from an "assignment." Under a transfer, the transferee itself becomes the beneficiary and acquires the right to draw. Whether a new, substitute credit is issued or the issuer advises the transferee of its status as such, the transfer constitutes a novation under which the transferee is the new, substituted beneficiary (but only to the extent of the transfer, in the case of a partial transfer).

Section 5-114(e) provides that the rights of a transferee beneficiary or nominated person are independent of the beneficiary's assignment of the proceeds of a letter of credit and are superior to the assignee's right to the proceeds. For this reason, transfer does not appear in this Article as a means of control or perfection. Section 9-109(c)(4) recognizes the independent and superior rights of a transferee beneficiary under Section 5-114(e); this Article does not apply to the rights of a transferee beneficiary or nominated person to the extent that those rights are independent and superior under Section 5-114.

5. Supporting Obligation: Automatic Attachment and Perfection. A letter-of-credit right is a type of "supporting obligation," as defined in Section 9-102. Under Sections 9-203 and 9-308, a security interest in a letter-of-credit right automatically attaches and is automatically perfected if the security interest in the supported obligation is a perfected security interest. However, unless the secured party has control of the letter-of-credit right or itself becomes a transferee beneficiary, it cannot obtain any rights against the issuer or a nominated person under Article 5. Consequently, as a practical matter, the secured party's rights would be limited to its ability to locate and identify proceeds distributed by the issuer or nominated person under the letter of credit.

§ 9-107A. Control of Controllable Electronic Record, Controllable Account, or Controllable Payment Intangible.

(a) [Control under Section 12-105.] A secured party has control of a controllable electronic record as provided in Section 12-105.

(b) [Control of controllable account and controllable payment intangible.] A secured party has control of a controllable account or controllable payment intangible if the secured party has control of the controllable electronic record that evidences the controllable account or controllable payment intangible.

Definitional Cross References:

Control	Section 12-105
Controllable account	Section 9-102(a)(27A)
Controllable electronic record	Section 12-102(a)(1)
Controllable payment intangible	Section 9-102(a)(27B)
Secured party	Section 9-102(a)(73)

Official Comment

1. Perfection by Control or Filing for Controllable Electronic Records. Perfection by filing and perfection by control are alternative methods of perfection for a controllable electronic record. See Sections 9-312, 9-314. Under this section, a secured party has control of a controllable electronic record as provided in Section 12-105. Under Section 9- 326A, a security interest in a controllable electronic record that is perfected by control has priority over a security interest perfected by another method.

2. Perfection by Control or Filing and Priority for Controllable Account or Controllable Payment Intangible. Perfection by filing and perfection by control also are alternative methods of perfection for a controllable account or controllable payment intangible. See Sections 9-312, 9-314. Under this section, a secured party would obtain control of a controllable account or controllable payment intangible by obtaining control of the controllable electronic record that evidences the controllable account or controllable payment intangible. Under Section 9-326A, a security interest in a controllable account or controllable payment intangible that is perfected by control has priority over a security interest perfected by another method.

By definition, a controllable account would be an Article 9 "account," and a controllable payment intangible would be an Article 9 "payment intangible." Section 9-102. The fact that an account or payment intangible is a controllable account or controllable payment intangible does not affect a secured party's alternative of perfection by filing. Moreover, that fact does not affect the applicability of other provisions of Article 9, including the provisions governing an account debtor's agreement not to assert defenses (Section 9-403) and the statutory overrides of legal and contractual restrictions on the assignability of accounts and payment intangibles (Sections 9-406 and 9-408).

§ 9-107B. No Requirement to Acknowledge or Confirm; No Duties.

(a) [No requirement to acknowledge.] A person that has control under Section 9-104, 9-105, or 9-105A is not required to acknowledge that it has control on behalf of another person.

(b) [No duties or confirmation.] If a person acknowledges that it has or will obtain control on behalf of another person, unless the person otherwise agrees or law other than this article otherwise provides, the person does not owe any duty to the other person and is not required to confirm the acknowledgment to any other person.

Definitional Cross References:

Person	Section 1-201(b)(27)
Control	Sections 9-104, 9-105, 9-105A

Official Comment

1. Source. Section 9-107B derives from Sections 8-106(g) and 9-313(f) and (g).

2. Purpose. Subsection (a) makes clear that a person that has control under the specified sections has no duty to acknowledge that it has or will obtain control on behalf of another person. Arrangements for a person to acknowledge that it has control on behalf of another person are not standardized. Accordingly, subsection (b) leaves to the agreement of the parties and to any other applicable law any duties of a person that does acknowledge that it has or will obtain control on behalf of any other person.

§ 9-108. Sufficiency of Description.

(a) [Sufficiency of description.] Except as otherwise provided in subsections (c), (d), and (e), a description of personal or real property is sufficient, whether or not it is specific, if it reasonably identifies what is described.

(b) [Examples of reasonable identification.] Except as otherwise provided in subsection (d), a description of collateral reasonably identifies the collateral if it identifies the collateral by:

(1) specific listing;

(2) category;

(3) except as otherwise provided in subsection (e), a type of collateral defined in [the Uniform Commercial Code];

(4) quantity;

(5) computational or allocational formula or procedure; or

(6) except as otherwise provided in subsection (c), any other method, if the identity of the collateral is objectively determinable.

(c) [Supergeneric description not sufficient.] A description of collateral as "all the debtor's assets" or "all the debtor's personal property" or using words of similar import does not reasonably identify the collateral.

(d) [Investment property.] Except as otherwise provided in subsection (e), a description of a security entitlement, securities account, or commodity account is sufficient if it describes:

(1) the collateral by those terms or as investment property; or

(2) the underlying financial asset or commodity contract.

(e) [When description by type insufficient.] A description only by type of collateral defined in [the Uniform Commercial Code] is an insufficient description of:

(1) a commercial tort claim; or

(2) in a consumer transaction, consumer goods, a security entitlement, a securities account, or a commodity account.

Definitional Cross References:

Collateral	Section 9-102(a)(12)
Commercial tort claim	Section 9-102(a)(13)
Commodity account	Section 9-102(a)(14)
Commodity contract	Section 9-102(a)(15)
Consumer goods	Section 9-102(a)(23)
Consumer transaction	Section 9-102(a)(26)
Debtor	Section 9-102(a)(28)
Financial asset	Section 8-102(a)(9)
Investment property	Section 9-102(a)(49)
Securities account	Section 8-501(a)
Security entitlement	Section 8-102(a)(17)

Comment References: 9-203 C5

Official Comment

1. Source. Former Sections 9-110, 9-115(3).

2. General Rules. Subsection (a) retains substantially the same formulation as former Section 9-110. Subsection (b) expands upon subsection (a) by indicating a variety of ways in which a description might reasonably identify collateral. Whereas a provision similar to subsection (b) was applicable only to investment property under former Section 9-115(3), subsection (b) applies to all types of collateral, subject to the limitation in subsection (d). Subsection (b) is subject to subsection (c), which follows prevailing case law and adopts the view that an "all assets" or "all personal property" description for purposes of a security agreement is not sufficient. Note, however, that under Section 9-504, a financing statement sufficiently indicates the collateral if it "covers all assets or all personal property."

The purpose of requiring a description of collateral in a security agreement under Section 9-203 is evidentiary. The test of sufficiency of a description under this section, as under former Section 9-110, is that the description do the job assigned to it: make possible the identification of the collateral described. This section rejects any requirement that a description is insufficient unless it is exact and detailed (the so-called "serial number" test).

3. After-Acquired Collateral. Much litigation has arisen over whether a description in a security agreement is sufficient to include after-acquired collateral if the agreement does not explicitly so provide. This question is one of contract interpretation and is not susceptible to a statutory rule (other than a rule to the effect that it is a question of contract interpretation). Accordingly, this section contains no reference to descriptions of after-acquired collateral.

4. Investment Property. Under subsection (d)(2), the use of the wrong Article 8 or commodities terminology does not render a description invalid (e.g., a security agreement intended to cover a debtor's "security entitlements" is sufficient if it refers to the debtor's "securities"); nor does subsection (d) require the use of the terms "security entitlement," "securities account," "commodity account," or "investment property" if the collateral description is otherwise sufficient under subsection (a). See PEB Commentary No. 28, dated January 16, 2024. The Commentary is available at https://www.ali.org/peb-ucc. Note also that given the broad definition of "securities account" in Section 8-501, a security interest in a securities account also includes all other rights of the debtor against the securities intermediary arising out of the securities account. For example, a security interest in a securities account would include credit balances due to the debtor from the securities intermediary, whether or not they are proceeds of a security entitlement. Moreover, describing collateral as a securities account is a simple way of describing all of the security entitlements carried in the account.

5. Consumer Investment Property; Commercial Tort Claims. Subsection (e) requires greater specificity of description in order to prevent debtors from inadvertently encumbering certain property. Subsection (e) provides that a description by defined "type" of collateral alone of a commercial tort claim or, in a consumer transaction, of a security entitlement, securities account, or commodity account, is not sufficient. For example, "all existing and after-acquired investment property" or "all existing and after-acquired security entitlements," without more, would be insufficient in a consumer transaction to describe a security entitlement, securities account, or commodity account. The reference to "only by type" in subsection (e) means that a description is sufficient if it satisfies subsection (a) and contains a descriptive component beyond the "type" alone. For example, a description such as "all goods now or hereafter sold by secured party to debtor" would suffice, but note that Section 9-204(b)(1) would apply except in the case of a purchase-money security interest. See Section 9- 204, Comment 3. Moreover, if the collateral consists of a securities account or commodity account, a description of the account is sufficient to cover all existing and future security entitlements or commodity contracts carried in the account. See Section 9-203(h), (i).

Under Section 9-204, an after-acquired collateral clause in a security agreement will not reach future commercial tort claims. It follows that when an effective security agreement (or amendment) covering a commercial tort claim as original collateral is entered into the claim already will exist. Subsection (e) does not require a description to be specific, so long as it extends beyond the "type." For example, a description such as "all tort claims arising out of the explosion of debtor's factory" would suffice, even if the exact amount of the claim, the theory on which it may be based, and the identity of the tortfeasor(s) are not described. (Indeed, those facts may not be known at the time.)

The enhanced specificity (beyond the "type") that subsection (e) requires does not apply to the attachment of security interests in commercial tort claims or collateral in consumer transactions that are identifiable proceeds of other collateral. A security interest automatically attaches to such property under Sections 9-203(f) and 9-315(a)(2). This point is confirmed by Section 9-204(b.1).

[Subpart 2. Applicability of Article]

§ 9-109. Scope.

(a) [General scope of article.] Except as otherwise provided in subsections (c) and (d), this article applies to:

(1) a transaction, regardless of its form, that creates a security interest in personal property or fixtures by contract;

(2) an agricultural lien;

(3) a sale of accounts, chattel paper, payment intangibles, or promissory notes;

(4) a consignment;

(5) a security interest arising under Section 2-401, 2-505, 2-711(3), or 2A-508(5), as provided in Section 9-110; and

(6) a security interest arising under Section 4-210 or 5-118.

(b) [Security interest in secured obligation.] The application of this article to a security interest in a secured obligation is not affected by the fact that the obligation is itself secured by a transaction or interest to which this article does not apply.

(c) [Extent to which article does not apply.] This article does not apply to the extent that:

(1) a statute, regulation, or treaty of the United States preempts this article;

(2) another statute of this State expressly governs the creation, perfection, priority, or enforcement of a security interest created by this State or a governmental unit of this State;

(3) a statute of another State, a foreign country, or a governmental unit of another State or a foreign country, other than a statute generally applicable to security interests, expressly governs creation, perfection, priority, or enforcement of a security interest created by the State, country, or governmental unit; or

(4) the rights of a transferee beneficiary or nominated person under a letter of credit are independent and superior under Section 5-114.

(d) [Inapplicability of article.] This article does not apply to:

(1) a landlord's lien, other than an agricultural lien;

(2) a lien, other than an agricultural lien, given by statute or other rule of law for services or materials, but Section 9-333 applies with respect to priority of the lien;

(3) an assignment of a claim for wages, salary, or other compensation of an employee;

(4) a sale of accounts, chattel paper, payment intangibles, or promissory notes as part of a sale of the business out of which they arose;

(5) an assignment of accounts, chattel paper, payment intangibles, or promissory notes which is for the purpose of collection only;

(6) an assignment of a right to payment under a contract to an assignee that is also obligated to perform under the contract;

(7) an assignment of a single account, payment intangible, or promissory note to an assignee in full or partial satisfaction of a preexisting indebtedness;

(8) a transfer of an interest in or an assignment of a claim under a policy of insurance, other than an assignment by or to a health-care provider of a health-care-insurance receivable and any subsequent assignment of the right to payment, but Sections 9-315 and 9-322 apply with respect to proceeds and priorities in proceeds;

(9) an assignment of a right represented by a judgment, other than a judgment taken on a right to payment that was collateral;

(10) a right of recoupment or set-off, but:

(A) Section 9-340 applies with respect to the effectiveness of rights of recoupment or set-off against deposit accounts; and

(B) Section 9-404 applies with respect to defenses or claims of an account debtor;

(11) the creation or transfer of an interest in or lien on real property, including a lease or rents thereunder, except to the extent that provision is made for:

(A) liens on real property in Sections 9-203 and 9-308;

(B) fixtures in Section 9-334;

(C) fixture filings in Sections 9-501, 9-502, 9-512, 9-516, and 9-519; and

(D) security agreements covering personal and real property in Section 9-604;

(12) an assignment of a claim arising in tort, other than a commercial tort claim, but Sections 9-315 and 9-322 apply with respect to proceeds and priorities in proceeds; or

(13) an assignment of a deposit account in a consumer transaction, but Sections 9-315 and 9-322 apply with respect to proceeds and priorities in proceeds.

Definitional Cross References:

Account	Section 9-102(a)(2)
Account debtor	Section 9-102(a)(3)
Agricultural lien	Section 9-102(a)(5)
Beneficiary	Section 5-102(a)(3)
Chattel paper	Section 9-102(a)(11)
Collateral	Section 9-102(a)(12)
Commercial tort claim	Section 9-102(a)(13)
Consignment	Section 9-102(a)(20)
Consumer transaction	Section 9-102(a)(26)
Contract	Section 1-201(b)(12)
Deposit account	Section 9-102(a)(29)
Fixture filing	Section 9-102(a)(40)
Fixtures	Section 9-102(a)(41)
Governmental unit	Section 9-102(a)(45)
Health-care-insurance receivable	Section 9-102(a)(46)
Lease	Section 2A-103(1)(j)
Letter of credit	Section 5-102(a)(10)
Nominated person	Section 5-102(a)(11)
Payment intangible	Section 9-102(a)(61)
Proceeds	Section 9-102(a)(64)
Promissory note	Section 9-102(a)(65)
Right	Section 1-201(b)(34)
Sale	Section 2-106(1)
Security agreement	Section 9-102(a)(74)
Security interest	Section 1-201(b)(35)
State	Section 9-102(a)(77)

Official Comment

1. Source. Former Sections 9-102, 9-104.

2. Basic Scope Provision. Subsection (a)(1) derives from former Section 9-102(1) and (2). These subsections have been combined and shortened. No change in meaning is intended. Under subsection (a)(1), all consensual security interests in personal property and fixtures are covered by this Article, except for transactions excluded by subsections (c) and (d). As to which transactions give rise to a "security interest," the definition of that term in Section 1-201 must be consulted. When a security interest is created, this Article applies regardless of the form of the transaction or the name that parties have given to it. Likewise, the subjective intention of the parties with respect to the legal characterization of their transaction is irrelevant to whether this Article applies, as it was to the application of former Article 9 under the proper interpretation of former Section 9-102.

3. Agricultural Liens. Subsection (a)(2) is new. It expands the scope of this Article to cover agricultural liens, as defined in Section 9-102.

4. Sales of Accounts, Chattel Paper, Payment Intangibles, Promissory Notes, and Other Receivables. Under subsection (a)(3), as under former Section 9-102, this Article applies to sales of accounts and chattel paper. This approach generally has been successful in avoiding difficult problems of distinguishing between transactions in which a receivable secures an obligation and those in which the receivable has been sold outright. In many commercial financing transactions the distinction is blurred.

Subsection (a)(3) added by the 1998 Revisions, expanded the scope of this Article by including the sale of a "payment intangible" (defined in Section 9-102 as "a general intangible under which the account debtor's principal obligation is a monetary obligation") and a "promissory note" (also defined in Section 9-102). To a considerable extent, this Article affords these transactions treatment identical to that given sales of accounts and chattel paper. In some respects, however, sales of payment intangibles and promissory notes are treated differently from sales of other receivables. See, e.g., Sections 9-309 (automatic perfection upon attachment), 9-408 (effect of restrictions on assignment). By virtue of the 1998 expanded definition of "account" (defined in Section 9-102), this Article covers sales of (and other security interests in) "health-care-insurance receivables" (also defined in Section 9-102). Although this Article occasionally distinguishes between outright sales of receivables and sales that secure an obligation, neither this Article nor the definition of "security interest" (Section 1-201(b)(35)) delineates how a particular transaction is to be classified. That issue is left to the courts.

5. Transfer of Ownership in Sales of Receivables. A "sale" of an account, chattel paper, a promissory note, or a payment intangible includes a sale of a right in the receivable, such as a sale of a participation interest. The term also includes the sale of an enforcement right. For example, a "[p]erson entitled to enforce" a negotiable promissory note (Section 3-301) may sell its ownership rights in the instrument. See Section 3-203, Comment 1 ("Ownership rights in instruments may be determined by principles of the law of property, independent of Article 3, which do not depend upon whether the instrument was transferred under Section 3-203."). Also, the right under Section 3-309 to enforce a lost, destroyed, or stolen negotiable promissory note may be sold to a purchaser who could enforce that right by causing the seller to provide the proof required under that section. This Article rejects decisions reaching a contrary result, e.g., *Dennis Joslin Co. v. Robinson Broadcasting*, 977 F. Supp. 491 (D.D.C. 1997).

Nothing in this section or any other provision of Article 9 prevents the transfer of full and complete ownership of an account, chattel paper, an instrument, or a payment intangible in a transaction of sale. However, as mentioned in Comment 4, neither this Article nor the definition of "security interest" in Section 1-201 provides rules for distinguishing sales transactions from those that create a security interest securing an obligation. This Article applies to both types of transactions. The principal effect of this coverage is to apply this Article's perfection and priority rules to these sales transactions. Use of terminology such as "security interest," "debtor," and "collateral" is merely a drafting convention adopted to reach this end, and its use has no relevance to distinguishing sales from other transactions. See PEB Commentary No. 14.

Following a debtor's outright sale and transfer of ownership of a receivable, the debtor-seller retains no legal or equitable rights in the receivable that has been sold. See Section 9-318(a). This is so whether or not the buyer's security interest is perfected. (A security interest arising from the sale of a promissory note or payment intangible is perfected upon attachment without further action. See Section 9-309.) However, if the buyer's interest in accounts or chattel paper is unperfected, a subsequent lien creditor, perfected secured party, or qualified buyer can reach the sold receivable and achieve priority over (or take free of) the buyer's unperfected security interest under Section 9-317. This is so not because the seller of a receivable retains rights in the property sold; it does not. Nor is this so because the seller of a receivable is a "debtor" and the buyer of a receivable is a "secured party" under this Article (they are). It is so for the simple reason that Sections 9-318(b), 9-317, and 9-322 make it so, as did former Sections 9-301 and 9-312. Because the buyer's security interest is unperfected, for purposes of determining the rights of creditors of and purchasers for value from the debtor-seller, under Section 9-318(b) the debtor-seller is deemed to have the rights and title it sold. Section 9-317 subjects the buyer's unperfected interest in accounts and chattel paper to that of the debtor-seller's lien creditor and other persons who qualify under that section.

6. Consignments. Subsection (a)(4) was added by the 1998 Revisions. This Article applies to every "consignment." The term, defined in Section 9-102, includes many but not all "true" consignments (i.e., bailments for the purpose of sale). If a transaction is a "sale or return," as defined in revised Section 2-326, it is not a "consignment." In a "sale or return" transaction, the buyer becomes the owner of the goods, and the seller may obtain an enforceable security interest in the goods only by satisfying the requirements of Section 9-203.

Under common law, creditors of a bailee were unable to reach the interest of the bailor (in the case of a consignment, the consignor-owner). Like former Section 2-326 and former Article 9, this Article changes the common-law result; however, it does so in a different manner. For purposes of determining the rights and interests of third-party creditors of, and purchasers of the goods from, the consignee, but not for other purposes, such as remedies of the consignor, the consignee is deemed to acquire under this Article whatever rights and title the consignor had or had power to transfer. See Section 9-319. The interest of a consignor is defined to be a security interest under revised Section 1-201(37), more specifically, a purchase-money security interest in the consignee's inventory. See Section 9-103(d). Thus, the rules pertaining to lien creditors, buyers, and attachment, perfection, and priority of competing security interests apply to consigned goods. The relationship between the consignor and consignee is left to other law. Consignors also have no duties under Part 6. See Section 9-601(g).

Sometimes parties characterize transactions that secure an obligation (other than the bailee's obligation to returned bailed goods) as "consignments." These transactions are not "consignments" as contemplated by Section 9-109(a)(4). See Section 9-102. This Article applies also to these transactions, by virtue of Section 9-109(a)(1). They create a security interest within the meaning of the first sentence of Section 1-201(b)(35).

This Article does not apply to a bailment for sale that falls outside the definition of "consignment" in Section 9-102. See PEB Commentary No. 20, dated January 24, 2019.

7. Security Interest in Obligation Secured by Non-Article 9 Transaction. Subsection (b) is unchanged in substance from former Section 9-102(3). The following example provides an illustration.

> **Example 1:** O borrows $10,000 from M and secures its repayment obligation, evidenced by a promissory note, by granting to M a mortgage on O's land. This Article does not apply to the creation of the real-property mortgage. However, if M sells the promissory note to X or gives a security interest in the note to secure M's own obligation to X, this Article applies to the security interest thereby created in favor of X. The security interest in the promissory note is covered by this Article even though the note is secured by a real-property mortgage. Also, X's security interest in the note gives X an attached security interest in the mortgage lien that secures the note and, if the security interest in the note is perfected, the security interest in the mortgage lien likewise is perfected. See Sections 9-203, 9-308.

It also follows from subsection (b) that an attempt to obtain or perfect a security interest in a secured obligation by complying with non-Article 9 law, as by an assignment of record of a real-property mortgage, would be ineffective. Finally, it is implicit from subsection (b) that one cannot obtain a security interest in a lien, such as a mortgage on real property, that is not also coupled with an equally effective security interest in the secured obligation. This Article rejects cases such as *In re Maryville Savings & Loan Corp.*, 743 F.2d 413 (6th Cir. 1984), clarified on reconsideration, 760 F.2d 119 (1985).

8. Federal Preemption. Former Section 9-104(a) excluded from Article 9 "a security interest subject to any statute of the United States, to the extent that such statute governs the rights of parties to and third parties affected by transactions in particular types of property." Some (erroneously) read the former section to suggest that Article 9 sometimes deferred to federal law even when federal law did not preempt Article 9. Subsection (c)(1) recognizes explicitly that this Article defers to federal law only when and to the extent that it must—i.e., when federal law preempts it.

9. Governmental Debtors. Former Section 9-104(e) excluded transfers by governmental debtors. It has been revised and replaced by the exclusions in new paragraphs (2) and (3) of subsection (c). These paragraphs reflect the view that Article 9 should apply to security interests created by a State, foreign country, or a "governmental unit" (defined in Section 9-102) of either except to the extent that another statute governs the issue in question. Under paragraph (2), this Article defers to all statutes of the forum State. (A forum cannot determine whether it should consult the choice-of-law rules in the forum's UCC unless it first determines that its UCC applies to the transaction before it.) Paragraph (3) defers to statutes of another State or a foreign country only to the extent that those statutes contain rules applicable specifically to security interests created by the governmental unit in question.

> **Example 2:** A New Jersey state commission creates a security interest in favor of a New York bank. The validity of the security interest is litigated in New York. The relevant security agreement provides that it is governed by New York law. To the extent that a New Jersey statute contains rules peculiar to creation of security interests by governmental units generally, to creation of security interests by state commissions, or to creation of security interests by this particular state commission, then that law will govern. On the other hand, to the extent that New Jersey law provides that security interests created by governmental units, state commissions, or this state commission are governed by the law generally applicable to secured transactions (i.e., New Jersey's Article 9), then New York's Article 9 will govern.

> **Example 3:** An airline that is an instrumentality of a foreign country creates a security interest in favor of a New York bank. The analysis used in the previous example would apply here. That is, if the matter is litigated in New York, New York law would govern except to the extent that the foreign country enacted a statute applicable to security interests created by governmental units generally or by the airline specifically.
>
> The fact that New York law applies does not necessarily mean that perfection is accomplished by filing in New York. Rather, it means that the court should apply New York's Article 9, including its choice-of-law provisions. Under New York's Section 9-301, perfection is governed by the law of the jurisdiction in which the debtor is located. Section 9-307 determines the debtor's location for choice-of-law purposes.

If a transaction does not bear an appropriate relation to the forum State, then that State's Article 9 will not apply, regardless of whether the transaction would be excluded by paragraph (3).

> **Example 4:** A Belgian governmental unit grants a security interest in its equipment to a Swiss secured party. The equipment is located in Belgium. A dispute arises and, for some reason, an action is brought in a New Mexico state court. Inasmuch as the transaction bears no "appropriate relation" to New Mexico, New Mexico's UCC, including its Article 9, is inapplicable. See Section 1-105(1). New Mexico's Section 9-109(c) on excluded transactions should not come into play. Even if the parties agreed that New Mexico law would govern, the parties' agreement would not be effective because the transaction does not bear a "reasonable relation" to New Mexico. See Section 1-105(1).

Conversely, Article 9 will come into play only if the litigation arises in a UCC jurisdiction or if a foreign choice-of-law rule leads a foreign court to apply the law of a UCC jurisdiction. For example, if issues concerning a security interest granted by a foreign airline to a New York bank are litigated overseas, the court may be bound to apply the law of the debtor's jurisdiction and not New York's Article 9.

10. Certain Statutory and Common-Law Liens; Interests in Real Property. With few exceptions (nonconsensual agricultural liens being one), this Article applies only to consensual security interests in personal property. Following former Section 9-104(b) and (j), paragraphs (1) and (11) of subsection (d) exclude landlord's liens and leases and most other interests in or liens on real property. These exclusions generally reiterate the limitations on coverage (i.e., "by contract," "in personal property and fixtures") made explicit in subsection (a)(1). Similarly, most jurisdictions provide special liens to suppliers of many types of services and materials, either by statute or by common law. With the exception of agricultural liens, it is not necessary for this Article to provide general codification of this lien structure, which is determined in large part by local conditions and which is far removed from ordinary commercial financing. As under former Section 9-104(c), subsection (d)(2) excludes these suppliers' liens (other than agricultural liens) from this Article. However, Section 9-333 provides a rule for determining priorities between certain possessory suppliers' liens and security interests covered by this Article.

11. Wage and Similar Claims. As under former Section 9-104(d), subsection (d)(3) excludes assignments of claims for wages and the like from this Article. These assignments present important social issues that other law addresses. The Federal Trade Commission has ruled that, with some exceptions, the taking of an assignment of wages or other earnings is an unfair act or practice under the Federal Trade Commission Act. See 16 C.F.R. Part 444. State statutes also may regulate such assignments.

12. Certain Sales and Assignments of Receivables; Judgments. In general this Article covers security interests in (including sales of) accounts, chattel paper, payment intangibles, and promissory notes. Paragraphs (4), (5), (6), and (7) of subsection (d) exclude from the Article certain sales and assignments of receivables that, by their nature, do not concern commercial financing transactions. These paragraphs add to the exclusions in former Section 9-104(f) analogous sales and assignments of payment intangibles and promissory notes. For similar reasons, subsection (d)(9) retains the exclusion of assignments of judgments under former Section 9-104(h) (other than judgments taken on a right to payment that itself was collateral under this Article).

13. Insurance. Subsection (d)(8) narrows somewhat the broad exclusion of interests in insurance policies under former Section 9-104(g). This Article now covers assignments by or to a health-care provider of "health-care-insurance receivables" (defined in Section 9-102).

14. Set-Off. Subsection (d)(10) adds two exceptions to the general exclusion of set-off rights from Article 9 under former Section 9-104(i). The first takes account of new Section 9-340, which regulates the effectiveness of a set-off against a deposit account that stands as collateral. The second recognizes Section 9-404, which affords the obligor on an account, chattel paper, or general intangible the right to raise claims and defenses against an assignee (secured party).

15. Tort Claims. Subsection (d)(12) narrows somewhat the broad exclusion of transfers of tort claims under former Section 9-104(k). This Article now applies to assignments of "commercial tort claims" (defined in Section 9-102) as well as to security interests in tort claims that constitute proceeds of other collateral (e.g., a right to payment for negligent destruction of the debtor's inventory). Note that once a claim arising in tort has been settled and reduced to a contractual obligation to pay, the right to payment becomes a payment intangible and ceases to be a claim arising in tort.

This Article contains two special rules governing creation of a security interest in tort claims. First, a description of collateral in a security agreement as "all tort claims" is insufficient to meet the requirement for attachment. See Section 9-108(e). Second, no security interest attaches under an after-acquired property clause to a tort claim. See Section 9-204(b). In addition, this Article does not determine whom the tortfeasor must pay to discharge its obligation. Inasmuch as a tortfeasor is not an "account debtor," the rules governing waiver of defenses and discharge of an obligation by an obligor (Sections 9-403, 9-404, 9-405, and 9-406) are inapplicable to tort-claim collateral.

16. Deposit Accounts. Except in consumer transactions, deposit accounts may be taken as original collateral under this Article. Under former Section 9-104(*l*), deposit accounts were excluded as original collateral, leaving security interests in deposit accounts to be governed by the common law. The common law is nonuniform, often difficult to discover and comprehend, and frequently costly to implement. As a consequence, debtors who wished to use deposit accounts as collateral sometimes were precluded from doing so as a practical matter. By excluding deposit accounts from the Article's scope as original collateral in consumer transactions, subsection (d)(13) leaves those transactions to law other than this Article. However, in both consumer and non-consumer transactions, sections 9-315 and 9-322 apply to deposit accounts as proceeds and with respect to priorities in proceeds.

This Article contains several safeguards to protect debtors against inadvertently encumbering deposit accounts and to reduce the likelihood that a secured party will realize a windfall from a debtor's deposit accounts. For example, because "deposit account" is a separate type of collateral, a security agreement covering general intangibles will not adequately describe deposit accounts. Rather, a security agreement must reasonably identify the deposit accounts that are the subject of a security interest, e.g., by using the term "deposit accounts." See Section 9-108.

To perfect a security interest in a deposit account as original collateral, a secured party (other than the bank with which the deposit account is maintained) must obtain "control" of the account either by obtaining the bank's signed agreement or by becoming the bank's customer with respect to the deposit account. See Sections 9-312(b)(1), 9-104. Either of these steps requires the debtor's consent.

This Article also contains new rules that determine which State's law governs perfection and priority of a security interest in a deposit account (Section 9-304), priority of conflicting security interests in and set-off rights against a deposit account (Sections 9-327, 9-340), the rights of transferees of funds from an encumbered deposit account (Section 9-332), the obligations of the bank (Section 9-341), enforcement of security interests in a deposit account (Section 9-607(c)), and the duty of a secured party to terminate control of a deposit account (Section 9-208(b)).

§ 9-110. Security Interests Arising Under Article 2 or 2A.

A security interest arising under Section 2-401, 2-505, 2-711(3), or 2A-508(5) is subject to this article. However, until the debtor obtains possession of the goods:

(1) the security interest is enforceable, even if Section 9-203(b)(3) has not been satisfied;

(2) filing is not required to perfect the security interest;

(3) the rights of the secured party after default by the debtor are governed by Article 2 or 2A; and

(4) the security interest has priority over a conflicting security interest created by the debtor.

Definitional Cross References:

Debtor	Section 9-102(a)(28)
Goods	Section 9-102(a)(44)
Right	Section 1-201(b)(34)
Secured party	Section 9-102(a)(73)
Security interest	Section 1-201(b)(35)

Official Comments

1. Source. Former Section 9-113.

2. Background. Former Section 9-113, from which this section derives, referred generally to security interests "arising solely under the Article on Sales (Article 2) or the Article on Leases (Article 2A)." Views differed as to the precise scope of that section. In contrast, Section 9-110 specifies the security interests to which it applies.

3. Security Interests Under Articles 2 and 2A. Section 2-505 explains how a seller of goods may reserve a security interest in them. Section 2-401 indicates that a reservation of title by the seller of goods, despite delivery to the buyer, is limited to reservation of a security interest. As did former Article 9, this Article governs a security interest arising solely under one of those sections; however, until the buyer obtains possession of the goods, the security interest is enforceable even in the absence of a security agreement, filing is not necessary to perfect the security interest, and the seller-secured party's rights on the buyer's default are governed by Article 2.

Sections 2-711(3) and 2A-508(5) create a security interest in favor of a buyer or lessee in possession of goods that were rightfully rejected or as to which acceptance was justifiably revoked. As did former Article 9, this Article governs a security interest arising solely under one of those sections; however, until the seller or lessor obtains possession of the goods, the security interest is enforceable even in the absence of a security agreement, filing is not necessary to perfect the security interest, and the secured party's (buyer's or lessee's) rights on the debtor's (seller's or lessor's) default are governed by Article 2 or 2A, as the case may be.

4. Priority. This section adds to former Section 9-113 a priority rule. Until the debtor obtains possession of the goods, a security interest arising under one of the specified sections of Article 2 or 2A has priority over conflicting security interests created by the debtor. Thus, a security interest arising under Section 2-401 or 2-505 has priority over a conflicting security interest in the buyer's after-acquired goods, even if the goods in question are inventory. Arguably, the same result would obtain under Section 9-322, but even if it would not, a purchase-money-like priority is appropriate. Similarly, a security interest under Section 2-711(3) or 2A-508(5) has priority over security interests claimed by the seller's or lessor's secured lender. This result is appropriate, inasmuch as the payments giving rise to the debt secured by the Article 2 or 2A security interest are likely to be included among the lender's proceeds.

> **Example:** Seller owns equipment subject to a security interest created by Seller in favor of Lender. Buyer pays for the equipment, accepts the goods, and then justifiably revokes acceptance. As long as Seller does not recover possession of the equipment, Buyer's security interest under Section 2-711(3) is senior to that of Lender.

In the event that a security interest referred to in this section conflicts with a security interest that is created by a person other than the debtor, Section 9-325 applies. Thus, if Lender's security interest in the example was created not by Seller but by the person from whom Seller acquired the goods, Section 9-325 would govern.

5. Relationship to Other Rights and Remedies Under Articles 2 and 2A. This Article does not specifically address the conflict between (i) a security interest created by a buyer or lessee and (ii) the seller's or lessor's right to withhold delivery under Section 2-702(1), 2-703(a), or 2A-525, the seller's or lessor's right to stop delivery under Section 2-705 or 2A-526, or the seller's right to reclaim under Section 2-507(2) or 2-702(2). These conflicts are governed by the first sentence of Section 2-403(1), under which the buyer's secured party obtains no greater rights in the goods than the buyer had or had power to convey, or Section 2A-307(1), under which creditors of the lessee take subject to the lease contract.

PART 2. EFFECTIVENESS OF SECURITY AGREEMENT; ATTACHMENT OF SECURITY INTEREST; RIGHTS OF PARTIES TO SECURITY AGREEMENT

[Subpart 1. Effectiveness and Attachment]

§ 9-201. General Effectiveness of Security Agreement.

(a) [General effectiveness.] Except as otherwise provided in [the Uniform Commercial Code], a security agreement is effective according to its terms between the parties, against purchasers of the collateral, and against creditors.

(b) [Applicable consumer laws and other law.] A transaction subject to this article is subject to any applicable rule of law which establishes a different rule for consumers and [insert reference to (i) any other statute or regulation that regulates the rates, charges, agreements, and practices for loans, credit sales, or other extensions of credit and (ii) any consumer-protection statute or regulation].

(c) [Other applicable law controls.] In case of conflict between this article and a rule of law, statute, or regulation described in subsection (b), the rule of law, statute, or regulation controls. Failure to comply with a statute or regulation described in subsection (b) has only the effect the statute or regulation specifies.

(d) [Further deference to other applicable law.] This article does not:

(1) validate any rate, charge, agreement, or practice that violates a rule of law, statute, or regulation described in subsection (b); or

(2) extend the application of the rule of law, statute, or regulation to a transaction not otherwise subject to it.

Definitional Cross References:

Agreement	Section 1-201(b)(3)
Collateral	Section 9-102(a)(12)
Creditor	Section 1-201(b)(13)
Purchaser	Section 1-201(b)(30)
Sale	Section 2-106(1)
Security agreement	Section 9-102(a)(74)
Term	Section 1-201(b)(40)

Official Comment

1. Source. Former Sections 9-201, 9-203(4).

2. Effectiveness of Security Agreement. Subsection (a) provides that a security agreement is generally effective. With certain exceptions, a security agreement is effective between the debtor and secured party and is likewise effective against third parties. Note that "security agreement" is used here (and elsewhere in this Article) as it is defined in Section 9-102: "an agreement that creates or provides for a security interest." It follows that subsection (a) does not provide that every term or provision contained in a record that contains a security agreement or that is so labeled is effective. Properly read, former Section 9-201 was to the same effect. Exceptions to the general rule of subsection (a) arise where there is an overriding provision in this Article or any other Article of the UCC. For example, Section 9-317 subordinates unperfected security interests to lien creditors and certain buyers, and several provisions in Part 3 subordinate some security interests to other security interests and interests of purchasers.

3. Law, Statutes, and Regulations Applicable to Certain Transactions. Subsection (b) makes clear that certain transactions, although subject to this Article, also are subject to other applicable laws relating to consumers or specified in that subsection. Subsection (c) provides that the other law is controlling in the event of a conflict, and that a violation of other law does not *ipso facto* constitute a violation of this Article. Subsection (d) provides that this Article does not validate violations under or extend the application of the other applicable laws.

§ 9-202. Title to Collateral Immaterial.

Except as otherwise provided with respect to consignments or sales of accounts, chattel paper, payment intangibles, or promissory notes, the provisions of this article with regard to rights and obligations apply whether title to collateral is in the secured party or the debtor.

Definitional Cross References:

Account	Section 9-102(a)(2)
Chattel paper	Section 9-102(a)(11)
Collateral	Section 9-102(a)(12)
Consignment	Section 9-102(a)(20)
Debtor	Section 9-102(a)(28)
Payment intangible	Section 9-102(a)(61)
Promissory note	Section 9-102(a)(65)
Right	Section 1-201(b)(34)
Sale	Section 2-106(1)
Secured party	Section 9-102(a)(73)

Official Comment

1. Source. Former Section 9-202.

2. Title Immaterial. The rights and duties of parties to a secured transaction and affected third parties are provided in this Article without reference to the location of "title" to the collateral. For example, the characteristics of a security interest that secures the purchase price of goods are the same whether the secured party appears to have retained title or the debtor appears to have obtained title and then conveyed title or a lien to the secured party.

3. When Title Matters.

a. Under This Article. This section explicitly acknowledges two circumstances in which the effect of certain Article 9 provisions turns on ownership (title). First, in some respects sales of accounts, chattel paper, payment intangibles, and promissory notes receive special treatment. See, e.g., Sections 9-207(a), 9-210(b), 9-615(e). Buyers of receivables under former Article 9 were treated specially, as well. See, e.g., former Section 9-502(2). Second, the remedies of a consignor under a true consignment and, for the most part, the remedies of a buyer of accounts, chattel paper, payment intangibles, or promissory notes are determined by other law and not by Part 6. See Section 9-601(g).

b. Under Other Law. This Article does not determine which line of interpretation (e.g., title theory or lien theory, retained title or conveyed title) should be followed in cases in which the applicability of another rule of law depends upon who has title. If, for example, a revenue law imposes a tax on the "legal" owner of goods or if a corporation law makes a vote of the stockholders prerequisite to a corporation "giving" a security interest but not if it acquires property "subject" to a security interest, this Article does not attempt to define whether the secured party is a "legal" owner or whether the transaction "gives" a security interest for the purpose of such laws. Other rules of law or the agreement of the parties determines the location and source of title for those purposes.

§ 9-203. Attachment and Enforceability of Security Interest; Proceeds; Supporting Obligations; Formal Requisites.

(a) [Attachment.] A security interest attaches to collateral when it becomes enforceable against the debtor with respect to the collateral, unless an agreement expressly postpones the time of attachment.

(b) [Enforceability.] Except as otherwise provided in subsections (c) through (i), a security interest is enforceable against the debtor and third parties with respect to the collateral only if:

(1) value has been given;

(2) the debtor has rights in the collateral or the power to transfer rights in the collateral to a secured party; and

(3) one of the following conditions is met:

(A) the debtor has signed a security agreement that provides a description of the collateral and, if the security interest covers timber to be cut, a description of the land concerned;

(B) the collateral is not a certificated security and is in the possession of the secured party under Section 9-313 pursuant to the debtor's security agreement;

(C) the collateral is a certificated security in registered form and the security certificate has been delivered to the secured party under Section 8-301 pursuant to the debtor's security agreement;

(D) the collateral is controllable accounts, controllable electronic records, controllable payment intangibles, deposit accounts, electronic documents, electronic money, investment property, or letter-of-credit rights, and the secured party has control under Sections 7-106, 9-104, 9-105A, 9-106, 9-107, or 9-107A pursuant to the debtor's security agreement.

(E) the collateral is chattel paper and the secured party has possession and control under Section 9-314A pursuant to the debtor's security agreement.

(c) [Other UCC provisions.] Subsection (b) is subject to Section 4-210 on the security interest of a collecting bank, Section 5-118 on the security interest of a letter-of-credit issuer or nominated person, Section 9-110 on a security interest arising under Article 2 or 2A, and Section 9-206 on security interests in investment property.

(d) [When person becomes bound by another person's security agreement.] A person becomes bound as debtor by a security agreement entered into by another person if, by operation of law other than this article or by contract:

(1) the security agreement becomes effective to create a security interest in the person's property; or

(2) the person becomes generally obligated for the obligations of the other person, including the obligation secured under the security agreement, and acquires or succeeds to all or substantially all of the assets of the other person.

(e) [Effect of new debtor becoming bound.] If a new debtor becomes bound as debtor by a security agreement entered into by another person:

(1) the agreement satisfies subsection (b)(3) with respect to existing or after-acquired

property of the new debtor to the extent the property is described in the agreement; and

(2) another agreement is not necessary to make a security interest in the property enforceable.

(f) [Proceeds and supporting obligations.] The attachment of a security interest in collateral gives the secured party the rights to proceeds provided by Section 9-315 and is also attachment of a security interest in a supporting obligation for the collateral.

(g) [Lien securing right to payment.] The attachment of a security interest in a right to payment or performance secured by a security interest or other lien on personal or real property is also attachment of a security interest in the security interest, mortgage, or other lien.

(h) [Security entitlement carried in securities account.] The attachment of a security interest in a securities account is also attachment of a security interest in the security entitlements carried in the securities account.

(i) [Commodity contracts carried in commodity account.] The attachment of a security interest in a commodity account is also attachment of a security interest in the commodity contracts carried in the commodity account.

Definitional Cross References:

Agreement	Section 1-201(b)(3)
Bank	Section 9-102(a)(8)
Certificated security	Section 8-102(a)(4)
Chattel paper	Section 9-102(a)(11)
Collateral	Section 9-102(a)(12)
Commodity account	Section 9-102(a)(14)
Commodity contract	Section 9-102(a)(15)
Contract	Section 1-201(b)(12)
Controllable account	Section 9-102(a)(27A)
Controllable electronic record	Section 12-102(a)(1)
Controllable payment intangible	Section 9-102(a)(27B)
Debtor	Section 9-102(a)(28)
Deposit account	Section 9-102(a)(29)
Document	Section 9-102(a)(30)
Electronic	Section 1-201(b)(16A)
Electronic money	Section 9-102(a)(31A)
Investment property	Section 9-102(a)(49)
Issuer (letter of credit/ letter-of-credit right)	Section 5-102(a)(9)
Letter-of-credit right	Section 9-102(a)(51)
Money	Section 9-102(a)(54A)
Mortgage	Section 9-102(a)(55)
New debtor	Section 9-102(a)(56)
Nominated person	Section 5-102(a)(11)
Proceeds	Section 9-102(a)(64)
Right	Section 1-201(b)(34)
Secured party	Section 9-102(a)(73)
Securities account	Section 8-501(a)
Security agreement	Section 9-102(a)(74)
Security certificate	Section 8-102(a)(16)
Security entitlement	Section 8-102(a)(17)
Security interest	Section 1-201(b)(35)
Sign	Section 1-201(b)(37)
Supporting obligation	Section 9-102(a)(78)
Value	Section 1-204

Comment References:

9-107 C5
9-108 C5
9-206 C4
9-322 C6

Official Comment

1. Source. Former Sections 9-203, 9-115(2), (6).

2. Creation, Attachment, and Enforceability. Subsection (a) states the general rule that a security interest attaches to collateral only when it becomes enforceable against the debtor. Subsection (b) specifies the circumstances under which a security interest becomes enforceable. Subsection (b) states three basic prerequisites to the existence of a security interest: value (paragraph (1)), rights or power to transfer rights in collateral (paragraph (2)), and agreement plus satisfaction of an evidentiary requirement (paragraph (3)). When all of these elements exist, a security interest becomes enforceable between the parties and attaches under subsection (a). Subsection (c) identifies certain exceptions to the general rule of subsection (b).

3. Security Agreement; Signed. Under subsection (b)(3), enforceability requires the debtor's security agreement and compliance with an evidentiary requirement in the nature of a Statute of Frauds. Paragraph (3)(A) represents the most basic of the evidentiary alternatives, under which the debtor must sign a security agreement that provides a description of the collateral. Under Section 9-102, a "security agreement" is "an agreement that creates or provides for a security interest." Neither that definition nor the requirement of paragraph (3)(A) rejects the deeply rooted doctrine that a bill of sale, although absolute in form, may be shown in fact to have been given as security. Under this Article, as under prior law, a debtor may show by parol evidence that a transfer purporting to be absolute was in fact for security. Similarly, a self-styled "lease" may serve as a security agreement if the agreement creates a security interest. See Section 1-203 (distinguishing security interest from lease). Consistent with the revised definition of "sign" in Section 1-201, the cognate terms "signed" and "signing" replace the references to "authenticated" and "authentication" in the pre-2022 text of this Section.

4. Possession, Delivery, or Control Pursuant to Security Agreement. The other alternatives in subsection (b)(3) dispense with the requirement of a signed security agreement and provide alternative evidentiary tests. Under paragraph (3)(B), the secured party's possession substitutes for the debtor's signed security agreement under paragraph (3)(A) if the secured party's possession is "pursuant to the debtor's security agreement." That phrase refers to the debtor's agreement to the secured party's possession in connection with the creation of a security interest. The phrase should not be confused with the phrase "debtor has signed a security agreement," used in paragraph (3)(A), which contemplates the debtor's signing of a record. In the unlikely event that possession is obtained without the debtor's agreement, possession would not suffice as a substitute for a signed security agreement. However, once the security interest has become enforceable and has attached, it is not impaired by the fact that the secured party's possession is maintained without the agreement of a subsequent debtor (e.g., a transferee). Possession as contemplated by Section 9-313 is possession for purposes of subsection (b)(3)(B), even though it may not constitute possession "pursuant to the debtor's agreement" and consequently might not serve as a substitute for a signed security agreement under subsection (b)(3)(A). Subsection (b)(3)(C) provides that delivery of a certificated security to the secured party under Section 8-301 pursuant to the debtor's security agreement is sufficient as a substitute for a signed security agreement. Similarly, under subsection (b)(3)(D), control of controllable accounts, controllable electronic records, controllable payment intangibles, deposit accounts, electronic documents, electronic money, investment property, or letter-of-credit rights satisfies the evidentiary test if control is pursuant to the debtor's security agreement, and under subsection (b)(3)(E), possession and control of chattel paper under Section 9-314A satisfies the evidentiary test if pursuant to the debtor's security agreement.

5. Collateral Covered by Other Statute or Treaty. One evidentiary purpose of the formal requisites stated in subsection (b) is to minimize the possibility of future disputes as to the terms of a security agreement (e.g., as to the property that stands as collateral for the obligation secured). One should distinguish the evidentiary functions of the formal requisites of attachment and enforceability (such as the requirement that a security agreement contain a description of the collateral) from the more limited goals of "notice filing" for financing statements under Part 5, explained in Section 9-502, Comment 2. When perfection is achieved by compliance with the requirements of a statute or treaty described in Section 9-311(a), such as a federal recording act or a certificate-of-title statute, the manner of describing the collateral in a registry imposed by the statute or treaty may or may not be adequate for purposes of this section and Section 9-108. However, the description contained in the security agreement, not the description in a public registry or on a certificate of title, controls for purposes of this section.

6. Debtor's Rights; Debtor's Power to Transfer Rights. Subsection (b)(2) conditions attachment on the debtor's having "rights in the collateral or the power to transfer rights in the collateral to a secured party." A debtor's limited rights in collateral, short of full ownership, are sufficient for a security interest to attach. However, in accordance with basic personal property conveyancing principles, the baseline rule is that a security interest attaches only to whatever rights a debtor may have, broad or limited as those rights may be.

Certain exceptions to the baseline rule enable a debtor to transfer, and a security interest to attach to, greater rights than the debtor has. See Part 3, Subpart 3 (priority rules). The phrase, "or the power to transfer rights in the collateral to a secured party," accommodates those exceptions. In some cases, a debtor may have power to transfer another person's rights only to a class of transferees that excludes secured parties. See, e.g., Section 2-403(2) (giving certain merchants power to transfer an entruster's rights to a buyer in ordinary course of business). Under those circumstances, the debtor would not have the power to create a security interest in the other person's rights, and the condition in subsection (b)(2) would not be satisfied.

7. New Debtors. Subsection (e) makes clear that the enforceability requirements of subsection (b)(3) are met when a new debtor becomes bound under an original debtor's security agreement. If a new debtor becomes bound as debtor by a security agreement entered into by another person, the security agreement satisfies the requirement of subsection (b)(3) as to the existing and after-acquired property of the new debtor to the extent the property is described in the agreement.

Subsection (d) explains when a new debtor becomes bound. Persons who become bound under paragraph (2) are limited to those who both become primarily liable for the original debtor's obligations and succeed to (or acquire) its assets. Thus, the paragraph excludes sureties and other secondary obligors as well as persons who become obligated through veil piercing and other non-successorship doctrines. In many cases, paragraph (2) will exclude successors to the assets and liabilities of a division of a debtor. See also Section 9-508, Comment 3.

8. Proceeds and Supporting Obligations. Under subsection (f), attachment of a security interest in original collateral also is attachment of a security interest in identifiable proceeds as provided in Section 9-315(a)(2). It is not necessary for a security agreement to mention "proceeds" or otherwise to describe collateral consisting of proceeds. See also Section 9-108, Comment 5. Also under subsection (f), a security interest in a "supporting obligation" (defined in Section 9-102) automatically follows from a security interest in the underlying, supported collateral. This result was implicit under pre-1998 Article 9. Implicit in subsection (f) is the principle that the secured party's interest in a supporting obligation extends to the supporting obligation only to the extent that it supports the collateral in which the secured party has a security interest. Complex issues may arise, however, if a supporting obligation supports many separate obligations of a particular account debtor and if the supported obligations are separately assigned as security to several secured parties. The problems may be exacerbated if a supporting obligation is limited to an aggregate amount that is less than the aggregate amount of the obligations it supports. This Article does not contain provisions dealing with competing claims to a limited supporting obligation. As under pre-1998 Article 9, the law of suretyship and the agreements of the parties will control.

9. Collateral Follows Right to Payment or Performance. Subsection (g) codifies the common-law rule that a transfer of an obligation secured by a security interest or other lien on personal or real property also transfers the security interest or lien. See Restatement (3d), Property (Mortgages) rule that a transfer of an obligation secured by a security interest or other lien on personal or real property also transfers the security interest or lien. See Restatement (3d), Property (Mortgages) § 5.4(a) (1997). See also Section 9-308(e) (analogous rule for perfection).

10. Investment Property. Subsections (h) and (i) make clear that attachment of a security interest in a securities account or commodity account is also attachment in security entitlements or commodity contracts carried in the accounts.

§ 9-204. After-Acquired Property; Future Advances.

(a) [After-Acquired Collateral.] Except as otherwise provided in subsection (b), a security agreement may create or provide for a security interest in after-acquired collateral.

(b) [When after-acquired property clause not effective.] Subject to subsection (b.1), a security interest does not attach under a term constituting an after-acquired property clause to:

(1) consumer goods, other than an accession when given as additional security, unless the debtor acquires rights in them within 10 days after the secured party gives value; or

(2) a commercial tort claim.

(b.1) [Limitation on subsection (b).] Subsection (b) does not prevent a security interest from attaching:

(1) to consumer goods as proceeds under Section 9-315(a) or commingled goods under Section 9-336(c);

(2) to a commercial tort claim as proceeds under Section 9-315(a); or

(3) under an after-acquired property clause to property that is proceeds of consumer goods or a commercial tort claim.

(c) [Future advances and other value.] A security agreement may provide that collateral secures, or that accounts, chattel paper, payment intangibles, or promissory notes are sold in connection with, future advances or other value, whether or not the advances or value are given pursuant to commitment.

Definitional Cross References:

Accession	Section 9-102(a)(1)
Account	Section 9-102(a)(2)
Chattel paper	Section 9-102(a)(11)
Collateral	Section 9-102(a)(12)
Commercial tort claim	Section 9-102(a)(13)
Consumer goods	Section 9-102(a)(23)
Debtor	Section 9-102(a)(28)
Goods	Section 9-102(a)(44)
Payment intangible	Section 9-102(a)(61)
Proceeds	Section 9-102(a)(64)
Promissory note	Section 9-102(a)(65)
Pursuant to commitment	Section 9-102(a)(69)
Right	Section 1-201(b)(34)
Secured party	Section 9-102(a)(73)
Security agreement	Section 9-102(a)(74)
Security interest	Section 1-201(b)(35)
Term	Section 1-201(b)(40)
Value	Section 1-204

Comment References:
9-108 C5
9-109 C15

Official Comment

1. Source. Former Section 9-204.

2. After-Acquired Property; Continuing General Lien. Subsection (a) makes clear that a security interest arising by virtue of an after-acquired property clause is no less valid than a security interest in collateral in which the debtor has rights at the time value is given. A security interest in after-acquired property is not merely an "equitable" interest; no further action by the secured party—such as a supplemental agreement covering the new collateral—is required. This section adopts the principle of a "continuing general lien" or "floating lien." It validates a security interest in the debtor's existing and (upon acquisition) future assets, even though the debtor has liberty to use or dispose of collateral without being required to account for proceeds or substitute new collateral. See Section 9-205. Subsection (a), together with subsection (c), also validates "cross-collateral" clauses under which collateral acquired at any time secures advances whenever made.

3. After-Acquired Consumer Goods. Subsection (b)(1) makes ineffective an after-acquired property clause covering consumer goods (defined in Section 9-102(a)(23)), except as accessions (see Section 9-335), acquired more than 10 days after the secured party gives value. Subsection (b)(1) is unchanged in substance from the corresponding provision in pre-1998 Section 9-204(2). However, a term granting a security interest in consumer goods that will be purchase-money collateral in the transaction is not "a term constituting an after-acquired property clause." Consequently, subsection (b)(1) does not prevent the security interest from attaching to the purchase-money collateral even if the collateral is not an accession and the debtor acquires rights in the collateral more than 10 days after the secured party gives value.

4. Commercial Tort Claims. Subsection (b)(2) provides that an after-acquired property clause in a security agreement does not reach future commercial tort claims. In order for a security interest in a tort claim as original collateral to attach, the claim must be in existence when the security agreement is signed. In addition, the security agreement must describe the tort claim with greater specificity than simply "all tort claims." See Section 9-108(e).

4A. Proceeds and Commingled Goods. Subsection (b.1) clarifies and makes explicit what is implicit in the pre-2022 text of subsection (b). Subsection (b) does not prevent a security interest from attaching to consumer goods as proceeds or as commingled goods, to commercial tort claims as proceeds, or under an after-acquired property clause to proceeds of consumer goods or commercial tort claims. This clarification corrects and rejects the erroneous holdings of several cases addressing commercial tort claims that are proceeds. As to proceeds, this result also follows from Section 9-203(f).

5. Future Advances; Obligations Secured. Under subsection (c) collateral may secure future as well as past or present advances if the security agreement so provides. This is in line with the policy of this Article toward security interests in after-acquired property under subsection (a). Indeed, the parties are free to agree that a security interest secures any obligation whatsoever. Determining the obligations secured by collateral is solely a matter of construing the parties' agreement under applicable law. This Article rejects the holdings of cases decided under former Article 9 that applied other tests, such as whether a future advance or other subsequently incurred obligation was of the same or a similar type or class as earlier advances and obligations secured by the collateral.

6. Sales of Receivables. Subsections (a) and (c) expressly validate after-acquired property and future advance clauses not only when the transaction is for security purposes but also when the transaction is the sale of accounts, chattel paper, payment intangibles, or promissory notes. This result was implicit under former Article 9.

7. Financing Statements. The effect of after-acquired property and future advance clauses as components of a security agreement should not be confused with the requirements applicable to financing statements under this Article's system of perfection by notice filing. The references to after-acquired property clauses and future advance clauses in this section are limited to security agreements. There is no need to refer to after-acquired property or future advances or other obligations secured in a financing statement. See Section 9-502, Comment 2.

§ 9-205. Use or Disposition of Collateral Permissible.

(a) [When security interest not invalid or fraudulent.] A security interest is not invalid or fraudulent against creditors solely because:

(1) the debtor has the right or ability to:

(A) use, commingle, or dispose of all or part of the collateral, including returned or repossessed goods;

(B) collect, compromise, enforce, or otherwise deal with collateral;

(C) accept the return of collateral or make repossessions; or

(D) use, commingle, or dispose of proceeds; or

(2) the secured party fails to require the debtor to account for proceeds or replace collateral.

(b) [Requirements of possession not relaxed.] This section does not relax the requirements of possession if attachment, perfection, or enforcement of a security interest depends upon possession of the collateral by the secured party.

Definitional Cross References:

Collateral	Section 9-102(a)(12)
Creditor	Section 1-201(b)(12)
Debtor	Section 9-102(a)(28)
Goods	Section 9-102(a)(44)
Proceeds	Section 9-102(a)(64)
Security interest	Section 1-201(b)(35)
Secured party	Section 9-102(a)(73)
Security agreement	Section 9-102(a)(74)

Official Comment

1. Source. Former Section 9-205.

2. Validity of Unrestricted "Floating Lien." This Article expressly validates the "floating lien" on shifting collateral. See Sections 9-201, 9-204 and Comment 2. This section provides that a security interest is not invalid or fraudulent by reason of the debtor's liberty to dispose of the collateral without being required to account to the secured party for proceeds or substitute new collateral. As did former Section 9-205, this section repeals the rule of *Benedict v. Ratner,* 268 U.S. 353 (1925), and other cases which held such arrangements void as a matter of law because the debtor was given unfettered dominion or control over collateral. The *Benedict* rule did not effectively discourage or eliminate security transactions in inventory and receivables. Instead, it forced financing arrangements to be self-liquidating. Although this section repeals *Benedict,* the filing and other perfection requirements (see Part 3, Subpart 2, and Part 5) provide for public notice that overcomes any potential misleading effects of a debtor's use and control of collateral. Moreover, nothing in this section prevents the debtor and secured party from agreeing to procedures by which the secured party polices or monitors collateral or to restrictions on the debtor's dominion. However, this Article leaves these matters to agreement based on business considerations, not on legal requirements.

3. Possessory Security Interests. Subsection (b) makes clear that this section does not relax the requirements for perfection by possession under Section 9-313. If a secured party allows the debtor access to and control over collateral its security interest may be or become unperfected.

4. Permissible Freedom for Debtor to Enforce Collateral. Former Section 9-205 referred to a debtor's "liberty . . . to collect or compromise accounts or chattel paper." This section recognizes the broader rights of a debtor to "enforce," as well as to "collect" and "compromise" collateral. This section's reference to collecting, compromising, and enforcing "collateral" instead of "accounts or chattel paper" contemplates the many other types of collateral that a debtor may wish to "collect, compromise, or enforce": e.g., deposit accounts, documents, general intangibles, instruments, investment property, and letter-of-credit rights.

§ 9-206. Security Interest Arising in Purchase or Delivery of Financial Asset.

(a) [Security interest when person buys through securities intermediary.] A security interest in favor of a securities intermediary attaches to a person's security entitlement if:

(1) the person buys a financial asset through the securities intermediary in a transaction in which the person is obligated to pay the purchase price to the securities intermediary at the time of the purchase; and

(2) the securities intermediary credits the financial asset to the buyer's securities account before the buyer pays the securities intermediary.

(b) [Security interest secures obligation to pay for financial asset.] The security interest described in subsection (a) secures the person's obligation to pay for the financial asset.

(c) [Security interest in payment against delivery transaction.] A security interest in favor of a person that delivers a certificated security or other financial asset represented by a writing attaches to the security or other financial asset if:

(1) the security or other financial asset:

(A) in the ordinary course of business is transferred by delivery with any necessary indorsement or assignment; and

(B) is delivered under an agreement between persons in the business of dealing with such securities or financial assets; and

(2) the agreement calls for delivery against payment.

(d) [Security interest secures obligation to pay for delivery.] The security interest described in subsection (c) secures the obligation to make payment for the delivery.

Definitional Cross References:

Agreement	Section 1-201(b)(3)
Certificated security	Section 8-102(a)(4)
Delivery	Section 1-201(b)(15)
Financial asset	Section 8-102(a)(9)
Purchase	Section 1-201(b)(29)
Securities account	Section 8-501(a)
Securities intermediary	Section 8-102(a)(14)
Security entitlement	Section 8-102(a)(17)
Security interest	Section 1-201(b)(35)
Security	Section 8-102(a)(15)
Writing	Section 1-201(b)(43)

Official Comment

1. Source. Former 9-116.

2. Codification of "Broker's Lien." Depending upon a securities intermediary's arrangements with its entitlement holders, the securities intermediary may treat the entitlement holder as entitled to financial assets before the entitlement holder has actually made payment for them. For example, many brokers permit retail customers to pay for financial assets by check.

The broker may not receive final payment of the check until several days after the broker has credited the customer's securities account for the financial assets. Thus, the customer will have acquired a security entitlement prior to payment. Subsection (a) provides that, in such circumstances, the securities intermediary has a security interest in the entitlement holder's security entitlement. Under subsection (b) the security interest secures the customer's obligation to pay for the financial asset in question. Subsections (a) and (b) codify and adapt to the indirect holding system the so-called "broker's lien," which has long been recognized. See Restatement, Security § 12.

3. Financial Assets Delivered Against Payment. Subsection (c) creates a security interest in favor of persons who deliver certificated securities or other financial assets in physical form, such as money market instruments, if the agreed payment is not received. In some arrangements for settlement of transactions in physical financial assets, the seller's securities custodian will deliver physical certificates to the buyer's securities custodian and receive a time-stamped delivery receipt. The buyer's securities custodian will examine the certificate to ensure that it is in good order, and that the delivery matches a trade in which the buyer has instructed the seller to deliver to that custodian. If all is in order, the receiving custodian will settle with the delivering custodian through whatever funds settlement system has been agreed upon or is used by custom and usage in that market. The understanding of the trade, however, is that the delivery is conditioned upon payment, so that if payment is not made for any reason, the security will be returned to the deliverer. Subsection (c) clarifies the rights of persons making deliveries in such circumstances. It provides the person making delivery with a security interest in the securities or other financial assets; under subsection (d), the security interest secures the seller's right to receive payment for the delivery. Section 8-301 specifies when delivery of a certificated security occurs; that section should be applied as well to other financial assets as well for purposes of this section.

4. Automatic Attachment and Perfection. Subsections (a) and (c) refer to attachment of a security interest. Attachment under this section has the same incidents (enforceability, right to proceeds, etc.) as attachment under Section 9-203. This section overrides the general attachment rules in Section 9-203. See Section 9-203(c). A securities intermediary's security interest under subsection (a) is perfected by control without further action. See Section 8-106 (control); 9-314 (perfection). Security interests arising under subsection (b) are automatically perfected. See Section 9-309(9).

[Subpart 2. Rights and Duties]

§ 9-207. Rights and Duties of Secured Party Having Possession or Control of Collateral.

(a) [Duty of care when secured party in possession.] Except as otherwise provided in subsection (d), a secured party shall use reasonable care in the custody and preservation of collateral in the secured party's possession. In the case of chattel paper or an instrument, reasonable care includes taking necessary steps to preserve rights against prior parties unless otherwise agreed.

(b) [Expenses, risks, duties, and rights when secured party in possession.] Except as otherwise provided in subsection (d), if a secured party has possession of collateral:

(1) reasonable expenses, including the cost of insurance and payment of taxes or other charges, incurred in the custody, preservation, use, or operation of the collateral are chargeable to the debtor and are secured by the collateral;

(2) the risk of accidental loss or damage is on the debtor to the extent of a deficiency in any effective insurance coverage;

(3) the secured party shall keep the collateral identifiable, but fungible collateral may be commingled; and

(4) the secured party may use or operate the collateral:

(A) for the purpose of preserving the collateral or its value;

(B) as permitted by an order of a court having competent jurisdiction; or

(C) except in the case of consumer goods, in the manner and to the extent agreed by the debtor.

(c) [Duties and rights when secured party in possession or control.] Except as otherwise provided in subsection (d), a secured party having possession of collateral or control of collateral under Sections 7-106, 9-104, 9-105, 9-105A, 9-106, 9-107, or 9-107A:

(1) may hold as additional security any proceeds, except money or funds, received from the collateral;

(2) shall apply money or funds received from the collateral to reduce the secured obligation, unless remitted to the debtor; and

(3) may create a security interest in the collateral.

(d) [Buyer of certain rights to payment.] If the secured party is a buyer of accounts, chattel paper, payment intangibles, or promissory notes or a consignor:

(1) subsection (a) does not apply unless the secured party is entitled under an agreement:

(A) to charge back uncollected collateral; or

(B) otherwise to full or limited recourse against the debtor or a secondary obligor based on the nonpayment or other default of an account debtor or other obligor on the collateral; and

(2) subsections (b) and (c) do not apply.

Definitional Cross References:

Account	Section 9-102(a)(2)
Account debtor	Section 9-102(a)(3)
Agreement	Section 1-201(b)(3)
Chattel paper	Section 9-102(a)(11)
Collateral	Section 9-102(a)(12)
Consignor	Section 9-102(a)(21)
Consumer goods	Section 9-102(a)(23)
Debtor	Section 9-102(a)(28)
Fungible goods	Section 1-201(b)(18)
Instrument	Section 9-102(a)(47)
Money	Section 1-201(b)(24)
Obligor	Section 9-102(a)(59)
Payment intangible	Section 9-102(a)(61)
Proceeds	Section 9-102(a)(64)
Promissory note	Section 9-102(a)(65)
Right	Section 1-201(b)(34)
Secondary obligor	Section 9-102(a)(72)
Secured party	Section 9-102(a)(73)
Security interest	Section 1-201(b)(35)
Security	Section 8-102(a)(15)
Value	Section 1-204

Comment References: 9-208 C4

Official Comment

1. Source. Former Section 9-207.

2. Duty of Care for Collateral in Secured Party's Possession. Like former section 9-207, subsection (a) imposes a duty of care, similar to that imposed on a pledgee at common law, on a secured party in possession of collateral. See Restatement, Security §§ 17, 18. In many cases a secured party in possession of collateral may satisfy this duty by notifying the debtor of action that should be taken and allowing the debtor to take the action itself. If the secured party itself takes action, its reasonable expenses may be added to the secured obligation. The revised definitions of "collateral," "debtor," and "secured party" in Section 9-102 make this section applicable to collateral subject to an agricultural lien if the collateral is in the lienholder's possession. Under Section 1-302 the duty to exercise reasonable care may not be disclaimed by agreement, although under that section the parties remain free to determine by agreement standards that are not manifestly unreasonable as to what constitutes reasonable care. Unless otherwise agreed, for a secured party in possession of chattel paper or an instrument, reasonable care includes the preservation of rights against prior parties. The secured party's right to have instruments or documents indorsed or transferred to it or its order is dealt with in the relevant sections of Articles 3, 7, and 8. See Sections 3-203(c), 7-506, 8-304(d).

3. Specific Rules When Secured Party in Possession or Control of Collateral. Subsections (b) and (c) provide rules following common-law precedents which apply unless the parties otherwise agree. The rules in subsection (b) apply to typical issues that may arise while a secured party is in possession of collateral, including expenses, insurance, and taxes, risk of loss or damage, identifiable and fungible collateral, and use or operation of collateral. Subsection (c) contains rules that apply in certain circumstances that may arise when a secured party is in either possession or control of collateral. These circumstances include the secured party's receiving proceeds from the collateral and the secured party's creation of a security interest in the collateral.

4. Applicability Following Default. This section applies when the secured party has possession of collateral either before or after default. See Sections 9-601(b), 9-609. Subsection (b)(4)(C) limits agreements concerning the use or operation of collateral to collateral other than consumer goods. Under Section 9-602(1), a debtor cannot waive or vary that limitation.

5. "Repledges" and Right of Redemption. Subsection (c)(3) eliminates the qualification in former Section 9-207 to the effect that the terms of a "repledge" may not "impair" a debtor's "right to redeem" collateral. The change is primarily for clarification. There is no basis on which to draw from subsection (c)(3) any inference concerning the debtor's right to redeem the collateral. The debtor enjoys that right under Section 9-623; this section need not address it. For example, if the collateral is a negotiable note that the secured party (SP-1) repledges to SP-2, nothing in this section suggests that the debtor (D) does not retain the right to redeem the note upon payment to SP-1 of all obligations secured by the note. But, as explained below, the debtor's unimpaired right to redeem as against the debtor's original secured party nevertheless may not be enforceable as against the new secured party.

In resolving questions that arise from the creation of a security interest by SP-1, one must take care to distinguish D's rights against SP-1 from D's rights against SP-2. Once D discharges the secured obligation,

D becomes entitled to the note; SP-1 has no legal basis upon which to withhold it. If, as a practical matter, SP-1 is unable to return the note because SP-2 holds it as collateral for SP-1's unpaid debt, then SP-1 is liable to D under the law of conversion.

Whether SP-2 would be liable to D depends on the relative priority of SP-2's security interest and D's interest. By permitting SP-1 to create a security interest in the collateral (repledge), subsection (c)(3) provides a statutory power for SP-1 to give SP-2 a security interest (subject, of course, to any agreement by SP-1 not to give a security interest). In the vast majority of cases where repledge rights are significant, the security interest of the second secured party, SP-2 in the example, will be senior to the debtor's interest. By virtue of the debtor's consent or applicable legal rules, SP-2 typically would cut off D's rights in investment property or be immune from D's claims. See Sections 9-331, 3-306 (holder in due course), 8-303 (protected purchaser), 8-502 (acquisition of a security entitlement), 8-503(e) (action by entitlement holder). Moreover, the expectations and business practices in some markets, such as the securities markets, are such that D's consent to SP-2's taking free of D's rights inheres in D's creation of SP-1's security interest which gives rise to SP-1's power under this section. In these situations, D would have no right to recover the collateral or recover damages from SP-2. Nevertheless, D would have a damage claim against SP-1 if SP-1 had given a security interest to SP-2 in breach of its agreement with D. Moreover, if SP-2's security interest secures an amount that is less than the amount secured by SP-1's security interest (granted by D), then D's exercise of its right to redeem would provide value sufficient to discharge SP-1's obligations to SP-2.

For the most part this section does not change the law under former Section 9-207, although eliminating the reference to the debtor's right of redemption may alter the secured party's right to repledge in one respect. Former Section 9-207 could have been read to limit the secured party's statutory right to repledge collateral to repledge transactions in which the collateral did not secure a greater obligation than that of the original debtor. Inasmuch as this is a matter normally dealt with by agreement between the debtor and secured party, any change would appear to have little practical effect.

6. "Repledges" of Investment Property. The following example will aid the discussion of "repledges" of investment property.

> **Example:** Debtor grants Alpha Bank a security interest in a security entitlement that includes 1000 shares of XYZ Co. stock that Debtor holds through an account with Able & Co. Alpha does not have an account with Able. Alpha uses Beta Bank as its securities custodian. Debtor instructs Able to transfer the shares to Beta, for the account of Alpha, and Able does so. Beta then credits Alpha's account. Alpha has control of the security entitlement for the 1000 shares under Section 8-106(d). (These are the facts of Example 2, Section 8-106, Comment 4.) Although, as between Debtor and Alpha, Debtor may have become the beneficial owner of the new securities entitlement with Beta, Beta has agreed to act on Alpha's entitlement orders because, as between Beta and Alpha, Alpha has become the entitlement holder.
>
> Next, Alpha grants Gamma Bank a security interest in the security entitlement with Beta that includes the 1000 shares of XYZ Co. stock. In order to afford Gamma control of the entitlement, Alpha instructs Beta to transfer the stock to Gamma's custodian, Delta Bank, which credits Gamma's account for 1000 shares. At this point Gamma holds its securities entitlement for its benefit as well as that of its debtor, Alpha. Alpha's derivative rights also are for the benefit of Debtor.

In many, probably most, situations and at any particular point in time, it will be impossible for Debtor or Alpha to "trace" Alpha's "repledge" to any particular securities entitlement or financial asset of Gamma or anyone else. Debtor would retain, of course, a right to redeem the collateral from Alpha upon satisfaction of the secured obligation. However, in the absence of a traceable interest, Debtor would retain only a personal claim against Alpha in the event Alpha failed to restore the security entitlement to Debtor. Moreover, even in the unlikely event that Debtor could trace a property interest, in the context of the financial markets, normally the operation of this section, Debtor's explicit agreement to permit Alpha to create a senior security interest, or legal rules permitting Gamma to cut off Debtor's rights or become immune from Debtor's claims would effectively subordinate Debtor's interest to the holder of a security interest created by Alpha. And, under the shelter principle, all subsequent transferees would obtain interests to which Debtor's interest also would be subordinate.

7. Buyers of Chattel Paper and Other Receivables; Consignors. This section has been revised to reflect the fact that a seller of accounts, chattel paper, payment intangibles, or promissory notes retains no interest in the collateral and so is not disadvantaged by the secured party's noncompliance with the requirements of this section. Accordingly, subsection (d) provides that subsection (a) applies only to security interests that secure an obligation and to sales of receivables in which the buyer has recourse against the debtor. (Of course, a buyer of accounts or payment intangibles could not have "possession" of original collateral, but might have possession of proceeds, such as promissory notes or checks.) The meaning of "recourse" in this respect is limited to recourse arising out of the account debtor's failure to pay or other default.

Subsection (d) makes subsections (b) and (c) inapplicable to buyers of accounts, chattel paper, payment intangibles, or promissory notes and consignors. Of course, there is no reason to believe that a buyer of receivables or a consignor could not, for example, create a security interest or otherwise transfer an interest in the collateral, regardless of who has possession of the collateral. However, this section leaves the rights of those owners to law other than Article 9.

§ 9-208. Additional Duties of Secured Party Having Control of Collateral.

(a) [Applicability of section.] This section applies to cases in which there is no outstanding secured obligation and the secured party is not committed to make advances, incur obligations, or otherwise give value.

(b) [Duties of secured party after receiving demand from debtor.] Within 10 days after receiving a signed demand by the debtor:

(1) a secured party having control of a deposit account under Section 9-104(a)(2) shall send to the bank with which the deposit account is maintained a signed record that releases the bank from any further obligation to comply with instructions originated by the secured party;

(2) a secured party having control of a deposit account under Section 9-104(a)(3) shall:

(A) pay the debtor the balance on deposit in the deposit account; or

(B) transfer the balance on deposit into a deposit account in the debtor's name;

(3) a secured party, other than a buyer, having control under Section 9-105 of an authoritative electronic copy of a record evidencing chattel paper shall transfer control of the electronic copy to the debtor or a person designated by the debtor;

(4) a secured party having control of investment property under Section 8-106(d)(2) or 9-106(b) shall send to the securities intermediary or commodity intermediary with which the security entitlement or commodity contract is maintained a signed record that releases the securities intermediary or commodity intermediary from any further obligation to comply with entitlement orders or directions originated by the secured party;

(5) a secured party having control of a letter-of-credit right under Section 9-107 shall send to each person having an unfulfilled obligation to pay or deliver proceeds of the letter of credit to the secured party a signed release from any further obligation to pay or deliver proceeds of the letter of credit to the secured party;

(6) a secured party having control under Section 7-106 of an authoritative electronic copy of an electronic document shall transfer control of the electronic copy to the debtor or a person designated by the debtor;

(7) a secured party having control under Section 9-105A of electronic money shall transfer control of the electronic money to the debtor or a person designated by the debtor; and

(8) a secured party having control under Section 12-105 of a controllable electronic record, other than a buyer of a controllable account or controllable payment intangible evidenced by the controllable electronic record, shall transfer control of the controllable electronic record to the debtor or a person designated by the debtor.

Definitional Cross References:

Action	Section 1-201(b)(1)
Bank	Section 9-102(a)(8)
Chattel paper	Section 9-102(a)(11)
Collateral	Section 9-102(a)(12)
Commodity contract	Section 9-102(a)(15)
Commodity intermediary	Section 9-102(a)(17)
Communicate	Section 9-102(a)(18)
Controllable account	Section 9-102(a)(27A)
Controllable electronic record	Section 12-102(a)(1)
Controllable payment intangible	Section 9-102(a)(27B)
Debtor	Section 9-102(a)(28)
Deposit account	Section 9-102(a)(29)
Document	Section 9-102(a)(30)
Electronic	Section 1-201(b)(16A)
Electronic money	Section 9-102(a)(31A)
Investment property	Section 9-102(a)(49)
Letter of credit	Section 5-102(a)(10)
Letter-of-credit right	Section 9-102(a)(51)
Person	Section 1-201(b)(27)
Proceeds	Section 9-102(a)(64)
Record	Section 9-102(a)(70)
Secured party	Section 9-102(a)(73)
Securities intermediary	Section 8-102(a)(14)
Security entitlement	Section 8-102(a)(17)
Send	Section 1-201(b)(36)
Sign	Section 1-201(b)(37)
Value	Section 1-204

Official Comment

1. Source. New.

2. Scope and Purpose. This section imposes duties on a secured party who has control of a deposit account, an electronic copy of a record evidencing chattel paper, investment property, a letter-of-credit right, an electronic document of title, electronic money, or a controllable electronic record. The duty to terminate the secured party's control is analogous to the duty to file a termination statement, imposed by Section 9-513. Under subsection (a), it applies only when there is no outstanding secured obligation and the secured party is not committed to give value. The requirements of this section can be varied by agreement under Section 1-102(3) [Ed. Note. New Article 1: Section 1-302(b)]. For example, a debtor could by contract agree that the secured party may comply with subsection (b) by releasing control more than 10 days after demand. Also, duties under this section should not be read to conflict with the terms of the collateral itself. For example, if the collateral is a time deposit account, subsection (b)(2) should not require a secured party with control to make an early withdrawal of the funds (assuming that were possible) in order to pay them over to the debtor or put them in an account in the debtor's name.

Note that subsection (b)(8) addresses secured parties that have control of a controllable electronic record. That control may have been obtained for the purpose of perfecting a security interest in a controllable account or controllable payment intangible evidenced by the controllable electronic record, even if the secured party did not have a security interest in the controllable electronic record itself.

This section does not explicitly impose duties on a secured party whose control is based on the acknowledgment under Section 7-106(g), 9-104(a)(4), or 9-105A(e) or under 9-107A and 12-105(e) by another person having control. Such a secured party would have control only while the other, acknowledging person retains control. This result necessarily follows because such a secured party's control derives solely from the other person's continued control. See, e.g., Section 9-314, Comment 2. Upon compliance with this section by an acknowledging person having control, the control of a person having control through such person's acknowledgment would cease.

3. Remedy for Failure to Relinquish Control. If a secured party fails to comply with the requirements of subsection (b), the debtor has the remedy set forth in Section 9-625(e). This remedy is identical to that applicable to failure to provide or file a termination statement under Section 9-513.

4. Duty to Relinquish Possession. Although Section 9-207 addresses directly the duties of a secured party in possession of collateral, that section does not require the secured party to relinquish possession when the secured party ceases to hold a security interest. Under common law, absent agreement to the contrary, the failure to relinquish possession of collateral upon satisfaction of the secured obligation would constitute a conversion. Inasmuch as problems apparently have not surfaced in the absence of statutory duties under former Article 9 and the common-law duty appears to have been sufficient, this Article does not impose a statutory duty to relinquish possession.

5. "Signed Replaces "Authenticated." Consistent with the revised definition of "sign" in Section 1-201, the cognate term "signed" replaces references to "authenticated" in the pre-2022 text of this section.

§ 9-209. Duties of Secured Party If Account Debtor Has Been Notified of Assignment.

(a) [Applicability of section.] Except as otherwise provided in subsection (c), this section applies if:

(1) there is no outstanding secured obligation; and

(2) the secured party is not committed to make advances, incur obligations, or otherwise give value.

(b) [Duties of secured party after receiving demand from debtor.] Within 10 days after receiving a signed demand by the debtor, a secured party shall send to an account debtor that has received notification under Section 9-406(a) or 12-106(b) of an assignment to the secured party as assignee a signed record that releases the account debtor from any further obligation to the secured party.

(c) [Inapplicability to sales.] This section does not apply to an assignment constituting the sale of an account, chattel paper, or payment intangible.

Definitional Cross References:

Account	Section 9-102(a)(2)
Account debtor	Section 9-102(a)(3)
Chattel paper	Section 9-102(a)(11)
Debtor	Section 9-102(a)(28)
Payment intangible	Section 9-102(a)(61)
Record	Section 9-102(a)(70)
Sale	Section 2-106(1)
Secured party	Section 9-102(a)(73)
Send	Section 1-201(b)(36)
Sign	Section 1-201(b)(37)
Value	Section 1-204

Official Comment

1. Source. New.

2. Scope and Purpose. Like Sections 9-208 and 9-513, which require a secured party to relinquish control of collateral and to file or provide a termination statement for a financing statement, this section requires a secured party to free up collateral when there no longer is any outstanding secured obligation or any commitment to give value in the future. This section addresses the case in which account debtors have been notified to pay a secured party to whom the receivables have been assigned. It requires the secured party (assignee) to inform the account debtors that they no longer are obligated to make payment to the secured party. See subsection (b). It does not apply to account debtors whose obligations on an account, chattel paper, or payment intangible have been sold. See subsection (c).

3. "Signed Replaces Authenticated." Consistent with the revised definition of "sign" in Section 1-201, the cognate term "signed" replaces references to "authenticated" in the pre-2022 text of this section.

§ 9-210. Request for Accounting; Request Regarding List of Collateral or Statement of Account.

(a) [Definitions.] In this section:

(1) "Request" means a record of a type described in paragraph (2), (3), or (4).

(2) "Request for an accounting" means a record signed by a debtor requesting that the recipient provide an accounting of the unpaid obligations secured by collateral and reasonably identifying the transaction or relationship that is the subject of the request.

(3) "Request regarding a list of collateral" means a record signed by a debtor requesting that the recipient approve or correct a list of what the debtor believes to be the collateral securing an obligation and reasonably identifying the transaction or relationship that is the subject of the request.

(4) "Request regarding a statement of account" means a record signed by a debtor requesting that the recipient approve or correct a statement indicating what the debtor believes to be the aggregate amount of unpaid obligations secured by collateral as of a specified date and reasonably identifying the transaction or relationship that is the subject of the request.

(b) [Duty to respond to requests.] Subject to subsections (c), (d), (e), and (f), a secured party, other than a buyer of accounts, chattel paper, payment intangibles, or promissory notes or a consignor, shall comply with a request within 14 days after receipt:

(1) in the case of a request for an accounting, by signing and sending to the debtor an accounting; and

(2) in the case of a request regarding a list of collateral or a request regarding a statement of account, by signing and sending to the debtor an approval or correction.

(c) [Request regarding list of collateral; statement concerning type of collateral.] A secured party that claims a security interest in all of a particular type of collateral owned by the debtor may comply with a request regarding a list of collateral by sending to the debtor a signed record including a statement to that effect within 14 days after receipt.

(d) [Request regarding list of collateral; no interest claimed.] A person that receives a request regarding a list of collateral, claims no interest in the collateral when it receives the request, and claimed an interest in the collateral at an earlier time shall comply with the request within 14 days after receipt by sending to the debtor a signed record:

(1) disclaiming any interest in the collateral; and

(2) if known to the recipient, providing the name and mailing address of any assignee of or successor to the recipient's interest in the collateral.

(e) [Request for accounting or regarding statement of account; no interest in obligation claimed.] A person that receives a request for an accounting or a request regarding a statement of account, claims no interest in the obligations when it receives the request, and claimed an interest in the obligations at an earlier time shall comply with the request within 14 days after receipt by sending to the debtor a signed record:

(1) disclaiming any interest in the obligations; and

(2) if known to the recipient, providing the name and mailing address of any assignee of or successor to the recipient's interest in the obligations.

(f) [Charges for responses.] A debtor is entitled without charge to one response to a request under this section during any six-month period. The secured party may require payment of a charge not exceeding $25 for each additional response.

Definitional Cross References:

Account	Section 9-102(a)(2)
Accounting	Section 9-102(a)(4)
Chattel paper	Section 9-102(a)(11)
Collateral	Section 9-102(a)(12)
Consignor	Section 9-102(a)(21)

Debtor	Section 9-102(a)(28)
Payment intangible	Section 9-102(a)(61)
Promissory note	Section 9-102(a)(65)
Record	Section 9-102(a)(70)
Secured party	Section 9-102(a)(73)
Security interest	Section 1-201(b)(35)
Send	Section 9-102(a)(75)
Sign	Section 1-201(b)(37)

Official Comment

1. Source. Former Section 9-208.

2. Scope and Purpose. This section provides a procedure whereby a debtor may obtain from a secured party information about the secured obligation and the collateral in which the secured party may claim a security interest. It clarifies and resolves some of the issues that arose under former Section 9-208 and makes information concerning the secured indebtedness readily available to debtors, both before and after default. It applies to agricultural lien transactions (see the definitions of "debtor," secured party," and "collateral" in Section 9-102), but generally not to sales of receivables. See subsection (b).

3. Requests by Debtors Only. A financing statement filed under Part 5 may disclose only that a secured party may have a security interest in specified types of collateral. In most cases the financing statement will contain no indication of the obligation (if any) secured, whether any security interest actually exists, or the particular property subject to a security interest. Because creditors of and prospective purchasers from a debtor may have legitimate needs for more detailed information, it is necessary to provide a procedure under which the secured party will be required to provide information. On the other hand, the secured party should not be under a duty to disclose any details of the debtor's financial affairs to any casual inquirer or competitor who may inquire. For this reason, this section gives the right to request information to the debtor only. The debtor may submit a request in connection with negotiations with subsequent creditors and purchasers, as well as for the purpose of determining the status of its credit relationship or demonstrating which of its assets are free of a security interest.

4. Permitted Types of Requests for Information. Subsection (a) contemplates that a debtor may request three types of information by submitting three types of "requests" to the secured party. First, the debtor may request the secured party to prepare and send an "accounting" (defined in Section 9-102). Second, the debtor may submit to the secured party a list of collateral for the secured party's approval or correction. Third, the debtor may submit to the secured party for its approval or correction a statement of the aggregate amount of unpaid secured obligations. Inasmuch as a secured party may have numerous transactions and relationships with a debtor, each request must identify the relevant transactions or relationships. Subsections (b) and (c) require the secured party to respond to a request within 14 days following receipt of the request.

5. Recipients Claiming No Interest in the Transaction. A debtor may be unaware that a creditor with whom it has dealt has assigned its security interest or the secured obligation. Subsections (d) and (e) impose upon recipients of requests under this section the duty to inform the debtor that they claim no interest in the collateral or secured obligation, respectively, and to inform the debtor of the name and mailing address of any known assignee or successor. As under subsections (b) and (c), a response to a request under subsection (d) or (e) is due 14 days following receipt.

6. Waiver; Remedy for Failure to Comply. The debtor's rights under this section may not be waived or varied. See Section 9-602(2). Section 9-625 sets forth the remedies for noncompliance with the requirements of this section.

7. Limitation on Free Responses to Requests. Under subsection (f), during a six-month period a debtor is entitled to receive from the secured party one free response to a request. The debtor is not entitled to a free response to each type of request (i.e., three free responses) during a six-month period.

8. "Signed and "Signing" Replaces "Authenticated" and "Authenticating." Consistent with the revised definition of "sign" in Section 1-201, the cognate terms "signed" and "signing" replaces references to "authenticated" and "authenticating" in the pre-2022 text of this section.

PART 3. PERFECTION AND PRIORITY

[Subpart 1. Law Governing Perfection and Priority]

§ 9-301. Law Governing Perfection and Priority of Security Interests.

Except as otherwise provided in Sections 9-303 through 9-306B, the following rules determine the law governing perfection, the effect of perfection or nonperfection, and the priority of a security interest in collateral:

(1) Except as otherwise provided in this section, while a debtor is located in a jurisdiction, the local law of that jurisdiction governs perfection, the effect of perfection or nonperfection, and the priority of a security interest in collateral.

(2) While collateral is located in a jurisdiction, the local law of that jurisdiction governs

perfection, the effect of perfection or nonperfection, and the priority of a possessory security interest in that collateral.

(3) Except as otherwise provided in paragraph (4), while negotiable tangible documents, goods, instruments, or tangible money is located in a jurisdiction, the local law of that jurisdiction governs:

(A) perfection of a security interest in the goods by filing a fixture filing;

(B) perfection of a security interest in timber to be cut; and

(C) the effect of perfection or nonperfection and the priority of a nonpossessory security interest in the collateral.

(4) The local law of the jurisdiction in which the wellhead or minehead is located governs perfection, the effect of perfection or nonperfection, and the priority of a security interest in as-extracted collateral.

Definitional Cross References:

As-extracted collateral	Section 9-102(a)(6)
Collateral	Section 9-102(a)(12)
Debtor	Section 9-102(a)(28)
Document	Section 9-102(a)(30)
Fixture filing	Section 9-102(a)(40)
Goods	Section 9-102(a)(44)
Instrument	Section 9-102(a)(47)
Money	Section 9-102(a)(54A)
Security interest	Section 1-201(b)(35)
Tangible money	Section 9-102(a)(79A)

Official Comment

1. Source. Former Sections 9-103(1)(a), (b), 9-103(3)(a), (b), 9-103(5), substantially modified.

2. Scope of This Subpart. Part 3, Subpart 1 (Sections 9-301 through 9-307) contains choice-of-law rules similar to those of former Section 9-103. Former Section 9-103 generally addresses which State's law governs "perfection and the effect of perfection or non-perfection of" security interests. See, e.g., former Section 9-103(1)(b). This Article follows the broader and more precise formulation in former Section 9-103(6)(b), which was revised in connection with the promulgation of Revised Article 8 in 1994: "perfection, the effect of perfection or non-perfection, and the priority of" security interests. Priority, in this context, subsumes all of the rules in Part 3, including "cut off" or "take free" rules such as Sections 9-317(b), (c), and (d), 9-320(a), (b), and (d), and 9-332. (The Hague Securities Convention may sometimes modify certain of this subpart's choice-of-law rules, as well as applying them to the requirements for foreclosure and the like, the characterization of a transfer as being outright or by way of security as it affects rights of third parties, and certain other issues. See Commentary No. 19, dated April 11, 2017. The Commentary is available at https://www.ali.org/peb-ucc.)

This subpart does not address choice of law for other purposes. For example, the law applicable to issues such as attachment, validity, characterization of a transaction (e.g., true lease or security interest) as it affects rights between the parties to the transaction, and enforcement is governed by the rules in Section 1-105(1) (Revised Section 1-301(a) and (b)); that governing law typically is specified in the same agreement that contains the security agreement. And, another jurisdiction's law may govern other third-party matters addressed in this Article. See Section 9-401, Comment 3. As to the law applicable to characterization, see PEB Commentary No. 24, dated August 12, 2022. The Commentary is available at https://www.ali.org/peb-ucc.

3. Scope of Referral. In designating the jurisdiction whose law governs, this Article directs the court to apply only the substantive ("local") law of a particular jurisdiction and not its choice-of-law rules.

Example 1: Litigation over the priority of a security interest in accounts arises in State X. State X has adopted the official text of this Article, which provides that priority is determined by the local law of the jurisdiction in which the debtor is located. See Section 9-301(1). The debtor is located in State Y. Even if State Y has retained former Article 9 or enacted a nonuniform choice-of-law rule (e.g., one that provides that perfection is governed by the law of State Z), a State X court should look only to the substantive law of State Y and disregard State Y's choice-of-law rule. State Y's substantive law (e.g., its Section 9-501) provides that financing statements should be filed in a filing office in State Y. Note, however, that if the identical perfection issue were to be litigated in State Y, the court would look to State Y's former Section 9-103 or nonuniform 9-301 and conclude that a filing in State Y is ineffective.

Example 2: In the preceding Example, assume that State X has adopted the official text of this Article, and State Y has adopted a nonuniform Section 9-301(1) under which perfection is governed by the whole law of State X, including its choice-of-law rules. If litigation occurs in State X, the court should look to the substantive law of State Y, which provides that financing statements are to be filed in a filing office in State Y. If litigation occurs in State Y, the court should look to the law of State X, whose choice-of-law rule requires that the court apply the substantive law of State Y. Thus, regardless of the jurisdiction in which the litigation arises, the financing statement should be filed in State Y.

4. Law Governing Perfection: General Rule. Paragraph (1) contains the general rule: the law governing perfection of security interests in both tangible and intangible collateral, whether perfected by filing or automatically, is the law of the jurisdiction of the debtor's location, as determined under Section 9-307.

Paragraph (1) substantially simplifies the choice-of-law rules. Former Section 9-103 contained different choice-of-law rules for different types of collateral. Under Section 9-301(1), the law of a single jurisdiction governs perfection with respect to most types of collateral, both tangible and intangible. Paragraph (1) eliminates the need for former Section 9-103(1)(c), which concerned purchase-money security interests in tangible collateral that is intended to move from one jurisdiction to the other. It is likely to reduce the frequency of cases in which the governing law changes after a financing statement is properly filed. (Presumably, debtors change their own location less frequently than they change the location of their collateral.) The approach taken in paragraph (1) also eliminates some difficult priority issues and the need to distinguish between "mobile" and "ordinary" goods, and it reduces the number of filing offices in which secured parties must file or search when collateral is located in several jurisdictions.

5. Law Governing Perfection: Exceptions. The general rule is subject to several exceptions. It does not apply to goods covered by a certificate of title (see Section 9-303), deposit accounts (see Section 9-304), investment property (see Section 9-305), letter-of-credit rights (see Section 9-306), chattel paper (see Section 9-306A), or controllable accounts, controllable electronic records, or controllable payment intangibles (see Section 9-306B). Nor does it apply to possessory security interests, i.e., security interests that the secured party has perfected by taking possession of the collateral (see paragraph (2)), security interests perfected by filing a fixture filing (see paragraph (4)), security interests in timber to be cut (paragraph (5)), or security interests in as-extracted collateral (see paragraph (6)). No exception is made for electronic money and the general rule applies (unless preempted by federal law).

a. Possessory Security Interests. Paragraph (2) applies to possessory security interests and provides that perfection and priority is governed by the local law of the jurisdiction in which the collateral is located. This is the rule of pre-1998 Section 9-103(1)(b), except paragraph (2) eliminates the troublesome "last event" test of former law.

The distinction between nonpossessory and possessory security interests creates the potential for the same jurisdiction to apply two different choice-of-law rules to determine perfection in the same collateral. For example, were a secured party in possession of an instrument or a tangible document to relinquish possession in reliance on temporary perfection, the applicable law immediately would change from that of the location of the collateral to that of the location of the debtor. The applicability of two different choice-of-law rules for perfection is unlikely to lead to any material practical problems. The perfection rules of one Article 9 jurisdiction are likely to be identical to those of another. Moreover, under paragraph (3), the relative priority of competing security interests in tangible collateral is resolved by reference to the law of the jurisdiction in which the collateral is located, regardless of how the security interests are perfected.

b. Fixtures Filings. Under the general rule in paragraph (1), a security interest in fixtures may be perfected by filing in the office specified by Section 9-501(a) as enacted in the jurisdiction in which the debtor is located. However, application of this rule to perfection of a security interest by filing a fixture filing could yield strange results. For example, perfection of a security interest in fixtures located in Arizona and owned by a Delaware corporation would be governed by the law of Delaware. Although Delaware law would send one to a filing office in Arizona for the place to file a financing statement as a fixture filing, see Section 9-501, Delaware law would not take account of local, nonuniform, real-property filing and recording requirements that Arizona law might impose. For this reason, paragraph (3)(A) contains a special rule for security interests perfected by a fixture filing; the law of the jurisdiction in which the fixtures are located governs perfection, including the formal requisites of a fixture filing. Under paragraph (3)(C), the same law governs priority. Fixtures are "goods" as defined in Section 9-102.

The filing of a financing statement to perfect a security interest in collateral of a transmitting utility constitutes a fixture filing with respect to goods that are or become fixtures. See Section 9-501(b). Accordingly, to perfect a security interest in goods of this kind by a fixture filing, a financing statement must be filed in the office specified by Section 9-501(b) as enacted in the jurisdiction in which the goods are located. If the fixtures collateral is located in more than one State, filing in all of those States will be necessary to perfect a security interest in all the fixtures collateral by a fixture filing. Of course, a security interest in nearly all types of collateral (including fixtures) of a transmitting utility may be perfected by filing in the office specified by Section 9-501(b) as enacted in the jurisdiction in which the transmitting utility is located. However, such a filing will not be effective as a fixture filing except with respect to goods that are located in that jurisdiction.

c. Timber to Be Cut. Application of the general rule in paragraph (1) to perfection of a security interest in timber to be cut would yield undesirable results analogous to those described with respect to fixtures.

Paragraph (3)(B) adopts a similar solution: perfection is governed by the law of the jurisdiction in which the timber is located. As with fixtures, under paragraph (3)(C), the same law governs priority. Timber to be cut also is "goods" as defined in Section 9-102.

Paragraph (3)(B) applies only to "timber to be cut," not to timber that has been cut. Consequently, once the timber is cut, the general choice-of-law rule in paragraph (1) becomes applicable. To ensure continued perfection, a secured party should file in both the jurisdiction in which the timber to be cut is located and in the state where the debtor is located. The former filing would be with the office in which a real property mortgage would be filed, and the latter would be a central filing. See Section 9-501.

d. As-Extracted Collateral. Paragraph (4) adopts the rule of former Section 9-103(5) with respect to certain security interests in minerals and related accounts. Like security interests in fixtures perfected by filing a fixture filing, security interests in minerals that are as-extracted collateral are perfected by filing in the office designated for the filing or recording of a mortgage on the real property. For the same reasons, the law governing perfection and priority is the law of the jurisdiction in which the wellhead or minehead is located.

6. Change in Law Governing Perfection. When the debtor changes its location to another jurisdiction, the jurisdiction whose law governs perfection under paragraph (1) changes, as well. Similarly, the law governing perfection of a possessory security interest in collateral under paragraph (2) changes when the collateral is removed to another jurisdiction. Nevertheless, these changes will not result in an immediate loss of perfection. See Section 9-316(a), (b).

7. Law Governing Effect of Perfection and Priority: Goods, Documents, Instruments, Money, Negotiable Documents, and Tangible Chattel Paper. Under former Section 9-103, the law of a single jurisdiction governed both questions of perfection and those of priority. This Article generally adopts that approach. See paragraph (1). But the approach may create problems if the debtor and collateral are located in different jurisdictions. For example, assume a security interest in equipment located in Pennsylvania is perfected by filing in Illinois, where the debtor is located. If the law of the jurisdiction in which the debtor is located were to govern priority, then the priority of an execution lien on goods located in Pennsylvania would be governed by rules enacted by the Illinois legislature.

To address this problem, paragraph (3)(C) divorces questions of perfection from questions of "the effect of perfection or nonperfection and the priority of a security interest." Under paragraph (3)(C), the rights of competing claimants to tangible collateral are resolved by reference to the law of the jurisdiction in which the collateral is located. A similar bifurcation applied to security interests in investment property under former Section 9-103(6). See Section 9-305.

Paragraph (3)(C) applies the law of the situs to determine priority only with respect to goods (including fixtures), instruments, money, tangible negotiable documents, and tangible chattel paper. Compare former Section 9-103(1), which applied the law of the location of the collateral to documents, instruments, and "ordinary" (as opposed to "mobile") goods. This Article does not distinguish among types of goods. The ordinary/mobile goods distinction appears to address concerns about where to file and search, rather than concerns about priority. There is no reason to preserve this distinction under the bifurcated approach.

Particularly serious confusion may arise when the choice-of-law rules of a given jurisdiction result in each of two competing security interests in the same collateral being governed by a different priority rule. The potential for this confusion existed under former Section 9-103(4) with respect to chattel paper: Perfection by possession was governed by the law of the location of the paper, whereas perfection by filing was governed by the law of the location of the debtor. Consider the mess that would have been created if the language or interpretation of former Section 9-308 were to differ in the two relevant States, or if one of the relevant jurisdictions (e.g., a foreign country) had not adopted Article 9. The potential for confusion could have been exacerbated when a secured party perfected both by taking possession in the State where the collateral is located (State A) and by filing in the State where the debtor is located (State B)—a common practice for some chattel paper financers. By providing that the law of the jurisdiction in which the collateral is located governs priority, paragraph (3) substantially diminishes this problem.

8. Non-U.S. Debtors. This Article applies the same choice-of-law rules to all debtors, foreign and domestic. For example, it adopts the bifurcated approach for determining the law applicable to security interests in goods and other tangible collateral. See Comment 5.a., above. The Article contains a new rule specifying the location of non-U.S. debtors for purposes of this Part. The rule appears in Section 9-307 and is explained in the Comments to that section. Former Section 9-103(3)(c), which contained a special choice-of-law rule governing security interests created by debtors located in a non-U.S. jurisdiction, proved unsatisfactory and was deleted.

§ 9-302. Law Governing Perfection and Priority of Agricultural Liens.

While farm products are located in a jurisdiction, the local law of that jurisdiction governs perfection, the effect of perfection or nonperfection, and the priority of an agricultural lien on the farm products.

Definitional Cross References:

Agricultural lien	Section 9-102(a)(5)
Farm products	Section 9-102(a)(34)

Official Comment

1. Source. New.

2. Agricultural Liens. This section provides choice-of-law rules for agricultural liens on farm products. Perfection, the effect of perfection or nonperfection, and priority all are governed by the law of the jurisdiction in which the farm products are located. Other choice-of-law rules, including Section 1-301, determine which jurisdiction's law governs other matters, such as the secured party's rights on default. See Section 9-301, Comment 2. Inasmuch as no agricultural lien on proceeds arises under this Article, this section does not expressly apply to proceeds of agricultural liens. However, if another statute creates an agricultural lien on proceeds, it may be appropriate for courts to apply the choice-of-law rule in this section to determine priority in the proceeds.

§ 9-303. Law Governing Perfection and Priority of Security Interests in Goods Covered by a Certificate of Title.

(a) [Applicability of section.] This section applies to goods covered by a certificate of title, even if there is no other relationship between the jurisdiction under whose certificate of title the goods are covered and the goods or the debtor.

(b) [When goods covered by certificate of title.] Goods become covered by a certificate of title when a valid application for the certificate of title and the applicable fee are delivered to the appropriate authority. Goods cease to be covered by a certificate of title at the earlier of the time the certificate of title ceases to be effective under the law of the issuing jurisdiction or the time the goods become covered subsequently by a certificate of title issued by another jurisdiction.

(c) [Applicable law.] The local law of the jurisdiction under whose certificate of title the goods are covered governs perfection, the effect of perfection or nonperfection, and the priority of a security interest in goods covered by a certificate of title from the time the goods become covered by the certificate of title until the goods cease to be covered by the certificate of title.

Definitional Cross References:

Certificate of title	Section 9-102(a)(10)
Debtor	Section 9-102(a)(28)
Goods	Section 9-102(a)(44)
Security interest	Section 1-201(b)(35)

Official Comment

1. Source. Former Section 9-103(2)(a), (b), substantially revised.

2. Scope of This Section. This section applies to "goods covered by a certificate of title." The new definition of "certificate of title" in Section 9-102 makes clear that this section applies not only to certificate-of-title statutes under which perfection occurs upon notation of the security interest on the certificate but also to those that contemplate notation but provide that perfection is achieved by another method, e.g., delivery of designated documents to an official. Subsection (a), which is new, makes clear that this section applies to certificates of a jurisdiction having no other contacts with the goods or the debtor. This result comports with most of the reported cases on the subject and with contemporary business practices in the trucking industry.

3. Law Governing Perfection and Priority. Subsection (c) is the basic choice-of-law rule for goods covered by a certificate of title. Perfection and priority of a security interest are governed by the law of the jurisdiction under whose certificate of title the goods are covered from the time the goods become covered by the certificate of title until the goods cease to be covered by the certificate of title.

Normally, under the law of the relevant jurisdiction, the perfection step would consist of compliance with that jurisdiction's certificate-of-title statute and a resulting notation of the security interest on the certificate of title. See Section 9-311(b). In the typical case of an automobile or over-the-road truck, a person who wishes to take a security interest in the vehicle can ascertain whether it is subject to any security interests by looking at the certificate of title. But certificates of title cover certain types of goods in some States but not in others. A secured party who does not realize this may extend credit and attempt to perfect by filing in the jurisdiction in which the debtor is located. If the goods had been titled in another jurisdiction, the lender would be unperfected.

Subsection (b) explains when goods become covered by a certificate of title and when they cease to be covered. Goods may become covered by a certificate of title, even though no certificate of title has issued. Former Section 9-103(2)(b) provided that the law of the jurisdiction issuing the certificate ceases to apply upon "surrender" of the certificate. This Article eliminates the concept of "surrender." However, if the certificate is surrendered in conjunction with an appropriate application for a certificate to be issued by another jurisdiction, the law of the original jurisdiction ceases to apply because the goods became covered subsequently by a certificate of title from another jurisdiction. Alternatively, the law of the original jurisdiction ceases to apply when the certificate "ceases to be effective" under the law of that jurisdiction. Given the diversity in certificate-of-title statutes, the term "effective" is not defined.

4. Continued Perfection. The fact that the law of one State ceases to apply under subsection (b) does not mean that a security interest perfected under that law becomes unperfected automatically. In most cases, the security interest will remain perfected. See Section 9-316(d), (e). Moreover, a perfected security interest may be subject to defeat by certain buyers and secured parties. See Section 9-337.

5. Inventory. Compliance with a certificate-of-title statute generally is not the method of perfecting security interests in inventory. Section 9-311(d) provides that a security interest created in inventory held by a person in the business of selling goods of that kind is subject to the normal filing rules; compliance with a certificate-of-title statute is not necessary or effective to perfect the security interest. Most certificate-of-title statutes are in accord.

The following example explains the subtle relationship between this rule and the choice-of-law rules in Section 9-303 and former Section 9-103(2):

> **Example:** Goods are located in State A and covered by a certificate of title issued under the law of State A. The State A certificate of title is "clean"; it does not reflect a security interest. Owner takes the goods to State B and sells (trades in) the goods to Dealer, who is in the business of selling goods of that kind and is located (within the meaning of Section 9-307) in State B. As is customary, Dealer retains the duly assigned State A certificate of title pending resale of the goods. Dealer's inventory financer, SP, obtains a security interest in the goods under its after-acquired property clause.
>
> Under Section 9-311(d) of both State A and State B, Dealer's inventory financer, SP, must perfect by filing instead of complying with a certificate-of-title statute. If Section 9-303 were read to provide that the law applicable to perfection of SP's security interest is that of State A, because the goods are covered by a State A certificate, then SP would be required to file in State A under State A's Section 9-501. That result would be anomalous, to say the least, since the principle underlying Section 9-311(d) is that the inventory should be treated as ordinary goods.
>
> Section 9-303 (and former Section 9-103(2)) should be read as providing that the law of State B, not State A, applies. A court looking to the forum's Section 9-303(a) would find that Section 9-303 applies only if two conditions are met: (i) the goods are covered by the certificate as explained in Section 9-303(b), i.e., application had been made for a State (here, State A) to issue a certificate of title covering the goods and (ii) the certificate is a "certificate of title" as defined in Section 9-102, i.e., "a statute provides for the security interest in question to be indicated on the certificate as a condition or result of the security interest's obtaining priority over the rights of a lien creditor." Stated otherwise, Section 9-303 applies only when compliance with a certificate-of-title statute, and not filing, is the appropriate method of perfection. Under the law of State A, *for purposes of perfecting SP's security interest in the dealer's inventory,* the proper method of perfection is filing—not compliance with State A's certificate-of-title statute. For that reason, the goods are not covered by a "certificate of title," and the second condition is not met. Thus, Section 9-303 does not apply to the goods. Instead, Section 9-301 applies, and the applicable law is that of State B, where the debtor (dealer) is located.

6. External Constraints on This Section. The need to coordinate Article 9 with a variety of nonuniform certificate-of-title statutes, the need to provide rules to take account of situations in which multiple certificates of title are outstanding with respect to particular goods, and the need to govern the transition from perfection by filing in one jurisdiction to perfection by notation in another all create pressure for a detailed and complex set of rules. In an effort to minimize complexity, this Article does not attempt to coordinate Article 9 with the entire array of certificate-of-title statutes. In particular, Sections 9-303, 9-311, and 9-316(d) and (e) assume that the certificate-of-title statutes to which they apply do not have relation-back provisions (i.e., provisions under which perfection is deemed to occur at a time earlier than when the perfection steps actually are taken). A Legislative Note to Section 9-311 recommends the elimination of relation-back provisions in certificate-of-title statutes affecting perfection of security interests.

Ideally, at any given time, only one certificate of title is outstanding with respect to particular goods. In fact, however, sometimes more than one jurisdiction issues more than one certificate of title with respect to the same goods. This situation results from defects in certificate-of-title laws and the interstate coordination of those laws, not from deficiencies in this Article. As long as the possibility of multiple certificates of title remains, the potential for innocent parties to suffer losses will continue. At best, this Article can identify clearly which innocent parties will bear the losses in familiar fact patterns.

§ 9-304. Law Governing Perfection and Priority of Security Interests in Deposit Accounts.

(a) [Law of bank's jurisdiction governs.] The local law of a bank's jurisdiction governs perfection, the effect of perfection or nonperfection, and the priority of a security interest in a deposit account maintained with that bank even if the transaction does not bear any relation to the bank's jurisdiction.

(b) [Bank's jurisdiction.] The following rules determine a bank's jurisdiction for purposes of this part:

(1) If an agreement between the bank and its customer governing the deposit account expressly provides that a particular jurisdiction is the bank's jurisdiction for purposes of this part, this article, or [the Uniform Commercial Code], that jurisdiction is the bank's jurisdiction.

(2) If paragraph (1) does not apply and an agreement between the bank and its customer governing the deposit account expressly provides that the agreement is governed by the law of a particular jurisdiction, that jurisdiction is the bank's jurisdiction.

(3) If neither paragraph (1) nor paragraph (2) applies and an agreement between the bank and its customer governing the deposit account expressly provides that the deposit account is maintained at an office in a particular jurisdiction, that jurisdiction is the bank's jurisdiction.

(4) If none of the preceding paragraphs applies, the bank's jurisdiction is the jurisdiction in which the office identified in an account statement as the office serving the customer's account is located.

(5) If none of the preceding paragraphs applies, the bank's jurisdiction is the jurisdiction in which the chief executive office of the bank is located.

Definitional Cross References:

Account	Section 9-102(a)(2)
Agreement	Section 1-201(b)(3)
Bank	Section 9-102(a)(8)
Customer	Section 4-104(a)(5)
Debtor	Section 9-102(a)(28)
Deposit account	Section 9-102(a)(29)
Security interest	Section 1-201(b)(35)

Official Comment

1. Source. New; derived from Section 8-110(e) and former Section 9-103(6).

2. Deposit Accounts. Under this section, the law of the "bank's jurisdiction" governs perfection and priority of a security interest in deposit accounts. Subsection (b) contains rules for determining the "bank's jurisdiction." The substance of these rules is substantially similar to that of the rules determining the "security intermediary's jurisdiction" under former Section 8-110(e), except that subsection (b)(1) provides more flexibility than the analogous provision in former Section 8-110(e)(1). Subsection (b)(1) permits the parties to choose the law of one jurisdiction to govern perfection and priority of security interests and a different governing law for other purposes. The parties' choice is effective, even if the jurisdiction whose law is chosen bears no relationship to the parties or the transaction. Section 8-110(e)(1) has been conformed to subsection (b)(1) of this section, and Section 9-305(b)(1), concerning a commodity intermediary's jurisdiction, makes a similar departure from former Section 9-103(6)(e)(i).

3. Change in Law Governing Perfection. When the bank's jurisdiction changes, the jurisdiction whose law governs perfection under subsection (a) changes, as well. Nevertheless, the change will not result in an immediate loss of perfection. See Section 9-316(f), (g).

4. No relation to Bank's Jurisdiction Required. As to the final clause of subsection (a), see Section 8-110, Comment 5A.

§ 9-305. Law Governing Perfection and Priority of Security Interests in Investment Property.

(a) [Governing law: general rules.] Except as otherwise provided in subsection (c), the following rules apply:

(1) While a security certificate is located in a jurisdiction, the local law of that jurisdiction governs perfection, the effect of perfection or nonperfection, and the priority of a security interest in the certificated security represented thereby.

(2) The local law of the issuer's jurisdiction as specified in Section 8-110(d) governs perfection, the effect of perfection or nonperfection, and the priority of a security interest in an uncertificated security.

(3) The local law of the securities intermediary's jurisdiction as specified in Section 8-110(e) governs perfection, the effect of perfection or nonperfection, and the priority of a security interest in a security entitlement or securities account.

(4) The local law of the commodity intermediary's jurisdiction governs perfection, the effect of perfection or nonperfection, and the priority of a security interest in a commodity contract or commodity account.

(5) Paragraphs (2), (3), and (4) apply even if the transaction does not bear any relation to the jurisdiction.

(b) [Commodity intermediary's jurisdiction.] The following rules determine a commodity intermediary's jurisdiction for purposes of this part:

(1) If an agreement between the commodity intermediary and commodity customer governing the commodity account expressly provides that a particular jurisdiction is the commodity intermediary's jurisdiction for purposes of this part, this article, or [the Uniform Commercial Code], that jurisdiction is the commodity intermediary's jurisdiction.

(2) If paragraph (1) does not apply and an agreement between the commodity intermediary and commodity customer governing the commodity account expressly provides that the agreement is governed by the law of a particular jurisdiction, that jurisdiction is the commodity intermediary's jurisdiction.

(3) If neither paragraph (1) nor paragraph (2) applies and an agreement between the commodity intermediary and commodity customer governing the commodity account expressly provides that the commodity account is maintained at an office in a particular jurisdiction, that jurisdiction is the commodity intermediary's jurisdiction.

(4) If none of the preceding paragraphs applies, the commodity intermediary's jurisdiction is the jurisdiction in which the office identified in an account statement as the office serving the commodity customer's account is located.

(5) If none of the preceding paragraphs applies, the commodity intermediary's jurisdiction is the jurisdiction in which the chief executive office of the commodity intermediary is located.

(c) [When perfection governed by law of jurisdiction where debtor located.] The local law of the jurisdiction in which the debtor is located governs:

(1) perfection of a security interest in investment property by filing;

(2) automatic perfection of a security interest in investment property created by a broker or securities intermediary; and

(3) automatic perfection of a security interest in a commodity contract or commodity account created by a commodity intermediary.

Definitional Cross References:

Account	Section 9-102(a)(2)
Agreement	Section 1-201(b)(3)
Broker	Section 8-102(a)(3)
Certificated security	Section 8-102(a)(4)
Commodity account	Section 9-102(a)(14)
Commodity contract	Section 9-102(a)(15)
Commodity customer	Section 9-102(a)(16)
Commodity intermediary	Section 9-102(a)(17)
Debtor	Section 9-102(a)(28)
Investment property	Section 9-102(a)(49)
Issuer (security)	Section 8-201(a)
Securities account	Section 8-501(a)
Securities intermediary	Section 8-102(a)(14)
Security certificate	Section 8-102(a)(16)
Security entitlement	Section 8-102(a)(17)
Security interest	Section 1-201(b)(35)
Uncertificated security	Section 8-102(a)(18)

Official Comment

1. Source. Former Section 9-103(6).

2. Investment Property: General Rules. This section specifies choice-of-law rules for perfection and priority of security interests in investment property. Subsection (a)(1) covers security interests in certificated securities. Subsection (a)(2) covers security interests in uncertificated securities. Subsection (a)(3) covers security interests in security entitlements and securities accounts, and where the Hague Securities Convention applies it may in occasional instances modify subsection (a)(3)'s results as discussed in Comments 3, 5 and 6 to Section 8-110. Subsection (a)(4) covers security interests in commodity contracts and commodity accounts. The approach of each of these paragraphs is essentially the same. They identify the jurisdiction's law that governs questions of perfection and priority by using the same principles that Article 8 uses to determine other questions concerning that form of investment property. Thus, for certificated securities, the law of the jurisdiction in which the certificate is located governs. Cf. Section 8-110(c). For uncertificated securities, the law of the issuer's jurisdiction governs. Cf. Section 8-110(a). For security entitlements and securities accounts, the law designated by the agreement between the securities intermediary and the entitlement holder governing the securities account generally governs. Cf. Section 8-110(b), (e)(1) and (2) and Convention article 4(1).

For commodity contracts and commodity accounts, the law of the commodity intermediary's jurisdiction governs, though if particular assets of this type qualify as securities held with an intermediary within the meaning of the Convention, the Convention would also apply. Commodity contracts and commodity accounts are not governed by Article 8, and for this reason subsection (b) contains rules that specify the commodity intermediary's jurisdiction that are analogous to the rules in Section 8-110(e) specifying a securities intermediary's jurisdiction. Subsection (b)(1) affords the parties greater flexibility than did former Section 9-103(6)(3). See also Section 9-304(b) (bank's jurisdiction); Revised Section 8-110(e)(1) and (2) (securities intermediary's jurisdiction).

3. Investment Property: Exceptions. Subsection (c) establishes an exception to the general rules discussed in the preceding Comment. It provides that perfection of a security interest by filing, automatic perfection of a security interest in investment property created by a debtor who is a broker or securities intermediary (see Section 9-309(10)), and automatic perfection of a security interest in a commodity contract or commodity account of a debtor who is a commodity intermediary (see Section 9-309(11)) are governed by the law of the jurisdiction in which the debtor is located, as determined under Section 9-307.

The Hague Securities Convention generally preserves these rules for perfection by filing. However, if the debtor is located in a non-U.S. jurisdiction, or if the account agreement designates the law of a non-U.S. jurisdiction, then filing may be appropriate only in a different jurisdiction or altogether unavailable. See Convention articles 12(2)(b) and 4(1), respectively, and PEB Commentary No. 19, particularly footnote 25.

4. Examples: The following examples illustrate the rules in this section:

Example 1: A customer residing in New Jersey maintains a securities account with Able & Co. The agreement between the customer and Able specifies that it is governed by Pennsylvania law but expressly provides that California is Able's jurisdiction for purposes of the Uniform Commercial Code. Through the account the customer holds securities of a Massachusetts corporation, which Able holds through a clearing corporation located in New York. The customer obtains a margin loan from Able. Subsection (a)(3) provides that California law—the law of the securities intermediary's jurisdiction—governs perfection and priority of the security interest, even if California has no other relationship to the parties or the transaction. Even if other facts cause the Hague Securities Convention to apply (see Comment 1 to Section 8-110), the Convention does not change this result, provided that the account agreement either was entered into before the Convention's effectiveness in the United States or expressly specifies that the law of California is applicable to all issues specified in Convention article 2(1), and also provided that at the time of the agreement Able had an office in the United States engaged in a regular activity of maintaining securities accounts.

Example 2: A customer residing in New Jersey maintains a securities account with Able & Co. The agreement between the customer and Able specifies that it is governed by Pennsylvania law. Through the account the customer holds securities of a Massachusetts corporation, which Able holds through a clearing corporation located in New York. The customer obtains a loan from a lender located in Illinois. The lender takes a security interest and perfects by obtaining an agreement among the debtor, itself, and Able, which satisfies the requirement of Section 8-106(d)(2) to give the lender control. Subsection (a)(3) provides that Pennsylvania law—the law of the securities intermediary's jurisdiction—governs perfection and priority of the security interest, even if Pennsylvania has no other relationship to the parties or the transaction. Even if other facts cause the Hague Securities Convention to apply, the Convention does not change this result, provided that, at the time of the agreement between the customer and Able, Able had an office in the United States engaged in a regular activity of maintaining securities accounts.

Example 3: A customer residing in New Jersey maintains a securities account with Able & Co. The agreement between the customer and Able specifies that it is governed by Pennsylvania law. Through the account, the customer holds securities of a Massachusetts corporation, which Able holds through a clearing corporation located in New York. The customer borrows from SP-1, and SP-1 files a financing statement in New Jersey. Later, the customer obtains a loan from SP-2. SP-2 takes a security interest and perfects by obtaining an agreement among the debtor, itself, and Able, which satisfies the requirement of Section 8-106(d)(2) to give SP-2 control. Subsection (c)(1) provides that perfection of SP-1's security interest by filing is governed by the location of the debtor, so the filing in New Jersey was appropriate. Even if other facts cause the Hague Securities Convention to apply, Convention article 12(2)(b) preserves this result. Subsection (a)(3), however, provides that Pennsylvania law—the law designated by the agreement between the customer and Able—governs all other questions of perfection and priority, and the Convention preserves this result, provided that at the time of the agreement between the customer and Able, Able had an office in the United States engaged in a regular activity of maintaining securities accounts. Thus, Pennsylvania law governs perfection of SP-2's security interest, and Pennsylvania law also governs the priority of the security interests of SP-1 and SP-2.

Example 4: A customer maintains a securities account with Able & Co. The customer is an Ontario, Canada corporation with its chief executive office in Toronto. The agreement between the customer and Able specifies that it is governed by New York law, and at the time of the agreement Able had an office in the United States engaged in a regular activity of maintaining securities accounts. The customer obtains a loan secured by the securities account, and the lender wishes to perfect by filing. Subsection (c)(1) provides that perfection of the security interest by filing is generally governed by the law of the location of the debtor (in this case Ontario), assuming that it has a filing system described by Section 9-307(c)); however, Convention article 12(2)(b) recognizes Article 9's place-of-filing rules only when they designate a U.S. jurisdiction for the filing. As a result, subsection (c)(1) does not govern filing for this transaction, and perfection of the security interest is governed by the substantive law of the jurisdiction designated by the account agreement (in this case New York).

Example 5: A customer maintains a securities account with Able & Co. The customer is a Texas corporation. The agreement between the customer and Able specifies that it is governed by English law, and at the time of the agreement Able had an office in England engaged in a regular activity of maintaining securities accounts. The customer obtains a loan secured by the securities account, and the lender wishes to perfect by filing. Subsection (c)(1), if it applied, would provide that perfection of the security interest by filing is governed by the law of the location of the debtor (in this case Texas); however, under Convention article 4(1), perfection of the security interest is governed by the law of the jurisdiction designated by the account agreement (in this case England), rather than by the law of any UCC jurisdiction.

5. Change in Law Governing Perfection. When the issuer's jurisdiction, the securities intermediary's jurisdiction, or commodity intermediary's jurisdiction changes, the jurisdiction whose law governs perfection under subsection (a) changes, as well. Similarly, the law governing perfection of a possessory security interest in a certificated security changes when the collateral is removed to another jurisdiction, see subsection (a)(1), and the law governing perfection by filing changes when the debtor changes its location. See subsection (c). Nevertheless, under the UCC these changes will not result in an immediate loss of perfection. See Section 9-316. Along generally similar lines in cases to which the Hague Securities Convention applies, article 7 provides that when the account agreement is amended to designate a new jurisdiction's law under article 4(1), the new law governs perfection, except that the old law continues to govern the perfection of security or other property interests that arose before the amendment and a limited number of other issues affecting such interests, without limitation as to time.

6. No Relation of Transaction to Issuer's, Securities intermediary's, or Commodity Intermediary Jurisdiction Required. As to subsection (a)(5), see Section 8-110, Comment 5A.

§ 9-306. Law Governing Perfection and Priority of Security Interests in Letter-of-Credit Rights.

(a) [Governing law: issuer's or nominated person's jurisdiction.] Subject to subsection (c), the local law of the issuer's jurisdiction or a nominated person's jurisdiction governs perfection, the effect of perfection or nonperfection, and the priority of a security interest in a letter-of-credit right if the issuer's jurisdiction or nominated person's jurisdiction is a State.

(b) [Issuer's or nominated person's jurisdiction.] For purposes of this part, an issuer's jurisdiction or nominated person's jurisdiction is the jurisdiction whose law governs the liability of the issuer or nominated person with respect to the letter-of-credit right as provided in Section 5-116.

(c) [When section not applicable.] This section does not apply to a security interest that is perfected only under Section 9-308(d).

Definitional Cross References:

Issuer (letter of credit/ letter-of-credit right)	Section 5-102(a)(9)
Letter-of-credit right	Section 9-102(a)(51)
Nominated person	Section 5-102(a)(11)
Security interest	Section 1-201(b)(35)
State	Section 9-102(a)(77)

Official Comment

1. Source. New; derived in part from Section 8-110(e) and former Section 9-103(6).

2. *Sui Generis* Treatment. This section governs the applicable law for perfection and priority of security interests in letter-of-credit rights, other than a security interest perfected only under Section 9-308(d) (i.e., as a supporting obligation). The treatment differs substantially from that provided in Section 9-304 for deposit accounts. The basic rule is that the law of the issuer's or nominated person's (e.g., confirmer's) jurisdiction, derived from the terms of the letter of credit itself, controls perfection and priority, but only if the issuer's or nominated person's jurisdiction is a State, as defined in Section 9-102. If the issuer's or nominated person's jurisdiction is not a State, the baseline rule of Section 9-301 applies—perfection and priority are governed by the law of the debtor's location, determined under Section 9-307. Export transactions typically involve a foreign issuer and a domestic nominated person, such as a confirmer, located in a State. The principal goal of this section is to reduce the likelihood that perfection and priority would be governed by the law of a foreign jurisdiction in a transaction that is essentially domestic from the standpoint of the debtor-beneficiary, its creditors, and a domestic nominated person.

3. Issuer's or Nominated Person's Jurisdiction. Subsection (b) defers to the rules established under Section 5-116 for determination of an issuer's or nominated person's jurisdiction.

> **Example:** An Italian bank issues a letter of credit that is confirmed by a New York bank. The beneficiary is a Connecticut corporation. The letter of credit provides that the issuer's liability is governed by Italian law, and the confirmation provides that the confirmer's liability is governed by the law of New York. Under Sections 9-306(b) and 5-116(a), Italy is the issuer's jurisdiction and New York is the confirmer's (nominated person's) jurisdiction. Because the confirmer's jurisdiction is a State, the law of New York governs perfection and priority of a security interest in the beneficiary's letter-of-credit right against the confirmer. See Section 9-306(a). However, because the issuer's jurisdiction is not a State, the law of that jurisdiction does not govern. See Section 9-306(a). Rather, the choice-of-law rule in Section 9-301(1) applies to perfection and priority of a security interest in the beneficiary's letter-of-credit right against the issuer. Under that section, perfection and priority are governed by the law of the jurisdiction in which the debtor (beneficiary) is located. That jurisdiction is Connecticut. See Section 9-307.

4. Scope of This Section. This section specifies only the law governing perfection, the effect of perfection or nonperfection, and priority of security interests. Section 5-116 specifies the law governing the liability of, and Article 5 (or other applicable law) deals with the rights and duties of, an issuer or nominated person. Perfection, nonperfection, and priority have no effect on those rights and duties.

5. Change in Law Governing Perfection. When the issuer's jurisdiction, or nominated person's jurisdiction changes, the jurisdiction whose law governs perfection under subsection (a) changes, as well. Nevertheless, this change will not result in an immediate loss of perfection. See Section 9-316(f), (g).

§ 9-306A. Law Governing Perfection and Priority of Security Interests in Chattel Paper.

(a) [Chattel paper evidenced by authoritative electronic copy.] Except as provided in subsection (d), if chattel paper is evidenced only by an authoritative electronic copy of the chattel paper or is evidenced by an authoritative electronic copy and an authoritative tangible copy, the local law of the chattel paper's jurisdiction governs perfection, the effect of perfection or nonperfection, and the priority of a security interest in the chattel paper, even if the transaction does not bear any relation to the chattel paper's jurisdiction.

(b) [Chattel paper's jurisdiction.] The following rules determine the chattel paper's jurisdiction under this section:

(1) If the authoritative electronic copy of the record evidencing chattel paper, or a record attached to or logically associated with the electronic copy and readily available for review, expressly provides that a particular jurisdiction is the chattel paper's jurisdiction for purposes of this part, this article, or [the Uniform Commercial Code], that jurisdiction is the chattel paper's jurisdiction.

(2) If paragraph (1) does not apply and the rules of the system in which the authoritative electronic copy is recorded are readily available for review and expressly provide that a particular jurisdiction is the chattel paper's jurisdiction for purposes of this part, this article, or [the Uniform Commercial Code], that jurisdiction is the chattel paper's jurisdiction.

(3) If paragraphs (1) and (2) do not apply and the authoritative electronic copy, or a record attached to or logically associated with the electronic copy and readily available for review, expressly provides that the chattel paper is governed by the law of a particular jurisdiction, that jurisdiction is the chattel paper's jurisdiction.

(4) If paragraphs (1), (2), and (3) do not apply and the rules of the system in which the authoritative electronic copy is recorded are readily available for review and expressly provide that the chattel paper or the system is governed by the law of a particular jurisdiction, that jurisdiction is the chattel paper's jurisdiction.

(5) If paragraphs (1) through (4) do not apply, the chattel paper's jurisdiction is the jurisdiction in which the debtor is located.

(c) [Chattel paper evidenced by authoritative tangible copy.] If an authoritative tangible copy of a record evidences chattel paper and the chattel paper is not evidenced by an authoritative electronic copy, while the authoritative tangible copy of the record evidencing chattel paper is located in a jurisdiction, the local law of that jurisdiction governs:

(1) perfection of a security interest in the chattel paper by possession under Section 9-314A; and

(2) the effect of perfection or nonperfection and the priority of a security interest in the chattel paper.

(d) [When perfection governed by law of jurisdiction where debtor located.] The local law of the jurisdiction in which the debtor is located governs perfection of a security interest in chattel paper by filing.

Definitional Cross References:

Chattel paper	Section 9-102(a)(11)
Debtor	Section 9-102(a)(28)
Electronic	Section 1-201(b)(16A)
Security interest	Section 1-201(b)(35)
Record	Section 9-102(a)(70)

Official Comment

1. Source. Section 9-306A(a) and (b) derive from Sections 8-110(e) and 9-305 on law governing perfection and priority of security interests in investment property (as do Sections 9-306B and 12-107).

2. Applicability of this Section. This section determines the law governing perfection and priority of security interests in chattel paper. Subsections (a) and (b) apply to chattel paper that is evidenced only by an authoritative electronic copy of the chattel paper or by an authoritative electronic copy and an authoritative tangible copy. Subsection (c) applies to chattel paper that is evidenced by an authoritative tangible copy but not evidenced by an authoritative electronic copy. Subsection (d) applies to perfection by filing for all chattel paper.

3. Authoritative Electronic Copy: Chattel Paper's Jurisdiction. Subsection (a) specifies the law governing perfection and priority of security interests in chattel paper evidenced by an authoritative electronic copy of the chattel paper, even if it is also evidenced by an authoritative tangible copy. Subject to subsection (d) on perfection by filing, the law governing perfection and priority is the local law of the chattel paper's jurisdiction. Drawing on Sections 8-110 and 9-305, it is the authoritative electronic copy itself, records attached thereto or associated therewith, or the system in which the authoritative electronic copy is recorded that determines the chattel paper's jurisdiction and, therefore, the governing law. Subsection (b) provides a "waterfall" of rules based on provisions that identify a particular jurisdiction as the chattel paper's jurisdiction or alternatively that provide the governing law of the chattel paper or of the system in which the electronic copy is recorded. When no such identification or provision is made, it is the debtor's location, determined under Section 9-307, that is the chattel paper's jurisdiction. As to the final clause of subsection (a), see Section 8-110, Comment 5A.

4. Rationale for Subsection (a). A buyer of, or secured lender against, chattel paper may arrange for authoritative electronic copies of chattel paper that it wishes to have assigned to it to be originated in or submitted into a system for the control and assignment of the chattel paper. The secured parties and lessors that will be assigning the chattel paper may be located in many different jurisdictions. As to assignments of the chattel paper by these secured parties and lessors (assignor-debtors), but for this section perfection and priority would be governed by the law of each assignor-debtor's location under Section 9-301(1). Under this section, however, the law of a single jurisdiction—the chattel paper's jurisdiction—could govern perfection and priority with respect to all of the assignments. By avoiding the application of the laws of multiple jurisdictions to perfection and priority, this rule could substantially reduce transaction costs.

5. Authoritative tangible copy. Subsection (c) ties the choice-of-law rules to the location of the authoritative tangible copy when no authoritative electronic copy exists. In that circumstance, the local law of the jurisdiction where the authoritative tangible copy is physically located governs perfection of a security interest in the chattel paper by possession, under Section 9-314A, and priority. Like its predecessor, subsection (c) assumes that all the authoritative tangible copies are located in the same jurisdiction. However, assuming the secured party is in possession of all the tangible copies, even if the copies are located in more than one jurisdiction the situation is unlikely to be problematic.

6. Perfection by filing. Subsection (d) provides that the local law of the jurisdiction where the debtor is located governs perfection by filing for all chattel paper.

§ 9-306B. Law Governing Perfection and Priority of Security Interests in Controllable Accounts, Controllable Electronic Records, and Controllable Payment Intangibles

(a) [Governing law: general rules.] Except as provided in subsection (b), the local law of the controllable electronic record's jurisdiction specified in Section 12-107(c) and (d) governs perfection, the effect of perfection or nonperfection, and the priority of a security interest in a controllable electronic record and a security interest in a controllable account or controllable payment intangible evidenced by the controllable electronic record.

(b) [When perfection governed by law of jurisdiction where debtor located.] The local law of the jurisdiction in which the debtor is located governs:

(1) perfection of a security interest in a controllable account, controllable electronic record, or controllable payment intangible by filing; and

(2) automatic perfection of a security interest in a controllable payment intangible created by a sale of the controllable payment intangible.

Definitional Cross References:

Controllable account	Section 9-102(a)(27A)
Controllable electronic record	Section 12-102(a)(1)
Controllable payment intangible	Section 9-102(a)(27B)
Debtor	Section 9-102(a)(28)
Sale	Section 2-106(1)
Security interest	Section 1-201(b)(35)

Official Comment

1. Perfection by control and priority. Subsection (a) deals with perfection of a security interest in a controllable account, controllable electronic record, or controllable payment intangible other than by filing—i.e., perfection by control under Section 12-105—and priority. For these purposes the governing law is that of the controllable electronic record's jurisdiction under Section 12-107(c) and (d).

2. Perfection by filing. Under subsection (b) the local law of the jurisdiction of the debtor's location governs perfection of a security interest in a controllable account, controllable electronic record, or controllable payment intangible by filing (but not priority, as to which subsection (a) would apply). Because controllable electronic records are general intangibles and controllable accounts and controllable payment intangibles are subsets of accounts and payment intangibles, this provision does not change prior law.

§ 9-307. Location of Debtor.

(a) ["Place of business."] In this section, "place of business" means a place where a debtor conducts its affairs.

(b) [Debtor's location: general rules.] Except as otherwise provided in this section, the following rules determine a debtor's location:

(1) A debtor who is an individual is located at the individual's principal residence.

(2) A debtor that is an organization and has only one place of business is located at its place of business.

(3) A debtor that is an organization and has more than one place of business is located at its chief executive office.

(c) [Limitation of applicability of subsection (b).] Subsection (b) applies only if a debtor's residence, place of business, or chief executive office, as applicable, is located in a jurisdiction whose law generally requires information concerning the existence of a nonpossessory security interest to be made generally available in a filing, recording, or registration system as a condition or result of the security interest's obtaining priority over the rights of a lien creditor with respect to the collateral. If subsection (b) does not apply, the debtor is located in the District of Columbia.

(d) [Continuation of location: cessation of existence, etc.] A person that ceases to exist, have a residence, or have a place of business continues to be located in the jurisdiction specified by subsections (b) and (c).

(e) [Location of registered organization organized under State law.] A registered organization that is organized under the law of a State is located in that State.

(f) [Location of registered organization organized under federal law; bank branches and agencies.] Except as otherwise provided in subsection (i), a registered organization that is organized under the law of the United States and a branch or agency of a bank that is not organized under the law of the United States or a State are located:

(1) in the State that the law of the United States designates, if the law designates a State of location;

(2) in the State that the registered organization, branch, or agency designates, if the law of the United States authorizes the registered organization, branch, or agency to designate its State of location, including by designating its main office, home office, or other comparable office; or

(3) in the District of Columbia, if neither paragraph (1) nor paragraph (2) applies.

(g) [Continuation of location: change in status of registered organization.] A registered organization continues to be located in the jurisdiction specified by subsection (e) or (f) notwithstanding:

(1) the suspension, revocation, forfeiture, or lapse of the registered organization's status as such in its jurisdiction of organization; or

(2) the dissolution, winding up, or cancellation of the existence of the registered organization.

(h) [Location of United States.] The United States is located in the District of Columbia.

(i) [Location of foreign bank branch or agency if licensed in only one state.] A branch or agency of a bank that is not organized under the law of the United States or a State is located in the State in which the branch or agency is licensed, if all branches and agencies of the bank are licensed in only one State.

(j) [Location of foreign air carrier.] A foreign air carrier under the Federal Aviation Act of 1958, as amended, is located at the designated office of the agent upon which service of process may be made on behalf of the carrier.

(k) [Section applies only to this part.] This section applies only for purposes of this part.

Definitional Cross References:

Bank	Section 9-102(a)(8)
Branch	Section 1-201(b)(7)
Collateral	Section 9-102(a)(12)
Debtor	Section 9-102(a)(28)
Jurisdiction of organization	Section 9-102(a)(50)
Lien creditor	Section 9-102(a)(52)
Organization	Section 1-201(b)(25)
Registered organization	Section 9-102(a)(71)
Right	Section 1-201(b)(34)
Security interest	Section 1-201(b)(35)
State	Section 9-102(a)(77)

Official Comment

1. Source. Former Section 9-103(3)(d), substantially revised.

2. General Rules. As a general matter, the location of the debtor determines the jurisdiction whose law governs perfection of a security interest. See Sections 9-301(1), 9-305(c). It also governs priority of a security interest in certain types of intangible collateral, such as accounts, electronic chattel paper, and general intangibles. This section determines the location of the debtor for choice-of-law purposes, but not for other purposes. See subsection (k).

Subsection (b) states the general rules: An individual debtor is deemed to be located at the individual's principal residence with respect to both personal and business assets. Any other debtor is deemed to be located at its place of business if it has only one, or at its chief executive office if it has more than one place of business.

As used in this section, a "place of business" means a place where the debtor conducts its affairs. See subsection (a). Thus, every organization, even eleemosynary institutions and other organizations that do not conduct "for profit" business activities, has a "place of business." Under subsection (d), a person who ceases to exist, have a residence, or have a place of business continues to be located in the jurisdiction determined by subsection (b).

The term "chief executive office" is not defined in this Section or elsewhere in the Uniform Commercial Code. "Chief executive office" means the place from which the debtor manages the main part of its business operations or other affairs. This is the place where persons dealing with the debtor would normally look for credit information, and is the appropriate place for filing. With respect to most multi-state debtors, it will be simple to determine which of the debtor's offices is the "chief executive office." Even when a doubt arises, it would be rare that there could be more than two possibilities. A secured party in such a case may protect itself by perfecting under the law of each possible jurisdiction.

Similarly, the term "principal residence" is not defined. If the security interest in question is a purchase-money security interest in consumer goods which is perfected upon attachment, see Section 9-309(1), the choice of law may make no difference. In other cases, when a doubt arises, prudence may dictate perfecting under the law of each jurisdiction that might be the debtor's "principal residence."

Questions sometimes arise about the location of the debtor with respect to collateral held in a common-law trust. A typical common-law trust is not itself a juridical entity capable of owning property and so would not be a "debtor" as defined in Section 9-102. Rather, the debtor with respect to property held in a common-law trust typically is the trustee of the trust acting in the capacity of trustee. (The beneficiary would be a "debtor" with respect to its beneficial interest in the trust, but not with respect to the property held in the trust.) If a common-law trust has multiple trustees located in different jurisdictions, a secured party who perfects by filing would be well advised to file a financing statement in each jurisdiction in which a trustee is located, as determined under Section 9-307. Filing in all relevant jurisdictions would insure perfection and minimize any priority complications that otherwise might arise.

The general rules are subject to several exceptions, each of which is discussed below.

3. Non-U.S. Debtors. Under the general rules of this section, a non-U.S. debtor normally would be located in a foreign jurisdiction and, as a consequence, foreign law would govern perfection. When foreign law affords no public notice of security interests, the general rule yields unacceptable results.

Accordingly, subsection (c) provides that the normal rules for determining the location of a debtor (i.e., the rules in subsection (b)) apply only if they yield a location that is "a jurisdiction whose law generally requires information concerning the existence of a nonpossessory security interest to be made generally available in a filing, recording, or registration system as a condition or result of the security interest's obtaining priority over the rights of a lien creditor with respect to the collateral." The phrase "generally requires" is meant to include legal regimes that generally require notice in a filing or recording system as a condition of perfecting nonpossessory security interests, but which permit perfection by another method (e.g., control, automatic perfection, temporary perfection) in limited circumstances. A jurisdiction that has adopted this Article or an earlier version of this Article is such a jurisdiction. If the rules in subsection (b) yield a jurisdiction whose law does not generally require notice in a filing or registration system and none of the special rules in subsections (e), (f), (i), and (j) applies, the debtor is located in the District of Columbia.

[Ed. Note. The remainder of this comment was deleted from the Official Text, probably inadvertently.]

Example 1: Debtor is an English corporation with 7 offices in the United States and its chief executive office in London, England. Debtor creates a security interest in its accounts. Under subsection (b)(3), Debtor would be located in England. However, subsection (c) provides that subsection (b) applies only if English law generally conditions perfection on giving public notice in a filing, recording, or registration system. Otherwise, Debtor is located in the District of Columbia. Under Section 9-301(1), perfection, the effect of perfection, and priority are governed by the law of the jurisdiction of the debtor's location—here, England or the District of Columbia (depending on the content of English law).

Example 2: Debtor is an English corporation with 7 offices in the United States and its chief executive office in London, England. Debtor creates a security interest in equipment located in London. Under subsection (b)(3) Debtor would be located in England. However, subsection (c) provides that subsection (b) applies only if English law generally conditions perfection on giving public notice in a filing, recording, or registration system. Otherwise, Debtor is located in the District of Columbia. Under Section 9-301(1), perfection is governed by the law of the jurisdiction of the debtor's location, whereas, under Section 9-301(3), the law of the jurisdiction in which the collateral is located—here, England—governs priority.

The foregoing discussion assumes that each transaction bears an appropriate relation to the forum State. In the absence of an appropriate relation, the forum State's entire UCC, including the choice-of-law provisions in Article 9 (Sections 9-301 through 9-307), will not apply. See Section 9-109, Comment 9.

4. Registered Organizations Organized Under Law of a State. Under subsection (e), a "registered organization" (defined in Section 9-102 so as to ordinarily include corporations, limited partnerships, limited liability companies, and statutory trusts) organized under the law of a "State" (defined in Section 9-102) is located in its State of organization. The term "registered organization" includes a business trust described in the second sentence of the term's definition. See Section 9-102. The trust's public organic record, typically the trust agreement, usually will indicate the jurisdiction under whose law the trust is organized. A protected series formed under the Uniform Protected Series Act (2017) is a registered organization. See PEB Commentary No. 23, dated February 24, 2021. The Commentary is available at https://www.ali.org/peb-ucc.

Subsection (g) makes clear that events affecting the status of a registered organization, such as the dissolution of a corporation or revocation of its charter, do not affect its location for purposes of subsection (e). However, certain of these events may result in, or be accompanied by, a transfer of collateral from the registered organization to another debtor. This section does not determine whether a transfer occurs, nor does it determine the legal consequences of any transfer.

Determining the registered organization-debtor's location by reference to the jurisdiction of organization could provide some important side benefits for the filing systems. A jurisdiction could structure its filing system so that it would be impossible to make a mistake in a registered organization-debtor's name on a financing statement. For example, a filer would be informed if a filed record designated an incorrect corporate name for the debtor. Linking filing to the jurisdiction of organization also could reduce pressure on the system imposed by transactions in which registered organizations cease to exist—as a consequence of merger or consolidation, for example. The jurisdiction of organization might prohibit such transactions unless steps were taken to ensure that existing filings were refiled against a successor or terminated by the secured party.

5. Registered Organizations Organized Under Law of United States; Branches and Agencies of Banks Not Organized Under Law of United States. Subsection (f) specifies the location of a debtor that is a registered organization organized under the law of the United States. It defers to the law of the United States, to the extent that that law determines, or authorizes the debtor to determine, the debtor's location. Thus, if the law of the United States designates a particular State as the debtor's location, that State is the debtor's location for purposes of this Article's choice-of-law rules. Similarly, if the law of the United States authorizes the registered organization to designate its State of location, the State that the registered organization designates is the State in which it is located for purposes of this Article's choice-of-law rules. In other cases, the debtor is located in the District of Columbia.

In some cases, the law of the United States authorizes the registered organization to designate a main office, home office, or other comparable office. See, e.g., 12 U.S.C. Sections 22 and 1464(a); 12 C.F.R. Section 552.3. Designation of such an office constitutes the designation of the State of location for purposes of Section 9-307(f)(2).

Subsection (f) also specifies the location of a branch or agency in the United States of a foreign bank that has one or more branches or agencies in the United States. The law of the United States authorizes a foreign bank (or, on behalf of the bank, a federal agency) to designate a single home state for all of the foreign bank's branches and agencies in the United States. See 12 U.S.C. Section 3-103(c) and 12 C.F.R. Section 211.22. As authorized, the designation constitutes the State of location for the branch or agency for purposes of Section 9-307(f), unless all of a foreign bank's branches or agencies that are in the United States are licensed in only one State, in which case the branches and agencies are located in that State. See subsection (i).

In cases not governed by subsection (f) or (i), the location of a foreign bank is determined by subsections (b) and (c).

6. United States. To the extent that Article 9 governs (see Sections 1-301, 9-109(c)), the United States is located in the District of Columbia for purposes of this Article's choice-of-law rules. See subsection (h).

7. Foreign Air Carriers. Subsection (j) follows former Section 9-103(3)(d). To the extent that it is applicable, the Convention on the International Recognition of Rights in Aircraft (Geneva Convention) supersedes state legislation on this subject, as set forth in Section 9-311(b), but some nations are not parties to that Convention.

[Subpart 2. Perfection]

§ 9-308. When Security Interest or Agricultural Lien Is Perfected; Continuity of Perfection.

(a) [Perfection of security interest.] Except as otherwise provided in this section and Section 9-309, a security interest is perfected if it has attached and all of the applicable requirements for perfection in Sections 9-310 through 9-316 have been satisfied. A security interest is perfected when it attaches if the applicable requirements are satisfied before the security interest attaches.

(b) [Perfection of agricultural lien.] An agricultural lien is perfected if it has become effective and all of the applicable requirements for perfection in Section 9-310 have been satisfied. An agricultural lien is perfected when it becomes effective if the applicable requirements are satisfied before the agricultural lien becomes effective.

(c) [Continuous perfection; perfection by different methods.] A security interest or agricultural lien is perfected continuously if it is originally perfected by one method under this article and is later perfected by another method under this article, without an intermediate period when it was unperfected.

(d) [Supporting obligation.] Perfection of a security interest in collateral also perfects a security interest in a supporting obligation for the collateral.

(e) [Lien securing right to payment.] Perfection of a security interest in a right to payment or performance also perfects a security interest in a security interest, mortgage, or other lien on personal or real property securing the right.

(f) [Security entitlement carried in securities account.] Perfection of a security interest in a securities account also perfects a security interest in the security entitlements carried in the securities account.

(g) [Commodity contract carried in commodity account.] Perfection of a security interest in a commodity account also perfects a security interest in the commodity contracts carried in the commodity account.

Legislative Note: *Any statute conflicting with subsection (e) must be made expressly subject to that subsection.*

Definitional Cross References:

Agricultural lien	Section 9-102(a)(5)
Collateral	Section 9-102(a)(12)
Commodity account	Section 9-102(a)(14)
Commodity contract	Section 9-102(a)(15)
Mortgage	Section 9-102(a)(55)
Securities account	Section 8-501(a)
Security entitlement	Section 8-102(a)(17)
Security interest	Section 1-201(b)(35)
Supporting obligation	Section 9-102(a)(78)

Comment References:

9-107 C5
9-322 C6

Official Comment

1. Source. Former Sections 9-303, 9-115(2).

2. General Rule. This Article uses the term "attach" to describe the point at which property becomes subject to a security interest. The requisites for attachment are stated in Section 9-203. When it attaches, a security interest may be either perfected or unperfected. "Perfected" means that the security interest has attached and the secured party has taken all the steps required by this Article as specified in Sections 9-310 through 9-316. A perfected security interest may still be or become subordinate to other interests. See, e.g., Sections 9-320, 9-322. However, in general, after perfection the secured party is protected against creditors and transferees of the debtor and, in particular, against any representative of creditors in insolvency proceedings instituted by or against the debtor. See, e.g., Section 9-317.

Subsection (a) explains that the time of perfection is when the security interest has attached and any necessary steps for perfection, such as taking possession or filing, have been taken. The "except" clause refers to the perfection-upon-attachment rules appearing in Section 9-309. It also reflects that other subsections of this section, e.g., subsection (d), contain automatic-perfection rules. If the steps for perfection have been taken in advance, as when the secured party files a financing statement before giving value or before the debtor acquires rights in the collateral, then the security interest is perfected when it attaches.

3. Agricultural Liens. Subsection (b) is new. It describes the elements of perfection of an agricultural lien.

4. Continuous Perfection. The following example illustrates the operation of subsection (c):

> **Example 1:** Debtor, an importer, creates a security interest in goods that it imports and the documents of title that cover the goods. The secured party, Bank, takes possession of a tangible negotiable bill of lading covering certain imported goods and thereby perfects its security interest in the bill of lading and the goods. See Sections 9-313(a), 9-312(c)(1). Bank releases the bill of lading to the debtor for the purpose of procuring the goods from the carrier and selling them. Under Section 9-312(f), Bank continues to have a perfected security interest in the document and goods for 20 days. Bank files a financing statement covering the collateral before the expiration of the 20-day period. Its security interest now continues perfected for as long as the filing is good.
>
> If the successive stages of Bank's security interest succeed each other without an intervening gap, the security interest is "perfected continuously," and the date of perfection is when the security interest first became perfected (i.e., when Bank received possession of the tangible bill of lading). If, however, there is a gap between stages—for example, if Bank does not file until after the expiration of the 20-day period specified in Section 9-312(f) and leaves the collateral in the debtor's possession—then, the chain being broken, the perfection is no longer continuous. The date of perfection would now be the date of filing (after expiration of the 20-day period). Bank's security interest would be vulnerable to any interests arising during the gap period which under Section 9-317 take priority over an unperfected security interest.

5. Supporting Obligations. Subsection (d) is new. It provides for automatic perfection of a security interest in a supporting obligation for collateral if the security interest in the collateral is perfected. This is unlikely to effect any change in the law prior to adoption of this Article.

> **Example 2:** Buyer is obligated to pay Debtor for goods sold. Buyer's president guarantees the obligation. Debtor creates a security interest in the right to payment (account) in favor of Lender. Under Section 9-203(f), the security interest attaches to Debtor's rights under the guarantee (supporting obligation). Under subsection (d), perfection of the security interest in the account constitutes perfection of the security interest in Debtor's rights under the guarantee.

6. Rights to Payment Secured by Lien. Subsection (e) is new. It deals with the situation in which a security interest is created in a right to payment that is secured by a security interest, mortgage, or other lien.

> **Example 3:** Owner gives to Mortgagee a mortgage on Blackacre to secure a loan. Owner's obligation to pay is evidenced by a promissory note. In need of working capital, Mortgagee borrows from Financer and creates a security interest in the note in favor of Financer. Section 9-203(g) adopts the traditional view that the mortgage follows the note; i.e., the transferee of the note acquires the mortgage, as well. This subsection adopts a similar principle: perfection of a security interest in the right to payment constitutes perfection of a security interest in the mortgage securing it.
>
> An important consequence of the rules in Section 9-203(g) and subsection (e) is that, by acquiring a perfected security interest in a mortgage (or other secured) note, the secured party acquires a security interest in the mortgage (or other lien) that is senior to the rights of a person who becomes a lien creditor of the mortgagee (Article 9 debtor). See Section 9-317(a)(2). This result helps prevent the separation of the mortgage (or other lien) from the note.

Under this Article, attachment and perfection of a security interest in a secured right to payment do not of themselves affect the obligation to pay. For example, if the obligation is evidenced by a negotiable note, then Article 3 dictates the person whom the maker must pay to discharge the note and any lien securing it. See Section 3-602. If the right to payment is a payment intangible, then Section 9-406 determines whom the account debtor must pay.

Similarly, this Article does not determine who has the power to release a mortgage of record. That issue is determined by real-property law.

7. Investment Property. Subsections (f) and (g) follow former Section 9-115(2).

§ 9-309. Security Interest Perfected upon Attachment.

The following security interests are perfected when they attach:

(1) a purchase-money security interest in consumer goods, except as otherwise provided in Section 9-311(b) with respect to consumer goods that are subject to a statute or treaty described in Section 9-311(a);

(2) an assignment of accounts or payment intangibles which does not by itself or in conjunction with other assignments to the same assignee transfer a significant part of the assignor's outstanding accounts or payment intangibles;

(3) a sale of a payment intangible;

(4) a sale of a promissory note;

(5) a security interest created by the assignment of a health-care-insurance receivable to the provider of the health-care goods or services;

(6) a security interest arising under Section 2-401, 2-505, 2-711(3), or 2A-508(5), until the debtor obtains possession of the collateral;

(7) a security interest of a collecting bank arising under Section 4-210;

(8) a security interest of an issuer or nominated person arising under Section 5-118;

(9) a security interest arising in the delivery of a financial asset under Section 9-206(c);

(10) a security interest in investment property created by a broker or securities intermediary;

(11) a security interest in a commodity contract or a commodity account created by a commodity intermediary;

(12) an assignment for the benefit of all creditors of the transferor and subsequent transfers by the assignee thereunder;

(13) a security interest created by an assignment of a beneficial interest in a decedent's estate; and

(14) a sale by an individual of an account that is a right to payment of winnings in a lottery or other game of chance.

Definitional Cross References:

Account	Section 9-102(a)(2)
Bank	Section 9-102(a)(8)
Broker	Section 8-102(a)(3)
Collateral	Section 9-102(a)(12)
Commodity account	Section 9-102(a)(14)
Commodity contract	Section 9-102(a)(15)
Commodity intermediary	Section 9-102(a)(17)
Consumer goods	Section 9-102(a)(23)
Creditor	Section 1-201(b)(13)
Debtor	Section 9-102(a)(28)
Delivery	Section 1-201(b)(15)
Financial asset	Section 8-102(a)(9)
Goods	Section 9-102(a)(44)
Investment property	Section 9-102(a)(49)
Issuer (letter of credit/ letter-of-credit right)	Section 5-102(a)(9)
Nominated person	Section 5-102(a)(11)
Payment intangible	Section 9-102(a)(61)
Promissory note	Section 9-102(a)(65)
Purchase Money Security Interest	Section 9-103
Sale	Section 2-106(1)
Securities intermediary	Section 8-102(a)(14)
Security interest	Section 1-201(b)(35)

Comment References: 9-323 C3

Official Comment

1. Source. Derived from former Sections 9-302(1), 9-115(4)(c), (d), 9-116.

2. Automatic Perfection. This section contains the perfection-upon-attachment rules previously located in former Sections 9-302(1), 9-115(4)(c), (d), and 9-116. Rather than continue to state the rule by indirection, this section explicitly provides for perfection upon attachment.

3. Purchase-Money Security Interest in Consumer Goods. Former Section 9-302(1)(d) has been revised and appears here as paragraph (1). No filing or other step is required to perfect a purchase-money security interest in consumer goods, other than goods, such as automobiles, that are subject to a statute or treaty described in Section 9-311(a). However, filing is required to perfect a non-purchase-money security interest in consumer goods and is necessary to prevent a buyer of consumer goods from taking free of a security interest under Section 9-320(b). A fixture filing is required for priority over conflicting interests in fixtures to the extent provided in Section 9-334.

4. Rights to Payment. Paragraph (2) expands upon former Section 9-302(1)(e) by affording automatic perfection to certain assignments of payment intangibles as well as accounts. The purpose of paragraph (2) is to save from ex post facto invalidation casual or isolated assignments—assignments which no one would think of filing. Any person who regularly takes assignments of any debtor's accounts or payment intangibles should file. In this connection Section 9-109(d)(4) through (7), which excludes certain transfers of accounts, chattel paper, payment intangibles, and promissory notes from this Article, should be consulted.

Paragraphs (3) and (4), which are new, afford automatic perfection to sales of payment intangibles and promissory notes, respectively. They reflect the practice under former Article 9. Under that Article, filing a financing statement did not affect the rights of a buyer of payment intangibles or promissory notes, inasmuch as the former Article did not cover those sales. To the extent that the exception in paragraph (2) covers outright sales of payment intangibles, which automatically are perfected under paragraph (3), the exception is redundant.

Paragraph (14), which is new, affords automatic perfection to sales by individuals of an "account" (as defined in Section 9-102) consisting of the right to winnings in a lottery or other game of chance. Payments on these accounts typically extend for periods of twenty years or more. It would be unduly burdensome for the secured party, who would have no other reason to maintain contact with the seller, to monitor the seller's whereabouts for such a length of time. This paragraph was added in 2001. It applies to a sale of an account described in it, even if the sale was entered into before the effective date of the paragraph. However, if the relative priorities of conflicting claims to the account were established before the paragraph took effect, Article 9 as in effect immediately prior to the date the paragraph took effect determines priority.

5. Health-Care-Insurance Receivables. Paragraph (5) extends automatic perfection to assignments of health-care-insurance receivables if the assignment is made to the health-care provider that provided the health-care goods or services. The primary effect is that, when an individual assigns a right to payment under an insurance policy to the person who provided health-care goods or services, the provider has no need to file a financing statement against the individual. The normal filing requirements apply to other assignments of health-care-insurance receivables covered by this Article, e.g., assignments from the health-care provider to a financer.

6. Investment Property. Paragraph (9) replaces the last clause of former Section 9-116(2), concerning security interests that arise in the delivery of a financial asset.

Paragraphs (10) and (11) replace former Section 9-115(4)(c) and (d), concerning secured financing of securities and commodity firms and clearing corporations. The former sections indicated that, with respect to certain security interests created by a securities intermediary or commodity intermediary, "[t]he filing of a financing statement . . . has no effect for purposes of perfection or priority with respect to that security interest." No change in meaning is intended by the deletion of the quoted phrase.

Secured financing arrangements for securities firms are currently implemented in various ways. In some circumstances, lenders may require that the transactions be structured as "hard pledges," where the securities are transferred on the books of a clearing corporation from the debtor's account to the lender's account or to a special pledge account for the lender where they cannot be disposed of without the specific consent of the lender. In other circumstances, lenders are content with so-called "agreement to pledge" or "agreement to deliver" arrangements, where the debtor retains the positions in its own account, but reflects on its books that the positions have been hypothecated and promises that the securities will be transferred to the secured party's account on demand.

The perfection and priority rules of this Article are designed to facilitate current secured financing arrangements for securities firms as well as to provide sufficient flexibility to accommodate new arrangements that develop in the future. Hard pledge arrangements are covered by the concept of control. See Sections 9-314, 9-106, 8-106. Non-control secured financing arrangements for securities firms are covered by the automatic perfection rule of paragraph (10). Before the 1994 revision of Articles 8 and 9, agreement to pledge arrangements could be implemented under a provision that a security interest in securities given for new value under a written security agreement was perfected without filing or possession for a period of 21 days. Although the security interests were temporary in legal theory, the financing arrangements could, in practice, be continued indefinitely by rolling over the loans at least every 21 days. Accordingly, a knowledgeable creditor of a securities firm realizes that the firm's securities may be subject to security interests that are not discoverable from any public records. The automatic-perfection rule of paragraph (10) makes it unnecessary to engage in the purely formal practice of rolling over these arrangements every 21 days.

In some circumstances, a clearing corporation may be the debtor in a secured financing arrangement. For example, a clearing corporation that settles delivery-versus-payment transactions among its participants on a net, same-day basis relies on timely payments from all participants with net obligations due to the system. If a participant that is a net debtor were to default on its payment obligation, the clearing corporation would not receive some of the funds needed to settle with participants that are net creditors to the system. To complete end-of-day settlement after a payment default by a participant, a clearing corporation that settles on a net, same-day basis may need to draw on credit lines and pledge securities of the defaulting participant or other securities pledged by participants in the clearing corporation to secure such drawings. The clearing corporation may be the top-tier securities intermediary for the securities pledged, so that it would not be practical for the lender to obtain control. Even where the clearing corporation holds some types of securities through other intermediaries, however, the clearing corporation is unlikely to be able to complete the arrangements necessary to convey "control" over the securities to be pledged in time to complete settlement in a timely manner. However, the term "securities intermediary" is defined in Section 8-102(a)(14) to include clearing corporations. Thus, the perfection rule of paragraph (10) applies to security interests in investment property granted by clearing corporations.

7. Beneficial Interests in Trusts. Under former Section 9-302(1)(c), filing was not required to perfect a security interest created by an assignment of a beneficial interest in a trust. Because beneficial interests in trusts are now used as collateral with greater frequency in commercial transactions, under this Article filing is required to perfect a security interest in a beneficial interest.

8. Assignments for Benefit of Creditors. No filing or other action is required to perfect an assignment for the benefit of creditors. These assignments are not financing transactions, and the debtor ordinarily will not be engaging in further credit transactions.

§ 9-310. When Filing Required to Perfect Security Interest or Agricultural Lien; Security Interests and Agricultural Liens to Which Filing Provisions Do Not Apply.

(a) [General rule: perfection by filing.] Except as otherwise provided in subsection (b) and Section 9-312(b), a financing statement must be filed to perfect all security interests and agricultural liens.

(b) [Exceptions: filing not necessary.] The filing of a financing statement is not necessary to perfect a security interest:

(1) that is perfected under Section 9-308(d), (e), (f), or (g);

(2) that is perfected under Section 9-309 when it attaches;

(3) in property subject to a statute, regulation, or treaty described in Section 9-311(a);

(4) in goods in possession of a bailee which is perfected under Section 9-312(d)(1) or (2);

(5) in certificated securities, documents, goods, or instruments which is perfected without filing, control, or possession under Section 9-312(e), (f), or (g);

(6) in collateral in the secured party's possession under Section 9-313;

(7) in a certificated security which is perfected by delivery of the security certificate to the secured party under Section 9-313;

(8) in controllable accounts, controllable electronic records, controllable payment intangibles, deposit accounts, electronic documents, investment property, or letter-of-credit rights which is perfected by control under Section 9-314;

(8.1) in chattel paper which is perfect by possession and control under Section 9-314A;

(9) in proceeds which is perfected under Section 9-315; or

(10) that is perfected under Section 9-316.

(c) [Assignment of perfected security interest.] If a secured party assigns a perfected security interest or agricultural lien, a filing under this article is not required to continue the perfected status of the security interest against creditors of and transferees from the original debtor.

Definitional Cross References:

Agricultural lien	Section 9-102(a)(5)
Certificated security	Section 8-102(a)(4)
Chattel paper	Section 9-102(a)(11)
Collateral	Section 9-102(a)(12)
Controllable account	Section 9-102(a)(27A)
Controllable electronic record	Section 12-102(a)(1)
Controllable payment intangible	Section 9-102(a)(27B)
Creditor	Section 1-201(b)(13)
Delivery	Section 1-201(b)(15)
Deposit account	Section 9-102(a)(29)
Document	Section 9-102(a)(30)
Electronic	Section 1-201(b)(16A)
Financing statement	Section 9-102(a)(39)
Goods	Section 9-102(a)(44)
Instrument	Section 9-102(a)(47)
Investment property	Section 9-102(a)(49)
Letter-of-credit right	Section 9-102(a)(51)
Original debtor	Section 9-102(a)(60)
Proceeds	Section 9-102(a)(64)
Secured party	Section 9-102(a)(73)
Security certificate	Section 8-102(a)(16)
Security interest	Section 1-201(b)(35)

Official Comment

1. Source. Former Section 9-302(1), (2).

2. General Rule. Subsection (a) establishes a central Article 9 principle: Filing a financing statement is necessary for perfection of security interests and agricultural liens. However, filing is not necessary to perfect a security interest that is perfected by another permissible method, see subsection (b), nor does filing ordinarily perfect a security interest in a deposit account, letter-of-credit right, or money. See Section 9-312(b). Part 5 of the Article deals with the office in which to file, mechanics of filing, and operations of the filing office.

3. Exemptions from Filing. Subsection (b) lists the security interests for which filing is not required as a condition of perfection, because they are perfected automatically upon attachment (subsections (b)(2) and (b)(9)) or upon the occurrence of another event (subsections (b)(1), (b)(5), and (b)(9)), because they are perfected under the law of another jurisdiction (subsection (b)(10)), or because they are perfected by another method, such as by the secured party's taking possession or control (subsections (b)(3), (b)(4), (b)(5), (b)(6), (b)(7), (b)(8), and (b)(8.1)).

4. Assignments of Perfected Security Interests. Subsection (c) concerns assignment of a perfected security interest or agricultural lien. It provides that no filing is necessary in connection with an assignment by a secured party to an assignee in order to maintain perfection as against creditors of and transferees from the original debtor.

> **Example 1:** Buyer buys goods from Seller, who retains a security interest in them. After Seller perfects the security interest by filing, Seller assigns the perfected security interest to X. The security interest, in X's hands and without further steps on X's part, continues perfected against *Buyer's* transferees and creditors.

> **Example 2:** Dealer creates a security interest in specific equipment in favor of Lender. After Lender perfects the security interest in the equipment by filing, Lender assigns the chattel paper (which includes the perfected security interest in Dealer's equipment) to X. The security interest in the equipment, in X's hands and without further steps on X's part, continues perfected against Dealer's transferees and creditors. However, regardless of whether Lender made the assignment to secure Lender's obligation to X or whether the assignment was an outright sale of the chattel paper, the assignment creates a security interest in the chattel paper in favor of X. Accordingly, X must take whatever steps may be required for perfection in order to be protected against Lender's transferees and creditors with respect to the chattel paper.

Subsection (c) applies not only to an assignment of a security interest perfected by filing but also to an assignment of a security interest perfected by a method other than by filing, such as by control or by possession. Although subsection (c) addresses explicitly only the absence of an additional filing requirement, the same result normally will follow in the case of an assignment of a security interest perfected by a method other than by filing. For example, as long as possession of collateral is maintained by an assignee or by the assignor or another person on behalf of the assignee, no further perfection steps need be taken on account of the assignment to continue perfection as against creditors and transferees of the original debtor. Of course, additional action may be required for perfection of the assignee's interest as against creditors and transferees of the *assignor*.

Similarly, subsection (c) applies to the assignment of a security interest perfected by compliance with a statute, regulation, or treaty under Section 9-311(b), such as a certificate-of-title statute. Unless the statute expressly provides to the contrary, the security interest will remain perfected against creditors of and transferees from the original debtor, even if the assignee takes no action to cause the certificate of title to reflect the assignment or to cause its name to appear on the certificate of title. See PEB Commentary No. 12, which discusses this issue under former Section 9-302(3). Compliance with the statute is "equivalent to filing" under Section 9-311(b).

§ 9-311. Perfection of Security Interests in Property Subject to Certain Statutes, Regulations, and Treaties.

(a) [Security interest subject to other law.] Except as otherwise provided in subsection (d), the filing of a financing statement is not necessary or effective to perfect a security interest in property subject to:

(1) a statute, regulation, or treaty of the United States whose requirements for a security interest's obtaining priority over the rights of a lien creditor with respect to the property preempt Section 9-310(a);

(2) [list any statute covering automobiles, trailers, mobile homes, boats, farm tractors, or the like, which provides for a security interest to be indicated on a certificate of title as a condition or result of perfection, and any non-Uniform Commercial Code central filing statute]; or

(3) a statute of another jurisdiction which provides for a security interest to be indicated on a certificate of title as a condition or result of the security interest's obtaining priority over

the rights of a lien creditor with respect to the property.

(b) [Compliance with other law.] Compliance with the requirements of a statute, regulation, or treaty described in subsection (a) for obtaining priority over the rights of a lien creditor is equivalent to the filing of a financing statement under this article. Except as otherwise provided in subsection (d) and Sections 9-313 and 9-316(d) and (e) for goods covered by a certificate of title, a security interest in property subject to a statute, regulation, or treaty described in subsection (a) may be perfected only by compliance with those requirements, and a security interest so perfected remains perfected notwithstanding a change in the use or transfer of possession of the collateral.

(c) [Duration and renewal of perfection.] Except as otherwise provided in subsection (d) and Section 9-316(d) and (e), duration and renewal of perfection of a security interest perfected by compliance with the requirements prescribed by a statute, regulation, or treaty described in subsection (a) are governed by the statute, regulation, or treaty. In other respects, the security interest is subject to this article.

(d) [Inapplicability to certain inventory.] During any period in which collateral subject to a statute specified in subsection (a)(2) is inventory held for sale or lease by a person or leased by that person as lessor and that person is in the business of selling goods of that kind, this section does not apply to a security interest in that collateral created by that person.

Legislative Note: *This Article contemplates that perfection of a security interest in goods covered by a certificate of title occurs upon receipt by appropriate State officials of a properly tendered application for a certificate of title on which the security interest is to be indicated, without a relation back to an earlier time. States whose certificate-of-title statutes provide for perfection at a different time or contain a relation-back provision should amend the statutes accordingly.*

Definitional Cross References:

Certificate of title	Section 9-102(a)(10)
Collateral	Section 9-102(a)(12)
Debtor	Section 9-102(a)(28)
Financing statement	Section 9-102(a)(39)
Goods	Section 9-102(a)(44)
Inventory	Section 9-102(a)(48)
Lease	Section 2A-103(1)(j)
Lessor	Section 2A-103(1)(p)
Lien creditor	Section 9-102(a)(52)
Right	Section 1-201(b)(34)
Sale	Section 2-106(1)
Security interest	Section 1-201(b)(35)
State	Section 9-102(a)(77)

Comment References:
9-203 C5
9-303 C5
9-303 C6

Official Comment

1. Source. Former Section 9-302(3), (4).

2. Federal Statutes, Regulations, and Treaties. Subsection (a)(1) exempts from the filing provisions of this Article transactions as to which a system of filing—state or federal—has been established under federal law. Subsection (b) makes clear that when such a system exists, perfection of a relevant security interest can be achieved only through compliance with that system (i.e., filing under this Article is not a permissible alternative).

An example of the type of federal statute referred to in subsection (a)(1) is 49 U.S.C. §§ 44107-11, for civil aircraft of the United States. The Assignment of Claims Act of 1940, as amended, provides for notice to contracting and disbursing officers and to sureties on bonds but does not establish a national filing system and therefore is not within the scope of subsection (a)(1). An assignee of a claim against the United States may benefit from compliance with the Assignment of Claims Act. But regardless of whether the assignee complies with that Act, the assignee must file under this Article in order to perfect its security interest against creditors and transferees of its assignor.

Subsection (a)(1) provides explicitly that the filing requirement of this Article defers only to federal statutes, regulations, or treaties whose requirements for a security interest's obtaining priority over the rights of a lien creditor preempt Section 9-310(a). The provision eschews reference to the term "perfection," inasmuch as Section 9-308 specifies the meaning of that term and a preemptive rule may use other terminology.

3. State Statutes. Subsections (a)(2) and (3) exempt from the filing requirements of this Article transactions covered by State certificate-of-title statutes covering motor vehicles and the like. The description of certificate-of-title statutes in subsections (a)(2) and (a)(3) tracks the language of the definition of "certificate of title" in Section 9-102. For a discussion of the operation of state certificate-of-title statutes in interstate contexts, see the Comments to Section 9-303.

Some states have enacted central filing statutes with respect to secured transactions in kinds of property that are of special importance in the local economy. Subsection (a)(2) defers to these statutes with respect to filing for that property.

4. Inventory Covered by Certificate of Title. Under subsection (d), perfection of a security interest in the inventory of a person in the business of selling goods of that kind is governed by the normal perfection rules, even if the inventory is subject to a certificate-of-title statute. Compliance with a certificate-of-title statute is both unnecessary and ineffective to perfect a security interest in inventory to which this subsection applies. Thus, a secured party who finances an automobile dealer that is in the business of selling and leasing its inventory of automobiles can perfect a security interest in all the automobiles by filing a financing statement but not by compliance with a certificate-of-title statute.

Subsection (d), and thus the filing and other perfection provisions of this Article, does not apply to inventory that is subject to a certificate-of-title statute and is of a kind that the debtor is not in the business of selling. For example, if goods are subject to a certificate-of-title statute and the debtor is in the business of leasing but not of selling, goods of that kind, the other subsections of this section govern perfection of a security interest in the goods. The fact that the debtor eventually sells the goods does not, of itself, mean that the debtor "is in the business of selling goods of that kind."

The filing and other perfection provisions of this Article apply to goods subject to a certificate-of-title statute only "during any period in which collateral is inventory held for sale or lease or leased." If the debtor takes goods of this kind out of inventory and uses them, say, as equipment, a filed financing statement would not remain effective to perfect a security interest.

5. Compliance with Perfection Requirements of Other Statute. Subsection (b) makes clear that compliance with the perfection requirements (i.e., the requirements for obtaining priority over a lien creditor), but not other requirements, of a statute, regulation, or treaty described in subsection (a) is sufficient for perfection under this Article. Perfection of a security interest under such a statute, regulation, or treaty has all the consequences of perfection under this Article.

The interplay of this section with certain certificate-of-title statutes may create confusion and uncertainty. For example, statutes under which perfection does not occur until a certificate of title is issued will create a gap between the time that the goods are covered by the certificate under Section 9-303 and the time of perfection. If the gap is long enough, it may result in turning some unobjectionable transactions into avoidable preferences under Bankruptcy Code Section 547. (The preference risk arises if more than 30 days passes between the time a security interest attaches (or the debtor receives possession of the collateral, in the case of a purchase-money security interest) and the time it is perfected.) Accordingly, the Legislative Note to this section instructs the legislature to amend the applicable certificate-of-title statute to provide that perfection occurs upon receipt by the appropriate State official of a properly tendered application for a certificate of title on which the security interest is to be indicated.

Under some certificate-of-title statutes, including the Uniform Motor Vehicle Certificate of Title and Anti-Theft Act, perfection generally occurs upon delivery of specified documents to a state official but may, under certain circumstances, relate back to the time of attachment. This relation-back feature can create great difficulties for the application of the rules in Sections 9-303 and 9-311(b). Accordingly, the Legislative Note also recommends to legislatures that they remove any relation-back provisions from certificate-of-title statutes affecting security interests.

6. Compliance with Perfection Requirements of Other Statute as Equivalent to Filing. Under Subsection (b), compliance with the perfection requirements (i.e., the requirements for obtaining priority over a lien creditor) of a statute, regulation, or treaty described in subsection (a) "is equivalent to the filing of a financing statement."

The quoted phrase appeared in former Section 9-302(3). Its meaning was unclear, and many questions arose concerning the extent to which and manner in which Article 9 rules referring to "filing" were applicable to perfection by compliance with a certificate-of-title statute. This Article takes a variety of approaches for applying Article 9's filing rules to compliance with other statutes and treaties. First, as discussed above in Comment 5, it leaves the determination of some rules, such as the rule establishing time of perfection (Section 9-516(a)), to the other statutes themselves. Second, this Article explicitly applies some Article 9 filing rules to perfection under other statutes or treaties. See, e.g., Section 9-505. Third, this Article makes other Article 9 rules applicable to security interests perfected by compliance with another statute through the "equivalent to . . . " provision in the first sentence of Section 9-311(b). The third approach is reflected for the most part in occasional Comments explaining how particular rules apply when perfection is accomplished under Section 9-311(b). See, e.g., Section 9-310, Comment 4; Section 9-315, Comment 6; Section 9-317, Comment 8. The absence of a Comment indicating that a particular filing provision applies to perfection pursuant to Section 9-311(b) does not mean the provision is inapplicable.

7. Perfection by Possession of Goods Covered by Certificate-of-Title Statute. A secured party who holds a security interest perfected under the law of State A in goods that subsequently are covered by a State B certificate of title may face a predicament. Ordinarily, the secured party will have four months under State B's Section 9-316(c) and (d) in which to (re)perfect as against a purchaser of the goods by having its security interest noted on a State B certificate. This procedure is likely to require the cooperation of the debtor and any competing secured party whose security interest has been noted on the certificate. Comment 4(e) to former Section 9-103 observed that "that cooperation is not likely to be forthcoming from an owner who wrongfully procured the issuance of a new certificate not showing the out-of-state security interest, or from a local secured party finding himself in a priority contest with the out-of-state secured party." According to that Comment, "[t]he only solution for the out-of-state secured party under present certificate of title statutes seems to be to reperfect by possession, i.e., by repossessing the goods." But the "solution" may not have worked: Former Section 9-302(4) provided that a security interest in property subject to a certificate-of-title statute "can be perfected only by compliance therewith."

Sections 9-316(d) and (e), 9-311(c), and 9-313(b) of this Article resolve the conflict by providing that a security interest that remains perfected solely by virtue of Section 9-316(e) can be (re)perfected by the secured party's taking possession of the collateral. These sections contemplate only that taking possession of goods covered by a certificate of title will work as a method of perfection. None of these sections creates a right to take possession. Section 9-609 and the agreement of the parties define the secured party's right to take possession.

§ 9-312. Perfection of Security Interests in Chattel Paper, Controllable Accounts, Controllable Electronic Records, Controllable Payment Intangibles, Deposit Accounts, Documents, Goods Covered by Documents, Instruments, Investment Property, Letter-of-Credit Rights, and Money; Perfection by Permissive Filing; Temporary Perfection Without Filing or Transfer of Possession.

(a) [Perfection by filing permitted.] A security interest in chattel paper, controllable accounts, controllable electronic records, controllable payment intangibles, instruments, investment property, or negotiable documents may be perfected by filing.

(b) [Control or possession of certain collateral.] Except as otherwise provided in Section 9-315(c) and (d) for proceeds:

(1) a security interest in a deposit account may be perfected only by control under Section 9-314;

(2) and except as otherwise provided in Section 9-308(d), a security interest in a letter-of-credit right may be perfected only by control under Section 9-314;

(3) a security interest in tangible money may be perfected only by the secured party's taking possession under Section 9-313; and

(4) a security interest in electronic money may be perfected only by control under Section 9-314.

(c) [Goods covered by negotiable document.] While goods are in the possession of a bailee that has issued a negotiable document covering the goods:

(1) a security interest in the goods may be perfected by perfecting a security interest in the document; and

(2) a security interest perfected in the document has priority over any security interest that becomes perfected in the goods by another method during that time.

(d) [Goods covered by nonnegotiable document.] While goods are in the possession of a bailee that has issued a nonnegotiable document covering the goods, a security interest in the goods may be perfected by:

(1) issuance of a document in the name of the secured party;

(2) the bailee's receipt of notification of the secured party's interest; or

(3) filing as to the goods.

(e) [Temporary perfection: new value.] A security interest in certificated securities, negotiable documents, or instruments is perfected without filing or the taking of possession or control for a period of 20 days from the time it attaches to the extent that it arises for new value given under a signed security agreement.

(f) [Temporary perfection: goods or documents made available to debtor.] A perfected security interest in a negotiable document or goods in possession of a bailee, other than one that has issued a negotiable document for the goods, remains perfected for 20 days without filing if the secured party makes available to the debtor the goods or documents representing the goods for the purpose of:

(1) ultimate sale or exchange; or

(2) loading, unloading, storing, shipping, transshipping, manufacturing, processing, or otherwise dealing with them in a manner preliminary to their sale or exchange.

(g) [Temporary perfection: delivery of security certificate or instrument to debtor.] A perfected security interest in a certificated security or instrument remains perfected for 20 days without filing if the secured party delivers the security certificate or instrument to the debtor for the purpose of:

(1) ultimate sale or exchange; or

(2) presentation, collection, enforcement, renewal, or registration of transfer.

(h) [Expiration of temporary perfection.] After the 20-day period specified in subsection (e), (f), or (g) expires, perfection depends upon compliance with this article.

Definitional Cross References:

Certificated security	Section 8-102(a)(4)
Chattel paper	Section 9-102(a)(11)
Collateral	Section 9-102(a)(12)
Controllable account	Section 9-102(a)(27A)
Controllable electronic Record	Section 12-102(a)(1)
Controllable payment intangible	Section 9-102(a)(27B)
Debtor	Section 9-102(a)(28)
Delivery	Section 1-201(b)(15)
Deposit account	Section 9-102(a)(29)
Document	Section 9-102(a)(30)
Electronic money	Section 9-102(a)(31A)
Goods	Section 9-102(a)(44)
Instrument	Section 9-102(a)(47)
Investment property	Section 9-102(a)(49)
Letter-of-credit right	Section 9-102(a)(51)
Money	Section 9-102(a)(54A)
New value	Section 9-102(a)(57)
Proceeds	Section 9-102(a)(64)
Sale	Section 2-106(1)
Secured party	Section 9-102(a)(73)
Security agreement	Section 9-102(a)(74)
Security certificate	Section 8-102(a)(16)
Security interest	Section 1-201(b)(35)
Sign	Section 1-201(b)(37)
Tangible money	Section 9-102(a)(79A)

Comment References: 9-323 C3

Official Comment

1. Source. Former Section 9-304, with additions and some changes.

2. Instruments. Under subsection (a), a security interest in instruments may be perfected by filing. This rule represents an important change from former Article 9, under which the secured party's taking possession of an instrument was the only method of achieving long-term perfection. The rule is likely to be particularly useful in transactions involving a large number of notes that a debtor uses as collateral but continues to collect from the makers. A security interest perfected by filing is subject to defeat by certain subsequent purchasers (including secured parties). Under Section 9-330(d), purchasers for value who take possession of an instrument without knowledge that the purchase violates the rights of the secured party generally would achieve priority over a security interest in the instrument perfected by filing. In addition, Section 9-331 provides that filing a financing statement does not constitute notice that would preclude a subsequent purchaser from becoming a holder in due course and taking free of all claims under Section 3-306.

3. Chattel Paper; Negotiable Documents. Subsection (a) further provides that filing is available as a method of perfection for security interests in chattel paper and negotiable documents. Tangible chattel paper is sometimes delivered to the assignee, and sometimes left in the hands of the assignor for collection. Subsection (a) allows the assignee to perfect its security interest by filing in the latter case. Alternatively, the assignee may perfect by taking possession. See Section 9-313(a). An assignee of electronic chattel paper may perfect by taking control. See Sections 9-314(a), 9-105. The security interest of an assignee who takes possession or control may qualify for priority over a competing security interest perfected by filing. See Section 9-330.

Negotiable documents may be, and usually are, delivered to the secured party. See Article 1, Section 1-201 (definition of "delivery"). The secured party's taking possession of a tangible document or control of an electronic document will suffice as a perfection step. See Sections 9-313(a), 9-314 and 7-106. However, as is the case with chattel paper, a security interest in a negotiable document may be perfected by filing.

4. Investment Property. A security interest in investment property, including certificated securities, uncertificated securities, security entitlements, and securities accounts, may be perfected by filing. However, security interests created by brokers, securities intermediaries, or commodity intermediaries are automatically perfected; filing is of no effect. See Section 9-309(10), (11). A security interest in all kinds of investment property also may be perfected by control, see Sections 9-314, 9-106, and a security interest in a certificated security also may be perfected by the secured party's taking delivery under Section 8-301. See Section 9-313(a). A security interest perfected only by filing is subordinate to a conflicting security interest perfected by control or delivery. See Section 9-328(1), (5). Thus, although filing is a permissible method of perfection, a secured party who perfects by filing takes the risk that the debtor has granted or will grant a security interest in the same collateral to another party who obtains control. Also, perfection by filing would not give the secured party protection against other types of adverse claims, since the Article 8 adverse claim cut-off rules require control. See Section 8-510.

4A. Controllable Accounts, Controllable Electronic Records, and Controllable Payment Intangibles. Consistent with the treatment of chattel paper, instruments, investment property, and negotiable documents, under subsection (a) a security interest in controllable accounts, controllable electronic records, and controllable payment intangibles may be perfected by filing. A security interest in that collateral also may be perfected by control. Section 9-314.

5. Deposit Accounts. Under new subsection (b)(1), the only method of perfecting a security interest in a deposit account as original collateral is by control. Filing is ineffective, except as provided in Section 9-315 with respect to proceeds. As explained in Section 9-104, "control" can arise as a result of an agreement among the secured party, debtor, and bank, whereby the bank agrees to comply with instructions of the secured party with respect to disposition of the funds on deposit, even though the debtor retains the right to direct disposition of the funds. Thus, subsection (b)(1) takes an intermediate position between certain non-UCC law, which conditions the effectiveness of a security interest on the secured party's enjoyment of such dominion and control over the deposit account that the debtor is unable to dispose of the funds, and the approach this Article takes to securities accounts, under which a secured party who is unable to reach the collateral without resort to judicial process may perfect by filing. By conditioning perfection on "control," rather than requiring the secured party to enjoy absolute dominion to the exclusion of the debtor, subsection (b)(1) permits perfection in a wide variety of transactions, including those in which the secured party actually relies on the deposit account in extending credit and maintains some meaningful dominion over it, but does not wish to deprive the debtor of access to the funds altogether.

6. Letter-of-Credit Rights. Letter-of-credit rights commonly are "supporting obligations," as defined in Section 9-102. Perfection as to the related account, chattel paper, document, general intangible, instrument, or investment property will perfect as to the letter-of-credit rights. See Section 9-308(d). Subsection (b)(2) provides that, in other cases, a security interest in a letter-of-credit right may be perfected only by control. "Control," for these purposes, is explained in Section 9-107.

6A. Money. Under subsection (b)(3), a security interest in tangible money may be perfected only by possession under Section 9-313. Similarly, under subsection (b)(4), a security interest in electronic money may be perfected only by control under Section 9-314.

7. Goods Covered by Document of Title. Subsection (c) applies to goods in the possession of a bailee who has issued a negotiable document covering the goods. Subsection (d) applies to goods in the possession of a bailee who has issued a nonnegotiable document of title, including a document of title that is "non-negotiable" under Section 7-104. Section 9-313 governs perfection of a security interest in goods in the possession of a bailee who has not issued a document of title.

Subsection (c) clarifies the perfection and priority rules in former Section 9-304(2). Consistently with the provisions of Article 7, subsection (c) takes the position that, as long as a negotiable document covering goods is outstanding, title to the goods is, so to say, locked up in the document. Accordingly, a security interest in goods covered by a negotiable document may be perfected by perfecting a security interest in the document. The security interest also may be perfected by another method, e.g., by filing. The priority rule in subsection (c) governs only priority between (i) a security interest in goods which is perfected by perfecting in the document and (ii) a security interest in the goods which becomes perfected by another method while the goods are covered by the document.

> **Example 1:** While wheat is in a grain elevator and covered by a negotiable warehouse receipt, Debtor creates a security interest in the wheat in favor of SP-1 and SP-2. SP-1 perfects by filing a financing statement covering "wheat." Thereafter, SP-2 perfects by filing a financing statement describing the warehouse receipt. Subsection (c)(1) provides that SP-2's security interest is perfected. Subsection (c)(2) provides that SP-2's security interest is senior to SP-1's.

> **Example 2:** The facts are as in Example 1, but SP-1's security interest attached and was perfected before the goods were delivered to the grain elevator. Subsection (c)(2) does not apply, because SP-1's security interest did not become perfected during the time that the wheat was in the possession of a bailee. Rather, the first-to-file-or-perfect priority rule applies. See Sections 7-503 and 9-322.

A secured party may become "a holder to whom a negotiable document of title has been duly negotiated" under Section 7-501. If so, the secured party acquires the rights specified by Article 7. Article 9 does not limit those rights, which may include the right to priority over an earlier-perfected security interest. See Section 9-331(a).

Subsection (d) takes a different approach to the problem of goods covered by a nonnegotiable document. Here, title to the goods is not looked on as being locked up in the document. For example, a transferee that takes delivery of a nonnegotiable document receives, under Section 7-504(a), "the title and rights" of the transferor, but the transferee would not thereby become a "person entitled under the document" with a right to receive delivery of the goods from the bailee. The secured party may perfect its security interest directly in the goods by filing as to them. The subsection provides two other methods of perfection: issuance of the document in the secured party's name (as consignee of a straight bill of lading or the person to whom delivery would be made under a non-negotiable warehouse receipt) and receipt of notification of the secured party's interest by the bailee. Issuance (or reissuance) of the nonnegotiable document in the secured party's name would allow the secured party to become a "person entitled under the document." However, the bailee's receipt of notification would not confer on the secured party the status of a person entitled unless the notification resulted from an instruction under the document. See Section 7-102(a)(9) (defining "person entitled under the document") and Comment 6. Perfection under subsection (d) occurs when the bailee receives notification of the secured party's interest in the goods, regardless of who sends the notification. Receipt of notification is effective to perfect, regardless of whether the bailee responds. Unlike pre-1998 Section 9-304(3), from which it derives, subsection (d) does not apply to goods in the possession of a bailee who has not issued a document of title. Section 9-313(c) covers that case and provides that perfection by possession as to goods not covered by a document requires the bailee's acknowledgment.

Subsection (a) makes clear that a security interest in negotiable documents (and other collateral mentioned there) may be perfected by filing, but it makes no mention of nonnegotiable documents. However, under the general rule of Section 9-310, a security interest in a nonnegotiable document can be perfected by filing. A security interest in an electronic document, negotiable or nonnegotiable, can be perfected by control under Section 7-106. Section 9-314(a). But a security interest in a nonnegotiable tangible document cannot be perfected by possession. Section 9-313(a). Although a perfected security interest in a nonnegotiable document might provide useful benefits for the secured party, it would not perfect a security interest in the goods. And by perfecting a security interest in the nonnegotiable document the secured party would not thereby become a "person entitled under the document." Indeed, unless the secured party also took delivery of the document (i.e., possession or control under Section 1-201(b)(15)), it would not obtain the rights of a transferee under Section 7-504(a).

8. Temporary Perfection Without Having First Otherwise Perfected. Subsection (e) follows pre-1998 Section 9-304(4) in giving perfected status to security interests in certificated securities, instruments, and negotiable documents for a short period (reduced from 21 to 20 days, which is the time period generally applicable in this Article), although there has been no filing and the collateral is in the debtor's possession or control. The 20-day temporary perfection runs from the date of attachment. There is no limitation on the purpose for which the debtor is in possession, but the secured party must have given "new value" (defined in Section 9-102) under a signed security agreement.

9. Maintaining Perfection After Surrendering Possession. There are a variety of legitimate reasons—many of them are described in subsections (f) and (g)—why certain types of collateral must be released temporarily to a debtor. No useful purpose would be served by cluttering the files with records of such exceedingly short term transactions.

Subsection (f) affords the possibility of 20-day perfection in negotiable documents and goods in the possession of a bailee but not covered by a negotiable document. Subsection (g) provides for 20-day perfection in certificated securities and instruments. These subsections derive from former Section 9-305(5). However, the period of temporary perfection has been reduced from 21 to 20 days, which is the time period generally applicable in this Article, and "enforcement" has been added in subsection (g) as one of the special and limited purposes for which a secured party can release an instrument or certificated security to the debtor and still remain perfected. The period of temporary perfection runs from the date a secured party who already has a perfected security interest turns over the collateral to the debtor. There is no new value requirement, but the turnover must be for one or more of the purposes stated in subsection (f) or (g). The 20-day period may be extended by perfecting as to the collateral by another method before the period expires. However, if the security interest is not perfected by another method until after the 20-day period expires, there will be a gap during which the security interest is unperfected.

Temporary perfection extends only to the negotiable document or goods under subsection (f) and only to the certificated security or instrument under subsection (g). It does not extend to proceeds. If the collateral is sold, the security interest will continue in the proceeds for the period specified in Section 9-315.

Subsections (f) and (g) deal only with perfection. Other sections of this Article govern the priority of a security interest in goods after surrender of possession or control of the document covering them. In the case of a purchase-money security interest in inventory, priority may be conditioned upon giving notification to a prior inventory financer. See Section 9-324.

10. "Signed" Replaces "Authenticated." Consistent with the revised definition of "sign" in Section 1-201, the cognate term "signed" replaces the reference to "authenticated" in the pre-2022 text of this section.

§ 9-313. When Possession by or Delivery to Secured Party Perfects Security Interest Without Filing.

(a) [Perfection by possession or delivery.] Except as otherwise provided in subsection (b), a secured party may perfect a security interest in goods, instruments, negotiable tangible documents, or tangible money by taking possession of the collateral. A secured party may perfect a security interest in certificated securities by taking delivery of the certificated securities under Section 8-301.

(b) [Goods covered by certificate of title.] With respect to goods covered by a certificate of title issued by this State, a secured party may perfect a security interest in the goods by taking possession of the goods only in the circumstances described in Section 9-316(d).

(c) [Collateral in possession of person other than debtor.] With respect to collateral other than certificated securities and goods covered by a document, a secured party takes possession of collateral in the possession of a person other than the debtor, the secured party, or a lessee of the collateral from the debtor in the ordinary course of the debtor's business, when:

(1) the person in possession signs a record acknowledging that it holds possession of the collateral for the secured party's benefit; or

(2) the person takes possession of the collateral after having signed a record acknowledging that it will hold possession of the collateral for the secured party's benefit.

(d) [Time of perfection by possession; continuation of perfection.] If perfection of a security interest depends upon possession of the collateral by a secured party, perfection occurs not earlier than the time the secured party takes possession and continues only while the secured party retains possession.

(e) [Time of perfection by delivery; continuation of perfection.] A security interest in a certificated security in registered form is perfected by delivery when delivery of the certificated security occurs under Section 8-301 and remains perfected by delivery until the debtor obtains possession of the security certificate.

(f) [Acknowledgment not required.] A person in possession of collateral is not required to acknowledge that it holds possession for a secured party's benefit.

(g) [Effectiveness of acknowledgment; no duties or confirmation.] If a person acknowledges that it holds possession for the secured party's benefit:

(1) the acknowledgment is effective under subsection (c) or Section 8-301(a), even if the acknowledgment violates the rights of a debtor; and

(2) unless the person otherwise agrees or law other than this article otherwise provides, the person does not owe any duty to the secured party and is not required to confirm the acknowledgment to another person.

(h) [Secured party's delivery to person other than debtor.] A secured party having possession of collateral does not relinquish possession by delivering the collateral to a person other than the debtor or a lessee of the collateral from the debtor in the ordinary course of the debtor's business if the person was instructed before the delivery or is instructed contemporaneously with the delivery:

(1) to hold possession of the collateral for the secured party's benefit; or

(2) to redeliver the collateral to the secured party.

(i) [Effect of delivery under subsection (h); no duties or confirmation.] A secured party does not relinquish possession, even if a delivery under subsection (h) violates the rights of a debtor. A person to which collateral is delivered under subsection (h) does not owe any duty to the secured party and is not required to confirm the delivery to another person unless the person otherwise agrees or law other than this article otherwise provides.

Definitional Cross References:

Certificate of title	Section 9-102(a)(10)
Certificated security	Section 8-102(a)(4)
Collateral	Section 9-102(a)(12)
Debtor	Section 9-102(a)(28)
Delivery	Section 1-201(b)(15)
Document	Section 9-102(a)(30)
Goods	Section 9-102(a)(44)
Instrument	Section 9-102(a)(47)
Lessee	Section 2A-103(1)(n)
Money	Section 9-102(a)(54A)
Person	Section 1-201(b)(27)
Record	Section 9-102(a)(70)
Right	Section 1-201(b)(34)
Secured party	Section 9-102(a)(73)
Security certificate	Section 8-102(a)(16)
Security interest	Section 1-201(b)(35)
Sign	Section 1-201(b)(37)
State	Section 9-102(a)(77)
Tangible money	Section 9-102(a)(79A)

Comment References: 9-203 C4

Official Comment

1. Source. Former Sections 9-305, 9-115(6).

2. Perfection by Possession. As under the common law of pledge, no filing is required by this Article to perfect a security interest if the secured party takes possession of the collateral. See Section 9-310(b)(6).

This section permits a security interest to be perfected by the taking of possession only when the collateral is goods, instruments, negotiable tangible documents, or tangible money. Accounts, commercial tort claims, deposit accounts, investment property, letter-of-credit rights, letters of credit, and oil, gas, or other minerals before extraction are excluded. (But see Comment 6, below, regarding certificated securities.) A security interest in accounts and payment intangibles—property not ordinarily represented by any writing whose delivery operates to transfer the right to payment—may under this Article be perfected only by filing. This rule would not be affected by the fact that a security agreement or other record described the assignment of such collateral as a "pledge." Section 9-309(2) exempts from filing certain assignments of accounts or payment intangibles which are out of the ordinary course of financing. These exempted assignments are perfected when they attach. Similarly, under Section 9-309(3), sales of payment intangibles are automatically perfected.

Perfection by possession of chattel paper evidenced by an authoritative tangible record (formerly defined as "tangible chattel paper") has been removed from this section. Instead, perfection by possession and control of chattel paper is governed by Section 9-314A.

3. "Possession." This section does not define "possession." It adopts the general concept as it developed under former Article 9. As under former Article 9, in determining whether a particular person has possession, the principles of agency apply. For example, if the collateral is in possession of an agent of the secured party for the purposes of possessing on behalf of the secured party, and if the agent is not also an agent of the debtor, the secured party has taken actual possession, and subsection (c) does not apply. Sometimes a person holds collateral both as an agent of the secured party and as an agent of the debtor. The fact of dual agency is not of itself inconsistent with the secured party's having taken possession (and thereby having rendered subsection (c) inapplicable). The debtor cannot qualify as an agent for the secured party for purposes of the secured party's taking possession. And, under appropriate circumstances, a court may determine that a person in possession is so closely connected to or controlled by the debtor that the debtor has retained effective possession, even though the person may have agreed to take possession on behalf of the secured party. If so, the person's taking possession would not constitute the secured party's taking possession and would not be sufficient for perfection. See also Section 9-205(b). In a typical escrow arrangement, where the escrowee has possession of collateral as agent for both the secured party and the debtor, the debtor's relationship to the escrowee is not such as to constitute retention of possession by the debtor.

4. Goods in Possession of Third Party: Perfection. Former Section 9-305 permitted perfection of a security interest by notification to a bailee in possession of collateral. This Article distinguishes between goods in the possession of a bailee who has issued a document of title covering the goods and goods in the possession of a third party who has not issued a document. Section 9-312(c) or (d) applies to the former, depending on whether the document is negotiable. Section 9-313(c) applies to the latter. It provides a method of perfection by possession when the collateral is possessed by a third person who is not the secured party's agent.

Notification of a third person does not suffice to perfect under Section 9-313(c). Rather, perfection does not occur unless the third person signs an acknowledgment that it holds possession of the collateral for the secured party's benefit. Compare Section 9-312(d), under which receipt of notification of the security party's interest by a bailee holding goods covered by a nonnegotiable document is sufficient to perfect, even if the bailee does not acknowledge receipt of the notification. A third person may acknowledge that it will hold for the secured party's benefit goods to be received in the future. Under these circumstances, perfection by possession occurs when the third person obtains possession of the goods.

Under subsection (c), acknowledgment of notification by a "lessee . . . in . . . ordinary course of . . . business" (defined in Section 2A-103) does not suffice for possession. The section thus rejects the reasoning of *In re Atlantic Systems, Inc.*, 135 B.R. 463 (Bankr. S.D.N.Y. 1992) (holding that notification to debtor-lessor's lessee sufficed to perfect security interest in leased goods). See Steven O. Weise, *Perfection by Possession: The Need for an Objective Test,* 29 Idaho Law Rev. 705 (1992-93) (arguing that lessee's possession in ordinary course of debtor-lessor's business does not provide adequate public notice of possible security interest in leased goods). Inclusion of a per se rule concerning lessees is not meant to preclude a court, under appropriate circumstances, from determining that a third person is so closely connected to or controlled by the debtor that the debtor has retained effective possession. If so, the third person's acknowledgment would not be sufficient for perfection.

In some cases, it may be uncertain whether a person who has possession of collateral is an agent of the secured party or a non-agent bailee. Under those circumstances, prudence might suggest that the secured party obtain the person's acknowledgment to avoid litigation and ensure perfection by possession regardless of how the relationship between the secured party and the person is characterized.

5. No Relation Back; time of perfection and continuation of perfection. Former Section 9-305 provided that a security interest is perfected by possession from the time possession is taken "without a relation back." As the Comment to pre-1998 Section 9-305 observed, the relation-back theory, under which the taking of possession was deemed to relate back to the date of the original security agreement, has had little vitality since the 1938 revision of the Federal Bankruptcy Act. The theory is inconsistent with pre-1998 Article 9 and with this Article. See Section 9-313(d). Accordingly, this Article deletes the quoted phrase as unnecessary. Under Subsection (d), where a pledge (perfection by possession) transaction is contemplated, perfection dates only from the time possession is taken. The only exceptions to this rule are the short, 20-day periods of perfection provided in Section 9-312(e), (f), and (g), during which a debtor may have possession of specified collateral in which there is a perfected security interest. Also under subsection (d), perfection continues only while the secured party retains possession. However, if a secured party's possession is based on an acknowledgment under Section 9-313(c) by another person in possession, the secured party remains perfected by possession only while the other person retains possession. This result necessarily follows because such a secured party's possession derives solely from the other person's continued possession.

6. Certificated Securities. The second sentence of subsection (a) reflects the traditional rule for perfection of a security interest in certificated securities. Compare Section 9-115(6) (1994 Official Text); Sections 8-321, 8-313(1)(a) (1978 Official Text); Section 9-305 (1972 Official Text). It has been modified to refer to "delivery" under Section 8-301. Corresponding changes appear in Section 9-203(b).

Subsection (e), which is new, applies to a secured party in possession of security certificates or another person who has taken delivery of security certificates and holds them for the secured party's benefit under Section 8-301. See Comment 8.

Under subsection (e), a possessory security interest in a certificated security remains perfected until the debtor obtains possession of the security certificate. This rule is analogous to that of Section 9-314(c), which deals with perfection of security interests in investment property by control. See Section 9-314, Comment 3.

7. Goods Covered by Certificate of Title. Subsection (b) is necessary to effect changes to the choice-of-law rules governing goods covered by a certificate of title. These changes are described in the Comments to Section 9-311. Subsection (b), like subsection (a), does not create a right to take possession. Rather, it indicates the circumstances under which the secured party's taking possession of goods covered by a certificate of title is effective to perfect a security interest in the goods: the goods become covered by a certificate of title issued by this State at a time when the security interest is perfected by any method under the law of another jurisdiction.

8. Goods in Possession of Third Party: No Duty to Acknowledge; Consequences of Acknowledgment. Subsections (f) and (g) are new and address matters as to which former Article 9 was silent. They derive in part from Section 8-106(g). Subsection (f) provides that a person in possession of collateral is not required to acknowledge that it holds for a secured party. Subsection (g)(1) provides that an acknowledgment is effective even if wrongful as to the debtor. Subsection (g)(2) makes clear that an acknowledgment does not give rise to any duties or responsibilities under this Article. Arrangements involving the possession of goods are hardly standardized. They include bailments for services to be performed on the goods (such as repair or processing), for use (leases), as security (pledges), for carriage, and for storage. This Article leaves to the agreement of the parties and to any other applicable law the imposition of duties and responsibilities upon a person who acknowledges under subsection (c). For example, by acknowledging, a third party does not become obliged to act on the secured party's direction or to remain in possession of the collateral unless it agrees to do so or other law so provides.

9. Delivery to Third Party by Secured Party. Subsections (h) and (i) address the practice of mortgage warehouse lenders. These lenders typically send mortgage notes to prospective purchasers under cover of letters advising the prospective purchasers that the lenders hold security interests in the notes. These lenders relied on notification to maintain perfection under pre-1998 Section 9-305. Requiring them to obtain signed acknowledgments from each prospective purchaser under subsection (c) could be unduly burdensome and disruptive of established practices. Under subsection (h), when a secured party in possession itself delivers the collateral to a third party, instructions to the third party would be sufficient to maintain perfection by possession; an acknowledgment would not be necessary. Under subsection (i), the secured party does not relinquish possession by making a delivery under subsection (h), even if the delivery violates the rights of the debtor. That subsection also makes clear that a person to whom collateral is delivered under subsection (h) does not owe any duty to the secured party and is not required to confirm the delivery to another person unless the person otherwise agrees or law other than this Article provides otherwise.

10. "Signs" and "Signed" Replaces "Authenticates" and "Authenticated." Consistent with the revised definition of "sign" in Section 1-201, the cognate terms "signs" and "signed" replace the references to "authenticates" and "authenticated" in the pre-2022 text of this section.

§ 9-314. Perfection by Control.

(a) [Perfection by control.] A security interest in controllable accounts, controllable electronic records, controllable payment intangibles, deposit accounts, electronic documents, electronic money, investment property, or letter-of-credit rights may be perfected by control of the collateral under Sections 7-106, 9-104, 9-105A, 9-106, 9-107, or 9-107A.

(b) [Specified collateral: time of perfection by control; continuation of perfection.] A security interest in controllable accounts, controllable electronic records, controllable payment intangibles, deposit accounts, electronic documents, electronic money, or letter-of-credit rights is perfected by control under Sections 7-106, 9-104, 9-105A, 9-107, or 9-107A not earlier than the time the secured party obtains control and remains perfected by control only while the secured party retains control.

(c) [Investment property: time of perfection by control; continuation of perfection.] A security interest in investment property is perfected by control under Section 9-106 not earlier than the time the secured party obtains control and remains perfected by control until:

(1) the secured party does not have control; and

(2) one of the following occurs:

(A) if the collateral is a certificated security, the debtor has or acquires possession of the security certificate;

(B) if the collateral is an uncertificated security, the issuer has registered or registers the debtor as the registered owner; or

(C) if the collateral is a security entitlement, the debtor is or becomes the entitlement holder.

Definitional Cross References:

Certificated security	Section 8-102(a)(4)
Collateral	Section 9-102(a)(12)
Controllable account	Section 9-102(a)(27A)
Controllable electronic Record	Section 12-102(a)(1)
Controllable payment intangible	Section 9-102(a)(27B)
Debtor	Section 9-102(a)(28)
Deposit account	Section 9-102(a)(29)
Document	Section 9-102(a)(30)
Electronic	Section 1-201(b)(16A)
Electronic money	Section 9-102(a)(31A)
Entitlement holder	Section 8-102(a)(7)
Investment property	Section 9-102(a)(49)
Issuer (security)	Section 8-201(a)
Letter-of-credit right	Section 9-102(a)(51)
Secured party	Section 9-102(a)(73)
Security certificate	Section 8-102(a)(16)
Security entitlement	Section 8-102(a)(17)
Security interest	Section 1-201(b)(35)
Uncertificated security	Section 8-102(a)(18)

Official Comment

1. Source. Substantially new; derived in part from former Section 9-115(4).

2. Control. This section provides for perfection by control with respect to controllable accounts, controllable electronic records, controllable payment intangibles, deposit accounts, electronic documents, electronic money, investment property, and letter-of-credit rights. Concerning how a secured party takes control of these types of collateral, see Sections 7-106, 9- 104, 9-105A, 9-107, and 9-107A, and Comments. Subsection (b) explains when a security interest is perfected by control and how long a security interest remains perfected by control. Like Section 9-313(d) and for the same reasons, subsection (b) makes no reference to the doctrine of "relation back." See Section 9-313, Comment 5. As to an electronic document that is reissued in a tangible medium, (see Section 7-105), a secured party that is perfected by control in the electronic document should file as to the document before relinquishing control in order to maintain continuous perfection in the document. See Section 9-308. If a secured party's control is based on an acknowledgment under Section 7-106(g), 9- 104(a)(4), or 9-105A(e) or under 9-107A and 12-105(e) by another person having control, the secured party remains perfected by control only while the other person retains control. This result necessarily follows because such a secured party's control derives solely from the other person's continued control.

Perfection by control of chattel paper evidenced by an authoritative electronic record (formerly defined as "electronic chattel paper") has been removed from this section. Instead, perfection by possession and control of chattel paper is governed by Section 9-314A.

3. Investment Property. Subsection (c) provides a special rule for investment property. Once a secured party has control, its security interest remains perfected by control until the secured party ceases to have control and the debtor receives possession of collateral that is a certificated security, becomes the registered owner of collateral that is an uncertificated security, or becomes the entitlement holder of collateral that is a security entitlement. The result is particularly important in the "repledge" context. See Section 9-207, Comment 5.

In a transaction in which a secured party who has control grants a security interest in investment property or sells outright the investment property, by virtue of the debtor's consent or applicable legal rules, a purchaser from the secured party typically will cut off the debtor's rights in the investment property or be immune from the debtor's claims. See Section 9-207, Comments 5 and 6. If the investment property is a security, the debtor normally would retain no interest in the security following the purchase from the secured party, and a claim of the debtor against the secured party for redemption (Section

9-623) or otherwise with respect to the security would be a purely personal claim. If the investment property transferred by the secured party is a financial asset in which the debtor had a security entitlement credited to a securities account maintained with the secured party as a securities intermediary, the debtor's claim against the secured party could arise as a part of its securities account notwithstanding its personal nature. (This claim would be analogous to a "credit balance" in the securities account, which is a component of the securities account even though it is a personal claim against the intermediary.) In the case in which the debtor may retain an interest in investment property notwithstanding a repledge or sale by the secured party, subsection (c) makes clear that the security interest will remain perfected by control. Notwithstanding subsection (c), if a secured party's control is based on an acknowledgment under Section 8-106(d)(3) by another person having control, the secured party remains perfected by control only while the other person retains control. This result necessarily follows because such a secured party's control derives solely from the other person's continued control. Although Section 8-106(d)(3) was amended by the 2022 Article 9 Revisions, this result also applied to a secured party in control under pre-2022 subsection (d)(3).

3A. Shared control between debtor and secured party (and other transferor and transferee) and control through another person. Sections 7-106 (control of electronic documents), 9-105 (control of authoritative electronic records evidencing chattel paper), 9-105A (control of electronic money), and 12-105 (control of controllable electronic records, on which control of controllable accounts and controllable payment intangibles under Section 9-107A depends) contemplate the possibility that both a debtor and a secured party may have control of the relevant collateral by sharing an exclusive power. Such shared control between a debtor and secured party does not necessarily impair perfection of a security interest under this section or Section 9-314A. On shared exclusive powers, see generally Section 12-105, Comment 5. However, if a secured party can exercise a power only if the power is exercised also by the debtor, the power would not be shared and, consequently, the secured party would not have control based on the exclusive power. This result follows from Section 12-105(c) and corresponding subsections in the other provisions on control cited above. Under Section 12- 105(c), because a debtor would be a "transferor of an interest" in a controllable electronic record or a controllable account or payment intangible evidenced by the record, the debtor's "blocking power" (i.e., the secured party can exercise the power only if the debtor also exercises the power) with respect to the secured party's exercise of the power would disqualify the secured party from sharing (and, consequently, enjoying) the exclusive power and perfection by control based on exclusive powers. Similarly, a purchaser in that situation would be disqualified from having control and thereby from enjoying the status and benefits of a qualifying purchaser (Section 12- 102(a)(2)) under Section 12-104(e) and (g) if the purchaser takes from a transferor of an interest and the transferor has such a blocking power (whether or not the transferor is a debtor).

Section 12-105(e) contains a similar limitation in connection with control through another person. An acknowledging person must be one "other than the transferor of an interest in the electronic record." The same or a similar limitation is found in the other provisions relating to control through another person. See Sections 7-106(g) (control of electronic document of title); 8-106(d)(3) (control of a security entitlement); 9-104(a)(4) (control of deposit accounts); 9-105(g) (control of authoritative electronic copy of record evidencing chattel paper); 9-105A)(e) (control of electronic money).

For a discussion of the rationale for these limitations on sharing exclusive control and control through another person, see Section 12-105, Comment 9.

§ 9-314A. Perfection by Possession and Control of Chattel Paper.

(a) [Perfection by possession and control.] A secured party may perfect a security interest in chattel paper by taking possession of each authoritative tangible copy of the record evidencing the chattel paper and obtaining control of each authoritative electronic copy of the electronic record evidencing the chattel paper.

(b) [Time of perfection; continuation of perfection.] A security interest is perfected under subsection (a) not earlier than the time the secured party takes possession and obtains control and remains perfected under subsection (a) only while the secured party retains possession and control.

(c) [Application of Section 9-313 to perfection by possession of chattel paper.] Section 9-313(c) and (f) through (i) applies to perfection by possession of an authoritative tangible copy of a record evidencing chattel paper.

Definitional Cross References:

Chattel paper	Section 9-102(a)(11)
Electronic	Section 1-201(b)(16A)
Record	Section 9-102(a)(70)
Secured party	Section 9-102(a)(73)
Security interest	Section 1-201(b)(35)

Official Comment

1. "Authoritative copy." To perfect a security interest in chattel paper other than by filing, this section provides that a secured party must obtain control of all authoritative electronic copies and take possession of all authoritative tangible copies.

Like the pre-2022 text, Section 9-105(b) distinguishes between authoritative and nonauthoritative copies of electronic chattel paper and refers to copies that are "authoritative." And, like its predecessor, Section 9-105(b) does not define the term "authoritative." However, it also applies this concept to tangible records that evidence chattel paper.

To show that it has possession of all authoritative tangible copies of a record evidencing chattel paper and all authoritative electronic copies of a record evidencing chattel paper, a purchaser can produce the tangible copies in its possession and prove control of the electronic copies and provide evidence that these are authoritative copies. The purchaser need not prove a negative—i.e., that no other tangible or electronic authoritative copies exist—to make a prima facie case. The purchaser's possession of the authoritative tangible copies and control of the authoritative electronic copies gives the purchaser the power to prevent others from taking possession or control of the copies and the power to transfer possession and control of the copies.

Perfection of a security interest in chattel paper by taking possession of the collateral generally has been understood to mean taking possession of the wet-ink "original." Experience has shown that the concept of an original breaks down when one allows for the possibility of the same monetary obligation being evidenced by different media over time, such as where electronic records evidencing the chattel paper are "papered out" (replaced with tangible records evidencing the same chattel paper) or tangible records are "converted" to electronic records.

Whether an electronic or tangible copy of a record evidencing chattel paper is authoritative depends on the facts and circumstances. The determination should turn on whether the copy provides reasonable notice to third parties that it is one that must be subject to control or possession for purposes of perfection and priority. To accommodate current practices and future technology, parties are allowed considerable flexibility in determining the method used to establish whether a particular copy is authoritative, provided that third parties are able to reasonably identify the authoritative copies that must be possessed or controlled to achieve perfection. For example, the parties could develop a system or protocol where each tangible or electronic copy is "watermarked" as authoritative or nonauthoritative or where the terms of the records themselves describe how to determine which copies are authoritative and which are not.

2. Time of perfection; continuation of perfection. Subsection (b) is modeled on Sections 9-313(d) and 9-314(b). If a secured party's possession or control is based on the acknowledgment under Section 9-313(c) or 9-105(g) by another person in possession or control, the secured party remains perfected by possession or control only while the other person retains possession or control. This result necessarily follows because such a secured party's possession or control derives solely from the other person's continued possession or control.

3. Applicability of Section 9-313. Subsection (c) makes specified subsections of Section 9-313 applicable to possession of authoritative tangible copies of records evidencing chattel paper.

4. Shared control. As to the sharing of powers over an authoritative electronic copy of a record evidencing chattel paper (see Section 9-105(c)(2)) by a debtor and a secured party (or by another transferor and transferee) and control through another person (see Section 9-105(g)), see Sections 9-314, Comment 3A; 12-105, Comment 9.

§ 9-315. Secured Party's Rights on Disposition of Collateral and in Proceeds.

(a) [Disposition of collateral: continuation of security interest or agricultural lien; proceeds.] Except as otherwise provided in this article and in Section 2-403(2):

(1) a security interest or agricultural lien continues in collateral notwithstanding sale, lease, license, exchange, or other disposition thereof unless the secured party authorized the disposition free of the security interest or agricultural lien; and

(2) a security interest attaches to any identifiable proceeds of collateral.

(b) [When commingled proceeds identifiable.] Proceeds that are commingled with other property are identifiable proceeds:

(1) if the proceeds are goods, to the extent provided by Section 9-336; and

(2) if the proceeds are not goods, to the extent that the secured party identifies the proceeds by a method of tracing, including application of equitable principles, that is permitted under law other than this article with respect to commingled property of the type involved.

(c) [Perfection of security interest in proceeds.] A security interest in proceeds is a perfected security interest if the security interest in the original collateral was perfected.

(d) [Continuation of perfection.] A perfected security interest in proceeds becomes unperfected on the 21st day after the security interest attaches to the proceeds unless:

(1) the following conditions are satisfied:

(A) a filed financing statement covers the original collateral;

(B) the proceeds are collateral in which a security interest may be perfected by filing in the office in which the financing statement has been filed; and

(C) the proceeds are not acquired with cash proceeds;

(2) the proceeds are identifiable cash proceeds; or

(3) the security interest in the proceeds is perfected other than under subsection (c) when the security interest attaches to the proceeds or within 20 days thereafter.

(e) [When perfected security interest in proceeds becomes unperfected.] If a filed financing statement covers the original collateral, a security interest in proceeds which remains perfected under subsection (d)(1) becomes unperfected at the later of:

(1) when the effectiveness of the filed financing statement lapses under Section 9-515 or is terminated under Section 9-513; or

(2) the 21st day after the security interest attaches to the proceeds.

Definitional Cross References:

Agricultural lien	Section 9-102(a)(5)
Cash proceeds	Section 9-102(a)(9)
Collateral	Section 9-102(a)(12)
Financing statement	Section 9-102(a)(39)
Goods	Section 9-102(a)(44)
Lease	Section 2A-103(1)(j)
Proceeds	Section 9-102(a)(64)
Right	Section 1-201(b)(34)
Sale	Section 2-106(1)
Secured party	Section 9-102(a)(73)
Security interest	Section 1-201(b)(35)

Comment References: 9-109 C16, 9-205 C3

Official Comment

1. Source. Former Section 9-306.

2. Continuation of Security Interest or Agricultural Lien Following Disposition of Collateral. Subsection (a)(1), which derives from former Section 9-306(2), contains the general rule that a security interest survives disposition of the collateral. In these cases, the secured party may repossess the collateral from the transferee or, in an appropriate case, maintain an action for conversion. The secured party may claim both any proceeds and the original collateral but, of course, may have only one satisfaction.

In many cases, a purchaser or other transferee of collateral will take free of a security interest, and the secured party's only right will be to proceeds. For example, the general rule does not apply, and a security interest does not continue in collateral, if the secured party authorized the disposition, in the agreement that contains the security agreement or otherwise. Subsection (a)(1) adopts the view of PEB Commentary No. 3 and makes explicit that the authorized disposition to which it refers is an authorized disposition "free of" the security interest or agricultural lien. The secured party's right to proceeds under this section or under the express terms of an agreement does not in itself constitute an authorization of disposition. The change in language from former Section 9-306(2) is not intended to address the frequently litigated situation in which the effectiveness of the secured party's consent to a disposition is conditioned upon the secured party's receipt of the proceeds. In that situation, subsection (a) leaves the determination of authorization to the courts, as under former Article 9.

This Article contains several provisions under which a transferee takes free of a security interest or agricultural lien. For example, Section 9-317 states when transferees take free of unperfected security interests; Sections 9-320 and 9-321 on goods, 9-321 on general intangibles, 9-330 on chattel paper and instruments, and 9-331 on negotiable instruments, negotiable documents, and securities state when purchasers of such collateral take free of a security interest, even though perfected and even though the disposition was not authorized. Section 9-332 enables most transferees (including non-purchasers) of funds from a deposit account and most transferees of money to take free of a perfected security interest in the deposit account or money.

Likewise, the general rule that a security interest survives disposition does not apply if the secured party entrusts goods collateral to a merchant who deals in goods of that kind and the merchant sells the collateral to a buyer in ordinary course of business. Section 2-403(2) gives the merchant the power to transfer all the secured party's rights to the buyer, even if the sale is wrongful as against the secured party. Thus, under subsection (a)(1), an entrusting secured party runs the same risk as any other entruster.

3. Secured Party's Right to Identifiable Proceeds. Under subsection (a)(2), which derives from former Section 9-306(2), a security interest attaches to any identifiable "proceeds," as defined in Section 9-102. See also Section 9-203(f). Subsection (b) is new. It indicates when proceeds commingled with other property are identifiable proceeds and permits the use of whatever methods of tracing other law permits with respect to the type of property involved. Among the "equitable principles" whose use other law may permit is the "lowest intermediate balance rule." See Restatement (2d), Trusts § 202.

4. Automatic Perfection in Proceeds: General Rule. Under subsection (c), a security interest in proceeds is a perfected security interest if the security interest in the original collateral was perfected. This Article extends the period of automatic perfection in proceeds from 10 days to 20 days. Generally, a security interest in proceeds becomes unperfected on the 21st day after the security interest attaches to the proceeds. See subsection (d). The loss of perfected status under subsection (d) is prospective only. Compare, e.g., Section 9-515(c) (deeming security interest unperfected retroactively).

5. Automatic Perfection in Proceeds: Proceeds Acquired with Cash Proceeds. Subsection (d)(1) derives from former Section 9-306(3)(a). It carries forward the basic rule that a security interest in proceeds remains perfected beyond the period of automatic perfection if a filed financing statement covers the original collateral (e.g., inventory) and the proceeds are collateral in which a security interest may be perfected by filing in the office where the financing statement has been filed (e.g., equipment). A different rule applies if the proceeds are acquired with cash proceeds, as is the case if the original collateral (inventory) is sold for cash (cash proceeds) that is used to purchase equipment (proceeds). Under these circumstances, the security interest in the equipment proceeds remains perfected only if the description in the filed financing indicates the type of property constituting the proceeds (e.g., "equipment").

This section reaches the same result but takes a different approach. It recognizes that the treatment of proceeds acquired with cash proceeds under former Section 9-306(3)(a) essentially was superfluous. In the example, had the filing covered "equipment" as well as "inventory," the security interest in the proceeds would have been perfected under the usual rules governing after-acquired equipment (see former Sections 9-302, 9-303); paragraph (3)(a) added only an exception to the general rule. Subsection (d)(1)(C) of this section takes a more direct approach. It makes the general rule of continued perfection inapplicable to proceeds acquired with cash proceeds, leaving perfection of a security interest in those proceeds to the generally applicable perfection rules under subsection (d)(3).

Example 1: Lender perfects a security interest in Debtor's inventory by filing a financing statement covering "inventory." Debtor sells the inventory and deposits the buyer's check into a deposit account. Debtor draws a check on the deposit account and uses it to pay for equipment. Under the "lowest intermediate balance rule," which is a permitted method of tracing in the relevant jurisdiction, see Comment 3, the funds used to pay for the equipment were identifiable proceeds of the inventory. Because the proceeds (equipment) were acquired with cash proceeds (deposit account), subsection (d)(1) does not extend perfection beyond the 20-day automatic period.

Example 2: Lender perfects a security interest in Debtor's inventory by filing a financing statement covering "all debtor's property." As in Example 1, Debtor sells the inventory, deposits the buyer's check into a deposit account, draws a check on the deposit account, and uses the check to pay for equipment. Under the "lowest intermediate balance rule," which is a permitted method of tracing in the relevant jurisdiction, see Comment 3, the funds used to pay for the equipment were identifiable proceeds of the inventory. Because the proceeds (equipment) were acquired with cash proceeds (deposit account), subsection (d)(1) does not extend perfection beyond the 20-day automatic period. However, because the financing statement is sufficient to perfect a security interest in debtor's equipment, under subsection (d)(3) the security interest in the equipment proceeds remains perfected beyond the 20-day period.

6. Automatic Perfection in Proceeds: Lapse or Termination of Financing Statement During 20-Day Period; Perfection under Other Statute or Treaty. Subsection (e) provides that a security interest in proceeds perfected under subsection (d)(1) ceases to be perfected when the financing statement covering the original collateral lapses or is terminated. If the lapse or termination occurs before the 21st day after the security interest attaches, however, the security interest in the proceeds remains perfected until the 21st day. Section 9-311(b) provides that compliance with the perfection requirements of a statute or treaty described in Section 9-311(a) "is equivalent to the filing of a financing statement." It follows that collateral subject to a security interest perfected by such compliance under Section 9-311(b) is covered by a "filed financing statement" within the meaning of Section 9-315(d) and (e).

7. Automatic Perfection in Proceeds: Continuation of Perfection in Cash Proceeds. Former Section 9-306(3)(b) provided that if a filed financing statement covered original collateral, a security interest in identifiable cash proceeds of the collateral remained perfected beyond the ten-day period of automatic perfection. Former Section 9-306(3)(c) contained a similar rule with respect to identifiable cash proceeds of investment property. Subsection (d)(2) extends the benefits of former Sections 9-306(3)(b) and (3)(c) to identifiable cash proceeds of all types of original collateral in which a security interest is perfected by any method. Under subsection (d)(2), if the security interest in the original collateral was perfected, a security interest in identifiable cash proceeds will remain perfected indefinitely, regardless of whether the security interest in the original collateral remains perfected. In many cases, however, a purchaser or other transferee of the cash proceeds will take free of the perfected security interest. See, e.g.,

Sections 9-330(d) (purchaser of check), 9-331 (holder in due course of check), 9-332 (transferee of money or funds from a deposit account).

8. Insolvency Proceedings; Returned and Repossessed Goods. This Article deletes former Section 9-306(4), which dealt with proceeds in insolvency proceedings. Except as otherwise provided by the Bankruptcy Code, the debtor's entering into bankruptcy does not affect a secured party's right to proceeds.

This Article also deletes former Section 9-306(5), which dealt with returned and repossessed goods. Section 9-330, Comments 9 to 11 explain and clarify the application of priority rules to returned and repossessed goods as proceeds of chattel paper.

9. Proceeds of Collateral Subject to Agricultural Lien. This Article does not determine whether a lien extends to proceeds of farm products encumbered by an agricultural lien. If, however, the proceeds are themselves farm products on which an "agricultural lien" (defined in Section 9-102) arises under other law, then the agricultural-lien provisions of this Article apply to the agricultural lien on the proceeds in the same way in which they would apply had the farm products not been proceeds.

§ 9-316. Continued Perfection of Security Interest Following Change in Governing Law

(a) [General rule: effect on perfection of change in governing law.] A security interest perfected pursuant to the law of the jurisdiction designated in Section 9-301(1), 9-305(c), 9-306A(d), or 9-306B(b) remains perfected until the earliest of:

(1) the time perfection would have ceased under the law of that jurisdiction;

(2) the expiration of four months after a change of the debtor's location to another jurisdiction; or

(3) the expiration of one year after a transfer of collateral to a person that thereby becomes a debtor and is located in another jurisdiction.

(b) [Security interest perfected or unperfected under law of new jurisdiction.] If a security interest described in subsection (a) becomes perfected under the law of the other jurisdiction before the earliest time or event described in that subsection, it remains perfected thereafter. If the security interest does not become perfected under the law of the other jurisdiction before the earliest time or event, it becomes unperfected and is deemed never to have been perfected as against a purchaser of the collateral for value.

(c) [Possessory security interest in collateral moved to new jurisdiction.] A possessory security interest in collateral, other than goods covered by a certificate of title and as-extracted collateral consisting of goods, remains continuously perfected if:

(1) the collateral is located in one jurisdiction and subject to a security interest perfected under the law of that jurisdiction;

(2) thereafter the collateral is brought into another jurisdiction; and

(3) upon entry into the other jurisdiction, the security interest is perfected under the law of the other jurisdiction.

(d) [Goods covered by certificate of title from this state.] Except as otherwise provided in subsection (e), a security interest in goods covered by a certificate of title which is perfected by any method under the law of another jurisdiction when the goods become covered by a certificate of title from this State remains perfected until the security interest would have become unperfected under the law of the other jurisdiction had the goods not become so covered.

(e) [When subsection (d) security interest becomes unperfected against purchasers.] A security interest described in subsection (d) becomes unperfected as against a purchaser of the goods for value and is deemed never to have been perfected as against a purchaser of the goods for value if the applicable requirements for perfection under Section 9-311(b) or 9-313 are not satisfied before the earlier of:

(1) the time the security interest would have become unperfected under the law of the other jurisdiction had the goods not become covered by a certificate of title from this State; or

(2) the expiration of four months after the goods had become so covered.

(f) [Change in jurisdiction of chattel paper, controllable electronic record, bank, issuer, nominated person, securities intermediary, or commodity intermediary.] A security interest in chattel paper, controllable accounts, controllable electronic records, controllable payment intangibles, deposit accounts, letter-of-credit rights, or investment property which is perfected under the law of the chattel paper's jurisdiction, the controllable electronic record's jurisdiction, the bank's jurisdiction, the issuer's jurisdiction, a nominated person's jurisdiction, the securities intermediary's jurisdiction, or the commodity intermediary's jurisdiction, as applicable, remains perfected until the earlier of:

(1) the time the security interest would have become unperfected under the law of that jurisdiction; or

(2) the expiration of four months after a change of the applicable jurisdiction to another jurisdiction.

(g) [Subsection (f) security interest perfected or unperfected under law of new jurisdiction.] If a security interest described in subsection (f) becomes perfected under the law of the other jurisdiction before the earlier of the time or the end of the period described in that subsection, it remains perfected thereafter. If the security interest does not become perfected under the law of the other jurisdiction before the earlier of that time or the end of that period, it becomes unperfected and is deemed never to have been perfected as against a purchaser of the collateral for value.

(h) [Effect on filed financing statement of change in governing law.] The following rules apply to collateral to which a security interest attaches within four months after the debtor changes its location to another jurisdiction:

(1) A financing statement filed before the change pursuant to the law of the jurisdiction designated in Section 9-301(1) or 9-305(c) is effective to perfect a security interest in the collateral if the financing statement would have been effective to perfect a security interest in the collateral had the debtor not changed its location.

(2) If a security interest perfected by a financing statement that is effective under paragraph (1) becomes perfected under the law of the other jurisdiction before the earlier of the time the financing statement would have become ineffective under the law of the jurisdiction designated in Section 9-301(1) or 9-305(c) or the expiration of the four-month period, it remains perfected thereafter. If the security interest does not become perfected under the law of the other jurisdiction before the earlier time or event, it becomes unperfected and is deemed never to have been perfected as against a purchaser of the collateral for value.

(i) [Effect of change in governing law on financing statement filed against original debtor.] If a financing statement naming an original debtor is filed pursuant to the law of the jurisdiction designated in Section 9-301(1) or 9-305(c) and the new debtor is located in another jurisdiction, the following rules apply:

(1) The financing statement is effective to perfect a security interest in collateral acquired by the new debtor before, and within four months after, the new debtor becomes bound under Section 9-203(d), if the financing statement would have been effective to perfect a security interest in the collateral had the collateral been acquired by the original debtor.

(2) A security interest perfected by the financing statement and which becomes perfected under the law of the other jurisdiction before the earlier of the time the financing statement would have become ineffective under the law of the jurisdiction designated in Section 9-301(1) or 9-305(c) or the expiration of the four-month period remains perfected thereafter. A security interest that is perfected by the financing statement but which does not become perfected under the law of the other jurisdiction before the earlier time or event becomes unperfected and is deemed never to have been perfected as against a purchaser of the collateral for value.

Definitional Cross References:

As-extracted collateral	Section 9-102(a)(6)
Bank	Section 9-102(a)(8)
Certificate of title	Section 9-102(a)(10)
Chattel paper	Section 9-102(a)(11)
Collateral	Section 9-102(a)(12)
Commodity intermediary	Section 9-102(a)(17)
Controllable account	Section 9-102(a)(27A)
Controllable electronic Record	Section 12-102(a)(1)
Controllable payment intangible	Section 9-102(a)(27B)
Debtor	Section 9-102(a)(28)
Deposit account	Section 9-102(a)(29)
Financing Statement	Section 9-102(a)(39)
Goods	Section 9-102(a)(44)
Investment property	Section 9-102(a)(49)
Issuer (letter of credit/ letter-of-credit right)	Section 5-102(a)(9)
Letter-of-credit right	Section 9-102(a)(51)
Nominated person	Section 5-102(a)(11)
Original debtor	Section 9-102(a)(60)
Person	Section 1-201(b)(27)
Purchaser	Section 1-201(b)(30)
Securities intermediary	Section 8-102(a)(14)
Security interest	Section 1-201(b)(35)
State	Section 9-102(a)(77)
Value	Section 1-204

Comment References: 9-303 C6

Official Comment

1. Source. Former Section 9-103(1)(d), (2)(b), (3)(e), as modified.

2. Continued Perfection. Subsections (a) through (g) deal with continued perfection of security interests that have been perfected under the law of another jurisdiction. The fact that the law of a particular jurisdiction ceases to govern perfection under Sections 9-301 through 9-307 does not necessarily mean that a security interest perfected under that law automatically becomes unperfected. To the contrary: This section generally provides that a security interest perfected under the law of one jurisdiction remains perfected for a fixed period of time (four months or one year, depending on the circumstances), even though the jurisdiction whose law governs perfection changes. However, cessation of perfection under the law of the original jurisdiction cuts short the fixed period. The four-month and one-year periods are long enough for a secured party to discover in most cases that the law of a different jurisdiction governs perfection and to reperfect (typically by filing) under the law of that jurisdiction. If a secured party properly reperfects a security interest before it becomes unperfected under subsection (a), then the security interest remains perfected continuously thereafter. See subsection (b).

Example 1: Debtor is a general partnership whose chief executive office is in Pennsylvania. Lender perfects a security interest in Debtor's equipment by filing in Pennsylvania on May 15, 2002. On April 1, 2005, without Lender's knowledge, Debtor moves its chief executive office to New Jersey. Lender's security interest remains perfected for four months after the move. See subsection (a)(2).

Example 2: Debtor is a general partnership whose chief executive office is in Pennsylvania. Lender perfects a security interest in Debtor's equipment by filing in Pennsylvania on May 15, 2002. On April 1, 2007, without Lender's knowledge, Debtor moves its chief executive office to New Jersey. Lender's security interest remains perfected only through May 14, 2007, when the effectiveness of the filed financing statement lapses. See subsection (a)(1). Although, under these facts, Lender would have only a short period of time to discover that Debtor had relocated and to reperfect under New Jersey law, Lender could have protected itself by filing a continuation statement in Pennsylvania before Debtor relocated. By doing so, Lender would have prevented lapse and allowed itself the full four months to discover Debtor's new location and refile there or, if Debtor is in default, to perfect by taking possession of the equipment.

Example 3: Under the facts of Example 2, Lender files a financing statement in New Jersey before the effectiveness of the Pennsylvania financing statement lapses. Under subsection (b), Lender's security interest is continuously perfected beyond May 14, 2007, for a period determined by New Jersey's Article 9.

Subsection (a)(3) allows a one-year period in which to reperfect. The longer period is necessary, because, even with the exercise of due diligence, the secured party may be unable to discover that the collateral has been transferred to a person located in another jurisdiction. In any event, the period is cut short if the financing statement becomes ineffective under the law of the jurisdiction in which it is filed.

Example 4: Debtor is a Pennsylvania corporation. On January 1, Lender perfects a security interest in Debtor's equipment by filing in Pennsylvania. Debtor's shareholders decide to "reincorporate" in Delaware. On March 1, they form a Delaware corporation (Newcorp) into which they merge Debtor. The merger effectuates a transfer of the collateral from Debtor to Newcorp, which thereby becomes a debtor and is located in another jurisdiction. Under subsection (a)(3), the security interest remains perfected for one year after the merger. If a financing statement is filed in Delaware against Newcorp within the year following the merger, then the security interest remains perfected thereafter for a period determined by Delaware's Article 9.

Note that although Newcorp is a "new debtor" as defined in Section 9-102, the application of subsection (a)(3) is not limited to transferees who are new debtors. Note also that, under Section 9-507, the financing statement naming Debtor remains effective even though Newcorp has become the debtor.

Subsection (a) addresses security interests that are perfected (i.e., that have attached and as to which any required perfection step has been taken) before the debtor changes its location. Subsection (h) applies to security interests that have not attached before the location changes. See Comment 7.

3. Retroactive Unperfection. Subsection (b) sets forth the consequences of the failure to reperfect before perfection ceases under subsection (a): the security interest becomes unperfected prospectively and, as against purchasers for value, including buyers and secured parties, but not as against donees or lien creditors, retroactively. The rule applies to agricultural liens, as well. See also Section 9-515 (taking the same approach with respect to lapse). Although this approach creates the potential for circular priorities, the alternative—retroactive unperfection against lien creditors—would create substantial and unjustifiable preference risks.

Example 5: Under the facts of Example 4, six months after the merger, Buyer bought from Newcorp some equipment formerly owned by Debtor. At the time of the purchase, Buyer took subject to Lender's perfected security interest, of which Buyer was unaware. See Section 9-315(a)(1). However, subsection (b) provides that if Lender fails to reperfect in Delaware within a year after the merger, its security interest becomes unperfected and is deemed never to have been perfected against Buyer. Having given value and received delivery of the equipment without knowledge of the security interest and before it was perfected, Buyer would take free of the security interest. See Section 9-317(b).

Example 6: Under the facts of Example 4, one month before the merger, Debtor created a security interest in certain equipment in favor of Financer, who perfected by filing in Pennsylvania. At that time, Financer's security interest is subordinate to Lender's. See Section 9-322(a)(1). Financer reperfects by filing in Delaware within a year after the merger, but Lender fails to do so. Under subsection (b), Lender's security interest is deemed never to have been perfected against Financer, a purchaser for value. Consequently, under Section 9-322(a)(2), Financer's security interest is now senior.

Of course, the expiration of the time period specified in subsection (a) does not of itself prevent the secured party from later reperfecting under the law of the new jurisdiction. If the secured party does so, however, there will be a gap in perfection, and the secured party may lose priority as a result. Thus, in Example 6, if Lender perfects by filing in Delaware more than one year under the merger, it will have a new date of filing and perfection for purposes of Section 9-322(a)(1). Financer's security interest, whose perfection dates back to the filing in Pennsylvania under subsection (b), will remain senior.

4. Possessory Security Interests. Subsection (c) deals with continued perfection of possessory security interests. It applies not only to security interests perfected solely by the secured party's having taken possession of the collateral. It also applies to security interests perfected by a method that includes as an element of perfection the secured party's having taken possession, such as perfection by taking delivery of a certificated security in registered form, see Section 9-313(a), perfection by obtaining control over a certificated security, see Section 9-314(a), and perfection by taking possession of and control over authoritative copies of records evidencing chattel paper, see Section 9-314A(a).

5. Goods Covered by Certificate of Title. Subsections (d) and (e) address continued perfection of a security interest in goods covered by a certificate of title. The following examples explain the operation of those subsections.

Example 7: Debtor's automobile is covered by a certificate of title issued by Illinois. Lender perfects a security interest in the automobile by complying with Illinois' certificate-of-title statute. Thereafter, Debtor applies for a certificate of title in Indiana. Six months thereafter, Creditor acquires a judicial lien on the automobile. Under Section 9-303(b), Illinois law ceases to govern perfection; rather, once Debtor delivers the application and applicable fee to the appropriate Indiana authority, Indiana law governs. Nevertheless, under Indiana's Section 9-316(d), Lender's security interest remains perfected until it would become unperfected under Illinois law had no certificate of title been issued by Indiana. (For example, Illinois' certificate-of-title statute may provide that the surrender of an Illinois certificate of title in connection with the issuance of a certificate of title by another jurisdiction causes a security interest noted thereon to become unperfected.) If Lender's security interest remains perfected, it is senior to Creditor's judicial lien.

Example 8: Under the facts in Example 8, five months after Debtor applies for an Indiana certificate of title, Debtor sells the automobile to Buyer. Under subsection (e)(2), because Lender did not reperfect within the four months after the goods became covered by the Indiana certificate of title, Lender's security interest is deemed never to have been perfected against Buyer. Under Section 9-317(b), Buyer is likely to take free of the security interest. Lender could have protected itself by perfecting its security interest either under Indiana's certificate-of-title statute, see Section 9-311, or, if it had a right to do so under an agreement or Section 9-609, by taking possession of the automobile. See Section 9-313(b).

The results in Examples 8 and 9 do not depend on the fact that the original perfection was achieved by notation on a certificate of title. Subsection (d) applies regardless of the method by which a security interest is perfected under the law of another jurisdiction when the goods became covered by a certificate of title from this State.

Section 9-337 affords protection to a limited class of persons buying or acquiring a security interest in the goods while a security interest is perfected under the law of another jurisdiction but after this State has issued a clean certificate of title.

6. Controllable Accounts, Controllable Electronic Records, Controllable Payment Intangibles, Chattel Paper, Deposit Accounts, Letter-of-Credit Rights, and Investment Property. Subsections (f) and (g) address changes in the jurisdiction of a bank, controllable electronic record, chattel paper, issuer of an uncertificated security, issuer of or nominated person under a letter of credit, securities intermediary, and commodity intermediary. The provisions are analogous to those of subsections (a) and (b).

7. Security Interests That Attach After Debtor Changes Location. In contrast to subsections (a) and (b), which address security interests that are perfected (i.e., that have attached and as to which any required perfection step has been taken) before the debtor changes its location, subsection (h) addresses security interests that attach within four months after the debtor changes its location. Under subsection (h), a filed financing statement that would have been effective to perfect a security interest in the collateral if the debtor had not changed its location is effective to perfect a security interest in collateral acquired within four months after the relocation.

> **Example 9:** Debtor, an individual whose principal residence is in Pennsylvania, grants to Lender a security interest in Debtor's existing and after-acquired inventory. Lender perfects the security interest by filing a proper financing statement in Pennsylvania on January 2, 2014. On March 31, 2014, Debtor's principal residence is relocated to New Jersey. Upon the relocation, New Jersey law governs perfection of a security interest in Debtor's inventory. See Sections 9-301, 9-307. Under New Jersey's Section 9-316(a), Lender's security interest in Debtor's inventory on hand at the time of the relocation remains perfected for four months thereafter. Had Debtor not relocated, the financing statement filed in Pennsylvania would have been effective to perfect Lender's security interest in inventory acquired by Debtor after March 31, 2014. Accordingly, under subsection (h), the financing statement is effective to perfect Lender's security interest in inventory that Debtor acquires within the four months after Debtor's location changed.

In Example 9, Lender's security interest in the inventory acquired within the four months after Debtor's relocation will be perfected when it attaches. It will remain perfected if, before the expiration of the four-month period, the security interest is perfected under the law of New Jersey. Otherwise, the security interest will become unperfected at the end of the four-month period and will be deemed never to have been perfected as against a purchaser for value. See subsection (h)(2).

8. Collateral Acquired by New Debtor. Subsection (i) is similar to subsection (h). Whereas subsection (h) addresses security interests that attach within four months after a debtor changes its location, subsection (i) addresses security interests that attach within four months after a new debtor becomes bound as debtor by a security agreement entered into by another person. Subsection (i) also addresses collateral acquired by the new debtor before it becomes bound.

> **Example 10:** Debtor, a Pennsylvania corporation, grants to Lender a security interest in Debtor's existing and after-acquired inventory. Lender perfects the security interest by filing a proper financing statement in Pennsylvania on January 2, 2014. On March 31, 2014, Debtor merges into Survivor, a Delaware corporation. Because Survivor is located in Delaware, Delaware law governs perfection of a security interest in Survivor's inventory. See Sections 9-301, 9-307. Under Delaware's Section 9-316(a), Lender's security interest in the inventory that Survivor acquired from Debtor remains perfected for one year after the transfer. See Comment 2. By virtue of the merger, Survivor becomes bound as debtor by Debtor's security agreement. See Section 9-203(d). As a consequence, Lender's security interest attaches to all of Survivor's inventory under Section 9-203, and Lender's collateral now includes inventory in which Debtor never had an interest. The financing statement filed in Pennsylvania against Debtor is effective under Delaware's Section 9-316(i) to perfect Lender's security interest in inventory that Survivor acquired before, and within the four months after, becoming bound as debtor by Debtor's security agreement. This is because the financing statement filed in Pennsylvania would have been effective to perfect Lender's security interest in this collateral had Debtor, rather than Survivor, acquired it.

If the financing statement is effective, Lender's security interest in the collateral that Survivor acquired before, and within four months after, Survivor became bound as debtor will be perfected upon attachment. It will remain perfected if, before the expiration of the four-month period, the security interest is perfected under Delaware law. Otherwise, the security interest will become unperfected at the end of the four-month period and will be deemed never to have been perfected as against a purchaser for value.

Section 9-325 contains special rules governing the priority of competing security interests in collateral that is transferred, by merger or otherwise, to a new debtor or other person who becomes a debtor with respect to the collateral. Section 9-326 contains special rules governing the priority of competing security interests in collateral acquired by a new debtor other than by transfer from the original debtor.

9. Agricultural Liens. This section does not apply to agricultural liens.

> **Example 11:** Supplier holds an agricultural lien on corn. The lien arises under an Iowa statute. Supplier perfects by filing a financing statement in Iowa, where the corn is located. See Section 9-302. Debtor stores the corn in Missouri. Assume the Iowa agricultural lien survives or an agricultural lien arises under Missouri law (matters that this Article does not govern). Once the corn is located in Missouri, Missouri becomes the jurisdiction whose law governs perfection. See Section 9-302. Thus, the agricultural lien will not be perfected unless Supplier files a financing statement in Missouri.

[Subpart 3. Priority]

§ 9-317. Interests That Take Priority Over or Take Free of Security Interest or Agricultural Lien.

(a) [Conflicting security interests and rights of lien creditors.] A security interest or agricultural lien is subordinate to the rights of:

(1) a person entitled to priority under Section 9-322; and

(2) except as otherwise provided in subsection (e), a person that becomes a lien creditor before the earlier of the time

(A) the security interest or agricultural lien is perfected; or

(B) one of the conditions specified in Section 9-203(b)(3) is met and a financing statement covering the collateral is filed.

(b) [Buyers that receive delivery.] Except as otherwise provided in subsection (e), a buyer, other than a secured party, of goods, instruments, tangible documents, or a certificated security takes free of a security interest or agricultural lien if the buyer gives value and receives delivery of the collateral without knowledge of the security interest or agricultural lien and before it is perfected.

(c) [Lessees that receive delivery.] Except as otherwise provided in subsection (e), a lessee of goods takes free of a security interest or agricultural lien if the lessee gives value and receives delivery of the collateral without knowledge of the security interest or agricultural lien and before it is perfected.

(d) [Licensees and buyers of certain collateral.] Subject to subsection (f) through (i), a licensee of a general intangible or a buyer, other than a secured party, of collateral other than electronic money, goods, instruments, tangible documents, or a certificated security takes free of a security interest if the licensee or buyer gives value without knowledge of the security interest and before it is perfected.

(e) [Purchase-money security interest.] Except as otherwise provided in Sections 9-320 and 9-321, if a person files a financing statement with respect to a purchase-money security interest before or within 20 days after the debtor receives delivery of the collateral, the security interest takes priority over the rights of a buyer, lessee, or lien creditor which arise between the time the security interest attaches and the time of filing.

(f) [Buyers of chattel paper.] A buyer, other than a secured party, of chattel paper takes free of a security interest if, without knowledge of the security interest and before it is perfected, the buyer gives value and:

(1) receives delivery of each authoritative tangible copy of the record evidencing the chattel paper; and

(2) if each authoritative electronic copy of the record evidencing the chattel paper can be subjected to control under Section 9-105, obtains control of each authoritative electronic copy.

(g) [Buyers of electronic documents.] A buyer of an electronic document takes free of a security interest if, without knowledge of the security interest and before it is perfected, the buyer gives value and, if each authoritative electronic copy of the document can be subjected to control under Section 7-106, obtains control of each authoritative electronic copy.

(h) [Buyers of controllable electronic records.] A buyer of a controllable electronic record takes free of a security interest if, without knowledge of the security interest and before it is perfected, the buyer gives value and obtains control of the controllable electronic record.

(i) [Buyers of controllable accounts and controllable payment intangibles.] A buyer, other than a secured party, of a controllable account or a controllable payment intangible takes free of a security interest if, without knowledge of the security interest and before it is perfected, the buyer gives value and obtains control of the controllable account or controllable payment intangible.

Definitional Cross References:

Account	Section 9-102(a)(2)
Agricultural lien	Section 9-102(a)(5)
Certificated security	Section 8-102(a)(4)
Chattel paper	Section 9-102(a)(11)
Collateral	Section 9-102(a)(12)
Controllable account	Section 9-102(a)(27A)
Controllable electronic record	Section 12-102(a)(1)
Controllable payment intangible	Section 9-102(a)(27B)
Debtor	Section 9-102(a)(28)
Delivery	Section 1-201(b)(15)
Document	Section 9-102(a)(30)
Electronic	Section 1-201(b)(16A)
Electronic money	Section 9-102(a)(31A)
Financing statement	Section 9-102(a)(39)
General intangible	Section 9-102(a)(42)
Goods	Section 9-102(a)(44)
Instrument	Section 9-102(a)(47)
Investment property	Section 9-102(a)(49)
Lessee	Section 2A-103(1)(n)
Lien creditor	Section 9-102(a)(52)
Person	Section 1-201(b)(27)
Purchase-money security interest	Section 9-103
Record	Section 9-102(a)(70)
Right	Section 1-201(b)(34)
Secured party	Section 9-102(a)(73)
Security certificate	Section 8-102(a)(16)
Security interest	Section 1-201(b)(35)
Value	Section 1-204

Comment References:
9-109 C5
9-323 C4

Official Comment

1. Source. Former Sections 9-301, 2A-307(2).

2. Scope of This Section. As did former Section 9-301, this section lists the classes of persons who take priority over, or take free of, an unperfected security interest. Section 9-308 explains when a security interest or agricultural lien is "perfected." A security interest that has attached (see Section 9-203) but as to which a required perfection step has not been taken is "unperfected." Certain provisions have been moved from former Section 9-301. The definition of "lien creditor" now appears in Section 9-102, and the rules governing priority in future advances are found in Section 9-323.

3. Competing Security Interests. Section 9-322 states general rules for determining priority among conflicting security interests and refers to other sections that state special rules of priority in a variety of situations. The security interests given priority under Section 9-322 and the other sections to which it refers take priority in general even over a perfected security interest. *A fortiori* they take priority over an unperfected security interest.

4. Filed But Unattached Security Interest vs. Lien Creditor. Under former Section 9-301(1)(b), a lien creditor's rights had priority over an unperfected security interest. Perfection required attachment (former Section 9-303) and attachment required the giving of value (former Section 9-203). It followed that, if a secured party had filed a financing statement, but the debtor had not entered into a security agreement and value had not yet been given, an intervening lien creditor whose lien arose after filing but before attachment of the security interest acquired rights that are senior to those of the secured party who later gives value. This result comported with the *nemo dat* concept: When the security interest attached, the collateral was already subject to the judicial lien.

On the other hand, this approach treated the first secured advance differently from all other advances, even in circumstances in which a security agreement covering the collateral had been entered into before the judicial lien attached. The special rule for future advances in former Section 9-301(4) (substantially reproduced in Section 9-323(b)) afforded priority to a discretionary advance made by a secured party within 45 days after the lien creditor's rights arose as long as the secured party was "perfected" when the lien creditor's lien arose—i.e., as long as the advance was not the first one and an earlier advance had been made.

Subsection (a)(2)(b) revises former Section 9-301(1)(b) and, in appropriate cases, treats the first advance the same as subsequent advances. More specifically, a judicial lien that arises after the security-agreement condition of Section 9-203(b)(3) is satisfied and a financing statement is filed but before the security interest attaches and becomes perfected is subordinate to all advances secured by the security interest, even the first advance, except as otherwise provided in Section 9-323(b). However, if the security interest becomes unperfected (e.g., because the effectiveness of the filed financing statement lapses) before the judicial lien arises, the security interest is subordinate. If a financing statement is filed but a security interest does not attach, then no priority contest arises. The lien creditor has the only enforceable claim to the property.

5. Security Interest of Consignor or Receivables Buyer vs. Lien Creditor. Section 1-201(b)(35) defines "security interest" to include the interest of most true consignors of goods and the interest of most buyers of certain receivables (including accounts, chattel paper, payment intangibles, and promissory notes). A consignee of goods or a seller of accounts or chattel paper each is deemed to have rights in the collateral which a lien creditor may reach, as long as the competing security interest of the consignor or buyer is unperfected. This is so even though, as between the consignor and the debtor-consignee, the latter has only limited rights, and, as between the buyer and debtor-seller, the latter does not have any rights in the collateral. See Sections 9-318 (seller), 9-319 (consignee). Security interests arising from sales of payment intangibles and promissory notes are automatically perfected. See Section 9-309. Accordingly, a subsequent judicial lien always would be subordinate to the rights of a buyer of those types of receivables.

6. Purchasers Other Than Secured Parties. Subsections (b), (c), (d), and (f) through (i) afford priority over an unperfected security interest to certain buyers (other than secured parties) of collateral. They derive in part from pre-1998 Sections 9-301(1)(c), 2A-307(2), and 9-301(d). Pre-1998 Section 9-301(1)(c) and (1)(d) provided that unperfected security interests are "subordinate" to the rights of certain purchasers. But, as pre-1998 Comment 9 suggested, the practical effect of subordination in this context is that the purchaser takes free of the security interest. To avoid any possible misinterpretation, these subsections now use the phrase "takes free."

Subsection (b) governs goods, as well as intangibles of the type whose transfer is effected by physical delivery of the representative piece of paper (tangible documents, instruments, and security certificates). To obtain priority, a buyer must both give value and receive delivery of the collateral without knowledge of the existing security interest and before perfection. Even if the buyer gave value without knowledge and before perfection, the buyer would take subject to the security interest if perfection occurred before physical delivery of the collateral to the buyer. Subsection (c) contains a similar rule with respect to lessees of goods. Note that a lessee of goods in ordinary course of business takes free of all security interests created by the lessor, even if perfected. See Section 9-321.

Normally, there will be no question when a buyer of tangible chattel paper, tangible documents, instruments, or security certificates "receives delivery" of the property. See Section 1-201 (defining "delivery"). However, sometimes a buyer or lessee of goods, such as complex machinery, takes delivery of the goods in stages and completes assembly at its own location. Under those circumstances, the buyer or lessee "receives delivery" within the meaning of subsections (b) and (c) when, after an inspection of the portion of the goods remaining with the seller or lessor, it would be apparent to a potential lender to the seller or lessor that another person might have an interest in the goods.

Subsection (b) no longer applies to chattel paper. The take-free rule in subsection (f) for buyers of chattel paper reflects the corresponding 2022 changes in the definition of chattel paper and in the methods of perfection. See Sections 9-102(a)(11) (defining "chattel paper"); 9-314A (perfection by possession and control). Note that subsection (f) applies only to a buyer of chattel paper "other than a secured party" and most buyers of chattel paper are secured parties. See Sections 9-102(a)(73) (defining "secured party" as including a person to which chattel paper has been sold); 9-109(a)(3) (Article 9 applies to a sale of chattel paper); 1-201(b)(35) (defining "security interest" to include the interest of a buyer of chattel paper). However, Article 9 does not apply to "a sale of... chattel paper... as part of a sale of the business out of which... [the chattel paper] arose" and, accordingly, subsection (f) could apply to a buyer of chattel paper in such a sale-of-business transaction. Subsection (f) provides that such a buyer of chattel paper takes free of a security interest if, without knowledge of the security interest and before it is perfected, the buyer gives value and receives delivery of each authoritative tangible copy of the record evidencing the chattel paper and, if the chattel paper can be subjected to control, the buyer obtains control of each authoritative electronic copy.

Although chattel paper has been removed from subsection (b), the phrase "other than a secured party" has been retained because buyers of instruments that are promissory notes, but not buyers of other instruments, are secured parties. See Sections 9-109(a)(3) (Article 9 applies to a sale of a promissory note); 1-201(b)(35) (defining "security interest" to include the interest of a buyer of a promissory note).

The rule of subsection (b) obviously is not appropriate where the collateral consists of intangibles and there is no representative piece of paper whose physical delivery is the only or the customary method of transfer or no means of taking control of the collateral as a functional equivalent of a delivery. Therefore, with respect to such intangibles (including accounts other than controllable accounts, electronic documents not subject to control, general intangibles other than controllable payment intangibles, and investment property other than certificated securities), subsection (d) gives priority to any buyer who gives value without knowledge, and before perfection, of the security interest. Buyers of electronic money also are excluded from the application of subsection (d) because transferees of electronic money which obtain control take free of security interests under Section 9-332(c), which provides a standard more generous to transferees than subsection (d). A licensee of a general intangible takes free of an unperfected security interest in the general intangible under the same circumstances. Note that a licensee of a general intangible in ordinary course of business takes rights under a nonexclusive license free of security interests created by the licensor, even if perfected. See Section 9-321.

Unless Section 9-109 excludes the transaction from this Article, a buyer of accounts, payment intangibles, or promissory notes is a "secured party" (defined in Section 9-102), and subsection (d) does not determine priority of the security interest created by the sale. Rather, the priority rules generally applicable to competing security interests apply. See, e.g., Section 9-322.

6A. [Buyers of Electronic Documents, Controllable Electronic Records, Controllable Accounts, and Controllable Payment Intangibles.] Subsection (g) provides a take-free rule for electronic documents, subsection (h) so provides for controllable electronic records, and subsection (i) so provides for controllable accounts and controllable payment intangibles. Subsection (g) conditions the take-free rule on the buyer obtaining control of authoritative electronic copies of the document only if the authoritative electronic copies can be subjected to control. Subsection (h) conditions the take-free rule for a buyer of a controllable electronic record on the buyer's obtaining control of the electronic record. Similarly, under subsection (i), the take-free rule for a buyer, other than a secured party, of a controllable account or controllable payment intangible is conditioned on the buyer's obtaining control of the account or payment intangible. Although in general a buyer of an account or a payment intangible is a secured party, there are limited exceptions. See Sections 1-201(b)(35) ("security interest" includes interest of buyer of accounts or payment intangibles); 9-109(d)(4) (inapplicability of Article 9 to sale of accounts or payment intangibles as a part of the sale of a business).

7. Agricultural Liens. Subsections (a), (b), and (c) subordinate unperfected agricultural liens in the same manner in which they subordinate unperfected security interests.

8. Purchase-Money Security Interests. Subsection (e) derives from former Section 9-301(2). It provides that, if a purchase-money security interest is perfected by filing no later than 20 days after the debtor receives delivery of the collateral, the security interest takes priority over the rights of buyers, lessees, or lien creditors which arise between the time the security interest attaches and the time of filing. Subsection (e) differs from former Section 9-301(2) in two significant respects. First, subsection (e) protects a purchase-money security interest against all buyers and lessees, not just against transferees in bulk. Second, subsection (e) conditions this protection on filing within 20, as opposed to ten, days after delivery.

Section 9-311(b) provides that compliance with the perfection requirements of a statute or treaty described in Section 9-311(a) "is equivalent to the filing of a financing statement." It follows that a person who perfects a security interest in goods covered by a certificate of title by complying with the perfection requirements of an applicable certificate-of-title statute "files a financing statement" within the meaning of subsection (e).

§ 9-318. No Interest Retained in Right to Payment That Is Sold; Rights and Title of Seller of Account or Chattel Paper with Respect to Creditors and Purchasers.

(a) [Seller retains no interest.] A debtor that has sold an account, chattel paper, payment intangible, or promissory note does not retain a legal or equitable interest in the collateral sold.

(b) [Deemed rights of debtor if buyer's security interest unperfected.] For purposes of determining the rights of creditors of, and purchasers for value of an account or chattel paper from, a debtor that has sold an account or chattel paper, while the buyer's security interest is unperfected, the debtor is deemed to have rights and title to the account or chattel paper identical to those the debtor sold.

Definitional Cross References:

Account	Section 9-102(a)(2)
Chattel paper	Section 9-102(a)(11)
Collateral	Section 9-102(a)(12)
Creditor	Section 1-201(b)(13)
Debtor	Section 9-102(a)(28)
Payment intangible	Section 9-102(a)(61)
Promissory note	Section 9-102(a)(65)
Purchaser	Section 1-201(b)(30)
Right	Section 1-201(b)(34)
Security interest	Section 1-201(b)(35)
Value	Section 1-204

Comment References: 9-109 C5

Official Comment

1. Source. New.

2. Sellers of Accounts, Chattel Paper, Payment Intangibles, and Promissory Notes. Section 1-201(b)(35) defines "security interest" to include the interest of a buyer of accounts, chattel paper, payment intangibles, or promissory notes. See also Section 9-109(a) and Comment 5. Subsection (a) makes explicit what was implicit, but perfectly obvious, under former Article 9: The fact that a sale of an account or chattel paper gives rise to a "security interest" does not imply that the seller retains an interest in the property that has been sold. To the contrary, a seller of an account or chattel paper retains no interest whatsoever in the property to the extent that it has been sold. Subsection (a) also applies to sales of payment intangibles and promissory notes, transactions that were not covered by former Article 9. Neither this Article nor the definition of "security interest" in Section 1-201 provides rules for distinguishing sales transactions from those that create a security interest securing an obligation.

3. Buyers of Accounts and Chattel Paper. Another aspect of sales of accounts and chattel paper also was implicit, and equally obvious, under former Article 9: If the buyer's security interest is unperfected, then for purposes of determining the rights of certain third parties, the seller (debtor) is deemed to have all rights and title that the seller sold. The seller is deemed to have these rights even though, as between the parties, it has sold all its rights to the buyer. Subsection (b) makes this explicit. As a consequence of subsection (b), if the buyer's security interest is unperfected, the seller can transfer, and the creditors of the seller can reach, the account or chattel paper as if it had not been sold.

> **Example:** Debtor sells accounts or chattel paper to Buyer-1 and retains no interest in them. Buyer-1 does not file a financing statement. Debtor then sells the same receivables to Buyer-2. Buyer-2 files a proper financing statement. Having sold the receivables to Buyer-1, Debtor would not have any rights in the collateral so as to permit Buyer-2's security (ownership) interest to attach. Nevertheless, under this section, for purposes of determining the rights of purchasers for value from Debtor, Debtor is deemed to have the rights that Debtor sold. Accordingly, Buyer-2's security interest attaches, is perfected by the filing, and, under Section 9-322, is senior to Buyer-1's interest.

4. Effect of Perfection. If the security interest of a buyer of accounts or chattel paper is perfected the usual result would take effect: transferees from and creditors of the seller could not acquire an interest in the sold accounts or chattel paper. The same result generally would occur if payment intangibles or promissory notes were sold, inasmuch as the buyer's security interest is automatically perfected under Section 9-309. However, in certain circumstances a purchaser who takes possession of a promissory note will achieve priority, under Sections 9-330 or 9-331, over the security interest of an earlier buyer of the promissory note. For this reason, the seller in those circumstances retains the power to transfer the promissory note, as if it had not been sold, to a purchaser who obtains priority under either of those sections. See Section 9-203(b)(3), Comment 6.

§ 9-319. Rights and Title of Consignee with Respect to Creditors and Purchasers.

(a) [Consignee has consignor's rights.] Except as otherwise provided in subsection (b), for purposes of determining the rights of creditors of, and purchasers for value of goods from, a consignee, while the goods are in the possession of the consignee, the consignee is deemed to have rights and title to the goods identical to those the consignor had or had power to transfer.

(b) [Applicability of other law.] For purposes of determining the rights of a creditor of a consignee, law other than this article determines the rights and title of a consignee while goods are in the consignee's possession if, under this part, a perfected security interest held by the consignor would have priority over the rights of the creditor.

Definitional Cross References:

Consignee	Section 9-102(a)(19)
Consignor	Section 9-102(a)(21)
Creditor	Section 1-201(b)(13)
Goods	Section 9-102(a)(44)
Purchaser	Section 1-201(b)(30)
Right	Section 1-201(b)(34)
Security interest	Section 1-201(b)(35)
Value	Section 1-204

Comment References: 9-109 C6

Official Comment

1. Source. New.

2. Consignments. This section takes an approach to consignments similar to that taken by Section 9-318 with respect to buyers of accounts and chattel paper. Revised Section 1-201(b)(35) defines "security interest" to include the interest of a consignor of goods under many true consignments. Section 9-319(a) provides that, for purposes of determining the rights of certain third parties, the consignee is deemed to acquire all rights and title that the consignor had, if the consignor's security interest is unperfected. The consignee acquires these rights even though, as between the parties, it purchases a limited interest in the goods (as would be the case in a true consignment, under which the consignee acquires only the interest of a bailee). As a consequence of this section, creditors of the consignee can acquire judicial liens and security interests in the goods while the goods are in the possession of the consignee.

The termination of a consignment does not ipso facto cause the consignee to lose its status as such with respect to the consignee's creditors whose claims to the goods arose before termination. Return of the goods to the consignor causes the consignee to lose its deemed rights and title, but it does not discharge a security interest or judicial lien that attached while the consignee was in possession. See PEB Commentary No. 20, dated January 24, 2019.

Insofar as creditors of the consignee are concerned, this Article to a considerable extent reformulates the former law, which appeared in former Sections 2-326 and 9-114, without changing the results. However, neither Article 2 nor former Article 9 specifically addresses the rights of non-ordinary course buyers from the consignee. Former Section 9-114 contained priority rules applicable to security interests in consigned goods.

Under this Article, the priority rules for purchase-money security interests in inventory apply to consignments. See Section 9-103(d). Accordingly, a special section containing priority rules for consignments no longer is needed. Section 9-317 determines whether the rights of a judicial lien creditor are senior to the interest of the consignor, Sections 9-322 and 9-324 govern competing security interests in consigned goods, and Sections 9-317, 9-315, and 9-320 determine whether a buyer takes free of the consignor's interest.

The following example explains the operation of this section:

> **Example 1:** SP-1 delivers goods to Debtor in a transaction constituting a "consignment" as defined in Section 9-102. SP-1 does not file a financing statement. Debtor then grants a security interest in the goods to SP-2. SP-2 files a proper financing statement. Assuming Debtor is a mere bailee, as in a "true" consignment, Debtor would not have any rights in the collateral (beyond those of a bailee) so as to permit SP-2's security interest to attach to any greater rights. Nevertheless, under this section, for purposes of determining the rights of Debtor's creditors, Debtor is deemed to acquire SP-1's rights. Accordingly, SP-2's security interest attaches, is perfected by the filing, and, under Section 9-322, is senior to SP-1's interest.

3. Effect of Perfection. Subsection (b) contains a special rule with respect to consignments that are perfected. If application of this Article would result in the consignor having priority over a competing creditor, then other law determines the rights and title of the consignee.

> **Example 2:** SP-1 delivers goods to Debtor in a transaction constituting a "consignment" as defined in Section 9-102. SP-1 files a proper financing statement. Debtor then grants a security interest in the goods to SP-2. Under Section 9-322, SP-1's security interest is senior to SP-2's. Subsection (b) indicates that, for purposes of determining SP-2's rights, other law determines the rights and title of the consignee. If, for example, a consignee obtains only the special property of a bailee, then SP-2's security interest would attach only to that special property.

> **Example 3:** SP-1 obtains a security interest in all Debtor's existing and after-acquired inventory. SP-1 perfects its security interest with a proper filing. Then SP-2 delivers goods to Debtor in a transaction constituting a "consignment" as defined in Section 9-102. SP-2 files a proper financing statement but does not send notification to SP-1 under Section 9-324(b). Accordingly, SP-2's security interest is junior to SP-1's under Section 9-322(a). Under Section 9-319(a), Debtor is deemed to have the consignor's rights and title, so that SP-1's security interest attaches to SP-2's ownership interest in the goods. Thereafter, Debtor grants a security interest in the goods to SP-3, and SP-3 perfects by filing. Because SP-2's perfected security interest is senior to SP-3's under Section 9-322(a), Section 9-319(b) applies: Other law determines Debtor's rights and title to the goods insofar as SP-3 is concerned, and SP-3's security interest attaches to those rights.

§ 9-320. Buyer of Goods.

(a) [Buyer in ordinary course of business.] Except as otherwise provided in subsection (e), a buyer in ordinary course of business, other than a person buying farm products from a person engaged in farming operations, takes free of a security interest created by the buyer's seller, even if the security interest is perfected and the buyer knows of its existence.

(b) [Buyer of consumer goods.] Except as otherwise provided in subsection (e), a buyer of goods from a person who used or bought the goods for use primarily for personal, family, or household purposes takes free of a security interest, even if perfected, if the buyer buys:

(1) without knowledge of the security interest;

(2) for value;

(3) primarily for the buyer's personal, family, or household purposes; and

(4) before the filing of a financing statement covering the goods.

(c) [Effectiveness of filing for subsection (b).] To the extent that it affects the priority of a security interest over a buyer of goods under subsection (b), the period of effectiveness of a filing made in the jurisdiction in which the seller is located is governed by Section 9-316(a) and (b).

(d) [Buyer in ordinary course of business at wellhead or minehead.] A buyer in ordinary course of business buying oil, gas, or other minerals at the wellhead or minehead or after extraction takes free of an interest arising out of an encumbrance.

(e) [Possessory security interest not affected.] Subsections (a) and (b) do not affect a security interest in goods in the possession of the secured party under Section 9-313.

Definitional Cross References:

Buyer in ordinary course of business	Section 1-201(b)(9)
Consumer goods	Section 9-102(a)(23)
Encumbrance	Section 9-102(a)(32)

Farm products	Section 9-102(a)(34)
Farming operation	Section 9-102(a)(35)
Financing statement	Section 9-102(a)(39)
Goods	Section 9-102(a)(44)
Person	Section 1-201(b)(27)
Secured party	Section 9-102(a)(73)
Security interest	Section 1-201(b)(35)
Value	Section 1-204

Comment References: 9-323 C6

Official Comment

1. Source. Former Section 9-307.

2. Scope of This Section. This section states when buyers of goods take free of a security interest even though perfected. Of course, a buyer who takes free of a perfected security interest takes free of an unperfected one. Section 9-317 should be consulted to determine what purchasers, in addition to the buyers covered in this section, take free of an unperfected security interest. Article 2 states general rules on purchase of goods from a seller with defective or voidable title (Section 2-403).

3. Buyers in Ordinary Course. Subsection (a) derives from former Section 9-307(1). The definition of "buyer in ordinary course of business" in Section 1-201 restricts its application to buyers "from a person, other than a pawnbroker, in the business of selling goods of that kind." Thus subsection (a) applies primarily to inventory collateral. The subsection further excludes from its operation buyers of "farm products" (defined in Section 9-102) from a person engaged in farming operations. The buyer in ordinary course of business is defined as one who buys goods "in good faith, without knowledge that the sale violates the rights of another person and in the ordinary course." Subsection (a) provides that such a buyer takes free of a security interest, even though perfected, and even though the buyer knows the security interest exists. Reading the definition together with the rule of law results in the buyer's taking free if the buyer merely knows that a security interest covers the goods but taking subject if the buyer knows, in addition, that the sale violates a term in an agreement with the secured party.

As did former Section 9-307(1), subsection (a) applies only to security interests created by the seller of the goods to the buyer in ordinary course. However, under certain circumstances a buyer in ordinary course who buys goods that were encumbered with a security interest created by a person other than the seller may take free of the security interest, as Example 2 explains. See also Comment 6, below.

Example 1: Manufacturer, who is in the business of manufacturing appliances, owns manufacturing equipment subject to a perfected security interest in favor of Lender. Manufacturer sells the equipment to Dealer, who is in the business of buying and selling used equipment. Buyer buys the equipment from Dealer. Even if Buyer qualifies as a buyer in the ordinary course of business, Buyer does not take free of Lender's security interest under subsection (a), because Dealer did not create the security interest; Manufacturer did.

Example 2: Manufacturer, who is in the business of manufacturing appliances, owns manufacturing equipment subject to a perfected security interest in favor of Lender. Manufacturer sells the equipment to Dealer, who is in the business of buying and selling used equipment. Lender learns of the sale but does nothing to assert its security interest. Buyer buys the equipment from Dealer. Inasmuch as Lender's acquiescence constitutes an "entrusting" of the goods to Dealer within the meaning of Section 2-403(3) Buyer takes free of Lender's security interest under Section 2-403(2) if Buyer qualifies as a buyer in ordinary course of business.

4. Buyers of Farm Products. This section does not enable a buyer of farm products to take free of a security interest created by the seller, even if the buyer is a buyer in ordinary course of business. However, a buyer of farm products may take free of a security interest under Section 1324 of the Food Security Act of 1985, 7 U.S.C. § 1631.

5. Buyers of Consumer Goods. Subsection (b), which derives from former Section 9-307(2), deals with buyers of collateral that the debtor-seller holds as "consumer goods" (defined in Section 9-102). Under Section 9-309(1), a purchase-money interest in consumer goods, except goods that are subject to a statute or treaty described in Section 9-311(a) (such as automobiles that are subject to a certificate-of-title statute), is perfected automatically upon attachment. There is no need to file to perfect. Under subsection (b) a buyer of consumer goods takes free of a security interest, even though perfected, if the buyer buys (1) without knowledge of the security interest, (2) for value, (3) primarily for the buyer's own personal, family, or household purposes, and (4) before a financing statement is filed.

As to purchase-money security interests which are perfected without filing under Section 9-309(1): A secured party may file a financing statement, although filing is not required for perfection. If the secured party does file, all buyers take subject to the security interest. If the secured party does not file, a buyer who meets the qualifications stated in the preceding paragraph takes free of the security interest.

As to security interests for which a perfection step is required: This category includes all non-purchase-money security interests, and all security interests, whether or not purchase-money, in goods subject to a statute or treaty described in Section 9-311(a), such as automobiles covered by a certificate-of-title statute. As long as the required perfection step has not been taken and the security interest remains unperfected, not only the buyers described in subsection (b) but also the purchasers described in Section 9-317 will take free of the security interest. After a financing statement has been filed or the perfection requirements of the applicable certificate-of-title statute have been complied with (compliance is the equivalent of filing a financing statement; see Section 9-311(b)), all subsequent buyers, under the rule of subsection (b), are subject to the security interest.

The rights of a buyer under subsection (b) turn on whether a financing statement has been filed against consumer goods. Occasionally, a debtor changes his or her location after a filing is made. Subsection (c), which derives from former Section 9-103(1)(d)(iii), deals with the continued effectiveness of the filing under those circumstances. It adopts the rules of Sections 9-316(a) and (b). These rules are explained in the Comments to that section.

6. Authorized Dispositions. The limitations that subsections (a) and (b) impose on the persons who may take free of a security interest apply of course only to unauthorized sales by the debtor. If the secured party authorized the sale in an express agreement or otherwise, the buyer takes free under Section 9-315(a) without regard to the limitations of this section. (That section also states the right of a secured party to the proceeds of a sale, authorized or unauthorized.) Moreover, the buyer also takes free if the secured party waived or otherwise is precluded from asserting its security interest against the buyer. See Section 1-103.

7. Oil, Gas, and Other Minerals. Under subsection (d), a buyer in ordinary course of business of minerals at the wellhead or minehead or after extraction takes free of a security interest created by the seller. Specifically, it provides that qualified buyers take free not only of Article 9 security interests but also of interests "arising out of an encumbrance." As defined in Section 9-102, the term "encumbrance" means "a right, other than an ownership interest, in real property." Thus, to the extent that a mortgage encumbers minerals not only before but also after extraction, subsection (d) enables a buyer in ordinary course of the minerals to take free of the mortgage. This subsection does not, however, enable these buyers to take free of interests arising out of ownership interests in the real property. This issue is significant only in a minority of states. Several of them have adopted special statutes and nonuniform amendments to Article 9 to provide special protections to mineral owners, whose interests often are highly fractionalized in the case of oil and gas. See Terry I. Cross, *Oil and Gas Product Liens—Statutory Security Interests for Producers and Royalty Owners Under the Statutes of Kansas, New Mexico, Oklahoma, Texas and Wyoming*, 50 Consumer Fin. L. Q. Rep. 418 (1996). Inasmuch as a complete resolution of the issue would require the addition of complex provisions to this Article, and there are good reasons to believe that a uniform solution would not be feasible, this Article leaves its resolution to other legislation.

8. Possessory Security Interests. Subsection (e) is new. It rejects the holding of *Tanbro Fabrics Corp. v. Deering Milliken, Inc.*, 350 N.E.2d 590 (N.Y. 1976) and, together with Section 9-317(b), prevents a buyer of goods collateral from taking free of a security interest if the collateral is in the possession of the secured party. "The secured party" referred in subsection (e) is the holder of the security interest referred to in subsection (a) or (b). Section 9-313 determines whether a secured party is in possession for purposes of this section. Under some circumstances, Section 9-313 provides that a secured party is in possession of collateral even if the collateral is in the physical possession of a third party.

§ 9-321. Licensee of General Intangible and Lessee of Goods in Ordinary Course of Business.

(a) ["Licensee in ordinary course of business."] In this section, "licensee in ordinary course of business" means a person that becomes a licensee of a general intangible in good faith, without knowledge that the license violates the rights of another person in the general intangible, and in the ordinary course from a person in the business of licensing general intangibles of that kind. A person becomes a licensee in the ordinary course if the license to the person comports with the usual or customary practices in the kind of business in which the licensor is engaged or with the licensor's own usual or customary practices.

(b) [Rights of licensee in ordinary course of business.] A licensee in ordinary course of business takes its rights under a nonexclusive license free of a security interest in the general intangible created by the licensor, even if the security interest is perfected and the licensee knows of its existence.

(c) [Rights of lessee in ordinary course of business.] A lessee in ordinary course of business takes its leasehold interest free of a security interest in the goods created by the lessor, even if the security interest is perfected and the lessee knows of its existence.

Definitional Cross References:

General intangible	Section 9-102(a)(42)
Good faith	Section 1-201(b)(20)
Goods	Section 9-102(a)(44)
Leasehold interest	Section 2A-103(1)(m)
Lessee in ordinary course of business	Section 2A-103(1)(o)

Lessee	Section 2A-103(1)(n)
Lessor	Section 2A-103(1)(p)
Person	Section 1-201(b)(27)
Right	Section 1-201(b)(34)
Security interest	Section 1-201(b)(35)

Comment References: 9-323 C6

Official Comment

1. Source. Derived from Sections 2A-103(1)(o), 2A-307(3).

2. Licensee in Ordinary Course. Like the analogous rules in Section 9-320(a) with respect to buyers in ordinary course and subsection (c) with respect to lessees in ordinary course, the new rule in subsection (b) reflects the expectations of the parties and the marketplace: a licensee under a nonexclusive license takes subject to a security interest unless the secured party authorizes the license free of the security interest or other, controlling law such as that of this section (protecting ordinary-course licensees) dictates a contrary result. See Sections 9-201, 9-315. The definition of "licensee in ordinary course of business" in subsection (a) is modeled upon that of "buyer in ordinary course of business."

3. Lessee in Ordinary Course. Subsection (c) contains the rule formerly found in Section 2A-307(3). The rule works in the same way as that of Section 9-320(a).

§ 9-322. Priorities Among Conflicting Security Interests in and Agricultural Liens on Same Collateral.

(a) [General priority rules.] Except as otherwise provided in this section, priority among conflicting security interests and agricultural liens in the same collateral is determined according to the following rules:

(1) Conflicting perfected security interests and agricultural liens rank according to priority in time of filing or perfection. Priority dates from the earlier of the time a filing covering the collateral is first made or the security interest or agricultural lien is first perfected, if there is no period thereafter when there is neither filing nor perfection.

(2) A perfected security interest or agricultural lien has priority over a conflicting unperfected security interest or agricultural lien.

(3) The first security interest or agricultural lien to attach or become effective has priority if conflicting security interests and agricultural liens are unperfected.

(b) [Time of perfection: proceeds and supporting obligations.] For the purposes of subsection (a)(1):

(1) the time of filing or perfection as to a security interest in collateral is also the time of filing or perfection as to a security interest in proceeds; and

(2) the time of filing or perfection as to a security interest in collateral supported by a supporting obligation is also the time of filing or perfection as to a security interest in the supporting obligation.

(c) [Special priority rules: proceeds and supporting obligations.] Except as otherwise provided in subsection (f), a security interest in collateral which qualifies for priority over a conflicting security interest under Section 9-327, 9-328, 9-329, 9-330, or 9-331 also has priority over a conflicting security interest in:

(1) any supporting obligation for the collateral; and

(2) proceeds of the collateral if:

(A) the security interest in proceeds is perfected;

(B) the proceeds are cash proceeds or of the same type as the collateral; and

(C) in the case of proceeds that are proceeds of proceeds, all intervening proceeds are cash proceeds, proceeds of the same type as the collateral, or an account relating to the collateral.

(d) [First-to-file priority rule for certain collateral.] Subject to subsection (e) and except as otherwise provided in subsection (f), if a security interest in chattel paper, deposit accounts, negotiable documents, instruments, investment property, or letter-of-credit rights is perfected by a method other than filing, conflicting perfected security interests in proceeds of the collateral rank according to priority in time of filing.

(e) [Applicability of subsection (d).] Subsection (d) applies only if the proceeds of the collateral are not cash proceeds, chattel paper, negotiable documents, instruments, investment property, or letter-of-credit rights.

(f) [Limitations on subsections (a) through (e).] Subsections (a) through (e) are subject to:

(1) subsection (g) and the other provisions of this part;

(2) Section 4-210 with respect to a security interest of a collecting bank;

(3) Section 5-118 with respect to a security interest of an issuer or nominated person; and

(4) Section 9-110 with respect to a security interest arising under Article 2 or 2A.

(g) [Priority under agricultural lien statute.] A perfected agricultural lien on collateral has priority over a conflicting security interest in or agricultural lien on the same collateral if the statute creating the agricultural lien so provides.

Definitional Cross References:

Account	Section 9-102(a)(2)
Agricultural lien	Section 9-102(a)(5)
Bank	Section 9-102(a)(8)
Cash proceeds	Section 9-102(a)(9)
Chattel paper	Section 9-102(a)(11)
Collateral	Section 9-102(a)(12)
Deposit account	Section 9-102(a)(29)
Document	Section 9-102(a)(30)
Instrument	Section 9-102(a)(47)
Investment property	Section 9-102(a)(49)
Issuer (letter of credit/ letter-of-credit right)	Section 5-102(a)(9)
Letter-of-credit right	Section 9-102(a)(51)
Nominated person	Section 5-102(a)(11)
Proceeds	Section 9-102(a)(64)
Security interest	Section 1-201(b)(35)
Supporting obligation	Section 9-102(a)(78)

Comment References:

9-109 C16
9-110 C4
9-323 C3

Official Comment

1. Source. Former Section 9-312(5), (6).

2. Scope of This Section. In a variety of situations, two or more people may claim a security interest in the same collateral. This section states general rules of priority among conflicting security interests. As subsection (f) provides, the general rules in subsections (a) through (e) are subject to the rule in subsection (g) governing perfected agricultural liens and to the other rules in this Part of this Article. Rules that override this section include those applicable to purchase-money security interests (Section 9-324) and those qualifying for special priority in particular types of collateral. See, e.g., Section 9-327 (deposit accounts); Section 9-328 (investment property); Section 9-329 (letter-of-credit rights); Section 9-330 (chattel paper and instruments); Section 9-334 (fixtures). In addition, the general rules of sections (a) through (e) are subject to priority rules governing security interests arising under Articles 2, 2A, 4, and 5.

3. General Rules. Subsection (a) contains three general rules. Subsection (a)(1) governs the priority of competing perfected security interests. Subsection (a)(2) governs the priority of competing security interests if one is perfected and the other is not. Subsection (a)(3) governs the priority of competing unperfected security interests. The rules may be regarded as adaptations of the idea, deeply rooted at common law, of a race of diligence among creditors. The first two rules are based on precedence in the time as of which the competing secured parties either filed their financing statements or obtained perfected security interests. Under subsection (a)(1), the first secured party who files or perfects has priority. Under subsection (a)(2), which is new, a perfected security interest has priority over an unperfected one. Under subsection (a)(3), if both security interests are unperfected, the first to attach has priority. Note that Section 9-709(b) may affect the application of subsection (a) to a filing that occurred before the effective date of this Article and which would be ineffective to perfect a security interest under former Article 9 but effective under this Article.

4. Competing Perfected Security Interests. When there is more than one perfected security interest, the security interests rank according to priority in time of filing or perfection. "Filing," of course, refers to the filing of an effective financing statement. "Perfection" refers to the acquisition of a perfected security interest, i.e., one that has attached and as to which any required perfection step has been taken. See Sections 9-308 and 9-309.

Example 1: On February 1, A files a financing statement covering a certain item of Debtor's equipment. On March 1, B files a financing statement covering the same equipment. On April 1, B makes a loan to Debtor and obtains a security interest in the equipment. On May 1, A makes a loan to Debtor and obtains a security interest in the same collateral. A has priority even though B's loan was made earlier and was perfected when made. It makes no difference whether A knew of B's security interest when A made its advance.

The problem stated in Example 1 is peculiar to a notice-filing system under which filing may occur before the security interest attaches (see Section 9-502). The justification for determining priority by order of filing lies in the necessity of protecting the filing system—that is, of allowing the first secured party who has filed to make subsequent advances without each time having to check for subsequent filings as a condition of protection. Note, however, that this first-to-file protection is not absolute. For example, Section 9-324 affords priority to certain purchase-money security interests, even if a competing secured party was the first to file or perfect.

Under a notice-filing system, a filed financing statement indicates to third parties that a person may have a security interest in the collateral indicated. With further inquiry, they may discover the complete state of affairs. When a financing statement that is ineffective when filed becomes effective thereafter, the policy underlying the notice-filing system determines the "time of filing" for purposes of subsection (a)(1). For example, the unauthorized filing of an otherwise sufficient initial financing statement becomes authorized, and the financing statement becomes effective, upon the debtor's post-filing authorization or ratification of the filing. See Section 9-509, Comment 3. Because the notice value of the financing statement is independent of the timing of authorization or ratification, the time of the unauthorized filing is the "time of filing" for purposes of subsection (a)(1). The same policy applies to the other priority rules in this part.

Example 2: A and B make non-purchase-money advances secured by the same collateral. The collateral is in Debtor's possession, and neither security interest is perfected when the second advance is made. Whichever secured party first perfects its security interest (by taking possession of the collateral or by filing) takes priority. It makes no difference whether that secured party knows of the other security interest at the time it perfects its own.

The rule of subsection (a)(1), affording priority to the first to file or perfect, applies to security interests that are perfected by any method, including temporarily (Section 9-312) or upon attachment (Section 9-309), even though there may be no notice to creditors or subsequent purchasers and notwithstanding any common-law rule to the contrary. The form of the claim to priority, i.e., filing or perfection, may shift from time to time, and the rank will be based on the first filing or perfection as long as there is no intervening period without filing or perfection. See Section 9-308(c).

Example 3: On October 1, A acquires a temporarily perfected (20-day) security interest, unfiled, in a tangible negotiable document in the debtor's possession under Section 9-312(e). On October 5, B files and thereby perfects a security interest that previously had attached to the same document. On October 10, A files. A has priority, even after the 20-day period expires, regardless of whether A knows of B's security interest when A files. A was the first to perfect and maintained continuous perfection or filing since the start of the 20-day period. However, the perfection of A's security interest extends only "to the extent it arises for new value given." To the extent A's security interest secures advances made by A beyond the 20-day period, its security interest would be subordinate to B's, inasmuch as B was the first to file.

In general, the rule in subsection (a)(1) does not distinguish among various advances made by a secured party. The priority of every advance dates from the earlier of filing or perfection. However, in rare instances, the priority of an advance dates from the time the advance is made. See Example 3 and Section 9-323.

5. Priority in After-Acquired Property. The application of the priority rules to after-acquired property must be considered separately for each item of collateral. Priority does not depend only on time of perfection but may also be based on priority in filing before perfection.

Example 4: On February 1, A makes advances to Debtor under a security agreement covering "all Debtor's machinery, both existing and after-acquired." A promptly files a financing statement. On April 1, B takes a security interest in all Debtor's machinery, existing and after-acquired, to secure an outstanding loan. The following day, B files a financing statement. On May 1, Debtor acquires a new machine. When Debtor acquires rights in the new machine, both A and B acquire security interests in the machine simultaneously. Both security interests are perfected simultaneously. However, A has priority because A filed before B.

When after-acquired collateral is encumbered by more than one security interest, one of the security interests often is a purchase-money security interest that is entitled to special priority under Section 9-324.

6. Priority in Proceeds: General Rule. Subsection (b)(1) follows former Section 9-312(6). It provides that the baseline rules of subsection (a) apply generally to priority conflicts in proceeds except where otherwise provided (e.g., as in subsections (c) through (e)). Under Section 9-203, attachment cannot occur (and therefore, under Section 9-308, perfection cannot occur) as to particular collateral until the collateral itself comes into existence and the debtor has rights in it. Thus, a security interest in proceeds of original collateral does not attach and is not perfected until the proceeds come into existence and the debtor acquires rights in them.

Example 5: On April 1, Debtor signs a security agreement granting to A a security interest in all Debtor's existing and after-acquired inventory. The same day, A files a financing statement covering inventory. On May 1, Debtor signs a security agreement granting B a security interest in all Debtor's existing and future accounts. On June 1, Debtor sells inventory to a customer on 30-day unsecured credit. When Debtor acquires the account, B's security interest attaches to it and is perfected by B's financing statement. At the very same time, A's security interest attaches to the account as proceeds of the inventory and is automatically perfected. See Section 9-315. Under subsection (b) of this section, for purposes of determining A's priority in the account, the time of filing as to the original collateral (April 1, as to inventory) is also the time of filing as to proceeds (account). Accordingly, A's security interest in the account has priority over B's. Of course, had B filed its financing statement before A filed (e.g., on March 1), then B would have priority in the accounts.

Section 9-324 governs the extent to which a special purchase-money priority in goods or software carries over into the proceeds of the original collateral.

7. Priority in Proceeds: Special Rules. Subsections (c), (d), and (e), which are new, provide additional priority rules for proceeds of collateral in situations where the temporal (first-in-time) rules of subsection (a)(1) are not appropriate. These new provisions distinguish what these Comments refer to as "non-filing collateral" from what they call "filing collateral." As used in these Comments, non-filing collateral is collateral of a type for which perfection may be achieved by a method other than filing (possession or control, mainly) and for which secured parties who so perfect generally do not expect or need to conduct a filing search. More specifically, non-filing collateral is chattel paper, deposit accounts, negotiable documents, instruments, investment property, and letter-of-credit rights. Other collateral—accounts, commercial tort claims, general intangibles, goods, nonnegotiable documents, and payment intangibles—is filing collateral.

8. Proceeds of Non-Filing Collateral: Non-Temporal Priority. Subsection (c)(2) provides a baseline priority rule for proceeds of non-filing collateral which applies if the secured party has taken the steps required for non-temporal priority over a conflicting security interest in non-filing collateral (e.g., control, in the case of deposit accounts, letter-of-credit rights, investment property, and in some cases, electronic negotiable documents, Section 9-331). This rule determines priority in proceeds of non-filing collateral whether or not there exists an actual conflicting security interest in the original non-filing collateral. Under subsection (c)(2), the priority in the original collateral continues in proceeds if the security interest in proceeds is perfected and the proceeds are cash proceeds or non-filing proceeds "of the same type" as the original collateral. As used in subsection (c)(2), "type" means a type of collateral defined in the Uniform Commercial Code and should be read broadly. For example, a security is "of the same type" as a security entitlement (i.e., investment property), and a promissory note is "of the same type" as a draft (i.e., an instrument).

Example 6: SP-1 perfects its security interest in investment property by filing. SP-2 perfects subsequently by taking control of a certificated security. Debtor receives cash proceeds of the security (e.g., dividends deposited into Debtor's deposit account). If the first-to-file-or-perfect rule of subsection (a)(1) were applied, SP-1's security interest in the cash proceeds would be senior, although SP-2's security interest continues perfected under Section 9-315 beyond the 20-day period of automatic perfection. This was the result under former Article 9. Under subsection (c), however, SP-2's security interest is senior.

Note that a different result would obtain in Example 6 (i.e., SP-1's security interest would be senior) if SP-1 were to obtain control of the deposit-account proceeds. This is so because subsection (c) is subject to subsection (f), which in turn provides that the priority rules under subsections (a) through (e) are subject to "the other provisions of this part." One of those "other provisions" is Section 9-327, which affords priority to a security interest perfected by control. See Section 9-327(1).

Example 7: SP-1 perfects its security interest in investment property by filing. SP-2 perfects subsequently by taking control of a certificated security. Debtor receives proceeds of the security consisting of a new certificated security issued as a stock dividend on the original collateral. Although the new security is of the same type as the original collateral (i.e., investment property), once the 20-day period of automatic perfection expires (see Section 9-315(d)), SP-2's security interest is unperfected. (SP-2 has not filed or taken delivery or control, and no temporary-perfection rule applies.) Consequently, once the 20-day period expires, subsection (c) does not confer priority, and, under subsection (a)(2), SP-1's security interest in the security is senior. This was the result under former Article 9.

Example 8: SP-1 perfects its security interest in investment property by filing. SP-2 perfects subsequently by taking control of a certificated security and also by filing against investment property. Debtor receives proceeds of the security consisting of a new certificated security issued as a stock dividend of the collateral. Because the new security is of the same type as the original collateral (i.e., investment property) and (unlike Example 7) SP-2's security interest is perfected by filing, SP-2's security interest is senior under subsection (c). If the new security were redeemed by the issuer upon surrender and yet another security were received by Debtor, SP-2's security interest would continue to enjoy priority under subsection (c). The new security would be proceeds of proceeds.

Example 9: SP-1 perfects its security interest in instruments by filing. SP-2 subsequently perfects its security interest in investment property by taking control of a certificated security and also by filing against investment property. Debtor receives proceeds of the security consisting of a dividend check that it deposits to a deposit account. Because the check and the deposit account are cash proceeds, SP-1's and SP-2's security interests in the cash proceeds are perfected under Section 9-315 beyond the 20-day period of automatic perfection. However, SP-2's security interest is senior under subsection (c).

Example 10: SP-1 perfects its security interest in investment property by filing. SP-2 perfects subsequently by taking control of a certificated security and also by filing against investment property. Debtor receives an instrument as proceeds of the security. (Assume that the instrument is not cash proceeds.) Because the instrument is not of the same type as the original collateral (i.e., investment property), SP-2's security interest, although perfected by filing, does not achieve priority under subsection (c). Under the first-to-file-or-perfect rule of subsection (a)(1), SP-1's security interest in the proceeds is senior.

The proceeds of proceeds are themselves proceeds. See Section 9-102 (defining "proceeds" and "collateral"). Sometimes competing security interests arise in proceeds that are several generations removed from the original collateral. As the following example explains, the applicability of subsection (c) may turn on the nature of the intervening proceeds.

Example 11: SP-1 perfects its security interest in Debtor's deposit account by obtaining control. Thereafter, SP-2 files against inventory, (presumably) searches, finds no indication of a conflicting security interest, and advances against Debtor's existing and after-acquired inventory. Debtor uses funds from the deposit account to purchase inventory, which SP-1 can trace as identifiable proceeds of its security interest in Debtor's deposit account, and which SP-2 claims as original collateral. The inventory is sold and the proceeds deposited into another deposit account, as to which SP-1 has not obtained control. Subsection (c) does not govern priority in this other deposit account. This deposit account is cash proceeds and is also the same type of collateral as SP-1's original collateral, as required by subsections (c)(2)(A) and (B). However, SP-1's security interest does not satisfy subsection (c)(2)(C) because the inventory proceeds, which intervened between the original deposit account and the deposit account constituting the proceeds at issue, are not cash proceeds, proceeds of the same type as the collateral (original deposit account), or an account relating to the collateral. Stated otherwise, once proceeds other than cash proceeds, proceeds of the same type as the original collateral, or an account relating to the original collateral intervene in the chain of proceeds, priority under subsection (c) is thereafter unavailable. The special priority rule in subsection (d) also is inapplicable to this case. See Comment 9, Example 13, below. Instead, the general first-to-file-or-perfect rule of subsections (a) and (b) apply. Under that rule, SP-1 has priority unless its security interest in the inventory proceeds became unperfected under Section 9-315(d). Had SP-2 filed against inventory before SP-1 obtained control of the original deposit account, then SP-2 would have had priority even if SP-1's security interest in the inventory proceeds remained perfected.

If two security interests in the same original collateral are entitled to priority in an item of proceeds under subsection (c)(2), the security interest having priority in the original collateral has priority in the proceeds.

9. Proceeds of Non-Filing Collateral: Special Temporal Priority. Under subsections (d) and (e), if a security interest in non-filing collateral is perfected by a method other than filing (e.g., control or possession), it does not retain its priority over a conflicting security interest in proceeds that are filing collateral. Moreover, it is not entitled to priority in proceeds under the first-to-file-or-perfect rule of subsections (a)(1) and (b). Instead, under subsection (d), priority is determined by a new first-to-file rule.

Example 12: SP-1 perfects its security interest in Debtor's deposit account by obtaining control. Thereafter, SP-2 files against equipment, (presumably) searches, finds no indication of a conflicting security interest, and advances against Debtor's equipment. SP-1 then files against Debtor's equipment. Debtor uses funds from the deposit account to purchase equipment, which SP-1 can trace as proceeds of its security interest in Debtor's deposit account. If the first-to-file-or-perfect rule were applied, SP-1's security interest would be senior under subsections (a)(1) and (b), because it was the first to perfect in the original collateral and there was no period during which its security interest was unperfected. Under subsection (d), however, SP-2's security interest would be senior because it filed first. This corresponds with the likely expectations of the parties.

Note that under subsection (e), the first-to-file rule of subsection (d) applies only if the proceeds in question are other than non-filing collateral (i.e., if the proceeds are filing collateral). If the proceeds are non-filing collateral, either the first-to-file-or-perfect rule under subsections (a) and (b) or the non-temporal priority rule in subsection (c) would apply, depending on the facts.

Example 13: SP-1 perfects its security interest in Debtor's deposit account by obtaining control. Thereafter, SP-2 files against inventory, (presumably) searches, finds no indication of a conflicting security interest, and advances against Debtor's existing and after-acquired inventory. Debtor uses funds from the deposit account to purchase inventory, which SP-1 can trace as identifiable proceeds of its security interest in Debtor's deposit account, and which SP-2 claims as original collateral. The inventory is sold and the proceeds deposited into another deposit account, as to which SP-1 has not obtained control. As discussed above in Comment 8, Example 11, subsection (c) does not govern priority in this deposit account. Subsection (d) also does not govern, because the proceeds at issue (the deposit account) are cash proceeds. See subsection (e). Rather, the general rules of subsections (a) and (b) govern.

10. Priority in Supporting Obligations. Under subsections (b)(2) and (c)(1), a security interest having priority in collateral also has priority in a supporting obligation for that collateral. However, the rules in these subsections are subject to the special rule in Section 9-329 governing the priority of security interests in a letter-of-credit right. See subsection (f). Under Section 9-329, a secured party's failure to obtain control (Section 9-107) of a letter-of-credit right that serves as supporting collateral leaves its security interest exposed to a priming interest of a party who does take control.

11. Unperfected Security Interests. Under subsection (a)(3), if conflicting security interests are unperfected, the first to attach has priority. This rule may be of merely theoretical interest, inasmuch as it is hard to imagine a situation where the case would come into litigation without either secured party's having perfected its security interest. If neither security interest had been perfected at the time of the filing of a petition in bankruptcy, ordinarily neither would be good against the trustee in bankruptcy under the Bankruptcy Code.

12. Agricultural Liens. Statutes other than this Article may purport to grant priority to an agricultural lien as against a conflicting security interest or agricultural lien. Under subsection (g), if another statute grants priority to an agricultural lien, the agricultural lien has priority only if the same statute creates the agricultural lien and the agricultural lien is perfected. Otherwise, subsection (a) applies the same priority rules to an agricultural lien as to a security interest, regardless of whether the agricultural lien conflicts with another agricultural lien or with a security interest.

Inasmuch as no agricultural lien on proceeds arises under this Article, subsections (b) through (e) do not apply to proceeds of agricultural liens. However, if an agricultural lien has priority under subsection (g) and the statute creating the agricultural lien gives the secured party a lien on proceeds of the collateral subject to the lien, a court should apply the principle of subsection (g) and award priority in the proceeds to the holder of the perfected agricultural lien.

§ 9-323. Future Advances.

(a) [When priority based on time of advance.] Except as otherwise provided in subsection (c), for purposes of determining the priority of a perfected security interest under Section 9-322(a)(1), perfection of the security interest dates from the time an advance is made to the extent that the security interest secures an advance that:

(1) is made while the security interest is perfected only:

(A) under Section 9-309 when it attaches; or

(B) temporarily under Section 9-312(e), (f), or (g); and

(2) is not made pursuant to a commitment entered into before or while the security interest is perfected by a method other than under Section 9-309 or 9-312(e), (f), or (g).

(b) [Lien creditor.] Except as otherwise provided in subsection (c), a security interest is subordinate to the rights of a person that becomes a lien creditor to the extent that the security interest secures an advance made more than 45 days after the person becomes a lien creditor unless the advance is made:

(1) without knowledge of the lien; or

(2) pursuant to a commitment entered into without knowledge of the lien.

(c) [Buyer of receivables.] Subsections (a) and (b) do not apply to a security interest held by a secured party that is a buyer of accounts, chattel paper, payment intangibles, or promissory notes or a consignor.

(d) [Buyer of goods.] Except as otherwise provided in subsection (e), a buyer of goods takes free of a security interest to the extent that it secures advances made after the earlier of:

(1) the time the secured party acquires knowledge of the buyer's purchase; or

(2) 45 days after the purchase.

(e) [Advances made pursuant to commitment: priority of buyer of goods.] Subsection (d) does not apply if the advance is made pursuant to a commitment entered into without knowledge of the buyer's purchase and before the expiration of the 45-day period.

(f) [Lessee of goods.] Except as otherwise provided in subsection (g), a lessee of goods, takes the leasehold interest free of a security interest to the extent that it secures advances made after the earlier of:

(1) the time the secured party acquires knowledge of the lease; or

(2) 45 days after the lease contract becomes enforceable.

(g) [Advances made pursuant to commitment: priority of lessee of goods.] Subsection (f) does not apply if the advance is made pursuant to a commitment entered into without knowledge of the lease and before the expiration of the 45-day period.

Definitional Cross References:

Account	Section 9-102(a)(2)
Buyer in ordinary course of business	Section 1-201(b)(9)
Chattel paper	Section 9-102(a)(11)
Consignor	Section 9-102(a)(21)
Goods	Section 9-102(a)(44)
Lease contract	Section 2A-103(1)(l)
Lease	Section 2A-103(1)(j)
Leasehold interest	Section 2A-103(1)(m)
Lessee	Section 2A-103(1)(n)
Lessee in ordinary course of business	Section 2A-103(1)(o)
Lien creditor	Section 9-102(a)(52)
Payment intangible	Section 9-102(a)(61)
Person	Section 1-201(b)(27)
Promissory note	Section 9-102(a)(65)
Purchase	Section 1-201(b)(29)
Pursuant to commitment	Section 9-102(a)(69)
Right	Section 1-201(b)(34)
Secured party	Section 9-102(a)(73)
Security interest	Section 1-201(b)(35)

Comment References:
9-317 C4
9-322 C4

Official Comment

1. Source. Former Sections 9-312(7), 9-301(4), 9-307(3), 2A-307(4).

2. Scope of This Section. A security agreement may provide that collateral secures future advances. See Section 9-204(c). This section collects all of the special rules dealing with the priority of advances made by a secured party after a third party acquires an interest in the collateral. Subsection (a) applies when the third party is a competing secured party. It replaces and clarifies former Section 9-312(7). Subsection (b) deals with lien creditors and replaces former Section 9-301(4). Subsections (d) and (e) deal with buyers and replace former Section 9-307(3). Subsections (f) and (g) deal with lessees and replace former Section 2A-307(4).

3. Competing Security Interests. Under a proper reading of the first-to-file-or-perfect rule of Section 9-322(a)(1) (and former Section 9-312(5)), it is abundantly clear that the time when an advance is made plays no role in determining priorities among conflicting security interests except when a financing statement was not filed and the advance is the giving of value as the last step for attachment and perfection. Thus, a secured party takes subject to all advances secured by a competing security interest having priority under Section 9-322(a)(1). This result generally obtains regardless of how the competing security interest is perfected and regardless of whether the advances are made "pursuant to commitment" (Section 9-102). Subsection (a) of this section states the only other instance when the time of an advance figures in the priority scheme in Section 9-322: when the security interest is perfected only automatically under Section 9-309 or temporarily under Section 9-312(e), (f), or (g), and the advance is not made pursuant to a commitment entered into while the security interest was perfected by another method. Thus, an advance has priority from the date it is made only in the rare case in which it is made without commitment and while the security interest is perfected only temporarily under Section 9-312.

The new formulation in subsection (a) clarifies the result when the initial advance is paid and a new ("future") advance is made subsequently. Under former Section 9-312(7), the priority of the new advance turned on whether it was "made while a security interest is perfected." This section resolves any ambiguity by omitting the quoted phrase.

> **Example 1:** On February 1, A makes an advance secured by machinery in the debtor's possession and files a financing statement. On March 1, B makes an advance secured by the same machinery and files a financing statement. On April 1, A makes a further advance, under the original security agreement, against the same machinery. A was the first to file and so, under the first-to-file-or-perfect rule of Section 9-322(a)(1), A's security interest has priority over B's, both as to the February 1 and as to the April 1 advance. It makes no difference whether A knows of B's intervening advance when A makes the second advance. Note that, as long as A was the first to

file or perfect, A would have priority with respect to both advances if either A or B had perfected by taking possession of the collateral. Likewise, A would have priority if A's April 1 advance was not made under the original agreement with the debtor, but was under a new agreement.

Example 2: On October 1, A acquires a temporarily perfected (20-day) security interest, unfiled, in a tangible negotiable document in the debtor's possession under Section 9-312(e) or (f). The security interest secures an advance made on that day as well as future advances. On October 5, B files and thereby perfects a security interest that previously had attached to the same document. On October 8, A makes an additional advance. On October 10, A files. Under Section 9-322(a)(1), because A was the first to perfect and maintained continuous perfection or filing since the start of the 20-day period, A has priority, even after the 20-day period expires. See Section 9-322, Comment 4, Example 3. However, under this section, for purposes of Section 9-322(a)(1), to the extent A's security interest secures the October 8 advance, the security interest was perfected on October 8. Inasmuch as B perfected on October 5, B has priority over the October 8 advance.

The rule in subsection (a) is more liberal toward the priority of future advances than the corresponding rules applicable to intervening lien creditors (subsection (b)), buyers (subsections (d) and (e)), and lessees (subsections (f) and (g)).

4. Competing Lien Creditors. Subsection (b) replaces former Section 9-301(4) and addresses the rights of a "lien creditor," as defined in Section 9-102. Under Section 9-317(a)(2), a security interest is senior to the rights of a person who becomes a lien creditor, unless the person becomes a lien creditor before the security interest is perfected and before a financing statement covering the collateral is filed and Section 9-203(b)(3) is satisfied. Subsection (b) of this section provides that a security interest is subordinate to those rights to the extent that the specified circumstances occur. Subsection (b) does not elevate the priority of a security interest that is subordinate to the rights of a lien creditor under Section 9-317(a)(2); it only subordinates.

As under former Section 9-301(4), a secured party's knowledge does not cut short the 45-day period during which future advances can achieve priority over an intervening lien creditor's interest. Rather, because of the impact of the rule in subsection (b) on the question whether the security interest for future advances is "protected" under Section 6323(c)(2) and (d) of the Internal Revenue Code as amended by the Federal Tax Lien Act of 1966, the priority of the security interest for future advances over a lien creditor is made absolute for 45 days regardless of knowledge of the secured party concerning the lien. If, however, the advance is made after the 45 days, the advance will not have priority unless it was made or committed without knowledge of the lien.

5. Sales of Receivables; Consignments. Subsections (a) and (b) do not apply to outright sales of accounts, chattel paper, payment intangibles, or promissory notes, nor do they apply to consignments.

6. Competing Buyers and Lessees. Under subsections (d) and (e), a buyer will not take subject to a security interest to the extent it secures advances made after the secured party has knowledge that the buyer has purchased the collateral or more than 45 days after the purchase unless the advances were made pursuant to a commitment entered into before the expiration of the 45-day period and without knowledge of the purchase. Subsections (f) and (g) provide an analogous rule for lessees. Subsections (d) and (e) replace pre-1998 Section 9-307(3), and subsections (f) and (g) replace pre-1998 Section 2A-307(4). No change in meaning is intended.

Of course, a buyer in ordinary course who takes free of the security interest under Section 9-320 and a lessee in ordinary course who takes free under Section 9-321 are not subject to any future advances. However, the exceptions for a buyer in ordinary course of business and a lessee in ordinary course of business in the 1998 text of subsections (d) and (f) have been deleted. Even if such a buyer or lessee does not meet the requirements under Section 9-320 or 9-321 to take free of a security interest, it should be entitled to the benefits of those subsections, which apply to buyers generally. This change is consistent with the intended result under the 1998 text.

§ 9-324. Priority of Purchase-Money Security Interests.

(a) [General rule: purchase-money priority.] Except as otherwise provided in subsection (g), a perfected purchase-money security interest in goods other than inventory or livestock has priority over a conflicting security interest in the same goods, and, except as otherwise provided in Section 9-327, a perfected security interest in its identifiable proceeds also has priority, if the purchase-money security interest is perfected when the debtor receives possession of the collateral or within 20 days thereafter.

(b) [Inventory purchase-money priority.] Subject to subsection (c) and except as otherwise provided in subsection (g), a perfected purchase-money security interest in inventory has priority over a conflicting security interest in the same inventory, has priority over a conflicting security interest in chattel paper or an instrument constituting proceeds of the inventory and in proceeds of the chattel paper, if so provided in Section 9-330, and, except as otherwise provided in Section 9-327, also has priority in identifiable cash proceeds of the inventory to the extent the identifiable cash proceeds are received on or before the delivery of the inventory to a buyer, if:

(1) the purchase-money security interest is perfected when the debtor receives possession of the inventory;

(2) the purchase-money secured party sends a signed notification to the holder of the conflicting security interest;

(3) the holder of the conflicting security interest receives the notification within five years before the debtor receives possession of the inventory; and

(4) the notification states that the person sending the notification has or expects to acquire a purchase-money security interest in inventory of the debtor and describes the inventory.

(c) [Holders of conflicting inventory security interests to be notified.] Subsections (b)(2) through (4) apply only if the holder of the conflicting security interest had filed a financing statement covering the same types of inventory:

(1) if the purchase-money security interest is perfected by filing, before the date of the filing; or

(2) if the purchase-money security interest is temporarily perfected without filing or possession under Section 9-312(f), before the beginning of the 20-day period thereunder.

(d) [Livestock purchase-money priority.] Subject to subsection (e) and except as otherwise provided in subsection (g), a perfected purchase-money security interest in livestock that are farm products has priority over a conflicting security interest in the same livestock, and, except as otherwise provided in Section 9-327, a perfected security interest in their identifiable proceeds and identifiable products in their unmanufactured states also has priority, if:

(1) the purchase-money security interest is perfected when the debtor receives possession of the livestock;

(2) the purchase-money secured party sends a signed notification to the holder of the conflicting security interest;

(3) the holder of the conflicting security interest receives the notification within six months before the debtor receives possession of the livestock; and

(4) the notification states that the person sending the notification has or expects to acquire a purchase-money security interest in livestock of the debtor and describes the livestock.

(e) [Holders of conflicting livestock security interests to be notified.] Subsections (d)(2) through (4) apply only if the holder of the conflicting security interest had filed a financing statement covering the same types of livestock:

(1) if the purchase-money security interest is perfected by filing, before the date of the filing; or

(2) if the purchase-money security interest is temporarily perfected without filing or possession under Section 9-312(f), before the beginning of the 20-day period thereunder.

(f) [Software purchase-money priority.] Except as otherwise provided in subsection (g), a perfected purchase-money security interest in software has priority over a conflicting security interest in the same collateral, and, except as otherwise provided in Section 9-327, a perfected security interest in its identifiable proceeds also has priority, to the extent that the purchase-money security interest in the goods in which the software was acquired for use has priority in the goods and proceeds of the goods under this section.

(g) [Conflicting purchase-money security interests.] If more than one security interest qualifies for priority in the same collateral under subsection (a), (b), (d), or (f):

(1) a security interest securing an obligation incurred as all or part of the price of the collateral has priority over a security interest securing an obligation incurred for value given to enable the debtor to acquire rights in or the use of collateral; and

(2) in all other cases, Section 9-322(a) applies to the qualifying security interests.

Definitional Cross References:

Cash proceeds	Section 9-102(a)(9)
Chattel paper	Section 9-102(a)(11)
Collateral	Section 9-102(a)(12)
Debtor	Section 9-102(a)(28)
Delivery	Section 1-201(b)(15)
Farm products	Section 9-102(a)(34)
Financing statement	Section 9-102(a)(39)
Goods	Section 9-102(a)(44)

Holder	Section 1-201(b)(21)
Instrument	Section 9-102(a)(47)
Inventory	Section 9-102(a)(48)
Person	Section 1-201(b)(27)
Proceeds	Section 9-102(a)(64)
Right	Section 1-201(b)(34)
Secured party	Section 9-102(a)(73)
Security interest	Section 1-201(b)(35)
Send	Section 1-201(b)(36)
Sign	Section 1-201(b)(37)
Software	Section 9-102(a)(76)
Value	Section 1-204

Official Comment

1. Source. Former Section 9-312(3), (4).

2. Priority of Purchase-Money Security Interests. This section contains the priority rules applicable to purchase-money security interests, as defined in Section 9-103. It affords a special, non-temporal priority to those purchase-money security interests that satisfy the statutory conditions. In most cases, priority will be over a security interest asserted under an after-acquired property clause. See Section 9-204 on the extent to which security interests in after-acquired property are validated.

A purchase-money security interest can be created only in goods and software. See Section 9-103. Section 9-324(a), which follows former Section 9-312(4), contains the general rule for purchase-money security interests in goods. It is subject to subsections (b) and (c), which derive from former Section 9-312(3) and apply to purchase-money security interests in inventory, and subsections (d) and (e), which apply to purchase-money security interests in livestock that are farm products. Subsection (f) applies to purchase-money security interests in software. Subsection (g) deals with the relatively unusual case in which a debtor creates two purchase-money security interests in the same collateral and both security interests qualify for special priority under one of the other subsections.

Former Section 9-312(2) contained a rule affording special priority to those who provided secured credit that enabled a debtor to produce crops. This rule proved unworkable and has been eliminated from this Article. Instead, model Section 9-324A contains a revised production-money priority rule. That section is a model, not uniform, provision. The sponsors of the UCC have taken no position as to whether it should be enacted, instead leaving the matter for state legislatures to consider if they are so inclined.

3. Purchase-Money Priority in Goods Other Than Inventory and Livestock. Subsection (a) states a general rule applicable to all types of goods except inventory and farm-products livestock: the purchase-money interest takes priority if it is perfected when the debtor receives possession of the collateral or within 20 days thereafter. (As to the 20-day "grace period," compare Section 9-317(e). Former Sections 9-312(4) and 9-301(2) contained a 10-day grace period.) The perfection requirement means that the purchase-money secured party either has filed a financing statement before that time or has a temporarily perfected security interest in goods covered by documents under Section 9-312(e) and (f) which is continued in a perfected status by filing before the expiration of the 20-day period specified in that section. A purchase-money security interest qualifies for priority under subsection (a), even if the purchase-money secured party knows that a conflicting security interest has been created and/or that the holder of the conflicting interest has filed a financing statement covering the collateral.

Normally, there will be no question when "the debtor receives possession of the collateral" for purposes of subsection (a). However, sometimes a debtor buys goods and takes possession of them in stages, and then assembly and testing are completed (by the seller or debtor-buyer) at the debtor's location. Under those circumstances, the buyer "takes possession" within the meaning of subsection (a) when, after an inspection of the portion of the goods in the debtor's possession, it would be apparent to a potential lender to the debtor that the debtor has acquired an interest in the goods taken as a whole.

A similar issue concerning the time when "the debtor receives possession" arises when a person acquires possession of goods under a transaction that is not governed by this Article and then later agrees to buy the goods on secured credit. For example, a person may take possession of goods as lessee under a lease contract and then exercise an option to purchase the goods from the lessor on secured credit. Under Section 2A-307(1), creditors of the lessee generally take subject to the lease contract; filing a financing statement against the lessee is unnecessary to protect the lessor's leasehold or residual interest. Once the lease is converted to a security interest, filing a financing statement is necessary to protect the seller's (former lessor's) security interest. Accordingly, the 20-day period in subsection (a) does not commence until the goods become "collateral" (defined in Section 9-102), i.e., until they are subject to a security interest.

4. Purchase-Money Security Interests in Inventory. Subsections (b) and (c) afford a means by which a purchase-money security interest in inventory can achieve priority over an earlier-filed security interest in the same collateral. To achieve priority, the purchase-money security interest must be perfected when the debtor receives possession of the inventory. For a discussion of when "the debtor receives possession," see Comment 3, above. The 20-day grace period of subsection (a) does not apply.

The arrangement between an inventory secured party and its debtor typically requires the secured party to make periodic advances against incoming inventory or periodic releases of old inventory as new inventory is received. A fraudulent debtor may apply to the secured party for advances even though it has already given a purchase-money security interest in the inventory to another secured party. For this reason, subsections (b)(2) through (4) and (c) impose a second condition for the purchase-money security interest's achieving priority: the purchase-money secured party must give notification to the holder of a conflicting security interest who filed against the same item or type of inventory before the purchase-money secured party filed or its security interest became perfected temporarily under Section 9-312(e) or (f). The notification requirement protects the non-purchase-money inventory secured party in such a situation: if the inventory secured party has received notification, it presumably will not make an advance; if it has not received notification (or if the other security interest does not qualify as purchase-money), any advance the inventory secured party may make ordinarily will have priority under Section 9-322. Inasmuch as an arrangement for periodic advances against incoming goods is unusual outside the inventory field, subsection (a) does not contain a notification requirement.

5. Notification to Conflicting Inventory Secured Party: Timing. Under subsection (b)(3), the perfected purchase-money security interest achieves priority over a conflicting security interest only if the holder of the conflicting security interest receives a notification within five years before the debtor receives possession of the purchase-money collateral. If the debtor never receives possession, the five-year period never begins, and the purchase-money security interest has priority, even if notification is not given. However, where the purchase-money inventory financing began by the purchase-money secured party's possession of a negotiable document of title, to retain priority the secured party must give the notification required by subsection (b) at or before the usual time, i.e., when the debtor gets possession of the inventory, even though the security interest remains perfected for 20 days under Section 9-312(e) or (f).

Some people have mistakenly read former Section 9-312(3)(b) to require, as a condition of purchase-money priority in inventory, that the purchase-money secured party give the notification before it files a financing statement. Read correctly, the "before" clauses compare (i) the time when the holder of the conflicting security interest filed a financing statement with (ii) the time when the purchase-money security interest becomes perfected by filing or automatically perfected temporarily. Only if (i) occurs before (ii) must notification be given to the holder of the conflicting security interest. Subsection (c) has been rewritten to clarify this point.

6. Notification to Conflicting Inventory Secured Party: Address. Inasmuch as the address provided as that of the secured party on a filed financing statement is an "address that is reasonable under the circumstances," the holder of a purchase-money security interest may satisfy the requirement to "send" notification to the holder of a conflicting security interest in inventory by sending a notification to that address, even if the address is or becomes incorrect. See Section 9-102 (definition of "send"). Similarly, because the address is "held out by [the holder of the conflicting security interest] as the place for receipt of such communications [i.e., communications relating to security interests]," the holder is deemed to have "received" a notification delivered to that address. See Section 1-202(e).

7. Consignments. Subsections (b) and (c) also determine the priority of a consignor's interest in consigned goods as against a security interest in the goods created by the consignee. Inasmuch as a consignment subject to this Article is defined to be a purchase-money security interest, see Section 9-103(d), no inference concerning the nature of the transaction should be drawn from the fact that a consignor uses the term "security interest" in its notice under subsection (b)(4). Similarly, a notice stating that the consignor has delivered or expects to deliver goods, properly described, "on consignment" meets the requirements of subsection (b)(4), even if it does not contain the term "security interest," and even if the transaction subsequently is determined to be a security interest. Cf. Section 9-505 (use of "consignor" and "consignee" in financing statement).

8. Priority in Proceeds: General. When the purchase-money secured party has priority over another secured party, the question arises whether this priority extends to the proceeds of the original collateral. Subsections (a), (d), and (f) give an affirmative answer, but only as to proceeds in which the security interest is perfected (see Section 9-315). Although this qualification did not appear in former Section 9-312(4), it was implicit in that provision.

In the case of inventory collateral under subsection (b), where financing frequently is based on the resulting accounts, chattel paper, or other proceeds, the special priority of the purchase-money secured interest carries over into only certain types of proceeds. As under former Section 9-312(3), the purchase-money priority in inventory under subsection (b) carries over into identifiable cash proceeds (defined in Section 9-102) received on or before the delivery of the inventory to a buyer.

As a general matter, also like former Section 9-312(3), the purchase-money priority in inventory does not carry over into proceeds consisting of accounts or chattel paper. Many parties financing inventory are quite content to protect their first-priority security interest in the inventory itself. They realize that when the inventory is sold, someone else will be financing the resulting receivables (accounts or chattel paper), and the priority for inventory will not run forward to the receivables constituting the proceeds. Indeed, the cash supplied by the receivables financer often will be used to pay the inventory financing. In some situations, the party financing the inventory on a purchase-money basis makes contractual arrangements that the proceeds of receivables financing by another be devoted to paying off the inventory security interest.

However, the purchase-money priority in inventory does carry over to proceeds consisting of chattel paper and its proceeds (and also to instruments) to the extent provided in Section 9-330. Under Section 9-330(e), the holder of a purchase-money security interest in inventory is deemed to give new value for proceeds consisting of chattel paper. Taken together, Sections 9-324(b) and 9-330(e) enable a purchase-money inventory secured party to obtain priority in chattel paper constituting proceeds of the inventory, even if the secured party does not actually give new value for the chattel paper, provided the purchase-money secured party satisfies the other conditions for achieving priority.

When the proceeds of original collateral (goods or software) consist of a deposit account, Section 9-327 governs priority to the extent it conflicts with the priority rules of this section.

9. Priority in Accounts Constituting Proceeds of Inventory. The application of the priority rules in subsection (b) is shown by the following examples:

Example 1: Debtor creates a security interest in its existing and after-acquired inventory in favor of SP-1, who files a financing statement covering inventory. SP-2 subsequently takes a purchase-money security interest in certain inventory and, under subsection (b), achieves priority in this inventory over SP-1. This inventory is then sold, producing accounts. Accounts are not cash proceeds, and so the special purchase-money priority in the inventory does not control the priority in the accounts. Rather, the first-to-file-or-perfect rule of Section 9-322(a)(1) applies. The time of SP-1's filing as to the inventory is also the time of filing as to the accounts under Section 9-322(b). Assuming that each security interest in the accounts proceeds remains perfected under Section 9-315, SP-1 has priority as to the accounts.

Example 2: In Example 1, if SP-2 had filed directly against accounts, the date of that filing as to accounts would be compared with the date of SP-1's filing as to the inventory. The first filed would prevail under Section 9-322(a)(1).

Example 3: If SP-3 had filed against accounts in Example 1 before either SP-1 or SP 2 filed against inventory, SP-3's filing against accounts would have priority over the filings of SP-1 and SP-2. This result obtains even though the filings against inventory are effective to continue the perfected status of SP-1's and SP-2's security interest in the accounts beyond the 20-day period of automatic perfection. See Section 9-315. SP-1's and SP-2's position as to the inventory does not give them a claim to accounts (as proceeds of the inventory) which is senior to someone who has filed earlier against accounts. If, on the other hand, either SP-1's or SP-2's filing against the inventory preceded SP-3's filing against accounts, SP-1 or SP-2 would outrank SP-3 as to the accounts.

10. Purchase-Money Security Interests in Livestock. New subsections (d) and (e) provide a purchase-money priority rule for farm-products livestock. They are patterned on the purchase-money priority rule for inventory found in subsections (b) and (c) and include a requirement that the purchase-money secured party notify earlier-filed parties. Two differences between subsections (b) and (d) are noteworthy. First, unlike the purchase-money inventory lender, the purchase-money livestock lender enjoys priority in all proceeds of the collateral. Thus, under subsection (d), the purchase-money secured party takes priority in accounts over an earlier-filed accounts financer. Second, subsection (d) affords priority in certain products of the collateral as well as proceeds.

11. Purchase-Money Security Interests in Aquatic Farm Products. Aquatic goods produced in aquacultural operations (e.g., catfish raised on a catfish farm) are farm products. See Section 9-102 (definition of "farm products"). The definition does not indicate whether aquatic goods are "crops," as to which the model production money security interest priority in Section 9-324A applies, or "livestock," as to which the purchase-money priority in subsection (d) of this section applies. This Article leaves courts free to determine the classification of particular aquatic goods on a case-by-case basis, applying whichever priority rule makes more sense in the overall context of the debtor's business.

12. Purchase-Money Security Interests in Software. Subsection (f) governs the priority of purchase-money security interests in software. Under Section 9-103(c), a purchase-money security interest arises in software only if the debtor acquires its interest in the software for the principal purpose of using the software in goods subject to a purchase-money security interest. Under subsection (f), a purchase-money security interest in software has the same priority as the purchase-money security interest in the goods in which the software was acquired for use. This priority is determined under subsections (b) and (c) (for inventory) or (a) (for other goods).

13. Multiple Purchase-Money Security Interests. New subsection (g) governs priority among multiple purchase-money security interests in the same collateral. It grants priority to purchase-money security interests securing the price of collateral (i.e., created in favor of the seller) over purchase-money security interests that secure enabling loans. Section 7.2(c) of the Restatement (3d) of the Law of Property (Mortgages) (1997) adopts this rule with respect to real property mortgages. As Comment *d* to that section explains:

> the equities favor the vendor. Not only does the vendor part with specific real estate rather than money, but the vendor would never relinquish it at all except on the understanding that the vendor will be able to use it to satisfy the obligation to pay the price. This is the case even though the vendor may know that the mortgagor is going to finance the transaction in part by borrowing from a third party and giving a mortgage to secure that obligation. In the final analysis, the law is more sympathetic to the vendor's hazard of losing real estate previously owned than to the third party lender's risk of being unable to collect from an interest in real estate that never previously belonged to it.

The first-to-file-or-perfect rule of Section 9-322 applies to multiple purchase-money security interests securing enabling loans.

14. "Signed Replaces "Authenticated." Consistent with the revised definition of "sign" in Section 1-201, the cognate term "signed" replaces the references to authenticated in the pre-2022 text of this section.

§ 9-325. Priority of Security Interests in Transferred Collateral.

(a) [Subordination of security interest in transferred collateral.] Except as otherwise provided in subsection (b), a security interest created by a debtor is subordinate to a security interest in the same collateral created by another person if:

(1) the debtor acquired the collateral subject to the security interest created by the other person;

(2) the security interest created by the other person was perfected when the debtor acquired the collateral; and

(3) there is no period thereafter when the security interest is unperfected.

(b) [Limitation of subsection (a) subordination.] Subsection (a) subordinates a security interest only if the security interest:

(1) otherwise would have priority solely under Section 9-322(a) or 9-324; or

(2) arose solely under Section 2-711(3) or 2A-508(5).

Definitional Cross References:

Collateral	Section 9-102(a)(12)
Debtor	Section 9-102(a)(28)
Person	Section 1-201(b)(27)
Security interest	Section 1-201(b)(35)

Comment References: 9-110 C4

Official Comment

1. Source. New.

2. "Double Debtor Problem." This section addresses the "double debtor" problem, which arises when a debtor acquires property that is subject to a security interest created by another debtor.

3. Taking Subject to Perfected Security Interest. Consider the following scenario:

> **Example 1:** A owns an item of equipment subject to a perfected security interest in favor of SP-A. A sells the equipment to B, not in the ordinary course of business. B acquires its interest subject to SP-A's security interest. See Sections 9-201, 9-315(a)(1). Under this section, if B creates a security interest in the equipment in favor of SP-B, SP-B's security interest is subordinate to SP-A's security interest, even if SP-B filed against B before SP-A filed against A, and even if SP-B took a purchase-money security interest. Normally, SP-B could have investigated the source of the equipment and discovered SP-A's filing before making an advance against the equipment, whereas SP-A had no reason to search the filings against someone other than its debtor, A.

4. Taking Subject to Unperfected Security Interest. This section applies only if the security interest in the transferred collateral was perfected when the transferee acquired the collateral. See subsection (a)(2). If this condition is not met, then the normal priority rules apply.

> **Example 2:** A owns an item of equipment subject to an unperfected security interest in favor of SP-A. A sells the equipment to B, who gives value and takes delivery of the equipment without knowledge of the security interest. B takes free of the security interest. See Section 9-317(b). If B then creates a security interest in favor of SP-B, no priority issue arises; SP-B has the only security interest in the equipment.

> **Example 3:** The facts are as in Example 2, except that B knows of SP-A's security interest and therefore takes the equipment subject to it. If B creates a security interest in the equipment in favor of SP-B, this section does not determine the relative priority of the security interests. Rather, the normal priority rules govern. If SP-B perfects its security interest, then, under Section 9-322(a)(2),

SP-A's unperfected security interest will be junior to SP-B's perfected security interest. The award of priority to SP-B is premised on the belief that SP-A's failure to file could have misled SP-B.

5. Taking Subject to Perfected Security Interest That Becomes Unperfected. This section applies only if the security interest in the transferred collateral did not become unperfected at any time after the transferee acquired the collateral. See subsection (a)(3). If this condition is not met, then the normal priority rules apply.

Example 4: As in Example 1, A owns an item of equipment subject to a perfected security interest in favor of SP-A. A sells the equipment to B, not in the ordinary course of business. B acquires its interest subject to SP-A's security interest. See Sections 9-201, 9-315(a)(1). B creates a security interest in favor of SP-B, and SP-B perfects its security interest. This section provides that SP-A's security interest is senior to SP-B's. However, if SP-A's financing statement lapses while SP-B's security interest is perfected, then the normal priority rules would apply, and SP-B's security interest would become senior to SP-A's security interest. See Sections 9-322(a)(2), 9-515(c).

6. Unusual Situations. The appropriateness of the rule of subsection (a) is most apparent when it works to subordinate security interests having priority under the basic priority rules of Section 9-322(a) or the purchase-money priority rules of Section 9-324. The rule also works properly when applied to the security interest of a buyer under Section 2-711(3) or a lessee under Section 2A-508(5). However, subsection (a) may provide an inappropriate resolution of the "double debtor" problem in some of the wide variety of other contexts in which the problem may arise. Although subsection (b) limits the application of subsection (a) to those cases in which subordination is known to be appropriate, courts should apply the rule in other settings, if necessary to promote the underlying purposes and policies of the Uniform Commercial Code. See Section 1-103(a).

§ 9-326. Priority of Security Interests Created by New Debtor.

(a) [Subordination of security interest created by new debtor.] Subject to subsection (b), a security interest that is created by a new debtor in collateral in which the new debtor has or acquires rights and is perfected solely by a filed financing statement that would be ineffective to perfect the security interest but for the application of Section 9-316(i)(1) or 9-508 is subordinate to a security interest in the same collateral which is perfected other than by such a filed financing statement.

(b) [Priority under other provisions; multiple original debtors.] The other provisions of this part determine the priority among conflicting security interests in the same collateral perfected by filed financing statements described in subsection (a). However, if the security agreements to which a new debtor became bound as debtor were not entered into by the same original debtor, the conflicting security interests rank according to priority in time of the new debtor's having become bound.

Definitional Cross References:

Collateral	Section 9-102(a)(12)
Debtor	Section 9-102(a)(28)
Financing statement	Section 9-102(a)(39)
New debtor	Section 9-102(a)(56)
Original debtor	Section 9-102(a)(60)
Right	Section 1-201(b)(34)
Security agreement	Section 9-102(a)(74)
Security interest	Section 1-201(b)(35)

Official Comment

1. Source. New.

2. Subordination of Security Interests Created by New Debtor. This section addresses the priority contests that may arise when a new debtor becomes bound by the security agreement of an *original debtor* and each debtor has a secured creditor.

Subsection (a) subordinates the original debtor's secured party's security interest perfected against the new debtor by a filed financing statement that would be ineffective to perfect the security interest but for Section 9-508 or, if the original debtor and new debtor are located in different jurisdictions, Section 9-316(i)(1). The security interest is subordinated to security interests in the same collateral perfected by another method, e.g., by filing against the new debtor. This section does not subordinate a security interest perfected by a new initial financing statement providing the name of the new debtor, even if the initial financing statement is filed to maintain the effectiveness of a financing statement under the circumstances described in Section 9-508(b). Nor does it subordinate a security interest perfected by a financing statement filed against the original debtor which remains effective against collateral transferred by the original debtor to the new debtor. See Section 9-508(c). Concerning priority contests involving transferred collateral, see Sections 9-325 and 9-507.

Example 1: SP-X holds a perfected-by-filing security interest in X Corp's existing and after-acquired inventory, and SP-Z holds a perfected-by-possession security interest in an item of Z Corp's inventory. Both X Corp and Z Corp are located in the same jurisdiction under Section 9-307. Z Corp becomes bound as debtor by X

Corp's security agreement (e.g., Z Corp buys X Corp's assets and assumes its security agreement). See Section 9-203(d). But for Section 9-508, SP-X's financing statement would be ineffective to perfect a security interest in the item of inventory in which Z Corp has rights. However, subsection (a) provides that SP-X's perfected security interest is subordinate to SP-Z's, regardless of whether SP-X's financing statement was filed before SP-Z perfected its security interest.

Example 2: SP-X holds a perfected-by-filing security interest in X Corp's existing and after-acquired inventory, and SP-Z holds a perfected-by-filing security interest in Z Corp's existing and after-acquired inventory. Both X Corp and Z Corp are located in the same jurisdiction under Section 9-307. Z Corp becomes bound as debtor by X Corp's security agreement. Immediately thereafter, and before the effectiveness of SP-X's financing statement lapses, Z Corp acquires a new item of inventory. But for Section 9-508, SP-X's financing statement would be ineffective to perfect a security interest in the new item of inventory in which Z Corp has rights. However, because SP-Z's security interest was perfected by a filing whose effectiveness does not depend on Section 9-316(i)(1) or 9-508, subsection (a) subordinates SP-X's perfected security interest to SP-Z's. This would be the case even if SP-Z filed after Z Corp became bound by X Corp's security agreement, and regardless of which financing statement was filed first.

The same result would obtain if X Corp and Z Corp were located in different jurisdictions. SP- X's security interest would be perfected by a financing statement that would be ineffective but for Section 9-316(i)(1), whereas the effectiveness of SP-Z's filing does not depend on Section 9-316(i)(1) or 9-508.

3. Other Priority Rules. Subsection (b) addresses the priority among security interests created by the original debtor (X Corp). By invoking the other priority rules of this subpart, as applicable, subsection (b) preserves the relative priority of security interests created by the original debtor.

Example 3: Under the facts of Example 2, SP-Y also holds a perfected-by-filing security interest in X Corp's existing and after-acquired inventory. SP-Y filed after SP-X. Inasmuch as both SP-X's and SP-Y's security interests in inventory acquired by Z Corp after it became bound would be unperfected but for the application of Section 9-508, the normal priority rules determine their relative priorities. Under the "first-to-file-or-perfect" rule of Section 9-322(a)(1), SP-X has priority over SP-Y.

Example 4: Under the facts of Example 3, after Z Corp became bound by X Corp's security agreement, SP-Y promptly filed a new initial financing statement against Z Corp. SP-X's security interest remains perfected only by virtue of its original filing against X Corp which "would be ineffective to perfect the security interest but for the application of Section 9-508." Because SP-Y's security interest is perfected by the filing of a financing statement whose effectiveness does not depend on Section 9-508 or 9-316(i)(1), subsection (a) subordinates SP-X's security interest to SP-Y's. If both SP-X and SP-Y file a new initial financing statement against Z Corp, then the "first-to-file-or-perfect" rule of Section 9-322(a)(1) governs their priority inter se as well as their priority against SP-Z.

The second sentence of subsection (b) effectively limits the applicability of the first sentence to situations in which a new debtor has become bound by more than one security agreement entered into by the same original debtor. When the new debtor has become bound by security agreements entered into by different original debtors, the second sentence provides that priority is based on priority in time of the new debtor's becoming bound.

Example 5: Under the facts of Example 2, SP-W holds a perfected-by-filing security interest in W Corp's existing and after-acquired inventory. After Z Corp became bound by X Corp's security agreement in favor of SP-X, Z Corp became bound by W Corp's security agreement. Under subsection (b), SP-W's security interest in inventory acquired by Z Corp is subordinate to that of SP-X, because Z Corp became bound under SP-X's security agreement before it became bound under SP-W's security agreement. This is the result regardless of which financing statement (SP-X's or SP-W's) was filed first.

The second sentence of subsection (b) reflects the generally accepted view that priority based on the first-to-file rule is inappropriate for resolving priority disputes when the filings were made against different debtors. Like subsection (a) and the first sentence of subsection (b), however, the second sentence of subsection (b) relates only to priority conflicts among security interests that would be unperfected but for the application of Section 9-316(i)(1) or 9-508.

Example 6: Under the facts of Example 5, after Z Corp became bound by W Corp's security agreement, SP-W promptly filed a new initial financing statement against Z Corp. At that time, SP-X's security interest was perfected only pursuant to its original filing against X Corp which "would be ineffective to perfect the security interest but for the application of Section 9-508." Because SP-W's security interest is perfected by the filing of a financing statement whose effectiveness does not depend on Section 9-316(i)(1) or 9-508, subsection (a) subordinates SP-X's security interest to SP-W's. If both SP-X and SP-W file a new initial financing statement against Z Corp, then the "first-to-file-or-perfect" rule of Section 9-322(a)(1) governs their priority inter se as well as their priority against SP-Z.

§ 9-326A. Priority of Security Interest in Controllable Account, Controllable Electronic Record, and Controllable Payment Intangible.

A security interest in a controllable account, controllable electronic record, or controllable payment intangible held by a secured party having control of the account, electronic record, or payment intangible has priority over a conflicting security interest held by a secured party that does not have control.

Definitional Cross References:

Account	Section 9-102(a)(2)
Controllable account	Section 9-102(a)(27A)
Controllable electronic record	Section 12-102(a)(1)
Controllable payment intangible	Section 9-102(a)(27B)
Electronic	Section 1-201(b)(16A)
Payment intangible	Section 9-102(a)(61)
Record	Section 9-102(a)(70)
Secured party	Section 9-102(a)(73)
Security interest	Section 1-201(b)(35)

Official Comment

1. [Control priority.] This section adopts an approach to priority in controllable accounts, controllable electronic records, and controllable payment intangibles that is similar to the approach of Sections 9-327 (deposit accounts) and 9-328 (investment property): A security interest perfected by control has priority over conflicting security interests that are not perfected by control.

2. [Multiple persons having control.] This section does not apply if more than one secured party has control of a controllable account, controllable electronic record, or controllable payment intangible, which may occur through shared control or a person in control acknowledging that it has control on behalf of another person. See Section 12-105(b)(2) (shared control), (e) (control through another person). In those situations, the residual first-to-file-or- perfect rule of Section 9-322(a)(1) would apply. However, affected persons may believe that the application of that first-in-time rule is not appropriate in some circumstances.

Example: A person (A) has a security interest in a controllable electronic record perfected by control (other than through an acknowledgment by another person under Section 12—105(e)) and A acknowledges that it has control on behalf of another person (B). B has a security interest perfected by a financing statement filed before A obtained control. Under Section 9-322(a) (the first-to-file-or-perfect rule), by obtaining control through A's acknowledgment B's security interest would have priority over A's previously senior security interest. To avoid that result, A might insist on B's subordination as a condition to A's acknowledgment. See Section 9-339 (subordination by agreement). In cases of multiple persons having control, it will be important for interested persons to adjust priorities by agreement, when appropriate. See also Section 12-105, Comment 5.

A secured party that relies on perfection by control resulting from the acknowledgment of another person under Section 12-105(e) need not prove a formal agency relationship with the acknowledging person. This is a principal rationale underlying the various provisions in Articles 7, 8, 9, and 12 which provide for a person to obtain control through another person's control and acknowledgment. However, a person obtaining control through an acknowledgment necessarily must rely on the integrity of the acknowledging person. In the case of perfection by control in the Example, the acknowledging person presumably also has control for the benefit of the debtor. The secured party's (B 's) control, and perfection, depends on the acknowledging person's (A's) continued control. The secured party's (B's) perfection would be lost if the acknowledging person (A) were to lose or give up control, as by transferring control to the debtor or any other person. See, e.g., Section 9-314, Comment 2.

An acknowledging person also might serially acknowledge over time that it holds for the benefit of multiple purchasers (secured parties or buyers). Putting aside perfection by filing as in the Example, secured parties so perfected would have priority based on priority of timing of control under Section 9-322(a). However, a transfer of control by the acknowledging person to a qualifying purchaser, or an acknowledgment by that the person that it has control on behalf of a buyer or secured party that is a qualifying purchaser, would allow the qualifying purchaser to take free of (or have priority over) earlier security interests or other interests. It follows that a first-to-control priority rule for security interests would not protect a secured party having control through another person's acknowledgment from having its interest cut off or subordinated by a later-in-time qualifying purchaser. Such a "first-to-control" priority rule would be illusory inasmuch as purchasers relying on control through another person's acknowledgment would have no reliable method of determining priority over subsequent transferees other than reliance on the acknowledging person's integrity.

§ 9-327. Priority of Security Interests in Deposit Account.

The following rules govern priority among conflicting security interests in the same deposit account:

(1) A security interest held by a secured party having control of the deposit account under Section 9-104 has priority over a conflicting security interest held by a secured party that does not have control.

(2) Except as otherwise provided in paragraphs (3) and (4), security interests perfected by control under Section 9-314 rank according to priority in time of obtaining control.

(3) Except as otherwise provided in paragraph (4), a security interest held by the bank with which the deposit account is maintained has priority over a conflicting security interest held by another secured party.

(4) A security interest perfected by control under Section 9-104(a)(3) has priority over a security interest held by the bank with which the deposit account is maintained.

Definitional Cross References:

Bank	Section 9-102(a)(8)
Deposit account	Section 9-102(a)(29)
Secured party	Section 9-102(a)(73)
Security interest	Section 1-201(b)(35)

Comment References: 9-322 C8

Official Comment

1. Source. New; derived from former Section 9-115(5).

2. Scope of This Section. This section contains the rules governing the priority of conflicting security interests in deposit accounts. It overrides conflicting priority rules. See Sections 9-322(f)(1), 9-324(a), (b), (d), (f). This section does not apply to accounts evidenced by an instrument (e.g., certain certificates of deposit), which by definition are not "deposit accounts."

3. Control. Under paragraph (1), security interests perfected by control (Sections 9-314, 9-104) take priority over those perfected otherwise, e.g., as identifiable cash proceeds under Section 9-315. Secured parties for whom the deposit account is an integral part of the credit decision will, at a minimum, insist upon the right to immediate access to the deposit account upon the debtor's default (i.e., control). Those secured parties for whom the deposit account is less essential will not take control, thereby running the risk that the debtor will dispose of funds on deposit (either outright or for collateral purposes) after default but before the account can be frozen by court order or the secured party can obtain control.

Paragraph (2) governs the case (expected to be very rare) in which a bank enters into a Section 9-104(a)(2) control agreement with more than one secured party. It provides that the security interests rank according to time of obtaining control. If the bank is solvent and the control agreements are well drafted, the bank will be liable to each secured party, and the priority rule will have no practical effect.

4. Priority of Bank. Under paragraph (3), the security interest of the bank with which the deposit account is maintained normally takes priority over all other conflicting security interests in the deposit account, regardless of whether the deposit account constitutes the competing secured party's original collateral or its proceeds. A rule of this kind enables banks to extend credit to their depositors without the need to examine either the public record or their own records to determine whether another party might have a security interest in the deposit account.

A secured party who takes a security interest in the deposit account as original collateral can protect itself against the results of this rule in one of two ways. It can take control of the deposit account by becoming the bank's customer. Under paragraph (4), this arrangement operates to subordinate the bank's security interest. Alternatively, the secured party can obtain a subordination agreement from the bank. See Section 9-339.

A secured party who claims the deposit account as proceeds of other collateral can reduce the risk of becoming junior by obtaining the debtor's agreement to deposit proceeds into a specific cash-collateral account and obtaining the agreement of that bank to subordinate all its claims to those of the secured party. But if the debtor violates its agreement and deposits funds into a deposit account other than the cash-collateral account, the secured party risks being subordinated.

5. Priority in Proceeds of, and Funds Transferred from, Deposit Account. The priority afforded by this section does not extend to proceeds of a deposit account. Rather, Section 9-322(c) through (e) and the provisions referred to in Section 9-322(f) govern priorities in proceeds of a deposit account. Section 9-315(d) addresses continuation of perfection in proceeds of deposit accounts. As to funds transferred from a deposit account that serves as collateral, see Section 9-332.

§ 9-328. Priority of Security Interests in Investment Property.

The following rules govern priority among conflicting security interests in the same investment property:

(1) A security interest held by a secured party having control of investment property under Section 9-106 has priority over a security interest held by a secured party that does not have control of the investment property.

(2) Except as otherwise provided in paragraphs (3) and (4), conflicting security interests held by secured parties each of which has control under Section 9-106 rank according to priority in time of:

(A) if the collateral is a security, obtaining control;

(B) if the collateral is a security entitlement carried in a securities account and:

(i) if the secured party obtained control under Section 8-106(d)(1), the secured party's becoming the person for which the securities account is maintained;

(ii) if the secured party obtained control under Section 8-106(d)(2), the securities intermediary's agreement to comply with the secured party's entitlement orders with respect to security entitlements carried or to be carried in the securities account; or

(iii) if the secured party obtained control through another person under Section 8-106(d)(3), the time on which priority would be based under this paragraph if the other person were the secured party; or

(C) if the collateral is a commodity contract carried with a commodity intermediary, the satisfaction of the requirement for control specified in Section 9-106(b)(2) with respect to commodity contracts carried or to be carried with the commodity intermediary.

(3) A security interest held by a securities intermediary in a security entitlement or a securities account maintained with the securities intermediary has priority over a conflicting security interest held by another secured party.

(4) A security interest held by a commodity intermediary in a commodity contract or a commodity account maintained with the commodity intermediary has priority over a conflicting security interest held by another secured party.

(5) A security interest in a certificated security in registered form which is perfected by taking delivery under Section 9-313(a) and not by control under Section 9-314 has priority over a conflicting security interest perfected by a method other than control.

(6) Conflicting security interests created by a broker, securities intermediary, or commodity intermediary which are perfected without control under Section 9-106 rank equally.

(7) In all other cases, priority among conflicting security interests in investment property is governed by Sections 9-322 and 9-323.

Definitional Cross References:

Agreement	Section 1-201(b)(3)
Broker	Section 8-102(a)(3)
Certificated security	Section 8-102(a)(4)
Collateral	Section 9-102(a)(12)
Commodity account	Section 9-102(a)(14)
Commodity contract	Section 9-102(a)(15)
Commodity intermediary	Section 9-102(a)(17)
Delivery	Section 1-201(b)(15)
Investment property	Section 9-102(a)(49)
Person	Section 1-201(b)(27)
Secured party	Section 9-102(a)(73)
Securities account	Section 8-501(a)
Securities intermediary	Section 8-102(a)(14)
Security entitlement	Section 8-102(a)(17)
Security interest	Section 1-201(b)(35)
Security	Section 8-102(a)(15)

Official Comment

1. Source. Former Section 9-115(5).

2. Scope of This Section. This section contains the rules governing the priority of conflicting security interests in investment property. Paragraph (1) states the most important general rule—that a secured party who obtains control has priority over a secured party who does not obtain control. Paragraphs (2) through (4) deal with conflicting security interests each of which is perfected by control. Paragraph (5) addresses the priority of a security interest in a certificated security which is perfected by delivery but not control. Paragraph (6) deals with the relatively unusual circumstance in which a broker, securities intermediary, or commodity intermediary has created conflicting security interests none of which is perfected by control. Paragraph (7) provides that the general priority rules of Sections 9-322 and 9-323 apply to cases not covered by the specific rules in this section. The principal application of this residual rule is that the usual first in time of filing rule applies to conflicting security interests that are perfected only by filing. Because the control priority rule of paragraph (1) provides for the ordinary cases in which persons purchase securities on margin credit from their brokers, there is no need for special rules for purchase-money security interests. See also Section 9-103 (limiting purchase-money collateral to goods and software).

3. General Rule: Priority of Security Interest Perfected by Control. Under paragraph (1), a secured party who obtains control has priority over a secured party who does not obtain control. The control priority rule does not turn on either temporal sequence or awareness of conflicting security interests. Rather, it is a structural rule, based on the principle that a lender should be able to rely on the collateral without question if the lender has taken the necessary steps to assure itself that it is in a position where it can foreclose on the collateral without further action by the debtor. The control priority rule is necessary because the perfection rules provide considerable flexibility in structuring secured financing arrangements. For example, at the "retail" level, a secured lender to an investor who wants the full measure of protection can obtain control, but the creditor may be willing to accept the greater measure of risk that follows from perfection by filing. Similarly, at the "wholesale" level, a lender to securities firms can leave the collateral with the debtor and obtain a perfected security interest under the automatic perfection rule of Section 9-309(a)(10), but a lender who wants to be entirely sure of its position will want to obtain control. The control priority rule of paragraph (1) is an essential part of this system of flexibility. It is feasible to provide more than one method of perfecting security interests only if the rules ensure that those who take the necessary steps to obtain the full measure of protection do not run the risk of subordination to those who have not taken such steps. A secured party who is unwilling to run the risk that the debtor has granted or will grant a conflicting control security interest should not make a loan without obtaining control of the collateral.

As applied to the retail level, the control priority rule means that a secured party who obtains control has priority over a conflicting security interest perfected by filing without regard to inquiry into whether the control secured party was aware of the filed security interest. Prior to the 1994 revisions to Articles 8 and 9, Article 9 did not permit perfection of security interests in securities by filing. Accordingly, parties who deal in securities never developed a practice of searching the UCC files before conducting securities transactions. Although filing is now a permissible method of perfection, in order to avoid disruption of existing practices in this business it is necessary to give perfection by filing a different and more limited effect for securities than for some other forms of collateral. The priority rules are not based on the assumption that parties who perfect by the usual method of obtaining control will search the files. Quite the contrary, the control priority rule is intended to ensure that, with respect to investment property, secured parties who do obtain control are entirely unaffected by filings. To state the point another way, perfection by filing is intended to affect only general creditors or other secured creditors who rely on filing. The rule that a security interest perfected by filing can be primed by a control security interest, without regard to awareness, is a consequence of the system of perfection and priority rules for investment property. These rules are designed to take account of the circumstances of the securities markets, where filing is not given the same effect as for some other forms of property. No implication is made about the effect of filing with respect to security interests in other forms of property, nor about other Article 9 rules, e.g., Section 9-330, which govern the circumstances in which security interests in other forms of property perfected by filing can be primed by subsequent perfected security interests.

The following examples illustrate the application of the priority rule in paragraph (1):

Example 1: Debtor borrows from Alpha and grants Alpha a security interest in a variety of collateral, including all of Debtor's investment property. At that time Debtor owns 1000 shares of XYZ Co. stock for which Debtor has a certificate. Alpha perfects by filing. Later, Debtor borrows from Beta and grants Beta a security interest in the 1000 shares of XYZ Co. stock. Debtor delivers the certificate, properly indorsed, to Beta. Alpha and Beta both have perfected security interests in the XYZ Co. stock. Beta has control, see Section 8-106(b)(1), and hence has priority over Alpha.

Example 2: Debtor borrows from Alpha and grants Alpha a security interest in a variety of collateral, including all of Debtor's investment property. At that time Debtor owns 1000 shares of XYZ Co. stock, held through a securities account with Able & Co. Alpha perfects by filing. Later, Debtor borrows from Beta and grants Beta a security interest in the 1000 shares of XYZ Co. stock. Debtor instructs Able to have the 1000 shares transferred through the clearing corporation to Custodian Bank, to be credited to Beta's account with Custodian Bank. Alpha and Beta both have perfected security interests in the XYZ Co. stock. Beta has control, see Section 8-106(d)(1), and hence has priority over Alpha.

Example 3: Debtor borrows from Alpha and grants Alpha a security interest in a variety of collateral, including all of Debtor's investment property. At that time Debtor owns 1000 shares of XYZ Co. stock, which is held through a securities account with Able & Co. Alpha perfects by filing.

Later, Debtor borrows from Beta and grants Beta a security interest in the 1000 shares of XYZ Co. stock. Debtor, Able, and Beta enter into an agreement under which Debtor will continue to receive dividends and distributions, and will continue to have the right to direct dispositions, but Beta will also have the right to direct dispositions and receive the proceeds. Alpha and Beta both have perfected security interests in the XYZ Co. stock (more precisely, in the Debtor's security entitlement to the financial asset consisting of the XYZ Co. stock). Beta has control, see Section 8-106(d)(2), and hence has priority over Alpha.

Example 4: Debtor borrows from Alpha and grants Alpha a security interest in a variety of collateral, including all of Debtor's investment property. At that time Debtor owns 1000 shares of XYZ Co. stock, held through a securities account with Able & Co. Alpha perfects by filing. Debtor's agreement with Able & Co. provides that Able has a security interest in all securities carried in the account as security for any obligations of Debtor to Able. Debtor incurs obligations to Able and later defaults on the obligations to Alpha and Able. Able has control by virtue of the rule of Section 8-106(e) that if a customer grants a security interest to its own intermediary, the intermediary has control. Since Alpha does not have control, Able has priority over Alpha under the general control priority rule of paragraph (1).

4. Conflicting Security Interests Perfected by Control: Priority of Securities Intermediary or Commodity Intermediary. Paragraphs (2) through (4) govern the priority of conflicting security interests each of which is perfected by control. The following example explains the application of the rules in paragraphs (3) and (4):

Example 5: Debtor holds securities through a securities account with Able & Co. Debtor's agreement with Able & Co. provides that Able has a security interest in all securities carried in the account as security for any obligations of Debtor to Able. Debtor borrows from Beta and grants Beta a security interest in 1000 shares of XYZ Co. stock carried in the account. Debtor, Able, and Beta enter into an agreement under which Debtor will continue to receive dividends and distributions and will continue to have the right to direct dispositions, but Beta will also have the right to direct dispositions and receive the proceeds. Debtor incurs obligations to Able and later defaults on the obligations to Beta and Able. Both Beta and Able have control, so the general control priority rule of paragraph (1) does not apply. Compare Example 4. Paragraph (3) provides that a security interest held by a securities intermediary in positions of its own customer has priority over a conflicting security interest of an external lender, so Able has priority over Beta. (Paragraph (4) contains a parallel rule for commodity intermediaries.) The agreement among Able, Beta, and Debtor could, of course, determine the relative priority of the security interests of Able and Beta, see Section 9-339, but the fact that the intermediary has agreed to act on the instructions of a secured party such as Beta does not itself imply any agreement by the intermediary to subordinate.

5. Conflicting Security Interests Perfected by Control: Temporal Priority. Former Section 9-115 introduced into Article 9 the concept of conflicting security interests that rank equally. Paragraph (2) of this section governs priority in those circumstances in which more than one secured party (other than a broker, securities intermediary, or commodity intermediary) has control. It replaces the equal-priority rule for conflicting security interests in investment property with a temporal rule. For securities, both certificated and uncertificated, under paragraph (2)(A) priority is based on the time that control is obtained. For security entitlements carried in securities accounts, the treatment is more complex. Paragraph (2)(B) bases priority on the timing of the steps taken to achieve control. The following example illustrates the application of paragraph (2).

Example 6: Debtor borrows from Alpha and grants Alpha a security interest in a variety of collateral, including all of Debtor's investment property. At that time Debtor owns a security entitlement that includes 1000 shares of XYZ Co. stock that Debtor holds through a securities account with Able & Co. Debtor, Able, and Alpha enter into an agreement under which Debtor will continue to receive dividends and distributions, and will continue to have the right to direct dispositions, but Alpha will also have the right to direct dispositions and receive the proceeds. Later, Debtor borrows from Beta and grants Beta a security interest in all its investment property, existing and after-acquired. Debtor, Able, and Beta enter into an agreement under which Debtor will continue to receive dividends and distributions, and will continue to have the right to direct dispositions, but Beta will also have the right to direct dispositions and receive the proceeds. Alpha and Beta both have perfected-by-control security interests in the security entitlement to the XYZ Co. stock by virtue of their agreements with Able. See Sections 9-314(a), 9-106(a), 8-106(d)(2). Under paragraph (2)(B)(ii), the priority of each security interest dates from the time of the secured party's agreement with Able. Because

Alpha's agreement was first in time, Alpha has priority. This priority applies equally to security entitlements to financial assets credited to the account after the agreement was entered into.

The priority rule is analogous to "first-to-file" priority under Section 9-322 with respect to after-acquired collateral. Paragraphs (2)(B)(i) and (2)(B)(iii) provide similar rules for security entitlements as to which control is obtained by other methods, and paragraph (2)(C) provides a similar rule for commodity contracts carried in a commodity account. Section 8-510 also has been revised to provide a temporal priority conforming to paragraph (2)(B).

6. Certificated Securities. A long-standing practice has developed whereby secured parties whose collateral consists of a security evidenced by a security certificate take possession of the security certificate. If the security certificate is in bearer form, the secured party's acquisition of possession constitutes "delivery" under Section 8-301(a)(1), and the delivery constitutes "control" under Section 8-106(a). Comment 5 discusses the priority of security interests perfected by control of investment property.

If the security certificate is in registered form, the secured party will not achieve control over the security unless the security certificate contains an appropriate indorsement or is (re)registered in the secured party's name. See Section 8-106(b). However, the secured party's acquisition of possession constitutes "delivery" of the security certificate under Section 8-301 and serves to perfect the security interest under Section 9-313(a), even if the security certificate has not been appropriately indorsed and has not been (re)registered in the secured party's name. A security interest perfected by this method has priority over a security interest perfected other than by control (e.g., by filing). See paragraph (5).

The priority rule stated in paragraph (5) may seem anomalous, in that it can afford less favorable treatment to purchasers who buy collateral outright that to those who take a security interest in it. For example, a buyer of a security certificate would cut off a security interest perfected by filing only if the buyer achieves the status of a protected purchaser under Section 8-303. The buyer would not be a protected purchaser, for example, if it does not obtain "control" under Section 8-106 (e.g., if it fails to obtain a proper indorsement of the certificate) or if it had notice of an adverse claim under Section 8-105. The apparent anomaly disappears, however, when one understands the priority rule not as one intended to protect careless or guilty parties, but as one that eliminates the need to conduct a search of the public records only insofar as necessary to serve the needs of the securities markets.

7. Secured Financing of Securities Firms. Priority questions concerning security interests granted by brokers and securities intermediaries are governed by the general control-beats-non-control priority rule of paragraph (1), as supplemented by the special rules set out in paragraphs (2) (temporal priority—first to control), (3) (special priority for securities intermediary), and (6) (equal priority for non-control). The following examples illustrate the priority rules as applied to this setting. (In all cases it is assumed that the debtor retains sufficient other securities to satisfy all customers' claims. This section deals with the relative rights of secured lenders to a securities firm. Disputes between a secured lender and the firm's own customers are governed by Section 8-511.)

Example 7: Able & Co., a securities dealer, enters into financing arrangements with two lenders, Alpha Bank and Beta Bank. In each case the agreements provide that the lender will have a security interest in the securities identified on lists provided to the lender on a daily basis, that the debtor will deliver the securities to the lender on demand, and that the debtor will not list as collateral any securities which the debtor has pledged to any other lender. Upon Able's insolvency it is discovered that Able has listed the same securities on the collateral lists provided to both Alpha and Beta. Alpha and Beta both have perfected security interests under the automatic-perfection rule of Section 9-309(10). Neither Alpha nor Beta has control. Paragraph (6) provides that the security interests of Alpha and Beta rank equally, because each of them has a non-control security interest granted by a securities firm. They share pro-rata.

Example 8: Able enters into financing arrangements, with Alpha Bank and Beta Bank as in Example 7. At some point, however, Beta decides that it is unwilling to continue to provide financing on a non-control basis. Able directs the clearing corporation where it holds its principal inventory of securities to move specified securities into Beta's account. Upon Able's insolvency it is discovered that a list of collateral provided to Alpha includes securities that had been moved to Beta's account. Both Alpha and Beta have perfected security interests; Alpha under the automatic-perfection rule of Section 9-309(10), and Beta under that rule and also the perfection-by-control rule in Section 9-314(a). Beta has control but Alpha does not. Beta has priority over Alpha under paragraph (1).

Example 9: Able & Co. carries its principal inventory of securities through Clearing Corporation, which offers a "shared control" facility whereby a participant securities firm can enter into an arrangement with a lender under which the securities firm will retain the power to trade and otherwise direct dispositions of securities carried in its account, but Clearing Corporation agrees that, at any time the lender so directs, Clearing Corporation will transfer any securities from the firm's account to the lender's account or otherwise dispose of them as directed by the lender. Able enters into financing arrangements with two lenders, Alpha and Beta, each of which obtains such a control agreement from Clearing Corporation. The agreement with each lender provides that Able will designate specific securities as collateral on lists provided to the lender on a daily or other periodic basis, and that it will not pledge the same securities to different lenders. Upon Able's insolvency, it is discovered that Able has listed the same securities on the collateral lists provided to both Alpha and Beta. Both Alpha and Beta have control over the disputed securities. Paragraph (2) awards priority to whichever secured party first entered into the agreement with Clearing Corporation.

8. Relation to Other Law. Section 1-103 provides that "unless displaced by particular provisions of this Act, the principles of law and equity . . . shall supplement its provision." There may be circumstances in which a secured party's action in acquiring a security interest that has priority under this section constitutes conduct that is wrongful under other law. Though the possibility of such resort to other law may provide an appropriate "escape valve" for cases of egregious conduct, care must be taken to ensure that this does not impair the certainty and predictability of the priority rules. Whether a court may appropriately look to other law to impose liability upon or estop a secured party from asserting its Article 9 priority depends on an assessment of the secured party's conduct under the standards established by such other law as well as a determination of whether the particular application of such other law is displaced by the UCC.

Some circumstances in which other law is clearly displaced by the UCC rules are readily identifiable. Common law "first in time, first in right" principles, or correlative tort liability rules such as common law conversion principles under which a purchaser may incur liability to a person with a prior property interest without regard to awareness of that claim, are necessarily displaced by the priority rules set out in this section since these rules determine the relative ranking of security interests in investment property. So too, Article 8 provides protections against adverse claims to certain purchasers of interests in investment property. In circumstances where a secured party not only has priority under Section 9-328, but also qualifies for protection against adverse claims under Section 8-303, 8-502, or 8-510, resort to other law would be precluded.

In determining whether it is appropriate in a particular case to look to other law, account must also be taken of the policies that underlie the commercial law rules on securities markets and security interests in securities. A principal objective of the 1994 revision of Article 8 and the provisions of Article 9 governing investment property was to ensure that secured financing transactions can be implemented on a simple, timely, and certain basis. One of the circumstances that led to the revision was the concern that uncertainty in the application of the rules on secured transactions involving securities and other financial assets could contribute to systemic risk by impairing the ability of financial institutions to provide liquidity to the markets in times of stress. The control priority rule is designed to provide a clear and certain rule to ensure that lenders who have taken the necessary steps to establish control do not face a risk of subordination to other lenders who have not done so.

The control priority rule does not turn on an inquiry into the state of a secured party's awareness of potential conflicting claims because a rule under which a person's rights depended on that sort of after-the-fact inquiry could introduce an unacceptable measure of uncertainty. If an inquiry into awareness could provide a complete and satisfactory resolution of the problem in all cases, the priority rules of this section would have incorporated that test. The fact that they do not necessarily means that resort to other law based solely on that factor is precluded, though the question whether a control secured party induced or encouraged its financing arrangement with actual knowledge that the debtor would be violating the rights of another secured party may, in some circumstances, appropriately be treated as a factor in determining whether the control party's action is the kind of egregious conduct for which resort to other law is appropriate.

§ 9-329. Priority of Security Interests in Letter-of-Credit Right.

The following rules govern priority among conflicting security interests in the same letter-of-credit right:

(1) A security interest held by a secured party having control of the letter-of-credit right under Section 9-107 has priority to the extent of its control over a conflicting security interest held by a secured party that does not have control.

(2) Security interests perfected by control under Section 9-314 rank according to priority in time of obtaining control.

Definitional Cross References:

Letter-of-credit right	Section 9-102(a)(51)
Secured party	Section 9-102(a)(73)
Security interest	Section 1-201(b)(35)

Comment References: 9-322 C10

Official Comment

1. Source. New; loosely modeled after former Section 9-115(5).

2. General Rule. Paragraph (1) awards priority to a secured party who perfects a security interest directly in letter-of-credit rights (i.e., one that takes an assignment of proceeds and obtains consent of the issuer or any nominated person under Section 5-114(c)) over another conflicting security interest (i.e., one that is perfected automatically in the letter-of-credit rights as supporting obligations under Section 9-308(d)). This is consistent with international letter-of-credit practice and provides finality to payments made to recognized assignees of letter-of-credit proceeds. If an issuer or nominated person recognizes multiple security interests in a letter-of-credit right, resulting in multiple parties having control (Section 9-107), under paragraph (2) the security interests rank according to the time of obtaining control.

3. Drawing Rights; Transferee Beneficiaries. Drawing under a letter of credit is personal to the beneficiary and requires the beneficiary to perform the conditions for drawing under the letter of credit. Accordingly, a beneficiary's grant of a security interest in a letter of credit includes the beneficiary's "letter-of-credit right" as defined in Section 9-102 and the right to "proceeds of [the] letter of credit" as defined in Section 5-114(a), but does not include the right to demand payment under the letter of credit.

Section 5-114(e) provides that the "[r]ights of a transferee beneficiary or nominated person are independent of the beneficiary's assignment of the proceeds of a letter of credit and are superior to the assignee's right to the proceeds." To the extent the rights of a transferee beneficiary or nominated person are independent and superior, this Article does not apply. See Section 9-109(c).

Under Article 5, there is in effect a novation upon the transfer with the issuer becoming bound on a new, independent obligation to the transferee. The rights of nominated persons and transferee beneficiaries under a letter of credit include the right to demand payment from the issuer. Under Section 5-114(e), their rights to payment are independent of their obligations to the beneficiary (or original beneficiary) and superior to the rights of assignees of letter of credit proceeds (Section 5-114(c)) and others claiming a security interest in the beneficiary's (or original beneficiary's) letter of credit rights.

A transfer of drawing rights under a transferable letter of credit establishes independent Article 5 rights in the transferee and does not create or perfect an Article 9 security interest in the transferred drawing rights. The definition of "letter-of-credit right" in Section 9-102 excludes a beneficiary's drawing rights. The exercise of drawing rights by a transferee beneficiary may breach a contractual obligation of the transferee to the original beneficiary concerning when and how much the transferee may draw or how it may use the funds received under the letter of credit. If, for example, drawing rights are transferred to support a sale or loan from the transferee to the original beneficiary, then the transferee would be obligated to the original beneficiary under the sale or loan agreement to account for any drawing and for the use of any funds received. The transferee's obligation would be governed by the applicable law of contracts or restitution.

4. Secured Party-Transferee Beneficiaries. As described in Comment 3, drawing rights under letters of credit are transferred in many commercial contexts in which the transferee is not a secured party claiming a security interest in an underlying receivable supported by the letter of credit. Consequently, a transfer of a letter of credit is not a method of "perfection" of a security interest. The transferee's independent right to draw under the letter of credit and to receive and retain the value thereunder (in effect, priority) is not based on Article 9 but on letter-of-credit law and the terms of the letter of credit. Assume, however, that a secured party does hold a security interest in a receivable that is owned by a beneficiary-debtor and supported by a transferable letter of credit. Assume further that the beneficiary-debtor causes the letter of credit to be transferred to the secured party, the secured party draws under the letter of credit, and, upon the issuer's payment to the secured party-transferee, the underlying account debtor's obligation to the original beneficiary-debtor is satisfied. In this situation, the payment to the secured party-transferee is proceeds of the receivable collected by the secured party-transferee. Consequently, the secured party-transferee would have certain duties to the debtor and third parties under Article 9. For example, it would be obliged to collect under the letter of credit in a commercially reasonable manner and to remit any surplus pursuant to Sections 9-607 and 9-608.

This scenario is problematic under letter-of-credit law and practice, inasmuch as a transferee beneficiary collects in its own right arising from its own performance. Accordingly, under Section 5-114, the independent and superior rights of a transferee control over any inconsistent duties under Article 9. A transferee beneficiary may take a transfer of drawing rights to avoid reliance on the original beneficiary's credit and collateral, and it may consider any Article 9 rights superseded by its Article 5 rights. Moreover, it will not always be clear (i) whether a transferee beneficiary has a security interest in the underlying collateral, (ii) whether any security interest is senior to the rights of others, or (iii) whether the transferee beneficiary is aware that it holds a security interest. There will be clear cases in which the role of a transferee beneficiary as such is merely incidental to a conventional secured financing. There also will be cases in which the existence of a security interest may have little to do with the position of a transferee beneficiary as such. In dealing with these cases and less clear cases involving the possible application of Article 9 to a nominated person or a transferee beneficiary, the right to demand payment under a letter of credit should be distinguished from letter-of-credit rights. The courts also should give appropriate consideration to the policies and provisions of Article 5 and letter-of-credit practice as well as Article 9.

§ 9-330. Priority of Purchaser of Chattel Paper or Instrument.

(a) [Purchaser's priority: security interest claimed merely as proceeds.] A purchaser of chattel paper has priority over a security interest in the chattel paper which is claimed merely as proceeds of inventory subject to a security interest if:

(1) in good faith and in the ordinary course of the purchaser's business, the purchaser gives new value, takes possession of each authoritative tangible copy of the record evidencing the chattel paper, and obtains control under Section 9-105 of each authoritative electronic copy of the record evidencing the chattel paper; and

(2) the authoritative copies of the record evidencing the chattel paper do not indicate that the chattel paper has been assigned to an identified assignee other than the purchaser.

(b) [Purchaser's priority: other security interests.] A purchaser of chattel paper has priority over a security interest in the chattel paper which is claimed other than merely as proceeds of inventory subject to a security interest if the purchaser gives new value, takes possession of each authoritative tangible copy of the record evidencing the chattel paper, and obtains control under Section 9-105 of each authoritative electronic copy of the record evidencing the chattel paper in good faith, in the ordinary course of the purchaser's business, and without knowledge that the purchase violates the rights of the secured party.

(c) [Chattel paper purchaser's priority in proceeds.] Except as otherwise provided in Section 9-327, a purchaser having priority in chattel paper under subsection (a) or (b) also has priority in proceeds of the chattel paper to the extent that:

(1) Section 9-322 provides for priority in the proceeds; or

(2) the proceeds consist of the specific goods covered by the chattel paper or cash proceeds of the specific goods, even if the purchaser's security interest in the proceeds is unperfected.

(d) [Instrument purchaser's priority.] Except as otherwise provided in Section 9-331(a), a purchaser of an instrument has priority over a security interest in the instrument perfected by a method other than possession if the purchaser gives value and takes possession of the instrument in good faith and without knowledge that the purchase violates the rights of the secured party.

(e) [Holder of purchase-money security interest gives new value.] For purposes of subsections (a) and (b), the holder of a purchase-money security interest in inventory gives new value for chattel paper constituting proceeds of the inventory.

(f) [Indication of assignment gives knowledge.] For purposes of subsections (b) and (d), if the authoritative copies of the record evidencing chattel paper or an instrument indicate that the chattel paper or instrument has been assigned to an identified secured party other than the purchaser, a purchaser of the chattel paper or instrument has knowledge that the purchase violates the rights of the secured party.

Definitional Cross References:

Assignee	Section 9-102(a)(7A)
Cash proceeds	Section 9-102(a)(9)
Chattel paper	Section 9-102(a)(11)
Electronic	Section 1-201(b)(16A)
Good faith	Section 1-201(b)(20)
Goods	Section 9-102(a)(44)
Holder	Section 1-201(b)(21)
Instrument	Section 9-102(a)(47)
Inventory	Section 9-102(a)(48)
New value	Section 9-102(a)(57)
Proceeds	Section 9-102(a)(64)
Purchase	Section 1-201(b)(29)
Purchase-money security interest	Section 9-103
Purchaser	Section 1-201(b)(30)
Record	Section 9-102(a)(70)
Right	Section 1-201(b)(34)
Secured party	Section 9-102(a)(72)
Security interest	Section 1-201(b)(35)
Value	Section 1-204

Comment References: 9-324C8.

Official Comment

1. Source. Former Section 9-308.

2. Non-Temporal Priority. This Article permits a security interest to be perfected in chattel paper either by filing or by the secured party's possession and control under Section 9-314A and in instruments either by filing or by the secured party's taking possession under Sections 9-312 and 9-313. This section enables secured parties and other purchasers of chattel paper (evidenced by either or both authoritative electronic and tangible records) and instruments to obtain priority over earlier-perfected security interests, thereby promoting the negotiability of these types of receivables.

3. Chattel Paper. Subsections (a) and (b) follow former Section 9-308 in distinguishing between earlier-perfected security interests in chattel paper that is claimed merely as proceeds of inventory subject to a security interest and chattel paper that is claimed other than merely as proceeds. Like former Section 9-308, this section does not elaborate upon the phrase "merely as proceeds." For an elaboration, see PEB Commentary No. 8.

This section makes explicit the "good faith" requirement and retains the pre-1998 requirements of "the ordinary course of the purchaser's business" and the giving of "new value" as conditions for priority. Concerning the last, this Article deletes pre-1998 Section 9-108 and adds to Section 9-102 a completely different definition of the term "new value." See Section 9-102, Comment 21 (discussing "new value"). Under subsection (e), the holder of a purchase-money security interest in inventory is deemed to give "new value" for chattel paper constituting the proceeds of the inventory. Accordingly, the purchase-money secured party may qualify for priority in the chattel paper under subsection (a) or (b), whichever is applicable, even if it does not make an additional advance against the chattel paper.

If a security interest in chattel paper that is perfected by possession and control under Section 9-314A does not qualify for priority under this section, it may be subordinate to a perfected-by-filing security interest under Section 9-322(a)(1).

4. Possession and Control. To qualify for priority under subsection (a) or (b), a purchaser must "take[] possession of each authoritative tangible copy of the record evidencing the chattel paper obtain[] control under Section 9-105 of each authoritative electronic copy of the record evidencing the chattel paper." Note that possession and control are methods of perfection under Section 9-314A. In determining which of several related records constitutes chattel paper and thus is relevant to possession or control, the form of the records is irrelevant. Rather, the possession-and-control requirement is based on the premise that it affords public notice. For example, because possession or control of an amendment extending the term of a lease would not afford the contemplated public notice, the amendment would not constitute a record evidencing chattel paper regardless of whether the amendment is in tangible form and the lease is in electronic form, the amendment is electronic and the lease is tangible, the amendment and lease are both tangible, or the amendment and lease are both electronic.

Two common practices have raised particular concerns with respect to the possession requirement. First, in some cases the parties create more than one copy or counterpart of chattel paper evidencing a single secured obligation or lease. This practice raises questions as to which counterpart is the "original" and whether it is necessary for a purchaser to take possession of all counterparts in order to "take possession" of the chattel paper. Second, parties sometimes enter into a single "master" agreement. The master agreement contemplates that the parties will enter into separate "schedules" from time to time, each evidencing chattel paper. Must a purchaser of an obligation or lease evidenced by a single schedule also take possession of the record evidencing the master agreement as well as the record evidencing the schedule in order to "take possession" of each authoritative tangible copy of the record evidencing the chattel paper?

The problem raised by the first practice is easily solved. The parties may in the terms of their agreement and by designation on the chattel paper identify only one counterpart as the original, authoritative tangible copy of the chattel paper for purposes of the possession requirement. Concerns about the second practice also are easily solved by careful drafting. Each schedule should provide that it incorporates the terms of the master agreement, not the other way around. This will make it clear that each schedule is a "stand alone" document.

A secured party may wish to convert chattel paper evidenced by authoritative tangible copies to chattel paper evidenced by electronic copies and vice versa. The priority of a security interest in chattel paper under subsection (a) or (b) may be preserved, even if the form of the chattel paper changes. The principle implied in the preceding paragraph, i.e., that not every copy of chattel paper is relevant, applies to "control" as well as to "possession." When there are multiple copies of chattel paper, a secured party may take "possession" or obtain "control" of the chattel paper if it acts with respect to the copy or copies that are reliably identified as the authoritative copy or copies. Concerning the identification of copies as authoritative or nonauthoritative, see Section 9-105(c) and Comment 3.

5. Chattel Paper Claimed Merely as Proceeds. Under subsection (a), purchaser who meets the possession-and-control, good faith, ordinary course, and new value requirements takes priority over a competing security interest claimed merely as proceeds of inventory unless the authoritative copies of the record evidencing the chattel paper indicate that it has been assigned to an identified assignee other than the purchaser. Thus subsection (a) recognizes the common practice of placing a "legend" on chattel paper to indicate that it has been assigned. This approach, under which the chattel paper purchaser who gives new value in ordinary course can rely on possession and control of unlegended, chattel paper without any concern for other facts that it may know, comports with the expectations of both inventory and chattel paper financers.

6. Chattel Paper Claimed Other Than Merely as Proceeds. Under subsection (b), a purchaser who meets the possession-and-control, good faith, ordinary course, and new value requirements takes priority over a competing security interest claimed other than merely as proceeds of inventory if it takes "without knowledge that the purchase violates the rights of the secured party." This standard derives from the definition of "buyer in ordinary course of business" in Section 1-201(b)(9). The source of the purchaser's knowledge is irrelevant. Note, however, that "knowledge" means "actual knowledge." Section 1-202(b).

In contrast to a junior secured party in accounts, who may be required in some special circumstances to undertake a search under the "good faith" requirement, see Comment 5 to Section 9-331, a purchaser of chattel paper under this section is not required as a matter of good faith to make a search in order to determine the existence of prior security interests. There may be circumstances where the purchaser undertakes a search nevertheless, either on its own volition or because other considerations make it advisable to do so, e.g., where the purchaser also is purchasing accounts. Without more, a purchaser of chattel paper who has seen a financing statement covering the chattel paper or who knows that the chattel paper is encumbered with a security interest, does not have knowledge that its purchase violates the secured party's rights. However, if a purchaser sees a statement in a financing statement to the effect that a purchase of chattel paper from the debtor would violate the rights of the filed secured party, the purchaser would have such knowledge. Likewise, under subsection (f), if the authoritative copies of the chattel paper indicate that it had been assigned to an identified secured party other than the purchaser, the purchaser would have wrongful knowledge for purposes of subsection (b), thereby preventing the purchaser from qualifying for priority under that subsection, even if the purchaser did not have actual knowledge. In the case of authoritative tangible copies of a record evidencing chattel paper, the indication normally would consist of a written legend on the copies. In the case of authoritative electronic copies of the record evidencing chattel paper, this Article leaves to developing market and technological practices the manner in which the copies would indicate an assignment.

Subsections (a) and (f) each refer to the possibility that authoritative copies of records evidencing chattel paper may indicate that the chattel paper has been assigned to an identified assignee. Those subsections should be read and interpreted in a manner consistent with Section 9-105 on control of authoritative electronic copies of records evidencing chattel paper. Accordingly, references in subsections (a) and (f) to an indication in a record evidencing chattel paper also embrace, for authoritative electronic copies of such records, records attached to or logically associated with the authoritative electronic copies and systems in which the authoritative electronic copies are recorded. See Section 9-105(c) and (d)(1).

7. Instruments. Subsection (d) contains a special priority rule for instruments. Under this subsection, a purchaser of an instrument has priority over a security interest perfected by a method other than possession (e.g., by filing, temporarily under Section 9-312(e) or (g), as proceeds under Section 9-315(d), or automatically upon attachment under Section 9-309(4) if the security interest arises out of a sale of the instrument) if the purchaser gives value and takes possession of the instrument in good faith and without knowledge that the purchase violates the rights of the secured party. Generally, to the extent subsection (d) conflicts with Section 3-306, subsection (d) governs. See Section 3-102(b). For example, notice of a conflicting security interest precludes a purchaser from becoming a holder in due course under Section 3-302 and thereby taking free of all claims to the instrument under Section 3-306. However, a purchaser who takes even with knowledge of the security interest qualifies for priority under subsection (d) if it takes without knowledge that the purchase violates the rights of the holder of the security interest. Likewise, a purchaser qualifies for priority under subsection (d) if it takes for "value" as defined in Section 1-201, even if it does not take for "value" as defined in Section 3-303. [Ed. Note. What was Section 1-201(44) is now Section 1-204 in the new Article 1.]

Subsection (d) is subject to Section 9-331(a), which provides that Article 9 does not limit the rights of a holder in due course under Article 3. Thus, in the rare case in which the purchaser of an instrument qualifies for priority under subsection (d), but another person has the rights of a holder in due course of the instrument, the other person takes free of the purchaser's claim. See Section 3-306.

The rule in subsection (d) is similar to the rules in subsections (a) and (b), which govern priority in chattel paper. The observations in Comment 6 concerning the requirement of good faith and the phrase "without knowledge that the purchase violates the rights of the secured party," including the operation of subsection (f) if an instrument indicates that it has been assigned to an identified secured party, apply equally to purchasers of instruments. However, unlike a purchaser of chattel paper, to qualify for priority under subsection (d) a purchaser of an instrument need only give "value" as defined in Section 1-204; it need not give "new value." Also, the purchaser need not purchase the instrument in the ordinary course of its business. [Ed. Note. What was Section 1-201(44) is now Section 1-204 in the new Article 1.]

Subsection (d) applies to checks as well as notes. For example, to collect and retain checks that are proceeds (collections) of accounts free of a senior secured party's claim to the same checks, a junior secured party must satisfy the good-faith requirement (honesty in fact and the observance of reasonable commercial standards of fair dealing) of this subsection. This is the same good-faith requirement applicable to holders in due course. See Section 9-331, Comment 5.

8. Priority in Proceeds of Chattel Paper. Subsection (c) sets forth the two circumstances under which the priority afforded to a purchaser of chattel paper under subsection (a) or (b) extends also to proceeds of the chattel paper. The first is if the purchaser would have priority under the normal priority rules applicable to proceeds. The second, which the following Comments discuss in greater detail, is if the proceeds consist of the specific goods covered by the chattel paper. Former Article 9 generally was silent as to the priority of a security interest in proceeds when a purchaser qualifies for priority under Section 9-308 (but see former Section 9-306(5)(b), concerning returned and repossessed goods).

9. Priority in Returned and Repossessed Goods. Returned and repossessed goods may constitute proceeds of chattel paper. The following Comments explain the treatment of returned and repossessed goods as proceeds of chattel paper. The analysis is consistent with that of PEB Commentary No. 5, which these Comments replace, and is based upon the following example:

> **Example:** SP-1 has a security interest in all the inventory of a dealer in goods (Dealer); SP-1's security interest is perfected by filing. Dealer sells some of its inventory to a buyer in the ordinary course of business (BIOCOB) pursuant to a conditional sales contract (chattel paper) that does not indicate that it has been assigned to SP-1. SP-2 purchases the chattel paper from Dealer and takes possession of the paper in good faith, in the ordinary course of business, and without knowledge that the purchase violates the rights of SP-1. Subsequently, BIOCOB returns the goods to Dealer because they are defective. Alternatively, Dealer acquires possession of the goods following BIOCOB's default.

10. Assignment of Non-Lease Chattel Paper.

a. Loan by SP-2 to Dealer Secured by Chattel Paper (or Functional Equivalent Pursuant to Recourse Arrangement).

(1) Returned Goods. If BIOCOB returns the goods to Dealer for repairs, Dealer is merely a bailee and acquires thereby no meaningful rights in the goods to which SP-1's security interest could attach. (Although SP-1's security interest could attach to Dealer's interest as a bailee, that interest is not likely to be of any particular value to SP-1.) Dealer is the owner of the chattel paper (i.e., the owner of a right to payment secured by a security interest in the goods); SP-2 has a security interest in the chattel paper, as does SP-1 (as proceeds of the goods under Section 9-315). Under Section 9-330, SP-2's security interest in the chattel paper is senior to that of SP-1. SP-2 enjoys this priority regardless of whether, or when, SP-2 filed a financing statement covering the chattel paper. Because chattel paper and goods represent different types of collateral, Dealer does not have any meaningful interest in goods to which either SP-1's or SP-2's security interest could attach in order to secure Dealer's obligations to either creditor. See Section 9-102 (defining "chattel paper" and "goods").

Now assume that BIOCOB returns the goods to Dealer under circumstances whereby Dealer once again becomes the owner of the goods. This would be the case, for example, if the goods were defective and BIOCOB was entitled to reject or revoke acceptance of the goods. See Sections 2-602 (rejection), 2-608 (revocation of acceptance). Unless BIOCOB has waived its defenses as against assignees of the chattel paper, SP-1's and SP-2's rights against BIOCOB would be subject to BIOCOB's claims and defenses. See Sections 9-403, 9-404. SP-1's security interest would attach again because the returned goods would be proceeds of the chattel paper. Dealer's acquisition of the goods easily can be characterized as "proceeds" consisting of an "in kind" collection on or distribution on account of the chattel paper. See Section 9-102 (definition of "proceeds"). Assuming that SP-1's security interest is perfected by filing against the goods and that the filing is made in the same office where a filing would be made against the chattel paper, SP-1's security interest in the goods would remain perfected beyond the 20-day period of automatic perfection. See Section 9-315(d).

Because Dealer's newly reacquired interest in the goods is proceeds of the chattel paper, SP-2's security interest also would attach in the goods as proceeds. If SP-2 had perfected its security interest in the chattel paper by filing (again, assuming that filing against the chattel paper was made in the same office where a filing would be made against the goods), SP-2's security interest in the reacquired goods would be perfected beyond 20 days. See Section 9-315(d). However, if SP-2 had relied only on its possession of the chattel paper for perfection and had not filed against the chattel paper or the goods, SP-2's security interest would be unperfected after the 20-day period. See Section 9-315(d). Nevertheless, SP-2's unperfected security interest in the goods would be senior to SP-1's security interest under Section 9-330(c). The result in this priority contest is not affected by SP-2's acquiescence or non-acquiescence in the return of the goods to Dealer.

(2) Repossessed Goods. As explained above, Dealer owns the chattel paper covering the goods, subject to security interests in favor of SP-1 and SP-2. In Article 9 parlance, Dealer has an interest in chattel paper, not goods. If Dealer, SP-1, or SP-2 repossesses the goods upon BIOCOB's default, whether the repossession is rightful or wrongful as among Dealer, SP-1, or SP-2, Dealer's interest will not change. The location of goods and the party who possesses them does not affect the fact that Dealer's interest is in chattel paper, not goods. The goods continue to be owned by BIOCOB. SP-1's security interest in the goods does not attach until such time as Dealer reacquires an interest (other than a bare possessory interest) in the goods. For example, Dealer might buy the goods at a foreclosure sale from SP-2 (whose security interest in the chattel paper is senior to that of SP-1); that disposition would cut off BIOCOB's rights in the goods. Section 9-617.

In many cases the matter would end upon sale of the goods to Dealer at a foreclosure sale and there would be no priority contest between SP-1 and SP-2; Dealer would be unlikely to buy the goods under circumstances whereby SP-2 would retain its security interest. There can be exceptions, however. For example, Dealer may be obliged to purchase the goods from SP-2 and SP-2 may be obliged to convey the goods to Dealer, but Dealer may fail to pay SP-2. Or, one could imagine that SP-2, like SP-1, has a general security interest in the inventory of Dealer. In the latter case, SP-2 should not receive the benefit of any special priority rule, since its interest in no way derives from priority under Section 9-330. In the former case, SP-2's security interest in the goods reacquired by Dealer is senior to SP-1's security interest under Section 9-330.

b. Dealer's Outright Sale of Chattel Paper to SP-2. Article 9 also applies to a transaction whereby SP-2 buys the chattel paper in an outright sale transaction without recourse against Dealer. Sections 1-201(b)(35), 9-109(a). Although Dealer does not, in such a transaction, retain any residual ownership interest in the chattel paper, the chattel paper constitutes proceeds of the goods to which SP-1's security interest will attach and continue following the sale of the goods. Section 9-315(a). Even though Dealer has not retained any interest in the chattel paper, as discussed above BIOCOB subsequently may return the goods to Dealer under circumstances whereby Dealer reacquires an interest in the goods. The priority contest between SP-1 and SP-2 will be resolved as discussed above; Section 9-330 makes no distinction among purchasers of chattel paper on the basis of whether the purchaser is an outright buyer of chattel paper or one whose security interest secures an obligation of Dealer.

11. Assignment of Lease Chattel Paper. As defined in Section 9-102, "chattel paper" includes not only rights to payment secured by specific goods but also rights to payment owed by a lessee under a true lease of goods.

The analysis with respect to lease chattel paper is similar to that set forth above with respect to non-lease chattel paper. It is complicated, however, by the fact that, unlike the case of chattel paper arising out of a sale, Dealer retains a residual interest in the *goods*. See Section 2A-103(1)(q) (defining "lessor's residual interest"); *In re Leasing Consultants, Inc.,* 486 F.2d 367 (2d Cir. 1973) (lessor's residual interest under true lease is an interest in goods and is a separate type of collateral from lessor's interest in the lease). If Dealer leases goods to a "lessee in ordinary course of business" (LIOCOB), then LIOCOB takes its interest under the lease (i.e., its "leasehold interest") free of the security interest of SP-1. See Sections 2A-307(3), 2A-103(1)(m) (defining "leasehold interest"), (1)(o) (defining "lessee in ordinary course of business"). SP-1 would, however, retain its security interest in the residual interest. In addition, SP-1 would acquire an interest in the lease chattel paper as proceeds. If Dealer then assigns the lease chattel paper to SP-2, Section 9-330 gives SP-2 priority over SP-1 with respect to the chattel paper, *but not* with respect to the residual interest in the *goods*. Consequently, assignees of lease chattel paper typically take a security interest in and file against the lessor's residual interest in goods, expecting their priority in the goods to be governed by the first-to-file-or-perfect rule of Section 9-322.

If the goods are returned to Dealer, other than upon expiration of the lease term, then the security interests of both SP-1 and SP-2 normally would attach to the goods as proceeds of the chattel paper. (If the goods are returned to Dealer at the expiration of the lease term and the lessee has made all payments due under the lease, however, then Dealer no longer has any rights under the chattel paper. Dealer's interest in the goods consists solely of its residual interest, as to which SP-2 has no claim.) This would be the case, for example, when the lessee rescinds the lease or when the lessor recovers possession in the exercise of its remedies under Article 2A. See, e.g., Section 2A-525. If SP-2 enjoyed priority in the chattel paper under Section 9-330, then SP-2 likewise would enjoy priority in the returned goods as proceeds. This does not mean that SP-2 necessarily is entitled to the entire value of the returned goods. The value of the goods represents the sum of the present value of (i) the value of their use for the term of the lease and (ii) the value of the residual interest. SP-2 has priority in the former, but SP-1 ordinarily would have priority in the latter. Thus, an allocation of a portion of the value of the goods to each component may be necessary. Where, as here, one secured party has a security interest in the lessor's residual interest and another has a priority security interest in the chattel paper, it may be advisable for the conflicting secured parties to establish a method for making such an allocation and otherwise to determine their relative rights in returned goods by agreement.

§ 9-331. Priority of Rights of Purchasers of Controllable Accounts, Controllable Electronic Records, Controllable Payment Intangibles, Documents, Instruments, and Securities Under Other Articles; Priority of Interests in Financial Assets and Security Entitlements and Protection Against Assertion of Claim Under Articles 8 and 12.

(a) [Rights under Articles 3, 7, 8, and 12 not limited.] This article does not limit the rights of a holder in due course of a negotiable instrument, a holder to which a negotiable document of title has been duly negotiated, a protected purchaser of a security, or a qualifying purchaser of a controllable account, controllable electronic record, or controllable payment intangible. These holders or purchasers take priority over an earlier security interest, even if perfected, to the extent provided in Articles 3, 7, 8, and 12.

(b) [Protection under Articles 8 and 12.] This article does not limit the rights of or impose liability on a person to the extent that the person is protected against the assertion of a claim under Article 8 or 12.

(c) [Filing not notice.] Filing under this article does not constitute notice of a claim or defense to the holders, or purchasers, or persons described in subsections (a) and (b).

Definitional Cross References:

Controllable account	Section 9-102(a)(27A)
Controllable electronic record	Section 12-102(a)(1)
Controllable payment intangible	Section 9-102(a)(27B)
Document	Section 9-102(a)(30)
Document of title	Section 1-201(b)(16)
Financial asset	Section 8-102(a)(9)
Holder	Section 1-201(b)(21)
Holder in due course	Section 3-302(a)
Instrument	Section 9-102(a)(47)
Negotiable instrument	Section 3-104(a)
Notice	Section 1-202(a)
Person	Section 1-201(b)(27)
Protected purchaser	Section 8-303(a)
Purchaser	Section 1-201(b)(30)
Qualifying purchaser	Section 12-102(a)(2)
Right	Section 1-201(b)(34)
Security	Section 8-102(a)(15)
Security entitlement	Section 8-102(a)(17)
Security interest	Section 1-201(b)(35)

Official Comment

1. Source. Former Section 9-309.

2. "Priority." In some provisions, this Article distinguishes between claimants that take collateral free of a security interest (in the sense that the security interest no longer encumbers the collateral) and those that take an interest in the collateral that is senior to a surviving security interest. See, e.g., Section 9-317. Whether a holder or purchaser referred to in this section takes free or is senior to a security interest depends on whether the purchaser is a buyer of the collateral or takes a security interest in it. The term "priority" is meant to encompass both scenarios, as it does in Section 9-330.

3. Rights Acquired by Purchasers. The rights to which this section refers are set forth in Sections 3-305 and 3-306 (holder in due course), 7-502 (holder to whom a negotiable document of title has been duly negotiated), and 8-303 (protected purchaser). The holders and purchasers referred to in this section do not always take priority over a security interest. See, e.g., Section 7-503 (affording paramount rights to certain owners and secured parties as against holder to whom a negotiable document of title has been duly negotiated). Accordingly, this section adds the clause, "to the extent provided in Articles 3, 7, and 8" to former Section 9-309.

The state-law Uniform Electronic Transactions Act (UETA) and the federal Electronic Signature in Global and National Commerce Act, 15 U.S.C. §§ 7001 et seq. (E-SIGN), provide certain rules for records referred to and defined as "transferable records." See UETA Section 16 and E-SIGN, 15 U.S.C. § 7021. When certain conditions have been met, those acts confer on a person the status of a "holder" (as defined in 1-201(b)(21), formerly Section 1-201(20)) of an "equivalent record" under pre-1998 Section 9-308 (now, in part, Section 9-330) and the rights and defenses of a "purchaser" under that section, among other effects. E-SIGN also refers to the rights and defenses of a purchaser under Section 9-330. As a matter of the application of the Uniform Commercial Code, those are not the only sections of the Uniform Commercial Code that would logically be affected by UETA and E-SIGN. For example, the rights of a holder in due course under Section 9-331(a) would also be covered by the application of those acts, when the conditions for applicability have been satisfied.

4. Financial Assets and Security Entitlements. New subsection (b) provides explicit protection for those who deal with financial assets and security entitlements and who are immunized from liability under Article 8. See, e.g., Sections 8-502, 8-503(e), 8-510, 8-511. The new subsection makes explicit in Article 9 what is implicit in former Article 9 and explicit in several provisions of Article 8. It does not change the law.

5. Collections by Junior Secured Party. Under this section, a secured party with a junior security interest in receivables (accounts, chattel paper, promissory notes, or payment intangibles) may collect and retain the proceeds of those receivables free of the claim of a senior secured party to the same receivables, if the junior secured party is a holder in due course of the proceeds. In order to qualify as a holder in due course, the junior must satisfy the requirements of Section 3-302, which include taking in "good faith." This means that the junior not only must act "honestly" but also must observe "reasonable commercial standards of fair dealing" under the particular circumstances. See Section 9-102(a). Although "good faith" does not impose a general duty of inquiry, e.g., a search of the records in filing offices, there may be circumstances in which "reasonable commercial standards of fair dealing" would require such a search.

Consider, for example, a junior secured party in the business of financing or buying accounts who fails to undertake a search to determine the existence of prior security interests. Because a search, under the usages of trade of that business, would enable it to know or learn upon reasonable inquiry that collecting the accounts violated the rights of a senior secured party, the junior may fail to meet the good-faith standard. See *Utility Contractors Financial Services, Inc. v. Amsouth Bank, NA*, 985 F.2d 1554 (11th Cir. 1993). Likewise, a junior secured party who collects accounts when it knows or should know under the particular circumstances that doing so would violate the rights of a senior secured party, because the debtor had agreed not to grant a junior security interest in, or sell, the accounts, may not meet the good-faith test. Thus, if a junior secured party conducted or should have conducted a search and a financing statement filed on behalf of the senior secured party states such a restriction, the junior's collection would not meet the good-faith standard. On the other hand, if there was a course of performance between the senior secured party and the debtor which placed no such restrictions on the debtor and allowed the debtor to collect and use the proceeds without any restrictions, the junior secured party may then satisfy the requirements for being a holder in due course. This would be more likely in those circumstances where the junior secured party was providing additional financing to the debtor on an on-going basis by lending against or buying the accounts and had no notice of any restrictions against doing so. Generally, the senior secured party would not be prejudiced because the practical effect of such payment to the junior secured party is little different than if the debtor itself had made the collections and subsequently paid the secured party from the debtor's general funds. Absent collusion, the junior secured party would take the funds free of the senior security interests. See Section 9-332. In contrast, the senior secured party is likely to be prejudiced if the debtor is going out of business and the junior secured party collects the accounts by notifying the account debtors to make payments directly to the junior. Those collections may not be consistent with "reasonable commercial standards of fair dealing."

Whether the junior secured party qualifies as a holder in due course is fact-sensitive and should be decided on a case-by-case basis in the light of those circumstances. Decisions such as *Financial Management Services Inc. v. Familian,* 905 P.2d 506 (Ariz. App. Div. 1995) (finding holder in due course status) could be determined differently under this application of the good- faith requirement.

The concepts addressed in this Comment are also applicable to junior secured parties as purchasers of instruments under Section 9-330(d). See Section 9-330, Comment 7.

§ 9-332. Transfer of Money; Transfer of Funds from Deposit Account.

(a) [Transferee of tangible money.] A transferee of tangible money takes the money free of a security interest if the transferee receives possession of the money without acting in collusion with the debtor in violating the rights of the secured party.

(b) [Transferee of funds from deposit account.] A transferee of funds from a deposit account takes the funds free of a security interest in the deposit account if the transferee receives the funds without acting in collusion with the debtor in violating the rights of the secured party.

(c) [Transferee of electronic money.] A transferee of electronic money takes the money free of a security interest if the transferee obtains control of the money without acting in collusion with the debtor in violating the rights of the secured party.

Definitional Cross References:

Debtor	Section 9-102(a)(28)
Deposit account	Section 9-102(a)(29)
Electronic money	Section 9-102(a)(31A)
Money	Section 9-102(a)(54A)
Right	Section 1-201(b)(34)
Secured party	Section 9-102(a)(73)
Security interest	Section 1-201(b)(35)
Tangible money	Section 9-102(a)(79A)

Official Comment

1. Source. New.

2. Scope of This Section. This section affords broad protection for transferees of money and of funds from a deposit account to take free of a security interest.

2A. Meaning of "Transfer." The term "transferee" is not defined; however, the debtor itself is not a transferee. Thus this section does not cover the case in which a debtor withdraws money (currency) from its deposit account or the case in which a bank debits an encumbered account and credits another account it maintains for the debtor.

A "transfer" of property occurs when the transferee has obtained a property interest in the relevant property. See Section 9-102, Comment 2.b.1 ("Several provisions of this Article and its official comments also refer to the 'transfer' of property interests." (emphasis added)). Other law determines when the transferee has acquired a property interest. See Section 9-408, Comment 3 ("Other law determines whether a debtor has a property interest ('rights in the collateral') and the nature of that interest."). Although the terms "transfer" and "transferee" are not defined in the UCC, the term "transfer" is broader in scope than "purchase," which requires taking in a "voluntary transaction creating an interest in property." Section 1-201(b)(29). For example, "transfer" includes an involuntary transfer such as the acquisition of a judicial lien by a lien creditor. See Section 9-102(a)(52) (defining "lien creditor"). However, many references to a "transfer" in the UCC and official comments relate to a voluntary transfer to a purchaser, as indicated by the context.

2B. Transferees of Tangible Money. Subsection (a) conditions the take-free rule on the transferee's receipt of possession of tangible money. This reflects what had always been assumed under the pre-2022 text—that a transfer of an interest in tangible money which is not accompanied by a physical transfer of possession would not impair the rights of third parties.

2C. Transferees of Funds from Deposit Account. Subsection (b) reflects the corresponding change for a transfer of funds from a deposit account. To qualify for the take-free protection under subsection (b), the transferee must "receive[] the funds without acting in collusion..." The amendments to subsections (a) and (b) clarify what was implicit under the original text. Although "funds" is not defined in the UCC, if deposit accounts with a central bank or another bank were to become money, as defined in Section 1-201(b)(24), transfers from such deposit accounts would be covered by subsection (b) and not subsection (c) (discussed in Comment 2.D.). See Section 9-102(a)(54A) (defining "money," for purposes of Article 9, to exclude deposit accounts).

A transfer of funds from a deposit account, to which subsection (b) applies, normally will be made by check, by funds transfer, or by debiting the debtor's deposit account and crediting another depositor's account.

Example 1: Debtor maintains a deposit account with Bank A. The deposit account is subject to a perfected security interest in favor of Lender. Debtor draws a check on the account, payable to Payee. Inasmuch as the check is not the proceeds of the deposit account (it is an order to pay funds from the deposit account), Lender's security interest in the deposit account does not give rise to a security interest in the check. Payee deposits the check into its own deposit account, and Bank A pays it. Unless Payee acted in collusion with Debtor in violating Lender's rights, Payee takes the funds (the credits running in favor of Payee) free of Lender's security interest. This is true regardless of whether Payee is a holder in due course of the check and even if Payee gave no value for the check.

Example 2: Debtor maintains a deposit account with Bank A. The deposit account is subject to a perfected security interest in favor of Lender. At Bank B's suggestion, Debtor moves the funds from the account at Bank A to Debtor's deposit account with Bank B. Unless Bank B acted in collusion with Debtor in violating Lender's rights, Bank B takes the funds (the credits running in favor of Bank B) free from Lender's security interest. See subsection (b). However, inasmuch as the deposit account maintained with Bank B constitutes the proceeds of the deposit account at Bank A, Lender's security interest would attach to that account as proceeds. See Section 9-315.

Subsection (b) also would apply if, in these examples, Bank A debited Debtor's deposit account in exchange for the issuance of Bank A's cashier's check. Lender's security interest would attach to the cashier's check as proceeds of the deposit account, and the rules applicable to instruments would govern any competing claims to the cashier's check. See, e.g., Sections 3-306, 9-322, 9-330, 9-331.

If Debtor withdraws funds from an encumbered deposit account, receives the funds in the form of tangible money, and transfers the money to a third party, then subsection (a), to the extent not displaced by federal law relating to money, applies to the transfer. It contains substantially the same rule as subsection (b).

Subsection (b) applies to transfers of funds from a deposit account; it does not apply to transfers of the deposit account itself or of an interest therein. Because a deposit account is a monetary obligation (debt) of the depositary bank to its depositor, a transfer of the deposit account itself does not transfer the funds credited to the deposit account. For example, this section does not apply to the creation of a security interest in a deposit account. Competing claims to the deposit account itself are dealt with by other Article 9 priority rules. See Sections 9-317(a), 9-327, 9-340, 9-341. Similarly, a corporate merger normally would not result in a transfer of funds from a deposit account. Rather, it might result in a transfer of the deposit account itself. If so, the normal rules applicable to transferred collateral would apply; this section would not.

The depositor's creditors (whether secured parties or lien creditors) do not have any interest in any funds (or any other assets of the depositary bank) as a result of having an interest in the deposit account (the right to payment of the bank's obligation). Consequently, a transferee of funds that takes free of a security interest under subsection (b) does so whether the security interest in the deposit account from which the funds were transferred arises as original collateral or as proceeds.

A transferee of an interest in the deposit account, such as a garnishing lien creditor, does not take free of a security interest in a deposit account under subsection (b). A transferee takes free under subsection (b) only upon the actual receipt of funds from the deposit account. The proper construction of subsection (b) rejects cases that treat garnishment of a deposit account as an immediate transfer of funds or an interest in funds credited to the deposit account.

The last event that provides a recovery for a creditor in a garnishment action virtually always would be a transfer of funds from a deposit account. However, this does not mean that a perfected security interest will always be cut off by a garnishing creditor. By intervening in the garnishment proceeding to assert its senior security interest before funds are disbursed, the secured party might assert and retain its priority. However, the relevant procedural law may not provide the secured party with adequate advance notice. In some cases, a control agreement that perfects a security interest in the deposit account may require the garnished bank to provide prompt notice to the secured party. But not all control agreements will so provide. Moreover, the secured party's priority is not absolute. See, e.g., Section 9-401, Comment 6 (explaining that the equitable doctrine of marshaling may be appropriate in the case of a lien creditor's interest in collateral when a senior secured party is oversecured).

2D. Transferees of Electronic Money. Because "electronic money" is new, no pattern of past practices or understandings exists. However, subsection (c) provides a take-free rule for electronic money that complements subsection (a) by conditioning the take-free rule on the transferee's obtaining control.

2E. Temporal Aspect of Collusion Test. For a transferee to take free of a security interest under this section the transferee must receive delivery of tangible money, receive funds from a deposit account, or obtain control of electronic money without acting in collusion. Whether the transferee is acting without collusion is determined as of the time of delivery to the transferee or receipt of funds or obtaining control by the transferee.

3. Policy. Broad protection for transferees helps to ensure that security interests in deposit accounts do not impair the free flow of funds. It also minimizes the likelihood that a secured party will enjoy a claim to whatever the transferee purchases with the funds. Rules concerning recovery of payments traditionally have placed a high value on finality. The opportunity to upset a completed transaction, or even to place a completed transaction in jeopardy by bringing suit against the transferee of funds, should be severely limited. Although the giving of value usually is a prerequisite for receiving the ability to take free from third-party claims, where payments are concerned the law is even more protective. Thus, Section 3-418(c) provides that, even where the law of restitution otherwise would permit recovery of funds paid by mistake, no recovery may be had from a person "who in good faith changed position in reliance on the payment." Rather than adopt this standard, this section eliminates all reliance requirements whatsoever. Payments made by mistake are relatively rare, but payments of funds from encumbered deposit accounts (e.g., deposit accounts containing collections from accounts receivable) occur with great regularity. In most cases, unlike payment by mistake, no one would object to these payments. In the vast proportion of cases, the transferee probably would be able to show a change of position in reliance on the payment. This section does not put the transferee to the burden of having to make this proof.

4. "Bad Actors." To deal with the question of the "bad actor," this section borrows "collusion" language from Article 8. See, e.g., Sections 8-115, 8-503(e). This is the most protective (i.e., least stringent) of the various standards now found in the UCC. Compare, e.g., Section 1-201(b)(9) ("without knowledge that the sale violates the rights of another person," in the definition of "buyer in ordinary course of business"); Section 1-201(b)(20) (defining "good faith" as "honesty in fact and the observance of reasonable commercial standards of fair dealing"); Section 3-302(a)(2)(v) ("without notice of any claim").

5. Transferee Who Does Not Take Free. This section sets forth the circumstances under which certain transferees of money or funds take free of security interests. It does not determine the rights of a transferee who does not take free of a security interest.

> **Example 3:** The facts are as in Example 2, but, in wrongfully moving the funds from the deposit account at Bank A to Debtor's deposit account with Bank B, Debtor acts in collusion with Bank B. Bank B does not take the funds

free of Lender's security interest under this section. If Debtor grants a security interest to Bank B, Section 9-327 governs the relative priorities of Lender and Bank B. Under Section 9-327(3), Bank B's security interest in the Bank B deposit account is senior to Lender's security interest in the deposit account as proceeds. However, Bank B's senior security interest does not protect Bank B against any liability to Lender that might arise from Bank B's wrongful conduct.

§ 9-333. Priority of Certain Liens Arising by Operation of Law.

(a) ["Possessory lien."] In this section, "possessory lien" means an interest, other than a security interest or an agricultural lien:

(1) which secures payment or performance of an obligation for services or materials furnished with respect to goods by a person in the ordinary course of the person's business;

(2) which is created by statute or rule of law in favor of the person; and

(3) whose effectiveness depends on the person's possession of the goods.

(b) [Priority of possessory lien.] A possessory lien on goods has priority over a security interest in the goods unless the lien is created by a statute that expressly provides otherwise.

Definitional Cross References:

Agricultural lien	Section 9-102(a)(5)
Goods	Section 9-102(a)(44)
Person	Section 1-201(b)(27)
Security interest	Section 1-201(b)(35)

Official Comment

1. Source. Former Section 9-310.

2. "Possessory Liens." This section governs the relative priority of security interests arising under this Article and "possessory liens," i.e., common-law and statutory liens whose effectiveness depends on the lienor's possession of goods with respect to which the lienor provided services or furnished materials in the ordinary course of its business. As under former Section 9-310, the possessory lien has priority over a security interest unless the possessory lien is created by a statute that expressly provides otherwise. If the statute creating the possessory lien is silent as to its priority relative to a security interest, this section provides a rule of interpretation that the possessory lien takes priority, even if the statute has been construed judicially to make the possessory lien subordinate.

§ 9-334. Priority of Security Interests in Fixtures and Crops.

(a) [Security interest in fixtures under this article.] A security interest under this article may be created in goods that are fixtures or may continue in goods that become fixtures. A security interest does not exist under this article in ordinary building materials incorporated into an improvement on land.

(b) [Security interest in fixtures under real-property law.] This article does not prevent creation of an encumbrance upon fixtures under real property law.

(c) [General rule: subordination of security interest in fixtures.] In cases not governed by subsections (d) through (h), a security interest in fixtures is subordinate to a conflicting interest of an encumbrancer or owner of the related real property other than the debtor.

(d) [Fixtures purchase-money priority.] Except as otherwise provided in subsection (h), a perfected security interest in fixtures has priority over a conflicting interest of an encumbrancer or owner of the real property if the debtor has an interest of record in or is in possession of the real property and:

(1) the security interest is a purchase-money security interest;

(2) the interest of the encumbrancer or owner arises before the goods become fixtures; and

(3) the security interest is perfected by a fixture filing before the goods become fixtures or within 20 days thereafter.

(e) [Priority of security interest in fixtures over interests in real property.] A perfected security interest in fixtures has priority over a conflicting interest of an encumbrancer or owner of the real property if:

(1) the debtor has an interest of record in the real property or is in possession of the real property and the security interest:

(A) is perfected by a fixture filing before the interest of the encumbrancer or owner is of record; and

(B) has priority over any conflicting interest of a predecessor in title of the encumbrancer or owner;

(2) before the goods become fixtures, the security interest is perfected by any method permitted by this article and the fixtures are readily removable:

(A) factory or office machines;

(B) equipment that is not primarily used or leased for use in the operation of the real property; or

(C) replacements of domestic appliances that are consumer goods;

(3) the conflicting interest is a lien on the real property obtained by legal or equitable proceedings after the security interest was perfected by any method permitted by this article; or

(4) the security interest is:

(A) created in a manufactured home in a manufactured-home transaction; and

(B) perfected pursuant to a statute described in Section 9-311(a)(2).

(f) [Priority based on consent, disclaimer, or right to remove.] A security interest in fixtures, whether or not perfected, has priority over a conflicting interest of an encumbrancer or owner of the real property if:

(1) the encumbrancer or owner has, in a signed record, consented to the security interest or disclaimed an interest in the goods as fixtures; or

(2) the debtor has a right to remove the goods as against the encumbrancer or owner.

(g) [Continuation of paragraph (f)(2) priority.] The priority of the security interest under paragraph (f)(2) continues for a reasonable time if the debtor's right to remove the goods as against the encumbrancer or owner terminates.

(h) [Priority of construction mortgage.] A mortgage is a construction mortgage to the extent that it secures an obligation incurred for the construction of an improvement on land, including the acquisition cost of the land, if a recorded record of the mortgage so indicates. Except as otherwise provided in subsections (e) and (f), a security interest in fixtures is subordinate to a construction mortgage if a record of the mortgage is recorded before the goods become fixtures and the goods become fixtures before the completion of the construction. A mortgage has this priority to the same extent as a construction mortgage to the extent that it is given to refinance a construction mortgage.

(i) [Priority of security interest in crops.] A perfected security interest in crops growing on real property has priority over a conflicting interest of an encumbrancer or owner of the real property if the debtor has an interest of record in or is in possession of the real property.

(j) [Subsection (i) prevails.] Subsection (i) prevails over any inconsistent provisions of the following statutes:

[List here any statutes containing provisions inconsistent with subsection (i).]

Legislative Note: *States that amend statutes to remove provisions inconsistent with subsection (i) need not enact subsection (j).*

Definitional Cross References:

Consumer goods	Section 9-102(a)(23)
Debtor	Section 9-102(a)(28)
Encumbrance	Section 9-102(a)(32)
Equipment	Section 9-102(a)(33)
Fixture filing	Section 9-102(a)(40)
Fixtures	Section 9-102(a)(41)
Goods	Section 9-102(a)(44)
Lease	Section 2A-103(1)(j)
Manufactured home	Section 9-102(a)(53)
Manufactured-home transaction	Section 9-102(a)(54)
Mortgage	Section 9-102(a)(55)
Purchase-money security interest	Section 9-103
Record	Section 9-102(a)(70)
Security interest	Section 1-201(b)(35)
Sign	Section 1-201(b)(37)
State	Section 9-102(a)(77)

Official Comment

1. Source. Former Section 9-313.

2. Scope of This Section. This section contains rules governing the priority of security interests in fixtures and crops as against persons who claim an interest in real property. Priority contests with other Article 9 security interests are governed by the other priority rules of this Article. The provisions with respect to fixtures follow those of former Section 9-313. However, they have been rewritten to conform to Section 2A-309 and to prevailing style conventions. Subsections (i) and (j), which apply to crops, are new.

3. Security Interests in Fixtures. Certain goods that are the subject of personal-property (chattel) financing become so affixed or otherwise so related to real property that they become part of the real property. These goods are called "fixtures." See Section 9-102 (definition of "fixtures"). Some fixtures retain their personal-property nature: a security interest under this Article may be created in fixtures and may continue in goods that become fixtures. See subsection (a). However, if the goods are ordinary building materials incorporated into an improvement on land, no security interest in them exists. Rather, the priority of claims to the building materials are determined by the law governing claims to real property. (Of course, the fact that no security interest exists in ordinary building materials incorporated into an improvement on land does not prejudice any rights the secured party may have against the debtor or any other person who violated the secured party's rights by wrongfully incorporating the goods into real property.)

Thus, this section recognizes three categories of goods: (1) those that retain their chattel character entirely and are not part of the real property; (2) ordinary building materials that have become an integral part of the real property and cannot retain their chattel character for purposes of finance; and (3) an intermediate class that has become real property for certain purposes, but as to which chattel financing may be preserved.

To achieve priority under certain provisions of this section, a security interest must be perfected by making a "fixture filing" (defined in Section 9-102) in the real-property records. Because the question whether goods have become fixtures often is a difficult one under applicable real-property law, a secured party may make a fixture filing as a precaution. Courts should not infer from a fixture filing that the secured party concedes that the goods are or will become fixtures.

4. Priority in Fixtures: General. In considering priority problems under this section, one must first determine whether real-property claimants per se have an interest in the crops or fixtures as part of real property. If not, it is immaterial, so far as concerns real property parties as such, whether a security interest arising under this Article is perfected or unperfected. In no event does a real-property claimant (e.g., owner or mortgagee) acquire an interest in a "pure" chattel just because a security interest therein is unperfected. If on the other hand real-property law gives real-property parties an interest in the goods, a conflict arises and this section states the priorities.

5. Priority in Fixtures: Residual Rule. Subsection (c) states the residual priority rule, which applies only if one of the other rules does not: A security interest in fixtures is subordinate to a conflicting interest of an encumbrancer or owner of the related real property other than the debtor.

6. Priority in Fixtures: First to File or Record. Subsection (e)(1), which follows former Section 9-313(4)(b), contains the usual priority rule of conveyancing, that is, the first to file or record prevails. In order to achieve priority under this rule, however, the security interest must be perfected by a "fixture filing" (defined in Section 9-102), i.e., a filing for record in the real property records and indexed therein, so that it will be found in a real-property search. The condition in subsection (e)(1)(B), that the security interest must have had priority over any conflicting interest of a predecessor in title of the conflicting encumbrancer or owner, appears to limit to the first-in-time principle. However, this apparent limitation is nothing other than an expression of the usual rule that a person must be entitled to transfer what he has. Thus, if the fixture security interest is subordinate to a mortgage, it is subordinate to an interest of an assignee of the mortgage, even though the assignment is a later recorded instrument. Similarly if the fixture security interest is subordinate to the rights of an owner, it is subordinate to a subsequent grantee of the owner and likewise subordinate to a subsequent mortgagee of the owner.

7. Priority in Fixtures: Purchase-Money Security Interests. Subsection (d), which follows former Section 9-313(4)(a), contains the principal exception to the first-to-file-or-record rule of subsection (e)(1). It affords priority to purchase-money security interests in fixtures as against prior recorded real-property interests, provided that the purchase-money security interest is filed as a fixture filing in the real-property records before the goods become fixtures or within 20 days thereafter. This priority corresponds to the purchase-money priority under Section 9-324(a). (Like other 10-day periods in former Article 9, the 10-day period in this section has been changed to 20 days.)

It should be emphasized that this purchase-money priority with the 20-day grace period for filing is limited to rights against real-property interests that arise before the goods become fixtures. There is no such priority with the 20-day grace period as against real-property interests that arise subsequently. The fixture security interest can defeat subsequent real-property interests only if it is filed first and prevails under the usual conveyancing rule in subsection (e)(1) or one of the other rules in this section.

8. Priority in Fixtures: Readily Removable Goods. Subsection (e)(2), which derives from Section 2A-309 and former Section 9-313(4)(d), contains another exception to the usual first-to-file-or-perfect rule. It affords priority to the holders of security interests in certain types of readily removable goods—factory and office machines, equipment that is not primarily used or leased for use in the operation of the real property, and (as discussed below) certain replacements of domestic appliances. This rule is made necessary by the confusion in the law as to whether certain machinery, equipment, and appliances become fixtures. It protects a secured party who, perhaps in the mistaken belief that the readily removable goods will not become fixtures, makes a UCC filing (or otherwise perfects under this Article) rather than making a fixture filing.

Frequently, under applicable law, goods of the type described in subsection (e)(2) will not be considered to have become part of the real property. In those cases, the fixture security interest does not conflict with a real-property interest, and resort to this section is unnecessary. However, if the goods have become part of the real property, subsection (e)(2) enables a fixture secured party to take priority over a conflicting real-property interest if the fixture security interest is perfected by a fixture filing or by any other method permitted by this Article. If perfection is by fixture filing, the fixture security interest would have priority over subsequently recorded real-property interests under subsection (e)(1) and, if the fixture security interest is a purchase-money security interest (a likely scenario), it would also have priority over most real property interests under the purchase-money priority of subsection (d). Note, however, that unlike the purchase-money priority rule in subsection (d), the priority rules in subsection (e) override the priority given to a construction mortgage under subsection (h).

The rule in subsection (e)(2) is limited to readily removable replacements of domestic appliances. It does not apply to original installations. Moreover, it is limited to appliances that are "consumer goods" (defined in Section 9-102) in the hands of the debtor. The principal effect of the rule is to make clear that a secured party financing occasional replacements of domestic appliances in noncommercial, owner-occupied contexts need not concern itself with real-property descriptions or records; indeed, for a purchase-money replacement of consumer goods, perfection without any filing will be possible. See Section 9-309(1).

9. Priority in Fixtures: Judicial Liens. Subsection (e)(3), which follows former Section 9-313(4)(d), adopts a first-in-time rule applicable to conflicts between a fixture security interest and a lien on the real property obtained by legal or equitable proceedings. Such a lien is subordinate to an earlier-perfected security interest, regardless of the method by which the security interest was perfected. Judgment creditors generally are not reliance creditors who search real-property records. Accordingly, a perfected fixture security interest takes priority over a subsequent judgment lien or other lien obtained by legal or equitable proceedings, even if no evidence of the security interest appears in the relevant real-property records. Subsection (e)(3) thus protects a perfected fixture security interest from avoidance by a trustee in bankruptcy under Bankruptcy Code Section 544(a), regardless of the method of perfection.

10. Priority in Fixtures: Manufactured Homes. A manufactured home may become a fixture. New subsection (e)(4) contains a special rule granting priority to certain security interests created in a "manufactured home" as part of a "manufactured-home transaction" (both defined in Section 9-102). Under this rule, a security interest in a manufactured home that becomes a fixture has priority over a conflicting interest of an encumbrancer or owner of the real property if the security interest is perfected under a certificate-of-title statute (see Section 9-311). Subsection (e)(4) is only one of the priority rules applicable to security interests in a manufactured home that becomes a fixture. Thus, a security interest in a manufactured home which does not qualify for priority under this subsection may qualify under another.

11. Priority in Fixtures: Construction Mortgages. The purchase-money priority presents a difficult problem in relation to construction mortgages. The latter ordinarily will have been recorded even before the commencement of delivery of materials to the job, and therefore would take priority over fixture security interests were it not for the purchase-money priority. However, having recorded first, the holder of a construction mortgage reasonably expects to have first priority in the improvement built using the mortgagee's advances. Subsection (g) [sic—should be (h)] expressly gives priority to the construction mortgage recorded before the filing of the purchase-money security interest in fixtures. A refinancing of a construction mortgage has the same priority as the construction mortgage itself. The phrase "an obligation incurred for the construction of an improvement" covers both optional advances and advances pursuant to commitment. Both types of advances have the same priority under subsection (g) [sic—should be (h)].

The priority under this subsection applies only to goods that become fixtures during the construction period leading to the completion of the improvement. The construction priority will not apply to additions to the building made long after completion of the improvement, even if the additions are financed by the real-property mortgagee under an open-end clause of the construction mortgage. In such case, subsections (d), (e), and (f) govern.

Although this subsection affords a construction mortgage priority over a purchase-money security interest that otherwise would have priority under subsection (d), the subsection is subject to the priority rules in subsections (e) and (f). Thus, a construction mortgage may be junior to a fixture security interest perfected by a fixture filing before the construction mortgage was recorded. See subsection (e)(1).

12. Crops. Growing crops are "goods" in which a security interest may be created and perfected under this Article. In some jurisdictions, a mortgage of real property may cover crops, as well. In the event that crops are encumbered by both a mortgage and an Article 9 security interest, subsection (i) provides that the security interest has priority. States whose real-property law provides otherwise should either amend that law directly or override it by enacting subsection (j).

13. "Signed" Replaces "Authenticated." Consistent with the revised definition of "sign" in Section 1-201, the cognate term "signed" replaces the reference to "authenticated" in the pre-2022 text of this section.

§ 9-335. Accessions.

(a) [Creation of security interest in accession.] A security interest may be created in an accession and continues in collateral that becomes an accession.

(b) [Perfection of security interest.] If a security interest is perfected when the collateral becomes an accession, the security interest remains perfected in the collateral.

(c) [Priority of security interest.] Except as otherwise provided in subsection (d), the other provisions of this part determine the priority of a security interest in an accession.

(d) [Compliance with certificate-of-title statute.] A security interest in an accession is subordinate to a security interest in the whole which is perfected by compliance with the requirements of a certificate-of-title statute under Section 9-311(b).

(e) [Removal of accession after default.] After default, subject to Part 6, a secured party may remove an accession from other goods if the security interest in the accession has priority over the claims of every person having an interest in the whole.

(f) [Reimbursement following removal.] A secured party that removes an accession from other goods under subsection (e) shall promptly reimburse any holder of a security interest or other lien on, or owner of, the whole or of the other goods, other than the debtor, for the cost of repair of any physical injury to the whole or the other goods. The secured party need not reimburse the holder or owner for any diminution in value of the whole or the other goods caused by the absence of the accession removed or by any necessity for replacing it. A person entitled to reimbursement may refuse permission to remove until the secured party gives adequate assurance for the performance of the obligation to reimburse.

Definitional Cross References:

Accession	Section 9-102(a)(1)
Collateral	Section 9-102(a)(12)
Debtor	Section 9-102(a)(28)
Goods	Section 9-102(a)(44)
Holder	Section 1-201(b)(21)
Person	Section 1-201(b)(27)
Secured party	Section 9-102(a)(73)
Security interest	Section 1-201(b)(35)
Value	Section 1-204

Official Comment

1. Source. Former Section 9-314.

2. "Accession." This section applies to an "accession," as defined in Section 9-102, regardless of the cost or difficulty of removing the accession from the other goods, and regardless of whether the original goods have come to form an integral part of the other goods. This section does not apply to goods whose identity has been lost. Goods of that kind are "commingled goods" governed by Section 9-336. Neither this section nor the following one addresses the case of collateral that changes form without the addition of other goods.

3. "Accession" vs. "Other Goods." This section distinguishes among the "accession," the "other goods," and the "whole." The last term refers to the combination of the "accession" and the "other goods." If one person's collateral becomes physically united with another person's collateral, each is an "accession."

> **Example 1:** SP-1 holds a security interest in the debtor's tractors (which are not subject to a certificate-of-title statute), and SP-2 holds a security interest in a particular tractor engine. The engine is installed in a tractor. From the perspective of SP-1, the tractor becomes an "accession" and the engine is the "other goods." From the perspective of SP-2, the engine is the "accession" and the tractor is the "other goods." The completed tractor—tractor cum engine—constitutes the "whole."

4. Scope. This section governs only a few issues concerning accessions. Subsection (a) contains rules governing continuation of a security interest in an accession. Subsection (b) contains a rule governing continued perfection of a security interest in goods that become an accession. Subsection (d) contains a special priority rule governing accessions that become part of a whole covered by a certificate of title. Subsections (e) and (f) govern enforcement of a security interest in an accession.

5. Matters Left to Other Provisions of This Article: Attachment and Perfection. Other provisions of this Article often govern accession-related issues. For example, this section does not address whether a secured party acquires a security interest in the whole if its collateral becomes an accession. Normally this will turn on the description of the collateral in the security agreement.

> **Example 2:** Debtor owns a computer subject to a perfected security interest in favor of SP-1. Debtor acquires memory and installs it in the computer. Whether SP-1's security interest attaches to the memory depends on whether the security agreement covers it.
>
> Similarly, this section does not determine whether perfection against collateral that becomes an accession is effective to perfect a security interest in the whole. Other provisions of this Article, including the requirements for indicating the collateral covered by a financing statement, resolve that question.

6. Matters Left to Other Provisions of This Article: Priority. With one exception, concerning goods covered by a certificate of title (see subsection (d)), the other provisions of this Part, including the rules governing purchase-money security interests, determine the priority of most security interests in an accession, including the relative priority of a security interest in an accession and a security interest in the whole. See subsection (c).

> **Example 3:** Debtor owns an office computer subject to a security interest in favor of SP-1. Debtor acquires memory and grants a perfected security interest in the memory to SP-2. Debtor installs the memory in the computer, at which time (one assumes) SP-1's security interest attaches to the memory. The first-to-file-or-perfect rule of Section 9-322 governs priority in the memory. If, however, SP-2's security interest is a purchase-money security interest, Section 9-324(a) would afford priority in the memory to SP-2, regardless of which security interest was perfected first.

7. Goods Covered by Certificate of Title. This section does govern the priority of a security interest in an accession that is or becomes part of a whole that is subject to a security interest perfected by compliance with a certificate-of-title statute. Subsection (d) provides that a security interest in the whole, perfected by compliance with a certificate-of-title statute, takes priority over a security interest in the accession. It enables a secured party to rely upon a certificate of title without having to check the UCC files to determine whether any components of the collateral may be encumbered. The subsection imposes a corresponding risk upon those who finance goods that may become part of goods covered by a certificate of title. In doing so, it reverses the priority that appeared reasonable to most pre-UCC courts.

> **Example 4:** Debtor owns an automobile subject to a security interest in favor of SP-1. The security interest is perfected by notation on the certificate of title. Debtor buys tires subject to a perfected-by-filing purchase-money security interest in favor of SP-2 and mounts the tires on the automobile's wheels. If the security interest in the automobile attaches to the tires, then SP-1 acquires priority over SP-2. The same result would obtain if SP-1's security interest attached to the automobile and was perfected after the tires had been mounted on the wheels.

§ 9-336. Commingled Goods.

(a) ["Commingled goods."] In this section, "commingled goods" means goods that are physically united with other goods in such a manner that their identity is lost in a product or mass.

(b) [No security interest in commingled goods as such.] A security interest does not exist in commingled goods as such. However, a security interest may attach to a product or mass that results when goods become commingled goods.

(c) [Attachment of security interest to product or mass.] If collateral becomes commingled goods, a security interest attaches to the product or mass.

(d) [Perfection of security interest.] If a security interest in collateral is perfected before the collateral becomes commingled goods, the security interest that attaches to the product or mass under subsection (c) is perfected.

(e) [Priority of security interest.] Except as otherwise provided in subsection (f), the other provisions of this part determine the priority of a security interest that attaches to the product or mass under subsection (c).

(f) [Conflicting security interests in product or mass] If more than one security interest attaches to the product or mass under subsection (c), the following rules determine priority:

(1) A security interest that is perfected under subsection (d) has priority over a security interest that is unperfected at the time the collateral becomes commingled goods.

(2) If more than one security interest is perfected under subsection (d), the security interests rank equally in proportion to value of the collateral at the time it became commingled goods.

Definitional Cross References:

Collateral	Section 9-102(a)(12)
Goods	Section 9-102(a)(44)
Security interest	Section 1-201(b)(35)
Value	Section 1-204

Official Comment

1. Source. Former Section 9-315.

2. "Commingled Goods." Subsection (a) defines "commingled goods." It is meant to include not only goods whose identity is lost through manufacturing or production (e.g., flour that has become part of baked goods) but also goods whose identity is lost by commingling with other goods from which they cannot be distinguished (e.g., ball bearings).

3. Consequences of Becoming "Commingled Goods." By definition, the identity of the original col lateral cannot be determined once the original collateral becomes commingled goods. Consequently, the security interest in the specific original collateral alone is lost once the collateral becomes commingled goods, and no security interest in the original collateral can be created thereafter except as a part of the resulting product or mass. See subsection (b).

Once collateral becomes commingled goods, the secured party's security interest is transferred from the original collateral to the product or mass. See subsection (c). If the security interest in the original collateral was perfected, the security interest in the product or mass is a perfected security interest. See subsection (d). This perfection continues until lapse.

4. Priority of Perfected Security Interests That Attach Under This Section. This section governs the priority of competing security interests in a product or mass only when both security interests arise under this section. In that case, if both security interests are perfected by operation of this section (see subsections (c) and (d)), then the security interests rank equally, in proportion to the value of the collateral at the time it became commingled goods. See subsection (f)(2).

> **Example 1:** SP-1 has a perfected security interest in Debtor's eggs, which have a value of $300 and secure a debt of $400, and SP-2 has a perfected security interest in Debtor's flour, which has a value of $500 and secures a debt of $700. Debtor uses the flour and eggs to make cakes, which have a value of $1000. The two security interests rank equally and share in the ratio of 3:5. Applying this ratio to the entire value of the product, SP-1 would be entitled to $375 (i.e., 3/ 8 $1000), and SP-2 would be entitled to $625 (i.e., 5/8 $1000).

> **Example 2:** Assume the facts of Example 1, except that SP-1's collateral, worth $300, secures a debt of $200. Recall that, if the cake is worth $1000, then applying the ratio of 3:5 would entitle SP 1 to $375 and SP-2 to $625. However, SP-1 is not entitled to collect from the product more than it is owed. Accordingly, SP-1's share would be only $200, SP-2 would receive the remaining value, up to the amount it is owed ($700).

> **Example 3:** Assume that the cakes in the previous examples have a value of only $600. Again, the parties share in the ratio of 3:5. If, as in Example 1, SP-1 is owed $400, then SP-1 is entitled to $225 (i.e., 3/8 $600), and SP-2 is entitled to $375 (i.e., 5/8 $600). Debtor receives nothing. If, however, as in Example 2, SP-1 is owed only $200, then SP-2 receives $400.

The results in the foregoing examples remain the same, regardless of whether SP-1 or SP-2 (or each) has a purchase-money security interest.

5. Perfection: Unperfected Security Interests. The rule explained in the preceding Comment applies only when both security interests in original collateral are perfected when the goods become commingled goods. If a security interest in original collateral is unperfected at the time the collateral becomes commingled goods, subsection (f)(1) applies.

> **Example 4:** SP-1 has a perfected security interest in the debtor's eggs, and SP-2 has an unperfected security interest in the debtor's flour. Debtor uses the flour and eggs to make cakes. Under subsection (c), both security interests attach to the cakes. But since SP-1's security interest was perfected at the time of commingling and SP-2's was not, only SP-1's security interest in the cakes is perfected. See subsection (d). Under subsection (f)(1) and Section 9-322(a)(2), SP-1's perfected security interest has priority over SP-2's unperfected security interest.

If both security interests are unperfected, the rule of Section 9-322(a)(3) would apply.

6. Multiple Security Interests. On occasion, a single input may be encumbered by more than one security interest. In those cases, the multiple secured parties should be treated like a single secured party for purposes of determining their collective share under subsection (f)(2). The normal priority rules would determine how that share would be allocated between them. Consider the following example, which is a variation on Example 1 above:

> **Example 5:** SP-1A has a perfected, first-priority security interest in Debtor's eggs. SP-1B has a perfected, second-priority security interest in the same collateral. The eggs have a value of $300. Debtor owes $200 to SP-1A and $200 to SP-1B. SP-2 has a perfected security interest in Debtor's flour, which has a value of $500 and secures a debt of $600. Debtor uses the flour and eggs to make cakes, which have a value of $1000.
>
> For purposes of subsection (f)(2), SP-1A and SP-1B should be treated like a single secured party. The collective security interest would rank equally with that of SP-2. Thus, the secured parties would share in the ratio of 3 (for SP-1A and SP-1B combined) to 5 (for SP-2). Applying this ratio to the entire value of the product, SP-1A and SP-1B in the aggregate would be entitled to $375 (i.e., 3/8 $1000), and SP-2 would be entitled to $625 (i.e., 5/8 $1000).
>
> SP-1A and SP-1B would share the $375 in accordance with their priority, as established under other rules. Inasmuch as SP-1A has first priority, it would receive $200, and SP-1B would receive $175.

7. Priority of Security Interests That Attach Other Than by Operation of This Section. Under subsection (e), the normal priority rules determine the priority of a security interest that attaches to the product or mass other than by operation of this section. For example, assume that SP-1 has a perfected security interest in Debtor's existing and after-acquired baked goods, and SP-2 has a perfected security interest in Debtor's flour. When the flour is processed into cakes, subsections (c) and (d) provide that SP-2 acquires a perfected security interest in the cakes. If SP-1 filed against the baked goods before SP-2 filed against the flour, then SP-1 will enjoy priority in the cakes. See Section 9-322 (first-to-file-or perfect). But if SP-2 filed against the flour before SP-1 filed against the baked goods, then SP-2 will enjoy priority in the cakes to the extent of its security interest.

§ 9-337. Priority of Security Interests in Goods Covered by Certificate of Title.

If, while a security interest in goods is perfected by any method under the law of another jurisdiction, this State issues a certificate of title that does not show that the goods are subject to the security interest or contain a statement that they may be subject to security interests not shown on the certificate:

(1) a buyer of the goods, other than a person in the business of selling goods of that kind, takes free of the security interest if the buyer gives value and receives delivery of the goods after issuance of the certificate and without knowledge of the security interest; and

(2) the security interest is subordinate to a conflicting security interest in the goods that attaches, and is perfected under Section 9-311(b), after issuance of the certificate and without the conflicting secured party's knowledge of the security interest.

Official Comment

1. Source. Derived from former Section 9-103(2)(d).

2. Protection for Buyers and Secured Parties. This section affords protection to certain good-faith purchasers for value who are likely to have relied on a "clean" certificate of title, i.e., one that neither shows that the goods are subject to a particular security interest nor contains a statement that they may be subject to security interests not shown on the certificate. Under this section, a buyer can take free of, and the holder of a conflicting security interest can acquire priority over, a security interest that is perfected by any method under the law of another jurisdiction. The fact that the security interest has been reperfected by possession under Section 9-313 does not of itself disqualify the holder of a conflicting security interest from protection under paragraph (2).

Definitional Cross References:

Certificate of title	Section 9-102(a)(10)
Delivery	Section 1-201(b)(15)
Goods	Section 9-102(a)(44)
Person	Section 1-201(b)(27)
Secured party	Section 9-102(a)(73)
Security interest	Section 1-201(b)(35)
State	Section 9-102(a)(77)
Value	Section 1-204

§ 9-338. Priority of Security Interest or Agricultural Lien Perfected by Filed Financing Statement Providing Certain Incorrect Information.

If a security interest or agricultural lien is perfected by a filed financing statement providing information described in Section 9-516(b)(5) which is incorrect at the time the financing statement is filed:

(1) the security interest or agricultural lien is subordinate to a conflicting perfected security interest in the collateral to the extent that the holder of the conflicting security interest gives value in reasonable reliance upon the incorrect information; and

(2) a purchaser, other than a secured party, of the collateral takes free of the security interest or agricultural lien to the extent that, in reasonable reliance upon the incorrect information, the purchaser gives value and, in the case of tangible chattel paper, tangible documents, goods, instruments, or a security certificate, receives delivery of the collateral.

Definitional Cross References:

Agricultural lien	Section 9-102(a)(5)
Chattel paper	Section 9-102(a)(11)
Collateral	Section 9-102(a)(12)
Delivery	Section 1-201(b)(15)
Document	Section 9-102(a)(30)
Financing statement	Section 9-102(a)(39)
Goods	Section 9-102(a)(44)
Holder	Section 1-201(b)(21)
Instrument	Section 9-102(a)(47)
Purchaser	Section 1-201(b)(30)
Secured party	Section 9-102(a)(73)
Security certificate	Section 8-102(a)(16)
Security interest	Section 1-201(b)(35)
Value	Section 1-204

Official Comment

1. Source. New.

2. Effect of Incorrect Information in Financing Statement. Section 9-520(a) requires the filing office to reject financing statements that do not contain information concerning the debtor as specified in Section 9-516(b)(5). An error in this information does not render the financing statement ineffective. On rare occasions, a subsequent purchaser of the collateral (i.e., a buyer or secured party) may rely on the misinformation to its detriment. This section subordinates a security interest or agricultural lien perfected by an effective, but flawed, financing statement to the rights of a buyer or holder of a perfected security interest to the extent that, in reasonable reliance on the incorrect information, the purchaser gives value and, in the case of tangible collateral, receives delivery of the collateral. A purchaser who has not made itself aware of the information in the filing office with respect to the debtor cannot act in "reasonable reliance" upon incorrect information.

3. Relationship to Section 9-507. This section applies to financing statements that contain information that is incorrect at the time of filing and imposes a small risk of subordination on the filer. In contrast, Section 9-507 deals with financing statements containing information that is correct at the time of filing but which becomes incorrect later. Except as provided in Section 9-507 with respect to changes in the name that is sufficient as the name of the debtor under Section 9-503(a), an otherwise effective financing statement does not become ineffective if the information contained in it becomes inaccurate.

§ 9-339. Priority Subject to Subordination.

This article does not preclude subordination by agreement by a person entitled to priority.

Definitional Cross References:

Agreement	Section 1-201(b)(3)
Person	Section 1-201(b)(27)

Official Comment

1. Source. Former Section 9-316.

2. Subordination by Agreement. The preceding sections deal elaborately with questions of priority. This section makes it entirely clear that a person entitled to priority may effectively agree to subordinate its claim. Only the person entitled to priority may make such an agreement: a person's rights cannot be adversely affected by an agreement to which the person is not a party.

[Subpart 4. Rights of Bank]

§ 9-340. Effectiveness of Right of Recoupment or Set-Off Against Deposit Account.

(a) [Exercise of recoupment or set-off.] Except as otherwise provided in subsection (c), a bank with which a deposit account is maintained may exercise any right of recoupment or set-off against a secured party that holds a security interest in the deposit account.

(b) [Recoupment or set-off not affected by security interest.] Except as otherwise provided in subsection (c), the application of this article to a security interest in a deposit account does not affect a right of recoupment or set-off of the secured party as to a deposit account maintained with the secured party.

(c) [When set-off ineffective.] The exercise by a bank of a set-off against a deposit account is ineffective against a secured party that holds a security interest in the deposit account which is perfected by control under Section 9-104(a)(3), if the set-off is based on a claim against the debtor.

Definitional Cross References:

Bank	Section 9-102(a)(8)
Debtor	Section 9-102(a)(28)
Deposit account	Section 9-102(a)(29)
Secured party	Section 9-102(a)(73)
Security interest	Section 1-201(b)(35)

Official Comment

1. Source. New; subsection (b) is based on a nonuniform Illinois amendment.

2. Set-Off vs. Security Interest. This section resolves the conflict between a security interest in a deposit account and the bank's rights of recoupment and set-off.

Subsection (a) states the general rule and provides that the bank may effectively exercise rights of recoupment and set-off against the secured party. Subsection (c) contains an exception: if the secured party has control under Section 9-104(a)(3) (i.e., if it has become the bank's customer), then any set-off exercised by the bank against a debt owed by the debtor (as opposed to a debt owed to the bank by the secured party) is ineffective. The bank may, however, exercise its recoupment rights effectively. This result is consistent with the priority rule in Section 9-327(4), under which the security interest of a bank in a deposit account is subordinate to that of a secured party who has control under Section 9-104(a)(3).

This section deals with rights of set-off and recoupment that a bank may have under other law. It does not create a right of set-off or recoupment, nor is it intended to override any limitations or restrictions that other law imposes on the exercise of those rights.

3. Preservation of Set-Off Right. Subsection (b) makes clear that a bank may hold both a right of set-off against, and an Article 9 security interest in, the same deposit account. By holding a security interest in a deposit account, a bank does not impair any right of set-off it would otherwise enjoy. This subsection does not pertain to accounts evidenced by an instrument (e.g., certain certificates of deposit), which are excluded from the definition of "deposit accounts."

§ 9-341. Bank's Rights and Duties with Respect to Deposit Account.

Except as otherwise provided in Section 9-340(c), and unless the bank otherwise agrees in a signed record, a bank's rights and duties with respect to a deposit account maintained with the bank are not terminated, suspended, or modified by:

(1) the creation, attachment, or perfection of a security interest in the deposit account;

(2) the bank's knowledge of the security interest; or

(3) the bank's receipt of instructions from the secured party.

Definitional Cross References:

Bank	Section 9-102(a)(8)
Deposit account	Section 9-102(a)(29)
Record	Section 9-102(a)(70)
Right	Section 1-201(b)(34)
Secured party	Section 9-102(a)(73)
Security interest	Section 1-201(b)(35)
Sign	Section 1-201(b)(37)

Official Comment

1. Source. New.

2. Free Flow of Funds. This section is designed to prevent security interests in deposit accounts from impeding the free flow of funds through the payment system. Subject to two exceptions, it leaves the bank's rights and duties with respect to the deposit account and the funds on deposit unaffected by the creation or perfection of a security interest or by the bank's knowledge of the security interest. In addition, the section permits the bank to ignore the instructions of the secured party unless it had agreed to honor them or unless other law provides to the contrary. A secured party who wishes to deprive the debtor of access to funds on deposit or to appropriate those funds for itself needs to obtain the agreement of the bank, utilize the judicial process, or comply with procedures set forth in other law. Section 4-303(a), concerning the effect of notice on a bank's right and duty to pay items, is not to the contrary. That section addresses only whether an otherwise effective notice comes too late; it does not determine whether a timely notice is otherwise effective.

3. Operation of Rule. The general rule of this section is subject to Section 9-340(c), under which a bank's right of set-off may not be exercised against a deposit account in the secured party's name if the right is based on a claim against the debtor. This result reflects current law in many jurisdictions and does not appear to have unduly disrupted banking practices or the payments system. The more important function of this section, which is not impaired by Section 9-340, is the bank's right to follow the debtor's (customer's) instructions (e.g., by honoring checks, permitting withdrawals, etc.) until such time as the depository institution is served with judicial process or receives instructions with respect to the funds on deposit from a secured party who has control over the deposit account.

4. Liability of Bank. This Article does not determine whether a bank that pays out funds from an encumbered deposit is liable to the holder of a security interest. Although the fact that a secured party has control over the deposit account and the manner by which control was achieved may be relevant to the imposition of liability, whatever rule applies generally when a bank pays out funds in which a third party has an interest would determine liability to a secured party. Often, this rule is found in a non-UCC adverse claim statute.

5. Certificates of Deposit. This section does not address the obligations of banks that issue instruments evidencing deposits (e.g., certain certificates of deposit).

6. "Signed" Replaces "Authenticated." Consistent with the revised definition of "sign" in Section 1-201, the cognate term "signed" replaces the reference to "authenticated" in the pre-2022 text of this section.

§ 9-342. Bank's Right to Refuse to Enter into or Disclose Existence of Control Agreement.

This article does not require a bank to enter into an agreement of the kind described in Section 9-104(a)(2), even if its customer so requests or directs. A bank that has entered into such an agreement is not required to confirm the existence of the agreement to another person unless requested to do so by its customer.

Definitional Cross References:

Agreement	Section 1-201(b)(3)
Bank	Section 9 102(a)(8)
Customer	Section 4-104(a)(5)
Person	Section 1-201(b)(27)

Official Comment

1. Source. New; derived from Section 8-106(g).

2. Protection for Bank. This section protects banks from the need to enter into agreements against their will and from the need to respond to inquiries from persons other than their customers.

PART 4. RIGHTS OF THIRD PARTIES

§ 9-401. Alienability of Debtor's Rights.

(a) [Other law governs alienability; exceptions.] Except as otherwise provided in subsection (b) and Sections 9-406, 9-407, 9-408, and 9-409, whether a debtor's rights in collateral may be voluntarily or involuntarily transferred is governed by law other than this article.

(b) [Agreement does not prevent transfer.] An agreement between the debtor and secured party which prohibits a transfer of the debtor's rights in collateral or makes the transfer a default does not prevent the transfer from taking effect.

Definitional Cross References:

Agreement	Section 1-201(b)(3)
Collateral	Section 9-102(a)(12)
Debtor	Section 9-102(a)(28)
Right	Section 1-201(b)(34)
Secured party	Section 9-102(a)(73)

Official Comment

1. Source. Former Section 9-311.

2. Scope of This Part. This Part deals with several issues affecting third parties (i.e., parties other than the debtor and the secured party). These issues are not addressed in Part 3, Subpart 3, which deals with priorities. This Part primarily addresses the rights and duties of account debtors and other persons obligated on collateral who are not, themselves, parties to a secured transaction.

3. Governing Law. There was some uncertainty under former Article 9 as to which jurisdiction's law (usually, which jurisdiction's version of Article 9) applied to the matters that this Part addresses. Part 3, Subpart 1, does not determine the law governing these matters because they do not relate to perfection, the effect of perfection or nonperfection, or priority. However, it might be inappropriate for a designation of applicable law by a debtor and secured party under Section 1-301 to control the law applicable to an independent transaction or relationship between the debtor and an account debtor.

Consider an example under Section 9-408.

Example 1: State X has adopted this Article; former Article 9 is the law of State Y. A general intangible (e.g., a franchise agreement) between a debtor-franchisee, D, and an account debtor-franchisor, AD, is governed by the law of State Y. D grants to SP a security interest in its rights under the franchise agreement. The franchise agreement contains a term prohibiting D's assignment of its rights under the agreement. D and SP agree that their secured transaction is governed by the law of State X. Under State X's Section 9-408, the restriction on D's assignment is ineffective to prevent the creation, attachment, or perfection of SP's security interest. State Y's former Section 9-318(4), however, does not address restrictions on the creation of security interests in general intangibles other than general intangibles for money due or to become due. Accordingly, it does not address restrictions on the assignment to SP of D's rights under the franchise agreement. The non-Article-9 law of State Y, which does address restrictions, provides that the prohibition on assignment is effective.

This Article does not provide a specific answer to the question of which State's law applies to the restriction on assignment in the example. However, assuming that under non-UCC choice-of-law principles the effectiveness of the restriction would be governed by the law of State Y, which governs the franchise agreement, the fact that State X's Article 9 governs the secured transaction between SP and D would not override the otherwise applicable law governing the agreement. Of course, to the extent that jurisdictions eventually adopt identical versions of this Article and courts interpret it consistently, the inability to identify the applicable law in circumstances such as those in the example may be inconsequential.

4. Inalienability Under Other Law. Subsection (a) addresses the question whether property necessarily is transferable by virtue of its inclusion (i.e., its eligibility as collateral) within the scope of Article 9. It gives a negative answer, subject to the identified exceptions. The substance of subsection (a) was implicit under former Article 9.

5. Negative Pledge Covenant. Subsection (b) is an exception to the general rule in subsection (a). It makes clear that in secured transactions under this Article the debtor has rights in collateral (whether legal title or equitable) which it can transfer and which its creditors can reach. It is best explained with an example.

Example 2: A debtor, D, grants to SP a security interest to secure a debt in excess of the value of the collateral. D agrees with SP that it will not create a subsequent security interest in the collateral and that any security interest purportedly granted in violation of the agreement will be void. Subsequently, in violation of its agreement with SP, D purports to grant a security interest in the same collateral to another secured party.

Subsection (b) validates D's creation of the subsequent (prohibited) security interest, which might even achieve priority over the earlier security interest. See Comment 7. However, unlike some other provisions of this Part, such as Section 9-406, subsection (b) does not provide that the agreement restricting assignment itself is "ineffective." Consequently, the debtor's breach may create a default.

6. Rights of Lien Creditors. Difficult problems may arise with respect to attachment, levy, and other judicial procedures under which a debtor's creditors may reach collateral subject to a security interest. For example, an obligation may be secured by collateral worth many times the amount of the obligation. If a lien creditor has caused all or a portion of the collateral to be seized under judicial process, it may be difficult to determine the amount of the debtor's "equity" in the collateral that has been seized. The section leaves resolution of this problem to the courts. The doctrine of marshaling may be appropriate.

7. Sale of Receivables. If a debtor sells an account, chattel paper, payment intangible, or promissory note outright, as against the buyer the debtor has no remaining rights to transfer. If, however, the buyer fails to perfect its interest, then solely insofar as the rights of certain third parties are concerned, the debtor is deemed to retain its rights and title. See Section 9-318. The debtor has the power to convey these rights to a subsequent purchaser. If the subsequent purchaser (buyer or secured lender) perfects its interest, it will achieve priority over the earlier, unperfected purchaser. See Section 9-322(a)(1).

8. Use of the Term "Assignment." The term "assignment," as used in this Article, refers to both an outright transfer of ownership and a transfer of an interest to secure an obligation. See Section 9-102, Comment 2.b.1; PEB Commentary No. 21.

§ 9-402. Secured Party Not Obligated on Contract of Debtor or in Tort.

The existence of a security interest, agricultural lien, or authority given to a debtor to dispose of or use collateral, without more, does not subject a secured party to liability in contract or tort for the debtor's acts or omissions.

Definitional Cross References:

Agricultural lien	Section 9-102(a)(5)
Collateral	Section 9-102(a)(12)
Contract	Section 1-201(b)(12)
Debtor	Section 9-102(a)(28)
Secured party	Section 9-102(a)(73)
Security interest	Section 1-201(b)(35)

Official Comment

1. Source. Former Section 9-317.

2. Nonliability of Secured Party. This section, like former Section 9-317, rejects theories on which a secured party might be held liable on a debtor's contracts or in tort merely because a security interest exists or because the debtor is entitled to dispose of or use collateral. This section expands former Section 9-317 to cover agricultural liens.

§ 9-403. Agreement Not to Assert Defenses Against Assignee.

(a) ["Value."] In this section, "value" has the meaning provided in Section 3-303(a).

(b) [Agreement not to assert claim or defense.] Except as otherwise provided in this section, an agreement between an account debtor and an assignor not to assert against an assignee any claim or defense that the account debtor may have against the assignor is enforceable by an assignee that takes an assignment:

(1) for value;

(2) in good faith;

(3) without notice of a claim of a property or possessory right to the property assigned; and

(4) without notice of a defense or claim in recoupment of the type that may be asserted against a person entitled to enforce a negotiable instrument under Section 3-305(a).

(c) [When subsection (b) not applicable.] Subsection (b) does not apply to defenses of a type that may be asserted against a holder in due course of a negotiable instrument under Section 3-305(b).

(d) [Omission of required statement in consumer transaction.] In a consumer transaction, if a record evidences the account debtor's obligation, law other than this article requires that the record include a statement to the effect that the rights of an assignee are subject to claims or defenses that the account debtor could assert against the original obligee, and the record does not include such a statement:

(1) the record has the same effect as if the record included such a statement; and

(2) the account debtor may assert against an assignee those claims and defenses that would have been available if the record included such a statement.

(e) [Rule for individual under other law.] This section is subject to law other than this article which establishes a different rule for an account debtor who is an individual and who incurred the obligation primarily for personal, family, or household purposes.

(f) [Other law not displaced.] Except as otherwise provided in subsection (d), this section does not displace law other than this article which gives effect to an agreement by an account debtor not to assert a claim or defense against an assignee.

Definitional Cross References:

Account debtor	Section 9-102(a)(3)
Agreement	Section 1-201(b)(3)
Assignee	Section 9-102(a)(7A)
Assignor	Section 9-102(a)(7B)
Consumer transaction	Section 9-102(a)(26)
Good faith	Section 1-201(b)(20)
Holder in due course	Section 3-302(a)
Negotiable instrument	Section 3-104(a)
Notice	Section 1-202(a)
Person	Section 1-201(b)(27)
Record	Section 9-102(a)(70)
Right	Section 1-201(b)(34)
Value	Section 3-303(a)

Comment References: 9-109 C15

Official Comment

1. Source. Former Section 9-206.

2. Scope and Purpose. Subsection (b), like former Section 9-206, generally validates an agreement between an account debtor and an assignor that the account debtor will not assert against an assignee claims and defenses that it may have against the assignor. These agreements are typical in installment sale agreements and leases. However, this section expands former Section 9-206 to apply to all account debtors; it is not limited to account debtors that have bought or leased goods. This section applies only to the obligations of an "account debtor," as defined in Section 9-102. Thus, it does not determine the circumstances under which and the extent to which a person who is obligated on a negotiable instrument is disabled from asserting claims and defenses. Rather, Article 3 must be consulted. See, e.g., Sections 3-305, 3-306. Article 3 governs even when the negotiable instrument constitutes part of chattel paper. See Section 9-102 (an obligor on a negotiable instrument constituting part of chattel paper is not an "account debtor").

3. Conditions of Validation; Relationship to Article 3. Subsection (b) validates an account debtor's agreement only if the assignee takes an assignment for value, in good faith, and without notice of conflicting claims to the property assigned or of certain claims or defenses of the account debtor. Like pre-1998 Section 9-206, this section is designed to put the assignee in a position that is no better and no worse than that of a holder in due course of a negotiable instrument under Article 3. However, pre-1998 Section 9-206 left open certain issues, e.g., whether the section incorporated the special Article 3 definition of "value" in Section 3-303 or the generally applicable definition in Article 1 (Section 1-204). Subsection (a) addresses this question; it provides that "value" has the meaning specified in Section 3-303(a). Similarly, subsection (c) provides that subsection (b) does not validate an agreement with respect to defenses that could be asserted against a holder in due course under Section 3-305(b) (the so-called "real" defenses). In 1990, the definition of "holder in due course" (Section 3-302) and the articulation of the rights of a holder in due course (Sections 3-305 and 3-306) were revised substantially. This section tracks more closely the rules of Sections 3-302, 3-305, and 3-306.

4. Relationship to Terms of Assigned Property. Former Section 9-206(2), concerning warranties accompanying the sale of goods, has been deleted as unnecessary. This Article does not regulate the terms of the account, chattel paper, or general intangible that is assigned, except insofar as the account, chattel paper, or general intangible itself creates a security interest (as often is the case with chattel paper). Thus, Article 2, and not this Article, determines whether a seller of goods makes or effectively disclaims warranties, even if the sale is secured. Similarly, other law, and not this Article, determines the effectiveness of an account debtor's undertaking to pay notwithstanding, and not to assert, any defenses or claims against an assignor—e.g., a "hell-or-high-water" provision in the underlying agreement that is assigned. If other law gives effect to this undertaking, then, under principles of nemo dat, the undertaking would be enforceable by the assignee (secured party). If other law prevents the assignor from enforcing the undertaking, this section nevertheless might permit the assignee to do so. The right of the assignee to enforce would depend upon whether, under the particular facts, the account debtor's undertaking fairly could be construed as an agreement that falls within the scope of this section and whether the assignee meets the requirements of this section.

5. Relationship to Federal Trade Commission Rule. Subsection (d) is new. It applies to rights evidenced by a record that is required to contain, but does not contain, the notice set forth in Federal Trade Commission Rule 433, 16 C.F.R. Part 433 (the "Holder-in-Due-Course Regulations"). Under this subsection, an assignee of such a record takes subject to the consumer account debtor's claims and defenses to the same extent as it would have if the writing had contained the required notice. Thus, subsection (d) effectively renders waiver-of-defense clauses ineffective in the transactions with consumers to which it applies.

6. Relationship to Other Law. Like former Section 9-206(1), this section takes no position on the enforceability of waivers of claims and defenses by consumer account debtors, leaving that question to other law. However, the reference to "law other than this article" in subsection (e) encompasses administrative rules and regulations; the reference in former Section 9-206(1) that it replaces ("statute or decision") arguably did not.

This section does not displace other law that gives effect to a non-consumer account debtor's agreement not to assert defenses against an assignee, even if the agreement would not qualify under subsection (b). See subsection (f). It validates, but does not invalidate, agreements made by a non-consumer account debtor. This section also does not displace other law to the extent that the other law permits an assignee, who takes an assignment with notice of a claim of a property or possessory right, a defense, or a claim in recoupment, to enforce an account debtor's agreement not to assert claims and defenses against the assignor (e.g., a "hell-or-high-water" agreement). See Comment 4. It also does not displace an assignee's right to assert that an account debtor is estopped from asserting a claim or defense. Nor does this section displace other law with respect to waivers of potential future claims and defenses that are the subject of an agreement between the account debtor and the assignee. Finally, it does not displace Section 1-107, concerning waiver of a breach that allegedly already has occurred. **[Ed. Note. New Article 1:** Section 1-306.]

§ 9-404. Rights Acquired by Assignee; Claims and Defenses Against Assignee.

(a) [Assignee's rights subject to terms, claims, and defenses; exceptions.] Unless an account debtor has made an enforceable agreement not to assert defenses or claims, and subject to subsections (b) through (e), the rights of an assignee are subject to:

(1) all terms of the agreement between the account debtor and assignor and any defense or claim in recoupment arising from the transaction that gave rise to the contract; and

(2) any other defense or claim of the account debtor against the assignor which accrues before the account debtor receives a notification of the assignment signed by the assignor or the assignee.

(b) [Account debtor's claim reduces amount owed to assignee.] Subject to subsection (c) and except as otherwise provided in subsection (d), the claim of an account debtor against an assignor may be asserted against an assignee under subsection (a) only to reduce the amount the account debtor owes.

(c) [Rule for individual under other law.] This section is subject to law other than this article which establishes a different rule for an account debtor who is an individual and who incurred the obligation primarily for personal, family, or household purposes.

(d) [Omission of required statement in consumer transaction.] In a consumer transaction, if a record evidences the account debtor's obligation, law other than this article requires that the record include a statement to the effect that the account debtor's recovery against an assignee with respect to claims and defenses against the assignor may not exceed amounts paid by the account debtor under the record, and the record does not include such a statement, the extent to which a claim of an account debtor against the assignor may be asserted against an assignee is determined as if the record included such a statement.

(e) [Inapplicability to health-care-insurance receivable.] This section does not apply to an assignment of a health-care-insurance receivable.

Definitional Cross References:

Account debtor	Section 9-102(a)(3)
Agreement	Section 1-201(b)(3)
Assignee	Section 9-102(a)(7A)
Assignor	Section 9-102(a)(7B)
Consumer transaction	Section 9-102(a)(26)
Contract	Section 1-201(b)(12)
Health-care-insurance receivable	Section 9-102(a)(46)
Record	Section 9-102(a)(70)
Right	Section 1-201(b)(34)
Sign	Section 1-201(b)(37)
Term	Section 1-201(b)(40)

Comment References: 9-109 C15

Official Comment

1. Source. Former Section 9-318(1).

2. Purpose; Rights of Assignee in General. Subsection (a), like former Section 9-318(1), provides that an assignee generally takes an assignment subject to defenses and claims of an account debtor. Under subsection (a)(1), if the account debtor's defenses on an assigned claim arise from the transaction that gave rise to the contract with the assignor, it makes no difference whether the defense or claim accrues before or after the account debtor is notified of the assignment. Under subsection (a)(2), the assignee takes subject to other defenses or claims only if they accrue before the account debtor has been notified of the assignment. Of course, an account debtor may waive its right to assert defenses or claims against an assignee under Section 9-403 or other applicable law. Subsection (a) tracks Section 3-305(a)(3) more closely than its predecessor.

3. Limitation on Affirmative Claims. Subsection (b) is new. It limits the claim that the account debtor may assert against an assignee. Borrowing from Section 3-305(a)(3) and cases construing former Section 9-318, subsection (b) generally does not afford the account debtor the right to an affirmative recovery from an assignee.

4. Consumer Account Debtors; Relationship to Federal Trade Commission Rule. Subsections (c) and (d) also are new. Subsection (c) makes clear that the rules of this section are subject to other law establishing special rules for consumer account debtors. An "account debtor who is an individual" as used in subsection (c) includes individuals who are jointly or jointly and severally obligated. Subsection (d) applies to rights evidenced by a record that is required to contain, but does not contain, the notice set forth in Federal Trade Commission Rule 433, 16 C.F.R. Part 433 (the "Holder-in-Due-Course Regulations"). Under subsection (d), a consumer account debtor has the same right to an affirmative recovery from an assignee of such a record as the consumer would have had against the assignee had the record contained the required notice.

5. Scope; Application to "Account Debtor." This section deals only with the rights and duties of "account debtors"—and for the most part only with account debtors on accounts, chattel paper, and payment intangibles. Subsection (e) provides that the obligation of an insurer with respect to a health-care-insurance receivable is governed by other law. References in this section to an "account debtor" include account debtors on collateral that is proceeds. Neither this section nor any other provision of this Article, including Sections 9-408 and 9-409, provides analogous regulation of the rights and duties of other obligors on collateral, such as the maker of a negotiable instrument (governed by Article 3), the issuer of or nominated person under a letter of credit (governed by Article 5), or the issuer of a security (governed by Article 8). Article 9 leaves those rights and duties untouched; however, Section 9-409 deals with the special case of letters of credit. When chattel paper is composed in part of a negotiable instrument, the obligor on the instrument is not an "account debtor," and Article 3 governs the rights of the assignee of the chattel paper with respect to the issues that this section addresses. See, e.g., Section 3-601 (dealing with discharge of an obligation to pay a negotiable instrument).

6. "Signed" Replaces "Authenticated." Consistent with the revised definition of "sign" in Section 1-201, the cognate term "signed" replaces the reference to "authenticated" in the pre-2022 text of this section.

§ 9-405. Modification of Assigned Contract.

(a) [Effect of modification on assignee.] A modification of or substitution for an assigned contract is effective against an assignee if made in good faith. The assignee acquires corresponding rights under the modified or substituted contract. The assignment may provide that the modification or substitution is a breach of contract by the assignor. This subsection is subject to subsections (b) through (d).

(b) [Applicability of subsection (a).] Subsection (a) applies to the extent that:

(1) the right to payment or a part thereof under an assigned contract has not been fully earned by performance; or

(2) the right to payment or a part thereof has been fully earned by performance and the account debtor has not received notification of the assignment under Section 9-406(a).

(c) [Rule for individual under other law.] This section is subject to law other than this article which establishes a different rule for an account debtor who is an individual and who incurred the obligation primarily for personal, family, or household purposes.

(d) [Inapplicability to health-care-insurance receivable.] This section does not apply to an assignment of a health-care-insurance receivable.

Definitional Cross References:

Account debtor	Section 9-102(a)(3)
Contract	Section 1-201(b)(12)
Good faith	Section 1-201(b)(20)
Health-care-insurance receivable	Section 9-102(a)(46)
Right	Section 1-201(b)(34)

Comment References: 9-109 C15

Official Comment

1. Source. Former Section 9-318(2).

2. Modification of Assigned Contract. The ability of account debtors and assignors to modify assigned contracts can be important, especially in the case of government contracts and complex contractual arrangements (e.g., construction contracts) with respect to which modifications are customary. Subsections (a) and (b) provide that good-faith modifications of assigned contracts are binding against an assignee to the extent that (i) the right to payment has not been fully earned or (ii) the right to payment has been earned and notification of the assignment has not been given to the account debtor. Former Section 9-318(2) did not validate modifications of fully-performed contracts under any circumstances, whether or not notification of the assignment had been given to the account debtor. Subsection (a) protects the interests of assignees by (i) limiting the effectiveness of modifications to those made in good faith, (ii) affording the assignee with corresponding rights under the contract as modified, and (iii) recognizing that the modification may be a breach of the assignor's agreement with the assignee.

3. Consumer Account Debtors. Subsection (c) is new. It makes clear that the rules of this section are subject to other law establishing special rules for consumer account debtors.

4. Account Debtors on Health-Care-Insurance Receivables. Subsection (d) also is new. It provides that this section does not apply to an assignment of a heath-care-insurance receivable. The obligation of an insurer with respect to a health-care-insurance receivable is governed by other law.

§ 9-406. Discharge of Account Debtor; Notification of Assignment; Identification and Proof of Assignment; Restrictions on Assignment of Accounts, Chattel Paper, Payment Intangibles, and Promissory Notes Ineffective.

(a) [Discharge of account debtor; effect of notification.] Subject to subsections (b) through (i) and (l), an account debtor on an account, chattel paper, or a payment intangible may discharge its obligation by paying the assignor until, but not after, the account debtor receives a notification, signed by the assignor or the assignee, that the amount due or to become due has been assigned and that payment is to be made to the assignee. After receipt of the notification, the account debtor may discharge its obligation by paying the assignee and may not discharge the obligation by paying the assignor.

(b) [When notification ineffective.] Subject to subsections (h) and (l), notification is ineffective under subsection (a):

(1) if it does not reasonably identify the rights assigned;

(2) to the extent that an agreement between an account debtor and a seller of a payment intangible limits the account debtor's duty to pay a person other than the seller and the limitation is effective under law other than this article; or

(3) at the option of an account debtor, if the notification notifies the account debtor to make less than the full amount of any installment or other periodic payment to the assignee, even if:

(A) only a portion of the account, chattel paper, or payment intangible has been assigned to that assignee;

(B) a portion has been assigned to another assignee; or

(C) the account debtor knows that the assignment to that assignee is limited.

(c) [Proof of assignment.] Subject to subsections (h) and (l), if requested by the account debtor, an assignee shall seasonably furnish reasonable proof that the assignment has been made. Unless the assignee complies, the account debtor may discharge its obligation by paying the assignor, even if the account debtor has received a notification under subsection (a).

(d) [Term restricting assignment generally ineffective.] In this subsection, "promissory note" includes a negotiable instrument that evidences chattel paper. Except as otherwise provided in subsections (e) and (k) and Sections 2A-303 and 9-407, and subject to subsection (h), a term in an agreement between an account debtor and an assignor or in a promissory note is ineffective to the extent that it:

(1) prohibits, restricts, or requires the consent of the account debtor or person obligated on the promissory note to the assignment or transfer of, or the creation, attachment, perfection, or enforcement of a security interest in, the account, chattel paper, payment intangible, or promissory note; or

(2) provides that the assignment or transfer or the creation, attachment, perfection, or enforcement of the security interest may give rise to a default, breach, right of recoupment, claim, defense, termination, right of termination, or remedy under the account, chattel paper, payment intangible, or promissory note.

(e) [Inapplicability of subsection (d) to certain sales.] Subsection (d) does not apply to the sale of a payment intangible or promissory note, other than a sale pursuant to a disposition under Section 9-610 or an acceptance of collateral under Section 9-620.

(f) [Legal restrictions on assignment generally ineffective.] Except as otherwise provided in subsection (k) and Sections 2A-303 and 9-407 and subject to subsections (h) and (i), a rule of law, statute, or regulation that prohibits, restricts, or requires the consent of a government, governmental body or official, or account debtor to the assignment or transfer of, or creation of a security interest in, an account or chattel paper is ineffective to the extent that the rule of law, statute, or regulation:

(1) prohibits, restricts, or requires the consent of the government, governmental body or official, or account debtor to the assignment or transfer of, or the creation, attachment, perfection, or enforcement of a security interest in the account or chattel paper; or

(2) provides that the assignment or transfer or the creation, attachment, perfection, or enforcement of the security interest may give rise to a default, breach, right of recoupment, claim, defense, termination, right of termination, or remedy under the account or chattel paper.

(g) [Subsection (b)(3) not waivable.] Subject to subsections (h) and (l), an account debtor may not waive or vary its option under subsection (b)(3).

(h) [Rule for individual under other law.] This section is subject to law other than this article which establishes a different rule for an account debtor who is an individual and who incurred the obligation primarily for personal, family, or household purposes.

(i) [Inapplicability to health-care-insurance receivable.] This section does not apply to an assignment of a health-care-insurance receivable.

(j) [Section prevails over specified inconsistent law.] This section prevails over any inconsistent provisions of the following statutes, rules, and regulations:

[List here any statutes, rules, and regulations containing provisions inconsistent with this section.]

(k) [Inapplicability to interests in certain entities.] Subsections (d), (f), and (j) do not apply to a security interest in an ownership interest in a general partnership, limited partnership, or limited liability company.

(l) [Inapplicability of certain subsections.] Subsections (a), (b), (c), and (g) do not apply to a controllable account or controllable payment intangible.

Legislative Note: *In 2018, a new subsection (k) was added to Section 9-406. A state that has not previously enacted that subsection should consider doing so in connection with the enactment of the 2022 Amendments.*

States that amend statutes, rules, and regulations to remove provisions inconsistent with this section need not enact subsection (j).

Definitional Cross References:

Account	Section 9-102(a)(2)
Account debtor	Section 9-102(a)(3)
Agreement	Section 1-201(b)(3)
Assignee	Section 9-102(a)(7A)
Assignor	Section 9-102(a)(7B)
Chattel paper	Section 9-102(a)(11)
Collateral	Section 9-102(a)(12)
Controllable account	Section 9-102(a)(27A)
Controllable payment intangible	Section 9-102(a)(27B)
Health-care-insurance receivable	Section 9-102(a)(46)
Negotiable instrument	Section 3-104(a)
Payment intangible	Section 9-102(a)(61)
Person	Section 1-201(b)(27)
Promissory note	Section 9-102(a)(65)
Remedy	Section 1-201(b)(32)
Right	Section 1-201(b)(34)
Sale	Section 2-106(1)
Security interest	Section 1-201(b)(35)
Sign	Section 1-201(b)(37)
State	Section 9-102(a)(77)
Term	Section 1-201(b)(40)

Comment References: 9-109 C15

Official Comment

1. Source. Former Section 9-318(3), (4).

2. Account Debtor's Right to Pay Assignor Until Notification. Subsection (a) provides the general rule concerning an account debtor's right to pay the assignor until the account debtor receives appropriate notification. The revision makes clear that once the account debtor receives the notification, the account debtor cannot discharge its obligation by paying the assignor. It also makes explicit that payment to the assignor before notification, or payment to the assignee after notification, discharges the obligation. No change in meaning from pre-1998 Section 9-318 is intended. Nothing in this section conditions the effectiveness of a notification on the identity of the person who gives it. An account debtor that doubts whether the right to payment has been assigned may avail itself of the procedures in subsection (c). See Comment 4. As to the rights and powers of an assignee generally, see Section 9-102(a)(7A) (defining "assignee"), (7B) (defining "assignor"), and Comment 2.b.1.

An effective notification under subsection (a) must be signed. This requirement normally could be satisfied by sending notification on the notifying person's letterhead or on a form on which the notifying person's name appears. In each case the printed name would be a symbol adopted by the notifying person for the purpose of identifying the person and adopting the notification. See Section 1-201(b)(37) (defining "sign").

Subsection (a) applies only to account debtors on accounts, chattel paper, and payment intangibles. (Section 9-102 defines the term "account debtor" more broadly, to include those obligated on all general intangibles.) Although subsection (a) is more precise than its predecessor, it probably does not change the rule that applied under former Article 9. Former Section 9-318(3) referred to the account debtor's obligation to "pay," indicating that the subsection was limited to account debtors on accounts, chattel paper, and other payment obligations.

3. Limitations on Effectiveness of Notification. Subsection (b) contains some special rules concerning the effectiveness of a notification under subsection (a).

Subsection (b)(1) tracks former Section 9-318(3) by making ineffective a notification that does not reasonably identify the rights assigned. A reasonable identification need not identify the right to payment with specificity, but what is reasonable also is not left to the arbitrary decision of the account debtor. If an account debtor has doubt as to the adequacy of a notification, it may not be safe in disregarding the notification unless it notifies the assignee with reasonable promptness as to the respects in which the account debtor considers the notification defective.

Subsection (b)(2), which is new, applies only to sales of payment intangibles. It makes a notification ineffective to the extent that other law gives effect to an agreement between an account debtor and a seller of a payment intangible that limits the account debtor's duty to pay a person other than the seller. Payment intangibles are substantially less fungible than accounts and chattel paper. In some (e.g., commercial bank loans), account debtors customarily and legitimately expect that they will not be required to pay any person other than the financial institution that has advanced funds.

It has become common in financing transactions to assign interests in a single obligation to more than one assignee. Requiring an account debtor that owes a single obligation to make multiple payments to multiple assignees would be unnecessarily burdensome. Thus, under subsection (b)(3), an account debtor that is notified to pay an assignee less than the full amount of any installment or other periodic payment has the option to treat the notification as ineffective, ignore the notice, and discharge the assigned obligation by paying the assignor. Some account debtors may not realize that the law affords them the right to ignore certain notices of assignment with impunity. By making the notification ineffective at the account debtor's option, subsection (b)(3) permits an account debtor to pay the assignee in accordance with the notice and thereby to satisfy its obligation *pro tanto*. Under subsection (g), the rights and duties created by subsection (b)(3) cannot be waived or varied.

4. Proof of Assignment. Subsection (c) links payment with discharge, as in subsection (a). It follows former Section 9-318(3) in referring to the right of the account debtor to pay the assignor if the requested proof of assignment is not seasonably forthcoming. Even if the proof is not forthcoming, the notification of assignment would remain effective, so that, in the absence of reasonable proof of the assignment, the account debtor could discharge the obligation by paying either the assignee or the assignor. Of course, if the assignee did not in fact receive an assignment, the account debtor cannot discharge its obligation by paying a putative assignee who is a stranger. The observations in Comment 3 concerning the reasonableness of an identification of a right to payment also apply here. An account debtor that questions the adequacy of proof submitted by an assignee would be well advised to promptly inform the assignee of the defects.

An account debtor may face another problem if its obligation becomes due while the account debtor is awaiting reasonable proof of the assignment that it has requested from the assignee. This section does not excuse the account debtor from timely compliance with its obligations. Consequently, an account debtor that has received a notification of assignment and who has requested reasonable proof of the assignment may discharge its obligation by paying the assignor at the time (or even earlier if reasonably necessary to avoid risk of default) when a payment is due, even if the account debtor has not yet received a response to its request for proof. On the other hand, after requesting reasonable proof of the assignment, an account debtor may not discharge its obligation by paying the assignor substantially in advance of the time that the payment is due unless the assignee has failed to provide the proof seasonably.

5. Contractual Restrictions on Assignment. Pre-1998 Section 9-318(4) rendered ineffective an agreement between an account debtor and an assignor which prohibited assignment of an account (whether outright or to secure an obligation) or prohibited a security assignment of a general intangible for the payment of money due or to become due. Subsection (d) essentially follows pre-1998 Section 9-318(4), but expands the rule of free assignability to chattel paper (subject to Sections 2A-303 and 9-407) and promissory notes and explicitly overrides both restrictions and prohibitions of assignment. The policies underlying the ineffectiveness of contractual restrictions under this section build on common-law developments that essentially have eliminated legal restrictions on assignments of rights to payment as security and other assignments of rights to payment such as accounts and chattel paper. Any that might linger for accounts and chattel paper are addressed by subsection (f). See Comment 6.

The first sentence of subsection (d) ensures that the subsection applies to a negotiable instrument that would be a promissory note but for (i) the exclusion of writings that evidence chattel paper from the definition of "instrument" (Section 9-102(a)(47), as revised in 2022) and (ii) the definition of "promissory note" (Section 9-102(a)(65)) as a subset of "instrument." That sentence also ensures that subsection (d) applies to an obligor on such a negotiable instrument, even though the obligor is not an "account debtor" (Section 9-102(a)(3)). The sentence restores the scope of subsection (d) to apply to all obligations and obligors on chattel paper, as was the case prior to the revision of the definition of "instrument".

Former Section 9-318(4) did not apply to a sale of a payment intangible (as described in the former provision, "a general intangible for money due or to become due") but did apply to an assignment of a payment intangible for security. Subsection (e) continues this approach and also makes subsection (d) inapplicable to sales of promissory notes. Section 9-408 addresses anti-assignment clauses with respect to sales of payment intangibles and promissory notes.

Like former Section 9-318(4), subsection (d) provides that anti-assignment clauses are "ineffective." The quoted term means that the clause is of no effect whatsoever; the clause does not prevent the assignment from taking effect between the parties and the prohibited assignment does not constitute a default under the agreement between the account debtor and assignor. However, subsection (d) does not override terms that do not directly prohibit, restrict, or require consent to an assignment but which might, nonetheless, present a practical impairment of the assignment. Properly read, however, subsection (d) reaches only covenants that prohibit, restrict, or require consents to assignments; it does not override all terms that might "impair" an assignment in fact.

Example: Buyer enters into an agreement with Seller to buy equipment that Seller is to manufacture according to Buyer's specifications. Buyer agrees to make a series of prepayments during the construction process. In return, Seller agrees to set aside the prepaid funds in a special account and to use the funds solely for the manufacture of the designated equipment. Seller also agrees that it will not assign any of its rights under the sale agreement with Buyer. Nevertheless, Seller grants to Secured Party a security interest in its accounts. Seller's anti-assignment agreement is ineffective under subsection (d); its agreement concerning the use of prepaid funds, which is not a restriction or prohibition on assignment, is not. However, if Secured Party notifies Buyer to make all future payments directly to Secured Party, Buyer will be obliged to do so under subsection (a) if it wishes the payments to discharge its obligation. Unless Secured Party releases the funds to Seller so that Seller can comply with its use-of-funds covenant, Seller will be in breach of that covenant.

In the example, there appears to be a plausible business purpose for the use-of-funds covenant. However, a court may conclude that a covenant with no business purpose other than imposing an impediment to an assignment actually is a direct restriction that is rendered ineffective by subsection (d).

6. Legal Restrictions on Assignment. Former Section 9-318(4), like subsection (d) of this section, addressed only contractual restrictions on assignment. The former section was grounded on the reality that legal, as opposed to contractual, restrictions on assignments of rights to payment had largely disappeared. New subsection (f) codifies this principle of free assignability for accounts and chattel paper. For the most part the discussion of contractual restrictions in Comment 5 applies as well to legal restrictions rendered ineffective under subsection (f).

7. Multiple Assignments. This section, like former Section 9-318, is not a complete codification of the law of assignments of rights to payment. In particular, it is silent concerning many of the ramifications for an account debtor in cases of multiple assignments of the same right. For example, an assignor might assign the same receivable to multiple assignees (which assignments could be either inadvertent or wrongful). Or, the assignor could assign the receivable to assignee-1, which then might reassign it to assignee-2, and so forth. The rights and duties of an account debtor in the face of multiple assignments and in other circumstances not resolved in the statutory text are left to the common-law rules. See, e.g., Restatement (2d), Contracts §§ 338(3), 339. The failure of former Article 9 to codify these rules does not appear to have caused problems.

8. Consumer Account Debtors. Subsection (h) is new. It makes clear that the rules of this section are subject to other law establishing special rules for consumer account debtors.

9. Account Debtors on Health-Care-Insurance Receivables. Subsection (i) also is new. The obligation of an insurer with respect to a health-care-insurance receivable is governed by other law. Section 9-408 addresses contractual and legal restrictions on the assignment of a health-care-insurance receivable.

10. Inapplicability to Certain Ownership Interests. Subsection (k) provides that subsections (d), (f), and (j) do not apply to a security interest in an ownership interest in a limited liability company, limited partnership, or general partnership, regardless of the name of the interest and whether the interest: (i) pertains to economic rights, governance rights, or both; (ii) arises under: (a) an operating agreement, the applicable limited liability company act, or both; or (b) a partnership agreement, the applicable partnership act, or both; or (iii) is owned by: (a) a member of a company or transferee or assignee of a member; or (b) a partner or a transferee or assignee of a partner; or (iv) comprises contractual, property, other rights, or some combination thereof. Ownership interests referred to in subsection (k) include interests in a series of a limited liability company, limited partnership, or general partnership, if the series is a "person" (Section 1-201(b)(27)).

11. Controllable Accounts and Controllable payment intangibles. For controllable accounts and controllable payment intangibles, subsection (l) recognizes that subsections (a), (b), (c) and (g) are replaced by analogous provisions in Section 12-106.

12. "Signed" Replaces "Authenticated." Consistent with the revised definition of "sign" in Section 1-201, the cognate term "signed" replaces the reference to "authenticated" in the pre-2022 text of this section.

§ 9-407. Restrictions on Creation or Enforcement of Security Interest in Leasehold Interest or in Lessor's Residual Interest.

(a) [Term restricting assignment generally ineffective.] Except as otherwise provided in subsection (b), a term in a lease agreement is ineffective to the extent that it:

(1) prohibits, restricts, or requires the consent of a party to the lease to the assignment or transfer of, or the creation, attachment, perfection, or enforcement of a security interest in an interest of a party under the lease contract or in the lessor's residual interest in the goods; or

(2) provides that the assignment or transfer or the creation, attachment, perfection, or enforcement of the security interest may give rise to a default, breach, right of recoupment, claim, defense, termination, right of termination, or remedy under the lease.

(b) [Effectiveness of certain terms.] Except as other-wise provided in Section 2A-303(7), a term described in subsection (a)(2) is effective to the extent that there is:

(1) a transfer by the lessee of the lessee's right of possession or use of the goods in violation of the term; or

(2) a delegation of a material performance of either party to the lease contract in violation of the term.

(c) [Security interest not material impairment.] The creation, attachment, perfection, or enforcement of a security interest in the lessor's interest under the lease contract or the lessor's residual interest in the goods is not a transfer that materially impairs the lessee's prospect of obtaining return performance or materially changes the duty of or materially increases the burden or risk imposed on the lessee within the purview of Section 2A-303(4) unless, and then only to the extent that, enforcement actually results in a delegation of material performance of the lessor.

Definitional Cross References:

Goods	Section 9-102(a)(44)
Lease	Section 2A-103(1)(j)
Lease agreement	Section 2A-103(1)(k)
Lease contract	Section 2A-103(1)(l)
Leasehold interest	Section 2A-103(1)(m)
Lessee	Section 2A-103(1)(n)
Lessor	Section 2A-103(1)(p)
Lessor's residual interest	Section 2A-103(1)(q)
Party	Section 1-201(b)(26)
Remedy	Section 1-201(b)(32)
Security interest	Section 1-201(b)(35)
Term	Section 1-201(b)(40)

Official Comment

1. Source. Section 2A-303.

2. Restrictions on Assignment Generally Ineffective. Under subsection (a), as under former Section 2A-303(3), a term in a lease agreement which prohibits or restricts the creation of a security interest generally is ineffective. This reflects the general policy of Section 9-406(d) and former Section 9-318(4). This section has been conformed in several respects to analogous provisions in Sections 9-406, 9-408, and 9-409, including the substitution of "ineffective" for "not enforceable" and the substitution of "assignment or transfer of, or the creation, attachment, perfection, or enforcement of a security interest" for "creation or enforcement of a security interest."

3. Exceptions for Certain Transfers and Delegations. Subsection (b) provides exceptions to the general ineffectiveness of restrictions under subsection (a). A term that otherwise is ineffective under subsection (a)(2) is effective to the extent that a lessee transfers its right to possession and use of goods or if either party delegates material performance of the lease contract in violation of the term. However, under subsection (c), as under former Section 2A-303(3), a lessor's creation of a security interest in its interest in a lease contract or its residual interest in the leased goods is not a material impairment under Section 2A-303(4) (former Section 2A-303(5)), absent an actual delegation of the lessor's material performance. The terms of the lease contract determine whether the lessor, in fact, has any remaining obligations to perform. If it does, it is then necessary to determine whether there has been an actual delegation of "material performance." See Section 2A-303, Comments 3 and 4.

§ 9-408. Restrictions on Assignment of Promissory Notes, Health-Care-Insurance Receivables, and Certain General Intangibles Ineffective.

(a) [Term restricting assignment generally ineffective.] Except as otherwise provided in subsections (b) and (f), a term in a promissory note or in an agreement between an account debtor and a debtor which relates to a health-care-insurance receivable or a general intangible, including a contract, permit, license, or franchise, and which term prohibits, restricts, or requires the consent of the person obligated on the promissory note or the account debtor to, the assignment or transfer of, or creation, attachment, or perfection of a security interest in, the promissory note, health-care-insurance receivable, or general intangible, is ineffective to the extent that the term:

(1) would impair the creation, attachment, or perfection of a security interest; or

(2) provides that the assignment or the transfer or the creation, attachment, or perfection of the security interest may give rise to a default, breach, right of recoupment, claim, defense, termination, right of termination, or remedy under the promissory note, health-care-insurance receivable, or general intangible.

(b) [Applicability of subsection (a) to sales of certain rights to payment.] Subsection (a) applies to a security interest in a payment intangible or promissory note only if the security interest arises out of a sale of the payment intangible or promissory note, other than a sale pursuant to a disposition under Section 9-610 or an acceptance of collateral under Section 9-620.

(c) [Legal restrictions on assignment generally ineffective.] Except as otherwise provided in subsection (f), a rule of law, statute, or regulation that prohibits, restricts, or requires the consent of a government, governmental body or official, person obligated on a promissory note, or account debtor to the assignment or transfer of, or creation of a security interest in, a promissory note, health-care-insurance receivable, or general intangible, including a contract, permit, license, or franchise between an account debtor and a debtor, is ineffective to the extent that the rule of law, statute, or regulation:

(1) would impair the creation, attachment, or perfection of a security interest; or

(2) provides that the assignment or the transfer or the creation, attachment, or perfection of the security interest may give rise to a default, breach, right of recoupment, claim, defense, termination, right of termination, or remedy under the promissory note, health-care-insurance receivable, or general intangible.

(d) [Limitation on ineffectiveness under subsections (a) and (c).] To the extent that a term in a promissory note or in an agreement between an account debtor and a debtor which relates to a health-care-insurance receivable or general intangible or a rule of law, statute, or regulation described in subsection (c) would be effective under law other than this article but is ineffective under subsection (a) or (c), the creation, attachment, or perfection of a security interest in the promissory note, health-care-insurance receivable, or general intangible:

(1) is not enforceable against the person obligated on the promissory note or the account debtor;

(2) does not impose a duty or obligation on the person obligated on the promissory note or the account debtor;

(3) does not require the person obligated on the promissory note or the account debtor to recognize the security interest, pay or render performance to the secured party, or accept payment or performance from the secured party;

(4) does not entitle the secured party to use or assign the debtor's rights under the promissory note, health-care-insurance receivable, or general intangible, including any related information or materials furnished to the debtor in the transaction giving rise to the promissory note, health-care-insurance receivable, or general intangible;

(5) does not entitle the secured party to use, assign, possess, or have access to any trade secrets or confidential information of the person obligated on the promissory note or the account debtor; and

(6) does not entitle the secured party to enforce the security interest in the promissory note, health-care-insurance receivable, or general intangible.

(e) [Section prevails over specified inconsistent law.] This section prevails over any inconsistent provisions of the following statutes, rules, and regulations:

[List here any statutes, rules, and regulations containing provisions inconsistent with this section.]

(f) [Inapplicability to interests in certain entities.] This section does not apply to a security interest in an ownership interest in a general partnership, limited partnership, or limited liability company.

(g) ["Promissory note."] In this section, "promissory note" includes a negotiable instrument that evidences chattel paper.

Legislative Note: *States that amend statutes, rules, and regulations to remove provisions inconsistent with this section need not enact subsection (e).*

In 2018, a new subsection (f) was added to Section 9-408. A state that has not previously enacted that subsection should consider doing so in connection with the enactment of the 2022 Amendments.

Definitional Cross References:

Account debtor	Section 9-102(a)(3)
Agreement	Section 1-201(b)(3)
Chattel paper	Section 9-102(a)(11)
Contract	Section 1-201(b)(12)
Collateral	Section 9-102(a)(12)
Debtor	Section 9-102(a)(28)
General intangible	Section 9-102(a)(42)
Health-care-insurance receivable	Section 9-102(a)(46)
Negotiable instrument	Section 3-104(a)
Payment intangible	Section 9-102(a)(61)
Person	Section 1-201(b)(27)
Promissory note	Section 9-102(a)(65)
Remedy	Section 1-201(b)(32)
Right	Section 1-201(b)(34)
Sale	Section 2-106(1)
Secured party	Section 9-102(a)(73)
Security interest	Section 1-201(b)(35)
State	Section 9-102(a)(77)
Term	Section 1-201(b)(40)

Official Comment

1. Source. New.

2. Free Assignability. This section makes ineffective any attempt to restrict the assignment of a general intangible, health-care-insurance receivable, or promissory note, whether the restriction appears in the terms of a promissory note or the agreement between an account debtor and a debtor (subsection (a)) or in a rule of law, including a statute or governmental rule or regulation (subsection (c)). This result allows the creation, attachment, and perfection of a security interest in a general intangible, such as an agreement for the nonexclusive license of software, as well as sales of certain receivables, such as a health-care-insurance receivable (which is an "account"), payment intangible, or promissory note, without giving rise to a default or breach by the assignor or from triggering a remedy of the account debtor or person obligated on a promissory note. This enhances the ability of certain debtors to obtain credit. On the other hand, subsection (d) protects the other party—the "account debtor" on a general intangible or the person obligated on a promissory note—from adverse effects arising from the security interest. It leaves the account debtor's or obligated person's rights and obligations unaffected in all material respects if a restriction rendered ineffective by subsection (a) or (c) would be effective under law other than Article 9.

Example 1: A term of an agreement for the nonexclusive license of computer software prohibits the licensee from assigning any of its rights as licensee with respect to the software. The agreement also provides that an attempt to assign rights in violation of the restriction is a default entitling the licensor to terminate the license agreement. The licensee, as debtor, grants to a secured party a security interest in its rights under the license and in the computers in which it is installed. Under this section, the term prohibiting assignment and providing for a default upon an attempted assignment is ineffective to prevent the creation, attachment, or perfection of the security interest or entitle the licensor to terminate the license agreement. However, under subsection (d), the secured party (absent the licensor's agreement) is not entitled to enforce the license or to use, assign, or otherwise enjoy the benefits of the licensed software, and the licensor need not recognize (or pay any attention to) the secured party. Even if the secured party takes possession of the computers on the debtor's default, the debtor would remain free to remove the software from the computer, load it on another computer, and continue to use it, if the license so permits. If the debtor does not remove the software, other law may require the secured party to remove it before disposing of the computer. Disposition of the software with the computer could violate an effective prohibition on enforcement of the security interest. See subsection (d).

3. Nature of Debtor's Interest. Neither this section nor any other provision of this Article determines whether a debtor has a property interest. The definition of the term "security interest" provides that it is an "interest in personal property." See Section 1-201(b)(35). Ordinarily, a debtor can create a security interest in collateral only if it has "rights in the collateral."

See Section 9-203(b). Other law determines whether a debtor has a property interest ("rights in the collateral") and the nature of that interest. For example, the nonexclusive license addressed in Example 1 may not create any property interest whatsoever in the intellectual property (e.g., copyright) that underlies the license and that effectively enables the licensor to grant the license. The debtor's property interest may be confined solely to its interest in the promises made by the licensor in the license agreement (e.g., a promise not to sue the debtor for its use of the software).

4. Scope: Sales of Payment Intangibles and Other General Intangibles; Assignments Unaffected by This Section. Subsections (a) and (c) render ineffective restrictions on assignments only "to the extent" that the assignments restrict the "creation, attachment, or perfection of a security interest," including sales of payment intangibles and promissory notes. This section does not render ineffective a restriction on an assignment that does not create a security interest. For example, if the debtor in Comment 2, Example 1 purported to assign the license to another entity that would use the computer software itself, other law would govern the effectiveness of the anti-assignment provisions.

Subsection (a) applies to a security interest in payment intangibles only if the security interest arises out of sale of the payment intangibles. Contractual restrictions directed to security interests in payment intangibles which secure an obligation are subject to Section 9-406(d). Subsection (a) also deals with sales of promissory notes which also create security interests. See Section 9-109(a). Subsection (c) deals with all security interests in payment intangibles or promissory notes, whether or not arising out of a sale.

Subsection (a) does not render ineffective any term, and subsection (c) does not render ineffective any law, statute or regulation, that restricts outright sales of general intangibles other than payment intangibles. They deal only with restrictions on security interests. The only sales of general intangibles that create security interests are sales of payment intangibles.

5. Terminology: "Account Debtor"; "Person Obligated on a Promissory Note." This section uses the term "account debtor" as it is defined in Section 9-102. The term refers to the party, other than the debtor, to a general intangible, including a permit, license, franchise, or the like, and the person obligated on a health-care-insurance receivable, which is a type of account. The definition of "account debtor" does not limit the term to persons who are obligated to pay under a general intangible. Rather, the term includes all persons who are obligated on a general intangible, including those who are obligated to render performance in exchange for payment. In some cases, e.g., the creation of a security interest in a franchisee's rights under a franchise agreement, the principal payment obligation may be owed by the debtor (franchisee) to the account debtor (franchisor). This section also refers to a "person obligated on a promissory note," inasmuch as those persons do not fall within the definition of "account debtor."

> **Example 2:** A licensor and licensee enter into an agreement for the nonexclusive license of computer software. The licensee's interest in the license agreement is a general intangible. If the licensee grants to a secured party a security interest in its rights under the license agreement, the licensee is the debtor and the licensor is the account debtor. On the other hand, if the licensor grants to a secured party a security interest in its right to payment (an account) under the license agreement, the licensor is the debtor and the licensee is the account debtor. (This section applies to the security interest in the general intangible but not to the security interest in the account, which is not a health-care-insurance receivable.)

6. Effects on Account Debtors and Persons Obligated on Promissory Notes. Subsections (a) and (c) affect two classes of persons. These subsections affect account debtors on general intangibles and health-care-insurance receivables and persons obligated on promissory notes. Subsection (c) also affects governmental entities that enact or determine rules of law. *However, subsection (d) ensures that these affected persons are not affected adversely.* That provision removes any burdens or adverse effects on these persons for which any rational basis could exist to restrict the effectiveness of an assignment or to exercise any remedies. For this reason, the effects of subsections (a) and (c) are immaterial insofar as those persons are concerned.

Subsection (a) does not override terms that do not directly prohibit, restrict, or require consent to an assignment but which might, nonetheless, present a practical impairment of the assignment. Properly read, however, this section, like Section 9-406(d), reaches only covenants that prohibit, restrict, or require consents to assignments; it does not override all terms that might "impair" an assignment in fact.

> **Example 3:** A licensor and licensee enter into an agreement for the nonexclusive license of valuable business software. The license agreement includes terms (i) prohibiting the licensee from assigning its rights under the license, (ii) prohibiting the licensee from disclosing to anyone certain information relating to the software and the licensor, and (iii) deeming prohibited assignments and prohibited disclosures to be defaults. The licensee wishes to obtain financing and, in exchange, is willing to grant a security interest in its rights under the license agreement. The secured party, reasonably, refuses to extend credit unless the licensee discloses the information that

it is prohibited from disclosing under the license agreement. The secured party cannot determine the value of the proposed collateral in the absence of this information. Under this section, the terms of the license prohibiting the assignment (grant of the security interest) and making the assignment a default are ineffective. However, the nondisclosure covenant is not a term that prohibits the assignment or creation of a security interest in the license. Consequently, the nondisclosure term is enforceable even though the practical effect is to restrict the licensee's ability to use its rights under the license agreement as collateral.

The nondisclosure term also would be effective in the factual setting of Comment 2, Example 1. If the secured party's possession of the computers loaded with software would put it in a position to discover confidential information that the debtor was prohibited from disclosing, the licensor should be entitled to enforce its rights against the secured party. Moreover, the licensor could have required the debtor to obtain the secured party's agreement that (i) it would immediately return all copies of software loaded on the computers and that (ii) it would not examine or otherwise acquire any information contained in the software. This section does not prevent an account debtor from protecting by agreement its independent interests that are unrelated to the "creation, attachment, or perfection" of a security interest. In Example 1, moreover, the secured party is not in possession of copies of software by virtue of its security interest or in connection with enforcing its security interest in the debtor's license of the software. Its possession is incidental to its possession of the computers, in which it has a security interest. Enforcing against the secured party a restriction relating to the software in no way interferes with its security interest in the computers.

7. Effect in Assignor's Bankruptcy. This section could have a substantial effect if the assignor enters bankruptcy. Roughly speaking, Bankruptcy Code Section 552 invalidates security interests in property acquired after a bankruptcy petition is filed, except to the extent that the postpetition property constitutes proceeds of prepetition collateral.

Example 4: A debtor is the owner of a cable television franchise that, under applicable law, cannot be assigned without the consent of the municipal franchisor. A lender wishes to extend credit to the debtor, provided that the credit is secured by the debtor's "going business" value. To secure the loan, the debtor grants a security interest in all its existing and after-acquired property. The franchise represents the principal value of the business. The municipality refuses to consent to any assignment for collateral purposes. If other law were given effect, the security interest in the franchise would not attach; and if the debtor were to enter bankruptcy and sell the business, the secured party would receive but a fraction of the business's value. Under this section, however, the security interest would attach to the franchise. As a result, the security interest would attach to the proceeds of any sale of the franchise while a bankruptcy is pending. However, this section would protect the interests of the municipality by preventing the secured party from enforcing its security interest to the detriment of the municipality.

8. Effect Outside of Bankruptcy. The principal effects of this section will take place outside of bankruptcy. Compared to the relatively few debtors that enter bankruptcy, there are many more that do not. By making available previously unavailable property as collateral, this section should enable debtors to obtain additional credit. For purposes of determining whether to extend credit, under some circumstances a secured party may ascribe value to the collateral to which its security interest has attached, even if this section precludes the secured party from enforcing the security interest without the agreement of the account debtor or person obligated on the promissory note. This may be the case where the secured party sees a likelihood of obtaining that agreement in the future. This may also be the case where the secured party anticipates that the collateral will give rise to a type of proceeds as to which this section would not apply.

Example 5: Under the facts of Example 4, the debtor does not enter bankruptcy. Perhaps in exchange for a fee, the municipality agrees that the debtor may transfer the franchise to a buyer. As consideration for the transfer, the debtor receives from the buyer its check for part of the purchase price and its promissory note for the balance. The security interest attaches to the check and promissory note as proceeds. See Section 9-315(a)(2). This section does not apply to the security interest in the check, which is not a promissory note, health-care-insurance receivable, or general intangible. Nor does it apply to the security interest in the promissory note, inasmuch as it was not sold to the secured party.

9. Contrary Federal Law. This section does not override federal law to the contrary. However, it does reflect an important policy judgment that should provide a template for future federal law reforms.

10. Inapplicability to Certain Ownership Interests. This section does not apply to an ownership interest in a limited liability company, limited partnership, or general partnership, regardless of the name of the interest and whether the interest: (i) pertains to economic rights, governance rights, or both; (ii) arises under: (a) an operating agreement, the applicable limited liability company act, or both; or (b) a partnership agreement, the applicable partnership act, or both; or (iii) is owned by: (a) a member of a company or transferee or assignee of a member; or (b) a partner or a transferee or assignee of a partner; or (iv) comprises contractual, property, other rights, or some combination thereof.

11. Subsection (g) ensures that this section applies to a negotiable instrument that would be a promissory note but for (i) the exclusion of writings that evidence chattel paper from the definition of "instrument" (Section 9-102(a)(47), as revised in 2022) and (ii) the definition of "promissory note" (Section 9-102(a)(65)) as a subset of "instrument." See Section 9-406, Comment 5.

§ 9-409. Restrictions on Assignment of Letter-of-Credit Rights Ineffective.

(a) [Term or law restricting assignment generally ineffective.] A term in a letter of credit or a rule of law, statute, regulation, custom, or practice applicable to the letter of credit which prohibits, restricts, or requires the consent of an applicant, issuer, or nominated person to a beneficiary's assignment of or creation of a security interest in a letter-of-credit right is ineffective to the extent that the term or rule of law, statute, regulation, custom, or practice:

(1) would impair the creation, attachment, or perfection of a security interest in the letter-of-credit right; or

(2) provides that the assignment or the creation, attachment, or perfection of the security interest may give rise to a default, breach, right of recoupment, claim, defense, termination, right of termination, or remedy under the letter-of-credit right.

(b) [Limitation on ineffectiveness under subsection (a).] To the extent that a term in a letter of credit is ineffective under subsection (a) but would be effective under law other than this article or a custom or practice applicable to the letter of credit, to the transfer of a right to draw or otherwise demand performance under the letter of credit, or to the assignment of a right to proceeds of the letter of credit, the creation, attachment, or perfection of a security interest in the letter-of-credit right:

(1) is not enforceable against the applicant, issuer, nominated person, or transferee beneficiary;

(2) imposes no duties or obligations on the applicant, issuer, nominated person, or transferee beneficiary; and

(3) does not require the applicant, issuer, nominated person, or transferee beneficiary to recognize the security interest, pay or render performance to the secured party, or accept payment or other performance from the secured party.

Definitional Cross References:

Applicant	Section 5-102(a)(2)
Beneficiary	Section 5-102(a)(3)
Issuer (letter of credit/ letter-of-credit right)	Section 5-102(a)(9)
Letter of credit	Section 5-102(a)(10)
Letter-of-credit right	Section 9-102(a)(51)
Nominated person	Section 5-102(a)(11)
Proceeds	Section 9-102(a)(64)
Remedy	Section 1-201(b)(32)
Secured party	Section 9-102(a)(73)
Security interest	Section 1-201(b)(35)
Term	Section 1-201(b)(40)

Official Comment

1. Source. New.

2. Purpose and Relevance. This section, patterned on Section 9-408, limits the effectiveness of attempts to restrict the creation, attachment, or perfection of a security interest in letter-of-credit rights, whether the restriction appears in the letter of credit or a rule of law, custom, or practice applicable to the letter of credit. It protects the creation, attachment, and perfection of a security interest while preventing these events from giving rise to a default or breach by the assignor or from triggering a remedy or defense of the issuer or other person obligated on a letter of credit. Letter-of-credit rights are a type of supporting obligation. See Section 9-102. Under Sections 9-203 and 9-308, a security interest in a supporting obligation attaches and is perfected automatically if the security interest in the supported obligation attaches and is perfected. See Section 9-107, Comment 5. The automatic attachment and perfection under Article 9 would be anomalous or misleading if, under other law (e.g., Article 5), a restriction on transfer or assignment were effective to block attachment and perfection.

3. Relationship to Letter-of-Credit Law. Although restrictions on an assignment of a letter of credit are ineffective to prevent creation, attachment, and perfection of a security interest, subsection (b) protects the issuer and other parties from any adverse effects of the security interest by preserving letter-of-credit law and practice that limits the right of a beneficiary to transfer its right to draw or otherwise demand performance

(Section 5-112) and limits the obligation of an issuer or nominated person to recognize a beneficiary's assignment of letter-of-credit proceeds (Section 5-114). Thus, this section's treatment of letter-of-credit rights differs from this Article's treatment of instruments and investment property. Moreover, under Section 9-109(c)(4), this Article does not apply to the extent that the rights of a transferee beneficiary or nominated person are independent and superior under Section 5-114, thereby preserving the "independence principle" of letter-of-credit law.

PART 5. FILING

[Subpart 1. Filing Office; Contents and Effectiveness of Financing Statement]

§ 9-501. Filing Office.

(a) Except as otherwise provided in subsection (b), if the local law of this State governs perfection of a security interest or agricultural lien, the office in which to file a financing statement to perfect the security interest or agricultural lien is:

(1) the office designated for the filing or recording of a record of a mortgage on the related real property, if:

(A) the collateral is as-extracted collateral or timber to be cut; or

(B) the financing statement is filed as a fixture filing and the collateral is goods that are or are to become fixtures; or

(2) the office of [] [or any office duly authorized by []], in all other cases, including a case in which the collateral is goods that are or are to become fixtures and the financing statement is not filed as a fixture filing.

(b) The office in which to file a financing statement to perfect a security interest in collateral, including fixtures, of a transmitting utility is the office of []. The financing statement also constitutes a fixture filing as to the collateral indicated in the financing statement which is or to become fixtures.

Legislative Note: *The State should designate the filing office where the brackets appear. The filing office may be that of a governmental official (e.g., the Secretary of State) or a private party that maintains the State's filing system.*

Definitional Cross References:

Agricultural lien	Section 9-102(a)(5)
As-extracted collateral	Section 9-102(a)(6)
Collateral	Section 9-102(a)(12)
Filing office	Section 9-102(a)(37)
Financing statement	Section 9-102(a)(39)
Fixture filing	Section 9-102(a)(40)
Fixtures	Section 9-102(a)(41)
Goods	Section 9-102(a)(44)
Mortgage	Section 9-102(a)(55)
Party	Section 1-201(b)(26)
Record	Section 9-102(a)(70)
Security interest	Section 1-201(b)(35)
State	Section 9-102(a)(77)
Transmitting utility	Section 9-102(a)(81)

Official Comment

1. Source. Derived from former Section 9-401.

2. Where to File. Subsection (a) indicates where in a given State a financing statement is to be filed. Former Article 9 afforded each State three alternative approaches, depending on the extent to which the State desires central filing (usually with the Secretary of State), local filing (usually with a county office), or both. As Comment 1 to former Section 9-401 observed, "The principal advantage of state-wide filing is ease of access to the credit information which the files exist to provide. Consider for example the national distributor who wishes to have current information about the credit standing of the thousands of persons he sells to on credit. The more completely the files are centralized on a state-wide basis, the easier and cheaper it becomes to procure credit information; the more the files are scattered in local filing units, the more burdensome and costly." Local filing increases the net costs of secured transactions also by increasing uncertainty and the number of required filings. Any benefit that local filing may have had in the 1950's is now insubstantial. Accordingly, this Article dictates central filing for most situations, while retaining local filing for real-estate-related collateral and special filing provisions for transmitting utilities.

3. Minerals and Timber. Under subsection (a)(1), a filing in the office where a record of a mortgage on the related real property would be filed will perfect a security interest in as-extracted collateral. Inasmuch as the security interest does not attach until extraction, the filing continues to be effective after extraction. A different result occurs with respect to timber to be cut, however. Unlike as-extracted collateral, standing timber may be goods before it is cut. See Section 9-102 (defining "goods"). Once cut, however, it is no longer timber to be cut, and the filing in the real-property-mortgage office ceases to be effective. The timber then becomes ordinary goods, and filing in the office specified in subsection (a)(2) is necessary for perfection. Note also that after the timber is cut the law of the debtor's location, not the location of the timber, governs perfection under Section 9-301.

4. Fixtures. There are two ways in which a secured party may file a financing statement to perfect a security interest in goods that are or are to become fixtures. It may file in the Article 9 records, as with most other goods. See subsection (a)(2). Or it may file the financing statement as a "fixture filing," defined in Section 9-102, in the office in which a record of a mortgage on the related real property would be filed. See subsection (a)(1)(B).

5. Transmitting Utilities. The usual filing rules do not apply well for a transmitting utility (defined in Section 9-102). Many pre-UCC statutes provided special filing rules for railroads and in some cases for other public utilities, to avoid the requirements for filing with legal descriptions in every county in which such debtors had property. Former Section 9-401(5) recreated and broadened these provisions, and subsection (b) follows this approach. The nature of the debtor will inform persons searching the record as to where to make a search.

A given State's subsection (b) applies only if the local law of that State governs perfection. As to most collateral, perfection by filing is governed by the law of the jurisdiction in which the debtor is located. See Section 9-301(1). However, the law of the jurisdiction in which goods that are or become fixtures are located governs perfection by filing a fixture filing. See Section 9-301(3)(A). As a consequence, filing in the filing office of more than one State may be necessary to perfect a security interest in fixtures collateral of a transmitting utility by filing a fixture filing. See Section 9-301, Comment 5.b.

§ 9-502. Contents of Financing Statement; Record of Mortgage as Financing Statement; Time of Filing Financing Statement.

(a) [Sufficiency of financing statement.] Subject to subsection (b), a financing statement is sufficient only if it:

(1) provides the name of the debtor;

(2) provides the name of the secured party or a representative of the secured party; and

(3) indicates the collateral covered by the financing statement.

(b) [Real-property-related financing statements.] Except as otherwise provided in Section 9-501(b), to be sufficient, a financing statement that covers as-extracted collateral or timber to be cut, or which is filed as a fixture filing and covers goods that are or are to become fixtures, must satisfy subsection (a) and also:

(1) indicate that it covers this type of collateral;

(2) indicate that it is to be filed [for record] in the real property records;

(3) provide a description of the real property to which the collateral is related [sufficient to give constructive notice of a mortgage under the law of this State if the description were contained in a record of the mortgage of the real property]; and

(4) if the debtor does not have an interest of record in the real property, provide the name of a record owner.

(c) [Record of mortgage as financing statement.] A record of a mortgage is effective, from the date of recording, as a financing statement filed as a fixture filing or as a financing statement covering as-extracted collateral or timber to be cut only if:

(1) the record indicates the goods or accounts that it covers;

(2) the goods are or are to become fixtures related to the real property described in the record or the collateral is related to the real property described in the record and is as-extracted collateral or timber to be cut;

(3) the record satisfies the requirements for a financing statement in this section, but:

(A) the record need not indicate that it is to be filed in the real property records; and

(B) the record sufficiently provides the name of a debtor who is an individual if it provides the individual name of the debtor or the surname and first personal name of the debtor, even if the debtor is an individual to whom Section 9-503(a)(4) applies; and

(4) the record is [duly] recorded.

(d) [Filing before security agreement or attachment.] A financing statement may be filed before a security agreement is made or a security interest otherwise attaches.

Legislative Note: *Language in brackets is optional. Where the State has any special recording system for real property other than the usual grantor-grantee index (as, for instance, a tract system or a title registration or Torrens system) local adaptations of subsection (b) and Section 9-519(d) and (e) may be necessary. See, e.g., Mass. Gen. Laws Chapter 106, Section 9-410. A State should enact the 2010 amendments to Section 9-502 only if the State enacts Alternative A of the 2010 amendments to Section 9-503.*

Definitional Cross References:

Account	Section 9-102(a)(2)
As-extracted collateral	Section 9-102(a)(6)
Collateral	Section 9-102(a)(12)
Debtor	Section 9-102(a)(28)
Financing statement	Section 9-102(a)(39)
Fixture filing	Section 9-102(a)(40)
Fixtures	Section 9-102(a)(41)
Goods	Section 9-102(a)(44)
Mortgage	Section 9-102(a)(55)

Notice	Section 1-202(a)
Record	Section 9-102(a)(70)
Representative	Section 1-201(b)(33)
Secured party	Section 9-102(a)(73)
Security agreement	Section 9-102(a)(74)
Security interest	Section 1-201(b)(35)
State	Section 9-102(a)(77)

Official Comment

1. Source. Former Section 9-402(1), (5), (6).

2. "Notice Filing." This section adopts the system of "notice filing." What is required to be filed is not, as under pre-UCC chattel mortgage and conditional sales acts, the security agreement itself, but only a simple record providing a limited amount of information (financing statement). The financing statement may be filed before the security interest attaches or thereafter. See subsection (d). See also Section 9-308(a) (contemplating situations in which a financing statement is filed before a security interest attaches).

The notice itself indicates merely that a person may have a security interest in the collateral indicated. Further inquiry from the parties concerned will be necessary to disclose the complete state of affairs. Section 9-210 provides a statutory procedure under which the secured party, at the debtor's request, may be required to make disclosure. However, in many cases, information may be forthcoming without the need to resort to the formalities of that section.

Notice filing has proved to be of great use in financing transactions involving inventory, accounts, and chattel paper, because it obviates the necessity of refiling on each of a series of transactions in a continuing arrangement under which the collateral changes from day to day. However, even in the case of filings that do not necessarily involve a series of transactions (e.g., a loan secured by a single item of equipment), a financing statement is effective to encompass transactions under a security agreement not in existence and not contemplated at the time the notice was filed, if the indication of collateral in the financing statement is sufficient to cover the collateral concerned. Similarly, a financing statement is effective to cover after-acquired property of the type indicated and to perfect with respect to future advances under security agreements, regardless of whether after-acquired property or future advances are mentioned in the financing statement and even if not in the contemplation of the parties at the time the financing statement was authorized to be filed.

3. Debtor's Signature; Required Authorization. Subsection (a) sets forth the simple formal requirements for an effective financing statement. These requirements are: (1) the debtor's name; (2) the name of a secured party or representative of the secured party; and (3) an indication of the collateral.

Whereas former Section 9-402(1) required the debtor's signature to appear on a financing statement, this Article contains no signature requirement. The elimination of the signature requirement facilitates paperless filing. (However, as PEB Commentary No. 15 indicates, a paperless financing statement was sufficient under former Article 9.) Elimination of the signature requirement also makes the exceptions provided by former Section 9-402(2) unnecessary.

The fact that this Article does not require that an authenticating symbol be contained in the public record does not mean that all filings are authorized. Rather, Section 9-509(a) entitles a person to file an initial financing statement, an amendment that adds collateral, or an amendment that adds a debtor only if the debtor authorizes the filing, and Section 9-509(d) entitles a person other than the debtor to file a termination statement only if the secured party of record authorizes the filing. Of course, a filing has legal effect only to the extent it is authorized. See Section 9-510.

Law other than this Article, including the law with respect to ratification of past acts, generally determines whether a person has the requisite authority to file a record under this Article. See Sections 1-103 and 9-509, Comment 3. However, under Section 9-509(b), the debtor's signing of (or becoming bound by) a security agreement *ipso facto* constitutes the debtor's authorization of the filing of a financing statement covering the collateral described in the security agreement. The secured party need not obtain a separate authorization. *Amendment approved by the Permanent Editorial Board for Uniform Commercial Code December 31, 2001.*

Section 9-625 provides a remedy for unauthorized filings. Making an unauthorized filing also may give rise to civil or criminal liability under other law. In addition, this Article contains provisions that assist in the discovery of unauthorized filings and the amelioration of their practical effect. For example, Section 9-518 provides a procedure whereby a person may add to the public record a statement to the effect that a financing statement indexed under the person's name was wrongfully filed, and Section 9-509(d) entitles any person to file a termination statement if the secured party of record fails to comply with its obligation to file or send one to the debtor, the debtor authorizes the filing, and the termination statement so indicates. However, the filing office is neither obligated nor permitted to inquire into issues of authorization. See Section 9-520(a).

4. Certain Other Requirements. Subsection (a) deletes other provisions of former Section 9-402(1) because they seems unwise (real-property description for financing statements covering crops), unnecessary (adequacy of copies of financing statements), or both (copy of security agreement as financing statement). In addition, the filing office must reject a financing statement lacking certain other information formerly required as a condition of perfection (e.g., an address for the debtor or secured party). See Sections 9-516(b), 9-520(a). However, if the filing office accepts the record, it is effective nevertheless. See Section 9-520(c).

5. Real-Property-Related Filings. Subsection (b) contains the requirements for financing statements filed as fixture filings and financing statements covering timber to be cut or minerals and minerals-related accounts constituting as-extracted collateral. A description of the related real property must be sufficient to reasonably identify it. See Section 9-108. This formulation rejects the view that the real property description must be by metes and bounds, or otherwise conforming to traditional real-property practice in conveyancing, but, of course, the incorporation of such a description by reference to the recording data of a deed, mortgage or other instrument containing the description should suffice under the most stringent standards. The proper test is that a description of real property must be sufficient so that the financing statement will fit into the real-property search system and be found by a real-property searcher. Under the optional language in subsection (b)(3), the test of adequacy of the description is whether it would be adequate in a record of a mortgage of the real property. As suggested in the Legislative Note, more detail may be required if there is a tract indexing system or a land registration system.

If the debtor does not have an interest of record in the real property, a real-property-related financing statement must show the name of a record owner, and Section 9-519(d) requires the financing statement to be indexed in the name of that owner. This requirement also enables financing statements covering as-extracted collateral or timber to be cut and financing statements filed as fixture filings to fit into the real-property search system.

6. Record of Mortgage Effective as Financing Statement. Subsection (c) explains when a record of a mortgage is effective as a financing statement filed as a fixture filing or to cover timber to be cut or as-extracted collateral. Use of the term "record of a mortgage" recognizes that in some systems the record actually filed is not the record pursuant to which a mortgage is created. Moreover, "mortgage" is defined in Section 9-102 as an "interest in real property," not as the record that creates or evidences the mortgage or the record that is filed in the public recording systems. A record creating a mortgage may also create a security interest with respect to fixtures (or other goods) in conformity with this Article. A single agreement creating a mortgage on real property and a security interest in chattels is common and useful for certain purposes. Under subsection (c), the recording of the record evidencing a mortgage (if it satisfies the requirements for a financing statement) constitutes the filing of a financing statement as to the fixtures (but not, of course, as to other goods). Section 9-515(g) makes the usual five-year maximum life for financing statements inapplicable to mortgages that operate as fixture filings under Section 9-502(c). Such mortgages are effective for the duration of the real-property recording.

Of course, if a combined mortgage covers chattels that are not fixtures, a regular financing statement filing is necessary with respect to the chattels, and subsection (c) is inapplicable. Likewise, a financing statement filed as a "fixture filing" is not effective to perfect a security interest in personal property other than fixtures.

In some cases it may be difficult to determine whether goods are or will become fixtures. Nothing in this Part prohibits the filing of a "precautionary" fixture filing, which would provide protection in the event goods are determined to be fixtures. The fact of filing should not be a factor in the determining whether goods are fixtures. Cf. Section 9-505(b).

§ 9-503. Name of Debtor and Secured Party.

(a) [Sufficiency of debtor's name.] A financing statement sufficiently provides the name of the debtor:

(1) except as otherwise provided in paragraph (3), if the debtor is a registered organization or the collateral is held in a trust that is a registered organization, only if the financing statement provides the name that is stated to be the registered organization's name on the public organic record most recently filed with or issued or enacted by the registered organization's jurisdiction of organization which purports to state, amend, or restate the registered organization's name;

(2) subject to subsection (f), if the collateral is being administered by the personal representative of a decedent, only if the financing statement provides, as the name of the debtor, the name of the decedent and, in a separate part of the financing statement, indicates that the collateral is being administered by a personal representative;

(3) if the collateral is held in a trust that is not a registered organization, only if the financing statement:

(A) provides, as the name of the debtor:

(i) if the organic record of the trust specifies a name for the trust, the name specified; or

(ii) if the organic record of the trust does not specify a name for the trust, the name of the settlor or testator; and

(B) in a separate part of the financing statement:

(i) if the name is provided in accordance with subparagraph (A)(i), indicates that the collateral is held in a trust; or

(ii) if the name is provided in accordance with subparagraph (A)(ii), provides additional information sufficient to distinguish the trust from other trusts having one or more of the same settlors or the same testator and indicates that the collateral is held in a trust, unless the additional information so indicates;

ALTERNATIVE A

(4) subject to subsection (g), if the debtor is an individual to whom this State has issued a [driver's license] that has not expired, only if the financing statement provides the name of the individual which is indicated on the [driver's license];

(5) if the debtor is an individual to whom paragraph (4) does not apply, only if the financing statement provides the individual name of the debtor or the surname and first personal name of the debtor; and

(6) in other cases:

(A) if the debtor has a name, only if the financing statement provides the organizational name of the debtor; and

(B) if the debtor does not have a name, only if it provides the names of the partners, members, associates, or other persons comprising the debtor, in a manner that each name provided would be sufficient if the person named were the debtor.

(b) [Additional debtor-related information.] A financing statement that provides the name of the debtor in accordance with subsection (a) is not rendered ineffective by the absence of:

(1) a trade name or other name of the debtor; or

(2) unless required under subsection (a)(6)(B), names of partners, members, associates, or other persons comprising the debtor.

ALTERNATIVE B

(4) if the debtor is an individual, only if the financing statement:

(A) provides the individual name of the debtor;

(B) provides the surname and first personal name of the debtor; or

(C) subject to subsection (g), provides the name of the individual which is indicated on a [driver's license] that this State has issued to the individual and which has not expired; and

(5) in other cases:

(A) if the debtor has a name, only if the financing statement provides the organizational name of the debtor; and

(B) if the debtor does not have a name, only if the financing statement provides the names of the partners, members, associates, or other persons comprising the debtor, in a manner that each name provided would be sufficient if the person named were the debtor.

(b) [Additional debtor-related information.] A financing statement that provides the name of the debtor in accordance with subsection (a) is not rendered ineffective by the absence of:

(1) a trade name or other name of the debtor; or

(2) unless required under subsection (a)(5)(B), names of partners, members, associates, or other persons comprising the debtor.

END OF ALTERNATIVES

(c) [Debtor's trade name insufficient.] A financing statement that provides only the debtor's trade name does not sufficiently provide the name of the debtor.

(d) [Representative capacity.] Failure to indicate the representative capacity of a secured party or representative of a secured party does not affect the sufficiency of a financing statement.

(e) [Multiple debtors and secured parties.] A financing statement may provide the name of more than one debtor and the name of more than one secured party.

(f) [Name of decedent.] The name of the decedent indicated on the order appointing the personal representative of the decedent issued by the court having jurisdiction over the collateral is sufficient as the "name of the decedent" under subsection (a)(2).

ALTERNATIVE A

(g) [Multiple driver's licenses.] If this State has issued to an individual more than one [driver's license] of a kind described in subsection (a)(4), the one that was issued most recently is the one to which subsection (a)(4) refers.

ALTERNATIVE B

(g) [Multiple driver's licenses.] If this State has issued to an individual more than one [driver's license] of a kind described in subsection (a)(4)(C), the one that was issued most recently is the one to which subsection (a)(4)(C) refers.

END OF ALTERNATIVES

(h) [Definition.] In this section, the "name of the settlor or testator" means:

(1) if the settlor is a registered organization, the name that is stated to be the settlor's name on the public organic record most recently filed with or issued or enacted by the settlor's jurisdiction of organization which purports to state, amend, or restate the settlor's name; or

(2) in other cases, the name of the settlor or testator indicated in the trust's organic record.

Legislative Note:

1. *This Act contains two alternative sets of amendments relating to the names of individual debtors. A State should enact the same Alternative, A or B, for both subsections (a) and (i) of Section 9-503. A State that enacts Alternative A of the amendments to this section should also enact the amendments to Section 9-502.*

2. *Both Alternatives refer, in part, to the name as shown on a debtor's driver's license. The Legislature should be aware that, in some States, certain characters that may be used by the State's department of motor vehicles (or similar agency) in the name on a driver's license may not be accepted by the State's central or local UCC filing offices under current regulations or internal protocols. This may occur because of technological limitations of the filing offices or merely as a result of inconsistent procedures. Similar issues may exist for field sizes as well. In these situations, perfection of a security interest granted by a debtor with such a driver's license may be impossible under Alternative A of the amendments and the utility of Alternative B, under which the name on the driver's license is one of the names that is sufficient, may be reduced. Accordingly, the State may wish to determine if one or more of these issues exist and, if so, to make certain that such issues have been resolved. A successful resolution might be accomplished by statute, agency regulation, or technological change effectuated before or as part of the enactment of this Act.*

3. *Regardless of which Alternative is enacted, in States in which a single agency issues driver's licenses and non-driver identification cards as an alternative to a driver's license, such that at any given time an individual may hold either a driver's license or an identification card but not both, the State should replace each use of the term "driver's license" with a phrase meaning "driver's license or identification card" but containing the analogous terms used in the enacting State. In other States, the State should replace the term "driver's license" with the analogous term used in the enacting State.*

Definitional Cross References:

Debtor	Section 9-102(a)(28)
Document	Section 9-102(a)(30)
Financing statement	Section 9-102(a)(39)
Jurisdiction of organization	Section 9-102(a)(50)
Organization	Section 1-201(b)(25)
Person	Section 1-201(b)(27)
Public organic record	Section 9-102(a)(68)
Record	Section 9-102(a)(70)
Registered organization	Section 9-102(a)(71)
Representative	Section 1-201(b)(33)
Secured party	Section 9-102(a)(73)

Official Comment

1. Source. Subsections (a)(4)(A), (b), and (c) derive from former Section 9-402(7); otherwise, new.

2. Debtor's Name. The requirement that a financing statement provide the debtor's name is particularly important. Financing statements are indexed under the name of the debtor, and those who wish to find financing statements search for them under the debtor's name. Subsection (a) explains what the debtor's name is for purposes of a financing statement.

a. Registered Organizations. As a general matter, if the debtor is a "registered organization" (defined in Section 9-102 so as to ordinarily include corporations, limited partnerships, limited liability companies, and statutory trusts), then the debtor's name is the name shown on the public organic record" of the debtor's "jurisdiction of organization" (both also defined in Section 9-102).

b. Collateral Held in a Trust. When a financing statement covers collateral that is held in a trust that is a registered organization, subsection (a)(1) governs the name of the debtor. If, however, the collateral is held in a trust that is not a registered organization, subsection (a)(3) applies. (As used in this Article, collateral "held in a trust" includes collateral as to which the trust is the debtor as well as collateral as to which the trustee is the debtor.) This subsection adopts a convention that generally results in the name of the trust or the name of the trust's settlor being provided as the name of the debtor on the financing statement, even if, as typically is the case with common-law trusts, the "debtor" (defined in Section 9-102) is a trustee acting with respect to the collateral. This convention provides more accurate information and eases the burden for searchers, who otherwise would have difficulty with respect to debtor trustees that are large financial institutions.

More specifically, if a trust's organic record specifies a name for the trust, subsection (a)(3) requires the financing statement to provide, as the name of the debtor, the name for the trust specified in the organic record. In addition, the financing statement must indicate, in a separate part of the financing statement, that the collateral is held in a trust.

If the organic record of the trust does not specify a name for the trust, the name required for the financing statement is the name of the settlor or, in the case of a testamentary trust, the testator, in each case as determined under subsection (h). In addition, the financing statement must provide sufficient additional information to distinguish the trust from other trusts having one or more of the same settlors or the same testator. In many cases an indication of the date on which the trust was settled will satisfy this requirement. If neither the name nor the additional information indicates that the collateral is held in a trust, the financing statement must indicate that fact, but not as part of the debtor's name.

Neither the indication that the collateral is held in a trust nor the additional information that distinguishes the trust from other trusts having one or more of the same settlors or the same testator is part of the debtor's name. Nevertheless, a financing statement that fails to provide, in a separate part of the financing statement, any required indication or additional information does not sufficiently provide the name of the debtor under Sections 9-502(a) and 9-503(a)(3), does not "substantially satisfy[] the requirements" of Part 5 within the meaning of Section 9-506(a), and so is ineffective.

c. Collateral Administered by a Personal Representative. Subsection (a)(2) deals with collateral that is being administered by an executor, administrator, or other personal representative of a decedent. Even if, as often is the case, the representative is the "debtor" (defined in Section 9-102), the financing statement must provide the name of the decedent as the name of the debtor. Subsection (f) provides a safe harbor, under which the name of the decedent indicated on the order appointing the personal representative issued by the court having jurisdiction over the collateral is sufficient as the name of the decedent. If the order indicates more than one name for the decedent, the first name in the list qualifies under subsection (f); however, other names in the list also may qualify as the "name of the decedent" within the meaning of subsection (a)(2). In addition to providing the name of the decedent, the financing statement must indicate, in a separate part of the financing statement, that the collateral is being administered by a personal representative. Although the indication is not part of the debtor's name, a financing statement that fails to provide the indication does not sufficiently provide the name of the debtor under Sections 9-502(a) and 9-503(a)(2), does not "substantially satisfy[] the requirements" of Part 5 within the meaning of Section 9-506(a), and so is ineffective.

d. Individuals. This Article provides alternative approaches towards the requirement for providing the name of a debtor who is an individual.

Alternative A. Alternative A distinguishes between two groups of individual debtors. For debtors holding an unexpired driver's license issued by the State where the financing statement is filed (ordinarily the State where the debtor maintains the debtor's principal residence), Alternative A requires that a financing statement provide the name indicated on the license. When a debtor does not hold an unexpired driver's license issued by the relevant State, the requirement can be satisfied in either of two ways. A financing statement is sufficient if it provides the "individual name" of the debtor. Alternatively, a financing statement is sufficient if it provides the debtor's surname (i.e., family name) and first personal name (i.e., first name other than the surname).

Alternative B. Alternative B provides three ways in which a financing statement may sufficiently provide the name of an individual who is a debtor. The "individual name" of the debtor is sufficient, as is the debtor's surname and first personal name. If the individual holds an unexpired driver's license issued by the State where the financing statement is filed (ordinarily the State of the debtor's principal residence), the name indicated on the driver's license also is sufficient.

Name indicated on the driver's license. A financing statement does not "provide the name of the individual which is indicated" on the debtor's driver's license unless the name it provides is the same as the name indicated on the license. This is the case even if the name indicated on the debtor's driver's license contains an error.

> **Example 1**: Debtor, an individual whose principal residence is in Illinois, grants a security interest to SP in certain business equipment. SP files a financing statement with the Illinois filing office. The financing statement provides the name appearing on Debtor's Illinois driver's license, "Joseph Allan Jones." Regardless of which Alternative is in effect in Illinois, this filing would be sufficient under Illinois' Section 9-503(a), even if Debtor's correct middle name is Alan, not Allan.

A filing against "Joseph A. Jones" or "Joseph Jones" would not "provide the name of the individual which is indicated" on the debtor's driver's license. However, these filings might be sufficient if Alternative A is in effect in Illinois and Jones has no current (i.e., unexpired) Illinois driver's license, or if Illinois has enacted Alternative B.

Determining the name that should be provided on the financing statement must not be done mechanically. The order in which the components of an individual's name appear on a driver's license differs among the States. Had the debtor in Example 1 obtained a driver's license from a different State, the license might have indicated the name as "Jones Joseph Allan." Regardless of the order on the driver's license, the debtor's surname must be provided in the part of the financing statement designated for the surname.

Alternatives A and B both refer to a license issued by "this State." Perfection of a security interest by filing ordinarily is determined by the law of the jurisdiction in which the debtor is located. See Section 9-301(1). (Exceptions to the general rule are found in Section 9-301(3) and (4), concerning fixture filings, timber to be cut, and as-extracted collateral.) A debtor who is an individual ordinarily is located at the individual's principal residence. See Section 9-307(b). (An exception appears in Section 9-307(c).) Thus, a given State's Section 9-503 ordinarily will apply during any period when the debtor's principal residence is located in that State, even if during that time the debtor holds or acquires a driver's license from another State.

When a debtor's principal residence changes, the location of the debtor under Section 9-307 also changes and perfection by filing ordinarily will be governed by the law of the debtor's new location. As a consequence of the application of that jurisdiction's Section 9-316, a security interest that is perfected by filing under the law of the debtor's former location will remain perfected for four months after the relocation, and thereafter if the secured party perfects under the law of the debtor's new location. Likewise, a financing statement filed in the former location may be effective to perfect a security interest that attaches after the debtor relocates. See Section 9-316(h).

Individual name of the debtor. Article 9 does not determine the "individual name" of a debtor. Nor does it determine which element or elements in a debtor's name constitute the surname. In some cases, determining the "individual name" of a debtor may be difficult, as may determining the debtor's surname. This is because in the case of individuals, unlike registered organizations, there is no public organic record to which reference can be made and from which the name and its components can be definitively determined.

Names can take many forms in the United States. For example, whereas a surname is often colloquially referred to as a "last name," the sequence in which the elements of a name are presented is not determinative. In some cultures, the surname appears first, while in others it may appear in a location that is neither first nor last. In addition, some surnames are composed of multiple elements that, taken together, constitute a single surname. These elements may or may not be separated by a space or connected by a hyphen, "i," or "y." In other instances, some or all of the same elements may not be part of the surname. In some cases, a debtor's entire name might be composed of only a single element, which should be provided in the part of the financing statement designated for the surname.

In disputes as to whether a financing statement sufficiently provides the "individual name" of a debtor, a court should refer to any non-UCC law concerning names. However, case law about names may have developed in contexts that implicate policies different from those of Article 9. A court considering an individual's name for purposes of determining the sufficiency of a financing statement is not necessarily bound by cases that were decided in other contexts and for other purposes.

Individuals are asked to provide their names on official documents such as tax returns and bankruptcy petitions. An individual may provide a particular name on an official document in response to instructions relating to the document rather than because the name is actually the individual's name. Accordingly, a court should not assume that the name an individual provides on an official document necessarily constitutes the "individual name" for purposes of the sufficiency of the debtor's name on a financing statement. Likewise, a court should not assume that the name as presented on an individual's birth certificate is necessarily the individual's current name.

In applying non-UCC law for purposes of determining the sufficiency of a debtor's name on a financing statement, a court should give effect to the instruction in Section 1-103(a)(1) that the UCC "must be liberally construed and applied to promote its underlying purposes and policies," which include simplifying and clarifying the law governing commercial transactions. Thus, determination of a debtor's name in the context of the Article 9 filing system must take into account the needs of both filers and searchers. Filers need a simple and predictable system in which they can have a reasonable degree of confidence that, without undue burden, they can determine a name that will be sufficient so as to permit their financing statements to be effective. Likewise, searchers need a simple and predictable system in which they can have a reasonable degree of confidence that, without undue burden, they will discover all financing statements pertaining to the debtor in question. The court also should take into account the purpose of the UCC to make the law uniform among the various jurisdictions. See Section 1-103(a)(3).

Of course, once an individual debtor's name has been determined to be sufficient for purposes of Section

9-503, a financing statement that provides a variation of that name, such as a "nickname" that does not constitute the debtor's name, does not sufficiently provide the name of the debtor under this section. Cf. Section 9-503(c) (a financing statement providing only a debtor's trade name is not sufficient).

If there is any doubt about an individual debtor's name, a secured party may choose to file one or more financing statements that provide a number of possible names for the debtor and a searcher may similarly choose to search under a number of possible names.

Note that, even if the name provided in an initial financing statement is correct, the filing office nevertheless must reject the financing statement if it does not identify an individual debtor's surname (e.g., if it is not clear whether the debtor's surname is Perry or Mason). See Section 9-516(b)(3)(C).

3. Secured Party's Name. New subsection (d) makes clear that when the secured party is a representative, a financing statement is sufficient if it names the secured party, whether or not it indicates any representative capacity. Similarly, a financing statement that names a representative of the secured party is sufficient, even if it does not indicate the representative capacity.

> **Example 2:** Debtor creates a security interest in favor of Bank X, Bank Y, and Bank Z, but not to their representative, the collateral agent (Bank A). The collateral agent is not itself a secured party. See Section 9-102. Under Sections 9-502(a) and 9-503(d), however, a financing statement is effective if it names as secured party Bank A and not the actual secured parties, even if it omits Bank A's representative capacity.

Each person whose name is provided in an initial financing statement as the name of the secured party or representative of the secured party is a secured party of record. See Section 9-511.

4. Multiple Names. Subsection (e) makes explicit what is implicit under former Article 9: a financing statement may provide the name of more than one debtor and secured party. See Section 1-106 (words in the singular include the plural). With respect to records relating to more than one debtor, see Section 9-520(d). With respect to financing statements providing the name of more than one secured party, see Sections 9-509(e) and 9-510(b).

§ 9-504. Indication of Collateral.

A financing statement sufficiently indicates the collateral that it covers if the financing statement provides:

(1) a description of the collateral pursuant to Section 9-108; or

(2) an indication that the financing statement covers all assets or all personal property.

Definitional Cross References:

Collateral	Section 9-102(a)(12)
Financing statement	Section 9-102(a)(39)

Official Comment

1. Source. Former Section 9-402(1).

2. Indication of Collateral. To comply with Section 9-502(a), a financing statement must "indicate" the collateral it covers. A financing statement sufficiently indicates collateral claimed to be covered by the financing statement if it satisfies the purpose of conditioning perfection on the filing of a financing statement, i.e., if it provides notice that a person may have a security interest in the collateral claimed. See Section 9-502, Comment 2. In particular, an indication of collateral that would have satisfied the requirements of former Section 9-402(1) (i.e., a "statement indicating the types, or describing the items, of collateral") suffices under Section 9-502(a). An indication may satisfy the requirements of Section 9-502(a), even if it would not have satisfied the requirements of former Section 9-402(1). A financing statement (including any attachments) that does not itself supply information satisfying Section(a) (3) or Section 9-504(a), but, rather, refers solely to a record not attached to the financing statement for information seeking to satisfy those provisions, does not satisfy the sufficiency requirement of Section 9-502(a)(3) that the financing statement indicate the collateral that it covers. See PEB Commentary No. 26, dated August 12, 2022. The Commentary is available at https://www.ali.org/peb-ucc.

This section provides two safe harbors. Under paragraph (1), a "description" of the collateral (as the term is explained in Section 9-108) suffices as an indication for purposes of the sufficiency of a financing statement.

Debtors sometimes create a security interest in all, or substantially all, of their assets. To accommodate this practice, paragraph (2) expands the class of sufficient collateral references to embrace "an indication that the financing statement covers all assets or all personal property." If the property in question belongs to the debtor and is personal property, any searcher will know that the property is covered by the financing statement. Of course, regardless of its breadth, a financing statement has no effect with respect to property indicated but to which a security interest has not attached. Note that a broad statement of this kind (e.g., "all debtor's personal property") would not be a sufficient "description" for purposes of a security agreement. See Sections 9-203(b)(3)(A), 9-108. It follows that a somewhat narrower description than "all assets," e.g., "all assets other than automobiles," is sufficient for purposes of this section, even if it does not suffice for purposes of a security agreement.

§ 9-505. Filing and Compliance with Other Statutes and Treaties for Consignments, Leases, Other Bailments, and Other Transactions.

(a) [Use of terms other than "debtor" and "secured party."] A consignor, lessor, or other bailor of goods, a licensor, or a buyer of a payment intangible or promissory note may file a financing statement, or may comply with a statute or treaty described in Section 9-311(a), using the terms "consignor", "consignee", "lessor", "lessee", "bailor", "bailee", "licensor", "licensee", "owner", "registered owner", "buyer", "seller", or words of similar import, instead of the terms "secured party" and "debtor".

(b) [Effect of financing statement under subsection (a).] This part applies to the filing of a financing statement under subsection (a) and, as appropriate, to compliance that is equivalent to filing a financing statement under Section 9-311(b), but the filing or compliance is not of itself a factor in determining whether the collateral secures an obligation. If it is determined for another reason that the collateral secures an obligation, a security interest held by the consignor, lessor, bailor, licensor, owner, or buyer which attaches to the collateral is perfected by the filing or compliance.

Definitional Cross References:

Collateral	Section 9-102(a)(12)
Consignee	Section 9-102(a)(19)
Consignment	Section 9-102(a)(20)
Consignor	Section 9-102(a)(21)
Debtor	Section 9-102(a)(28)
Financing statement	Section 9-102(a)(39)
Goods	Section 9-102(a)(44)
Lease	Section 2A-103(1)(j)
Lessee	Section 2A-103(1)(n)
Lessor	Section 2A-103(1)(p)
Payment intangible	Section 9-102(a)(61)
Promissory note	Section 9-102(a)(65)
Secured party	Section 9-102(a)(73)
Security interest	Section 1-201(b)(35)
Term	Section 1-201(b)(40)

Official Comment

1. Source. Former Section 9-408.

2. Precautionary Filing. Occasionally, doubts arise concerning whether a transaction creates a relationship to which this Article or its filing provisions apply. For example, questions may arise over whether a "lease" of equipment in fact creates a security interest or whether the "sale" of payment intangibles in fact secures an obligation, thereby requiring action to perfect the security interest. This section, which derives from former Section 9-408, affords the option of filing of a financing statement with appropriate changes of terminology but without affecting the substantive question of classification of the transaction.

3. Changes from Former Section 9-408. This section expands the rule of former Section 9-408 to embrace more generally other bailments and transactions, as well as sales transactions, primarily sales of payment intangibles and promissory notes. It provides the same benefits for compliance with a statute or treaty described in Section 9-311(a) that former Section 9-408 provided for filing, in connection with the use of terms such as "lessor," consignor," etc. The references to "owner" and "registered owner" are intended to address, for example, the situation where a putative lessor is the registered owner of an automobile covered by a certificate of title and the transaction is determined to create a security interest. Although this section provides that the security interest is perfected, the relevant certificate-of-title statute may expressly provide to the contrary or may be ambiguous. If so, it may be necessary or advisable to amend the certificate-of-title statute to ensure that perfection of the security interest will be achieved.

As did former Section 1-201, former Article 9 referred to transactions, including leases and consignments, "intended as security." [Ed. Note. the new Article 1 does not include "intent" as part of its test for distinguishing a lease from a security interest. See Article 1-203.] This misleading phrase created the erroneous impression that the parties to a transaction can dictate how the law will classify it (e.g., as a bailment or as a security interest) and thus affect the rights of third parties. This Article deletes the phrase wherever it appears. Subsection (b) expresses the principle more precisely by referring to a security interest that "secures an obligation."

4. Consignments. Although a "true" consignment is a bailment, the filing and priority provisions of former Article 9 applied to "true" consignments. See former Sections 2-326(3), 9-114. A consignment "intended as security" created a security interest that was in all respects subject to former Article 9. This Article subsumes most true consignments under the rubric of "security interest." See Sections 9-102 (definition of "consignment"), 9-109(a)(4), 1-201(b)(35) (definition of "security interest"). Nevertheless, it maintains the distinction between a (true) "consignment," as to which only certain aspects of Article 9 apply, and a so-called consignment that actually "secures an obligation," to which Article 9 applies in full. The revisions to this section reflect the change in terminology.

§ 9-506. Effect of Errors or Omissions.

(a) [Minor errors and omissions.] A financing statement substantially satisfying the requirements of this part is effective, even if it has minor errors or omissions, unless the errors or omissions make the financing statement seriously misleading.

(b) [Financing statement seriously misleading.] Except as otherwise provided in subsection (c), a financing statement that fails sufficiently to provide the name of the debtor in accordance with Section 9-503(a) is seriously misleading.

(c) [Financing statement not seriously misleading.] If a search of the records of the filing office under the debtor's correct name, using the filing office's standard search logic, if any, would disclose a financing statement that fails sufficiently to provide the name of the debtor in accordance with Section 9-503(a), the name provided does not make the financing statement seriously misleading.

(d) ["Debtor's correct name."] For purposes of Section 9-508(b), the "debtor's correct name" in subsection (c) means the correct name of the new debtor.

Definitional Cross References:

Debtor	Section 9-102(a)(28)
Filing office	Section 9-102(a)(37)
Financing statement	Section 9-102(a)(39)
New debtor	Section 9-102(a)(56)
Record	Section 9-102(a)(70)

Official Comment

1. Source. Former Section 9-402(8).

2. Errors and Omissions. Like former Section 9-402(8), subsection (a) is in line with the policy of this Article to simplify formal requisites and filing requirements. It is designed to discourage the fanatical and impossibly refined reading of statutory requirements in which courts occasionally have indulged themselves. Subsection (a) provides the standard applicable to indications of collateral. Subsections (b) and (c), which are new, concern the effectiveness of financing statements in which the debtor's name is incorrect. Subsection (b) contains the general rule: a financing statement that fails sufficiently to provide the debtor's name in accordance with Section 9-503(a) is seriously misleading as a matter of law. Subsection (c) provides an exception: If the financing statement nevertheless would be discovered in a search under the debtor's correct name, using the filing office's standard search logic, if any, then as a matter of law the incorrect name does not make the financing statement seriously misleading. A financing statement that is seriously misleading under this section is ineffective even if it is disclosed by (i) using a search logic other than that of the filing office to search the official records, or (ii) using the filing office's standard search logic to search a data base other than that of the filing office. For purposes of subsection (c), any name that satisfies Section 9-503(a) at the time of the search is a "correct name."

This section and Section 9-503 balance the interests of filers and searchers. Searchers are not expected to ascertain nicknames, trade names, and the like by which the debtor may be known and then search under each of them. Rather, it is the secured party's responsibility to provide the name of the debtor sufficiently in a filed financing statement. Subsection (c) sets forth the only situation in which a financing statement that fails sufficiently to provide the name of the debtor is not seriously misleading. As stated in subsection (b), if the name of the debtor provided on a financing statement is insufficient and subsection (c) is not satisfied, the financing statement is seriously misleading. Such a financing statement is ineffective even if the debtor is known in some contexts by the name provided on the financing statement and even if searchers know or have reason to know that the name provided on the financing statement refers to the debtor. Any suggestion to the contrary in a judicial opinion is incorrect.

To satisfy the requirements of Section 9-503(a)(2), a financing statement must indicate that the collateral is being administered by a personal representative. To satisfy the requirements of Section 9-503(a)(3), a financing statement must indicate that the collateral is held in a trust and provide additional information that distinguishes the trust from certain other trusts. The indications and additional information are not part of the debtor's name. Nevertheless, a financing statement that fails to provide an indication or the additional information when required does not sufficiently provide the name of the debtor under Sections 9-502(a) and 9-503(a), does not "substantially satisfy[] the requirements" of Part 5 within the meaning of this section and so is ineffective.

In addition to requiring the debtor's name and an indication of the collateral, Section 9-502(a) requires a financing statement to provide the name of the secured party or a representative of the secured party. Inasmuch as searches are not conducted under the secured party's name, and no filing is needed to continue the perfected status of security interest after it is assigned, an error in the name of the secured party or its representative will not be seriously misleading. However, in an appropriate case, an error of this kind may give rise to an estoppel in favor of a particular holder of a conflicting claim to the collateral. See Section 1-103.

3. New Debtors. Subsection (d) provides that, in determining the extent to which a financing statement naming an original debtor is effective against a new debtor, the sufficiency of the financing statement should be tested against the name of the new debtor.

§ 9-507. Effect of Certain Events on Effectiveness of Financing Statement.

(a) [Disposition.] A filed financing statement remains effective with respect to collateral that is sold, exchanged, leased, licensed, or otherwise disposed of and in which a security interest or agricultural lien continues, even if the secured party knows of or consents to the disposition.

(b) [Information becoming seriously misleading.] Except as otherwise provided in subsection (c) and Section 9-508, a financing statement is not rendered ineffective if, after the financing statement is filed, the information provided in the financing statement becomes seriously misleading under Section 9-506.

(c) [Change in debtor's name.] If the name that a filed financing statement provides for a debtor becomes insufficient as the name of the debtor under Section 9-503(a) so that the financing statement becomes seriously misleading under Section 9-506:

(1) the financing statement is effective to perfect a security interest in collateral acquired by the debtor before, or within four months after, the filed financing statement becomes seriously misleading; and

(2) the financing statement is not effective to perfect a security interest in collateral acquired by the debtor more than four months after the filed financing statement becomes seriously misleading, unless an amendment to the financing statement which renders the financing statement not seriously misleading is filed within four months after the filed financing statement becomes seriously misleading.

Definitional Cross References:

Agricultural lien	Section 9-102(a)(5)
Collateral	Section 9-102(a)(12)
Debtor	Section 9-102(a)(28)
Financing statement	Section 9-102(a)(39)
Secured party	Section 9-102(a)(73)
Security interest	Section 1-201(b)(35)

Official Comment

1. Source. Former Section 9-402(7).

2. Scope of Section. This section deals with situations in which the information in a proper financing statement becomes inaccurate after the financing statement is filed. Compare Section 9-338, which deals with situations in which a financing statement contains a particular kind of information concerning the debtor (i.e., the information described in Section 9-516(b)(5)) that is incorrect at the time it is filed.

3. Post-Filing Disposition of Collateral. Under subsection (a), a financing statement remains effective even if the collateral is sold or otherwise disposed of. This subsection clarifies the third sentence of former Section 9-402(7) by providing that a financing statement remains effective following the disposition of collateral only when the security interest or agricultural lien continues in that collateral. This result is consistent with the conclusion of PEB Commentary No. 3. Normally, a security interest does continue after disposition of the collateral. See Section 9-315(a). Law other than this Article determines whether an agricultural lien survives disposition of the collateral.

As a consequence of the disposition, the collateral may be owned by a person other than the debtor against whom the financing statement was filed. Under subsection (a), the secured party remains perfected even if it does not correct the public record. For this reason, any person seeking to determine whether a debtor owns collateral free of security interests must inquire as to the debtor's source of title and, if circumstances seem to require it, search in the name of a former owner. Subsection (a) addresses only the sufficiency of the information contained in the financing statement. A disposition of collateral may result in loss of perfection for other reasons. See Section 9-316.

> **Example:** Dee Corp. is an Illinois corporation. It creates a security interest in its equipment in favor of Secured Party. Secured Party files a proper financing statement in Illinois. Dee Corp. sells an item of equipment to Bee Corp., a Pennsylvania corporation, subject to the security interest. The security interest continues, see Section 9-315(a), and remains perfected, see Section 9-507(a), notwithstanding that the financing statement is filed under "D" (for Dee Corp.) and not under "B." However, because Bee Corp. is located in Pennsylvania and not Illinois, see Section 9-307, unless Secured Party perfects under Pennsylvania law within one year after the transfer, its security interest will become unperfected and will be deemed to have been unperfected against purchasers of the collateral. See Section 9-316.

4. Other Post-Filing Changes. Subsection (b) provides that, as a general matter, post- filing changes that render a financing statement seriously misleading have no effect on a financing statement. The financing statement remains effective. It is subject to two exceptions: Section 9-508 and Section 9-507(c). Section 9-508 addresses the effectiveness of a financing statement filed against an original debtor when a new debtor becomes bound by the original debtor's security agreement. It is discussed in the Comments to that section. Section 9-507(c) addresses cases in which a filed financing statement provides a name that, at the time of filing, satisfies the requirements of Section 9-503(a) with respect to the named debtor but, at a later time, no longer does so.

Example 1: Debtor, an individual whose principal residence is in California, grants a security interest to SP in certain business equipment. SP files a financing statement with the California filing office. Alternative A is in effect in California. The financing statement provides the name appearing on Debtor's California driver's license, "James McGinty." Debtor obtains a court order changing his name to "Roger McGuinn" but does not change his driver's license. Even after the court order issues, the name provided for the debtor in the financing statement is sufficient under Section 9-503(a). Accordingly, Section 9-507(c) does not apply.

The same result would follow if Alternative B is in effect in California.

Under Section 9-503(a)(4) (Alternative A), if the debtor holds a current (i.e., unexpired) driver's license issued by the State where the financing statement is filed, the name required for the financing statement is the name indicated on the license that was issued most recently by that State. If the debtor does not have a current driver's license issued by that State, then the debtor's name is determined under subsection (a)(5). It follows that a debtor's name may change, and a financing statement providing the name on the debtor's then-current driver's license may become seriously misleading, if the license expires and the debtor's name under subsection (a)(5) is different. The same consequences may follow if a debtor's driver's license is renewed and the names on the licenses differ.

Example 2: The facts are as in Example 1. Debtor's driver's license expires one year after the entry of the court order changing Debtor's name. Debtor does not renew the license. Upon expiration of the license, the name required for sufficiency by Section 9-503(a) is the individual name of the debtor or the debtor's surname and first personal name. The name "James McGinty" has become insufficient.

Example 3: The facts are as in Example 1. Before the license expires, Debtor renews the license. The name indicated on the new license is "Roger McGuinn." Upon issuance of the new license, "James McGinty" becomes insufficient as the debtor's name under Section 9-503(a).

The same results would follow if Alternative B is in effect in California (assuming that, following the issuance of the court order, "James McGinty" is neither the individual name of the debtor nor the debtor's surname and first personal name).

Even if the name provided as the name of the debtor becomes insufficient under Section 9-503(a), the filed financing statement does not become seriously misleading, and Section 9-507(c) does not apply, if the financing statement can be found by searching under the debtor's "correct" name, using the filing office's standard search logic. See Section 9-506. Any name that satisfies Section 9-503(a) at the time of the search is a "correct name" for these purposes. Thus, assuming that a search of the records of the California filing office under "Roger McGuinn," using the filing office's standard search logic, would not disclose a financing statement naming "James McGinty," the financing statement in Examples 2 and 3 has become seriously misleading and Section 9-507(c) applies.

If a filed financing statement becomes seriously misleading because the name it provides for a debtor becomes insufficient, the financing statement, unless amended to provide a sufficient name for the debtor, is effective only to perfect a security interest in collateral acquired by the debtor before, or within four months after, the change. If an amendment that provides a sufficient name is filed within four months after the change, the financing statement as amended would be effective also with respect to collateral acquired more than four months after the change. If an amendment that provides a sufficient name is filed more than four months after the change, the financing statement as amended would be effective also with respect to collateral acquired more than four months after the change, but only from the time of the filing of the amendment.

§ 9-508. Effectiveness of Financing Statement If New Debtor Becomes Bound by Security Agreement.

(a) [Financing statement naming original debtor.] Except as otherwise provided in this section, a filed financing statement naming an original debtor is effective to perfect a security interest in collateral in which a new debtor has or acquires rights to the extent that the financing statement would have been effective had the original debtor acquired rights in the collateral.

(b) [Financing statement becoming seriously misleading.] If the difference between the name of the original debtor and that of the new debtor causes a filed financing statement that is effective under subsection (a) to be seriously misleading under Section 9-506:

(1) the financing statement is effective to perfect a security interest in collateral acquired

by the new debtor before, and within four months after, the new debtor becomes bound under Section 9-203(d); and

(2) the financing statement is not effective to perfect a security interest in collateral acquired by the new debtor more than four months after the new debtor becomes bound under Section 9-203(d) unless an initial financing statement providing the name of the new debtor is filed before the expiration of that time.

(c) [When section not applicable.] This section does not apply to collateral as to which a filed financing statement remains effective against the new debtor under Section 9-507(a).

Definitional Cross References:

Collateral	Section 9-102(a)(12)
Financing statement	Section 9-102(a)(39)
New debtor	Section 9-102(a)(56)
Original debtor	Section 9-102(a)(60)
Right	Section 1-201(b)(34)
Security agreement	Section 9-102(a)(74)
Security interest	Section 1-201(b)(35)

Official Comment

1. Source. New.

2. The Problem. Section 9-203(d) and (e) and this section deal with situations where one party (the "new debtor") becomes bound as debtor by a security agreement entered into by another person (the "original debtor"). These situations often arise as a consequence of changes in business structure. For example, the original debtor may be an individual debtor who operates a business as a sole proprietorship and then incorporates it. Or, the original debtor may be a corporation that is merged into another corporation. Under both former Article 9 and this Article, collateral that is transferred in the course of the incorporation or merger normally would remain subject to a perfected security interest. See Sections 9-315(a), 9-507(a). Former Article 9 was less clear with respect to whether an after-acquired property clause in a security agreement signed by the original debtor would be effective to create a security interest in property acquired by the new corporation or the merger survivor and, if so, whether a financing statement filed against the original debtor would be effective to perfect the security interest. This section and Sections 9-203(d) and (e) are a clarification.

3. How New Debtor Becomes Bound. Normally, a security interest is unenforceable unless the debtor has signed a security agreement describing the collateral. See Section 9-203(b). Section 9-203(e) creates an exception, under which a security agreement entered into by one person is effective with respect to the property of another. This exception comes into play if a "new debtor" becomes bound as debtor by a security agreement entered into by another person (the "original debtor"). (The quoted terms are defined in Section 9-102.) If a new debtor does become bound, then the security agreement entered into by the original debtor satisfies the security-agreement requirement of Section 9-203(b)(3) as to existing or after-acquired property of the new debtor to the extent the property is described in the security agreement. In that case, no other agreement is necessary to make a security interest enforceable in that property. See Section 9-203(e).

Section 9-203(d) explains when a new debtor becomes bound by an original debtor's security agreement. Under Section 9-203(d)(1), a new debtor becomes bound as debtor if, by contract or operation of other law, the security agreement becomes effective to create a security interest in the new debtor's property. For example, if the applicable corporate law of mergers provides that when A Corp merges into B Corp, B Corp becomes a debtor under A Corp's security agreement, then B Corp would become bound as debtor following such a merger. Similarly, B Corp would become bound as debtor if B Corp contractually assumes A's obligations under the security agreement.

Under certain circumstances, a new debtor becomes bound for purposes of this Article even though it would not be bound under other law. Under Section 9-203(d)(2), a new debtor becomes bound when, by contract or operation of other law, it (i) becomes obligated not only for the secured obligation but also generally for the obligations of the original debtor and (ii) acquires or succeeds to substantially all the assets of the original debtor. For example, some corporate laws provide that, when two corporations merge, the surviving corporation succeeds to the assets of its merger partner and "has all liabilities" of both corporations. In the case where, for example, A Corp merges into B Corp (and A Corp ceases to exist), some people have questioned whether A Corp's grant of a security interest in its existing and after-acquired property becomes a "liability" of B Corp, such that B Corp's existing and after-acquired property becomes subject to a security interest in favor of A Corp's lender. Even if corporate law were to give a negative answer, under Section 9-203(d)(2), B Corp would become bound for purposes of Section 9-203(e) and this section. The "substantially all of the assets" requirement of Section 9-203(d)(2) excludes sureties and other secondary obligors as well as persons who become obligated through veil piercing and other non-successorship doctrines. In most cases, it will exclude successors to the assets and liabilities of a division of a debtor.

4. When Financing Statement Effective Against New Debtor. Subsection (a) provides that a filing against the original debtor generally is effective to perfect a security interest in collateral that a new debtor has at the time it becomes bound by the original debtor's security agreement and collateral that it acquires after the new debtor becomes bound. Under subsection (b), however, if the filing against the original debtor is seriously misleading as to the new debtor's name, the filing is effective as to collateral acquired by the new debtor more than four months after the new debtor becomes bound only if a person files during the four-month period an initial financing statement providing the name of the new debtor. Compare Section 9-507(c) (four-month period of effectiveness with respect to collateral acquired by a debtor after the name provided for the debtor becomes insufficient as the name of the debtor). As to the meaning of "initial financing statement" in this context, see Section 9-512, Comment 5.

5. Transferred Collateral. This section does not apply to collateral transferred by the original debtor to a new debtor. See subsection (c). Under those circumstances, the filing against the original debtor continues to be effective until it lapses or perfection is lost for another reason. See Sections 9-316, 9-507(a).

6. Priority. Section 9-326 governs the priority contest between a secured creditor of the original debtor and a secured creditor of the new debtor.

§ 9-509. Persons Entitled to File a Record.

(a) [Person entitled to file record.] A person may file an initial financing statement, amendment that adds collateral covered by a financing statement, or amendment that adds a debtor to a financing statement only if:

(1) the debtor authorizes the filing in a signed record or pursuant to subsection (b) or (c); or

(2) the person holds an agricultural lien that has become effective at the time of filing and the financing statement covers only collateral in which the person holds an agricultural lien.

(b) [Security agreement as authorization.] By signing or becoming bound as debtor by a security agreement, a debtor or new debtor authorizes the filing of an initial financing statement, and an amendment, covering:

(1) the collateral described in the security agreement; and

(2) property that becomes collateral under Section 9-315(a)(2), whether or not the security agreement expressly covers proceeds.

(c) [Acquisition of collateral as authorization.] By acquiring collateral in which a security interest or agricultural lien continues under Section 9-315(a)(1), a debtor authorizes the filing of an initial financing statement, and an amendment, covering the collateral and property that becomes collateral under Section 9-315(a)(2).

(d) [Person entitled to file certain amendments.] A person may file an amendment other than an amendment that adds collateral covered by a financing statement or an amendment that adds a debtor to a financing statement only if:

(1) the secured party of record authorizes the filing; or

(2) the amendment is a termination statement for a financing statement as to which the secured party of record has failed to file or send a termination statement as required by Section 9-513(a) or (c), the debtor authorizes the filing, and the termination statement indicates that the debtor authorized it to be filed.

(e) [Multiple secured parties of record.] If there is more than one secured party of record for a financing statement, each secured party of record may authorize the filing of an amendment under subsection (d).

Definitional Cross References:

Agricultural lien	Section 9-102(a)(5)
Collateral	Section 9-102(a)(12)
Debtor	Section 9-102(a)(28)
Financing statement	Section 9-102(a)(39)
New debtor	Section 9-102(a)(56)
Person	Section 1-201(b)(27)
Proceeds	Section 9-102(a)(64)
Record	Section 9-102(a)(70)
Secured party	Section 9-102(a)(73)
Security agreement	Section 9-102(a)(74)
Security interest	Section 1-201(b)(35)
Send	Section 1-201(b)(36)
Sign	Section 1-201(b)(37)
Termination statement	Section 9-102(a)(80)

Official Comment

1. Source. New.

2. Scope and Approach of This Section. This section collects in one place most of the rules determining whether a record may be filed. Section 9-510 explains the extent to which a filed record is effective. Under these sections, the identity of the person who effects a filing is immaterial. The filing scheme contemplated by this Part does not contemplate that the identity of a "filer" will be a part of the searchable records. This is consistent with, and a necessary aspect of, eliminating signatures or other evidence of authorization from the system. (Note that the 1972 amendments to this Article eliminated the requirement that a financing statement contain the signature of the secured party.) As long as the appropriate person authorizes the filing, or, in the case of a termination statement, the debtor is entitled to the termination, it is insignificant whether the secured party or another person files any given record. The question of authorization is one for the court, not the filing office. However, a filing office may choose to employ authentication procedures in connection with electronic communications, e.g., to verify the identity of a filer who seeks to charge the filing fee.

3. Unauthorized Filings. Records filed in the filing office do not require signatures for their effectiveness. Subsection (a)(1) substitutes for the debtor's signature on a financing statement the requirement that the debtor authorize in a signed record the filing of an initial financing statement or an amendment that adds collateral. Also, under subsection (a)(1), if an amendment adds a debtor, the debtor who is added must authorize the amendment. A person who files an unauthorized record in violation of subsection (a)(1) is liable under Section 9-625(a) and (e) for actual and statutory damages. Of course, a filed financing statement is ineffective to perfect a security interest if the filing is not authorized. See Section 9-510(a). Law other than this Article, including the law with respect to ratification of past acts, generally determines whether a person has the requisite authority to file a record under this section. See Sections 1-103, 9-502, Comment 3. This Article applies to other issues, such as the priority of a security interest perfected by the filing of a financing statement. See Section 9-322, Comment 4. *Amendment approved by the Permanent Editorial Board for Uniform Commercial Code December 31, 2001.*

4. *Ipso Facto* Authorization. Under subsection (b), the signing of a security agreement *ipso facto* constitutes the debtor's authorization of the filing of a financing statement covering the collateral described in the security agreement. The secured party need not obtain a separate authorization. Similarly, a new debtor's becoming bound by a security agreement *ipso facto* constitutes the new debtor's authorization of the filing of a financing statement covering the collateral described in the security agreement by which the new debtor has become bound. And, under subsection (c), the acquisition of collateral in which a security interest continues after disposition under Section 9-315(a)(1) *ipso facto* constitutes an authorization to file an initial financing statement against the person who acquired the collateral. The authorization to file an initial financing statement also constitutes an authorization to file a record covering actual proceeds of the original collateral, even if the security agreement is silent as to proceeds.

Example 1: Debtor signs a security agreement creating a security interest in Debtor's inventory in favor of Secured Party. Secured Party files a financing statement covering inventory and accounts. The financing statement is authorized insofar as it covers inventory and unauthorized insofar as it covers accounts. (Note, however, that the financing statement will be effective to perfect a security interest in accounts constituting proceeds of the inventory to the same extent as a financing statement covering only inventory.)

Example 2: Debtor signs a security agreement creating a security interest in Debtor's inventory in favor of Secured Party. Secured Party files a financing statement covering inventory. Debtor sells some inventory, deposits the buyer's payment into a deposit account, and withdraws the funds to purchase equipment. As long as the equipment can be traced to the inventory, the security interest continues in the equipment. See Section 9-315(a)(2). However, because the equipment was acquired with cash proceeds, the financing statement becomes ineffective to perfect the security interest in the equipment on the 21st day after the security interest attaches to the equipment unless Secured Party continues perfection beyond the 20-day period by filing a financing statement against the equipment or amending the filed financing statement to cover equipment. See Section 9-315(d). Debtor's signing of the security agreement authorizes the filing of an initial financing statement or amendment covering the equipment, which is "property that becomes collateral under Section 9-315(a)(2)." See Section 9-509(b)(2).

5. Agricultural Liens. Under subsection (a)(2), the holder of an agricultural lien may file a financing statement covering collateral subject to the lien without obtaining the debtor's authorization. Because the lien arises as matter of law, the debtor's consent is not required. A person who files an unauthorized record in violation of this subsection is liable under Section 9-625(e) for a statutory penalty and damages.

6. Amendments; Termination Statements Authorized by Debtor. Most amendments may not be filed unless the secured party of record, as determined under Section 9-511, authorizes the filing. See subsection (d)(1). However, under subsection (d)(2), the authorization of the secured party of record is not required for the filing of a termination statement if the secured party of record failed to send or file a termination statement as required by Section 9-513, the debtor authorizes it to be filed, and the termination statement so indicates. An authorization to file a record under subsection (d) is effective even if the authorization is not in a signed record. Compare subsection (a)(1). However, both the person filing the record and the person giving the authorization may wish to obtain and retain a record indicating that the filing was authorized.

7. Multiple Secured Parties of Record. Subsection (e) deals with multiple secured parties of record. It permits each secured party of record to authorize the filing of amendments. However, Section 9-510(b) protects the rights and powers of one secured party of record from the effects of filings made by another secured party of record. See Section 9-510, Comment 3.

8. Successor to Secured Party of Record. A person may succeed to the powers of the secured party of record by operation of other law, e.g., the law of corporate mergers. In that case, the successor has the power to authorize filings within the meaning of this section.

9. "Signed" and "Signing" Replace "Authenticated" and "Authenticating." Consistent with the revised definition of "sign" in Section 1-201, the cognate terms "signed" and "signing" replace the references to "authenticated" and "authenticating" in the pre-2022 text of this section.

§ 9-510. Effectiveness of Filed Record.

(a) [Filed record effective if authorized.] A filed record is effective only to the extent that it was filed by a person that may file it under Section 9-509.

(b) [Authorization by one secured party of record.] A record authorized by one secured party of record does not affect the financing statement with respect to another secured party of record.

(c) [Continuation statement not timely filed.] A continuation statement that is not filed within the six-month period prescribed by Section 9-515(d) is ineffective.

Definitional Cross References:

Continuation statement	Section 9-102(a)(27)
Financing statement	Section 9-102(a)(39)
Person	Section 1-201(b)(27)
Record	Section 9-102(a)(70)
Secured party	Section 9-102(a)(73)

Official Comment

1. Source. New.

2. Ineffectiveness of Unauthorized or Overbroad Filings. Subsection (a) provides that a filed financing statement is effective only to the extent it was filed by a person entitled to file it.

Example 1: Debtor authorizes the filing of a financing statement covering inventory. Under Section 9-509, the secured party may file a financing statement covering only inventory; it may not file a financing statement covering other collateral. The secured party files a financing statement covering inventory and equipment. This section provides that the financing statement is effective only to the extent the secured party may file it. Thus, the financing statement is effective to perfect a security interest in inventory but ineffective to perfect a security interest in equipment.

3. Multiple Secured Parties of Record. Section 9-509(e) permits any secured party of record to authorize the filing of most amendments. Subsection (b) of this section prevents a filing authorized by one secured party of record from affecting the rights and powers of another secured party of record without the latter's consent.

Example 2: Debtor creates a security interest in favor of A and B. The filed financing statement names A and B as the secured parties. An amendment deleting some collateral covered by the financing statement is filed pursuant to B's authorization. Although B's security interest in the deleted collateral becomes unperfected, A's security interest remains perfected in all the collateral.

Example 3: Debtor creates a security interest in favor of A and B. The financing statement names A and B as the secured parties. A termination statement is filed pursuant to B's authorization. Although the effectiveness of the financing statement terminates with respect to B's security interest, A's rights are unaffected. That is, the financing statement continues to be effective to perfect A's security interest.

4. Continuation Statements. A continuation statement may be filed only within the six months immediately before lapse. See Section 9-515(d). The filing office is obligated to reject a continuation statement that is filed outside the six-month period. See Sections 9-520(a), 9-516(b)(7). Subsection (c) provides that if the filing office fails to reject a continuation statement that is not filed in a timely manner, the continuation statement is ineffective nevertheless.

§ 9-511. Secured Party of Record.

(a) [Secured party of record.] A secured party of record with respect to a financing statement is a person whose name is provided as the name of the secured party or a representative of the secured party in an initial financing statement that has been filed. If an initial financing statement is filed under Section 9-514(a), the assignee named in the initial financing statement is the secured party of record with respect to the financing statement.

(b) [Amendment naming secured party of record.] If an amendment of a financing statement which provides the name of a person as a secured party or a representative of a secured party is filed, the person named in the amendment is a secured party of record. If an amendment is filed under Section 9-514(b), the assignee named in the amendment is a secured party of record.

(c) [Amendment deleting secured party of record.] A person remains a secured party of record until the filing of an amendment of the financing statement which deletes the person.

Definitional Cross References:

Financing statement	Section 9-102(a)(39)
Person	Section 1-201(b)(27)
Representative	Section 1-201(b)(33)
Secured party	Section 9-102(a)(73)

Official Comment

1. Source. New.

2. Secured Party of Record. This new section explains how the secured party of record is to be determined. If SP-1 is named as the secured party in an initial financing statement, it is the secured party of record. Similarly, if an initial financing statement reflects a total assignment from SP-0 to SP-1, then SP-1 is the secured party of record. See subsection (a). If, subsequently, an amendment is filed assigning SP-1's status to SP-2, then SP-2 becomes the secured party of record in place of SP-1. The same result obtains if a subsequent amendment deletes the reference to SP-1 and substitutes therefor a reference to SP-2. If, however, a subsequent amendment adds SP-2 as a secured party but does not purport to remove SP-1 as a secured party, then SP-2 and SP-1 each is a secured party of record. See subsection (b). An amendment purporting to remove the only secured party of record without providing a successor is ineffective. See Section 9-512(e). At any point in time, all effective records that comprise a financing statement must be examined to determine the person or persons that have the status of secured party of record.

3. Successor to Secured Party of Record. Application of other law may result in a person succeeding to the powers of a secured party of record. For example, if the secured party of record (A) merges into another corporation (B) and the other corporation (B) survives, other law may provide that B has all of A's powers. In that case, B is authorized to take all actions under this Part that A would have been authorized to take. Similarly, acts taken by a person who is authorized under generally applicable principles of agency to act on behalf of the secured party of record are effective under this Part.

§ 9-512. Amendment of Financing Statement.

ALTERNATIVE A

(a) [Amendment of information in financing statement.] Subject to Section 9-509, a person may add or delete collateral covered by, continue or terminate the effectiveness of, or, subject to subsection (e), otherwise amend the information provided in, a financing statement by filing an amendment that:

(1) identifies, by its file number, the initial financing statement to which the amendment relates; and

(2) if the amendment relates to an initial financing statement filed [or recorded] in a filing office described in Section 9-501(a)(1), provides the information specified in Section 9-502(b).

ALTERNATIVE B

(a) [Amendment of information in financing statement.] Subject to Section 9-509, a person may add or delete collateral covered by, continue or terminate the effectiveness of, or, subject to subsection (e), otherwise amend the information provided in, a financing statement by filing an amendment that:

(1) identifies, by its file number, the initial financing statement to which the amendment relates; and

(2) if the amendment relates to an initial financing statement filed [or recorded] in a filing office described in Section 9-501(a)(1), provides the date [and time] that the initial financing statement was filed [or recorded] and the information specified in Section 9-502(b).

END OF ALTERNATIVES

(b) [Period of effectiveness not affected.] Except as otherwise provided in Section 9-515, the filing of an amendment does not extend the period of effectiveness of the financing statement.

(c) [Effectiveness of amendment adding collateral.] A financing statement that is amended by an amendment that adds collateral is effective as to the added collateral only from the date of the filing of the amendment.

(d) [Effectiveness of amendment adding debtor.] A financing statement that is amended by an amendment that adds a debtor is effective as to the added debtor only from the date of the filing of the amendment.

(e) [Certain amendments ineffective.] An amendment is ineffective to the extent it:

(1) purports to delete all debtors and fails to provide the name of a debtor to be covered by the financing statement; or

(2) purports to delete all secured parties of record and fails to provide the name of a new secured party of record.

Legislative Note: *States whose real-estate filing offices require additional information in amendments and cannot search their records by both the name of the debtor and the file number should enact Alternative B to Sections 9-512(a), 9-518(b), 9-518(d), 9-519(f), and 9-522(a).*

Definitional Cross References:

Collateral	Section 9-102(a)(12)
Debtor	Section 9-102(a)(28)
File number	Section 9-102(a)(36)
Filing office	Section 9-102(a)(37)
Financing statement	Section 9-102(a)(39)
Person	Section 1-201(b)(27)
Record	Section 9-102(a)(70)
State	Section 9-102(a)(77)

Official Comment

1. Source. Former 9-402(4).

2. Changes to Financing Statements. This section addresses changes to financing statements, including addition and deletion of collateral. Although termination statements, assignments, and continuation statements are types of amendment, this Article follows former Article 9 and contains separate sections containing additional provisions applicable to particular types of amendments. See Section 9-513 (termination statements); 9-514 (assignments); 9-515 (continuation statements). One should not infer from this separate treatment that this Article requires a separate amendment to accomplish each change. Rather, a single amendment would be legally sufficient to, e.g., add collateral and continue the effectiveness of the financing statement.

3. Amendments. An amendment under this Article may identify only the information contained in a financing statement that is to be changed; alternatively, it may take the form of an amended and restated financing statement. The latter would state, for example, that the financing statement "is amended and restated to read as follows:" References in this Part to an "amended financing statement" are to a financing statement as amended by an amendment using either technique.

This section revises former Section 9-402(4) to permit secured parties of record to make changes in the public record without the need to obtain the debtor's signature. However, the filing of an amendment that adds collateral or adds a debtor must be authorized by the debtor or it will not be effective. See Sections 9-509(a), 9-510(a).

4. Amendment Adding Debtor. An amendment that adds a debtor is effective, provided that the added debtor authorizes the filing. See Section 9-509(a). However, filing an amendment adding a debtor to a previously filed financing statement affords no advantage over filing an initial financing statement against that debtor and may be disadvantageous. With respect to the added debtor, for purposes of determining the priority of the security interest, the time of filing is the time of the filing of the amendment, not the time of the filing of the initial financing statement. See subsection (d). However, the effectiveness of the financing statement lapses with respect to added debtor at the time it lapses with respect to the original debtor. See subsection (b).

5. Amendment Adding Debtor Name. Many states have enacted statutes governing the "conversion" of one organization organized under the law of that state, e.g., a corporation, into another such organization, e.g., a limited liability company. This Article defers to those statutes to determine whether the resulting organization is the same legal person as the initial, converting organization (albeit with a different name) or whether the resulting organization is a different legal person. When the governing statute does not clearly resolve the question, a secured party whose debtor is the converting organization may wish to proceed as if the statute provides for both results. In these circumstances, an amendment adding to the initial financing statement the name of the resulting organization may be preferable to an amendment substituting that name for the name of the debtor provided on the initial financing statement. In the event the governing statute is construed as providing that the resulting organization is the same legal person as the converting organization, but with a different name, the timely filing of such an amendment would satisfy the requirement of Section 9-507(c)(2). If, however, the governing statute is construed as providing that the resulting organization is a different legal person, the financing statement (which continues to provide the name of the original debtor) would be effective as to collateral acquired by the resulting organization ("new debtor") before, and within four months after, the conversion. See Section 9-508(b)(1). Inasmuch as it is the first financing statement filed against the resulting organization by the secured party, the record adding the name of the resulting organization as a debtor would constitute "an initial financing statement providing the name of the new debtor" under Section 9-508(b)(2). The secured party also may wish to file another financing statement naming the resulting organization as debtor. See Comment 4.

6. Deletion of All Debtors or Secured Parties of Record. Subsection (e) assures that there will be a debtor and secured party of record for every financing statement.

Example: A filed financing statement names A and B as secured parties of record and covers inventory and equipment. An amendment deletes equipment and purports to delete A and B as secured parties of record without adding a substitute secured party. The amendment is ineffective to the extent it purports to delete the secured parties of record but effective with respect to the deletion of collateral. As a consequence, the financing statement, as amended, covers only inventory, but A and B remain as secured parties of record.

§ 9-513. Termination Statement.

(a) [Consumer goods.] A secured party shall cause the secured party of record for a financing statement to file a termination statement for the financing statement if the financing statement covers consumer goods and:

(1) there is no obligation secured by the collateral covered by the financing statement and no commitment to make an advance, incur an obligation, or otherwise give value; or

(2) the debtor did not authorize the filing of the initial financing statement.

(b) [Time for compliance with subsection (a).] To comply with subsection (a), a secured party shall cause the secured party of record to file the termination statement:

(1) within one month after there is no obligation secured by the collateral covered by the financing statement and no commitment to make an advance, incur an obligation, or otherwise give value; or

(2) if earlier, within 20 days after the secured party receives a signed demand from a debtor.

(c) [Other collateral.] In cases not governed by subsection (a), within 20 days after a secured party receives a signed demand from a debtor, the secured party shall cause the secured party of record for a financing statement to send to the debtor a termination statement for the financing statement or file the termination statement in the filing office if:

(1) except in the case of a financing statement covering accounts or chattel paper that has been sold or goods that are the subject of a consignment, there is no obligation secured by the collateral covered by the financing statement and no commitment to make an advance, incur an obligation, or otherwise give value;

(2) the financing statement covers accounts or chattel paper that has been sold but as to which the account debtor or other person obligated has discharged its obligation;

(3) the financing statement covers goods that were the subject of a consignment to the debtor but are not in the debtor's possession; or

(4) the debtor did not authorize the filing of the initial financing statement.

(d) [Effect of filing termination statement.] Except as otherwise provided in Section 9-510, upon the filing of a termination statement with the filing office, the financing statement to which the termination statement relates ceases to be effective. Except as otherwise provided in Section 9-510, for purposes of Sections 9-519(g), 9-522(a), and 9-523(c), the filing with the filing office of a termination statement relating to a financing statement that indicates that the debtor is a transmitting utility also causes the effectiveness of the financing statement to lapse.

Definitional Cross References:

Account	Section 9-102(a)(2)
Account debtor	Section 9-102(a)(3)
Chattel paper	Section 9-102(a)(11)
Collateral	Section 9-102(a)(12)
Consignment	Section 9-102(a)(20)
Consumer goods	Section 9-102(a)(23)
Debtor	Section 9-102(a)(28)
Filing office	Section 9-102(a)(37)
Financing statement	Section 9-102(a)(39)
Goods	Section 9-102(a)(44)
Secured party	Section 9-102(a)(73)
Send	Section 1-201(b)(36)
Sign	Section 1-201(b)(37)
Termination statement	Section 9-102(a)(80)
Value	Section 1-204

Official Comment

1. Source. Former Section 9-404.

2. Duty to File or Send. This section specifies when a secured party must cause the secured party of record to file or send to the debtor a termination statement for a financing statement. Because most financing statements expire in five years unless a continuation statement is filed (Section 9-515), no compulsion is placed on the secured party to file a termination statement unless demanded by the debtor, except in the case of consumer goods. Because many consumers will not realize the importance to them of clearing the public record, an affirmative duty is put on the secured party in that case. But many purchase-money security interests in consumer goods will not be filed, except for motor vehicles. See Section 9-309(1). Under Section 9-311(b), compliance with a certificate-of-title statute is "equivalent to the filing of a financing statement under this article." Thus, this section applies to a certificate of title unless the section is superseded by a certificate-of-title statute that contains a specific rule addressing a secured party's duty to cause a notation of a security interest to be removed from a certificate of title. In the context of a certificate of title, however, the secured party could comply with this section by causing the removal itself or providing the debtor with documentation sufficient to enable the debtor to effect the removal.

Subsections (a) and (b) apply to a financing statement covering consumer goods. Subsection (c) applies to other financing statements. Subsection (a) and (c) each makes explicit what was implicit under former Article 9: If the debtor did not authorize the filing of a financing statement in the first place, the secured party of record should file or send a termination statement. The liability imposed upon a secured party that fails to comply with subsection (a) or (c) is identical to that imposed for the filing of an unauthorized financing statement or amendment. See Section 9-625(e).

References to a "termination statement" in this section and in Part 5 generally should be interpreted functionally, based on the purposes of the termination. A termination statement includes any amendment that meets the definition of that term by containing an indication that the amendment "is a termination statement" or that the identified financing statement "is no longer effective." Section 9-102(a)(80). The amendment may terminate the effectiveness of a financing statement in whole or in part. For example, if a person did not authorize the filing of a financing statement against it as debtor, under subsection (a)(2) and (c)(4) the person may demand that the financing statement be terminated as to that person, even if the financing statement remains of record and effective as to one or more other persons named as debtors in the financing statement. Such a termination statement may take the form of an amendment that deletes the person as a debtor. Similarly, if a person authorized the filing of a financing statement as to some collateral but not as to other property identified as collateral on the financing statement, the person may demand that the financing statement be terminated as to the unauthorized identified collateral, even if the financing statement remains of record and effective as to other identified collateral. Such a termination statement may take the form of an amendment that deletes the unauthorized identified collateral from coverage of the financing statement. Even if such amendments do not indicate explicitly that they are termination statements, they would nonetheless indicate that the financing statement "is no longer effective" to the extent specified and fall within the definition of "termination statement."

3. "Bogus" Filings. A secured party's duty to send a termination statement arises when the secured party "receives" a signed demand from the debtor. In the case of an unauthorized financing statement, the person named as debtor in the financing statement may have no relationship with the named secured party and no reason to know the secured party's address. Inasmuch as the address in the financing statement is "held out by [the person named as secured party in the financing statement] as the place for receipt of such communications [i.e., communications relating to security interests]," the putative secured party is deemed to have "received" a notification delivered to that address. See Section 1-202(e). If a termination statement is not forthcoming, the person named as debtor itself may authorize the filing of a termination statement, which will be effective if it indicates that the person authorized it to be filed. See Sections 9-509(d)(2), 9-510(a).

4. Buyers of Receivables. Applied literally, former Section 9-404(1) would have required many buyers of receivables to file a termination statement immediately upon filing a financing statement because "there is no outstanding secured obligation and no commitment to make advances, incur obligations, or otherwise give value." Subsections (c)(1) and (2) remedy this problem. While the security interest of a buyer of accounts or chattel paper (B-1) is perfected, the debtor is not deemed to retain an interest in the sold receivables and thus could transfer no interest in them to another buyer (B-2) or to a lien creditor (LC). However, for purposes of determining the rights of the debtor's creditors and certain purchasers of accounts or chattel paper from the debtor, while B-1's security interest is unperfected, the debtor-seller is deemed to have rights in the sold receivables, and a competing security interest or judicial lien may attach to those rights. See Sections 9-318, 9-109, Comment 5. Suppose that B-1's security interest in certain accounts and chattel paper is perfected by filing, but the effectiveness of the financing statement lapses. Both before and after lapse, B-1 collects some of the receivables. After lapse, LC acquires a lien on the accounts and chattel paper. B-1's unperfected security interest in the accounts and chattel paper is subordinate to LC's rights. See Section 9-317(a)(2). But collections on accounts and chattel paper are not "accounts" or "chattel paper." Even if B-1's security interest in the accounts and chattel paper is or becomes unperfected, neither the debtor nor LC acquires rights to the collections that B-1 collects (and owns) before LC acquires a lien.

5. Effect of Filing. Subsection (d) states the effect of filing a termination statement: the related financing statement ceases to be effective. If one of several secured parties of record files a termination statement, subsection (d) applies only with respect to the rights of the person who authorized the filing of the termination statement. See Section 9-510(b). The financing statement remains effective with respect to the rights of the others. However, even if a financing statement is terminated (and thus no longer is effective) with respect to all secured parties of record, the financing statement, including the termination statement, will remain of record until at least one year after it lapses with respect to all secured parties of record. See Section 9-519(g).

6. "Signed" Replaces "Authenticated." Consistent with the revised definition of "sign" in Section 1-201, the cognate term "signed" replaces the references to "authenticated" in the pre-2022 text of this section.

§ 9-514. Assignment of Powers of Secured Party of Record.

(a) [Assignment reflected on initial financing statement.] Except as otherwise provided in subsection (c), an initial financing statement may reflect an assignment of all of the secured party's power to authorize an amendment to the financing statement by providing the name and mailing address of the assignee as the name and address of the secured party.

(b) [Assignment of filed financing statement.] Except as otherwise provided in subsection (c), a secured party of record may assign of record all or part of its power to authorize an amendment to a financing statement by filing in the filing office an amendment of the financing statement which:

(1) identifies, by its file number, the initial financing statement to which it relates;

(2) provides the name of the assignor; and

(3) provides the name and mailing address of the assignee.

(c) [Assignment of record of mortgage.] An assignment of record of a security interest in a fixture covered by a record of a mortgage which is effective as a financing statement filed as a fixture filing under Section 9-502(c) may be made only by an assignment of record of the mortgage in the manner provided by law of this State other than [the Uniform Commercial Code].

Definitional Cross References:

File number	Section 9-102(a)(36)
Filing office	Section 9-102(a)(37)
Financing statement	Section 9-102(a)(39)
Fixture filing	Section 9-102(a)(40)
Fixtures	Section 9-102(a)(41)
Mortgage	Section 9-102(a)(55)
Secured party	Section 9-102(a)(73)
Security interest	Section 1-201(b)(35)
State	Section 9-102(a)(77)

Official Comment

1. Source. Former Section 9-405.

2. Assignments. This section provides a permissive device whereby a secured party of record may effectuate an assignment of its power to affect a financing statement. It may also be useful for a secured party who has assigned all or part of its security interest or agricultural lien and wishes to have the fact noted of record, so that inquiries concerning the transaction would be addressed to the assignee. See Section 9-502, Comment 2. Upon the filing of an assignment, the assignee becomes the "secured party of record" and may authorize the filing of a continuation statement, termination statement, or other amendment. Note that under Section 9-310(c) no filing of an assignment is required as a condition of continuing the perfected status of the security interest against creditors and transferees of the original debtor. However, if an assignment is not filed, the assignor remains the secured party of record, with the power (even if not the right) to authorize the filing of effective amendments. See Sections 9-511(c), 9-509(d).

Where a record of a mortgage is effective as a financing statement filed as a fixture filing (Section 9-502(c)), then an assignment of record of the security interest may be made only in the manner in which an assignment of record of the mortgage may be made under local real-property law.

3. Comparison to Prior Law. Most of the changes reflected in this section are for clarification or to embrace medium-neutral drafting. As a general matter, this section preserves the opportunity given by former Section 9-405 to assign a security interest of record in one of two different ways. Under subsection (a), a secured party may assign all of its power to affect a financing statement by naming an assignee in the initial financing statement. The secured party of record may accomplish the same result under subsection (b) by making a subsequent filing. Subsection (b) also may be used for an assignment of only some of the secured party of record's power to affect a financing statement, e.g., the power to affect the financing statement as it relates to particular items of collateral or as it relates to an undivided interest in a security interest in all the collateral. An initial financing statement may not be used to change the secured party of record under these circumstances. However, an amendment adding the assignee as a secured party of record may be used.

§ 9-515. Duration and Effectiveness of Financing Statement; Effect of Lapsed Financing Statement.

(a) [Five-year effectiveness.] Except as otherwise provided in subsections (b), (e), (f), and (g), a filed financing statement is effective for a period of five years after the date of filing.

(b) [Public-finance or manufactured-home transaction.] Except as otherwise provided in subsections (e), (f), and (g), an initial financing statement filed in connection with a public-finance transaction or manufactured-home transaction is effective for a period of 30 years after the date of filing if it indicates that it is filed in connection with a public-finance transaction or manufactured-home transaction.

(c) [Lapse and continuation of financing statement.] The effectiveness of a filed financing statement lapses on the expiration of the period of its effectiveness unless before the lapse a continuation statement is filed pursuant to subsection (d). Upon lapse, a financing statement ceases to be effective and any security interest or agricultural lien that was perfected by the financing statement becomes unperfected, unless the security interest is perfected otherwise. If the security interest or agricultural lien becomes unperfected upon lapse, it is deemed never to have been perfected as against a purchaser of the collateral for value.

(d) [When continuation statement may be filed.] A continuation statement may be filed only within six months before the expiration of the five-year period specified in subsection (a) or the 30-year period specified in subsection (b), whichever is applicable.

(e) [Effect of filing continuation statement.] Except as otherwise provided in Section 9-510, upon timely filing of a continuation statement, the effectiveness of the initial financing statement continues for a period of five years commencing on the day on which the financing statement would have become ineffective in the absence of the filing. Upon the expiration of the five-year period, the financing statement lapses in the same manner as provided in subsection (c), unless, before the lapse, another continuation statement is filed pursuant to subsection (d). Succeeding continuation statements may be filed in the same manner to continue the effectiveness of the initial financing statement.

(f) [Transmitting utility financing statement.] If a debtor is a transmitting utility and a filed initial financing statement so indicates, the financing statement is effective until a termination statement is filed.

(g) [Record of mortgage as financing statement.] A record of a mortgage that is effective as a financing statement filed as a fixture filing under Section 9-502(c) remains effective as a financing statement filed as a fixture filing until the mortgage is released or satisfied of record or its effectiveness otherwise terminates as to the real property.

Definitional Cross References:

Agricultural lien	Section 9-102(a)(5)
Collateral	Section 9-102(a)(12)
Continuation statement	Section 9-102(a)(27)
Debtor	Section 9-102(a)(28)
Financing statement	Section 9-102(a)(39)
Fixture filing	Section 9-102(a)(40)
Manufactured-home transaction	Section 9-102(a)(54)
Mortgage	Section 9-102(a)(55)
Public-finance transaction	Section 9-102(a)(67)
Purchaser	Section 1-201(b)(30)
Record	Section 9-102(a)(70)
Security interest	Section 1-201(b)(35)
Termination statement	Section 9-102(a)(80)
Transmitting utility	Section 9-102(a)(81)
Value	Section 1-204

Official Comment

1. Source. Former Section 9-403(2), (3), (6).

2. Period of Financing Statement's Effectiveness. Subsection (a) states the general rule: a financing statement is effective for a five-year period unless its effectiveness is continued under this section or terminated under Section 9-513. Subsection (b) provides that if the financing statement relates to a public-finance transaction or a manufactured-home transaction and so indicates, the financing statement is effective for 30 years. These financings typically extend well beyond the standard, five-year period. Under subsection (f), a financing statement filed against a transmitting utility remains effective indefinitely, until a termination statement is filed. Likewise, under subsection (g), a mortgage effective as a fixture filing remains effective until its effectiveness terminates under real-property law.

3. Lapse. When the period of effectiveness under subsection (a) or (b) expires, the effectiveness of the financing statement lapses. The last sentence of subsection (c) addresses the effect of lapse. The deemed retroactive unperfection applies only with respect to purchasers for value; unlike former Section 9-403(2), it does not apply with respect to lien creditors.

Example 1: SP-1 and SP-2 both hold security interests in the same collateral. Both security interests are perfected by filing. SP-1 filed first and has priority under Section 9-322(a)(1). The effectiveness of SP-1's filing lapses. As long as SP-2's security interest remains perfected thereafter, SP-2 is entitled to priority over SP-1's security interest, which is deemed never to have been perfected as against a purchaser for value (SP-2). See Section 9-322(a)(2).

Example 2: SP holds a security interest perfected by filing. On July 1, LC acquires a judicial lien on the collateral. Two weeks later, the effectiveness of the financing statement lapses. Although the security interest becomes unperfected upon lapse, it was perfected when LC acquired its lien. Accordingly, notwithstanding the lapse, the perfected security interest has priority over the rights of LC, who is not a purchaser. See Section 9-317(a)(2).

4. Effect of Debtor's Bankruptcy. Under former Section 9-403(2), lapse was tolled if the debtor entered bankruptcy or another insolvency proceeding. Nevertheless, being unaware that insolvency proceedings had been commenced, filing offices routinely removed records from the files as if lapse had not been tolled. Subsection (c) deletes the former tolling provision and thereby imposes a new burden on the secured party: to be sure that a financing statement does not lapse during the debtor's bankruptcy. The secured party can prevent lapse by filing a continuation statement, even without first obtaining relief from the automatic stay. See Bankruptcy Code Section 362(b)(3). Of course, if the debtor enters bankruptcy before lapse, the provisions of this Article with respect to lapse would be of no effect to the extent that federal bankruptcy law dictates a contrary result (e.g., to the extent that the Bankruptcy Code determines rights as of the date of the filing of the bankruptcy petition).

5. Continuation Statements. Subsection (d) explains when a continuation statement may be filed. A continuation statement filed at a time other than that prescribed by subsection (d) is ineffective, see Section 9-510(c), and the filing office may not accept it. See Sections 9-520(a), 9-516(b). Subsection (e) specifies the effect of a continuation statement and provides for successive continuation statements.

§ 9-516. What Constitutes Filing; Effectiveness of Filing.

(a) [What constitutes filing.] Except as otherwise provided in subsection (b), communication of a record to a filing office and tender of the filing fee or acceptance of the record by the filing office constitutes filing.

(b) [Refusal to accept record; filing does not occur.] Filing does not occur with respect to a record that a filing office refuses to accept because:

(1) the record is not communicated by a method or medium of communication authorized by the filing office;

(2) an amount equal to or greater than the applicable filing fee is not tendered;

(3) the filing office is unable to index the record because:

(A) in the case of an initial financing statement, the record does not provide a name for the debtor;

(B) in the case of an amendment or information statement, the record:

(i) does not identify the initial financing statement as required by Section 9-512 or 9-518, as applicable; or

(ii) identifies an initial financing statement whose effectiveness has lapsed under Section 9-515;

(C) in the case of an initial financing statement that provides the name of a debtor identified as an individual or an amendment that provides a name of a debtor identified as an individual which was not previously provided in the financing statement to which the record relates, the record does not identify the debtor's surname; or

(D) in the case of a record filed [or recorded] in the filing office described in Section 9-501(a)(1), the record does not provide a sufficient description of the real property to which it relates;

(4) in the case of an initial financing statement or an amendment that adds a secured party of record, the record does not provide a name and mailing address for the secured party of record;

(5) in the case of an initial financing statement or an amendment that provides a name of a debtor which was not previously provided in the financing statement to which the amendment relates, the record does not:

(A) provide a mailing address for the debtor; or

(B) indicate whether the name provided as the name of the debtor is the name of an individual or an organization;

(6) in the case of an assignment reflected in an initial financing statement under Section 9-514(a) or an amendment filed under Section 9-514(b), the record does not provide a name and mailing address for the assignee; or

(7) in the case of a continuation statement, the record is not filed within the six-month period prescribed by Section 9-515(d).

(c) [Rules applicable to subsection (b).] For purposes of subsection (b):

(1) a record does not provide information if the filing office is unable to read or decipher the information; and

(2) a record that does not indicate that it is an amendment or identify an initial financing statement to which it relates, as required by Section 9-512, 9-514, or 9-518, is an initial financing statement.

(d) [Refusal to accept record; record effective as filed record.] A record that is communicated to the filing office with tender of the filing fee, but which the filing office refuses to accept for a reason other than one set forth in subsection (b), is effective as a filed record except as against a purchaser of the collateral which gives value in reasonable reliance upon the absence of the record from the files.

Definitional Cross References:

Collateral	Section 9-102(a)(12)
Communicate	Section 9-102(a)(18)
Continuation statement	Section 9-102(a)(27)
Debtor	Section 9-102(a)(28)
Filing office	Section 9-102(a)(37)
Financing statement	Section 9-102(a)(39)
Jurisdiction of organization	Section 9-102(a)(50)
Organization	Section 1-201(b)(25)
Purchaser	Section 1-201(b)(30)
Record	Section 9-102(a)(70)
Secured party	Section 9-102(a)(73)
Value	Section 1-204

Official Comment

1. Source. Subsection (a): former Section 9-403(1); the remainder is new.

2. What Constitutes Filing. Subsection (a) deals generically with what constitutes filing of a record, including an initial financing statement and amendments of all kinds (e.g., assignments, termination statements, and continuation statements). It follows former Section 9-403(1), under which either acceptance of a record by the filing office or presentation of the record and tender of the filing fee constitutes filing.

3. Effectiveness of Rejected Record. Subsection (b) provides an exclusive list of grounds upon which the filing office may reject a record. See Section 9-520(a). Although some of these grounds would also be grounds for rendering a filed record ineffective (e.g., an initial financing statement does not provide a name for the debtor), many others would not be (e.g., an initial financing statement does not provide a mailing address for the debtor or secured party of record). Neither this section nor Section 9-520 requires or authorizes the filing office to determine, or even consider, the accuracy of information provided in a record.

A financing statement or other record that is communicated to the filing office but which the filing office refuses to accept provides no public notice, regardless of the reason for the rejection. However, this section distinguishes between records that the filing office rightfully rejects and those that it wrongfully rejects. A filer is able to prevent a rightful rejection by complying with the requirements of subsection (b). No purpose is served by giving effect to records that justifiably never find their way into the system, and subsection (b) so provides.

Subsection (d) deals with the filing office's unjustified refusal to accept a record. Here, the filer is in no position to prevent the rejection and as a general matter should not be prejudiced by it. Although wrongfully rejected records generally are effective, subsection (d) contains a special rule to protect a third-party purchaser of the collateral (e.g., a buyer or competing secured party) who gives value in reliance upon the apparent absence of the record from the files. As against a person who searches the public record and reasonably relies on what the public record shows, subsection (d) imposes upon the filer the risk that a record failed to make its way into the filing system because of the filing office's wrongful rejection of it. (Compare Section 9-517, under which a mis-indexed financing statement is fully effective.) This risk is likely to be small, particularly when a record is presented electronically, and the filer can guard against this risk by conducting a post-filing search of the records. Moreover, Section 9-520(b) requires the filing office to give prompt notice of its refusal to accept a record for filing.

4. Method or Medium of Communication. Rejection pursuant to subsection (b)(1) for failure to communicate a record properly should be understood to mean noncompliance with procedures relating to security, signing, or other communication-related requirements that the filing office may impose. Subsection (b)(1) does not authorize a filing office to impose additional substantive requirements. See Section 9-520, Comment 2.

5. Address for Secured Party of Record. Under subsection (b)(4) and Section 9-520(a), the lack of a mailing address for the secured party of record requires the filing office to reject an initial financing statement. The failure to include an address for the secured party of record no longer renders a financing statement ineffective. See Section 9-502(a). The function of the address is not to identify the secured party of record but rather to provide an address to which others can send required notifications, e.g., of a purchase-money security interest in inventory or of the disposition of collateral. Inasmuch as the address shown on a filed financing statement is an "address that is reasonable under the circumstances," a person required to send a notification to the secured party may satisfy the requirement by sending a notification to that address, even if the address is or becomes incorrect. See Section 9-102 (definition of "send"). Similarly, because the address is "held out by [the secured party] as the place for receipt of such communications [i.e., communications relating to security interests]," the secured party is deemed to have received a notification delivered to that address. See Section 1-202(e).

6. Uncertainty Concerning Individual Debtor's Surname. Subsection (b)(3)(C) requires the filing office to reject an initial financing statement or amendment adding an individual debtor if the office cannot index the record because it does not identify the debtor's surname (e.g., it is unclear whether the debtor's surname is Elton or John).

7. Inability of Filing Office to Read or Decipher Information. Under subsection (c)(1), if the filing office cannot read or decipher information, the information is not provided by a record for purposes of subsection (b).

8. Classification of Records. For purposes of subsection (b), a record that does not indicate it is an amendment or identify an initial financing statement to which it relates is deemed to be an initial financing statement. See subsection (c)(2).

9. Effectiveness of Rejectable But Unrejected Record. Section 9-520(a) requires the filing office to refuse to accept an initial financing statement for a reason set forth in subsection (b). However, if the filing office accepts such a financing statement nevertheless, the financing statement generally is effective if it complies with the requirements of Section 9-502(a) and (b). See Section 9-520(c). Similarly, an otherwise effective financing statement generally remains so even though the information in the financing statement becomes incorrect. See Section 9-507(b). (Note that if the information required by subsection (b)(5) is incorrect when the financing statement is filed, Section 9-338 applies.)

§ 9-517. Effect of Indexing Errors.

The failure of the filing office to index a record correctly does not affect the effectiveness of the filed record.

Definitional Cross References:

Filing office	Section 9-102(a)(37)
Record	Section 9-102(a)(70)

Official Comment

1. Source. New.

2. Effectiveness of Mis-Indexed Records. This section provides that the filing office's error in mis-indexing a record does not render ineffective an otherwise effective record. As did former Section 9-401, this section imposes the risk of filing-office error on those who search the files rather than on those who file.

§ 9-518. Claim Concerning Inaccurate or Wrongfully Filed Record.

(a) [Statement with respect to record indexed under person's name.] A person may file in the filing office an information statement with respect to a record indexed there under the person's name if the person believes that the record is inaccurate or was wrongfully filed.

ALTERNATIVE A

(b) [Contents of statement under subsection (a).] An information statement under subsection (a) must:

(1) identify the record to which it relates by the file number assigned to the initial financing statement to which the record relates;

(2) indicate that it is an information statement; and

(3) provide the basis for the person's belief that the record is inaccurate and indicate the manner in which the person believes the record should be amended to cure any inaccuracy or provide the basis for the person's belief that the record was wrongfully filed.

ALTERNATIVE B

(b) [Contents of statement under subsection (a).] An information statement under subsection (a) must:

(1) identify the record to which it relates by:

(A) the file number assigned to the initial financing statement to which the record relates; and

(B) if the information statement relates to a record filed [or recorded] in a filing office described in Section 9-501(a)(1), the date [and time] that the initial financing statement was filed [or recorded] and the information specified in Section 9-502(b);

(2) indicate that it is an information statement; and

(3) provide the basis for the person's belief that the record is inaccurate and indicate the manner in which the person believes the record should be amended to cure any inaccuracy or provide the basis for the person's belief that the record was wrongfully filed.

END OF ALTERNATIVES

(c) [Statement by secured party of record.] A person may file in the filing office an information statement with respect to a record filed there if the person is a secured party of record with respect to the financing statement to which the record relates and believes that the person that filed the record was not entitled to do so under Section 9-509(d).

ALTERNATIVE A

(d) [Contents of statement under subsection (c).] An information statement under subsection (c) must:

(1) identify the record to which it relates by the file number assigned to the initial financing statement to which the record relates;

(2) indicate that it is an information statement; and

(3) provide the basis for the person's belief that the person that filed the record was not entitled to do so under Section 9-509(d).

ALTERNATIVE B

(d) [Contents of statement under subsection (c).] An information statement under subsection (c) must:

(1) identify the record to which it relates by:

(A) the file number assigned to the initial financing statement to which the record relates; and

(B) if the information statement relates to a record filed [or recorded] in a filing office described in Section 9-501(a)(1), the date [and time] that the initial financing statement was filed [or recorded] and the information specified in Section 9-502(b);

(2) indicate that it is an information statement; and

(3) provide the basis for the person's belief that the person that filed the record was not entitled to do so under Section 9-509(d).

END OF ALTERNATIVES

(e) [Record not affected by information statement.] The filing of a correction statement does not affect the effectiveness of an initial financing statement or other filed record.

Legislative Note: *States whose real-estate filing offices require additional information in amendments and cannot search their records by both the name of the debtor and the file number should enact Alternative B to Sections 9-512(a), 9-518(b), 9-518(d), 9-519(f), and 9-522(a).*

Definitional Cross References:

Debtor	Section 9-102(a)(28)
File number	Section 9-102(a)(36)
Filing office	Section 9-102(a)(37)
Financing statement	Section 9-102(a)(39)
Person	Section 1-201(b)(27)
Record	Section 9-102(a)(70)
State	Section 9-102(a)(77)

Official Comment

1. Source. New.

2. Information Statements. Former Article 9 did not afford a nonjudicial means for a debtor to indicate that financing statement or other record was inaccurate or wrongfully filed. Subsection (a) affords the debtor the right to file an information statement. Among other requirements, the information statement must provide the basis for the debtor's belief that the public record should be corrected. See subsection (b). These provisions, which resemble the analogous remedy in the Fair Credit Reporting Act, 15 U.S.C. § 1681i, afford an aggrieved person the opportunity to state its position on the public record. They do not permit an aggrieved person to change the legal effect of the public record. Thus, although a filed information statement becomes part of the "financing statement," as defined in Section 9-102, the filing does not affect the effectiveness of the initial financing statement or any other filed record. See subsection (e).

Sometimes a person files a termination statement or other record relating to a filed financing statement without being entitled to do so. A secured party of record with respect to the financing statement who believes that such a record has been filed may, but need not, file an information statement indicating that the person that filed the record was not entitled to do so. See subsection (c). An information statement has no legal effect. Its sole purpose is to provide some limited public notice that the efficacy of a filed record is disputed. If the person that filed the record was not entitled to do so, the filed record is ineffective, regardless of whether the secured party of record files an information statement. Likewise, if the person that filed the record was entitled to do so, the filed record is effective, even if the secured party of record files an information statement. See Section 9-510(a), 9-518(e). Because an information statement filed under subsection (c) has no legal effect, a secured party of record—even one who is aware of the unauthorized filing of a record—has no duty to file one. Just as searchers bear the burden of determining whether the filing of initial financing statement was authorized, searchers bear the burden of determining whether the filing of every subsequent record was authorized.

Inasmuch as the filing of an information statement has no legal effect, this section does not provide a mechanism by which a secured party can correct an error that it discovers in its own financing statement.

This section does not displace other provisions of this Article that impose liability for making unauthorized filings or failing to file or send a termination statement (see Section 9-625(e)), nor does it displace any available judicial remedies.

3. Resort to Other Law. This Article cannot provide a satisfactory or complete solution to problems caused by misuse of the public records. The problem of "bogus" filings is not limited to the UCC filing system but extends to the real-property records, as well. A summary judicial procedure for correcting the public record and criminal penalties for those who misuse the filing and recording systems are likely to be more effective and put less strain on the filing system than provisions authorizing or requiring action by filing and recording offices.

[Subpart 2. Duties and Operation of Filing Office]

§ 9-519. Numbering, Maintaining, and Indexing Records; Communicating Information Provided in Records.

(a) [Filing office duties.] For each record filed in a filing office, the filing office shall:

(1) assign a unique number to the filed record;

(2) create a record that bears the number assigned to the filed record and the date and time of filing;

(3) maintain the filed record for public inspection; and

(4) index the filed record in accordance with subsections (c), (d), and (e).

(b) [File number.] A file number [assigned after January 1, 2002,] must include a digit that:

(1) is mathematically derived from or related to the other digits of the file number; and

(2) aids the filing office in determining whether a number communicated as the file number includes a single-digit or transpositional error.

(c) [Indexing: general.] Except as otherwise provided in subsections (d) and (e), the filing office shall:

(1) index an initial financing statement according to the name of the debtor and index all filed records relating to the initial financing statement in a manner that associates with one another an initial financing statement and all filed records relating to the initial financing statement; and

(2) index a record that provides a name of a debtor which was not previously provided in the financing statement to which the record relates also according to the name that was not previously provided.

(d) [Indexing: real-property-related financing statement.] If a financing statement is filed as a fixture filing or covers as-extracted collateral or timber to be cut, [it must be filed for record and] the filing office shall index it:

(1) under the names of the debtor and of each owner of record shown on the financing

statement as if they were the mortgagors under a mortgage of the real property described; and

(2) to the extent that the law of this State provides for indexing of records of mortgages under the name of the mortgagee, under the name of the secured party as if the secured party were the mortgagee thereunder, or, if indexing is by description, as if the financing statement were a record of a mortgage of the real property described.

(e) [Indexing: real-property-related assignment.] If a financing statement is filed as a fixture filing or covers as-extracted collateral or timber to be cut, the filing office shall index an assignment filed under Section 9-514(a) or an amendment filed under Section 9-514(b):

(1) under the name of the assignor as grantor; and

(2) to the extent that the law of this State provides for indexing a record of the assignment of a mortgage under the name of the assignee, under the name of the assignee.

ALTERNATIVE A

(f) [Retrieval and association capability.] The filing office shall maintain a capability:

(1) to retrieve a record by the name of the debtor and by the file number assigned to the initial financing statement to which the record relates; and

(2) to associate and retrieve with one another an initial financing statement and each filed record relating to the initial financing statement.

ALTERNATIVE B

(f) [Retrieval and association capability.] The filing office shall maintain a capability:

(1) to retrieve a record by the name of the debtor and:

(A) if the filing office is described in Section 9-501(a)(1), by the file number assigned to the initial financing statement to which the record relates and the date [and time] that the record was filed [or recorded]; or

(B) if the filing office is described in Section 9-501(a)(2), by the file number assigned to the initial financing statement to which the record relates; and

(2) to associate and retrieve with one another an initial financing statement and each filed record relating to the initial financing statement.

END OF ALTERNATIVES

(g) [Removal of debtor's name.] The filing office may not remove a debtor's name from the index until one year after the effectiveness of a financing statement naming the debtor lapses under Section 9-515 with respect to all secured parties of record.

(h) [Timeliness of filing office performance.] The filing office shall perform the acts required by subsections (a) through (e) at the time and in the manner prescribed by filing-office rule, but not later than two business days after the filing office receives the record in question.

[(i) [Inapplicability to real-property-related filing office.] Subsection[s] [(b)] [and] [(h)] do[es] not apply to a filing office described in Section 9-501(a)(1).]

Legislative Notes:

1. *States whose filing offices currently assign file numbers that include a verification number, commonly known as a "check digit," or can implement this requirement before the effective date of this Article should omit the bracketed language in subsection (b).*

2. *In States in which writings will not appear in the real property records and indices unless actually recorded the bracketed language in subsection (d) should be used.*

3. *States whose real-estate filing offices require additional information in amendments and cannot search their records by both the name of the debtor and the file number should enact Alternative B to Sections 9-512(a), 9-518(b), 9-518(d), 9-519(f), and 9-522(a).*

4. *A State that elects not to require real-estate filing offices to comply with either or both of subsections (b) and (h) may adopt an applicable*

variation of subsection (i) and add "Except as otherwise provided in subsection (i)," to the appropriate subsection or subsections.

Definitional Cross References:

As-extracted collateral	Section 9-102(a)(6)
Communicate	Section 9-102(a)(18)
Debtor	Section 9-102(a)(28)
File number	Section 9-102(a)(36)
Filing office	Section 9-102(a)(37)
Filing-office rule	Section 9-102(a)(38)
Financing statement	Section 9-102(a)(39)
Fixture filing	Section 9-102(a)(40)
Mortgage	Section 9-102(a)(55)
Record	Section 9-102(a)(70)
Secured party	Section 9-102(a)(73)
State	Section 9-102(a)(77)
Writing	Section 1-201(b)(43)

Official Comment

1. Source. Former Sections 9-403(4), (7), 9-405(2).

2. Filing Office's Duties. Subsections (a) through (e) set forth the duties of the filing office with respect to filed records. Subsection (h), which is new, imposes a minimum standard of performance for those duties. Prompt indexing is crucial to the effectiveness of any filing system. An accepted but un-indexed record affords no public notice. Subsection (f) requires the filing office to maintain appropriate storage and retrieval facilities, and subsection (g) contains minimum requirements for the retention of records.

3. File Number. Subsection (a)(1) requires the filing office to assign a unique number to each filed record. That number is the "file number" only if the record is an initial financing statement. See Section 9-102.

4. Time of Filing. Subsection (a)(2) and Section 9-523 refer to the "date and time" of filing. The statutory text does not contain any instructions to a filing office as to how the time of filing is to be determined. The method of determining or assigning a time of filing is an appropriate matter for filing-office rules to address.

5. Related Records. Subsections (c) and (f) are designed to ensure that an initial financing statement and all filed records relating to it are associated with one another, indexed under the name of the debtor, and retrieved together. To comply with subsection (f), a filing office (other than a real-property recording office in a State that enacts subsection (f), Alternative B) must be capable of retrieving records in each of two ways: by the name of the debtor and by the file number of the initial financing statement to which the record relates.

6. Prohibition on Deleting Names from Index. This Article contemplates that the filing office will not delete the name of a debtor from the index until at least one year passes after the effectiveness of the financing statement lapses as to all secured parties of record. See subsection (g). This rule applies even if the filing office accepts an amendment purporting to delete or modify the name of a debtor or terminate the effectiveness of the financing statement. If an amendment provides a modified name for a debtor, the amended name should be added to the index, see subsection (c)(2), but the pre-amendment name should remain in the index.

Compared to former Article 9, the rule in subsection (g) increases the amount of information available to those who search the public records. The rule also contemplates that searchers—not the filing office—will determine the significance and effectiveness of filed records.

§ 9-520. Acceptance and Refusal to Accept Record.

(a) [Mandatory refusal to accept record.] A filing office shall refuse to accept a record for filing for a reason set forth in Section 9-516(b) and may refuse to accept a record for filing only for a reason set forth in Section 9-516(b).

(b) [Communication concerning refusal.] If a filing office refuses to accept a record for filing, it shall communicate to the person that presented the record the fact of and reason for the refusal and the date and time the record would have been filed had the filing office accepted it. The communication must be made at the time and in the manner prescribed by filing-office rule but [, in the case of a filing office described in Section 9-501(a)(2),] in no event more than two business days after the filing office receives the record.

(c) [When filed financing statement effective.] A filed financing statement satisfying Section 9-502(a) and (b) is effective, even if the filing office is required to refuse to accept it for filing under subsection (a). However, Section 9-338 applies to a filed financing statement providing information described in Section 9-516(b)(5) which is incorrect at the time the financing statement is filed.

(d) [Separate application to multiple debtors.] If a record communicated to a filing office provides information that relates to more than one debtor, this part applies as to each debtor separately.

Legislative Note: A State that elects not to require real-property filing offices to comply with subsection (b) should include the bracketed language.

Definitional Cross References:

Communicate	Section 9-102(a)(18)
Debtor	Section 9-102(a)(28)
Filing office	Section 9-102(a)(37)
Filing-office rule	Section 9-102(a)(38)
Financing statement	Section 9-102(a)(39)
Person	Section 1-201(b)(27)
Record	Section 9-102(a)(70)
State	Section 9-102(a)(77)

Official Comment

1. Source. New.

2. Refusal to Accept Record for Filing. In some States, filing offices considered themselves obligated by former Article 9 to review the form and content of a financing statement and to refuse to accept those that they determine are legally insufficient. Some filing offices imposed requirements for or conditions to filing that do not appear in the statute. Under this section, the filing office is not expected to make legal judgments and is not permitted to impose additional conditions or requirements.

Subsection (a) both prescribes and limits the bases upon which the filing office must and may reject records by reference to the reasons set forth in Section 9-516(b). For the most part, the bases for rejection are limited to those that prevent the filing office from dealing with a record that it receives—because some of the requisite information (e.g., the debtor's name) is missing or cannot be deciphered, because the record is not communicated by a method (e.g., it is MIME- rather than UU-encoded) or medium (e.g., it is written rather than electronic) that the filing office accepts, or because the filer fails to tender an amount equal to or greater than the filing fee.

3. Consequences of Accepting Rejectable Record. Section 9-516(b) includes among the reasons for rejecting an initial financing statement the failure to give certain information that is not required as a condition of effectiveness. In conjunction with Section 9-516(b)(5), this section requires the filing office to refuse to accept a financing statement that is legally sufficient to perfect a security interest under Section 9-502 but does not contain a mailing address for the debtor or disclose whether the debtor is an individual or an organization. The information required by Section 9-516(b)(5) assists searchers in weeding out "false positives," i.e., records that a search reveals but which do not pertain to the debtor in question. It assists filers by helping to ensure that the debtor's name is correct and that the financing statement is filed in the proper jurisdiction.

If the filing office accepts a financing statement that does not give this information at all, the filing is fully effective. Section 9-520(c). The financing statement also generally is effective if the information is given but is incorrect; however, Section 9-338 affords protection to buyers and holders of perfected security interests who give value in reasonable reliance upon the incorrect information.

4. Filing Office's Duties with Respect to Rejected Record. Subsection (b) requires the filing office to communicate the fact of rejection and the reason therefor within a fixed period of time. Inasmuch as a rightfully rejected record is ineffective and a wrongfully rejected record is not fully effective, prompt communication concerning any rejection is important.

5. Partial Effectiveness of Record. Under subsection (d), the provisions of this Part apply to each debtor separately. Thus, a filing office may reject an initial financing statement or other record as to one named debtor but accept it as to the other.

> **Example:** An initial financing statement is communicated to the filing office. The financing statement names two debtors, John Smith and Jane Smith. It contains all of the information described in Section 9-516(b)(5) with respect to John but lacks some of the information with respect to Jane. The filing office must accept the financing statement with respect to John, reject it with respect to Jane, and notify the filer of the rejection.

§ 9-521. Uniform Form of Written Financing Statement and Amendment.

(a) [Initial financing statement form.] A filing office that accepts written records may not refuse to accept a written initial financing statement in the following form and format except for a reason set forth in Section 9-516(b):

UCC FINANCING STATEMENT

FOLLOW INSTRUCTIONS

A. NAME & PHONE OF CONTACT AT FILER (optional)

B. E-MAIL CONTACT AT FILER (optional)

C. SEND ACKNOWLEDGMENT TO: (Name and Address)

THE ABOVE SPACE IS FOR FILING OFFICE USE ONLY

1. DEBTOR'S NAME: Provide only one Debtor name (1a or 1b) (use exact, full name; do not omit, modify, or abbreviate any part of the Debtor's name); if any part of the Individual Debtor's name will not fit in line 1b, leave all of item 1 blank, check here ☐ and provide the Individual Debtor information in item 10 of the Financing Statement Addendum (Form UCC1Ad)

	1a. ORGANIZATION'S NAME				
OR	1b. INDIVIDUAL'S SURNAME	FIRST PERSONAL NAME	ADDITIONAL NAME(S)/INITIAL(S)		SUFFIX
1c.	MAILING ADDRESS	CITY	STATE	POSTAL CODE	COUNTRY

2. DEBTOR'S NAME: Provide only one Debtor name (2a or 2b) (use exact, full name; do not omit, modify, or abbreviate any part of the Debtor's name); if any part of the Individual Debtor's name will not fit in line 2b, leave all of item 2 blank, check here ☐ and provide the Individual Debtor information in item 10 of the Financing Statement Addendum (Form UCC1Ad)

	2a. ORGANIZATION'S NAME				
OR	2b. INDIVIDUAL'S SURNAME	FIRST PERSONAL NAME	ADDITIONAL NAME(S)/INITIAL(S)		SUFFIX
2c.	MAILING ADDRESS	CITY	STATE	POSTAL CODE	COUNTRY

3. SECURED PARTY'S NAME (or NAME of ASSIGNEE of ASSIGNOR SECURED PARTY): Provide only one Secured Party name (3a or 3b)

	3a. ORGANIZATION'S NAME				
OR	3b. INDIVIDUAL'S SURNAME	FIRST PERSONAL NAME	ADDITIONAL NAME(S)/INITIAL(S)		SUFFIX
3c.	MAILING ADDRESS	CITY	STATE	POSTAL CODE	COUNTRY

4. COLLATERAL: This financing statement covers the following collateral:

5. Check only if applicable and check only one box: Collateral is ☐ held in a Trust (see UCC1Ad, item 17 and Instructions) ☐ being administered by a Decedent's Personal Representative

6a. Check only if applicable and check only one box:
☐ Public-Finance Transaction ☐ Manufactured-Home Transaction ☐ A Debtor is a Transmitting Utility

6b. Check only if applicable and check only one box:
☐ Agricultural Lien ☐ Non-UCC Filing

7. ALTERNATIVE DESIGNATION (if applicable): ☐ Lessee/Lessor ☐ Consignee/Consignor ☐ Seller/Buyer ☐ Bailee/Bailor ☐ Licensee/Licensor

8. OPTIONAL FILER REFERENCE DATA:

UCC FINANCING STATEMENT (Form UCC1) (Rev. 04/20/11)

UCC FINANCING STATEMENT ADDENDUM

FOLLOW INSTRUCTIONS

9. NAME OF FIRST DEBTOR: Same as line 1a or 1b on Financing Statement; if line 1b was left blank because Individual Debtor name did not fit, check here ☐

9a. ORGANIZATION'S NAME

OR

9b. INDIVIDUAL'S SURNAME

FIRST PERSONAL NAME

ADDITIONAL NAME(S)/INITIAL(S) | SUFFIX

THE ABOVE SPACE IS FOR FILING OFFICE USE ONLY

10. DEBTOR'S NAME: Provide (10a or 10b) only one additional Debtor name or Debtor name that did not fit in line 1b or 2b of the Financing Statement (Form UCC1) (use exact, full name; do not omit, modify, or abbreviate any part of the Debtor's name) and enter the mailing address in line 10c

10a. ORGANIZATION'S NAME

OR

10b. INDIVIDUAL'S SURNAME

INDIVIDUAL'S FIRST PERSONAL NAME

INDIVIDUAL'S ADDITIONAL NAME(S)/INITIAL(S) | SUFFIX

10c. MAILING ADDRESS	CITY	STATE	POSTAL CODE	COUNTRY

11. ☐ ADDITIONAL SECURED PARTY'S NAME or ☐ ASSIGNOR SECURED PARTY'S NAME: Provide only one name (11a or 11b)

11a. ORGANIZATION'S NAME

OR

11b. INDIVIDUAL'S SURNAME	FIRST PERSONAL NAME	ADDITIONAL NAME(S)/INITIAL(S)	SUFFIX

11c. MAILING ADDRESS	CITY	STATE	POSTAL CODE	COUNTRY

12. ADDITIONAL SPACE FOR ITEM 4 (Collateral):

13. ☐ This FINANCING STATEMENT is to be filed [for record] (or recorded) in the REAL ESTATE RECORDS (if applicable)

14. This FINANCING STATEMENT:
☐ covers timber to be cut ☐ covers as-extracted collateral ☐ is filed as a fixture filing

15. Name and address of a RECORD OWNER of real estate described in item 16 (if Debtor does not have a record interest):

16. Description of real estate:

17. MISCELLANEOUS:

UCC FINANCING STATEMENT ADDENDUM (Form UCC1Ad) (Rev. 04/20/11)

(b) [Amendment form.] A filing office that accepts written records may not refuse to accept a written record in the following form and format except for a reason set forth in Section 9-516(b):

UCC FINANCING STATEMENT AMENDMENT

FOLLOW INSTRUCTIONS

A. NAME & PHONE OF CONTACT AT FILER (optional)

B. E-MAIL CONTACT AT FILER (optional)

C. SEND ACKNOWLEDGMENT TO: (Name and Address)

THE ABOVE SPACE IS FOR FILING OFFICE USE ONLY

1a. INITIAL FINANCING STATEMENT FILE NUMBER

1b. ☐ This FINANCING STATEMENT AMENDMENT is to be filed [for record] (or recorded) in the REAL ESTATE RECORDS
Filer: attach Amendment Addendum (Form UCC3Ad) and provide Debtor's name in item 13

2. ☐ TERMINATION: Effectiveness of the Financing Statement identified above is terminated with respect to the security interest(s) of Secured Party authorizing this Termination Statement

3. ☐ ASSIGNMENT (full or partial): Provide name of Assignee in item 7a or 7b, and address of Assignee in item 7c and name of Assignor in item 9
For partial assignment, complete items 7 and 9 and also indicate affected collateral in item 8

4. ☐ CONTINUATION: Effectiveness of the Financing Statement identified above with respect to the security interest(s) of Secured Party authorizing this Continuation Statement is continued for the additional period provided by applicable law

5. ☐ PARTY INFORMATION CHANGE:

Check one of these two boxes:
This Change affects ☐ Debtor or ☐ Secured Party of record

AND Check one of these three boxes to:
☐ CHANGE name and/or address: Complete item 6a or 6b; and item 7a or 7b and item 7c
☐ ADD name: Complete item 7a or 7b, and item 7c
☐ DELETE name: Give record name to be deleted in item 6a or 6b

6. CURRENT RECORD INFORMATION: Complete for Party Information Change - provide only one name (6a or 6b)

6a. ORGANIZATION'S NAME

OR

6b. INDIVIDUAL'S SURNAME	FIRST PERSONAL NAME	ADDITIONAL NAME(S)/INITIAL(S)	SUFFIX

7. CHANGED OR ADDED INFORMATION: Complete for Assignment or Party Information Change - provide only one name (7a or 7b) (use exact, full name; do not omit, modify, or abbreviate any part of the Debtor's name)

7a. ORGANIZATION'S NAME

OR

7b. INDIVIDUAL'S SURNAME

INDIVIDUAL'S FIRST PERSONAL NAME

INDIVIDUAL'S ADDITIONAL NAME(S)/INITIAL(S) SUFFIX

7c. MAILING ADDRESS	CITY	STATE	POSTAL CODE	COUNTRY

8. ☐ COLLATERAL CHANGE: Also check one of these four boxes: ☐ ADD collateral ☐ DELETE collateral ☐ RESTATE covered collateral ☐ ASSIGN collateral

Indicate collateral:

9. NAME OF SECURED PARTY OF RECORD AUTHORIZING THIS AMENDMENT: Provide only one name (9a or 9b) (name of Assignor, if this is an Assignment)
If this is an Amendment authorized by a DEBTOR, check here ☐ and provide name of authorizing Debtor

9a. ORGANIZATION'S NAME

OR

9b. INDIVIDUAL'S SURNAME	FIRST PERSONAL NAME	ADDITIONAL NAME(S)/INITIAL(S)	SUFFIX

10. OPTIONAL FILER REFERENCE DATA:

UCC FINANCING STATEMENT AMENDMENT (Form UCC3) (Rev. 04/20/11)

UCC FINANCING STATEMENT AMENDMENT ADDENDUM

FOLLOW INSTRUCTIONS

11. INITIAL FINANCING STATEMENT FILE NUMBER: Same as item 1a on Amendment form

12. NAME OF PARTY AUTHORIZING THIS AMENDMENT: Same as item 9 on Amendment form

12a. ORGANIZATION'S NAME

OR 12b. INDIVIDUAL'S SURNAME

FIRST PERSONAL NAME

ADDITIONAL NAME(S)/INITIAL(S) | SUFFIX

THE ABOVE SPACE IS FOR FILING OFFICE USE ONLY

13. Name of DEBTOR on related financing statement (Name of a current Debtor of record required for indexing purposes only in some filing offices - see Instruction item 13): Provide only one Debtor name (13a or 13b) (use exact, full name; do not omit, modify, or abbreviate any part of the Debtor's name); see Instructions if name does not fit

13a. ORGANIZATION'S NAME

OR 13b. INDIVIDUAL'S SURNAME	FIRST PERSONAL NAME	ADDITIONAL NAME(S)/INITIAL(S)	SUFFIX

14. ADDITIONAL SPACE FOR ITEM 8 (Collateral):

15. This FINANCING STATEMENT AMENDMENT:

☐ covers timber to be cut ☐ covers as-extracted collateral ☐ is filed as a fixture filing

16. Name and address of a RECORD OWNER of real estate described in item 17 (if Debtor does not have a record interest):

17. Description of real estate:

18. MISCELLANEOUS:

UCC FINANCING STATEMENT AMENDMENT ADDENDUM (Form UCC3Ad) (Rev. 04/20/11)

Definitional Cross References:

Filing office	Section 9-102(a)(37)
Financing statement	Section 9-102(a)(39)
Record	Section 9-102(a)(70)
Writing	Section 1-201(b)(43)

Official Comment

1. Source. New.

2. "Safe Harbor" Written Forms. Although Section 9-520 limits the bases upon which the filing office can refuse to accept records, this section provides sample written forms that must be accepted in every filing office in the country, as long as the filing office's rules permit it to accept written communications. By completing one of the forms in this section, a secured party can be certain that the filing office is obligated to accept it.

The forms in this section are based upon national financing statement forms that were in use under former Article 9. Those forms were developed over an extended period and reflect the comments and suggestions of filing officers, secured parties and their counsel, and service companies. The formatting of those forms and of the ones in this section has been designed to reduce error by both filers and filing offices.

A filing office that accepts written communications may not reject, on grounds of form or format, a filing using these forms. Although filers are not required to use the forms, they are encouraged and can be expected to do so, inasmuch as the forms are well designed and avoid the risk of rejection on the basis of form or format. As their use expands, the forms will rapidly become familiar to both filers and filing-office personnel. Filing offices may and should encourage the use of these forms by declaring them to be the "standard" (but not exclusive) forms for each jurisdiction, albeit without in any way suggesting that alternative forms are unacceptable.

The multi-purpose form in subsection (b) covers changes with respect to the debtor, the secured party, the collateral, and the status of the financing statement (termination and continuation). A single form may be used for several different types of amendments at once (e.g., both to change a debtor's name and continue the effectiveness of the financing statement).

§ 9-522. Maintenance and Destruction of Records.

ALTERNATIVE A

(a) [Post-lapse maintenance and retrieval of information.] The filing office shall maintain a record of the information provided in a filed financing statement for at least one year after the effectiveness of the financing statement has lapsed under Section 9-515 with respect to all secured parties of record. The record must be retrievable by using the name of the debtor and by using the file number assigned to the initial financing statement to which the record relates.

ALTERNATIVE B

(a) [Post-lapse maintenance and retrieval of information.] The filing office shall maintain a record of the information provided in a filed financing statement for at least one year after the effectiveness of the financing statement has lapsed under Section 9-515 with respect to all secured parties of record. The record must be retrievable by using the name of the debtor and:

(1) if the record was filed [or recorded] in the filing office described in Section 9-501(a)(1), by using the file number assigned to the initial financing statement to which the record relates and the date [and time] that the record was filed [or recorded]; or

(2) if the record was filed in the filing office described in Section 9-501(a)(2), by using the file number assigned to the initial financing statement to which the record relates.

END OF ALTERNATIVES

(b) [Destruction of written records.] Except to the extent that a statute governing disposition of public records provides otherwise, the filing office immediately may destroy any written record evidencing a financing statement. However, if the filing office destroys a written record, it shall maintain another record of the financing statement which complies with subsection (a).

Legislative Note: *States whose real-estate filing offices require additional information in amendments and cannot search their records by both the name of the debtor and the file number should enact Alternative B to Sections 9-512(a), 9-518(b), 9-518(d), 9-519(f), and 9-522(a).*

Definitional Cross References:

Debtor	Section 9-102(a)(28)
File number	Section 9-102(a)(36)
Filing office	Section 9-102(a)(37)
Financing statement	Section 9-102(a)(39)
Record	Section 9-102(a)(70)
State	Section 9-102(a)(77)
Writing	Section 1-201(b)(43)

Official Comment

1. Source. Former Section 9-403(3), revised substantially.

2. Maintenance of Records. Section 9-523 requires the filing office to provide information concerning certain lapsed financing statements. Accordingly, subsection (a) requires the filing office to maintain a record of the information in a financing statement for at least one year after lapse. During that time, the filing office may not delete any information with respect to a filed financing statement; it may only add information. This approach relieves the filing office from any duty to determine whether to substitute or delete information upon receipt of an amendment. It also assures searchers that they will receive all information with respect to financing statements filed against a debtor and thereby be able themselves to determine the state of the public record.

The filing office may maintain this information in any medium. Subsection (b) permits the filing office immediately to destroy written records evidencing a financing statement, provided that the filing office maintains another record of the information contained in the financing statement as required by subsection (a).

§ 9-523. Information from Filing Office; Sale or License of Records.

(a) [Acknowledgment of filing written record.] If a person that files a written record requests an acknowledgment of the filing, the filing office shall send to the person an image of the record showing the number assigned to the record pursuant to Section 9-519(a)(1) and the date and time of the filing of the record. However, if the person furnishes a copy of the record to the filing office, the filing office may instead:

(1) note upon the copy the number assigned to the record pursuant to Section 9-519(a)(1) and the date and time of the filing of the record; and

(2) send the copy to the person.

(b) [Acknowledgment of filing other record.] If a person files a record other than a written record, the filing office shall communicate to the person an acknowledgment that provides:

(1) the information in the record;

(2) the number assigned to the record pursuant to Section 9-519(a)(1); and

(3) the date and time of the filing of the record.

(c) [Communication of requested information.] The filing office shall communicate or otherwise make available in a record the following information to any person that requests it:

(1) whether there is on file on a date and time specified by the filing office, but not a date earlier than three business days before the filing office receives the request, any financing statement that:

(A) designates a particular debtor [or, if the request so states, designates a particular debtor at the address specified in the request];

(B) has not lapsed under Section 9-515 with respect to all secured parties of record; and

(C) if the request so states, has lapsed under Section 9-515 and a record of which is maintained by the filing office under Section 9-522(a);

(2) the date and time of filing of each financing statement; and

(3) the information provided in each financing statement.

(d) [Medium for communicating information.] In complying with its duty under subsection (c), the filing office may communicate information in any medium. However, if requested, the filing office shall communicate information by issuing [its written certificate] [a record that can be admitted into evidence in the courts of this State without extrinsic evidence of its authenticity].

(e) [Timeliness of filing office performance.] The filing office shall perform the acts required by subsections (a) through (d) at the time and in the manner prescribed by filing-office rule, but not later than two business days after the filing office receives the request.

(f) [Public availability of records.] At least weekly, the [insert appropriate official or governmental agency] [filing office] shall offer to sell or license to the public on a nonexclusive basis, in bulk, copies of all records filed in it under this part, in every medium from time to time available to the filing office.

Legislative Notes:

1. *States whose filing office does not offer the additional service of responding to search requests limited to a particular address should omit the bracketed language in subsection (c)(1)(A).*

2. *A State that elects not to require real-estate filing offices to comply with either or both of*

subsections (e) and (f) should specify in the appropriate subsection(s) only the filing office described in Section 9-501(a)(2).

Definitional Cross References:

Communicate	Section 9-102(a)(18)
Debtor	Section 9-102(a)(28)
Filing office	Section 9-102(a)(37)
Filing-office rule	Section 9-102(a)(38)
Financing statement	Section 9-102(a)(39)
Person	Section 1-201(b)(27)
Record	Section 9-102(a)(70)
Sale	Section 2-106(1)
Send	Section 1-201(b)(36)
State	Section 9-102(a)(77)
Writing	Section 1-201(b)(43)

Official Comment

1. Source. Former Section 9-407; subsections (d) and (e) are new.

2. Filing Office's Duty to Provide Information. Former Section 9-407, dealing with obtaining information from the filing office, was bracketed to suggest to legislatures that its enactment was optional. Experience has shown that the method by which interested persons can obtain information concerning the public records should be uniform. Accordingly, the analogous provisions of this Article are not in brackets.

Most of the other changes from former Section 9-407 are for clarification, to embrace medium-neutral drafting, or to impose standards of performance on the filing office.

3. Acknowledgments of Filing. Subsections (a) and (b) require the filing office to acknowledge the filing of a record. Under subsection (a), the filing office is required to acknowledge the filing of a written record only upon request of the filer. Subsection (b) requires the filing office to acknowledge the filing of a non-written record even in the absence of a request from the filer.

4. Response to Search Request. Subsection (c)(3) requires the filing office to provide "the information contained in each financing statement" to a person who requests it. This requirement can be satisfied by providing copies, images, or reports. The requirement does not in any manner inhibit the filing office from also offering to provide less than all of the information (presumably for a lower fee) to a person who asks for less. Thus, subsection (c) accommodates the practice of providing only the type of record (e.g., initial financing statement, continuation statement), number assigned to the record, date and time of filing, and names and addresses of the debtor and secured party when a requesting person asks for no more (i.e., when the person does not ask for copies of financing statements). In contrast, the filing office's obligation under subsection (b) to provide an acknowledgment containing "the information contained in the record" is not defined by a customer's request. Thus unless the filer stipulates otherwise, to comply with subsection (b) the filing office's acknowledgment must contain all of the information in a record.

Subsection (c) assures that a minimum amount of information about filed records will be available to the public. It does not preclude a filing office from offering additional services.

5. Lapsed and Terminated Financing Statements. This section reflects the policy that terminated financing statements will remain part of the filing office's data base. The filing office may remove from the data base only lapsed financing statements, and then only when at least a year has passed after lapse. See Section 9-519(g). Subsection (c)(1)(C) requires a filing office to conduct a search and report as to lapsed financing statements that have not been removed from the data base, when requested.

6. Search by Debtor's Address. Subsection (c)(1)(A) contemplates that, by making a single request, a searcher will receive the results of a search of the entire public record maintained by any given filing office. Addition of the bracketed language in subsection (c)(1)(A) would permit a search report limited to financing statements showing a particular address for the debtor, but only if the search request is so limited. With or without the bracketed language, this subsection does not permit the filing office to compel a searcher to limit a request by address.

7. Medium of Communication; Certificates. Former Article 9 provided that the filing office respond to a request for information by providing a certificate. The principle of medium-neutrality would suggest that the statute not require a written certificate. Subsection (d) follows this principle by permitting the filing office to respond by communicating "in any medium." By permitting communication "in any medium," subsection (d) is not inconsistent with a system in which persons other than filing office staff conduct searches of the filing office's (computer) records.

Some searchers find it necessary to introduce the results of their search into evidence. Because official written certificates might be introduced into evidence more easily than official communications in another medium, subsection (d) affords States the option of requiring the filing office to issue written certificates upon request. The alternative bracketed language in subsection (d) recognizes that some States may prefer to permit the filing office to respond in another medium, as long as the response can be admitted into evidence in the courts of that State without extrinsic evidence of its authenticity.

8. Performance Standard. The utility of the filing system depends on the ability of searchers to get current information quickly. Accordingly, subsection

(e) requires that the filing office respond to a request for information no later than two business days after it receives the request. The information contained in the response must be current as of a date no earlier than three business days before the filing office receives the request. See subsection (c)(1). The failure of the filing office to comply with performance standards, such as subsection (e), has no effect on the private rights of persons affected by the filing of records.

9. Sales of Records in Bulk. Subsection (f), which is new, mandates that the appropriate official or the filing office sell or license the filing records to the public in bulk, on a nonexclusive basis, in every medium available to the filing office. The details of implementation are left to filing-office rules.

§ 9-524. Delay by Filing Office.

Delay by the filing office beyond a time limit prescribed by this part is excused if:

(1) the delay is caused by interruption of communication or computer facilities, war, emergency conditions, failure of equipment, or other circumstances beyond control of the filing office; and

(2) the filing office exercises reasonable diligence under the circumstances.

Definitional Cross References:

Equipment Section 9-102(a)(33)
Filing office Section 9-102(a)(37)

Official Comment

Source. New; derived from Section 4-109.

§ 9-525. Fees.

(a) [Initial financing statement or other record: general rule.] Except as otherwise provided in subsection (e), the fee for filing and indexing a record under this part, other than an initial financing statement of the kind described in subsection (b), is [the amount specified in subsection (c), if applicable, plus]:

(1) $ [X] if the record is communicated in writing and consists of one or two pages;

(2) $ [2X] if the record is communicated in writing and consists of more than two pages; a

(3) $ [1/2X] if the record is communicated by another medium authorized by filing-office rule.

(b) [Initial financing statement: public-finance and manufactured-housing transactions.] Except as otherwise provided in subsection (e), the fee for filing and indexing an initial financing statement of the following kind is [the amount specified in subsection (c), if applicable, plus]:

(1) $ if the financing statement indicates that it is filed in connection with a public-finance transaction;

(2) $ if the financing statement indicates that it is filed in connection with a manufactured-home transaction.

ALTERNATIVE A

(c) [Number of names.] The number of names required to be indexed does not affect the amount of the fee in subsections (a) and (b).

ALTERNATIVE B

(c) [Number of names.] Except as otherwise provided in subsection (e), if a record is communicated in writing, the fee for each name more than two required to be indexed is $.

END OF ALTERNATIVES

(d) [Response to information request.] The fee for responding to a request for information from the filing office, including for [issuing a certificate showing] [communicating] whether there is on file any financing statement naming a particular debtor, is:

(1) $ if the request is communicated in writing; and

(2) $ if the request is communicated by another medium authorized by filing-office rule.

(e) [Record of mortgage.] This section does not require a fee with respect to a record of a mortgage which is effective as a financing statement filed as a fixture filing or as a financing statement covering as-extracted collateral or timber to be cut under Section 9-502(c). However, the recording and satisfaction fees that otherwise would be applicable to the record of the mortgage apply.

Legislative Notes:

1. *To preserve uniformity, a State that places the provisions of this section together with statutes setting fees for other services should do so without modification.*

2. *A State should enact subsection (c), Alternative A, and omit the bracketed language in subsections (a) and (b) unless its indexing system entails a substantial additional cost when indexing additional names.*

Definitional Cross References:

As-extracted collateral	Section 9-102(a)(6)
Communicate	Section 9-102(a)(18)
Debtor	Section 9-102(a)(28)
Filing office	Section 9-102(a)(37)
Financing statement	Section 9-102(a)(39)
Fixture filing	Section 9-102(a)(40)
Mortgage	Section 9-102(a)(55)
Public-finance transaction	Section 9-102(a)(67)
Record	Section 9-102(a)(70)
State	Section 9-102(a)(77)
Writing	Section 1-201(b)(43)

Official Comment

1. Source. Various sections of former Part 4.

2. Fees. This section contains all fee requirements for filing, indexing, and responding to requests for information. Uniformity in the fee structure (but not necessarily in the amount of fees) makes this Article easier for secured parties to use and reduces the likelihood that a filed record will be rejected for failure to pay at least the correct amount of the fee. See Section 9-516(b)(2).

The costs of processing electronic records are less than those with respect to written records. Accordingly, this section mandates a lower fee as an incentive to file electronically and imposes the additional charge (if any) for multiple debtors only with respect to written records. When written records are used, this Article encourages the use of the uniform forms in Section 9-521. The fee for filing these forms should be no greater than the fee for other written records.

To make the relevant information included in a filed record more accessible once the record is found, this section mandates a higher fee for longer written records than for shorter ones. Finally, recognizing that financing statements naming more than one debtor are most often filed against a husband and wife, any additional charge for multiple debtors applies to records filed with respect to more than two debtors, rather than with respect to more than one.

§ 9-526. Filing-Office Rules.

(a) [Adoption of filing-office rules.] The [insert appropriate governmental official or agency] shall adopt and publish rules to implement this article. The filing-office rules must be:

(1) consistent with this article; and

(2) adopted and published in accordance with the [insert any applicable state administrative procedure act].

(b) [Harmonization of rules.] To keep the filing-office rules and practices of the filing office in harmony with the rules and practices of filing offices in other jurisdictions that enact substantially this part, and to keep the technology used by the filing office compatible with the technology used by filing offices in other jurisdictions that enact substantially this part, the [insert appropriate governmental official or agency], so far as is consistent with the purposes, policies, and provisions of this article, in adopting, amending, and repealing filing-office rules, shall:

(1) consult with filing offices in other jurisdictions that enact substantially this part; and

(2) consult the most recent version of the Model Rules promulgated by the International Association of Corporate Administrators or any successor organization; and

(3) take into consideration the rules and practices of, and the technology used by, filing offices in other jurisdictions that enact substantially this part.

Definitional Cross References:

Filing office	Section 9-102(a)(37)
Filing-office rule	Section 9-102(a)(38)
Organization	Section 1-201(b)(25)
State	Section 9-102(a)(77)

Official Comment

1. Source. New; subsection (b) derives in part from the Uniform Consumer Credit Code (1974).

2. Rules Required. Operating a filing office is a complicated business, requiring many more rules and procedures than this Article can usefully provide. Subsection (a) requires the adoption of rules to carry out the provisions of Article 9. The filing-office rules must be consistent with the provisions of the statute and adopted in accordance with local procedures. The publication requirement informs secured parties about filing-office practices, aids secured parties in evaluating filing-related risks and costs, and promotes regularity of application within the filing office.

3. Importance of Uniformity. In today's national economy, uniformity of the policies and practices of the filing offices will reduce the costs of secured transactions substantially. The International Association of Corporate Administrators (IACA), referred to in subsection (b), is an organization whose membership includes filing officers from every State. These individuals are responsible for the proper functioning of the Article 9 filing system and have worked diligently to develop model filing-office rules, with a view toward efficiency and uniformity.

Although uniformity is an important desideratum, subsection (a) affords considerable flexibility in the adoption of filing-office rules. Each State may adopt a version of subsection (a) that reflects the desired relationship between the statewide filing office described in Section 9-501(a)(2) and the local filing offices described in Section 9-501(a)(1) and that takes into account the practices of its filing offices. Subsection (a) need not designate a single official or agency to adopt rules applicable to all filing offices, and the rules applicable to the statewide filing office need not be identical to those applicable to the local filing office. For example, subsection (a) might provide for the statewide filing office to adopt filing-office rules, and, if not prohibited by other law, the filing office might adopt one set of rules for itself and another for local offices. Or, subsection (a) might designate one official or agency to adopt rules for the statewide filing office and another to adopt rules for local filing offices.

§ 9-527. Duty to Report.

The [insert appropriate governmental official or agency] shall report [annually on or before] to the [Governor and Legislature] on the operation of the filing office. The report must contain a statement of the extent to which:

(1) the filing-office rules are not in harmony with the rules of filing offices in other jurisdictions that enact substantially this part and the reasons for these variations; and

(2) the filing-office rules are not in harmony with the most recent version of the Model Rules promulgated by the International Association of Corporate Administrators, or any successor organization, and the reasons for these variations.

Definitional Cross References:

Filing office	Section 9-102(a)(37)
Filing-office rule	Section 9-102(a)(38)
Organization	Section 1-201(b)(25)

Official Comment

1. Source. New; derived in part from the Uniform Consumer Credit Code (1974).

2. Duty to Report. This section is designed to promote compliance with the standards of performance imposed upon the filing office and with the requirement that the filing office's policies, practices, and technology be consistent and compatible with the policies, practices, and technology of other filing offices.

PART 6. DEFAULT

[Subpart 1. Default and Enforcement of Security Interest]

§ 9-601. Rights After Default; Judicial Enforcement; Consignor or Buyer of Accounts, Chattel Paper, Payment Intangibles, or Promissory Notes.

(a) [Rights of secured party after default.] After default, a secured party has the rights provided in this part and, except as otherwise provided in Section 9-602, those provided by agreement of the parties. A secured party:

(1) may reduce a claim to judgment, foreclose, or otherwise enforce the claim, security interest, or agricultural lien by any available judicial procedure; and

(2) if the collateral is documents, may proceed either as to the documents or as to the goods they cover.

(b) [Rights and duties of secured party in possession or control.] A secured party in possession of collateral or control of collateral under Sections 7-106, 9-104, 9-105, 9-105A, 9-106, 9-107, or 9-107A has the rights and duties provided in Section 9-207.

(c) [Rights cumulative; simultaneous exercise.] The rights under subsections (a) and (b) are cumulative and may be exercised simultaneously.

(d) [Rights of debtor and obligor.] Except as otherwise provided in subsection (g) and Section 9-605, after default, a debtor and an obligor have the rights provided in this part and by agreement of the parties.

(e) [Lien of levy after judgment.] If a secured party has reduced its claim to judgment, the lien of any levy that may be made upon the collateral by virtue of an execution based upon the judgment relates back to the earliest of:

(1) the date of perfection of the security interest or agricultural lien in the collateral;

(2) the date of filing a financing statement covering the collateral; or

(3) any date specified in a statute under which the agricultural lien was created.

(f) [Execution sale.] A sale pursuant to an execution is a foreclosure of the security interest or agricultural lien by judicial procedure within the meaning of this section. A secured party may purchase at the sale and thereafter hold the collateral free of any other requirements of this article.

(g) [Consignor or buyer of certain rights to payment.] Except as otherwise provided in Section 9-607(c), this part imposes no duties upon a secured party that is a consignor or is a buyer of accounts, chattel paper, payment intangibles, or promissory notes.

Definitional Cross References:

Account	Section 9-102(a)(2)
Agreement	Section 1-201(b)(3)
Agricultural lien	Section 9-102(a)(5)
Chattel paper	Section 9-102(a)(11)
Collateral	Section 9-102(a)(12)
Consignor	Section 9-102(a)(21)
Debtor	Section 9-102(a)(28)
Document	Section 9-102(a)(30)
Financing statement	Section 9-102(a)(39)
Goods	Section 9-102(a)(44)
Obligor	Section 9-102(a)(59)
Payment intangible	Section 9-102(a)(61)
Promissory note	Section 9-102(a)(65)
Purchase	Section 1-201(b)(29)
Right	Section 1-201(b)(34)
Sale	Section 2-106(1)
Secured party	Section 9-102(a)(73)
Security interest	Section 1-201(b)(35)

Comment References: 9-109 C6

Official Comment

1. Source. Former Section 9-501(1), (2), (5).

2. Enforcement: In General. The rights of a secured party to enforce its security interest in collateral after the debtor's default are an important feature of a secured transaction. (Note that the term "rights," as defined in Section 1-201, includes "remedies.") This Part provides those rights as well as certain limitations on their exercise for the protection of the defaulting debtor, other creditors, and other affected persons. However, subsections (a) and (d) make clear that the rights provided in this Part do not exclude other rights provided by agreement.

3. When Remedies Arise. Under subsection (a) the secured party's rights arise "[a]fter default." As did former Section 9-501, this Article leaves to the agreement of the parties the circumstances giving rise to a default. This Article does not determine whether a secured party's post-default conduct can constitute a waiver of default in the face of an agreement stating that such conduct shall not constitute a waiver. Rather, it continues to leave to the parties' agreement, as supplemented by law other than this Article, the determination whether a default has occurred or has been waived. See Section 1-103.

4. Possession of Collateral; Section 9-207. After a secured party takes possession of collateral following a default, there is no longer any distinction between a security interest that before default was nonpossessory and a security interest that was possessory before default, as under a common-law pledge. This Part generally does not distinguish between the rights of a secured party with a nonpossessory security interest and those of a secured party with a possessory security interest. However, Section 9-207 addresses rights and duties with respect to collateral in a secured party's possession. Under subsection (b) of this section, Section 9-207 applies not only to possession before default but also to possession after default. Subsection (b) also has been conformed to Section 9-207, which, unlike former Section 9-207, applies to secured parties having control of collateral.

5. Cumulative Remedies. Former Section 9-501(1) provided that the secured party's remedies were cumulative, but it did not explicitly provide whether the remedies could be exercised simultaneously. Subsection (c) permits the simultaneous exercise of remedies if the secured party acts in good faith. The liability scheme of Subpart 2 affords redress to an aggrieved debtor or obligor. Moreover, permitting the simultaneous exercise of remedies under subsection (c) does not override any non-UCC law, including the law of tort and statutes regulating collection of debts, under which the simultaneous exercise of remedies in a particular case constitutes abusive behavior or harassment giving rise to liability.

6. Judicial Enforcement. Under subsection (a) a secured party may reduce its claim to judgment or foreclose its interest by any available procedure outside this Article under applicable law. Subsection (e) generally follows former Section 9-501(5). It makes clear that any judicial lien that the secured party may acquire against the collateral effectively is a continuation of the original security interest (if perfected) and not the acquisition of a new interest or a transfer of property on account of a preexisting obligation. Under former Section 9-501(5), the judicial lien was stated to relate back to the date of perfection of the security interest. Subsection (e), however, provides that the lien relates back to the earlier of the date of filing or the date of perfection. This provides a secured party who enforces a security interest by judicial process with the benefit of the "first-to-file-or-perfect" priority rule of Section 9-322(a)(1).

7. Agricultural Liens. Part 6 provides parallel treatment for the enforcement of agricultural liens and security interests. Because agricultural liens are statutory rather than consensual, this Article does draw a few distinctions between these liens and security interests. Under subsection (e), the statute creating an agricultural lien would govern whether and the date to which an execution lien relates back. Section 9-606 explains when a "default" occurs in the agricultural lien context.

8. Execution Sales. Subsection (f) also follows former Section 9-501(5). It makes clear that an execution sale is an appropriate method of foreclosure contemplated by this Part. However, the sale is governed by other law and not by this Article, and the limitations under Section 9-610 on the right of a secured party to purchase collateral do not apply.

9. Sales of Receivables; Consignments. Subsection (g) provides that, except as provided in Section 9-607(c), the duties imposed on secured parties do not apply to buyers of accounts, chattel paper, payment intangibles, or promissory notes. Although denominated "secured parties," these buyers own the entire interest in the property sold and so may enforce their rights without regard to the seller ("debtor") or the seller's creditors. Likewise, a true consignor may enforce its ownership interest under other law without regard to the duties that this Part imposes on secured parties. Note, however, that Section 9-615 governs cases in which a consignee's secured party (other than a consignor) is enforcing a security interest that is senior to the security interest (i.e., ownership interest) of a true consignor.

§ 9-602. Waiver and Variance of Rights and Duties.

Except as otherwise provided in Section 9-624, to the extent that they give rights to a debtor or obligor and impose duties on a secured party, the debtor or obligor may not waive or vary the rules stated in the following listed sections:

(1) Section 9-207(b)(4)(C), which deals with use and operation of the collateral by the secured party;

(2) Section 9-210, which deals with requests for an accounting and requests concerning a list of collateral and statement of account;

(3) Section 9-607(c), which deals with collection and enforcement of collateral;

(4) Sections 9-608(a) and 9-615(c) to the extent that they deal with application or payment of noncash proceeds of collection, enforcement, or disposition;

(5) Sections 9-608(a) and 9-615(d) to the extent that they require accounting for or payment of surplus proceeds of collateral;

(6) Section 9-609 to the extent that it imposes upon a secured party that takes possession of collateral without judicial process the duty to do so without breach of the peace;

(7) Sections 9-610(b), 9-611, 9-613, and 9-614, which deal with disposition of collateral;

(8) Section 9-615(f), which deals with calculation of a deficiency or surplus when a disposition is made to the secured party, a person related to the secured party, or a secondary obligor;

(9) Section 9-616, which deals with explanation of the calculation of a surplus or deficiency;

(10) Sections 9-620, 9-621, and 9-622, which deal with acceptance of collateral in satisfaction of obligation;

(11) Section 9-623, which deals with redemption of collateral;

(12) Section 9-624, which deals with permissible waivers; and

(13) Sections 9-625 and 9-626, which deal with the secured party's liability for failure to comply with this article.

Definitional Cross References:

Account	Section 9-102(a)(2)
Accounting	Section 9-102(a)(4)
Collateral	Section 9-102(a)(12)
Debtor	Section 9-102(a)(28)
Noncash proceeds	Section 9-102(a)(58)
Obligor	Section 9-102(a)(59)
Person related to individual	Section 9-102(a)(62)
Person related to organization	Section 9-102(a)(63)
Proceeds	Section 9-102(a)(64)
Right	Section 1-201(b)(34)
Secondary obligor	Section 9-102(a)(72)
Secured party	Section 9-102(a)(73)

Official Comment

1. Source. Former Section 9-501(3).

2. Waiver: In General. Section 1-102(3) addresses which provisions of the UCC are mandatory and which may be varied by agreement. With exceptions relating to good faith, diligence, reasonableness, and care, immediate parties, as between themselves, may vary its provisions by agreement. However, in the context of rights and duties after default, our legal system traditionally has looked with suspicion on agreements that limit the debtor's rights and free the secured party of its duties. As stated in former Section 9-501, Comment 4, "no mortgage clause has ever been allowed to clog the equity of redemption." The context of default offers great opportunity for overreaching. The suspicious attitudes of the courts have been grounded in common sense. This section, like former Section 9-501(3), codifies this long-standing and deeply rooted attitude. The specified rights of the debtor and duties of the secured party may not be waived or varied except as stated. Provisions that are not specified in this section are subject to the general rules in Section 1-102(3). [Ed. Note. Both references to 9-102(3) are now to Section 1-302 of the new Article 1.]

3. Nonwaivable Rights and Duties. This section revises former Section 9-501(3) by restricting the ability to waive or modify additional specified rights and duties: (i) duties under Section 9-207(b)(4)(C), which deals with the use and operation of consumer goods, (ii) the right to a response to a request for an accounting, concerning a list of collateral, or concerning a statement of account (Section 9-210), (iii) the duty to collect collateral in a commercially reasonable manner (Section 9-607), (iv) the implicit duty to refrain from a breach of the peace in taking possession of collateral under Section 9-609, (v) the duty to apply noncash proceeds of collection or disposition in a commercially reasonable manner (Sections 9-608 and 9-615), (vi) the right to a special method of calculating a surplus or deficiency in certain dispositions to a secured party, a person related to secured party, or a secondary obligor (Section 9-615), (vii) the duty to give an explanation of the calculation of a surplus or deficiency (Section 9-616), (viii) the right to limitations on the effectiveness of certain waivers (Section 9-624), and (ix) the right to hold a secured party liable for failure to comply with this Article (Sections 9-625 and 9-626). For clarity and consistency, this Article uses the term "waive or vary" instead of "renounc[e] or modify[]," which appeared in former Section 9-504(3).

This section provides generally that the specified rights and duties "may not be waived or varied." However, it does not restrict the ability of parties to agree to settle, compromise, or renounce claims for past conduct that may have constituted a violation or breach of those rights and duties, even if the settlement involves an express "waiver."

Section 9-610(c) limits the circumstances under which a secured party may purchase at its own private disposition. Transactions of this kind are equivalent to "strict foreclosures" and are governed by Sections 9-620, 9-621, and 9-622. The provisions of these sections can be waived only to the extent provided in Section 9-624(b). See Section 9-602.

4. Waiver by Debtors and Obligors. The restrictions on waiver contained in this section apply to obligors as well as debtors. This resolves a question under former Article 9 as to whether secondary obligors, assuming that they were "debtors" for purposes of former Part 5, were permitted to waive, under the law of suretyship, rights and duties under that Part.

5. Certain Post-Default Waivers. Section 9-624 permits post-default waivers in limited circumstances. These waivers must be made in agreements that are signed. Under Section 1-201, an "'agreement' means "the bargain of the parties in fact." In considering waivers under Section 9-624 and analogous agreements in other contexts, courts should carefully scrutinize putative agreements that appear in records that also address many additional or unrelated matters.

§ 9-603. Agreement on Standards Concerning Rights and Duties.

(a) [Agreed standards.] The parties may determine by agreement the standards measuring the fulfillment of the rights of a debtor or obligor and the duties of a secured party under a rule stated in Section 9-602 if the standards are not manifestly unreasonable.

(b) [Agreed standards inapplicable to breach of peace.] Subsection (a) does not apply to the duty under Section 9-609 to refrain from breaching the peace.

Definitional Cross References:

Agreement	Section 1-201(b)(3)
Debtor	Section 9-102(a)(28)
Obligor	Section 9-102(a)(59)
Right	Section 1-201(b)(34)
Secured party	Section 9-102(a)(73)

Official Comment

1. Source. Former Section 9-501(3).

2. Limitation on Ability to Set Standards. Subsection (a), like former Section 9-501(3), permits the parties to set standards for compliance with the rights and duties under this Part if the standards are not "manifestly unreasonable." Under subsection (b), the parties are not permitted to set standards measuring fulfillment of the secured party's duty to take collateral without breaching the peace.

§ 9-604. Procedure If Security Agreement Covers Real Property or Fixtures.

(a) [Enforcement: personal and real property.] If a security agreement covers both personal and real property, a secured party may proceed:

(1) under this part as to the personal property without prejudicing any rights with respect to the real property; or

(2) as to both the personal property and the real property in accordance with the rights with respect to the real property, in which case the other provisions of this part do not apply.

(b) [Enforcement: fixtures.] Subject to subsection (c), if a security agreement covers goods that are or become fixtures, a secured party may proceed:

(1) under this part; or

(2) in accordance with the rights with respect to real property, in which case the other provisions of this part do not apply.

(c) [Removal of fixtures.] Subject to the other provisions of this part, if a secured party holding a security interest in fixtures has priority over all owners and encumbrancers of the real property, the secured party, after default, may remove the collateral from the real property.

(d) [Injury caused by removal.] A secured party that removes collateral shall promptly reimburse any encumbrancer or owner of the real property, other than the debtor, for the cost of repair of any physical injury caused by the removal. The secured party need not reimburse the encumbrancer or owner for any diminution in value of the real property caused by the absence of the goods removed or by any necessity of replacing them. A person entitled to reimbursement may refuse permission to remove until the secured party gives adequate assurance for the performance of the obligation to reimburse.

Definitional Cross References:

Collateral	Section 9-102(a)(12)
Debtor	Section 9-102(a)(28)
Fixtures	Section 9-102(a)(41)
Goods	Section 9-102(a)(44)
Person	Section 1-201(b)(27)
Right	Section 1-201(b)(34)
Secured party	Section 9-102(a)(73)
Security agreement	Section 9-102(a)(74)
Security interest	Section 1-201(b)(35)
Value	Section 1-204

Official Comment

1. Source. Former Sections 9-501(4), 9-313(8).

2. Real-Property-Related Collateral. The collateral in many transactions consists of both real and personal property. In the interest of simplicity, speed, and economy, subsection (a), like former Section 9-501(4), permits (but does not require) the secured party to proceed as to both real and personal property in accordance with its rights and remedies with respect to the real property. Subsection (a) also makes clear that a secured party who exercises rights under Part 6 with respect to personal property does not prejudice any rights under real-property law.

This Article does not address certain other real-property-related problems. In a number of States, the exercise of remedies by a creditor who is secured by both real property and non-real property collateral is governed by special legal rules. For example, under some anti-deficiency laws, creditors risk loss of rights against personal property collateral if they err in enforcing their rights against the real property. Under a "one-form-of-action" rule (or rule against splitting a cause of action), a creditor who judicially enforces a real property mortgage and does not proceed in the same action to enforce a security interest in personalty may (among other consequences) lose the right to proceed against the personalty. Although statutes of this kind create impediments to enforcement of security interests, this Article does not override these limitations under other law.

3. Fixtures. Subsection (b) is new. It makes clear that a security interest in fixtures may be enforced either under real-property law or under any of the applicable provisions of Part 6, including sale or other disposition either before or after removal of the fixtures (see subsection (c)). Subsection (b) also serves to overrule cases holding that a secured party's only remedy after default is the removal of the fixtures from the real property. See, e.g., *Maplewood Bank & Trust v. Sears, Roebuck & Co.*, 625 A.2d 537 (N.J. Super. Ct. App. Div. 1993).

Subsection (c) generally follows former Section 9-313(8). It gives the secured party the right to remove fixtures under certain circumstances. A secured party whose security interest in fixtures has priority over owners and encumbrancers of the real property may remove the collateral from the real property. However, subsection (d) requires the secured party to reimburse any owner (other than the debtor) or encumbrancer for the cost of repairing any physical injury caused by the removal. This right to reimbursement is implemented by the last sentence of subsection (d), which gives the owner or encumbrancer a right to security or indemnity as a condition for giving permission to remove.

§ 9-605. Unknown Debtor or Secondary Obligor.

(a) [In general: No duty owed by secured party.] Except as provided in subsection (b), a secured party does not owe a duty based on its status as secured party:

(1) to a person that is a debtor or obligor, unless the secured party knows:

(A) that the person is a debtor or obligor;

(B) the identity of the person; and

(C) how to communicate with the person; or

(2) to a secured party or lienholder that has filed a financing statement against a person, unless the secured party knows:

(A) that the person is a debtor; and

(B) the identity of the person.

(b) [Exception: Secured party owes duty to debtor or obligor.] A secured party owes a duty based on its status as a secured party to a person if, at the time the secured party obtains control of collateral that is a controllable account, controllable electronic record, or controllable payment intangible or at the time the security interest attaches to the collateral, whichever is later:

(1) the person is a debtor or obligor; and

(2) the secured party knows that the information in subsection (a)(1)(A), (B), or (C) relating to the person is not provided by the collateral, a record attached to or logically associated with the collateral, or the system in which the collateral is recorded.

Definitional Cross References:

Collateral	Section 9-102(a)(12)
Communicate	Section 9-102(a)(18)
Controllable account	Section 9-102(a)(27A)
Controllable electronic record	Section 12-102(a)(1)
Controllable payment intangible	Section 9-102(a)(27B)
Debtor	Section 9-102(a)(28)
Financing statement	Section 9-102(a)(39)
Obligor	Section 9-102(a)(59)
Person	Section 1-201(b)(27)
Record	Section 9-102(a)(70)
Secondary obligor	Section 9-102(a)(72)
Secured party	Section 9-102(a)(73)
Security interest	Section 1-201(b)(35)

Official Comment

1. Source. New.

2. Duties to Unknown Persons and Limitation of Liability. This section relieves a secured party from duties owed to a debtor or obligor, if the secured party does not know about the debtor or obligor. Similarly, it relieves a secured party from duties owed to a secured party or lienholder who has filed a financing statement against the debtor, if the secured party does not know about the debtor. Section 9-628(a) and (b) provide analogous limitations of liability. For example, a secured party may be unaware that the original debtor has sold the collateral subject to the security interest and that the new owner has become the debtor. If so, the secured party owes no duty to the new owner (debtor) or to a secured party who has filed a financing statement against the new owner. Note that it relieves a secured party not only from duties arising under this Article but also from duties arising under other law by virtue of the secured party's status as such under this Article, unless the other law otherwise provides.

This section should be read in conjunction with the limitations on liability contained in the exculpatory provisions in subsections (a), (b), and (c) of Section 9-628. Without this group of provisions, a secured party could incur liability to unknown persons and under circumstances that would not allow the secured party to protect itself. The broadened definition of the term "debtor" underscores the need for these provisions. For example, as noted above, a debtor may dispose of collateral subject to a security interest, resulting in the transferee becoming a debtor, but the secured party may have no knowledge of the disposition or that the transferee has become a debtor. In that situation the secured party will have no means of giving notice to or accounting to the transferee debtor. Sections 9-605 and 9-628 contemplate such situations by relieving the secured party of its duties to the debtor and limiting the secured party's liability to the debtor.

3. Exceptions to Relief from Duties and Limitation of Liability. In some cases, lenders may extend secured credit without knowing, or having the ability to discover, the identity of their borrowers. Pre-2022 Sections 9-605(a) and 9-628(a) and (b) would excuse these secured parties from having duties to their debtors and obligors, including, for example, the duty to notify the debtor or secondary obligor before disposing of the collateral and the duty to account to the debtor for any surplus arising from a disposition, and would limit the secured parties' liability to their debtors and obligors. In many cases these debtors and obligors may be aware that their identities are unknown to their secured parties. By failing to make their identities and contact information known, these debtors and obligors may be impairing the ability of their secured parties to comply with their duties under Article 9. However, such debtor complicity notwithstanding, if secured parties were relieved of their duties in these circumstances, it would conflict with the policy of Section 9-602, which prohibits a waiver or variance of many rights of debtors and obligors and duties of secured parties.

Sections 9-605(b) and 9-628(f) reflect the policy that a secured party should not be free to avoid statutory duties or absolve itself from liability to a debtor or obligor when the secured party knows that the collateral, records attached to or logically associated with the collateral, and the system in which the collateral is recorded do not provide the secured party with the information necessary to fulfill its statutory duties. As discussed in the following paragraph, the secured party's knowledge that it may not be able to comply with its duties enables the secured party to protect itself from being in breach of these duties. (A person has knowledge of or knows a fact if it has "actual knowledge." Section 1-202(b).) The exceptions from the exculpatory protections otherwise afforded to secured parties are determined by the secured party's knowledge at the later of the time the secured party obtains control of a controllable account, controllable electronic record, or controllable payment intangible or the time that the security interest attaches to the collateral.

Obtaining control or attachment of the security interest serves as a rough proxy for the context in which a secured party may know that it may be unable to comply with its duties, usually because the transferor is pseudonymous. The carve-out from the exculpatory protection is limited to duties owed to and liability to a debtor—the transferor of a controllable account, controllable electronic record, or controllable payment intangible over which the secured party obtains control—or obligor. The secured party in such situations could protect itself by choosing not to enter into a transaction in which it might be unable to comply with its statutory duties or by conditioning its participation on disclosure of the debtor's or obligor's identity and contact information. Ideally, systems providing for the transfer of controllable electronic records would provide mechanisms that would permit compliance with such duties (such as methods of communication and making payments that would preserve a debtor's or obligor's pseudonymity, where that is desired). The amendments to Sections 9-605 and 9-628 provide incentives for system design that would allow for compliance with Article 9 duties.

Secured parties that enter into transactions with knowledge that they may not be able to comply with their Article 9 duties do so at their own peril. Of course, if a secured party possesses, or can obtain, the information necessary to comply with its duties, there is no need for the exculpation from those duties. Note, however, that the limitation on a secured party's relief from duties and liability relates only to secured transactions involving controllable accounts, controllable electronic records, or controllable payment intangibles. Designing systems for these assets that would afford secured parties with opportunities to comply with their Article 9 duties, as suggested above, could eliminate the risks to secured parties and also provide for the protection of debtors' and obligors' rights.

§ 9-606. Time of Default for Agricultural Lien.

For purposes of this part, a default occurs in connection with an agricultural lien at the time the secured party becomes entitled to enforce the lien in accordance with the statute under which it was created.

Definitional Cross References:

Agricultural lien	Section 9-102(a)(5)
Secured party	Section 9-102(a)(73)

Official Comment

1. Source. New.

2. Time of Default. Remedies under this Part become available upon the debtor's "default." See Section 9-601. This section explains when "default" occurs in the agricultural-lien context. It requires one to consult the enabling statute to determine when the lienholder is entitled to enforce the lien.

§ 9-607. Collection and Enforcement by Secured Party.

(a) [Collection and enforcement generally.] If so agreed, and in any event after default, a secured party:

(1) may notify an account debtor or other person obligated on collateral to make payment or otherwise render performance to or for the benefit of the secured party;

(2) may take any proceeds to which the secured party is entitled under Section 9-315;

(3) may enforce the obligations of an account debtor or other person obligated on collateral and exercise the rights of the debtor with respect to the obligation of the account debtor or other person obligated on collateral to make payment or otherwise render performance to the debtor, and with respect to any property that secures the obligations of the account debtor or other person obligated on the collateral;

(4) if it holds a security interest in a deposit account perfected by control under Section 9-104(a)(1), may apply the balance of the deposit account to the obligation secured by the deposit account; and

(5) if it holds a security interest in a deposit account perfected by control under Section 9-104(a)(2) or (3), may instruct the bank to pay the balance of the deposit account to or for the benefit of the secured party.

(b) [Nonjudicial enforcement of mortgage.] If necessary to enable a secured party to exercise under subsection (a)(3) the right of a debtor to enforce a mortgage nonjudicially, the secured party may record in the office in which a record of the mortgage is recorded:

(1) a copy of the security agreement that creates or provides for a security interest in the obligation secured by the mortgage; and

(2) the secured party's sworn affidavit in recordable form stating that:

(A) a default has occurred with respect to the obligation secured by the mortgage; and

(B) the secured party is entitled to enforce the mortgage nonjudicially.

(c) [Commercially reasonable collection and enforcement.] A secured party shall proceed in a commercially reasonable manner if the secured party:

(1) undertakes to collect from or enforce an obligation of an account debtor or other person obligated on collateral; and

(2) is entitled to charge back uncollected collateral or otherwise to full or limited recourse against the debtor or a secondary obligor.

(d) [Expenses of collection and enforcement.] A secured party may deduct from the collections made pursuant to subsection (c) reasonable expenses of collection and enforcement, including reasonable attorney's fees and legal expenses incurred by the secured party.

(e) [Duties to secured party not affected.] This section does not determine whether an account debtor, bank, or other person obligated on collateral owes a duty to a secured party.

Definitional Cross References:

Account debtor	Section 9-102(a)(3)
Bank	Section 9-102(a)(8)
Collateral	Section 9-102(a)(12)
Debtor	Section 9-102(a)(28)
Deposit account	Section 9-102(a)(29)
Mortgage	Section 9-102(a)(55)
Notify	Section 1-202(d)
Proceeds	Section 9-102(a)(64)
Right	Section 1-201(b)(34)
Secondary obligor	Section 9-102(a)(72)
Secured party	Section 9-102(a)(73)
Security agreement	Section 9-102(a)(74)
Security interest	Section 1-201(b)(35)

Official Comment

1. Source. Former Section 9-502; subsections (b), (d), and (e) are new.

2. Collections: In General. Collateral consisting of rights to payment is not only the most liquid asset of a typical debtor's business but also is property that may be collected without any interruption of the debtor's business. This situation is far different from that in which collateral is inventory or equipment, whose removal may bring the business to a halt. Furthermore, problems of valuation and identification, present with collateral that is tangible personal property, frequently are not as serious in the case of rights to payment and other intangible collateral. Consequently, this section, like former Section 9-502, recognizes that financing through assignments of intangibles lacks many of the complexities that arise after default in other types of financing. This section allows the assignee to liquidate collateral by collecting whatever may become due on the collateral, whether or not the method of collection contemplated by the security arrangement before default was direct (i.e., payment by the account debtor to the assignee, "notification" financing) or indirect (i.e., payment by the account debtor to the assignor, "nonnotification" financing).

3. Scope. The scope of this section is broader than that of former Section 9-502. It applies not only to collections from account debtors and obligors on instruments but also to enforcement more generally against all persons obligated on collateral. It explicitly provides for the secured party's enforcement of the debtor's rights in respect of the account debtor's (and other third parties') obligations and for the secured party's enforcement of supporting obligations with respect to those obligations. (Supporting obligations are components of the collateral under Section 9-203(f).) The rights of a secured party under subsection (a) include the right to enforce claims that the debtor may enjoy against others. For example, the claims might include a breach-of-warranty claim arising out of a defect in equipment that is collateral or a secured party's action for an injunction against infringement of a patent that is collateral. Those claims typically would be proceeds of original collateral under Section 9-315.

4. Collection and Enforcement Before Default. Like Part 6 generally, this section deals with the rights and duties of secured parties following default. However, as did former Section 9-502 with respect to collection rights, this section also applies to the collection and enforcement rights of secured parties even if a default has not occurred, as long as the debtor has so agreed. It is not unusual for debtors to agree that secured parties are entitled to collect and enforce rights against account debtors prior to default.

5. Collections by Junior Secured Party. A secured party who holds a security interest in a right to payment may exercise the right to collect and enforce under this section, even if the security interest is subordinate to a conflicting security interest in the same right to payment. Whether the junior secured party has priority in the collected proceeds depends on whether the junior secured party qualifies for priority as a purchaser of an instrument (e.g., the account debtor's check) under Section 9-330(d), as a holder in due course of an instrument under Sections 3-305 and 9-331(a), or as a transferee of money under Section 9-332(a). See Sections 9-330, Comment 7; 9-331, Comment 5; and 9-332.

6. Relationship to Rights and Duties of Persons Obligated on Collateral. This section permits a secured party to collect and enforce obligations included in collateral in its capacity as a secured party. It is not necessary for a secured party first to become the owner of the collateral pursuant to a disposition or acceptance. However, the secured party's rights, as between it and the debtor, to collect from and enforce collateral against account debtors and others obligated on collateral under subsection (a) are subject to Section 9-341, Part 4, and other applicable law. Neither this section nor former Section 9-502 should be understood to regulate the duties of an account debtor or other person obligated on collateral. Subsection (e) makes this explicit. For example, the secured party may be unable to exercise the debtor's rights under an instrument if the debtor is in possession of the instrument, or under a non-transferable letter of credit if the debtor is the beneficiary. Unless a secured party has control over a letter-of-credit right and is entitled to receive payment or performance from the issuer or a nominated person under Article 5, its remedies with respect to the letter-of-credit right may be limited to the recovery of any identifiable proceeds from the debtor. This section establishes only the baseline rights of the secured party vis-à-vis the debtor—the secured party is entitled to enforce and collect after default or earlier if so agreed.

7. Deposit Account Collateral. Subsections (a)(4) and (5) set forth the self-help remedy for a secured party whose collateral is a deposit account. Subsection (a)(4) addresses the rights of a secured party that is the bank with which the deposit account is maintained. That secured party automatically has control of the deposit account under Section 9-104(a)(1). After default, and otherwise if so agreed, the bank/secured party may apply the funds on deposit to the secured obligation.

If a security interest of a third party is perfected by control (Section 9-104(a)(2) or (a)(3)), then after default, and otherwise if so agreed, the secured party may instruct the bank to pay out the funds in the account. If the third party has control under Section 9-104(a)(3), the depositary institution is obliged to obey the instruction because the secured party is its customer. See Section 4-401. If the third party has control under Section 9-104(a)(2), the control agreement determines the depositary institution's obligation to obey.

If a security interest in a deposit account is unperfected, or is perfected by filing by virtue of the proceeds rules of Section 9-315, the depositary institution ordinarily owes no obligation to obey the secured party's instructions. See Section 9-341. To reach the funds without the debtor's cooperation, the secured party must use an available judicial procedure.

8. Rights Against Mortgagor of Real Property. Subsection (b) addresses the situation in which the collateral consists of a mortgage note (or other obligation secured by a mortgage on real property). After the debtor's (mortgagee's) default, the secured party (assignee) may wish to proceed with a nonjudicial foreclosure of the mortgage securing the note but may be unable to do so because it has not become the assignee of record. The assignee/secured party may not have taken a recordable assignment at the commencement of the transaction (perhaps the mortgage note in question was one of hundreds assigned to the secured party as collateral). Having defaulted, the mortgagee may be unwilling to sign a recordable assignment. This section enables the secured party (assignee) to become the assignee of record by recording in the applicable real-property records the security agreement and an affidavit certifying default. Of course, the secured party's rights derive from those of its debtor. Subsection (b) would not entitle the secured party to proceed with a foreclosure unless the mortgagor also were in default or the debtor (mortgagee) otherwise enjoyed the right to foreclose.

9. Commercial Reasonableness. Subsection (c) provides that the secured party's collection and enforcement rights under subsection (a) must be exercised in a commercially reasonable manner. These rights include the right to settle and compromise claims against the account debtor. The secured party's failure to observe the standard of commercial reasonableness could render it liable to an aggrieved person under Section 9-625, and the secured party's recovery of a deficiency would be subject to Section 9-626. Subsection (c) does not apply if, as is characteristic of most sales of accounts, chattel paper, payment intangibles, and promissory notes, the secured party (buyer) has no right of recourse against the debtor (seller) or a secondary obligor. However, if the secured party does have a right of recourse, the commercial-reasonableness standard applies to collection and enforcement even though the assignment to the secured party was a "true" sale. The obligation to proceed in a commercially reasonable manner arises because the collection process affects the extent of the seller's recourse liability, not because the seller retains an interest in the sold collateral (the seller does not). Concerning classification of a transaction, see Section 9-109, Comment 4.

10. Attorney's Fees and Legal Expenses. The phrase "reasonable attorney's fees and legal expenses," which appears in subsection (d), includes only those fees and expenses incurred in proceeding against account debtors or other third parties. The secured party's right to recover these expenses from the collections arises automatically under this section. The secured party also may incur other attorney's fees and legal expenses in proceeding against the debtor or obligor. Whether the secured party has a right to recover those fees and expenses depends on whether the debtor or obligor has agreed to pay them, as is the case with respect to attorney's fees and legal expenses under Sections 9-608(a)(1)(A) and 9-615(a)(1). The parties also may agree to allocate a portion of the secured party's overhead to collection and enforcement under subsection (d) or Section 9-608(a).

§ 9-608. Application of Proceeds of Collection or Enforcement; Liability for Deficiency and Rights to Surplus.

(a) [Application of proceeds, surplus, and deficiency if obligation secured.] If a security interest or agricultural lien secures payment or performance of an obligation, the following rules apply:

(1) A secured party shall apply or pay over for application the cash proceeds of collection

or enforcement under Section 9-607 in the following order to:

(A) the reasonable expenses of collection and enforcement and, to the extent provided for by agreement and not prohibited by law, reasonable attorney's fees and legal expenses incurred by the secured party;

(B) the satisfaction of obligations secured by the security interest or agricultural lien under which the collection or enforcement is made; and

(C) the satisfaction of obligations secured by any subordinate security interest in or other lien on the collateral subject to the security interest or agricultural lien under which the collection or enforcement is made if the secured party receives a signed demand for proceeds before distribution of the proceeds is completed.

(2) If requested by a secured party, a holder of a subordinate security interest or other lien shall furnish reasonable proof of the interest or lien within a reasonable time. Unless the holder complies, the secured party need not comply with the holder's demand under paragraph (1)(C).

(3) A secured party need not apply or pay over for application noncash proceeds of collection and enforcement under Section 9-607 unless the failure to do so would be commercially unreasonable. A secured party that applies or pays over for application noncash proceeds shall do so in a commercially reasonable manner.

(4) A secured party shall account to and pay a debtor for any surplus, and the obligor is liable for any deficiency.

(b) [No surplus or deficiency in sales of certain rights to payment.] If the underlying transaction is a sale of accounts, chattel paper, payment intangibles, or promissory notes, the debtor is not entitled to any surplus, and the obligor is not liable for any deficiency.

Definitional Cross References:

Account	Section 9-102(a)(2)
Agreement	Section 1-201(b)(3)
Agricultural lien	Section 9-102(a)(5)
Chattel paper	Section 9-102(a)(11)
Collateral	Section 9-102(a)(12)
Debtor	Section 9-102(a)(28)
Holder	Section 1-201(b)(21)
Noncash proceeds	Section 9-102(a)(58)
Obligor	Section 9-102(a)(59)
Payment intangible	Section 9-102(a)(61)
Proceeds	Section 9-102(a)(64)
Promissory note	Section 9-102(a)(65)
Right	Section 1-201(b)(34)
Sale	Section 2-106(1)
Secured party	Section 9-102(a)(73)
Security interest	Section 1-201(b)(35)
Sign	Section 1-201(b)(37)

Official Comment

1. Source. Subsection (a) is new; subsection (b) derives from former Section 9-502(2).

2. Modifications of Prior Law. Subsections (a) and (b) modify former Section 9-502(2) by explicitly providing for the application of proceeds recovered by the secured party in substantially the same manner as provided in Section 9-615(a) and (e) for dispositions of collateral.

3. Surplus and Deficiency. Subsections (a)(4) and (b) omit, as unnecessary, the references contained in former Section 9-502(2) to agreements varying the baseline rules on surplus and deficiency. The parties are always free to agree that an obligor will not be liable for a deficiency, even if the collateral secures an obligation, and that an obligor is liable for a deficiency, even if the transaction is a sale of receivables. For parallel provisions, see Section 9-615(d) and (e).

4. Noncash Proceeds. Subsection (a)(3) addresses the situation in which an enforcing secured party receives noncash proceeds.

> **Example:** An enforcing secured party receives a promissory note from an account debtor who is unable to pay an account when it is due. The secured party accepts the note in exchange for extending the date on which the account debtor's obligation is due. The secured party may wish to credit its debtor (the assignor) with the principal amount of the note upon receipt of the note, but probably will prefer to credit the debtor only as and when the note is paid.

Under subsection (a)(3), the secured party is under no duty to apply the note or its value to the outstanding obligation unless its failure to do so would be commercially unreasonable. If the secured party does apply the note to the outstanding obligation, however, it must do so in a commercially reasonable manner. The parties may provide for the method of application of noncash proceeds by agreement, if the method is not manifestly unreasonable. See Section 9-603. This section does not explain when the failure to apply noncash proceeds would be commercially unreasonable; it leaves that determination to case-by-case adjudication. In the example, the secured party appears to have accepted the account debtor's note in order to increase the likelihood of payment and decrease the likelihood that the account debtor would dispute its obligation. Under these circumstances, it may well be commercially reasonable for the secured party to credit its debtor's obligations only as and when cash proceeds are collected from the account debtor, especially given the uncertainty that attends the account debtor's eventual payment. For an example of a secured party's receipt of noncash proceeds in which it may well be commercially unreasonable for the secured party to delay crediting its debtor's obligations with the value of noncash proceeds, see Section 9-615, Comment 3.

When the secured party is not required to "apply or pay over for application noncash proceeds," the proceeds nonetheless remain collateral subject to this Article. If the secured party were to dispose of them, for example, appropriate notification would be required (see Section 9-611), and the disposition would be subject to the standards provided in this Part (see Section 9-610). Moreover, a secured party in possession of the noncash proceeds would have the duties specified in Section 9-207.

5. No Effect on Priority of Senior Security Interest. The application of proceeds required by subsection (a) does not affect the priority of a security interest in collateral which is senior to the interest of the secured party who is collecting or enforcing collateral under Section 9-607. Although subsection (a) imposes a duty to apply proceeds to the enforcing secured party's expenses and to the satisfaction of the secured obligations owed to it and to subordinate secured parties, that duty applies only among the enforcing secured party and those persons. Concerning the priority of a junior secured party who collects and enforces collateral, see Section 9-607, Comment 5.

6. "Signed" Replaces "Authenticated." Consistent with the revised definition of "sign" in Section 1-201, the cognate term "signed" replaces the reference to "authenticated" in the pre-2022 text of this section.

§ 9-609. Secured Party's Right to Take Possession After Default.

(a) [Possession; rendering equipment unusable; disposition on debtor's premises.] After default, a secured party:

(1) may take possession of the collateral; and

(2) without removal, may render equipment unusable and dispose of collateral on a debtor's premises under Section 9-610.

(b) [Judicial and nonjudicial process.] A secured party may proceed under subsection (a):

(1) pursuant to judicial process; or

(2) without judicial process, if it proceeds without breach of the peace.

(c) [Assembly of collateral.] If so agreed, and in any event after default, a secured party may require the debtor to assemble the collateral and make it available to the secured party at a place to be designated by the secured party which is reasonably convenient to both parties.

Definitional Cross References:

Collateral	Section 9-102(a)(12)
Debtor	Section 9-102(a)(28)
Equipment	Section 9-102(a)(33)
Proceeds	Section 9-102(a)(64)
Secured party	Section 9-102(a)(73)

Official Comment

1. Source. Former Section 9-503.

2. Secured Party's Right to Possession. This section follows former Section 9-503 and earlier uniform legislation. It provides that the secured party is entitled to take possession of collateral after default.

3. Judicial Process; Breach of Peace. Subsection (b) permits a secured party to proceed under this section without judicial process if it does so "without breach of the peace." Although former Section 9-503 placed the same condition on a secured party's right to take possession of collateral, subsection (b) extends the condition to the right provided in subsection (a)(2) as well. Like former Section 9-503, this section does not define or explain the conduct that will constitute a breach of the peace, leaving that matter for continuing development by the courts. In considering whether a secured party has engaged in a breach of the peace, however, courts should hold the secured party responsible for the actions of others taken on the secured party's behalf, including independent contractors engaged by the secured party to take possession of collateral.

This section does not authorize a secured party who repossesses without judicial process to utilize the assistance of a law-enforcement officer. A number of cases have held that a repossessing secured party's use of a law-enforcement officer without benefit of judicial process constituted a failure to comply with former Section 9-503.

4. Damages for Breach of Peace. Concerning damages that may be recovered based on a secured party's breach of the peace in connection with taking possession of collateral, see Section 9-625, Comment 3.

5. Multiple Secured Parties. More than one secured party may be entitled to take possession of collateral under this section. Conflicting rights to possession among secured parties are resolved by the priority rules of this Article. Thus, a senior secured party is entitled to possession as against a junior claimant. Non-UCC law governs whether a junior secured party in possession of collateral is liable to the senior in conversion. Normally, a junior who refuses to relinquish possession of collateral upon the demand of a secured party having a superior possessory right to the collateral would be liable in conversion.

6. Secured Party's Right to Disable and Dispose of Equipment on Debtor's Premises. In the case of some collateral, such as heavy equipment, the physical removal from the debtor's plant and the storage of the collateral pending disposition may be impractical or unduly expensive. This section follows former Section 9-503 by providing that, in lieu of removal, the secured party may render equipment unusable or may dispose of collateral on the debtor's premises. Unlike former Section 9-503, however, this section explicitly conditions these rights on the debtor's default. Of course, this section does not validate unreasonable action by a secured party. Under Section 9-610, all aspects of a disposition must be commercially reasonable.

7. Debtor's Agreement to Assemble Collateral. This section follows former Section 9-503 also by validating a debtor's agreement to assemble collateral and make it available to a secured party at a place that the secured party designates. Similar to the treatment of agreements to permit collection prior to default under Section 9-607 and former 9-502, however, this section validates these agreements whether or not they are conditioned on the debtor's default. For example, a debtor might agree to make available to a secured party, from time to time, any instruments or negotiable documents that the debtor receives on account of collateral. A court should not infer from this section's validation that a debtor's agreement to assemble and make available collateral would not be enforceable under other applicable law.

8. Agreed Standards. Subject to the limitation imposed by Section 9-603(b), this section's provisions concerning agreements to assemble and make available collateral and a secured party's right to disable equipment and dispose of collateral on a debtor's premises are likely topics for agreement on standards as contemplated by Section 9-603.

§ 9-610. Disposition of Collateral After Default.

(a) [Disposition after default.] After default, a secured party may sell, lease, license, or otherwise dispose of any or all of the collateral in its present condition or following any commercially reasonable preparation or processing.

(b) [Commercially reasonable disposition.] Every aspect of a disposition of collateral, including the method, manner, time, place, and other terms, must be commercially reasonable. If commercially reasonable, a secured party may dispose of collateral by public or private proceedings, by one or more contracts, as a unit or in parcels, and at any time and place and on any terms.

(c) [Purchase by secured party.] A secured party may purchase collateral:

(1) at a public disposition; or

(2) at a private disposition only if the collateral is of a kind that is customarily sold on a recognized market or the subject of widely distributed standard price quotations.

(d) [Warranties on disposition.] A contract for sale, lease, license, or other disposition includes the warranties relating to title, possession, quiet enjoyment, and the like which by operation of law accompany a voluntary disposition of property of the kind subject to the contract.

(e) [Disclaimer of warranties.] A secured party may disclaim or modify warranties under subsection (d):

(1) in a manner that would be effective to disclaim or modify the warranties in a voluntary disposition of property of the kind subject to the contract of disposition; or

(2) by communicating to the purchaser a record evidencing the contract for disposition and including an express disclaimer or modification of the warranties.

(f) [Record sufficient to disclaim warranties.] A record is sufficient to disclaim warranties under subsection (e) if it indicates "There is no warranty relating to title, possession, quiet enjoyment, or the like in this disposition" or uses words of similar import.

Definitional Cross References:

Collateral	Section 9-102(a)(12)
Contract	Section 1-201(b)(12)
Contract for sale	Section 2-106(1)
Lease	Section 2A-103(1)(j)
Purchase	Section 1-201(b)(29)
Purchaser	Section 1-201(b)(30)
Record	Section 9-102(a)(70)
Secured party	Section 9-102(a)(73)
Term	Section 1-201(b)(40)

Official Comment

1. Source. Former Section 9-504(1), (3).

2. Commercially Reasonable Dispositions. Subsection (a) follows former Section 9-504 by permitting a secured party to dispose of collateral in a commercially reasonable manner following a default. Although subsection (b) permits both public and private dispositions, including public and private dispositions conducted over the Internet, "every aspect of a disposition . . . must be commercially reasonable." This section encourages private dispositions on the assumption that they frequently will result in higher realization on collateral for the benefit of all concerned. Subsection (a) does not restrict dispositions to sales; collateral may be sold, leased, licensed, or otherwise disposed. Section 9-627 provides guidance for determining the circumstances under which a disposition is "commercially reasonable."

3. Time of Disposition. This Article does not specify a period within which a secured party must dispose of collateral. This is consistent with this Article's policy to encourage private dispositions through regular commercial channels. It may, for example, be prudent not to dispose of goods when the market has collapsed. Or, it might be more appropriate to sell a large inventory in parcels over a period of time instead of in bulk. Of course, under subsection (b) every aspect of a disposition of collateral must be commercially reasonable. This requirement explicitly includes the "method, manner, time, place and other terms." For example, if a secured party does not proceed under Section 9-620 and holds collateral for a long period of time without disposing of it, and if there is no good reason for not making a prompt disposition, the secured party may be determined not to have acted in a "commercially reasonable" manner. See also Section 1-203 (general obligation of good faith). [Ed. Note. The good faith obligation is now contained in Section 1-304.]

4. Pre-Disposition Preparation and Processing. Former Section 9-504(1) appeared to give the secured party the choice of disposing of collateral either "in its then condition or following any commercially reasonable preparation or processing." Some courts held that the "commercially reasonable" standard of former Section 9-504(3) nevertheless could impose an affirmative duty on the secured party to process or prepare the collateral prior to disposition. Subsection (a) retains the substance of the quoted language. Although courts should not be quick to impose a duty of preparation or processing on the secured party, subsection (a) does not grant the secured party the right to dispose of the collateral "in its then condition" under all circumstances. A secured party may not dispose of collateral "in its then condition" when, taking into account the costs and probable benefits of preparation or processing and the fact that the secured party would be advancing the costs at its risk, it would be commercially unreasonable to dispose of the collateral in that condition.

5. Disposition by Junior Secured Party. Disposition rights under subsection (a) are not limited to first-priority security interests. Rather, any secured party as to whom there has been a default enjoys the right to dispose of collateral under this subsection. The exercise of this right by a secured party whose security interest is subordinate to that of another secured party does not of itself constitute a conversion or otherwise give rise to liability in favor of the holder of the senior security interest. Section 9-615 addresses application of the proceeds of a disposition by a junior secured party. Under Section 9-615(a), a junior secured party owes no obligation to apply the proceeds of disposition to the satisfaction of obligations secured by a senior security interest. Section 9-615(g) builds on this general rule by protecting certain juniors from claims of a senior concerning cash proceeds of the disposition. Even if a senior were to have a non-Article 9 claim to proceeds of a junior's disposition, Section 9-615(g) would protect a junior that acts in good faith and without knowledge that its actions violate the rights of a senior party. Because the disposition by a junior would not cut off a senior's security interest or other lien (see Section 9-617), in many (probably most) cases the junior's receipt of the cash proceeds would not violate the rights of the senior.

The holder of a senior security interest is entitled, by virtue of its priority, to take possession of collateral from the junior secured party and conduct its own disposition, provided that the senior enjoys the right to take possession of the collateral from the debtor. See Section 9-609. The holder of a junior security interest normally must notify the senior secured party of an impending disposition. See Section 9-611. Regardless of whether the senior receives a notification from the junior, the junior's disposition does not of itself discharge the senior's security interest. See Section 9-617. Unless the senior secured party has authorized the disposition free and clear of its security interest, the senior's security interest ordinarily will survive the disposition by the junior and continue under Section 9-315(a). If the senior enjoys the right to repossess the collateral from the debtor, the senior likewise may recover the collateral from the transferee.

When a secured party's collateral is encumbered by another security interest or other lien, one of the claimants may seek to invoke the equitable doctrine of marshaling. As explained by the Supreme Court, that doctrine "rests upon the principle that a creditor having two funds to satisfy his debt, may not by his application of them to his demand, defeat another creditor, who may resort to only one of the funds." *Meyer v. United States,* 375 U.S. 233, 236 (1963), quoting *Sowell v. Federal Reserve Bank,* 268 U.S. 449, 456-57 (1925). The purpose of the doctrine is "to prevent the arbitrary action of a senior lienor from destroying the rights of a junior lienor or a creditor having less security." Id. at 237. Because it is an equitable doctrine, marshaling "is applied only when it can be equitably fashioned as to all of the parties" having an interest in the property. Id. This Article leaves courts free to determine whether marshaling is appropriate in any given case. See Section 1-103.

6. Security Interests of Equal Rank. Sometimes two security interests enjoy the same priority. This situation may arise by contract, e.g., pursuant to "equal and ratable" provisions in indentures, or by operation of law. See Section 9-328(6). This Article treats a security interest having equal priority like a senior security interest in many respects. Assume, for example, that SP-X and SP-Y enjoy equal priority, SP-W is senior to them, and SP-Z is junior. If SP-X disposes of the collateral under this section, then (i) SP-W's and SP-Y's security interests survive the disposition but SP-Z's does not, see Section 9-617, and (ii) neither SP-W nor SP-Y is entitled to receive a distribution of proceeds, but SP-Z is. See Section 9-615(a)(3).

When one considers the ability to obtain possession of the collateral, a secured party with equal priority is unlike a senior secured party. As the senior secured party, SP-W should enjoy the right to possession as against SP-X. See Section 9-609, Comment 5. If SP-W takes possession and disposes of the collateral under this section, it is entitled to apply the proceeds to satisfy its secured claim. SP-Y, however, should not have such a right to take possession from SP-X; otherwise, once SP-Y took possession from SP-X, SP-X would have the right to get possession from SP-Y, which would be obligated to redeliver possession to SP-X, and so on. Resolution of this problem is left to the parties and, if necessary, the courts.

7. Public vs. Private Dispositions. This Part maintains two distinctions between "public" and other dispositions: (i) the secured party may buy at the former, but normally not at the latter (Section 9-610(c)), and (ii) the debtor is entitled to notification of "the time and place of a public disposition" and notification of "the time after which" a private disposition or other intended disposition is to be made (Section 9-613(1)(E)). It does not retain the distinction under former Section 9-504(4), under which transferees in a noncomplying public disposition could lose protection more easily than transferees in other noncomplying dispositions. Instead, Section 9-617(b) adopts a unitary standard. Although the term is not defined, as used in this Article, a "public disposition" is one at which the price is determined after the public has had a meaningful opportunity for competitive bidding. "Meaningful opportunity" is meant to imply that some form of advertisement or public notice must precede the sale (or other disposition) and that the public must have access to the sale (disposition).

A secured party's purchase of collateral at its own private disposition is equivalent to a "strict foreclosure" and is governed by Sections 9-620, 9-621, and 9-622. The provisions of these sections can be waived only to the extent provided in Section 9-624(b). See Section 9-602.

8. Investment Property. Dispositions of investment property may be regulated by the federal securities laws. Although a "public" disposition of securities under this Article may implicate the registration requirements of the Securities Act of 1933, it need not do so. A disposition that qualifies for a "private placement" exemption under the Securities Act of 1933 nevertheless may constitute a "public" disposition within the meaning of this section. Moreover, the "commercially reasonable" requirements of subsection (b) need not prevent a secured party from conducting a foreclosure sale without the issuer's compliance with federal registration requirements.

9. "Recognized Market." A "recognized market," as used in subsection (c)(2), Section 9-611(d), and Section 9-627(b)(1) and (2), is one in which the items sold are fungible and which generally produces market prices that are not lower than those that would be expected to result from, as applicable, (i) commercially reasonable dispositions to persons other than the secured party, (ii) commercially reasonable dispositions made with otherwise required notifications to the debtor or other affected persons, or (iii) dispositions otherwise made in a commercially reasonable manner. (As used here, "fungible" items are those that are considered interchangeable in the relevant market and not only items that are strictly "identical" to the other items.) The intended goals of the recognized market exceptions are to ensure that neither the debtor nor other affected parties would be disadvantaged by the special treatment given to recognized markets and to facilitate the efficiencies and cost savings that the special treatment may provide. The purpose of including in subsection (c)(2) collateral that is "the subject of widely distributed standard price quotations" and the criteria for determining whether price quotations meet this standard in subsection (c)(2) are the same as for a recognized market, although the availability of such standard price quotations may be based on, but distributed independently of, a "market" in which acquisitions and dispositions are made. Although a recognized market need not be subject to direct or indirect (e.g., self-regulatory) regulation or supervision, the existence of regulatory requirements or guidelines that are designed to arrive at prices consistent with those contemplated by subsection (c)(2) may provide useful guidance for applying the regulated market standard.

Traditionally, it has been understood that a market in which prices are individually negotiated is not a recognized market, even if the items are the subject of widely disseminated price guides (such as the Kelly Blue Book for automobiles) or are disposed of through specialized auctions (such as those conducted for dealers in livestock and automobiles). However, this does not suggest that, for example, dispositions at prices reflected in such guides or of livestock or automobiles at such auctions could not be commercially reasonable.

The New York Stock Exchange, NASDAQ, the Chicago Mercantile Exchange, and ICE Futures U.S., Inc. are examples of recognized markets. Such exchanges match buy and sell orders submitted by or on behalf of buyers and sellers that are not typically known to each other and do not involve individual negotiations. Other parties, such as inter-dealer brokers in the on-the-run U.S. Treasury market and broker-dealers in the equities market, often operate similar trading facilities that would likewise not involve known buyers or sellers or individual negotiations and may constitute recognized markets. These markets provide for robust trading with active bidding on fungible assets. There is no reason to believe that prices obtained on these markets would be less favorable to debtors, other obligors, and other interested persons than if collateral were disposed of in an off-market public or private disposition.

Trading environments generally referred to as "over-the-counter" or "OTC" markets, however, typically have involved prospective buyers and sellers that can know each other and have direct communication in order to make trades. Unlike typical exchanges, OTC markets normally do involve the individual negotiation of a price. See Carl S. Bjerre, *Investment Securities*, 71 Bus. Law. 1311, 1316-17 (2016) (contrasting exchanges and typical OTC markets for equity securities and explaining that OTC markets have tended to feature thinner markets with less liquidity and more variability of pricing).

In considering the recognized market exceptions, it is important to appreciate that recognized markets and other systems that produce equivalent "widely distributed standard price quotations" are not limited to traditional exchanges, such as those mentioned above. In particular, the exchange-OTC dichotomy no longer offers such a reliable, bright-line test for determining status as a recognized market or as a source of widely distributed standard price quotations. To be sure, some OTC markets do not qualify for the exceptions. However, recent years have witnessed a variety of new trading platforms, the use of new technologies, and new sources of providing and consuming information. There now exist markets, in particular for debt securities (including United States Treasury securities), that might be classified as OTC markets under the traditional taxonomy, but which qualify for the exceptions as recognized markets or as sources of data for widely distributed standard price quotations. Market participants rely on prices provided by these markets to the same extent and for the same purposes (including in connection with default and enforcement of security interests) as they rely on prices generated by traditional securities and commodities exchanges. These prices are widely available from business publications and online sources as well as from private subscription-based service providers. It can safely be assumed that these financial markets and the data that they provide to the public will continue to evolve. The touchstone for determining whether a market structure is a recognized market or one that produces equivalent price quotations is a functional one. It is not based on the "type" of market (e.g., "exchange," "OTC," or other classification). It is based on whether the market or distribution of price quotations provides reliable and trusted data on prices consistent with the purposes of subsection (c)(2) and the corresponding provisions of Sections 9- 611 and 9-627.

10. Relevance of Price. While not itself sufficient to establish a violation of this Part, a low price suggests that a court should scrutinize carefully all aspects of a disposition to ensure that each aspect was commercially reasonable. Note also that even if the disposition is commercially reasonable, Section 9-615(f) provides a special method for calculating a deficiency or surplus if (i) the transferee in the disposition is the secured party, a person related to the secured party, or a secondary obligor, and (ii) the amount of proceeds of the disposition is significantly below the range of proceeds that a complying disposition to a person other than the secured party, a person related to the secured party, or a secondary obligor would have brought.

11. Warranties. Subsection (d) affords the transferee in a disposition under this section the benefit of any title, possession, quiet enjoyment, and similar warranties that would have accompanied the disposition by operation of non-Article 9 law had the disposition been conducted under other circumstances. For example, the Article 2 warranty of title would apply to a sale of goods, the analogous warranties of Article 2A would apply to a lease of goods, and any common-law warranties of title would apply to dispositions of other types of collateral. See, e.g., Restatement (2d), Contracts § 333, the analogous warranties of Article 2A would apply to a lease of goods, and any common-law warranties of title would apply to dispositions of other types of collateral.

Subsection (e) explicitly provides that these warranties can be disclaimed either under other applicable law or by communicating a record containing an express disclaimer. The record need not be written, but an oral communication would not be sufficient. See Section 9-102 (definition of "record"). Subsection (f) provides a sample of wording that will effectively exclude the warranties in a disposition under this section, whether or not the exclusion would be effective under non-Article 9 law.

The warranties incorporated by subsection (d) are those relating to "title, possession, quiet enjoyment, and the like." Depending on the circumstances, a disposition under this section also may give rise to other statutory or implied warranties, e.g., warranties of quality or fitness for purpose. Law other than this Article determines whether such other warranties apply to a disposition under this section. Other law also determines issues relating to disclaimer of such warranties. For example, a foreclosure sale of a car by a car dealer could give rise to an implied warranty of merchantability (Section 2-314) unless effectively disclaimed or modified (Section 2-316).

This section's approach to these warranties conflicts with the former Comment to Section 2-312. This Article rejects the baseline assumption that commercially reasonable dispositions under this section are out of the ordinary commercial course or peculiar. The Comment to Section 2-312 has been revised accordingly.

§ 9-611. Notification Before Disposition of Collateral.

(a) ["Notification date."] In this section, "notification date" means the earlier of the date on which:

(1) a secured party sends to the debtor and any secondary obligor a signed notification of disposition; or

(2) the debtor and any secondary obligor waive the right to notification.

(b) [Notification of disposition required.] Except as otherwise provided in subsection (d), a secured party that disposes of collateral under Section 9-610 shall send to the persons specified in subsection (c) a reasonable signed notification of disposition.

(c) [Persons to be notified.] To comply with subsection (b), the secured party shall send a signed notification of disposition to:

(1) the debtor;

(2) any secondary obligor; and

(3) if the collateral is other than consumer goods:

(A) any other person from which the secured party has received, before the notification date, a signed notification of a claim of an interest in the collateral;

(B) any other secured party or lienholder that, 10 days before the notification date, held a security interest in or other lien on the collateral perfected by the filing of a financing statement that:

(i) identified the collateral;

(ii) was indexed under the debtor's name as of that date; and

(iii) was filed in the office in which to file a financing statement against the debtor covering the collateral as of that date; and

(C) any other secured party that, 10 days before the notification date, held a security interest in the collateral perfected by compliance with a statute, regulation, or treaty described in Section 9-311(a).

(d) [Subsection (b) inapplicable: perishable collateral; recognized market.] Subsection (b) does not apply if the collateral is perishable or threatens to decline speedily in value or is of a type customarily sold on a recognized market.

(e) [Compliance with subsection (c)(3)(B).] A secured party complies with the requirement for notification prescribed by subsection (c)(3)(B) if:

(1) not later than 20 days or earlier than 30 days before the notification date, the secured party requests, in a commercially reasonable manner, information concerning financing statements indexed under the debtor's name in the office indicated in subsection (c)(3)(B); and

(2) before the notification date, the secured party:

(A) did not receive a response to the request for information; or

(B) received a response to the request for information and sent a signed notification of disposition to each secured party or other lienholder named in that response whose financing statement covered the collateral.

Definitional Cross References:

Collateral	Section 9-102(a)(12)
Consumer goods	Section 9-102(a)(23)
Debtor	Section 9-102(a)(28)
Financing statement	Section 9-102(a)(39)
Person	Section 1-201(b)(27)
Secondary obligor	Section 9-102(a)(72)
Secured party	Section 9-102(a)(73)
Security interest	Section 1-201(b)(35)
Send	Section 1-201(b)(36)
Sign	Section 1-201(b)(37)
Value	Section 1-204

Official Comment

1. Source. Former Section 9-504(3).

2. Reasonable Notification. This section requires a secured party who wishes to dispose of collateral under Section 9-610 to send "a reasonable signed notification of disposition" to specified interested persons, subject to certain exceptions. The notification must be reasonable as to the manner in which it is sent, its timeliness (i.e., a reasonable time before the disposition is to take place), and its content. See Sections 9-612 (timeliness of notification), 9-613 (contents of notification generally),

9-614 (contents of notification in consumer-goods transactions).

3. Notification to Debtors and Secondary Obligors. This section imposes a duty to send notification of a disposition not only to the debtor but also to any secondary obligor. Subsections (b) and (c) resolve an uncertainty under former Article 9 by providing that secondary obligors (sureties) are entitled to receive notification of an intended disposition of collateral, regardless of who created the security interest in the collateral. If the surety created the security interest, it would be the debtor. If it did not, it would be a secondary obligor. (This Article also resolves the question of the secondary obligor's ability to waive, pre-default, the right to notification—waiver generally is not permitted. See Section 9-602.) Section 9-605 relieves a secured party from any duty to send notification to a debtor or secondary obligor unknown to the secured party.

Under subsection (b), the principal obligor (borrower) is not always entitled to notification of disposition.

> **Example:** Behnfeldt borrows on an unsecured basis, and Bruno grants a security interest in her car to secure the debt. Behnfeldt is a primary obligor, not a secondary obligor. As such, she is not entitled to notification of disposition under this section.

4. Notification to Other Secured Parties. Prior to the 1972 amendments to Article 9, former Section 9-504(3) required the enforcing secured party to send reasonable notification of the disposition:

> except in the case of consumer goods to any other person who has a security interest in the collateral and who has duly filed a financing statement indexed in the name of the debtor in this State or who is known by the secured party to have a security interest in the collateral.

The 1972 amendments eliminated the duty to give notice to secured parties other than those from whom the foreclosing secured party had received written notice of a claim of an interest in the collateral.

Many of the problems arising from dispositions of collateral encumbered by multiple security interests can be ameliorated or solved by informing all secured parties of an intended disposition and affording them the opportunity to work with one another. To this end, subsection (c)(3)(B) expands the duties of the foreclosing secured party to include the duty to notify (and the corresponding burden of searching the files to discover) certain competing secured parties. The subsection imposes a search burden that in some cases may be greater than the pre-1972 burden on foreclosing secured parties but certainly is more modest than that faced by a new secured lender.

To determine who is entitled to notification, the foreclosing secured party must determine the proper office for filing a financing statement as of a particular date, measured by reference to the "notification date," as defined in subsection (a). This determination requires reference to the choice-of-law provisions of Part 3. The secured party must ascertain whether any financing statements covering the collateral and indexed under the debtor's name, as the name existed as of that date, in fact were filed in that office. The foreclosing secured party generally need not notify secured parties whose effective financing statements have become more difficult to locate because of changes in the location of the debtor, proceeds rules, or changes in the name that is sufficient as the name of the debtor under Section 9-503(a).

Under subsection (c)(3)(C), the secured party also must notify a secured party who has perfected a security interest by complying with a statute or treaty described in Section 9-311(a), such as a certificate-of-title statute.

Subsection (e) provides a "safe harbor" that takes into account the delays that may be attendant to receiving information from the public filing offices. It provides, generally, that the secured party will be deemed to have satisfied its notification duty under subsection (c)(3)(B) if it requests a search from the proper office at least 20 but not more than 30 days before sending notification to the debtor and if it also sends a notification to all secured parties (and other lienholders) reflected on the search report. The secured party's duty under subsection (c)(3)(B) also will be satisfied if the secured party requests but does not receive a search report before the notification is sent to the debtor. Thus, if subsection (e) applies, a secured party who is entitled to notification under subsection (c)(3)(B) has no remedy against a foreclosing secured party who does not send the notification. The foreclosing secured party has complied with the notification requirement. Subsection (e) has no effect on the requirements of the other paragraphs of subsection (c). For example, if the foreclosing secured party received a notification from the holder of a conflicting security interest in accordance with subsection (c)(3)(A) but failed to send to the holder a notification of the disposition, the holder of the conflicting security interest would have the right to recover any loss under Section 9-625(b).

5. Signature Requirement. Subsections (b), (c), and (e) explicitly provide that notifications must be "signed." Some cases read pre-1998 Section 9-504(3) as validating oral notification. Consistent with the revised definition of "sign" in Section 1-201, the cognate term "signed" replaces the references to "authenticated" in the pre-2022 text of this section.

6. Second Try. This Article leaves to judicial resolution, based upon the facts of each case, the question whether the requirement of "reasonable notification" requires a "second try," i.e., whether a secured party who sends notification and learns that the debtor did not receive it must attempt to locate the debtor and send another notification.

7. Recognized Market; Perishable Collateral. Subsection (d) makes it clear that there is no obligation to give notification of a disposition in the case of perishable collateral or collateral customarily sold on a recognized market (e.g., marketable securities). As to what constitutes a recognized market, see Section 9-610, Comment 9.

8. Failure to Conduct Notified Disposition. Nothing in this Article prevents a secured party from electing not to conduct a disposition after sending a notification. Nor does this Article prevent a secured party from electing to send a revised notification if its plans for disposition change. This assumes, however, that the secured party acts in good faith, the revised notification is reasonable, and the revised plan for disposition and any attendant delay are commercially reasonable.

9. Waiver. A debtor or secondary obligor may waive the right to notification under this section only by a post-default signed agreement. See Section 9-624(a).

10. Other Law. Other State or federal law may contain requirements concerning notification of a disposition of property by a secured party. For example, federal law imposes notification requirements with respect to the enforcement of mortgages on federally documented vessels. Principles of statutory interpretation and, in the context of federal law, supremacy and preemption determine whether and to what extent law other than this Article supplements, displaces, or is displaced by this Article. See Sections 1-103, 1-104, 9-109(c)(1).

§ 9-612. Timeliness of Notification Before Disposition of Collateral.

(a) [Reasonable time is question of fact.] Except as otherwise provided in subsection (b), whether a notification is sent within a reasonable time is a question of fact.

(b) [10-day period sufficient in non-consumer transaction.] In a transaction other than a consumer transaction, a notification of disposition sent after default and 10 days or more before the earliest time of disposition set forth in the notification is sent within a reasonable time before the disposition.

Definitional Cross References:

Collateral	Section 9-102(a)(12)
Consumer transaction	Section 9-102(a)(26)

Official Comment

1. Source. New.

2. Reasonable Notification. Section 9-611(b) requires the secured party to send a "reasonable signed notification." Under that section, as under pre-1998 Section 9-504(3), one aspect of a reasonable notification is its timeliness. This generally means that the notification must be sent at a reasonable time in advance of the date of a public disposition or the date after which a private disposition is to be made. A notification that is sent so near to the disposition date that a notified person could not be expected to act on or take account of the notification would be unreasonable.

3. Timeliness of Notification: Safe Harbor. The 10-day notice period in subsection (b) is intended to be a "safe harbor" and not a minimum requirement. To qualify for the "safe harbor" the notification must be sent after default. A notification also must be sent in a commercially reasonable manner. See Section 9-611(b) ("reasonable signed notification"). These requirements prevent a secured party from taking advantage of the "safe harbor" by, for example, giving the debtor a notification at the time of the original extension of credit or sending the notice by surface mail to a debtor overseas.

§ 9-613. Contents and Form of Notification Before Disposition of Collateral: General.

(a) [Contents and form of notification] Except in a consumer-goods transaction, the following rules apply:

(1) The contents of a notification of disposition are sufficient if the notification:

(A) describes the debtor and the secured party;

(B) describes the collateral that is the subject of the intended disposition;

(C) states the method of intended disposition;

(D) states that the debtor is entitled to an accounting of the unpaid indebtedness and states the charge, if any, for an accounting; and

(E) states the time and place of a public disposition or the time after which any other disposition is to be made.

(2) Whether the contents of a notification that lacks any of the information specified in paragraph (1) are nevertheless sufficient is a question of fact.

(3) The contents of a notification providing substantially the information specified in paragraph (1) are sufficient, even if the notification includes:

(A) information not specified by that paragraph; or

(B) minor errors that are not seriously misleading.

(4) A particular phrasing of the notification is not required.

(5) The following form of notification and the form appearing in Section 9-614(a)(3), when completed in accordance with the instructions in subsection (b) and Section 9-614(b), each provides sufficient information:

NOTIFICATION OF DISPOSITION OF COLLATERAL

To: (*Name of debtor, obligor, or other person to which the notification is sent*)

From: (*Name, address, and telephone number of secured party*)

{1} Name of any debtor that is not an addressee: (*Name of each debtor*)

{2} We will sell (*describe collateral*) (to the highest qualified bidder) at public sale. A sale could include a lease or license. The sale will be held as follows:

(Date) ________________

(Time) ________________

(Place) ________________

{3} We will sell (*describe collateral*) at private sale sometime after (*date*). A sale could include a lease or license.

{4} You are entitled to an accounting of the unpaid indebtedness secured by the property that we intend to sell or, as applicable, lease or license.

{5} If you request an accounting you must pay a charge of $ (*amount*).

{6} You may request an accounting by calling us at (*telephone number*).

[End of Form]

(b) [Instructions for form of notification.] The following instructions apply to the form of notification in subsection (a)(5):

(1) The instructions in this subsection refer to the numbers in braces before items in the form of notification in subsection (a)(5). Do not include the numbers or braces in the notification. The numbers and braces are used only for the purpose of these instructions.

(2) Include and complete item {1} only if there is a debtor that is not an addressee of the notification and list the name or names.

(3) Include and complete either item {2}, if the notification relates to a public disposition of the collateral, or item {3}, if the notification relates to a private disposition of the collateral. If item {2} is included, include the words "to the highest qualified bidder" only if applicable.

(4) Include and complete items {4} and {6}

(5) Include and complete item {5} only if the sender will charge the recipient for an accounting.

Definitional Cross References:

Accounting	Section 9-102(a)(4)
Collateral	Section 9-102(a)(12)
Consumer-goods transaction	Section 9-102(a)(24)
Debtor	Section 9-102(a)(28)
Lease	Section 2A-103(1)(j)
Obligor	Section 9-102(a)(59)
Sale	Section 2-106(1)
Secured party	Section 9-102(a)(73)

Official Comment

1. Source. New.

2. Contents of Notification. To comply with the "reasonable signed notification" requirement of Section 9-611(b), the contents of a notification must be reasonable. Except in a consumer-goods transaction, the contents of a notification that includes the information set forth in paragraph (1) are sufficient as a matter of law, unless the parties agree otherwise. (The reference to "time" of disposition means here, as it did in former Section 9-504(3), not only the hour of the day but also the date.) Although a secured party may choose to include additional information concerning the transaction or the debtor's rights and obligations, no additional information is required unless the parties agree otherwise. A notification that lacks some of the information set forth in paragraph (1) nevertheless may be sufficient if found to be reasonable by the trier of fact, under paragraph (2). A properly completed sample form of notification in paragraph (5) or in Section 9-614(a)(3) is an example of a notification that would contain the information set forth in paragraph (1). Under paragraph (4), however, no particular phrasing of the notification is required.

This section applies to a notification of a public disposition conducted electronically. A notification of an electronic disposition satisfies paragraph (1)(E) if it states the time when the disposition is scheduled to begin and states the electronic location. For example, under the technology current in 2010, the Uniform Resource Locator (URL) or other Internet address where the site of the public disposition can be accessed suffices as an electronic location.

3. [Style Changes in Safe-Harbor Form and Medium Netrality] No change in substance is intended by the changes in style to the form provided in paragraph (5) of the pre- 2022 text of this section. However, the presentation and explanation of how to use the form has been simplified and clarified.

§ 9-614. Contents and Form of Notification Before Disposition of Collateral: Consumer-Goods Transaction.

(a) [Contents and form of notification] In a consumer-goods transaction, the following rules apply:

(1) A notification of disposition must provide the following information:

(A) the information specified in Section 9-613(a)(1);

(B) a description of any liability for a deficiency of the person to which the notification is sent;

(C) a telephone number from which the amount that must be paid to the secured party to redeem the collateral under Section 9-623 is available; and

(D) a telephone number or mailing address from which additional information concerning the disposition and the obligation secured is available.

(2) A particular phrasing of the notification is not required.

(3) The following form of notification, when completed in accordance with the instructions in subsection (b), provides sufficient information:

(*Name and address of secured party*)

(*Date*)

NOTICE OF OUR PLAN TO SELL PROPERTY

(*Name and address of any obligor who is also a debtor*)

Subject: (*Identify Transaction*)

We have your (*describe collateral*), because you broke promises in our agreement.

{1} We will sell (*describe collateral*) at public sale. A sale could include a lease or license. The sale will be held as follows:

(Date) ____________________

(Time) ____________________

(Place) ____________________

You may attend the sale and bring bidders if you want.

{2} We will sell (*describe collateral*) at private sale sometime after (date). A sale could include a lease or license.

{3} The money that we get from the sale, after paying our costs, will reduce the amount you owe. If we get less money than you owe, you (*will or will not, as applicable*) still owe us the difference. If we get more money than you owe, you will get the extra money, unless we must pay it to someone else.

{4} You can get the property back at any time before we sell it by paying us the full amount you owe, not just the past due payments, including our expenses. To learn the exact amount you must pay, call us at (*telephone number*).

{5} If you want us to explain to you (in writing or in (*description of electronic record*)) how we have figured the amount that you owe us, you may

{6} call us at (*telephone number*) or write us at (*secured party's address*) (or contact us by (*description of electronic communication method*))

{7} and request a (written explanation) (a written explanation or an explanation in (description of electronic record)) (an explanation in (description of electronic record)).

{8} (We will charge you $ (*amount*) for the explanation if we sent you another written explanation of the amount you owe us within the last six months.)

{9} If you need more information about the sale call us at (*telephone number*) or write us at (*secured party's address*).

{10} We are sending this notice to the following other people who have an interest in (*describe collateral*) or who owe money under your agreement:

(*Names of all other debtors and obligors, if any*)

(4) A notification in the form of paragraph (3) is sufficient, even if additional information appears at the end of the form.

(5) A notification in the form of paragraph (3) is sufficient, even if it includes errors in information not required by paragraph (1), unless the error is misleading with respect to rights arising under this article.

(6) If a notification under this section is not in the form of paragraph (3), law other than this article determines the effect of including information not required by paragraph (1).

(b) [Instructions for form of notification.] The following instructions apply to the form of notification in subsection (a)(3):

(1) The instructions in this subsection refer to the numbers in braces before items in the form of notification in subsection (a)(3). Do not include the numbers or braces in the notification. The numbers and braces are used only for the purpose of these instructions.

(2) Include and complete either item {1}, if the notification relates to a public disposition of the collateral, or item {2}, if the notification relates to a private disposition of the collateral.

(3) Include and complete items {3}, {4}, {5}, {6}, and {7}.

(4) In item {5}, include and complete any one of the three alternative methods for the explanation—writing, writing or electronic record, or electronic record.

(5) In item {6}, include the telephone number. In addition, the sender may include and complete either or both of the two additional alternative methods of communication—writing or electronic communication—for the recipient of the notification to communicate with the sender. Neither of the two additional

methods of communication is required to be included.

(6) In item {7}, include and complete the method or methods for the explanation—writing, writing or electronic record, or electronic record—included in item {5}.

(7) Include and complete item {8} only if a written explanation is included in item {5} as a method for communicating the explanation and the sender will charge the recipient for another written explanation.

(8) In item {9}, include either the telephone number or the address or both the telephone number and the address. In addition, the sender may include and complete the additional method of communication—electronic communication—for the recipient of the notification to communicate with the sender. The additional method of electronic communication is not required to be included.

(9) If item {10} does not apply, insert "None" after "agreement:".

Definitional Cross References:

Agreement	Section 1-201(b)(3)
Collateral	Section 9-102(a)(12)
Consumer-goods transaction	Section 9-102(a)(24)
Debtor	Section 9-102(a)(28)
Electronic	Section 1-201(b)(16A)
Lease	Section 2A-103(1)(j)
Money	Section 9-102(a)(54A)
Notice	Section 1-202(a)
Notification	Section 1-202(d)
Obligor	Section 9-102(a)(59)
Person	Section 1-201(b)(27)
Record	Section 9-102(a)(70)
Right	Section 1-201(b)(34)
Sale	Section 2-106(1)
Secured party	Section 9-102(a)(73)
Send	Section 1-201(b)(36)
Written or writing	Section 1-201(b)(43)

Official Comment

1. Source. New.

2. Notification in Consumer-Goods Transactions. Paragraph (1) sets forth the information required for a reasonable notification in a consumer-goods transaction. A notification that lacks any of the information set forth in paragraph (1) is insufficient as a matter of law. Compare Section 9-613(2), under which the trier of fact may find a notification to be sufficient even if it lacks some information listed in paragraph (1) of that section.

3. Safe-Harbor Form of Notification; Errors in Information. Although paragraph (2) provides that a particular phrasing of a notification is not required, paragraph (3) specifies a safe-harbor form that, when properly completed, satisfies paragraph (1). Paragraphs (4), (5), and (6) contain special rules applicable to erroneous and additional information. Under paragraph (4), a notification in the safe-harbor form specified in paragraph (3) is not rendered insufficient if it contains additional information at the end of the form. Paragraph (5) provides that non-misleading errors in information contained in a notification are permitted if the safe-harbor form is used and if the errors are in information not required by paragraph (1). Finally, if a notification is in a form other than the paragraph (3) safe-harbor form, other law determines the effect of including in the notification information other than that required by paragraph (1).

4. [Style Changes in Safe-harbor Form and medium Neutrality] No change in substance is intended by the changes in style to the form provided in paragraph (3) of the pre- 2022 text of this section, except that in furtherance of medium neutrality references to "electronic record" and "electronic communication method" have been added to the form. However, the presentation and explanation of how to use the form has been simplified and clarified.

§ 9-615. Application of Proceeds of Disposition; Liability for Deficiency and Rights to Surplus.

(a) [Application of proceeds.] A secured party shall apply or pay over for application the cash proceeds of disposition under Section 9-610 in the following order to:

(1) the reasonable expenses of retaking, holding, preparing for disposition, processing, and disposing, and, to the extent provided for by agreement and not prohibited by law, reasonable attorney's fees and legal expenses incurred by the secured party;

(2) the satisfaction of obligations secured by the security interest or agricultural lien under which the disposition is made;

(3) the satisfaction of obligations secured by any subordinate security interest in or other subordinate lien on the collateral if:

(A) the secured party receives from the holder of the subordinate security interest or other lien a signed demand for proceeds before distribution of the proceeds is completed; and

(B) in a case in which a consignor has an interest in the collateral, the subordinate security interest or other lien is senior to the interest of the consignor; and

(4) a secured party that is a consignor of the collateral if the secured party receives from the consignor a signed demand for proceeds before distribution of the proceeds is completed.

(b) [Proof of subordinate interest.] If requested by a secured party, a holder of a subordinate security interest or other lien shall furnish reasonable proof of the interest or lien within a reasonable time. Unless the holder does so, the secured party need not comply with the holder's demand under subsection (a)(3).

(c) [Application of noncash proceeds.] A secured party need not apply or pay over for application noncash proceeds of disposition under Section 9-610 unless the failure to do so would be commercially unreasonable. A secured party that applies or pays over for application noncash proceeds shall do so in a commercially reasonable manner.

(d) [Surplus or deficiency if obligation secured.] If the security interest under which a disposition is made secures payment or performance of an obligation, after making the payments and applications required by subsection (a) and permitted by subsection (c):

(1) unless subsection (a)(4) requires the secured party to apply or pay over cash proceeds to a consignor, the secured party shall account to and pay a debtor for any surplus; and

(2) the obligor is liable for any deficiency.

(e) [No surplus or deficiency in sales of certain rights to payment.] If the underlying transaction is a sale of accounts, chattel paper, payment intangibles, or promissory notes:

(1) the debtor is not entitled to any surplus; and

(2) the obligor is not liable for any deficiency.

(f) [Calculation of surplus or deficiency in disposition to person related to secured party.] The surplus or deficiency following a disposition is calculated based on the amount of proceeds that would have been realized in a disposition complying with this part to a transferee other than the secured party, a person related to the secured party, or a secondary obligor if:

(1) the transferee in the disposition is the secured party, a person related to the secured party, or a secondary obligor; and

(2) the amount of proceeds of the disposition is significantly below the range of proceeds that a complying disposition to a person other than the secured party, a person related to the secured party, or a secondary obligor would have brought.

(g) [Cash proceeds received by junior secured party.] A secured party that receives cash proceeds of a disposition in good faith and without knowledge that the receipt violates the rights of the holder of a security interest or other lien that is not subordinate to the security interest or agricultural lien under which the disposition is made:

(1) takes the cash proceeds free of the security interest or other lien;

(2) is not obligated to apply the proceeds of the disposition to the satisfaction of obligations secured by the security interest or other lien; and

(3) is not obligated to account to or pay the holder of the security interest or other lien for any surplus.

Definitional Cross References:

Account	Section 9-102(a)(2)
Agreement	Section 1-201(b)(3)
Agricultural lien	Section 9-102(a)(5)
Cash proceeds	Section 9-102(a)(9)
Chattel paper	Section 9-102(a)(11)
Collateral	Section 9-102(a)(12)
Consignor	Section 9-102(a)(21)
Debtor	Section 9-102(a)(28)
Good faith	Section 1-201(b)(20)
Holder	Section 1-201(b)(21)
Noncash proceeds	Section 9-102(a)(58)
Obligor	Section 9-102(a)(59)
Payment intangible	Section 9-102(a)(61)
Person related to individual	Section 9-102(a)(62)
Person related to organization	Section 9-102(a)(63)
Proceeds	Section 9-102(a)(64)
Promissory note	Section 9-102(a)(65)
Right	Section 1-201(b)(34)
Sale	Section 2-106(1)
Secondary obligor	Section 9-102(a)(72)
Secured party	Section 9-102(a)(73)
Security interest	Section 1-201(b)(35)
Sign	Section 1-201(b)(37)

Comment Reference: 9-610 C5

Official Comment

1. Source. Former Section 9-504(1), (2).

2. Application of Proceeds. This section contains the rules governing application of proceeds and the debtor's liability for a deficiency following a disposition of collateral. Subsection (a) sets forth the basic order of application. The proceeds are applied first to the expenses of disposition, second to the obligation secured by the security interest that is being enforced, and third, in the specified circumstances, to interests that are subordinate to that security interest.

Subsections (a) and (d) also address the right of a consignor to receive proceeds of a disposition by a secured party whose interest is senior to that of the consignor. Subsection (a) requires the enforcing secured party to pay excess proceeds first to subordinate secured parties or lienholders whose interests are senior to that of a consignor and, finally, to a consignor. Inasmuch as a consignor is the owner of the collateral, secured parties and lienholders whose interests are junior to the consignor's interest will not be entitled to any proceeds. In like fashion, under subsection (d)(1) the debtor is not entitled to a surplus when the enforcing secured party is required to pay over proceeds to a consignor.

3. Noncash Proceeds. Subsection (c) addresses the application of noncash proceeds of a disposition, such as a note or lease. The explanation in Section 9-608, Comment 4, generally applies to this subsection.

> **Example:** A secured party in the business of selling or financing automobiles takes possession of collateral (an automobile) following its debtor's default. The secured party decides to sell the automobile in a private disposition under Section 9-610 and sends appropriate notification under Section 9-611. After undertaking its normal credit investigation and in accordance with its normal credit policies, the secured party sells the automobile on credit, on terms typical of the credit terms normally extended by the secured party in the ordinary course of its business. The automobile stands as collateral for the remaining balance of the price. The noncash proceeds received by the secured party are chattel paper. The secured party may wish to credit its debtor (the assignor) with the principal amount of the chattel paper or may wish to credit the debtor only as and when the payments are made on the chattel paper by the buyer.

Under subsection (c), the secured party is under no duty to apply the noncash proceeds (here, the chattel paper) or their value to the secured obligation unless its failure to do so would be commercially unreasonable. If a secured party elects to apply the chattel paper to the outstanding obligation, however, it must do so in a commercially reasonable manner. The facts in the example indicate that it would be commercially unreasonable for the secured party to fail to apply the value of the chattel paper to the original debtor's secured obligation. Unlike the example in Comment 4 to Section 9-608, the noncash proceeds received in this example are of the type that the secured party regularly generates in the ordinary course of its financing business in nonforeclosure transactions. The original debtor should not be exposed to delay or uncertainty in this situation. Of course, there will be many situations that fall between the examples presented in the Comment to Section 9-608 and in this Comment. This Article leaves their resolution to the court based on the facts of each case.

One would expect that where noncash proceeds are or may be material, the secured party and debtor would agree to more specific standards in an agreement entered into before or after default. The parties may agree to the method of application of noncash proceeds if the method is not manifestly unreasonable. See Section 9-603.

When the secured party is not required to "apply or pay over for application noncash proceeds," the proceeds nonetheless remain collateral subject to this Article. See Section 9-608, Comment 4.

4. Surplus and Deficiency. Subsection (d) deals with surplus and deficiency. It revises former Section 9-504(2) by imposing an explicit requirement that the secured party "pay" the debtor for any surplus, while retaining the secured party's duty to "account." Inasmuch as the debtor may not be an obligor, subsection (d) provides that the obligor (not the debtor) is liable for the deficiency. The special rule governing surplus and deficiency when receivables have been sold likewise takes into account the distinction between a debtor and an obligor. Subsection (d) also addresses the situation in which a consignor has an interest that is subordinate to the security interest being enforced.

5. Collateral Under New Ownership. When the debtor sells collateral subject to a security interest, the original debtor (creator of the security interest) is no longer a debtor inasmuch as it no longer has a property interest in the collateral; the buyer is the debtor. See Section 9-102. As between the debtor (buyer of the collateral) and the original debtor (seller of the collateral), the debtor (buyer) normally would be entitled to the surplus following a disposition. Subsection (d) therefore requires the secured party to pay the surplus to the debtor (buyer), not to the original debtor (seller) with which it has dealt. But, because this situation typically arises as a result of the debtor's wrongful act, this Article does not expose the secured party to the risk of determining ownership of the collateral. If the secured party does not know about the buyer and accordingly pays the surplus to the original debtor, the exculpatory provisions of this Article exonerate the secured party from liability to the buyer. See Sections 9-605, 9-628(a), (b). If a debtor sells collateral free of a security interest, as in a sale to a buyer in ordinary course of business (see Section 9-320(a)), the property is no longer collateral and the buyer is not a debtor.

6. Certain "Low-Price" Dispositions. Subsection (f) provides a special method for calculating a deficiency or surplus when the secured party, a person related to the secured party (defined in Section 9-102), or a secondary obligor acquires the collateral at a foreclosure disposition. It recognizes that when the foreclosing secured party or a related party is the transferee of the collateral, the secured party sometimes lacks the incentive to maximize the proceeds of disposition. As a consequence, the disposition may comply with the procedural requirements of this Article (e.g., it is conducted in a commercially reasonable manner following reasonable notice) but nevertheless fetch a low price.

Subsection (f) adjusts for this lack of incentive. If the proceeds of a disposition of collateral to a secured party, a person related to the secured party, or a secondary obligor are "significantly below the range of proceeds that a complying disposition to a person other than the secured party, a person related to the secured party, or a secondary obligor would have brought," then instead of calculating a deficiency (or surplus) based on the actual net proceeds, the calculation is based upon the amount that would have been received in a commercially reasonable disposition to a person other than the secured party, a person related to the secured party, or a secondary obligor. Subsection (f) thus rejects the view that the secured party's receipt of such a price necessarily constitutes noncompliance with Part 6. However, such a price may suggest the need for greater judicial scrutiny. See Section 9-610, Comment 10.

7. "Person Related To." Section 9-102 defines "person related to." That term is a key element of the system provided in subsection (f) for low-price dispositions. One part of the definition applies when the secured party is an individual, and the other applies when the secured party is an organization. The definition is patterned closely on the corresponding definition in Section 1.301(32) of the Uniform Consumer Credit Code.

8. "Signed" Replaces "Authenticated." Consistent with the revised definition of "sign" in Section 1-201, the cognate term "signed" replaces the reference to "authenticated" in the pre-2022 text of this section.

§ 9-616. Explanation of Calculation of Surplus or Deficiency.

(a) [Definitions.] In this section:

(1) "Explanation" means a record that:

(A) states the amount of the surplus or deficiency;

(B) provides an explanation in accordance with subsection (c) of how the secured party calculated the surplus or deficiency;

(C) states, if applicable, that future debits, credits, charges, including additional credit service charges or interest, rebates, and expenses may affect the amount of the surplus or deficiency; and

(D) provides a telephone number or mailing address from which additional information concerning the transaction is available.

(2) "Request" means a record:

(A) signed by a debtor or consumer obligor;

(B) requesting that the recipient provide an explanation; and

(C) sent after disposition of the collateral under Section 9-610.

(b) [Explanation of calculation.] In a consumer-goods transaction in which the debtor is entitled to a surplus or a consumer obligor is liable for a deficiency under Section 9-615, the secured party shall:

(1) send an explanation to the debtor or consumer obligor, as applicable, after the disposition and:

(A) before or when the secured party accounts to the debtor and pays any surplus or first makes demand in a record on the consumer obligor after the disposition for payment of the deficiency; and

(B) within 14 days after receipt of a request; or

(2) in the case of a consumer obligor who is liable for a deficiency, within 14 days after receipt of a request, send to the consumer obligor a record waiving the secured party's right to a deficiency.

(c) [Required information.] To comply with subsection (a)(1)(B), an explanation must provide the following information in the following order:

(1) the aggregate amount of obligations secured by the security interest under which the disposition was made, and, if the amount reflects a rebate of unearned interest or credit service charge, an indication of that fact, calculated as of a specified date:

(A) if the secured party takes or receives possession of the collateral after default, not more than 35 days before the secured party takes or receives possession; or

(B) if the secured party takes or receives possession of the collateral before default or does not take possession of the collateral, not more than 35 days before the disposition;

(2) the amount of proceeds of the disposition;

(3) the aggregate amount of the obligations after deducting the amount of proceeds;

(4) the amount, in the aggregate or by type, and types of expenses, including expenses of retaking, holding, preparing for disposition, processing, and disposing of the collateral, and attorney's fees secured by the collateral which are known to the secured party and relate to the current disposition;

(5) the amount, in the aggregate or by type, and types of credits, including rebates of interest or credit service charges, to which the obligor is known to be entitled and which are not reflected in the amount in paragraph (1); and

(6) the amount of the surplus or deficiency.

(d) [Substantial compliance.] A particular phrasing of the explanation is not required. An explanation complying substantially with the requirements of subsection (a) is sufficient, even if it includes minor errors that are not seriously misleading.

(e) [Charges for responses.] A debtor or consumer obligor is entitled without charge to one response to a request under this section during any six-month period in which the secured party did not send to the debtor or consumer obligor an explanation pursuant to subsection (b)(1). The secured party may require payment of a charge not exceeding $25 for each additional response.

Definitional Cross References:

Collateral	Section 9-102(a)(12)
Consumer-goods transaction	Section 9-102(a)(24)
Consumer obligor	Section 9-102(a)(25)
Debtor	Section 9-102(a)(28)
Obligor	Section 9-102(a)(59)
Proceeds	Section 9-102(a)(64)
Record	Section 9-102(a)(70)
Secured party	Section 9-102(a)(73)
Security interest	Section 1-201(b)(35)
Send	Section 1-201(b)(36)
Sign	Section 1-201(b)(37)

Official Comment

1. Source. New.

2. Duty to Send Information Concerning Surplus or Deficiency. This section reflects the view that, in every consumer-goods transaction, the debtor or obligor is entitled to know the amount of a surplus or deficiency and the basis upon which the surplus or deficiency was calculated. Under subsection (b)(1)(B), a secured party is obligated to provide this information (an "explanation," defined in subsection (a)(1)) no later than the time that it accounts for and pays a surplus or the time of its first demand in a record in an attempt to collect the deficiency. The obligor need not make a request for an accounting in order to receive an explanation. A secured party who does not attempt to collect a deficiency in a demand in a record or account for and pay a surplus has no obligation to send an explanation under subsection (b)(1) and, consequently, cannot be liable for noncompliance.

A debtor or secondary obligor need not wait until the secured party commences collection efforts in a demand in a record in order to receive an explanation of how a deficiency or surplus was calculated. Subsection (b)(1)(B) obliges the secured party to send an explanation within 14 days after it receives a "request" (defined in subsection (a)(2)).

3. Explanation of Calculation of Surplus or Deficiency. Subsection (c) contains the requirements for how a calculation of a surplus or deficiency must be explained in order to satisfy subsection (a)(1)(B). It gives a secured party some discretion concerning rebates of interest or credit service charges. The secured party may include these rebates in the aggregate amount of obligations secured, under subsection (c)(1), or may include them with other types of rebates and credits under subsection (c)(5). Rebates of interest or credit service charges are the only types of rebates for which this discretion is provided. If the secured party provides an explanation that includes rebates of pre-computed interest, its explanation must so indicate. The expenses and attorney's fees to be described pursuant to subsection (c)(4) are those relating to the most recent disposition, not those that may have been incurred in connection with earlier enforcement efforts and which have been resolved by the parties.

4. Liability for Noncompliance. A secured party who fails to comply with subsection (b)(2) is liable for any loss caused plus $500. See Section 9-625(b), (c), (e)(6). A secured party who fails to send an explanation under subsection (b)(1) is liable for any loss caused plus, if the noncompliance was "part of a pattern, or consistent with a practice of noncompliance," $500. See Section 9-625(b), (c), (e)(5). However, a secured party who fails to comply with this section is not liable for statutory minimum damages under Section 9-625(c)(2). See Section 9-628(d).

5. "Signed" Replaces "Authenticated"; Medium Neutrality. Consistent with the revised definition of "sign" in Section 1-201, the cognate term "signed" replaces the reference to "authenticated" in the pre-2022 text of this section. In furtherance of medium neutrality, the reference in the pre-2022 text of this section to a "written demand" has been replaced by a reference to a "demand in a record" and the reference to a "writing" has been replaced by a reference to a "record."

§ 9-617. Rights of Transferee of Collateral.

(a) [Effects of disposition.] A secured party's disposition of collateral after default:

(1) transfers to a transferee for value all of the debtor's rights in the collateral;

(2) discharges the security interest under which the disposition is made; and

(3) discharges any subordinate security interest or other subordinate lien [other than liens created under [cite acts or statutes providing for liens, if any, that are not to be discharged]].

(b) [Rights of good-faith transferee.] A transferee that acts in good faith takes free of the rights and interests described in subsection (a), even if the secured party fails to comply with this article or the requirements of any judicial proceeding.

(c) [Rights of other transferee.] If a transferee does not take free of the rights and interests described in subsection (a), the transferee takes the collateral subject to:

(1) the debtor's rights in the collateral;

(2) the security interest or agricultural lien under which the disposition is made; and

(3) any other security interest or other lien.

Definitional Cross References:

Agricultural lien	Section 9-102(a)(5)
Collateral	Section 9-102(a)(12)
Debtor	Section 9-102(a)(28)
Good faith	Section 1-201(b)(20)
Right	Section 1-201(b)(34)
Secured party	Section 9-102(a)(73)
Security interest	Section 1-201(b)(35)
Value	Section 1-204

Official Comment

1. Source. Former Section 9-504(4).

2. Title Taken by Good-Faith Transferee. Subsection (a) sets forth the rights acquired by persons who qualify under subsection (b)—transferees who act in good faith. Such a person is a "transferee," inasmuch as a buyer at a foreclosure sale does not meet the definition of "purchaser" in Section 1-201 (the transfer is not, vis-à-vis the debtor, "voluntary"). By virtue of the expanded definition of the term "debtor" in Section 9-102, subsection (a) makes clear that the ownership interest of a person who bought the collateral subject to the security interest is terminated by a subsequent disposition under this Part. Such a person is a debtor under this Article. Under former Article 9, the result arguably was the same, but the statute was less clear. Under subsection (a), a disposition normally discharges the security interest being foreclosed and any subordinate security interests and other liens.

A disposition has the effect specified in subsection (a), even if the secured party fails to comply with this Article. An aggrieved person (e.g., the holder of a subordinate security interest to whom a notification required by Section 9-611 was not sent) has a right to recover any loss under Section 9-625(b).

3. Unitary Standard in Public and Private Dispositions. Subsection (b) now contains a unitary standard that applies to transferees in both private and public dispositions—acting in good faith. However, this change from former Section 9-504(4) should not be interpreted to mean that a transferee acts in good faith even though it has knowledge of defects or buys in collusion, standards applicable to public dispositions under the former section. Properly understood, those standards were specific examples of the absence of good faith.

4. Title Taken by Nonqualifying Transferee. Subsection (c) specifies the consequences for a transferee who does not qualify for protection under subsections (a) and (b) (i.e., a transferee who does not act in good faith). The transferee takes subject to the rights of the debtor, the enforcing secured party, and other security interests or other liens. In such a case the disposition is ineffective to the extent that it would otherwise have cut off the debtor's rights in the collateral, and the debtor retains those rights, including the debtor's right of redemption under Section 9-623, albeit subject to the security interest under which the disposition was made and any other security interests or liens. See PEB Commentary No. 22, dated August 24, 2020. The Commentary is available at https://www.ali.org/peb-ucc.

§ 9-618. Rights and Duties of Certain Secondary Obligors.

(a) [Rights and duties of secondary obligor.] A secondary obligor acquires the rights and becomes obligated to perform the duties of the secured party after the secondary obligor:

(1) receives an assignment of a secured obligation from the secured party;

(2) receives a transfer of collateral from the secured party and agrees to accept the rights and assume the duties of the secured party; or

(3) is subrogated to the rights of a secured party with respect to collateral.

(b) [Effect of assignment, transfer, or subrogation.] An assignment, transfer, or subrogation described in subsection (a):

(1) is not a disposition of collateral under Section 9-610; and

(2) relieves the secured party of further duties under this article.

Definitional Cross References:

Collateral	Section 9-102(a)(12)
Right	Section 1-201(b)(34)
Secondary obligor	Section 9-102(a)(72)
Secured party	Section 9-102(a)(73)

Official Comment

1. Source. Former Section 9-504(5).

2. Scope of This Section. Under this section, assignments of secured obligations and other transactions (regardless of form) that function like assignments of secured obligations are not dispositions to which Part 6 applies. Rather, they constitute assignments of rights and (occasionally) delegations of duties. Application of this section may require an investigation into the agreement of the parties, which may not be reflected in the words of the repurchase agreement (e.g., when the agreement requires a recourse party to "purchase the collateral" but contemplates that the purchaser will then conduct an Article 9 foreclosure disposition).

This section, like former Section 9-504(5), does not constitute a general and comprehensive rule for allocating rights and duties upon assignment of a secured obligation. Rather, it applies only in situations involving a secondary obligor described in subsection (a). In other contexts, the agreement of the parties and applicable law other than Article 9 determine whether the assignment imposes upon the assignee any duty to the debtor and whether the assignor retains its duties to the debtor after the assignment.

Subsection (a)(1) applies when there has been an assignment of an obligation that is secured at the time it is assigned. Thus, if a secondary obligor acquires the collateral at a disposition under Section 9-610 and simultaneously or subsequently discharges the unsecured deficiency claim, subsection (a)(1) is not implicated. Similarly, subsection (a)(3) applies only when the secondary obligor is subrogated to the secured party's rights with respect to collateral. Thus, this subsection will not be implicated if a secondary obligor discharges the debtor's unsecured obligation for a post-disposition deficiency. Similarly, if the secured party disposes of some of the collateral and the secondary obligor thereafter discharges the remaining obligation, subsection (a) applies only with respect to rights and duties concerning the remaining collateral, and, under subsection (b), the subrogation is not a disposition of the remaining collateral.

As discussed more fully in Comment 3, a secondary obligor may receive a transfer of collateral in a disposition under Section 9-610 in exchange for a payment that is applied against the secured obligation. However, a secondary obligor who pays and receives a transfer of collateral does not necessarily become subrogated to the rights of the secured party as contemplated by subsection (a)(3). Only to the extent the secondary obligor makes a payment in satisfaction of its secondary obligation would it become subrogated. To the extent its payment constitutes the price of the collateral in a Section 9-610 disposition by the secured party, the secondary obligor would not be subrogated. Thus, if the amount paid by the secondary obligor for the collateral in a Section 9-610 disposition is itself insufficient to discharge the secured obligation, but the secondary obligor makes an additional payment that satisfies the remaining balance, the secondary obligor would be subrogated to the secured party's deficiency claim. However, the duties of the secured party as such would have come to an end with respect to that collateral. In some situations the capacity in which the payment is made may be unclear. Accordingly, the parties should in their relationship provide clear evidence of the nature and circumstances of the payment by the secondary obligor.

3. Transfer of Collateral to Secondary Obligor. It is possible for a secured party to transfer collateral to a secondary obligor in a transaction that is a disposition under Section 9-610 and that establishes a surplus or deficiency under Section 9-615. Indeed, this Article includes a special rule, in Section 9-615(f), for establishing a deficiency in the case of some dispositions to, *inter alia,* secondary obligors. This Article rejects the view, which some may have ascribed to former Section 9-504(5), that a transfer of collateral to a recourse party can never constitute a disposition of collateral which discharges a security interest. Inasmuch as a secured party could itself buy collateral at its own public sale, it makes no sense to prohibit a recourse party ever from buying at the sale.

4. Timing and Scope of Obligations. Under subsection (a), a recourse party acquires rights and incurs obligations only "after" one of the specified circumstances occurs. This makes clear that when a successor assignee, transferee, or subrogee becomes obligated it does not assume any liability for earlier actions or inactions of the secured party whom it has succeeded unless it agrees to do so. Once the successor becomes obligated, however, it is responsible for complying with the secured party's duties thereafter. For example, if the successor is in possession of collateral, then it has the duties specified in Section 9-207.

Under subsection (b), the same event (assignment, transfer, or subrogation) that gives rise to rights to, and imposes obligations on, a successor relieves its predecessor of any further duties under this Article. For example, if the security interest is enforced after the secured obligation is assigned, the assignee—but not the assignor—has the duty to comply with this Part. Similarly, the assignment does not excuse the assignor from liability for failure to comply with duties that arose before the event or impose liability on the assignee for the assignor's failure to comply.

§ 9-619. Transfer of Record or Legal Title.

(a) ["Transfer statement."] In this section, "transfer statement" means a record signed by a secured party stating:

(1) that the debtor has defaulted in connection with an obligation secured by specified collateral;

(2) that the secured party has exercised its post-default remedies with respect to the collateral;

(3) that, by reason of the exercise, a transferee has acquired the rights of the debtor in the collateral; and

(4) the name and mailing address of the secured party, debtor, and transferee.

(b) [Effect of transfer statement.] A transfer statement entitles the transferee to the transfer of record of all rights of the debtor in the collateral specified in the statement in any official filing, recording, registration, or certificate-of-title system covering the collateral. If a transfer statement is presented with the applicable fee and request form to the official or office responsible for maintaining the system, the official or office shall:

(1) accept the transfer statement;

(2) promptly amend its records to reflect the transfer; and

(3) if applicable, issue a new appropriate certificate of title in the name of the transferee.

(c) [Transfer not a disposition; no relief of secured party's duties.] A transfer of the record or legal title to collateral to a secured party under subsection (b) or otherwise is not of itself a disposition of collateral under this article and does not of itself relieve the secured party of its duties under this article.

Definitional Cross References:

Certificate of title	Section 9-102(a)(10)
Collateral	Section 9-102(a)(12)
Debtor	Section 9-102(a)(28)
Record	Section 9-102(a)(70)
Remedy	Section 1-201(b)(32)
Right	Section 1-201(b)(34)
Secured party	Section 9-102(a)(73)
Sign	Section 1-201(b)(37)

Official Comment

1. Source. New.

2. Transfer of Record or Legal Title. Potential buyers of collateral that is covered by a certificate of title (e.g., an automobile) or is subject to a registration system (e.g., a copyright) typically require as a condition of their purchase that the certificate or registry reflect their ownership. In many cases, this condition can be met only with the consent of the record owner. If the record owner is the debtor and, as may be the case after the default, the debtor refuses to cooperate, the secured party may have great difficulty disposing of the collateral.

Subsection (b) provides a simple mechanism for obtaining record or legal title, for use primarily when other law does not provide one. Of course, use of this mechanism will not be effective to clear title to the extent that subsection (b) is preempted by federal law. Subsection (b) contemplates a transfer of record or legal title to a third party, following a secured party's exercise of its disposition or acceptance remedies under this Part, as well as a transfer by a debtor to a secured party prior to the secured party's exercise of those remedies. Under subsection (c), a transfer of record or legal title (under subsection (b) or under other law) to a secured party prior to the exercise of those remedies merely puts the secured party in a position to pass legal or record title to a transferee at foreclosure. A secured party who has obtained record or legal title retains its duties with respect to enforcement of its security interest, and the debtor retains its rights as well.

3. Title-Clearing Systems under Other Law. Applicable non-UCC law (e.g., a certificate-of-title statute, federal registry rules, or the like) may provide a means by which the secured party may obtain or transfer record or legal title for the purpose of a disposition of the property under this Article. The mechanism provided by this section is in addition to any title-clearing provision under law other than this Article.

4. "Signed" Replaced "Authenticated." Consistent with the revised definition of "sign" in Section 1-201, the cognate term "signed" replaces the reference to "authenticated" in the pre-2022 text of this section.

§ 9-620. Acceptance of Collateral in Full or Partial Satisfaction of Obligation; Compulsory Disposition of Collateral.

(a) [Conditions to acceptance in satisfaction.] Except as otherwise provided in subsection (g), a secured party may accept collateral in full or partial satisfaction of the obligation it secures only if:

(1) the debtor consents to the acceptance under subsection (c);

(2) the secured party does not receive, within the time set forth in subsection (d),

a notification of objection to the proposal signed by:

(A) a person to which the secured party was required to send a proposal under Section 9-621; or

(B) any other person, other than the debtor, holding an interest in the collateral subordinate to the security interest that is the subject of the proposal;

(3) if the collateral is consumer goods, the collateral is not in the possession of the debtor when the debtor consents to the acceptance; and

(4) subsection (e) does not require the secured party to dispose of the collateral or the debtor waives the requirement pursuant to Section 9-624.

(b) [Purported acceptance ineffective.] A purported or apparent acceptance of collateral under this section is ineffective unless:

(1) the secured party consents to the acceptance in a signed record or sends a proposal to the debtor; and

(2) the conditions of subsection (a) are met.

(c) [Debtor's consent.] For purposes of this section:

(1) a debtor consents to an acceptance of collateral in partial satisfaction of the obligation it secures only if the debtor agrees to the terms of the acceptance in a record signed after default; and

(2) a debtor consents to an acceptance of collateral in full satisfaction of the obligation it secures only if the debtor agrees to the terms of the acceptance in a record signed after default or the secured party:

(A) sends to the debtor after default a proposal that is unconditional or subject only to a condition that collateral not in the possession of the secured party be preserved or maintained;

(B) in the proposal, proposes to accept collateral in full satisfaction of the obligation it secures; and

(C) does not receive a notification of objection signed by the debtor within 20 days after the proposal is sent.

(d) [Effectiveness of notification.] To be effective under subsection (a)(2), a notification of objection must be received by the secured party:

(1) in the case of a person to which the proposal was sent pursuant to Section 9-621, within 20 days after notification was sent to that person; and

(2) in other cases:

(A) within 20 days after the last notification was sent pursuant to Section 9-621; or

(B) if a notification was not sent, before the debtor consents to the acceptance under subsection (c).

(e) [Mandatory disposition of consumer goods.] A secured party that has taken possession of collateral shall dispose of the collateral pursuant to Section 9-610 within the time specified in subsection (f) if:

(1) 60 percent of the cash price has been paid in the case of a purchase-money security interest in consumer goods; or

(2) 60 percent of the principal amount of the obligation secured has been paid in the case of a non-purchase-money security interest in consumer goods.

(f) [Compliance with mandatory disposition requirement.] To comply with subsection (e), the secured party shall dispose of the collateral:

(1) within 90 days after taking possession; or

(2) within any longer period to which the debtor and all secondary obligors have agreed in an agreement to that effect entered into and signed after default.

(g) [No partial satisfaction in consumer transaction.] In a consumer transaction, a secured party may not accept collateral in partial satisfaction of the obligation it secures.

Definitional Cross References:

Agreement	Section 1-201(b)(3)
Collateral	Section 9-102(a)(12)
Consumer goods	Section 9-102(a)(23)
Consumer transaction	Section 9-102(a)(26)
Debtor	Section 9-102(a)(28)
Proposal	Section 9-102(a)(66)
Person	Section 1-201(b)(27)
Record	Section 9-102(a)(70)
Secondary obligor	Section 9-102(a)(72)
Secured party	Section 9-102(a)(73)
Security interest	Section 1-201(b)(35)
Send	Section 1-201(b)(36)
Sign	Section 1-201(b)(37)
Term	Section 1-201(b)(40)

Official Comment

1. Source. Former Section 9-505.

2. Overview. This section and the two sections following deal with strict foreclosure, a procedure by which the secured party acquires the debtor's interest in the collateral without the need for a sale or other disposition under Section 9-610. Although these provisions derive from former Section 9-505, they have been entirely reorganized and substantially rewritten. The more straightforward approach taken in this Article eliminates the fiction that the secured party always will present a "proposal" for the retention of collateral and the debtor will have a fixed period to respond. By eliminating the need (but preserving the possibility) for proceeding in that fashion, this section eliminates much of the awkwardness of former Section 9-505. It reflects the belief that strict foreclosures should be encouraged and often will produce better results than a disposition for all concerned.

Subsection (a) sets forth the conditions necessary to an effective acceptance (formerly, retention) of collateral in full or partial satisfaction of the secured obligation. Section 9-621 requires in addition that a secured party who wishes to proceed under this section notify certain other persons who have or claim to have an interest in the collateral. Unlike the failure to meet the conditions in subsection (a), under Section 9-622(b) the failure to comply with the notification requirement of Section 9-621 does not render the acceptance of collateral ineffective. Rather, the acceptance can take effect notwithstanding the secured party's noncompliance. A person to whom the required notice was not sent has the right to recover damages under Section 9-625(b). Section 9-622(a) sets forth the effect of an acceptance of collateral.

3. Conditions to Effective Acceptance. Subsection (a) contains the conditions necessary to the effectiveness of an acceptance of collateral. Subsection (a)(1) requires the debtor's consent. Under subsections (c)(1) and (c)(2), the debtor may consent by agreeing to the acceptance in writing after default. Subsection (c)(2) contains an alternative method by which to satisfy the debtor's-consent condition in subsection (a)(1). It follows the proposal-and-objection model found in pre-1998 Section 9-505: The debtor consents if the secured party sends a proposal to the debtor and does not receive an objection within 20 days. Under subsection (c)(1), however, that silence is not deemed to be consent with respect to acceptances in partial satisfaction. Thus, a secured party who wishes to conduct a "partial strict foreclosure" must obtain the debtor's agreement in a record signed after default. In all other respects, the conditions necessary to an effective partial strict foreclosure are the same as those governing acceptance of collateral in full satisfaction. (But see subsection (g), prohibiting partial strict foreclosure of a security interest in consumer transactions.)

The time when a debtor consents to a strict foreclosure is significant in several circumstances under this section and the following one. See Sections 9-620(a)(1), (d)(2), 9-621(a)(1), (a)(2), (a)(3). For purposes of determining the time of consent, a debtor's conditional consent constitutes consent.

Subsection (a)(2) contains the second condition to the effectiveness of an acceptance under this section: the absence of a timely objection from a person holding a junior interest in the collateral or from a secondary obligor. Any junior party—secured party or lienholder—is entitled to lodge an objection to a proposal, even if that person was not entitled to notification under Section 9-621. Subsection (d), discussed below, indicates when an objection is timely.

Subsections (a)(3) and (a)(4) contain special rules for transactions in which consumers are involved. See Comment 12.

4. Proposals. Section 9-102 defines the term "proposal." It is necessary to send a "proposal" to the debtor only if the debtor does not agree to an acceptance in a signed record as described in subsection (c)(1) or (c)(2). Section 9-621(a) determines whether it is necessary to send a proposal to third parties. A proposal need not take any particular form as long as it sets forth the terms under which the secured party is willing to accept collateral in satisfaction. A proposal to accept collateral should specify the amount (or a means of calculating the amount, such as by including a per diem accrual figure) of the secured obligations to be satisfied, state the conditions (if any) under which the proposal may be revoked, and describe any other applicable conditions. Note, however, that a conditional proposal generally requires the debtor's agreement in order to take effect. See subsection (c).

5. Secured Party's Agreement; No "Constructive" Strict Foreclosure. The conditions of subsection (a) relate to actual or implied consent by the debtor and any secondary obligor or holder of a junior security interest or lien. To ensure that the debtor cannot unilaterally cause an acceptance of collateral, subsection (b) provides that compliance with these conditions is necessary but not sufficient to cause an acceptance of collateral. Rather, under subsection (b), acceptance does not occur unless, in addition, the secured party consents to the acceptance in a signed record or sends to the debtor a proposal. For this reason, a mere delay in collection or disposition of collateral does not constitute a "constructive" strict foreclosure. Instead, delay is a factor relating to whether the secured party acted in a commercially reasonable manner for purposes of Section 9-607 or 9-610. A debtor's voluntary surrender of collateral to a secured party and the secured party's acceptance of possession of the collateral does not, of itself, necessarily raise an implication that the secured party intends or is proposing to accept the collateral in satisfaction of the secured obligation under this section.

6. When Acceptance Occurs. This section does not impose any formalities or identify any steps that a secured party must take in order to accept collateral once the conditions of subsections (a) and (b) have been met. Absent facts or circumstances indicating a contrary intention, the fact that the conditions have been met provides a sufficient indication that the secured party has accepted the collateral on the terms to which the secured party has consented or proposed and the debtor has consented or failed to object. Following a proposal, acceptance of the collateral normally is automatic upon the secured party's becoming bound and the time for objection passing. As a matter of good business practice, an enforcing secured party may wish to memorialize its acceptance following a proposal, such as by notifying the debtor that the strict foreclosure is effective or by placing a written record to that effect in its files. The secured party's agreement to accept collateral is self-executing and cannot be breached. The secured party is bound by its agreement to accept collateral and by any proposal to which the debtor consents.

7. No Possession Requirement. This section eliminates the requirement in former Section 9-505 that the secured party be "in possession" of collateral. It clarifies that intangible collateral, which cannot be possessed, may be subject to a strict foreclosure under this section. However, under subsection (a)(3), if the collateral is consumer goods, acceptance does not occur unless the debtor is not in possession.

8. When Objection Timely. Subsection (d) explains when an objection is timely and thus prevents an acceptance of collateral from taking effect. An objection by a person to which notification was sent under Section 9-621 is effective if it is received by the secured party within 20 days from the date the notification was sent to that person. Other objecting parties (i.e., third parties who are not entitled to notification) may object at any time within 20 days after the last notification is sent under Section 9-621. If no such notification is sent, third parties must object before the debtor agrees to the acceptance in writing or is deemed to have consented by silence. The former may occur any time after default, and the latter requires a 20-day waiting period. See subsection (c).

9. Applicability of Other Law. This section does not purport to regulate all aspects of the transaction by which a secured party may become the owner of collateral previously owned by the debtor. For example, a secured party's acceptance of a motor vehicle in satisfaction of secured obligations may require compliance with the applicable motor vehicle certificate-of-title law. State legislatures should conform those laws so that they mesh well with this section and Section 9-610, and courts should construe those laws and this section harmoniously. A secured party's acceptance of collateral in the possession of the debtor also may implicate statutes dealing with a seller's retention of possession of goods sold.

10. Accounts, Chattel Paper, Payment Intangibles, and Promissory Notes. If the collateral is accounts, chattel paper, payment intangibles, or promissory notes, then a secured party's acceptance of the collateral in satisfaction of secured obligations would constitute a sale to the secured party. That sale normally would give rise to a new security interest (the ownership interest) under Sections 1-201(b)(35) and 9-109. [Ed. Note. New Article 1: Section 1-201(b)(35).] In the case of accounts and chattel paper, the new security interest would remain perfected by a filing that was effective to perfect the secured party's original security interest. In the case of payment intangibles or promissory notes, the security interest would be perfected when it attaches. See Section 9-309. However, the procedures for acceptance of collateral under this section satisfy all necessary formalities and a new security agreement signed by the debtor would not be necessary.

11. Role of Good Faith. Section 1-304 imposes an obligation of good faith on a secured party's enforcement under this Article. This obligation may not be disclaimed by agreement. See Section 1-302. Thus, a proposal and acceptance made under this section in bad faith would not be effective. For example, a secured party's proposal to accept marketable securities worth $1,000 in full satisfaction of indebtedness in the amount of $100, made in the hopes that the debtor might inadvertently fail to object, would be made in bad faith. On the other hand, in the normal case proposals and acceptances should be not second-guessed on the basis of the "value" of the collateral involved. Disputes about valuation or even a clear excess of collateral value over the amount of obligations satisfied do not necessarily demonstrate the absence of good faith.

12. Special Rules in Consumer Cases. Subsection (e) imposes an obligation on the secured party to dispose of consumer goods under certain circumstances. Subsection (f) explains when a disposition that is required under subsection (e) is timely. An effective acceptance of collateral cannot occur if subsection (e) requires a disposition unless the debtor waives this requirement pursuant to Section 9-624(b). Moreover, a secured party who takes possession of collateral and unreasonably delays disposition violates subsection (e), if applicable, and may also violate Section 9-610 or other provisions of this Part. Subsection (e) eliminates as superfluous the express statutory reference to "conversion" found in former Section 9-505. Remedies available under other law, including conversion, remain available under this Article in appropriate cases. See Sections 1-103, 1-305.

Subsection (g) prohibits the secured party in consumer transactions from accepting collateral in partial satisfaction of the obligation it secures. If a secured party attempts an acceptance in partial satisfaction in a consumer transaction, the attempted acceptance is void.

13. "Signed" Replaces "Authenticated." Consistent with the revised definition of "sign" in Section 1-201, the cognate term "signed" replaces the references to "authenticated" in the pre-2022 text of this section.

§ 9-621. Notification of Proposal to Accept Collateral.

(a) [Persons to which proposal to be sent.] A secured party that desires to accept collateral in full or partial satisfaction of the obligation it secures shall send its proposal to:

(1) any person from which the secured party has received, before the debtor consented to the acceptance, a signed notification of a claim of an interest in the collateral;

(2) any other secured party or lienholder that, 10 days before the debtor consented to the acceptance, held a security interest in or other lien on the collateral perfected by the filing of a financing statement that:

(A) identified the collateral;

(B) was indexed under the debtor's name as of that date; and

(C) was filed in the office or offices in which to file a financing statement against the debtor covering the collateral as of that date; and

(3) any other secured party that, 10 days before the debtor consented to the acceptance, held a security interest in the collateral perfected by compliance with a statute, regulation, or treaty described in Section 9-311(a).

(b) [Proposal to be sent to secondary obligor in partial satisfaction.] A secured party that desires to accept collateral in partial satisfaction of the obligation it secures shall send its proposal to any secondary obligor in addition to the persons described in subsection (a).

Definitional Cross References:

Collateral	Section 9-102(a)(12)
Debtor	Section 9-102(a)(28)
Financing statement	Section 9-102(a)(39)
Person	Section 1-201(b)(27)
Proposal	Section 9-102(a)(66)
Secondary obligor	Section 9-102(a)(72)
Secured party	Section 9-102(a)(73)
Security interest	Section 1-201(b)(35)
Send	Section 1-201(b)(36)
Sign	Section 1-201(b)(37)

Official Comment

1. Source. Former Section 9-505.

2. Notification Requirement. Subsection (a) specifies three classes of competing claimants to whom the secured party must send notification of its proposal: (i) those who notify the secured party that they claim an interest in the collateral, (ii) holders of certain security interests and liens who have filed against the debtor, and (iii) holders of certain security interests who have perfected by compliance with a statute (including a certificate-of-title statute), regulation, or treaty described in Section 9-311(a). With regard to (ii), see Section 9-611, Comment 4. Subsection (b) also requires notification to any secondary obligor if the proposal is for acceptance in partial satisfaction.

Unlike Section 9-611, this section contains no "safe harbor," which excuses an enforcing secured party from notifying certain secured parties and other lienholders. This is because, unlike Section 9-610, which requires that a disposition of collateral be commercially reasonable, Section 9-620 permits the debtor and secured party to set the amount of credit the debtor will receive for the collateral subject only to the requirement of good faith. An effective acceptance discharges subordinate security interests and other subordinate liens. See Section 9-622. If collateral is subject to several liens securing debts much larger than the value of the collateral, the debtor may be disinclined to refrain from consenting to an acceptance by the holder of the senior security interest, even though, had the debtor objected and the senior disposed of the collateral under Section 9-610, the collateral may have yielded more than enough to satisfy the senior security interest (but not enough to satisfy all the liens). Accordingly, this section imposes upon the enforcing secured party the risk of the filing office's errors and delay. The holder of a security interest who is entitled to notification under this section but to whom the enforcing secured party does not send notification has the right to recover under Section 9-625(b) any loss resulting from the secured party's noncompliance with this section.

3. "Signed" Replaces "Authenticated." Consistent with the revised definition of "sign" in Section 1-201, the cognate term "signed" replaces the reference to "authenticated" in the pre-2022 text of this section.

§ 9-622. Effect of Acceptance of Collateral.

(a) [Effect of acceptance.] A secured party's acceptance of collateral in full or partial satisfaction of the obligation it secures:

(1) discharges the obligation to the extent consented to by the debtor;

(2) transfers to the secured party all of a debtor's rights in the collateral;

(3) discharges the security interest or agricultural lien that is the subject of the debtor's consent and any subordinate security interest or other subordinate lien; and

(4) terminates any other subordinate interest.

(b) [Discharge of subordinate interest notwithstanding noncompliance.] A subordinate interest is discharged or terminated under subsection (a), even if the secured party fails to comply with this article.

Definitional Cross References:

Agricultural lien	Section 9-102(a)(5)
Collateral	Section 9-102(a)(12)
Debtor	Section 9-102(a)(28)
Right	Section 1-201(b)(34)
Secured party	Section 9-102(a)(73)
Security interest	Section 1-201(b)(35)

Official Comment

1. Source. New.

2. Effect of Acceptance. Subsection (a) specifies the effect of an acceptance of collateral in full or partial satisfaction of the secured obligation. The acceptance to which it refers is an effective acceptance. If a purported acceptance is ineffective under Section 9-620, e.g., because the secured party receives a timely objection from a person entitled to notification, then neither this subsection nor subsection (b) applies. Paragraph (1) expresses the fundamental consequence of accepting collateral in full or partial satisfaction of the secured obligation—the obligation is discharged to the extent consented to by the debtor. Unless otherwise agreed, the obligor remains liable for any deficiency. Paragraphs (2) through (4) indicate the effects of an acceptance on various property rights and interests. Paragraph (2) follows Section 9-617(a) in providing that the secured party acquires "all of a debtor's rights in the collateral." Under paragraph (3), the effect of strict foreclosure on holders of junior security interests and other liens is the same regardless of whether the collateral is accepted in full or partial satisfaction of the secured obligation: all junior encumbrances are discharged. Paragraph (4) provides for the termination of other subordinate interests.

Subsection (b) makes clear that subordinate interests are discharged under subsection (a) regardless of whether the secured party complies with this Article. Thus, subordinate interests are discharged regardless of whether a proposal was required to be sent or, if required, was sent. However, a secured party's failure to send a proposal or otherwise to comply with this Article may subject the secured party to liability under Section 9-625.

§ 9-623. Right to Redeem Collateral.

(a) [Persons that may redeem.] A debtor, any secondary obligor, or any other secured party or lienholder may redeem collateral.

(b) [Requirements for redemption.] To redeem collateral, a person shall tender:

(1) fulfillment of all obligations secured by the collateral; and

(2) the reasonable expenses and attorney's fees described in Section 9-615(a)(1).

(c) [When redemption may occur.] A redemption may occur at any time before a secured party:

(1) has collected collateral under Section 9-607;

(2) has disposed of collateral or entered into a contract for its disposition under Section 9-610; or

(3) has accepted collateral in full or partial satisfaction of the obligation it secures under Section 9-622.

Definitional Cross References:

Collateral	Section 9-102(a)(12)
Contract	Section 1-201(b)(12)
Debtor	Section 9-102(a)(28)
Person	Section 1-201(b)(27)
Right	Section 1-201(b)(34)
Secondary obligor	Section 9-102(a)(72)
Secured party	Section 9-102(a)(73)

Official Comment

1. Source. Former Section 9-506.

2. Redemption Right. Under this section, as under former Section 9-506, the debtor or another secured party may redeem collateral as long as the secured party has not collected (Section 9-607), disposed of or contracted for the disposition of (Section 9-610), or accepted (Section 9-620) the collateral. Although this section generally follows former Section 9-506, it extends the right of redemption to holders of nonconsensual liens. To redeem the collateral a person must tender fulfillment of all obligations secured, plus certain expenses. If the entire balance of a secured obligation has been accelerated, it would be necessary to tender the entire balance. A tender of fulfillment obviously means more than a new promise to perform an existing promise. It requires payment in full of all monetary obligations then due and performance in full of all other obligations then matured. If unmatured secured obligations remain, the security interest continues to secure them (i.e., as if there had been no default).

3. Redemption of Remaining Collateral Following Partial Enforcement. Under Section 9-610 a secured party may make successive dispositions of portions of its collateral. These dispositions would not affect the debtor's, another secured party's, or a lienholder's right to redeem the remaining collateral.

4. Effect of "Repledging." Section 9-207 generally permits a secured party having possession or control of collateral to create a security interest in the collateral. As explained in the Comments to that section, the debtor's right (as opposed to its practical ability) to redeem collateral is not affected by, and does not affect, the priority of a security interest created by the debtor's secured party.

§ 9-624. Waiver.

(a) [Waiver of disposition notification.] A debtor or secondary obligor may waive the right to notification of disposition of collateral under Section 9-611 only by an agreement to that effect entered into and signed after default.

(b) [Waiver of mandatory disposition.] A debtor may waive the right to require disposition of collateral under Section 9-620(e) only by an agreement to that effect entered into and signed after default.

(c) [Waiver of redemption right.] Except in a consumer-goods transaction, a debtor or secondary obligor may waive the right to redeem collateral under Section 9-623 only by an agreement to that effect entered into and signed after default.

Definitional Cross References:

Agreement	Section 1-201(b)(3)
Collateral	Section 9-102(a)(12)
Consumer-goods transaction	Section 9-102(a)(24)
Debtor	Section 9-102(a)(28)
Secondary obligor	Section 9-102(a)(72)
Sign	Section 1-201(b)(37)

Official Comment

1. Source. Former Sections 9-504(3), 9-505, 9-506.

2. Waiver. This section is a limited exception to Section 9-602, which generally prohibits waiver by debtors and obligors. It makes no provision for waiver of the rule prohibiting a secured party from buying at its own private disposition. Transactions of this kind are equivalent to "strict foreclosures" and are governed by Sections 9-620, 9-621, and 9-622.

3. "Signed" Replaces "Authenticated." Consistent with the revised definition of "sign" in Section 1-201, the cognate term "signed" replaces the references to "authenticated" in the pre-2022 text of this section.

[Subpart 2. Noncompliance with Article]

§ 9-625. Remedies for Secured Party's Failure to Comply with Article.

(a) [Judicial orders concerning noncompliance.] If it is established that a secured party is not proceeding in accordance with this article, a court may order or restrain collection, enforcement, or disposition of collateral on appropriate terms and conditions.

(b) [Damages for noncompliance.] Subject to subsections (c), (d), and (f), a person is liable for damages in the amount of any loss caused by a failure to comply with this article. Loss caused by a failure to comply may include loss resulting from the debtor's inability to obtain, or increased costs of, alternative financing.

(c) [Persons entitled to recover damages; statutory damages if collateral is consumer goods.] Except as otherwise provided in Section 9-628:

(1) a person that, at the time of the failure, was a debtor, was an obligor, or held a security interest in or other lien on the collateral may recover damages under subsection (b) for its loss; and

(2) if the collateral is consumer goods, a person that was a debtor or a secondary obligor at the time a secured party failed to comply with this part may recover for that failure in any event an amount not less than the credit service charge plus 10 percent of the principal amount of the obligation or the time-price differential plus 10 percent of the cash price.

(d) [Recovery when deficiency eliminated or reduced.] A debtor whose deficiency is eliminated under Section 9-626 may recover damages for the loss of any surplus. However, a debtor or secondary obligor whose deficiency is eliminated or reduced under Section 9-626 may not otherwise recover under subsection (b) for noncompliance with the provisions of this part relating to collection, enforcement, disposition, or acceptance.

(e) [Statutory damages: noncompliance with specified provisions.] In addition to any damages recoverable under subsection (b), the debtor, consumer obligor, or person named as a debtor in a filed record, as applicable, may recover $500 in each case from a person that:

(1) fails to comply with Section 9-208;

(2) fails to comply with Section 9-209;

(3) files a record that the person is not entitled to file under Section 9-509(a);

(4) fails to cause the secured party of record to file or send a termination statement as required by Section 9-513(a) or (c);

(5) fails to comply with Section 9-616(b)(1) and whose failure is part of a pattern, or consistent with a practice, of noncompliance; or

(6) fails to comply with Section 9-616(b)(2).

(f) [Statutory damages: noncompliance with Section 9-210.] A debtor or consumer obligor may recover damages under subsection (b) and, in addition, $500 in each case from a person that, without reasonable cause, fails to comply with a request under Section 9-210. A recipient of a request under Section 9-210 which never claimed an interest in the collateral or obligations that are the subject of a request under that section has a reasonable excuse for failure to comply with the request within the meaning of this subsection.

(g) [Limitation of security interest: noncompliance with Section 9-210.] If a secured party fails to comply with a request regarding a list of collateral or a statement of account under Section 9-210, the secured party may claim a security interest only as shown in the list or statement included in the request as against a person that is reasonably misled by the failure.

Definitional Cross References:

Account	Section 9-102(a)(2)
Collateral	Section 9-102(a)(12)
Consumer goods	Section 9-102(a)(23)
Consumer-goods transaction	Section 9-102(a)(24)
Consumer obligor	Section 9-102(a)(25)
Debtor	Section 9-102(a)(28)
Obligor	Section 9-102(a)(59)
Person	Section 1-201(b)(27)
Record	Section 9-102(a)(70)
Remedy	Section 1-201(b)(32)
Secondary obligor	Section 9-102(a)(72)
Secured party	Section 9-102(a)(73)
Security interest	Section 1-201(b)(35)
Send	Section 1-201(b)(36)
Term	Section 1-201(b)(40)
Termination statement	Section 9-102(a)(80)

Official Comment

1. Source. Former Section 9-507.

2. Remedies for Noncompliance; Scope. Subsections (a) and (b) provide the basic remedies afforded to those aggrieved by a secured party's failure to comply with this Article. Like all provisions that create liability, they are subject to Section 9-628, which should be read in conjunction with Section 9-605. The principal limitations under this Part on a secured party's right to enforce its security interest against collateral are the requirements that it proceed in good faith (Section 1-203), in a commercially reasonable manner (Sections 9-607 and 9-610), and, in most cases, with reasonable notification (Sections 9-611 through 9-614). [Ed. Note. New Article 1: Section 1-304; unofficially, see also 1-201(b)(20) (definition of good faith).] Following former Section 9-507, under subsection (a) an aggrieved person may seek injunctive relief, and under subsection (b) the person may recover damages for losses caused by noncompliance. Unlike former Section 9-507, however, subsections (a) and (b) are not limited to noncompliance with provisions of this Part of Article 9. Rather, they apply to noncompliance with any provision of this Article. The change makes this section applicable to noncompliance with Sections 9-207 (duties of secured party in possession of collateral), 9-208 (duties of secured party having control over deposit account), 9-209 (duties of secured party if account debtor has been notified of an assignment), 9-210 (duty to comply with request for accounting, etc.), 9-509(a) (duty to refrain from filing unauthorized financing statement), and 9-513(a) or (c) (duty to provide termination statement). Subsection (a) also modifies the first sentence of former Section 9-507(1) by adding the references to "collection" and "enforcement." Subsection (c)(2), which gives a minimum damage recovery in consumer-goods transactions, applies only to noncompliance with the provisions of this Part.

Subsection (a) displaces other state law governing availability of the types of relief addressed in that subsection to the extent that the other state law would preclude the availability of injunctive relief in an otherwise appropriate case solely because the aggrieved party would be able to obtain a collectible money judgment for noncompliance with the rules of this Article. Rather, under subsection (a), in an appropriate case the aggrieved party should be able obtain relief of the sort described in that subsection even if it would be possible for the aggrieved party to obtain such a judgment. See PEB Commentary No. 27, dated December 16, 2022, discussing the issue in the context of a noncomplying disposition under Section 9-610. The Commentary is available at https://www.ali.org/peb-ucc.

3. Damages for Noncompliance with This Article. Subsection (b) sets forth the basic remedy for failure to comply with the requirements of this Article: a damage recovery in the amount of loss caused by the noncompliance. Subsection (c) identifies who may recover under subsection (b). It affords a remedy to any aggrieved person who is a debtor or obligor. However, a principal obligor who is not a debtor may recover damages only for noncompliance with Section 9-616, inasmuch as none of the other rights and duties in this Article run in favor of such a principal obligor. Such a principal obligor could not suffer any loss or damage on account of noncompliance with rights or duties of which it is not a beneficiary. Subsection (c) also affords a remedy to an aggrieved person who holds a competing security interest or other lien, regardless of whether the aggrieved person is entitled to notification under Part 6. The remedy is available even to holders of senior security interests and other liens. The exercise of this remedy is subject to the normal rules of pleading and proof. A person who has delegated the duties of a secured party but who remains obligated to perform them is liable under this subsection. The last sentence of subsection (d) eliminates the possibility of double recovery or other over-compensation arising out of a reduction or elimination of a deficiency under Section 9-626, based on noncompliance with the provisions of this Part relating to collection, enforcement, disposition, or acceptance. Assuming no double recovery, a debtor whose deficiency is eliminated under Section 9-626 may pursue a claim for a surplus. Because Section 9-626 does not apply to consumer transactions, the statute is silent as to whether a double recovery or other over-compensation is possible in a consumer transaction.

Damages for violation of the requirements of this Article, including Section 9-609, are those reasonably calculated to put an eligible claimant in the position that it would have occupied had no violation occurred. See Section 1-106. Subsection (b) supports the recovery of actual damages for committing a breach of the peace in violation of Section 9-609, and principles of tort law supplement this subsection. [Ed. Note. New Article 1: Section 103. See Section 1-103.] However, to the extent that damages in tort compensate the debtor for the same loss dealt with by this Article, the debtor should be entitled to only one recovery.

4. Minimum Damages in Consumer-Goods Transactions. Subsection (c)(2) provides a minimum, statutory, damage recovery for a debtor and secondary obligor in a consumer-goods transaction. It is patterned on former Section 9-507(1) and is designed to ensure that every noncompliance with the requirements of Part 6 in a consumer-goods transaction results in liability, regardless of any injury that may have resulted. Subsection (c)(2) leaves the treatment of statutory damages as it was under former Article 9. A secured party is not liable for statutory damages under this subsection more than once with respect to any one secured obligation (see Section 9-628(e)), nor is a secured party liable under this subsection for failure to comply with Section 9-616 (see Section 9-628(d)).

Following former Section 9-507(1), this Article does not include a definition or explanation of the terms "credit service charge," "principal amount," "time-price differential," or "cash price," as used in subsection (c)(2). It leaves their construction and application to the court, taking into account the subsection's purpose of providing a minimum recovery in consumer-goods transactions.

5. Supplemental Damages. Subsections (e) and (f) provide damages that supplement the recovery, if any, under subsection (b). Subsection (e) imposes an additional $500 liability upon a person who fails to comply with the provisions specified in that subsection, and subsection (f) imposes like damages on a person who, without reasonable excuse, fails to comply with a request for an accounting or a request regarding a list of collateral or statement of account under Section 9-210. However, under subsection (f), a person has a reasonable excuse for the failure if the person never claimed an interest in the collateral or obligations that were the subject of the request.

6. Estoppel. Subsection (g) limits the extent to which a secured party who fails to comply with a request regarding a list of collateral or statement of account may claim a security interest.

§ 9-626. Action in Which Deficiency or Surplus Is in Issue.

(a) [Applicable rules if amount of deficiency or surplus in issue.] In an action arising from a transaction, other than a consumer transaction, in which the amount of a deficiency or surplus is in issue, the following rules apply:

(1) A secured party need not prove compliance with the provisions of this part relating to collection, enforcement, disposition, or acceptance unless the debtor or a secondary obligor places the secured party's compliance in issue.

(2) If the secured party's compliance is placed in issue, the secured party has the burden of establishing that the collection, enforcement, disposition, or acceptance was conducted in accordance with this part.

(3) Except as otherwise provided in Section 9-628, if a secured party fails to prove that the collection, enforcement, disposition, or acceptance was conducted in accordance with the provisions of this part relating to collection, enforcement, disposition, or acceptance, the liability of a debtor or a secondary obligor for a deficiency is limited to an amount by which the sum of the secured obligation, expenses, and attorney's fees exceeds the greater of:

(A) the proceeds of the collection, enforcement, disposition, or acceptance; or

(B) the amount of proceeds that would have been realized had the noncomplying secured party proceeded in accordance with the provisions of this part relating to collection, enforcement, disposition, or acceptance.

(4) For purposes of paragraph (3)(B), the amount of proceeds that would have been realized is equal to the sum of the secured obligation, expenses, and attorney's fees unless the secured party proves that the amount is less than that sum.

(5) If a deficiency or surplus is calculated under Section 9-615(f), the debtor or obligor has the burden of establishing that the amount of proceeds of the disposition is significantly below the range of prices that a complying disposition to a person other than the secured party, a person related to the secured party, or a secondary obligor would have brought.

(b) [Non-consumer transactions; no inference.] The limitation of the rules in subsection (a) to transactions other than consumer transactions is intended to leave to the court the determination of the proper rules in consumer transactions. The court may not infer from that limitation the nature of the proper rule in consumer transactions and may continue to apply established approaches.

Definitional Cross References:

Action	Section 1-201(b)(1)
Burden of establishing	Section 1-201(b)(8)
Consumer transaction	Section 9-102(a)(26)
Debtor	Section 9-102(a)(28)
Obligor	Section 9-102(a)(59)
Person	Section 1-201(b)(27)
Person related to individual	Section 9-102(a)(62)
Person related to organization	Section 9-102(a)(63)
Proceeds	Section 9-102(a)(64)
Prove	Section 3-103(a)(10)
Secondary obligor	Section 9-102(a)(72)
Secured party	Section 9-102(a)(73)

Official Comment

1. Source. New.

2. Scope. The basic damage remedy under Section 9-625(b) is subject to the special rules in this section for transactions other than consumer transactions. This section addresses situations in which the amount of a deficiency or surplus is in issue, i.e., situations in which the secured party has collected, enforced, disposed of, or accepted the collateral. It contains special rules applicable to a determination of the amount of a deficiency or surplus. Because this section affects a person's liability for a deficiency, it is subject to Section 9-628, which should be read in conjunction with Section 9-605. The rules in this section apply only to noncompliance in connection with the "collection, enforcement, disposition, or acceptance" under Part 6. For other types of noncompliance with Part 6, the general liability rule of Section 9-625(b)—recovery of actual damages—applies. Consider, for example, a repossession that does not comply with Section 9-609 for want of a default. The debtor's remedy is under Section 9-625(b). In a proper case, the secured party also may be liable for conversion under non-UCC law. If the secured party thereafter disposed of the collateral, however, it would violate Section 9-610 at that time, and this section would apply.

3. Rebuttable Presumption Rule. Subsection (a) establishes the rebuttable presumption rule for transactions other than consumer transactions. Under paragraph (1), the secured party need not prove compliance with the relevant provisions of this Part as part of its prima facie case. If, however, the debtor or a secondary obligor raises the issue (in accordance with the forum's rules of pleading and practice), then the secured party bears the burden of proving that the collection, enforcement, disposition, or acceptance complied. In the event the secured party is unable to meet this burden, then paragraph (3) explains how to calculate the deficiency. Under this rebuttable presumption rule, the debtor or obligor is to be credited with the greater of the actual proceeds of the disposition or the proceeds that would have been realized had the secured party complied with the relevant provisions. If a deficiency remains, then the secured party is entitled to recover it. The references to "the secured obligation, expenses, and attorney's fees" in paragraphs (3) and (4) embrace the application rules in Sections 9-608(a) and 9-615(a).

Unless the secured party proves that compliance with the relevant provisions would have yielded a smaller amount, under paragraph (4) the amount that a complying collection, enforcement, or disposition would have yielded is deemed to be equal to the amount of the secured obligation, together with expenses and attorney's fees. Thus, the secured party may not recover any deficiency unless it meets this burden.

4. Consumer Transactions. Although subsection (a) adopts a version of the rebuttable presumption rule for transactions other than consumer transactions, with certain exceptions Part 6 does not specify the effect of a secured party's noncompliance in consumer transactions. (The exceptions are the provisions for the recovery of damages in Section 9-625.) Subsection (b) provides that the limitation of subsection (a) to transactions other than consumer transactions is intended to leave to the court the determination of the proper rules in consumer transactions. It also instructs the court not to draw any inference from the limitation as to the proper rules for consumer transactions and leaves the court free to continue to apply established approaches to those transactions.

Courts construing former Section 9-507 disagreed about the consequences of a secured party's failure to comply with the requirements of former Part 5. Three general approaches emerged. Some courts have held that a noncomplying secured party may not recover a deficiency (the "absolute bar" rule). A few courts held that the debtor can offset against a claim to a deficiency all damages recoverable under former Section 9-507 resulting from the secured party's noncompliance (the "offset" rule). A plurality of courts considering the issue held that the noncomplying secured party is barred from recovering a deficiency unless it overcomes a rebuttable presumption that compliance with former Part 5 would have yielded an amount sufficient to satisfy the secured debt. In addition to the nonuniformity resulting from court decisions, some States enacted special rules governing the availability of deficiencies.

5. Burden of Proof When Section 9-615(f) Applies. In a non-consumer transaction, subsection (a)(5) imposes upon a debtor or obligor the burden of proving that the proceeds of a disposition are so low that, under Section 9-615(f), the actual proceeds should not serve as the basis upon which a deficiency or surplus is calculated. Were the burden placed on the secured party, then debtors might be encouraged to challenge the price received in every disposition to the secured party, a person related to the secured party, or a secondary obligor.

6. Delay in Applying This Section. There is an inevitable delay between the time a secured party engages in a noncomplying collection, enforcement, disposition, or acceptance and the time of a subsequent judicial determination that the secured party did not comply with Part 6. During the interim, the secured party, believing that the secured obligation is larger than it ultimately is determined to be, may continue to enforce its security interest in collateral. If some or all of the secured indebtedness ultimately is discharged under this section, a reasonable application of this section would impose liability on the secured party for the amount of any excess, unwarranted recoveries but would not make the enforcement efforts wrongful.

§ 9-627. Determination of Whether Conduct Was Commercially Reasonable.

(a) [Greater amount obtainable under other circumstances; no preclusion of commercial reasonableness.] The fact that a greater amount could have been obtained by a collection, enforcement, disposition, or acceptance at a different time or in a different method from that selected by the secured party is not of itself sufficient to preclude the secured party from establishing that the collection, enforcement, disposition, or acceptance was made in a commercially reasonable manner.

(b) [Dispositions that are commercially reasonable.] A disposition of collateral is made in a commercially reasonable manner if the disposition is made:

(1) in the usual manner on any recognized market;

(2) at the price current in any recognized market at the time of the disposition; or

(3) otherwise in conformity with reasonable commercial practices among dealers in the type of property that was the subject of the disposition.

(c) [Approval by court or on behalf of creditors.] A collection, enforcement, disposition, or acceptance is commercially reasonable if it has been approved:

(1) in a judicial proceeding;

(2) by a bona fide creditors' committee;

(3) by a representative of creditors; or

(4) by an assignee for the benefit of creditors.

(d) [Approval under subsection (c) not necessary; absence of approval has no effect.] Approval under subsection (c) need not be obtained, and lack of approval does not mean that the collection, enforcement, disposition, or acceptance is not commercially reasonable.

Definitional Cross References:

Collateral	Section 9-102(a)(12)
Creditor	Section 1-201(b)(13)
Representative	Section 1-201(b)(33)
Secured party	Section 9-102(a)(73)

Official Comment

1. Source. Former Section 9-507(2).

2. Relationship of Price to Commercial Reasonableness. Some observers have found the notion contained in subsection (a) (derived from former Section 9-507(2)) (the fact that a better price could have been obtained does not establish lack of commercial reasonableness) to be inconsistent with that found in Section 9-610(b) (derived from former Section 9-504(3)) (every aspect of the disposition, including its terms, must be commercially reasonable). There is no such inconsistency. While not itself sufficient to establish a violation of this Part, a low price suggests that a court should scrutinize carefully all aspects of a disposition to ensure that each aspect was commercially reasonable.

The law long has grappled with the problem of dispositions of personal and real property which comply with applicable procedural requirements (e.g., advertising, notification to interested persons, etc.) but which yield a price that seems low. This Article addresses that issue in Section 9-615(f). That section applies only when the transferee is the secured party, a person related to the secured party, or a secondary obligor. It contains a special rule for calculating a deficiency or surplus in a complying disposition that yields a price that is "significantly below the range of proceeds that a complying disposition to a person other than the secured party, a person related to the secured party, or a secondary obligor would have brought."

3. Determination of Commercial Reasonableness; Advance Approval. It is important to make clear the conduct and procedures that are commercially reasonable and to provide a secured party with the means of obtaining, by court order or negotiation with a creditors' committee or a representative of creditors, advance approval of a proposed method of enforcement as commercially reasonable. This section contains rules that assist in that determination and provides for advance approval in appropriate situations. However, none of the specific methods of disposition specified in subsection (b) is required or exclusive.

4. "Recognized Market." As in Sections 9-610(c) and 9-611(d), the concept of a "recognized market" in subsections (b)(1) and (2) is quite limited; it applies only to markets in which there are standardized price quotations for property that is essentially fungible, such as (but not limited to) securities and commodities exchanges. See Section 9-610, Comment 9 (discussing standard for a "recognized market").

§ 9-628. Nonliability and Limitation on Liability of Secured Party; Liability of Secondary Obligor.

(a) [Limitation of liability of secured party for noncompliance with article.] Subject to subsection (f), unless a secured party knows that a person is a debtor or obligor, knows the identity of the person, and knows how to communicate with the person:

(1) the secured party is not liable to the person, or to a secured party or lienholder that has filed a financing statement against the person, for failure to comply with this article; and

(2) the secured party's failure to comply with this article does not affect the liability of the person for a deficiency.

(b) [Limitation of liability based on status as secured party.] Subject to subsection (f), a secured party is not liable because of its status as secured party:

(1) to a person that is a debtor or obligor, unless the secured party knows:

(A) that the person is a debtor or obligor;

(B) the identity of the person; and

(C) how to communicate with the person; or

(2) to a secured party or lienholder that has filed a financing statement against a person, unless the secured party knows:

(A) that the person is a debtor; and

(B) the identity of the person.

(c) [Limitation of liability if reasonable belief that transaction not a consumer-goods transaction or consumer transaction.] A secured party is not liable to any person, and a person's liability for a deficiency is not affected, because of any act or omission arising out of the secured party's reasonable belief that a transaction is not a consumer-goods transaction or a consumer transaction or that goods are not consumer goods, if the secured party's belief is based on its reasonable reliance on:

(1) a debtor's representation concerning the purpose for which collateral was to be used, acquired, or held; or

(2) an obligor's representation concerning the purpose for which a secured obligation was incurred.

(d) [Limitation of liability for statutory damages.] A secured party is not liable to any person under Section 9-625(c)(2) for its failure to comply with Section 9-616.

(e) [Limitation of multiple liability for statutory damages.] A secured party is not liable under Section 9-625(c)(2) more than once with respect to any one secured obligation.

(f) [Exception: Limitation of liability under subsections (a) and (b) does not apply.] Subsections (a) and (b) do not apply to limit the liability of a secured party to a person if, at the time the secured party obtains control of collateral that is a controllable account, controllable electronic record, or controllable payment intangible or at the time the security interest attaches to the collateral, whichever is later:

(1) the person is a debtor or obligor; and

(2) the secured party knows that the information in subsection (b)(1)(A), (B), or (C) relating to the person is not provided by the collateral, a record attached to or logically

associated with the collateral, or the system in which the collateral is recorded.

Definitional Cross References:

Collateral	Section 9-102(a)(12)
Communicate	Section 9-102(a)(18)
Consumer goods	Section 9-102(a)(23)
Consumer-goods transaction	Section 9-102(a)(24)
Consumer transaction	Section 9-102(a)(26)
Controllable account	Section 9-102(a)(27A)
Controllable electronic record	Section 12-102(a)(1)
Controllable payment intangible	Section 9-102(a)(27B)
Debtor	Section 9-102(a)(28)
Financing statement	Section 9-102(a)(39)
Goods	Section 9-102(a)(44)
Obligor	Section 9-102(a)(59)
Person	Section 1-201(b)(27)
Record	Section 9-102(a)(70)
Secondary obligor	Section 9-102(a)(72)
Secured party	Section 9-102(a)(73)
Security interest	Section 1-201(b)(35)

Official Comment

1. Source. New.

2. Exculpatory Provisions. With respect to subsection (f), see Section 9-605, Comments 2 and 3.

If a secured party reasonably, but mistakenly, believes that a consumer transaction or consumer-goods transaction is a non-consumer transaction or non-consumer-goods transaction, and if the secured party's belief is based on its reasonable reliance on a representation of the type specified in subsection (c)(1) or (c)(2), then this Article should be applied as if the facts reasonably believed and the representation reasonably relied upon were true. For example, if a secured party reasonably believed that a transaction was a non-consumer transaction and its belief was based on reasonable reliance on the debtor's representation that the collateral secured an obligation incurred for business purposes, the secured party is not liable to any person, and the debtor's liability for a deficiency is not affected, because of any act or omission of the secured party which arises out of the reasonable belief. Of course, if the secured party's belief is not reasonable or, even if reasonable, is not based on reasonable reliance on the debtor's representation, this limitation on liability is inapplicable.

3. Inapplicability of Statutory Damages to Section 9-616. Subsection (d) excludes noncompliance with Section 9-616 entirely from the scope of statutory damage liability under Section 9-625(c)(2).

4. Single Liability for Statutory Minimum Damages. Subsection (e) ensures that a secured party will incur statutory damages only once in connection with any one secured obligation.

PART 7. TRANSITION

§ 9-701. Effective Date.

This [Act] takes effect on July 1, 2001.

Official Comment

A uniform law as complex as Article 9 necessarily gives rise to difficult problems and uncertainties during the transition to the new law. As is customary for uniform laws, this Article is based on the general assumption that all States will have enacted substantially identical versions. While always important, uniformity is essential to the success of this Article. If former Article 9 is in effect in some jurisdictions, and this Article is in effect in others, horrendous complications may arise. For example, the proper place in which to file to perfect a security interest (and thus the status of a particular security interest as perfected or unperfected) would depend on whether the matter was litigated in a State in which former Article 9 was in effect or a State in which this Article was in effect. Accordingly, this section contemplates that States will adopt a uniform effective date for this Article. Any one State's failure to adopt the uniform effective date will greatly increase the cost and uncertainty surrounding the transition.

Other problems arise from transactions and relationships that were entered into under former Article 9 or under non-UCC law and which remain outstanding on the effective date of this Article. The difficulties arise primarily because this Article expands the scope of former Article 9 to cover additional types of collateral and transactions and because it provides new methods of perfection for some types of collateral, different priority rules, and different choice-of-law rules governing perfection and priority. This Section and the other sections in this Part address primarily this second set of problems.

§ 9-702. Savings Clause.

(a) [Pre-effective-date transactions or liens.] Except as otherwise provided in this part, this [Act] applies to a transaction or lien within its scope, even if the transaction or lien was entered into or created before this [Act] takes effect.

(b) [Continuing validity.] Except as otherwise provided in subsection (c) and Sections 9-703 through 9-709:

(1) transactions and liens that were not governed by [former Article 9], were validly entered into or created before this [Act] takes effect, and would be subject to this [Act] if they

had been entered into or created after this [Act] takes effect, and the rights, duties, and interests flowing from those transactions and liens remain valid after this [Act] takes effect; and

(2) the transactions and liens may be terminated, completed, consummated, and enforced as required or permitted by this [Act] or by the law that otherwise would apply if this [Act] had not taken effect.

(c) [Pre-effective-date proceedings.] This [Act] does not affect an action, case, or proceeding commenced before this [Act] takes effect.

Definitional Cross References:

Action	Section 1-201(b)(1)
Right	Section 1-201(b)(34)

Official Comment

1. Pre-Effective-Date Transactions. Subsection (a) contains the general rule that this Article applies to transactions, security interests, and other liens within its scope (see Section 9-109), even if the transaction or lien was entered into or created before the effective date. Thus, secured transactions entered into under former Article 9 must be terminated, completed, consummated, and enforced under this Article. Subsection (b) is an exception to the general rule. It applies to valid, pre-effective-date transactions and liens that were not governed by former Article 9 but would be governed by this Article if they had been entered into or created after this Article takes effect. Under subsection (b), these valid transactions, such as the creation of agricultural liens and security interests in commercial tort claims, retain their validity under this Article and may be terminated, completed, consummated, and enforced under this Article. However, these transactions also may be terminated, completed, consummated, and enforced by the law that otherwise would apply had this Article not taken effect.

2. Judicial Proceedings Commenced Before Effective Date. As is usual in transition provisions, subsection (c) provides that this Article does not affect litigation pending on the effective date.

§ 9-703. Security Interest Perfected Before Effective Date.

(a) [Continuing priority over lien creditor: perfection requirements satisfied.] A security interest that is enforceable immediately before this [Act] takes effect and would have priority over the rights of a person that becomes a lien creditor at that time is a perfected security interest under this [Act] if, when this [Act] takes effect, the applicable requirements for enforceability and perfection under this [Act] are satisfied without further action.

(b) [Continuing priority over lien creditor: perfection requirements not satisfied.] Except as otherwise provided in Section 9-705, if, immediately before this [Act] takes effect, a security interest is enforceable and would have priority over the rights of a person that becomes a lien creditor at that time, but the applicable requirements for enforceability or perfection under this [Act] are not satisfied when this [Act] takes effect, the security interest:

(1) is a perfected security interest for one year after this [Act] takes effect;

(2) remains enforceable thereafter only if the security interest becomes enforceable under Section 9-203 before the year expires; and

(3) remains perfected thereafter only if the applicable requirements for perfection under this [Act] are satisfied before the year expires.

Definitional Cross References:

Action	Section 1-201(b)(1)
Lien creditor	Section 9-102(a)(52)
Person	Section 1-201(b)(27)
Right	Section 1-201(b)(34)
Security interest	Section 1-201(b)(35)

Official Comment

1. Perfected Security Interests Under Former Article 9 and This Article. This section deals with security interests that are perfected (i.e., that are enforceable and have priority over the rights of a lien creditor) under former Article 9 or other applicable law immediately before this Article takes effect. Subsection (a) provides, not surprisingly, that if the security interest would be a perfected security interest under this Article (i.e., if the transaction satisfies this Article's requirements for enforceability (attachment) and perfection), no further action need be taken for the security interest to be a perfected security interest.

2. Security Interests Enforceable and Perfected Under Former Article 9 but Unenforceable or Unperfected Under This Article. Subsection (b) deals with security interests that are enforceable and perfected under former Article 9 or other applicable law immediately before this Article takes effect but do not satisfy the requirements for enforceability (attachment) or perfection under this Article. Except as otherwise provided in Section 9-705, these security interests are perfected security interests for one year after the effective date. If the security interest satisfies the requirements for attachment and perfection within that period, the security interest remains perfected thereafter. If the security interest satisfies only the requirements for attachment within that period, the security interest becomes unperfected at the end of the one-year period.

Example 1: A pre-effective-date security agreement in a consumer transaction covers "all securities accounts." The security interest is properly perfected. The collateral description was adequate under former Article 9 (see former Section 9-115(3)) but is insufficient under this Article (see Section 9-108(e)(2)). Unless the debtor authenticates a new security agreement describing the collateral other than by "type" (or Section 9-203(b)(3) otherwise is satisfied) within the one-year period following the effective date, the security interest becomes unenforceable at the end of that period.

Other examples under former Article 9 or other applicable law that may be effective as attachment or enforceability steps but may be ineffective under this Article include an oral agreement to sell a payment intangible or possession by virtue of a notification to a bailee under former Section 9-305. Neither the oral agreement nor the notification would satisfy the revised Section 9-203 requirements for attachment.

Example 2: A pre-effective-date possessory security interest in instruments is perfected by a bailee's receipt of notification under former 9-305. The bailee has not, however, acknowledged that it holds for the secured party's benefit under revised Section 9-313. Unless the bailee authenticates a record acknowledging that it holds for the secured party (or another appropriate perfection step is taken) within the one-year period following the effective date, the security interest becomes unperfected at the end of that period.

3. Interpretation of Pre-Effective-Date Security Agreements. Section 9-102 defines "security agreement" as "an agreement that creates or provides for a security interest." Under Section 1-201(3), an "agreement" is a "bargain of the parties in fact." [Ed. Note. New Article 1: Section 1-201(b)(3).] If parties to a pre-effective-date security agreement describe the collateral by using a term defined in former Article 9 in one way and defined in this Article in another way, in most cases it should be presumed that the bargain of the parties contemplated the meaning of the term under former Article 9.

Example 3: A pre-effective-date security agreement covers "all accounts" of a debtor. As defined under former Article 9, an "account" did not include a right to payment for lottery winnings. These rights to payment are "accounts" under this Article, however. The agreement of the parties presumptively created a security interest in "accounts" as defined in former Article 9. A different result might be appropriate, for example, if the security agreement explicitly contemplated future changes in the Article 9 definitions of types of collateral—e.g., " 'Accounts' means 'accounts' as defined in the UCC Article 9 of [State X], as that definition may be amended from time to time." Whether a different approach is appropriate in any given case depends on the bargain of the parties, as determined by applying ordinary principles of contract construction.

§ 9-704. Security Interest Unperfected Before Effective Date.

A security interest that is enforceable immediately before this [Act] takes effect but which would be subordinate to the rights of a person that becomes a lien creditor at that time:

(1) remains an enforceable security interest for one year after this [Act] takes effect;

(2) remains enforceable thereafter if the security interest becomes enforceable under Section 9-203 when this [Act] takes effect or within one year thereafter; and

(3) becomes perfected:

(A) without further action, when this [Act] takes effect if the applicable requirements for perfection under this [Act] are satisfied before or at that time; or

(B) when the applicable requirements for perfection are satisfied if the requirements are satisfied after that time.

Definitional Cross References:

Action	Section 1-201(b)(1)
Lien creditor	Section 9-102(a)(52)
Person	Section 1-201(b)(27)
Right	Section 1-201(b)(34)
Security interest	Section 1-201(b)(35)

Official Comment

This section deals with security interests that are enforceable but unperfected (i.e., subordinate to the rights of a person who becomes a lien creditor) under former Article 9 or other applicable law immediately before this Article takes effect. These security interests remain enforceable for one year after the effective date, and thereafter if the appropriate steps for attachment under this Article are taken before the one-year period expires. (This section's treatment of enforceability is the same as that of Section 9-703.) The security interest becomes a perfected security interest on the effective date if, at that time, the security interest satisfies the requirements for perfection under this Article. If the security interest does not satisfy the requirements for perfection until sometime thereafter, it becomes a perfected security interest at that later time.

Example: A security interest has attached under former Article 9 but is unperfected because the filed financing statement covers "all of debtor's personal property" and controlling case law in the applicable jurisdiction has determined that this identification of collateral in a financing statement is insufficient. Upon the effective date of this Article, the financing statement becomes sufficient under Section 9-504(2). On that date the security interest becomes perfected. (This assumes, of course, that the financing statement is filed in the proper filing office under this Article.)

§ 9-705. Effectiveness of Action Taken Before Effective Date.

(a) [Pre-effective-date action; one-year perfection period unless reperfected.] If action, other than the filing of a financing statement, is taken before this [Act] takes effect and the action would have resulted in priority of a security interest over the rights of a person that becomes a lien creditor had the security interest become enforceable before this [Act] takes effect, the action is effective to perfect a security interest that attaches under this [Act] within one year after this [Act] takes effect. An attached security interest becomes unperfected one year after this [Act] takes effect unless the security interest becomes a perfected security interest under this [Act] before the expiration of that period.

(b) [Pre-effective-date filing.] The filing of a financing statement before this [Act] takes effect is effective to perfect a security interest to the extent the filing would satisfy the applicable requirements for perfection under this [Act].

(c) [Pre-effective-date filing in jurisdiction formerly governing perfection.] This [Act] does not render ineffective an effective financing statement that, before this [Act] takes effect, is filed and satisfies the applicable requirements for perfection under the law of the jurisdiction governing perfection as provided in [former Section 9-103]. However, except as otherwise provided in subsections (d) and (e) and Section 9-706, the financing statement ceases to be effective at the earlier of:

(1) the time the financing statement would have ceased to be effective under the law of the jurisdiction in which it is filed; or

(2) June 30, 2006.

(d) [Continuation statement.] The filing of a continuation statement after this [Act] takes effect does not continue the effectiveness of the financing statement filed before this [Act] takes effect. However, upon the timely filing of a continuation statement after this [Act] takes effect and in accordance with the law of the jurisdiction governing perfection as provided in Part 3, the effectiveness of a financing statement filed in the same office in that jurisdiction before this [Act] takes effect continues for the period provided by the law of that jurisdiction.

(e) [Application of subsection (c)(2) to transmitting utility financing statement.] Subsection (c)(2) applies to a financing statement that, before this [Act] takes effect, is filed against a transmitting utility and satisfies the applicable requirements for perfection under the law of the jurisdiction governing perfection as provided in [former Section 9-103] only to the extent that Part 3 provides that the law of a jurisdiction other than the jurisdiction in which the financing statement is filed governs perfection of a security interest in collateral covered by the financing statement.

(f) [Application of Part 5.] A financing statement that includes a financing statement filed before this [Act] takes effect and a continuation statement filed after this [Act] takes effect is effective only to the extent that it satisfies the requirements of Part 5 for an initial financing statement.

Definitional Cross References:

Action	Section 1-201(b)(1)
Collateral	Section 9-102(a)(12)
Continuation statement	Section 9-102(a)(27)
Financing statement	Section 9-102(a)(39)
Lien creditor	Section 9-102(a)(52)
Person	Section 1-201(b)(27)
Right	Section 1-201(b)(34)
Security interest	Section 1-201(b)(35)
Transmitting utility	Section 9-102(a)(81)

Official Comment

1. General. This section addresses primarily the situation in which the perfection step is taken under former Article 9 or other applicable law before the effective date of this Article, but the security interest does not attach until after that date.

2. Perfection Other Than by Filing. Subsection (a) applies when the perfection step is a step other than the filing of a financing statement. If the step that would be a valid perfection step under former Article 9 or other law is taken before this Article takes effect, and if a security interest attaches within one year after this Article takes effect, then the security interest becomes a perfected security interest upon attachment. However, the security interest becomes unperfected one year after the effective date unless the requirements for attachment and perfection under this Article are satisfied within that period.

3. Perfection by Filing: Ineffective Filings Made Effective. Subsection (b) deals with financing statements that were filed under former Article 9 and which would not have perfected a security interest under the former Article (because, e.g., they did not accurately describe the collateral or were filed in the wrong place), but which would perfect a security interest under this Article. Under subsection (b), such a financing statement is effective to perfect a security interest to the extent it complies with this Article. Subsection (b) applies regardless of the reason for the filing. For example, a secured party need not wait until the effective date to respond to the change this Article makes with respect to the jurisdiction whose law governs perfection of certain security interests. Rather, a secured party may wish to prepare for this change by filing a financing statement before the effective date in the jurisdiction whose law governs perfection under this Article. When this Article takes effect, the filing becomes effective to perfect a security interest (assuming the filing satisfies the perfection requirements of this Article). Note, however, that Section 9-706 determines whether a financing statement filed before the effective date operates to continue the effectiveness of a financing statement filed in another office before the effective date.

4. Perfection by Filing: Change in Applicable Law or Filing Office. Subsection (c) provides that a financing statement filed in the proper jurisdiction under former Section 9-103 remains effective for all purposes, despite the fact that Part 3 of this Article would require filing of a financing statement in a different jurisdiction or in a different office in the same jurisdiction. This means that, during the early years of this Article's effectiveness, it may be necessary to search not only in the filing office of the jurisdiction whose law governs perfection under this Article but also (if different) in the jurisdiction(s) and filing office(s) designated by former Article 9. To limit this burden, subsection (c) provides that a financing statement filed in the jurisdiction determined by former Section 9-103 becomes ineffective at the earlier of the time it would become ineffective under the law of that jurisdiction or June 30, 2006. The June 30, 2006, limitation addresses some nonuniform versions of former Article 9 that extended the effectiveness of a financing statement beyond five years. Note that a financing statement filed before the effective date may remain effective beyond June 30, 2006, if subsection (d) (concerning continuation statements) or (e) (concerning transmitting utilities) or Section 9-706 (concerning initial financing statements that operate to continue pre-effective-date financing statements) so provides.

Subsection (c) is an exception to Section 9-703(b). Under the general rule in Section 9-703(b), a security interest that is enforceable and perfected on the effective date of this Article is a perfected security interest for one year after this Article takes effect, even if the security interest is not enforceable under this Article and the applicable requirements for perfection under this Article have not been met. However, in some cases subsection (c) may shorten the one-year period of perfection; in others, if the security interest is enforceable under Section 9-203, it may extend the period of perfection.

> **Example 1:** On July 3, 1996, D, a State X corporation, creates a security interest in certain manufacturing equipment located in State Y. On July 6, 1996, SP perfects a security interest in the equipment under former Article 9 by filing in the office of the State Y Secretary of State. See former Section 9-103(1)(b). This Article takes effect in States X and Y on July 1, 2001. Under Section 9-705(c), the financing statement remains effective until it lapses in July 2001. See former Section 9-403. Had SP continued the effectiveness of the financing statement by filing a continuation statement in State Y under former Article 9 before July 1, 2001, the financing statement would have remained effective to perfect the security interest through June 30, 2006. See subsection (c)(2). Alternatively, SP could have filed an initial financing statement in State X under subsection (b) or Section 9-706 before the State Y financing statement lapsed. Had SP done so, the security interest would have remained perfected without interruption until the State X financing statement lapsed.

5. Continuing Effectiveness of Filed Financing Statement. A financing statement filed before the effective date of this Article may be continued only by filing in the State and office designated by this Article. This result is accomplished in the following manner: Subsection (d) indicates that, as a general matter, a continuation statement filed after the effective date of this Article does not continue the effectiveness of a financing statement filed under the law designated by former Section 9-103. Instead, an initial financing statement must be filed under Section 9-706. The second sentence of subsection (d) contains an exception to the general rule. It provides that a continuation statement is effective to continue the effectiveness of a financing statement filed before this Article takes effect if this Article prescribes not only the same jurisdiction but also the same filing office.

> **Example 2:** On November 8, 2000, D, a State X corporation, creates a security interest in certain manufacturing equipment located in State Y. On November 15, 2000, SP perfects a security interest in the equipment under former Article 9 by filing in office of the State Y Secretary of State.

See former Section 9-103(1)(b). This Article takes effect in States X and Y on July 1, 2001. Under Section 9-705(c), the financing statement ceases to be effective in November, 2005, when it lapses. See Section 9-515. Under this Article, the law of D's location (State X, see Section 9-307) governs perfection. See Section 9-301. Thus, the filing of a continuation statement in State Y after the effective date would not continue the effectiveness of the financing statement. See subsection (d). However, the effectiveness of the financing statement could be continued under Section 9-706.

Example 3: The facts are as in Example 2, except that D is a State Y corporation. Assume State Y adopted former Section 9-401(1) (second alternative). State Y law governs perfection under Part 3 of this Article. (See Sections 9-301, 9-307.) Under the second sentence of subsection (d), the timely filing of a continuation statement in accordance with the law of State Y continues the effectiveness of the financing statement.

Example 4: The facts are as in Example 3, except that the collateral is equipment used in farming operations and, in accordance with former Section 9-401(1) (second alternative) as enacted in State Y, the financing statement was filed in State Y, in the office of the Shelby County Recorder of Deeds. Under this Article, a continuation statement must be filed in the office of the State Y Secretary of State. See Section 9-501(a)(2). Under the second sentence of subsection (d), the timely filing of a continuation statement in accordance with the law of State Y operates to continue a pre-effective-date financing statement only if the continuation statement is filed in the same office as the financing statement. Accordingly, the continuation statement is not effective in this case, but the financing statement may be continued under Section 9-706.

Example 5: The facts are as in Example 3, except that State Y enacted former Section 9-401(1) (third alternative). As required by former Section 9-401(1), SP filed financing statements in both the office of the State Y Secretary of State and the office of the Shelby County Recorder of Deeds. Under this Article, a continuation statement must be filed in the office of the State Y Secretary of State. See Section 9-501(a)(2). The timely filing of a continuation statement in that office after this Article takes effect would be effective to continue the effectiveness of the financing statement (and thus continue the perfection of the security interest), even if the financing statement filed with the County Recorder lapses.

6. Continuation Statements. In some cases, this Article reclassifies collateral covered by a financing statement filed under former Article 9. For example, collateral consisting of the right to payment for real property sold would be a "general intangible" under the former Article but an "account" under this Article. To continue perfection under those circumstances, a continuation statement must comply with the normal requirements for a continuation statement. See Section 9-515. In addition, the pre-effective-date financing statement and continuation statement, taken together, must satisfy the requirements of this Article concerning the sufficiency of the debtor's name, secured party's name, and indication of collateral. See subsection (f).

Example 6: A pre-effective-date financing statement covers "all general intangibles" of a debtor. As defined under former Article 9, a "general intangible," would include rights to payment for lottery winnings. These rights to payment are "accounts" under this Article, however. A post-effective-date continuation statement will not continue the effectiveness of the pre-effective-date financing statement with respect to lottery winnings unless it amends the indication of collateral covered to include lottery winnings (e.g., by adding "accounts," "rights to payment for lottery winnings," or the like). If the continuation statement does not amend the indication of collateral, the continuation statement will be effective to continue the effectiveness of the financing statement only with respect to "general intangibles" as defined in this Article.

Example 7: The facts are as in Example 6, except that the pre-effective-date financing statement covers "all accounts and general intangibles." Even though rights to payment for lottery winnings are "general intangibles" under former Article 9 and "accounts" under this Article, a post-effective-date continuation statement would continue the effectiveness of the pre-effective-date financing statement with respect to lottery winnings. There would be no need to amend the indication of collateral covered, inasmuch as the indication ("accounts") satisfies the requirements of this Article.

§ 9-706. When Initial Financing Statement Suffices to Continue Effectiveness of Financing Statement.

(a) [Initial financing statement in lieu of continuation statement.] The filing of an initial financing statement in the office specified in Section 9-501 continues the effectiveness of a financing statement filed before this [Act] takes effect if:

(1) the filing of an initial financing statement in that office would be effective to perfect a security interest under this [Act];

(2) the pre-effective-date financing statement was filed in an office in another State or another office in this State; and

(3) the initial financing statement satisfies subsection (c).

(b) [Period of continued effectiveness.] The filing of an initial financing statement under subsection (a) continues the effectiveness of the pre-effective-date financing statement:

(1) if the initial financing statement is filed before this [Act] takes effect, for the period provided in [former Section 9-403] with respect to a financing statement; and

(2) if the initial financing statement is filed after this [Act] takes effect, for the period provided in Section 9-515 with respect to an initial financing statement.

(c) [Requirements for initial financing statement under subsection (a).] To be effective for purposes of subsection (a), an initial financing statement must:

(1) satisfy the requirements of Part 5 for an initial financing statement;

(2) identify the pre-effective-date financing statement by indicating the office in which the financing statement was filed and providing the dates of filing and file numbers, if any, of the financing statement and of the most recent continuation statement filed with respect to the financing statement; and

(3) indicate that the pre-effective-date financing statement remains effective.

Definitional Cross References:

Continuation statement	Section 9-102(a)(27)
File number	Section 9-102(a)(36)
Financing statement	Section 9-102(a)(39)
Security interest	Section 1-201(b)(35)
State	Section 9-102(a)(77)

Official Comment

1. Continuation of Financing Statements Not Filed in Proper Filing Office Under This Article. This section deals with continuing the effectiveness of financing statements that are filed in the proper State and office under former Article 9, but which would be filed in the wrong State or in the wrong office of the proper State under this Article. Section 9-705(d) provides that, under these circumstances, filing a continuation statement after the effective date of this Article in the office designated by former Article 9 would not be effective. This section provides the means by which the effectiveness of such a financing statement can be continued if this Article governs perfection under the applicable choice-of-law rule: filing an initial financing statement in the office specified by Section 9-501.

Although it has the effect of continuing the effectiveness of a pre-effective-date financing statement, an initial financing statement described in this section is not a continuation statement. Rather, it is governed by the rules applicable to initial financing statements. (However, the debtor need not authorize the filing. See Section 9-708.) Unlike a continuation statement, the initial financing statement described in this section may be filed any time during the effectiveness of the pre-effective-date financing statement—even before this Article is enacted—and not only within the six months immediately prior to lapse. In contrast to a continuation statement, which extends the lapse date of a filed financing statement for five years, the initial financing statement has its own lapse date, which bears no relation to the lapse date of the pre-effective-date financing statement whose effectiveness the initial financing statement continues. See subsection (b).

As subsection (a) makes clear, the filing of an initial financing statement under this section continues the effectiveness of a pre-effective-date financing statement. If the effectiveness of a pre-effective-date financing statement lapses before the initial financing statement is filed, the effectiveness of the pre-effective-date financing statement cannot be continued. Rather, unless the security interest is perfected otherwise, there will be a period during which the security interest is unperfected before becoming perfected again by the filing of the initial financing statement under this section.

If an initial financing statement is filed under this section before the effective date of this Article, it takes effect when this Article takes effect (assuming that it is ineffective under former Article 9). Note, however, that former Article 9 determines whether the filing office is obligated to accept such an initial financing statement. For the reason given in the preceding paragraph, an initial financing statement filed before the effective date of this Article does not continue the effectiveness of a pre-effective-date financing statement unless the latter remains effective on the effective date of this Article. Thus, for example, if the effectiveness of the pre-effective-date financing statement lapses before this Article takes effect, the initial financing statement would not continue its effectiveness.

2. Requirements of Initial Financing Statement Filed in Lieu of Continuation Statement. Subsection (c) sets forth the requirements for the initial financing statement under subsection (a). These requirements are needed to inform searchers that the initial financing statement operates to continue a financing statement filed elsewhere and to enable searchers to locate and discover the attributes of the other financing statement. The notice-filing policy of this Article applies to the initial financing statements described in this section. Accordingly, an initial financing statement that substantially satisfies the requirements of subsection (c) is effective, even if it has minor errors or omissions, unless the errors or omissions make the financing statement seriously misleading. See Section 9-506.

A single initial financing statement may continue the effectiveness of more than one financing statement filed before this Article's effective date. See Section 1-106 (words in the singular include the plural). If a financing statement has been filed in more than one office in a given jurisdiction, as may be the case if the jurisdiction had adopted former Section 9-401(l), the third alternative, then an identification of the filing in the central filing office suffices for purposes of subsection (c)(2). If under this Article the collateral is of a type different from its type under former Article 9—as would be the case, e.g., with a right to payment of lottery winnings (a "general intangible" under former Article 9 and an "account" under this Article), then subsection (c) requires that the initial financing statement indicate the type under this Article.

§ 9-707. Amendment of Pre-Effective-Date Financing Statement.

(a) ["Pre-effective-date financing statement".] In this section, "pre-effective-date financing statement" means a financing statement filed before this [Act] takes effect.

(b) [Applicable law.] After this [Act] takes effect, a person may add or delete collateral covered by, continue or terminate the effectiveness of, or otherwise amend the information provided in, a pre-effective-date financing statement only in accordance with the law of the jurisdiction governing perfection as provided in Part 3. However, the effectiveness of a pre-effective-date financing statement also may be terminated in accordance with the law of the jurisdiction in which the financing statement is filed.

(c) [Method of amending: general rule.] Except as otherwise provided in subsection (d), if the law of this State governs perfection of a security interest, the information in a pre-effective-date financing statement may be amended after this [Act] takes effect only if:

(1) the pre-effective-date financing statement and an amendment are filed in the office specified in Section 9-501;

(2) an amendment is filed in the office specified in Section 9-501 concurrently with, or after the filing in that office of, an initial financing statement that satisfies Section 9-706(c); or

(3) an initial financing statement that provides the information as amended and satisfies Section 9-706(c) is filed in the office specified in Section 9-501.

(d) [Method of amending: continuation.] If the law of this State governs perfection of a security interest, the effectiveness of a pre-effective-date financing statement may be continued only under Section 9-705(d) and (f) or 9-706.

(e) [Method of amending: additional termination rule.] Whether or not the law of this State governs perfection of a security interest, the effectiveness of a pre-effective-date financing statement filed in this State may be terminated after this [Act] takes effect by filing a termination statement in the office in which the pre-effective-date financing statement is filed, unless an initial financing statement that satisfies Section 9-706(c) has been filed in the office specified by the law of the jurisdiction governing perfection as provided in Part 3 as the office in which to file a financing statement.

Definitional Cross References:

Collateral	Section 9-102(a)(12)
Continuation statement	Section 9-102(a)(27)
Financing statement	Section 9-102(a)(39)
Person	Section 1-201(b)(27)
Secured party	Section 9-102(a)(73)
Security interest	Section 1-201(b)(35)

Official Comment

1. Scope of This Section. This section addresses post-effective date amendments to pre-effective-date financing statements.

2. Applicable Law. Determining how to amend a pre-effective-date financing statement requires one first to determine the jurisdiction whose law applies. Subsection (b) provides that, as a general matter, post-effective-date amendments to pre-effective-date financing statements are effective only if they are accomplished in accordance with the substantive (or local) law of the jurisdiction governing perfection under Part 3 of this Article. However, under certain circumstances, the effectiveness of a financing statement may be terminated in accordance with the substantive law of the jurisdiction in which the financing statement is filed. See Comment 5, below.

Example 1: D is a corporation organized under the law of State Y. It owns equipment located in State X. Under former Article 9, SP properly perfected a security interest in the equipment by filing a financing statement in State X. Under this Article, the law of State Y governs perfection of the security interest. See Sections 9-301, 9-307. After this Article takes effect, SP wishes to amend the financing statement to reflect a change in D's name. Under subsection (b), the financing statement may be amended in accordance with the law of State Y, i.e., in accordance with subsection (c) as enacted in State Y.

Example 2: The facts are as in Example 1, except that SP wishes to terminate the effectiveness of the State X filing. The first sentence of subsection (b) provides that the financing statement may be terminated after the effective date of this Article in accordance with the law of State Y, i.e., in accordance with subsection (c) as enacted in State Y. However, the second sentence provides that the financing statement also may be terminated in accordance with the law of the jurisdiction in which it is filed, i.e., in accordance with subsection (e) as enacted in State X. If the pre-effective-date financing statement is filed in the jurisdiction whose law governs perfection (here, State Y), then both sentences would designate the law of State Y as applicable to the termination of the financing statement. That is, the financing statement could be terminated in accordance with subsection (c) or (e) as enacted in State Y.

3. Method of Amending. Subsection (c) provides three methods of effectuating a post-effective-date amendment to a pre-effective-date financing statement. Under subsection (c)(1), if the financing statement is filed in the jurisdiction and office determined by this Article, then an effective amendment may be filed in the same office.

Example 3: D is a corporation organized under the law of State Z. It owns equipment located in State Z. Before the effective date of this Article, SP perfected a security interest in the equipment by filing in two offices in State Z, a local filing office and the office of the Secretary of State. See former Section 9-401(1) (third alternative). State Z enacts this Article and specifies in Section 9-501 that a financing statement covering equipment is to be filed in the office of the Secretary of State. SP wishes to assign its power as secured party of record. Under subsection (b), the substantive law of State Z applies. Because the pre-effective-date financing statement is filed in the office specified in subsection (c)(1) as enacted by State Z, SP may effectuate the assignment by filing an amendment under Section 9-514 with the office of the Secretary of State. SP need not amend the local filing, and the priority of the security interest perfected by the filing of the financing statement would not be affected by the failure to amend the local filing.

If a pre-effective-date financing statement is filed in an office other than the one specified by Section 9-501 of the relevant jurisdiction, then ordinarily an amendment filed in that office is ineffective. (Subsection (e) provides an exception for termination statements.) Rather, the amendment must be effectuated by a filing in the jurisdiction and office determined by this Article. That filing may consist of an initial financing statement followed by an amendment, an initial financing statement together with an amendment, or an initial financing statement that indicates the information provided in the financing statement, as amended. Subsection (c)(2) encompasses the first two options; subsection (c)(3) contemplates the last. In each instance, the initial financing statement must satisfy Section 9-706(c).

4. Continuation. Subsection (d) refers to the two methods by which a secured party may continue the effectiveness of a pre-effective-date financing statement under this Part. The Comments to Sections 9-705 and 9-706 explain these methods.

5. Termination. The effectiveness of a pre-effective-date financing statement may be terminated pursuant to subsection (c). This section also provides an alternative method for accomplishing this result: filing a termination statement in the office in which the financing statement is filed. The alternative method becomes unavailable once an initial financing statement that relates to the pre-effective-date financing statement and satisfies Section 9-706(c) is filed in the jurisdiction and office determined by this Article.

Example 4: The facts are as in Example 1, except that SP wishes to terminate a financing statement filed in State X. As explained in Example 1, the financing statement may be amended in accordance with the law of the jurisdiction governing perfection under this Article, i.e., in accordance with the substantive law of State Y. As enacted in State Y, subsection (c)(1) is inapplicable because the financing statement was not filed in the State Y filing office specified in Section 9-501. Under subsection (c)(2), the financing statement may be amended by filing in the State Y filing office an initial financing statement followed by a termination statement. The filing of an initial financing statement together with a termination statement also would be legally sufficient under subsection (c)(2), but Section 9-512(a)(1) may render this method impractical. The financing statement also may be amended under subsection (c)(3), but the resulting initial financing statement is likely to be very confusing. In each instance, the initial financing statement must satisfy Section 9-706(c). Applying the law of State Y, subsection (e) is inapplicable, because the financing statement was not filed in "this State," i.e., State Y.

This section affords another option to SP. Subsection (b) provides that the effectiveness of a financing statement may be terminated either in accordance with the law of the jurisdiction governing perfection (here, State Y) or in accordance with the substantive law of the jurisdiction in which the financing statement is filed (here, State X). Applying the law of State X, the financing statement is filed in "this State," i.e., State X, and subsection (e) applies. Accordingly, the effectiveness of the financing statement can be terminated by filing a termination statement in the State X office in which the financing statement is filed, unless an initial financing statement that relates to the financing statement and satisfies Section 9-706(c) as enacted in State X has been filed in the jurisdiction and office determined by this Article (here, the State Y filing office).

§ 9-708. Persons Entitled to File Initial Financing Statement or Continuation Statement.

A person may file an initial financing statement or a continuation statement under this part if:

(1) the secured party of record authorizes the filing; and

(2) the filing is necessary under this part:

(A) to continue the effectiveness of a financing statement filed before this [Act] takes effect; or

(B) to perfect or continue the perfection of a security interest.

Definitional Cross References:

Financing statement	Section 9-102(a)(39)
Person	Section 1-201(b)(27)
Security interest	Section 1-201(b)(35)
Secured party	Section 9-102(a)(73)

Official Comment

This section permits a secured party to file an initial financing statement or continuation statement necessary under this Part to continue the effectiveness of a financing statement filed before this Article takes effect or to perfect or otherwise continue the perfection of a security interest. Because a filing described in this section typically operates to continue the effectiveness of a financing statement whose filing the debtor already has authorized, this section does not require authorization from the debtor.

§ 9-709. Priority.

(a) [Law governing priority.] This [Act] determines the priority of conflicting claims to collateral. However, if the relative priorities of the claims were established before this [Act] takes effect, [former Article 9] determines priority.

(b) [Priority if security interest becomes enforceable under Section 9-203.] For purposes of Section 9-322(a), the priority of a security interest that becomes enforceable under Section 9-203 of this [Act] dates from the time this [Act] takes effect if the security interest is perfected under this [Act] by the filing of a financing statement before this [Act] takes effect which would not have been effective to perfect the security interest under [former Article 9]. This subsection does not apply to conflicting security interests each of which is perfected by the filing of such a financing statement.

Definitional Cross References:

Collateral	Section 9-102(a)(12)
Financing statement	Section 9-102(a)(39)
Security interest	Section 1-201(b)(35)

Official Comment

1. Law Governing Priority. Ordinarily, this Article determines the priority of conflicting claims to collateral. However, when the relative priorities of the claims were established before this Article takes effect, former Article 9 governs.

Example 1: In 1999, SP-1 obtains a security interest in a right to payment for goods sold ("account"). SP-1 fails to file a financing statement. This Article takes effect on July 1, 2001. Thereafter, on August 1, 2001, D creates a security interest in the same account in favor of SP-2, who files a financing statement. This Article determines the relative priorities of the claims. SP-2's security interest has priority under Section 9-322(a)(1).

Example 2: In 1999, SP-1 obtains a security interest in a right to payment for goods sold ("account"). SP-1 fails to file a financing statement. In 2000, D creates a security interest in the same account in favor of SP-2, who likewise fails to file a financing statement. This Article takes effect on July 1, 2001. Because the relative priorities of the security interests were established before the effective date of this Article, former

Article 9 governs priority, and SP-1's security interest has priority under former Section 9-312(5)(b).

Example 3: The facts are as in Example 2, except that, on August 1, 2001, SP-2 files a proper financing statement under this Article. Until August 1, 2001, the relative priorities of the security interests were established before the effective date of this Article, as in Example 2. However, by taking the affirmative step of filing a financing statement, SP-2 established anew the relative priority of the conflicting claims after the effective date. Thus, this Article determines priority. SP-2's security interest has priority under Section 9-322(a)(1).

As Example 3 illustrates, relative priorities that are "established" before the effective date do not necessarily remain unchanged following the effective date. Of course, unlike priority contests among unperfected security interests, some priorities are established permanently, e.g., the rights of a buyer of property who took free of a security interest under former Article 9.

One consequence of the rule in subsection (a) is that the mere taking effect of this Article does not of itself adversely affect the priority of conflicting claims to collateral.

Example 4: In 1999, SP-1 obtains a security interest in a right to payment for lottery winnings (a "general intangible" as defined in former Article 9 but an "account" as defined in this Article). SP-1's security interest is unperfected because its filed financing statement covers only "accounts." In 2000, D creates a security interest in the same right to payment in favor of SP-2, who files a financing statement covering "accounts and general intangibles." Before this Article takes effect on July 1, 2001, SP-2's perfected security interest has priority over SP-1's unperfected security interest under former Section 9-312(5). Because the relative priorities of the security interests were established before the effective date of this Article, former Article 9 continues to govern priority after this Article takes effect. Thus, SP-2's priority is not adversely affected by this Article's having taken effect.

Note that were this Article to govern priority, SP-2 would become subordinated to SP-1 under Section 9-322(a)(1), even though nothing changes other than this Article's having taken effect. Under Section 9-704, SP-1's security interest would become perfected; the financing statement covering "accounts" adequately covers the lottery winnings and complies with the other perfection requirements of this Article, e.g., it is filed in the proper office.

Example 5: In 1999, SP-1 obtains a security interest in a right to payment for lottery winnings—a "general intangible" (as defined under former Article 9). SP-1's security interest is unperfected because its filed financing statement covers only "accounts." In 2000, D creates a security interest in the same right to payment in favor of SP-2, who makes the same mistake and also files a financing statement covering only "accounts." Before this Article takes effect on July 1, 2001, SP-1's unperfected security interest has priority over SP-2's unperfected security interest, because SP-1's security interest was the first to attach. See former Section 9-312(5)(b). Because the relative priorities of the security interests were established before the effective date of this Article, former Article 9 continues to govern priority after this Article takes effect. Although Section 9-704 makes both security interests perfected for purposes of this Article, both are unperfected under former Article 9, which determines their relative priorities.

2. Financing Statements Ineffective Under Former Article 9 But Effective Under This Article. If this Article determines priority, subsection (b) may apply. It deals with the case in which a filing that occurs before the effective date of this Article would be ineffective to perfect a security interest under former Article 9 but effective under this Article. For purposes of Section 9-322(a), the priority of a security interest that attaches after this Article takes effect and is perfected in this manner dates from the time this Article takes effect.

Example 6: In 1999, SP-1 obtains a security interest in D's existing and after-acquired instruments and files a financing statement covering "instruments." In 2000, D grants a security interest in its existing and after-acquired accounts in favor of SP-2, who files a financing statement covering "accounts." After this Article takes effect on July 1, 2001, one of D's account debtors gives D a negotiable note to evidence its obligation to pay an overdue account. Under the first-to-file-or-perfect rule in Section 9-322(a), SP-1 would have priority in the instrument, which constitutes SP-2's proceeds. SP-1's filing in 1999 was earlier than SP-2's in 2000. However, subsection (b) provides that, for purposes of Section 9-322(a), SP-1's priority dates from the time this Article takes effect (July 1, 2001). Under Section 9-322(b), SP-2's priority with respect to the proceeds (instrument) dates from its filing as to the original collateral (accounts). Accordingly, SP-2's security interest would be senior.

Subsection (b) does not apply to conflicting security interests each of which is perfected by a pre-effective-date filing that was not effective under former Article 9 but is effective under this Article.

Example 7: In 1999, SP-1 obtains a security interest in D's existing and after-acquired instruments and files a financing statement covering "instruments." In 2000, D grants a security interest in its existing and after-acquired instruments in favor of SP-2, who files a financing statement covering "instruments." After this Article takes effect on July 1, 2001, one of D's account debtors gives D a negotiable note to evidence its obligation to pay an overdue account. Under the first-to-file-or-perfect rule in Section 9-322(a), SP-1 would have priority in the instrument. Both filings are effective under this Article, see Section 9-705(b), and SP-1's filing in 1999 was earlier than SP-2's in 2000. Subsection (b) does not change this result.

PART 8 TRANSITION PROVISIONS FOR 2010 AMENDMENTS

§ 9-801. Effective Date.

This [Act] takes effect on July 1, 2013.

Legislative Note: *Because these amendments change the proper place in which to file to perfect certain security interests, it is particularly important that States adopt a uniform effective date. Otherwise, the status of a particular security interest as perfected or unperfected would depend on whether the matter was litigated in a State in which the amendments were in effect or a State in which the amendments were not in effect. Any one State's failure to adopt the uniform effective date will significantly increase the cost and uncertainty surrounding the affected transactions.*

Official Comment

These transition provisions largely track the provisions of Part 7, which govern the transition to the 1998 revision of this Article. The Comments to the sections of Part 7 generally are relevant to the corresponding sections of Part 8. The 2010 amendments are less far-reaching than the 1998 revision. Although Part 8 does not carry forward those Part 7 provisions that clearly would have no application to the transition to the amendments, as a matter of prudence Part 8 does carry forward all Part 7 provisions that are even arguably relevant to the transition.

The most significant transition problem raised by the 2010 amendments arises from changes to Section 9-503(a), concerning the name of the debtor that must be provided for a financing statement to be sufficient. Sections 9-805 and 9-806 address this problem.

Example: On November 8, 2012, Debtor, an individual whose "individual name" is "Lon Debtor" and whose principal residence is located in State A, creates a security interest in certain manufacturing equipment. On November 15, 2012, SP perfects a security interest in the equipment under Article 9 (as in effect prior to the 2010 amendments) by filing a financing statement against "Lon Debtor" in the State A filing office. On July 1, 2013, the 2010 amendments, including Alternative A to Section 9-503(a), take effect in State A. Debtor's unexpired State A driver's indicates that Debtor's name is "Polonius Debtor." Assuming that a search under "Polonius Debtor" using the filing office's standard search logic would not disclose the filed financing statement, the financing statement would be insufficient under amended Section 9-503(a)(4) (Alt. A). However, Section 9-805(b) provides that the 2010 amendments do not render the financing statement ineffective. Rather, the financing statement remains effective—even if it has become seriously misleading—until it would have ceased to be effective had the amendments not taken effect. See Section 9-805(b)(1). SP can continue the effectiveness of the financing statement by filing a continuation statement with the State A filing office. To do so, however, SP must amend Debtor's name on the financing statement to provide the name that is sufficient under Section 9-503(a)(4) (Alt. A) at the time the continuation statement is filed. See Section 9-805(c), (e).

The most significant transition problem addressed by the 1998 revision arose from the change in the choice-of-law rules governing where to file a financing statement. The 2010 amendments do not change the choice-of-law rules. Even so, the amendments will change the place to file in a few cases, because certain entities that were not previously classified as "registered organizations" would fall within that category under the amendments.

§ 9-802. Savings Clause.

(a) [Pre-effective-date transactions or liens.] Except as otherwise provided in this part, this [Act] applies to a transaction or lien within its scope, even if the transaction or lien was entered into or created before this [Act] takes effect.

(b) [Pre-effective-date proceedings.] This [Act] does not affect an action, case, or proceeding commenced before this [Act] takes effect.

§ 9-803. Security Interest Perfected Before Effective Date.

(a) [Continuing perfection: perfection requirements satisfied.] A security interest that is a perfected security interest immediately before this [Act] takes effect is a perfected security interest under [Article 9 as amended by this [Act]] if, when this [Act] takes effect, the applicable requirements for attachment and perfection under [Article 9 as amended by this [Act]] are satisfied without further action.

(b) [Continuing perfection: perfection requirements not satisfied.] Except as otherwise provided in Section 9-805, if, immediately before this [Act] takes effect, a security interest is a perfected security interest, but the applicable requirements for perfection under [Article 9 as amended by this [Act]] are not satisfied when this [Act] takes effect, the security interest remains perfected thereafter only if the applicable requirements for perfection under [Article 9 as amended by this [Act]] are satisfied within one year after this [Act] takes effect.]

§ 9-804. Security Interest Unperfected Before Effective Date.

A security interest that is an unperfected security interest immediately before this [Act] takes effect becomes a perfected security interest:

(1) without further action, when this [Act] takes effect if the applicable requirements for perfection under [Article 9 as amended by this [Act]] are satisfied before or at that time; or

(2) when the applicable requirements for perfection are satisfied if the requirements are satisfied after that time.

§ 9-805. Effectiveness of Action Taken Before Effective Date.

(a) [Pre-effective-date filing effective.] The filing of a financing statement before this [Act] takes effect is effective to perfect a security interest to the extent the filing would satisfy the applicable requirements for perfection under [Article 9 as amended by this [Act]].

(b) [When pre-effective-date filing becomes ineffective.] This [Act] does not render ineffective an effective financing statement that, before this [Act] takes effect, is filed and satisfies the applicable requirements for perfection under the law of the jurisdiction governing perfection as provided in [Article 9 as it existed before amendment]. However, except as otherwise provided in subsections (c) and (d) and Section 9-806, the financing statement ceases to be effective:

(1) if the financing statement is filed in this State, at the time the financing statement would have ceased to be effective had this [Act] not taken effect; or

(2) if the financing statement is filed in another jurisdiction, at the earlier of:

(A) the time the financing statement would have ceased to be effective under the law of that jurisdiction; or

(B) June 30, 2018.

(c) [Continuation statement.] The filing of a continuation statement after this [Act] takes effect does not continue the effectiveness of a financing statement filed before this [Act] takes effect. However, upon the timely filing of a continuation statement after this [Act] takes effect and in accordance with the law of the jurisdiction governing perfection as provided in [Article 9 as amended by this [Act]], the effectiveness of a financing statement filed in the same office in that jurisdiction before this [Act] takes effect continues for the period provided by the law of that jurisdiction.

(d) [Application of subsection (b)(2)(B) to transmitting utility financing statement.] Subsection (b)(2)(B) applies to a financing statement that, before this [Act] takes effect, is filed against a transmitting utility and satisfies the applicable requirements for perfection under the law of the jurisdiction governing perfection as provided in [Article 9 as it existed before amendment], only to the extent that [Article 9 as amended by this [Act]] provides that the law of a jurisdiction other than the jurisdiction in which the financing statement is filed governs perfection of a security interest in collateral covered by the financing statement.

(e) [Application of Part 5.] A financing statement that includes a financing statement filed before this [Act] takes effect and a continuation statement filed after this [Act] takes effect is effective only to the extent that it satisfies the requirements of [Part 5 as amended by this [Act]] for an initial financing statement. A financing statement that indicates that the debtor is a decedent's estate indicates that the collateral is being administered by a personal representative within the meaning of Section 9-503(a)(2) as amended by this [Act]. A financing statement that indicates that the debtor is a trust or is a trustee acting with respect to property held in trust indicates that the collateral is held in a trust within the meaning of Section 9-503(a)(3) as amended by this [Act].

§ 9-806. When Initial Financing Statement Suffices to Continue Effectiveness of Financing Statement.

(a) [Initial financing statement in lieu of continuation statement.] The filing of an initial financing statement in the office specified in Section 9-501 continues the effectiveness of a financing statement filed before this [Act] takes effect if:

(1) the filing of an initial financing statement in that office would be effective to perfect a security interest under [Article 9 as amended by this [Act]];

(2) the pre-effective-date financing statement was filed in an office in another State; and

(3) the initial financing statement satisfies subsection (c).

(b) [Period of continued effectiveness.] The filing of an initial financing statement under subsection (a) continues the effectiveness of the pre-effective-date financing statement:

(1) if the initial financing statement is filed before this [Act] takes effect, for the period provided in [unamended Section 9-515] with respect to an initial financing statement; and

(2) if the initial financing statement is filed after this [Act] takes effect, for the period provided in Section 9-515 as amended by this [Act] with respect to an initial financing statement.

(c) [Requirements for initial financing statement under subsection (a).] To be effective for purposes of subsection (a), an initial financing statement must:

(1) satisfy the requirements of [Part 5 as amended by this [Act]] for an initial financing statement;

(2) identify the pre-effective-date financing statement by indicating the office in which the financing statement was filed and providing the dates of filing and file numbers, if any, of the financing statement and of the most recent continuation statement filed with respect to the financing statement; and

(3) indicate that the pre-effective-date financing statement remains effective.

§ 9-807. Amendment of Pre-Effective-Date Financing Statement.

(a) ["Pre-effective-date financing statement".] In this section, "pre-effective-date financing statement" means a financing statement filed before this [Act] takes effect.

(b) [Applicable law.] After this [Act] takes effect, a person may add or delete collateral covered by, continue or terminate the effectiveness of, or otherwise amend the information provided in, a pre-effective-date financing statement only in accordance with the law of the jurisdiction governing perfection as provided in [Article 9 as amended by this [Act]]. However, the effectiveness of a pre-effective-date financing statement also may be terminated in accordance with the law of the jurisdiction in which the financing statement is filed.

(c) [Method of amending: general rule.] Except as otherwise provided in subsection

(d) , if the law of this State governs perfection of a security interest, the information in a pre-effective-date financing statement may be amended after this [Act] takes effect only if:

(1) the pre-effective-date financing statement and an amendment are filed in the office specified in Section 9-501;

(2) an amendment is filed in the office specified in Section 9-501 concurrently with, or after the filing in that office of, an initial financing statement that satisfies Section 9-806(c); or

(3) an initial financing statement that provides the information as amended and satisfies Section 9-806(c) is filed in the office specified in Section 9-501.

(d) [Method of amending: continuation.] If the law of this State governs perfection of a security interest, the effectiveness of a pre-effective-date financing statement may be continued only under Section 9-805(c) and (e) or 9-806.

(e) [Method of amending: additional termination rule.] Whether or not the law of this State governs perfection of a security interest, the effectiveness of a pre-effective-date financing statement filed in this State may be terminated after this [Act] takes effect by filing a termination statement in the office in which the pre-effective-date financing statement is filed, unless an initial financing statement that satisfies Section 9-806(c) has been filed in the office specified by the law of the jurisdiction governing perfection as provided in [Article 9 as amended by this [Act]] as the office in which to file a financing statement.

§ 9-808. Person Entitled to File Initial Financing Statement or Continuation Statement. A person may file an initial financing statement or a continuation statement under this part if:

(1) the secured party of record authorizes the filing; and

(2) the filing is necessary under this part:

(A) to continue the effectiveness of a financing statement filed before this [Act] takes effect; or

(B) to perfect or continue the perfection of a security interest.

§ 9-809. Priority. This [Act] determines the priority of conflicting claims to collateral. However, if the relative priorities of the claims were established before this [Act] takes effect, [Article 9 as it existed before amendment] determines priority.

Legislative Note: *The term "this [Act]" as used in this part refers to the legislation enacting these amendments to Article 9, not to the legislation that enacted Article 9. States should substitute appropriate references.*

APPENDIX I. CONFORMING AMENDMENTS TO OTHER ARTICLES

[omitted]

APPENDIX II. MODEL PROVISIONS FOR PRODUCTION-MONEY PRIORITY

Legislative Note: *States that enact these model provisions should add the following definitions to Section 9-102(a) following the definition of "proceeds," and preceding the definition of "promissory note", renumbering paragraphs in Section 9-102(a) accordingly:*

(xx) "Production-money crops" means crops that secure a production-money obligation incurred with respect to the production of those crops.

(xx) "Production-money obligation" means an obligation of an obligor incurred for new value given to enable the debtor to produce crops if the value is in fact used for the production of the crops.

(xx) "Production of crops" includes tilling and otherwise preparing land for growing, planting, cultivating, fertilizing, irrigating, harvesting, and gathering crops, and protecting them from damage or disease.

[Model §[9-103A]. "Production-Money Crops"; "Production-Money Obligation"; Production-Money Security Interest; Burden of Establishing.

(a) A security interest in crops is a production-money security interest to the extent that the crops are production-money crops.

(b) If the extent to which a security interest is a production-money security interest depends on the application of a payment to a particular obligation, the payment must be applied:

(1) in accordance with any reasonable method of application to which the parties agree;

(2) in the absence of the parties' agreement to a reasonable method, in accordance with any intention of the obligor manifested at or before the time of payment; or

(3) in the absence of an agreement to a reasonable method and a timely manifestation of the obligor's intention, in the following order:

(A) to obligations that are not secured; and

(B) if more than one obligation is secured, to obligations secured by production-money security interests in the order in which those obligations were incurred.

(c) A production-money security interest does not lose its status as such, even if:

(1) the production-money crops also secure an obligation that is not a production-money obligation;

(2) collateral that is not production-money crops also secures the production-money obligation; or

(3) the production-money obligation has been renewed, refinanced, or restructured.

(d) A secured party claiming a production-money security interest has the burden of establishing the extent to which the security interest is a production-money security interest.]

Legislative Note: *This section is optional. States that enact this section should place it between Sections 9-103 and 9-104 and number it accordingly, e.g., as Section 9-103A or 9-103.1.*

Official Comment

1. Source. New.

2. Production-Money Priority; "Production-Money Security Interest." This section is patterned closely on Section 9-103, which defines "purchase-money security interest." Subsection (b) makes clear that a security interest can obtain production-money status only to the extent that it secures value that actually can be traced to the direct production of crops. To the extent that a security interest is not entitled to production-money treatment.

[Model §[9-324A]. Priority of Production-Money Security Interests and Agricultural Liens.

(a) Except as otherwise provided in subsections (c), (d), and (e), if the requirements of subsection (b) are met, a perfected production-money security interest in production-money crops has priority over a conflicting security interest in the same crops and, except as otherwise provided in Section 9-327, also has priority in their identifiable proceeds.

(b) A production-money security interest has priority under subsection (a) if:

(1) the production-money security interest is perfected by filing when the production-money secured party first gives new value to enable the debtor to produce the crops;

(2) the production-money secured party sends an authenticated notification to the holder of the conflicting security interest not less than 10 or more than 30 days before the production-money secured party first gives new value to enable the debtor to produce the crops if the holder had filed a financing statement covering the crops before the date of the filing made by the production-money secured party; and

(3) the notification states that the production-money secured party has or expects to acquire a production-money security interest in the debtor's crops and provides a description of the crops.

(c) Except as otherwise provided in subsection (d) or (e), if more than one security interest qualifies for priority in the same collateral under subsection (a), the security interests rank according to priority in time of filing under Section 9-322(a).

(d) To the extent that a person holding a perfected security interest in production-money crops that are the subject of a production-money security interest gives new value to enable the debtor to produce the production-money crops and the value is in fact used for the production of the production-money crops, the security interests rank according to priority in time of filing under Section 9-322(a).

(e) To the extent that a person holds both an agricultural lien and a production-money security interest in the same collateral securing the same obligations, the rules of priority applicable to agricultural liens govern priority.

Legislative Note: *This section is optional. States that enact this section should place it between Sections 9-324 and 9-325 and number it accordingly, e.g., as Section 9-324A or 9-324.1.*

Official Comment

1. Source. New; replaces former Section 9-312(2).

2. Priority of Production-Money Security Interests and Conflicting Security Interests. This section replaces the limited priority in crops afforded by former Section 9-312(2). That priority generally has been though to be of little value for its intended beneficiaries. This section attempts to balance the interests of the production-money secured party with those of a secured party who has previously filed a financing statement covering the crops that are to be produced. For example, to qualify for priority under this section, the production-money secured party must notify the earlier-filed secured party prior to extending the production-money credit. The notification affords the earlier secured party the opportunity to prevent subordination by extending the credit itself. Subsection (d) makes this explicit. If the holder of a security interest in production-money crops which conflicts with a production-money security interest gives new value for the production of the crops, the security interests rank according to priority in time of filing under Section 9-322(a).

3. Multiple Production-Money Security Interests. In the case of multiple production-money security interests that qualify for priority under subsection (a), the first to file has priority. See subsection (c). Note that only a security interest perfected by filing is entitled to production-money priority. See subsection (b)(1). Consequently, subsection (c) does not adopt the first-to-file-or-perfect formulation.

4. Holder of Agricultural Lien and Production-Money Security Interest. Subsection (e) deals with a creditor who holds both an agricultural lien and an Article 9 production-money security interest in the same collateral. In these cases, the priority rules applicable to agricultural liens govern. The creditor can avoid this result by waiving its agricultural lien.

TABLE OF DISPOSITION OF SECTIONS IN FORMER ARTICLE 9 AND OTHER CODE SECTIONS

Old Article 9	New Article 9
9-101	9-101
9-102	9-109
9-103(1)(a), (b); (c) omitted	9-301
9-103(1)(d)	9-316
9-103(2)(a), (b); (c) omitted	9-303, 9-316
9-103(2)(d)	9-337
9-103(3)(a), (b); (c) omitted	9-301
9-103(3)(d)	9-307
9-103(3)(e)	9-316
9-103(4)	9-301
9-103(5)	9-301
9-103(6)	9-304, 9-305, 9-306
9-104	9-109
9-105	9-102
9-106	9-102
9-107	9-103
9-108	Omitted as no longer needed
9-109	9-102
9-110	9-108
9-111	Deleted as unnecessary
	Omitted (see 9-102(a)(28))
9-113	9-110
9-114	Omitted (see 9-103 and 9-324)
9-115(1)	9-102, 9-106
9-115(2)	9-203, 9-308
9-115(3)	9-108
9-115(4)	9-309, 9-312, 9-314
9-115(5)	9-327, 9-328, 9-329
9-115(6)	9-203, 9-313
9-115(e)	9-106
9-116	9-206, 9-309
9-201	9-201
9-202	9-202
9-203(1)-(3)	9-203
9-203(4)	9-201
9-204	9-204
9-205	9-205
9-206	9-403
9-207	9-207
9-208	9-210
9-301(1)-(2)	9-317
9-301(3)	9-102
9-301(4)	9-323
9-302(1)	9-309, 9-310
9-302(2)	9-310
9-302(3), (4)	9-311
9-303	9-308
9-304	9-312
9-305	9-306, 9-313
9-306	9-315
9-307(1)-(2)	9-320
9-307(3)	9-323
9-308	9-330
9-309	9-331
9-310	9-333
9-311	9-401
9-312(1)	9-322
9-312(2) omitted	See Appendix II
9-312(3), (4)	9-324
9-312(5), (6)	9-322
9-312(7)	9-323
9-313(1)-(7)	9-334
9-313(8)	9-604
9-314	9-335
9-315	9-336
9-316	9-339
9-317	9-402
9-318(1)	9-404
9-318(2)	9-405
9-318(3), (4)	9-406
9-401	9-501
9-402(1)	9-504, 9-502
9-402(2)	Omitted as unnecessary
9-402(3)	9-521
9-402(4)	9-512
9-402(5), (6)	9-502
9-402(7)	9-503(a)(4), 9-507
9-402(8)	9-506
9-403(1)	9-516(a)
9-403(2)	9-515
9-403(3)	9-515, 9-522
9-403(4)	9-519
9-403(5)	9-525
9-403(6)	9-515
9-403(7)	9-519
9-404	9-513
9-405	9-514, 9-519
9-406	9-512
9-407	9-523
9-408	9-505
9-501(1), (2)	9-601
9-501(3)	9-602, 9-603
9-501(4)	9-604
9-501 (5)	9-601
9-502	9-607, 9-608
9-503	9-609
9-504(1)	9-610, 9-615
9-504(2)	9-615
9-504(3)	9-610, 9-611, 9-624
9-504(4)	9-617
9-504(5)	9-618
9-505	9-620, 9-621, 9-624
9-506	9-623, 9-624

TABLE INDICATING SOURCES OR DERIVATIONS OF NEW ARTICLE 9 SECTIONS AND CONFORMING AMENDMENTS

New Article 9 sections	Old Article 9, and other code sections (Note: Many sections contain some new coverage)
9-101	9-101
9-102	9-105, 9-106, 9-109,9-301(3), 9-306(1),
9-103	9-115, 2-326(3)
9-103	9-107
9-104 (New)	Derived from 8-106
9-105 (New)	Derived from 8-106
9-106	8-106 and 9-115(e)
9-107 (New)	Derived from 8-106
9-108	9-110, 9-115(3)
9-109	9-102, 9-104
9-110	9-113
9-201	9-201, 9-203(4)
9-202	9-202
9-203	9-203, 9-115(2), (6)
9-204	9-204
9-205	9-205
9-206	9-116
9-207	9-207
9-208 (New)	
9-209 (New)	
9-210	9-208
9-301	9-103(1)(a),(b), 9-103(3) (a), (b), 9-103(4),
9-302	9-103(5) substantially modified
9-302 (New)	
9-303	9-103(2)(a), (b), substantially revised
9-304 (New)	Derived from 8-110(e) and former 9-103(6)
9-305	9-103(6)
9-306 (New)	Derived in part from 8-110(e) and 9-305 and former 9-103(6)
9-307	9-103(3)(d), as substantially revised
9-308	9-303, 9-115(2)
9-309	9-302(1), 9-115(4)(c), (d), 9-116
9-310	9-302(1), (2)
9-311	9-302(3), (4)
9-312	9-115(4) and 9-304, with additions and some changes
9-313	9-305, 9-115(6)
9-314 (New in part)	9-115(4) and derived from 8-106
9-315	9-306
9-316	9-103(1)(d), (2)(b), (3)(e), as modified
9-317	9-301, 2A-307(2)
9-318 (New)	
9-319 (New)	
9-320	9-307
9-321	2A-103(1)(o), 2A-307(3)
9-322	9-312(5), (6)
9-323	9-312(7), 9-301(4), 9-307(3), 2A-307(4)
9-324	9-312(3), (4)
9-325 (New)	But see 9-402(7)
9-326 (New)	But see 9-402(7)
9-327	Derived from 9-115(5)
9-328	9-115(5)
9-329 (New)	Loosely modeled after former 9-115(5). See also 5-114 and 5-118
9-330	9-308
9-331	9-309
9-332 (New)	But see Comment 2(c) to 9-306
9-333	9-310
9-334	9-313
9-335 (New)	Section replaces former 9-314
9-336 (New)	Section replaces former 9-315
9-337	Derived from 9-103(2)(d)
9-338 (New)	
9-339	9-316
9-340 (New)	
9-341 (New)	
9-342 (New)	Derived from 8-106(g)
9-401	9-311
9-402	9-317
9-403	9-206
9-404	9-318(1)
9-405	9-318(2)
9-406	9-318(3), (4)
9-407	2A-303
9-408 (New)	
9-409 (New)	See also 5-114
9-501	Derived from former 9-401
9-502	9-402(1), (5), (6)
9-503 (New)	Subsection (a)(4), (b) and (c) derive from former 9-402(7); otherwise, new
9-504	9-402(1)
9-505	9-408
9-506	9-402(8)
9-507	9-402(7)
9-508 (New)	But see 9-402(7)
9-509 (New)	
9-510 (New)	
9-511 (New)	
9-512	9-402(4)
9-513	9-404
9-514	9-405
9-515	9-403(2), (3), (6)

9-516 (Basically New)	Subsection (a) is former 9-403(1); the remainder is new
9-517 (New)	
9-518 (New)	
9-519	9-403(4), (7); 9-405(2)
9-520 (New)	
9-521 (New)	
9-522	9-403(3), revised substantially
9-523	9-407; subsections (d) and (e) are new
9-524 (New)	Derived from 4-109
9-525	Various sections of former Part 4
9-526 (New)	Subsection (b) derives in part from the Uniform Consumer Credit Code (1974)
9-527 (New)	Derived in part from the Uniform Consumer Credit Code (1974)
9-601	9-501(1), (2), (5)
9-602	9-501(3)
9-603	9-501(3)
9-604	9-501(4), 9-313(8)
9-605 (New)	
9-606 (New)	
9-607	9-502, subsections (b), (d), and (e) are new
9-608	Subsection (a) is new. Subsection (b) derives from former 9-502(2)
9-609	9-503
9-610	9-504(1), (3)
9-611	9-504(3)
9-612 (New)	
9-613 (New)	
9-614 (New)	
9-615	9-504(1), (2)
9-616 (New)	
9-617	9-504(4)
9-618	9-504(5)
9-619 (New)	
9-620	9-505
9-621	9-505
9-622 (New)	
9-623	9-506
9-624	9-504(3), 9-505, 9-506
9-625	9-507
9-626 (New)	
9-627	9-507(2)
9-628 (New)	
9-701	No comparable provision in Article 9 (See Article 10)
9-702	No comparable provision in Article 9 (See Article 10)
9-703	No comparable provision in Article 9 (See Article 10)
9-704	No comparable provision in Article 9 (See Article 10)
9-705	No comparable provision in Article 9 (See Article 10)
9-706	No comparable provision in Article 9 (See Article 10)
9-707	No comparable provision in Article 9 (See Article 10)
9-708	No comparable provision in Article 9 (See Article 10)
9-709	No comparableprovision in Article 9(See Article 10)

UNIFORM COMMERCIAL CODE

Article 12—Controllable Electronic Records

PREFATORY NOTE TO ARTICLE 12

Section

12-101. Title.

12-102. Definitions.

12-103. Relation to Article 9 and Consumer Laws.

12-104. Rights in Controllable Account, Controllable Electronic Record, and Controllable Payment Intangible.

12-105. Control of Controllable Electronic Record.

12-106. Discharge of Account Debtor on Controllable Account or Controllable Payment Intangible.

12-107. Governing Law

ARTICLE 12

CONTROLLABLE ELECTRONIC RECORDS

Prefatory Note to Article 12

1. Introduction to Controllable Electronic Records. Article 12, which deals with controllable electronic records, and the conforming amendments to Articles 1 and 9, in particular, are a major part of the effort to adapt the UCC to emerging technologies as they might affect electronic commerce.

Article 12 creates a legal regime that is meant to apply more broadly than to electronic (intangible) assets that are created using existing technologies such as distributed ledger technology (DLT), including blockchain technology, which records transactions in bitcoin and other digital assets. It also aspires to apply to electronic assets that may be created using technologies that have yet to be developed, or even imagined.

The adoption of DLT has underscored two important trends in electronic commerce. First, people have begun to assign economic value to some electronic records that bear no relationship to extrinsic rights and interests. For example, without any law or legally enforceable agreement, people around the world have agreed to treat virtual currencies such as bitcoin (or, more precisely "transaction outputs" generated by the Bitcoin protocol) as a medium of exchange and store of value. Second, people are using the creation or transfer of electronic records to transfer rights to receive payment, rights to receive performance of other obligations (e.g., services or delivery of goods), and other rights and interests in personal and real property.

These trends will inevitably result in disputes among claimants to electronic records and their related rights and other benefits. Uncertainty as to the criteria for resolving these claims creates commercial risk. The magnitude of these risks will grow as these trends continue.

As explained in more detail below, Article 12 is designed to reduce these risks by providing legal rules governing the transfer—both outright and for security—of interests in some, but not all, electronic records (controllable electronic records). These rules specify certain rights in a controllable electronic record that a purchaser would acquire. Many systems for transferring controllable electronic records are pseudonymous, so that the transferee of a controllable electronic record may be unable to verify the identity of the transferor or the source of the transferor's title. Accordingly, the Article 12 rules would make controllable electronic records negotiable, in the sense that a qualifying good faith purchaser for value could take a controllable electronic record free of third-party claims of a property interest in the controllable electronic record.

Experience with DLT and other records-management systems has established some general functions required for electronic records to serve as an effective and reliable means of transferring economic value.

- The electronic record must have some "use" or benefit that one person can enjoy and can exclude all others from enjoying, e.g., the power to "spend" a bitcoin (or, more precisely, the power to include an unspent transaction output (a UTXO) in a message that the Bitcoin protocol will record to its blockchain).
- A person must be able to transfer to another person this exclusive power to use and the exclusive power to transfer the electronic record. To remain exclusive, the transfer must divest the transferor of the power to use the electronic record.
- A person must be able to demonstrate to others that the person has the power to use and transfer control of the electronic record.

As discussed in the Comments to Section 12-105, these functions form the basis of the Article 12 concept of control. To receive the benefits of negotiability and take free of third-party claims of a property interest in a controllable electronic record, a person must have control of the controllable electronic record. In addition, control serves as a method of perfection of a security interest in a controllable electronic record and as a condition for achieving a non-temporal priority of a security interest. In this context, it may be useful to think of control as the functional analogue of possession of tangible personal property such as goods. Note that the concept of control allows for certain exceptions to the exclusivity of powers.

Article 12 governs certain rights (primarily property rights) of transacting parties and other persons that might be affected by the transactions. Article 12 does not govern assets other than controllable electronic records except, in coordination with Article 9, controllable accounts and controllable payment intangibles evidenced by controllable electronic records (discussed below). Like the UCC in general, Article 12 is not a regulatory statute. The fact that an asset is or is not a controllable electronic record under the UCC would not necessarily affect the application of laws regulating, for example, banking, securities, commodities, money transmission, and taxation.

2. Scope of Article 12. Article 12 applies to controllable electronic records. Controllable electronic records are a subset of what often are referred to as digital assets. Article 12 is designed to work for both technologies that are known and those that may be developed in the future. Whether an asset is a controllable electronic record (and therefore within the scope of Article 12) depends on whether the characteristics of the asset and the protocols of any system on which the asset is recorded make it suitable for the application of Article 12's substantive rules. The nature of electronic commerce is constantly changing. For this reason, the technology on which an asset depends, the type of asset, and the prevailing use of the asset should all be irrelevant to whether the asset is a controllable electronic record.

To determine whether Article 12 applies to a particular asset, for example, bitcoin, one must determine whether the asset falls within the definition of controllable electronic record. A controllable electronic record is a record, as the UCC defines the term. A record is information that is retrievable in perceivable form. Section 1-201(b)(31) (defining "record"). A controllable electronic record is a record that is stored in an electronic medium and that can be subjected to control, as defined in Section 12-105. Sections 1-201(b)(16A) (defining "electronic"); 12- 102(a)(1) (defining "controllable electronic record"). An electronic record that cannot be subjected to control under Section 12-105 is outside the scope of Article 12. As already mentioned, Article 12 addresses primarily certain property rights in controllable electronic records. Of course, that an electronic record is not subject to control does not imply that it does not have commercial utility. Businesses generate and sell or license large quantities of electronic records that do not require the attributes of negotiability that Article 12 affords to controllable electronic records.

The meaning of control in the UCC depends on the type of property involved. See Sections 7-106 (electronic documents of title); 8-106 (four different types of investment property, each with a different definition of "control"); 9-104 (deposit accounts); 9-105 (chattel paper); 9-105A (electronic money). The Comments to Section 12-105 explain the requirements for obtaining control of a controllable electronic record. For present purposes of exposition, it is sufficient to think of bitcoin and other virtual currencies as prototypical controllable electronic records. The provisions under other law that govern control and other matters for other types of electronic records (some of which are modified by these amendments) are not addressed by Article 12.

3. Substantive Provisions of Article 12. The principal function of Article 12 is to specify certain rights of a purchaser of a controllable electronic record. A purchaser is a person that acquires an interest in property by a voluntary transaction, such as a sale. Section 1-201(b)(29) (defining "purchase"), (30) (defining "purchaser"). Purchasers include both buyers and secured parties. Law other than Article 12 would determine whether a person acquires any rights in a controllable electronic record and so would be eligible to be a purchaser. Section 12-104(c).

Section 12-104 adopts the "shelter" principle, under which a purchaser of a controllable electronic record acquires whatever rights the transferor had or had power to transfer. Section 12-104(d). A similar rule appears in Articles 2, 3, 7, and 8. See Sections 2-403(1) (goods); 3- 203(b) (negotiable instruments); 7-504(a) (documents of title); 8-302(a) (certificated and uncertificated securities).

The ability to take a controllable electronic record free of third-party property claims appears to be necessary for a controllable electronic record to have commercial utility. As is the case with Articles 2, 3, 7, and 9, Article 12 would facilitate commerce by affording to certain good-faith purchasers for value (buyers as well as secured parties) greater rights than their transferors had or had power to transfer. (Article 8 also provides for certain purchasers for value to take greater rights than their transferors had, but does not contain an explicit good-faith requirement. See Section 8-303.) Article 12 refers to these purchasers as qualifying purchasers. Qualifying purchasers are purchasers that obtain control of a controllable electronic record for value, in good faith, and without notice of any claim of a property interest in the controllable electronic record. Section 12-102(a)(2). Like a holder in due course of a negotiable instrument, a qualifying purchaser of a controllable electronic record takes the controllable electronic record free of property claims. Section 12-104(e).

Consider an example in which B contracts to buy bitcoin from S.

- Law other than Article 12 generally would determine whether S is the owner of the bitcoin.
- Law other than Article 12 would resolve issues concerning the formation of the contract of sale between B and S and the obligations of the parties under the contract.
- Except to the extent provided by Article 12, law other than Article 12 would determine what steps are necessary for B to acquire rights in the bitcoin.
- By acquiring rights in the bitcoin by sale, B would become a purchaser of the bitcoin within the meaning of UCC Article 1.
- Article 12 provides that if B becomes a purchaser, B will acquire whatever rights S had or had power to transfer. As a general matter, law other than Article 12 would define these rights. B would acquire these rights regardless of whether B obtained control of the bitcoin.

In this example, law other than Article 12 includes UCC Article 9, which determines the steps necessary for a security interest to attach to a controllable electronic record. More generally, Article 9 governs any conflict between Article 9 and Article 12. Section 12-103(a).

Now assume that O is the owner of the bitcoin and that S is a hacker, who acquired control of the bitcoin illegally from O.

- Just as a buyer of goods can obtain possession from a seller that has no rights in the goods, B can obtain control of the bitcoin, even if S "stole" it from O.
- If B obtains control of the bitcoin for value, in good faith, and without notice of any claim of a property interest, B would be a qualifying purchaser.
- Even if B would not have acquired any rights in the bitcoin under non-Article 12 law (for example, because S, a "thief," had no rights to give), as an Article 12 qualifying purchaser, B would acquire the bitcoin free of all claims of a property interest in the bitcoin. S's control of the bitcoin gave S the power to transfer rights to a qualifying purchaser, such as B. Even if O could locate B, B would defeat O's claim of ownership and own the bitcoin free and clear. (The same result would obtain if B bought a negotiable instrument from a thief under circumstances where B became a holder in due course. This distinguishes "negotiable" property from property such as goods, as to which a buyer from a thief normally obtains no rights.)

4. Rights or Property Linked to a Controllable Electronic Record.

a. General Rules. Recall that a controllable electronic record is a record, i.e., information. Some records have what one might call "inherent value" solely because the market treats them as having value. Bitcoin would be an example of such a record. Bitcoin can be exchanged (sold) for cash or other valuable assets. Or, the owner of bitcoin can hold the bitcoin as an investment.

The value of many records, however, is as evidence of the rights of the parties to a transaction or of the rights of a party in other property. In these situations, it is essential to differentiate between the record and the rights that are evidenced by the record.

Suppose, for example, that S and B enter into a written contract for the sale of 100 air purifiers. The contract provides that at a specified time in the future, S is to deliver the goods and B is to pay for them. B may sell (assign) to P the right to receive delivery of the goods from S. P has acquired a valuable asset, i.e., the right to receive delivery.

In contrast, if B sells to P only the paper (record) on which the contract is written, P might or might not acquire the right to delivery of the goods, depending on whether applicable law treats the sale of the paper as an assignment of the right to delivery (as can be the case with a negotiable document of title under UCC Article 7). P would become the owner of the paper in any event, but the paper itself may be of little value.

If the contract for the sale of air purifiers were electronic rather than written, the same analysis would apply. The right evidenced by the electronic record (i.e., B's right to receive delivery from S) would be the valuable asset, not the record itself.

Suppose that the contract of sale between B and S is evidenced by a controllable electronic record that B sells to P. Under Section 12-104(d), P would acquire all rights in the controllable electronic record that the transferor (B) had or had power to transfer. If P obtains control of the controllable electronic record for value, in good faith, and without notice of any claim of a property right in the controllable electronic record, P will become a qualifying purchaser and, as such, would acquire its rights in the controllable electronic record free of any claim of a property right under Section 12-104.

But the controllable electronic record itself may or may not be a valuable asset. In this example, unlike bitcoin, the record would have value to P only if by virtue of acquiring rights in the controllable electronic record, P would also acquire the right to receive delivery of the goods from S.

Except to the extent provided by Article 12, that Article leaves to other law the question whether P's acquisition of rights in the controllable electronic record gives P the right to receive delivery of the goods. Section 12-104(f). We would typically expect that under other law P would not acquire the right to receive the goods merely by acquiring rights in the controllable electronic record, any more than P would have acquired the right to receive the goods if the record were in paper form, the paper were physically delivered to P, and P acquired rights in the paper.

Suppose, however, that other law does provide that, by acquiring the controllable electronic record, P would acquire the right to receive delivery of the goods from S. Suppose also that P becomes a qualifying purchaser of the controllable electronic record. As we have seen, as a qualifying purchaser, P would take its rights in the controllable electronic record free of property claims. But even though under non-Article 12 law P would (as posited) acquire the right to receive delivery of the goods, P would not acquire that right free of property claims unless non-Article 12 law also were to provide otherwise. Section 12-104(f).

b. Exceptions: Controllable Accounts and Controllable Payment Intangibles. As a general rule, Article 12 applies to records and not to rights evidenced by records (or to rights that records are purported to evidence). And, in general, law other than Article 12 would govern what steps must be taken or conditions must be satisfied for a person to acquire an interest in a controllable electronic record and the rights, if any, that the person acquires in other property (including a right to payment or performance of an obligation) as a result of acquiring an interest in the record. This "other" law includes UCC Article 9.

Article 12 provides an important exception to this general rule. The exception concerns rights to payment (specifically, accounts and payment intangibles) that are evidenced by a controllable electronic record and as to which the obligor (account debtor) undertakes to pay the person that has control of the controllable electronic record. These rights to payment are referred to as "controllable accounts" and "controllable payment intangibles." See Section 9-102(a)(27A) (defining "controllable account") and (27B) (defining "controllable payment intangible"). A qualifying purchaser of a controllable account or controllable payment intangible takes free of property claims and is protected from certain actions. See Section 12-104(a) through (e), (g), and (h), and Comments 6 through 10. As to the feasibility and rationale for this exception for controllable accounts and controllable payment intangibles, see Section 12-104, Comments 9 and 10.

The 2022 Article 9 Revisions amend several sections of Article 9 to deal with various aspects of security interests in controllable accounts, controllable electronic records, and controllable payment intangibles. See Sections 9-101, Comment 4.a.; 9-102, Comment 5.d.1.

5. Governing Law for Article 12. Section 12-107 provides rules on governing law. The general rule under subsection (a) is that the local law of a "controllable electronic record's jurisdiction" governs matters covered by Article 12. The controllable electronic record's jurisdiction is determined by an express provision in the record or in the system in which the record is recorded. If not so designated, it is determined based on the designation of the law governing the record or the system generally.

Absent any such designations, at the bottom of this "waterfall" of alternatives, the governing law will be that of the District of Columbia. Subsection (b) provides an exception for the rights and duties of account debtors under Section 12-106 if an agreement between the account debtor and an assignor of the record provides for the law of another jurisdiction to govern those rights and duties.

The law of the controllable electronic record's jurisdiction also governs perfection and priority of security interests in controllable electronic records, controllable accounts, and controllable payment intangibles. Perfection by filing, however, is governed by the law of the location of the debtor. See Section 9-306B.

§ 12-101. Title.

This article may be cited as Uniform Commercial Code—Controllable Electronic Records.

Official Comment

Subsection headings. Subsection headings are not a part of the official text itself and have not been approved by the sponsors. See Section 1-107, Comment 1.

§ 12-102. Definitions.

(a) [Article 12 definitions.] In this article:

(1) "Controllable electronic record" means a record stored in an electronic medium that can be subjected to control under Section 12-105. The term does not include a controllable account, a controllable payment intangible, a deposit account, an electronic copy of a record evidencing chattel paper, an electronic document of title, electronic money, investment property, or a transferable record.

(2) "Qualifying purchaser" means a purchaser of a controllable electronic record or an interest in a controllable electronic record that obtains control of the controllable electronic record for value, in good faith, and without notice of a claim of a property right in the controllable electronic record.

(3) "Transferable record" has the meaning provided for that term in:

(A) Section 201(a)(1) of the Electronic Signatures in Global and National Commerce Act, 15 U.S.C. Section 7021(a)(1)[, as amended]; or

(B) [cite to Uniform Electronic Transactions Act Section 16(a)].

(4) "Value" has the meaning provided in Section 3-303(a), as if references in that subsection to an "instrument" were references to a controllable account, controllable electronic record, or controllable payment intangible.

(b) [Definitions in Article 9.] The definitions in Article 9 of "account debtor", "controllable account", "controllable payment intangible", "chattel paper", "deposit account", "electronic money", and "investment property" apply to this article.

(c) [Article 1 definitions and principles.] Article 1 contains general definitions and principles of construction and interpretation applicable throughout this article.

Legislative Note: *It is the intent of this act to incorporate future amendments to the federal law cited in subsection (a)(3)(A). A state in which the constitution or other law does not permit incorporation of future amendments when a federal statute is incorporated into state law should omit the phrase "[as amended]". A state in which, in the absence of a legislative declaration, future amendments are incorporated into state law also should omit the phrase.*

In subsection (a)(3)(B), the state should cite to the state's version of the Uniform Electronic Transactions Act Section 16(a) or comparable state law.

Official Comment

1. **Source.** Subsection (a)(2), defining "qualifying purchaser," derives from Section 3-302(a)(2), which defines "holder in due course" of a negotiable instrument.

2. **"Controllable electronic record."** To be a "controllable electronic record" (CER) within the scope of Article 12, an electronic record must be susceptible of control under Section 12-105. Unlike "transferable records" under the Electronic Signatures in Global and National Commerce Act (E-SIGN) or a "transferable record" under the Uniform Electronic Transactions Act (UETA), a record can be a CER under Article 12 in the absence of an agreement to that effect.

This definition uses the term "record," defined in Section 1-201 to include "information... that is stored in an electronic or other medium and is retrievable in perceivable form." The term "electronic" also is defined in Section 1-201. These broad definitions of "record" and "electronic" necessarily produce an expansive meaning of "electronic record." An electronic record would include, for example, music stored on compact disks, email messages, digital photos, personal and other information stored on a social media platform, and all types of databases stored on in an electronic medium. But most of these electronic records typically would not fall within the definition of a CER in subsection (a)(1), which includes only those electronic records "that can be subjected to control under Section 12-105." See generally Prefatory Note 2.

Consider, for example, a so-called "page" on a social media platform. Generalizations about social media/social networking platforms are difficult and these systems no doubt will continue to evolve. But these platforms typically involve licensing arrangements with users that do not permit the users (or anyone) to acquire the exclusive powers contemplated by the definition of "control" in Section 12-105. Consequently, these electronic records are not controllable electronic records as defined.

The provisions of Article 12 also do not apply to certain specified types of electronic records, and the definition has been limited accordingly. For example, the definition does not include a "transferable record" under E-SIGN or UETA. It also does not include "investment property," as defined in Section 9-102(a)(49). For this reason, the rights of an entitlement holder in a controllable electronic record that is a financial asset with respect to which the entitlement holder has a security entitlement are excluded from the definition (although the entitlement holder's securities intermediary may hold directly an interest in a controllable electronic record that it has credited to a securities account). See Sections 8-102(a)(9) (defining "financial asset"), (a)(14) (defining "securities intermediary"), (a)(17) (defining "security entitlement"), and Comment 9; 9-102(a)(49) (defining "investment property"). See also Section 8-103(h), clarifying that a controllable electronic record is not a "financial asset" except pursuant to Section 8- 102(a)(9)(iii).

A controllable electronic record is not itself a "security," defined in part in Section 8- 102(a)(15) as "an obligation of an issuer or a share, participation, or other interest in an issuer or in property or an enterprise of an issuer." It also is not "a share or similar equity interest," an "investment company security," or "an interest in a partnership or limited liability company." See Section 8-103(a), (b), and (c). For a discussion of the roles that controllable electronic records may play in transactions involving uncertificated securities, see Section 8-102, Comment 18.

3. "Qualifying purchaser." The conditions for becoming a qualifying purchaser were drawn from Article 3. More specifically, the conditions for becoming a qualifying purchaser were drawn from Section 3-302(a)(2), which defines "holder in due course" of a negotiable instrument. Among these conditions is that a person take the instrument "for value."

See subsection (a)(4) (defining "value") and Comment 5. To meet the requirements for a qualifying purchaser under subsection (a)(2) there must be a time at which all of the requirements are satisfied. For example, if a purchaser obtains notice of a claim of a property right before giving value or satisfying the requirements for control, the purchaser cannot be a qualifying purchaser.

Under Section 12-104(a), not only a purchaser of a controllable electronic record but also a purchaser of a controllable account or controllable payment intangible may be a qualifying purchaser. Moreover, a purchaser of a controllable account or a controllable payment intangible may be a qualifying purchaser even if the purchaser does not also purchase the controllable electronic record that evidences the account or payment intangible. For example, a secured party having a security interest in all of a debtor's accounts and payment intangibles would be a purchaser of those rights to payment, which would include the debtor's controllable accounts and payment intangibles. If the secured party were to obtain control of the debtor's controllable account or payment intangible, it would become a qualifying purchaser if it also met the other conditions for that status. However, to obtain control of the controllable account or controllable payment intangible, a requirement for qualifying purchaser status, the purchaser must obtain control of the controllable electronic record evidencing the controllable account or controllable payment intangible. Section 12-104(b); see also Section 9-107A. A person need not be a purchaser, however, to obtain control of a controllable electronic record.

4. "Transferable record." This definition facilitates the exclusion of transferable records from the definition of controllable electronic record.

5. "Value." This definition adopts the concept of value in Section 3-303, which is narrower than the generally applicable concept in Section 1-204. Comment 10 to Section 12-104 explains the difference between the two concepts.

§ 12-103. Relation to Article 9 and Consumer Laws.

(a) [Article 9 governs in case of conflict.] If there is conflict between this article and Article 9, Article 9 governs.

(b) [Applicable consumer law and other laws.] A transaction subject to this article is subject to any applicable rule of law that establishes a different rule for consumers and [insert reference to (i) any other statute or regulation that regulates the rates, charges, agreements, and practices for loans, credit sales, or other extensions of credit and (ii) any consumer-protection statute or regulation].

Official Comment

Source. Subsection (a) follows Section 3-102(b). Notwithstanding subsection (a), as is the case with respect to Article 3, Article 9 explicitly defers to Article 12 in some instances. See, e.g., Section 9-331. Subsection (b) is copied from Section 9-201(b). To the extent that Article 9 contains provisions described in subsection (b), subsections (a) and (b) are not mutually exclusive.

§ 12-104. Rights in Controllable Account, Controllable Electronic Record, and Controllable Payment Intangible.

(a) [Applicability of section to controllable account and controllable payment intangible.] This section applies to the acquisition and purchase of rights in a controllable account or controllable payment intangible, including the rights and benefits under subsections (c), (d), (e), (g), and (h) of a purchaser and qualifying purchaser, in the same manner this section applies to a controllable electronic record.

(b) [Control of controllable account and controllable payment intangible.] To determine whether a purchaser of a controllable account or a controllable payment intangible is a qualifying purchaser, the purchaser obtains control of the account or payment intangible if it obtains control of the controllable electronic record that evidences the account or payment intangible.

(c) [Applicability of other law to acquisition of rights.] Except as provided in this section, law other than this article determines whether a person acquires a right in a controllable electronic record and the right the person acquires.

(d) [Shelter principle and purchase of limited interest.] A purchaser of a controllable electronic record acquires all rights in the controllable electronic record that the transferor had or had power to transfer, except that a purchaser of a limited interest in a controllable electronic record acquires rights only to the extent of the interest purchased.

(e) [Rights of qualifying purchaser.] A qualifying purchaser acquires its rights in the controllable electronic record free of a claim of a property right in the controllable electronic record.

(f) [Limitation of rights of qualifying purchaser in other property.] Except as provided in subsections (a) and (e) for a controllable account and a controllable payment intangible or law other than this article, a qualifying purchaser takes a right to payment, right to performance, or other interest in property evidenced by the controllable electronic record subject to a claim of a property right in the right to payment, right to performance, or other interest in property.

(g) [No-action protection for qualifying purchaser.] An action may not be asserted against a qualifying purchaser based on both a purchase by the qualifying purchaser of a controllable electronic record and a claim of a property right in another controllable electronic record, whether the action is framed in conversion, replevin, constructive trust, equitable lien, or other theory.

(h) [Filing not notice.] Filing of a financing statement under Article 9 is not notice of a claim of a property right in a controllable electronic record.

Official Comment

1. Source. Subsection (d) derives from Section 2-403(1) (concerning the rights of a purchaser).

Subsection (e) derives from Sections 3-306 (concerning the rights of a holder in due course of an instrument) and 8-303 (concerning rights of a protected purchaser of a security).

Subsection (g) derives from Section 8-502 (protecting entitlement holders).

Subsection (h) derives from Section 9-331(c) (filing under Article 9 does not provide notice for purposes of protections of purchasers under other articles).

2. Applicability of section to controllable accounts and controllable payment intangibles. Under subsection (a), the provisions of this section apply to controllable accounts and controllable payment intangibles in the same manner that they apply to controllable electronic records. For example, a qualifying purchaser of a controllable account that obtains control of the controllable electronic record that evidences the account (and who thereby obtains control of the account under subsection (b) and Section 9-107A) would take the account free of conflicting claims of a property right in the account under subsection (e). Under subsection (b), for purposes of determining whether a purchaser of a controllable account or controllable payment intangible obtains control, the purchaser obtains control by obtaining control of the controllable electronic record that evidences the account or payment intangible. Unless otherwise specified or the context otherwise requires, references to a controllable electronic record in the official comments in this Article also refer to a controllable account or controllable payment intangible.

3. Applicability of other law. As a general matter, subsection (c) leaves to other law the resolution of questions concerning the transfer of rights in a controllable electronic record, such as the acts that must be taken to effectuate a transfer of rights and the scope of the rights that a transferee acquires. Subsections (d) through (h) contain important exceptions to subsection (c).

> **Example 1:** A creates a controllable electronic record. Although the system in which the electronic record is recorded may determine how the electronic record can be used and control may be transferred, other law would determine what rights A has in the controllable electronic record.

If, for example, A created the electronic record in the scope of its employment, A's rights would be subject to the terms of A's employment contract.

A and B agree to the sale of the controllable electronic record to B. Other law would determine what steps need to be taken for B to acquire rights in the controllable electronic record. Once B acquires those rights under other law, B would be a purchaser (as defined in Section 1-201), whose rights also would be determined by subsection (d) (i.e., the shelter principle, discussed below in Comment 4). However, even if B did not acquire rights under other law, if B met the requirements for a qualifying purchaser, its rights would be determined by subsections (e) and (g). See Comments 7 and 8, below.

The "law other than this article" that may apply to the transfer of rights in a controllable electronic record under subsection (c) includes UCC Article 9. Section 9-203 would apply, for example, to determine whether a purported secured party acquired an enforceable security interest in a controllable electronic record.

4. Purchaser and transferor under subsection (d): shelter principle and resulting controllable electronic records. Subsection (d) sets forth the familiar "shelter" principle, under which a purchaser of a controllable electronic record acquires whatever rights the transferor had or had power to transfer. However, in some cases the controllable electronic record that is acquired by the purchaser will not be the "same" controllable electronic record that was transferred by the transferor. Such a transfer might involve the elimination of a "transferred" controllable electronic record and the resulting and corresponding derivative creation and acquisition of a new controllable electronic record. An example of such a resulting controllable electronic record is the unspent transaction output (UTXO) generated by a transaction in bitcoin.

The Bitcoin protocol operates by allowing users to "spend" their UTXOs to create one or more new UTXOs for the same amount of bitcoin, so each transfer produces new UTXOs controlled by the transferees (one of which may be the transferor—spender—of the bitcoin). Subsection (d) should be construed broadly to encompass such transfers and resulting derivative controllable electronic records acquired by a purchaser. Because subsection (d) addresses the rights of a purchaser in the "purchased" asset and not the "transferred" asset, this construction is wholly consistent with the statutory text.

Notwithstanding the broad subsection (d) shelter principle, which provides that a purchaser acquires "all rights" of the transferor, those rights are subject to the reach of Section 1- 304. Under that section a contract or duty under the UCC imposes an overarching "obligation of good faith in its performance and enforcement." Section 1-304. In this context, "performance and enforcement" include the exercise of rights under the UCC, such as the rights conferred on a purchaser by the subsection (d) shelter principle. See Section 1-304, Comment 2. For example, consider a qualifying purchaser of a controllable electronic record, controllable account, or controllable payment intangible who then sells that asset to a person who is not a qualifying purchaser. If the second purchaser had previously engaged in fraudulent or illegal activity in connection with the purchased asset or an asset to which the purchased asset is attributable, the purchaser's exercise of rights under subsection (d) as to the purchased asset may be in breach of its obligation of good faith. Section 3-203(b) states this result directly with respect to a transferee of a negotiable instrument if the transferee previously engaged in fraud or illegality with respect to the same instrument. Section 3-203(b). The same result would apply under subsection (d).

Subsection (d) relies on the application of the general obligation of good faith under Section 1- 304 to reach the appropriate result. However, unlike negotiable instruments, many controllable electronic records are fungible. For this reason, in some cases it might not be possible to establish that an acquired controllable electronic record has a sufficient nexus with a transferee's earlier fraud or illegality.

5. Nonpurchaser having control. Under Section 12-105, a person may have control of a controllable electronic record even if the person has no property interest in the controllable electronic record. A person that has control of, but no property interest in, a controllable electronic record would not be a purchaser of the controllable electronic record and so would not be eligible to be a qualifying purchaser under this section.

> **Example 2:** Debtor granted to Secured Party a security interest in all Debtor's existing and after-acquired accounts, chattel paper, and payment intangibles. Secured Party perfected its security interest in a specific controllable account by obtaining control of the controllable electronic record that evidences the controllable account. See Section 9- 107A.

Because Debtor's security agreement does not cover controllable electronic records, Secured Party would have no interest in the controllable electronic record. Accordingly, Secured Party would not be a purchaser of the controllable electronic record. However, as a purchaser of the controllable accounts and controllable payment intangibles, Secured Party could benefit from the take-free rule in subsection (e) (discussed in Comment 7).

6. Distinction between controllable electronic record and controllable account or controllable payment intangible evidenced by the controllable electronic record. Even though a controllable electronic record evidences a controllable account or controllable payment intangible, the controllable electronic record is distinct from the account or payment intangible that it evidences. The account or payment intangible is connected with (or "tethered" to) the electronic record by virtue of the relevant account debtor's obligation to pay the person in control of the controllable electronic record. Moreover, control of the controllable account or payment intangible is achieved only by obtaining control of the controllable electronic record that evidences the account or payment intangible. Example 2 explains that a purchaser may obtain a property interest in the controllable account or controllable payment intangible even if it does not acquire any interest in the controllable electronic record that evidences the account or payment intangible. (On the other hand, merely obtaining control of a controllable electronic record does not result in the acquisition of an interest in the record.) This approach is intended to avoid a trap for the unwary purchaser that obtains an interest in the account or payment intangible (which is the asset that has stand-alone value) but might fail to acquire an interest in the related controllable electronic record. However, good practice may encourage a purchaser to acquire an interest in the controllable electronic record as well, which would eliminate any potential confusion.

7. The take-free rule. Subsection (e) makes controllable electronic records and, under subsection (a), controllable accounts and controllable payment intangibles, highly negotiable. Subsection (e) derives from Section 3-306, under which a holder in due course takes a negotiable instrument free of a claim of a property right in the instrument. A qualifying purchaser of a controllable electronic record, controllable account, or controllable payment intangible takes free of all claims of a property right in the purchased controllable electronic record, account, or payment intangible.

> **Example 3:** Hacker, a thief, "steals" and obtains control of a controllable electronic record. Hacker then sells the controllable electronic record to Buyer, who obtains control and otherwise meets the requirements for a qualifying purchaser (by obtaining control and purchasing for value, in good faith, and without notice of a claim of a property right).

As a general matter, law other than Article 12 would determine whether any particular transaction creates a property interest in a controllable electronic record. Section 12- 104(c). However, even if under other applicable law Hacker has no rights in, and no right to transfer, the "stolen" controllable electronic record, subsection (e) enables Buyer, a qualifying purchaser, to take the controllable electronic record (or any purchased controllable account or controllable payment intangible evidenced by the controllable electronic record) free of claims of a property right—including that of the rightful owner.

As Example 3 illustrates, a person in control of a controllable electronic record, such as Hacker, has the power, even if not the right, to transfer rights in the record to a qualifying purchaser. Of course, if the qualifying purchaser is a secured party whose security interest secures an obligation, the purchaser would take free of the conflicting property right only to the extent of the obligation secured. See Section 12-104(d) (purchaser of a limited interest); cf. Section 3- 302(e). Moreover, even if a secured party were not a qualifying purchaser of a controllable electronic record, controllable account, or controllable payment intangible, its security interest in the collateral over which it obtained control would, however, have priority over a conflicting security interest that was perfected by a method other than control. Section 9-326A.

8. Subsection (g)—the "no-action" rule. Subsection (g) applies in the situation (explained in Comment 4) in which the "resulting" controllable electronic record (or controllable account or controllable payment intangible) purchased by a qualifying purchaser is not the "same" record, account, or payment intangible that was transferred. In such a situation, a person claiming a property right in the transferred asset may assert a claim against a purchaser of the "resulting" asset even though the claimant is not asserting a claim of a property right in the purchased asset. If the claim is based on both the purchaser's purchase of the acquired asset and the claimant's claim of a property right in the transferred asset, subsection (g) protects the qualifying purchaser from liability to the claimant based on any theory. The qualifying purchaser's protection from the assertion of such a claim does not depend on any proof that the purchased asset is somehow "traceable" to the transferred asset.

If instead, such a claimant were to assert a claim based on a property right in the purchased asset, then the qualifying purchaser would take free of that claim under subsection (e). Subsection (e) applies whether or not the acquired asset is the same asset that was transferred.

9. "Tethered" assets. Certain controllable electronic records may carry with them rights to other assets, for example, goods or rights to payment. By its terms, the take-free rule in subsection (e) applies to controllable electronic records (and, under subsection (a), controllable accounts and controllable payment intangibles evidenced by a controllable electronic record). One might argue that the inclusion of controllable accounts and controllable payment intangibles in the scope of subsection (e) is unnecessary. By taking a controllable electronic record free of property claims, the argument would be that a person takes not only the controllable electronic record itself but also all rights that are "carried" in the controllable electronic record free and clear.

Subsection (f) defeats that argument. It limits the application of the take-free rule in subsection (e) to controllable electronic records and, through the application of subsection (a), controllable accounts and controllable payment intangibles evidenced by a controllable electronic record. Under subsection (f), except as provided in subsections (a) and (e), a qualifying purchaser takes rights to payment (other than controllable accounts and controllable payment intangibles), rights to performance, and interests in property that are evidenced by a controllable electronic record subject to third-party property claims, unless law other than Article 12 provides to the contrary. The reference in subsection (f) to "law other than this article" contemplates that another article of the UCC might provide a contrary rule for some types of property that might be tethered to a controllable electronic record.

The treatment of controllable accounts and controllable payment intangibles in Articles 9 and 12 is feasible because Article 9 already provides the legal framework for assignments of accounts and payment intangibles. In addition, because accounts and payment intangibles are rights to payment of monetary obligations, tethering of an account or payment intangible to a controllable electronic record is straightforward. The account debtor is obligated to pay the person that has control of the relevant controllable electronic record (subject to the qualifications imposed by Section 12-106).

10. Creating the functional equivalent of a negotiable instrument. Two defining characteristics of an Article 3 negotiable instrument are that a holder in due course (i) takes free of claims of a property or possessory right to the instrument (Section 3-306) and (ii) takes free of most defenses and claims in recoupment (Section 3-305). Article 3 applies only to written instruments. Article 12 and the revisions to Article 9 provide a method for reaching a similar result with respect to controllable accounts and controllable payment intangibles.

As regards the first characteristic, a qualifying purchaser could acquire the controllable account or controllable payment intangible free of any claim of a property interest. As regards the second characteristic, the definition of "qualifying purchaser" omits some of the conditions for becoming a holder in due course. For example, to qualify as a holder in due course, a holder must take "without notice that any party has a defense or claim in recoupment " Section 3-302(a)(2)(vi). A controllable electronic record is information; there are no parties to a controllable electronic record. However, there are parties to a controllable account or controllable payment intangible. Accordingly, Sections 9-404 and 9-403 would determine whether a purchaser of the controllable account or controllable payment intangible takes free of a defense. Section 9-403 ordinarily would give effect to the account debtor's agreement not to assert claims or defenses.

Section 9-403 adopts the meaning of value in Section 3-303, as does Article 12. The concept of value in Section 3-303 is narrower than the concept in Section 1-204, which applies generally to UCC transactions. Under Section 1-204, a person gives value for rights if the person acquires them in return for a promise. However, under Section 3-303, if a negotiable instrument is issued or transferred for a promise of performance, the instrument is transferred for value only to the extent that the promise has been performed.

§ 12-105. Control of Controllable Electronic Record.

(a) [General rule: control of controllable electronic record.] A person has control of a controllable electronic record if the electronic record, a record attached to or logically associated with the electronic record, or a system in which the electronic record is recorded:

(1) gives the person:

(A) power to avail itself of substantially all the benefit from the electronic record; and

(B) exclusive power, subject to subsection (b), to:

(i) prevent others from availing themselves of substantially all the benefit from the electronic record; and

(ii) transfer control of the electronic record to another person or cause another person to obtain control of another controllable electronic record as a result of the transfer of the electronic record; and

(2) enables the person readily to identify itself in any way, including by name, identifying number, cryptographic key, office, or account number, as having the powers specified in paragraph (1).

(b) [Meaning of exclusive.] Subject to subsection (c), a power is exclusive under subsection (a)(1)(B)(i) and (ii) even if:

(1) the controllable electronic record, a record attached to or logically associated with the electronic record, or a system in which the electronic record is recorded limits the use of the electronic record or has a protocol programmed to cause a change, including a transfer or loss of control or a modification of benefits afforded by the electronic record; or

(2) the power is shared with another person.

(c) [When power not shared with another person.] A power of a person is not shared with another person under subsection (b)(2) and the person's power is not exclusive if:

(1) the person can exercise the power only if the power also is exercised by the other person; and

(2) the other person:

(A) can exercise the power without exercise of the power by the person; or

(B) is the transferor to the person of an interest in the controllable electronic record or a controllable account or controllable payment intangible evidenced by the controllable electronic record.

(d) [Presumption of exclusivity of certain powers.] If a person has the powers specified in subsection (a)(1)(B)(i) and (ii), the powers are presumed to be exclusive.

(e) [Control through another person.] A person has control of a controllable electronic record if another person, other than the transferor to the person of an interest in the controllable electronic record or a controllable account or controllable payment intangible evidenced by the controllable electronic record:

(1) has control of the electronic record and acknowledges that it has control on behalf of the person; or

(2) obtains control of the electronic record after having acknowledged that it will obtain control of the electronic record on behalf of the person.

(f) [No requirement to acknowledge.] A person that has control under this section is not required to acknowledge that it has control on behalf of another person.

(g) [No duties or confirmation.] If a person acknowledges that it has or will obtain control on behalf of another person, unless the person otherwise agrees or law other than this article or Article 9 otherwise provides, the person does not owe any duty to the other person and is not required to confirm the acknowledgment to any other person.

Official Comment

1. Why "control" matters. Control serves two major functions in Article 12. An electronic record is a "controllable electronic record" and is subject to the provisions of this Article only if it can be subjected to control under this section. See Section 12-102(a)(1) (defining "controllable electronic record"). And only a person having control of a controllable electronic record is eligible to become a qualifying purchaser and so to take free of claims of a property interest in the controllable electronic record, or any controllable account or controllable payment intangible evidenced by the controllable electronic record, and to be protected by the "no-action" rule. See Section 12-104(e) and (g).

Article 9 provides that obtaining control of a controllable electronic record is one method by which to perfect a security interest in the controllable electronic record or in any controllable account or controllable payment intangible evidenced by the controllable electronic record. See Sections 9-107A; 9-314. Moreover, a security interest perfected by control has priority over a conflicting security interest that was perfected by a method other than control and "control... pursuant to the debtor's agreement" may substitute for an authenticated a signed security agreement as an element of attachment. See Sections 9-326A; 9-203(b)(3)(D).

2. Powers and sources of powers; inability to exercise a power. This section conditions control on a person's having the three powers specified in subsection (a)(1). A person would have the powers described in that subsection if the controllable electronic record, a record attached to or logically associated with the controllable electronic record, or any system in which it is recorded gives the person those powers. This description of the source of the relevant powers should be construed broadly and functionally. For example, a person would have a power even if the characteristics of the particular purchaser disable the person from exercising the power. This would be the case, for example, when the purchaser holds the private key required to access the benefit of the controllable electronic record but lacks the hardware required to use it. In addition, a system in which the person in control is identified is a permissible source of a power even if it is related to but not precisely the "same" system in which the controllable electronic record is recorded. Moreover, this broad and functional construction is particularly important for references to "a record attached to or logically associated with the electronic record, or a system in which the electronic record is recorded," as used in Section 12-105(a) and (b) (and elsewhere). For example, overly literal or technical interpretations of the terminology "attached to" or "logically associated" are inappropriate. The statutory language must be adapted and applied in a functional manner to technology, systems, and infrastructure that may be developed and employed in the future. The goal is to embrace records and systems that are connected to a particular electronic record in such a manner that the information contained in or the functions performed by those "attached" or "associated" records are appropriately and reasonably attributable to and identifiable as connected with the electronic record itself. See also, e.g., Sections 7-106, 9-105, 9-105A, 9-306A, 9-605, 9-628, and 12-107.

3. "Benefit." Subsection (a)(1)(A) and (a)(1)(B)(i) condition control of a controllable electronic record on a person's relationship to the benefit of the controllable electronic record.

As used in this section, the "benefit" of a controllable electronic record refers to the rights that are afforded by the controllable electronic record and the uses to which the controllable electronic record can be put. These, in turn, depend on the characteristics of the controllable electronic record in question. For example, the benefit afforded by control of a bitcoin is that it can be held or disposed of (sold or spent). And control of a controllable electronic record evidencing a controllable account or controllable payment intangible affords the benefit of the right to collect from the account debtor (obligor).

The system in which a controllable electronic record is recorded may limit the benefit from the controllable electronic record that is available to those who interact with the system. In determining whether a person has the power to avail itself of substantially all the benefit from a controllable electronic record under subsection (a)(1)(A), or to prevent others from availing themselves of substantially all the benefit from a controllable electronic record under subsection (a)(1)(B)(i), only the benefit that the system makes available (subject to the system's inherent limitations) should be considered.

4. Power to retrieve information. By definition, the information constituting an electronic record must be "retrievable in perceivable form." Section 1-201(b)(31) (defining "record"). The power to retrieve the record in perceivable form is included in the benefit of a controllable electronic record. "Perceivable form" means that the contents of the record are intelligible; the ability to perceive the indecipherable jumble of an encrypted record does not give a person the power to retrieve the record in perceivable form.

To have control of a controllable electronic record under subsection (a)(1)(A), a person must have at least the nonexclusive power to avail itself of this benefit. If a person also has the exclusive power to decrypt the encrypted record, the person will have the exclusive power to prevent others from availing themselves of substantially all the benefit from the controllable electronic record and thereby will satisfy the condition in subsection (a)(1)(B)(i).

5. Exclusive powers. Unlike the power in subsection (a)(1)(A), the powers in subsection (a)(1)(B)(i) and (a)(1)(B)(ii) must be held exclusively by the person claiming control in order to establish control. However, once it is established that a person has received those powers, subsection (d) provides a presumption of exclusivity. Consequently, a person asserting control need not prove exclusivity in order to make out a prima facie case. Application of the presumption will be governed also by Section 1-206 (effects of a presumption under the UCC) and applicable non-UCC law (including rules of procedure and evidence). In addition, subsection (b) contains two qualifications of the term "exclusive" as used in subsection (a)(1)(B). A power can be "exclusive" under subsection (a)(1)(B) even if one or both of these qualifications apply.

Subsection (b)(1) takes account of the fact that the powers of a purchaser of a controllable electronic record necessarily are subject to the attributes of the controllable electronic record, records associated with the controllable electronic record, and the protocols of any system in which the controllable electronic record is recorded. For example, a transfer of control resulting from a program that is a part of a system's protocol is inherent in the controllable electronic record and does not impair the exclusivity of the power of the person in control of the record. Subsection (b)(1) also contemplates that the potential for the system to otherwise modify (or even destroy) controllable electronic records would not impair the exclusivity.

> **Example 1:** Pursuant to the governance apparatus of a system (Propofolium) for a cryptocurrency (propofol), an upgrade to the system was made that modified the consensus mechanism for determining the effectiveness of transfers of propofols within the system. Although this change did not divest any holder of propofols of its control, it prospectively modified the system for all propofols. The adoption of this change and the potential for such a change (or any other change) are functions of the attributes of the system and, consequently, of all propofols. Neither this change nor such potential impaired the exclusivity, for purposes of subsection (a)(1)(B), of the powers of a person in control of propofols.

Subsection (b)(2) allows for a power to be shared with another person without impairing the exclusivity of the power. One effect of subsection (b)(2) is that, under a multi-signature (multi-sig) agreement, any person that is readily identifiable under subsection (a)(2) and shares the relevant power would be eligible to have control, even if the action of another person is a condition for the exercise of the power. For example, a person in control may agree that another person's action on the relevant system would be required to effect a transfer of control without impairing the requisite exclusivity.

> **Example 2:** Pursuant to a multi-sig arrangement, control of propofols (in the system described in Example 1) is shared by Campbell, Elizabeth, Mia, and Natasha. Under the multi-sig arrangement, the exercise of powers over the propofols requires action by three of the four persons having control. None of the participants acting alone has the power to exercise the relevant powers. Subsection (b)(2) makes clear that all four participants have control over the propofols and exclusivity is not impaired by the shared control under the multi-sig arrangement.

Although all four persons in Example 2 have control, that may leave many questions as to the rights of the four as among themselves. For example, if more than one of the four were secured parties, it would be important for them to settle by agreement issues such as relative priorities and enforcement rights. Similar situations can arise in other contexts and with respect to other types of collateral.

A multi-sig arrangement for a controllable electronic record, such as that described in Example 2, may provide enhanced security. For example, if the power of one participant is compromised by a "hacker," the required actions by the other participants would prevent the hacker from exercising unauthorized power over the record. Although the hacker might possess the power along with the remaining multi-sig participants, those participants would continue to have control. A multi-sig structure also may protect against the misuse of a record by ensuring that actions by multiple persons are required for exercising power over the record.

Subsection (c) provides that in certain circumstances a power is not shared within the meaning of subsection (b)(2), the relaxation of the exclusivity requirement provided by subsection (b)(2) does not apply, and, consequently, a person's power is not exclusive.

Subsection (c) provides that a person does not share an exclusive power with another person if the person can exercise the power only with the other person's cooperation (subsection (c)(1)) but the other person either (i) can exercise the power without the person's cooperation (subsection (c)(2)(A)) or (ii) is the transferor to the person (transferee) of an interest in the controllable electronic record or a controllable account or controllable payment intangible evidenced by the controllable electronic record (subsection (c)(2)(B)). It follows that a person to which subsection (c) applies does not have control based on its exclusive powers (although it might have control through another person under subsection (e), discussed below, or if another person having control is acting as the person's agent).

Comment 9 addresses the rationale for disqualifying the transferee from a transferor under subsection (c)(2)(B) from the benefit of sharing a power under subsection (b)(2).

The following examples illustrate the application of subsection (c):

> **Example 3:** Under a multi-sig arrangement, exercise by any two of Campbell, Elizabeth, and Mia is required to exercise a power with respect to a controllable electronic record (CER). None of the three can exercise a power without the cooperation of another, so all three have control because they share the power. Even if Campbell were the transferor of the CER to Elizabeth, Elizabeth's power is shared, and therefore treated as exclusive, because Campbell cannot block Elizabeth's exercise of the power if Mia acts with Elizabeth. It follows that subsection (c)(1) does not apply, subsection (b)(2) does apply, and Elizabeth shares the power with Campbell. (The same result would apply with respect to Mia's power if Campbell were the transferor of the CER to Mia.)

> **Example 4:** Under a multi-sig arrangement, exercise by both Campbell and Elizabeth are required to exercise a power, so subsection (c)(1) applies with respect to each person. However, neither Campbell nor Elizabeth can exercise the power without cooperation of the other and neither is the transferor to the other, so subsection (c)(2)(A) and (2)(B) does not apply with respect to either person. It follows that Campbell and Elizabeth each share the power.

> **Example 5:** The facts are the same as in Example 4, but Campbell is the transferor of an interest in the CER to Elizabeth. Elizabeth does not share the power with Campbell and Elizabeth's power is not exclusive because subsection (c)(1) and (2)(B) applies.

> **Example 6:** Under a multi-sig arrangement, Mia or Natasha can exercise a power only with the exercise by Campbell, but Campbell can exercise the power unilaterally without the exercise by either Mia or Natasha. Neither Mia nor Natasha shares the power with Campbell because subsection (c)(1) and (2)(A) apply, so neither Mia's nor Natasha's power is treated as exclusive. Campbell's power is exclusive in fact

and Campbell need not rely on subsection (b)(2) for shared power.

Example 7: Under a multi-sig arrangement, Mia can exercise a power only with exercise by Elizabeth or Natasha, but Elizabeth and Natasha each can exercise the power unilaterally without the exercise by the other or by Mia. Elizabeth and Natasha share the power, but Mia does not share the power with Elizabeth or Natasha. Mia's power is not exclusive because subsection (c)(1) and (2)(A) applies.

Although the presumption in subsection (d) is not expressly made subject to subsection (c), it is functionally so. Under Section 1-206, once evidence is introduced that subsection (c) applies and that, accordingly, a person relying on the presumption cannot rely on the relaxation of the exclusivity requirement provided by subsection (b)(2), the presumption would no longer apply.

6. Transfer of control. The power to transfer control of a controllable electronic record under subsection (a)(1)(B)(ii) includes the power to cause another person to obtain control of another derivative and resulting controllable electronic record that results from the transfer of the controllable electronic record. See Section 12-104, Comment 4.

7. Readily identify itself. Subsection (a)(2) provides that a person does not have control of a controllable electronic record unless the controllable electronic record, a record attached to or logically associated with the controllable electronic record, or any system in which the controllable electronic record is recorded enables the person readily to identify itself as the person having the requisite powers. The identification need not be by a "name," but also may be by "identifying number, cryptographic key, office, or account number"—language derived from Section 3-110(c). The reference to "office" means a public office. See Section 3-110, Comment 3. This subsection does not obligate a person to identify itself as having control. However, to prove that it has control, a person would need to prove that the relevant records or any system in which the controllable electronic record is recorded readily identifies the person as such.

Consistent with the subsection (d) presumption of exclusivity, proof that a person has the powers specified in section (a)(1) does not require proof of exclusivity—i.e., proof of a negative (that no one else has such powers). The means of identification mentioned in subsection (a)(2) derive from Section 3-110(c). Subsection (a)(2) adds "cryptographic key" as an example of a way in which a person may be identified.

8. Control through another person. Neither Article 12 nor any other provision of the UCC would restrict or render ineffective any agreement of a person in control of a controllable electronic record to hold control on behalf of another person. This result is implicit from subsection (b)(2) dealing with sharing of control. It also would follow under principles of agency. But such an arrangement should be effective regardless of any agency or fiduciary relationship.

This concept is expressly addressed in Section 8-106(d)(3), on control of a security entitlement, which achieves perfection of a security interest under Sections 9-106(a) and 9- 314(a). It also applies to perfection by possession under Section 9-313(c) if a person other than the debtor or the secured party (or the secured party's agent) is in possession of collateral. Under those provisions, however, effectiveness is conditioned in some circumstances on an "acknowledgment" by the person in control or possession. Under Section 9-313(c) the acknowledgment must be in a signed record. These provisions appear to derive from practices involving bailees of tangible property, such as goods, chattel paper, and certificated securities. See Section 9-313, Comment 4.

Subsection (e) likewise provides for control by a person through another person's acknowledgment that it has control on behalf of the person. Subsection (e) is patterned on Section 9-313(c), but like Section 8-106(d)(3), subsection (e) omits the requirement in Section 9- 313(c) that an acknowledgment be made in a signed record. Although best practices might suggest the wisdom of relying on a signed record to evidence such an acknowledgment, subsection (e) would permit proof by other means. Under subsection (e) for an acknowledgment by another person to be effective to confer control on a person, the other person making the acknowledgment must be one "other than the transferor of an interest in the electronic record" to the person. The rationale for this limitation is discussed in Comment 9. Control based on an acknowledgment under subsection (e) by another person having control continues only while the other person retains control. This result necessarily follows because such control derives solely from the other person's continued control.

The combined operation of subsections (b)(2) and (e) ensure that the continuance of various existing practices would not prevent or cause the loss of control. For example, a person in control may wish to grant another person the power to approve or disapprove a transfer of control on the system. Alternatively, a person in control may wish to permit a system administrator, the system itself, or a prearranged operation to transfer control to another person under specified conditions without participation by the person in control. And, of course, a person in control may wish to delegate the power to transfer control to an agent or fiduciary.

Provisions substantially similar to subsection (e) are included in Section 7-106 (control of electronic documents of title), Section 8-106(d)(3) (control of security entitlement), 9-104 (control of deposit accounts), 9-105 (control of authoritative electronic copies of records evidencing chattel paper), and 9-105A (control of electronic money).

9. Shared powers under subsection (b)(2) and control through another person under subsection (e). Limitations related to transferors and transferees of interests in controllable electronic records. Subsection (c)(2)(B) disqualifies a transferee (which includes a secured party in a secured transaction) of an interest in a controllable electronic record (or controllable account or controllable payment intangible) from the benefit of a shared power under subsection (b)(2) when the transferor retains a blocking power (i.e., when the transferee cannot exercise the power unless the transferor also exercises the power). In similar fashion, under subsection (e), an acknowledgment by a transferor of an interest in a controllable electronic record (or controllable account or controllable payment intangible) that the transferor has control for the benefit of a person is ineffective to confer control on the person. Each of these limitations is premised on the view that the transferor has not been divested sufficiently of its powers over the relevant controllable electronic record so as to warrant treating the transferee as a secured party having a security interest perfected by control or as having the requisite control to be a qualifying purchaser.

Subsection (c)(1) and (c)(2)(B) contemplates that the transferor has retained a blocking power over the transferee's exercise of a power. Subsection (e) contemplates that the transferor remains in control and has merely acknowledged that its control is for the transferee's benefit and that the acknowledgment is ineffective to confer control on the transferee. Although the concept of shared control is newly introduced in the UCC, holding possession or control for another is not. Section 9-313(c) expressly provides in this context that an acknowledging person having possession of goods must be a person "other than the debtor" for a secured party to take possession through the acknowledging person. The official comments to Section 8-106 are to the same effect in the context of control of a security entitlement. See Section 8-106(d)(3), Comment 4A and pre-2022 Comment 4. The same policy that underpins the inapplicability of this method of control to an acknowledgment by a debtor applies as well to a transferor that is not an Article 9 debtor. Control is intended to be a proxy for and a functional equivalent of the transfer of physical possession of goods. In general, a person can obtain control through control by an agent, but under subsection (e) an acknowledgment by a debtor or transferor (even "as agent") that acknowledges control on behalf of a secured party or other transferee would be ineffective. This corresponds to the policy underlying Section 9-313 that "the debtor cannot qualify as an agent for the secured party for purposes of the secured party's taking possession." Section 9-313, Comment 3.

Notwithstanding these limitations, they would not impair the continued perfection by control upon a secured party's assignment of a perfected-by-control security interest in a controllable electronic record to a successor secured party. The following example illustrates.

> **Example 8:** Debtor (D) buys a CER and obtains control. D then grants a security interest in the CER to Secured Party A (SPA) to secure D's obligation to SPA and transfers to SPA control of the CER (not pursuant to shared control with D or pursuant to subsection (e)). SPA then assigns to Secured Party B (SPB) the secured obligation owed by D to SPA.

As to perfection of the security interest granted by D, perfection by control is not affected even if SPA retains powers over the CER (as between SPA and SPB) following the assignment to SPB. The security interest remains perfected. This is consistent with the policy underlying 9-310(c)—an assignment of a security interest should not require the assignee to refile or take an assignment of record of a filed financing statement in favor of the assignor for protection against a debtor's creditors and transferees.

The economic interest being assigned by SPA to SPB in Example 8 is primarily the right to payment or performance of the obligation of D that is secured by the CER. If the transfer of the secured obligation by SPA to SPB itself creates a security interest securing an obligation (e.g., owed by SPA to SPB), then SPB should perfect the security interest granted by SPA (which is distinct from the security interest in the CER granted by D and assigned by SPA to SPB). The method of perfection will depend on the nature of the secured obligation—the type of collateral—being assigned. Is the right to payment an instrument, an account, or a payment intangible? Or is performance of the secured obligation pursuant to another type of general intangible? SPB should file a financing statement against SPA, as debtor, or take possession of the instrument, if applicable. However, as to the underlying collateral securing the assigned obligation—the CER—attachment and perfection of SPB's security interest in the obligation of D owed to SPA would also constitute attachment and perfection as to the security interest in the CER securing that obligation. Sections 9-203(g); 9-308(e); see also 1 Restatement (Second) of Contracts § 340, Comment b ("b. Security follows the debt. Where a secured claim is assigned, the collateral is ordinarily assigned as well.").

If the transfer by SPA to SPB is an outright transfer (a sale) of an account, a payment intangible, or a promissory note, the transfer creates a security interest and the analysis in the preceding paragraph applies (except that the security interest arising from the sale of a payment intangible or promissory note is automatically perfected under Section 9-309(a)(3) and (4)). If the transfer is a sale of another type of general intangible or instrument that is secured by the CER, then non-Article 9 law applies to the transfer. However, the same result may occur under the common-law rule that the collateral (the CER) follows a secured obligation that is transferred. See Sections 9-203, Comment 9; 9-308, Comment 6.

For obvious business reasons, SPB may not wish to allow SPA to remain in control of the CER and may require SPA to transfer control to it as a condition to the transaction. Alternatively, SPB may obtain control through sharing powers with SPA or through SPA's acknowledgment pursuant to subsection (e). It is true that SPA's assignment to SPB of D's secured obligation carried with it the collateral—the CER—securing the obligation. But such a derivative acquisition (through the operation of Sections 9-203(g) and 9-308(e)) by SPB would not be a transfer by SPA of "an interest in" the CER within the meaning of the limitations imposed in subsections (c)(2)(B) or (e). The operation of these rules, providing that collateral follows the transfer of a secured obligation, are based on the premise that any necessary public notice provided in connection with the assignment of the obligation provides, in turn, sufficient public notice with respect to the underlying collateral. It follows that the policy to be implemented by subsections (c)(2)(B) and (e) is not implicated by such an assignment.

10. No requirement to acknowledge, no duties, and no requirement to confirm acknowledgment. Subsections (f) and (g) derive from Section 9-313(f) and (g). Subsection (f) makes clear that a person that has control under this section has no duty to acknowledge that it has or will obtain control on behalf of another person. Arrangements for a person to acknowledge that it has or will obtain control on behalf of another person are not standardized. Accordingly, subsection (g) leaves to the agreement of the parties and to any other applicable law (other than this Article or Article 9) any duties of a person that does acknowledge that it has or will obtain control on behalf of another person and provides that a person making an acknowledgment is not required to confirm the acknowledgment to another person.

For example, subsection (e) would apply to give control to a person, Alpha, when another person, Beta, has control of a controllable electronic record and acknowledges that it has control on behalf of Alpha. However, under subsection (f), Beta is not required to so acknowledge. And under subsection (g), even if Beta does so acknowledge, Beta owes no duty to Alpha unless Beta agrees or other law so provides, and Beta is not required to confirm its acknowledgment to any other person.

§ 12-106. Discharge of Account Debtor on Controllable Account or Controllable Payment Intangible.

(a) [Discharge of account debtor.] An account debtor on a controllable account or controllable payment intangible may discharge its obligation by paying:

(1) the person having control of the controllable electronic record that evidences the controllable account or controllable payment intangible; or

(2) except as provided in subsection (b), a person that formerly had control of the controllable electronic record.

(b) [Content and effect of notification.] Subject to subsection (d), the account debtor may not discharge its obligation by paying a person that formerly had control of the controllable electronic record if the account debtor receives a notification that:

(1) is signed by a person that formerly had control or the person to which control was transferred;

(2) reasonably identifies the controllable account or controllable payment intangible;

(3) notifies the account debtor that control of the controllable electronic record that evidences the controllable account or controllable payment intangible was transferred;

(4) identifies the transferee, in any reasonable way, including by name, identifying number, cryptographic key, office, or account number; and

(5) provides a commercially reasonable method by which the account debtor is to pay the transferee.

(c) [Discharge following effective notification.] After receipt of a notification that complies with subsection (b), the account debtor may discharge its obligation by paying in accordance with the notification and may not discharge the obligation by paying a person that formerly had control.

(d) [When notification ineffective.] Subject to subsection (h), notification is ineffective under subsection (b):

(1) unless, before the notification is sent, the account debtor and the person that, at that time, had control of the controllable electronic record that evidences the controllable account or controllable payment intangible agree in a signed record to a commercially reasonable method by which a person may furnish reasonable proof that control has been transferred;

(2) to the extent an agreement between the account debtor and seller of a payment intangible limits the account debtor's duty to pay a

person other than the seller and the limitation is effective under law other than this article; or

(3) at the option of the account debtor, if the notification notifies the account debtor to:

(A) divide a payment;

(B) make less than the full amount of an installment or other periodic payment; or

(C) pay any part of a payment by more than one method or to more than one person.

(e) [Proof of transfer of control.] Subject to subsection (h), if requested by the account debtor, the person giving the notification under subsection (b) seasonably shall furnish reasonable proof, using the method in the agreement referred to in subsection (d)(1), that control of the controllable electronic record has been transferred. Unless the person complies with the request, the account debtor may discharge its obligation by paying a person that formerly had control, even if the account debtor has received a notification under subsection (b).

(f) [What constitutes reasonable proof.] A person furnishes reasonable proof under subsection (e) that control has been transferred if the person demonstrates, using the method in the agreement referred to in subsection (d)(1), that the transferee has the power to:

(1) avail itself of substantially all the benefit from the controllable electronic record;

(2) prevent others from availing themselves of substantially all the benefit from the controllable electronic record; and

(3) transfer the powers specified in paragraphs (1) and (2) to another person.

(g) [Rights not waivable.] Subject to subsection (h), an account debtor may not waive or vary its rights under subsections (d)(1) and (e) or its option under subsection (d)(3).

(h) [Rule for individual under other law.] This section is subject to law other than this article which establishes a different rule for an account debtor who is an individual and who incurred the obligation primarily for personal, family, or household purposes.

Official Comment

1. Source. These provisions derive from Section 3-602, which governs the discharge of a person obligated on a negotiable instrument, and Section 9-406(a), (b) and (c), which governs the discharge of an account debtor, including a person obligated on an account or payment intangible.

2. The basic rules. This section applies only to an account debtor that has undertaken to pay the person that has control of the controllable electronic record that evidences the obligation to pay. See Section 9-102 (defining "controllable account" and "controllable payment intangible"). Section 9-406 would continue to apply in other respects and to all other account debtors. As to the relationship between this section and Section 9-406, see Comment 5.

Under subsection (a)(1), an account debtor may discharge its obligation on the controllable account or controllable payment intangible by paying the person that has control of the related controllable electronic record at the time of payment. Subsections (a)(2) and (b) would remove from an account debtor the burden of determining who has control of the related controllable electronic record at any given time—a burden that, with respect to some controllable electronic records, an account debtor may be unable to satisfy. Under subsection (a)(2), subject to subsection (b), an account debtor may discharge its obligation by paying a person that formerly had control of the related controllable electronic record, which presumably would include the initial obligee.

Subsection (b) reflects the fact that a person to which control has been transferred may not wish to take the risk that the account debtor will discharge its obligation by paying the transferor. Subsection (b) protects the transferee by providing that, if the account debtor receives an effective notification that control has been transferred, the account debtor may discharge its obligation by paying in accordance with the notification and may not discharge its obligation by paying a person that formerly had control. The notification must be signed by a person formerly having control or by the transferee.

To be effective under subsection (b), a notification must reasonably identify the controllable account or controllable payment intangible, notify the account debtor that control of the controllable electronic record that evidences the controllable account or controllable payment intangible was transferred, identify the transferee in any reasonable way, and provide a commercially reasonable method by which the account debtor is to make payments to the transferee. A change in the identity of the person to which the account debtor must make payment should not, and typically will not, impose a significant burden on the account debtor.

However, one can imagine a method of making payment that would be burdensome, for example, making a payment through a trading platform or payment service with which the account debtor does not have an account. For this reason, the designated method of making payment must be "commercially reasonable."

3. "Reasonable proof." As noted above, this section derives in large part from Section 9-406, which provides for notification that an account or payment intangible has been assigned. Experience suggests that account debtors that have received notification of an assignment under Section 9-406 typically make payments in accordance with the notice. Recognizing that an account debtor may be uncertain whether a notification is legitimate, Section 9-406 affords to an account debtor the right to request proof that the account or payment intangible was assigned. See generally, Section 9-406, Comment 4.

Subsection (e) contains a similar provision. On the account debtor's request, the person giving the notification must seasonably furnish reasonable proof that control of the controllable electronic record has been transferred. If the person does not comply with the request, the account debtor may ignore the notification and discharge its obligation by paying a person formerly in control.

"Reasonable proof" requires evidence that would be understood by a typical account debtor to whom it is proffered as demonstrating to a reasonably high probability that control of the controllable electronic record has been transferred to the transferee. Subsection (f) provides a safe harbor for providing reasonable proof. It enables a person to satisfy the account debtor's request by demonstrating that the transferee has the power to avail itself of substantially all the benefit from the controllable electronic record, to prevent others from availing themselves of substantially all the benefit from the controllable electronic record, and to transfer these powers to another person. This demonstration would not necessarily prove that a person actually has control of a controllable electronic record because it need not show that the transferee held the last two powers exclusively. Nevertheless, such a demonstration would constitute "reasonable proof" under subsection (f). A person that has control should have little difficulty providing this proof, as a person cannot have control unless it can readily identify itself as having the requisite powers. See Section 12-105(a)(2). Reasonable proof that is seasonably furnished by a person other than the person that gave the notification would constitute compliance with the account debtor's request.

Subsection (e) requires that reasonable proof be provided "using the agreed method." Subsection (f) requires that a person use "the agreed method" to demonstrate that the transferee has the specified powers. "Agreed method" refers to the commercially reasonable method to which the parties agreed, in a signed record, before the notification was sent. If parties did not so agree, the notification is ineffective under subsection (d)(1).

An account debtor may agree to participate in a system providing for the control of controllable accounts or controllable payment intangibles. If the system is programmed to provide for notification to the account debtor upon the transfer of control, the account debtor's agreement and the operation of the system may satisfy the requirements of subsections (d)(1), (e), and (f).

4. Additional considerations for account debtors. The requirement in subsection (e) that reasonable proof be furnished using the "agreed method" provides considerable protection for account debtors upon receipt of a notification of assignment and making a request for proof. There are, however, other considerations that are of importance to account debtors but are beyond the scope of the frameworks provided by Articles 9 and 12. One such consideration is the potential involvement of pseudonymous payees, which may raise issues such as compliance with anti-money laundering regulations and sanctions compliance. These are examples of issues that a well-structured program for controllable accounts and controllable payment intangibles might address.

5. Relationship to Section 9-406. Section 9-406 governs the discharge of the obligation of an account debtor. Section 9-406 carves out of its scope transactions to the extent covered by this section. See Section 9-406(l).

§ 12-107. Governing Law.

(a) [Governing law: general rule.] Except as provided in subsection (b), the local law of a controllable electronic record's jurisdiction governs a matter covered by this article.

(b) [Governing law: Section 12-106.] For a controllable electronic record that evidences a controllable account or controllable payment intangible, the local law of the controllable electronic record's jurisdiction governs a matter covered by Section 12-106 unless an effective agreement determines that the local law of another jurisdiction governs.

(c) [Controllable electronic record's jurisdiction.] The following rules determine a controllable electronic record's jurisdiction under this section:

(1) If the controllable electronic record, or a record attached to or logically associated with the controllable electronic record and readily available for review, expressly provides that a particular jurisdiction is the controllable electronic record's jurisdiction for purposes of this article or [the Uniform Commercial Code], that jurisdiction is the controllable electronic record's jurisdiction.

(2) If paragraph (1) does not apply and the rules of the system in which the controllable electronic record is recorded are readily available for review and expressly provide that a particular jurisdiction is the controllable electronic record's jurisdiction for purposes of this article or [the Uniform Commercial Code], that jurisdiction is the controllable electronic record's jurisdiction.

(3) If paragraphs (1) and (2) do not apply and the controllable electronic record, or a record attached to or logically associated with the controllable electronic record and readily available for review, expressly provides that the controllable electronic record is governed by the law of a particular jurisdiction, that jurisdiction is the controllable electronic record's jurisdiction.

(4) If paragraphs (1), (2), and (3) do not apply and the rules of the system in which the controllable electronic record is recorded are readily available for review and expressly provide that the controllable electronic record or the system is governed by the law of a particular jurisdiction, that jurisdiction is the controllable electronic record's jurisdiction.

(5) If paragraphs (1) through (4) do not apply, the controllable electronic record's jurisdiction is the District of Columbia.

(d) [Applicability of Article 12.] If subsection (c)(5) applies and Article 12 is not in effect in the District of Columbia without material modification, the governing law for a matter covered by this article is the law of the District of Columbia as though Article 12 were in effect in the District of Columbia without material modification. In this subsection, "Article 12" means Article 12 of Uniform Commercial Code Amendments (2022).

(e) [Relation of matter or transaction to controllable electronic record's jurisdiction not necessary.] To the extent subsections (a) and (b) provide that the local law of the controllable electronic record's jurisdiction governs a matter covered by this article, that law governs even if the matter or a transaction to which the matter relates does not bear any relation to the controllable electronic record's jurisdiction.

(f) [Rights of purchasers determined at time of purchase.] The rights acquired under Section 12-104 by a purchaser or qualifying purchaser are governed by the law applicable under this section at the time of purchase.

Official Comment

1. Source. The provisions of Section 12-107 (as well as Sections 9-306A and 9- 306B) derive from Sections 8-110 and 9-305 on law governing perfection and priority of security interests in investment property and the relevance of a securities intermediary's jurisdiction and a commodity intermediary's jurisdiction.

2. The basic rule. Law governing matters covered by Article 12. Subsection (a) states the basic rule that the local law of the controllable electronic record's jurisdiction governs the matters covered by this Article. The "matters covered by" this Article are relatively narrow and discrete, albeit enormously important. If the choice-of-law rule provided by this section points to a jurisdiction that has adopted Article 12, those matters would include the interpretation and application of Article 12, including its definitions. In general, issues that would be determined by the provisions of this Article are to be determined under the law that is applicable as determined by this section. These include the rights of purchasers and property claimants more generally with respect to controllable electronic records, controllable accounts, and controllable payment intangibles to the extent dealt with by this Article—issues addressed by section 12-104. The rights and obligations of account debtors, to the extent dealt with by section 12-106, are also matters covered. Matters not covered by this Article, including matters as to which this Article expressly provides are covered by other law, are not within the scope of this section.

3. Practical considerations on determination of governing law. This section relating to the law governing the matters covered by this Article must confront substantial practical considerations. These considerations arise primarily from two factors. First, as described below, this section relies primarily on a "waterfall" of alternatives for determining a controllable electronic record's jurisdiction. The first four elements of the waterfall require for their applicability express provisions of a controllable electronic record, an attached or logically associated record, or the system in which a controllable electronic record is recorded. However, many controllable electronic records and systems existing at the time of the 2022 Amendments do not contain these provisions. As explained in Comment 6, the expectation is that over time electronic records and related systems will adopt these provisions in reliance on this section, thereby satisfying at least one of the first four elements of the waterfall. Second, in the absence of these provisions, at the bottom of the waterfall the controllable electronic record's jurisdiction is the District of Columbia. See Comment 6.

4. Governing law for Section 12-106. Subsection (b) provides an exception to the general rule of subsection (a) that "the local law of a controllable electronic record's jurisdiction governs the matters covered by this Article." The exception recognizes that an account debtor's rights and duties generally are governed by the law applicable to the underlying obligation of the account debtor, and not by the law applicable to the agreement between the assignor (debtor) and the assignee (secured party)—a security agreement. See Section 9-401, Comment 3. Subsection (b) recognizes that an effective agreement (i.e., one effective under Section 1-301(a)) between the account debtor and assignor may choose a different law to cover the matters covered by Section 12-106 (i.e., the account debtor's rights and duties addressed in that section). Such an agreement may, of course, address matters other than those covered by Section 12-106 (for example, an agreement that all obligations of the account debtor are governed by the laws of State X).

5. Determination of controllable electronic record's jurisdiction. The basic rule that the law of a controllable electronic record's jurisdiction governs the matters covered by Article 12 may be viewed as a rough proxy for the traditional role of the location of tangible asset (e.g., goods) in determining the applicable law (lex rei sitae). Drawing on the analogous provisions in Sections 8-110 and 9-305 in the context of a security entitlement or securities account or a commodity contract or commodity account, under subsection (c) it is the controllable electronic record itself, records attached thereto or associated therewith, or the system in which the controllable electronic record is recorded that determines the controllable electronic record's jurisdiction and, thereby, the governing law. Subsection (c) provides a "waterfall" of rules based on provisions that identify a particular jurisdiction as the controllable electronic record's jurisdiction or alternatively that provide the governing law for a controllable electronic record or the system in which the record is recorded. As to subsection (e), see Section 8-110, Comment 5A.

Paragraphs (1) through (4) of the subsection (c) waterfall each relies on information available from a controllable electronic record, an attached or logically associated record, or rules of a system in which the record is recorded. A controllable electronic record's jurisdiction is determined by one of these sources that "expressly provide[s]" that a jurisdiction is the controllable electronic record's jurisdiction or that a particular jurisdiction's law is the governing law. These paragraphs refer to attached or logically associated records or system rules that are "readily available." They also assume that the controllable electronic record is itself readily available to anyone choosing to deal with the record. These provisions are based on the assumption that the relevant express provision will be available to an interested person without the imposition of unreasonable burdens.

6. Bottom of the waterfall. District of Columbia. Many controllable electronic records, attached or logically associated records, and systems in which controllable electronic records are recorded that exist at the time of the 2022 Amendments do not identify the "controllable electronic record's jurisdiction" or the governing law (some permissioned systems being exceptions). (It is anticipated that, upon widespread adoption of Article 12 and accompanying amendments, systems will adapt and the first four elements of the waterfall will become more generally applicable for identifying a controllable electronic record's jurisdiction.) Consequently, subsection (c)(5) addresses an issue that does not normally exist in the context of Sections 8-110 and 9-305. It might be thought that the logical choice for the residual rule for designating the controllable electronic record's jurisdiction at bottom of the waterfall would be, the location of the debtor. That approach would follow the role of the location of a debtor under Sections 9-301 and 9-307. However, that location may not readily be determined by parties to a transaction, primarily because in many cases involving controllable electronic records the transferor is not known to or easily discoverable by a purchaser. See Prefatory Note 1 to Article 12. Consequently, Subsection (c)(5) resolves this issue by providing that the controllable electronic record's jurisdiction is the District of Columbia.

7. District of Columbia as controllable electronic record's jurisdiction. The designation of the District of Columbia as the controllable electronic record's jurisdiction follows Section 9-307(c), which designates the District of Columbia as the location of a debtor that otherwise would be located in a jurisdiction whose law does not provide for a generally applicable system of public notice (such a filing or registration) for nonpossessory security interests. This designation also assumes that the District of Columbia will have adopted Article 12 and the conforming amendments to Articles 1 and 9 in substantially the uniform version—i.e., without material modification of the official text. This is a plausible assumption based on the history of adoptions in that jurisdiction. Because the controllable electronic record's jurisdiction does not govern perfection of a security interest by filing, the designation of the District of Columbia at the bottom of the waterfall will not confer on that jurisdiction any economic benefits of fees for filing of financing statements. See Section 9-306B(b). Subsection (d) addresses the unlikely situation that the District of Columbia does not adopt Article 12 without material modification of the official text or later adopts materially non-uniform amendments. Subsection (d) is patterned loosely (but as closely as feasible) on the TRADES Regulations, 31 CFR § 357.11(e), for U.S. Treasury securities.

The term "Article 12" is defined in subsection (d) as the officially promulgated 2022 version of Article 12 and conforming amendments. In determining whether the District of Columbia has enacted Article 12 without material modification, a court or other tribunal should consider the materiality of any provision in the context of the issue or issues before it. A modification of a provision that would be material in another context should be disregarded if it has no bearing on the issue or issues before the tribunal. In connection with any future revision of the Article 12 official text, it will be important for transitional provisions to address the situations in which the District of Columbia may or may not have adopted the revised official text.

8. Relevant time for determination of governing law. Subsection (f) provides that the rights of purchasers are governed by the applicable law as of the time of purchase. Note that Sections 8-110 and 9-305 do not contain an analogous rule with respect to a securities intermediary's jurisdiction. However, Section 8-110(c) does provide a similar rule for the delivery of a security certificate and adverse claims. As to the timing of the determination of the governing law for other issues under Article 12, such as the rights and duties of account debtors under Section 12-106, the section does not specify a time. As with most statutory provisions relating to governing law, courts are free to determine the appropriate relevant time taking into account the relevant facts and the nature of the issues involved.

UNIFORM COMMERCIAL CODE

Article A—Transitional Provisions for Uniform Commercial Code Amendments (2022)

PREFATORY NOTE TO ARTICLE A—TRANSITIONAL PROVISIONS

PART 1. GENERAL PROVISIONS AND DEFINITIONS

Section

A-101. Short Title.
A-102. Definitions.

PART 2. GENERAL TRANSITIONAL PROVISION

Section

A-201. Saving Clause.

PART 3. TRANSITIONAL PROVISIONS FOR ARTICLES 9 AND 12

Section

A-301. Saving Clause.
A-302. Security Interest Perfected Before Effective Date.
A-303. Security Interest Unperfected Before Effective Date
A-304. Effectiveness of Actions Taken Before Effective Date
A-305. Priority.
A-306. Priority of Claims When Priority Rules of Article 9 Do Not Apply.

PART 4. EFFECTIVE DATE

Section

A-401. Effective Date

ARTICLE A

TRANSITIONAL PROVISIONS FOR UNIFORM COMMERCIAL CODE AMENDMENTS (2022)

Prefatory Note to Article A—Transitional Provisions

The Uniform Commercial Code Amendments (2022) (2022 Amendments) pose special challenges. The amendments add a new Article 12, covering new classes of property, and provide extensive revisions to Article 9. They also include amendments to every other UCC article (save Article 6). Earlier transitional provisions do not provide an adequate template for addressing such a broad set of amendments. However, this article draws substantially on Article 9, Part 7, the transitional provisions applicable to the 1998 Article 9 Revisions. In particular, the substantial amendments to Article 9 and the new Article 12 contained in the 2022 Amendments require that special attention be given to post-effective date perfection and priority issues.

A uniform law as complex as the 2022 Amendments necessarily gives rise to difficult problems and uncertainties during the transition to the new law. As is customary for uniform laws, these amendments are based on the general assumption that all States will have enacted substantially identical versions. While always important, uniformity is particularly important to the success of these amendments, especially those to Article 9 and the new Article 12 and conforming amendments to other articles relating to each.

Article 9, Part 7, provided that several material changes in the law would be given effect one year after a "uniform" effective date. (As it turned out, all but a few states enacted the 1998 Article 9 Revisions with the uniform effective date.). However, for practical reasons many states may wish to provide an effective date for this act that is consistent with their usual timing for effectiveness of legislation. Consequently, this article does not provide for a uniform effective date but does provide for a uniform adjustment date (Adjustment Date), which is July 1, 2025, on which several material provisions (in particular, new priority rules that would override pre- effective-date established priorities) would apply. However, if the uniform Adjustment Date would be less than one year after the effective date for a state's adoption of these amendments, then the state should adopt an Adjustment Date that is one year after the state's effective date.

The minimum of a one-year period between the effective date and the Adjustment Date is important. It is intended primarily to provide sufficient time for a person to achieve perfection or priority of a security interest under the 2022 Amendments following the effective date, or for a person with an established priority in property to protect its priority before the priority might otherwise be lost on the Adjustment Date.

The law, other than the Uniform Commercial Code, of a state adopting the 2022 Amendments determines the time of day on the state's effective date on which the amendments take effect.

Legislative Note: *A state should codify Parts 1, 2 and 3 of this article as a part of the state's [Uniform Commercial Code].*

In its codification of this article a state should provide a title that is conducive to its usual methods of codification, which is likely to ensure that it is called to the attention of users of the state's [Uniform Commercial Code], and which will avoid misunderstandings as to the relationship of this article to the other provisions of the state's [Uniform Commercial Code]. The designation of "Article" indicates that this article is a part of the state's [Uniform Commercial Code] as are the other articles. A state that uses a designation other than "article" may adopt for this article that other designation (such as "division"). Alternatively, a state may wish to adopt for this article a distinctive designation, such as "annex," which would distinguish its focus on transitional provisions from the content of other articles.

PART 1. GENERAL PROVISIONS AND DEFINITIONS.

§ A-101. Short Title.

This article may be cited as Transitional Provisions for Uniform Commercial Code Amendments (2022).

§ A-102. Definitions.

(a) [Article A Definitions.] In this article:

(1) "Adjustment date" means July 1, 2025, or the date that is one year after [the effective date of this [act]], whichever is later.

(2) "Article 12" means Article 12 of [the Uniform Commercial Code].

(3) "Article 12 property" means a controllable account, controllable electronic record, or controllable payment intangible.

(b) [Definitions in other articles.] The following definitions in other articles of [the Uniform Commercial Code] apply to this article.

"Controllable account". Section 9-102.

"Controllable electronic record". Section 12-102.

"Controllable payment intangible". Section 9-102.

"Electronic money". Section 9-102.

"Financing statement". Section 9-102.

(c) [Article 1 definitions and principles.] Article 1 contains general definitions and principles of construction and interpretation applicable throughout this article.

Official Comment

Subsection headings. Subsection headings are not a part of the official text itself and have not been approved by the sponsors.

PART 2. GENERAL TRANSITIONAL PROVISION.

§ A-201. Saving Clause.

Except as provided in Part 3, a transaction validly entered into before [the effective date of this [act]] and the rights, duties, and interests flowing from the transaction remain valid thereafter and may be terminated, completed, consummated, or enforced as required or permitted by law other than [the Uniform Commercial Code] or, if applicable, [the Uniform Commercial Code], as though this [act] had not taken effect.

Official Comment

1. Source. This Section is drawn from pre-2022 Section 10-102(2) (now withdrawn).

2. In general: Prospective application. This section is a savings clause that provides in general for the prospective application of the 2022 Amendments and the preservation of the validity of pre-effective-date transactions and the rights, duties, and interests flowing from those transactions. Part 3 provides important exceptions to this prospective application for Articles 9 and new Article 12.

3. Prospective application: Examples.

"Conspicuous." 2022 section 1-201(b)(10) provides a revised definition of "conspicuous" and revised Comment 10 provides extensive new commentary. The revised definition applies to a record that becomes a part of the relevant transaction after the effective date.

"Hybrid transaction" and "hybrid lease." The 2022 revisions of Sections 2-102 and 2A- 102 address a sale of goods that is a part of a "hybrid transaction" and a lease of goods that is part of a "hybrid lease." See Sections 2-106(5) (defining "hybrid transaction") and 2A- 103(1)(h.1) (defining "hybrid lease"). These revisions apply to transactions entered into after the effective date.

4. Revisions reflecting continuation of pre-effective-date precedents. Several revisions are intended to clarify and reaffirm understandings of pre-effective-date interpretations of the Uniform Commercial Code and are intended to modify some pre-effective-date judicial interpretations. Examples include (i) the amendment to Section 3-104, which clarifies that neither a choice-of-law nor a choice-of-forum clause prevents a promise from being a negotiable instrument, (ii) the amendments to Section 4A-201, which indicate that a security procedure may impose an obligation on both the receiving bank and the customer and may involve the use of symbols, sounds, or biometrics, (iii) the clarifying revision of Section 5-116, (iv) the new definitions of "assignee" and "assignor" in Section 9-102(a)(7A) and (7B), and (v) clarification in Section 9-204(b.1) as to the attachment of a security interest in consumer goods as proceeds or commingled goods and in a commercial tort claim as proceeds. However, this transitional rule will be important in situations in which the controlling pre-effective-date case law is not consistent with the amended provisions.

PART 3. TRANSITIONAL PROVISIONS FOR ARTICLES 9 AND 12.

§ A-301. Saving Clause.

(a) [Pre-effective-date transaction, lien, or interest.] Except as provided in this part, Article 9 as amended by this [act] and Article 12 apply to a transaction, lien, or other interest in property, even if the transaction, lien, or interest was entered into, created, or acquired before [the effective date of this [act]].

(b) [Continuing validity.] Except as provided in subsection (c) and Sections A-302 through A-306:

(1) a transaction, lien, or interest in property that was validly entered into, created, or transferred before [the effective date of this [act]] and was not governed by [the Uniform Commercial Code], but would be subject to Article 9 as amended by this [act] or Article 12 if it had been entered into, created, or transferred on or after [the effective date of this [act]], including the rights, duties, and interests flowing from the transaction, lien, or interest, remains valid on and after [the effective date of this [act]]; and

(2) the transaction, lien, or interest may be terminated, completed, consummated, and enforced as required or permitted by this [act] or by the law that would apply if this [act] had not taken effect.

(c) [Pre-effective-date proceeding.] This [act] does not affect an action, case, or proceeding commenced before [the effective date of this [act]].

Official Comment

1. Source. This section derives from Section 9-702.

2. Pre-effective-date transactions, liens, and interests. Subsection (a) contains the general rule that Article 9 as amended by this act (2022 Article 9) and Article 12 generally apply to transactions, liens (including security interests), and interests in property, even if entered into, created, or acquired before the effective date. Thus, for example, secured transactions entered into under Article 9 before amendment by this act (as used in these official comments to Article A, "pre-2022 Article 9") must be terminated, completed, consummated, and enforced under this act. However, other provisions in this part provide exceptions to this general rule.

3. Pre-effective-date transactions not governed by pre-effective-date Uniform Commercial Code. Subsection (b) is an exception to the general rule. It applies to valid, pre- effective-date transactions, liens, and other interests in property that were not governed by the pre-2022 Uniform Commercial Code but would be governed by this act if they had been entered into or created after this act takes effect. Under subsection (b), these valid transactions, such as the sale of a controllable electronic record, retain their validity under this act and may be terminated, completed, consummated, and enforced as required or permitted by the law that would apply had this act not taken effect or, to the extent not inconsistent with that law, this act.

4. Judicial proceedings commenced before effective date. As is usual in transitional provisions, subsection (c) provides that this act does not affect litigation pending on the effective date.

§ A-302. Security Interest Perfected Before Effective Date.

(a) [Continuing perfection: perfection requirements satisfied.] A security interest that is enforceable and perfected immediately before [the effective date of this [act]] is a perfected security interest under this [act] if, on [the effective date of this [act]], the requirements for enforceability and perfection under this [act] are satisfied without further action.

(b) [Continuing perfection: enforceability or perfection requirements not satisfied.] If a security interest is enforceable and perfected immediately before [the effective date of this [act]], but the requirements for enforceability or perfection under this [act] are not satisfied on [the effective date of this [act]], the security interest:

(1) is a perfected security interest until the earlier of the time perfection would have ceased under the law in effect immediately before [the effective date of this [act]] or the adjustment date;

(2) remains enforceable thereafter only if the security interest satisfies the requirements for enforceability under Section 9-203, as amended by this [act], before the adjustment date; and

(3) remains perfected thereafter only if the requirements for perfection under this [act] are satisfied before the time specified in paragraph (1).

Official Comment

1. Source. This section derives from Section 9-703.

2. Perfected security interests under pre-2022 Article 9 and 2022 Article 9. This section deals with security interests that are perfected under pre-2022 Article 9 immediately before this act takes effect. Subsection (a) provides, not surprisingly, that if the security interest would be a perfected security interest under 2022 Article 9 (i.e., if the transaction satisfies 2022 Article 9's requirements for enforceability (attachment) and perfection), no further action need be taken for the security interest to be a perfected security interest.

Example 1: A pre-effective-date security agreement and financing statement covered "all accounts and general intangibles now owned or hereafter acquired." After the effective date the debtor acquired controllable accounts, controllable electronic records, and controllable payment intangibles. The security interest in the after-acquired collateral is enforceable and perfected under both pre-2022 and 2022 Article 9. The controllable accounts are accounts, the controllable electronic records and controllable payment intangibles are general intangibles, and filing is an appropriate method of perfection for that collateral under both versions of Article 9.

Other examples of methods of perfection under pre-2022 Article 9 that also would achieve perfection under 2022 Article 9 include filing a financing statement and perfection by control in electronic documents under pre-2022 and amended Section 7-106, in chattel paper under pre- 2022 Section 9-105, and in chattel paper evidenced by authoritative electronic records under 2022 Section 9-105.

3. Security interests enforceable and perfected under pre-2022 Article 9 but unenforceable or unperfected under 2022 Article 9. Subsection (b) deals with security interests that are enforceable and perfected under pre-2022 Article 9 immediately before this act takes effect but do not satisfy the requirements for enforceability (attachment) or perfection under 2022 Article 9. These security interests are perfected security interests until the earlier of the time perfection would have ceased under the law in effect immediately before this act takes effect and the adjustment date. If the security interest satisfies the requirements for attachment and perfection within that period, the security interest remains continuously perfected thereafter. If the security interest satisfies only the requirements for attachment within that period, the security interest becomes unperfected on the adjustment date.

Example 2: A pre-effective-date security agreement signed by Debtor in favor of Secured Party covers, among other things, "all money... and general intangibles now owned or hereafter acquired." Secured Party filed a proper financing statement in the appropriate filing office covering "All personal property." Debtor owns electronic money, spitcoin, issued by the government of El Cuspidouro. Under pre-2022 Article 9 the electronic money might be characterized as a general intangible if "money" were to be construed (at least for purposes of Article 9) to include only tangible money as to which perfection is possible only by possession. See pre-2022 Section 9-312(b)(3).

Alternatively, even if the spitcoin is money, perfection might be possible by filing under the baseline rule of Section 9-310, inasmuch as the spitcoin (an intangible) cannot be possessed. Assume, therefore, that under pre-2022 Article 9 Secured Party's security interest in the spitcoin is perfected by filing. Assume also that spitcoin can be subjected to control under Section 9-105A. As to the spitcoin owned by the debtor before the effective date, under subsection (b) the security interest would remain perfected until the adjustment date but would become unperfected under 2022 Article 9 on the adjustment date unless earlier perfected by control. This is so because a security interest in electronic money that can be subject to control under Section 9-105A, such as spitcoin, may be perfected only by control under 2022 Article 9. Sections 9-312(b)(4); 9-314(a). The security interest in any spitcoin acquired by the debtor after the effective date would be unperfected until the secured party obtains control.

Example 3: Secured Party has a pre-effective-date security interest in a security entitlement perfected by control pursuant to Sections 9-106 and 8-106(d)(3), based on control held by Kontroal Phreeque LLC (KP) on behalf of Secured Party. Even in the highly unlikely event that following the effective date the secured party could not prove that KP acknowledged its control on behalf of the secured party in conformity with 2022 Section 8-106(d)(3), its security interest would nevertheless remain perfected beyond the adjustment date. Perfection by control for a security entitlement under Section 9-106 depends on control under 8-106 and, under Section A-301(a), Part 3 of this article, including subsection (b), does not apply to transactions under Article 8 because Section A-301(a) applies only to Articles 9 and 12. The rules under pre-effective date Article 8 continue to apply to the pre-effective date transaction. As to financial assets acquired and becoming a part of the security entitlement after the effective date, however, 2022 Articles 8 and 9 would apply. Secured Party could perfect its security interest in those financial assets through a complying acknowledgment by KP or by filing. This means for a securities account involving active trading, for example, the secured party should ensure compliance with the 2022 Article 8 control requirements at or before the effective date so as to ensure perfection in post-effective date-acquired financial assets.

4. Interpretation of pre-effective-date security agreements. Section 9-102 defines "security agreement" as "an agreement that creates or provides for a security interest." Under Section 1-201(b)(3), an "agreement" is a "bargain of the parties in fact." If parties to a pre- effective-date security agreement describe the collateral by using a term defined in pre-2022 Article 9 in one way and defined in 2022 Article 9 in another way, in most cases it should be presumed that the bargain of the parties contemplated the meaning of the term under pre-2022 Article 9. Definitions of terms relating to collateral which have been amended in 2022 Article 9 are "account," "chattel paper," "instrument," "money," and "general intangible." A different result might be appropriate, for example, if a security agreement explicitly contemplated future changes in the Article 9 definitions of types of collateral–for example, " 'Accounts' means 'accounts' as defined in the Uniform Commercial Code Article 9 of [State X], as that definition may be amended from time to time." Whether a different interpretive approach is appropriate in any given case depends on the bargain of the parties, as determined by applying ordinary principles of contract law.

§ A-303. Security Interest Unperfected Before Effective Date.

A security interest that is enforceable immediately before [the effective date of this [act]] but is unperfected at that time:

(1) remains an enforceable security interest until the adjustment date;

(2) remains enforceable thereafter if the security interest becomes enforceable under Section 9-203, as amended by this [act], on [the effective date of this [act]] or before the adjustment date; and

(3) becomes perfected:

(A) without further action, on [the effective date of this [act]] if the requirements for perfection under this [act] are satisfied before or at that time; or

(B) when the requirements for perfection are satisfied if the requirements are satisfied after that time.

Official Comment

1. Source. This Section derives from Section 9-704.

2. Pre-effective-date enforceable but unperfected security interests. This section deals with security interests that are enforceable but unperfected (i.e., subordinate to the rights of a person who becomes a lien creditor) under pre-2022 Article 9 or other applicable law immediately before this act takes effect. These security interests remain enforceable until the adjustment date, and thereafter if the appropriate steps for attachment under 2022 Article 9 are taken before the adjustment date. See Section A-304(c) (This section's treatment of enforceability is the same as that of Section A-302.) The security interest becomes a perfected security interest on the effective date if, at that time, the security interest satisfies the requirements for perfection (which include the requirements for attachment) under 2022 Article 9. If the security interest does not satisfy the requirements for perfection until sometime thereafter, it becomes a perfected security interest at that later time.

Example 1: Prior to the effective date Debtor obtained a loan from Secured Party and signed a security agreement covering "all cryptocurrencies now owned or hereafter acquired." The security interest attached to various cryptocurrencies owned by Debtor, including 1,000 happicoins held by debtor on the happicoins blockchain platform. Debtor then transferred the 1,000 happicoins to Secured Party on the blockchain. Although the happicoins are general intangibles, Secured Party failed to file a financing statement necessary to perfect its security interest under pre-2022 Article 9.

Under 2022 Article 9, the happicoins would be controllable electronic records and the transfer of the happicoins to Secured Party would give Secured Party "control" of the happicoins as provided in Section 12-105. Before 2022 Article 9 (i.e., including 2022 Sections 9-107A and 9-314) and Article 12 became effective, Secured Party's security interest was unperfected as noted above. Upon the effective date, however, the security interest became perfected by control as a result of the pre-effective-date transfer of control to Secured Party.

Example 2: Prior to the effective date Debtor obtained a loan from Secured Party and signed a security agreement covering certain specified deposit accounts and "all documents and chattel paper now owned or hereafter acquired by Debtor." The security interest attached to the deposit accounts and to various documents and chattel paper owned by Debtor. Persons in control of certain electronic chattel paper, electronic documents, and deposit accounts included in the collateral acknowledged that they had control of that collateral on behalf of Secured Party. Assuming that an agency relationship cannot be established between these acknowledging persons and Secured Party, it is perhaps arguable that Secured Party's security interest in the relevant collateral was unperfected because Secured Party did not have control under pre-2022 Sections 7- 106, 9-104, and 9-105. However, because the pre-effective-date acknowledgments would give Secured Party control under the relevant 2022 sections, its security interest, even if not perfected pre-effective date, became perfected by control on the effective date.

§ A-304. Effectiveness of Actions Taken Before Effective Date.

(a) [Pre-effective-date action; attachment and perfection before adjustment date.] If action, other than the filing of a financing statement, is taken before [the effective date of this [act]] and the action would have resulted in perfection of the security interest had the security interest become enforceable before [the effective date of this [act]], the action is effective to perfect a security interest that attaches under this [act] before the adjustment date. An attached security interest becomes unperfected on the adjustment date unless the security interest becomes a perfected security interest under this [act] before the adjustment date.

(b) [Pre-effective-date filing.] The filing of a financing statement before [the effective date of this [act]] is effective to perfect a security interest on [the effective date of this [act]] to the extent the filing would satisfy the requirements for perfection under this [act].

(c) [Pre-effective-date enforceability action.] The taking of an action before [the effective date of this [act]] is sufficient for the enforceability of a security interest on [the effective date of this [act]] if the action would satisfy the requirements for enforceability under this [act].

Official Comment

1. Source. Subsections (a) and (b) of this Section derive from Section 9-705. Subsection (c) is new.

2. General. This section addresses primarily the situation in which the perfection step or requirement for enforceability is taken under pre-2022 Article 9 or other applicable law before the effective date of this act, but the security interest does not attach until after that date.

3. Perfection other than by filing. Subsection (a) applies when the perfection step is a step other than the filing of a financing statement. If the step that would be a valid perfection step under pre-2022 Article 9 or other law is taken before this act takes effect, and if a security interest attaches before the adjustment date, then the security interest becomes a perfected security interest upon attachment. However, the security interest becomes unperfected on the adjustment date unless the requirements for attachment and perfection under 2022 Article 9 are satisfied within that period.

4. Perfection by filing: ineffective filings made effective. Subsection (b) deals with financing statements that were filed under pre-2022 Article 9 and which would not have perfected a security interest under the pre-2022 Article, but which would perfect a security interest under 2022 Article 9. Under subsection (b), such a financing statement is effective to perfect a security interest to the extent it complies with 2022 Article 9. Subsection (b) applies regardless of the reason for the filing. When this act takes effect, the filing becomes effective to perfect a security interest assuming the filing satisfies the perfection requirements under 2022 Article 9.

Example 1. Prior to the effective date Debtor obtained a loan from Secured Party and signed a security agreement covering, among other collateral, "money," "accounts," "chattel paper," and "general intangibles." Secured Party filed a financing statement covering "all assets." If, under the applicable pre-2022 Article 9 as interpreted by the courts, electronic currency was "money" as defined in pre-2022 Section 1-201 even though as an intangible it could not be possessed, then under the applicable pre-2022 Section 9-312(b)(3), filing a financing statement was not an effective method of perfection. Assume, however, that under 2022 Articles 1 and 9, the electronic currency is not "money," and is instead a general intangible. Under 2022 Article 9, filing is an effective method of perfection. Upon the effective date of 2022 Article 9, the security interest became perfected by the pre-effective-date filed financing statement.

Example 2. Prior to the effective date Debtor obtained a loan from Secured Party and signed a security agreement covering, among other collateral, "accounts," "chattel paper," and "general intangibles." Secured Party filed a financing statement covering "accounts." Under the applicable pre-2022 Article 9, a certain right to payment was chattel paper because it was a lease of specific goods, even though the transaction also covered, and the lessee's monetary obligation also related to, various other assets and various services. Because the filed financing statement covered only accounts, the security interest in the chattel paper was unperfected. Under 2022 Article 9, however, the right to payment was an "account," and not chattel paper, assuming that the lessee's right to possession and use of the goods was not "the predominant purpose of the transaction." Section 9-102(a)(11)(B)(ii). On that assumption, upon the effective date the security interest became perfected by the pre-effective-date filed financing statement covering accounts.

5. Enforceability of security interest: unenforceable security interest made enforceable.

Example 3. Under the facts of Example 1, Section A-303, Comment 2, instead of signing a security agreement Debtor agreed orally to grant to Secured Party a security interest in the happicoins. It follows that under pre-2022 Article 9 Secured Party's security interest was unenforceable and did not attach to the happicoins for want of a signed security agreement. Pre-2022 Section 9-203(b)(3)(A). However, upon the effective date of 2022 Article 9, Secured Party had control of the happicoins under 2022 Article 9. Sections 12- 105. At that time the security interest became enforceable and attached under Sections 9- 107A and 9-203(b)(3)(D) and also was perfected by control.

§ A-305. Priority.

(a) [Determination of priority.] Subject to subsections (b) and (c), this [act] determines the priority of conflicting claims to collateral.

(b) [Established priorities.] Subject to subsection (c), if the priorities of claims to collateral were established before [the effective date of this [act]], Article 9 as in effect before [the effective date of this [act]] determines priority.

(c) [Determination of certain priorities on adjustment date.] On the adjustment date, to the extent the priorities determined by Article 9 as amended by this [act] modify the priorities established before [the effective date of this [act]], the priorities of claims to Article 12 property and electronic money established before [the effective date of this [act]] cease to apply.

Official Comment

1. Source. This section derives from Section 9-709.

2. Law governing priority and established priorities. Ordinarily, 2022 Article 9 determines the priority of conflicting claims to collateral under subsection (a). However, when the relative priorities of the claims were established before the effective date, pre-2022 Article 9 governs under subsection (b). Subsection (c) provides an exception to subsection (b).

Example 1. In 2021, prior to the effective date, Debtor obtained a loan from Secured Party and signed a security agreement covering "all cryptocurrency and money now owned or hereafter acquired." The security interest attached to various cryptocurrencies owned by Debtor, including 1,000 happicoins held by Debtor on the happicoins blockchain platform. Secured Party promptly filed a financing statement covering "all general intangibles, including cryptocurrencies." In 2022, also prior to the effective date, Debtor obtained a loan from Lender and signed a security agreement covering "all cryptocurrency." Although the happicoins are general intangibles, Lender failed to file a financing statement. Because the priorities of the claims were established before the effective date, pre-2022 Article 9 governs. Secured Party's perfected security interest has priority over Lender's unperfected security interest under pre-2022 Section 9-322(a)(2).

Example 2. The facts are the same as in Example 1, except that Debtor transferred control of the 1,000 happicoins to Lender on the blockchain in 2022 before the effective date. Because Lender failed to file a financing statement and control was not a method of perfection under pre-2022 Article 9, Lender's security interest was unperfected immediately prior to the effective date. However, because under 2022 Article 9 the happicoins are controllable electronic records and Lender has "control" of the happicoins under Section 12-105, Lender's security interest became perfected on the effective date. Nevertheless, because the priorities of Secured Party's and

Lender's security interests were established before the effective date, Secured Party's security interest continues to have priority after the effective date. (However, see Example 4 for the shift of priority on the adjustment date.)

Example 3. The facts are the same as in Example 1, except that in 2023, after the effective date, Debtor transferred control of the 1,000 happicoins to Lender on the blockchain. Under 2022 Article 9, the happicoins were controllable electronic records and the transfer of control of the happicoins gave Lender "control" of the happicoins as provided in Section 12-105. The affirmative step of transferring control established anew the relative priority of the conflicting claims after the effective date. 2022 Article 9 determines priority and Lender's security interest has priority under Section 9-326A (without any deferral until the adjustment date). Moreover, Lender also may have priority over other property claims as a qualifying purchaser under Section 12-104(e).

One consequence of the rule on established priorities in subsection (b) is that the mere taking effect of this act does not of itself adversely affect the priority of conflicting claims to collateral, as Example 2 illustrates. However, as Example 3 illustrates, relative priorities that are "established" before the effective date do not necessarily remain unchanged following the effective date. Of course, unlike priority contests among security interests, some priorities are established permanently, for example, the rights of a buyer of property who took free of a security interest under pre-2022 Article 9.

3. Modification of established priorities on adjustment date. Subsection (c) provides an exception to the respect that subsection (b) affords to pre- effective-date established priorities, but only for security interests in Article 12 property— controllable accounts, controllable electronic records, and controllable payment intangibles—and electronic money.

Example 4. The facts are the same as in Example 2. Lender's security interest became perfected by control on the effective date, Secured Party's established priority continued to apply under subsection (b). Under subsection (c), however, on the adjustment date the priorities shifted. Secured Party's established priority ceased to apply and Lender's perfection by control gave Lender priority under 2022 Section 9-326A.

4. Transfers of collateral after the effective date.

Example 5. The facts are the same as in Example 2. In 2023, after the effective date, Debtor acquired an additional 500 happicoins. The security interests of both Secured Party and Lender attached to the happicoins pursuant to the after-acquired property clauses in their respective security agreements. Secured Party's security interest was perfected by its earlier financing statement filing. Lender then perfected its security interest by Debtor's transfer of control of the happicoins to Lender. Lender's security interest in the additional happicoins perfected by control gave Lender priority as to those happicoins under Section 9-326A. Unlike the situation in Example 2, however, as to the newly acquired happicoins the priorities were not established prior to the effective date. Before the effective date neither creditor could have had a "perfected" security interest in happicoins in which Debtor had not yet acquired rights.

Example 6. The facts are the same as in Example 1. In 2023, after the effective date, Debtor transferred 750 spitcoins, an electronic money, to Beier. Beier then obtained control of the spitcoins under Section 9-105A. Secured Party's security interest in the spitcoins, which were either money not capable of being possessed or general intangibles under pre-2022 Article 9, are assumed to be perfected by filing. See Section A-302, Comment 3, Example 2. Because there was no wrongful collusion with Debtor (indeed, Beier had no knowledge or notice of Secured Party's security interest), Beier took the spitcoin free of Secured Party's security interest under Section 9-332(c).

§ A-306. Priority of Claims When Priority Rules of Article 9 Do Not Apply.

(a) [Determination of priority.] Subject to subsections (b) and (c), Article 12 determines the priority of conflicting claims to Article 12 property when the priority rules of Article 9 as amended by this [act] do not apply.

(b) [Established priorities.] Subject to subsection (c), when the priority rules of Article 9 as amended by this [act] do not apply and the priorities of claims to Article 12 property were established before [the effective date of this [act]], law other than Article 12 determines priority.

(c) [Determination of certain priorities on adjustment date.] When the priority rules of Article 9 as amended by this [act] do not apply, to the extent the priorities determined by this [act] modify the priorities established before [the effective date of this [act]], the priorities of claims to Article 12 property established before [the effective date of this [act]] cease to apply on the adjustment date.

Official Comment

1. Source. This section derives from Section 9-709 and, in part, from Section 8-510.

2. Applicability of this section to Article 12 property. Although this section applies to Article 12 property (controllable accounts, controllable electronic records, and controllable payment intangibles) when the priority rules of Article 9 do not apply, it applies primarily to controllable electronic records. Its application to controllable accounts and controllable payment intangibles is quite limited because Article 9 applies to most sales of accounts and payment intangibles (as well as to the use of that property to secure an obligation). Section 9-109(a)(3). There is a very limited exclusion from the scope of Article 9 for a sale of accounts and payment intangibles in connection with a sale of the business out of which they arose. Section 9-109(d)(4).

3. Law governing priority and established priorities. Ordinarily, when the priority rules of Article 9 do not apply, Article 12 determines the priority of conflicting claims to Article 12 property under subsection (a). However, when the relative priorities of the claims were established before the effective date, under subsection (b) law other than Article 12 governs. Subsection (c) provides an exception to subsection (b).

4. Law governing priority and established priorities.

> **Example 1.** In 2021, prior to the effective date, Aiko owned 500 happicoins (a cryptocurrency consisting of controllable electronic records) over which Aiko had control (within the meaning of Section 12-105, which was not yet effective) on the happicoin blockchain. In December 2021 Aiko sold the 500 happicoins to Barbara for $10,000 cash. Aiko provided Barbara with a signed memorandum acknowledging the sale and Aiko's receipt of the purchase price and agreeing to hold the happicoins for Barbara pending Barbara's further instructions.
>
> In January 2022 (also prior to the effective date), Aiko sold the same 500 happicoins to Molly for $12,000 cash. Aiko provided Molly with a signed memorandum similar to the one Aiko had provided to Barbara. Assume that, under the non-Uniform Commercial Code applicable law, Barbara remained the owner of the happicoins and under that law Molly obtained no interest in the happicoins pursuant to the purported sale because Aiko had retained no interest and had nothing to transfer to Molly. Because the priorities of the claims of Aiko, Barbara, and Molly were established before the effective date, under subsection (a) those priorities remained in effect after the effective date and Barbara remains the owner of the happicoins.
>
> **Example 2.** The facts are the same as in Example 1, except that before the effective date, Aiko transferred control of the happicoins to Molly on the happicoins blockchain. Again, assume that under the non-Uniform Commercial Code applicable law that transfer of control had no legal effect. After the effective date the relative priorities are unchanged from those described in Example 1 because the relative priorities were established before the effective date and subsection (b) applies.
>
> **Example 3.** The facts are the same as in Example 1, except that after the effective date, Aiko transferred control of the happicoins to Molly on the happicoins blockchain. Under Article 12, the happicoins were controllable electronic records and the transfer of control of the happicoins gave Molly "control" of the happicoins as provided in Section 12-105. Because (it is assumed) Molly met the requirements for a "qualifying purchaser" under Section 12-104(e), Molly acquired the happicoins free of Barbara's property claim. The affirmative step of transferring control after the effective date established anew the relative priority of the conflicting claims after the effective date. Under Section A-301(a), Article 12 applies to the pre-effective-date transactions and property interests and subsection (a) of this section applies.

5. Modification of established priorities on adjustment date. Subsection (c) provides an exception to the respect that subsection (b) affords to pre-effective-date established priorities.

> **Example 4.** The facts are the same as in Example 2. However, on the adjustment date the established priorities change. Because (it is assumed) Molly met the requirements for a "qualifying purchaser" under Section 12-104(e), on the adjustment date Molly acquired the happicoins free of Barbara's property claim. Under Section A-301(a), Article 12 applies to the pre-effective-date transactions and property interests and subsection (a) of this section applies.

6. Transfers after the effective date.

> **Example 5.** The facts are the same as in Example 1, except that after the effective date Aiko sold the happicoins to Jacob, for value, and also transferred control of the happicoins to Jacob on the happicoins blockchain. Because (it is assumed) Jacob met the requirements for a "qualifying purchaser" under Section 12-104(e), Jacob acquired the happicoins free of both Barbara's and Molly's property claims. Note that Jacob took the happicoins free of conflicting claims in the post-effective date acquisition immediately upon

acquisition as a qualifying purchaser. Jacob's priority was established after the effective date and was not deferred until the adjustment date, as was the case for Molly's rights in Example 4.

PART 4. EFFECTIVE DATE.

§ A-401. Effective Date.

This [act] takes effect on…

UNIFORM FRAUDULENT TRANSFER ACT

Section

1. Definitions
2. Insolvency
3. Value
4. Transfers Fraudulent as to Present and Future Creditors
5. Transfers Fraudulent as to Present Creditors
6. When Transfer Is Made or Obligation Is Incurred
7. Remedies of Creditors
8. Defenses, Liability, and Protection of Transferee
9. Extinguishment of [Claim for Relief] [Cause of Action]
10. Supplementary Provisions
11. Uniformity of Application and Construction
12. Short Title
13. Repeal

§ 1. Definitions.

As used in this [Act]:

(1) "Affiliate" means:

(i) a person who directly or indirectly owns, controls, or holds with power to vote, 20 percent or more of the outstanding voting securities of the debtor, other than a person who holds the securities,

(A) as a fiduciary or agent without sole discretionary power to vote the securities; or

(B) solely to secure a debt, if the person has not exercised the power to vote;

(ii) a corporation 20 percent or more of whose outstanding voting securities are directly or indirectly owned, controlled, or held with power to vote, by the debtor or a person who directly or indirectly owns, controls, or holds with power to vote, 20 percent or more of the outstanding voting securities of the debtor, other than a person who holds the securities,

(A) as a fiduciary or agent without sole power to vote the securities; or

(B) solely to secure a debt, if the person has not in fact exercised the power to vote;

(iii) a person whose business is operated by the debtor under a lease or other agreement, or a person substantially all of whose assets are controlled by the debtor; or

(iv) a person who operates the debtor's business under a lease or other agreement or controls substantially all of the debtor's assets.

(2) "Asset" means property of a debtor, but the term does not include:

(i) property to the extent it is encumbered by a valid lien;

(ii) property to the extent it is generally exempt under nonbankruptcy law; or

(iii) an interest in property held in tenancy by the entireties to the extent it is not subject to process by a creditor holding a claim against only one tenant.

(3) "Claim" means a right to payment, whether or not the right is reduced to judgment, liquidated, unliquidated, fixed, contingent, matured, unmatured, disputed, undisputed, legal, equitable, secured, or unsecured.

(4) "Creditor" means a person who has a claim.

(5) "Debt" means liability on a claim.

(6) "Debtor" means a person who is liable on a claim.

(7) "Insider" includes:

(i) if the debtor is an individual,

(A) a relative of the debtor or of a general partner of the debtor;

(B) a partnership in which the debtor is a general partner;

(C) a general partner in a partnership described in clause (B); or

(D) a corporation of which the debtor is a director, officer, or person in control;

(ii) if the debtor is a corporation,

(A) a director of the debtor;

(B) an officer of the debtor;

(C) a person in control of the debtor;

(D) a partnership in which the debtor is a general partner;

(E) a general partner in a partnership described in clause (D); or

(F) a relative of a general partner, director, officer, or person in control of the debtor;

(iii) if the debtor is a partnership,

(A) a general partner in the debtor;

(B) a relative of a general partner in, or a general partner of, or a person in control of the debtor;

(C) another partnership in which the debtor is a general partner;

(D) a general partner in a partnership described in clause (C); or

(E) a person in control of the debtor;

(iv) an affiliate, or an insider of an affiliate as if the affiliate were the debtor; and

(v) a managing agent of the debtor.

(8) "Lien" means a charge against or an interest in property to secure payment of a debt or performance of an obligation, and includes a security interest created by agreement, a judicial lien obtained by legal or equitable process or proceedings, a common-law lien, or a statutory lien.

(9) "Person" means an individual, partnership, corporation, association, organization, government or governmental subdivision or agency, business trust, estate, trust, or any other legal or commercial entity.

(10) "Property" means anything that may be the subject of ownership.

(11) "Relative" means an individual related by consanguinity within the third degree as determined by the common law, a spouse, or an individual related to a spouse within the third degree as so determined, and includes an individual in an adoptive relationship within the third degree.

(12) "Transfer" means every mode, direct or indirect, absolute or conditional, voluntary or involuntary, of disposing of or parting with an asset or an interest in an asset, and includes payment of money, release, lease, and creation of a lien or other encumbrance.

(13) "Valid lien" means a lien that is effective against the holder of a judicial lien subsequently obtained by legal or equitable process or proceedings.

§ 2. Insolvency.

(a) A debtor is insolvent if the sum of the debtor's debts is greater than all of the debtor's assets at a fair valuation.

(b) A debtor who is generally not paying his [or her] debts as they become due is presumed to be insolvent.

(c) A partnership is insolvent under subsection (a) if the sum of the partnership's debts is greater than the aggregate, at a fair valuation, of all of the partnership's assets and the sum of the excess of the value of each general partner's nonpartnership assets over the partner's nonpartnership debts.

(d) Assets under this section do not include property that has been transferred, concealed, or removed with intent to hinder, delay, or defraud creditors or that has been transferred in a manner making the transfer voidable under this [Act].

(e) Debts under this section do not include an obligation to the extent it is secured by a valid lien on property of the debtor not included as an asset.

§ 3. Value.

(a) Value is given for a transfer or an obligation if, in exchange for the transfer or obligation, property is transferred or an antecedent debt is secured or satisfied, but value does not include an unperformed promise made otherwise than in the ordinary course of the promisor's business to furnish support to the debtor or another person.

(b) For the purposes of Sections 4(a)(2) and 5, a person gives a reasonably equivalent value if the person acquires an interest of the debtor in an asset pursuant to a regularly conducted, noncollusive foreclosure sale or execution of a power of sale for the acquisition or disposition of the interest of the debtor upon default under a mortgage, deed of trust, or security agreement.

(c) A transfer is made for present value if the exchange between the debtor and the transferee is intended by them to be contemporaneous and is in fact substantially contemporaneous.

§ 4. Transfers Fraudulent as to Present and Future Creditors.

(a) A transfer made or obligation incurred by a debtor is fraudulent as to a creditor, whether the creditor's claim arose before or after the transfer was made or the obligation was incurred, if the debtor made the transfer or incurred the obligation:

(1) with actual intent to hinder, delay, or defraud any creditor of the debtor; or

(2) without receiving a reasonably equivalent value in exchange for the transfer or obligation, and the debtor:

(i) was engaged or was about to engage in a business or a transaction for which the remaining assets of the debtor were unreasonably small in relation to the business or transaction; or

(ii) intended to incur, or believed or reasonably should have believed that he [or she] would incur, debts beyond his [or her] ability to pay as they became due.

(b) In determining actual intent under subsection (a)(1), consideration may be given, among other factors, to whether:

(1) the transfer or obligation was to an insider;

(2) the debtor retained possession or control of the property transferred after the transfer;

(3) the transfer or obligation was disclosed or concealed;

(4) before the transfer was made or obligation was incurred, the debtor had been sued or threatened with suit;

(5) the transfer was of substantially all the debtor's assets;

(6) the debtor absconded;

(7) the debtor removed or concealed assets;

(8) the value of the consideration received by the debtor was reasonably equivalent to the value of the asset transferred or the amount of the obligation incurred;

(9) the debtor was insolvent or became insolvent shortly after the transfer was made or the obligation was incurred;

(10) the transfer occurred shortly before or shortly after a substantial debt was incurred; and

(11) the debtor transferred the essential assets of the business to a lienor who transferred the assets to an insider of the debtor.

§ 5. Transfers Fraudulent as to Present Creditors.

(a) A transfer made or obligation incurred by a debtor is fraudulent as to a creditor whose claim arose before the transfer was made or the obligation was incurred if the debtor made the transfer or incurred the obligation without receiving a reasonably equivalent value in exchange for the transfer or obligation and the debtor was insolvent at that time or the debtor became insolvent as a result of the transfer or obligation.

(b) A transfer made by a debtor is fraudulent as to a creditor whose claim arose before the transfer was made if the transfer was made to an insider for an antecedent debt, the debtor was insolvent at that time, and the insider had reasonable cause to believe that the debtor was insolvent.

§ 6. When Transfer Is Made or Obligation Is Incurred.

For the Purposes of this [Act]:

(1) a transfer is made:

(i) with respect to an asset that is real property other than a fixture, but including the interest of a seller or purchaser under a contract for the sale of the asset, when the transfer is so far perfected that a good-faith purchaser of the asset from the debtor against whom applicable law permits the transfer to be perfected cannot acquire an interest in the asset that is superior to the interest of the transferee; and

(ii) with respect to an asset that is not real property or that is a fixture, when the transfer is so far perfected that a creditor on a simple contract cannot acquire a judicial lien otherwise than under this [Act] that is superior to the interest of the transferee;

(2) if applicable law permits the transfer to be perfected as provided in paragraph (1) and the transfer is not so perfected before the commencement of an action for relief under this [Act], the transfer is deemed made immediately before the commencement of the action;

(3) if applicable law does not permit the transfer to be perfected as provided in paragraph (1), the transfer is made when it becomes effective between the debtor and the transferee;

(4) a transfer is not made until the debtor has acquired rights in the asset transferred;

(5) an obligation is incurred:

(i) if oral, when it becomes effective between the parties; or

(ii) if evidenced by a writing, when the writing executed by the obligor is delivered to or for the benefit of the obligee.

§ 7. Remedies of Creditors.

(a) In an action for relief against a transfer or obligation under this [Act], a creditor, subject to the limitations in Section 8, may obtain:

(1) avoidance of the transfer or obligation to the extent necessary to satisfy the creditor's claim;

[(2) an attachment or other provisional remedy against the asset transferred or other property of the transferee in accordance with the procedure prescribed by [];]

(3) subject to applicable principles of equity and in accordance with applicable rules of civil procedure,

(i) an injunction against further disposition by the debtor or a transferee, or both, of the asset transferred or of other property;

(ii) appointment of a receiver to take charge of the asset transferred or of other property of the transferee; or

(iii) any other relief the circumstances may require.

(b) If a creditor has obtained a judgment on a claim against the debtor, the creditor, if the court so orders, may levy execution on the asset transferred or its proceeds.

§ 8. Defenses, Liability, and Protection of Transferee.

(a) A transfer or obligation is not voidable under Section 4(a)(1) against a person who took in good faith and for a reasonably equivalent value or against any subsequent transferee or obligee.

(b) Except as otherwise provided in this section, to the extent a transfer is voidable in an action by a creditor under Section 7(a)(1), the creditor may recover judgment for the value of the asset transferred, as adjusted under subsection (c), or the amount necessary to satisfy the creditor's claim, whichever is less. The judgment may be entered against:

(1) the first transferee of the asset or the person for whose benefit the transfer was made; or

(2) any subsequent transferee other than a good-faith transferee or obligee who took for value or from any subsequent transferee or obligee.

(c) If the judgment under subsection (b) is based upon the value of the asset transferred, the judgment must be for an amount equal to the value of the asset at the time of the transfer, subject to adjustment as the equities may require.

(d) Notwithstanding voidability of a transfer or an obligation under this [Act], a good-faith transferee or obligee is entitled, to the extent of the value given the debtor for the transfer or obligation, to

(1) a lien on or a right to retain any interest in the asset transferred;

(2) enforcement of any obligation incurred; or

(3) a reduction in the amount of the liability on the judgment.

(e) A transfer is not voidable under Section 4(a)(2) or Section 5 if the transfer results from:

(1) termination of a lease upon default by the debtor when the termination is pursuant to the lease and applicable law; or

(2) enforcement of a security interest in compliance with Article 9 of the Uniform Commercial Code.

(f) A transfer is not voidable under Section 5(b):

(1) to the extent the insider gave new value to or for the benefit of the debtor after the transfer was made unless the new value was secured by a valid lien;

(2) if made in the ordinary course of business or financial affairs of the debtor and the insider; or

(3) if made pursuant to a good-faith effort to rehabilitate the debtor and the transfer secured present value given for that purpose as well as an antecedent debt of the debtor.

§ 9. Extinguishment of [Claim for Relief] [Cause of Action].

A [claim for relief] [cause of action] with respect to a fraudulent transfer or obligation under this [Act] is extinguished unless action is brought:

(a) under Section 4(a)(1), within 4 years after the transfer was made or the obligation was incurred or, if later, within one year after the transfer or obligation was or could reasonably have been discovered by the claimant;

(b) under Section 4(a)(2) or 5(a), within 4 years after the transfer was made or the obligation was incurred; or

(c) under Section 5(b), within one year after the transfer was made or the obligation was incurred.

§ 10. Supplementary Provisions.

Unless displaced by the provisions of this [Act], the principles of law and equity, including the law merchant and the law relating to principal and agent, estoppel, laches, fraud, misrepresentation, duress, coercion, mistake, insolvency, or other validating or invalidating cause, supplement its provisions.

§ 11. Uniformity of Application and Construction.

This [Act] shall be applied and construed to effectuate its general purpose to make uniform the law with respect to the subject of this [Act] among states enacting it.

§ 12. Short Title.

This [Act] may be cited as the Uniform Fraudulent Transfer Act.

§ 13. Repeal.

The following acts and all other acts and parts of acts inconsistent herewith are hereby repealed:

UNIFORM VOIDABLE TRANSACTIONS ACT

(Formerly Uniform Fraudulent Transfer Act)

(As Amended in 2014)

§ 1. Definitions
§ 2. Insolvency.
§ 3. Value.
§ 4. Transfer or Obligation Voidable as to Present or Future Creditor.
§ 5. Transfer or Obligation Voidable as to Present Creditor.
§ 6. When Transfer Is Made or Obligation is Incurred.
§ 7. Remedies of Creditor.
§ 8. Defenses, Liability, and Protection of Transferee or Obligee.
§ 9. Extinguishment of Claim for Relief.
§ 10. Governing Law.
§ 11. Application to Series Organization.
§ 12. Supplementary Provisions.
§ 13. Uniformity of Application and Construction.
§ 14. Relation to Electronic Signature in Global and National Commerce Act.
§ 15. Short Title.
§ 16. Repeals; Conforming Amendments.

§ 1. Definitions

As used in this [Act]:

(1) "Affiliate" means:

(i) a person that directly or indirectly owns, controls, or holds with power to vote, 20 percent or more of the outstanding voting securities of the debtor, other than a person that holds the securities:

(A) as a fiduciary or agent without sole discretionary power to vote the securities; or

(B) solely to secure a debt, if the person has not in fact exercised the power to vote;

(ii) a corporation 20 percent or more of whose outstanding voting securities are directly or indirectly owned, controlled, or held with power to vote, by the debtor or a person that directly or indirectly owns, controls, or holds, with power to vote, 20 percent or more of the outstanding voting securities of the debtor, other than a person that holds the securities:

(A) as a fiduciary or agent without sole discretionary power to vote the securities; or

(B) solely to secure a debt, if the person has not in fact exercised the power to vote;

(iii) a person whose business is operated by the debtor under a lease or other agreement, or a person substantially all of whose assets are controlled by the debtor; or

(iv) a person that operates the debtor's business under a lease or other agreement or controls substantially all of the debtor's assets.

(2) "Asset" means property of a debtor, but the term does not include:

(i) property to the extent it is encumbered by a valid lien;

(ii) property to the extent it is generally exempt under nonbankruptcy law; or

(iii) an interest in property held in tenancy by the entireties to the extent it is not subject to process by a creditor holding a claim against only one tenant.

(3) "Claim", except as used in "claim for relief", means a right to payment, whether or not the right is reduced to judgment, liquidated, unliquidated, fixed, contingent, matured, unmatured, disputed, undisputed, legal, equitable, secured, or unsecured.

(4) "Creditor" means a person that has a claim.

(5) "Debt" means liability on a claim.

(6) "Debtor" means a person that is liable on a claim.

(7) "Electronic" means relating to technology having electrical, digital, magnetic, wireless, optical, electromagnetic, or similar capabilities.

(8) "Insider" includes:

(i) if the debtor is an individual:

(A) a relative of the debtor or of a general partner of the debtor;

(B) a partnership in which the debtor is a general partner;
(C) a general partner in a partnership described in clause (B); or
(D) a corporation of which the debtor is a director, officer, or person in control;
(ii) if the debtor is a corporation:
(A) a director of the debtor;
(B) an officer of the debtor;
(C) a person in control of the debtor;
(D) a partnership in which the debtor is a general partner;
(E) a general partner in a partnership described in clause (D); or
(F) a relative of a general partner, director, officer, or person in control of the debtor;
(iii) if the debtor is a partnership:
(A) a general partner in the debtor;
(B) a relative of a general partner in, a general partner of, or a person in control of the debtor;
(C) another partnership in which the debtor is a general partner;
(D) a general partner in a partnership described in clause (C); or
(E) a person in control of the debtor;
(iv) an affiliate, or an insider of an affiliate as if the affiliate were the debtor; and
(v) a managing agent of the debtor.

(9) "Lien" means a charge against or an interest in property to secure payment of a debt or performance of an obligation, and includes a security interest created by agreement, a judicial lien obtained by legal or equitable process or proceedings, a common-law lien, or a statutory lien.

(10) "Organization" means a person other than an individual.

(11) "Person" means an individual, estate, partnership, association, trust, business or nonprofit entity, public corporation, government or governmental subdivision, agency, or instrumentality, or other legal entity.

(12) "Property" means anything that may be the subject of ownership.

(13) "Record" means information that is inscribed on a tangible medium or that is stored in an electronic or other medium and is retrievable in perceivable form.

(14) "Relative" means an individual related by consanguinity within the third degree as determined by the common law, a spouse, or an individual related to a spouse within the third degree as so determined, and includes an individual in an adoptive relationship within the third degree.

(15) "Sign" means, with present intent to authenticate or adopt a record:
(i) to execute or adopt a tangible symbol; or
(ii) to attach to or logically associate with the record an electronic symbol, sound, or process.

(16) "Transfer" means every mode, direct or indirect, absolute or conditional, voluntary or involuntary, of disposing of or parting with an asset or an interest in an asset, and includes payment of money, release, lease, license, and creation of a lien or other encumbrance.

(17) "Valid lien" means a lien that is effective against the holder of a judicial lien subsequently obtained by legal or equitable process or proceedings.

§ 2. Insolvency.

(a) A debtor is insolvent if, at a fair valuation, the sum of the debtor's debts is greater than the sum of the debtor's assets.

(b) A debtor that is generally not paying the debtor's debts as they become due other than as a result of a bona fide dispute is presumed to be insolvent. The presumption imposes on the party against which the presumption is directed the burden of proving that the nonexistence of insolvency is more probable than its existence.

(c) Assets under this section do not include property that has been transferred, concealed, or removed with intent to hinder, delay, or defraud creditors or that has been transferred in a manner making the transfer voidable under this [Act].

(d) Debts under this section do not include an obligation to the extent it is secured by a valid lien on property of the debtor not included as an asset.

§ 3. Value.

(a) Value is given for a transfer or an obligation if, in exchange for the transfer or obligation, property is transferred or an antecedent debt is secured or satisfied, but value does not include an unperformed promise made otherwise than in the ordinary course of the promisor's business to furnish support to the debtor or another person.

(b) For the purposes of Section 4(a)(2) and Section 5, a person gives a reasonably equivalent value if the person acquires an interest of the debtor in an asset pursuant to a regularly conducted, non-collusive foreclosure sale or execution of a power of sale for the acquisition or disposition of the interest of the debtor upon default under a mortgage, deed of trust, or security agreement.

(c) A transfer is made for present value if the exchange between the debtor and the transferee is intended by them to be contemporaneous and is in fact substantially contemporaneous.

§ 4. Transfer or Obligation Voidable as to Present or Future Creditor.

(a) A transfer made or obligation incurred by a debtor is voidable as to a creditor, whether the creditor's claim arose before or after the transfer was made or the obligation was incurred, if the debtor made the transfer or incurred the obligation:

(1) with actual intent to hinder, delay, or defraud any creditor of the debtor; or

(2) without receiving a reasonably equivalent value in exchange for the transfer or obligation, and the debtor:

(i) was engaged or was about to engage in a business or a transaction for which the remaining assets of the debtor were unreasonably small in relation to the business or transaction; or

(ii) intended to incur, or believed or reasonably should have believed that the debtor would incur, debts beyond the debtor's ability to pay as they became due.

(b) In determining actual intent under subsection (a)(1), consideration may be given, among other factors, to whether:

(1) the transfer or obligation was to an insider;

(2) the debtor retained possession or control of the property transferred after the transfer;

(3) the transfer or obligation was disclosed or concealed;

(4) before the transfer was made or obligation was incurred, the debtor had been sued or threatened with suit;

(5) the transfer was of substantially all the debtor's assets;

(6) the debtor absconded;

(7) the debtor removed or concealed assets;

(8) the value of the consideration received by the debtor was reasonably equivalent to the value of the asset transferred or the amount of the obligation incurred;

(9) the debtor was insolvent or became insolvent shortly after the transfer was made or the obligation was incurred;

(10) the transfer occurred shortly before or shortly after a substantial debt was incurred; and

(11) the debtor transferred the essential assets of the business to a lienor that transferred the assets to an insider of the debtor.

(c) A creditor making a claim for relief under subsection (a) has the burden of proving the elements of the claim for relief by a preponderance of the evidence.

§ 5. Transfer or Obligation Voidable as to Present Creditor.

(a) A transfer made or obligation incurred by a debtor is voidable as to a creditor whose claim arose before the transfer was made or the obligation was incurred if the debtor made the transfer or incurred the obligation without receiving a reasonably equivalent value in exchange for the transfer or obligation and the debtor was insolvent at that time or the debtor became insolvent as a result of the transfer or obligation.

(b) A transfer made by a debtor is voidable as to a creditor whose claim arose before the transfer was made if the transfer was made to an insider for an antecedent debt, the debtor was insolvent at that time, and the insider had reasonable cause to believe that the debtor was insolvent.

(c) Subject to Section 2(b), a creditor making a claim for relief under subsection (a) or (b) has the burden of proving the elements of the claim for relief by a preponderance of the evidence.

§ 6. When Transfer Is Made or Obligation is Incurred.

For the purposes of this [Act]:

(1) a transfer is made:

(i) with respect to an asset that is real property other than a fixture, but including the interest of a seller or purchaser under a contract for the sale of the asset, when the transfer is so far perfected that a good-faith purchaser of the asset from the debtor against which applicable law permits the transfer to be perfected cannot acquire an interest in the asset that is superior to the interest of the transferee; and

(ii) with respect to an asset that is not real property or that is a fixture, when the transfer is so far perfected that a creditor on a simple contract cannot acquire a judicial lien otherwise than under this [Act] that is superior to the interest of the transferee;

(2) if applicable law permits the transfer to be perfected as provided in paragraph (1) and the transfer is not so perfected before the commencement of an action for relief under this [Act], the transfer is deemed made immediately before the commencement of the action;

(3) if applicable law does not permit the transfer to be perfected as provided in paragraph (1), the transfer is made when it becomes effective between the debtor and the transferee;

(4) a transfer is not made until the debtor has acquired rights in the asset transferred; and

(5) an obligation is incurred:

(i) if oral, when it becomes effective between the parties; or

(ii) if evidenced by a record, when the record signed by the obligor is delivered to or for the benefit of the obligee.

§ 7. Remedies of Creditor.

(a) In an action for relief against a transfer or obligation under this [Act], a creditor, subject to the limitations in Section 8, may obtain:

(1) avoidance of the transfer or obligation to the extent necessary to satisfy the creditor's claim;

(2) an attachment or other provisional remedy against the asset transferred or other property of the transferee if available under applicable law; and

(3) subject to applicable principles of equity and in accordance with applicable rules of civil procedure:

(i) an injunction against further disposition by the debtor or a transferee, or both, of the asset transferred or of other property;

(ii) appointment of a receiver to take charge of the asset transferred or of other property of the transferee; or

(iii) any other relief the circumstances may require.

(b) If a creditor has obtained a judgment on a claim against the debtor, the creditor, if the court so orders, may levy execution on the asset transferred or its proceeds.

§ 8. Defenses, Liability, and Protection of Transferee or Obligee.

(a) A transfer or obligation is not voidable under Section 4(a)(1) against a person that took in good faith and for a reasonably equivalent value given the debtor or against any subsequent transferee or obligee.

(b) To the extent a transfer is avoidable in an action by a creditor under Section 7(a)(1), the following rules apply:

(1) Except as otherwise provided in this section, the creditor may recover judgment for the value of the asset transferred, as adjusted under subsection (c), or the amount necessary to satisfy the creditor's claim, whichever is less. The judgment may be entered against:

(i) the first transferee of the asset or the person for whose benefit the transfer was made; or

(ii) an immediate or mediate transferee of the first transferee, other than:

(A) a good-faith transferee that took for value; or

(B) an immediate or mediate good-faith transferee of a person described in clause (A).

(2) Recovery pursuant to Section 7(a)(1) or (b) of or from the asset transferred or its proceeds, by levy or otherwise, is available only against a person described in paragraph (1)(i) or (ii).

(c) If the judgment under subsection (b) is based upon the value of the asset transferred, the judgment must be for an amount equal to the value of the asset at the time of the transfer, subject to adjustment as the equities may require.

(d) Notwithstanding voidability of a transfer or an obligation under this [Act], a good-faith transferee or obligee is entitled, to the extent of the value given the debtor for the transfer or obligation, to:

(1) a lien on or a right to retain an interest in the asset transferred;

(2) enforcement of an obligation incurred; or

(3) a reduction in the amount of the liability on the judgment.

(e) A transfer is not voidable under Section 4(a)(2) or Section 5 if the transfer results from:

(1) termination of a lease upon default by the debtor when the termination is pursuant to the lease and applicable law; or

(2) enforcement of a security interest in compliance with Article 9 of the Uniform Commercial Code, other than acceptance of collateral in full or partial satisfaction of the obligation it secures.

(f) A transfer is not voidable under Section 5(b):

(1) to the extent the insider gave new value to or for the benefit of the debtor after the transfer was made, except to the extent the new value was secured by a valid lien;

(2) if made in the ordinary course of business or financial affairs of the debtor and the insider; or

(3) if made pursuant to a good-faith effort to rehabilitate the debtor and the transfer secured present value given for that purpose as well as an antecedent debt of the debtor.

(g) The following rules determine the burden of proving matters referred to in this section:

(1) A party that seeks to invoke subsection (a), (d), (e), or (f) has the burden of proving the applicability of that subsection.

(2) Except as otherwise provided in paragraphs (3) and (4), the creditor has the burden of proving each applicable element of subsection (b) or (c).

(3) The transferee has the burden of proving the applicability to the transferee of subsection (b)(1)(ii)(A) or (B).

(4) A party that seeks adjustment under subsection (c) has the burden of proving the adjustment.

(h) The standard of proof required to establish matters referred to in this section is preponderance of the evidence.

§ 9. Extinguishment of Claim for Relief.

A claim for relief with respect to a transfer or obligation under this [Act] is extinguished unless action is brought:

(a) under Section 4(a)(1), not later than four years after the transfer was made or the obligation was incurred or, if later, not later than one year after the transfer or obligation was or could reasonably have been discovered by the claimant;

(b) under Section 4(a)(2) or 5(a), not later than four years after the transfer was made or the obligation was incurred; or

(c) under Section 5(b), not later than one year after the transfer was made.

§ 10. Governing Law.

(a) In this section, the following rules determine a debtor's location:

(1) A debtor who is an individual is located at the individual's principal residence.

(2) A debtor that is an organization and has only one place of business is located at its place of business.

(3) A debtor that is an organization and has more than one place of business is located at its chief executive office.

(b) A claim for relief in the nature of a claim for relief under this [Act] is governed by the local law of the jurisdiction in which the debtor is located when the transfer is made or the obligation is incurred.

§ 11. Application to Series Organization.

(a) In this section:

(1) "Protected series" means an arrangement, however denominated, created by a series organization that, pursuant to the law under which the series organization is organized, has the characteristics set forth in paragraph (2).

(2) "Series organization" means an organization that, pursuant to the law under which it is organized, has the following characteristics:

(i) The organic record of the organization provides for creation by the organization of one or more protected series, however denominated, with respect to specified property of the organization, and for records to be maintained for each protected series that identify the property of or associated with the protected series.

(ii) Debt incurred or existing with respect to the activities of, or property of or associated with, a particular protected series is enforceable against the property of or associated with the protected series only, and not against the property of or associated with the organization or other protected series of the organization.

(iii) Debt incurred or existing with respect to the activities or property of the organization is enforceable against the property of the organization only, and not against the property of or associated with a protected series of the organization.

(b) A series organization and each protected series of the organization is a separate person for purposes of this [Act], even if for other purposes a protected series is not a person separate from the organization or other protected series of the organization.

Legislative Note: *This section should be enacted even if the enacting jurisdiction does not itself have legislation enabling the creation of protected series. For example, in such an enacting jurisdiction this section will apply if a protected series of a series organization organized under the law of a different jurisdiction makes a transfer to another protected series of that organization and, under applicable choice of law rules, the voidability of the transfer is governed by the law of the enacting jurisdiction.*

§ 12. Supplementary Provisions.

Unless displaced by the provisions of this [Act], the principles of law and equity, including the law merchant and the law relating to principal and agent, estoppel, laches, fraud, misrepresentation, duress, coercion, mistake, insolvency, or other validating or invalidating cause, supplement its provisions.

§ 13. Uniformity of Application and Construction.

This [Act] shall be applied and construed to effectuate its general purpose to make uniform the law with respect to the subject of this [Act] among states enacting it.

§ 14. Relation to Electronic Signature in Global and National Commerce Act.

This [Act] modifies, limits, or supersedes the Electronic Signatures in Global and National Commerce Act, 15 U.S.C. Section 7001 et seq., but does not modify, limit, or supersede Section 101(c) of that act, 15 U.S.C. Section 7001(c), or authorize electronic delivery of any of the notices described in Section 103(b) of that act, 15 U.S.C. Section 7003(b).

§ 15. Short Title.

This [Act], which was formerly cited as the Uniform Fraudulent Transfer Act, may be cited as the Uniform Voidable Transactions Act.

§ 16. Repeals; Conforming Amendments.

(a) ....

(b) ....

(c) ....

Legislative Note: *The legislation enacting the 2014 amendments in a jurisdiction in which the act is already in force should provide as follows: (i) the amendments apply to a transfer made or obligation incurred on or after the effective date of the enacting legislation, (ii) the amendments do not apply to a transfer made or obligation incurred before the effective date of the enacting legislation, (iii) the amendments do not apply to a right of action that has accrued before the effective date of the enacting legislation, and (iv) for the foregoing purposes a transfer is made and an obligation is incurred at the time provided in Section 6 of the act. In addition, the enacting legislation should revise any reference to the act by its former title in other permanent legislation of the enacting jurisdiction.*

UNIFORM MOTOR VEHICLE CERTIFICATE OF TITLE AND ANTI-THEFT ACT

PART 1. DEFINITIONS AND EXCLUSIONS

Section

1. Definitions
2. Exclusions
3. Excepted Liens and Security Interests; Buyer from Manufacturer or Dealer

PART 2. CERTIFICATES OF TITLE

4. Certificate of Title Required
5. Optional Certificates of Title
6. Application for First Certificate of Title
7. Examination of Records
8. Issuance and Records
9. Contents and Effect
10. Delivery
11. Registration Without Certificate of Title; Bond
12. Refusing Certificate of Title
13. Lost, Stolen or Mutilated Certificates
14. Transfer
15. Transfer to or from Dealer; Records
16. Transfer by Operation of Law
17. Fees; Registration Cards; License Plates
18. When Department to Issue New Certificate
19. Scrapping, Dismantling or Destroying Vehicle
20. Perfection of Security Interests
21. Security Interest
22. Assignment by Lienholder
23. Release of Security Interest
24. Duty of Lienholder
25. Exclusiveness of Procedure
26. Suspension or Revocation of Certificates
27. Fees
28. Powers of Department
29. Hearings
30. Court Review

PART 1. DEFINITIONS AND EXCLUSIONS

§ 1. [Definitions].

Except when the context otherwise requires, as used in this act:

(a) "Dealer" means a person engaged in the business of buying, selling, or exchanging vehicles who has an established place of business in this state [and to whom current dealer registration plates have been issued by the Department].

(b) "Department" means the [Department of Motor Vehicles] of this state. [The term includes a [County Clerk] when authorized by the Department to receive a document [or article] on its behalf.]

(c) "Identifying number" means the numbers, and letters if any, on a vehicle designated by the Department for the purpose of identifying the vehicle.

(d) "Implement of husbandry" means a vehicle designed and adapted exclusively for agricultural, horticultural or livestock raising operations or for lifting or carrying an implement of husbandry and in either case not subject to registration if used upon the highways.

(e) "Lienholder" means a person holding a security interest in a vehicle.

(f) To "mail" means to deposit in the United States mail properly addressed and with postage prepaid.

(g) "Owner" means a person, other than a lienholder, having the property in or title to a vehicle. The term includes a person entitled to the use and possession of a vehicle subject to a security interest in another person, but excludes a lessee under a lease not intended as security.

(h) "Person" means a natural person, firm, copartnership, association or corporation.

[(i) "Pole trailer" means a vehicle without motive power designed to be drawn by another vehicle and attached to the towing vehicle by means of a reach, or pole, or by being boomed or otherwise secured to the towing vehicle, and ordinarily used for transporting long or irregularly shaped loads such as logs, poles, pipes, or structural members capable, generally, of sustaining themselves as beams between the supporting connections.]

(j) "Security agreement" means a written agreement which reserves or creates a security interest.

(k) "Security interest" means an interest in a vehicle reserved or created by agreement and which secures payment or performance of an obligation.

The term includes the interest of a lessor under a lease intended as security. A security interest is "perfected" when it is valid against third parties generally, subject only to specific statutory exceptions.

(l) "Special mobile equipment" means a vehicle not designed for the transportation of persons or property upon a highway and only incidentally operated or moved over a highway, including but not limited to: ditch digging apparatus, well boring apparatus and road construction and maintenance machinery such as asphalt spreaders, bituminous mixers, bucket loaders, tractors other than truck tractors, ditchers, levelling graders, finishing machines, motor graders, road rollers, scarifiers, earth moving carry-alls and scrapers, power shovels and drag lines, and self-propelled cranes and earth moving equipment. The term does not include house trailers, dump trucks, truck mounted transit mixers, cranes or shovels, or other vehicles designed for the transportation of persons or property to which machinery has been attached.

(m) "State" means a state, territory or possession of the United States, the District of Columbia, the Commonwealth of Puerto Rico, or a province of the Dominion of Canada.

(n) "Vehicle" means a device in, upon, or by which a person or property is or may be transported or drawn upon a highway, except a device moved by human power or used exclusively upon stationary rails or tracks.

§ 2. [Exclusions].

(a) No certificate of title need be obtained for:

(1) A vehicle owned by the United States unless it is registered in this state;

(2) A vehicle owned by a manufacturer or dealer and held for sale, even though incidentally moved on the highway or used for purposes of testing or demonstration; or a vehicle used by a manufacturer solely for testing;

(3) A vehicle owned by a non-resident of this state and not required by law to be registered in this state;

(4) A vehicle regularly engaged in the interstate transportation of persons or property for which a currently effective certificate of title has been issued in another state;

(5) A vehicle moved solely by animal power;

(6) An implement of husbandry;

(7) Special mobile equipment;

[(8) A self-propelled wheel chair or invalid tricycle;]

[(9) A pole trailer.]

(b) Part 3 of this act does not apply to:

(1) A vehicle moved solely by animal power;

(2) An implement of husbandry;

(3) Special mobile equipment;

(4) A self-propelled wheel chair or invalid tricycle.

§ 3. [Excepted Liens and Security Interests[; Buyer from Manufacturer or Dealer]].

This act does not apply to or affect:

(a) A lien given by statute or rule of law to a supplier of services or materials for the vehicle;

(b) A lien given by statute to the United States, this state, or any political subdivision of this state;

(c) A security interest in a vehicle created by a manufacturer or dealer who holds the vehicle for sale [but a buyer in the ordinary course of trade from the manufacturer or dealer takes free of the security interest].

PART 2. CERTIFICATES OF TITLE

§ 4. [Certificate of Title Required].

(a) Except as provided in Section 2, every owner of a vehicle which is in this state and for which no certificate of title has been issued by the Department shall make application to the Department for a certificate of title of the vehicle.

(b) The Department shall not register or renew the registration of a vehicle unless an application for a certificate of title has been delivered to the Department.

§ 5. [Optional Certificates of Title].

The owner of an implement of husbandry or special mobile equipment may apply for and obtain a certificate of title on it. All of the provisions of this Part are applicable to a certificate of title so issued, except that a person who receives a transfer of an interest in the vehicle without knowledge of the certificate of title is not prejudiced by reason of the existence of the certificate, and the perfection of a security interest under this act is not effective until the lienholder has complied with the provisions of applicable law which otherwise relate to the perfection of security interests in personal property.

§ 6. [Application for First Certificate of Title].

(a) The application for the first certificate of title of a vehicle in this state shall be made by the owner to the Department on the form it prescribes and shall contain:

(1) The name, residence and mail address of the owner;

(2) A description of the vehicle including, so far as the following data exists: its make, model, identifying number, type of body, the number of cylinders, and whether new or used;

(3) The date of purchase by applicant, the name and address of the person from whom the vehicle was acquired and the names and addresses of any lienholders in the order of their priority and the dates of their security agreements; and

(4) Any further information the Department reasonably requires to identify the vehicle and to enable it to determine whether the owner is entitled to a certificate of title and the existence or non-existence of security interests in the vehicle.

(b) If the application refers to a vehicle purchased from a dealer, it shall contain the name and address of any lienholder holding a security interest created or reserved at the time of the sale and the date of his security agreement and be signed by the dealer as well as the owner, and the dealer shall promptly mail or deliver the application to the Department.

(c) If the application refers to a vehicle last previously registered in another state or country, the application shall contain or be accompanied by:

(1) Any certificate of title issued by the other state or country;

(2) Any other information and documents the Department reasonably requires to establish the ownership of the vehicle and the existence or non-existence of security interests in it; and

(3) The certificate of a person authorized by the Department that the identifying number of the vehicle has been inspected and found to conform to the description given in the application, or any other proof of the identity of the vehicle the Department reasonably requires.

§ 7. [Examination of Records].

The Department, upon receiving application for a first certificate of title, shall check the identifying number of the vehicle shown in the application against the records of vehicles required to be maintained by Section 8 and against the record of stolen and converted vehicles required to be maintained by Section 35.

§ 8. [Issuance and Records].

(a) The Department shall file each application received and, when satisfied as to its genuineness and regularity and that the applicant is entitled to the issuance of a certificate of title, shall issue a certificate of title of the vehicle.

(b) The Department shall maintain a record of all certificates of title issued by it:

(1) Under a distinctive title number assigned to the vehicle;

(2) Under the identifying number of the vehicle;

[(3) Alphabetically, under the name of the owner;]

and, in the discretion of the Department, in any other method it determines.

§ 9. [Contents and Effect].

(a) Each certificate of title issued by the Department shall contain:

(1) The date issued;

(2) The name and address of the owner;

(3) The names and addresses of any lienholders, in the order of priority as shown on the application or, if the application is based on a certificate of title, as shown on the certificate;

(4) The title number assigned to the vehicle;

(5) A description of the vehicle including, so far as the following data exists: its make, model, identifying number, type of body, number of cylinders, whether new or used, and, if a new vehicle, the date of the first sale of the vehicle for use; and

(6) Any other data the Department prescribes.

(b) Unless a bond is filed as provided in Section 11(b), a distinctive certificate of title shall be issued for a vehicle last previously registered in another state or country the laws of which do not require that lienholders be named on a certificate of title to perfect their security interests. The certificate shall contain the legend "This vehicle may be subject to an undisclosed lien" and may contain any other information the Department prescribes. If no notice of a security interest in the vehicle is received by the Department within four (4) months from the issuance of the distinctive certificate of title, it shall, upon application and surrender of the distinctive certificate, issue a certificate of title in ordinary form.

(c) The certificate of title shall contain forms for assignment and warranty of title by the owner, and for assignment and warranty of title by a dealer, and may contain forms for applications for a certificate of title by a transferee, the naming of a lienholder and the assignment or release of the security interest of a lienholder;

(d) A certificate of title issued by the Department is prima facie evidence of the facts appearing on it.

(e) A certificate of title for a vehicle is not subject to garnishment, attachment, execution or other judicial process, but this Subsection does not prevent a lawful levy upon the vehicle.

§ 10. [Delivery].

The certificate of title shall be mailed to the first lienholder named in it or, if none, to the owner.

§ 11. [Registration Without Certificate of Title; Bond].

If the Department is not satisfied as to the ownership of the vehicle or that there are no undisclosed security interests in it, the Department may register the vehicle but shall either:

(a) Withhold issuance of a certificate of title until the applicant presents documents reasonably sufficient to satisfy the Department as to the applicant's ownership of the vehicle and that there are no undisclosed security interests in it; or

(b) As a condition of issuing a certificate of title, require the applicant to file with the Department a bond in the form prescribed by the Department and executed by the application, and either accompanied by the deposit of cash with the Department or also executed by a person authorized to conduct a surety business in this state. The bond shall be in an amount equal to one and one-half times the value of the vehicle as determined by the Department and conditioned to indemnify any prior owner and lienholder and any subsequent purchaser of the vehicle or person acquiring any security interest in it, and their respective successors in interest, against any expense, loss or damage, including reasonable attorney's fees, by reason of the issuance of the certificate of title of the vehicle or on account of any defect in or undisclosed security interest upon the right, title and interest of the applicant in and to the vehicle. Any such interested person has a right of action to recover on the bond for any breach of its conditions, but the aggregate liability of the surety to all persons shall not exceed the amount of the bond. The bond, and any deposit accompanying it, shall be returned at the end of three (3) years or prior thereto if the vehicle is no longer registered in this state and the currently valid certificate of title is surrendered to the Department, unless the Department has been notified of the pendency of an action to recover on the bond.

§ 12. [Refusing Certificate of Title].

The Department shall refuse issuance of a certificate of title if any required fee is not paid or if it has reasonable grounds to believe that:

(a) The applicant is not the owner of the vehicle;

(b) The application contains a false or fraudulent statement; or

(c) The applicant fails to furnish required information or documents or any additional information the Department reasonably requires.

§ 13. [Lost, Stolen, or Mutilated Certificates].

(a) If a certificate of title is lost, stolen, mutilated or destroyed or becomes illegible, the first lienholder or, if none, the owner or legal representative of the owner named in the certificate, as shown by the records of the Department, shall promptly make application for and may obtain a duplicate upon furnishing information satisfactory, to the Department. The duplicate certificate of title shall contain the legend "This is a duplicate certificate and may be subject to the rights of a person under the original certificate." It shall be mailed to the first lienholder named in it or, if none, to the owner.

(b) The Department shall not issue a new certificate of title to a transferee upon application made on a duplicate until fifteen (15) days after receipt of the application.

(c) A person recovering an original certificate of title for which a duplicate has been issued shall promptly surrender the original certificate to the Department.

§ 14. [Transfer].

(a) If an owner transfers his interest in a vehicle, other than by the creation of a security interest, he shall, at the time of the delivery of the vehicle, execute an assignment and warranty of title to the transferee in the space provided therefore on the certificate or as the Department prescribes, and cause the certificate and assignment to be mailed or delivered to the transferee or to the Department.

(b) Except as provided in Section 15, the transferee shall, promptly after delivery to him of the vehicle, execute the application for a new certificate of title in the space provided therefore on the certificate or as the Department prescribes, and cause the certificate and application to be mailed or delivered to the Department.

(c) Upon request of the owner or transferee, a lienholder in possession of the certificate of title shall, unless the transfer was a breach of his security agreement, either deliver the certificate to the transferee for delivery to the Department or, upon receipt from the transferee of the owner's assignment, the transferee's application for a new certificate[, the registration card] [, license plates] and the required fee, mail or deliver them to the Department. The delivery of the certificate does not affect the rights of the lienholder under his security agreement.

(d) If a security interest is reserved or created at the time of the transfer, the certificate of title shall be retained by or delivered to the person who becomes the lienholder, and the parties shall comply with the provisions of Section 21.

(e) Except as provided in Section 15 and as between the parties, a transfer by an owner is not effective until the provisions of this Section [and Section 17] have been complied with [; however, an owner who has delivered possession of the vehicle of the transferee and has complied with the provisions of this Section [and Section 17] requiring action by him is not liable as owner for any damages thereafter resulting from op-eration of the vehicle].

§ 15. [Transfer to or from Dealer; Records].

(a) If a dealer buys a vehicle and holds it for resale and procures the certificate of title from the owner or the lienholder within ten (10) days after delivery to him of the vehicle, he need not send the certificate to the Department but, upon transferring the vehicle to another person other than by the creation of a security interest, shall promptly execute the assignment and warranty of title by a dealer, showing the names and addresses of the transferee and of any lienholder holding a security interest created or reserved at the time of the resale and the date of his security agreement, in the spaces provided therefore on the certificate or as the Department prescribes, and mail or deliver the certificate to the Department with the transferee's application for a new certificate.

(b) Every dealer shall maintain for five (5) years a record in the form the Department prescribes of every vehicle bought, sold or exchanged by him, or received by him for sale or exchange, which shall be open to inspection by a representative of the Department or peace officer during reasonable business hours.

§ 16. [Transfer by Operation of Law].

(a) If the interest of an owner in a vehicle passes to another other than by voluntary transfer, the transferee shall, except as provided in Subsection (b), promptly mail or deliver to the Department the last certificate of title, if available, proof of the transfer, and his application for a new certificate in the form the Department prescribes.

(b) If the interest of the owner is terminated or the vehicle is sold under a security agreement by a lienholder named in the certificate of title, the transferee shall promptly mail or deliver to the Department the last certificate of title, his application for a new certificate in the form the Department prescribes, and an affidavit made by or on behalf of the lienholder that the vehicle was repossessed and that the interest of the owner was lawfully terminated or sold pursuant to the terms of the security agreement. If the lienholder succeeds to the interest of the owner and holds the vehicle for resale, he need not secure a new certificate of title but, upon transfer to another person, shall promptly mail or deliver to the transferee or to the Department the certificate, affidavit and other documents [and articles] required to be sent to the Department by the transferee.

(c) A person holding a certificate of title whose interest in the vehicle has been extinguished or transferred other than by voluntary transfer shall mail or deliver the certificate to the Department upon request of the Department. The delivery of the certificate pursuant to the request of the Department does not affect the rights of the person surrendering the certificate, and the action of the Department in issuing a new certificate of title as provided herein is not conclusive upon the rights of an owner or lienholder named the old certificate.

§ 17. [Fees[; Registration Cards][; License Plates]].

(a) An application for a certificate of title shall be accompanied by [the registration card][,] [license plates] [and] the required fee when mailed or delivered to the Department.

(b) An application for the naming of a lienholder or his assignee on a certificate of title shall be accompanied by [the registration card and] the required fee when mailed or delivered to the Department.

[(c) A transferor of a vehicle, other than a dealer transferring a new vehicle, shall deliver to the transferee at the time of the delivery of possession of the vehicle [the registration card] [and] [license plates] for the vehicle.]

§ 18. [When Department to Issue New Certificate].

(a) The Department, upon receipt of a properly assigned certificate of title, with an application for a new certificate of title, the required fee and any other documents [and articles] required by law, shall issue a new certificate of title in the name of the transferee as owner and mail it to the first lienholder named in it or, if none, to the owner.

(b) The Department, upon receipt of an application for a new certificate of title by a transferee other than by voluntary transfer, with proof of the transfer, the required fee and any other documents [and articles] required by law, shall issue a new certificate of title in the name of the transferee as owner. If the outstanding certificate of title is not delivered to it, the Department shall make demand therefore from the holder thereof.

(c) The Department shall file and retain for [five (5)] years every surrendered I certificate of title, the file to be maintained so as to permit the tracing of title of the vehicle designated therein.

§ 19. [Scrapping, Dismantling, or Destroying Vehicle].

An owner who scraps, dismantles or destroys a vehicle and a person who purchases a vehicle as scrap or to be dismantled or destroyed shall immediately cause the certificate of title to be mailed or delivered to the Department for cancellation. A certificate of title of the vehicle shall not again be issued except upon application containing the information the Department requires accompanied by a certificate of inspection in the form and content specified in Section 6(c)(3).

§ 20. [Perfection of Security Interests].

(a) Unless excepted by Section 3, a security interest in a vehicle of a type for which a certificate of title is required is not valid against creditors of the owner or subsequent transferees or lienholders of the vehicle unless perfected as provided in this act.

(b) A security interest is perfected by the delivery to the Department of the existing certificate of title, if any, an application for a certificate of title containing the name and address of the lienholder and the date of his security agreement and the required fee [and registration card]. It is perfected as of the time of its creation if the delivery is completed within ten (10) days thereafter, otherwise, as of the time of the delivery.

(c) If a vehicle is subject to a security interest when brought into this state, the validity of the security interest is determined by the law of the jurisdiction where the vehicle was when the security interest attached, subject to the following:

(1) If the parties understood at the time the security interest attached that the vehicle would be kept in this state and it was brought into this state within thirty (30) days thereafter for purposes other than transportation through this state, the validity of the security interest in this state is determined by the law of this state.

(2) If the security interest was perfected under the law of the jurisdiction where the vehicle was when the security interest attached, the following rules apply:

(A) If the name of the lienholder is shown on an existing certificate of title issued by that jurisdiction, his security interest continues perfected in this state.

(B) If the name of the lienholder is not shown on an existing certificate of title issued by that jurisdiction, the security interest continues perfected in this state for four (4) months after a first certificate of title of the vehicle is issued in this state, and also, thereafter if, within the four (4) month period, it is perfected in this state. This security interest may also be perfected in this state after the expiration of the four (4) month period; in that case perfection dates from the time of perfection in this state.

(3) If the security interest was not perfected under the law of the jurisdiction where the vehicle was when the security interest attached, it may be perfected in this state; in that case, perfection dates from the time of perfection in this state.

(4) A security interest may be perfected under paragraph (2)(B) or paragraph (3) of this Subsection either as provided in Subsection (b) or by the lienholder delivering to the Department a notice of security interest in the form the Department prescribes and the required fee.

§ 21. [Security Interest].

If an owner creates a security interest in a vehicle:

(a) The owner shall immediately execute the application, in the space provided lienholder on the certificate of title or on a separate form the Department prescribes, to name the lienholder on the certificate, showing the name and address of the lienholder and the date of his security agreement, and cause the certificate, application and the required fee [and registration card] to be delivered to the lienholder.

(b) The lienholder shall immediately cause the certificate, application and the required fee [and registration card] to be mailed or delivered to the Department.

(c) Upon request of the owner or subordinate lienholder, a lienholder in possession of the certificate of title shall either mail or deliver the certificate to the subordinate lienholder for delivery to the Department or, upon receipt from the subordinate lienholder of the owner's application and the required fee [and registration card], mail or deliver them to the Department with the certificate. The delivery of the certificate does not affect the rights of the first lienholder under his security agreement.

(d) Upon receipt of the certificate of title, application and the required fee [and registration card], the Department shall either endorse on the certificate or issue a new certificate containing the name and address of the new lienholder, and mail the certificate to the first lienholder named in it.

§ 22. [Assignment by Lienholder].

(a) A lienholder may assign, absolutely or otherwise, his security interest in the vehicle to a person other than the owner without affecting the interest of the owner or the validity of the security interest, but any person without notice of the assignment is protected in dealing with the lienholder as the holder of the security interest and the lienholder remains liable for any obligations as lienholder until the assignee is named as lienholder on the certificate.

(b) The assignee may, but need not to perfect the assignment, have the certificate of title endorsed or issued with the assignee named as lienholder, upon delivering to the Department the certificate and an assignment by the lienholder named in the certificate in the form the Department prescribes.

§ 23. [Release of Security Interest].

(a) Upon the satisfaction of a security interest in a vehicle for which the certificate of title is in the possession of the lienholder, he shall, within ten (10) days after demand and, in any event, within thirty (30) days, execute a release of his security interest, in the space provided therefore on the certificate or as the Department prescribes, and mail or deliver the certificate and release to the next lienholder named therein, or, if none, to the owner or any person who delivers to the lienholder an authorization from the owner to receive the certificate. The owner, other than a dealer holding the vehicle for resale, shall promptly cause the certificate and release to be mailed or delivered to the Department, which shall release the lienholder's rights on the certificate or issue a new certificate.

(b) Upon the satisfaction of a security interest in a vehicle for which the certificate of title is in the possession of a prior lienholder, the lienholder whose security interest is satisfied shall within ten (10) days after demand and, in any event, within thirty (30) days execute a release in the form the Department prescribes and deliver the release to the owner or any person who delivers to the lienholder an authorization from the owner to receive it. The lienholder in possession of the certificate of title shall either deliver the certificate to the owner, or the person authorized by him, for delivery to the Department, or, upon receipt of the release [and registration card], mail or deliver it [them] with the certificate to the Department, which shall release the subordinate lienholder's rights on the certificate or issue a new certificate.

§ 24. [Duty of Lienholder].

A lienholder named in a certificate of title shall, upon written request of the owner or of another lienholder named on the certificate, disclose any pertinent information as to his security agreement and the indebtedness secured by it.

§ 25. [Exclusiveness of Procedure].

The method provided in this act of perfecting and giving notice of security interests subject to this act is exclusive. Security interests subject to this act are hereby exempted from the provisions of law which otherwise require or relate to the [[recording] [filing] of instruments creating or evidencing security interests . . .].

§ 26. [Suspension or Revocation of Certificates].

(a) The Department shall suspend or revoke a certificate of title, upon notice and reasonable opportunity to be heard in accordance with Section 29, when authorized by any other provision of law or if it finds:

(1) The certificate of title was fraudulently procured or erroneously issued, or

(2) The vehicle has been scrapped, dismantled or destroyed.

(b) Suspension or revocation of a certificate of title does not, in itself, affect the validity of a security interest noted on it.

(c) When the Department suspends or revokes a certificate of title, the owner or person in possession of it shall, immediately upon receiving notice of the suspension or revocation, mail or deliver the certificate to the Department.

(d) The Department may seize and impound any certificate of title which has been suspended or revoked.

§ 27. [Fees].

(a) The Department shall be paid the following fees:

(1) For filing an application for a first certificate of title, $________;

(2) For each security interest noted upon a certificate of title, $________;

(3) For a certificate of title after a transfer, $________;

(4) For each assignment of a security interest noted upon a certificate of title, $________;

(5) For a duplicate certificate of title, $________;

(6) For an ordinary certificate of title issued upon surrender of a distinctive certificate, $________;

(7) For filing a notice of security interest, $________; and

(8) For a certificate of search of its records for each name or identifying number searched against, $________.

(b) If an application, certificate of title or other document [or article] required to be mailed or delivered to the Department under any provision of this act is not delivered to the Department within ten (10) days from the time it is required to be mailed or delivered, the Department shall collect, as a penalty, an amount equal to the fee required for the transaction.

§ 28. [Powers of Department].

(a) The Department shall prescribe and provide suitable forms of applications, certificates of title, notices of security interests, and all other notices and forms necessary to carry out the provisions of this act.

(b) The Department may:

(1) Make necessary investigations to procure information required to carry out the provisions of this act;

(2) Adopt and enforce reasonable rules and regulations to carry out the provisions of this act;

(3) Assign a new identifying number to a vehicle if it has none, or its identifying number is destroyed or obliterated, or its motor is changed, and shall either issue a new certificate of title showing the new identifying number or make an appropriate indorsement on the original certificate.

§ 29. [Hearings].

A person aggrieved by an act or omission to act of the Department under this act is entitled, upon request, to a hearing in accordance with [the Administrative Procedure Act of this state] [law].

§ 30. [Court Review].

A person aggrieved by an act or omission to act of the Department under this act is also entitled to a review thereof by the [] Court in accordance with [the Administrative Procedure Act of this state] [law].

TITLE 11—BANKRUPTCY

Chapter
1 GENERAL PROVISIONS
3 CASE ADMINISTRATION
5 CREDITORS, THE DEBTOR, AND THE ESTATE
7 LIQUIDATION
9 ADJUSTMENT OF DEBTS OF A MUNICIPALITY
11 REORGANIZATION
12 ADJUSTMENT OF DEBTS OF A FAMILY FARMER OR FISHERMAN WITH REGULAR INCOME
13 ADJUSTMENT OF DEBTS OF AN INDIVIDUAL WITH REGULAR INCOME
15 ANCILLARY AND OTHER CROSS-BORDER CASES

This Title was Enacted by Pub. L. 109-8.

CHAPTER 1. GENERAL PROVISIONS

Section

101. Definitions
102. Rules of Construction
103. Applicability of Chapters
104. Adjustment of Dollar Amounts
105. Power of Court
106. Waiver of Sovereign Immunity
107. Public Access to Papers
108. Extension of Time
109. Who May Be a Debtor
110. Penalty for Persons Who Negligently or Fraudulently Prepare Bankruptcy Petitions
111. Nonprofit Budget and Credit Counseling Agencies; Financial Management Instructional Courses
112. Prohibition on Disclosure of Name of Minor Children

§ 101. Definitions

In this title the following definitions shall apply:

(1) The term "accountant" means accountant authorized under applicable law to practice public accounting, and includes professional accounting association, corporation, or partnership, if so authorized.

(2) The term "affiliate" means—

(A) entity that directly or indirectly owns, controls, or holds with power to vote, 20 percent or more of the outstanding voting securities of the debtor, other than an entity that holds such securities—

(i) in a fiduciary or agency capacity without sole discretionary power to vote such securities; or

(ii) solely to secure a debt, if such entity has not in fact exercised such power to vote;

(B) corporation 20 percent or more of whose outstanding voting securities are directly or indirectly owned, controlled, or held with power to vote, by the debtor, or by an entity that directly or indirectly owns, controls, or holds with power to vote, 20 percent or more of the outstanding voting securities of the debtor, other than an entity that holds such securities—

(i) in a fiduciary or agency capacity without sole discretionary power to vote such securities; or

(ii) solely to secure a debt, if such entity has not in fact exercised such power to vote;

(C) person whose business is operated under a lease or operating agreement by a debtor, or person substantially all of whose property is operated under an operating agreement with the debtor; or

(D) entity that operates the business or substantially all of the property of the debtor under a lease or operating agreement.

(3) The term "assisted person" means any person whose debts consist primarily of consumer debts and the value of whose nonexempt property is less than $226,850.[1]

(4) The term "attorney" means attorney, professional law association, corporation, or partnership, authorized under applicable law to practice law.

(4A) The term "bankruptcy assistance" means any goods or services sold or otherwise provided to an assisted person with the express Uor implied purpose of providing information,

[1] Dollar amounts will change again on April 1, 2025.

advice, counsel, document preparation, or filing, or attendance at a creditors' meeting or appearing in a case or proceeding on behalf of another or providing legal representation with respect to a case or proceeding under this title.

(5) The term "claim" means—

(A) right to payment, whether or not such right is reduced to judgment, liquidated, unliquidated, fixed, contingent, matured, unmatured, disputed, undisputed, legal, equitable, secured, or unsecured; or

(B) right to an equitable remedy for breach of performance if such breach gives rise to a right to payment, whether or not such right to an equitable remedy is reduced to judgment, fixed, contingent, matured, unmatured, disputed, undisputed, secured, or unsecured.

(6) The term "commodity broker" means futures commission merchant, foreign futures commission merchant, clearing organization, leverage transaction merchant, or commodity options dealer, as defined in section 761 of this title, with respect to which there is a customer, as defined in section 761 of this title.

(7) The term "community claim" means claim that arose before the commencement of the case concerning the debtor for which property of the kind specified in section 541(a)(2) of this title is liable, whether or not there is any such property at the time of the commencement of the case.

(7A) The term "commercial fishing operation" means—

(A) the catching or harvesting of fish, shrimp, lobsters, urchins, seaweed, shellfish, or other aquatic species or products of such species; or

(B) for purposes of section 109 and chapter 12, aquaculture activities consisting of raising for market any species or product described in subparagraph (A).

(7B) The term "commercial fishing vessel" means a vessel used by a family fisherman to carry out a commercial fishing operation.

(8) The term "consumer debt" means debt incurred by an individual primarily for a personal, family, or household purpose.

(9) The term "corporation"—

(A) includes—

(i) association having a power or privilege that a private corporation, but not an individual or a partnership, possesses;

(ii) partnership association organized under a law that makes only the capital subscribed responsible for the debts of such association;

(iii) joint-stock company;

(iv) unincorporated company or association; or

(v) business trust; but

(B) does not include limited partnership.

(10) The term "creditor" means—

(A) entity that has a claim against the debtor that arose at the time of or before the order for relief concerning the debtor;

(B) entity that has a claim against the estate of a kind specified in section 348(d), 502(f), 502(g), 502(h) or 502(i) of this title; or

(C) entity that has a community claim.

(10A) The term "current monthly income"—

(A) means the average monthly income from all sources that the debtor receives (or in a joint case the debtor and the debtor's spouse receive) without regard to whether such income is taxable income, derived during the 6-month period ending on—

(i) the last day of the calendar month immediately preceding the date of the commencement of the case if the debtor files the schedule of current income required by section 521(a)(1)(B)(ii); or

(ii) the date on which current income is determined by the court for purposes of this title if the debtor does not file the schedule of current income required by section 521(a)(1)(B)(ii); and

(B) (i) includes any amount paid by any entity other than the debtor (or in a joint case the debtor and the debtor's spouse), on a regular basis for the household expenses of the debtor or the debtor's dependents (and, in a joint case, the debtor's spouse if not otherwise a dependent); and

(ii) excludes—

(I) benefits received under the Social Security Act (42 U.S.C. 301 et seq.);

(II) payments to victims of war crimes or crimes against humanity on account of their status as victims of such crimes;

(III) payments to victims of international terrorism or domestic terrorism, as those terms are defined in section 2331 of title 18, on account of their status as victims of such terrorism;

(IV) any monthly compensation, pension, pay, annuity, or allowance paid under title 10, 37, or 38 in connection with a disability, combat-related injury or disability, or death of a member of the uniformed services, except that any retired pay excluded under this subclause shall include retired pay paid under chapter 61 of title 10 only to the extent that such retired pay exceeds the amount of retired pay to which the debtor would otherwise be entitled if retired under any provision of title 10 other than chapter 61 of that title.

(11) The term "custodian" means—

(A) receiver or trustee of any of the property of the debtor, appointed in a case or proceeding not under this title;

(B) assignee under a general assignment for the benefit of the debtor's creditors; or

(C) trustee, receiver, or agent under applicable law, or under a contract, that is appointed or authorized to take charge of property of the debtor for the purpose of enforcing a lien against such property, or for the purpose of general administration of such property for the benefit of the debtor's creditors.

(12) The term "debt" means liability on a claim.

(12A) The term "debt relief agency" means any person who provides any bankruptcy assistance to an assisted person in return for the payment of money or other valuable consideration, or who is a bankruptcy petition preparer under section 110, but does not include—

(A) any person who is an officer, director, employee, or agent of a person who provides such assistance or of the bankruptcy petition preparer;

(B) a nonprofit organization that is exempt from taxation under section 501(c)(3) of the Internal Revenue Code of 1986;

(C) a creditor of such assisted person, to the extent that the creditor is assisting such assisted person to restructure any debt owed by such assisted person to the creditor;

(D) a depository institution (as defined in section 3 of the Federal Deposit Insurance Act) or any Federal credit union or State credit union (as those terms are defined in section 101 of the Federal Credit Union Act), or any affiliate or subsidiary of such depository institution or credit union; or

(E) an author, publisher, distributor, or seller of works subject to copyright protection under title 17, when acting in such capacity.

(13) The term "debtor" means person or municipality concerning which a case under this title has been commenced.

(13A) The term "debtor's principal residence"—

(A) means a residential structure if used as the principal residence by the debtor, including incidental property, without regard to whether that structure is attached to real property; and

(B) includes an individual condominium or cooperative unit, a mobile or manufactured home, or trailer if used as the principal residence by the debtor.

(14) The term "disinterested person" means a person that—

(A) is not a creditor, an equity security holder, or an insider;

(B) is not and was not, within 2 years before the date of the filing of the petition, a director, officer, or employee of the debtor; and

(C) does not have an interest materially adverse to the interest of the estate or of any class of creditors or equity security holders, by reason of any direct or indirect relationship to, connection with, or interest in, the debtor, or for any other reason.

(14A) The term "domestic support obligation" means a debt that accrues before, on, or after the date of the order for relief in a case under this title, including interest that accrues on that debt as provided under applicable nonbankruptcy law notwithstanding any other provision of this title, that is—

(A) owed to or recoverable by—

(i) a spouse, former spouse, or child of the debtor or such child's parent, legal guardian, or responsible relative; or

(ii) a governmental unit;

(B) in the nature of alimony, maintenance, or support (including assistance provided by a governmental unit) of such spouse, former spouse, or child of the debtor or such child's parent, without regard to whether such debt is expressly so designated;

(C) established or subject to establishment before, on, or after the date of the order for relief in a case under this title, by reason of applicable provisions of—

(i) a separation agreement, divorce decree, or property settlement agreement;

(ii) an order of a court of record; or

(iii) a determination made in accordance with applicable nonbankruptcy law by a governmental unit; and

(D) not assigned to a nongovernmental entity, unless that obligation is assigned voluntarily by the spouse, former spouse, child of the debtor, or such child's parent, legal guardian, or responsible relative for the purpose of collecting the debt.

(15) The term "entity" includes person, estate, trust, governmental unit, and United States trustee.

(16) The term "equity security" means—

(A) share in a corporation, whether or not transferable or denominated "stock", or similar security;

(B) interest of a limited partner in a limited partnership; or

(C) warrant or right, other than a right to convert, to purchase, sell, or subscribe to a share, security, or interest of a kind specified in subparagraph (A) or (B) of this paragraph.

(17) The term "equity security holder" means holder of an equity security of the debtor.

(18) The term "family farmer" means —

(A) individual or individual and spouse engaged in a farming operation whose aggregate debts do not exceed $11,097,350 and not less than 50 percent of whose aggregate noncontingent, liquidated debts (excluding a debt for the principal residence of such individual or such individual and spouse unless such debt arises out of a farming operation), on the date the case is filed, arise out of a farming operation owned or operated by such individual or such individual and spouse, and such individual or such individual and spouse receive from such farming operation more than 50 percent of such individual's or such individual and spouse's gross income for—

(i) the taxable year preceding; or

(ii) each of the 2d and 3d taxable years preceding; the taxable year in which the case concerning such individual or such individual and spouse was filed; or

(B) corporation or partnership in which more than 50 percent of the outstanding stock or equity is held by one family, or by one family and the relatives of the members of such family, and such family or such relatives conduct the farming operation, and

(i) more than 80 percent of the value of its assets consists of assets related to the farming operation;

(ii) its aggregate debts do not exceed $11,097,350 and not less than 50 percent of its aggregate noncontingent, liquidated debts (excluding a debt for one dwelling which is owned by such corporation or partnership and which a shareholder or partner maintains as a principal residence, unless such debt arises out of a farming operation), on the date the case is filed, arise out of the farming operation owned or operated by such corporation or such partnership; and

(iii) if such corporation issues stock, such stock is not publicly traded.

(19) The term "family farmer with regular annual income" means family farmer whose annual income is sufficiently stable and regular to enable such family farmer to make payments under a plan under chapter 12 of this title.

(19A) The term "family fisherman" means—

(A) an individual or individual and spouse engaged in a commercial fishing operation—

(i) whose aggregate debts do not exceed $2,268,550 and not less than 80 percent of whose aggregate noncontingent, liquidated debts (excluding a debt for the principal residence of such individual or such individual and spouse, unless such debt arises out of a commercial fishing operation), on the date the case is filed, arise out of a commercial fishing operation owned or operated by such individual or such individual and spouse; and

(ii) who receive from such commercial fishing operation more than 50 percent of such individual's or such individual's and spouse's gross income for the taxable year preceding the taxable year in which the case concerning such individual or such individual and spouse was filed; or

(B) a corporation or partnership—

(i) in which more than 50 percent of the outstanding stock or equity is held by—

(I) 1 family that conducts the commercial fishing operation; or

(II) 1 family and the relatives of the members of such family, and such family or such relatives conduct the commercial fishing operation; and

(ii) (I) more than 80 percent of the value of its assets consists of assets related to the commercial fishing operation;

(II) its aggregate debts do not exceed $2,268,550 and not less than 80 percent of its aggregate noncontingent, liquidated debts (excluding a debt for 1 dwelling which is owned by such corporation or partnership and which a shareholder or partner maintains as a principal residence, unless such debt arises out of a commercial fishing operation), on the date the case is filed, arise out of a commercial fishing operation owned or operated by such corporation or such partnership; and

(III) if such corporation issues stock, such stock is not publicly traded.

(19B) The term "family fisherman with regular annual income" means a family fisherman whose annual income is sufficiently stable and regular to enable such family fisherman to make payments under a plan under chapter 12 of this title.

(20) The term "farmer" means (except when such term appears in the term "family farmer") person that received more than 80 percent of such person's gross income during the taxable year of such person immediately preceding the taxable year of such person during which the case under this title concerning such person was commenced from a farming operation owned or operated by such person.

(21) The term "farming operation" includes farming, tillage of the soil, dairy farming, ranching, production or raising of crops, poultry, or livestock, and production of poultry or livestock products in an unmanufactured state.

(21A) The term "farmout agreement" means a written agreement in which—

(A) the owner of a right to drill, produce, or operate liquid or gaseous hydrocarbons on property agrees or has agreed to transfer or assign all or a part of such right to another entity; and

(B) such other entity (either directly or through its agents or its assigns), as consideration, agrees to perform drilling, reworking, recompleting, testing, or similar or related operations, to develop or produce liquid or gaseous hydrocarbons on the property.

(21B) The term "Federal depository institutions regulatory agency" means—

(A) with respect to an insured depository institution (as defined in section 3(c)(2) of the Federal Deposit Insurance Act) for which no conservator or receiver has been appointed, the appropriate Federal banking agency (as defined in section 3(q) of such Act);

(B) with respect to an insured credit union (including an insured credit union for which the National Credit Union Administration has been appointed conservator or liquidating agent), the National Credit Union Administration;

(C) with respect to any insured depository institution for which the Resolution Trust Corporation has been appointed conservator or receiver, the Resolution Trust Corporation; and

(D) with respect to any insured depository institution for which the Federal Deposit Insurance Corporation has been appointed conservator or receiver, the Federal Deposit Insurance Corporation.

(22) The term "financial institution" means—

(A) a Federal reserve bank, or an entity that is a commercial or savings bank, industrial savings bank, savings and loan association, trust company, federally-insured credit union, or receiver, liquidating agent, or conservator for such entity and, when any such Federal reserve bank, receiver, liquidating agent, conservator or entity is acting as agent or custodian for a customer (whether or not a "customer", as defined in section 741) in connection with a securities contract (as defined in section 741) such customer; or

(B) in connection with a securities contract (as defined in section 741) an investment company registered under the Investment Company Act of 1940.

(22A) The term "financial participant" means—

(A) an entity that, at the time it enters into a securities contract, commodity contract, swap agreement, repurchase agreement, or forward contract, or at the time of the date of the filing of the petition, has one or more agreements or transactions described in paragraph (1), (2), (3), (4), (5), or (6) of section 561(a) with the debtor or any other entity (other than an affiliate) of a total gross dollar value of not less than $1,000,000,000 in notional or actual principal amount outstanding (aggregated across counterparties) at such time or on any day during the 15-month period preceding the date of the filing of the petition, or has gross mark-to-market positions of not less than $100,000,000 (aggregated across counterparties) in one or more such agreements or transactions with the debtor or any other entity (other than an affiliate) at such time or on any day during the 15-month period preceding the date of the filing of the petition; or

(B) a clearing organization (as defined in section 402 of the Federal Deposit Insurance Corporation Improvement Act of 1991).

(23) The term "foreign proceeding" means a collective judicial or administrative proceeding in a foreign country, including an interim proceeding, under a law relating to insolvency or adjustment of debt in which proceeding the assets and affairs of the debtor are subject to control or supervision by a foreign court, for the purpose of reorganization or liquidation.

(24) The term "foreign representative" means a person or body, including a person or body appointed on an interim basis, authorized in a foreign proceeding to administer the reorganization or the liquidation of the debtor's assets or affairs or to act as a representative of such foreign proceeding.

(25) The term "forward contract" means—

(A) a contract (other than a commodity contract, as defined in Section 761) for the purchase, sale, or transfer of a commodity, as defined in section 761(8) of this title, or any similar good, article, service, right, or interest which is presently or in the future becomes the subject of dealing in the forward contract trade, or product or byproduct thereof, with a maturity date more than two days after the date the contract is entered into, including, but not limited to, a repurchase or reverse repurchase transaction (whether or not such repurchase or reverse repurchase transaction is a "repurchase agreement", as defined in this section)[2] consignment, lease, swap, hedge transaction, deposit, loan, option, allocated transaction, unallocated transaction, or any other similar agreement;

(B) any combination of agreements or transactions referred to in subparagraphs (A) and (C);

(C) any option to enter into an agreement or transaction referred to in subparagraph (A) or (B);

(D) a master agreement that provides for an agreement or transaction referred to in subparagraph (A), (B), or (C), together with all supplements to any such master agreement, without regard to whether such master agreement provides for an agreement or transaction that is not a forward contract under this paragraph, except that such master agreement shall be considered to be a forward contract under this paragraph only with respect to each agreement or transaction under such master agreement that is referred to in subparagraph (A), (B), or (C); or

(E) any security agreement or arrangement, or other credit enhancement related to

[2] So in original. Probably should be followed by a comma.

any agreement or transaction referred to in subparagraph (A), (B), (C), or (D), including any guarantee or reimbursement obligation by or to a forward contract merchant or financial participant in connection with any agreement or transaction referred to in any such subparagraph, but not to exceed the damages in connection with any such agreement or transaction, measured in accordance with section 562.

(26) The term "forward contract merchant" means a Federal reserve bank, or an entity the business of which consists in whole or in part of entering into forward contracts as or with merchants in a commodity (as defined in section 761) or any similar good, article, service, right, or interest which is presently or in the future becomes the subject of dealing in the forward contract trade.

(27) The term "governmental unit" means United States; State; Commonwealth; District; Territory; municipality; foreign state; department, agency, or instrumentality of the United States (but not a United States trustee while serving as a trustee in a case under this title), a State, a Commonwealth, a District, a Territory, a municipality, or a foreign state; or other foreign or domestic government.

(27A) The term "health care business"—

(A) means any public or private entity (without regard to whether that entity is organized for profit or not for profit) that is primarily engaged in offering to the general public facilities and services for—

(i) the diagnosis or treatment of injury, deformity, or disease; and

(ii) surgical, drug treatment, psychiatric, or obstetric care; and

(B) includes—

(i) any—

(I) general or specialized hospital;

(II) ancillary ambulatory, emergency, or surgical treatment facility;

(III) hospice;

(IV) home health agency; and

(V) other health care institution that is similar to an entity referred to in subclause (I), (II), (III), or (IV); and

(ii) any long-term care facility, including any—

(I) skilled nursing facility;

(II) intermediate care facility;

(III) assisted living facility;

(IV) home for the aged;

(V) domiciliary care facility; and

(VI) health care institution that is related to a facility referred to in subclause (I), (II), (III), (IV), or (V), if that institution is primarily engaged in offering room, board, laundry, or personal assistance with activities of daily living and incidentals to activities of daily living.

(27B) The term "incidental property" means, with respect to a debtor's principal residence—

(A) property commonly conveyed with a principal residence in the area where the real property is located;

(B) all easements, rights, appurtenances, fixtures, rents, royalties, mineral rights, oil or gas rights or profits, water rights, escrow funds, or insurance proceeds; and

(C) all replacements or additions.

(28) The term "indenture" means mortgage, deed of trust, or indenture, under which there is outstanding a security, other than a voting-trust certificate, constituting a claim against the debtor, a claim secured by a lien on any of the debtor's property, or an equity security of the debtor.

(29) The term "indenture trustee" means trustee under an indenture.

(30) The term "individual with regular income" means individual whose income is sufficiently stable and regular to enable such individual to make payments under a plan under chapter 13 of this title, other than a stockbroker or a commodity broker.

(31) The term "insider" includes—

(A) if the debtor is an individual—

(i) relative of the debtor or of a general partner of the debtor;

(ii) partnership in which the debtor is a general partner;

(iii) general partner of the debtor; or

(iv) corporation of which the debtor is a director, officer, or person in control;

(B) if the debtor is a corporation—

(i) director of the debtor;

(ii) officer of the debtor;

(iii) person in control of the debtor;

(iv) partnership in which the debtor is a general partner;

(v) general partner of the debtor; or

(vi) relative of a general partner, director, officer, or person in control of the debtor;

(C) if the debtor is a partnership—

(i) general partner in the debtor;

(ii) relative of a general partner in, general partner of, or person in control of the debtor;

(iii) partnership in which the debtor is a general partner;

(iv) general partner of the debtor; or

(v) person in control of the debtor;

(D) if the debtor is a municipality, elected official of the debtor or relative of an elected official of the debtor;

(E) affiliate, or insider of an affiliate as if such affiliate were the debtor; and

(F) managing agent of the debtor.

(32) The term "insolvent" means—

(A) with reference to an entity other than a partnership and a municipality, financial condition such that the sum of such entity's debts is greater than all of such entity's property, at a fair valuation, exclusive of—

(i) property transferred, concealed, or removed with intent to hinder, delay, or defraud such entity's creditors; and

(ii) property that may be exempted from property of the estate under section 522 of this title;

(B) with reference to a partnership, financial condition such that the sum of such partnership's debts is greater than the aggregate of, at a fair valuation—

(i) all of such partnership's property, exclusive of property of the kind specified in subparagraph (A)(i) of this paragraph; and

(ii) the sum of the excess of the value of each general partner's nonpartnership property, exclusive of property of the kind specified in subparagraph (A) of this paragraph, over such partner's nonpartnership debts; and

(C) with reference to a municipality, financial condition such that the municipality is—

(i) generally not paying its debts as they become due unless such debts are the subject of a bona fide dispute; or

(ii) unable to pay its debts as they become due.

(33) The term "institution-affiliated party"—

(A) with respect to an insured depository institution (as defined in section 3(c)(2) of the Federal Deposit Insurance Act), has the meaning given it in section 3(u) of the Federal Deposit Insurance Act; and

(B) with respect to an insured credit union, has the meaning given it in section 206(r) of the Federal Credit Union Act.

(34) The term "insured credit union" has the meaning given it in section 101(7) of the Federal Credit Union Act.

(35) The term "insured depository institution"—

(A) has the meaning given it in section 3(c)(2) of the Federal Deposit Insurance Act; and

(B) includes an insured credit union (except in the case of paragraphs (21B) and (33)(A) of this subsection).

(35A) The term "intellectual property" means—

(A) trade secret;

(B) invention, process, design, or plant protected under title 35;

(C) patent application;

(D) plant variety;

(E) work of authorship protected under title 17; or

(F) mask work protected under chapter 9 of title 17; to the extent protected by applicable nonbankruptcy law.

(36) The term "judicial lien" means lien obtained by judgment, levy, sequestration, or other legal or equitable process or proceeding.

(37) The term "lien" means charge against or interest in property to secure payment of a debt or performance of an obligation.

(38) The term "margin payment" means, for purposes of the forward contract provisions of this title, payment or deposit of cash, a security or other property, that is commonly known in the forward contract trade as original margin, initial margin, maintenance margin, or variation

margin, including mark-to-market payments, or variation payments.

(38A) The term "master netting agreement"—

(A) means an agreement providing for the exercise of rights, including rights of netting, setoff, liquidation, termination, acceleration, or close out, under or in connection with one or more contracts that are described in any one or more of paragraphs (1) through (5) of section 561(a), or any security agreement or arrangement or other credit enhancement related to one or more of the foregoing, including any guarantee or reimbursement obligation related to 1 or more of the foregoing; and

(B) if the agreement contains provisions relating to agreements or transactions that are not contracts described in paragraphs (1) through (5) of section 561(a), shall be deemed to be a master netting agreement only with respect to those agreements or transactions that are described in any one or more of paragraphs (1) through (5) of section 561(a).

(38B) The term "master netting agreement participant" means an entity that, at any time before the date of the filing of the petition, is a party to an outstanding master netting agreement with the debtor.

(39) The term "mask work" has the meaning given it in section 901(a)(2) of title 17.

(39A) The term "median family income" means for any year—

(A) the median family income both calculated and reported by the Bureau of the Census in the then most recent year; and

(B) if not so calculated and reported in the then current year, adjusted annually after such most recent year until the next year in which median family income is both calculated and reported by the Bureau of the Census, to reflect the percentage change in the Consumer Price Index for All Urban Consumers during the period of years occurring after such most recent year and before such current year.

(40) The term "municipality" means political subdivision or public agency or instrumentality of a State.

(40A) The term "patient" means any individual who obtains or receives services from a health care business.

(40B) The term "patient records" means any record relating to a patient, including a written document or a record recorded in a magnetic, optical, or other form of electronic medium.

(41) The term "person" includes individual, partnership, and corporation, but does not include governmental unit, except that a governmental unit that—

(A) acquires an asset from a person—

(i) as a result of the operation of a loan guarantee agreement; or

(ii) as receiver or liquidating agent of a person;

(B) is a guarantor of a pension benefit payable by or on behalf of the debtor or an affiliate of the debtor; or

(C) is the legal or beneficial owner of an asset of—

(i) an employee pension benefit plan that is a governmental plan, as defined in section 414(d) of the Internal Revenue Code of 1986; or

(ii) an eligible deferred compensation plan, as defined in section 457(b) of the Internal Revenue Code of 1986;

shall be considered, for purposes of section 1102 of this title, to be a person with respect to such asset or such benefit.

(41A) The term "personally identifiable information" means—

(A) if provided by an individual to the debtor in connection with obtaining a product or a service from the debtor primarily for personal, family, or household purposes—

(i) the first name (or initial) and last name of such individual, whether given at birth or time of adoption, or resulting from a lawful change of name;

(ii) the geographical address of a physical place of residence of such individual;

(iii) an electronic address (including an e-mail address) of such individual;

(iv) a telephone number dedicated to contacting such individual at such physical place of residence;

(v) a social security account number issued to such individual; or

(vi) the account number of a credit card issued to such individual; or

(B) if identified in connection with 1 or more of the items of information specified in subparagraph (A)—

(i) a birth date, the number of a certificate of birth or adoption, or a place of birth; or

(ii) any other information concerning an identified individual that, if disclosed, will result in contacting or identifying such individual physically or electronically.

(42) The term "petition" means petition filed under section 301, 302, 303 and[3] 1504 of this title, as the case may be, commencing a case under this title.

(42A) The term "production payment" means a term overriding royalty satisfiable in cash or in kind—

(A) contingent on the production of a liquid or gaseous hydrocarbon from particular real property; and

(B) from a specified volume, or a specified value, from the liquid or gaseous hydrocarbon produced from such property, and determined without regard to production costs.

(43) The term "purchaser" means transferee of a voluntary transfer, and includes immediate or mediate transferee of such a transferee.

(44) The term "railroad" means common carrier by railroad engaged in the transportation of individuals or property or owner of trackage facilities leased by such a common carrier.

(45) The term "relative" means individual related by affinity or consanguinity within the third degree as determined by the common law, or individual in a step or adoptive relationship within such third degree.

(46) The term "repo participant" means an entity that, at any time before the filing of the petition, has an outstanding repurchase agreement with the debtor.

(47) The term "repurchase agreement" (which definition also applies to a reverse repurchase agreement)—

(A) means—

(i) an agreement, including related terms, which provides for the transfer of one or more certificates of deposit, mortgage related securities (as defined in section 3 of the Securities Exchange Act of 1934), mortgage loans, interests in mortgage related securities or mortgage loans, eligible bankers' acceptances, qualified foreign government securities (defined as a security that is a direct obligation of, or that is fully guaranteed by, the central government of a member of the Organization for Economic Cooperation and Development), or securities that are direct obligations of, or that are fully guaranteed by, the United States or any agency of the United States against the transfer of funds by the transferee of such certificates of deposit, eligible bankers' acceptances, securities, mortgage loans, or interests, with a simultaneous agreement by such transferee to transfer to the transferor thereof certificates of deposit, eligible bankers' acceptance, securities, mortgage loans, or interests of the kind described in this clause, at a date certain not later than 1 year after such transfer or on demand, against the transfer of funds;

(ii) any combination of agreements or transactions referred to in clauses (i) and (iii);

(iii) an option to enter into an agreement or transaction referred to in clause (i) or (ii);

(iv) a master agreement that provides for an agreement or transaction referred to in clause (i), (ii), or (iii), together with all supplements to any such master agreement, without regard to whether such master agreement provides for an agreement or transaction that is not a repurchase agreement under this paragraph, except that such master agreement shall be considered to be a repurchase agreement under this paragraph only with respect to each agreement or transaction under the master agreement that is referred to in clause (i), (ii), or (iii); or

(v) any security agreement or arrangement or other credit enhancement

[3] So in original. Probably should be "or".

related to any agreement or transaction referred to in clause (i), (ii), (iii), or (iv), including any guarantee or reimbursement obligation by or to a repo participant or financial participant in connection with any agreement or transaction referred to in any such clause, but not to exceed the damages in connection with any such agreement or transaction, measured in accordance with section 562 of this title; and

(B) does not include a repurchase obligation under a participation in a commercial mortgage loan.

(48) The term "securities clearing agency" means person that is registered as a clearing agency under section 17A of the Securities Exchange Act of 1934, or exempt from such registration under such section pursuant to an order of the Securities and Exchange Commission, or whose business is confined to the performance of functions of a clearing agency with respect to exempted securities, as defined in section 3(a)(12) of such Act for the purposes of such section 17A.

(48A) The term "securities self regulatory organization" means either a securities association registered with the Securities and Exchange Commission under section 15A of the Securities Exchange Act of 1934 or a national securities exchange registered with the Securities and Exchange Commission under section 6 of the Securities Exchange Act of 1934.

(49) The term "security"—

(A) includes—

(i) note;

(ii) stock;

(iii) treasury stock;

(iv) bond;

(v) debenture;

(vi) collateral trust certificate;

(vii) pre-organization certificate or subscription;

(viii) transferable share;

(ix) voting-trust certificate;

(x) certificate of deposit;

(xi) certificate of deposit for security;

(xii) investment contract or certificate of interest or participation in a profit-sharing agreement or in an oil, gas, or mineral royalty or lease, if such contract or interest is required to be the subject of a registration statement filed with the Securities and Exchange Commission under the provisions of the Securities Act of 1933, or is exempt under section 3(b) of such Act from the requirement to file such a statement;

(xiii) interest of a limited partner in a limited partnership;

(xiv) other claim or interest commonly known as "security"; and

(xv) certificate of interest or participation in, temporary or interim certificate for, receipt for, or warrant or right to subscribe to or purchase or sell, a security; but

(B) does not include—

(i) currency, check, draft, bill of exchange, or bank letter of credit;

(ii) leverage transaction, as defined in section 761 of this title;

(iii) commodity futures contract or forward contract;

(iv) option, warrant, or right to subscribe to or purchase or sell a commodity futures contract;

(v) option to purchase or sell a commodity;

(vi) contract or certificate of a kind specified in subparagraph (A)(xii) of this paragraph that is not required to be the subject of a registration statement filed with the Securities and Exchange Commission and is not exempt under section 3(b) of the Securities Act of 1933 from the requirement to file such a statement; or

(vii) debt or evidence of indebtedness for goods sold and delivered or services rendered.

(50) The term "security agreement" means agreement that creates or provides for a security interest.

(51) The term "security interest" means lien created by an agreement.

(51A) The term "settlement payment" means, for purposes of the forward contract provisions of this title, a preliminary settlement payment, a partial settlement payment, an interim settlement payment, a settlement payment on account, a final settlement payment, a net settlement payment, or any other similar payment commonly used in the forward contract trade.

(51B) The term "single asset real estate" means real property constituting a single property or project, other than residential real property with fewer than 4 residential units, which generates substantially all of the gross income of a debtor who is not a family farmer and on which no substantial business is being conducted by a debtor other than the business of operating the real property and activities incidental thereto.

(51C) The term "small business case" means a case filed under chapter 11 of this title in which the debtor is a small business debtor and has not elected that subchapter V of chapter 11 of this title shall apply.

(51D) The term "small business debtor"—

(A) subject to subparagraph (B), means a person engaged in commercial or business activities (including any affiliate of such person that is also a debtor under this title and excluding a person whose primary activity is the business of owning single asset real estate) that has aggregate noncontingent liquidated secured and unsecured debts as of the date of the filing of the petition or the date of the order for relief in an amount not more than $3,024,725 (excluding debts owed to 1 or more affiliates or insiders) not less than 50 percent of which arose from the commercial or business activities of the debtor; and

(B) does not include—

(i) any member of a group of affiliated debtors under this title that has aggregate noncontingent liquidated secured and unsecured debts in an amount greater than $3,024,725 (excluding debt owed to 1 or more affiliates or insiders);

(ii) any debtor that is a corporation subject to the reporting requirements under section 13 or 15(d) of the Securities Exchange Act of 1934 (15 U.S.C. 78m, 78o(d)); or

(iii) any debtor that is an affiliate of a corporation described in clause (ii).

(52) The term "State" includes the District of Columbia and Puerto Rico, except for the purpose of defining who may be a debtor under chapter 9 of this title.

(53) The term "statutory lien" means lien arising solely by force of a statute on specified circumstances or conditions, or lien of distress for rent, whether or not statutory, but does not include security interest or judicial lien, whether or not such interest or lien is provided by or is dependent on a statute and whether or not such interest or lien is made fully effective by statute.

(53A) The term "stockbroker" means person—

(A) with respect to which there is a customer, as defined in section 741 of this title; and

(B) that is engaged in the business of effecting transactions in securities—

(i) for the account of others; or

(ii) with members of the general public, from or for such person's own account.

(53B) The term "swap agreement"—

(A) means—

(i) any agreement, including the terms and conditions incorporated by reference in such agreement, which is—

(I) an interest rate swap, option, future, or forward agreement, including a rate floor, rate cap, rate collar, cross-currency rate swap, and basis swap;

(II) a spot, same day-tomorrow, tomorrow-next, forward, or other foreign exchange, precious metals, or other commodity agreement;

(III) a currency swap, option, future, or forward agreement;

(IV) an equity index or equity swap, option, future, or forward agreement;

(V) a debt index or debt swap, option, future, or forward agreement;

(VI) a total return, credit spread or credit swap, option, future, or forward agreement;

(VII) a commodity index or a commodity swap, option, future, or forward agreement;

(VIII) a weather swap, option, future, or forward agreement;

(IX) an emissions swap, option, future, or forward agreement; or

(X) an inflation swap, option, future, or forward agreement;

(ii) any agreement or transaction that is similar to any other agreement or transaction referred to in this paragraph and that—

(I) is of a type that has been, is presently, or in the future becomes, the subject of recurrent dealings in the swap or other derivatives markets (including terms and conditions incorporated by reference therein); and

(II) is a forward, swap, future, option, or spot transaction on one or more rates, currencies, commodities, equity securities, or other equity instruments, debt securities or other debt instruments, quantitative measures associated with an occurrence, extent of an occurrence, or contingency associated with a financial, commercial, or economic consequence, or economic or financial indices or measures of economic or financial risk or value;

(iii) any combination of agreements or transactions referred to in this subparagraph;

(iv) any option to enter into an agreement or transaction referred to in this subparagraph;

(v) a master agreement that provides for an agreement or transaction referred to in clause (i), (ii), (iii), or (iv), together with all supplements to any such master agreement, and without regard to whether the master agreement contains an agreement or transaction that is not a swap agreement under this paragraph, except that the master agreement shall be considered to be a swap agreement under this paragraph only with respect to each agreement or transaction under the master agreement that is referred to in clause (i), (ii), (iii), or (iv); or

(vi) any security agreement or arrangement or other credit enhancement related to any agreements or transactions referred to in clause (i) through (v), including any guarantee or reimbursement obligation by or to a swap participant or financial participant in connection with any agreement or transaction referred to in any such clause, but not to exceed the damages in connection with any such agreement or transaction, measured in accordance with section 562; and

(B) is applicable for purposes of this title only, and shall not be construed or applied so as to challenge or affect the characterization, definition, or treatment of any swap agreement under any other statute, regulation, or rule, including the Gramm-Leach-Bliley Act, the Legal Certainty for Bank Products Act of 2000, the securities laws (as such term is defined in section 3(a)(47) of the Securities Exchange Act of 1934) and the Commodity Exchange Act.

(53C) The term "swap participant" means an entity that, at any time before the filing of the petition, has an outstanding swap agreement with the debtor.

(56A) [4]The term "term overriding royalty" means an interest in liquid or gaseous hydrocarbons in place or to be produced from particular real property that entitles the owner thereof to a share of production, or the value thereof, for a term limited by time, quantity, or value realized.

(53D) The term "timeshare plan" means and shall include that interest purchased in any arrangement, plan, scheme, or similar device, but not including exchange programs, whether by membership, agreement, tenancy in common, sale, lease, deed, rental agreement, license, right to use agreement, or by any other means, whereby a purchaser, in exchange for consideration, receives a right to use accommodations, facilities, or recreational sites, whether improved or unimproved, for a specific period of time less than a full year during any given year, but not necessarily for consecutive years, and which extends for a period of more than three years. A "timeshare interest" is that interest purchased in a timeshare plan which grants the purchaser the right to use and occupy accommodations, facilities, or recreational sites, whether improved or unimproved, pursuant to a timeshare plan.

---

[4] So in original.

(54) The term "transfer" means—

(A) the creation of a lien;

(B) the retention of title as a security interest;

(C) the foreclosure of a debtor's equity of redemption; or

(D) each mode, direct or indirect, absolute or conditional, voluntary or involuntary, of disposing of or parting with—

(i) property; or

(ii) an interest in property.

(54A) The term "uninsured State member bank" means a State member bank (as defined in section 3 of the Federal Deposit Insurance Act) the deposits of which are not insured by the Federal Deposit Insurance Corporation.

(55) The term "United States", when used in a geographical sense, includes all locations where the judicial jurisdiction of the United States extends, including territories and possessions of the United States.

§ 102. Rules of Construction

In this title—

(1) "after notice and a hearing", or a similar phrase—

(A) means after such notice as is appropriate in the particular circumstances, and such opportunity for a hearing as is appropriate in the particular circumstances; but

(B) authorizes an act without an actual hearing if such notice is given properly and if—

(i) such a hearing is not requested timely by a party in interest; or

(ii) there is insufficient time for a hearing to be commenced before such act must be done, and the court authorizes such act;

(2) "claim against the debtor" includes claim against property of the debtor;

(3) "includes" and "including" are not limiting;

(4) "may not" is prohibitive, and not permissive;

(5) "or" is not exclusive;

(6) "order for relief" means entry of an order for relief;

(7) the singular includes the plural;

(8) a definition, contained in a section of this title that refers to another section of this title, does not, for the purpose of such reference, affect the meaning of a term used in such other section; and

(9) "United States trustee" includes a designee of the United States trustee.

§ 103. Applicability of Chapters

(a) Except as provided in section 1161 of this title, chapters 1, 3, and 5 of this title apply in a case under chapter 7, 11, 12, or 13 of this title, and this chapter, sections 307, 362(o), 555 through 557, and 559 through 562 apply in a case under chapter 15.

(b) Subchapters I and II of chapter 7 of this title apply only in a case under such chapter.

(c) Subchapter III of chapter 7 of this title applies only in a case under such chapter concerning a stockbroker.

(d) Subchapter IV of chapter 7 of this title applies only in a case under such chapter concerning a commodity broker.

(e) Scope of application.—Subchapter V of chapter 7 of this title shall apply only in a case under such chapter concerning the liquidation of an uninsured State member bank, or a corporation organized under section 25A of the Federal Reserve Act, which operates, or operates as, a multilateral clearing organization pursuant to section 409 of the Federal Deposit Insurance Corporation Improvement Act of 1991.

(f) Except as provided in section 901 of this title, only chapters 1 and 9 of this title apply in a case under such chapter 9.

(g) Except as provided in section 901 of this title, subchapters I, II, and III of chapter 11 of this title apply only in a case under such chapter.

(h) Subchapter IV of chapter 11 of this title applies only in a case under such chapter concerning a railroad.

(i) Subchapter V of chapter 11 of this title applies only in a case under chapter 11 in which a debtor (as defined in section 1182) elects that subchapter V of chapter 11 shall apply.

(j) Chapter 13 of this title applies only in a case under such chapter.

(k) Chapter 12 of this title applies only in a case under such chapter.

(l) Chapter 15 applies only in a case under such chapter, except that—

(1) sections 1505, 1513, and 1514 apply in all cases under this title; and

(2) section 1509 applies whether or not a case under this title is pending.

§ 104. Adjustment of Dollar Amounts

(a) On April 1, 1998, and at each 3-year interval ending on April 1 thereafter, each dollar amount in effect under sections 101(3), 101(18), 101(19A), 101(51D), 109(e), 303(b), 507(a), 522(d), 522(f)(3) and 522(f)(4), 522(n), 522(p), 522(q), 523(a)(2)(C), 541(b), 547(c)(9), 707(b), 1182(1), 1322(d), 1325(b), and 1326(b)(3) of this title and section 1409(b) of title 28 immediately before such April 1 shall be adjusted—

(1) to reflect the change in the Consumer Price Index for All Urban Consumers, published by the Department of Labor, for the most recent 3-year period ending immediately before January 1 preceding such April 1, and

(2) to round to the nearest $25 the dollar amount that represents such change.

(b) Not later than March 1, 1998, and at each 3-year interval ending on March 1 thereafter, the Judicial Conference of the United States shall publish in the Federal Register the dollar amounts that will become effective on such April 1 under sections 101(3), 101(18), 101(19A), 101(51D), 109(e), 303(b), 507(a), 522(d), 522(f)(3) and 522(f)(4), 522(n), 522(p), 522(q), 523(a)(2)(C), 541(b), 547(c)(9), 707(b), 1182(1), 1322(d), 1325(b), and 1326(b)(3) of this title and section 1409(b) of title 28.

(c) Adjustments made in accordance with subsection (a) shall not apply with respect to cases commenced before the date of such adjustments.

§ 105. Power of Court

(a) The court may issue any order, process, or judgment that is necessary or appropriate to carry out the provisions of this title. No provision of this title providing for the raising of an issue by a party in interest shall be construed to preclude the court from, sua sponte, taking any action or making any determination necessary or appropriate to enforce or implement court orders or rules, or to prevent an abuse of process.

(b) Notwithstanding subsection (a) of this section, a court may not appoint a receiver in a case under this title.

(c) The ability of any district judge or other officer or employee of a district court to exercise any of the authority or responsibilities conferred upon the court under this title shall be determined by reference to the provisions relating to such judge, officer, or employee set forth in title 28. This subsection shall not be interpreted to exclude bankruptcy judges and other officers or employees appointed pursuant to chapter 6 of title 28 from its operation.

(d) The court, on its own motion or on the request of a party in interest—

(1) shall hold such status conferences as are necessary to further the expeditious and economical resolution of the case; and

(2) unless inconsistent with another provision of this title or with applicable Federal Rules of Bankruptcy Procedure, may issue an order at any such conference prescribing such limitations and conditions as the court deems appropriate to ensure that the case is handled expeditiously and economically, including an order that—

(A) sets the date by which the trustee must assume or reject an executory contract or unexpired lease; or

(B) in a case under chapter 11 of this title—

(i) sets a date by which the debtor, or trustee if one has been appointed, shall file a disclosure statement and plan;

(ii) sets a date by which the debtor, or trustee if one has been appointed, shall solicit acceptances of a plan;

(iii) sets the date by which a party in interest other than a debtor may file a plan;

(iv) sets a date by which a proponent of a plan, other than the debtor, shall solicit acceptances of such plan;

(v) fixes the scope and format of the notice to be provided regarding the hearing on approval of the disclosure statement; or

(vi) provides that the hearing on approval of the disclosure statement may be combined with the hearing on confirmation of the plan.

§ 106. Waiver of Sovereign Immunity

(a) Notwithstanding an assertion of sovereign immunity, sovereign immunity is abrogated as to a governmental unit to the extent set forth in this section with respect to the following:

(1) Sections 105, 106, 107, 108, 303, 346, 362, 363, 364, 365, 366, 502, 503, 505, 506, 510, 522, 523, 524, 525, 542, 543, 544, 545, 546, 547, 548, 549, 550, 551, 552, 553, 722, 724, 726, 744, 749, 764, 901, 922, 926, 928, 929, 944, 1107, 1141, 1142, 1143, 1146, 1201, 1203, 1205, 1206, 1227, 1231, 1301, 1303, 1305, and 1327 of this title.

(2) The court may hear and determine any issue arising with respect to the application of such sections to governmental units.

(3) The court may issue against a governmental unit an order, process, or judgment under such sections or the Federal Rules of Bankruptcy Procedure, including an order or judgment awarding a money recovery, but not including an award of punitive damages. Such order or judgment for costs or fees under this title or the Federal Rules of Bankruptcy Procedure against any governmental unit shall be consistent with the provisions and limitations of section 2412(d)(2)(A) of title 28.

(4) The enforcement of any such order, process, or judgment against any governmental unit shall be consistent with appropriate nonbankruptcy law applicable to such governmental unit and, in the case of a money judgment against the United States, shall be paid as if it is a judgment rendered by a district court of the United States.

(5) Nothing in this section shall create any substantive claim for relief or cause of action not otherwise existing under this title, the Federal Rules of Bankruptcy Procedure, or nonbankruptcy law.

(b) A governmental unit that has filed a proof of claim in the case is deemed to have waived sovereign immunity with respect to a claim against such governmental unit that is property of the estate and that arose out of the same transaction or occurrence out of which the claim of such governmental unit arose.

(c) Notwithstanding any assertion of sovereign immunity by a governmental unit, there shall be offset against a claim or interest of a governmental unit any claim against such governmental unit that is property of the estate.

§ 107. Public Access to Papers

(a) Except as provided in subsections (b) and (c) and subject to section 112, a paper filed in a case under this title and the dockets of a bankruptcy court are public records and open to examination by an entity at reasonable times without charge.

(b) On request of a party in interest, the bankruptcy court shall, and on the bankruptcy court's own motion, the bankruptcy court may—

(1) protect an entity with respect to a trade secret or confidential research, development, or commercial information; or

(2) protect a person with respect to scandalous or defamatory matter contained in a paper filed in a case under this title.

(c)(1) The bankruptcy court, for cause, may protect an individual, with respect to the following types of information to the extent the court finds that disclosure of such information would create undue risk of identity theft or other unlawful injury to the individual or the individual's property:

(A) Any means of identification (as defined in section 1028(d) of title 18) contained in a paper filed, or to be filed, in a case under this title.

(B) Other information contained in a paper described in subparagraph (A).

(2) Upon ex parte application demonstrating cause, the court shall provide access to information protected pursuant to paragraph (1) to an entity acting pursuant to the police or regulatory power of a domestic governmental unit.

(3) The United States trustee, bankruptcy administrator, trustee, and any auditor serving under section 586(f) of title 28—

(A) shall have full access to all information contained in any paper filed or submitted in a case under this title; and

(B) shall not disclose information specifically protected by the court under this title.

§ 108. Extension of Time

(a) If applicable nonbankruptcy law, an order entered in a nonbankruptcy proceeding, or an agreement fixes a period within which the debtor may commence an action, and such period has not expired before the date of the filing of the petition, the trustee may commence such action only before the later of—

(1) the end of such period, including any suspension of such period occurring on or after the commencement of the case; or

(2) two years after the order for relief.

(b) Except as provided in subsection (a) of this section, if applicable nonbankruptcy law, an order entered in a nonbankruptcy proceeding, or an agreement fixes a period within which the debtor or an individual protected under section 1201 or 1301 of this title may file any pleading, demand, notice, or proof of claim or loss, cure a default, or perform any other similar act, and such period has not expired before the date of the filing of the petition, the trustee may only file, cure, or perform, as the case may be, before the later of—

(1) the end of such period, including any suspension of such period occurring on or after the commencement of the case; or

(2) 60 days after the order for relief.

(c) Except as provided in section 524 of this title, if applicable nonbankruptcy law, an order entered in a nonbankruptcy proceeding, or an agreement fixes a period for commencing or continuing a civil action in a court other than a bankruptcy court on a claim against the debtor, or against an individual with respect to which such individual is protected under section 1201 or 1301 of this title, and such period has not expired before the date of the filing of the petition, then such period does not expire until the later of—

(1) the end of such period, including any suspension of such period occurring on or after the commencement of the case; or

(2) 30 days after notice of the termination or expiration of the stay under section 362, 922, 1201, or 1301 of this title, as the case may be, with respect to such claim.

§ 109. Who May Be a Debtor

(a) Notwithstanding any other provision of this section, only a person that resides or has a domicile, a place of business, or property in the United States, or a municipality, may be a debtor under this title.

(b) A person may be a debtor under chapter 7 of this title only if such person is not—

(1) a railroad;

(2) a domestic insurance company, bank, savings bank, cooperative bank, savings and loan association, building and loan association, homestead association, a New Markets Venture Capital company as defined in section 351 of the Small Business Investment Act of 1958, a small business investment company licensed by the Small Business Administration under section 301 of the Small Business Investment Act of 1958, credit union, or industrial bank or similar institution which is an insured bank as defined in section 3(h) of the Federal Deposit Insurance Act, except that an uninsured State member bank, or a corporation organized under section 25A of the Federal Reserve Act, which operates, or operates as, a multilateral clearing organization pursuant to section 409 of the Federal Deposit Insurance Corporation Improvement Act of 1991 may be a debtor if a petition is filed at the direction of the Board of Governors of the Federal Reserve System; or

(3) (A) a foreign insurance company, engaged in such business in the United States; or

(B) a foreign bank, savings bank, cooperative bank, savings and loan association, building and loan association, or credit union, that has a branch or agency (as defined in section 1(b) of the International Banking Act of 1978) in the United States.

(c) An entity may be a debtor under chapter 9 of this title if and only if such entity—

(1) is a municipality;

(2) is specifically authorized, in its capacity as a municipality or by name, to be a debtor under such chapter by State law, or by a governmental officer or organization empowered by State law to authorize such entity to be a debtor under such chapter;

(3) is insolvent;

(4) desires to effect a plan to adjust such debts; and

(5) (A) has obtained the agreement of creditors holding at least a majority in amount of the claims of each class that such entity intends to impair under a plan in a case under such chapter;

(B) has negotiated in good faith with creditors and has failed to obtain the agreement of creditors holding at least a majority in amount of the claims of each class that such entity intends to impair under a plan in a case under such chapter;

(C) is unable to negotiate with creditors because such negotiation is impracticable; or

(D) reasonably believes that a creditor may attempt to obtain a transfer that is avoidable under section 547 of this title.

(d) Only a railroad, a person that may be a debtor under chapter 7 of this title (except a stockbroker or a commodity broker), and an uninsured State member bank, or a corporation organized under section 25A of the Federal Reserve Act, which operates, or operates as, a multilateral clearing organization pursuant to section 409 of the Federal Deposit Insurance Corporation Improvement Act of 1991 may be a debtor under chapter 11 of this title.

(e) Only an individual with regular income that owes, on the date of the filing of the petition, noncontingent, liquidated debts of less than $2,750,000 or an individual with regular income and such individual's spouse, except a stockbroker or a commodity broker, that owe, on the date of the filing of the petition, noncontingent, liquidated debts that aggregate less than $2,750,000 may be a debtor under chapter 13 of this title.

(f) Only a family farmer or family fisherman with regular annual income may be a debtor under chapter 12 of this title.

(g) Notwithstanding any other provision of this section, no individual or family farmer may be a debtor under this title who has been a debtor in a case pending under this title at any time in the preceding 180 days if—

(1) the case was dismissed by the court for willful failure of the debtor to abide by orders of the court, or to appear before the court in proper prosecution of the case; or

(2) the debtor requested and obtained the voluntary dismissal of the case following the filing of a request for relief from the automatic stay provided by section 362 of this title.

(h)(1) Subject to paragraphs (2) and (3), and notwithstanding any other provision of this section other than paragraph (4) of this subsection, an individual may not be a debtor under this title unless such individual has, during the 180-day period ending on the date of filing of the petition by such individual, received from an approved nonprofit budget and credit counseling agency described in section 111(a) an individual or group briefing (including a briefing conducted by telephone or on the Internet) that outlined the opportunities for available credit counseling and assisted such individual in performing a related budget analysis.

(2) (A) Paragraph (1) shall not apply with respect to a debtor who resides in a district (for which the United States trustee or the bankruptcy administrator, if any) determines that the approved nonprofit budget and credit counseling agencies for such district are not reasonably able to provide adequate services to the additional individuals who would otherwise seek credit counseling from such agencies by reason of the requirements of paragraph (1).

(B) The United States trustee (or the bankruptcy administrator, if any) who makes a determination described in subparagraph (A) shall review such determination not later than 1 year after the date of such determination, and not less frequently than annually thereafter. Notwithstanding the preceding sentence, a nonprofit budget and credit counseling agency may be disapproved by the United States trustee (or the bankruptcy administrator, if any) at any time.

(3) (A) Subject to subparagraph (B), the requirements of paragraph (1) shall not apply with respect to a debtor who submits to the court a certification that—

(i) describes exigent circumstances that merit a waiver of the requirements of paragraph (1);

(ii) states that the debtor requested credit counseling services from an approved nonprofit budget and credit counseling agency, but was unable to obtain the services referred to in paragraph (1) during the 7-day period beginning on the date on which the debtor made that request; and

(iii) is satisfactory to the court.

(B) With respect to a debtor, an exemption under subparagraph (A) shall cease to apply to that debtor on the date on which the debtor meets the requirements of paragraph (1), but in no case may the exemption apply to that debtor after the date that is 30 days after the debtor files a petition, except that the court, for cause, may order an additional 15 days.

(4) The requirements of paragraph (1) shall not apply with respect to a debtor whom the court determines, after notice and hearing, is unable to complete those requirements because of incapacity, disability, or active military duty in a military combat zone. For the purposes of this paragraph, incapacity means that the debtor is impaired by reason of mental illness or mental deficiency so that he is incapable of realizing and making rational decisions with respect to his financial responsibilities; and "disability"

means that the debtor is so physically impaired as to be unable, after reasonable effort, to participate in an in person, telephone, or Internet briefing required under paragraph (1).

[Editor's note: Section 109(e) reverts to previous language on June 21, 2024.]

§ 110. Penalty for Persons Who Negligently or Fraudulently Prepare Bankruptcy Petitions

(a) In this section—

(1) "bankruptcy petition preparer" means a person, other than an attorney for the debtor or an employee of such attorney under the direct supervision of such attorney, who prepares for compensation a document for filing; and

(2) "document for filing" means a petition or any other document prepared for filing by a debtor in a United States bankruptcy court or a United States district court in connection with a case under this title.

(b)(1) A bankruptcy petition preparer who prepares a document for filing shall sign the document and print on the document the preparer's name and address. If a bankruptcy petition preparer is not an individual, then an officer, principal, responsible person, or partner of the bankruptcy petition preparer shall be required to—

(A) sign the document for filing; and

(B) print on the document the name and address of that officer, principal, responsible person, or partner.

(2) (A) Before preparing any document for filing or accepting any fees from or on behalf of a debtor, the bankruptcy petition preparer shall provide to the debtor a written notice which shall be on an official form prescribed by the Judicial Conference of the United States in accordance with rule 9009 of the Federal Rules of Bankruptcy Procedure.

(B) The notice under subparagraph (A)—

(i) shall inform the debtor in simple language that a bankruptcy petition preparer is not an attorney and may not practice law or give legal advice;

(ii) may contain a description of examples of legal advice that a bankruptcy petition preparer is not authorized to give, in addition to any advice that the preparer may not give by reason of subsection (e)(2); and

(iii) shall—

(I) be signed by the debtor and, under penalty of perjury, by the bankruptcy petition preparer; and

(II) be filed with any document for filing.

(c)(1) A bankruptcy petition preparer who prepares a document for filing shall place on the document, after the preparer's signature, an identifying number that identifies individuals who prepared the document.

(2) (A) Subject to subparagraph (B), for purposes of this section, the identifying number of a bankruptcy petition preparer shall be the Social Security account number of each individual who prepared the document or assisted in its preparation.

(B) If a bankruptcy petition preparer is not an individual, the identifying number of the bankruptcy petition preparer shall be the Social Security account number of the officer, principal, responsible person, or partner of the bankruptcy petition preparer.

(d) A bankruptcy petition preparer shall, not later than the time at which a document for filing is presented for the debtor's signature, furnish to the debtor a copy of the document.

(e)(1) A bankruptcy petition preparer shall not execute any document on behalf of a debtor.

(2) (A) A bankruptcy petition preparer may not offer a potential bankruptcy debtor any legal advice, including any legal advice described in subparagraph (B).

(B) The legal advice referred to in subparagraph (A) includes advising the debtor—

(i) whether—

(I) to file a petition under this title; or

(II) commencing a case under chapter 7, 11, 12, or 13 is appropriate;

(ii) whether the debtor's debts will be discharged in a case under this title;

(iii) whether the debtor will be able to retain the debtor's home, car, or other property after commencing a case under this title;

(iv) concerning—

(I) the tax consequences of a case brought under this title; or

(II) the dischargeability of tax claims;

(v) whether the debtor may or should promise to repay debts to a creditor or enter into a reaffirmation agreement with a creditor to reaffirm a debt;

(vi) concerning how to characterize the nature of the debtor's interests in property or the debtor's debts; or

(vii) concerning bankruptcy procedures and rights.

(f) A bankruptcy petition preparer shall not use the word "legal" or any similar term in any advertisements, or advertise under any category that includes the word "legal" or any similar term.

(g) A bankruptcy petition preparer shall not collect or receive any payment from the debtor or on behalf of the debtor for the court fees in connection with filing the petition.

(h)(1) The Supreme Court may promulgate rules under section 2075 of title 28, or the Judicial Conference of the United States may prescribe guidelines, for setting a maximum allowable fee chargeable by a bankruptcy petition preparer. A bankruptcy petition preparer shall notify the debtor of any such maximum amount before preparing any document for filing for the debtor or accepting any fee from or on behalf of the debtor.

(2) A declaration under penalty of perjury by the bankruptcy petition preparer shall be filed together with the petition, disclosing any fee received from or on behalf of the debtor within 12 months immediately prior to the filing of the case, and any unpaid fee charged to the debtor. If rules or guidelines setting a maximum fee for services have been promulgated or prescribed under paragraph (1), the declaration under this paragraph shall include a certification that the bankruptcy petition preparer complied with the notification requirement under paragraph (1).

(3) (A) The court shall disallow and order the immediate turnover to the bankruptcy trustee any fee referred to in paragraph (2)—

(i) found to be in excess of the value of any services rendered by the bankruptcy petition preparer during the 12-month period immediately preceding the date of the filing of the petition; or

(ii) found to be in violation of any rule or guideline promulgated or prescribed under paragraph (1).

(B) All fees charged by a bankruptcy petition preparer may be forfeited in any case in which the bankruptcy petition preparer fails to comply with this subsection or subsection (b), (c), (d), (e), (f), or (g).

(C) An individual may exempt any funds recovered under this paragraph under section 522(b).

(4) The debtor, the trustee, a creditor, the United States trustee (or the bankruptcy administrator, if any) or the court, on the initiative of the court, may file a motion for an order under paragraph (3).

(5) A bankruptcy petition preparer shall be fined not more than $500 for each failure to comply with a court order to turn over funds within 30 days of service of such order.

(i)(1) If a bankruptcy petition preparer violates this section or commits any act that the court finds to be fraudulent, unfair, or deceptive, on the motion of the debtor, trustee, United States trustee (or the bankruptcy administrator, if any), and after notice and a hearing, the court shall order the bankruptcy petition preparer to pay to the debtor—

(A) the debtor's actual damages;

(B) the greater of—

(i) $2,000; or

(ii) twice the amount paid by the debtor to the bankruptcy petition preparer for the preparer's services; and

(C) reasonable attorneys' fees and costs in moving for damages under this subsection.

(2) If the trustee or creditor moves for damages on behalf of the debtor under this subsection, the bankruptcy petition preparer shall be ordered to pay the movant the additional amount of $1,000 plus reasonable attorneys' fees and costs incurred.

(j)(1) A debtor for whom a bankruptcy petition preparer has prepared a document for filing, the trustee, a creditor, or the United States trustee in the district in which the bankruptcy petition preparer resides, has conducted business, or the United States trustee in any other district in which the debtor resides may bring a civil action to enjoin a bankruptcy petition preparer from engaging in any conduct in violation of this section or from further acting as a bankruptcy petition preparer.

(2) (A) In an action under paragraph (1), if the court finds that—

(i) a bankruptcy petition preparer has—

(I) engaged in conduct in violation of this section or of any provision of this title;

(II) misrepresented the preparer's experience or education as a bankruptcy petition preparer; or

(III) engaged in any other fraudulent, unfair, or deceptive conduct; and

(ii) injunctive relief is appropriate to prevent the recurrence of such conduct,

the court may enjoin the bankruptcy petition preparer from engaging in such conduct.

(B) If the court finds that a bankruptcy petition preparer has continually engaged in conduct described in subclause (I), (II), or (III) of clause (i) and that an injunction prohibiting such conduct would not be sufficient to prevent such person's interference with the proper administration of this title, has not paid a penalty imposed under this section, or failed to disgorge all fees ordered by the court, the court may enjoin the person from acting as a bankruptcy petition preparer.

(3) The court, as part of its contempt power, may enjoin a bankruptcy petition preparer that has failed to comply with a previous order issued under this section. The injunction under this paragraph may be issued on the motion of the court, the trustee, or the United States trustee (or the bankruptcy administrator, if any).

(4) The court shall award to a debtor, trustee, or creditor that brings a successful action under this subsection reasonable attorneys' fees and costs of the action, to be paid by the bankruptcy petition preparer.

(k) Nothing in this section shall be construed to permit activities that are otherwise prohibited by law, including rules and laws that prohibit the unauthorized practice of law.

(l)(1) A bankruptcy petition preparer who fails to comply with any provision of subsection (b), (c), (d), (e), (f), (g), or (h) may be fined not more than $500 for each such failure.

(2) The court shall triple the amount of a fine assessed under paragraph (1) in any case in which the court finds that a bankruptcy petition preparer—

(A) advised the debtor to exclude assets or income that should have been included on applicable schedules;

(B) advised the debtor to use a false Social Security account number;

(C) failed to inform the debtor that the debtor was filing for relief under this title; or

(D) prepared a document for filing in a manner that failed to disclose the identity of the bankruptcy petition preparer.

(3) A debtor, trustee, creditor, or United States trustee (or the bankruptcy administrator, if any) may file a motion for an order imposing a fine on the bankruptcy petition preparer for any violation of this section.

(4)(A) Fines imposed under this subsection in judicial districts served by United States trustees shall be paid to the United States trustees, who shall deposit an amount equal to such fines in the United States Trustee Fund.

(B) Fines imposed under this subsection in judicial districts served by bankruptcy administrators shall be deposited as offsetting receipts to the fund established under section 1931 of title 28, and shall remain available until expended to reimburse any appropriation for the amount paid out of such appropriation for expenses of the operation and maintenance of the courts of the United States.

§ 111. Nonprofit Budget and Credit Counseling Agencies; Financial Management Instructional Courses

(a) The clerk shall maintain a publicly available list of—

(1) nonprofit budget and credit counseling agencies that provide 1 or more services described in section 109(h) currently approved by the United States trustee (or the bankruptcy administrator, if any); and

(2) instructional courses concerning personal financial management currently approved by the United States trustee (or the bankruptcy administrator, if any), as applicable.

(b) The United States trustee (or bankruptcy administrator, if any) shall only approve a nonprofit budget and credit counseling agency or an instructional course concerning personal financial management as follows:

(1) The United States trustee (or bankruptcy administrator, if any) shall have thoroughly reviewed the qualifications of the nonprofit budget and credit counseling agency or of

the provider of the instructional course under the standards set forth in this section, and the services or instructional courses that will be offered by such agency or such provider, and may require such agency or such provider that has sought approval to provide information with respect to such review.

(2) The United States trustee (or bankruptcy administrator, if any) shall have determined that such agency or such instructional course fully satisfies the applicable standards set forth in this section.

(3) If a nonprofit budget and credit counseling agency or instructional course did not appear on the approved list for the district under subsection (a) immediately before approval under this section, approval under this subsection of such agency or such instructional course shall be for a probationary period not to exceed 6 months.

(4) At the conclusion of the applicable probationary period under paragraph (3), the United States trustee (or bankruptcy administrator, if any) may only approve for an additional 1-year period, and for successive 1-year periods thereafter, an agency or instructional course that has demonstrated during the probationary or applicable subsequent period of approval that such agency or instructional course—

(A) has met the standards set forth under this section during such period; and

(B) can satisfy such standards in the future.

(5) Not later than 30 days after any final decision under paragraph (4), an interested person may seek judicial review of such decision in the appropriate district court of the United States.

(c)(1) The United States trustee (or the bankruptcy administrator, if any) shall only approve a nonprofit budget and credit counseling agency that demonstrates that it will provide qualified counselors, maintain adequate provision for safekeeping and payment of client funds, provide adequate counseling with respect to client credit problems, and deal responsibly and effectively with other matters relating to the quality, effectiveness, and financial security of the services it provides.

(2) To be approved by the United States trustee (or the bankruptcy administrator, if any), a nonprofit budget and credit counseling agency shall, at a minimum—

(A) have a board of directors the majority of which—

(i) are not employed by such agency; and

(ii) will not directly or indirectly benefit financially from the outcome of the counseling services provided by such agency;

(B) if a fee is charged for counseling services, charge a reasonable fee, and provide services without regard to ability to pay the fee;

(C) provide for safekeeping and payment of client funds, including an annual audit of the trust accounts and appropriate employee bonding;

(D) provide full disclosures to a client, including funding sources, counselor qualifications, possible impact on credit reports, and any costs of such program that will be paid by such client and how such costs will be paid;

(E) provide adequate counseling with respect to a client's credit problems that includes an analysis of such client's current financial condition, factors that caused such financial condition, and how such client can develop a plan to respond to the problems without incurring negative amortization of debt;

(F) provide trained counselors who receive no commissions or bonuses based on the outcome of the counseling services provided by such agency, and who have adequate experience, and have been adequately trained to provide counseling services to individuals in financial difficulty, including the matters described in subparagraph (E);

(G) demonstrate adequate experience and background in providing credit counseling; and

(H) have adequate financial resources to provide continuing support services for budgeting plans over the life of any repayment plan.

(d) The United States trustee (or the bankruptcy administrator, if any) shall only approve an instructional course concerning personal financial management—

(1) for an initial probationary period under subsection (b)(3) if the course will provide at a minimum—

(A) trained personnel with adequate experience and training in providing effective instruction and services;

(B) learning materials and teaching methodologies designed to assist debtors in understanding personal financial management and that are consistent with stated objectives directly related to the goals of such instructional course;

(C) adequate facilities situated in reasonably convenient locations at which such instructional course is offered, except that such facilities may include the provision of such instructional course by telephone or through the Internet, if such instructional course is effective;

(D) the preparation and retention of reasonable records (which shall include the debtor's bankruptcy case number) to permit evaluation of the effectiveness of such instructional course, including any evaluation of satisfaction of instructional course requirements for each debtor attending such instructional course, which shall be available for inspection and evaluation by the Executive Office for United States Trustees, the United States trustee (or the bankruptcy administrator, if any), or the chief bankruptcy judge for the district in which such instructional course is offered; and

(E) if a fee is charged for the instructional course, charge a reasonable fee, and provide services without regard to ability to pay the fee; and

(2) for any 1-year period if the provider thereof has demonstrated that the course meets the standards of paragraph (1) and, in addition—

(A) has been effective in assisting a substantial number of debtors to understand personal financial management; and

(B) is otherwise likely to increase substantially the debtor's understanding of personal financial management.

(e) The district court may, at any time, investigate the qualifications of a nonprofit budget and credit counseling agency referred to in subsection (a), and request production of documents to ensure the integrity and effectiveness of such agency. The district court may, at any time, remove from the approved list under subsection (a) a nonprofit budget and credit counseling agency upon finding such agency does not meet the qualifications of subsection (b).

(f) The United States trustee (or the bankruptcy administrator, if any) shall notify the clerk that a nonprofit budget and credit counseling agency or an instructional course is no longer approved, in which case the clerk shall remove it from the list maintained under subsection (a).

(g)(1) No nonprofit budget and credit counseling agency may provide to a credit reporting agency information concerning whether a debtor has received or sought instruction concerning personal financial management from such agency.

(2) A nonprofit budget and credit counseling agency that willfully or negligently fails to comply with any requirement under this title with respect to a debtor shall be liable for damages in an amount equal to the sum of—

(A) any actual damages sustained by the debtor as a result of the violation; and

(B) any court costs or reasonable attorneys' fees (as determined by the court) incurred in an action to recover those damages.

§ 112. Prohibition on Disclosure of Name of Minor Children

The debtor may be required to provide information regarding a minor child involved in matters under this title but may not be required to disclose in the public records in the case the name of such minor child. The debtor may be required to disclose the name of such minor child in a nonpublic record that is maintained by the court and made available by the court for examination by the United States trustee, the trustee, and the auditor (if any) serving under section 586(f) of title 28, in the case. The court, the United States trustee, the trustee, and such auditor shall not disclose the name of such minor child maintained in such nonpublic record.

CHAPTER 3. CASE ADMINISTRATION

SUBCHAPTER I—COMMENCEMENT OF A CASE

Section

301. Voluntary Cases
302. Joint Cases

303. Involuntary Cases
305. Abstention
306. Limited Appearance
307. United States Trustee
308. Debtor Reporting Requirements

§ 301. Voluntary Cases

(a) A voluntary case under a chapter of this title is commenced by the filing with the bankruptcy court of a petition under such chapter by an entity that may be a debtor under such chapter.

(b) The commencement of a voluntary case under a chapter of this title constitutes an order for relief under such chapter.

§ 302. Joint Cases

(a) A joint case under a chapter of this title is commenced by the filing with the bankruptcy court of a single petition under such chapter by an individual that may be a debtor under such chapter and such individual's spouse. The commencement of a joint case under a chapter of this title constitutes an order for relief under such chapter.

(b) After the commencement of a joint case, the court shall determine the extent, if any, to which the debtors' estates shall be consolidated.

§ 303. Involuntary Cases

(a) An involuntary case may be commenced only under chapter 7 or 11 of this title, and only against a person, except a farmer, family farmer, or a corporation that is not a moneyed, business, or commercial corporation, that may be a debtor under the chapter under which such case is commenced.

(b) An involuntary case against a person is commenced by the filing with the bankruptcy court of a petition under chapter 7 or 11 of this title—

(1) by three or more entities, each of which is either a holder of a claim against such person that is not contingent as to liability or the subject of a bona fide dispute as to liability or amount, or an indenture trustee representing such a holder, if such noncontingent, undisputed claims aggregate at least $18,600 more than the value of any lien on property of the debtor securing such claims held by the holders of such claims;

(2) if there are fewer than 12 such holders, excluding any employee or insider of such person and any transferee of a transfer that is voidable under section 544, 545, 547, 548, 549, or 724(a) of this title, by one or more of such holders that hold in the aggregate at least $18,600 of such claims;

(3) if such person is a partnership—

(A) by fewer than all of the general partners in such partnership; or

(B) if relief has been ordered under this title with respect to all of the general partners in such partnership, by a general partner in such partnership, the trustee of such a general partner, or a holder of a claim against such partnership; or

(4) by a foreign representative of the estate in a foreign proceeding concerning such person.

(c) After the filing of a petition under this section but before the case is dismissed or relief is ordered, a creditor holding an unsecured claim that is not contingent, other than a creditor filing under subsection (b) of this section, may join in the petition with the same effect as if such joining creditor were a petitioning creditor under subsection (b) of this section.

(d) The debtor, or a general partner in a partnership debtor that did not join in the petition, may file an answer to a petition under this section.

(e) After notice and a hearing, and for cause, the court may require the petitioners under this section to file a bond to indemnify the debtor for such amounts as the court may later allow under subsection (i) of this section.

(f) Notwithstanding section 363 of this title, except to the extent that the court orders otherwise, and until an order for relief in the case, any business of the debtor may continue to operate, and the debtor may continue to use, acquire, or dispose of property as if an involuntary case concerning the debtor had not been commenced.

(g) At any time after the commencement of an involuntary case under chapter 7 of this title but before an order for relief in the case, the court, on request of a party in interest, after notice to the debtor and a hearing, and if necessary to preserve the property of the estate or to prevent loss to the estate, may order the United States trustee to appoint an interim trustee under section 701 of this title to take possession of the property of the estate and to operate any business of the debtor. Before an order for relief, the debtor may regain possession of property in the possession of a trustee ordered appointed under this subsection if the debtor files such bond as the court requires, conditioned on the debtor's accounting for and delivering to the trustee, if there is an order for relief in the case, such property, or the value, as of the date the debtor regains possession, of such property.

(h) If the petition is not timely controverted, the court shall order relief against the debtor in an involuntary case under the chapter under which the petition was filed. Otherwise, after trial, the court shall order relief against the debtor in an involuntary case under the chapter under which the petition was filed, only if—

(1) the debtor is generally not paying such debtor's debts as such debts become due unless such debts are the subject of a bona fide dispute as to liability or amount; or

(2) within 120 days before the date of the filing of the petition, a custodian, other than a trustee, receiver, or agent appointed or authorized to take charge of less than substantially all of the property of the debtor for the purpose of enforcing a lien against such property, was appointed or took possession.

(i) If the court dismisses a petition under this section other than on consent of all petitioners and the debtor, and if the debtor does not waive the right to judgment under this subsection, the court may grant judgment—

(1) against the petitioners and in favor of the debtor for—

(A) costs; or

(B) a reasonable attorney's fee; or

(2) against any petitioner that filed the petition in bad faith, for—

(A) any damages proximately caused by such filing; or

(B) punitive damages.

(j) Only after notice to all creditors and a hearing may the court dismiss a petition filed under this section—

(1) on the motion of a petitioner;

(2) on consent of all petitioners and the debtor; or

(3) for want of prosecution.

(k)(1) If—

(A) the petition under this section is false or contains any materially false, fictitious, or fraudulent statement;

(B) the debtor is an individual; and

(C) the court dismisses such petition, the court, upon the motion of the debtor, shall seal all the records of the court relating to such petition, and all references to such petition.

(2) If the debtor is an individual and the court dismisses a petition under this section, the court may enter an order prohibiting all consumer reporting agencies (as defined in section 603(f) of the Fair Credit Reporting Act (15 U.S.C. 1681a(f)) from making any consumer report (as defined in section 603(d) of that Act) that contains any information relating to such petition or to the case commenced by the filing of such petition.

(3) Upon the expiration of the statute of limitations described in section 3282 of title 18, for a violation of section 152 or 157 of such title, the court, upon the motion of the debtor and for good cause, may expunge any records relating to a petition filed under this section.

§ 305. Abstention

(a) The court, after notice and a hearing, may dismiss a case under this title, or may suspend all proceedings in a case under this title, at any time if—

(1) the interests of creditors and the debtor would be better served by such dismissal or suspension; or

(2) (A) a petition under section 1515 for recognition of a foreign proceeding has been granted; and

(B) the purposes of chapter 15 of this title would be best served by such dismissal or suspension.

(b) A foreign representative may seek dismissal or suspension under subsection (a)(2) of this section.

(c) An order under subsection (a) of this section dismissing a case or suspending all proceedings in a case, or a decision not so to dismiss or suspend, is not reviewable by appeal or otherwise by the court of appeals under section 158(d), 1291, or 1292 of title 28 or by the Supreme Court of the United States under section 1254 of title 28.

§ 306. Limited Appearance

An appearance in a bankruptcy court by a foreign representative in connection with a petition or request under section 303 or 305 of this title does not submit such foreign representative to the jurisdiction of any court in the United States for any other purpose, but the bankruptcy court may condition any order under section 303 or 305 of this title on compliance by such foreign representative with the orders of such bankruptcy court.

§ 307. United States Trustee

The United States trustee may raise and may appear and be heard on any issue in any case or proceeding under this title but may not file a plan pursuant to section 1121(c) of this title.

§ 308. Debtor Reporting Requirements

(a) For purposes of this section, the term "profitability" means, with respect to a debtor, the amount of money that the debtor has earned or lost during current and recent fiscal periods.

(b) A debtor in a small business case shall file periodic financial and other reports containing information including—

(1) the debtor's profitability;

(2) reasonable approximations of the debtor's projected cash receipts and cash disbursements over a reasonable period;

(3) comparisons of actual cash receipts and disbursements with projections in prior reports;

(4) whether the debtor is—

(A) in compliance in all material respects with postpetition requirements imposed by this title and the Federal Rules of Bankruptcy Procedure; and

(B) timely filing tax returns and other required government filings and paying taxes and other administrative expenses when due;

(5) if the debtor is not in compliance with the requirements referred to in paragraph (4)(A) or filing tax returns and other required government filings and making the payments referred to in paragraph (4)(B), what the failures are and how, at what cost, and when the debtor intends to remedy such failures; and

(6) such other matters as are in the best interests of the debtor and creditors, and in the public interest in fair and efficient procedures under chapter 11 of this title.

SUBCHAPTER II—OFFICERS

Section

321. Eligibility to Serve as Trustee
322. Qualification of Trustee
323. Role and Capacity of Trustee
324. Removal of Trustee or Examiner
325. Effect of Vacancy
326. Limitation on Compensation of Trustee
327. Employment of Professional Persons
328. Limitation on Compensation of Professional Persons
329. Debtor's Transactions with Attorneys
330. Compensation of Officers
331. Interim Compensation
332. Consumer Privacy Ombudsman
333. Appointment of Patient Care Ombudsman

§ 321. Eligibility to Serve as Trustee

(a) A person may serve as trustee in a case under this title only if such person is—

(1) an individual that is competent to perform the duties of trustee and, in a case under chapter 7, 12, or 13 of this title, resides or has an office in the judicial district within which the case is pending, or in any judicial district adjacent to such district; or

(2) a corporation authorized by such corporation's charter or bylaws to act as trustee, and, in a case under chapter 7, 12, or 13 of this title, having an office in at least one of such districts.

(b) A person that has served as an examiner in the case may not serve as trustee in the case.

(c) The United States trustee for the judicial district in which the case is pending is eligible to serve as trustee in the case if necessary.

§ 322. Qualification of Trustee

(a) Except as provided in subsection (b)(1), a person selected under section 701, 702, 703, 1104, 1163, 1183, 1202, or 1302 of this title to serve as trustee in a case under this title qualifies if before seven days after such selection, and before beginning official duties, such person has filed with the court a bond in favor of the United States conditioned on the faithful performance of such official duties.

(b)(1) The United States trustee qualifies wherever such trustee serves as trustee in a case under this title.

(2) The United States trustee shall determine—

(A) the amount of a bond required to be filed under subsection (a) of this section; and

(B) the sufficiency of the surety on such bond.

(c) A trustee is not liable personally or on such trustee's bond in favor of the United States for any penalty or forfeiture incurred by the debtor.

(d) A proceeding on a trustee's bond may not be commenced after two years after the date on which such trustee was discharged.

§ 323. Role and Capacity of Trustee

(a) The trustee in a case under this title is the representative of the estate.

(b) The trustee in a case under this title has capacity to sue and be sued.

§ 324. Removal of Trustee or Examiner

(a) The court, after notice and a hearing, may remove a trustee, other than the United States trustee, or an examiner, for cause.

(b) Whenever the court removes a trustee or examiner under subsection (a) in a case under this title, such trustee or examiner shall thereby be removed in all other cases under this title in which such trustee or examiner is then serving unless the court orders otherwise.

§ 325. Effect of Vacancy

A vacancy in the office of trustee during a case does not abate any pending action or proceeding, and the successor trustee shall be substituted as a party in such action or proceeding.

§ 326. Limitation on Compensation of Trustee

(a) In a case under chapter 7 or 11, other than a case under subchapter V of chapter 11, the court may allow reasonable compensation under section 330 of this title of the trustee for the trustee's services, payable after the trustee renders such services, not to exceed 25 percent on the first $5,000 or less, 10 percent on any amount in excess of $5,000 but not in excess of $50,000, 5 percent on any amount in excess of $50,000 but not in excess of $1,000,000, and reasonable compensation not to exceed 3 percent of such moneys in excess of $1,000,000, upon all moneys disbursed or turned over in the case by the trustee to parties in interest, excluding the debtor, but including holders of secured claims.

(b) In a case under subchapter V of chapter 11 or chapter 12 or 13 of this title, the court may not allow compensation for services or reimbursement of expenses of the United States trustee or of a standing trustee appointed under section 586(b) of title 28, but may allow reasonable compensation under section 330 of this title of a trustee appointed under section 1202(a) or 1302(a) of this title for the trustee's services, payable after the trustee renders such services, not to exceed five percent upon all payments under the plan.

(c) If more than one person serves as trustee in the case, the aggregate compensation of such persons for such service may not exceed the maximum compensation prescribed for a single trustee by subsection (a) or (b) of this section, as the case may be.

(d) The court may deny allowance of compensation for services or reimbursement of expenses of the trustee if the trustee failed to make diligent inquiry into facts that would permit denial of allowance under section 328(c) of this title or, with knowledge of such facts, employed a professional person under section 327 of this title.

§ 327. Employment of Professional Persons

(a) Except as otherwise provided in this section, the trustee, with the court's approval, may employ one or more attorneys, accountants, appraisers, auctioneers, or other professional persons, that do not hold or represent an interest adverse to the estate, and that are disinterested persons, to represent or assist the trustee in carrying out the trustee's duties under this title.

(b) If the trustee is authorized to operate the business of the debtor under section 721, 1202, or 1108 of this title, and if the debtor has regularly employed attorneys, accountants, or other professional persons on salary, the trustee may retain or replace such professional persons if necessary in the operation of such business.

(c) In a case under chapter 7, 12, or 11 of this title, a person is not disqualified for employment under this section solely because of such person's employment by or representation of a creditor, unless there is objection by another creditor or the United States trustee, in which case the court shall disapprove such employment if there is an actual conflict of interest.

(d) The court may authorize the trustee to act as attorney or accountant for the estate if such authorization is in the best interest of the estate.

(e) The trustee, with the court's approval, may employ, for a specified special purpose, other than to represent the trustee in conducting the case, an attorney that has represented the debtor, if in the best interest of the estate, and if such attorney does not represent or hold any interest adverse to the debtor or to the estate with respect to the matter on which such attorney is to be employed.

(f) The trustee may not employ a person that has served as an examiner in the case.

§ 328. Limitation on Compensation of Professional Persons

(a) The trustee, or a committee appointed under section 1102 of this title, with the court's approval, may employ or authorize the employment of a professional person under section 327 or 1103 of this title, as the case may be, on any reasonable terms and conditions of employment, including on a retainer, on an hourly basis, on a fixed or percentage fee basis, or on a contingent fee basis. Notwithstanding such terms and conditions, the court may allow compensation different from the compensation provided under such terms and conditions after the conclusion of such employment, if such terms and conditions prove to have been improvident in light of developments not capable of being anticipated at the time of the fixing of such terms and conditions.

(b) If the court has authorized a trustee to serve as an attorney or accountant for the estate under section 327(d) of this title, the court may allow compensation for the trustee's services as such attorney or accountant only to the extent that the trustee performed services as attorney or accountant for the estate and not for performance of any of the trustee's duties that are generally performed by a trustee without the assistance of an attorney or accountant for the estate.

(c) Except as provided in section 327(c), 327(e), or 1107(b) of this title, the court may deny allowance of compensation for services and reimbursement of expenses of a professional person employed under section 327 or 1103 of this title if, at any time during such professional person's employment under section 327 or 1103 of this title, such professional person is not a disinterested person, or represents or holds an interest adverse to the interest of the estate with respect to the matter on which such professional person is employed.

§ 329. Debtor's Transactions with Attorneys

(a) Any attorney representing a debtor in a case under this title, or in connection with such a case, whether or not such attorney applies for compensation under this title, shall file with the court a statement of the compensation paid or agreed to be paid, if such payment or agreement was made after one year before the date of the filing of the petition, for services rendered or to be rendered in contemplation of or in connection with the case by such attorney, and the source of such compensation.

(b) If such compensation exceeds the reasonable value of any such services, the court may cancel any such agreement, or order the return of any such payment, to the extent excessive, to—

(1) the estate, if the property transferred—

(A) would have been property of the estate; or

(B) was to be paid by or on behalf of the debtor under a plan under chapter 11, 12, or 13 of this title; or

(2) the entity that made such payment.

§ 330. Compensation of Officers

(a)(1) After notice to the parties in interest and the United States Trustee and a hearing, and subject to sections 326, 328, and 329, the court may award to a trustee, a consumer privacy ombudsman appointed under section 332, an examiner, an ombudsman appointed under section 333, or a professional person employed under section 327 or 1103—

(A) reasonable compensation for actual, necessary services rendered by the trustee, examiner, ombudsman, professional person, or attorney and by any paraprofessional person employed by any such person; and

(B) reimbursement for actual, necessary expenses.

(2) The court may, on its own motion or on the motion of the United States Trustee, the United States Trustee for the District or Region, the trustee for the estate, or any other party in interest, award compensation that is less than the amount of compensation that is requested.

(3) In determining the amount of reasonable compensation to be awarded to an examiner, trustee under chapter 11, or professional person, the court shall consider the nature, the extent, and the value of such services, taking into account all relevant factors, including—

(A) the time spent on such services;

(B) the rates charged for such services;

(C) whether the services were necessary to the administration of, or beneficial at the time at which the service was rendered toward the completion of, a case under this title;

(D) whether the services were performed within a reasonable amount of time commensurate with the complexity, importance, and nature of the problem, issue, or task addressed;

(E) with respect to a professional person, whether the person is board certified or otherwise has demonstrated skill and experience in the bankruptcy field; and

(F) whether the compensation is reasonable based on the customary compensation charged by comparably skilled practitioners in cases other than cases under this title.

(4) (A) Except as provided in subparagraph (B), the court shall not allow compensation for—

(i) unnecessary duplication of services; or

(ii) services that were not—

(I) reasonably likely to benefit the debtor's estate; or

(II) necessary to the administration of the case.

(B) In a chapter 12 or chapter 13 case in which the debtor is an individual, the court may allow reasonable compensation to the debtor's attorney for representing the interests of the debtor in connection with the bankruptcy case based on a consideration of the benefit and necessity of such services to the debtor and the other factors set forth in this section.

(5) The court shall reduce the amount of compensation awarded under this section by the amount of any interim compensation awarded under section 331, and, if the amount of such interim compensation exceeds the amount of compensation awarded under this section, may order the return of the excess to the estate.

(6) Any compensation awarded for the preparation of a fee application shall be based on the level and skill reasonably required to prepare the application.

(7) In determining the amount of reasonable compensation to be awarded to a trustee, the court shall treat such compensation as a commission, based on section 326.

(b)(1) There shall be paid from the filing fee in a case under chapter 7 of this title $45 to the trustee serving in such case, after such trustee's services are rendered.

(2) The Judicial Conference of the United States—

(A) shall prescribe additional fees of the same kind as prescribed under section 1914(b) of title 28; and

(B) may prescribe notice of appearance fees and fees charged against distributions in cases under this title;

to pay $15 to trustees serving in cases after such trustees' services are rendered. Beginning 1 year after the date of the enactment of the Bankruptcy Reform Act of 1994, such $15 shall be paid in addition to the amount paid under paragraph (1).

(c) Unless the court orders otherwise, in a case under chapter 12 or 13 of this title the compensation paid to the trustee serving in the case shall not be less than $5 per month from any distribution under the plan during the administration of the plan.

(d) In a case in which the United States trustee serves as trustee, the compensation of the trustee under this section shall be paid to the clerk of the bankruptcy court and deposited by the clerk into the United States Trustee System Fund established by section 589a of title 28.

(e)(1) There is established a fund in the Treasury of the United States to be known as the "Chapter 7 Trustee Fund", which shall be administered by the Director of the Administrative Office of the United States Courts.

(2) Deposits into the Chapter 7 Trustee Fund under section 589a(f)(l)(C) of title 28 shall be available until expended for the purposes described in paragraph (3).

(3) For fiscal years 2021 through 2026, the Chapter 7 Trustee Fund shall be available to pay the trustee serving in a case that is filed under chapter 7 or a case that is converted to a chapter 7 case in the most recent fiscal year (referred to in this subsection as a "chapter 7 case") the amount described in paragraph (4) for the chapter 7 case in which the trustee has rendered services.

(4) The amount described in this paragraph shall be the lesser of—

(A) $60; or

(B) a pro rata share, for each chapter 7 case, of the fees collected under section 1930(a)(6) of title 28 and deposited to the United States Trustee System Fund under section 589a(f)(l) of title 28, less the amounts specified in section 589a(f)(l)(A) and (B) of title 28.

(5) The payment received by a trustee under paragraph (3) shall be paid in addition to the amount paid under subsection (b).

(6) Not later than September 30, 2021, the Director of the Administrative Office of the United States Courts shall promulgate regulations for the administration of this subsection.

§ 331. Interim Compensation

A trustee, an examiner, a debtor's attorney, or any professional person employed under section 327 or 1103 of this title may apply to the court not more than once every 120 days after an order for relief in a case under this title, or more often if the court permits, for such compensation for services rendered before the date of such an application or reimbursement for expenses incurred before such date as is provided under section 330 of this title. After notice and a hearing, the court may allow and disburse to such applicant such compensation or reimbursement.

§ 332. Consumer Privacy Ombudsman

(a) If a hearing is required under section 363(b)(1)(B), the court shall order the United States trustee to appoint, not later than 7 days before the commencement of the hearing, 1 disinterested person (other than the United States trustee) to serve as the consumer privacy ombudsman in the case and shall require that notice of such hearing be timely given to such ombudsman.

(b) The consumer privacy ombudsman may appear and be heard at such hearing and shall provide to the court information to assist the court in its consideration of the facts, circumstances, and conditions of the proposed sale or lease of personally identifiable information under section 363(b)(1)(B). Such information may include presentation of—

(1) the debtor's privacy policy;

(2) the potential losses or gains of privacy to consumers if such sale or such lease is approved by the court;

(3) the potential costs or benefits to consumers if such sale or such lease is approved by the court; and

(4) the potential alternatives that would mitigate potential privacy losses or potential costs to consumers.

(c) A consumer privacy ombudsman shall not disclose any personally identifiable information obtained by the ombudsman under this title.

§ 333. Appointment of Patient Care Ombudsman

(a)(1) If the debtor in a case under chapter 7, 9, or 11 is a health care business, the court shall order, not later than 30 days after the commencement of the case, the appointment of an ombudsman to monitor the quality of patient care and to represent the interests of the patients of the health care business unless the court finds that the appointment of such ombudsman is not necessary for the protection of patients under the specific facts of the case.

(2) (A) If the court orders the appointment of an ombudsman under paragraph (1), the United States trustee shall appoint 1 disinterested person (other than the United States trustee) to serve as such ombudsman.

(B) If the debtor is a health care business that provides long-term care, then the United States trustee may appoint the State Long-Term Care Ombudsman appointed under the Older Americans Act of 1965 for the State in which the case is pending to serve as the ombudsman required by paragraph (1).

(C) If the United States trustee does not appoint a State Long-Term Care Ombudsman under subparagraph (B), the court shall notify the State Long-Term Care Ombudsman appointed under the Older Americans Act of 1965 for the State in which the case is pending, of the name and address of the person who is appointed under subparagraph (A).

(b) An ombudsman appointed under subsection (a) shall—

(1) monitor the quality of patient care provided to patients of the debtor, to the extent necessary under the circumstances, including interviewing patients and physicians;

(2) not later than 60 days after the date of appointment, and not less frequently than at 60-day intervals thereafter, report to the court after notice to the parties in interest, at a hearing or in writing, regarding the quality of patient care provided to patients of the debtor; and

(3) if such ombudsman determines that the quality of patient care provided to patients of the debtor is declining significantly or is otherwise being materially compromised, file with the court a motion or a written report, with notice to the parties in interest immediately upon making such determination.

(c)(1) An ombudsman appointed under subsection (a) shall maintain any information obtained by such ombudsman under this section that relates to patients (including information relating to patient records) as confidential information. Such ombudsman may not review confidential patient records unless the court approves such review in advance and imposes restrictions on such ombudsman to protect the confidentiality of such records.

(2) An ombudsman appointed under subsection (a)(2)(B) shall have access to patient records consistent with authority of such ombudsman under the Older Americans Act of 1965 and under non-Federal laws governing the State Long-Term Care Ombudsman program.

SUBCHAPTER III—ADMINISTRATION

Section

341. Meetings of Creditors and Equity Security Holders
342. Notice
343. Examination of the Debtor
344. Self-incrimination; Immunity
345. Money of Estates
346. Special Provisions Related to the Treatment of State and Local Taxes
347. Unclaimed Property
348. Effect of Conversion
349. Effect of Dismissal
350. Closing and Reopening Cases
351. Disposal of Patient Records

§ 341. Meetings of Creditors and Equity Security Holders

(a) Within a reasonable time after the order for relief in a case under this title, the United States trustee shall convene and preside at a meeting of creditors.

(b) The United States trustee may convene a meeting of any equity security holders.

(c) The court may not preside at, and may not attend, any meeting under this section including any final meeting of creditors. Notwithstanding any local court rule, provision of a State constitution, any otherwise applicable nonbankruptcy law, or any other requirement that representation at the meeting of creditors under subsection (a) be by an attorney, a creditor holding a consumer debt or any representative of the creditor (which may include an entity or an employee of an entity and may be a representative for more than 1 creditor) shall be permitted to appear at and participate in the meeting of creditors in a case under chapter 7 or 13, either alone or in conjunction with an attorney for the creditor. Nothing in this subsection shall be construed to require any creditor to be represented by an attorney at any meeting of creditors.

(d) Prior to the conclusion of the meeting of creditors or equity security holders, the trustee shall orally examine the debtor to ensure that the debtor in a case under chapter 7 of this title is aware of—

(1) the potential consequences of seeking a discharge in bankruptcy, including the effects on credit history;

(2) the debtor's ability to file a petition under a different chapter of this title;

(3) the effect of receiving a discharge of debts under this title; and

(4) the effect of reaffirming a debt, including the debtor's knowledge of the provisions of section 524(d) of this title.

(e) Notwithstanding subsections (a) and (b), the court, on the request of a party in interest and after notice and a hearing, for cause may order that the United States trustee not convene a meeting of creditors or equity security holders if the debtor has filed a plan as to which the debtor solicited acceptances prior to the commencement of the case.

§ 342. Notice

(a) There shall be given such notice as is appropriate, including notice to any holder of a community claim, of an order for relief in a case under this title.

(b) Before the commencement of a case under this title by an individual whose debts are primarily consumer debts, the clerk shall give to such individual written notice containing—

(1) a brief description of—

(A) chapters 7, 11, 12, and 13 and the general purpose, benefits, and costs of proceeding under each of those chapters; and

(B) the types of services available from credit counseling agencies; and

(2) statements specifying that—

(A) a person who knowingly and fraudulently conceals assets or makes a false oath or statement under penalty of perjury in connection with a case under this title shall be subject to fine, imprisonment, or both; and

(B) all information supplied by a debtor in connection with a case under this title is subject to examination by the Attorney General.

(c)(1) If notice is required to be given by the debtor to a creditor under this title, any rule, any applicable law, or any order of the court, such notice shall contain the name, address, and last 4 digits of the taxpayer identification number of the debtor. If the notice concerns an amendment that adds a creditor to the schedules of assets and liabilities, the debtor shall include the full taxpayer identification number in the notice sent to that creditor, but the debtor shall include only the last 4 digits of the taxpayer identification number in the copy of the notice filed with the court.

(2) (A) If, within the 90 days before the commencement of a voluntary case, a creditor supplies the debtor in at least 2 communications sent to the debtor with the current account number of the debtor and the address at which such creditor requests to receive correspondence, then any notice required by this title to be sent by the debtor to such creditor shall be sent to such address and shall include such account number.

(B) If a creditor would be in violation of applicable nonbankruptcy law by sending any such communication within such 90-day period and if such creditor supplies the debtor in the last 2 communications with the current account number of the debtor and the address at which such creditor requests to receive correspondence, then any notice required by this title to be sent by the debtor to such creditor shall be sent to such address and shall include such account number.

(d) In a case under chapter 7 of this title in which the debtor is an individual and in which the presumption of abuse arises under section 707(b), the clerk shall give written notice to all creditors not later than 10 days after the date of the filing of the petition that the presumption of abuse has arisen.

(e)(1) In a case under chapter 7 or 13 of this title of a debtor who is an individual, a creditor at any time may both file with the court and serve on the debtor a notice of address to be used to provide notice in such case to such creditor.

(2) Any notice in such case required to be provided to such creditor by the debtor or the court later than 7 days after the court and the debtor receive such creditor's notice of address, shall be provided to such address.

(f)(1) An entity may file with any bankruptcy court a notice of address to be used by all the bankruptcy courts or by particular bankruptcy courts, as so specified by such entity at the time such notice is filed, to provide notice to such entity in all cases under chapters 7 and 13 pending in the courts with respect to which such notice is filed, in which such entity is a creditor.

(2) In any case filed under chapter 7 or 13, any notice required to be provided by a court with respect to which a notice is filed under paragraph (1), to such entity later than 30 days after the filing of such notice under paragraph (1) shall be provided to such address unless with respect to a particular case a different address is specified in a notice filed and served in accordance with subsection (e).

(3) A notice filed under paragraph (1) may be withdrawn by such entity.

(g)(1) Notice provided to a creditor by the debtor or the court other than in accordance with this section (excluding this subsection) shall not be effective notice until such notice is brought to the attention of such creditor. If such creditor designates a person or an organizational subdivision of such creditor to be responsible for receiving notices under this title and establishes reasonable procedures so that such notices receivable by such creditor are to be delivered to such person or such subdivision, then a notice provided to such creditor other than in accordance with this section (excluding this subsection) shall not be considered to have been brought to the attention of such creditor until such notice is received by such person or such subdivision.

(2) A monetary penalty may not be imposed on a creditor for a violation of a stay in effect under section 362(a) (including a monetary penalty imposed under section 362(k)) or for failure to comply with section 542 or 543 unless the conduct that is the basis of such violation or of such failure occurs after such creditor receives notice effective under this section of the order for relief.

§ 343. Examination of the Debtor

The debtor shall appear and submit to examination under oath at the meeting of creditors under section 341(a) of this title. Creditors, any indenture trustee, any trustee or examiner in the case, or the United States trustee may examine the debtor. The United States trustee may administer the oath required under this section.

§ 344. Self-Incrimination; Immunity

Immunity for persons required to submit to examination, to testify, or to provide information in a case under this title may be granted under part V of title 18.

§ 345. Money of Estates

(a) A trustee in a case under this title may make such deposit or investment of the money of the estate for which such trustee serves as will yield the maximum reasonable net return on such money, taking into account the safety of such deposit or investment.

(b) Except with respect to a deposit or investment that is insured or guaranteed by the United States or by a department, agency, or instrumentality of the United States or backed by the full faith and credit of the United States, the trustee shall require from an entity with which such money is deposited or invested—

(1) a bond—

(A) in favor of the United States;

(B) secured by the undertaking of a corporate surety approved by the United States trustee for the district in which the case is pending; and

(C) conditioned on—

(i) a proper accounting for all money so deposited or invested and for any return on such money;

(ii) prompt repayment of such money and return; and

(iii) faithful performance of duties as a depository; or

(2) the deposit of securities of the kind specified in section 9303 of title 31; unless the court for cause orders otherwise.

(c) An entity with which such moneys are deposited or invested is authorized to deposit or invest such moneys as may be required under this section.

§ 346. Special Provisions Related to the Treatment of State and Local Taxes

(a) Whenever the Internal Revenue Code of 1986 provides that a separate taxable estate or entity is created in a case concerning a debtor under this title, and the income, gain, loss, deductions, and credits of such estate shall be taxed to or claimed by the estate, a separate taxable estate is also created for purposes of any State and local law imposing a tax on or measured by income and such income, gain, loss, deductions, and credits shall be taxed to or claimed by the estate and may not be taxed to or claimed by the debtor. The preceding sentence shall not apply if the case is dismissed. The trustee shall make tax returns of income required under any such State or local law.

(b) Whenever the Internal Revenue Code of 1986 provides that no separate taxable estate shall be created in a case concerning a debtor under this title, and the income, gain, loss, deductions, and credits of an estate shall be taxed to or claimed by the debtor, such income, gain, loss, deductions, and credits shall be taxed to or claimed by the debtor under a State or local law imposing a tax on or measured by income and may not be taxed to or claimed by the estate. The trustee shall make such tax returns of income of corporations and of partnerships as are required under any State or local law, but with respect to partnerships, shall make such returns only to the extent such returns are also required to be made under such Code. The estate shall be liable for any tax imposed on such corporation or partnership, but not for any tax imposed on partners or members.

(c) With respect to a partnership or any entity treated as a partnership under a State or local law imposing a tax on or measured by income that is a debtor in a case under this title, any gain or loss resulting from a distribution of property from such partnership, or any distributive share of any income, gain, loss, deduction, or credit of a partner or member that is distributed, or considered distributed, from such partnership, after the commencement of the case, is gain, loss, income, deduction, or credit, as the case may be, of the partner or member, and if such partner or member is a debtor in a case under this title, shall be subject to tax in accordance with subsection (a) or (b).

(d) For purposes of any State or local law imposing a tax on or measured by income, the taxable period of a debtor in a case under this title shall terminate only if and to the extent that the taxable period of such debtor terminates under the Internal Revenue Code of 1986.

(e) The estate in any case described in subsection (a) shall use the same accounting method as the debtor used immediately before the commencement of the case, if such method of accounting complies with applicable nonbankruptcy tax law.

(f) For purposes of any State or local law imposing a tax on or measured by income, a transfer of property from the debtor to the estate or from the estate to the debtor shall not be treated as a disposition for purposes of any provision assigning tax consequences to a disposition, except to the extent that such transfer is treated as a disposition under the Internal Revenue Code of 1986.

(g) Whenever a tax is imposed pursuant to a State or local law imposing a tax on or measured by income pursuant to subsection (a) or (b), such tax shall be imposed at rates generally applicable to the same types of entities under such State or local law.

(h) The trustee shall withhold from any payment of claims for wages, salaries, commissions, dividends, interest, or other payments, or collect, any amount required to be withheld or collected under applicable State or local tax law, and shall pay such withheld or collected amount to the appropriate governmental unit at the time and in the manner required by such tax law, and with the same priority as the claim from which such amount was withheld or collected was paid.

(i)(1) To the extent that any State or local law imposing a tax on or measured by income provides for the carryover of any tax attribute from one taxable period to a subsequent taxable period, the estate shall succeed to such tax attribute in any case in which such estate is subject to tax under subsection (a).

(2) After such a case is closed or dismissed, the debtor shall succeed to any tax attribute to which the estate succeeded under paragraph (1) to the extent consistent with the Internal Revenue Code of 1986.

(3) The estate may carry back any loss or tax attribute to a taxable period of the debtor that ended before the date of the order for relief under this title to the extent that—

(A) applicable State or local tax law provides for a carryback in the case of the debtor; and

(B) the same or a similar tax attribute may be carried back by the estate to such a taxable period of the debtor under the Internal Revenue Code of 1986.

(j)(1) For purposes of any State or local law imposing a tax on or measured by income, income is not realized by the estate, the debtor, or a successor to the debtor by reason of discharge of indebtedness in a case under this title, except to the extent, if any, that such income is subject to tax under the Internal Revenue Code of 1986.

(2) Whenever the Internal Revenue Code of 1986 provides that the amount excluded from gross income in respect of the discharge of indebtedness in a case under this title shall be applied to reduce the tax attributes of the debtor or the estate, a similar reduction shall be made under any State or local law imposing a tax on or measured by income to the extent such State or local law recognizes such attributes. Such State or local law may also provide for the reduction of other attributes to the extent that the full amount of income from the discharge of indebtedness has not been applied.

(k)(1) Except as provided in this section and section 505, the time and manner of filing tax returns and the items of income, gain, loss, deduction, and credit of any taxpayer shall be determined under applicable nonbankruptcy law.

(2) For Federal tax purposes, the provisions of this section are subject to the Internal Revenue Code of 1986 and other applicable Federal nonbankruptcy law.

§ 347. Unclaimed Property

(a) Ninety days after the final distribution under section 726, 1194, 1226, or 1326 of this title in a case under chapter 7, subchapter V of chapter 11, 12, or 13 of this title, as the case may be, the trustee shall stop payment on any check remaining unpaid, and any remaining property of the estate shall be paid into the court and disposed of under chapter 129 of title 28.

(b) Any security, money, or other property remaining unclaimed at the expiration of the time allowed in a case under chapter 9, 11, or 12 of this title for the presentation of a security or the performance of any other act as a condition to participation in the distribution under any plan confirmed under section 943(b), 1129, 1173, 1191, or 1225 of this title, as the case may be, becomes the property of the debtor or of the entity acquiring the assets of the debtor under the plan, as the case may be.

§ 348. Effect of Conversion

(a) Conversion of a case from a case under one chapter of this title to a case under another chapter of this title constitutes an order for relief under the chapter to which the case is converted, but, except as provided in subsections (b) and (c) of this section, does not effect a change in the date of the filing of the petition, the commencement of the case, or the order for relief.

(b) Unless the court for cause orders otherwise, in sections 701(a), 727(a)(10), 727(b), 1102(a), 1110(a)(1), 1121(b), 1121(c), 1141(d)(4), 1201(a), 1221, 1228(a), 1301(a), and 1305(a) of this title, "the order for relief under this chapter" in a chapter to which a case has been converted under section 706, 1112, 1208, or 1307 of this title means the conversion of such case to such chapter.

(c) Sections 342 and 365(d) of this title apply in a case that has been converted under section 706, 1112, 1208, or 1307 of this title, as if the conversion order were the order for relief.

(d) A claim against the estate or the debtor that arises after the order for relief but before conversion in a case that is converted under section 1112, 1208, or 1307 of this title, other than a claim specified in section 503(b) of this title, shall be treated for all purposes as if such claim had arisen immediately before the date of the filing of the petition.

(e) Conversion of a case under section 706, 1112, 1208, or 1307 of this title terminates the service of any trustee or examiner that is serving in the case before such conversion.

(f)(1) Except as provided in paragraph (2), when a case under chapter 13 of this title is converted to a case under another chapter under this title—

(A) property of the estate in the converted case shall consist of property of the estate, as of the date of filing of the petition, that remains in the possession of or is under the control of the debtor on the date of conversion;

(B) valuations of property and of allowed secured claims in the chapter 13 case shall apply only in a case converted to a case under chapter 11 or 12, but not in a case converted to a case under chapter 7, with allowed secured claims in cases under chapters 11 and 12 reduced to the extent that they have been paid in accordance with the chapter 13 plan; and

(C) with respect to cases converted from chapter 13—

(i) the claim of any creditor holding security as of the date of the filing of the petition shall continue to be secured by that security unless the full amount of such claim determined under applicable nonbankruptcy law has been paid in full as of the date of conversion, notwithstanding any valuation or determination of the amount of an allowed secured claim made for the purposes of the case under chapter 13; and

(ii) unless a prebankruptcy default has been fully cured under the plan at the time of conversion, in any proceeding under this title or otherwise, the default shall have the effect given under applicable nonbankruptcy law.

(2) If the debtor converts a case under chapter 13 of this title to a case under another chapter under this title in bad faith, the property of the estate in the converted case shall consist of the property of the estate as of the date of conversion.

§ 349. Effect of Dismissal

(a) Unless the court, for cause, orders otherwise, the dismissal of a case under this title does not bar the discharge, in a later case under this title, of debts that were dischargeable in the case dismissed; nor does the dismissal of a case under this title prejudice the debtor with regard to the filing of a subsequent petition under this title, except as provided in section 109(g) of this title.

(b) Unless the court, for cause, orders otherwise, a dismissal of a case other than under section 742 of this title—

(1) reinstates—

(A) any proceeding or custodianship superseded under section 543 of this title;

(B) any transfer avoided under section 522, 544, 545, 547, 548, 549, or 724(a) of this title, or preserved under section 510(c)(2), 522(i)(2), or 551 of this title; and

(C) any lien voided under section 506(d) of this title;

(2) vacates any order, judgment, or transfer ordered, under section 522(i)(1), 542, 550, or 553 of this title; and

(3) revests the property of the estate in the entity in which such property was vested immediately before the commencement of the case under this title.

§ 350. Closing and Reopening Cases

(a) After an estate is fully administered and the court has discharged the trustee, the court shall close the case.

(b) A case may be reopened in the court in which such case was closed to administer assets, to accord relief to the debtor, or for other cause.

§ 351. Disposal of Patient Records

If a health care business commences a case under chapter 7, 9, or 11, and the trustee does not have a sufficient amount of funds to pay for the storage of patient records in the manner required under applicable Federal or State law, the following requirements shall apply:

(1) The trustee shall—

(A) promptly publish notice, in 1 or more appropriate newspapers, that if patient records are not claimed by the patient or an insurance provider (if applicable law permits the insurance provider to make that claim) by the date that is 365 days after the date of that notification, the trustee will destroy the patient records; and

(B) during the first 180 days of the 365-day period described in subparagraph (A), promptly attempt to notify directly each patient that is the subject of the patient records and appropriate insurance carrier concerning the patient records by mailing to the most recent known address of that patient, or a family member or contact person for that patient, and to the appropriate insurance carrier an appropriate notice regarding the claiming or disposing of patient records.

(2) If, after providing the notification under paragraph (1), patient records are not claimed during the 365-day period described under that paragraph, the trustee shall mail, by certified mail, at the end of such 365-day period a written request to each appropriate Federal agency to request permission from that agency to deposit the patient records with that agency, except that no Federal agency is required to accept patient records under this paragraph.

(3) If, following the 365-day period described in paragraph (2) and after providing the notification under paragraph (1), patient records are not claimed by a patient or insurance provider, or request is not granted by a Federal agency to deposit such records with that agency, the trustee shall destroy those records by—

(A) if the records are written, shredding or burning the records; or

(B) if the records are magnetic, optical, or other electronic records, by otherwise destroying those records so that those records cannot be retrieved.

SUBCHAPTER IV—ADMINISTRATIVE POWERS

Section

361. Adequate Protection
362. Automatic Stay
363. Use, Sale, or Lease of Property
364. Obtaining Credit
365. Executory Contracts and Unexpired Leases
366. Utility Service

§ 361. Adequate Protection

When adequate protection is required under section 362, 363, or 364 of this title of an interest of an entity in property, such adequate protection may be provided by—

(1) requiring the trustee to make a cash payment or periodic cash payments to such entity, to the extent that the stay under section 362 of this title, use, sale, or lease under section 363 of this title, or any grant of a lien under section 364 of this title results in a decrease in the value of such entity's interest in such property;

(2) providing to such entity an additional or replacement lien to the extent that such stay, use, sale, lease, or grant results in a decrease in the value of such entity's interest in such property; or

(3) granting such other relief, other than entitling such entity to compensation allowable under section 503(b)(1) of this title as an administrative expense, as will result in the realization by such entity of the indubitable equivalent of such entity's interest in such property.

§ 362. Automatic Stay

(a) Except as provided in subsection (b) of this section, a petition filed under section 301, 302, or 303 of this title, or an application filed under section 5(a)(3) of the Securities Investor Protection Act of 1970, operates as a stay, applicable to all entities, of—

(1) the commencement or continuation, including the issuance or employment of process, of a judicial, administrative, or other action or proceeding against the debtor that was or could have been commenced before the commencement of the case under this title, or to recover a claim against the debtor that arose before the commencement of the case under this title;

(2) the enforcement, against the debtor or against property of the estate, of a judgment obtained before the commencement of the case under this title;

(3) any act to obtain possession of property of the estate or of property from the estate or to exercise control over property of the estate;

(4) any act to create, perfect, or enforce any lien against property of the estate;

(5) any act to create, perfect, or enforce against property of the debtor any lien to the extent that such lien secures a claim that arose before the commencement of the case under this title;

(6) any act to collect, assess, or recover a claim against the debtor that arose before the commencement of the case under this title;

(7) the setoff of any debt owing to the debtor that arose before the commencement of the case under this title against any claim against the debtor; and

(8) the commencement or continuation of a proceeding before the United States Tax Court concerning a tax liability of a debtor that is a corporation for a taxable period the bankruptcy court may determine or concerning the tax liability of a debtor who is an individual for a taxable period ending before the date of the order for relief under this title.

(b) The filing of a petition under section 301, 302, or 303 of this title, or of an application under section 5(a)(3) of the Securities Investor Protection Act of 1970, does not operate as a stay—

(1) under subsection (a) of this section, of the commencement or continuation of a criminal action or proceeding against the debtor;

(2) under subsection (a)—

(A) of the commencement or continuation of a civil action or proceeding—

(i) for the establishment of paternity;

(ii) for the establishment or modification of an order for domestic support obligations;

(iii) concerning child custody or visitation;

(iv) for the dissolution of a marriage, except to the extent that such proceeding seeks to determine the division of property that is property of the estate; or

(v) regarding domestic violence;

(B) of the collection of a domestic support obligation from property that is not property of the estate;

(C) with respect to the withholding of income that is property of the estate or property of the debtor for payment of a domestic support obligation under a judicial or administrative order or a statute;

(D) of the withholding, suspension, or restriction of a driver's license, a professional or occupational license, or a recreational license, under State law, as specified in section 466(a)(16) of the Social Security Act;

(E) of the reporting of overdue support owed by a parent to any consumer reporting agency as specified in section 466(a)(7) of the Social Security Act;

(F) of the interception of a tax refund, as specified in sections 464 and 466(a)(3) of the Social Security Act or under an analogous State law; or

(G) of the enforcement of a medical obligation, as specified under title IV of the Social Security Act;

(3) under subsection (a) of this section, of any act to perfect, or to maintain or continue the perfection of, an interest in property to the extent that the trustee's rights and powers are subject to such perfection under section 546(b) of this title or to the extent that such act is accomplished within the period provided under section 547(e)(2)(A) of this title;

(4) under paragraph (1), (2), (3), or (6) of subsection (a) of this section, of the commencement or continuation of an action or proceeding by a governmental unit or any organization exercising authority under the Convention on the Prohibition of the Development, Production, stockpiling and Use of Chemical Weapons and on Their Destruction, opened for signature on January 13, 1993, to enforce such governmental unit's or organization's police and regulatory power, including the enforcement of a judgment

other than a money judgment, obtained in an action or proceeding by the governmental unit to enforce such governmental unit's or organization's police or regulatory power;

[(5) Repealed. Pub. L. 105–277, div. I, title VI, § 603(1), Oct. 21, 1998, 112 Stat. 2681–866;]

(6) under subsection (a) of this section, of the exercise by a commodity broker, forward contract merchant, stockbroker, financial institution, financial participant, or securities clearing agency of any contractual right (as defined in section 555 or 556) under any security agreement or arrangement or other credit enhancement forming a part of or related to any commodity contract, forward contract or securities contract, or of any contractual right (as defined in section 555 or 556) to offset or net out any termination value, payment amount, or other transfer obligation arising under or in connection with 1 or more such contracts, including any master agreement for such contracts;

(7) under subsection (a) of this section, of the exercise by a repo participant or financial participant of any contractual right (as defined in section 559) under any security agreement or arrangement or other credit enhancement forming a part of or related to any repurchase agreement, or of any contractual right (as defined in section 559) to offset or net out any termination value, payment amount, or other transfer obligation arising under or in connection with 1 or more such agreements, including any master agreement for such agreements;

(8) under subsection (a) of this section, of the commencement of any action by the Secretary of Housing and Urban Development to foreclose a mortgage or deed of trust in any case in which the mortgage or deed of trust held by the Secretary is insured or was formerly insured under the National Housing Act and covers property, or combinations of property, consisting of five or more living units;

(9) under subsection (a), of—

(A) an audit by a governmental unit to determine tax liability;

(B) the issuance to the debtor by a governmental unit of a notice of tax deficiency;

(C) a demand for tax returns; or

(D) the making of an assessment for any tax and issuance of a notice and demand for payment of such an assessment (but any tax lien that would otherwise attach to property of the estate by reason of such an assessment shall not take effect unless such tax is a debt of the debtor that will not be discharged in the case and such property or its proceeds are transferred out of the estate to, or otherwise revested in, the debtor).

(10) under subsection (a) of this section, of any act by a lessor to the debtor under a lease of nonresidential real property that has terminated by the expiration of the stated term of the lease before the commencement of or during a case under this title to obtain possession of such property;

(11) under subsection (a) of this section, of the presentment of a negotiable instrument and the giving of notice of and protesting dishonor of such an instrument;

(12) under subsection (a) of this section, after the date which is 90 days after the filing of such petition, of the commencement or continuation, and conclusion to the entry of final judgment, of an action which involves a debtor subject to reorganization pursuant to chapter 11 of this title and which was brought by the Secretary of Transportation under section 31325 of title 46 (including distribution of any proceeds of sale) to foreclose a preferred ship or fleet mortgage, or a security interest in or relating to a vessel or vessel under construction, held by the Secretary of Transportation under chapter 537 of title 46 or section 109(h) of title 49, or under applicable state law;

(13) under subsection (a) of this section, after the date which is 90 days after the filing of such petition, of the commencement or continuation, and conclusion to the entry of final judgment, of an action which involves a debtor subject to reorganization pursuant to chapter 11 of this title and which was brought by the Secretary of Commerce under section 31325 of title 46 (including distribution of any proceeds of sale) to foreclose a preferred ship or fleet mortgage in a vessel or a mortgage, deed of trust, or other security interest in a fishing facility held by the Secretary of Commerce under chapter 537 of title 46;

(14) under subsection (a) of this section, of any action by an accrediting agency regarding

the accreditation status of the debtor as an educational institution;

(15) under subsection (a) of this section, of any action by a state licensing body regarding the licensure of the debtor as an educational institution;

(16) under subsection (a) of this section, of any action by a guaranty agency, as defined in section 435(j) of the Higher Education Act of 1965 or the Secretary of Education regarding the eligibility of the debtor to participate in programs authorized under such Act;

(17) under subsection (a) of this section, of the exercise by a swap participant or financial participant of any contractual right (as defined in section 560) under any security agreement or arrangement or other credit enhancement forming a part of or related to any swap agreement, or of any contractual right (as defined in section 560) to offset or net out any termination value, payment amount, or other transfer obligation arising under or in connection with 1 or more such agreements, including any master agreement for such agreements;

(18) under subsection (a) of the creation or perfection of a statutory lien for an ad valorem property tax, or a special tax or special assessment on real property whether or not ad valorem, imposed by a governmental unit, if such tax or assessment comes due after the date of the filing of the petition;

(19) under subsection (a), of withholding of income from a debtor's wages and collection of amounts withheld, under the debtor's agreement authorizing that withholding and collection for the benefit of a pension, profit-sharing, stock bonus, or other plan established under section 401, 403, 408, 408A, 414, 457, or 501(c) of the Internal Revenue Code of 1986, that is sponsored by the employer of the debtor, or an affiliate, successor, or predecessor of such employer—

(A) to the extent that the amounts withheld and collected are used solely for payments relating to a loan from a plan under section 408(b)(1) of the Employee Retirement Income Security Act of 1974 or is subject to section 72(p) of the Internal Revenue Code of 1986; or

(B) a loan from a thrift savings plan permitted under subchapter III of chapter 84 of title 5, that satisfies the requirements of section 8433(g) of such title; but nothing in this paragraph may be construed to provide that any loan made under a governmental plan under section 414(d), or a contract or account under section 403(b), of the Internal Revenue Code of 1986 constitutes a claim or a debt under this title;

(20) under subsection (a), of any act to enforce any lien against or security interest in real property following entry of the order under subsection (d)(4) as to such real property in any prior case under this title, for a period of 2 years after the date of the entry of such an order, except that the debtor, in a subsequent case under this title, may move for relief from such order based upon changed circumstances or for other good cause shown, after notice and a hearing;

(21) under subsection (a), of any act to enforce any lien against or security interest in real property—

(A) if the debtor is ineligible under section 109(g) to be a debtor in a case under this title; or

(B) if the case under this title was filed in violation of a bankruptcy court order in a prior case under this title prohibiting the debtor from being a debtor in another case under this title;

(22) subject to subsection (l), under subsection (a)(3), of the continuation of any eviction, unlawful detainer action, or similar proceeding by a lessor against a debtor involving residential property in which the debtor resides as a tenant under a lease or rental agreement and with respect to which the lessor has obtained before the date of the filing of the bankruptcy petition, a judgment for possession of such property against the debtor;

(23) subject to subsection (m), under subsection (a)(3), of an eviction action that seeks possession of the residential property in which the debtor resides as a tenant under a lease or rental agreement based on endangerment of such property or the illegal use of controlled substances on such property, but only if the lessor files with the court, and serves upon the debtor, a certification under penalty of perjury that such an eviction action has been filed, or that the debtor, during the 30-day period

preceding the date of the filing of the certification, has endangered property or illegally used or allowed to be used a controlled substance on the property;

(24) under subsection (a), of any transfer that is not avoidable under section 544 and that is not avoidable under section 549;

(25) under subsection (a), of—

(A) the commencement or continuation of an investigation or action by a securities self regulatory organization to enforce such organization's regulatory power;

(B) the enforcement of an order or decision, other than for monetary sanctions, obtained in an action by such securities self regulatory organization to enforce such organization's regulatory power; or

(C) any act taken by such securities self regulatory organization to delist, delete, or refuse to permit quotation of any stock that does not meet applicable regulatory requirements;

(26) under subsection (a), of the setoff under applicable nonbankruptcy law of an income tax refund, by a governmental unit, with respect to a taxable period that ended before the date of the order for relief against an income tax liability for a taxable period that also ended before the date of the order for relief, except that in any case in which the setoff of an income tax refund is not permitted under applicable nonbankruptcy law because of a pending action to determine the amount or legality of a tax liability, the governmental unit may hold the refund pending the resolution of the action, unless the court, on the motion of the trustee and after notice and a hearing, grants the taxing authority adequate protection (within the meaning of section 361) for the secured claim of such authority in the setoff under section 506(a);

(27) under subsection (a) of this section, of the exercise by a master netting agreement participant of any contractual right (as defined in section 555, 556, 559, or 560) under any security agreement or arrangement or other credit enhancement forming a part of or related to any master netting agreement, or of any contractual right (as defined in section 555, 556, 559, or 560) to offset or net out any termination value, payment amount, or other transfer obligation arising under or in connection with 1 or more such master netting agreements to the extent that such participant is eligible to exercise such rights under paragraph (6), (7), or (17) for each individual contract covered by the master netting agreement in issue;

(28) under subsection (a), of the exclusion by the Secretary of Health and Human Services of the debtor from participation in the medicare program or any other Federal health care program (as defined in section 1128B(f) of the Social Security Act pursuant to title XI or XVIII of such Act); and

(29) under subsection (a)(1) of this section, of any action by—

(A) an amateur sports organization, as defined in section 220501(b) of title 36, to replace a national governing body, as defined in that section, under section 220528 of that title; or

(B) the corporation, as defined in section 220501(b) of title 36, to revoke the certification of a national governing body, as defined in that section, under section 220521 of that title.

The provisions of paragraphs (12) and (13) of this subsection shall apply with respect to any such petition filed on or before December 31, 1989.

(c) Except as provided in subsections (d), (e), (f), and (h) of this section—

(1) the stay of an act against property of the estate under subsection (a) of this section continues until such property is no longer property of the estate;

(2) the stay of any other act under subsection (a) of this section continues until the earliest of—

(A) the time the case is closed;

(B) the time the case is dismissed; or

(C) if the case is a case under chapter 7 of this title concerning an individual or a case under chapter 9, 11, 12, or 13 of this title, the time a discharge is granted or denied;

(3) if a single or joint case is filed by or against a debtor who is an individual in a case under chapter 7, 11, or 13, and if a single or joint case of the debtor was pending within the preceding 1-year period but was dismissed, other than a case refiled under a chapter other than chapter 7 after dismissal under section 707(b)—

(A) the stay under subsection (a) with respect to any action taken with respect to a debt or property securing such debt or with respect to any lease shall terminate with respect to the debtor on the 30th day after the filing of the later case;

(B) on the motion of a party in interest for continuation of the automatic stay and upon notice and a hearing, the court may extend the stay in particular cases as to any or all creditors (subject to such conditions or limitations as the court may then impose) after notice and a hearing completed before the expiration of the 30-day period only if the party in interest demonstrates that the filing of the later case is in good faith as to the creditors to be stayed; and

(C) for purposes of subparagraph (B), a case is presumptively filed not in good faith (but such presumption may be rebutted by clear and convincing evidence to the contrary)—

(i) as to all creditors, if—

(I) more than 1 previous case under any of chapters 7, 11, and 13 in which the individual was a debtor was pending within the preceding 1-year period;

(II) a previous case under any of chapters 7, 11, and 13 in which the individual was a debtor was dismissed within such 1-year period, after the debtor failed to—

(aa) file or amend the petition or other documents as required by this title or the court without substantial excuse (but mere inadvertence or negligence shall not be a substantial excuse unless the dismissal was caused by the negligence of the debtor's attorney);

(bb) provide adequate protection as ordered by the court; or

(cc) perform the terms of a plan confirmed by the court; or

(III) there has not been a substantial change in the financial or personal affairs of the debtor since the dismissal of the next most previous case under chapter 7, 11, or 13 or any other reason to conclude that the later case will be concluded—

(aa) if a case under chapter 7, with a discharge; or

(bb) if a case under chapter 11 or 13, with a confirmed plan that will be fully performed; and

(ii) as to any creditor that commenced an action under subsection (d) in a previous case in which the individual was a debtor if, as of the date of dismissal of such case, that action was still pending or had been resolved by terminating, conditioning, or limiting the stay as to actions of such creditor; and

(4) (A)(i) if a single or joint case is filed by or against a debtor who is an individual under this title, and if 2 or more single or joint cases of the debtor were pending within the previous year but were dismissed, other than a case refiled under a chapter other than chapter 7 after dismissal under section 707(b), the stay under subsection (a) shall not go into effect upon the filing of the later case; and

(ii) on request of a party in interest, the court shall promptly enter an order confirming that no stay is in effect;

(B) if, within 30 days after the filing of the later case, a party in interest requests the court may order the stay to take effect in the case as to any or all creditors (subject to such conditions or limitations as the court may impose), after notice and a hearing, only if the party in interest demonstrates that the filing of the later case is in good faith as to the creditors to be stayed;

(C) a stay imposed under subparagraph (B) shall be effective on the date of the entry of the order allowing the stay to go into effect; and

(D) for purposes of subparagraph (B), a case is presumptively filed not in good faith (but such presumption may be rebutted by clear and convincing evidence to the contrary)—

(i) as to all creditors if—

(I) 2 or more previous cases under this title in which the individual was a debtor were pending within the 1-year period;

(II) a previous case under this title in which the individual was a debtor was dismissed within the time period stated in this paragraph after the debtor failed to file or amend the petition or other documents as required by this title or the court without substantial excuse (but mere inadvertence or negligence shall not be substantial excuse unless the dismissal was caused by the negligence of the debtor's attorney), failed to provide adequate protection as ordered by the court, or failed to perform the terms of a plan confirmed by the court; or

(III) there has not been a substantial change in the financial or personal affairs of the debtor since the dismissal of the next most previous case under this title, or any other reason to conclude that the later case will not be concluded, if a case under chapter 7, with a discharge, and if a case under chapter 11 or 13, with a confirmed plan that will be fully performed; or

(ii) as to any creditor that commenced an action under subsection (d) in a previous case in which the individual was a debtor if, as of the date of dismissal of such case, such action was still pending or had been resolved by terminating, conditioning, or limiting the stay as to such action of such creditor.

(d) On request of a party in interest and after notice and a hearing, the court shall grant relief from the stay provided under subsection (a) of this section, such as by terminating, annulling, modifying, or conditioning such stay—

(1) for cause, including the lack of adequate protection of an interest in property of such party in interest;

(2) with respect to a stay of an act against property under subsection (a) of this section, if—

(A) the debtor does not have an equity in such property; and

(B) such property is not necessary to an effective reorganization;

(3) with respect to a stay of an act against single asset real estate under subsection (a), by a creditor whose claim is secured by an interest in such real estate, unless, not later than the date that is 90 days after the entry of the order for relief (or such later date as the court may determine for cause by order entered within that 90-day period) or 30 days after the court determines that the debtor is subject to this paragraph, whichever is later—

(A) the debtor has filed a plan of reorganization that has a reasonable possibility of being confirmed within a reasonable time; or

(B) the debtor has commenced monthly payments that—

(i) may, in the debtor's sole discretion, notwithstanding section 363(c)(2), be made from rents or other income generated before, on, or after the date of the commencement of the case by or from the property to each creditor whose claim is secured by such real estate (other than a claim secured by a judgment lien or by an unmatured statutory lien); and

(ii) are in an amount equal to interest at the then applicable nondefault contract rate of interest on the value of the creditor's interest in the real estate; or

(4) with respect to a stay of an act against real property under subsection (a), by a creditor whose claim is secured by an interest in such real property, if the court finds that the filing of the petition was part of a scheme to delay, hinder, or defraud creditors that involved either—

(A) transfer of all or part ownership of, or other interest in, such real property without the consent of the secured creditor or court approval; or

(B) multiple bankruptcy filings affecting such real property. If recorded in compliance with applicable State laws governing notices of interests or liens in real property, an order entered under paragraph (4) shall be binding in any other case under this title purporting to affect such real property filed not later than 2 years after the date of the entry of such order by the court, except that a debtor in a subsequent case under this title may move for relief from such order based upon changed circumstances or for good cause shown, after notice and a hearing. Any Federal, State, or local governmental unit that accepts notices of interests or liens in real property shall accept any certified copy of an order described in this subsection for indexing and recording.

(e)(1) Thirty days after a request under subsection (d) of this section for relief from the stay of any act against property of the estate under subsection (a) of this section, such stay is terminated with respect to the party in interest making such request, unless the court, after notice and a hearing, orders such stay continued in effect pending the conclusion of, or as a result of, a final hearing and determination under subsection (d) of this section. A hearing under this subsection may be a preliminary hearing, or may be consolidated with the final hearing under subsection (d) of this section. The court shall order such stay continued in effect pending the conclusion of the final hearing under subsection (d) of this section if there is a reasonable likelihood that the party opposing relief from such stay will prevail at the conclusion of such final hearing. If the hearing under this subsection is a preliminary hearing, then such final hearing shall be concluded not later than thirty days after the conclusion of such preliminary hearing, unless the 30-day period is extended with the consent of the parties in interest or for a specific time which the court finds is required by compelling circumstances.

(2) Notwithstanding paragraph (1), in a case under chapter 7, 11, or 13 in which the debtor is an individual, the stay under subsection (a) shall terminate on the date that is 60 days after a request is made by a party in interest under subsection (d), unless—

(A) a final decision is rendered by the court during the 60- day period beginning on the date of the request; or

(B) such 60-day period is extended—

(i) by agreement of all parties in interest; or

(ii) by the court for such specific period of time as the court finds is required for good cause, as described in findings made by the court.

(f) Upon request of a party in interest, the court, with or without a hearing, shall grant such relief from the stay provided under subsection (a) of this section as is necessary to prevent irreparable damage to the interest of an entity in property, if such interest will suffer such damage before there is an opportunity for notice and a hearing under subsection (d) or (e) of this section.

(g) In any hearing under subsection (d) or (e) of this section concerning relief from the stay of any act under subsection (a) of this section—

(1) the party requesting such relief has the burden of proof on the issue of the debtor's equity in property; and

(2) the party opposing such relief has the burden of proof on all other issues.

(h)(1) In a case in which the debtor is an individual, the stay provided by subsection (a) is terminated with respect to personal property of the estate or of the debtor securing in whole or in part a claim, or subject to an unexpired lease, and such personal property shall no longer be property of the estate if the debtor fails within the applicable time set by section 521(a)(2)—

(A) to file timely any statement of intention required under section 521(a)(2) with respect to such personal property or to indicate in such statement that the debtor will either surrender such personal property or retain it and, if retaining such personal property, either redeem such personal property pursuant to section 722, enter into an agreement of the kind specified in section 524(c) applicable to the debt secured by such personal property, or assume such unexpired lease pursuant to section 365(p) if the trustee does not do so, as applicable; and

(B) to take timely the action specified in such statement, as it may be amended before expiration of the period for taking action, unless such statement specifies the debtor's intention to reaffirm such debt on the original contract terms and the creditor refuses to agree to the reaffirmation on such terms.

(2) Paragraph (1) does not apply if the court determines, on the motion of the trustee filed before the expiration of the applicable time set by section 521(a)(2), after notice and a hearing, that such personal property is of consequential value or benefit to the estate, and orders appropriate adequate protection of the creditor's interest, and orders the debtor to deliver any collateral in the debtor's possession to the trustee. If the court does not so determine, the stay provided by subsection (a) shall terminate upon the conclusion of the hearing on the motion.

(i) If a case commenced under chapter 7, 11, or 13 is dismissed due to the creation of a debt repayment plan, for purposes of subsection (c)(3), any subsequent case commenced by the debtor under any such chapter shall not be presumed to be filed not in good faith.

(j) On request of a party in interest, the court shall issue an order under subsection (c) confirming that the automatic stay has been terminated.

(k)(1) Except as provided in paragraph (2), an individual injured by any willful violation of a stay provided by this section shall recover actual damages, including costs and attorneys' fees, and, in appropriate circumstances, may recover punitive damages.

(2) If such violation is based on an action taken by an entity in the good faith belief that subsection (h) applies to the debtor, the recovery under paragraph (1) of this subsection against such entity shall be limited to actual damages.

(l)(1) Except as otherwise provided in this subsection, subsection (b)(22) shall apply on the date that is 30 days after the date on which the bankruptcy petition is filed, if the debtor files with the petition and serves upon the lessor a certification under penalty of perjury that—

(A) under nonbankruptcy law applicable in the jurisdiction, there are circumstances under which the debtor would be permitted to cure the entire monetary default that gave rise to the judgment for possession, after that judgment for possession was entered; and

(B) the debtor (or an adult dependent of the debtor) has deposited with the clerk of the court, any rent that would become due during the 30-day period after the filing of the bankruptcy petition.

(2) If, within the 30-day period after the filing of the bankruptcy petition, the debtor (or an adult dependent of the debtor) complies with paragraph (1) and files with the court and serves upon the lessor a further certification under penalty of perjury that the debtor (or an adult dependent of the debtor) has cured, under nonbankruptcy law applicable in the jurisdiction, the entire monetary default that gave rise to the judgment under which possession is sought by the lessor, subsection (b)(22) shall not apply, unless ordered to apply by the court under paragraph (3).

(3) (A) If the lessor files an objection to any certification filed by the debtor under paragraph (1) or (2), and serves such objection upon the debtor, the court shall hold a hearing within 10 days after the filing and service of such objection to determine if the certification filed by the debtor under paragraph (1) or (2) is true.

(B) If the court upholds the objection of the lessor filed under subparagraph (A)—

(i) subsection (b)(22) shall apply immediately and relief from the stay provided under subsection (a)(3) shall not be required to enable the lessor to complete the process to recover full possession of the property; and

(ii) the clerk of the court shall immediately serve upon the lessor and the debtor a certified copy of the court's order upholding the lessor's objection.

(4) If a debtor, in accordance with paragraph (5), indicates on the petition that there was a judgment for possession of the residential rental property in which the debtor resides and does not file a certification under paragraph (1) or (2)—

(A) subsection (b)(22) shall apply immediately upon failure to file such certification, and relief from the stay provided under subsection (a)(3) shall not be required to enable the lessor to complete the process to recover full possession of the property; and

(B) the clerk of the court shall immediately serve upon the lessor and the debtor a certified copy of the docket indicating the absence of a filed certification and the applicability of the exception to the stay under subsection (b)(22).

(5) (A) Where a judgment for possession of residential property in which the debtor resides as a tenant under a lease or rental agreement has been obtained by the lessor, the debtor shall so indicate on the bankruptcy petition and shall provide the name and address of the lessor that obtained that pre-petition judgment on the petition and on any certification filed under this subsection.

(B) The form of certification filed with the petition, as specified in this subsection, shall provide for the debtor to certify, and the debtor shall certify—

(i) whether a judgment for possession of residential rental housing in which the debtor resides has been obtained against the debtor before the date of the filing of the petition; and

(ii) whether the debtor is claiming under paragraph (1) that under nonbankruptcy law applicable in the jurisdiction, there are circumstances under which the debtor would be permitted to cure the entire monetary default that gave rise to the judgment for possession, after that judgment of possession was entered, and has made the appropriate deposit with the court.

(C) The standard forms (electronic and otherwise) used in a bankruptcy proceeding shall be amended to reflect the requirements of this subsection.

(D) The clerk of the court shall arrange for the prompt transmittal of the rent deposited in accordance with paragraph (1)(B) to the lessor.

(m)(1) Except as otherwise provided in this subsection, subsection (b)(23) shall apply on the date that is 15 days after the date on which the lessor files and serves a certification described in subsection (b)(23).

(2) (A) If the debtor files with the court an objection to the truth or legal sufficiency of the certification described in subsection (b)(23) and serves such objection upon the lessor, subsection (b)(23) shall not apply, unless ordered to apply by the court under this subsection.

(B) If the debtor files and serves the objection under subparagraph (A), the court shall hold a hearing within 10 days after the filing and service of such objection to determine if the situation giving rise to the lessor's certification under paragraph (1) existed or has been remedied.

(C) If the debtor can demonstrate to the satisfaction of the court that the situation giving rise to the lessor's certification under paragraph (1) did not exist or has been remedied, the stay provided under subsection (a)(3) shall remain in effect until the termination of the stay under this section.

(D) If the debtor cannot demonstrate to the satisfaction of the court that the situation giving rise to the lessor's certification under paragraph (1) did not exist or has been remedied—

(i) relief from the stay provided under subsection (a)(3) shall not be required to enable the lessor to proceed with the eviction; and

(ii) the clerk of the court shall immediately serve upon the lessor and the debtor a certified copy of the court's order upholding the lessor's certification.

(3) If the debtor fails to file, within 15 days, an objection under paragraph (2)(A)—

(A) subsection (b)(23) shall apply immediately upon such failure and relief from the stay provided under subsection (a)(3) shall not be required to enable the lessor to complete the process to recover full possession of the property; and

(B) the clerk of the court shall immediately serve upon the lessor and the debtor a certified copy of the docket indicating such failure.

(n)(1) Except as provided in paragraph (2), subsection (a) does not apply in a case in which the debtor—

(A) is a debtor in a small business case pending at the time the petition is filed;

(B) was a debtor in a small business case that was dismissed for any reason by an order that became final in the 2-year period ending on the date of the order for relief entered with respect to the petition;

(C) was a debtor in a small business case in which a plan was confirmed in the 2-year period ending on the date of the order for relief entered with respect to the petition; or

(D) is an entity that has acquired substantially all of the assets or business of a small business debtor described in subparagraph (A), (B), or (C), unless such entity establishes by a preponderance of the evidence that such entity acquired substantially all of the assets or business of such small business debtor in good faith and not for the purpose of evading this paragraph.

(2) Paragraph (1) does not apply—

(A) to an involuntary case involving no collusion by the debtor with creditors; or

(B) to the filing of a petition if—

(i) the debtor proves by a preponderance of the evidence that the filing of the petition resulted from circumstances beyond the control of the debtor not foreseeable at the time the case then pending was filed; and

(ii) it is more likely than not that the court will confirm a feasible plan, but not a liquidating plan, within a reasonable period of time.

(o) The exercise of rights not subject to the stay arising under subsection (a) pursuant to paragraph (6), (7), (17), or (27) of subsection (b) shall not be stayed by any order of a court or administrative agency in any proceeding under this title.

§ 363. Use, Sale, or Lease of Property

(a) In this section, "cash collateral" means cash, negotiable instruments, documents of title, securities, deposit accounts, or other cash equivalents whenever acquired in which the estate and an entity other than the estate have an interest and includes the proceeds, products, offspring, rents, or profits of property and the fees, charges, accounts or other payments for the use or occupancy of rooms and other public facilities in hotels, motels, or other lodging properties subject to a security interest as provided in section 552(b) of this title, whether existing before or after the commencement of a case under this title.

(b)(1) The trustee, after notice and a hearing, may use, sell, or lease, other than in the ordinary course of business, property of the estate, except that if the debtor in connection with offering a product or a service discloses to an individual a policy prohibiting the transfer of personally identifiable information about individuals to persons that are not affiliated with the debtor and if such policy is in effect on the date of the commencement of the case, then the trustee may not sell or lease personally identifiable information to any person unless—

(A) such sale or such lease is consistent with such policy; or

(B) after appointment of a consumer privacy ombudsman in accordance with section 332, and after notice and a hearing, the court approves such sale or such lease—

(i) giving due consideration to the facts, circumstances, and conditions of such sale or such lease; and

(ii) finding that no showing was made that such sale or such lease would violate applicable nonbankruptcy law.

(2) If notification is required under subsection (a) of section 7A of the Clayton Act in the case of a transaction under this subsection, then—

(A) notwithstanding subsection (a) of such section, the notification required by such subsection to be given by the debtor shall be given by the trustee; and

(B) notwithstanding subsection (b) of such section, the required waiting period shall end on the 15th day after the date of the receipt, by the Federal Trade Commission and the Assistant Attorney General in charge of the Antitrust Division of the Department of Justice, of the notification required under such subsection (a), unless such waiting period is extended—

(i) pursuant to subsection (e)(2) of such section, in the same manner as such subsection (e)(2) applies to a cash tender offer;

(ii) pursuant to subsection (g)(2) of such section; or

(iii) by the court after notice and a hearing.

(c)(1) If the business of the debtor is authorized to be operated under section 721, 1108, 1183, 1184, 1203, 1204, or 1304 of this title and unless the court orders otherwise, the trustee may enter into transactions, including the sale or lease of property of the estate, in the ordinary course of business, without notice or a hearing, and may use property of the estate in the ordinary course of business without notice or a hearing.

(2) The trustee may not use, sell, or lease cash collateral under paragraph (1) of this subsection unless—

(A) each entity that has an interest in such cash collateral consents; or

(B) the court, after notice and a hearing, authorizes such use, sale, or lease in accordance with the provisions of this section.

(3) Any hearing under paragraph (2)(B) of this subsection may be a preliminary hearing or may be consolidated with a hearing under subsection (e) of this section, but shall be scheduled in accordance with the needs of the debtor. If the hearing under paragraph (2)(B) of this subsection is a preliminary hearing, the court may authorize such use, sale, or lease only if there is a reasonable likelihood that the trustee will prevail at the final hearing under subsection (e) of this section. The court shall act promptly on any request for authorization under paragraph (2)(B) of this subsection.

(4) Except as provided in paragraph (2) of this subsection, the trustee shall segregate and account for any cash collateral in the trustee's possession, custody, or control.

(d) The trustee may use, sell, or lease property under subsection (b) or (c) of this section—

(1) in the case of a debtor that is a corporation or trust that is not a moneyed business, commercial corporation, or trust, only in accordance with nonbankruptcy law applicable to the transfer of property by a debtor that is such a corporation or trust; and

(2) only to the extent not inconsistent with any relief granted under subsection (c), (d), (e), or (f) of section 362.

(e) Notwithstanding any other provision of this section, at any time, on request of an entity that has an interest in property used, sold, or leased, or proposed to be used, sold, or leased, by the trustee, the court, with or without a hearing, shall prohibit or condition such use, sale, or lease as is necessary to provide adequate protection of such interest. This subsection also applies to property that is subject to any unexpired lease of personal property (to the exclusion of such property being subject to an order to grant relief from the stay under section 362).

(f) The trustee may sell property under subsection (b) or (c) of this section free and clear of any interest in such property of an entity other than the estate, only if—

(1) applicable nonbankruptcy law permits sale of such property free and clear of such interest;

(2) such entity consents;

(3) such interest is a lien and the price at which such property is to be sold is greater than the aggregate value of all liens on such property;

(4) such interest is in bona fide dispute; or

(5) such entity could be compelled, in a legal or equitable proceeding, to accept a money satisfaction of such interest.

(g) Notwithstanding subsection (f) of this section, the trustee may sell property under subsection (b) or (c) of this section free and clear of any vested or contingent right in the nature of dower or curtesy.

(h) Notwithstanding subsection (f) of this section, the trustee may sell both the estate's interest, under subsection (b) or (c) of this section, and the interest of any co-owner in property in which the debtor had, at the time of the commencement of the case, an undivided interest as a tenant in common, joint tenant, or tenant by the entirety, only if—

(1) partition in kind of such property among the estate and such co-owners is impracticable;

(2) sale of the estate's undivided interest in such property would realize significantly less for the estate than sale of such property free of the interests of such co-owners;

(3) the benefit to the estate of a sale of such property free of the interests of co-owners outweighs the detriment, if any, to such co-owners; and

(4) such property is not used in the production, transmission, or distribution, for sale, of electric energy or of natural or synthetic gas for heat, light, or power.

(i) Before the consummation of a sale of property to which subsection (g) or (h) of this section applies, or of property of the estate that was community property of the debtor and the debtor's spouse immediately before the commencement of the case, the debtor's spouse, or a co-owner of such property, as the case may be, may purchase such property at the price at which such sale is to be consummated.

(j) After a sale of property to which subsection (g) or (h) of this section applies, the trustee shall distribute to the debtor's spouse or the co-owners of such property, as the case may be, and to the estate, the proceeds of such sale, less the costs and expenses, not including any compensation of the trustee, of such sale, according to the interests of such spouse or co-owners, and of the estate.

(k) At a sale under subsection (b) of this section of property that is subject to a lien that secures an allowed claim, unless the court for cause orders otherwise the holder of such claim may bid at such sale, and, if the holder of such claim purchases such property, such holder may offset such claim against the purchase price of such property.

(l) Subject to the provisions of section 365, the trustee may use, sell, or lease property under subsection (b) or (c) of this section, or a plan under chapter 11, 12, or 13 of this title may provide for the use, sale, or lease of property, notwithstanding any provision in a contract, a lease, or applicable law that is conditioned on the insolvency or financial condition of the debtor, on the commencement of a case under this title concerning the debtor, or on the appointment of or the taking possession by a trustee in a case under this title or a custodian, and that effects, or gives an option to effect, a forfeiture, modification, or termination of the debtor's interest in such property.

(m) The reversal or modification on appeal of an authorization under subsection (b) or (c) of this section of a sale or lease of property does not affect the validity of a sale or lease under such authorization to an entity that purchased or leased such property in good faith, whether or not such entity knew of the pendency of the appeal, unless such authorization and such sale or lease were stayed pending appeal.

(n) The trustee may avoid a sale under this section if the sale price was controlled by an agreement among potential bidders at such sale, or may recover from a party to such agreement any amount by which the value of the property sold exceeds the price at which such sale was consummated, and may recover any costs, attorneys' fees, or expenses incurred in avoiding such sale or recovering such amount. In addition to any recovery under the preceding sentence, the court may grant judgment for punitive damages in favor of the estate and against any such party that entered into such an agreement in willful disregard of this subsection.

(o) Notwithstanding subsection (f), if a person purchases any interest in a consumer credit transaction that is subject to the Truth in Lending Act or any interest in a consumer credit contract (as defined in section 433.1 of title 16 of the Code of Federal Regulations (January 1, 2004), as amended from time to time), and if such interest is purchased through a sale under this section, then such person shall remain subject to all claims and defenses that are related to such consumer credit transaction or such consumer credit contract, to the same extent as such person would be subject to such claims and defenses of the consumer had such interest been purchased at a sale not under this section.

(p) In any hearing under this section—

(1) the trustee has the burden of proof on the issue of adequate protection; and

(2) the entity asserting an interest in property has the burden of proof on the issue of the validity, priority, or extent of such interest.

§ 364. Obtaining Credit

(a) If the trustee is authorized to operate the business of the debtor under section 721, 1108, 1183, 1184, 1203, 1204, or 1304 of this title, unless the court orders otherwise, the trustee may obtain unsecured credit and incur unsecured debt in the ordinary course of business allowable under section 503(b)(1) of this title as an administrative expense.

(b) The court, after notice and a hearing, may authorize the trustee to obtain unsecured credit or to incur unsecured debt other than under subsection (a) of this section, allowable under section 503(b)(1) of this title as an administrative expense.

(c) If the trustee is unable to obtain unsecured credit allowable under section 503(b)(1) of this title as an administrative expense, the court, after notice and a hearing, may authorize the obtaining of credit or the incurring of debt—

(1) with priority over any or all administrative expenses of the kind specified in section 503(b) or 507(b) of this title;

(2) secured by a lien on property of the estate that is not otherwise subject to a lien; or

(3) secured by a junior lien on property of the estate that is subject to a lien.

(d)(1) The court, after notice and a hearing, may authorize the obtaining of credit or the incurring of debt secured by a senior or equal lien on property of the estate that is subject to a lien only if—

(A) the trustee is unable to obtain such credit otherwise; and

(B) there is adequate protection of the interest of the holder of the lien on the property of the estate on which such senior or equal lien is proposed to be granted.

(2) In any hearing under this subsection, the trustee has the burden of proof on the issue of adequate protection.

(e) The reversal or modification on appeal of an authorization under this section to obtain credit or incur debt, or of a grant under this section of a priority or a lien, does not affect the validity of any debt so incurred, or any priority or lien so granted, to an entity that extended such credit in good faith, whether or not such entity knew of the pendency of the appeal, unless such authorization and the incurring of such debt, or the granting of such priority or lien, were stayed pending appeal.

(f) Except with respect to an entity that is an underwriter as defined in section 1145(b) of this title, section 5 of the Securities Act of 1933, the Trust Indenture Act of 1939, and any state or local law requiring registration for offer or sale of a security or registration or licensing of an issuer of, underwriter of, or broker or dealer in, a security does not apply to the offer or sale under this section of a security that is not an equity security.

§ 365. Executory Contracts and Unexpired Leases

(a) Except as provided in sections 765 and 766 of this title and in subsections (b), (c), and (d) of this section, the trustee, subject to the court's approval, may assume or reject any executory contract or unexpired lease of the debtor.

(b)(1) If there has been a default in an executory contract or unexpired lease of the debtor, the trustee may not assume such contract or lease unless, at the time of assumption of such contract or lease, the trustee—

(A) cures, or provides adequate assurance that the trustee will promptly cure, such default other than a default that is a breach of a provision relating to the satisfaction of any provision (other than a penalty rate or penalty provision) relating to a default arising from any failure to perform nonmonetary obligations under an unexpired lease of real property, if it is impossible for the trustee to cure such default by performing nonmonetary acts at and after the time of assumption, except that if such default arises from a failure to operate in accordance with a nonresidential real property lease, then such default shall be cured by performance at and after the time of assumption in accordance with such lease, and pecuniary losses resulting from such default shall be compensated in accordance with the provisions of this paragraph;

(B) compensates, or provides adequate assurance that the trustee will promptly compensate, a party other than the debtor to such contract or lease, for any actual pecuniary loss to such party resulting from such default; and

(C) provides adequate assurance of future performance under such contract or lease.

(2) Paragraph (1) of this subsection does not apply to a default that is a breach of a provision relating to—

(A) the insolvency or financial condition of the debtor at any time before the closing of the case;

(B) the commencement of a case under this title;

(C) the appointment of or taking possession by a trustee in a case under this title or a custodian before such commencement; or

(D) the satisfaction of any penalty rate or penalty provision relating to a default arising from any failure by the debtor to perform nonmonetary obligations under the executory contract or unexpired lease.

(3) (A) For the purposes of paragraph (1) of this subsection and paragraph (2)(B) of subsection (f), adequate assurance of future performance of a lease of real property in a shopping center includes adequate assurance—

(A) of the source of rent and other consideration due under such lease, and in the case of an assignment, that the financial condition and operating performance of the proposed assignee and its guarantors, if any, shall be similar to the financial condition and operating performance of the debtor and its guarantors, if any, as of the time the debtor became the lessee under the lease;

(B) that any percentage rent due under such lease will not decline substantially;

(C) that assumption or assignment of such lease is subject to all the provisions thereof, including (but not limited to) provisions such as a radius, location, use, or exclusivity provision, and will not breach any such provision contained in any other lease, financing agreement, or master agreement relating to such shopping center; and

(D) that assumption or assignment of such lease will not disrupt any tenant mix or balance in such shopping center.

(4) Notwithstanding any other provision of this section, if there has been a default in an unexpired lease of the debtor, other than a default of a kind specified in paragraph (2) of this subsection, the trustee may not require a lessor to provide services or supplies incidental to such lease before assumption of such lease unless the lessor is compensated under the terms of such lease for any services and supplies provided under such lease before assumption of such lease.

(c) The trustee may not assume or assign any executory contract or unexpired lease of the debtor, whether or not such contract or lease prohibits or restricts assignment of rights or delegation of duties, if—

(1) (A) applicable law excuses a party, other than the debtor, to such contract or lease from accepting performance from or rendering

performance to an entity other than the debtor or the debtor in possession, whether or not such contract or lease prohibits or restricts assignment of rights or delegation of duties; and

(B) such party does not consent to such assumption or assignment; or

(2) such contract is a contract to make a loan, or extend other debt financing or financial accommodations, to or for the benefit of the debtor, or to issue a security of the debtor; or

(3) such lease is of nonresidential real property and has been terminated under applicable nonbankruptcy law prior to the order for relief.

(d)(1) In a case under chapter 7 of this title, if the trustee does not assume or reject an executory contract or unexpired lease of residential real property or of personal property of the debtor within 60 days after the order for relief, or within such additional time as the court, for cause, within such 60-day period, fixes, then such contract or lease is deemed rejected.

(2) In a case under chapter 9, 11, 12, or 13 of this title, the trustee may assume or reject an executory contract or unexpired lease of residential real property or of personal property of the debtor at any time before the confirmation of a plan but the court, on the request of any party to such contract or lease, may order the trustee to determine within a specified period of time whether to assume or reject such contract or lease.

(3) The trustee shall timely perform all the obligations of the debtor, except those specified in section 365(b)(2), arising from and after the order for relief under any unexpired lease of nonresidential real property, until such lease is assumed or rejected, notwithstanding section 503(b)(1) of this title. The court may extend, for cause, the time for performance of any such obligation that arises within 60 days after the date of the order for relief, but the time for performance shall not be extended beyond such 60-day period, except as provided in subparagraph (B). This subsection shall not be deemed to affect the trustee's obligations under the provisions of subsection (b) or (f) of this section. Acceptance of any such performance does not constitute waiver or relinquishment of the lessor's rights under such lease or under this title.

(4) (A) Subject to subparagraph (B), an unexpired lease of nonresidential real property under which the debtor is the lessee shall be deemed rejected, and the trustee shall immediately surrender that nonresidential real property to the lessor, if the trustee does not assume or reject the unexpired lease by the earlier of—

(i) the date that is 120 days after the date of the order for relief; or

(ii) the date of the entry of an order confirming a plan.

(B) (i) The court may extend the period determined under subparagraph (A), prior to the expiration of the 120-day period, for 90 days on the motion of the trustee or lessor for cause.

(ii) If the court grants an extension under clause (i), the court may grant a subsequent extension only upon prior written consent of the lessor in each instance.

(5) The trustee shall timely perform all of the obligations of the debtor, except those specified in section 365(b)(2), first arising from or after 60 days after the order for relief in a case under chapter 11 of this title under an unexpired lease of personal property (other than personal property leased to an individual primarily for personal, family, or household purposes), until such lease is assumed or rejected notwithstanding section 503(b)(1) of this title, unless the court, after notice and a hearing and based on the equities of the case, orders otherwise with respect to the obligations or timely performance thereof. This subsection shall not be deemed to affect the trustee's obligations under the provisions of subsection (b) or (f). Acceptance of any such performance does not constitute waiver or relinquishment of the lessor's rights under such lease or under this title.

(e)(1) Notwithstanding a provision in an executory contract or unexpired lease, or in applicable law, an executory contract or unexpired lease of the debtor may not be terminated or modified, and any right or obligation under such contract or lease may not be terminated or modified, at any time after the commencement of the case solely because of a provision in such contract or lease that is conditioned on—

(A) the insolvency or financial condition of the debtor at any time before the closing of the case;

(B) the commencement of a case under this title; or

(C) the appointment of or taking possession by a trustee in a case under this title or a custodian before such commencement.

(2) Paragraph (1) of this subsection does not apply to an executory contract or unexpired lease of the debtor, whether or not such contract or lease prohibits or restricts assignment of rights or delegation of duties, if—

(A) (i) applicable law excuses a party, other than the debtor, to such contract or lease from accepting performance from or rendering performance to the trustee or to an assignee of such contract or lease, whether or not such contract or lease prohibits or restricts assignment of rights or delegation of duties; and

(ii) such party does not consent to such assumption or assignment; or

(B) such contract is a contract to make a loan, or extend other debt financing or financial accommodations, to or for the benefit of the debtor, or to issue a security of the debtor.

(f)(1) Except as provided in subsections (b) and (c) of this section, notwithstanding a provision in an executory contract or unexpired lease of the debtor, or in applicable law, that prohibits, restricts, or conditions the assignment of such contract or lease, the trustee may assign such contract or lease under paragraph (2) of this subsection.

(2) The trustee may assign an executory contract or unexpired lease of the debtor only if—

(A) the trustee assumes such contract or lease in accordance with the provisions of this section; and

(B) adequate assurance of future performance by the assignee of such contract or lease is provided, whether or not there has been a default in such contract or lease.

(3) Notwithstanding a provision in an executory contract or unexpired lease of the debtor, or in applicable law that terminates or modifies, or permits a party other than the debtor to terminate or modify, such contract or lease or a right or obligation under such contract or lease on account of an assignment of such contract or lease, such contract, lease, right, or obligation may not be terminated or modified under such provision because of the assumption or assignment of such contract or lease by the trustee.

(g) Except as provided in subsections (h)(2) and (i)(2) of this section, the rejection of an executory contract or unexpired lease of the debtor constitutes a breach of such contract or lease—

(1) if such contract or lease has not been assumed under this section or under a plan confirmed under chapter 9, 11, 12, or 13 of this title, immediately before the date of the filing of the petition; or

(2) if such contract or lease has been assumed under this section or under a plan confirmed under chapter 9, 11, 12, or 13 of this title—

(A) if before such rejection the case has not been converted under section 1112, 1208, or 1307 of this title, at the time of such rejection; or

(B) if before such rejection the case has been converted under section 1112, 1208, or 1307 of this title—

(i) immediately before the date of such conversion, if such contract or lease was assumed before such conversion; or

(ii) at the time of such rejection, if such contract or lease was assumed after such conversion.

(h)(1)(A) If the trustee rejects an unexpired lease of real property under which the debtor is the lessor and—

(i) if the rejection by the trustee amounts to such a breach as would entitle the lessee to treat such lease as terminated by virtue of its terms, applicable nonbankruptcy law, or any agreement made by the lessee, then the lessee under such lease may treat such lease as terminated by the rejection; or

(ii) if the term of such lease has commenced, the lessee may retain its rights under such lease (including rights such as those relating to the amount and timing of payment of rent and other amounts payable by the lessee and any right of use, possession, quiet enjoyment, subletting, assignment, or hypothecation) that are in or appurtenant to the real property for the balance of the term of such lease and for any renewal or extension of such rights to the extent that such rights are enforceable under applicable nonbankruptcy law.

(B) If the lessee retains its rights under subparagraph (A)(ii), the lessee may offset against the rent reserved under such lease for the balance of the term after the date of the rejection of such lease and for the term of any renewal or extension of such lease, the value of any damage caused by the nonperformance after the date of such rejection, of any obligation of the debtor under such lease, but the lessee shall not have any other right against the estate or the debtor on account of any damage occurring after such date caused by such nonperformance.

(C) The rejection of a lease of real property in a shopping center with respect to which the lessee elects to retain its rights under subparagraph (A)(ii) does not affect the enforceability under applicable nonbankruptcy law of any provision in the lease pertaining to radius, location, use, exclusivity, or tenant mix or balance.

(D) In this paragraph, "lessee" includes any successor, assign, or mortgagee permitted under the terms of such lease.

(2) (A) If the trustee rejects a timeshare interest under a timeshare plan under which the debtor is the timeshare interest seller and—

(i) if the rejection amounts to such a breach as would entitle the timeshare interest purchaser to treat the timeshare plan as terminated under its terms, applicable nonbankruptcy law, or any agreement made by timeshare interest purchaser, the timeshare interest purchaser under the timeshare plan may treat the timeshare plan as terminated by such rejection; or

(ii) if the term of such timeshare interest has commenced, then the timeshare interest purchaser may retain its rights in such timeshare interest for the balance of such term and for any term of renewal or extension of such timeshare interest to the extent that such rights are enforceable under applicable nonbankruptcy law.

(B) If the timeshare interest purchaser retains its rights under subparagraph (A), such timeshare interest purchaser may offset against the moneys due for such timeshare interest for the balance of the term after the date of the rejection of such timeshare interest, and the term of any renewal or extension of such timeshare interest, the value of any damage caused by the nonperformance after the date of such rejection, of any obligation of the debtor under such timeshare plan, but the timeshare interest purchaser shall not have any right against the estate or the debtor on account of any damage occurring after such date caused by such nonperformance.

(i)(1) If the trustee rejects an executory contract of the debtor for the sale of real property or for the sale of a timeshare interest under a timeshare plan, under which the purchaser is in possession, such purchaser may treat such contract as terminated, or, in the alternative, may remain in possession of such real property or timeshare interest.

(2) If such purchaser remains in possession—

(A) such purchaser shall continue to make all payments due under such contract, but may, offset against such payments any damages occurring after the date of the rejection of such contract caused by the nonperformance of any obligation of the debtor after such date, but such purchaser does not have any rights against the estate on account of any damages arising after such date from such rejection, other than such offset; and

(B) the trustee shall deliver title to such purchaser in accordance with the provisions of such contract, but is relieved of all other obligations to perform under such contract.

(j) A purchaser that treats an executory contract as terminated under subsection (i) of this section, or a party whose executory contract to purchase real property from the debtor is rejected and under which such party is not in possession, has a lien on the interest of the debtor in such property for the recovery of any portion of the purchase price that such purchaser or party has paid.

(k) Assignment by the trustee to an entity of a contract or lease assumed under this section relieves the trustee and the estate from any liability for any breach of such contract or lease occurring after such assignment.

(l) If an unexpired lease under which the debtor is the lessee is assigned pursuant to this section, the lessor of the property may require a deposit or other security for the performance of the debtor's obligations under the lease substantially the same as would have been required by the landlord upon the initial leasing to a similar tenant.

(m) For purposes of this section 365 and sections 541(b)(2) and 362(b)(10), leases of real property shall include any rental agreement to use real property.

(n)(1) If the trustee rejects an executory contract under which the debtor is a licensor of a right to intellectual property, the licensee under such contract may elect—

(A) to treat such contract as terminated by such rejection if such rejection by the trustee amounts to such a breach as would entitle the licensee to treat such contract as terminated by virtue of its own terms, applicable nonbankruptcy law, or an agreement made by the licensee with another entity; or

(B) to retain its rights (including a right to enforce any exclusivity provision of such contract, but excluding any other right under applicable nonbankruptcy law to specific performance of such contract) under such contract and under any agreement supplementary to such contract, to such intellectual property (including any embodiment of such intellectual property to the extent protected by applicable nonbankruptcy law), as such rights existed immediately before the case commenced, for—

(i) the duration of such contract; and

(ii) any period for which such contract may be extended by the licensee as of right under applicable nonbankruptcy law.

(2) If the licensee elects to retain its rights, as described in paragraph (1)(B) of this subsection, under such contract—

(A) the trustee shall allow the licensee to exercise such rights;

(B) the licensee shall make all royalty payments due under such contract for the duration of such contract and for any period described in paragraph (1)(B) of this subsection for which the licensee extends such contract; and

(C) the licensee shall be deemed to waive—

(i) any right of setoff it may have with respect to such contract under this title or applicable nonbankruptcy law; and

(ii) any claim allowable under section 503(b) of this title arising from the performance of such contract.

(3) If the licensee elects to retain its rights, as described in paragraph (1)(B) of this subsection, then on the written request of the licensee the trustee shall—

(A) to the extent provided in such contract, or any agreement supplementary to such contract, provide to the licensee any intellectual property (including such embodiment) held by the trustee; and

(B) not interfere with the rights of the licensee as provided in such contract, or any agreement supplementary to such contract, to such intellectual property (including such embodiment) including any right to obtain such intellectual property (or such embodiment) from another entity.

(4) Unless and until the trustee rejects such contract, on the written request of the licensee the trustee shall—

(A) to the extent provided in such contract or any agreement supplementary to such contract—

(i) perform such contract; or

(ii) provide to the licensee such intellectual property (including any embodiment of such intellectual property to the extent protected by applicable nonbankruptcy law) held by the trustee; and

(B) not interfere with the rights of the licensee as provided in such contract, or any agreement supplementary to such contract, to such intellectual property (including such embodiment), including any right to obtain such intellectual property (or such embodiment) from another entity.

(o) In a case under chapter 11 of this title, the trustee shall be deemed to have assumed (consistent with the debtor's other obligations under section 507), and shall immediately cure any deficit under, any commitment by the debtor to a Federal depository institutions regulatory agency (or predecessor to such agency) to maintain the capital of an insured depository institution, and any claim for a subsequent breach of the obligations thereunder shall be entitled to priority under section 507. This subsection shall not extend any commitment that would otherwise be terminated by any act of such an agency.

(p)(1) If a lease of personal property is rejected or not timely assumed by the trustee under subsection (d), the leased property is no longer property of the estate and the stay under section 362(a) is automatically terminated.

(2) (A) If the debtor in a case under chapter 7 is an individual, the debtor may notify the creditor in writing that the debtor desires to assume the lease. Upon being so notified, the creditor may, at its option, notify the debtor that it is willing to have the lease assumed by the debtor and may condition such assumption on cure of any outstanding default on terms set by the contract.

(B) If, not later than 30 days after notice is provided under subparagraph (A), the debtor notifies the lessor in writing that the lease is assumed, the liability under the lease will be assumed by the debtor and not by the estate.

(C) The stay under section 362 and the injunction under section 524(a)(2) shall not be violated by notification of the debtor and negotiation of cure under this subsection.

(3) In a case under chapter 11 in which the debtor is an individual and in a case under chapter 13, if the debtor is the lessee with respect to personal property and the lease is not assumed in the plan confirmed by the court, the lease is deemed rejected as of the conclusion of the hearing on confirmation. If the lease is rejected, the stay under section 362 and any stay under section 1301 is automatically terminated with respect to the property subject to the lease.

§ 366. Utility Service

(a) Except as provided in subsections (b) and (c) of this section, a utility may not alter, refuse, or discontinue service to, or discriminate against, the trustee or the debtor solely on the basis of the commencement of a case under this title or that a debt owed by the debtor to such utility for service rendered before the order for relief was not paid when due.

(b) Such utility may alter, refuse, or discontinue service if neither the trustee nor the debtor, within 20 days after the date of the order for relief, furnishes adequate assurance of payment, in the form of a deposit or other security, for service after such date. On request of a party in interest and after notice and a hearing, the court may order reasonable modification of the amount of the deposit or other security necessary to provide adequate assurance of payment.

(c)(1)(A) For purposes of this subsection, the term "assurance of payment" means—

(i) a cash deposit;

(ii) a letter of credit;

(iii) a certificate of deposit;

(iv) a surety bond;

(v) a prepayment of utility consumption; or

(vi) another form of security that is mutually agreed on between the utility and the debtor or the trustee.

(B) For purposes of this subsection an administrative expense priority shall not constitute an assurance of payment.

(2) Subject to paragraphs (3) and (4), with respect to a case filed under chapter 11, a utility referred to in subsection (a) may alter, refuse, or discontinue utility service, if during the 30-day period beginning on the date of the filing of the petition, the utility does not receive from the debtor or the trustee adequate assurance of payment for utility service that is satisfactory to the utility.

(3) (A) On request of a party in interest and after notice and a hearing, the court may order modification of the amount of an assurance of payment under paragraph (2).

(B) In making a determination under this paragraph whether an assurance of payment is adequate, the court may not consider—

(i) the absence of security before the date of the filing of the petition;

(ii) the payment by the debtor of charges for utility service in a timely manner before the date of the filing of the petition; or

(iii) the availability of an administrative expense priority.

(4) Notwithstanding any other provision of law, with respect to a case subject to this subsection, a utility may recover or set off against a security deposit provided to the utility by the debtor before the date of the filing of the petition without notice or order of the court.

CHAPTER 5. CREDITORS, THE DEBTOR, AND THE ESTATE

SUBCHAPTER I—CREDITORS AND CLAIMS

Section

501. Filing of Proofs of Claims or Interest
502. Allowance of Claims or Interest
503. Allowance of Administrative Expenses
504. Sharing of Compensation
505. Determination of Tax Liability
506. Determination of Secured Status
507. Priorities
508. Effect of Distribution Other Than under This Title
509. Claims of Codebtors
510. Subordination
511. Rate of Interest on Tax Claims

§ 501. Filing of Proofs of Claims or Interests

(a) A creditor or an indenture trustee may file a proof of claim. An equity security holder may file a proof of interest.

(b) If a creditor does not timely file a proof of such creditor's claim, an entity that is liable to such creditor with the debtor, or that has secured such creditor, may file a proof of such claim.

(c) If a creditor does not timely file a proof of such creditor's claim, the debtor or the trustee may file a proof of such claim.

(d) A claim of a kind specified in section 502(e)(2), 502(f), 502(g), 502(h) or 502(i) of this title may be filed under subsection (a), (b), or (c) of this section the same as if such claim were a claim against the debtor and had arisen before the date of the filing of the petition.

(e) A claim arising from the liability of a debtor for fuel use tax assessed consistent with the requirements of section 31705 of title 49 may be filed by the base jurisdiction designated pursuant to the International Fuel Tax Agreement (as defined in section 31701 of title 49) and, if so filed, shall be allowed as a single claim.

§ 502. Allowance of Claims or Interests

(a) A claim or interest, proof of which is filed under section 501 of this title, is deemed allowed, unless a party in interest, including a creditor of a general partner in a partnership that is a debtor in a case under chapter 7 of this title, objects.

(b) Except as provided in subsections (e)(2), (f), (g), (h) and (i) of this section, if such objection to a claim is made, the court, after notice and a hearing, shall determine the amount of such claim in lawful currency of the United States as of the date of the filing of the petition, and shall allow such claim in such amount, except to the extent that—

(1) such claim is unenforceable against the debtor and property of the debtor, under any agreement or applicable law for a reason other than because such claim is contingent or unmatured;

(2) such claim is for unmatured interest;

(3) if such claim is for a tax assessed against property of the estate, such claim exceeds the value of the interest of the estate in such property;

(4) if such claim is for services of an insider or attorney of the debtor, such claim exceeds the reasonable value of such services;

(5) such claim is for a debt that is unmatured on the date of the filing of the petition and that is excepted from discharge under section 523(a)(5) of this title;

(6) if such claim is the claim of a lessor for damages resulting from the termination of a lease of real property, such claim exceeds—

(A) the rent reserved by such lease, without acceleration, for the greater of one year, or 15 percent, not to exceed three years, of the remaining term of such lease, following the earlier of—

(i) the date of the filing of the petition; and

(ii) the date on which such lessor repossessed, or the lessee surrendered, the leased property; plus

(B) any unpaid rent due under such lease, without acceleration, on the earlier of such dates;

(7) if such claim is the claim of an employee for damages resulting from the termination of an employment contract, such claim exceeds—

(A) the compensation provided by such contract, without acceleration, for one year following the earlier of—

(i) the date of the filing of the petition; or

(ii) the date on which the employer directed the employee to terminate, or such employee terminated, performance under such contract; plus

(B) any unpaid compensation due under such contract, without acceleration, on the earlier of such dates;

(8) such claim results from a reduction, due to late payment, in the amount of an otherwise applicable credit available to the debtor in connection with an employment tax on wages, salaries, or commissions earned from the debtor; or

(9) proof of such claim is not timely filed, except to the extent tardily filed as permitted under paragraph (1), (2), or (3) of section 726(a) of this title or under the Federal Rules of Bankruptcy Procedure, except that—

(A) a claim of a governmental unit shall be timely filed if it is filed before 180 days after the date of the order for relief or such later time as the Federal Rules of Bankruptcy Procedure may provide; and

(B) in a case under chapter 13, a claim of a governmental unit for a tax with respect to a return filed under section 1308 shall be timely if the claim is filed on or before the date that is 60 days after the date on which such return was filed as required.

(c) There shall be estimated for purpose of allowance under this section—

(1) any contingent or unliquidated claim, the fixing or liquidation of which, as the case may be, would unduly delay the administration of the case; or

(2) any right to payment arising from a right to an equitable remedy for breach of performance.

(d) Notwithstanding subsections (a) and (b) of this section, the court shall disallow any claim of any entity from which property is recoverable under section 542, 543, 550, or 553 of this title or that is a transferee of a transfer avoidable under section 522(f), 522(h), 544, 545, 547, 548, 549, or 724(a) of this title, unless such entity or transferee has paid the amount, or turned over any such property, for which such entity or transferee is liable under section 522(i), 542, 543, 550, or 553 of this title.

(e)(1) Notwithstanding subsections (a), (b), and (c) of this section and paragraph (2) of this subsection, the court shall disallow any claim for reimbursement or contribution of an entity that is liable with the debtor on or has secured the claim of a creditor, to the extent that—

(A) such creditor's claim against the estate is disallowed;

(B) such claim for reimbursement or contribution is contingent as of the time of allowance or disallowance of such claim for reimbursement or contribution; or

(C) such entity asserts a right of subrogation to the rights of such creditor under section 509 of this title.

(2) A claim for reimbursement or contribution of such an entity that becomes fixed after the commencement of the case shall be determined, and shall be allowed under subsection (a), (b), or (c) of this section, or disallowed under subsection (d) of this section, the same as if such claim had become fixed before the date of the filing of the petition.

(f) In an involuntary case, a claim arising in the ordinary course of the debtor's business or financial affairs after the commencement of the case but before the earlier of the appointment of a trustee and the order for relief shall be determined as of the date such claim arises, and shall be allowed under subsection (a), (b), or (c) of this section or disallowed under subsection (d) or (e) of this section, the same as if such claim had arisen before the date of the filing of the petition.

(g)(1) A claim arising from the rejection, under section 365 of this title or under a plan under chapter 9, 11, 12, or 13 of this title, of an executory contract or unexpired lease of the debtor that has not been assumed shall be determined, and shall be allowed under subsection (a), (b), or (c) of this section or disallowed under subsection (d) or (e) of this section, the same as if such claim had arisen before the date of the filing of the petition.

(2) A claim for damages calculated in accordance with section 562 shall be allowed under subsection (a), (b), or (c), or disallowed under subsection (d) or (e), as if such claim had arisen before the date of the filing of the petition.

(h) A claim arising from the recovery of property under section 522, 550, or 553 of this title shall be determined, and shall be allowed under subsection (a), (b), or (c) of this section, or disallowed under subsection (d) or (e) of this section, the same as if such claim had arisen before the date of the filing of the petition.

(i) A claim that does not arise until after the commencement of the case for a tax entitled to priority under section 507(a)(8) of this title shall be determined, and shall be allowed under subsection (a), (b), or (c) of this section, or disallowed under subsection (d) or (e) of this section, the same as if such claim had arisen before the date of the filing of the petition.

(j) A claim that has been allowed or disallowed may be reconsidered for cause. A reconsidered claim may be allowed or disallowed according to the equities of the case. Reconsideration of a claim under this subsection does not affect the validity of any payment or transfer from the estate made to a holder of an allowed claim on account of such allowed claim that is not reconsidered, but if a reconsidered claim is allowed and is of the same class as such holder's claim, such holder may not receive any additional payment or transfer from the estate on account of such holder's allowed claim until the holder of such reconsidered and allowed claim receives payment on account of such claim proportionate in value to that already received by such other holder. This subsection does not alter or modify the trustee's right to recover from a creditor any excess payment or transfer made to such creditor.

(k)(1) The court, on the motion of the debtor and after a hearing, may reduce a claim filed under this section based in whole on an unsecured consumer debt by not more than 20 percent of the claim, if—

(A) the claim was filed by a creditor who unreasonably refused to negotiate a reasonable alternative repayment schedule proposed on behalf of the debtor by an approved nonprofit budget and credit counseling agency described in section 111;

(B) the offer of the debtor under subparagraph (A)—

(i) was made at least 60 days before the date of the filing of the petition; and

(ii) provided for payment of at least 60 percent of the amount of the debt over a period not to exceed the repayment period of the loan, or a reasonable extension thereof; and

(C) no part of the debt under the alternative repayment schedule is nondischargeable.

(2) The debtor shall have the burden of proving, by clear and convincing evidence, that—

(A) the creditor unreasonably refused to consider the debtor's proposal; and

(B) the proposed alternative repayment schedule was made prior to expiration of the 60-day period specified in paragraph (1)(B)(i).

§ 503. Allowance of Administrative Expenses

(a) An entity may timely file a request for payment of an administrative expense, or may tardily file such request if permitted by the court for cause.

(b) After notice and a hearing, there shall be allowed administrative expenses, other than claims allowed under section 502(f) of this title, including—

(1) (A) the actual, necessary costs and expenses of preserving the estate including—

(i) wages, salaries, and commissions for services rendered after the commencement of the case; and

(ii) wages and benefits awarded pursuant to a judicial proceeding or a proceeding of the National Labor Relations Board as back pay attributable to any period of time occurring after commencement of the case under this title, as a result of a violation of Federal or State law by the debtor, without regard to the time of the occurrence of unlawful conduct on which such award is based or to whether any services were rendered, if the court determines that payment of wages and benefits by reason of the operation of this clause will not substantially increase the probability of layoff or termination of current employees, or of nonpayment of domestic support obligations, during the case under this title;

(B) any tax—

(i) incurred by the estate, whether secured or unsecured, including property taxes for which liability is in rem, in personam, or both, except a tax of a kind specified in section 507(a)(8) of this title; or

(ii) attributable to an excessive allowance of a tentative carryback adjustment that the estate received, whether the taxable year to which such adjustment relates ended before or after the commencement of the case;

(C) any fine, penalty, or reduction in credit relating to a tax of a kind specified in subparagraph (B) of this paragraph; and

(D) notwithstanding the requirements of subsection (a), a governmental unit shall not be required to file a request for the payment of an expense described in subparagraph (B) or (C), as a condition of its being an allowed administrative expense;

(2) compensation and reimbursement awarded under section 330(a) of this title;

(3) the actual, necessary expenses, other than compensation and reimbursement specified in paragraph (4) of this subsection, incurred by—

(A) a creditor that files a petition under section 303 of this title;

(B) a creditor that recovers, after the court's approval, for the benefit of the estate any property transferred or concealed by the debtor;

(C) a creditor in connection with the prosecution of a criminal offense relating to the case or to the business or property of the debtor;

(D) a creditor, an indenture trustee, an equity security holder, or a committee representing creditors or equity security holders other than a committee appointed under section 1102 of this title, in making a substantial contribution in a case under chapter 9 or 11 of this title;

(E) a custodian superseded under section 543 of this title, and compensation for the services of such custodian; or

(F) a member of a committee appointed under section 1102 of this title, if such expenses are incurred in the performance of the duties of such committee;

(4) reasonable compensation for professional services rendered by an attorney or an accountant of an entity whose expense is allowable under subparagraph (A), (B), (C), (D), or (E) of paragraph (3) of this subsection, based on the time, the nature, the extent, and the value of such services, and the cost of comparable services other than in a case under this title, and reimbursement for actual, necessary expenses incurred by such attorney or accountant;

(5) reasonable compensation for services rendered by an indenture trustee in making a substantial contribution in a case under chapter 9 or 11 of this title, based on the time, the nature, the extent, and the value of such services, and the cost of comparable services other than in a case under this title;

(6) the fees and mileage payable under chapter 119 of title 28;

(7) with respect to a nonresidential real property lease previously assumed under section 365, and subsequently rejected, a sum equal to all monetary obligations due, excluding those arising from or relating to a failure to operate or a penalty provision, for the period of 2 years following the later of the rejection date or the date of actual turnover of the premises, without reduction or setoff for any reason whatsoever except for sums actually received or to be received from an entity other than the debtor, and the claim for remaining sums due for the balance of the term of the lease shall be a claim under section 502(b)(6);

(8) the actual, necessary costs and expenses of closing a health care business incurred by a trustee or by a Federal agency (as defined in section 551(1) of title 5) or a department or agency of a State or political subdivision thereof, including any cost or expense incurred—

(A) in disposing of patient records in accordance with section 351; or

(B) in connection with transferring patients from the health care business that is in the process of being closed to another health care business;

(9) the value of any goods received by the debtor within 20 days before the date of commencement of a case under this title in which the goods have been sold to the debtor in the ordinary course of such debtor's business.

(c) Notwithstanding subsection (b), there shall neither be allowed, nor paid—

(1) a transfer made to, or an obligation incurred for the benefit of, an insider of the debtor for the purpose of inducing such person to remain with the debtor's business, absent a finding by the court based on evidence in the record that—

(A) the transfer or obligation is essential to retention of the person because the individual has a bona fide job offer from another business at the same or greater rate of compensation;

(B) the services provided by the person are essential to the survival of the business; and

(C) either—

(i) the amount of the transfer made to, or obligation incurred for the benefit of, the person is not greater than an amount equal to 10 times the amount of the mean transfer or obligation of a similar kind given to nonmanagement employees for any purpose during the calendar year in which the transfer is made or the obligation is incurred; or

(ii) if no such similar transfers were made to, or obligations were incurred for the benefit of, such nonmanagement employees during such calendar year, the amount of the transfer or obligation is not greater than an amount equal to 25 percent of the amount of any similar transfer or obligation made to or incurred for the benefit of such insider for any purpose during the calendar year before the year in which such transfer is made or obligation is incurred;

(2) a severance payment to an insider of the debtor, unless—

(A) the payment is part of a program that is generally applicable to all full-time employees; and

(B) the amount of the payment is not greater than 10 times the amount of the mean severance pay given to nonmanagement employees during the calendar year in which the payment is made; or

(3) other transfers or obligations that are outside the ordinary course of business and not justified by the facts and circumstances of the case, including transfers made to, or obligations incurred for the benefit of, officers, managers, or consultants hired after the date of the filing of the petition.

§ 504. Sharing of Compensation

(a) Except as provided in subsection (b) of this section, a person receiving compensation or reimbursement under section 503(b)(2) or 503(b)(4) of this title may not share or agree to share—

(1) any such compensation or reimbursement with another person; or

(2) any compensation or reimbursement received by another person under such sections.

(b)(1) A member, partner, or regular associate in a professional association, corporation, or partnership may share compensation or reimbursement received under section 503(b)(2) or 503(b)(4) of this title with another member, partner, or regular associate in such association, corporation, or partnership, and may share in any compensation or reimbursement received under such sections by another member, partner, or regular associate in such association, corporation, or partnership.

(2) An attorney for a creditor that files a petition under section 303 of this title may share compensation and reimbursement received under section 503(b)(4) of this title with any other attorney contributing to the services rendered or expenses incurred by such creditor's attorney.

(c) This section shall not apply with respect to sharing, or agreeing to share, compensation with a bona fide public service attorney referral program that operates in accordance with non-Federal law regulating attorney referral services and with rules of professional responsibility applicable to attorney acceptance of referrals.

§ 505. Determination of Tax Liability

(a)(1) Except as provided in paragraph (2) of this subsection, the court may determine the amount or legality of any tax, any fine or penalty relating to a tax, or any addition to tax, whether or not previously assessed, whether or not paid, and whether or not contested before and adjudicated by a judicial or administrative tribunal of competent jurisdiction.

(2) The court may not so determine—

(A) the amount or legality of a tax, fine, penalty, or addition to tax if such amount or legality was contested before and adjudicated by a judicial or administrative tribunal of competent jurisdiction before the commencement of the case under this title;

(B) any right of the estate to a tax refund, before the earlier of—

(i) 120 days after the trustee properly requests such refund from the governmental unit from which such refund is claimed; or

(ii) a determination by such governmental unit of such request; or

(C) the amount or legality of any amount arising in connection with an ad valorem tax on real or personal property of the estate, if the applicable period for contesting or redetermining that amount under applicable nonbankruptcy law has expired.

(b)(1)(A) The clerk shall maintain a list under which a Federal, State, or local governmental unit responsible for the collection of taxes within the district may—

(i) designate an address for service of requests under this subsection; and

(ii) describe where further information concerning additional requirements for filing such requests may be found.

(B) If such governmental unit does not designate an address and provide such address to the clerk under subparagraph (A), any request made under this subsection may be served at the address for the filing of a tax return or protest with the appropriate taxing authority of such governmental unit.

(2) A trustee may request a determination of any unpaid liability of the estate for any tax incurred during the administration of the case by submitting a tax return for such tax and a request for such a determination to the governmental unit charged with responsibility for collection or determination of such tax at the address and in the manner designated in paragraph (1). Unless such return is fraudulent, or contains a material misrepresentation, the estate, the trustee, the debtor, and any successor to the debtor are discharged from any liability for such tax—

(A) upon payment of the tax shown on such return, if—

(i) such governmental unit does not notify the trustee, within 60 days after such request, that such return has been selected for examination; or

(ii) such governmental unit does not complete such an examination and notify the trustee of any tax due, within 180 days after such request or within such additional time as the court, for cause, permits;

(B) upon payment of the tax determined by the court, after notice and a hearing, after completion by such governmental unit of such examination; or

(C) upon payment of the tax determined by such governmental unit to be due.

(c) Notwithstanding section 362 of this title, after determination by the court of a tax under this section, the governmental unit charged with responsibility for collection of such tax may assess such tax against the estate, the debtor, or a successor to the debtor, as the case may be, subject to any otherwise applicable law.

§ 506. Determination of Secured Status

(a)(1) An allowed claim of a creditor secured by a lien on property in which the estate has an interest, or that is subject to setoff under section 553 of this title, is a secured claim to the extent of the value of such creditor's interest in the estate's interest in such property, or to the extent of the amount subject to setoff, as the case may be, and is an unsecured claim to the extent that the value of such creditor's interest or the amount so subject to setoff is less than the amount of such allowed claim. Such value shall be determined in light of the purpose of the valuation and of the proposed disposition or use of such property, and in conjunction with any hearing on such disposition or use or on a plan affecting such creditor's interest.

(2) If the debtor is an individual in a case under chapter 7 or 13, such value with respect to personal property securing an allowed claim shall be determined based on the replacement value of such property as of the date of the filing of the petition without deduction for costs of sale or marketing. With respect to property acquired for personal, family, or household purposes, replacement value shall mean the price a retail merchant would charge for property of that kind considering the age and condition of the property at the time value is determined.

(b) To the extent that an allowed secured claim is secured by property the value of which, after any recovery under subsection (c) of this section, is greater than the amount of such claim, there shall be allowed to the holder of such claim, interest on such claim, and any reasonable fees, costs, or charges provided for under the agreement or state statute under which such claim arose.

(c) The trustee may recover from property securing an allowed secured claim the reasonable, necessary costs and expenses of preserving, or disposing of, such property to the extent of any benefit to the holder of such claim, including the payment of all ad valorem property taxes with respect to the property.

(d) To the extent that a lien secures a claim against the debtor that is not an allowed secured claim, such lien is void, unless—

(1) such claim was disallowed only under section 502(b)(5) or 502(e) of this title; or

(2) such claim is not an allowed secured claim due only to the failure of any entity to file a proof of such claim under section 501 of this title.

§ 507. Priorities

(a) The following expenses and claims have priority in the following order:

(1) First:

(A) Allowed unsecured claims for domestic support obligations that, as of the date of the filing of the petition in a case under this title, are owed to or recoverable by a spouse, former spouse, or child of the debtor, or such child's parent, legal guardian, or responsible relative, without regard to whether the claim is filed by such person or is filed by a governmental unit on behalf of such person, on the condition that funds received under this paragraph by a governmental unit under this title after the date of the filing of the petition shall be applied and distributed in accordance with applicable nonbankruptcy law.

(B) Subject to claims under subparagraph (A), allowed unsecured claims for domestic support obligations that, as of the date of the filing of the petition, are assigned by a spouse, former spouse, child of the debtor, or such child's parent, legal guardian, or responsible relative to a governmental unit (unless such obligation is assigned voluntarily by the spouse, former spouse, child, parent, legal guardian, or responsible relative of the child for the purpose of collecting the debt) or are owed directly to or recoverable by a governmental unit under applicable nonbankruptcy law, on the condition that funds received under this paragraph by a governmental unit under this title after the date of the filing of the petition be applied and distributed in accordance with applicable nonbankruptcy law.

(C) If a trustee is appointed or elected under section 701, 702, 703, 1104, 1202, or 1302, the administrative expenses of the trustee allowed under paragraphs (1)(A), (2), and (6) of section 503(b) shall be paid before payment of claims under subparagraphs (A) and (B), to the extent that the trustee administers assets that are otherwise available for the payment of such claims.

(2) Second, administrative expenses allowed under section 503(b) of this title, unsecured claims of any Federal reserve bank related to loans made through programs or facilities authorized under section 13(3) of the Federal Reserve Act (12 U.S.C. 343), and any fees and charges assessed against the estate under chapter 123 of title 28.

(3) Third, unsecured claims allowed under section 502(f) of this title.

(4) Fourth, allowed unsecured claims, but only to the extent of $15,150 for each individual or corporation, as the case may be, earned within 180 days before the date of the filing of the petition or the date of the cessation of the debtor's business, whichever occurs first, for—

(A) wages, salaries, or commissions, including vacation, severance, and sick leave pay earned by an individual; or

(B) sales commissions earned by an individual or by a corporation with only 1 employee, acting as an independent contractor in the sale of goods or services for the debtor in the ordinary course of the debtor's business if, and only if, during the 12 months preceding that date, at least 75 percent of the amount that the individual or corporation earned by acting as an independent contractor in the sale of goods or services was earned from the debtor.

(5) Fifth, allowed unsecured claims for contributions to an employee benefit plan—

(A) arising from services rendered within 180 days before the date of the filing of the petition or the date of the cessation of the debtor's business, whichever occurs first; but only

(B) for each such plan, to the extent of—

(i) the number of employees covered by each such plan multiplied by $15,150; less

(ii) the aggregate amount paid to such employees under paragraph (4) of this subsection, plus the aggregate amount paid by the estate on behalf of such employees to any other employee benefit plan.

(6) Sixth, allowed unsecured claims of persons—

(A) engaged in the production or raising of grain, as defined in section 557(b) of this title, against a debtor who owns or operates a grain storage facility, as defined in section 557(b) of this title, for grain or the proceeds of grain, or

(B) engaged as a United States fisherman against a debtor who has acquired fish or fish produce from a fisherman through a sale or conversion, and who is engaged in operating a fish produce storage or processing facility—

but only to the extent of $7,475 for each such individual.

(7) Seventh, allowed unsecured claims of individuals, to the extent of $3,350 for each such individual, arising from the deposit, before the commencement of the case, of money in connection with the purchase, lease, or rental of property, or the purchase of services, for the personal, family, or household use of such individuals, that were not delivered or provided.

(8) Eighth, allowed unsecured claims of governmental units, only to the extent that such claims are for—

(A) a tax on or measured by income or gross receipts for a taxable year ending on or before the date of the filing of the petition—

(i) for which a return, if required, is last due, including extensions, after three years before the date of the filing of the petition;

(ii) assessed within 240 days before the date of the filing of the petition, exclusive of—

(I) any time during which an offer in compromise with respect to that tax was pending or in effect during that 240-day period, plus 30 days; and

(II) any time during which a stay of proceedings against collections was in effect in a prior case under this title during that 240-day period, plus 90 days; or

(iii) other than a tax of a kind specified in section 523(a)(1)(B) or 523(a)(1)(C) of this title, not assessed before, but assessable, under applicable law or by agreement, after, the commencement of the case;

(B) a property tax incurred before the commencement of the case and last payable without penalty after one year before the date of the filing of the petition;

(C) a tax required to be collected or withheld and for which the debtor is liable in whatever capacity;

(D) an employment tax on a wage, salary, or commission of a kind specified in paragraph (4) of this subsection earned from the debtor before the date of the filing of the petition, whether or not actually paid before such date, for which a return is last due, under applicable law or under any extension, after three years before the date of the filing of the petition;

(E) an excise tax on—

(i) a transaction occurring before the date of the filing of the petition for which a return, if required, is last due, under applicable law or under any extension, after three years before the date of the filing of the petition; or

(ii) if a return is not required, a transaction occurring during the three years immediately preceding the date of the filing of the petition;

(F) a customs duty arising out of the importation of merchandise—

(i) entered for consumption within one year before the date of the filing of the petition;

(ii) covered by an entry liquidated or reliquidated within one year before the date of the filing of the petition; or

(iii) entered for consumption within four years before the date of the filing of the petition but unliquidated on such date, if the Secretary of the Treasury certifies that failure to liquidate such entry was due to an investigation pending on such date into assessment of antidumping or countervailing duties or fraud, or if information needed for the proper appraisement or classification of such merchandise was not available to the appropriate customs officer before such date; or

(G) a penalty related to a claim of a kind specified in this paragraph and in compensation for actual pecuniary loss. An otherwise applicable time period specified in this paragraph shall be suspended for any period during which a governmental unit is prohibited under applicable nonbankruptcy law from collecting a tax as a result of a request by the debtor for a hearing and an appeal of any collection action taken or proposed against the debtor, plus 90 days; plus any time during which the stay of proceedings was in effect in a prior case under this title or during which collection was precluded by the existence of 1 or more confirmed plans under this title, plus 90 days.

(9) Ninth, allowed unsecured claims based upon any commitment by the debtor to a Federal depository institutions regulatory agency (or predecessor to such agency) to maintain the capital of an insured depository institution.

(10) Tenth, allowed claims for death or personal injury resulting from the operation of a motor vehicle or vessel if such operation was unlawful because the debtor was intoxicated from using alcohol, a drug, or another substance.

(b) If the trustee, under section 362, 363, or 364 of this title, provides adequate protection of the interest of a holder of a claim secured by a lien on property of the debtor and if, notwithstanding such protection, such creditor has a claim allowable under subsection (a)(2) of this section arising from the stay of action against such property under section 362 of this title, from the use, sale, or lease of such property under section 363 of this title, or from the granting of a lien under section 364(d) of this title, then such creditor's claim under such subsection shall have priority over every other claim allowable under such subsection.

(c) For the purpose of subsection (a) of this section, a claim of a governmental unit arising from an erroneous refund or credit of a tax has the same priority as a claim for the tax to which such refund or credit relates.

(d) An entity that is subrogated to the rights of a holder of a claim of a kind specified in subsection (a)(1), (a)(4), (a)(5), (a)(6), (a)(7), (a)(8) excluding subparagraph (F), or (a)(9) of this section is not subrogated to the right of the holder of such claim to priority under such subsection.

§ 508. Effect of Distribution Other Than Under This Title

If a creditor of a partnership debtor receives, from a general partner that is not a debtor in a case under chapter 7 of this title, payment of, or a transfer of property on account of, a claim that is allowed under this title and that is not secured by a lien on property of such partner, such creditor may not receive any payment under this title on account of such claim until each of the other holders of claims on account of which such holders are entitled to share equally with such creditor under this title has received payment under this title equal in value to the consideration received by such creditor from such general partner.

§ 509. Claims of Codebtors

(a) Except as provided in subsection (b) or (c) of this section, an entity that is liable with the debtor on, or that has secured, a claim of a creditor against the debtor, and that pays such claim, is subrogated to the rights of such creditor to the extent of such payment.

(b) such entity is not subrogated to the rights of such creditor to the extent that—

(1) a claim of such entity for reimbursement or contribution on account of such payment of such creditor's claim is—

(A) allowed under section 502 of this title;

(B) disallowed other than under section 502(e) of this title; or

(C) subordinated under section 510 of this title; or

(2) as between the debtor and such entity, such entity received the consideration for the claim held by such creditor.

(c) the court shall subordinate to the claim of a creditor and for the benefit of such creditor an allowed claim, by way of subrogation under this section, or for reimbursement or contribution, of an entity that is liable with the debtor on, or that has secured, such creditor's claim, until such creditor's claim is paid in full, either through payments under this title or otherwise.

§ 510. Subordination

(a) A subordination agreement is enforceable in a case under this title to the same extent that such agreement is enforceable under applicable nonbankruptcy law.

(b) For the purpose of distribution under this title, a claim arising from rescission of a purchase or sale of a security of the debtor or of an affiliate of the debtor, for damages arising from the purchase or sale of such a security, or for reimbursement or contribution allowed under section 502 on account of such a claim, shall be subordinated to all claims or interests that are senior to or equal the claim or interest represented by such security, except that if such security is common stock, such claim has the same priority as common stock.

(c) Notwithstanding subsections (a) and (b) of this section, after notice and a hearing, the court may—

(1) under principles of equitable subordination, subordinate for purposes of distribution all or part of an allowed claim to all or part of another allowed claim or all or part of an allowed interest to all or part of another allowed interest; or

(2) order that any lien securing such a subordinated claim be transferred to the estate.

§ 511. Rate of Interest on Tax Claims

(a) If any provision of this title requires the payment of interest on a tax claim or on an administrative expense tax, or the payment of interest to enable a creditor to receive the present value of the allowed amount of a tax claim, the rate of interest shall be the rate determined under applicable nonbankruptcy law.

(b) In the case of taxes paid under a confirmed plan under this title, the rate of interest shall be determined as of the calendar month in which the plan is confirmed.

SUBCHAPTER II—DEBTOR'S DUTIES AND BENEFITS

Section

521. Debtor's Duties
522. Exemptions
523. Exceptions to Discharge
524. Effect of Discharge
525. Protection Against Discriminatory Treatment
526. Restrictions on Debt Relief Agencies
527. Disclosures
528. Requirements for Debt Relief Agencies

§ 521. Debtor's Duties

(a) The debtor shall—

(1) file—

(A) a list of creditors; and

(B) unless the court orders otherwise—

(i) a schedule of assets and liabilities;

(ii) a schedule of current income and current expenditures;

(iii) a statement of the debtor's financial affairs and, if section 342(b) applies, a certificate—

(I) of an attorney whose name is indicated on the petition as the attorney for the debtor, or a bankruptcy petition preparer signing the petition under section 110(b)(1), indicating that such attorney or the bankruptcy petition preparer delivered to the debtor the notice required by section 342(b); or

(II) if no attorney is so indicated, and no bankruptcy petition preparer signed the petition, of the debtor that such notice was received and read by the debtor;

(iv) copies of all payment advices or other evidence of payment received within 60 days before the date of the filing of the petition, by the debtor from any employer of the debtor;

(v) a statement of the amount of monthly net income, itemized to show how the amount is calculated; and

(vi) a statement disclosing any reasonably anticipated increase in income or expenditures over the 12-month period following the date of the filing of the petition;

(2) if an individual debtor's schedule of assets and liabilities includes debts which are secured by property of the estate—

(A) within thirty days after the date of the filing of a petition under chapter 7 of this title or on or before the date of the meeting of creditors, whichever is earlier, or within such additional time as the court, for cause, within such period fixes, file with the clerk a statement of his intention with respect to the retention or surrender of such property and, if applicable, specifying that such property is claimed as exempt, that the debtor intends to redeem such property, or that the debtor intends to reaffirm debts secured by such property; and

(B) within 30 days after the first date set for the meeting of creditors under section 341(a), or within such additional time as the court, for cause, within such 30-day period fixes, perform his intention with respect to such property, as specified by subparagraph (A) of this paragraph;

except that nothing in subparagraphs (A) and (B) of this paragraph shall alter the debtor's or the trustee's rights with regard to such property under this title, except as provided in section 362(h);

(3) if a trustee is serving in the case or an auditor is serving under section 586(f) of title 28, cooperate with the trustee as necessary to enable the trustee to perform the trustee's duties under this title;

(4) if a trustee is serving in the case or an auditor is serving under section 586(f) of title 28, surrender to the trustee all property of the estate and any recorded information, including books, documents, records, and papers, relating to property of the estate, whether or not immunity is granted under section 344 of this title;

(5) appear at the hearing required under section 524(d) of this title;

(6) in a case under chapter 7 of this title in which the debtor is an individual, not retain possession of personal property as to which a creditor has an allowed claim for the purchase price secured in whole or in part by an interest in such personal property unless the debtor, not later than 45 days after the first meeting of creditors under section 341(a), either—

(A) enters into an agreement with the creditor pursuant to section 524(c) with respect to the claim secured by such property; or

(B) redeems such property from the security interest pursuant to section 722; and

(7) unless a trustee is serving in the case, continue to perform the obligations required of the administrator (as defined in section 3 of the Employee Retirement Income Security Act of 1974) of an employee benefit plan if at the time of the commencement of the case the debtor (or any entity designated by the debtor) served as such administrator.

If the debtor fails to so act within the 45-day period referred to in paragraph (6), the stay under section 362(a) is terminated with respect to the personal property of the estate or of the debtor which is affected, such property shall no longer be property of the estate, and the creditor may take whatever action as to such property as is permitted by applicable nonbankruptcy law, unless the court determines on the motion of the trustee filed before the expiration of such 45-day period, and after notice and a hearing, that such property is of consequential value or benefit to the estate, orders appropriate adequate protection of the creditor's interest, and orders the debtor to deliver any collateral in the debtor's possession to the trustee.

(b) In addition to the requirements under subsection (a), a debtor who is an individual shall file with the court—

(1) a certificate from the approved nonprofit budget and credit counseling agency that provided the debtor services under section 109(h) describing the services provided to the debtor; and

(2) a copy of the debt repayment plan, if any, developed under section 109(h) through the approved nonprofit budget and credit counseling agency referred to in paragraph (1).

(c) In addition to meeting the requirements under subsection (a), a debtor shall file with the court a record of any interest that a debtor has in an education individual retirement account (as defined in section 530(b)(1) of the Internal Revenue Code of 1986), an interest in an account in a qualified ABLE program (as defined in section 529A(b) of such Code, or under a qualified State tuition program (as defined in section 529(b)(1) of such Code).

(d) If the debtor fails timely to take the action specified in subsection (a)(6) of this section, or in paragraphs (1) and (2) of section 362(h), with respect to property which a lessor or bailor owns and has leased, rented, or bailed to the debtor or as to which a creditor holds a security interest not otherwise voidable under section 522(f), 544, 545, 547, 548, or 549, nothing in this title shall prevent or limit the operation of a provision in the underlying lease or agreement that has the effect of placing the debtor in default under such lease or agreement by reason of the occurrence, pendency, or existence of a proceeding under this title or the insolvency of the debtor. Nothing in this subsection shall be deemed to justify limiting such a provision in any other circumstance.

(e)(1) If the debtor in a case under chapter 7 or 13 is an individual and if a creditor files with the court at any time a request to receive a copy of the petition, schedules, and statement of financial affairs filed by the debtor, then the court shall make such petition, such schedules, and such statement available to such creditor.

(2)(A) The debtor shall provide—

(i) not later than 7 days before the date first set for the first meeting of creditors, to the trustee a copy of the Federal income tax return required under applicable law (or at the election of the debtor, a transcript of such return) for the most recent tax year ending immediately before the commencement of the case and for which a Federal income tax return was filed; and

(ii) at the same time the debtor complies with clause (i), a copy of such return (or if elected under clause (i), such transcript) to any creditor that timely requests such copy.

(B) If the debtor fails to comply with clause (i) or (ii) of subparagraph (A), the court shall dismiss the case unless the debtor demonstrates that the failure to so comply is due to circumstances beyond the control of the debtor.

(C) If a creditor requests a copy of such tax return or such transcript and if the debtor fails to provide a copy of such tax return or such transcript to such creditor at the time the debtor provides such tax return or such transcript to the trustee, then the court shall dismiss the case unless the debtor demonstrates that the failure to provide a copy of such tax return or such transcript is due to circumstances beyond the control of the debtor.

(3) If a creditor in a case under chapter 13 files with the court at any time a request to receive a copy of the plan filed by the debtor, then the court shall make available to such creditor a copy of the plan—

(A) at a reasonable cost; and

(B) not later than 7 days after such request is filed.

(f) At the request of the court, the United States trustee, or any party in interest in a case under chapter 7, 11, or 13, a debtor who is an individual shall file with the court—

(1) at the same time filed with the taxing authority, a copy of each Federal income tax return required under applicable law (or at the election of the debtor, a transcript of such tax return) with respect to each tax year of the debtor ending while the case is pending under such chapter;

(2) at the same time filed with the taxing authority, each Federal income tax return required under applicable law (or at the election of the debtor, a transcript of such tax return) that had not been filed with such authority as of the date of the commencement of the case and that was subsequently filed for any tax year of the debtor ending in the 3-year period ending on the date of the commencement of the case;

(3) a copy of each amendment to any Federal income tax return or transcript filed with the court under paragraph (1) or (2); and

(4) in a case under chapter 13—

(A) on the date that is either 90 days after the end of such tax year or 1 year after the date of the commencement of the case, whichever is later, if a plan is not confirmed before such later date; and

(B) annually after the plan is confirmed and until the case is closed, not later than the date that is 45 days before the anniversary of the confirmation of the plan; a statement, under penalty of perjury, of the income and expenditures of the debtor during the tax year of the debtor most recently concluded before such statement is filed under this paragraph, and of the monthly income of the debtor, that shows how income, expenditures, and monthly income are calculated.

(g)(1) A statement referred to in subsection (f)(4) shall disclose—

(A) the amount and sources of the income of the debtor;

(B) the identity of any person responsible with the debtor for the support of any dependent of the debtor; and

(C) the identity of any person who contributed, and the amount contributed, to the household in which the debtor resides.

(2) The tax returns, amendments, and statement of income and expenditures described in subsections (e)(2)(A) and (f) shall be available to the United States trustee (or the bankruptcy administrator, if any), the trustee, and any party in interest for inspection and copying, subject to the requirements of section 315(c) of the Bankruptcy Abuse Prevention and Consumer Protection Act of 2005.

(h) If requested by the United States trustee or by the trustee, the debtor shall provide—

(1) a document that establishes the identity of the debtor, including a driver's license, passport, or other document that contains a photograph of the debtor; or

(2) such other personal identifying information relating to the debtor that establishes the identity of the debtor.

(i)(1) Subject to paragraphs (2) and (4) and notwithstanding section 707(a), if an individual debtor in a voluntary case under chapter 7 or 13 fails to file all of the information required under subsection (a)(1) within 45 days after the date of the filing of the petition, the case shall be automatically dismissed effective on the 46th day after the date of the filing of the petition.

(2) Subject to paragraph (4) and with respect to a case described in paragraph (1), any party in interest may request the court to enter an order dismissing the case. If requested, the court shall enter an order of dismissal not later than 7 days after such request.

(3) Subject to paragraph (4) and upon request of the debtor made within 45 days after the date of the filing of the petition described in paragraph (1), the court may allow the debtor an additional period of not to exceed 45 days to file the information required under subsection (a)(1) if the court finds justification for extending the period for the filing.

(4) Notwithstanding any other provision of this subsection, on the motion of the trustee filed before the expiration of the applicable period of time specified in paragraph (1), (2), or (3), and after notice and a hearing, the court may decline to dismiss the case if the court finds that the debtor attempted in good faith to file all the information required by subsection (a)(1)(B)(iv) and that the best interests of creditors would be served by administration of the case.

(j)(1) Notwithstanding any other provision of this title, if the debtor fails to file a tax return that becomes due after the commencement of the case or to properly obtain an extension of the due date for filing such return, the taxing authority may request that the court enter an order converting or dismissing the case.

(2) If the debtor does not file the required return or obtain the extension referred to in paragraph (1) within 90 days after a request is filed by the taxing authority under that paragraph, the court shall convert or dismiss the case, whichever is in the best interests of creditors and the estate.

§ 522. Exemptions

(a) In this section—

(1) "dependent" includes spouse, whether or not actually dependent; and

(2) "value" means fair market value as of the date of the filing of the petition or, with respect to property that becomes property of the estate after such date, as of the date such property becomes property of the estate.

(b)(1) Notwithstanding section 541 of this title, an individual debtor may exempt from property of the estate the property listed in either paragraph (2) or, in the alternative, paragraph (3) of this subsection. In joint cases filed under section 302 of this title and individual cases filed under section 301 or 303 of this title by or against debtors who are husband and wife, and whose estates are ordered to be jointly administered under Rule 1015(b) of the Federal Rules of Bankruptcy Procedure, one debtor may not elect to exempt property listed in paragraph (2) and the other debtor elect to exempt property listed in paragraph (3) of this subsection. If the parties cannot agree on the alternative to be elected, they shall be deemed to elect paragraph (2), where such election is permitted under the law of the jurisdiction where the case is filed.

(2) Property listed in this paragraph is property that is specified under subsection (d), unless the State law that is applicable to the debtor under paragraph (3)(A) specifically does not so authorize.

(3) Property listed in this paragraph is—

(A) subject to subsections (o) and (p), any property that is exempt under Federal law, other than subsection (d) of this section, or state or local law that is applicable on the date of the filing of the petition to the place in which the debtor's domicile has been located for the 730 days immediately preceding the date of the filing of the petition or if the debtor's domicile has not been located in a single State for such 730-day period, the place in which the debtor's domicile was located for 180 days immediately preceding the 730-day period or for a longer portion of such 180-day period than in any other place;

(B) any interest in property in which the debtor had, immediately before the commencement of the case, an interest as a tenant by the entirety or joint tenant to the extent that such interest as a tenant by the entirety or joint tenant is exempt from process under applicable nonbankruptcy law; and

(C) retirement funds to the extent that those funds are in a fund or account that is exempt from taxation under section 401, 403, 408, 408A, 414, 457, or 501(a) of the Internal Revenue Code of 1986.

If the effect of the domiciliary requirement under subparagraph (A) is to render the debtor ineligible for any exemption, the debtor may elect to exempt property that is specified under subsection (d).

(4) For purposes of paragraph (3)(C) and subsection (d)(12), the following shall apply:

(A) If the retirement funds are in a retirement fund that has received a favorable determination under section 7805 of the Internal Revenue Code of 1986, and that determination is in effect as of the date of the filing of the petition in a case under this title, those funds shall be presumed to be exempt from the estate.

(B) If the retirement funds are in a retirement fund that has not received a favorable determination under such section 7805, those funds are exempt from the estate if the debtor demonstrates that—

(i) no prior determination to the contrary has been made by a court or the Internal Revenue Service; and

(ii) (I) the retirement fund is in substantial compliance with the applicable requirements of the Internal Revenue Code of 1986; or

(II) the retirement fund fails to be in substantial compliance with the applicable requirements of the Internal Revenue Code of 1986 and the debtor is not materially responsible for that failure.

(C) A direct transfer of retirement funds from 1 fund or account that is exempt from taxation under section 401, 403, 408, 408A, 414, 457, or 501(a) of the Internal Revenue Code of 1986, under section 401(a)(31) of the Internal Revenue Code of 1986, or otherwise, shall not cease to qualify for exemption under paragraph (3)(C) or subsection (d)(12) by reason of such direct transfer.

(D) (i) Any distribution that qualifies as an eligible rollover distribution within the meaning of section 402(c) of the Internal Revenue Code of 1986 or that is described in clause (ii) shall not cease to qualify for exemption under paragraph (3)(C) or subsection (d)(12) by reason of such distribution.

(ii) A distribution described in this clause is an amount that—

(I) has been distributed from a fund or account that is exempt from taxation under section 401, 403, 408, 408A, 414, 457, or 501(a) of the Internal Revenue Code of 1986; and

(II) to the extent allowed by law, is deposited in such a fund or account not later than 60 days after the distribution of such amount.

(c) Unless the case is dismissed, property exempted under this section is not liable during or after the case for any debt of the debtor that arose, or that is determined under section 502 of this title as if such debt had arisen, before the commencement of the case, except—

(1) a debt of a kind specified in paragraph (1) or (5) of section 523(a) (in which case, notwithstanding any provision of applicable nonbankruptcy law to the contrary, such property shall be liable for a debt of a kind specified in such paragraph);

(2) a debt secured by a lien that is—

(A) (i) not avoided under subsection (f) or (g) of this section or under section 544, 545, 547, 548, 549, or 724(a) of this title; and

(ii) not void under section 506(d) of this title; or

(B) a tax lien, notice of which is properly filed;

(3) a debt of a kind specified in section 523(a)(4) or 523(a)(6) of this title owed by an institution-affiliated party of an insured depository institution to a Federal depository institutions regulatory agency acting in its capacity as conservator, receiver, or liquidating agent for such institution; or

(4) a debt in connection with fraud in the obtaining or providing of any scholarship, grant, loan, tuition, discount, award, or other financial assistance for purposes of financing an education at an institution of higher education (as that term is defined in section 101 of the Higher Education Act of 1965 (20 U.S.C. 1001)).

(d) The following property may be exempted under subsection (b)(2) of this section:

(1) The debtor's aggregate interest, not to exceed $27,900 in value, in real property or personal property that the debtor or a dependent of the debtor uses as a residence, in a cooperative that owns property that the debtor or a dependent of the debtor uses as a residence, or in a burial plot for the debtor or a dependent of the debtor.

(2) The debtor's interest, not to exceed $4,450 in value, in one motor vehicle.

(3) The debtor's interest, not to exceed $700 in value in any particular item or $14,875 in aggregate value, in household furnishings, household goods, wearing apparel, appliances, books, animals, crops, or musical instruments, that are held primarily for the personal, family, or household use of the debtor or a dependent of the debtor.

(4) The debtor's aggregate interest, not to exceed $1,875 in value, in jewelry held primarily for the personal, family, or household use of the debtor or a dependent of the debtor.

(5) The debtor's aggregate interest in any property, not to exceed in value $1,475 plus up to $13,950 of any unused amount of the exemption provided under paragraph (1) of this subsection.

(6) The debtor's aggregate interest, not to exceed $2,800 in value, in any implements, professional books, or tools, of the trade of the debtor or the trade of a dependent of the debtor.

(7) Any unmatured life insurance contract owned by the debtor, other than a credit life insurance contract.

(8) The debtor's aggregate interest, not to exceed in value $14,875 less any amount of property of the estate transferred in the manner specified in section 542(d) of this title, in any accrued dividend or interest under, or loan value of, any unmatured life insurance contract owned by the debtor under which the insured is the debtor or an individual of whom the debtor is a dependent.

(9) Professionally prescribed health aids for the debtor or a dependent of the debtor.

(10) The debtor's right to receive—

(A) a social security benefit, unemployment compensation, or a local public assistance benefit;

(B) a veterans' benefit;

(C) a disability, illness, or unemployment benefit;

(D) alimony, support, or separate maintenance, to the extent reasonably necessary for the support of the debtor and any dependent of the debtor;

(E) a payment under a stock bonus, pension, profitsharing, annuity, or similar plan or contract on account of illness, disability, death, age, or length of service, to the extent reasonably necessary for the support of the debtor and any dependent of the debtor, unless—

(i) such plan or contract was established by or under the auspices of an insider that employed the debtor at the time the debtor's rights under such plan or contract arose;

(ii) such payment is on account of age or length of service; and

(iii) such plan or contract does not qualify under section 401(a), 403(a), 403(b), or 408 of the Internal Revenue Code of 1986.

(11) The debtor's right to receive, or property that is traceable to—

(A) an award under a crime victim's reparation law;

(B) a payment on account of the wrongful death of an individual of whom the debtor was a dependent, to the extent reasonably necessary for the support of the debtor and any dependent of the debtor;

(C) a payment under a life insurance contract that insured the life of an individual of whom the debtor was a dependent on the date of such individual's death, to the extent reasonably necessary for the support of the debtor and any dependent of the debtor;

(D) a payment, not to exceed $27,900, on account of personal bodily injury, not including pain and suffering or compensation for actual pecuniary loss, of the debtor or an individual of whom the debtor is a dependent; or

(E) a payment in compensation of loss of future earnings of the debtor or an individual of whom the debtor is or was a dependent, to the extent reasonably necessary for the support of the debtor and any dependent of the debtor.

(12) Retirement funds to the extent that those funds are in a fund or account that is exempt from taxation under section 401, 403, 408, 408A, 414, 457, or 501(a) of the Internal Revenue Code of 1986.

(e) A waiver of an exemption executed in favor of a creditor that holds an unsecured claim against the debtor is unenforceable in a case under this title with respect to such claim against property that the debtor may exempt under subsection (b) of this section. A waiver by the debtor of a power under subsection (f) or (h) of this section to avoid a transfer, under subsection (g) or (i) of this section to exempt property, or under subsection (i) of this section to recover property or to preserve a transfer, is unenforceable in a case under this title.

(f)(1) Notwithstanding any waiver of exemptions but subject to paragraph (3), the debtor may avoid the fixing of a lien on an interest of the debtor in property to the extent that such lien impairs an exemption to which the debtor would have been entitled under subsection (b) of this section, if such lien is—

(A) a judicial lien, other than a judicial lien that secures a debt of a kind that is specified in section 523(a)(5); or

(B) a nonpossessory, nonpurchase-money security interest in any—

(i) household furnishings, household goods, wearing apparel, appliances, books, animals, crops, musical instruments, or jewelry that are held primarily for the personal, family, or household use of the debtor or a dependent of the debtor;

(ii) implements, professional books, or tools, of the trade of the debtor or the trade of a dependent of the debtor; or

(iii) professionally prescribed health aids for the debtor or a dependent of the debtor.

(2) (A) For the purposes of this subsection, a lien shall be considered to impair an exemption to the extent that the sum of—

(i) the lien;

(ii) all other liens on the property; and

(iii) the amount of the exemption that the debtor could claim if there were no liens on the property;

exceeds the value that the debtor's interest in the property would have in the absence of any liens.

(B) In the case of a property subject to more than 1 lien, a lien that has been avoided shall not be considered in making the calculation under subparagraph (A) with respect to other liens.

(C) This paragraph shall not apply with respect to a judgment arising out of a mortgage foreclosure.

(3) In a case in which state law that is applicable to the debtor—

(A) permits a person to voluntarily waive a right to claim exemptions under subsection (d) or prohibits a debtor from claiming exemptions under subsection (d); and

(B) either permits the debtor to claim exemptions under state law without limitation in amount, except to the extent that the debtor has permitted the fixing of a consensual lien on any property or prohibits avoidance of a consensual lien on property otherwise eligible to be claimed as exempt property;

the debtor may not avoid the fixing of a lien on an interest of the debtor or a dependent of the debtor in property if the lien is a nonpossessory, nonpurchase-money security interest in implements, professional books, or tools of the trade of the debtor or a dependent of the debtor or farm animals or crops of the debtor or a dependent of the debtor to the extent the value of such implements, professional books, tools of the trade, animals, and crops exceeds $7,575.

(4) (A) Subject to subparagraph (B), for purposes of paragraph (1)(B), the term "household goods" means—

(i) clothing;

(ii) furniture;

(iii) appliances;

(iv) 1 radio;

(v) 1 television;

(vi) 1 VCR;

(vii) linens;

(viii) china;

(ix) crockery;

(x) kitchenware;

(xi) educational materials and educational equipment primarily for the use of minor dependent children of the debtor;

(xii) medical equipment and supplies;

(xiii) furniture exclusively for the use of minor children, or elderly or disabled dependents of the debtor;

(xiv) personal effects (including the toys and hobby equipment of minor dependent children and wedding rings) of the debtor and the dependents of the debtor; and

(xv) 1 personal computer and related equipment.

(B) The term "household goods" does not include—

(i) works of art (unless by or of the debtor, or any relative of the debtor);

(ii) electronic entertainment equipment with a fair market value of more than $800 in the aggregate (except 1 television, 1 radio, and 1 VCR);

(iii) items acquired as antiques with a fair market value of more than $800 in the aggregate;

(iv) jewelry with a fair market value of more than $800 in the aggregate (except wedding rings); and

(v) a computer (except as otherwise provided for in this section), motor vehicle (including a tractor or lawn tractor), boat, or a motorized recreational device, conveyance, vehicle, watercraft, or aircraft.

(g) Notwithstanding sections 550 and 551 of this title, the debtor may exempt under subsection (b) of this section property that the trustee recovers under section 510(c)(2), 542, 543, 550, 551, or 553 of this title, to the extent that the debtor could have exempted such property under subsection (b) of this section if such property had not been transferred, if—

(1) (A) such transfer was not a voluntary transfer of such property by the debtor; and

(B) the debtor did not conceal such property; or

(2) the debtor could have avoided such transfer under subsection (f)(1)(B) of this section.

(h) The debtor may avoid a transfer of property of the debtor or recover a setoff to the extent that the debtor could have exempted such property under subsection (g)(1) of this section if the trustee had avoided such transfer, if—

(1) such transfer is avoidable by the trustee under section 544, 545, 547, 548, 549, or 724(a) of this title or recoverable by the trustee under section 553 of this title; and

(2) the trustee does not attempt to avoid such transfer.

(i)(1) If the debtor avoids a transfer or recovers a setoff under subsection (f) or (h) of this section, the debtor may recover in the manner prescribed by, and subject to the limitations of, section 550 of this title, the same as if the trustee had avoided such transfer, and may exempt any property so recovered under subsection (b) of this section.

(2) Notwithstanding section 551 of this title, a transfer avoided under section 544, 545, 547, 548, 549, or 724(a) of this title, under subsection (f) or (h) of this section, or property recovered under section 553 of this title, may be preserved for the benefit of the debtor to the extent that the debtor may exempt such property under subsection (g) of this section or paragraph (1) of this subsection.

(j) Notwithstanding subsections (g) and (i) of this section, the debtor may exempt a particular kind of property under subsections (g) and (i) of this section only to the extent that the debtor has exempted less property in value of such kind than that to which the debtor is entitled under subsection (b) of this section.

(k) Property that the debtor exempts under this section is not liable for payment of any administrative expense except—

(1) the aliquot share of the costs and expenses of avoiding a transfer of property that

the debtor exempts under subsection (g) of this section, or of recovery of such property, that is attributable to the value of the portion of such property exempted in relation to the value of the property recovered; and

(2) any costs and expenses of avoiding a transfer under subsection (f) or (h) of this section, or of recovery of property under subsection (i)(1) of this section, that the debtor has not paid.

(l) The debtor shall file a list of property that the debtor claims as exempt under subsection (b) of this section. If the debtor does not file such a list, a dependent of the debtor may file such a list, or may claim property as exempt from property of the estate on behalf of the debtor. Unless a party in interest objects, the property claimed as exempt on such list is exempt.

(m) Subject to the limitation in subsection (b), this section shall apply separately with respect to each debtor in a joint case.

(n) For assets in individual retirement accounts described in section 408 or 408A of the Internal Revenue Code of 1986, other than a simplified employee pension under section 408(k) of such Code or a simple retirement account under section 408(p) of such Code, the aggregate value of such assets exempted under this section, without regard to amounts attributable to rollover contributions under section 402(c), 402(e)(6), 403(a)(4), 403(a)(5), and 403(b)(8) of the Internal Revenue Code of 1986, and earnings thereon, shall not exceed $1,512,350 in a case filed by a debtor who is an individual, except that such amount may be increased if the interests of justice so require.

(o) For purposes of subsection (b)(3)(A), and notwithstanding subsection (a), the value of an interest in—

(1) real or personal property that the debtor or a dependent of the debtor uses as a residence;

(2) a cooperative that owns property that the debtor or a dependent of the debtor uses as a residence;

(3) a burial plot for the debtor or a dependent of the debtor; or

(4) real or personal property that the debtor or a dependent of the debtor claims as a homestead; shall be reduced to the extent that such value is attributable to any portion of any property that the debtor disposed of in the 10-year period ending on the date of the filing of the petition with the intent to hinder, delay, or defraud a creditor and that the debtor could not exempt, or that portion that the debtor could not exempt, under subsection (b), if on such date the debtor had held the property so disposed of.

(p)(1) Except as provided in paragraph (2) of this subsection and sections 544 and 548, as a result of electing under subsection (b)(3)(A) to exempt property under State or local law, a debtor may not exempt any amount of interest that was acquired by the debtor during the 1215-day period preceding the date of the filing of the petition that exceeds in the aggregate $189,050 in value in—

(A) real or personal property that the debtor or a dependent of the debtor uses as a residence;

(B) a cooperative that owns property that the debtor or a dependent of the debtor uses as a residence;

(C) a burial plot for the debtor or a dependent of the debtor; or

(D) real or personal property that the debtor or dependent of the debtor claims as a homestead.

(2) (A) The limitation under paragraph (1) shall not apply to an exemption claimed under subsection (b)(3)(A) by a family farmer for the principal residence of such farmer.

(B) For purposes of paragraph (1), any amount of such interest does not include any interest transferred from a debtor's previous principal residence (which was acquired prior to the beginning of such 1215-day period) into the debtor's current principal residence, if the debtor's previous and current residences are located in the same State.

(q)(1) As a result of electing under subsection (b)(3)(A) to exempt property under State or local law, a debtor may not exempt any amount of an interest in property described in subparagraphs (A), (B), (C), and (D) of subsection (p)(1) which exceeds in the aggregate $189,050 if—

(A) the court determines, after notice and a hearing, that the debtor has been convicted of a felony (as defined in section 3156 of title 18), which under the circumstances, demonstrates that the filing of the case was an abuse of the provisions of this title; or

(B) the debtor owes a debt arising from—

(i) any violation of the Federal securities laws (as defined in section

3(a)(47) of the Securities Exchange Act of 1934), any State securities laws, or any regulation or order issued under Federal securities laws or State securities laws;

(ii) fraud, deceit, or manipulation in a fiduciary capacity or in connection with the purchase or sale of any security registered under section 12 or 15(d) of the Securities Exchange Act of 1934 or under section 6 of the Securities Act of 1933;

(iii) any civil remedy under section 1964 of title 18; or

(iv) any criminal act, intentional tort, or willful or reckless misconduct that caused serious physical injury or death to another individual in the preceding 5 years.

(2) Paragraph (1) shall not apply to the extent the amount of an interest in property described in subparagraphs (A), (B), (C), and (D) of subsection (p)(1) is reasonably necessary for the support of the debtor and any dependent of the debtor.

§ 523. Exceptions to Discharge

(a) A discharge under section 727, 1141, 1192, 1228(a), 1228(b), or 1328(b) of this title does not discharge an individual debtor from any debt—

(1) for a tax or a customs duty—

(A) of the kind and for the periods specified in section 507(a)(3) or 507(a)(8) of this title, whether or not a claim for such tax was filed or allowed;

(B) with respect to which a return, or equivalent report or notice, if required—

(i) was not filed or given; or

(ii) was filed or given after the date on which such return, report, or notice was last due, under applicable law or under any extension, and after two years before the date of the filing of the petition; or

(C) with respect to which the debtor made a fraudulent return or willfully attempted in any manner to evade or defeat such tax;

(2) for money, property, services, or an extension, renewal, or refinancing of credit, to the extent obtained by—

(A) false pretenses, a false representation, or actual fraud, other than a statement respecting the debtor's or an insider's financial condition;

(B) use of a statement in writing—

(i) that is materially false;

(ii) respecting the debtor's or an insider's financial condition;

(iii) on which the creditor to whom the debtor is liable for such money, property, services, or credit reasonably relied; and

(iv) that the debtor caused to be made or published with intent to deceive; or

(C)(i) for purposes of subparagraph (A)—

(I) consumer debts owed to a single creditor and aggregating more than $800 for luxury goods or services incurred by an individual debtor on or within 90 days before the order for relief under this title are presumed to be nondischargeable; and

(II) cash advances aggregating more than $1,100 that are extensions of consumer credit under an open end credit plan obtained by an individual debtor on or within 70 days before the order for relief under this title, are presumed to be nondischargeable; and

(ii) for purposes of this subparagraph—

(I) the terms "consumer", "credit", and "open end credit plan" have the same meanings as in section 103 of the Truth in Lending Act; and

(II) the term "luxury goods or services" does not include goods or services reasonably necessary for the support or maintenance of the debtor or a dependent of the debtor;

(3) neither listed nor scheduled under section 521(a)(1) of this title, with the name, if known to the debtor, of the creditor to whom such debt is owed, in time to permit—

(A) if such debt is not of a kind specified in paragraph (2), (4), or (6) of this subsection, timely filing of a proof of claim, unless such creditor had notice or actual knowledge of the case in time for such timely filing; or

(B) if such debt is of a kind specified in paragraph (2), (4), or (6) of this subsection, timely filing of a proof of claim and timely request for a determination of dischargeability of such debt under one of such paragraphs, unless such creditor had notice or actual knowledge of the case in time for such timely filing and request;

(4) for fraud or defalcation while acting in a fiduciary capacity, embezzlement, or larceny;

(5) for a domestic support obligation;

(6) for willful and malicious injury by the debtor to another entity or to the property of another entity;

(7) to the extent such debt is for a fine, penalty, or forfeiture payable to and for the benefit of a governmental unit, and is not compensation for actual pecuniary loss, other than a tax penalty—

(A) relating to a tax of a kind not specified in paragraph (1) of this subsection; or

(B) imposed with respect to a transaction or event that occurred before three years before the date of the filing of the petition;

(8) unless excepting such debt from discharge under this paragraph would impose an undue hardship on the debtor and the debtor's dependents, for—

(A) (i) an educational benefit overpayment or loan made, insured, or guaranteed by a governmental unit, or made under any program funded in whole or in part by a governmental unit or nonprofit institution; or

(ii) an obligation to repay funds received as an educational benefit, scholarship, or stipend; or

(B) any other educational loan that is a qualified education loan, as defined in section 221(d)(1) of the Internal Revenue Code of 1986, incurred by a debtor who is an individual;

(9) for death or personal injury caused by the debtor's operation of a motor vehicle, vessel, or aircraft if such operation was unlawful because the debtor was intoxicated from using alcohol, a drug, or another substance;

(10) that was or could have been listed or scheduled by the debtor in a prior case concerning the debtor under this title or under the Bankruptcy Act in which the debtor waived discharge, or was denied a discharge under section 727(a)(2), (3), (4), (5), (6), or (7) of this title, or under section 14c(1), (2), (3), (4), (6), or (7) of such Act;

(11) provided in any final judgment, unreviewable order, or consent order or decree entered in any court of the United States or of any state, issued by a Federal depository institutions regulatory agency, or contained in any settlement agreement entered into by the debtor, arising from any act of fraud or defalcation while acting in a fiduciary capacity committed with respect to any depository institution or insured credit union;

(12) for malicious or reckless failure to fulfill any commitment by the debtor to a Federal depository institutions regulatory agency to maintain the capital of an insured depository institution, except that this paragraph shall not extend any such commitment which would otherwise be terminated due to any act of such agency;

(13) for any payment of an order of restitution issued under title 18, United States Code;

(14) incurred to pay a tax to the United States that would be nondischargeable pursuant to paragraph (1);

(14A) incurred to pay a tax to a governmental unit, other than the United States, that would be nondischargeable under paragraph (1);

(14B) incurred to pay fines or penalties imposed under Federal election law;

(15) to a spouse, former spouse, or child of the debtor and not of the kind described in paragraph (5) that is incurred by the debtor in the course of a divorce or separation or in connection with a separation agreement, divorce decree or other order of a court of record, or a determination made in accordance with state or territorial law by a governmental unit;

(16) for a fee or assessment that becomes due and payable after the order for relief to a membership association with respect to the debtor's interest in a unit that has condominium ownership, in a share of a cooperative corporation, or a lot in a homeowners association, for as long as the debtor or the trustee has a legal, equitable, or possessory ownership interest in such unit, such corporation, or such lot, but nothing in this paragraph shall except from discharge the debt of a debtor for a membership association fee or assessment for a period

arising before entry of the order for relief in a pending or subsequent bankruptcy case.

(17) for a fee imposed on a prisoner by any court for the filing of a case, motion, complaint, or appeal, or for other costs and expenses assessed with respect to such filing, regardless of an assertion of poverty by the debtor under subsection (b) or (f)(2) of section 1915 of title 28 (or a similar non-Federal law), or the debtor's status as a prisoner, as defined in section 1915(h) of title 28 (or a similar non-Federal law);

(18) owed to a pension, profit-sharing, stock bonus, or other plan established under section 401, 403, 408, 408A, 414, 457, or 501(c) of the Internal Revenue Code of 1986, under—

(A) a loan permitted under section 408(b)(1) of the Employee Retirement Income Security Act of 1974, or subject to section 72(p) of the Internal Revenue Code of 1986; or

(B) a loan from a thrift savings plan permitted under subchapter III of chapter 84 of title 5, that satisfies the requirements of section 8433(g) of such title; but nothing in this paragraph may be construed to provide that any loan made under a governmental plan under section 414(d), or a contract or account under section 403(b), of the Internal Revenue Code of 1986 constitutes a claim or a debt under this title; or

(19) that—

(A) is for—

(i) the violation of any of the Federal securities laws (as that term is defined in section 3(a)(47) of the Securities Exchange Act of 1934), any of the State securities laws, or any regulation or order issued under such Federal or State securities laws; or

(ii) common law fraud, deceit, or manipulation in connection with the purchase or sale of any security; and

(B) results, before, on, or after the date on which the petition was filed, from—

(i) any judgment, order, consent order, or decree entered in any Federal or State judicial or administrative proceeding;

(ii) any settlement agreement entered into by the debtor;

(iii) any court or administrative order for any damages, fine, penalty, citation, restitutionary payment, disgorgement payment, attorney fee, cost, or other payment owed by the debtor; or

(20) for injury to an individual by the debtor relating to a violation of chapter 77 of title 18, including injury caused by an instance in which the debtor knowingly benefitted financially, or by receiving anything of value, from participation in a venture that the debtor knew or should have known engaged in an act in violation of chapter 77 of title 18.

For purposes of this subsection, the term "return" means a return that satisfies the requirements of applicable nonbankruptcy law (including applicable filing requirements). Such term includes a return prepared pursuant to section 6020(a) of the Internal Revenue Code of 1986, or similar State or local law, or a written stipulation to a judgment or a final order entered by a nonbankruptcy tribunal, but does not include a return made pursuant to section 6020(b) of the Internal Revenue Code of 1986, or a similar State or local law.

(b) Notwithstanding subsection (a) of this section, a debt that was excepted from discharge under subsection (a)(1), (a)(3), or (a)(8) of this section, under section 17a(1), 17a(3), or 17a(5) of the Bankruptcy Act, under section 439A of the Higher Education Act of 1965, or under section 733(g) of the Public Health Service Act in a prior case concerning the debtor under this title, or under the Bankruptcy Act, is dischargeable in a case under this title unless, by the terms of subsection (a) of this section, such debt is not dischargeable in the case under this title.

(c)(1) Except as provided in subsection (a)(3)(B) of this section, the debtor shall be discharged from a debt of a kind specified in paragraph (2), (4), or (6) of subsection (a) of this section, unless, on request of the creditor to whom such debt is owed, and after notice and a hearing, the court determines such debt to be excepted from discharge under paragraph (2), (4), or (6), as the case may be, of subsection (a) of this section.

(2) Paragraph (1) shall not apply in the case of a Federal depository institutions regulatory agency seeking, in its capacity as conservator, receiver, or liquidating agent for

an insured depository institution, to recover a debt described in subsection (a)(2), (a)(4), (a)(6), or (a)(11) owed to such institution by an institution-affiliated party unless the receiver, conservator, or liquidating agent was appointed in time to reasonably comply, or for a Federal depository institutions regulatory agency acting in its corporate capacity as a successor to such receiver, conservator, or liquidating agent to reasonably comply, with subsection (a)(3)(B) as a creditor of such institution-affiliated party with respect to such debt.

(d) If a creditor requests a determination of dischargeability of a consumer debt under subsection (a)(2) of this section, and such debt is discharged, the court shall grant judgment in favor of the debtor for the costs of, and a reasonable attorney's fee for, the proceeding if the court finds that the position of the creditor was not substantially justified, except that the court shall not award such costs and fees if special circumstances would make the award unjust.

(e) Any institution-affiliated party of an insured depository institution shall be considered to be acting in a fiduciary capacity with respect to the purposes of subsection (a)(4) or (11).

§ 524. Effect of Discharge

(a) A discharge in a case under this title—

(1) voids any judgment at any time obtained, to the extent that such judgment is a determination of the personal liability of the debtor with respect to any debt discharged under section 727, 944, 1141, 1192, 1228, or 1328 of this title, whether or not discharge of such debt is waived;

(2) operates as an injunction against the commencement or continuation of an action, the employment of process, or an act, to collect, recover or offset any such debt as a personal liability of the debtor, whether or not discharge of such debt is waived; and

(3) operates as an injunction against the commencement or continuation of an action, the employment of process, or an act, to collect or recover from, or offset against, property of the debtor of the kind specified in section 541(a)(2) of this title that is acquired after the commencement of the case, on account of any allowable community claim, except a community claim that is excepted from discharge under section 523, 1192, 1228(a)(1), or 1328(a)(1), or that would be so excepted, determined in accordance with the provisions of sections 523(c) and 523(d) of this title, in a case concerning the debtor's spouse commenced on the date of the filing of the petition in the case concerning the debtor, whether or not discharge of the debt based on such community claim is waived.

(b) Subsection (a)(3) of this section does not apply if—

(1) (A) the debtor's spouse is a debtor in a case under this title, or a bankrupt or a debtor in a case under the Bankruptcy Act, commenced within six years of the date of the filing of the petition in the case concerning the debtor; and

(B) the court does not grant the debtor's spouse a discharge in such case concerning the debtor's spouse; or

(2) (A) the court would not grant the debtor's spouse a discharge in a case under chapter 7 of this title concerning such spouse commenced on the date of the filing of the petition in the case concerning the debtor; and

(B) a determination that the court would not so grant such discharge is made by the bankruptcy court within the time and in the manner provided for a determination under section 727 of this title of whether a debtor is granted a discharge.

(c) An agreement between a holder of a claim and the debtor, the consideration for which, in whole or in part, is based on a debt that is dischargeable in a case under this title is enforceable only to any extent enforceable under applicable nonbankruptcy law, whether or not discharge of such debt is waived, only if—

(1) such agreement was made before the granting of the discharge under section 727, 1192, 1141, 1228, or 1328 of this title;

(2) the debtor received the disclosures described in subsection (k) at or before the time at which the debtor signed the agreement;

(3) such agreement has been filed with the court and, if applicable, accompanied by a declaration or an affidavit of the attorney that represented the debtor during the course of negotiating an agreement under this subsection, which states that—

(A) such agreement represents a fully informed and voluntary agreement by the debtor;

(B) such agreement does not impose an undue hardship on the debtor or a dependent of the debtor; and

(C) the attorney fully advised the debtor of the legal effect and consequences of—

(i) an agreement of the kind specified in this subsection; and

(ii) any default under such an agreement;

(4) the debtor has not rescinded such agreement at any time prior to discharge or within sixty days after such agreement is filed with the court, whichever occurs later, by giving notice of rescission to the holder of such claim;

(5) the provisions of subsection (d) of this section have been complied with; and

(6) (A) in a case concerning an individual who was not represented by an attorney during the course of negotiating an agreement under this subsection, the court approves such agreement as—

(i) not imposing an undue hardship on the debtor or a dependent of the debtor; and

(ii) in the best interest of the debtor.

(B) Subparagraph (A) shall not apply to the extent that such debt is a consumer debt secured by real property.

(d) In a case concerning an individual, when the court has determined whether to grant or not to grant a discharge under section 727, 1141, 1192, 1228, or 1328 of this title, the court may hold a hearing at which the debtor shall appear in person. At any such hearing, the court shall inform the debtor that a discharge has been granted or the reason why a discharge has not been granted. If a discharge has been granted and if the debtor desires to make an agreement of the kind specified in subsection (c) of this section and was not represented by an attorney during the course of negotiating such agreement, then the court shall hold a hearing at which the debtor shall appear in person and at such hearing the court shall—

(1) inform the debtor—

(A) that such an agreement is not required under this title, under nonbankruptcy law, or under any agreement not made in accordance with the provisions of subsection (c) of this section; and

(B) of the legal effect and consequences of—

(i) an agreement of the kind specified in subsection (c) of this section; and

(ii) a default under such an agreement; and

(2) determine whether the agreement that the debtor desires to make complies with the requirements of subsection (c)(6) of this section, if the consideration for such agreement is based in whole or in part on a consumer debt that is not secured by real property of the debtor.

(e) Except as provided in subsection (a)(3) of this section, discharge of a debt of the debtor does not affect the liability of any other entity on, or the property of any other entity for, such debt.

(f) Nothing contained in subsection (c) or (d) of this section prevents a debtor from voluntarily repaying any debt.

(g)(1)(A) After notice and hearing, a court that enters an order confirming a plan of reorganization under chapter 11 may issue, in connection with such order, an injunction in accordance with this subsection to supplement the injunctive effect of a discharge under this section.

(B) An injunction may be issued under subparagraph (A) to enjoin entities from taking legal action for the purpose of directly or indirectly collecting, recovering, or receiving payment or recovery with respect to any claim or demand that, under a plan of reorganization, is to be paid in whole or in part by a trust described in paragraph (2)(B)(i), except such legal actions as are expressly allowed by the injunction, the confirmation order, or the plan of reorganization.

(2) (A) Subject to subsection (h), if the requirements of subparagraph (B) are met at the time an injunction described in paragraph (1) is entered, then after entry of such injunction, any proceeding that involves the validity, application, construction, or modification of such injunction, or of this subsection with respect to such injunction, may be commenced only in the district court in which such injunction was entered, and such court shall have exclusive jurisdiction over any such proceeding without regard to the amount in controversy.

(B) The requirements of this subparagraph are that—

(i) the injunction is to be implemented in connection with a trust that, pursuant to the plan of reorganization—

(I) is to assume the liabilities of a debtor which at the time of entry of the order for relief has been named as a defendant in personal injury, wrongful death, or property-damage actions seeking recovery for damages allegedly caused by the presence of, or exposure to, asbestos or asbestos-containing products;

(II) is to be funded in whole or in part by the securities of 1 or more debtors involved in such plan and by the obligation of such debtor or debtors to make future payments, including dividends;

(III) is to own, or by the exercise of rights granted under such plan would be entitled to own if specified contingencies occur, a majority of the voting shares of—

(aa) each such debtor;

(bb) the parent corporation of each such debtor; or

(cc) a subsidiary of each such debtor that is also a debtor; and

(IV) is to use its assets or income to pay claims and demands; and

(ii) subject to subsection (h), the court determines that—

(I) the debtor is likely to be subject to substantial future demands for payment arising out of the same or similar conduct or events that gave rise to the claims that are addressed by the injunction;

(II) the actual amounts, numbers, and timing of such future demands cannot be determined;

(III) pursuit of such demands outside the procedures prescribed by such plan is likely to threaten the plan's purpose to deal equitably with claims and future demands;

(IV) as part of the process of seeking confirmation of such plan—

(aa) the terms of the injunction proposed to be issued under paragraph (1)(A), including any provisions barring actions against third parties pursuant to paragraph (4)(A), are set out in such plan and in any disclosure statement supporting the plan; and

(bb) a separate class or classes of the claimants whose claims are to be addressed by a trust described in clause (i) is established and votes, by at least 75 percent of those voting, in favor of the plan; and

(V) subject to subsection (h), pursuant to court orders or otherwise, the trust will operate through mechanisms such as structured, periodic, or supplemental payments, pro rata distributions, matrices, or periodic review of estimates of the numbers and values of present claims and future demands, or other comparable mechanisms, that provide reasonable assurance that the trust will value, and be in a financial position to pay, present claims and future demands that involve similar claims in substantially the same manner.

(3) (A) If the requirements of paragraph (2)(B) are met and the order confirming the plan of reorganization was issued or affirmed by the district court that has jurisdiction over the reorganization case, then after the time for appeal of the order that issues or affirms the plan—

(i) the injunction shall be valid and enforceable and may not be revoked or modified by any court except through appeal in accordance with paragraph (6);

(ii) no entity that pursuant to such plan or thereafter becomes a direct or indirect transferee of, or successor to any assets of, a debtor or trust that is the subject of the injunction shall be liable with respect to any claim or demand made against such entity by reason of its becoming such a transferee or successor; and

(iii) no entity that pursuant to such plan or thereafter makes a loan to such a debtor or trust or to such a successor or transferee shall, by reason of making the loan, be liable with respect to any claim or demand made against such entity, nor shall any pledge of assets made in connection with such a loan be upset or impaired for that reason;

(B) Subparagraph (A) shall not be construed to—

(i) imply that an entity described in subparagraph (A)(ii) or (iii) would, if this paragraph were not applicable, necessarily be liable to any entity by reason of any of the acts described in subparagraph (A);

(ii) relieve any such entity of the duty to comply with, or of liability under, any Federal or state law regarding the making of a fraudulent conveyance in a transaction described in subparagraph (A)(ii) or (iii); or

(iii) relieve a debtor of the debtor's obligation to comply with the terms of the plan of reorganization, or affect the power of the court to exercise its authority under sections 1141 and 1142 to compel the debtor to do so.

(4) (A)(i) Subject to subparagraph (B), an injunction described in paragraph (1) shall be valid and enforceable against all entities that it addresses.

(ii) Notwithstanding the provisions of section 524(e), such an injunction may bar any action directed against a third party who is identifiable from the terms of such injunction (by name or as part of an identifiable group) and is alleged to be directly or indirectly liable for the conduct of, claims against, or demands on the debtor to the extent such alleged liability of such third party arises by reason of—

(I) the third party's ownership of a financial interest in the debtor, a past or present affiliate of the debtor, or a predecessor in interest of the debtor;

(II) the third party's involvement in the management of the debtor or a predecessor in interest of the debtor, or service as an officer, director or employee of the debtor or a related party;

(III) the third party's provision of insurance to the debtor or a related party; or

(IV) the third party's involvement in a transaction changing the corporate structure, or in a loan or other financial transaction affecting the financial condition, of the debtor or a related party, including but not limited to—

(aa) involvement in providing financing (debt or equity), or advice to an entity involved in such a transaction; or

(bb) acquiring or selling a financial interest in an entity as part of such a transaction.

(iii) As used in this subparagraph, the term "related party" means—

(I) a past or present affiliate of the debtor;

(II) a predecessor in interest of the debtor; or

(III) any entity that owned a financial interest in—

(aa) the debtor;

(bb) a past or present affiliate of the debtor; or

(cc) a predecessor in interest of the debtor.

(B) Subject to subsection (h), if, under a plan of reorganization, a kind of demand described in such plan is to be paid in whole or in part by a trust described in paragraph (2)(B)(i) in connection with which an injunction described in paragraph (1) is to be implemented, then such injunction shall be valid and enforceable with respect to a demand of such kind made, after such plan is confirmed, against the debtor or debtors involved, or against a third party described in subparagraph (A)(ii), if—

(i) as part of the proceedings leading to issuance of such injunction, the court appoints a legal representative for the purpose of protecting the rights of persons that might subsequently assert demands of such kind, and

(ii) the court determines, before entering the order confirming such plan, that identifying such debtor or debtors, or such third party (by name or as part of an identifiable group), in such injunction with respect to such demands for purposes of this subparagraph is fair and equitable with respect to the persons that might subsequently assert such demands, in light of the benefits provided, or to be provided, to such trust on behalf of such debtor or debtors or such third party.

(5) In this subsection, the term "demand" means a demand for payment, present or future, that—

(A) was not a claim during the proceedings leading to the confirmation of a plan of reorganization;

(B) arises out of the same or similar conduct or events that gave rise to the claims addressed by the injunction issued under paragraph (1); and

(C) pursuant to the plan, is to be paid by a trust described in paragraph (2)(B)(i).

(6) Paragraph (3)(A)(i) does not bar an action taken by or at the direction of an appellate court on appeal of an injunction issued under paragraph (1) or of the order of confirmation that relates to the injunction.

(7) This subsection does not affect the operation of section 1144 or the power of the district court to refer a proceeding under section 157 of title 28 or any reference of a proceeding made prior to the date of the enactment of this subsection.

(h) Application to existing injunctions.—For purposes of subsection (g)—

(1) subject to paragraph (2), if an injunction of the kind described in subsection (g)(1)(B) was issued before the date of the enactment of this Act, as part of a plan of reorganization confirmed by an order entered before such date, then the injunction shall be considered to meet the requirements of subsection (g)(2)(B) for purposes of subsection (g)(2)(A), and to satisfy subsection (g)(4)(A)(ii), if—

(A) the court determined at the time the plan was confirmed that the plan was fair and equitable in accordance with the requirements of section 1129(b);

(B) as part of the proceedings leading to issuance of such injunction and confirmation of such plan, the court had appointed a legal representative for the purpose of protecting the rights of persons that might subsequently assert demands described in subsection (g)(4)(B) with respect to such plan; and

(C) such legal representative did not object to confirmation of such plan or issuance of such injunction; and

(2) for purposes of paragraph (1), if a trust described in subsection (g)(2)(B)(i) is subject to a court order on the date of the enactment of this Act staying such trust from settling or paying further claims—

(A) the requirements of subsection (g)(2)(B)(ii)(V) shall not apply with respect to such trust until such stay is lifted or dissolved; and

(B) if such trust meets such requirements on the date such stay is lifted or dissolved, such trust shall be considered to have met such requirements continuously from the date of the enactment of this Act.

(i) The willful failure of a creditor to credit payments received under a plan confirmed under this title, unless the order confirming the plan is revoked, the plan is in default, or the creditor has not received payments required to be made under the plan in the manner required by the plan (including crediting the amounts required under the plan), shall constitute a violation of an injunction under subsection (a)(2) if the act of the creditor to collect and failure to credit payments in the manner required by the plan caused material injury to the debtor.

(j) Subsection (a)(2) does not operate as an injunction against an act by a creditor that is the holder of a secured claim, if—

(1) such creditor retains a security interest in real property that is the principal residence of the debtor;

(2) such act is in the ordinary course of business between the creditor and the debtor; and

(3) such act is limited to seeking or obtaining periodic payments associated with a valid security interest in lieu of pursuit of in rem relief to enforce the lien.

(k)(1) The disclosures required under subsection (c)(2) shall consist of the disclosure statement described in paragraph (3), completed as required in that paragraph, together with the agreement specified in subsection (c), statement, declaration, motion and order described, respectively, in paragraphs (4) through (8), and shall be the only disclosures required in connection with entering into such agreement.

(2) Disclosures made under paragraph (1) shall be made clearly and conspicuously and in writing. The terms "Amount Reaffirmed" and "Annual Percentage Rate" shall be disclosed more conspicuously than other terms,

data or information provided in connection with this disclosure, except that the phrases "Before agreeing to reaffirm a debt, review these important disclosures" and "Summary of Reaffirmation Agreement" may be equally conspicuous. Disclosures may be made in a different order and may use terminology different from that set forth in paragraphs (2) through (8), except that the terms "Amount Reaffirmed" and "Annual Percentage Rate" must be used where indicated.

(3) The disclosure statement required under this paragraph shall consist of the following:

(A) The statement: "Part A: Before agreeing to reaffirm a debt, review these important disclosures:";

(B) Under the heading "Summary of Reaffirmation Agreement", the statement: "This Summary is made pursuant to the requirements of the Bankruptcy Code";

(C) The "Amount Reaffirmed", using that term, which shall be—

(i) the total amount of debt that the debtor agrees to reaffirm by entering into an agreement of the kind specified in subsection (c), and

(ii) the total of any fees and costs accrued as of the date of the disclosure statement, related to such total amount.

(D) In conjunction with the disclosure of the "Amount Reaffirmed", the statements—

(i) "The amount of debt you have agreed to reaffirm"; and

(ii) "Your credit agreement may obligate you to pay additional amounts which may come due after the date of this disclosure. Consult your credit agreement.".

(E) The "Annual Percentage Rate", using that term, which shall be disclosed as—

(i) if, at the time the petition is filed, the debt is an extension of credit under an open end credit plan, as the terms "credit" and "open end credit plan" are defined in section 103 of the Truth in Lending Act, then—

(I) the annual percentage rate determined under paragraphs (5) and (6) of section 127(b) of the Truth in Lending Act, as applicable, as disclosed to the debtor in the most recent periodic statement prior to entering into an agreement of the kind specified in subsection (c) or, if no such periodic statement has been given to the debtor during the prior 6 months, the annual percentage rate as it would have been so disclosed at the time the disclosure statement is given to the debtor, or to the extent this annual percentage rate is not readily available or not applicable, then

(II) the simple interest rate applicable to the amount reaffirmed as of the date the disclosure statement is given to the debtor, or if different simple interest rates apply to different balances, the simple interest rate applicable to each such balance, identifying the amount of each such balance included in the amount reaffirmed, or

(III) if the entity making the disclosure elects, to disclose the annual percentage rate under subclause (I) and the simple interest rate under subclause (II); or

(ii) if, at the time the petition is filed, the debt is an extension of credit other than under an open end credit plan, as the terms "credit" and "open end credit plan" are defined in section 103 of the Truth in Lending Act, then—

(I) the annual percentage rate under section 128(a)(4) of the Truth in Lending Act, as disclosed to the debtor in the most recent disclosure statement given to the debtor prior to the entering into an agreement of the kind specified in subsection (c) with respect to the debt, or, if no such disclosure statement was given to the debtor, the annual percentage rate as it would have been so disclosed at the time the disclosure statement is given to the debtor, or to the extent this annual percentage rate is not readily available or not applicable, then

(II) the simple interest rate applicable to the amount reaffirmed as of the date the disclosure statement is given to the debtor, or if different simple interest rates apply to different balances, the simple interest rate applicable to each such balance, identifying the amount of such balance included in the amount reaffirmed, or

(III) if the entity making the disclosure elects, to disclose the annual percentage rate under (I) and the simple interest rate under (II).

(F) If the underlying debt transaction was disclosed as a variable rate transaction on the most recent disclosure given under the Truth in Lending Act, by stating "The interest rate on your loan may be a variable interest rate which changes from time to time, so that the annual percentage rate disclosed here may be higher or lower.".

(G) If the debt is secured by a security interest which has not been waived in whole or in part or determined to be void by a final order of the court at the time of the disclosure, by disclosing that a security interest or lien in goods or property is asserted over some or all of the debts the debtor is reaffirming and listing the items and their original purchase price that are subject to the asserted security interest, or if not a purchase-money security interest then listing by items or types and the original amount of the loan.

(H) At the election of the creditor, a statement of the repayment schedule using 1 or a combination of the following—

(i) by making the statement: "Your first payment in the amount of $______ is due on ______ but the future payment amount may be different. Consult your reaffirmation agreement or credit agreement, as applicable.", and stating the amount of the first payment and the due date of that payment in the places provided;

(ii) by making the statement: "Your payment schedule will be:", and describing the repayment schedule with the number, amount, and due dates or period of payments scheduled to repay the debts reaffirmed to the extent then known by the disclosing party; or

(iii) by describing the debtor's repayment obligations with reasonable specificity to the extent then known by the disclosing party.

(I) The following statement:

"Note: When this disclosure refers to what a creditor 'may' do, it does not use the word 'may' to give the creditor specific permission. The word 'may' is used to tell you what might occur if the law permits the creditor to take the action. If you have questions about your reaffirming a debt or what the law requires, consult with the attorney who helped you negotiate this agreement reaffirming a debt. If you don't have an attorney helping you, the judge will explain the effect of your reaffirming a debt when the hearing on the reaffirmation agreement is held.".

(J) (i) The following additional statements:

"Reaffirming a debt is a serious financial decision. The law requires you to take certain steps to make sure the decision is in your best interest. If these steps are not completed, the reaffirmation agreement is not effective, even though you have signed it.

"1. Read the disclosures in this Part A carefully. Consider the decision to reaffirm carefully. Then, if you want to reaffirm, sign the reaffirmation agreement in Part B (or you may use a separate agreement you and your creditor agree on).

"2. Complete and sign Part D and be sure you can afford to make the payments you are agreeing to make and have received a copy of the disclosure statement and a completed and signed reaffirmation agreement.

"3. If you were represented by an attorney during the negotiation of your reaffirmation agreement, the attorney must have signed the certification in Part C.

"4. If you were not represented by an attorney during the negotiation of your reaffirmation agreement, you must have completed and signed Part E.

"5. The original of this disclosure must be filed with the court by you or your creditor. If a separate reaffirmation agreement (other than the one in Part B) has been signed, it must be attached.

"6. If you were represented by an attorney during the negotiation of your reaffirmation agreement, your reaffirmation agreement becomes effective upon filing with the court unless the reaffirmation is presumed to be an undue hardship as explained in Part D.

"7. If you were not represented by an attorney during the negotiation of your reaffirmation agreement, it will not be effective unless the court approves it. The court will notify you of the hearing on your reaffirmation agreement. You must attend this hearing in bankruptcy court where the judge will review your reaffirmation agreement. The bankruptcy court must approve your reaffirmation agreement as consistent with your best interests, except that no court approval is required if your reaffirmation agreement is for a consumer debt secured by a mortgage, deed of trust, security deed, or other lien on your real property, like your home.

"Your right to rescind (cancel) your reaffirmation agreement. You may rescind (cancel) your reaffirmation agreement at any time before the bankruptcy court enters a discharge order, or before the expiration of the 60-day period that begins on the date your reaffirmation agreement is filed with the court, whichever occurs later. To rescind (cancel) your reaffirmation agreement, you must notify the creditor that your reaffirmation agreement is rescinded (or canceled).

"What are your obligations if you reaffirm the debt? A reaffirmed debt remains your personal legal obligation. It is not discharged in your bankruptcy case. That means that if you default on your reaffirmed debt after your bankruptcy case is over, your creditor may be able to take your property or your wages. Otherwise, your obligations will be determined by the reaffirmation agreement which may have changed the terms of the original agreement. For example, if you are reaffirming an open end credit agreement, the creditor may be permitted by that agreement or applicable law to change the terms of that agreement in the future under certain conditions.

"Are you required to enter into a reaffirmation agreement by any law? No, you are not required to reaffirm a debt by any law. Only agree to reaffirm a debt if it is in your best interest. Be sure you can afford the payments you agree to make.

"What if your creditor has a security interest or lien? Your bankruptcy discharge does not eliminate any lien on your property. A 'lien' is often referred to as a security interest, deed of trust, mortgage or security deed. Even if you do not reaffirm and your personal liability on the debt is discharged, because of the lien your creditor may still have the right to take the property securing the lien if you do not pay the debt or default on it. If the lien is on an item of personal property that is exempt under your State's law or that the trustee has abandoned, you may be able to redeem the item rather than reaffirm the debt. To redeem, you must make a single payment to the creditor equal to the amount of the allowed secured claim, as agreed by the parties or determined by the court.".

(ii) In the case of a reaffirmation under subsection (m)(2), numbered paragraph 6 in the disclosures required by clause (i) of this subparagraph shall read as follows:

"6. If you were represented by an attorney during the negotiation of your reaffirmation agreement, your reaffirmation agreement becomes effective upon filing with the court.".

(4) The form of such agreement required under this paragraph shall consist of the following:

"**Part B:** Reaffirmation Agreement. I (we) agree to reaffirm the debts arising under the credit agreement described below.

"Brief description of credit agreement:

"Description of any changes to the credit agreement made as part of this reaffirmation agreement:

"Signature:

Date:

"Borrower:

"Co-borrower, if also reaffirming these debts:

"Accepted by creditor:

"Date of creditor acceptance:".

(5) The declaration shall consist of the following:

(A) The following certification:

"**Part C:** Certification by Debtor's Attorney (If Any)."I hereby certify that (1) this agreement represents a fully informed and voluntary agreement by the debtor;

(2) this agreement does not impose an undue hardship on the debtor or any dependent of the debtor; and

(3) I have fully advised the debtor of the legal effect and consequences of this agreement and any default under this agreement.

"Signature of Debtor's Attorney:

Date:".

(B) If a presumption of undue hardship has been established with respect to such agreement, such certification shall state that, in the opinion of the attorney, the debtor is able to make the payment.

(C) In the case of a reaffirmation agreement under subsection (m)(2), subparagraph (B) is not applicable.

(6) (A) The statement in support of such agreement, which the debtor shall sign and date prior to filing with the court, shall consist of the following:

"Part D: Debtor's Statement in Support of Reaffirmation Agreement.

"1. I believe this reaffirmation agreement will not impose an undue hardship on my dependents or me. I can afford to make the payments on the reaffirmed debt because my monthly income (take home pay plus any other income received) is $______, and my actual current monthly expenses including monthly payments on postbankruptcy debt and other reaffirmation agreements total $______, leaving $______ to make the required payments on this reaffirmed debt. I understand that if my income less my monthly expenses does not leave enough to make the payments, this reaffirmation agreement is presumed to be an undue hardship on me and must be reviewed by the court. However, this presumption may be overcome if I explain to the satisfaction of the court how I can afford to make the payments here: ______.

"2. I received a copy of the Reaffirmation Disclosure Statement in Part A and a completed and signed reaffirmation agreement.".

(B) Where the debtor is represented by an attorney and is reaffirming a debt owed to a creditor defined in section 19(b)(1)(A)(iv) of the Federal Reserve Act, the statement of support of the reaffirmation agreement, which the debtor shall sign and date prior to filing with the court, shall consist of the following:

"I believe this reaffirmation agreement is in my financial interest. I can afford to make the payments on the reaffirmed debt. I received a copy of the Reaffirmation Disclosure Statement in Part A and a completed and signed reaffirmation agreement.".

(7) The motion that may be used if approval of such agreement by the court is required in order for it to be effective, shall be signed and dated by the movant and shall consist of the following:

"Part E: Motion for Court Approval (To be completed only if the debtor is not represented by an attorney.). I (we), the debtor(s), affirm the following to be true and correct:

"I am not represented by an attorney in connection with this reaffirmation agreement.

"I believe this reaffirmation agreement is in my best interest based on the income and expenses I have disclosed in my Statement in Support of this reaffirmation agreement, and because (provide any additional relevant reasons the court should consider):

"Therefore, I ask the court for an order approving this reaffirmation agreement.".

(8) The court order, which may be used to approve such agreement, shall consist of the following:

"Court Order: The court grants the debtor's motion and approves the reaffirmation agreement described above.".

(l) Notwithstanding any other provision of this title the following shall apply:

(1) A creditor may accept payments from a debtor before and after the filing of an agreement of the kind specified in subsection (c) with the court.

(2) A creditor may accept payments from a debtor under such agreement that the creditor believes in good faith to be effective.

(3) The requirements of subsections (c)(2) and (k) shall be satisfied if disclosures required under those subsections are given in good faith.

(m)(1) Until 60 days after an agreement of the kind specified in subsection (c) is filed with the court (or such additional period as the court, after notice and a hearing and for cause, orders before the expiration of such period), it shall be presumed that such agreement is an undue hardship on the debtor if the debtor's monthly income less the debtor's monthly expenses as shown on the debtor's completed and signed statement in support of such agreement required under subsection (k)(6)(A) is less than the scheduled payments on the reaffirmed debt. This presumption shall be reviewed by the court. The presumption may be rebutted in writing by the debtor if the statement includes an explanation that identifies additional sources of funds to make the payments as agreed upon under the terms of such agreement. If the presumption is not rebutted to the satisfaction of the court, the court may disapprove such agreement. No agreement shall be disapproved without notice and a hearing to the debtor and creditor, and such hearing shall be concluded before the entry of the debtor's discharge.

(2) This subsection does not apply to reaffirmation agreements where the creditor is a credit union, as defined in section 19(b)(1)(A)(iv) of the Federal Reserve Act.

§ 525. Protection Against Discriminatory Treatment

(a) Except as provided in the Perishable Agricultural Commodities Act, 1930, the Packers and Stockyards Act, 1921, and section 1 of the Act entitled "An Act making appropriations for the Department of Agriculture for the fiscal year ending June 30, 1944, and for other purposes," approved July 12, 1943, a governmental unit may not deny, revoke, suspend, or refuse to renew a license, permit, charter, franchise, or other similar grant to, condition such a grant to, discriminate with respect to such a grant against, deny employment to, terminate the employment of, or discriminate with respect to employment against, a person that is or has been a debtor under this title or a bankrupt or a debtor under the Bankruptcy Act, or another person with whom such bankrupt or debtor has been associated, solely because such bankrupt or debtor is or has been a debtor under this title or a bankrupt or debtor under the Bankruptcy Act, has been insolvent before the commencement of the case under this title, or during the case but before the debtor is granted or denied a discharge, or has not paid a debt that is dischargeable in the case under this title or that was discharged under the Bankruptcy Act.

(b) No private employer may terminate the employment of, or discriminate with respect to employment against, an individual who is or has been a debtor under this title, a debtor or bankrupt under the Bankruptcy Act, or an individual associated with such debtor or bankrupt, solely because such debtor or bankrupt—

(1) is or has been a debtor under this title or a debtor or bankrupt under the Bankruptcy Act;

(2) has been insolvent before the commencement of a case under this title or during the case but before the grant or denial of a discharge; or

(3) has not paid a debt that is dischargeable in a case under this title or that was discharged under the Bankruptcy Act.

(c)(1) A governmental unit that operates a student grant or loan program and a person engaged in a business that includes the making of loans guaranteed or insured under a student loan program may not deny a student grant, loan, loan guarantee, or loan insurance to a person that is or has been a debtor under this title or a bankrupt or debtor under the Bankruptcy Act, or another person with whom the debtor or bankrupt has been associated, because the debtor or bankrupt is or has been a debtor under this title or a bankrupt or debtor under the Bankruptcy Act, has been insolvent before the commencement of a case under this title or during the pendency of the case but before the debtor is granted or denied a discharge, or has not paid a debt that is dischargeable in the case under this title or that was discharged under the Bankruptcy Act.

(2) In this section, "student loan program" means any program operated under title IV of the Higher Education Act of 1965 or a similar program operated under state or local law.

§ 526. Restrictions on Debt Relief Agencies

(a) A debt relief agency shall not—

(1) fail to perform any service that such agency informed an assisted person or prospective assisted person it would provide in connection with a case or proceeding under this title;

(2) make any statement, or counsel or advise any assisted person or prospective assisted person to make a statement in a document filed in a case or proceeding under this title, that is untrue or misleading, or that upon the exercise of reasonable care, should have been known by such agency to be untrue or misleading;

(3) misrepresent to any assisted person or prospective assisted person, directly or indirectly, affirmatively or by material omission, with respect to—

(A) the services that such agency will provide to such person; or

(B) the benefits and risks that may result if such person becomes a debtor in a case under this title; or

(4) advise an assisted person or prospective assisted person to incur more debt in contemplation of such person filing a case under this title or to pay an attorney or bankruptcy petition preparer a fee or charge for services performed as part of preparing for or representing a debtor in a case under this title.

(b) Any waiver by any assisted person of any protection or right provided under this section shall not be enforceable against the debtor by any Federal or State court or any other person, but may be enforced against a debt relief agency.

(c)(1) Any contract for bankruptcy assistance between a debt relief agency and an assisted person that does not comply with the material requirements of this section, section 527, or section 528 shall be void and may not be enforced by any Federal or State court or by any other person, other than such assisted person.

(2) Any debt relief agency shall be liable to an assisted person in the amount of any fees or charges in connection with providing bankruptcy assistance to such person that such debt relief agency has received, for actual damages, and for reasonable attorneys' fees and costs if

such agency is found, after notice and a hearing, to have—

(A) intentionally or negligently failed to comply with any provision of this section, section 527, or section 528 with respect to a case or proceeding under this title for such assisted person;

(B) provided bankruptcy assistance to an assisted person in a case or proceeding under this title that is dismissed or converted to a case under another chapter of this title because of such agency's intentional or negligent failure to file any required document including those specified in section 521; or

(C) intentionally or negligently disregarded the material requirements of this title or the Federal Rules of Bankruptcy Procedure applicable to such agency.

(3) In addition to such other remedies as are provided under State law, whenever the chief law enforcement officer of a State, or an official or agency designated by a State, has reason to believe that any person has violated or is violating this section, the State—

(A) may bring an action to enjoin such violation;

(B) may bring an action on behalf of its residents to recover the actual damages of assisted persons arising from such violation, including any liability under paragraph (2); and

(C) in the case of any successful action under subparagraph (A) or (B), shall be awarded the costs of the action and reasonable attorneys' fees as determined by the court.

(4) The district courts of the United States for districts located in the State shall have concurrent jurisdiction of any action under subparagraph (A) or (B) of paragraph (3).

(5) Notwithstanding any other provision of Federal law and in addition to any other remedy provided under Federal or State law, if the court, on its own motion or on the motion of the United States trustee or the debtor, finds that a person intentionally violated this section, or engaged in a clear and consistent pattern or practice of violating this section, the court may—

(A) enjoin the violation of such section; or

(B) impose an appropriate civil penalty against such person.

(d) No provision of this section, section 527, or section 528 shall—

(1) annul, alter, affect, or exempt any person subject to such sections from complying with any law of any State except to the extent that such law is inconsistent with those sections, and then only to the extent of the inconsistency; or

(2) be deemed to limit or curtail the authority or ability—

(A) of a State or subdivision or instrumentality thereof, to determine and enforce qualifications for the practice of law under the laws of that State; or

(B) of a Federal court to determine and enforce the qualifications for the practice of law before that court.

§ 527. Disclosures

(a) A debt relief agency providing bankruptcy assistance to an assisted person shall provide—

(1) the written notice required under section 342(b)(1); and

(2) to the extent not covered in the written notice described in paragraph (1), and not later than 3 business days after the first date on which a debt relief agency first offers to provide any bankruptcy assistance services to an assisted person, a clear and conspicuous written notice advising assisted persons that—

(A) all information that the assisted person is required to provide with a petition and thereafter during a case under this title is required to be complete, accurate, and truthful;

(B) all assets and all liabilities are required to be completely and accurately disclosed in the documents filed to commence the case, and the replacement value of each asset as defined in section 506 must be stated in those documents where requested after reasonable inquiry to establish such value;

(C) current monthly income, the amounts specified in section 707(b)(2), and, in a case under chapter 13 of this title, disposable income (determined in accordance with section 707(b)(2)), are required to be stated after reasonable inquiry; and

(D) information that an assisted person provides during their case may be audited pursuant to this title, and that failure to provide such information may result in dismissal of the case under this title or other sanction, including a criminal sanction.

(b) A debt relief agency providing bankruptcy assistance to an assisted person shall provide each assisted person at the same time as the notices required under subsection (a)(1) the following statement, to the extent applicable, or one substantially similar. The statement shall be clear and conspicuous and shall be in a single document separate from other documents or notices provided to the assisted person:

"IMPORTANT INFORMATION ABOUT BANKRUPTCY ASSISTANCE SERVICES FROM AN ATTORNEY OR BANKRUPTCY PETITION PREPARER.

"If you decide to seek bankruptcy relief, you can represent yourself, you can hire an attorney to represent you, or you can get help in some localities from a bankruptcy petition preparer who is not an attorney. THE LAW REQUIRES AN ATTORNEY OR BANKRUPTCY PETITION PREPARER TO GIVE YOU A WRITTEN CONTRACT SPECIFYING WHAT THE ATTORNEY OR BANKRUPTCY PETITION PREPARER WILL DO FOR YOU AND HOW MUCH IT WILL COST. Ask to see the contract before you hire anyone.

"The following information helps you understand what must be done in a routine bankruptcy case to help you evaluate how much service you need. Although bankruptcy can be complex, many cases are routine.

"Before filing a bankruptcy case, either you or your attorney should analyze your eligibility for different forms of debt relief available under the Bankruptcy Code and which form of relief is most likely to be beneficial for you. Be sure you understand the relief you can obtain and its limitations. To file a bankruptcy case, documents called a Petition, Schedules, and Statement of Financial Affairs, and in some cases a Statement of Intention, need to be prepared correctly and filed with the bankruptcy court. You will have to pay a filing fee to the bankruptcy court. Once your case starts, you will have to attend the required first meeting of creditors where you may be questioned by a court official called a 'trustee' and by creditors.

"If you choose to file a chapter 7 case, you may be asked by a creditor to reaffirm a debt. You may want help deciding whether to do so. A creditor is not permitted to coerce you into reaffirming your debts.

"If you choose to file a chapter 13 case in which you repay your creditors what you can afford over 3 to 5 years, you may also want help with preparing your chapter 13 plan and with the confirmation hearing on your plan which will be before a bankruptcy judge.

"If you select another type of relief under the Bankruptcy Code other than chapter 7 or chapter 13, you will want to find out what should be done from someone familiar with that type of relief.

"Your bankruptcy case may also involve litigation. You are generally permitted to represent yourself in litigation in bankruptcy court, but only attorneys, not bankruptcy petition preparers, can give you legal advice."

(c) Except to the extent the debt relief agency provides the required information itself after reasonably diligent inquiry of the assisted person or others so as to obtain such information reasonably accurately for inclusion on the petition, schedules or statement of financial affairs, a debt relief agency providing bankruptcy assistance to an assisted person, to the extent permitted by nonbankruptcy law, shall provide each assisted person at the time required for the notice required under subsection (a)(1) reasonably sufficient information (which shall be provided in a clear and conspicuous writing) to the assisted person on how to provide all the information the assisted person is required to provide under this title pursuant to section 521, including—

(1) how to value assets at replacement value, determine current monthly income, the amounts specified in section 707(b)(2) and, in a chapter 13 case, how to determine disposable income in accordance with section 707(b)(2) and related calculations;

(2) how to complete the list of creditors, including how to determine what amount is owed and what address for the creditor should be shown; and

(3) how to determine what property is exempt and how to value exempt property at replacement value as defined in section 506.

(d) A debt relief agency shall maintain a copy of the notices required under subsection (a) of this section for 2 years after the date on which the notice is given the assisted person.

§ 528. Requirements for Debt Relief Agencies

(a) A debt relief agency shall—

(1) not later than 5 business days after the first date on which such agency provides any bankruptcy assistance services to an assisted person, but prior to such assisted person's petition under this title being filed, execute a written contract with such assisted person that explains clearly and conspicuously—

(A) the services such agency will provide to such assisted person; and

(B) the fees or charges for such services, and the terms of payment;

(2) provide the assisted person with a copy of the fully executed and completed contract;

(3) clearly and conspicuously disclose in any advertisement of bankruptcy assistance services or of the benefits of bankruptcy directed to the general public (whether in general media, seminars or specific mailings, telephonic or electronic messages, or otherwise) that the services or benefits are with respect to bankruptcy relief under this title; and

(4) clearly and conspicuously use the following statement in such advertisement: "We are a debt relief agency. We help people file for bankruptcy relief under the Bankruptcy Code." or a substantially similar statement.

(b)(1) An advertisement of bankruptcy assistance services or of the benefits of bankruptcy directed to the general public includes—

(A) descriptions of bankruptcy assistance in connection with a chapter 13 plan whether or not chapter 13 is specifically mentioned in such advertisement; and

(B) statements such as "federally supervised repayment plan" or "Federal debt restructuring help" or other similar statements that could lead a reasonable consumer to believe that debt counseling was being offered when in fact the services were directed to providing bankruptcy assistance with a chapter 13 plan or other form of bankruptcy relief under this title.

(2) An advertisement, directed to the general public, indicating that the debt relief agency provides assistance with respect to credit defaults, mortgage foreclosures, eviction proceedings, excessive debt, debt collection pressure, or inability to pay any consumer debt shall—

(A) disclose clearly and conspicuously in such advertisement that the assistance may involve bankruptcy relief under this title; and

(B) include the following statement: "We are a debt relief agency. We help people file for bankruptcy relief under the Bankruptcy Code." or a substantially similar statement.

SUBCHAPTER III—THE ESTATE

Section

541. Property of the Estate
542. Turnover of Property to the Estate
543. Turnover of Property by a Custodian
544. Trustee as Lien Creditor and as Successor to Certain Creditors and Purchasers
545. Statutory Liens
546. Limitations on Avoiding Powers
547. Preferences
548. Fraudulent Transfers and Obligations
549. Postpetition Transactions
550. Liability of Transferee of Avoided Transfer
551. Automatic Preservation of Avoided Transfer
552. Postpetition Effect of Security Interest
553. Setoff
554. Abandonment of Property of the Estate
555. Contractual Right to Liquidate, Terminate, or Accelerate a Securities Contract
556. Contractual Right to Liquidate, Terminate, or Accelerate a Commodities Contract or Forward Contract
557. Expedited Determination of Interests in, and Abandonment or Other Disposition of, Grain Assets
558. Defenses of the Estate
559. Contractual Right to Liquidate, Terminate, or Accelerate a Repurchase Agreement
560. Contractual Right to Liquidate, Terminate, or Accelerate a Swap Agreement
561. Contractual Right to Terminate, Liquidate, Accelerate, or Offset under a Master Netting Agreement and across Contracts; Proceedings under Chapter 15
562. Timing of Damage Measure in Connection with Swap Agreements, Securities Contracts, Forward Contracts, Commodity Contracts, Repurchase Agreements, and Master Netting Agreements

§ 541. Property of the Estate

(a) The commencement of a case under section 301, 302, or 303 of this title creates an estate. Such estate is comprised of all the following property, wherever located and by whomever held:

(1) Except as provided in subsections (b) and (c)(2) of this section, all legal or equitable interests of the debtor in property as of the commencement of the case.

(2) All interests of the debtor and the debtor's spouse in community property as of the commencement of the case that is—

(A) under the sole, equal, or joint management and control of the debtor; or

(B) liable for an allowable claim against the debtor, or for both an allowable claim against the debtor and an allowable claim against the debtor's spouse, to the extent that such interest is so liable.

(3) Any interest in property that the trustee recovers under section 329(b), 363(n), 543, 550, 553, or 723 of this title.

(4) Any interest in property preserved for the benefit of or ordered transferred to the estate under section 510(c) or 551 of this title.

(5) Any interest in property that would have been property of the estate if such interest had been an interest of the debtor on the date of the filing of the petition, and that the debtor acquires or becomes entitled to acquire within 180 days after such date—

(A) by bequest, devise, or inheritance;

(B) as a result of a property settlement agreement with the debtor's spouse, or of an interlocutory or final divorce decree; or

(C) as a beneficiary of a life insurance policy or of a death benefit plan.

(6) Proceeds, product, offspring, rents, or profits of or from property of the estate, except such as are earnings from services performed by an individual debtor after the commencement of the case.

(7) Any interest in property that the estate acquires after the commencement of the case.

(b) Property of the estate does not include—

(1) any power that the debtor may exercise solely for the benefit of an entity other than the debtor;

(2) any interest of the debtor as a lessee under a lease of nonresidential real property that has terminated at the expiration of the stated term of such lease before the commencement of the case under this title, and ceases to include any interest of the debtor as a lessee under a lease of nonresidential real property that has terminated at the expiration of the stated term of such lease during the case;

(3) any eligibility of the debtor to participate in programs authorized under the Higher Education Act of 1965 (20 U.S.C. 1001 et seq.; 42 U.S.C. 2751 et seq.), or any accreditation status or state licensure of the debtor as an educational institution;

(4) any interest of the debtor in liquid or gaseous hydrocarbons to the extent that—

(A) (i) the debtor has transferred or has agreed to transfer such interest pursuant to a farmout agreement or any written agreement directly related to a farmout agreement; and

(ii) but for the operation of this paragraph, the estate could include the interest referred to in clause (i) only by virtue of section 365 or 544(a)(3) of this title; or

(B) (i) the debtor has transferred such interest pursuant to a written conveyance of a production payment to an entity that does not participate in the operation of the property from which such production payment is transferred; and

(ii) but for the operation of this paragraph, the estate could include the interest referred to in clause (i) only by virtue of section 365 or 542 of this title;

(5) funds placed in an education individual retirement account (as defined in section 530(b)(1) of the Internal Revenue Code of 1986) not later than 365 days before the date of the filing of the petition in a case under this title, but—

(A) only if the designated beneficiary of such account was a child, stepchild, grandchild, or stepgrandchild of the debtor for the taxable year for which funds were placed in such account;

(B) only to the extent that such funds—

(i) are not pledged or promised to any entity in connection with any extension of credit; and

(ii) are not excess contributions (as described in section 4973(e) of the Internal Revenue Code of 1986); and

(C) in the case of funds placed in all such accounts having the same designated beneficiary not earlier than 720 days nor later than 365 days before such date, only so much of such funds as does not exceed $7,575;

(6) funds used to purchase a tuition credit or certificate or contributed to an account in accordance with section 529(b)(1)(A) of the Internal Revenue Code of 1986 under a qualified State tuition program (as defined in section 529(b)(1) of such Code) not later than 365 days before the date of the filing of the petition in a case under this title, but—

(A) only if the designated beneficiary of the amounts paid or contributed to such tuition program was a child, stepchild, grandchild, or stepgrandchild of the debtor for the taxable year for which funds were paid or contributed;

(B) with respect to the aggregate amount paid or contributed to such program having the same designated beneficiary, only so much of such amount as does not exceed the total contributions permitted under section 529(b)(6) of such Code with respect to such beneficiary, as adjusted beginning on the date of the filing of the petition in a case under this title by the annual increase or decrease (rounded to the nearest tenth of 1 percent) in the education expenditure category of the Consumer Price Index prepared by the Department of Labor; and

(C) in the case of funds paid or contributed to such program having the same designated beneficiary not earlier than 720 days nor later than 365 days before such date, only so much of such funds as does not exceed $7,575;

(7) any amount—

(A) withheld by an employer from the wages of employees for payment as contributions—

(i) to—

(I) an employee benefit plan that is subject to title I of the Employee Retirement Income Security Act of 1974 or under an employee benefit plan which is a governmental plan under section 414(d) of the Internal Revenue Code of 1986;

(II) a deferred compensation plan under section 457 of the Internal Revenue Code of 1986; or

(III) a tax-deferred annuity under section 403(b) of the Internal Revenue Code of 1986; except that such amount under this subparagraph shall not constitute disposable income as defined in section 1325(b)(2); or

(ii) to a health insurance plan regulated by State law whether or not subject to such title; or

(B) received by an employer from employees for payment as contributions—

(i) to—

(I) an employee benefit plan that is subject to title I of the Employee Retirement Income Security Act of 1974 or under an employee benefit plan which is a governmental plan under section 414(d) of the Internal Revenue Code of 1986;

(II) a deferred compensation plan under section 457 of the Internal Revenue Code of 1986; or

(III) a tax-deferred annuity under section 403(b) of the Internal Revenue Code of 1986; except that such amount under this subparagraph shall not constitute disposable income, as defined in section 1325(b)(2); or

(ii) to a health insurance plan regulated by State law whether or not subject to such title;

(8) subject to subchapter III of chapter 5, any interest of the debtor in property where the debtor pledged or sold tangible personal property (other than securities or written or printed evidences of indebtedness or title) as collateral for a loan or advance of money given by a person licensed under law to make such loans or advances, where—

(A) the tangible personal property is in the possession of the pledgee or transferee;

(B) the debtor has no obligation to repay the money, redeem the collateral, or buy back the property at a stipulated price; and

(C) neither the debtor nor the trustee have exercised any right to redeem provided under the contract or State law, in a timely manner as provided under State law and section 108(b);

(9) any interest in cash or cash equivalents that constitute proceeds of a sale by the debtor of a money order that is made—

(A) on or after the date that is 14 days prior to the date on which the petition is filed; and

(B) under an agreement with a money order issuer that prohibits the commingling of such proceeds with property of the debtor (notwithstanding that, contrary to the agreement, the proceeds may have been commingled with property of the debtor),

unless the money order issuer had not taken action, prior to the filing of the petition, to require compliance with the prohibition, or

(10) funds placed in an account of a qualified ABLE program (as defined in section 529A(b) of the Internal Revenue Code of 1986) not later than 365 days before the date of the filing of the petition in a case under this title, but—

(A) only if the designated beneficiary of such account was a child, stepchild, grandchild, or stepgrandchild of the debtor for the taxable year for which funds were placed in such account;

(B) only to the extent that such funds—

(i) are not pledged or promised to any entity in connection with any extension of credit; and

(ii) are not excess contributions (as described in section 4973(h) of the Internal Revenue Code of 1986); and

(C) in the case of funds placed in all such accounts having the same designated beneficiary not earlier than 720 days nor later than 365 days before such date, only so much of such funds as does not exceed $7,575

(c)(1) Except as provided in paragraph (2) of this subsection, an interest of the debtor in property becomes property of the estate under subsection (a)(1), (a)(2), or (a)(5) of this section notwithstanding any provision in an agreement, transfer instrument, or applicable nonbankruptcy law—

(A) that restricts or conditions transfer of such interest by the debtor; or

(B) that is conditioned on the insolvency or financial condition of the debtor, on the commencement of a case under this title, or on the appointment of or taking possession by a trustee in a case under this title or a custodian before such commencement, and that effects or gives an option to effect a forfeiture, modification, or termination of the debtor's interest in property.

(2) A restriction on the transfer of a beneficial interest of the debtor in a trust that is enforceable under applicable nonbankruptcy law is enforceable in a case under this title.

(d) Property in which the debtor holds, as of the commencement of the case, only legal title and not an equitable interest, such as a mortgage secured by real property, or an interest in such a mortgage, sold by the debtor but as to which the debtor retains legal title to service or supervise the servicing of such mortgage or interest, becomes property of the estate under subsection (a)(1) or (2) of this section only to the extent of the debtor's legal title to such property, but not to the extent of any equitable interest in such property that the debtor does not hold.

(e) In determining whether any of the relationships specified in paragraph (5)(A) or (6)(A) of subsection (b) exists, a legally adopted child of an individual (and a child who is a member of an individual's household, if placed with such individual by an authorized placement agency for legal adoption by such individual), or a foster child of an individual (if such child has as the child's principal place of abode the home of the debtor and is a member of the debtor's household) shall be treated as a child of such individual by blood.

(f) Notwithstanding any other provision of this title, property that is held by a debtor that is a corporation described in section 501(c)(3) of the Internal Revenue Code of 1986 and exempt from tax under section 501(a) of such Code may be transferred to an entity that is not such a corporation, but only under the same conditions as would apply if the debtor had not filed a case under this title.

§ 542. Turnover of Property to the Estate

(a) Except as provided in subsection (c) or (d) of this section, an entity, other than a custodian, in possession, custody, or control, during the case, of property that the trustee may use, sell, or lease under section 363 of this title, or that the debtor may exempt under section 522 of this title, shall deliver to the trustee, and account for, such property or the value of such property, unless such property is of inconsequential value or benefit to the estate.

(b) Except as provided in subsection (c) or (d) of this section, an entity that owes a debt that is property of the estate and that is matured, payable on demand, or payable on order, shall pay such debt to, or on the order of, the trustee, except to the extent that such debt may be offset under section 553 of this title against a claim against the debtor.

(c) Except as provided in section 362(a)(7) of this title, an entity that has neither actual notice nor actual knowledge of the commencement of the case concerning the debtor may transfer property of the estate, or pay a debt owing to the debtor, in good faith and other than in the manner specified in subsection (d) of this section, to an entity other than the trustee, with the same effect as to the entity making such transfer or payment as if the case under this title concerning the debtor had not been commenced.

(d) A life insurance company may transfer property of the estate or property of the debtor to such company in good faith, with the same effect with respect to such company as if the case under this title concerning the debtor had not been commenced, if such transfer is to pay a premium or to carry out a nonforfeiture insurance option, and is required to be made automatically, under a life insurance contract with such company that was entered into before the date of the filing of the petition and that is property of the estate.

(e) Subject to any applicable privilege, after notice and a hearing, the court may order an attorney, accountant, or other person that holds recorded information, including books, documents, records, and papers, relating to the debtor's property or financial affairs, to turn over or disclose such recorded information to the trustee.

§ 543. Turnover of Property by a Custodian

(a) A custodian with knowledge of the commencement of a case under this title concerning the debtor may not make any disbursement from, or take any action in the administration of, property of the debtor, proceeds, product, offspring, rents, or profits of such property, or property of the estate, in the possession, custody, or control of such custodian, except such action as is necessary to preserve such property.

(b) A custodian shall—

(1) deliver to the trustee any property of the debtor held by or transferred to such custodian, or proceeds, product, offspring, rents, or profits of such property, that is in such custodian's possession, custody, or control on the date that such custodian acquires knowledge of the commencement of the case; and

(2) file an accounting of any property of the debtor, or proceeds, product, offspring, rents, or profits of such property, that, at any time, came into the possession, custody, or control of such custodian.

(c) The court, after notice and a hearing, shall—

(1) protect all entities to which a custodian has become obligated with respect to such property or proceeds, product, offspring, rents, or profits of such property;

(2) provide for the payment of reasonable compensation for services rendered and costs and expenses incurred by such custodian; and

(3) surcharge such custodian, other than an assignee for the benefit of the debtor's creditors that was appointed or took possession more than 120 days before the date of the filing of the petition, for any improper or excessive disbursement, other than a disbursement that has been made in accordance with applicable law or that has been approved, after notice and a hearing, by a court of competent jurisdiction before the commencement of the case under this title.

(d) After notice and hearing, the bankruptcy court—

(1) may excuse compliance with subsection (a), (b), or (c) of this section if the interests of creditors and, if the debtor is not insolvent, of equity security holders would be better served by permitting a custodian to continue in possession, custody, or control of such property, and

(2) shall excuse compliance with subsections (a) and (b)(1) of this section if the custodian is an assignee for the benefit of the debtor's creditors that was appointed or took possession more than 120 days before the date of the filing of the petition, unless compliance with such subsections is necessary to prevent fraud or injustice.

§ 544. Trustee as Lien Creditor and as Successor to Certain Creditors and Purchasers

(a) The trustee shall have, as of the commencement of the case, and without regard to any knowledge of the trustee or of any creditor, the rights and powers of, or may avoid any transfer of property of the debtor or any obligation incurred by the debtor that is voidable by—

(1) a creditor that extends credit to the debtor at the time of the commencement of the case, and that obtains, at such time and with respect to such credit, a judicial lien on all property on which a creditor on a simple contract could have obtained such a judicial lien, whether or not such a creditor exists;

(2) a creditor that extends credit to the debtor at the time of the commencement of the case, and obtains, at such time and with respect to such credit, an execution against the debtor that is returned unsatisfied at such time, whether or not such a creditor exists; or

(3) a bona fide purchaser of real property, other than fixtures, from the debtor, against whom applicable law permits such transfer to be perfected, that obtains the status of a bona fide purchaser and has perfected such transfer at the time of the commencement of the case, whether or not such a purchaser exists.

(b)(1) Except as provided in paragraph (2), the trustee may avoid any transfer of an interest of the debtor in property or any obligation incurred by the debtor that is voidable under applicable law by a creditor holding an unsecured claim that is allowable under section 502 of this title or that is not allowable only under section 502(e) of this title.

(2) Paragraph (1) shall not apply to a transfer of a charitable contribution (as that term is defined in section 548(d)(3)) that is not covered under section 548(a)(1)(B), by reason of section 548(a)(2). Any claim by any person to recover a transferred contribution described in the preceding sentence under Federal or state law in a Federal or state court shall be preempted by the commencement of the case.

§ 545. Statutory Liens

The trustee may avoid the fixing of a statutory lien on property of the debtor to the extent that such lien—

(1) first becomes effective against the debtor—

(A) when a case under this title concerning the debtor is commenced;

(B) when an insolvency proceeding other than under this title concerning the debtor is commenced;

(C) when a custodian is appointed or authorized to take or takes possession;

(D) when the debtor becomes insolvent;

(E) when the debtor's financial condition fails to meet a specified standard; or

(F) at the time of an execution against property of the debtor levied at the instance of an entity other than the holder of such statutory lien;

(2) is not perfected or enforceable at the time of the commencement of the case against a bona fide purchaser that purchases such property at the time of the commencement of the case, whether or not such a purchaser exists, except in any case in which a purchaser is a purchaser described in section 6323 of the Internal Revenue Code of 1986, or in any other similar provision of State or local law;

(3) is for rent; or

(4) is a lien of distress for rent.

§ 546. Limitations on Avoiding Powers

(a) An action or proceeding under section 544, 545, 547, 548, or 553 of this title may not be commenced after the earlier of—

(1) the later of—

(A) 2 years after the entry of the order for relief; or

(B) 1 year after the appointment or election of the first trustee under section 702, 1104, 1163, 1202, or 1302 of this title if such appointment or such election occurs before the expiration of the period specified in subparagraph (A); or

(2) the time the case is closed or dismissed.

(b)(1) The rights and powers of a trustee under sections 544, 545, and 549 of this title are subject to any generally applicable law that—

(A) permits perfection of an interest in property to be effective against an entity that acquires rights in such property before the date of perfection; or

(B) provides for the maintenance or continuation of perfection of an interest in property to be effective against an entity that acquires rights in such property before the date on which action is taken to effect such maintenance or continuation.

(2) If—

(A) a law described in paragraph (1) requires seizure of such property or commencement of an action to accomplish such perfection, or maintenance or continuation of perfection of an interest in property; and

(B) such property has not been seized or such an action has not been commenced before the date of the filing of the petition;

such interest in such property shall be perfected, or perfection of such interest shall be maintained or continued, by giving notice within the time fixed by such law for such seizure or such commencement.

(c)(1) Except as provided in subsection (d) of this section and in section 507(c), and subject to the prior rights of a holder of a security interest in such goods or the proceeds thereof, the rights and powers of the trustee under sections 544(a), 545, 547, and 549 are subject to the right of a seller of goods that has sold goods to the debtor, in the ordinary course of such seller's business, to reclaim such goods if the debtor has received such goods while insolvent, within 45 days before the date of the commencement of a case under this title, but such seller may not reclaim such goods unless such seller demands in writing reclamation of such goods—

(A) not later than 45 days after the date of receipt of such goods by the debtor; or

(B) not later than 20 days after the date of commencement of the case, if the 45-day period expires after the commencement of the case.

(2) If a seller of goods fails to provide notice in the manner described in paragraph (1), the seller still may assert the rights contained in section 503(b)(9).

(d) In the case of a seller who is a producer of grain sold to a grain storage facility, owned or operated by the debtor, in the ordinary course of such seller's business (as such terms are defined in section 557 of this title) or in the case of a United States fisherman who has caught fish sold to a fish processing facility owned or operated by the debtor in the ordinary course of such fisherman's business, the rights and powers of the trustee under sections 544(a), 545, 547, and 549 of this title are subject to any statutory or common law right of such producer or fisherman to reclaim such grain or fish if the debtor has received such grain or fish while insolvent, but—

(1) such producer or fisherman may not reclaim any grain or fish unless such producer or fisherman demands, in writing, reclamation of such grain or fish before ten days after receipt thereof by the debtor; and

(2) the court may deny reclamation to such a producer or fisherman with a right of reclamation that has made such a demand only if the court secures such claim by a lien.

(e) Notwithstanding sections 544, 545, 547, 548(a)(1)(B), and 548(b) of this title, the trustee may not avoid a transfer that is a margin payment, as defined in section 101, 741, or 761 of this title, or settlement payment, as defined in section 101 or 741 of this title, made by or to (or for the benefit of) a commodity broker, forward contract merchant, stockbroker, financial institution, financial participant, or securities clearing agency, or that is a transfer made by or to (or for the benefit of) a commodity broker, forward contract merchant, stockbroker, financial institution, financial participant, or securities clearing agency, in connection with a securities contract, as defined in section 741(7), commodity contract, as defined in section 761(4), or forward contract, that is made before the commencement of the case, except under section 548(a)(1)(A) of this title.

(f) Notwithstanding sections 544, 545, 547, 548(a)(1)(B), and 548(b) of this title, the trustee may not avoid a transfer made by or to (or for the benefit of) a repo participant or financial participant, in connection with a repurchase agreement and that is made before the commencement of the case, except under section 548(a)(1)(A) of this title.

(g) Notwithstanding sections 544, 545, 547, 548(a)(1)(B) and 548(b) of this title, the trustee may not avoid a transfer, made by or to (or for the benefit of) a swap participant or financial participant, under or in connection with any swap agreement and that is made before the commencement of the case, except under section 548(a)(1)(A) of this title.

(h) Notwithstanding the rights and powers of a trustee under sections 544(a), 545, 547, 549, and 553, if the court determines on a motion by the trustee made not later than 120 days after the date of the order for relief in a case under chapter 11 of this title and after notice and a hearing, that a return is in the best interests of the estate, the debtor, with the consent of a creditor and subject to the prior rights of holders of security interests in such goods or the proceeds of such goods, may return goods shipped to the debtor by the creditor before the commencement of the case, and the creditor may offset the purchase price of such goods against any claim of the creditor against the debtor that arose before the commencement of the case.

(i)(1) Notwithstanding paragraphs (2) and (3) of section 545, the trustee may not avoid a warehouseman's lien for storage, transportation, or other costs incidental to the storage and handling of goods.

(2) The prohibition under paragraph (1) shall be applied in a manner consistent with any State statute applicable to such lien that is similar to section 7–209 of the Uniform Commercial Code, as in effect on the date of enactment of the Bankruptcy Abuse Prevention and Consumer Protection Act of 2005, or any successor to such section 7–209.

(j) Notwithstanding sections 544, 545, 547, 548(a)(1)(B), and 548(b) the trustee may not avoid a transfer made by or to (or for the benefit of) a master netting agreement participant under or in connection with any master netting agreement or any individual contract covered thereby that is made before the commencement of the case, except under section 548(a)(1)(A) and except to the extent that the trustee could otherwise avoid such a transfer made under an individual contract covered by such master netting agreement.

§ 547. Preferences

(a) In this section—

(1) "inventory" means personal property leased or furnished, held for sale or lease, or to be furnished under a contract for service, raw materials, work in process, or materials used or consumed in a business, including farm products such as crops or livestock, held for sale or lease;

(2) "new value" means money or money's worth in goods, services, or new credit, or release by a transferee of property previously transferred to such transferee in a transaction that is neither void nor voidable by the debtor or the trustee under any applicable law, including proceeds of such property, but does not include an obligation substituted for an existing obligation;

(3) "receivable" means right to payment, whether or not such right has been earned by performance; and

(4) a debt for a tax is incurred on the day when such tax is last payable without penalty, including any extension.

(b) Except as provided in subsections (c), (i), and (j) of this section, the trustee may, based on reasonable due diligence in the circumstances of the case and taking into account a party's known or reasonably knowable affirmative defenses under subsection (c), avoid any transfer of an interest of the debtor in property—

(1) to or for the benefit of a creditor;

(2) for or on account of an antecedent debt owed by the debtor before such transfer was made;

(3) made while the debtor was insolvent;

(4) made—

(A) on or within 90 days before the date of the filing of the petition; or

(B) between ninety days and one year before the date of the filing of the petition, if such creditor at the time of such transfer was an insider; and

(5) that enables such creditor to receive more than such creditor would receive if—

(A) the case were a case under chapter 7 of this title;

(B) the transfer had not been made; and

(C) such creditor received payment of such debt to the extent provided by the provisions of this title.

(c) The trustee may not avoid under this section a transfer—

(1) to the extent that such transfer was—

(A) intended by the debtor and the creditor to or for whose benefit such transfer was made to be a contemporaneous exchange for new value given to the debtor; and

(B) in fact a substantially contemporaneous exchange;

(2) to the extent that such transfer was in payment of a debt incurred by the debtor in the ordinary course of business or financial affairs of the debtor and the transferee, and such transfer was—

(A) made in the ordinary course of business or financial affairs of the debtor and the transferee; or

(B) made according to ordinary business terms;

(3) that creates a security interest in property acquired by the debtor—

(A) to the extent such security interest secures new value that was—

(i) given at or after the signing of a security agreement that contains a description of such property as collateral;

(ii) given by or on behalf of the secured party under such agreement;

(iii) given to enable the debtor to acquire such property; and

(iv) in fact used by the debtor to acquire such property; and

(B) that is perfected on or before 30 days after the debtor receives possession of such property;

(4) to or for the benefit of a creditor, to the extent that, after such transfer, such creditor gave new value to or for the benefit of the debtor—

(A) not secured by an otherwise unavoidable security interest; and

(B) on account of which new value the debtor did not make an otherwise unavoidable transfer to or for the benefit of such creditor;

(5) that creates a perfected security interest in inventory or a receivable or the proceeds of either, except to the extent that the aggregate of all such transfers to the transferee caused a reduction, as of the date of the filing of the petition and to the prejudice of other creditors holding unsecured claims, of any amount by which the debt secured by such security interest exceeded the value of all security interests for such debt on the later of—

(A) (i) with respect to a transfer to which subsection (b)(4)(A) of this section applies, 90 days before the date of the filing of the petition; or

(ii) with respect to a transfer to which subsection (b)(4)(B) of this section applies, one year before the date of the filing of the petition; or

(B) the date on which new value was first given under the security agreement creating such security interest;

(6) that is the fixing of a statutory lien that is not avoidable under section 545 of this title;

(7) to the extent such transfer was a bona fide payment of a debt for a domestic support obligation;

(8) if, in a case filed by an individual debtor whose debts are primarily consumer debts, the aggregate value of all property that constitutes or is affected by such transfer is less than $600; or

(9) if, in a case filed by a debtor whose debts are not primarily consumer debts, the aggregate value of all property that constitutes or is affected by such transfer is less than $7,575.

(d) The trustee may avoid a transfer of an interest in property of the debtor transferred to or for the benefit of a surety to secure reimbursement of such a surety that furnished a bond or other obligation to dissolve a judicial lien that would have been avoidable by the trustee under subsection (b) of this section. The liability of such surety under such bond or obligation shall be discharged to the extent of the value of such property recovered by the trustee or the amount paid to the trustee.

(e)(1) For the purposes of this section—

(A) a transfer of real property other than fixtures, but including the interest of a seller or purchaser under a contract for the sale of real property, is perfected when a bona fide purchaser of such property from the debtor against whom applicable law permits such transfer to be perfected cannot acquire an interest that is superior to the interest of the transferee; and

(B) a transfer of a fixture or property other than real property is perfected when a creditor on a simple contract cannot acquire a judicial lien that is superior to the interest of the transferee.

(2) For the purposes of this section, except as provided in paragraph (3) of this subsection, a transfer is made—

(A) at the time such transfer takes effect between the transferor and the transferee, if such transfer is perfected at, or within 30 days after, such time, except as provided in subsection (c)(3)(B);

(B) at the time such transfer is perfected, if such transfer is perfected after such 30 days; or

(C) immediately before the date of the filing of the petition, if such transfer is not perfected at the later of—

(i) the commencement of the case; or

(ii) 30 days after such transfer takes effect between the transferor and the transferee.

(3) For the purposes of this section, a transfer is not made until the debtor has acquired rights in the property transferred.

(f) For the purposes of this section, the debtor is presumed to have been insolvent on and during the 90 days immediately preceding the date of the filing of the petition.

(g) For the purposes of this section, the trustee has the burden of proving the avoidability of a transfer under subsection (b) of this section, and the creditor or party in interest against whom recovery or avoidance is sought has the burden of proving the nonavoidability of a transfer under subsection (c) of this section.

(h) The trustee may not avoid a transfer if such transfer was made as a part of an alternative repayment schedule between the debtor and any creditor of the debtor created by an approved nonprofit budget and credit counseling agency.

(i) If the trustee avoids under subsection (b) a transfer made between 90 days and 1 year before the date of the filing of the petition, by the debtor to an entity that is not an insider for the benefit of a creditor that is an insider, such transfer shall be considered to be avoided under this section only with respect to the creditor that is an insider.

§ 548. Fraudulent Transfers and Obligations

(a)(1) The trustee may avoid any transfer (including any transfer to or for the benefit of an insider under an employment contract) of an interest of the debtor in property, or any obligation (including any obligation to or for the benefit of an insider under an employment contract) incurred by the debtor, that was made or incurred on or within 2 years before the date of the filing of the petition, if the debtor voluntarily or involuntarily—

(A) made such transfer or incurred such obligation with actual intent to hinder, delay, or defraud any entity to which the debtor was or became, on or after the date that such transfer was made or such obligation was incurred, indebted; or

(B) (i) received less than a reasonably equivalent value in exchange for such transfer or obligation; and

(ii) (I) was insolvent on the date that such transfer was made or such obligation was incurred, or became insolvent as a result of such transfer or obligation;

(II) was engaged in business or a transaction, or was about to engage in business or a transaction, for which any property remaining with the debtor was an unreasonably small capital;

(III) intended to incur, or believed that the debtor would incur, debts that would be beyond the debtor's ability to pay as such debts matured; or

(IV) made such transfer to or for the benefit of an insider, or incurred such obligation to or for the benefit of an insider, under an employment contract and not in the ordinary course of business.

(2) A transfer of a charitable contribution to a qualified religious or charitable entity or organization shall not be considered to be a transfer covered under paragraph (1)(B) in any case in which—

(A) the amount of that contribution does not exceed 15 percent of the gross annual income of the debtor for the year in which the transfer of the contribution is made; or

(B) the contribution made by a debtor exceeded the percentage amount of gross annual income specified in subparagraph (A), if the transfer was consistent with the practices of the debtor in making charitable contributions.

(b) The trustee of a partnership debtor may avoid any transfer of an interest of the debtor in property, or any obligation incurred by the debtor, that was made or incurred on or within 2 years before the date of the filing of the petition, to a general partner in the debtor, if the debtor was insolvent on the date such transfer was made or such obligation was incurred, or became insolvent as a result of such transfer or obligation.

(c) Except to the extent that a transfer or obligation voidable under this section is voidable under section 544, 545, or 547 of this title, a transferee or obligee of such a transfer or obligation that takes for value and in good faith has a lien on or may retain any interest transferred or may enforce any obligation incurred, as the case may be, to the extent that such transferee or obligee gave value to the debtor in exchange for such transfer or obligation.

(d)(1) For the purposes of this section, a transfer is made when such transfer is so perfected that a bona fide purchaser from the debtor against whom applicable law permits such transfer to be perfected cannot acquire an interest in the property transferred that is superior to the interest in such property of the transferee, but if such transfer is not so perfected before the commencement of the case, such transfer is made immediately before the date of the filing of the petition.

(2) In this section—

(A) "value" means property, or satisfaction or securing of a present or antecedent debt of the debtor, but does not include an unperformed promise to furnish support to the debtor or to a relative of the debtor;

(B) a commodity broker, forward contract merchant, stockbroker, financial institution, financial participant, or securities clearing agency that receives a margin payment, as defined in section 101, 741, or 761 of this title, or settlement payment, as defined in section 101 or 741 of this title, takes for value to the extent of such payment;

(C) a repo participant or financial participant that receives a margin payment, as defined in section 741 or 761 of this title, or settlement payment, as defined in section 741 of this title, in connection with a repurchase agreement, takes for value to the extent of such payment;

(D) a swap participant or financial participant that receives a transfer in connection with a swap agreement takes for value to the extent of such transfer; and

(E) a master netting agreement participant that receives a transfer in connection with a master netting agreement or any individual contract covered thereby takes for value to the extent of such transfer, except that, with respect to a transfer under any individual contract covered thereby, to the extent that such master netting agreement participant otherwise did not take (or is otherwise not deemed to have taken) such transfer for value.

(3) In this section, the term "charitable contribution" means a charitable contribution, as that term is defined in section 170(c) of the Internal Revenue Code of 1986, if that contribution—

(A) is made by a natural person; and

(B) consists of—

(i) a financial instrument (as that term is defined in section 731(c)(2)(C) of the Internal Revenue Code of 1986); or

(ii) cash.

(4) In this section, the term "qualified religious or charitable entity or organization" means—

(A) an entity described in section 170(c)(1) of the Internal Revenue Code of 1986; or

(B) an entity or organization described in section 170(c)(2) of the Internal Revenue Code of 1986.

(e)(1) In addition to any transfer that the trustee may otherwise avoid, the trustee may avoid any transfer of an interest of the debtor in property that was made on or within 10 years before the date of the filing of the petition, if—

(A) such transfer was made to a self-settled trust or similar device;

(B) such transfer was by the debtor;

(C) the debtor is a beneficiary of such trust or similar device; and

(D) the debtor made such transfer with actual intent to hinder, delay, or defraud any entity to which the debtor was or became, on or after the date that such transfer was made, indebted.

(2) For the purposes of this subsection, a transfer includes a transfer made in anticipation of any money judgment, settlement, civil penalty, equitable order, or criminal fine incurred by, or which the debtor believed would be incurred by—

(A) any violation of the securities laws (as defined in section 3(a)(47) of the Securities Exchange Act of 1934 (15 U.S.C. 78c(a)(47))), any State securities laws, or any regulation or order issued under Federal securities laws or State securities laws; or

(B) fraud, deceit, or manipulation in a fiduciary capacity or in connection with the purchase or sale of any security registered under section 12 or 15(d) of the Securities Exchange Act of 1934 (15 U.S.C. 78l and 78o(d)) or under section 6 of the Securities Act of 1933 (15 U.S.C. 77f).

§ 549. Postpetition Transactions

(a) Except as provided in subsection (b) or (c) of this section, the trustee may avoid a transfer of property of the estate—

(1) that occurs after the commencement of the case; and

(2) (A) that is authorized only under section 303(f) or 542(c) of this title; or

(B) that is not authorized under this title or by the court.

(b) In an involuntary case, the trustee may not avoid under subsection (a) of this section a transfer made after the commencement of such case but before the order for relief to the extent any value, including services, but not including satisfaction or securing of a debt that arose before the commencement of the case, is given after the commencement of the case in exchange for such transfer, notwithstanding any notice or knowledge of the case that the transferee has.

(c) The trustee may not avoid under subsection (a) of this section a transfer of an interest in real property to a good faith purchaser without knowledge of the commencement of the case and for present fair equivalent value unless a copy or notice of the petition was filed, where a transfer of an interest in such real property may be recorded to perfect such transfer, before such transfer is so perfected that a bona fide purchaser of such real property, against whom applicable law permits such transfer to be perfected, could not acquire an interest that is superior to such interest of such good faith purchaser. A good faith purchaser without knowledge of the commencement of the case and for less than present fair equivalent value has a lien on the property transferred to the extent of any present value given, unless a copy or notice of the petition was so filed before such transfer was so perfected.

(d) An action or proceeding under this section may not be commenced after the earlier of—

(1) two years after the date of the transfer sought to be avoided; or

(2) the time the case is closed or dismissed.

§ 550. Liability of Transferee of Avoided Transfer

(a) Except as otherwise provided in this section, to the extent that a transfer is avoided under section 544, 545, 547, 548, 549, 553(b), or 724(a) of this title, the trustee may recover, for the benefit of the estate, the property transferred, or, if the court so orders, the value of such property, from—

(1) the initial transferee of such transfer or the entity for whose benefit such transfer was made; or

(2) any immediate or mediate transferee of such initial transferee.

(b) The trustee may not recover under section (a)(2) of this section from—

(1) a transferee that takes for value, including satisfaction or securing of a present or antecedent debt, in good faith, and without knowledge of the voidability of the transfer avoided; or

(2) any immediate or mediate good faith transferee of such transferee.

(c) If a transfer made between 90 days and one year before the filing of the petition—

(1) is avoided under section 547(b) of this title; and

(2) was made for the benefit of a creditor that at the time of such transfer was an insider;

the trustee may not recover under subsection (a) from a transferee that is not an insider.

(d) The trustee is entitled to only a single satisfaction under subsection (a) of this section.

(e)(1) A good faith transferee from whom the trustee may recover under subsection (a) of this section has a lien on the property recovered to secure the lesser of—

(A) the cost, to such transferee, of any improvement made after the transfer, less the amount of any profit realized by or accruing to such transferee from such property; and

(B) any increase in the value of such property as a result of such improvement, of the property transferred.

(2) In this subsection, "improvement" includes—

(A) physical additions or changes to the property transferred;

(B) repairs to such property;

(C) payment of any tax on such property;

(D) payment of any debt secured by a lien on such property that is superior or equal to the rights of the trustee; and

(E) preservation of such property.

(f) An action or proceeding under this section may not be commenced after the earlier of—

(1) one year after the avoidance of the transfer on account of which recovery under this section is sought; or

(2) the time the case is closed or dismissed.

§ 551. Automatic Preservation of Avoided Transfer

Any transfer avoided under section 522, 544, 545, 547, 548, 549, or 724(a) of this title, or any lien void under section 506(d) of this title, is preserved for the benefit of the estate but only with respect to property of the estate.

§ 552. Postpetition Effect of Security Interest

(a) Except as provided in subsection (b) of this section, property acquired by the estate or by the debtor after the commencement of the case is not subject to any lien resulting from any security agreement entered into by the debtor before the commencement of the case.

(b)(1) Except as provided in sections 363, 506(c), 522, 544, 545, 547, and 548 of this title, if the debtor and an entity entered into a security agreement before the commencement of the case and if the security interest created by such security agreement extends to property of the debtor acquired before the commencement of the case and to proceeds, products, offspring, or profits of such property, then such security interest extends to such proceeds, products, offspring, or profits acquired by the estate after the commencement of the case to the extent provided by such security agreement and by applicable nonbankruptcy law, except to any extent that the court, after notice and a hearing and based on the equities of the case, orders otherwise.

(2) Except as provided in sections 363, 506(c), 522, 544, 545, 547, and 548 of this title, and notwithstanding section 546(b) of this title, if the debtor and an entity entered into a security agreement before the commencement of the case and if the security interest created by such security agreement extends to property of the debtor acquired before the commencement of the case and to amounts paid as rents of such property or the fees, charges, accounts, or other payments for the use or occupancy of rooms and other public facilities in hotels, motels, or other lodging properties, then such security interest extends to such rents and such fees, charges, accounts, or other payments acquired by the estate after the commencement of the case to the extent provided in such security agreement, except to any extent that the court, after notice and a hearing and based on the equities of the case, orders otherwise.

§ 553. Setoff

(a) Except as otherwise provided in this section and in sections 362 and 363 of this title, this title does not affect any right of a creditor to offset a mutual debt owing by such creditor to the debtor that arose before the commencement of the case under this title against a claim of such creditor against the debtor that arose before the commencement of the case, except to the extent that—

(1) the claim of such creditor against the debtor is disallowed;

(2) such claim was transferred, by an entity other than the debtor, to such creditor—

(A) after the commencement of the case; or

(B) (i) after 90 days before the date of the filing of the petition; and

(ii) while the debtor was insolvent (except for a setoff of a kind described in section 362(b)(6), 362(b)(7), 362(b)(17), 362(b)(27), 555, 556, 559, 560, or 561); or

(3) the debt owed to the debtor by such creditor was incurred by such creditor—

(A) after 90 days before the date of the filing of the petition;

(B) while the debtor was insolvent; and

(C) for the purpose of obtaining a right of setoff against the debtor (except for a setoff of a kind described in section 362(b)(6), 362(b)(7), 362(b)(17), 362(b)(27), 555, 556, 559, 560, or 561).

(b)(1) Except with respect to a setoff of a kind described in section 362(b)(6), 362(b)(7), 362(b)(17), 362(b)(27), 555, 556, 559, 560, 561, 365(h), 546(h), or 365(i)(2) of this title, if a creditor offsets a mutual debt owing to the debtor against a claim against the debtor on or within 90 days before the date of the filing of the petition, then the trustee may recover from such creditor the amount so offset to the extent that any insufficiency on the date of such setoff is less than the insufficiency on the later of—

(A) 90 days before the date of the filing of the petition; and

(B) the first date during the 90 days immediately preceding the date of the filing of the petition on which there is an insufficiency.

(2) In this subsection, "insufficiency" means amount, if any, by which a claim against the

debtor exceeds a mutual debt owing to the debtor by the holder of such claim.

(c) For the purposes of this section, the debtor is presumed to have been insolvent on and during the 90 days immediately preceding the date of the filing of the petition.

§ 554. Abandonment of Property of the Estate

(a) After notice and a hearing, the trustee may abandon any property of the estate that is burdensome to the estate or that is of inconsequential value and benefit to the estate.

(b) On request of a party in interest and after notice and a hearing, the court may order the trustee to abandon any property of the estate that is burdensome to the estate or that is of inconsequential value and benefit to the estate.

(c) Unless the court orders otherwise, any property scheduled under section 521(a)(1) of this title not otherwise administered at the time of the closing of a case is abandoned to the debtor and administered for purposes of section 350 of this title.

(d) Unless the court orders otherwise, property of the estate that is not abandoned under this section and that is not administered in the case remains property of the estate.

§ 555. Contractual Right to Liquidate, Terminate, or Accelerate a Securities Contract

The exercise of a contractual right of a stockbroker, financial institution, financial participant, or securities clearing agency to cause the liquidation, termination, or acceleration of a securities contract, as defined in section 741 of this title, because of a condition of the kind specified in section 365(e)(1) of this title shall not be stayed, avoided, or otherwise limited by operation of any provision of this title or by order of a court or administrative agency in any proceeding under this title unless such order is authorized under the provisions of the Securities Investor Protection Act of 1970 or any statute administered by the Securities and Exchange Commission. As used in this section, the term "contractual right" includes a right set forth in a rule or bylaw of a derivatives clearing organization (as defined in the Commodity Exchange Act), a multilateral clearing organization (as defined in the Federal Deposit Insurance Corporation Improvement Act of 1991), a national securities exchange, a national securities association, a securities clearing agency, a contract market designated under the Commodity Exchange Act, a derivatives transaction execution facility registered under the Commodity Exchange Act, or a board of trade (as defined in the Commodity Exchange Act), or in a resolution of the governing board thereof, and a right, whether or not in writing, arising under common law, under law merchant, or by reason of normal business practice.

§ 556. Contractual Right to Liquidate, Terminate, or Accelerate a Commodities Contract or Forward Contract

The contractual right of a commodity broker, financial participant, or forward contract merchant to cause the liquidation, termination, or acceleration of a commodity contract, as defined in section 761 of this title, or forward contract because of a condition of the kind specified in section 365(e)(1) of this title, and the right to a variation or maintenance margin payment received from a trustee with respect to open commodity contracts or forward contracts, shall not be stayed, avoided, or otherwise limited by operation of any provision of this title or by the order of a court in any proceeding under this title. As used in this section, the term "contractual right" includes a right set forth in a rule or bylaw of a derivatives clearing organization (as defined in the Commodity Exchange Act), a multilateral clearing organization (as defined in the Federal Deposit Insurance Corporation Improvement Act of 1991), a national securities exchange, a national securities association, a securities clearing agency, a contract market designated under the Commodity Exchange Act, a derivatives transaction execution facility registered under the Commodity Exchange Act, or a board of trade (as defined in the Commodity Exchange Act) or in a resolution of the governing board thereof and a right, whether or not evidenced in writing, arising under common law, under law merchant or by reason of normal business practice.

§ 557. Expedited Determination of Interests in, and Abandonment or Other Disposition of Grain Assets

(a) This section applies only in a case concerning a debtor that owns or operates a grain storage facility and only with respect to grain and the proceeds of grain. This section does not affect the application of any other section of this title to property other than grain and proceeds of grain.

(b) In this section—

(1) "grain" means wheat, corn, flaxseed, grain sorghum, barley, oats, rye, soybeans, other dry edible beans, or rice;

(2) "grain storage facility" means a site or physical structure regularly used to store grain for producers, or to store grain acquired from producers for resale; and

(3) "producer" means an entity which engages in the growing of grain.

(c)(1) Notwithstanding sections 362, 363, 365, and 554 of this title, on the court's own motion the court may, and on the request of the trustee or an entity that claims an interest in grain or the proceeds of grain the court shall, expedite the procedures for the determination of interests in and the disposition of grain and the proceeds of grain, by shortening to the greatest extent feasible such time periods as are otherwise applicable for such procedures and by establishing, by order, a timetable having a duration of not to exceed 120 days for the completion of the applicable procedure specified in subsection (d) of this section. Such time periods and such timetable may be modified by the court, for cause, in accordance with subsection (f) of this section.

(2) The court shall determine the extent to which such time periods shall be shortened, based upon—

(A) any need of an entity claiming an interest in such grain or the proceeds of grain for a prompt determination of such interest;

(B) any need of such entity for a prompt disposition of such grain;

(C) the market for such grain;

(D) the conditions under which such grain is stored;

(E) the costs of continued storage or disposition of such grain;

(F) the orderly administration of the estate;

(G) the appropriate opportunity for an entity to assert an interest in such grain; and

(H) such other considerations as are relevant to the need to expedite such procedures in the case.

(d) The procedures that may be expedited under subsection (c) of this section include—

(1) the filing of and response to—

(A) a claim of ownership;

(B) a proof of claim;

(C) a request for abandonment;

(D) a request for relief from the stay of action against property under section 362(a) of this title;

(E) a request for determination of secured status;

(F) a request for determination of whether such grain or the proceeds of grain—

(i) is property of the estate;

(ii) must be turned over to the estate; or

(iii) may be used, sold, or leased; and

(G) any other request for determination of an interest in such grain or the proceeds of grain;

(2) the disposition of such grain or the proceeds of grain, before or after determination of interests in such grain or the proceeds of grain, by way of—

(A) sale of such grain;

(B) abandonment;

(C) distribution; or

(D) such other method as is equitable in the case;

(3) subject to sections 701, 702, 703, 1104, 1183, 1202, and 1302 of this title, the appointment of a trustee or examiner and the retention and compensation of any professional person required to assist with respect to matters relevant to the determination of interests in or disposition of such grain or the proceeds of grain; and

(4) the determination of any dispute concerning a matter specified in paragraph (1), (2), or (3) of this subsection.

(e)(1) Any governmental unit that has regulatory jurisdiction over the operation or liquidation of the debtor or the debtor's business shall be given notice of any request made or order entered under subsection (c) of this section.

(2) Any such governmental unit may raise, and may appear and be heard on, any issue relating to grain or the proceeds of grain in a case in which a request is made, or an order is entered, under subsection (c) of this section.

(3) The trustee shall consult with such governmental unit before taking any action relating to the disposition of grain in the possession, custody, or control of the debtor or the estate.

(f) The court may extend the period for final disposition of grain or the proceeds of grain under this section beyond 120 days if the court finds that—

(1) the interests of justice so require in light of the complexity of the case; and

(2) the interests of those claimants entitled to distribution of grain or the proceeds of grain will not be materially injured by such additional delay.

(g) Unless an order establishing an expedited procedure under subsection (c) of this section, or determining any interest in or approving any disposition of grain or the proceeds of grain, is stayed pending appeal—

(1) the reversal or modification of such order on appeal does not affect the validity of any procedure, determination, or disposition that occurs before such reversal or modification, whether or not any entity knew of the pendency of the appeal; and

(2) neither the court nor the trustee may delay, due to the appeal of such order, any proceeding in the case in which such order is issued.

(h)(1) The trustee may recover from grain and the proceeds of grain the reasonable and necessary costs and expenses allowable under section 503(b) of this title attributable to preserving or disposing of grain or the proceeds of grain, but may not recover from such grain or the proceeds of grain any other costs or expenses.

(2) Notwithstanding section 326(a) of this title, the dollar amounts of money specified in such section include the value, as of the date of disposition, of any grain that the trustee distributes in kind.

(i) In all cases where the quantity of a specific type of grain held by a debtor operating a grain storage facility exceeds ten thousand bushels, such grain shall be sold by the trustee and the assets thereof distributed in accordance with the provisions of this section.

§ 558. Defenses of the Estate

The estate shall have the benefit of any defense available to the debtor as against any entity other than the estate, including statutes of limitation, statutes of frauds, usury, and other personal defenses. A waiver of any such defense by the debtor after the commencement of the case does not bind the estate.

§ 559. Contractual Right to Liquidate, Terminate, or Accelerate a Repurchase Agreement

The exercise of a contractual right of a repo participant or financial participant to cause the liquidation, termination, or acceleration of a repurchase agreement because of a condition of the kind specified in section 365(e)(1) of this title shall not be stayed, avoided, or otherwise limited by operation of any provision of this title or by order of a court or administrative agency in any proceeding under this title, unless, where the debtor is a stockbroker or securities clearing agency, such order is authorized under the provisions of the Securities Investor Protection Act of 1970 or any statute administered by the Securities and Exchange Commission. In the event that a repo participant or financial participant liquidates one or more repurchase agreements with a debtor and under the terms of one or more such agreements has agreed to deliver assets subject to repurchase agreements to the debtor, any excess of the market prices received on liquidation of such assets (or if any such assets are not disposed of on the date of liquidation of such repurchase agreements, at the prices available at the time of liquidation of such repurchase agreements from a generally recognized source or the most recent closing bid quotation from such a source) over the sum of the stated repurchase prices and all expenses in connection with the liquidation of such repurchase agreements shall be deemed property of the estate, subject to the available rights of setoff. As used in this section, the term "contractual right" includes a right set forth in a rule or bylaw of a derivatives clearing organization (as defined in the Commodity Exchange Act), a multilateral clearing organization (as defined in the Federal Deposit Insurance Corporation Improvement Act of 1991), a national securities exchange, a national securities association, a securities clearing agency, a contract market designated under the Commodity Exchange Act, a derivatives transaction execution facility registered under the Commodity Exchange Act, or a board of trade (as defined in the Commodity Exchange Act) or in a resolution of the governing board thereof and a right, whether or not evidenced in writing, arising under common law, under law merchant or by reason of normal business practice.

§ 560. Contractual Right to Liquidate, Terminate, or Accelerate a Swap Agreement

The exercise of any contractual right of any swap participant or financial participant to cause the liquidation, termination, or acceleration of one or more swap agreements because of a condition of the kind specified in section 365(e)(1) of this title or to offset or net out any termination values or payment amounts arising under or in connection with the termination, liquidation, or acceleration of one or more swap agreements shall not be stayed, avoided, or otherwise limited by operation of any provision of this title or by order of a court or administrative agency in any proceeding under this title. As used in this section, the term "contractual right" includes a right set forth in a rule or bylaw of a derivatives clearing organization (as defined in the Commodity Exchange Act), a multilateral clearing organization (as defined in the Federal Deposit Insurance Corporation Improvement Act of 1991), a national securities exchange, a national securities association, a securities clearing agency, a contract market designated under the Commodity Exchange Act, a derivatives transaction execution facility registered under the Commodity Exchange Act, or a board of trade (as defined in the Commodity Exchange Act) or in a resolution of the governing board thereof and a right, whether or not evidenced in writing, arising under common law, under law merchant, or by reason of normal business practice.

§ 561. Contractual Right to Terminate, Liquidate, Accelerate, or Offset Under a Master Netting Agreement and Across Contracts; Proceedings Under Chapter 15

(a) Subject to subsection (b), the exercise of any contractual right, because of a condition of the kind specified in section 365(e)(1), to cause the termination, liquidation, or acceleration of or to offset or net termination values, payment amounts, or other transfer obligations arising under or in connection with one or more (or the termination, liquidation, or acceleration of one or more)—

(1) securities contracts, as defined in section 741(7);

(2) commodity contracts, as defined in section 761(4);

(3) forward contracts;

(4) repurchase agreements;

(5) swap agreements; or

(6) master netting agreements,

shall not be stayed, avoided, or otherwise limited by operation of any provision of this title or by any order of a court or administrative agency in any proceeding under this title.

(b)(1) A party may exercise a contractual right described in subsection (a) to terminate, liquidate, or accelerate only to the extent that such party could exercise such a right under section 555, 556, 559, or 560 for each individual contract covered by the master netting agreement in issue.

(2) If a debtor is a commodity broker subject to subchapter IV of chapter 7—

(A) a party may not net or offset an obligation to the debtor arising under, or in connection with, a commodity contract traded on or subject to the rules of a contract market designated under the Commodity Exchange Act or a derivatives transaction execution facility registered under the Commodity Exchange Act against any claim arising under, or in connection with, other instruments, contracts, or agreements listed in subsection (a) except to the extent that the party has positive net equity in the commodity accounts at the debtor, as calculated under such subchapter; and

(B) another commodity broker may not net or offset an obligation to the debtor arising under, or in connection with, a commodity contract entered into or held on behalf of a customer of the debtor and traded on or subject to the rules of a contract market designated under the Commodity Exchange Act or a derivatives transaction execution facility registered under the Commodity Exchange Act against any claim arising under, or in connection with, other instruments, contracts, or agreements listed in subsection (a).

(3) No provision of subparagraph (A) or (B) of paragraph (2) shall prohibit the offset of claims and obligations that arise under—

(A) a cross-margining agreement or similar arrangement that has been approved by the Commodity Futures Trading Commission or submitted to the Commodity Futures Trading Commission under paragraph (1) or (2) of section 5c(c) of the Commodity Exchange Act and has not been abrogated or rendered ineffective by the Commodity Futures Trading Commission; or

(B) any other netting agreement between a clearing organization (as defined in section 761) and another entity that has been approved by the Commodity Futures Trading Commission.

(c) As used in this section, the term "contractual right" includes a right set forth in a rule or bylaw of a derivatives clearing organization (as defined in the Commodity Exchange Act), a multilateral clearing organization (as defined in the Federal Deposit Insurance Corporation Improvement Act of 1991), a national securities exchange, a national securities association, a securities clearing agency, a contract market designated under the Commodity Exchange Act, a derivatives transaction execution facility registered under the Commodity Exchange Act, or a board of trade (as defined in the Commodity Exchange Act) or in a resolution of the governing board thereof, and a right, whether or not evidenced in writing, arising under common law, under law merchant, or by reason of normal business practice.

(d) Any provisions of this title relating to securities contracts, commodity contracts, forward contracts, repurchase agreements, swap agreements, or master netting agreements shall apply in a case under chapter 15, so that enforcement of contractual provisions of such contracts and agreements in accordance with their terms will not be stayed or otherwise limited by operation of any provision of this title or by order of a court in any case under this title, and to limit avoidance powers to the same extent as in a proceeding under chapter 7 or 11 of this title (such enforcement not to be limited based on the presence or absence of assets of the debtor in the United States).

§ 562. Timing of Damage Measurement in Connection with Swap Agreements, Securities Contracts, Forward Contracts, Commodity Contracts, Repurchase Agreements, and Master Netting Agreements

(a) If the trustee rejects a swap agreement, securities contract (as defined in section 741), forward contract, commodity contract (as defined in section 761), repurchase agreement, or master netting agreement pursuant to section 365(a), or if a forward contract merchant, stockbroker, financial institution, securities clearing agency, repo participant, financial participant, master netting agreement participant, or swap participant liquidates, terminates, or accelerates such contract or agreement, damages shall be measured as of the earlier of—

(1) the date of such rejection; or

(2) the date or dates of such liquidation, termination, or acceleration.

(b) If there are not any commercially reasonable determinants of value as of any date referred to in paragraph (1) or (2) of subsection (a), damages shall be measured as of the earliest subsequent date or dates on which there are commercially reasonable determinants of value.

(c) For the purposes of subsection (b), if damages are not measured as of the date or dates of rejection, liquidation, termination, or acceleration, and the forward contract merchant, stockbroker, financial institution, securities clearing agency, repo participant, financial participant, master netting agreement participant, or swap participant or the trustee objects to the timing of the measurement of damages—

(1) the trustee, in the case of an objection by a forward contract merchant, stockbroker, financial institution, securities clearing agency, repo participant, financial participant, master netting agreement participant, or swap participant; or

(2) the forward contract merchant, stockbroker, financial institution, securities clearing agency, repo participant, financial participant, master netting agreement participant, or swap participant, in the case of an objection by the trustee, has the burden of proving that there were no commercially reasonable determinants of value as of such date or dates.

CHAPTER 7. LIQUIDATION

SUBCHAPTER I—OFFICERS AND ADMINISTRATION

Section

701. Interim Trustee
702. Election of Trustee
703. Successor Trustee
704. Duties of Trustee
705. Creditors' Committee
706. Conversion
707. Dismissal of a Case or Conversion to a Case under Chapter 11 or 13

§ 701. Interim Trustee

(a)(1) Promptly after the order for relief under this chapter, the United States trustee shall appoint one disinterested person that is a member of the panel of private trustees established under section 586(a)(1) of title 28 or that is serving as trustee in the case immediately before the order for relief under this chapter to serve as interim trustee in the case.

(2) If none of the members of such panel is willing to serve as interim trustee in the case, then the United States trustee may serve as interim trustee in the case.

(b) The service of an interim trustee under this section terminates when a trustee elected or designated under section 702 of this title to serve as trustee in the case qualifies under section 322 of this title.

(c) An interim trustee serving under this section is a trustee in a case under this title.

§ 702. Election of Trustee

(a) A creditor may vote for a candidate for trustee only if such creditor—

(1) holds an allowable, undisputed, fixed, liquidated, unsecured claim of a kind entitled to

distribution under section 726(a)(2), 726(a)(3), 726(a)(4), 752(a), 766(h), or 766(i) of this title;

(2) does not have an interest materially adverse, other than an equity interest that is not substantial in relation to such creditor's interest as a creditor, to the interest of creditors entitled to such distribution; and

(3) is not an insider.

(b) At the meeting of creditors held under section 341 of this title, creditors may elect one person to serve as trustee in the case if election of a trustee is requested by creditors that may vote under subsection (a) of this section, and that hold at least 20 percent in amount of the claims specified in subsection (a)(1) of this section that are held by creditors that may vote under subsection (a) of this section.

(c) A candidate for trustee is elected trustee if—

(1) creditors holding at least 20 percent in amount of the claims of a kind specified in subsection (a)(1) of this section that are held by creditors that may vote under subsection (a) of this section vote; and

(2) such candidate receives the votes of creditors holding a majority in amount of claims specified in subsection (a)(1) of this section that are held by creditors that vote for a trustee.

(d) If a trustee is not elected under this section, then the interim trustee shall serve as trustee in the case.

§ 703. Successor Trustee

(a) If a trustee dies or resigns during a case, fails to qualify under section 322 of this title, or is removed under section 324 of this title, creditors may elect, in the manner specified in section 702 of this title, a person to fill the vacancy in the office of trustee.

(b) Pending election of a trustee under subsection (a) of this section, if necessary to preserve or prevent loss to the estate, the United States trustee may appoint an interim trustee in the manner specified in section 701(a).

(c) If creditors do not elect a successor trustee under subsection (a) of this section or if a trustee is needed in a case reopened under section 350 of this title, then the United States trustee—

(1) shall appoint one disinterested person that is a member of the panel of private trustees established under section 586(a)(1) of title 28 to serve as trustee in the case; or

(2) may, if none of the disinterested members of such panel is willing to serve as trustee, serve as trustee in the case.

§ 704. Duties of Trustee

(a) The trustee shall—

(1) collect and reduce to money the property of the estate for which such trustee serves, and close such estate as expeditiously as is compatible with the best interests of parties in interest;

(2) be accountable for all property received;

(3) ensure that the debtor shall perform his intention as specified in section 521(a)(2)(B) of this title;

(4) investigate the financial affairs of the debtor;

(5) if a purpose would be served, examine proofs of claims and object to the allowance of any claim that is improper;

(6) if advisable, oppose the discharge of the debtor;

(7) unless the court orders otherwise, furnish such information concerning the estate and the estate's administration as is requested by a party in interest;

(8) if the business of the debtor is authorized to be operated, file with the court, with the United States trustee, and with any governmental unit charged with responsibility for collection or determination of any tax arising out of such operation, periodic reports and summaries of the operation of such business, including a statement of receipts and disbursements, and such other information as the United States trustee or the court requires;

(9) make a final report and file a final account of the administration of the estate with the court and with the United States trustee;

(10) if with respect to the debtor there is a claim for a domestic support obligation, provide the applicable notice specified in subsection (c);

(11) if, at the time of the commencement of the case, the debtor (or any entity designated by the debtor) served as the administrator (as defined in section 3 of the Employee Retirement Income Security Act of 1974) of an employee benefit plan, continue to perform the obligations required of the administrator; and

(12) use all reasonable and best efforts to transfer patients from a health care business

that is in the process of being closed to an appropriate health care business that—

(A) is in the vicinity of the health care business that is closing;

(B) provides the patient with services that are substantially similar to those provided by the health care business that is in the process of being closed; and

(C) maintains a reasonable quality of care.

(b)(1) With respect to a debtor who is an individual in a case under this chapter—

(A) the United States trustee (or the bankruptcy administrator, if any) shall review all materials filed by the debtor and, not later than 10 days after the date of the first meeting of creditors, file with the court a statement as to whether the debtor's case would be presumed to be an abuse under section 707(b); and

(B) not later than 7 days after receiving a statement under subparagraph (A), the court shall provide a copy of the statement to all creditors.

(2) The United States trustee (or bankruptcy administrator, if any) shall, not later than 30 days after the date of filing a statement under paragraph (1), either file a motion to dismiss or convert under section 707(b) or file a statement setting forth the reasons the United States trustee (or the bankruptcy administrator, if any) does not consider such a motion to be appropriate, if the United States trustee (or the bankruptcy administrator, if any) determines that the debtor's case should be presumed to be an abuse under section 707(b) and the product of the debtor's current monthly income, multiplied by 12 is not less than—

(A) in the case of a debtor in a household of 1 person, the median family income of the applicable State for 1 earner; or

(B) in the case of a debtor in a household of 2 or more individuals, the highest median family income of the applicable State for a family of the same number or fewer individuals.

(c)(1) In a case described in subsection (a)(10) to which subsection (a)(10) applies, the trustee shall—

(A) (i) provide written notice to the holder of the claim described in subsection (a)(10) of such claim and of the right of such holder to use the services of the State child support enforcement agency established under sections 464 and 466 of the Social Security Act for the State in which such holder resides, for assistance in collecting child support during and after the case under this title;

(ii) include in the notice provided under clause (i) the address and telephone number of such State child support enforcement agency; and

(iii) include in the notice provided under clause (i) an explanation of the rights of such holder to payment of such claim under this chapter;

(B) (i) provide written notice to such State child support enforcement agency of such claim; and

(ii) include in the notice provided under clause (i) the name, address, and telephone number of such holder; and

(C) at such time as the debtor is granted a discharge under section 727, provide written notice to such holder and to such State child support enforcement agency of—

(i) the granting of the discharge;

(ii) the last recent known address of the debtor;

(iii) the last recent known name and address of the debtor's employer; and

(iv) the name of each creditor that holds a claim that—

(I) is not discharged under paragraph (2), (4), or (14A) of section 523(a); or

(II) was reaffirmed by the debtor under section 524(c).

(2) (A) The holder of a claim described in subsection (a)(10) or the State child support enforcement agency of the State in which such holder resides may request from a creditor described in paragraph (1)(C)(iv) the last known address of the debtor.

(B) Notwithstanding any other provision of law, a creditor that makes a disclosure of a last known address of a debtor in connection with a request made under subparagraph (A) shall not be liable by reason of making such disclosure.

§ 705. Creditors' Committee

(a) At the meeting under section 341(a) of this title, creditors that may vote for a trustee under section 702(a) of this title may elect a committee of not fewer than three, and not more than eleven, creditors, each of whom holds an allowable unsecured claim of a kind entitled to distribution under section 726(a)(2) of this title.

(b) A committee elected under subsection (a) of this section may consult with the trustee or the United States trustee in connection with the administration of the estate, make recommendations to the trustee or the United States trustee respecting the performance of the trustee's duties, and submit to the court or the United States trustee any question affecting the administration of the estate.

§ 706. Conversion

(a) The debtor may convert a case under this chapter to a case under chapter 11, 12, or 13 of this title at any time, if the case has not been converted under section 1112, 1208, or 1307 of this title. Any waiver of the right to convert a case under this subsection is unenforceable.

(b) On request of a party in interest and after notice and a hearing, the court may convert a case under this chapter to a case under chapter 11 of this title at any time.

(c) The court may not convert a case under this chapter to a case under chapter 12 or 13 of this title unless the debtor requests or consents to such conversion.

(d) Notwithstanding any other provision of this section, a case may not be converted to a case under another chapter of this title unless the debtor may be a debtor under such chapter.

§ 707. Dismissal of a Case or Conversion to a Case under Chapter 11 or 13

(a) The court may dismiss a case under this chapter only after notice and a hearing and only for cause, including—

(1) unreasonable delay by the debtor that is prejudicial to creditors;

(2) nonpayment of any fees or charges required under chapter 123 of title 28; and

(3) failure of the debtor in a voluntary case to file, within fifteen days or such additional time as the court may allow after the filing of the petition commencing such case, the information required by paragraph (1) of section 521(a), but only on a motion by the United States trustee.

(b)(1) After notice and a hearing, the court, on its own motion or on a motion by the United States trustee, trustee (or bankruptcy administrator, if any), or any party in interest, may dismiss a case filed by an individual debtor under this chapter whose debts are primarily consumer debts, or, with the debtor's consent, convert such a case to a case under chapter 11 or 13 of this title, if it finds that the granting of relief would be an abuse of the provisions of this chapter. In making a determination whether to dismiss a case under this section, the court may not take into consideration whether a debtor has made, or continues to make, charitable contributions (that meet the definition of "charitable contribution" under section 548(d)(3)) to any qualified religious or charitable entity or organization (as that term is defined in section 548(d)(4)).

(2) (A)(i) In considering under paragraph (1) whether the granting of relief would be an abuse of the provisions of this chapter, the court shall presume abuse exists if the debtor's current monthly income reduced by the amounts determined under clauses (ii), (iii), and (iv), and multiplied by 60 is not less than the lesser of—

(I) 25 percent of the debtor's nonpriority unsecured claims in the case, or $9,075, whichever is greater; or

(II) $15,150.

(ii) (I) The debtor's monthly expenses shall be the debtor's applicable monthly expense amounts specified under the National Standards and Local Standards, and the debtor's actual monthly expenses for the categories specified as Other Necessary Expenses issued by the Internal Revenue Service for the area in which the debtor resides, as in effect on the date of the order for relief, for the debtor, the dependents of the debtor, and the spouse of the debtor in a joint case, if the spouse is not otherwise a dependent. Such expenses shall include reasonably necessary health insurance, disability insurance, and health savings account expenses for the debtor, the spouse of the debtor, or the dependents of the debtor. Notwithstanding any other provision of this clause, the monthly expenses of the debtor shall not include any payments for debts. In addition, the debtor's monthly expenses shall include the debtor's reasonably necessary expenses incurred to maintain the safety of the debtor and the family of the debtor from family violence as identified under section 302 of the Family Violence Prevention and Services Act, or other applicable Federal law. The expenses included in the debtor's monthly expenses described in the preceding sentence shall be kept confidential by the court. In addition, if it is demonstrated that it is reasonable and necessary, the debtor's monthly expenses may also include an additional allowance for food and clothing of up to 5 percent of the food and clothing categories as specified by the National Standards issued by the Internal Revenue Service.

(II) In addition, the debtor's monthly expenses may include, if applicable, the continuation of actual expenses paid by the debtor that are reasonable and necessary for care and support of an elderly, chronically ill, or disabled household member or member of the debtor's immediate family (including parents, grandparents, siblings, children, and grandchildren of the debtor, the dependents of the debtor, and the spouse of the debtor in a joint case who is not a dependent) and who is unable to pay for such reasonable and necessary expenses. Such monthly expenses may include, if applicable, contributions to an account of a qualified ABLE program to the extent such contributions are not excess contributions (as described in section 4973(h) of the Internal Revenue Code of 1986) and if the designated beneficiary of such account is a child, stepchild, grandchild, or stepgrandchild of the debtor.

(III) In addition, for a debtor eligible for chapter 13, the debtor's monthly expenses may include the actual administrative expenses of administering a chapter 13 plan for the district in which the debtor resides, up to an amount of 10 percent of the projected plan payments, as determined under schedules issued by the Executive Office for United States Trustees.

(IV) In addition, the debtor's monthly expenses may include the actual expenses for each dependent child less than 18 years of age, not to exceed $2,275[5] per year per child, to attend a private or public elementary or secondary school if the debtor provides documentation of such expenses and a detailed explanation of why such expenses are reasonable and necessary, and why such expenses are not already accounted for in the National Standards, Local Standards, or Other Necessary Expenses referred to in subclause (I).

(V) In addition, the debtor's monthly expenses may include an allowance for housing and utilities, in excess of the allowance specified by the Local Standards for housing and utilities issued by the Internal Revenue Service, based on the actual expenses for home energy costs if the debtor provides documentation of such actual expenses and demonstrates that such actual expenses are reasonable and necessary.

(iii) The debtor's average monthly payments on account of secured debts shall be calculated as the sum of—

(I) the total of all amounts scheduled as contractually due to secured creditors in each month of the 60 months following the date of the filing of the petition; and

(II) any additional payments to secured creditors necessary for the debtor, in filing a plan under chapter 13 of this title, to maintain possession of the debtor's primary residence, motor vehicle, or other property necessary for the support of the debtor and the debtor's dependents, that serves as collateral for secured debts; divided by 60.

---

[5] Dollar amounts will change again on April 1, 2025.

(iv) The debtor's expenses for payment of all priority claims (including priority child support and alimony claims) shall be calculated as the total amount of debts entitled to priority, divided by 60.

(B) (i) In any proceeding brought under this subsection, the presumption of abuse may only be rebutted by demonstrating special circumstances, such as a serious medical condition or a call or order to active duty in the Armed Forces, to the extent such special circumstances that justify additional expenses or adjustments of current monthly income for which there is no reasonable alternative.

(ii) In order to establish special circumstances, the debtor shall be required to itemize each additional expense or adjustment of income and to provide—

(I) documentation for such expense or adjustment to income; and

(II) a detailed explanation of the special circumstances that make such expenses or adjustment to income necessary and reasonable.

(iii) The debtor shall attest under oath to the accuracy of any information provided to demonstrate that additional expenses or adjustments to income are required.

(iv) The presumption of abuse may only be rebutted if the additional expenses or adjustments to income referred to in clause (i) cause the product of the debtor's current monthly income reduced by the amounts determined under clauses (ii), (iii), and (iv) of subparagraph (A) when multiplied by 60 to be less than the lesser of—

(I) 25 percent of the debtor's nonpriority unsecured claims, or $9,075, whichever is greater; or

(II) $15,150.

(C) As part of the schedule of current income and expenditures required under section 521, the debtor shall include a statement of the debtor's current monthly income, and the calculations that determine whether a presumption arises under subparagraph (A)(i), that show how each such amount is calculated.

(D) Subparagraphs (A) through (C) shall not apply, and the court may not dismiss or convert a case based on any form of means testing—

(i) if the debtor is a disabled veteran (as defined in section 3741(1) of title 38), and the indebtedness occurred primarily during a period during which he or she was—

(I) on active duty (as defined in section 101(d)(1) of title 10); or

(II) performing a homeland defense activity (as defined in section 901(1) of title 32); or

(ii) with respect to the debtor, while the debtor is—

(I) on, and during the 540-day period beginning immediately after the debtor is released from, a period of active duty (as defined in section 101(d)(1) of title 10) of not less than 90 days; or

(II) performing, and during the 540-day period beginning immediately after the debtor is no longer performing, a homeland defense activity (as defined in section 901(1) of title 32) performed for a period of not less than 90 days; if after September 11, 2001, the debtor while a member of a reserve component of the Armed Forces or a member of the National Guard, was called to such active duty or performed such homeland defense activity.

(3) In considering under paragraph (1) whether the granting of relief would be an abuse of the provisions of this chapter in a case in which the presumption in paragraph (2)(A)(i) does not arise or is rebutted, the court shall consider—

(A) whether the debtor filed the petition in bad faith; or

(B) the totality of the circumstances (including whether the debtor seeks to reject a personal services contract and the financial need for such rejection as sought by the debtor) of the debtor's financial situation demonstrates abuse.

(4) (A) The court, on its own initiative or on the motion of a party in interest, in accordance with the procedures described in rule 9011 of the Federal Rules of Bankruptcy Procedure, may order the attorney for the debtor to reimburse the trustee for all reasonable costs in prosecuting a motion filed under section 707(b), including reasonable attorneys' fees, if—

(i) a trustee files a motion for dismissal or conversion under this subsection; and

(ii) the court—

(I) grants such motion; and

(II) finds that the action of the attorney for the debtor in filing a case under this chapter violated rule 9011 of the Federal Rules of Bankruptcy Procedure.

(B) If the court finds that the attorney for the debtor violated rule 9011 of the Federal Rules of Bankruptcy Procedure, the court, on its own initiative or on the motion of a party in interest, in accordance with such procedures, may order—

(i) the assessment of an appropriate civil penalty against the attorney for the debtor; and

(ii) the payment of such civil penalty to the trustee, the United States trustee (or the bankruptcy administrator, if any).

(C) The signature of an attorney on a petition, pleading, or written motion shall constitute a certification that the attorney has—

(i) performed a reasonable investigation into the circumstances that gave rise to the petition, pleading, or written motion; and

(ii) determined that the petition, pleading, or written motion—

(I) is well grounded in fact; and

(II) is warranted by existing law or a good faith argument for the extension, modification, or reversal of existing law and does not constitute an abuse under paragraph (1).

(D) The signature of an attorney on the petition shall constitute a certification that the attorney has no knowledge after an inquiry that the information in the schedules filed with such petition is incorrect.

(5) (A) Except as provided in subparagraph (B) and subject to paragraph (6), the court, on its own initiative or on the motion of a party in interest, in accordance with the procedures described in rule 9011 of the Federal Rules of Bankruptcy Procedure, may award a debtor all reasonable costs (including reasonable attorneys' fees) in contesting a motion filed by a party in interest (other than a trustee or United States trustee (or bankruptcy administrator, if any)) under this subsection if—

(i) the court does not grant the motion; and

(ii) the court finds that—

(I) the position of the party that filed the motion violated rule 9011 of the Federal Rules of Bankruptcy Procedure; or

(II) the attorney (if any) who filed the motion did not comply with the requirements of clauses (i) and (ii) of paragraph (4)(C), and the motion was made solely for the purpose of coercing a debtor into waiving a right guaranteed to the debtor under this title.

(B) A small business that has a claim of an aggregate amount less than $1,525 shall not be subject to subparagraph (A)(ii)(I).

(C) For purposes of this paragraph—

(i) the term "small business" means an unincorporated business, partnership, corporation, association, or organization that—

(I) has fewer than 25 full-time employees as determined on the date on which the motion is filed; and

(II) is engaged in commercial or business activity; and

(ii) the number of employees of a wholly owned subsidiary of a corporation includes the employees of—

(I) a parent corporation; and

(II) any other subsidiary corporation of the parent corporation.

(6) Only the judge or United States trustee (or bankruptcy administrator, if any) may file a motion under section 707(b), if the current monthly income of the debtor, or in a joint case, the debtor and the debtor's spouse, as of the date of the order for relief, when multiplied by 12, is equal to or less than—

(A) in the case of a debtor in a household of 1 person, the median family income of the applicable State for 1 earner;

(B) in the case of a debtor in a household of 2, 3, or 4 individuals, the highest median family income of the applicable State for a family of the same number or fewer individuals; or

(C) in the case of a debtor in a household exceeding 4 individuals, the highest median family income of the applicable State for a family of 4 or fewer individuals, plus $825 per month for each individual in excess of 4.

(7) (A) No judge, United States trustee (or bankruptcy administrator, if any), trustee, or other party in interest may file a motion under paragraph (2) if the current monthly income of the debtor, including a veteran (as that term is defined in section 101 of title 38), and the debtor's spouse combined, as of the date of the order for relief when multiplied by 12, is equal to or less than—

(i) in the case of a debtor in a household of 1 person, the median family income of the applicable State for 1 earner;

(ii) in the case of a debtor in a household of 2, 3, or 4 individuals, the highest median family income of the applicable State for a family of the same number or fewer individuals; or

(iii) in the case of a debtor in a household exceeding 4 individuals, the highest median family income of the applicable State for a family of 4 or fewer individuals, plus $825 per month for each individual in excess of 4.

(B) In a case that is not a joint case, current monthly income of the debtor's spouse shall not be considered for purposes of subparagraph (A) if—

(i) (I) the debtor and the debtor's spouse are separated under applicable nonbankruptcy law; or

(II) the debtor and the debtor's spouse are living separate and apart, other than for the purpose of evading subparagraph (A); and

(ii) the debtor files a statement under penalty of perjury—

(I) specifying that the debtor meets the requirement of subclause (I) or (II) of clause (i); and

(II) disclosing the aggregate, or best estimate of the aggregate, amount of any cash or money payments received from the debtor's spouse attributed to the debtor's current monthly income.

(c)(1) In this subsection—

(A) the term "crime of violence" has the meaning given such term in section 16 of title 18; and

(B) the term "drug trafficking crime" has the meaning given such term in section 924(c)(2) of title 18.

(2) Except as provided in paragraph (3), after notice and a hearing, the court, on a motion by the victim of a crime of violence or a drug trafficking crime, may when it is in the best interest of the victim dismiss a voluntary case filed under this chapter by a debtor who is an individual if such individual was convicted of such crime.

(3) The court may not dismiss a case under paragraph (2) if the debtor establishes by a preponderance of the evidence that the filing of a case under this chapter is necessary to satisfy a claim for a domestic support obligation.

SUBCHAPTER II—COLLECTION, LIQUIDATION, AND DISTRIBUTION OF THE ESTATE

Section

721. Authorization to Operate Business
722. Redemption
723. Rights of Partnership Trustee Against General Partners
724. Treatment of Certain Liens
725. Disposition of Certain Property
726. Distribution of Property of the Estate
727. Discharge

§ 721. Authorization to Operate Business

The court may authorize the trustee to operate the business of the debtor for a limited period, if such operation is in the best interest of the estate and consistent with the orderly liquidation of the estate.

§ 722. Redemption

An individual debtor may, whether or not the debtor has waived the right to redeem under this section, redeem tangible personal property intended primarily for personal, family, or household use, from a lien securing a dischargeable consumer debt, if such property is exempted under section 522 of this title or has been abandoned under section 554 of this title, by paying the holder of such lien the amount of the allowed secured claim of such holder that is secured by such lien in full at the time of redemption.

§ 723. Rights of Partnership Trustee Against General Partners

(a) If there is a deficiency of property of the estate to pay in full all claims which are allowed in a case under this chapter concerning a partnership and with respect to which a general partner of the partnership is personally liable, the trustee shall have a claim against such general partner to the extent that under applicable nonbankruptcy law such general partner is personally liable for such deficiency.

(b) To the extent practicable, the trustee shall first seek recovery of such deficiency from any general partner in such partnership that is not a debtor in a case under this title. Pending determination of such deficiency, the court may order any such partner to provide the estate with indemnity for, or assurance of payment of, any deficiency recoverable from such partner, or not to dispose of property.

(c) The trustee has a claim against the estate of each general partner in such partnership that is a debtor in a case under this title for the full amount of all claims of creditors allowed in the case concerning such partnership. Notwithstanding section 502 of this title, there shall not be allowed in such partner's case a claim against such partner on which both such partner and such partnership are liable, except to any extent that such claim is secured only by property of such partner and not by property of such partnership. The claim of the trustee under this subsection is entitled to distribution in such partner's case under section 726(a) of this title the same as any other claim of a kind specified in such section.

(d) If the aggregate that the trustee recovers from the estates of general partners under subsection (c) of this section is greater than any deficiency not recovered under subsection (b) of this section, the court, after notice and a hearing, shall determine an equitable distribution of the surplus so recovered, and the trustee shall distribute such surplus to the estates of the general partners in such partnership according to such determination.

§ 724. Treatment of Certain Liens

(a) The trustee may avoid a lien that secures a claim of a kind specified in section 726(a)(4) of this title.

(b) Property in which the estate has an interest and that is subject to a lien that is not avoidable under this title (other than to the extent that there is a properly perfected unavoidable tax lien arising in connection with an ad valorem tax on real or personal property of the estate) and that secures an allowed claim for a tax, or proceeds of such property, shall be distributed—

(1) first, to any holder of an allowed claim secured by a lien on such property that is not avoidable under this title and that is senior to such tax lien;

(2) second, to any holder of a claim of a kind specified in section 507(a)(1)(c) or 507(a)(2) (except that such expenses under each such section, other than claims for wages, salaries, or commissions that arise after the date of the filing of the petition, shall be limited to expenses incurred under this chapter and shall not include expenses incurred under chapter 11 of this title), 507(a)(1)(A), 507(a)(1)(B), 507(a)(3), 507(a)(4), 507(a)(5), 507(a)(6), or 507(a)(7) of this title, to the extent of the amount of such allowed tax claim that is secured by such tax lien;

(3) third, to the holder of such tax lien, to any extent that such holder's allowed tax claim that is secured by such tax lien exceeds any amount distributed under paragraph (2) of this subsection;

(4) fourth, to any holder of an allowed claim secured by a lien on such property that is not avoidable under this title and that is junior to such tax lien;

(5) fifth, to the holder of such tax lien, to the extent that such holder's allowed claim secured by such tax lien is not paid under paragraph (3) of this subsection; and

(6) sixth, to the estate.

(c) If more than one holder of a claim is entitled to distribution under a particular paragraph of subsection (b) of this section, distribution to such holders under such paragraph shall be in the same order as distribution to such holders would have been other than under this section.

(d) A statutory lien the priority of which is determined in the same manner as the priority of a tax lien under section 6323 of the Internal Revenue

Code of 1986 shall be treated under subsection (b) of this section the same as if such lien were a tax lien.

(e) Before subordinating a tax lien on real or personal property of the estate, the trustee shall—

(1) exhaust the unencumbered assets of the estate; and

(2) in a manner consistent with section 506(c), recover from property securing an allowed secured claim the reasonable, necessary costs and expenses of preserving or disposing of such property.

(f) Notwithstanding the exclusion of ad valorem tax liens under this section and subject to the requirements of subsection (e), the following may be paid from property of the estate which secures a tax lien, or the proceeds of such property:

(1) Claims for wages, salaries, and commissions that are entitled to priority under section 507(a)(4).

(2) Claims for contributions to an employee benefit plan entitled to priority under section 507(a)(5).

§ 725. Disposition of Certain Property

After the commencement of a case under this chapter, but before final distribution of property of the estate under section 726 of this title, the trustee, after notice and a hearing, shall dispose of any property in which an entity other than the estate has an interest, such as a lien, and that has not been disposed of under another section of this title.

§ 726. Distribution of Property of the Estate

(a) Except as provided in section 510 of this title, property of the estate shall be distributed—

(1) first, in payment of claims of the kind specified in, and in the order specified in, section 507 of this title, proof of which is timely filed under section 501 of this title or tardily filed on or before the earlier of—

(A) the date that is 10 days after the mailing to creditors of the summary of the trustee's final report; or

(B) the date on which the trustee commences final distribution under this section;

(2) second, in payment of any allowed unsecured claim, other than a claim of a kind specified in paragraph (1), (3), or (4) of this subsection, proof of which is—

(A) timely filed under section 501(a) of this title;

(B) timely filed under section 501(b) or 501(c) of this title; or

(C) tardily filed under section 501(a) of this title, if—

(i) the creditor that holds such claim did not have notice or actual knowledge of the case in time for timely filing of a proof of such claim under section 501(a) of this title; and

(ii) proof of such claim is filed in time to permit payment of such claim;

(3) third, in payment of any allowed unsecured claim proof of which is tardily filed under section 501(a) of this title, other than a claim of the kind specified in paragraph (2)(C) of this subsection;

(4) fourth, in payment of any allowed claim, whether secured or unsecured, for any fine, penalty, or forfeiture, or for multiple, exemplary, or punitive damages, arising before the earlier of the order for relief or the appointment of a trustee, to the extent that such fine, penalty, forfeiture, or damages are not compensation for actual pecuniary loss suffered by the holder of such claim;

(5) fifth, in payment of interest at the legal rate from the date of the filing of the petition, on any claim paid under paragraph (1), (2), (3), or (4) of this subsection; and

(6) sixth, to the debtor.

(b) Payment on claims of a kind specified in paragraph (1), (2), (3), (4), (5), (6), (7), (8), (9), or (10) of section 507(a) of this title, or in paragraph (2), (3), (4), or (5) of subsection (a) of this section, shall be made pro rata among claims of the kind specified in each such particular paragraph, except that in a case that has been converted to this chapter under section 1112, 1208, or 1307 of this title, a claim allowed under section 503(b) of this title incurred under this chapter after such conversion has priority over a claim allowed under section 503(b) of this title incurred under any other chapter of this title or under this chapter before such conversion and over any expenses of a custodian superseded under section 543 of this title.

(c) Notwithstanding subsections (a) and (b) of this section, if there is property of the kind specified in section 541(a)(2) of this title, or proceeds of such property, in the estate, such property or proceeds shall be segregated from other property of the estate, and such property or proceeds and other property of the estate shall be distributed as follows:

(1) Claims allowed under section 503 of this title shall be paid either from property of the kind specified in section 541(a)(2) of this title, or from other property of the estate, as the interest of justice requires.

(2) Allowed claims, other than claims allowed under section 503 of this title, shall be paid in the order specified in subsection (a) of this section, and, with respect to claims of a kind specified in a particular paragraph of section 507 of this title or subsection (a) of this section, in the following order and manner:

(A) First, community claims against the debtor or the debtor's spouse shall be paid from property of the kind specified in section 541(a)(2) of this title, except to the extent that such property is solely liable for debts of the debtor.

(B) Second, to the extent that community claims against the debtor are not paid under subparagraph (A) of this paragraph, such community claims shall be paid from property of the kind specified in section 541(a)(2) of this title that is solely liable for debts of the debtor.

(C) Third, to the extent that all claims against the debtor including community claims against the debtor are not paid under subparagraph (A) or (B) of this paragraph such claims shall be paid from property of the estate other than property of the kind specified in section 541(a)(2) of this title.

(D) Fourth, to the extent that community claims against the debtor or the debtor's spouse are not paid under subparagraph (A), (B), or (C) of this paragraph, such claims shall be paid from all remaining property of the estate.

§ 727. Discharge

(a) The court shall grant the debtor a discharge, unless—

(1) the debtor is not an individual;

(2) the debtor, with intent to hinder, delay, or defraud a creditor or an officer of the estate charged with custody of property under this title, has transferred, removed, destroyed, mutilated, or concealed, or has permitted to be transferred, removed, destroyed, mutilated, or concealed—

(A) property of the debtor, within one year before the date of the filing of the petition; or

(B) property of the estate, after the date of the filing of the petition;

(3) the debtor has concealed, destroyed, mutilated, falsified, or failed to keep or preserve any recorded information, including books, documents, records, and papers, from which the debtor's financial condition or business transactions might be ascertained, unless such act or failure to act was justified under all of the circumstances of the case;

(4) the debtor knowingly and fraudulently, in or in connection with the case—

(A) made a false oath or account;

(B) presented or used a false claim;

(C) gave, offered, received, or attempted to obtain money, property, or advantage, or a promise of money, property, or advantage, for acting or forbearing to act; or

(D) withheld from an officer of the estate entitled to possession under this title, any recorded information, including books, documents, records, and papers, relating to the debtor's property or financial affairs;

(5) the debtor has failed to explain satisfactorily, before determination of denial of discharge under this paragraph, any loss of assets or deficiency of assets to meet the debtor's liabilities;

(6) the debtor has refused, in the case—

(A) to obey any lawful order of the court, other than an order to respond to a material question or to testify;

(B) on the ground of privilege against self-incrimination, to respond to a material question approved by the court or to testify, after the debtor has been granted immunity with respect to the matter concerning which such privilege was invoked; or

(C) on a ground other than the properly invoked privilege against self-incrimination, to respond to a material question approved by the court or to testify;

(7) the debtor has committed any act specified in paragraph (2), (3), (4), (5), or (6) of this subsection, on or within one year before the date of the filing of the petition, or during the

case, in connection with another case, under this title or under the Bankruptcy Act, concerning an insider;

(8) the debtor has been granted a discharge under this section, under section 1141 of this title, or under section 14, 371, or 476 of the Bankruptcy Act, in a case commenced within 8 years before the date of the filing of the petition;

(9) the debtor has been granted a discharge under section 1228 or 1328 of this title, or under section 660 or 661 of the Bankruptcy Act, in a case commenced within six years before the date of the filing of the petition, unless payments under the plan in such case totaled at least—

(A) 100 percent of the allowed unsecured claims in such case; or

(B) (i) 70 percent of such claims; and

(ii) the plan was proposed by the debtor in good faith, and was the debtor's best effort;

(10) the court approves a written waiver of discharge executed by the debtor after the order for relief under this chapter;

(11) after filing the petition, the debtor failed to complete an instructional course concerning personal financial management described in section 111, except that this paragraph shall not apply with respect to a debtor who is a person described in section 109(h)(4) or who resides in a district for which the United States trustee (or the bankruptcy administrator, if any) determines that the approved instructional courses are not adequate to service the additional individuals who would otherwise be required to complete such instructional courses under this section (The United States trustee (or the bankruptcy administrator, if any) who makes a determination described in this paragraph shall review such determination not later than 1 year after the date of such determination, and not less frequently than annually thereafter.); or

(12) the court after notice and a hearing held not more than 10 days before the date of the entry of the order granting the discharge finds that there is reasonable cause to believe that—

(A) section 522(q)(1) may be applicable to the debtor; and

(B) there is pending any proceeding in which the debtor may be found guilty of a felony of the kind described in section 522(q)(1)(A) or liable for a debt of the kind described in section 522(q)(1)(B).

(b) Except as provided in section 523 of this title, a discharge under subsection (a) of this section discharges the debtor from all debts that arose before the date of the order for relief under this chapter, and any liability on a claim that is determined under section 502 of this title as if such claim had arisen before the commencement of the case, whether or not a proof of claim based on any such debt or liability is filed under section 501 of this title, and whether or not a claim based on any such debt or liability is allowed under section 502 of this title.

(c) (1) The trustee, a creditor, or the United States trustee may object to the granting of a discharge under subsection (a) of this section.

(2) On request of a party in interest, the court may order the trustee to examine the acts and conduct of the debtor to determine whether a ground exists for denial of discharge.

(d) On request of the trustee, a creditor, or the United States trustee, and after notice and a hearing, the court shall revoke a discharge granted under subsection (a) of this section if—

(1) such discharge was obtained through the fraud of the debtor, and the requesting party did not know of such fraud until after the granting of such discharge;

(2) the debtor acquired property that is property of the estate, or became entitled to acquire property that would be property of the estate, and knowingly and fraudulently failed to report the acquisition of or entitlement to such property, or to deliver or surrender such property to the trustee;

(3) the debtor committed an act specified in subsection (a)(6) of this section; or

(4) the debtor has failed to explain satisfactorily—

(A) a material misstatement in an audit referred to in section 586(f) of title 28; or

(B) a failure to make available for inspection all necessary accounts, papers, documents, financial records, files, and all other papers, things, or property belonging to the debtor that are requested for an audit referred to in section 586(f) of title 28.

(e) The trustee, a creditor, or the United States trustee may request a revocation of a discharge—

(1) under subsection (d)(1) of this section within one year after such discharge is granted; or

(2) under subsection (d)(2) or (d)(3) of this section before the later of—

(A) one year after the granting of such discharge; and

(B) the date the case is closed.

CHAPTER 9. ADJUSTMENT OF DEBTS OF A MUNICIPALITY

SUBCHAPTER I—GENERAL PROVISIONS

Section

901. Applicability of Other Sections of This Title
902. Definitions for This Chapter
903. Reservation of State Power to Control Municipalities
904. Limitation on Jurisdiction and Powers of Court

§ 901. Applicability of Other Sections of This Title

(a) Sections 301, 333, 344, 347(b), 349, 350(b), 351, 361, 362, 364(c), 364(d), 364(e), 364(f), 365, 366, 501, 502, 503, 504, 506, 507(a)(2), 509, 510, 524(a)(1), 524(a)(2), 544, 545, 546, 547, 548, 549(a), 549(c), 549(d), 550, 551, 552, 553, 555, 556, 557, 559, 560, 561, 562, 1102, 1103, 1109, 1111(b), 1122, 1123(a)(1), 1123(a)(2), 1123(a)(3), 1123(a)(4), 1123(a)(5), 1123(b), 1123(d), 1124, 1125, 1126(a), 1126(b), 1126(c), 1126(e), 1126(f), 1126(g), 1127(d), 1128, 1129(a)(2), 1129(a)(3), 1129(a)(6), 1129(a)(8), 1129(a)(10), 1129(b)(1), 1129(b)(2)(A), 1129(b)(2)(B), 1142(b), 1143, 1144, and 1145 of this title apply in a case under this chapter.

(b) A term used in a section of this title made applicable in a case under this chapter by subsection (a) of this section or section 103(e) of this title has the meaning defined for such term for the purpose of such applicable section, unless such term is otherwise defined in section 902 of this title.

(c) A section made applicable in a case under this chapter by subsection (a) of this section that is operative if the business of the debtor is authorized to be operated is operative in a case under this chapter.

§ 902. Definitions for This Chapter

In this chapter—

(1) "property of the estate", when used in a section that is made applicable in a case under this chapter by section 103(e) or 901 of this title, means property of the debtor;

(2) "special revenues" means—

(A) receipts derived from the ownership, operation, or disposition of projects or systems of the debtor that are primarily used or intended to be used primarily to provide transportation, utility, or other services, including the proceeds of borrowings to finance the projects or systems;

(B) special excise taxes imposed on particular activities or transactions;

(C) incremental tax receipts from the benefited area in the case of tax-increment financing;

(D) other revenues or receipts derived from particular functions of the debtor, whether or not the debtor has other functions; or

(E) taxes specifically levied to finance one or more projects or systems, excluding receipts from general property, sales, or income taxes (other than tax-increment financing) levied to finance the general purposes of the debtor;

(3) "special tax payer" means record owner or holder of legal or equitable title to real property against which a special assessment or special tax has been levied the proceeds of which are the sole source of payment of an obligation issued by the debtor to defray the cost of an improvement relating to such real property;

(4) "special tax payer affected by the plan" means special tax payer with respect to whose real property the plan proposes to increase the proportion of special assessments or special taxes referred to in paragraph (2) of this section assessed against such real property; and

(5) "trustee", when used in a section that is made applicable in a case under this chapter by section 103(e) or 901 of this title, means debtor, except as provided in section 926 of this title.

§ 903. Reservation of State Power to Control Municipalities

This chapter does not limit or impair the power of a state to control, by legislation or otherwise, a municipality of or in such state in the exercise of the political or governmental powers of such municipality, including expenditures for such exercise, but—

(1) a state law prescribing a method of composition of indebtedness of such municipality may not bind any creditor that does not consent to such composition; and

(2) a judgment entered under such a law may not bind a creditor that does not consent to such composition.

§ 904. Limitation on Jurisdiction and Powers of Court

Notwithstanding any power of the court, unless the debtor consents or the plan so provides, the court may not, by any stay, order, or decree, in the case or otherwise, interfere with—

(1) any of the political or governmental powers of the debtor;

(2) any of the property or revenues of the debtor; or

(3) the debtor's use or enjoyment of any income-producing property.

SUBCHAPTER II—ADMINISTRATION

Section

921. Petition and Proceedings Relating to Petition
922. Automatic Stay of Enforcement of Claims Against the Debtor
923. Notice
924. List of Creditors
925. Effect of List of Claims
926. Avoiding Powers
927. Limitation on Recourse
928. Post Petition Effect of Security Interest
929. Municipal Leases
930. Dismissal

§ 921. Petition and Proceedings Relating to Petition

(a) Notwithstanding sections 109(d) and 301 of this title, a case under this chapter concerning an unincorporated tax or special assessment district that does not have such district's own officials is commenced by the filing under section 301 of this title of a petition under this chapter by such district's governing authority or the board or body having authority to levy taxes or assessments to meet the obligations of such district.

(b) The chief judge of the court of appeals for the circuit embracing the district in which the case is commenced shall designate the bankruptcy judge to conduct the case.

(c) After any objection to the petition, the court, after notice and a hearing, may dismiss the petition if the debtor did not file the petition in good faith or if the petition does not meet the requirements of this title.

(d) If the petition is not dismissed under subsection (c) of this section, the court shall order relief under this chapter notwithstanding section 301(b).

(e) The court may not, on account of an appeal from an order for relief, delay any proceeding under this chapter in the case in which the appeal is being taken; nor shall any court order a stay of such proceeding pending such appeal. The reversal on appeal of a finding of jurisdiction does not affect the validity of any debt incurred that is authorized by the court under section 364(c) or 364(d) of this title.

§ 922. Automatic Stay of Enforcement of Claims Against the Debtor

(a) A petition filed under this chapter operates as a stay, in addition to the stay provided by section 362 of this title, applicable to all entities, of—

(1) the commencement or continuation, including the issuance or employment of process, of a judicial, administrative, or other action or proceeding against an officer or inhabitant of the debtor that seeks to enforce a claim against the debtor; and

(2) the enforcement of a lien on or arising out of taxes or assessments owed to the debtor.

(b) Subsections (c), (d), (e), (f), and (g) of section 362 of this title apply to a stay under subsection (a) of this section the same as such subsections apply to a stay under section 362(a) of this title.

(c) If the debtor provides, under section 362, 364, or 922 of this title, adequate protection of the interest of the holder of a claim secured by a lien on property of the debtor and if, notwithstanding such protection such creditor has a claim arising from the stay of action against such property under section 362 or 922 of this title or from the granting of a lien under section 364(d) of this title, then such claim shall be allowable as an administrative expense under section 503(b) of this title.

(d) Notwithstanding section 362 of this title and subsection (a) of this section, a petition filed under this chapter does not operate as a stay of application of pledged special revenues in a manner consistent with section 927 of this title to payment of indebtedness secured by such revenues.

§ 923. Notice

There shall be given notice of the commencement of a case under this chapter, notice of an order for relief under this chapter, and notice of the dismissal of a case under this chapter. Such notice shall also be published at least once a week for three successive weeks in at least one newspaper of general circulation published within the district in which the case is commenced, and in such other newspaper having a general circulation among bond dealers and bondholders as the court designates.

§ 924. List of Creditors

The debtor shall file a list of creditors.

§ 925. Effect of List of Claims

A proof of claim is deemed filed under section 501 of this title for any claim that appears in the list filed under section 924 of this title, except a claim that is listed as disputed, contingent, or unliquidated.

§ 926. Avoiding Powers

(a) If the debtor refuses to pursue a cause of action under section 544, 545, 547, 548, 549(a), or 550 of this title, then on request of a creditor, the court may appoint a trustee to pursue such cause of action.

(b) A transfer of property of the debtor to or for the benefit of any holder of a bond or note, on account of such bond or note, may not be avoided under section 547 of this title.

§ 927. Limitation on Recourse

The holder of a claim payable solely from special revenues of the debtor under applicable nonbankruptcy law shall not be treated as having recourse against the debtor on account of such claim pursuant to section 1111(b) of this title.

§ 928. Post Petition Effect of Security Interest

(a) Notwithstanding section 552(a) of this title and subject to subsection (b) of this section, special revenues acquired by the debtor after the commencement of the case shall remain subject to any lien resulting from any security agreement entered into by the debtor before the commencement of the case.

(b) Any such lien on special revenues, other than municipal betterment assessments, derived from a project or system shall be subject to the necessary operating expenses of such project or system, as the case may be.

§ 929. Municipal Leases

A lease to a municipality shall not be treated as an executory contract or unexpired lease for the purposes of section 365 or 502(b)(6) of this title solely by reason of its being subject to termination in the event the debtor fails to appropriate rent.

§ 930. Dismissal

(a) After notice and a hearing, the court may dismiss a case under this chapter for cause, including—

(1) want of prosecution;

(2) unreasonable delay by the debtor that is prejudicial to creditors;

(3) failure to propose a plan within the time fixed under section 941 of this title;

(4) if a plan is not accepted within any time fixed by the court;

(5) denial of confirmation of a plan under section 943(b) of this title and denial of additional time for filing another plan or a modification of a plan; or

(6) if the court has retained jurisdiction after confirmation of a plan—

(A) material default by the debtor with respect to a term of such plan; or

(B) termination of such plan by reason of the occurrence of a condition specified in such plan.

(b) The court shall dismiss a case under this chapter if confirmation of a plan under this chapter is refused.

SUBCHAPTER III—THE PLAN

Section

941. Filing of Plan
942. Modification of Plan
943. Confirmation
944. Effect of Confirmation
945. Continuing Jurisdiction and Closing of the Case
946. Effect of Exchange of Securities Before the Date of the Filing of the Petition

§ 941. Filing of Plan

The debtor shall file a plan for the adjustment of the debtor's debts. If such a plan is not filed with the petition, the debtor shall file such a plan at such later time as the court fixes.

§ 942. Modification of Plan

The debtor may modify the plan at any time before confirmation, but may not modify the plan so that the plan as modified fails to meet the requirements of this chapter. After the debtor files a modification, the plan as modified becomes the plan.

§ 943. Confirmation

(a) A special tax payer may object to confirmation of a plan.

(b) The court shall confirm the plan if—

(1) the plan complies with the provisions of this title made applicable by sections 103(e) and 901 of this title;

(2) the plan complies with the provisions of this chapter;

(3) all amounts to be paid by the debtor or by any person for services or expenses in the case or incident to the plan have been fully disclosed and are reasonable;

(4) the debtor is not prohibited by law from taking any action necessary to carry out the plan;

(5) except to the extent that the holder of a particular claim has agreed to a different treatment of such claim, the plan provides that on the effective date of the plan each holder of a claim of a kind specified in section 507(a)(2) of this title will receive on account of such claim cash equal to the allowed amount of such claim;

(6) any regulatory or electoral approval necessary under applicable nonbankruptcy law in order to carry out any provision of the plan has been obtained, or such provision is expressly conditioned on such approval; and

(7) the plan is in the best interests of creditors and is feasible.

§ 944. Effect of Confirmation

(a) The provisions of a confirmed plan bind the debtor and any creditor, whether or not—

(1) a proof of such creditor's claim is filed or deemed filed under section 501 of this title;

(2) such claim is allowed under section 502 of this title; or

(3) such creditor has accepted the plan.

(b) Except as provided in subsection (c) of this section, the debtor is discharged from all debts as of the time when—

(1) the plan is confirmed;

(2) the debtor deposits any consideration to be distributed under the plan with a disbursing agent appointed by the court; and

(3) the court has determined—

(A) that any security so deposited will constitute, after distribution, a valid legal obligation of the debtor; and

(B) that any provision made to pay or secure payment of such obligation is valid.

(c) The debtor is not discharged under subsection (b) of this section from any debt—

(1) excepted from discharge by the plan or order confirming the plan; or

(2) owed to an entity that, before confirmation of the plan, had neither notice nor actual knowledge of the case.

§ 945. Continuing Jurisdiction and Closing of the Case

(a) The court may retain jurisdiction over the case for such period of time as is necessary for the successful implementation of the plan.

(b) Except as provided in subsection (a) of this section, the court shall close the case when administration of the case has been completed.

§ 946. Effect of Exchange of Securities Before the Date of the Filing of the Petition.

The exchange of a new security under the plan for a claim covered by the plan, whether such exchange occurred before or after the date of the filing of the petition, does not limit or impair the effectiveness of the plan or of any provision of this chapter. The amount and number specified in section 1126(c) of this title include the amount and number of claims formerly held by a creditor that has participated in any such exchange.

CHAPTER 11. REORGANIZATION

SUBCHAPTER I—OFFICERS AND ADMINISTRATION

Section

1101. Definitions for This Chapter
1102. Creditors' and Equity Security Holders' Committees
1103. Powers and Duties of Committees
1104. Appointment of Trustee or Examiner
1105. Termination of Trustee's Appointment
1106. Duties of Trustee and Examiner

1107. Rights, Powers, and Duties of Debtor in Possession
1108. Authorization to Operate Business
1109. Right to Be Heard
1110. Aircraft Equipment and Vessels
1111. Claims and Interests
1112. Conversion or Dismissal
1113. Rejection of Collective Bargaining Agreements
1114. Payment of Insurance Benefits to Retired Employees
1115. Property of the Estate
1116. Duties of Trustee or Debtor in Possession in Small Business Cases

§ 1101. Definitions for This Chapter

In this chapter—

(1) "debtor in possession" means debtor except when a person that has qualified under section 322 of this title is serving as trustee in the case;

(2) "substantial consummation" means—

(A) transfer of all or substantially all of the property proposed by the plan to be transferred;

(B) assumption by the debtor or by the successor to the debtor under the plan of the business or of the management of all or substantially all of the property dealt with by the plan; and

(C) commencement of distribution under the plan.

§ 1102. Creditors' and Equity Security Holders' Committees

(a)(1) Except as provided in paragraph (3), as soon as practicable after the order for relief under chapter 11 of this title, the United States trustee shall appoint a committee of creditors holding unsecured claims and may appoint additional committees of creditors or of equity security holders as the United States trustee deems appropriate.

(2) On request of a party in interest, the court may order the appointment of additional committees of creditors or of equity security holders if necessary to assure adequate representation of creditors or of equity security holders. The United States trustee shall appoint any such committee.

(3) Unless the court for cause orders otherwise, a committee of creditors may not be appointed in a small business case or a case under subchapter V of this chapter.

(4) On request of a party in interest and after notice and a hearing, the court may order the United States trustee to change the membership of a committee appointed under this subsection, if the court determines that the change is necessary to ensure adequate representation of creditors or equity security holders. The court may order the United States trustee to increase the number of members of a committee to include a creditor that is a small business concern (as described in section 3(a)(1) of the Small Business Act), if the court determines that the creditor holds claims (of the kind represented by the committee) the aggregate amount of which, in comparison to the annual gross revenue of that creditor, is disproportionately large.

(b)(1) A committee of creditors appointed under subsection (a) of this section shall ordinarily consist of the persons, willing to serve, that hold the seven largest claims against the debtor of the kinds represented on such committee, or of the members of a committee organized by creditors before the commencement of the case under this chapter, if such committee was fairly chosen and is representative of the different kinds of claims to be represented.

(2) A committee of equity security holders appointed under subsection (a)(2) of this section shall ordinarily consist of the persons, willing to serve, that hold the seven largest amounts of equity securities of the debtor of the kinds represented on such committee.

(3) A committee appointed under subsection (a) shall—

(A) provide access to information for creditors who—

(i) hold claims of the kind represented by that committee; and

(ii) are not appointed to the committee;

(B) solicit and receive comments from the creditors described in subparagraph (A); and

(C) be subject to a court order that compels any additional report or disclosure to be made to the creditors described in subparagraph (A).

§ 1103. Powers and Duties of Committees

(a) At a scheduled meeting of a committee appointed under section 1102 of this title, at which a majority of the members of such committee are present, and with the court's approval, such committee may select and authorize the employment by such committee of one or more attorneys, accountants, or other agents, to represent or perform services for such committee.

(b) An attorney or accountant employed to represent a committee appointed under section 1102 of this title may not, while employed by such committee, represent any other entity having an adverse interest in connection with the case. Representation of one or more creditors of the same class as represented by the committee shall not per se constitute the representation of an adverse interest.

(c) A committee appointed under section 1102 of this title may—

(1) consult with the trustee or debtor in possession concerning the administration of the case;

(2) investigate the acts, conduct, assets, liabilities, and financial condition of the debtor, the operation of the debtor's business and the desirability of the continuance of such business, and any other matter relevant to the case or to the formulation of a plan;

(3) participate in the formulation of a plan, advise those represented by such committee of such committee's determinations as to any plan formulated, and collect and file with the court acceptances or rejections of a plan;

(4) request the appointment of a trustee or examiner under section 1104 of this title; and

(5) perform such other services as are in the interest of those represented.

(d) As soon as practicable after the appointment of a committee under section 1102 of this title, the trustee shall meet with such committee to transact such business as may be necessary and proper.

§ 1104. Appointment of Trustee or Examiner

(a) At any time after the commencement of the case but before confirmation of a plan, on request of a party in interest or the United States trustee, and after notice and a hearing, the court shall order the appointment of a trustee—

(1) for cause, including fraud, dishonesty, incompetence, or gross mismanagement of the affairs of the debtor by current management, either before or after the commencement of the case, or similar cause, but not including the number of holders of securities of the debtor or the amount of assets or liabilities of the debtor; or

(2) if such appointment is in the interests of creditors, any equity security holders, and other interests of the estate, without regard to the number of holders of securities of the debtor or the amount of assets or liabilities of the debtor.

(b)(1) Except as provided in section 1163 of this title, on the request of a party in interest made not later than 30 days after the court orders the appointment of a trustee under subsection (a), the United States trustee shall convene a meeting of creditors for the purpose of electing one disinterested person to serve as trustee in the case. The election of a trustee shall be conducted in the manner provided in subsections (a), (b), and (c) of section 702 of this title.

(2) (A) If an eligible, disinterested trustee is elected at a meeting of creditors under paragraph (1), the United States trustee shall file a report certifying that election.

(B) Upon the filing of a report under subparagraph (A)—

(i) the trustee elected under paragraph (1) shall be considered to have been selected and appointed for purposes of this section; and

(ii) the service of any trustee appointed under subsection (a) shall terminate.

(C) The court shall resolve any dispute arising out of an election described in subparagraph (A).

(c) If the court does not order the appointment of a trustee under this section, then at any time before the confirmation of a plan, on request of a party in interest or the United States trustee, and after notice and a hearing, the court shall order the appointment of an examiner to conduct such an investigation of the debtor as is appropriate, including an investigation of any allegations of fraud, dishonesty, incompetence, misconduct, mismanagement, or irregularity in the management of the affairs of the debtor of or by current or former management of the debtor, if—

(1) such appointment is in the interests of creditors, any equity security holders, and other interests of the estate; or

(2) the debtor's fixed, liquidated, unsecured debts, other than debts for goods, services,

or taxes, or owing to an insider, exceed $5,000,000.

(d) If the court orders the appointment of a trustee or an examiner, if a trustee or an examiner dies or resigns during the case or is removed under section 324 of this title, or if a trustee fails to qualify under section 322 of this title, then the United States trustee, after consultation with parties in interest, shall appoint, subject to the court's approval, one disinterested person other than the United States trustee to serve as trustee or examiner, as the case may be, in the case.

(e) The United States trustee shall move for the appointment of a trustee under subsection (a) if there are reasonable grounds to suspect that current members of the governing body of the debtor, the debtor's chief executive or chief financial officer, or members of the governing body who selected the debtor's chief executive or chief financial officer, participated in actual fraud, dishonesty, or criminal conduct in the management of the debtor or the debtor's public financial reporting.

§ 1105. Termination of Trustee's Appointment

At any time before confirmation of a plan, on request of a party in interest or the United States trustee, and after notice and a hearing, the court may terminate the trustee's appointment and restore the debtor to possession and management of the property of the estate and of the operation of the debtor's business.

§ 1106. Duties of Trustee and Examiner

(a) A trustee shall—

(1) perform the duties of the trustee, as specified in paragraphs (2), (5), (7), (8), (9), (10), (11), and (12) of section 704(a);

(2) if the debtor has not done so, file the list, schedule, and statement required under section 521(a)(1) of this title;

(3) except to the extent that the court orders otherwise, investigate the acts, conduct, assets, liabilities, and financial condition of the debtor, the operation of the debtor's business and the desirability of the continuance of such business, and any other matter relevant to the case or to the formulation of a plan;

(4) as soon as practicable—

(A) file a statement of any investigation conducted under paragraph (3) of this subsection, including any fact ascertained pertaining to fraud, dishonesty, incompetence, misconduct, mismanagement, or irregularity in the management of the affairs of the debtor, or to a cause of action available to the estate; and

(B) transmit a copy or a summary of any such statement to any creditors' committee or equity security holders' committee, to any indenture trustee, and to such other entity as the court designates;

(5) as soon as practicable, file a plan under section 1121 of this title, file a report of why the trustee will not file a plan, or recommend conversion of the case to a case under chapter 7, 12, or 13 of this title or dismissal of the case;

(6) for any year for which the debtor has not filed a tax return required by law, furnish, without personal liability, such information as may be required by the governmental unit with which such tax return was to be filed, in light of the condition of the debtor's books and records and the availability of such information;

(7) after confirmation of a plan, file such reports as are necessary or as the court orders; and

(8) if with respect to the debtor there is a claim for a domestic support obligation, provide the applicable notice specified in subsection (c).

(b) An examiner appointed under section 1104(d) of this title shall perform the duties specified in paragraphs (3) and (4) of subsection (a) of this section, and, except to the extent that the court orders otherwise, any other duties of the trustee that the court orders the debtor in possession not to perform.

(c)(1) In a case described in subsection (a)(8) to which subsection (a)(8) applies, the trustee shall—

(A) (i) provide written notice to the holder of the claim described in subsection (a)(8) of such claim and of the right of such holder to use the services of the State child support enforcement agency established under sections 464 and 466 of the Social Security Act for the State in which such holder resides, for assistance in collecting child support during and after the case under this title; and

(ii) include in the notice required by clause (i) the address and telephone number of such State child support enforcement agency;

(B) (i) provide written notice to such State child support enforcement agency of such claim; and

(ii) include in the notice required by clause (i) the name, address, and telephone number of such holder; and

(C) at such time as the debtor is granted a discharge under section 1141, provide written notice to such holder and to such State child support enforcement agency of—

(i) the granting of the discharge;

(ii) the last recent known address of the debtor;

(iii) the last recent known name and address of the debtor's employer; and

(iv) the name of each creditor that holds a claim that—

(I) is not discharged under paragraph (2), (4), or (14A) of section 523(a); or

(II) was reaffirmed by the debtor under section 524(c).

(2) (A) The holder of a claim described in subsection (a)(8) or the State child enforcement support agency of the State in which such holder resides may request from a creditor described in paragraph (1)(C)(iv) the last known address of the debtor.

(B) Notwithstanding any other provision of law, a creditor that makes a disclosure of a last known address of a debtor in connection with a request made under subparagraph (A) shall not be liable by reason of making such disclosure.

§ 1107. Rights, Powers, and Duties of Debtor in Possession

(a) Subject to any limitations on a trustee serving in a case under this chapter, and to such limitations or conditions as the court prescribes, a debtor in possession shall have all the rights, other than the right to compensation under section 330 of this title, and powers, and shall perform all the functions and duties, except the duties specified in sections 1106(a)(2), (3), and (4) of this title, of a trustee serving in a case under this chapter.

(b) Notwithstanding section 327(a) of this title, a person is not disqualified for employment under section 327 of this title by a debtor in possession solely because of such person's employment by or representation of the debtor before the commencement of the case.

§ 1108. Authorization to Operate Business

Unless the court, on request of a party in interest and after notice and a hearing, orders otherwise, the trustee may operate the debtor's business.

§ 1109. Right to Be Heard

(a) The Securities and Exchange Commission may raise and may appear and be heard on any issue in a case under this chapter, but the Securities and Exchange Commission may not appeal from any judgment, order, or decree entered in the case.

(b) A party in interest, including the debtor, the trustee, a creditors' committee, an equity security holders' committee, a creditor, an equity security holder, or any indenture trustee, may raise and may appear and be heard on any issue in a case under this chapter.

§ 1110. Aircraft Equipment and Vessels

(a)(1) Except as provided in paragraph (2) and subject to subsection (b), the right of a secured party with a security interest in equipment described in paragraph (3), or of a lessor or conditional vendor of such equipment, to take possession of such equipment in compliance with a security agreement, lease, or conditional sale contract, and to enforce any of its other rights or remedies, under such security agreement, lease, or conditional sale contract, to sell, lease, or otherwise retain or dispose of such equipment, is not limited or otherwise affected by any other provision of this title or by any power of the court.

(2) The right to take possession and to enforce the other rights and remedies described in paragraph (1) shall be subject to section 362 if—

(A) before the date that is 60 days after the date of the order for relief under this chapter, the trustee, subject to the approval of the court, agrees to perform all obligations of the debtor under such security agreement, lease, or conditional sale contract; and

(B) any default, other than a default of a kind specified in section 365(b)(2), under such security agreement, lease, or conditional sale contract—

(i) that occurs before the date of the order is cured before the expiration of such 60-day period;

(ii) that occurs after the date of the order and before the expiration of such 60-day period is cured before the later of—

(I) the date that is 30 days after the date of the default; or

(II) the expiration of such 60-day period; and

(iii) that occurs on or after the expiration of such 60-day period is cured in compliance with the terms of such security agreement, lease, or conditional sale contract, if a cure is permitted under that agreement, lease, or contract.

(3) The equipment described in this paragraph—

(A) is—

(i) an aircraft, aircraft engine, propeller, appliance, or spare part (as defined in section 40102 of title 49) that is subject to a security interest granted by, leased to, or conditionally sold to a debtor that, at the time such transaction is entered into, holds an air carrier operating certificate issued pursuant to chapter 447 of title 49 for aircraft capable of carrying 10 or more individuals or 6,000 pounds or more of cargo; or

(ii) a vessel documented under chapter 121 of title 46 that is subject to a security interest granted by, leased to, or conditionally sold to a debtor that is a water carrier that, at the time such transaction is entered into, holds a certificate of public convenience and necessity or permit issued by the Department of Transportation; and

(B) includes all records and documents relating to such equipment that are required, under the terms of the security agreement, lease, or conditional sale contract, to be surrendered or returned by the debtor in connection with the surrender or return of such equipment.

(4) Paragraph (1) applies to a secured party, lessor, or conditional vendor acting in its own behalf or acting as trustee or otherwise in behalf of another party.

(b) The trustee and the secured party, lessor, or conditional vendor whose right to take possession is protected under subsection (a) may agree, subject to the approval of the court, to extend the 60-day period specified in subsection (a)(1).

(c)(1) In any case under this chapter, the trustee shall immediately surrender and return to a secured party, lessor, or conditional vendor, described in subsection (a)(1), equipment described in subsection (a)(3), if at any time after the date of the order for relief under this chapter such secured party, lessor, or conditional vendor is entitled pursuant to subsection (a)(1) to take possession of such equipment and makes a written demand for such possession to the trustee.

(2) At such time as the trustee is required under paragraph (1) to surrender and return equipment described in subsection (a)(3), any lease of such equipment, and any security agreement or conditional sale contract relating to such equipment, if such security agreement or conditional sale contract is an executory contract, shall be deemed rejected.

(d) With respect to equipment first placed in service on or before October 22, 1994, for purposes of this section—

(1) the term "lease" includes any written agreement with respect to which the lessor and the debtor, as lessee, have expressed in the agreement or in a substantially contemporaneous writing that the agreement is to be treated as a lease for Federal income tax purposes; and

(2) the term "security interest" means a purchase-money equipment security interest.

§ 1111. Claims and Interests

(a) A proof of claim or interest is deemed filed under section 501 of this title for any claim or interest that appears in the schedules filed under section 521(a)(1) or 1106(a)(2) of this title, except a claim or interest that is scheduled as disputed, contingent, or unliquidated.

(b)(1)(A) A claim secured by a lien on property of the estate shall be allowed or disallowed under section 502 of this title the same as if the holder of such claim had recourse against the debtor on account of such claim, whether or not such holder has such recourse, unless—

(i) the class of which such claim is a part elects, by at least two-thirds in amount and more than half in number of allowed claims of such class, application of paragraph (2) of this subsection; or

(ii) such holder does not have such recourse and such property is sold under section 363 of this title or is to be sold under the plan.

(B) A class of claims may not elect application of paragraph (2) of this subsection if—

(i) the interest on account of such claims of the holders of such claims in such property is of inconsequential value; or

(ii) the holder of a claim of such class has recourse against the debtor on account of such claim and such property is sold under section 363 of this title or is to be sold under the plan.

(2) If such an election is made, then notwithstanding section 506(a) of this title, such claim is a secured claim to the extent that such claim is allowed.

§ 1112. Conversion or Dismissal

(a) The debtor may convert a case under this chapter to a case under chapter 7 of this title unless—

(1) the debtor is not a debtor in possession;

(2) the case originally was commenced as an involuntary case under this chapter; or

(3) the case was converted to a case under this chapter other than on the debtor's request.

(b)(1) Except as provided in paragraph (2) and subsection (c), on request of a party in interest, and after notice and a hearing, the court shall convert a case under this chapter to a case under chapter 7 or dismiss a case under this chapter, whichever is in the best interests of creditors and the estate, for cause unless the court determines that the appointment under section 1104(a) of a trustee or an examiner is in the best interests of creditors and the estate.

(2) The court may not convert a case under this chapter to a case under chapter 7 or dismiss a case under this chapter if the court finds and specifically identifies unusual circumstances establishing that converting or dismissing the case is not in the best interests of creditors and the estate, and the debtor or any other party in interest establishes that—

(A) there is a reasonable likelihood that a plan will be confirmed within the timeframes established in sections 1121(e) and 1129(e) of this title, or if such sections do not apply, within a reasonable period of time; and

(B) the grounds for converting or dismissing the case include an act or omission of the debtor other than under paragraph (4)(A)—

(i) for which there exists a reasonable justification for the act or omission; and

(ii) that will be cured within a reasonable period of time fixed by the court.

(3) The court shall commence the hearing on a motion under this subsection not later than 30 days after filing of the motion, and shall decide the motion not later than 15 days after commencement of such hearing, unless the movant expressly consents to a continuance for a specific period of time or compelling circumstances prevent the court from meeting the time limits established by this paragraph.

(4) For purposes of this subsection, the term "cause" includes—

(A) substantial or continuing loss to or diminution of the estate and the absence of a reasonable likelihood of rehabilitation;

(B) gross mismanagement of the estate;

(C) failure to maintain appropriate insurance that poses a risk to the estate or to the public;

(D) unauthorized use of cash collateral substantially harmful to 1 or more creditors;

(E) failure to comply with an order of the court;

(F) unexcused failure to satisfy timely any filing or reporting requirement established by this title or by any rule applicable to a case under this chapter;

(G) failure to attend the meeting of creditors convened under section 341(a) or an examination ordered under rule 2004 of the Federal Rules of Bankruptcy Procedure without good cause shown by the debtor;

(H) failure timely to provide information or attend meetings reasonably requested by the United States trustee (or the bankruptcy administrator, if any);

(I) failure timely to pay taxes owed after the date of the order for relief or to file tax returns due after the date of the order for relief;

(J) failure to file a disclosure statement, or to file or confirm a plan, within the time fixed by this title or by order of the court;

(K) failure to pay any fees or charges required under chapter 123 of title 28;

(L) revocation of an order of confirmation under section 1144;

(M) inability to effectuate substantial consummation of a confirmed plan;

(N) material default by the debtor with respect to a confirmed plan;

(O) termination of a confirmed plan by reason of the occurrence of a condition specified in the plan; and

(P) failure of the debtor to pay any domestic support obligation that first becomes payable after the date of the filing of the petition.

(c) The court may not convert a case under this chapter to a case under chapter 7 of this title if the debtor is a farmer or a corporation that is not a moneyed, business, or commercial corporation, unless the debtor requests such conversion.

(d) The court may convert a case under this chapter to a case under chapter 12 or 13 of this title only if—

(1) the debtor requests such conversion;

(2) the debtor has not been discharged under section 1141(d) of this title; and

(3) if the debtor requests conversion to chapter 12 of this title, such conversion is equitable.

(e) Except as provided in subsections (c) and (f), the court, on request of the United States trustee, may convert a case under this chapter to a case under chapter 7 of this title or may dismiss a case under this chapter, whichever is in the best interest of creditors and the estate if the debtor in a voluntary case fails to file, within fifteen days after the filing of the petition commencing such case or such additional time as the court may allow, the information required by paragraph (1) of section 521(a), including a list containing the names and addresses of the holders of the twenty largest unsecured claims (or of all unsecured claims if there are fewer than twenty unsecured claims), and the approximate dollar amounts of each of such claims.

(f) Notwithstanding any other provision of this section, a case may not be converted to a case under another chapter of this title unless the debtor may be a debtor under such chapter.

§ 1113. Rejection of Collective Bargaining Agreements

(a) The debtor in possession, or the trustee if one has been appointed under the provisions of this chapter, other than a trustee in a case covered by subchapter IV of this chapter and by title I of the Railway Labor Act, may assume or reject a collective bargaining agreement only in accordance with the provisions of this section.

(b)(1) Subsequent to filing a petition and prior to filing an application seeking rejection of a collective bargaining agreement, the debtor in possession or trustee (hereinafter in this section "trustee" shall include a debtor in possession), shall—

(A) make a proposal to the authorized representative of the employees covered by such agreement, based on the most complete and reliable information available at the time of such proposal, which provides for those necessary modifications in the employees benefits and protections that are necessary to permit the reorganization of the debtor and assures that all creditors, the debtor and all of the affected parties are treated fairly and equitably; and

(B) provide, subject to subsection (d)(3), the representative of the employees with such relevant information as is necessary to evaluate the proposal.

(2) During the period beginning on the date of the making of a proposal provided for in paragraph (1) and ending on the date of the hearing provided for in subsection (d)(1), the trustee shall meet, at reasonable times, with the authorized representative to confer in good faith in attempting to reach mutually satisfactory modifications of such agreement.

(c) The court shall approve an application for rejection of a collective bargaining agreement only if the court finds that—

(1) the trustee has, prior to the hearing, made a proposal that fulfills the requirements of subsection (b)(1);

(2) the authorized representative of the employees has refused to accept such proposal without good cause; and

(3) the balance of the equities clearly favors rejection of such agreement.

(d)(1) Upon the filing of an application for rejection the court shall schedule a hearing to be held not later than fourteen days after the date of the filing of such application. All interested parties may appear and be heard at such hearing. Adequate notice shall be provided to such parties at least ten days before the date of such hearing. The court may extend the time for the commencement of such hearing for a period not exceeding seven days where the circumstances of the case, and the interests of justice require such extension, or for additional periods of time to which the trustee and representative agree.

(2) The court shall rule on such application for rejection within thirty days after the date of the commencement of the hearing. In the interests of justice, the court may extend such time for ruling for such additional period as the trustee and the employees' representative may agree to. If the court does not rule on such application within thirty days after the date of the commencement of the hearing, or within such additional time as the trustee and the employees' representative may agree to, the trustee may terminate or alter any provisions of the collective bargaining agreement pending the ruling of the court on such application.

(3) The court may enter such protective orders, consistent with the need of the authorized representative of the employee to evaluate the trustee's proposal and the application for rejection, as may be necessary to prevent disclosure of information provided to such representative where such disclosure could compromise the position of the debtor with respect to its competitors in the industry in which it is engaged.

(e) If during a period when the collective bargaining agreement continues in effect, and if essential to the continuation of the debtor's business, or in order to avoid irreparable damage to the estate, the court, after notice and a hearing, may authorize the trustee to implement interim changes in the terms, conditions, wages, benefits, or work rules provided by a collective bargaining agreement. Any hearing under this paragraph shall be scheduled in accordance with the needs of the trustee. The implementation of such interim changes shall not render the application for rejection moot.

(f) No provision of this title shall be construed to permit a trustee to unilaterally terminate or alter any provisions of a collective bargaining agreement prior to compliance with the provisions of this section.

§ 1114. Payment of Insurance Benefits to Retired Employees

(a) For purposes of this section, the term "retiree benefits" means payments to any entity or person for the purpose of providing or reimbursing payments for retired employees and their spouses and dependents, for medical, surgical, or hospital care benefits, or benefits in the event of sickness, accident, disability, or death under any plan, fund, or program (through the purchase of insurance or otherwise) maintained or established in whole or in part by the debtor prior to filing a petition commencing a case under this title.

(b)(1) For purposes of this section, the term "authorized representative" means the authorized representative designated pursuant to subsection (c) for persons receiving any retiree benefits covered by a collective bargaining agreement or subsection (d) in the case of persons receiving retiree benefits not covered by such an agreement.

(2) Committees of retired employees appointed by the court pursuant to this section shall have the same rights, powers, and duties as committees appointed under sections 1102 and 1103 of this title for the purpose of carrying out the purposes of sections 1114 and 1129(a)(13) and, as permitted by the court, shall have the power to enforce the rights of persons under this title as they relate to retiree benefits.

(c)(1) A labor organization shall be, for purposes of this section, the authorized representative of those persons receiving any retiree benefits covered by any collective bargaining agreement to which that labor organization is signatory, unless (A) such labor organization elects not to serve as the authorized representative of such persons, or (B) the court, upon a motion by any party in interest, after notice and hearing, determines that different representation of such persons is appropriate.

(2) In cases where the labor organization referred to in paragraph (1) elects not to serve as the authorized representative of those persons receiving any retiree benefits covered by any collective bargaining agreement to which that labor organization is signatory, or in cases where the court, pursuant to paragraph (1) finds different representation of such persons appropriate, the court, upon a motion by any party in interest, and after notice and a hearing, shall appoint a committee of retired employees if the debtor seeks to modify or not pay the retiree

benefits or if the court otherwise determines that it is appropriate, from among such persons, to serve as the authorized representative of such persons under this section.

(d) The court, upon a motion by any party in interest, and after notice and a hearing, shall order the appointment of a committee of retired employees if the debtor seeks to modify or not pay the retiree benefits or if the court otherwise determines that it is appropriate, to serve as the authorized representative, under this section, of those persons receiving any retiree benefits not covered by a collective bargaining agreement. The United States trustee shall appoint any such committee.

(e)(1) Notwithstanding any other provision of this title, the debtor in possession, or the trustee if one has been appointed under the provisions of this chapter (hereinafter in this section "trustee" shall include a debtor in possession), shall timely pay and shall not modify any retiree benefits, except that—

(A) the court, on motion of the trustee or authorized representative, and after notice and a hearing, may order modification of such payments, pursuant to the provisions of subsections (g) and (h) of this section, or

(B) the trustee and the authorized representative of the recipients of those benefits may agree to modification of such payments, after which such benefits as modified shall continue to be paid by the trustee.

(2) Any payment for retiree benefits required to be made before a plan confirmed under section 1129 of this title is effective has the status of an allowed administrative expense as provided in section 503 of this title.

(f)(1) Subsequent to filing a petition and prior to filing an application seeking modification of the retiree benefits, the trustee shall—

(A) make a proposal to the authorized representative of the retirees, based on the most complete and reliable information available at the time of such proposal, which provides for those necessary modifications in the retiree benefits that are necessary to permit the reorganization of the debtor and assures that all creditors, the debtor and all of the affected parties are treated fairly and equitably; and

(B) provide, subject to subsection (k)(3), the representative of the retirees with such relevant information as is necessary to evaluate the proposal.

(2) During the period beginning on the date of the making of a proposal provided for in paragraph (1), and ending on the date of the hearing provided for in subsection (k)(1), the trustee shall meet, at reasonable times, with the authorized representative to confer in good faith in attempting to reach mutually satisfactory modifications of such retiree benefits.

(g) The court shall enter an order providing for modification in the payment of retiree benefits if the court finds that—

(1) the trustee has, prior to the hearing, made a proposal that fulfills the requirements of subsection (f);

(2) the authorized representative of the retirees has refused to accept such proposal without good cause; and

(3) such modification is necessary to permit the reorganization of the debtor and assures that all creditors, the debtor, and all of the affected parties are treated fairly and equitably, and is clearly favored by the balance of the equities;

except that in no case shall the court enter an order providing for such modification which provides for a modification to a level lower than that proposed by the trustee in the proposal found by the court to have complied with the requirements of this subsection and subsection (f): *Provided, however,* That at any time after an order is entered providing for modification in the payment of retiree benefits, or at any time after an agreement modifying such benefits is made between the trustee and the authorized representative of the recipients of such benefits, the authorized representative may apply to the court for an order increasing those benefits which order shall be granted if the increase in retiree benefits sought is consistent with the standard set forth in paragraph (3): *Provided further,* That neither the trustee nor the authorized representative is precluded from making more than one motion for a modification order governed by this subsection.

(h)(1) Prior to a court issuing a final order under subsection (g) of this section, if essential to the continuation of the debtor's business, or in order to avoid irreparable damage to the estate, the court, after notice and a hearing, may authorize the trustee to implement interim modifications in retiree benefits.

(2) Any hearing under this subsection shall be scheduled in accordance with the needs of the trustee.

(3) The implementation of such interim changes does not render the motion for modification moot.

(i) No retiree benefits paid between the filing of the petition and the time a plan confirmed under section 1129 of this title becomes effective shall be deducted or offset from the amounts allowed as claims for any benefits which remain unpaid, or from the amounts to be paid under the plan with respect to such claims for unpaid benefits, whether such claims for unpaid benefits are based upon or arise from a right to future unpaid benefits or from any benefits not paid as a result of modifications allowed pursuant to this section.

(j) No claim for retiree benefits shall be limited by section 502(b)(7) of this title.

(k)(1) Upon the filing of an application for modifying retiree benefits, the court shall schedule a hearing to be held not later than fourteen days after the date of the filing of such application. All interested parties may appear and be heard at such hearing. Adequate notice shall be provided to such parties at least ten days before the date of such hearing. The court may extend the time for the commencement of such hearing for a period not exceeding seven days where the circumstances of the case, and the interests of justice require such extension, or for additional periods of time to which the trustee and the authorized representative agree.

(2) The court shall rule on such application for modification within ninety days after the date of the commencement of the hearing. In the interests of justice, the court may extend such time for ruling for such additional period as the trustee and the authorized representative may agree to. If the court does not rule on such application within ninety days after the date of the commencement of the hearing, or within such additional time as the trustee and the authorized representative may agree to, the trustee may implement the proposed modifications pending the ruling of the court on such application.

(3) The court may enter such protective orders, consistent with the need of the authorized representative of the retirees to evaluate the trustee's proposal and the application for modification, as may be necessary to prevent disclosure of information provided to such representative where such disclosure could compromise the position of the debtor with respect to its competitors in the industry in which it is engaged.

(l) If the debtor, during the 180-day period ending on the date of the filing of the petition—

(1) modified retiree benefits; and

(2) was insolvent on the date such benefits were modified; the court, on motion of a party in interest, and after notice and a hearing, shall issue an order reinstating as of the date the modification was made, such benefits as in effect immediately before such date unless the court finds that the balance of the equities clearly favors such modification.

(m) This section shall not apply to any retiree, or the spouse or dependents of such retiree, if such retiree's gross income for the twelve months preceding the filing of the bankruptcy petition equals or exceeds $250,000, unless such retiree can demonstrate to the satisfaction of the court that he is unable to obtain health, medical, life, and disability coverage for himself, his spouse, and his dependents who would otherwise be covered by the employer's insurance plan, comparable to the coverage provided by the employer on the day before the filing of a petition under this title.

§ 1115. Property of the Estate

(a) In a case in which the debtor is an individual, property of the estate includes, in addition to the property specified in section 541—

(1) all property of the kind specified in section 541 that the debtor acquires after the commencement of the case but before the case is closed, dismissed, or converted to a case under chapter 7, 12, or 13, whichever occurs first; and

(2) earnings from services performed by the debtor after the commencement of the case but before the case is closed, dismissed, or converted to a case under chapter 7, 12, or 13, whichever occurs first.

(b) Except as provided in section 1104 or a confirmed plan or order confirming a plan, the debtor shall remain in possession of all property of the estate.

§ 1116. Duties of Trustee or Debtor in Possession in Small Business Cases

In a small business case, a trustee or the debtor in possession, in addition to the duties provided in this title and as otherwise required by law, shall—

(1) append to the voluntary petition or, in an involuntary case, file not later than 7 days after the date of the order for relief—

(A) its most recent balance sheet, statement of operations, cash-flow statement, and Federal income tax return; or

(B) a statement made under penalty of perjury that no balance sheet, statement of operations, or cash-flow statement has been prepared and no Federal tax return has been filed;

(2) attend, through its senior management personnel and counsel, meetings scheduled by the court or the United States trustee, including initial debtor interviews, scheduling conferences, and meetings of creditors convened under section 341 unless the court, after notice and a hearing, waives that requirement upon a finding of extraordinary and compelling circumstances;

(3) timely file all schedules and statements of financial affairs, unless the court, after notice and a hearing, grants an extension, which shall not extend such time period to a date later than 30 days after the date of the order for relief, absent extraordinary and compelling circumstances;

(4) file all postpetition financial and other reports required by the Federal Rules of Bankruptcy Procedure or by local rule of the district court;

(5) subject to section 363(c)(2), maintain insurance customary and appropriate to the industry;

(6) (A) timely file tax returns and other required government filings; and

(B) subject to section 363(c)(2), timely pay all taxes entitled to administrative expense priority except those being contested by appropriate proceedings being diligently prosecuted; and

(7) allow the United States trustee, or a designated representative of the United States trustee, to inspect the debtor's business premises, books, and records at reasonable times, after reasonable prior written notice, unless notice is waived by the debtor.

SUBCHAPTER II—THE PLAN

Section

1121. Who May File a Plan
1122. Classification of Claims or Interests
1123. Contents of Plan
1124. Impairment of Claims or Interests
1125. Postpetition Disclosure and Solicitation
1126. Acceptance of Plan
1127. Modification of Plan
1128. Confirmation Hearing
1129. Confirmation of Plan

§ 1121. Who May File a Plan

(a) The debtor may file a plan with a petition commencing a voluntary case, or at any time in a voluntary case or an involuntary case.

(b) Except as otherwise provided in this section, only the debtor may file a plan until after 120 days after the date of the order for relief under this chapter.

(c) Any party in interest, including the debtor, the trustee, a creditors' committee, an equity security holders' committee, a creditor, an equity security holder, or any indenture trustee, may file a plan if and only if—

(1) a trustee has been appointed under this chapter;

(2) the debtor has not filed a plan before 120 days after the date of the order for relief under this chapter; or

(3) the debtor has not filed a plan that has been accepted, before 180 days after the date of the order for relief under this chapter, by each class of claims or interests that is impaired under the plan.

(d)(1) Subject to paragraph (2), on request of a party in interest made within the respective periods specified in subsections (b) and (c) of this section and after notice and a hearing, the court may for cause reduce or increase the 120-day period or the 180-day period referred to in this section.

(2) (A) The 120-day period specified in paragraph (1) may not be extended beyond a date that is 18 months after the date of the order for relief under this chapter.

(B) The 180-day period specified in paragraph (1) may not be extended beyond a date that is 20 months after the date of the order for relief under this chapter.

(e) In a small business case—

(1) only the debtor may file a plan until after 180 days after the date of the order for relief, unless that period is—

(A) extended as provided by this subsection, after notice and a hearing; or

(B) the court, for cause, orders otherwise;

(2) the plan and a disclosure statement (if any) shall be filed not later than 300 days after the date of the order for relief; and

(3) the time periods specified in paragraphs (1) and (2), and the time fixed in section 1129(e) within which the plan shall be confirmed, may be extended only if—

(A) the debtor, after providing notice to parties in interest (including the United States trustee), demonstrates by a preponderance of the evidence that it is more likely than not that the court will confirm a plan within a reasonable period of time;

(B) a new deadline is imposed at the time the extension is granted; and

(C) the order extending time is signed before the existing deadline has expired.

§ 1122. Classification of Claims or Interests

(a) Except as provided in subsection (b) of this section, a plan may place a claim or an interest in a particular class only if such claim or interest is substantially similar to the other claims or interests of such class.

(b) A plan may designate a separate class of claims consisting only of every unsecured claim that is less than or reduced to an amount that the court approves as reasonable and necessary for administrative convenience.

§ 1123. Contents of Plan

(a) Notwithstanding any otherwise applicable nonbankruptcy law, a plan shall—

(1) designate, subject to section 1122 of this title, classes of claims, other than claims of a kind specified in section 507(a)(2), 507(a)(3), or 507(a)(8) of this title, and classes of interests;

(2) specify any class of claims or interests that is not impaired under the plan;

(3) specify the treatment of any class of claims or interests that is impaired under the plan;

(4) provide the same treatment for each claim or interest of a particular class, unless the holder of a particular claim or interest agrees to a less favorable treatment of such particular claim or interest;

(5) provide adequate means for the plan's implementation, such as—

(A) retention by the debtor of all or any part of the property of the estate;

(B) transfer of all or any part of the property of the estate to one or more entities, whether organized before or after the confirmation of such plan;

(C) merger or consolidation of the debtor with one or more persons;

(D) sale of all or any part of the property of the estate, either subject to or free of any lien, or the distribution of all or any part of the property of the estate among those having an interest in such property of the estate;

(E) satisfaction or modification of any lien;

(F) cancellation or modification of any indenture or similar instrument;

(G) curing or waiving of any default;

(H) extension of a maturity date or a change in an interest rate or other term of outstanding securities;

(I) amendment of the debtor's charter; or

(J) issuance of securities of the debtor, or of any entity referred to in subparagraph (B) or (C) of this paragraph, for cash, for property, for existing securities, or in exchange for claims or interests, or for any other appropriate purpose;

(6) provide for the inclusion in the charter of the debtor, if the debtor is a corporation, or of any corporation referred to in paragraph (5)(B) or (5)(C) of this subsection, of a provision prohibiting the issuance of nonvoting equity securities, and providing, as to the several classes of securities possessing voting power, an appropriate distribution of such power among such classes, including, in the case of any class of equity securities having a preference over another class of equity securities with respect to dividends, adequate provisions for the election of directors representing such preferred class in the event of default in the payment of such dividends;

(7) contain only provisions that are consistent with the interests of creditors and equity security holders and with public policy with respect to the manner of selection of any officer,

director, or trustee under the plan and any successor to such officer, director, or trustee; and

(8) in a case in which the debtor is an individual, provide for the payment to creditors under the plan of all or such portion of earnings from personal services performed by the debtor after the commencement of the case or other future income of the debtor as is necessary for the execution of the plan.

(b) Subject to subsection (a) of this section, a plan may—

(1) impair or leave unimpaired any class of claims, secured or unsecured, or of interests;

(2) subject to section 365 of this title, provide for the assumption, rejection, or assignment of any executory contract or unexpired lease of the debtor not previously rejected under such section;

(3) provide for—

(A) the settlement or adjustment of any claim or interest belonging to the debtor or to the estate; or

(B) the retention and enforcement by the debtor, by the trustee, or by a representative of the estate appointed for such purpose, of any such claim or interest;

(4) provide for the sale of all or substantially all of the property of the estate, and the distribution of the proceeds of such sale among holders of claims or interests;

(5) modify the rights of holders of secured claims, other than a claim secured only by a security interest in real property that is the debtor's principal residence, or of holders of unsecured claims, or leave unaffected the rights of holders of any class of claims; and

(6) include any other appropriate provision not inconsistent with the applicable provisions of this title.

(c) In a case concerning an individual, a plan proposed by an entity other than the debtor may not provide for the use, sale, or lease of property exempted under section 522 of this title, unless the debtor consents to such use, sale, or lease.

(d) Notwithstanding subsection (a) of this section and sections 506(b), 1129(a)(7), and 1129(b) of this title, if it is proposed in a plan to cure a default the amount necessary to cure the default shall be determined in accordance with the underlying agreement and applicable nonbankruptcy law.

§ 1124. Impairment of Claims or Interests

Except as provided in section 1123(a)(4) of this title, a class of claims or interests is impaired under a plan unless, with respect to each claim or interest of such class, the plan—

(1) leaves unaltered the legal, equitable, and contractual rights to which such claim or interest entitles the holder of such claim or interest; or

(2) notwithstanding any contractual provision or applicable law that entitles the holder of such claim or interest to demand or receive accelerated payment of such claim or interest after the occurrence of a default—

(A) cures any such default that occurred before or after the commencement of the case under this title, other than a default of a kind specified in section 365(b)(2) of this title or of a kind that section 365(b)(2) expressly does not require to be cured;

(B) reinstates the maturity of such claim or interest as such maturity existed before such default;

(C) compensates the holder of such claim or interest for any damages incurred as a result of any reasonable reliance by such holder on such contractual provision or such applicable law;

(D) if such claim or such interest arises from any failure to perform a nonmonetary obligation, other than a default arising from failure to operate a nonresidential real property lease subject to section 365(b)(1)(A), compensates the holder of such claim or such interest (other than the debtor or an insider) for any actual pecuniary loss incurred by such holder as a result of such failure; and

(E) does not otherwise alter the legal, equitable, or contractual rights to which such claim or interest entitles the holder of such claim or interest.

§ 1125. Postpetition Disclosure and Solicitation

(a) In this section—

(1) "adequate information" means information of a kind, and in sufficient detail, as far as is reasonably practicable in light of the nature and history of the debtor and the condition of the debtor's books and records, including a discussion of the potential material Federal tax

consequences of the plan to the debtor, any successor to the debtor, and a hypothetical investor typical of the holders of claims or interests in the case, that would enable such a hypothetical investor of the relevant class to make an informed judgment about the plan, but adequate information need not include such information about any other possible or proposed plan and in determining whether a disclosure statement provides adequate information, the court shall consider the complexity of the case, the benefit of additional information to creditors and other parties in interest, and the cost of providing additional information; and

(2) "investor typical of holders of claims or interests of the relevant class" means investor having—

(A) a claim or interest of the relevant class;

(B) such a relationship with the debtor as the holders of other claims or interests of such class generally have; and

(C) such ability to obtain such information from sources other than the disclosure required by this section as holders of claims or interests in such class generally have.

(b) An acceptance or rejection of a plan may not be solicited after the commencement of the case under this title from a holder of a claim or interest with respect to such claim or interest, unless, at the time of or before such solicitation, there is transmitted to such holder the plan or a summary of the plan, and a written disclosure statement approved, after notice and a hearing, by the court as containing adequate information. The court may approve a disclosure statement without a valuation of the debtor or an appraisal of the debtor's assets.

(c) The same disclosure statement shall be transmitted to each holder of a claim or interest of a particular class, but there may be transmitted different disclosure statements, differing in amount, detail, or kind of information, as between classes.

(d) Whether a disclosure statement required under subsection (b) of this section contains adequate information is not governed by any otherwise applicable nonbankruptcy law, rule, or regulation, but an agency or official whose duty is to administer or enforce such a law, rule, or regulation may be heard on the issue of whether a disclosure statement contains adequate information. Such an agency or official may not appeal from, or otherwise seek review of, an order approving a disclosure statement.

(e) A person that solicits acceptance or rejection of a plan, in good faith and in compliance with the applicable provisions of this title, or that participates, in good faith and in compliance with the applicable provisions of this title, in the offer, issuance, sale, or purchase of a security, offered or sold under the plan, of the debtor, of an affiliate participating in a joint plan with the debtor, or of a newly organized successor to the debtor under the plan, is not liable, on account of such solicitation or participation, for violation of any applicable law, rule, or regulation governing solicitation of acceptance or rejection of a plan or the offer, issuance, sale, or purchase of securities.

(f) Notwithstanding subsection (b), in a small business case—

(1) the court may determine that the plan itself provides adequate information and that a separate disclosure statement is not necessary;

(2) the court may approve a disclosure statement submitted on standard forms approved by the court or adopted under section 2075 of title 28; and

(3) (A) the court may conditionally approve a disclosure statement subject to final approval after notice and a hearing;

(B) acceptances and rejections of a plan may be solicited based on a conditionally approved disclosure statement if the debtor provides adequate information to each holder of a claim or interest that is solicited, but a conditionally approved disclosure statement shall be mailed not later than 25 days before the date of the hearing on confirmation of the plan; and

(C) the hearing on the disclosure statement may be combined with the hearing on confirmation of a plan.

(g) Notwithstanding subsection (b), an acceptance or rejection of the plan may be solicited from a holder of a claim or interest if such solicitation complies with applicable nonbankruptcy law and if such holder was solicited before the commencement of the case in a manner complying with applicable nonbankruptcy law.

§ 1126. Acceptance of Plan

(a) The holder of a claim or interest allowed under section 502 of this title may accept or reject a plan. If the United States is a creditor or equity security holder, the Secretary of the Treasury may accept or reject the plan on behalf of the United States.

(b) For the purposes of subsections (c) and (d) of this section, a holder of a claim or interest that has accepted or rejected the plan before the commencement of the case under this title is deemed to have accepted or rejected such plan, as the case may be, if—

(1) the solicitation of such acceptance or rejection was in compliance with any applicable nonbankruptcy law, rule, or regulation governing the adequacy of disclosure in connection with such solicitation; or

(2) if there is not any such law, rule, or regulation, such acceptance or rejection was solicited after disclosure to such holder of adequate information, as defined in section 1125(a) of this title.

(c) A class of claims has accepted a plan if such plan has been accepted by creditors, other than any entity designated under subsection (e) of this section, that hold at least two-thirds in amount and more than one-half in number of the allowed claims of such class held by creditors, other than any entity designated under subsection (e) of this section, that have accepted or rejected such plan.

(d) A class of interests has accepted a plan if such plan has been accepted by holders of such interests, other than any entity designated under subsection (e) of this section, that hold at least two-thirds in amount of the allowed interests of such class held by holders of such interests, other than any entity designated under subsection (e) of this section, that have accepted or rejected such plan.

(e) On request of a party in interest, and after notice and a hearing, the court may designate any entity whose acceptance or rejection of such plan was not in good faith, or was not solicited or procured in good faith or in accordance with the provisions of this title.

(f) Notwithstanding any other provision of this section, a class that is not impaired under a plan, and each holder of a claim or interest of such class, are conclusively presumed to have accepted the plan, and solicitation of acceptances with respect to such class from the holders of claims or interests of such class is not required.

(g) Notwithstanding any other provision of this section, a class is deemed not to have accepted a plan if such plan provides that the claims or interests of such class do not entitle the holders of such claims or interests to receive or retain any property under the plan on account of such claims or interests.

§ 1127. Modification of Plan

(a) The proponent of a plan may modify such plan at any time before confirmation, but may not modify such plan so that such plan as modified fails to meet the requirements of sections 1122 and 1123 of this title. After the proponent of a plan files a modification of such plan with the court, the plan as modified becomes the plan.

(b) The proponent of a plan or the reorganized debtor may modify such plan at any time after confirmation of such plan and before substantial consummation of such plan, but may not modify such plan so that such plan as modified fails to meet the requirements of sections 1122 and 1123 of this title. Such plan as modified under this subsection becomes the plan only if circumstances warrant such modification and the court, after notice and a hearing, confirms such plan as modified, under section 1129 of this title.

(c) The proponent of a modification shall comply with section 1125 of this title with respect to the plan as modified.

(d) Any holder of a claim or interest that has accepted or rejected a plan is deemed to have accepted or rejected, as the case may be, such plan as modified, unless, within the time fixed by the court, such holder changes such holder's previous acceptance or rejection.

(e) If the debtor is an individual, the plan may be modified at any time after confirmation of the plan but before the completion of payments under the plan, whether or not the plan has been substantially consummated, upon request of the debtor, the trustee, the United States trustee, or the holder of an allowed unsecured claim, to—

(1) increase or reduce the amount of payments on claims of a particular class provided for by the plan;

(2) extend or reduce the time period for such payments; or

(3) alter the amount of the distribution to a creditor whose claim is provided for by the plan to the extent necessary to take account of any payment of such claim made other than under the plan.

(f)(1) Sections 1121 through 1128 and the requirements of section 1129 apply to any modification under subsection (e).

(2) The plan, as modified, shall become the plan only after there has been disclosure under section 1125 as the court may direct, notice and a hearing, and such modification is approved.

§ 1128. Confirmation Hearing

(a) After notice, the court shall hold a hearing on confirmation of a plan.

(b) A party in interest may object to confirmation of a plan.

§ 1129. Confirmation of Plan

(a) The court shall confirm a plan only if all of the following requirements are met:

(1) The plan complies with the applicable provisions of this title.

(2) The proponent of the plan complies with the applicable provisions of this title.

(3) The plan has been proposed in good faith and not by any means forbidden by law.

(4) Any payment made or to be made by the proponent, by the debtor, or by a person issuing securities or acquiring property under the plan, for services or for costs and expenses in or in connection with the case, or in connection with the plan and incident to the case, has been approved by, or is subject to the approval of, the court as reasonable.

(5) (A)(i) The proponent of the plan has disclosed the identity and affiliations of any individual proposed to serve, after confirmation of the plan, as a director, officer, or voting trustee of the debtor, an affiliate of the debtor participating in a joint plan with the debtor, or a successor to the debtor under the plan; and

(ii) the appointment to, or continuance in, such office of such individual, is consistent with the interests of creditors and equity security holders and with public policy; and

(B) the proponent of the plan has disclosed the identity of any insider that will be employed or retained by the reorganized debtor, and the nature of any compensation for such insider.

(6) Any governmental regulatory commission with jurisdiction, after confirmation of the plan, over the rates of the debtor has approved any rate change provided for in the plan, or such rate change is expressly conditioned on such approval.

(7) With respect to each impaired class of claims or interests—

(A) each holder of a claim or interest of such class—

(i) has accepted the plan; or

(ii) will receive or retain under the plan on account of such claim or interest property of a value, as of the effective date of the plan, that is not less than the amount that such holder would so receive or retain if the debtor were liquidated under chapter 7 of this title on such date; or

(B) if section 1111(b)(2) of this title applies to the claims of such class, each holder of a claim of such class will receive or retain under the plan on account of such claim property of a value, as of the effective date of the plan, that is not less than the value of such holder's interest in the estate's interest in the property that secures such claims.

(8) With respect to each class of claims or interests—

(A) such class has accepted the plan; or

(B) such class is not impaired under the plan.

(9) Except to the extent that the holder of a particular claim has agreed to a different treatment of such claim, the plan provides that—

(A) with respect to a claim of a kind specified in section 507(a)(2) or 507(a)(3) of this title, on the effective date of the plan, the holder of such claim will receive on account of such claim cash equal to the allowed amount of such claim;

(B) with respect to a class of claims of a kind specified in section 507(a)(1), 507(a)(4), 507(a)(5), 507(a)(6), or 507(a)(7) of this title, each holder of a claim of such class will receive—

(i) if such class has accepted the plan, deferred cash payments of a value, as of the effective date of the plan, equal to the allowed amount of such claim; or

(ii) if such class has not accepted the plan, cash on the effective date of the plan equal to the allowed amount of such claim;

(C) with respect to a claim of a kind specified in section 507(a)(8) of this title, the holder of such claim will receive on account of such claim regular installment payments in cash—

(i) of a total value, as of the effective date of the plan, equal to the allowed amount of such claim;

(ii) over a period ending not later than 5 years after the date of the order for relief under section 301, 302, or 303; and

(iii) in a manner not less favorable than the most favored nonpriority unsecured claim provided for by the plan (other than cash payments made to a class of creditors under section 1122(b)); and

(D) with respect to a secured claim which would otherwise meet the description of an unsecured claim of a governmental unit under section 507(a)(8), but for the secured status of that claim, the holder of that claim will receive on account of that claim, cash payments, in the same manner and over the same period, as prescribed in subparagraph (C).

(10) If a class of claims is impaired under the plan, at least one class of claims that is impaired under the plan has accepted the plan, determined without including any acceptance of the plan by any insider.

(11) Confirmation of the plan is not likely to be followed by the liquidation, or the need for further financial reorganization, of the debtor or any successor to the debtor under the plan, unless such liquidation or reorganization is proposed in the plan.

(12) All fees payable under section 1930 of title 28, as determined by the court at the hearing on confirmation of the plan, have been paid or the plan provides for the payment of all such fees on the effective date of the plan.

(13) The plan provides for the continuation after its effective date of payment of all retiree benefits, as that term is defined in section 1114 of this title, at the level established pursuant to subsection (e)(1)(B) or (g) of section 1114 of this title, at any time prior to confirmation of the plan, for the duration of the period the debtor has obligated itself to provide such benefits.

(14) If the debtor is required by a judicial or administrative order, or by statute, to pay a domestic support obligation, the debtor has paid all amounts payable under such order or such statute for such obligation that first become payable after the date of the filing of the petition.

(15) In a case in which the debtor is an individual and in which the holder of an allowed unsecured claim objects to the confirmation of the plan—

(A) the value, as of the effective date of the plan, of the property to be distributed under the plan on account of such claim is not less than the amount of such claim; or

(B) the value of the property to be distributed under the plan is not less than the projected disposable income of the debtor (as defined in section 1325(b)(2)) to be received during the 5-year period beginning on the date that the first payment is due under the plan, or during the period for which the plan provides payments, whichever is longer.

(16) All transfers of property under the plan shall be made in accordance with any applicable provisions of nonbankruptcy law that govern the transfer of property by a corporation or trust that is not a moneyed, business, or commercial corporation or trust.

(b)(1) Notwithstanding section 510(a) of this title, if all of the applicable requirements of subsection (a) of this section other than paragraph (8) are met with respect to a plan, the court, on request of the proponent of the plan, shall confirm the plan notwithstanding the requirements of such paragraph if the plan does not discriminate unfairly, and is fair and equitable, with respect to each class of claims or interests that is impaired under, and has not accepted, the plan.

(2) For the purpose of this subsection, the condition that a plan be fair and equitable with respect to a class includes the following requirements:

(A) With respect to a class of secured claims, the plan provides—

(i) (I) that the holders of such claims retain the liens securing such claims, whether the property subject to such liens is retained by the debtor or transferred to another entity, to the extent of the allowed amount of such claims; and

(II) that each holder of a claim of such class receive on account of such claim deferred cash payments totaling at least the allowed amount of such claim, of a value, as of the effective date of the plan, of at least the value of such holder's interest in the estate's interest in such property;

(ii) for the sale, subject to section 363(k) of this title, of any property that is subject to the liens securing such claims, free and clear of such liens, with such liens to attach to the proceeds of such sale, and the treatment of such liens on proceeds under clause (i) or (iii) of this subparagraph; or

(iii) for the realization by such holders of the indubitable equivalent of such claims.

(B) With respect to a class of unsecured claims—

(i) the plan provides that each holder of a claim of such class receive or retain on account of such claim property of a value, as of the effective date of the plan, equal to the allowed amount of such claim; or

(ii) the holder of any claim or interest that is junior to the claims of such class will not receive or retain under the plan on account of such junior claim or interest any property, except that in a case in which the debtor is an individual, the debtor may retain property included in the estate under section 1115, subject to the requirements of subsection (a)(14) of this section.

(C) With respect to a class of interests—

(i) the plan provides that each holder of an interest of such class receive or retain on account of such interest property of a value, as of the effective date of the plan, equal to the greatest of the allowed amount of any fixed liquidation preference to which such holder is entitled, any fixed redemption price to which such holder is entitled, or the value of such interest; or

(ii) the holder of any interest that is junior to the interests of such class will not receive or retain under the plan on account of such junior interest any property.

(c) Notwithstanding subsections (a) and (b) of this section and except as provided in section 1127(b) of this title, the court may confirm only one plan, unless the order of confirmation in the case has been revoked under section 1144 of this title. If the requirements of subsections (a) and (b) of this section are met with respect to more than one plan, the court shall consider the preferences of creditors and equity security holders in determining which plan to confirm.

(d) Notwithstanding any other provision of this section, on request of a party in interest that is a governmental unit, the court may not confirm a plan if the principal purpose of the plan is the avoidance of taxes or the avoidance of the application of section 5 of the Securities Act of 1933. In any hearing under this subsection, the governmental unit has the burden of proof on the issue of avoidance.

(e) In a small business case, the court shall confirm a plan that complies with the applicable provisions of this title and that is filed in accordance with section 1121(e) not later than 45 days after the plan is filed unless the time for confirmation is extended in accordance with section 1121(e)(3).

SUBCHAPTER III— POSTCONFIRMATION MATTERS

Section

1141. Effect of Confirmation
1142. Implementation of Plan
1143. Distribution
1144. Revocation of an Order of Confirmation
1145. Exemption from Securities Laws
1146. Special Tax Provisions

§ 1141. Effect of Confirmation

(a) Except as provided in subsections (d)(2) and (d)(3) of this section, the provisions of a confirmed plan bind the debtor, any entity issuing securities under the plan, any entity acquiring property under the plan, and any creditor, equity security holder, or general partner in the debtor, whether or not the claim or interest of such creditor, equity security holder, or general partner is impaired under the plan and whether or not such creditor, equity security holder, or general partner has accepted the plan.

(b) Except as otherwise provided in the plan or the order confirming the plan, the confirmation of a plan vests all of the property of the estate in the debtor.

(c) Except as provided in subsections (d)(2) and (d)(3) of this section and except as otherwise provided in the plan or in the order confirming the plan, after confirmation of a plan, the property dealt with by the plan is free and clear of all claims and interests of creditors, equity security holders, and of general partners in the debtor.

(d)(1) Except as otherwise provided in this subsection, in the plan, or in the order confirming the plan, the confirmation of a plan—

(A) discharges the debtor from any debt that arose before the date of such confirmation, and any debt of a kind specified in section 502(g), 502(h), or 502(i) of this title, whether or not—

(i) a proof of the claim based on such debt is filed or deemed filed under section 501 of this title;

(ii) such claim is allowed under section 502 of this title; or

(iii) the holder of such claim has accepted the plan; and

(B) terminates all rights and interests of equity security holders and general partners provided for by the plan.

(2) A discharge under this chapter does not discharge a debtor who is an individual from any debt excepted from discharge under section 523 of this title.

(3) The confirmation of a plan does not discharge a debtor if—

(A) the plan provides for the liquidation of all or substantially all of the property of the estate;

(B) the debtor does not engage in business after consummation of the plan; and

(C) the debtor would be denied a discharge under section 727(a) of this title if the case were a case under chapter 7 of this title.

(4) The court may approve a written waiver of discharge executed by the debtor after the order for relief under this chapter.

(5) In a case in which the debtor is an individual—

(A) unless after notice and a hearing the court orders otherwise for cause, confirmation of the plan does not discharge any debt provided for in the plan until the court grants a discharge on completion of all payments under the plan;

(B) at any time after the confirmation of the plan, and after notice and a hearing, the court may grant a discharge to the debtor who has not completed payments under the plan if—

(i) the value, as of the effective date of the plan, of property actually distributed under the plan on account of each allowed unsecured claim is not less than the amount that would have been paid on such claim if the estate of the debtor had been liquidated under chapter 7 on such date;

(ii) modification of the plan under section 1127 is not practicable; and

(iii) subparagraph (c) permits the court to grant a discharge; and

(C) the court may grant a discharge if, after notice and a hearing held not more than 10 days before the date of the entry of the order granting the discharge, the court finds that there is no reasonable cause to believe that—

(i) section 522(q)(1) may be applicable to the debtor; and

(ii) there is pending any proceeding in which the debtor may be found guilty of a felony of the kind described in section 522(q)(1)(A) or liable for a debt of the kind described in section 522(q)(1)(B); and if the requirements of subparagraph (A) or (B) are met.

(6) Notwithstanding paragraph (1), the confirmation of a plan does not discharge a debtor that is a corporation from any debt—

(A) of a kind specified in paragraph (2)(A) or (2)(B) of section 523(a) that is owed to a domestic governmental unit, or owed to a person as the result of an action filed under subchapter III of chapter 37 of title 31 or any similar State statute; or

(B) for a tax or customs duty with respect to which the debtor—

(i) made a fraudulent return; or

(ii) willfully attempted in any manner to evade or to defeat such tax or such customs duty.

§ 1142. Implementation of Plan

(a) Notwithstanding any otherwise applicable nonbankruptcy law, rule, or regulation relating to financial condition, the debtor and any entity organized or to be organized for the purpose of carrying out the plan shall carry out the plan and shall comply with any orders of the court.

(b) The court may direct the debtor and any other necessary party to execute or deliver or to join in the execution or delivery of any instrument required to effect a transfer of property dealt with by a confirmed plan, and to perform any other act, including the satisfaction of any lien, that is necessary for the consummation of the plan.

§ 1143. Distribution

If a plan requires presentment or surrender of a security or the performance of any other act as a condition to participation in distribution under the plan, such action shall be taken not later than five years after the date of the entry of the order of confirmation. Any entity that has not within such time presented or surrendered such entity's security or taken any such other action that the plan requires may not participate in distribution under the plan.

§ 1144. Revocation of an Order of Confirmation

On request of a party in interest at any time before 180 days after the date of the entry of the order of confirmation, and after notice and a hearing, the court may revoke such order if and only if such order was procured by fraud. An order under this section revoking an order of confirmation shall—

(1) contain such provisions as are necessary to protect any entity acquiring rights in good faith reliance on the order of confirmation; and

(2) revoke the discharge of the debtor.

§ 1145. Exemption from Securities Laws

(a) Except with respect to an entity that is an underwriter as defined in subsection (b) of this section, section 5 of the Securities Act of 1933 and any state or local law requiring registration for offer or sale of a security or registration or licensing of an issuer of, underwriter of, or broker or dealer in, a security do not apply to—

(1) the offer or sale under a plan of a security of the debtor, of an affiliate participating in a joint plan with the debtor, or of a successor to the debtor under the plan—

(A) in exchange for a claim against, an interest in, or a claim for an administrative expense in the case concerning, the debtor or such affiliate; or

(B) principally in such exchange and partly for cash or property;

(2) the offer of a security through any warrant, option, right to subscribe, or conversion privilege that was sold in the manner specified in paragraph (1) of this subsection, or the sale of a security upon the exercise of such a warrant, option, right, or privilege;

(3) the offer or sale, other than under a plan, of a security of an issuer other than the debtor or an affiliate, if—

(A) such security was owned by the debtor on the date of the filing of the petition;

(B) the issuer of such security is—

(i) required to file reports under section 13 or 15(d) of the Securities Exchange Act of 1934; and

(ii) in compliance with the disclosure and reporting provision of such applicable section; and

(C) such offer or sale is of securities that do not exceed—

(i) during the two-year period immediately following the date of the filing of the petition, four percent of the securities of such class outstanding on such date; and

(ii) during any 180-day period following such two-year period, one percent of the securities outstanding at the beginning of such 180-day period; or

(4) a transaction by a stockbroker in a security that is executed after a transaction of a kind specified in paragraph (1) or (2) of this subsection in such security and before the expiration of 40 days after the first date on which such security was bona fide offered to the public by the issuer or by or through an underwriter, if such stockbroker provides, at the time of or before such transaction by such stockbroker, a disclosure statement approved under section 1125 of this title, and, if the court orders, information supplementing such disclosure statement.

(b)(1) Except as provided in paragraph (2) of this subsection and except with respect to ordinary trading transactions of an entity that is not an issuer, an entity is an underwriter under section 2(a)(11) of the Securities Act of 1933, if such entity—

(A) purchases a claim against, interest in, or claim for an administrative expense in the case concerning, the debtor, if such purchase is with a view to distribution of any security received or to be received in exchange for such a claim or interest;

(B) offers to sell securities offered or sold under the plan for the holders of such securities;

(C) offers to buy securities offered or sold under the plan from the holders of such securities, if such offer to buy is—

(i) with a view to distribution of such securities; and

(ii) under an agreement made in connection with the plan, with the consummation of the plan, or with the offer or sale of securities under the plan; or

(D) is an issuer, as used in such section 2(a)(11), with respect to such securities.

(2) An entity is not an underwriter under section 2(a)(11) of the Securities Act of 1933 or under paragraph (1) of this subsection with respect to an agreement that provides only for—

(A) (i) the matching or combining of fractional interests in securities offered or sold under the plan into whole interests; or

(ii) the purchase or sale of such fractional interests from or to entities receiving such fractional interests under the plan; or

(B) the purchase or sale for such entities of such fractional or whole interests as are necessary to adjust for any remaining fractional interests after such matching.

(3) An entity other than an entity of the kind specified in paragraph (1) of this subsection is not an underwriter under section 2(a)(11) of the Securities Act of 1933 with respect to any securities offered or sold to such entity in the manner specified in subsection (a)(1) of this section.

(c) An offer or sale of securities of the kind and in the manner specified under subsection (a)(1) of this section is deemed to be a public offering.

(d) The Trust Indenture Act of 1939 does not apply to a note issued under the plan that matures not later than one year after the effective date of the plan.

§ 1146. Special Tax Provisions

(a) The issuance, transfer, or exchange of a security, or the making or delivery of an instrument of transfer under a plan confirmed under section 1129 or 1191 of this title, may not be taxed under any law imposing a stamp tax or similar tax.

(b) The court may authorize the proponent of a plan to request a determination, limited to questions of law, by a state or local governmental unit charged with responsibility for collection or determination of a tax on or measured by income, of the tax effects, under section 346 of this title and under the law imposing such tax, of the plan. In the event of an actual controversy, the court may declare such effects after the earlier of—

(1) the date on which such governmental unit responds to the request under this subsection; or

(2) 270 days after such request.

SUBCHAPTER IV—RAILROAD REORGANIZATION

Section

1161. Inapplicability of Other Sections
1162. Definition
1163. Appointment of Trustee
1164. Right to Be Heard
1165. Protection of the Public Interest
1166. Effect of Subtitle IV of Title 49 and of Federal, State, or Local Regulations
1167. Collective Bargaining Agreements
1168. Rolling Stock Equipment
1169. Effect of Rejection of Lease of Railroad Line
1170. Abandonment of Railroad Line
1171. Priority Claims
1172. Contents of Plan
1173. Confirmation of Plan
1174. Liquidation

§ 1161. Inapplicability of Other Sections

Sections 341, 343, 1102(a)(1), 1104, 1105, 1107, 1129(a)(7), and 1129(c) of this title do not apply in a case concerning a railroad.

§ 1162. Definition

In this subchapter, "Board" means the "Surface Transportation Board".

§ 1163. Appointment of Trustee

As soon as practicable after the order for relief the Secretary of Transportation shall submit a list of five disinterested persons that are qualified and willing to serve as trustees in the case. The United States trustee shall appoint one of such persons to serve as trustee in the case.

§ 1164. Right to Be Heard

The Board, the Department of Transportation, and any State or local commission having regulatory jurisdiction over the debtor may raise and may appear and be heard on any issue in a case under this chapter, but may not appeal from any judgment, order, or decree entered in the case.

§ 1165. Protection of the Public Interest

In applying sections 1166, 1167, 1169, 1170, 1171, 1172, 1173, and 1174 of this title, the court and the trustee shall consider the public interest in addition to the interests of the debtor, creditors, and equity security holders.

§ 1166. Effect of Subtitle IV of Title 49 and of Federal, State, or Local Regulations

Except with respect to abandonment under section 1170 of this title, or merger, modification of the financial structure of the debtor, or issuance or sale of securities under a plan, the trustee and the debtor are subject to the provisions of subtitle IV of title 49 that are applicable to railroads, and the trustee is subject to orders of any Federal, state, or local regulatory body to the same extent as the debtor would be if a petition commencing the case under this chapter had not been filed, but—

(1) any such order that would require the expenditure, or the incurring of an obligation for the expenditure, of money from the estate is not effective unless approved by the court; and

(2) the provisions of this chapter are subject to section 601(b) of the Regional Rail Reorganization Act of 1973.

§ 1167. Collective Bargaining Agreements

Notwithstanding section 365 of this title, neither the court nor the trustee may change the wages or working conditions of employees of the debtor established by a collective bargaining agreement that is subject to the Railway Labor Act except in accordance with section 6 of such Act.

§ 1168. Rolling Stock Equipment

(a)(1) The right of a secured party with a security interest in or of a lessor or conditional vendor of equipment described in paragraph (2) to take possession of such equipment in compliance with an equipment security agreement, lease, or conditional sale contract, and to enforce any of its other rights or remedies under such security agreement, lease, or conditional sale contract, to sell, lease, or otherwise retain or dispose of such equipment, is not limited or otherwise affected by any other provision of this title or by any power of the court, except that right to take possession and enforce those other rights and remedies shall be subject to section 362, if—

(A) before the date that is 60 days after the date of commencement of a case under this chapter, the trustee, subject to the court's approval, agrees to perform all obligations of the debtor under such security agreement, lease, or conditional sale contract; and

(B) any default, other than a default of a kind described in section 365(b)(2), under such security agreement, lease, or conditional sale contract—

(i) that occurs before the date of commencement of the case and is an event of default therewith is cured before the expiration of such 60-day period;

(ii) that occurs or becomes an event of default after the date of commencement of the case and before the expiration of such 60-day period is cured before the later of—

(I) the date that is 30 days after the date of the default or event of the default; or

(II) the expiration of such 60-day period; and

(iii) that occurs on or after the expiration of such 60-day period is cured in accordance with the terms of such security agreement, lease, or conditional sale contract, if cure is permitted under that agreement, lease, or conditional sale contract.

(2) The equipment described in this paragraph—

(A) is rolling stock equipment or accessories used on rolling stock equipment, including superstructures or racks, that is subject to a security interest granted by, leased to, or conditionally sold to a debtor; and

(B) includes all records and documents relating to such equipment that are required, under the terms of the security agreement, lease, or conditional sale contract, that is to be surrendered or returned by the debtor in connection with the surrender or return of such equipment.

(3) Paragraph (1) applies to a secured party, lessor, or conditional vendor acting in its own behalf or acting as trustee or otherwise in behalf of another party.

(b) The trustee and the secured party, lessor, or conditional vendor whose right to take possession is protected under subsection (a) may agree, subject to the court's approval, to extend the 60-day period specified in subsection (a)(1).

(c)(1) In any case under this chapter, the trustee shall immediately surrender and return to a secured party, lessor, or conditional vendor, described in subsection (a)(1), equipment described in subsection (a)(2), if at any time after the date of commencement of the case under this chapter such secured party, lessor, or conditional vendor is entitled pursuant to subsection (a)(1) to take possession of such equipment and makes a written demand for such possession of the trustee.

(2) At such time as the trustee is required under paragraph (1) to surrender and return equipment described in subsection (a)(2), any lease of such equipment, and any security agreement or conditional sale contract relating to such equipment, if such security agreement or conditional sale contract is an executory contract, shall be deemed rejected.

(d) With respect to equipment first placed in service on or prior to October 22, 1994, for purposes of this section—

(1) the term "lease" includes any written agreement with respect to which the lessor and the debtor, as lessee, have expressed in the agreement or in a substantially contemporaneous writing that the agreement is to be treated as a lease for Federal income tax purposes; and

(2) the term "security interest" means a purchase-money equipment security interest.

(e) With respect to equipment first placed in service after October 22, 1994, for purposes of this section, the term "rolling stock equipment" includes rolling stock equipment that is substantially rebuilt and accessories used on such equipment.

§ 1169. Effect of Rejection of Lease of Railroad Line

(a) Except as provided in subsection (b) of this section, if a lease of a line of railroad under which the debtor is the lessee is rejected under section 365 of this title, and if the trustee, within such time as the court fixes, and with the court's approval, elects not to operate the leased line, the lessor under such lease, after such approval, shall operate the line.

(b) If operation of such line by such lessor is impracticable or contrary to the public interest, the court, on request of such lessor, and after notice and a hearing, shall order the trustee to continue operation of such line for the account of such lessor until abandonment is ordered under section 1170 of this title, or until such operation is otherwise lawfully terminated, whichever occurs first.

(c) During any such operation, such lessor is deemed a carrier subject to the provisions of subtitle IV of title 49 that are applicable to railroads.

§ 1170. Abandonment of Railroad Line

(a) The court, after notice and a hearing, may authorize the abandonment of all or a portion of a railroad line if such abandonment is—

(1) (A) in the best interest of the estate; or

(B) essential to the formulation of a plan; and

(2) consistent with the public interest.

(b) If, except for the pendency of the case under this chapter, such abandonment would require approval by the Board under a law of the United States, the trustee shall initiate an appropriate application for such abandonment with the Board. The court may fix a time within which the Board shall report to the court on such application.

(c) After the court receives the report of the Board, or the expiration of the time fixed under subsection (b) of this section, whichever occurs first, the court may authorize such abandonment, after notice to the Board, the Secretary of Transportation, the trustee, any party in interest that has requested notice, any affected shipper or community, and any other entity prescribed by the court, and a hearing.

(d)(1) Enforcement of an order authorizing such abandonment shall be stayed until the time for taking an appeal has expired, or, if an appeal is timely taken, until such order has become final.

(2) If an order authorizing such abandonment is appealed, the court, on request of a party in interest, may authorize suspension of service on a line or a portion of a line pending the determination of such appeal, after notice to the Board, the Secretary of Transportation, the trustee, any party in interest that has requested notice, any affected shipper or community, and any other entity prescribed by the court, and a hearing. An appellant may not obtain a stay of the enforcement of an order authorizing such suspension by the giving of a supersedeas bond or otherwise, during the pendency of such appeal.

(e)(1) In authorizing any abandonment of a railroad line under this section, the court shall require the rail carrier to provide a fair arrangement at least as protective of the interests of employees as that established under section 11326(a) of title 49.

(2) Nothing in this subsection shall be deemed to affect the priorities or timing of payment of employee protection which might have existed in the absence of this subsection.

§ 1171. Priority Claims

(a) There shall be paid as an administrative expense any claim of an individual or of the personal representative of a deceased individual against the debtor or the estate, for personal injury to or death of such individual arising out of the operation of the debtor or the estate, whether such claim arose before or after the commencement of the case.

(b) Any unsecured claim against the debtor that would have been entitled to priority if a receiver in equity of the property of the debtor had been appointed by a Federal court on the date of the order for relief under this title shall be entitled to the same priority in the case under this chapter.

§ 1172. Contents of Plan

(a) In addition to the provisions required or permitted under section 1123 of this title, a plan—

(1) shall specify the extent to and the means by which the debtor's rail service is proposed to be continued, and the extent to which any of the debtor's rail service is proposed to be terminated; and

(2) may include a provision for—

(A) the transfer of any or all of the operating railroad lines of the debtor to another operating railroad; or

(B) abandonment of any railroad line in accordance with section 1170 of this title.

(b) If, except for the pendency of the case under this chapter, transfer of, or operation of or over, any of the debtor's rail lines by an entity other than the debtor or a successor to the debtor under the plan would require approval by the Board under a law of the United States, then a plan may not propose such a transfer or such operation unless the proponent of the plan initiates an appropriate application for such a transfer or such operation with the Board and, within such time as the court may fix, not exceeding 180 days, the Board, with or without a hearing, as the Board may determine, and with or without modification or condition, approves such application, or does not act on such application. Any action or order of the Board approving, modifying, conditioning, or disapproving such application is subject to review by the court only under sections 706(2)(A), 706(2)(B), 706(2)(C), and 706(2)(D) of title 5.

(c)(1) In approving an application under subsection (b) of this section, the Board shall require the rail carrier to provide a fair arrangement at least as protective of the interests of employees as that established under section 11326(a) of title 49.

(2) Nothing in this subsection shall be deemed to affect the priorities or timing of payment of employee protection which might have existed in the absence of this subsection.

§ 1173. Confirmation of Plan

(a) The court shall confirm a plan if—

(1) the applicable requirements of section 1129 of this title have been met;

(2) each creditor or equity security holder will receive or retain under the plan property of a value, as of the effective date of the plan, that is not less than the value of property that each such creditor or equity security holder would so receive or retain if all of the operating railroad lines of the debtor were sold, and the proceeds of such sale, and the other property of the estate, were distributed under chapter 7 of this title on such date;

(3) in light of the debtor's past earnings and the probable prospective earnings of the reorganized debtor, there will be adequate coverage by such prospective earnings of any fixed charges, such as interest on debt, amortization of funded debt, and rent for leased railroads, provided for by the plan; and

(4) the plan is consistent with the public interest.

(b) If the requirements of subsection (a) of this section are met with respect to more than one plan, the court shall confirm the plan that is most likely to maintain adequate rail service in the public interest.

§ 1174. Liquidation

On request of a party in interest and after notice and a hearing, the court may, or, if a plan has not been confirmed under section 1173 of this title before five years after the date of the order for relief, the court shall, order the trustee to cease the debtor's operation and to collect and reduce to money all of the property of the estate in the same manner as if the case were a case under chapter 7 of this title.

SUBCHAPTER V—SMALL BUSINESS DEBTOR REORGANIZATION

Section

1181. Inapplicability of Other Sections
1182. Definitions
1183. Trustee
1184. Rights and Powers of a Debtor in Possession
1185. Removal of Debtor in Possession
1186. Property of the Estate
1187. Duties and Reporting Requirements of Debtors
1188. Status Conference
1189. Filing of the Plan
1190. Contents of Plan
1191. Confirmation of Plan
1192. Discharge
1193. Modification of Plan
1194. Payments
1195. Transactions with Professionals

§ 1181. Inapplicability of Other Sections

(a) In general.—Sections 105(d), 1101(1), 1104, 1105, 1106, 1107, 1108, 1115, 1116, 1121, 1123(a)(8), 1123(c), 1127, 1129(a)(15), 1129(b), 1129(c), 1129(e), and 1141(d)(5) of this title do not apply in a case under this subchapter.

(b) Court authority.—Unless the court for cause orders otherwise, paragraphs (1), (2), and (4) of section 1102(a) and sections 1102(b), 1103, and 1125 of this title do not apply in a case under this subchapter

(c) Special rule for discharge.—If a plan is confirmed under section 1191(b) of this title, section 1141(d) of this title shall not apply, except as provided in section 1192 of this title.

§ 1182. Definitions

In this subchapter:

(1) Debtor.—The term "debtor"—

(A) subject to subparagraph (B), means a person engaged in commercial or business activities (including any affiliate of such person that is also a debtor under this title and excluding a person whose primary activity is the business of owning single asset real estate) that has aggregate noncontingent liquidated secured and unsecured debts as of the date of the filing of the petition or the date of the order for relief in an amount not more than $7,500,000 (excluding debts owed to 1 or more affiliates or insiders) not less than 50 percent of which arose from the commercial or business activities of the debtor; and

(B) does not include—

(i) any member of a group of affiliated debtors under this title that has aggregate noncontingent liquidated secured and unsecured debts in an amount greater than $7,500,000 (excluding debt owed to 1 or more affiliates or insiders);

(ii) any debtor that is a corporation subject to the reporting requirements under section 13 or 15(d) of the Securities Exchange Act of 1934 (15 U.S.C. 78m, 78o(d)); or

(iii) any debtor that is an affiliate of a corporation described in clause (ii).

(2) Debtor in possession.—The term "debtor in possession" means the debtor, unless removed as debtor in possession under section 1185(a) of this title.

[Editor's note: Section 1182(1) reverts to previous language on June 21, 2024.]

§ 1183. Trustee

(a) In general.—If the United States trustee has appointed an individual under section 586(b) of title 28 to serve as standing trustee in cases under this subchapter, and if such individual qualifies as a trustee under section 322 of this title, then that individual shall serve as trustee in any case under this subchapter. Otherwise, the United States trustee shall appoint one disinterested person to serve as trustee in the case or the United States trustee may serve as trustee in the case, as necessary.

(b) Duties.—The trustee shall—

(1) perform the duties specified in paragraphs (2), (5), (6), (7), and (9) of section 704(a) of this title;

(2) perform the duties specified in paragraphs (3), (4), and (7) of section 1106(a) of this title, if the court, for cause and on request of a party in interest, the trustee, or the United States trustee, so orders;

(3) appear and be heard at the status conference under section 1188 of this title and any hearing that concerns—

(A) the value of property subject to a lien;

(B) confirmation of a plan filed under this subchapter;

(C) modification of the plan after confirmation; or

(D) the sale of property of the estate;

(4) ensure that the debtor commences making timely payments required by a plan confirmed under this subchapter;

(5) if the debtor ceases to be a debtor in possession—

(A) perform the duties specified in section 704(a)(8) and paragraphs (1), (2), and (6) of section 1106(a) of this title; and

(B) be authorized to operate the business of the debtor;

(6) if there is a claim for a domestic support obligation with respect to the debtor, perform the duties specified in section 704(c) of this title; and

(7) facilitate the development of a consensual plan of reorganization.

(c) Termination of trustee service.—

(1) In general.—If the plan of the debtor is confirmed under section 1191(a) of this title, the service of the trustee in the case shall terminate when the plan has been substantially consummated, except that the United States trustee may reappoint a trustee as needed for performance of duties under subsection (b)(3)(C) of this section and section 1185(a) of this title.

(2) Service of notice of substantial consummation.—Not later than 14 days after the plan of the debtor is substantially consummated, the debtor shall file with the court and serve on the trustee, the United States trustee, and all parties in interest notice of such substantial consummation.

§ 1184. Rights and Powers of a Debtor in Possession

Subject to such limitations or conditions as the court may prescribe, a debtor in possession shall have all the rights, other than the right to compensation under section 330 of this title, and powers, and shall perform all functions and duties, except the duties specified in paragraphs (2), (3), and (4) of section 1106(a) of this title, of a trustee serving in a case under this chapter, including operating the business of the debtor.

§ 1185. Removal of Debtor in Possession

(a) In general.—On request of a party in interest, and after notice and a hearing, the court shall order that the debtor shall not be a debtor in possession for cause, including fraud, dishonesty, incompetence, or gross mismanagement of the affairs of the debtor, either before or after the date of commencement of the case, or for failure to perform the obligations of the debtor under a plan confirmed under this subchapter.

(b) Reinstatement.—On request of a party in interest, and after notice and a hearing, the court may reinstate the debtor in possession.

§ 1186. Property of the Estate

(a) Inclusions.—If a plan is confirmed under section 1191(b) of this title, property of the estate includes, in addition to the property specified in section 541 of this title—

(1) all property of the kind specified in that section that the debtor acquires after the date of commencement of the case but before the case is closed, dismissed, or converted to a case under chapter 7, 12, or 13 of this title, whichever occurs first; and

(2) earnings from services performed by the debtor after the date of commencement of the case but before the case is closed, dismissed, or converted to a case under chapter 7, 12, or 13 of this title, whichever occurs first.

(b) Debtor remaining in possession.—Except as provided in section 1185 of this title, a plan confirmed under this subchapter, or an order confirming a plan under this subchapter, the debtor shall remain in possession of all property of the estate.

§ 1187. Duties and Reporting Requirements of Debtors

(a) Filing requirements.—Upon electing to be a debtor under this subchapter, the debtor shall file the documents required by subparagraphs (A) and (B) of section 1116(1) of this title.

(b) Other applicable provisions.—A debtor, in addition to the duties provided in this title and as otherwise required by law, shall comply with the requirements of section 308 and paragraphs (2), (3), (4), (5), (6), and (7) of section 1116 of this title.

(c) Separate disclosure statement exemption.—If the court orders under section 1181(b) of this title that section 1125 of this title applies, section 1125(f) of this title shall apply.

§ 1188. Status Conference

(a) In general.—Except as provided in subsection (b), not later than 60 days after the entry of the order for relief under this chapter, the court shall hold a status conference to further the expeditious and economical resolution of a case under this subchapter.

(b) Exception.—The court may extend the period of time for holding a status conference under subsection (a) if the need for an extension is attributable to circumstances for which the debtor should not justly be held accountable.

(c) Report.—Not later than 14 days before the date of the status conference under subsection (a), the debtor shall file with the court and serve on the trustee and all parties in interest a report that details the efforts the debtor has undertaken and will undertake to attain a consensual plan of reorganization.

§ 1189. Filing of the Plan

(a) Who may file a plan.—Only the debtor may file a plan under this subchapter.

(b) Deadline.—The debtor shall file a plan not later than 90 days after the order for relief under this chapter, except that the court may extend the period if the need for the extension is attributable to circumstances for which the debtor should not justly be held accountable.

§ 1190. Contents of Plan

A plan filed under this subchapter—

(1) shall include—

(A) a brief history of the business operations of the debtor;

(B) a liquidation analysis; and

(C) projections with respect to the ability of the debtor to make payments under the proposed plan of reorganization;

(2) shall provide for the submission of all or such portion of the future earnings or other future income of the debtor to the supervision and control of the trustee as is necessary for the execution of the plan; and

(3) notwithstanding section 1123(b)(5) of this title, may modify the rights of the holder of a claim secured only by a security interest in real property that is the principal residence of the debtor if the new value received in connection with the granting of the security interest was—

(A) not used primarily to acquire the real property; and

(B) used primarily in connection with the small business of the debtor.

§ 1191. Confirmation of Plan

(a) Terms.—The court shall confirm a plan under this subchapter only if all of the requirements of section 1129(a), other than paragraph (15) of that section, of this title are met.

(b) Exception.—Notwithstanding section 510(a) of this title, if all of the applicable requirements of section 1129(a) of this title, other than paragraphs (8), (10), and (15) of that section, are met with respect to a plan, the court, on request of the debtor, shall confirm the plan notwithstanding the requirements of such paragraphs if the plan does not discriminate unfairly, and is fair and equitable, with respect to each class of claims or interests that is impaired under, and has not accepted, the plan.

(c) Rule of construction.—For purposes of this section, the condition that a plan be fair and equitable with respect to each class of claims or interests includes the following requirements:

(1) With respect to a class of secured claims, the plan meets the requirements of section 1129(b)(2)(A) of this title.

(2) As of the effective date of the plan—

(A) the plan provides that all of the projected disposable income of the debtor to be received in the 3-year period, or such longer period not to exceed 5 years as the court may fix, beginning on the date that the first payment is due under the plan will be applied to make payments under the plan; or

(B) the value of the property to be distributed under the plan in the 3-year period, or such longer period not to exceed 5 years as the court may fix, beginning on the date on which the first distribution is due under the plan is not less than the projected disposable income of the debtor.

(3) (A)The debtor will be able to make all payments under the plan; or

(B) (i) there is a reasonable likelihood that the debtor will be able to make all payments under the plan; and

(ii) the plan provides appropriate remedies, which may include the liquidation of nonexempt assets, to protect the holders of claims or interests in the event that the payments are not made.

(d) Disposable income.—For purposes of this section, the term "disposable income" means the income that is received by the debtor and that is not reasonably necessary to be expended—

(1) for—

(A) the maintenance or support of the debtor or a dependent of the debtor; or

(B) a domestic support obligation that first becomes payable after the date of the filing of the petition; or

(2) for the payment of expenditures necessary for the continuation, preservation, or operation of the business of the debtor.

(e) Special rule.—Notwithstanding section 1129(a)(9)(A) of this title, a plan that provides for the payment through the plan of a claim of a kind specified in paragraph (2) or (3) of section 507(a) of this title may be confirmed under subsection (b) of this section.

§ 1192. Discharge

If the plan of the debtor is confirmed under section 1191(b) of this title, as soon as practicable after completion by the debtor of all payments due within the first 3 years of the plan, or such longer period not to exceed 5 years as the court may fix, unless the court approves a written waiver of discharge executed by the debtor after the order for relief under this chapter, the court shall grant the debtor a discharge of all debts provided in section 1141(d)(1)(A) of this title, and all other debts allowed under section 503 of this title and provided for in the plan, except any debt—

(1) on which the last payment is due after the first 3 years of the plan, or such other time not to exceed 5 years fixed by the court; or

(2) of the kind specified in section 523(a) of this title.

§ 1193. Modification of Plan

(a) Modification before confirmation.—The debtor may modify a plan at any time before confirmation, but may not modify the plan so that the plan as modified fails to meet the requirements of sections 1122 and 1123 of this title, with the exception of subsection (a)(8) of such section 1123. After the modification is filed with the court, the plan as modified becomes the plan.

(b) Modification after confirmation.—If a plan has been confirmed under section 1191(a) of this title, the debtor may modify the plan at any time after confirmation of the plan and before substantial consummation of the plan, but may not modify the plan so that the plan as modified fails to meet the requirements of sections 1122 and 1123 of this title, with the exception of subsection (a)(8) of such section 1123. The plan, as modified under this subsection, becomes the plan only if circumstances warrant the modification and the court, after notice and a hearing, confirms the plan as modified under section 1191(a) of this title.

(c) Certain other modifications.—If a plan has been confirmed under section 1191(b) of this title, the debtor may modify the plan at any time within 3 years, or such longer time not to exceed 5 years, as fixed by the court, but may not modify the plan so that the plan as modified fails to meet the requirements of section 1191(b) of this title. The plan as modified under this subsection becomes the plan only if circumstances warrant such modification and the court, after notice and a hearing, confirms such plan, as modified, under section 1191(b) of this title.

(d) Holders of a claim or interest.—If a plan has been confirmed under section 1191(a) of this title, any holder of a claim or interest that has accepted or rejected the plan is deemed to have accepted or rejected, as the case may be, the plan as modified, unless, within the time fixed by the court, such holder changes the previous acceptance or rejection of the holder.

§ 1194. Payments

(a) Retention and distribution by trustee.—Payments and funds received by the trustee shall be retained by the trustee until confirmation or denial of confirmation of a plan. If a plan is confirmed, the trustee shall distribute any such payment in accordance with the plan. If a plan is not confirmed, the trustee shall return any such payments to the debtor after deducting—

(1) any unpaid claim allowed under section 503(b) of this title;

(2) any payment made for the purpose of providing adequate protection of an interest in property due to the holder of a secured claim; and

(3) any fee owing to the trustee.

(b) Other plans.— If a plan is confirmed under section 1191(b) of this title, except as otherwise provided in the plan or in the order confirming the plan, the trustee shall make payments to creditors under the plan.

(c) Payments prior to confirmation.— Prior to confirmation of a plan, the court, after notice and a hearing, may authorize the trustee to make payments to the holder of a secured claim for the purpose of providing adequate protection of an interest in property.

§ 1195. Transactions with Professionals

Notwithstanding section 327(a) of this title, a person is not disqualified for employment under section 327 of this title, by a debtor solely because that person holds a claim of less than $10,000 that arose prior to commencement of the case.

CHAPTER 12. ADJUSTMENT OF DEBTS OF A FAMILY FARMER OR FISHERMAN WITH REGULAR INCOME

SUBCHAPTER I—OFFICERS, ADMINISTRATION, AND THE ESTATE

Section

1201. Stay of Action Against Codebtor
1202. Trustee
1203. Rights and Powers of Debtor
1204. Removal of Debtor as Debtor in Possession
1205. Adequate Protection
1206. Sales Free of Interests
1207. Property of the Estate
1208. Conversion or Dismissal

§ 1201. Stay of Action Against Codebtor

(a) Except as provided in subsections (b) and (c) of this section, after the order for relief under this chapter, a creditor may not act, or commence or continue any civil action, to collect all or any part of a consumer debt of the debtor from any individual that is liable on such debt with the debtor, or that secured such debt, unless—

(1) such individual became liable on or secured such debt in the ordinary course of such individual's business; or

(2) the case is closed, dismissed, or converted to a case under chapter 7 of this title.

(b) A creditor may present a negotiable instrument, and may give notice of dishonor of such an instrument.

(c) On request of a party in interest and after notice and a hearing, the court shall grant relief from the stay provided by subsection (a) of this section with respect to a creditor, to the extent that—

(1) as between the debtor and the individual protected under subsection (a) of this section, such individual received the consideration for the claim held by such creditor;

(2) the plan filed by the debtor proposes not to pay such claim; or

(3) such creditor's interest would be irreparably harmed by continuation of such stay.

(d) Twenty days after the filing of a request under subsection (c)(2) of this section for relief from the stay provided by subsection (a) of this section, such stay is terminated with respect to the party in interest making such request, unless the debtor or any individual that is liable on such debt with the debtor files and serves upon such party in interest a written objection to the taking of the proposed action.

§ 1202. Trustee

(a) If the United States trustee has appointed an individual under section 586(b) of title 28 to serve as standing trustee in cases under this chapter and if such individual qualifies as a trustee under section 322 of this title, then such individual shall serve as trustee in any case filed under this chapter. Otherwise, the United States trustee shall appoint one disinterested person to serve as trustee in the case or the United States trustee may serve as trustee in the case if necessary.

(b) The trustee shall—

(1) perform the duties specified in sections 704(a)(2), 704(a)(3), 704(a)(5), 704(a)(6), 704(a)(7), and 704(a)(9) of this title;

(2) perform the duties specified in section 1106(a)(3) and 1106(a)(4) of this title if the court, for cause and on request of a party in interest, the trustee, or the United States trustee, so orders;

(3) appear and be heard at any hearing that concerns—

(A) the value of property subject to a lien;

(B) confirmation of a plan;

(C) modification of the plan after confirmation; or

(D) the sale of property of the estate;

(4) ensure that the debtor commences making timely payments required by a confirmed plan;

(5) if the debtor ceases to be a debtor in possession, perform the duties specified in sections 704(a)(8), 1106(a)(1), 1106(a)(2), 1106(a)(6), 1106(a)(7), and 1203; and

(6) if with respect to the debtor there is a claim for a domestic support obligation, provide the applicable notice specified in subsection (c).

(c)(1) In a case described in subsection (b)(6) to which subsection (b)(6) applies, the trustee shall—

(A) (i) provide written notice to the holder of the claim described in subsection (b)(6) of such claim and of the right of such holder to use the services of the State child support enforcement agency established under sections 464 and 466 of the Social Security Act for the State in which such holder resides, for assistance in collecting child support during and after the case under this title; and

(ii) include in the notice provided under clause (i) the address and telephone number of such State child support enforcement agency;

(B) (i) provide written notice to such State child support enforcement agency of such claim; and

(ii) include in the notice provided under clause (i) the name, address, and telephone number of such holder; and

(C) at such time as the debtor is granted a discharge under section 1228, provide written notice to such holder and to such State child support enforcement agency of—

(i) the granting of the discharge;

(ii) the last recent known address of the debtor;

(iii) the last recent known name and address of the debtor's employer; and

(iv) the name of each creditor that holds a claim that—

(I) is not discharged under paragraph (2), (4), or (14A) of section 523(a); or

(II) was reaffirmed by the debtor under section 524(c).

(2) (A) The holder of a claim described in subsection (b)(6) or the State child support enforcement agency of the State in which such holder resides may request from a creditor described in paragraph (1)(C)(iv) the last known address of the debtor.

(B) Notwithstanding any other provision of law, a creditor that makes a disclosure of a last known address of a debtor in connection with a request made under subparagraph (A) shall not be liable by reason of making that disclosure.

§ 1203. Rights and Powers of Debtor

Subject to such limitations as the court may prescribe, a debtor in possession shall have all the rights, other than the right to compensation under section 330, and powers, and shall perform all the functions and duties, except the duties specified in paragraphs (3) and (4) of section 1106(a), of a trustee serving in a case under chapter 11, including operating the debtor's farm or commercial fishing operation.

§ 1204. Removal of Debtor as Debtor in Possession

(a) On request of a party in interest, and after notice and a hearing, the court shall order that the debtor shall not be a debtor in possession for cause, including fraud, dishonesty, incompetence, or gross mismanagement of the affairs of the debtor, either before or after the commencement of the case.

(b) On request of a party in interest, and after notice and a hearing, the court may reinstate the debtor in possession.

§ 1205. Adequate Protection

(a) Section 361 does not apply in a case under this chapter.

(b) In a case under this chapter, when adequate protection is required under section 362, 363, or 364 of this title of an interest of an entity in property, such adequate protection may be provided by—

(1) requiring the trustee to make a cash payment or periodic cash payments to such entity, to the extent that the stay under section 362 of this title, use, sale, or lease under section 363 of this title, or any grant of a lien under section 364 of this title results in a decrease in the value of property securing a claim or of an entity's ownership interest in property;

(2) providing to such entity an additional or replacement lien to the extent that such stay, use, sale, lease, or grant results in a decrease in the value of property securing a claim or of an entity's ownership interest in property;

(3) paying to such entity for the use of farmland the reasonable rent customary in the community where the property is located, based

upon the rental value, net income, and earning capacity of the property; or

(4) granting such other relief, other than entitling such entity to compensation allowable under section 503(b)(1) of this title as an administrative expense, as will adequately protect the value of property securing a claim or of such entity's ownership interest in property.

§ 1206. Sales Free of Interests

After notice and a hearing, in addition to the authorization contained in section 363(f), the trustee in a case under this chapter may sell property under section 363(b) and (c) free and clear of any interest in such property of an entity other than the estate if the property is farmland, farm equipment, or property used to carry out a commercial fishing operation (including a commercial fishing vessel), except that the proceeds of such sale shall be subject to such interest.

§ 1207. Property of the Estate

(a) Property of the estate includes, in addition to the property specified in section 541 of this title—

(1) all property of the kind specified in such section that the debtor acquires after the commencement of the case but before the case is closed, dismissed, or converted to a case under chapter 7 of this title, whichever occurs first; and

(2) earnings from services performed by the debtor after the commencement of the case but before the case is closed, dismissed, or converted to a case under chapter 7 of this title, whichever occurs first.

(b) Except as provided in section 1204, a confirmed plan, or an order confirming a plan, the debtor shall remain in possession of all property of the estate.

§ 1208. Conversion or Dismissal

(a) The debtor may convert a case under this chapter to a case under chapter 7 of this title at any time. Any waiver of the right to convert under this subsection is unenforceable.

(b) On request of the debtor at any time, if the case has not been converted under section 706 or 1112 of this title, the court shall dismiss a case under this chapter. Any waiver of the right to dismiss under this subsection is unenforceable.

(c) On request of a party in interest, and after notice and a hearing, the court may dismiss a case under this chapter for cause, including—

(1) unreasonable delay, or gross mismanagement, by the debtor that is prejudicial to creditors;

(2) nonpayment of any fees and charges required under chapter 123 of title 28;

(3) failure to file a plan timely under section 1221 of this title;

(4) failure to commence making timely payments required by a confirmed plan;

(5) denial of confirmation of a plan under section 1225 of this title and denial of a request made for additional time for filing another plan or a modification of a plan;

(6) material default by the debtor with respect to a term of a confirmed plan;

(7) revocation of the order of confirmation under section 1230 of this title, and denial of confirmation of a modified plan under section 1229 of this title;

(8) termination of a confirmed plan by reason of the occurrence of a condition specified in the plan;

(9) continuing loss to or diminution of the estate and absence of a reasonable likelihood of rehabilitation; and

(10) failure of the debtor to pay any domestic support obligation that first becomes payable after the date of the filing of the petition.

(d) On request of a party in interest, and after notice and a hearing, the court may dismiss a case under this chapter or convert a case under this chapter to a case under chapter 7 of this title upon a showing that the debtor has committed fraud in connection with the case.

(e) Notwithstanding any other provision of this section, a case may not be converted to a case under another chapter of this title unless the debtor may be a debtor under such chapter.

SUBCHAPTER II—THE PLAN

Section

1221. Filing of Plan
1222. Contents of Plan
1223. Modification of Plan Before Confirmation
1224. Confirmation Hearing
1225. Confirmation of Plan
1226. Payments
1227. Effect of Confirmation
1228. Discharge
1229. Modification of Plan After Confirmation
1230. Revocation of an Order of Confirmation
1231. Special Tax Provisions

§ 1221. Filing of Plan

The debtor shall file a plan not later than 90 days after the order for relief under this chapter, except that the court may extend such period if the need for an extension is attributable to circumstances for which the debtor should not justly be held accountable.

§ 1222. Contents of Plan

(a) The plan shall—

(1) provide for the submission of all or such portion of future earnings or other future income of the debtor to the supervision and control of the trustee as is necessary for the execution of the plan;

(2) provide for the full payment, in deferred cash payments, of all claims entitled to priority under section 507, unless—

(A) the claim is a claim owed to a governmental unit that arises as a result of the sale, transfer, exchange, or other disposition of any farm asset used in the debtor's farming operation, in which case the claim shall be treated as an unsecured claim that is not entitled to priority under section 507, but the debt shall be treated in such manner only if the debtor receives a discharge; or

(B) the holder of a particular claim agrees to a different treatment of that claim;

(3) if the plan classifies claims and interests, provide the same treatment for each claim or interest within a particular class unless the holder of a particular claim or interest agrees to less favorable treatment; and

(4) notwithstanding any other provision of this section, a plan may provide for less than full payment of all amounts owed for a claim entitled to priority under section 507(a)(1)(B) only if the plan provides that all of the debtor's projected disposable income for a 5-year period beginning on the date that the first payment is due under the plan will be applied to make payments under the plan; and

(5) subject to section 1232, provide for the treatment of any claim by a governmental unit of a kind described in section 1232(a).

(b) Subject to subsections (a) and (c) of this section, the plan may—

(1) designate a class or classes of unsecured claims, as provided in section 1122 of this title, but may not discriminate unfairly against any class so designated; however, such plan may treat claims for a consumer debt of the debtor if an individual is liable on such consumer debt with the debtor differently than other unsecured claims;

(2) modify the rights of holders of secured claims, or of holders of unsecured claims, or leave unaffected the rights of holders of any class of claims;

(3) provide for the curing or waiving of any default;

(4) provide for payments on any unsecured claim to be made concurrently with payments on any secured claim or any other unsecured claim;

(5) provide for the curing of any default within a reasonable time and maintenance of payments while the case is pending on any unsecured claim or secured claim on which the last payment is due after the date on which the final payment under the plan is due;

(6) subject to section 365 of this title, provide for the assumption, rejection, or assignment of any executory contract or unexpired lease of the debtor not previously rejected under such section;

(7) provide for the payment of all or part of a claim against the debtor from property of the estate or property of the debtor;

(8) provide for the sale of all or any part of the property of the estate or the distribution of all or any part of the property of the estate among those having an interest in such property;

(9) provide for payment of allowed secured claims consistent with section 1225(a)(5) of this title, over a period exceeding the period permitted under section 1222(c);

(10) provide for the vesting of property of the estate, on confirmation of the plan or at a later time, in the debtor or in any other entity;

(11) provide for the payment of interest accruing after the date of the filing of the petition on unsecured claims that are nondischargeable under section 1228(a), except that such interest may be paid only to the extent that the debtor has disposable income available to pay such interest after making provision for full payment of all allowed claims; and

(12) include any other appropriate provision not inconsistent with this title.

(c) Except as provided in subsections (b)(5) and (b)(9), the plan may not provide for payments over a period that is longer than three years unless the court for cause approves a longer period, but the court may not approve a period that is longer than five years.

(d) Notwithstanding subsection (b)(2) of this section and sections 506(b) and 1225(a)(5) of this title, if it is proposed in a plan to cure a default, the amount necessary to cure the default, shall be determined in accordance with the underlying agreement and applicable nonbankruptcy law.

§ 1223. Modification of Plan Before Confirmation

(a) The debtor may modify the plan at any time before confirmation, but may not modify the plan so that the plan as modified fails to meet the requirements of section 1222 of this title.

(b) After the debtor files a modification under this section, the plan as modified becomes the plan.

(c) Any holder of a secured claim that has accepted or rejected the plan is deemed to have accepted or rejected, as the case may be, the plan as modified, unless the modification provides for a change in the rights of such holder from what such rights were under the plan before modification, and such holder changes such holder's previous acceptance or rejection.

§ 1224. Confirmation Hearing

After expedited notice, the court shall hold a hearing on confirmation of the plan. A party in interest, the trustee, or the United States trustee may object to the confirmation of the plan. Except for cause, the hearing shall be concluded not later than 45 days after the filing of the plan.

§ 1225. Confirmation of Plan

(a) Except as provided in subsection (b), the court shall confirm a plan if—

(1) the plan complies with the provisions of this chapter and with the other applicable provisions of this title;

(2) any fee, charge, or amount required under chapter 123 of title 28, or by the plan, to be paid before confirmation, has been paid;

(3) the plan has been proposed in good faith and not by any means forbidden by law;

(4) the value, as of the effective date of the plan, of property to be distributed under the plan on account of each allowed unsecured claim is not less than the amount that would be paid on such claim if the estate of the debtor were liquidated under chapter 7 of this title on such date;

(5) with respect to each allowed secured claim provided for by the plan—

(A) the holder of such claim has accepted the plan;

(B) (i) the plan provides that the holder of such claim retain the lien securing such claim; and

(ii) the value, as of the effective date of the plan, of property to be distributed by the trustee or the debtor under the plan on account of such claim is not less than the allowed amount of such claim; or

(C) the debtor surrenders the property securing such claim to such holder;

(6) the debtor will be able to make all payments under the plan and to comply with the plan; and

(7) the debtor has paid all amounts that are required to be paid under a domestic support obligation and that first become payable after the date of the filing of the petition if the debtor is required by a judicial or administrative order, or by statute, to pay such domestic support obligation.

(b)(1) If the trustee or the holder of an allowed unsecured claim objects to the confirmation of the plan, then the court may not approve the plan unless, as of the effective date of the plan—

(A) the value of the property to be distributed under the plan on account of such claim is not less than the amount of such claim;

(B) the plan provides that all of the debtor's projected disposable income to be received in the three-year period, or such longer period as the court may approve under section 1222(c), beginning on the date that the first payment is due under the plan will be applied to make payments under the plan; or

(C) the value of the property to be distributed under the plan in the 3-year period, or such longer period as the court may approve under section 1222(c), beginning on the date that the first distribution is due under the plan is not less than the debtor's projected disposable income for such period.

(2) For purposes of this subsection, "disposable income" means income which is received by the debtor and which is not reasonably necessary to be expended—

(A) for the maintenance or support of the debtor or a dependent of the debtor or for a domestic support obligation that first becomes payable after the date of the filing of the petition; or

(B) for the payment of expenditures necessary for the continuation, preservation, and operation of the debtor's business.

(c) After confirmation of a plan, the court may order any entity from whom the debtor receives income to pay all or any part of such income to the trustee.

§ 1226. Payments

(a) Payments and funds received by the trustee shall be retained by the trustee until confirmation or denial of confirmation of a plan. If a plan is confirmed, the trustee shall distribute any such payment in accordance with the plan. If a plan is not confirmed, the trustee shall return any such payments to the debtor, after deducting—

(1) any unpaid claim allowed under section 503(b) of this title; and

(2) if a standing trustee is serving in the case, the percentage fee fixed for such standing trustee.

(b) Before or at the time of each payment to creditors under the plan, there shall be paid—

(1) any unpaid claim of the kind specified in section 507(a)(2) of this title; and

(2) if a standing trustee appointed under section 1202(c) of this title is serving in the case, the percentage fee fixed for such standing trustee under section 1202(d) of this title.

(c) Except as otherwise provided in the plan or in the order confirming the plan, the trustee shall make payments to creditors under the plan.

§ 1227. Effect of Confirmation

(a) Except as provided in section 1228(a) of this title, the provisions of a confirmed plan bind the debtor, each creditor, each equity security holder, and each general partner in the debtor, whether or not the claim of such creditor, such equity security holder, or such general partner in the debtor is provided for by the plan, and whether or not such creditor, such equity security holder, or such general partner in the debtor has objected to, has accepted, or has rejected the plan.

(b) Except as otherwise provided in the plan or the order confirming the plan, the confirmation of a plan vests all of the property of the estate in the debtor.

(c) Except as provided in section 1228(a) of this title and except as otherwise provided in the plan or in the order confirming the plan, the property vesting in the debtor under subsection (b) of this section is free and clear of any claim or interest of any creditor provided for by the plan.

§ 1228. Discharge

(a) Subject to subsection (d), as soon as practicable after completion by the debtor of all payments under the plan, and in the case of a debtor who is required by a judicial or administrative order, or by statute, to pay a domestic support obligation, after such debtor certifies that all amounts payable under such order or such statute that are due on or before the date of the certification (including amounts due before the petition was filed, but only to the extent provided for by the plan) have been paid, other than payments to holders of allowed claims provided for under section 1222(b)(5) or 1222(b)(9) of this title, unless the court approves a written waiver of discharge executed by the debtor after the order for relief under this chapter, the court shall grant the debtor a discharge of all debts provided for by the plan allowed under section 503 of this title or disallowed under section 502 of this title, except any debt—

(1) provided for under section 1222(b)(5) or 1222(b)(9) of this title; or

(2) of the kind specified in section 523(a) of this title.

(b) Subject to subsection (d), at any time after the confirmation of the plan and after notice and a hearing, the court may grant a discharge to a debtor that has not completed payments under the plan only if—

(1) the debtor's failure to complete such payments is due to circumstances for which the debtor should not justly be held accountable;

(2) the value, as of the effective date of the plan, of property actually distributed under the plan on account of each allowed unsecured claim is not less than the amount that would have been paid on such claim if the estate of the debtor had been liquidated under chapter 7 of this title on such date; and

(3) modification of the plan under section 1229 of this title is not practicable.

(c) A discharge granted under subsection (b) of this section discharges the debtor from all unsecured debts provided for by the plan or disallowed under section 502 of this title, except any debt—

(1) provided for under section 1222(b)(5) or 1222(b)(9) of this title; or

(2) of a kind specified in section 523(a) of this title.

(d) On request of a party in interest before one year after a discharge under this section is granted, and after notice and a hearing, the court may revoke such discharge only if—

(1) such discharge was obtained by the debtor through fraud; and

(2) the requesting party did not know of such fraud until after such discharge was granted.

(e) After the debtor is granted a discharge, the court shall terminate the services of any trustee serving in the case.

(f) The court may not grant a discharge under this chapter unless the court after notice and a hearing held not more than 10 days before the date of the entry of the order granting the discharge finds that there is no reasonable cause to believe that—

(1) section 522(q)(1) may be applicable to the debtor; and

(2) there is pending any proceeding in which the debtor may be found guilty of a felony of the kind described in section 522(q)(1)(A) or liable for a debt of the kind described in section 522(q)(1)(B).

§ 1229. Modification of Plan After Confirmation

(a) At any time after confirmation of the plan but before the completion of payments under such plan, the plan may be modified, on request of the debtor, the trustee, or the holder of an allowed unsecured claim, to—

(1) increase or reduce the amount of payments on claims of a particular class provided for by the plan;

(2) extend or reduce the time for such payments; or

(3) alter the amount of the distribution to a creditor whose claim is provided for by the plan to the extent necessary to take account of any payment of such claim other than under the plan.

(b)(1) Sections 1222(a), 1222(b), and 1223(c) of this title and the requirements of section 1225(a) of this title apply to any modification under subsection (a) of this section.

(2) The plan as modified becomes the plan unless, after notice and a hearing, such modification is disapproved.

(c) A plan modified under this section may not provide for payments over a period that expires after three years after the time that the first payment under the original confirmed plan was due, unless the court, for cause, approves a longer period, but the court may not approve a period that expires after five years after such time.

(d) A plan may not be modified under this section—

(1) to increase the amount of any payment due before the plan as modified becomes the plan;

(2) by anyone except the debtor, based on an increase in the debtor's disposable income, to increase the amount of payments to unsecured creditors required for a particular month so that the aggregate of such payments exceeds the debtor's disposable income for such month; or

(3) in the last year of the plan by anyone except the debtor, to require payments that would leave the debtor with insufficient funds to carry on the farming operation after the plan is completed.

§ 1230. Revocation of an Order of Confirmation

(a) On request of a party in interest at any time within 180 days after the date of the entry of an order of confirmation under section 1225 of this title, and after notice and a hearing, the court may revoke such order if such order was procured by fraud.

(b) If the court revokes an order of confirmation under subsection (a) of this section, the court shall dispose of the case under section 1207 of this title, unless, within the time fixed by the court, the debtor proposes and the court confirms a modification of the plan under section 1229 of this title.

§ 1231. Special Tax Provisions

(a) The issuance, transfer, or exchange of a security, or the making or delivery of an instrument of transfer under a plan confirmed under section 1225 of this title, may not be taxed under any law imposing a stamp tax or similar tax.

(b) The court may authorize the proponent of a plan to request a determination, limited to questions of law, by any governmental unit charged with responsibility for collection or determination of a tax on or measured by income, of the tax effects, under section 346 of this title and under the law imposing such tax, of the plan. In the event of an actual controversy, the court may declare such effects after the earlier of—

(1) the date on which such governmental unit responds to the request under this subsection; or

(2) 270 days after such request.

CHAPTER 13. ADJUSTMENT OF DEBTS OF AN INDIVIDUAL WITH REGULAR INCOME

SUBCHAPTER I—OFFICERS, ADMINISTRATION, AND THE ESTATE

Section

1301. Stay of Action Against Codebtor
1302. Trustee
1303. Rights and Powers of Debtor
1304. Debtor Engaged in Business
1305. Filing and Allowance of Postpetition Claims
1306. Property of the Estate
1307. Conversion or Dismissal
1308. Filing of Prepetition Tax Returns

§ 1301. Stay of Action Against Codebtor

(a) Except as provided in subsections (b) and (c) of this section, after the order for relief under this chapter, a creditor may not act, or commence or continue any civil action, to collect all or any part of a consumer debt of the debtor from any individual that is liable on such debt with the debtor, or that secured such debt, unless—

(1) such individual became liable on or secured such debt in the ordinary course of such individual's business; or

(2) the case is closed, dismissed, or converted to a case under chapter 7 or 11 of this title.

(b) A creditor may present a negotiable instrument, and may give notice of dishonor of such an instrument.

(c) On request of a party in interest and after notice and a hearing, the court shall grant relief from the stay provided by subsection (a) of this section with respect to a creditor, to the extent that—

(1) as between the debtor and the individual protected under subsection (a) of this section, such individual received the consideration for the claim held by such creditor;

(2) the plan filed by the debtor proposes not to pay such claim; or

(3) such creditor's interest would be irreparably harmed by continuation of such stay.

(d) Twenty days after the filing of a request under subsection (c)(2) of this section for relief from the stay provided by subsection (a) of this section, such stay is terminated with respect to the party in interest making such request, unless the debtor or any individual that is liable on such debt with the debtor files and serves upon such party in interest a written objection to the taking of the proposed action.

§ 1302. Trustee

(a) If the United States trustee appoints an individual under section 586(b) of title 28 to serve as standing trustee in cases under this chapter and if such individual qualifies under section 322 of this title, then such individual shall serve as trustee in the case. Otherwise, the United States trustee shall appoint one disinterested person to serve as trustee in the case or the United States trustee may serve as a trustee in the case.

(b) The trustee shall—

(1) perform the duties specified in sections 704(a)(2), 704(a)(3), 704(a)(4), 704(a)(5), 704(a)(6), 704(a)(7), and 704(a)(9) of this title;

(2) appear and be heard at any hearing that concerns—

(A) the value of property subject to a lien;

(B) confirmation of a plan; or

(C) modification of the plan after confirmation;

(3) dispose of, under regulations issued by the Director of the Administrative Office of the United States Courts, moneys received or to be received in a case under chapter XIII of the Bankruptcy Act;

(4) advise, other than on legal matters, and assist the debtor in performance under the plan;

(5) ensure that the debtor commences making timely payments under section 1326 of this title; and

(6) if with respect to the debtor there is a claim for a domestic support obligation, provide the applicable notice specified in subsection (d).

(c) If the debtor is engaged in business, then in addition to the duties specified in subsection (b) of this section, the trustee shall perform the duties specified in sections 1106(a)(3) and 1106(a)(4) of this title.

(d)(1) In a case described in subsection (b)(6) to which subsection (b)(6) applies, the trustee shall—

(A) (i) provide written notice to the holder of the claim described in subsection (b)(6) of such claim and of the right of such holder to use the services of the State child support enforcement agency established under sections 464 and 466 of the Social Security Act for the State in which such holder resides, for assistance in collecting child support during and after the case under this title; and

(ii) include in the notice provided under clause (i) the address and telephone number of such State child support enforcement agency;

(B) (i) provide written notice to such State child support enforcement agency of such claim; and

(ii) include in the notice provided under clause (i) the name, address, and telephone number of such holder; and

(C) at such time as the debtor is granted a discharge under section 1328, provide written notice to such holder and to such State child support enforcement agency of—

(i) the granting of the discharge;

(ii) the last recent known address of the debtor;

(iii) the last recent known name and address of the debtor's employer; and

(iv) the name of each creditor that holds a claim that—

(I) is not discharged under paragraph (2) or (4) of section 523(a); or

(II) was reaffirmed by the debtor under section 524(c).

(2) (A) The holder of a claim described in subsection (b)(6) or the State child support enforcement agency of the State in which such holder resides may request from a creditor described in paragraph (1)(C)(iv) the last known address of the debtor.

(B) Notwithstanding any other provision of law, a creditor that makes a disclosure of a last known address of a debtor in connection with a request made under subparagraph (A) shall not be liable by reason of making that disclosure.

§ 1303. Rights and Powers of Debtor

Subject to any limitations on a trustee under this chapter, the debtor shall have, exclusive of the trustee, the rights and powers of a trustee under sections 363(b), 363(d), 363(e), 363(f), and 363(l), of this title.

§ 1304. Debtor Engaged in Business

(a) A debtor that is self-employed and incurs trade credit in the production of income from such employment is engaged in business.

(b) Unless the court orders otherwise, a debtor engaged in business may operate the business of the debtor and, subject to any limitations on a trustee under sections 363(c) and 364 of this title and to such limitations or conditions as the court prescribes, shall have, exclusive of the trustee, the rights and powers of the trustee under such sections.

(c) A debtor engaged in business shall perform the duties of the trustee specified in section 704(a)(8) of this title.

§ 1305. Filing and Allowance of Postpetition Claims

(a) A proof of claim may be filed by any entity that holds a claim against the debtor—

(1) for taxes that become payable to a governmental unit while the case is pending; or

(2) that is a consumer debt, that arises after the date of the order for relief under this chapter, and that is for property or services necessary for the debtor's performance under the plan.

(b) Except as provided in subsection (c) of this section, a claim filed under subsection (a) of this section shall be allowed or disallowed under section 502 of this title, but shall be determined as of the date such claim arises, and shall be allowed under section 502(a), 502(b), or 502(c) of this title, or disallowed under section 502(d) or 502(e) of this title, the same as if such claim had arisen before the date of the filing of the petition.

(c) A claim filed under subsection (a)(2) of this section shall be disallowed if the holder of such claim knew or should have known that prior approval by the trustee of the debtor's incurring the obligation was practicable and was not obtained.

§ 1306. Property of the Estate

(a) Property of the estate includes, in addition to the property specified in section 541 of this title—

(1) all property of the kind specified in such section that the debtor acquires after the commencement of the case but before the case is closed, dismissed, or converted to a case under chapter 7, 11, or 12 of this title, whichever occurs first; and

(2) earnings from services performed by the debtor after the commencement of the case but before the case is closed, dismissed, or converted to a case under chapter 7, 11, or 12 of this title, whichever occurs first.

(b) Except as provided in a confirmed plan or order confirming a plan, the debtor shall remain in possession of all property of the estate.

§ 1307. Conversion or Dismissal

(a) The debtor may convert a case under this chapter to a case under chapter 7 of this title at any time. Any waiver of the right to convert under this subsection is unenforceable.

(b) On request of the debtor at any time, if the case has not been converted under section 706, 1112, or 1208 of this title, the court shall dismiss a case under this chapter. Any waiver of the right to dismiss under this subsection is unenforceable.

(c) Except as provided in subsection (f) of this section, on request of a party in interest or the United States trustee and after notice and a hearing, the court may convert a case under this chapter to a case under chapter 7 of this title, or may dismiss a case under this chapter, whichever is in the best interests of creditors and the estate, for cause, including—

(1) unreasonable delay by the debtor that is prejudicial to creditors;

(2) nonpayment of any fees and charges required under chapter 123 of title 28;

(3) failure to file a plan timely under section 1321 of this title;

(4) failure to commence making timely payments under section 1326 of this title;

(5) denial of confirmation of a plan under section 1325 of this title and denial of a request made for additional time for filing another plan or a modification of a plan;

(6) material default by the debtor with respect to a term of a confirmed plan;

(7) revocation of the order of confirmation under section 1330 of this title, and denial of confirmation of a modified plan under section 1329 of this title;

(8) termination of a confirmed plan by reason of the occurrence of a condition specified in the plan other than completion of payments under the plan;

(9) only on request of the United States trustee, failure of the debtor to file, within fifteen days, or such additional time as the court may allow, after the filing of the petition commencing such case, the information required by paragraph (1) of section 521(a);

(10) only on request of the United States trustee, failure to timely file the information required by paragraph (2) of section 521(a); or

(11) failure of the debtor to pay any domestic support obligation that first becomes payable after the date of the filing of the petition.

(d) Except as provided in subsection (f) of this section, at any time before the confirmation of a plan under section 1325 of this title, on request of a party in interest or the United States trustee and after notice and a hearing, the court may convert a case under this chapter to a case under chapter 11 or 12 of this title.

(e) Upon the failure of the debtor to file a tax return under section 1308, on request of a party in interest or the United States trustee and after notice and a hearing, the court shall dismiss a case or convert a case under this chapter to a case under chapter 7 of this title, whichever is in the best interest of the creditors and the estate.

(f) The court may not convert a case under this chapter to a case under chapter 7, 11, or 12 of this title if the debtor is a farmer, unless the debtor requests such conversion.

(g) Notwithstanding any other provision of this section, a case may not be converted to a case under another chapter of this title unless the debtor may be a debtor under such chapter.

§ 1308. Filing of Prepetition Tax Returns

(a) Not later than the day before the date on which the meeting of the creditors is first scheduled to be held under section 341(a), if the debtor was required to file a tax return under applicable nonbankruptcy law, the debtor shall file with appropriate tax authorities all tax returns for all taxable periods ending during the 4-year period ending on the date of the filing of the petition.

(b)(1) Subject to paragraph (2), if the tax returns required by subsection (a) have not been filed by the date on which the meeting of creditors is first scheduled to be held under section 341(a), the trustee may hold open that meeting for a reasonable period of time to allow the debtor an additional period of time to file any unfiled returns, but such additional period of time shall not extend beyond—

(A) for any return that is past due as of the date of the filing of the petition, the date that is 120 days after the date of that meeting; or

(B) for any return that is not past due as of the date of the filing of the petition, the later of—

(i) the date that is 120 days after the date of that meeting; or

(ii) the date on which the return is due under the last automatic extension of time for filing that return to which the debtor is entitled, and for which request is timely made, in accordance with applicable nonbankruptcy law.

(2) After notice and a hearing, and order entered before the tolling of any applicable filing period determined under paragraph (1), if the debtor demonstrates by a preponderance of the evidence that the failure to file a return as required under paragraph (1) is attributable to circumstances beyond the control of the debtor, the court may extend the filing period established by the trustee under paragraph (1) for—

(A) a period of not more than 30 days for returns described in paragraph (1)(a); and

(B) a period not to extend after the applicable extended due date for a return described in paragraph (1)(b).

(c) For purposes of this section, the term "return" includes a return prepared pursuant to subsection (a) or (b) of section 6020 of the Internal Revenue Code of 1986, or a similar State or local law, or a written stipulation to a judgment or a final order entered by a nonbankruptcy tribunal.

SUBCHAPTER II—THE PLAN

Section

1321. Filing of Plan
1322. Contents of Plan
1323. Modification of Plan Before Confirmation
1324. Confirmation Hearing
1325. Confirmation of Plan
1326. Payments
1327. Effect of Confirmation
1328. Discharge
1329. Modification of Plan After Confirmation
1330. Revocation of an Order of Confirmation

§ 1321. Filing of Plan

The debtor shall file a plan.

§ 1322. Contents of Plan

(a) The plan—

(1) shall provide for the submission of all or such portion of future earnings or other future income of the debtor to the supervision and control of the trustee as is necessary for the execution of the plan;

(2) shall provide for the full payment, in deferred cash payments, of all claims entitled to priority under section 507 of this title, unless the holder of a particular claim agrees to a different treatment of such claim;

(3) if the plan classifies claims, shall provide the same treatment for each claim within a particular class; and

(4) notwithstanding any other provision of this section, may provide for less than full payment of all amounts owed for a claim entitled to priority under section 507(a)(1)(B) only if the plan provides that all of the debtor's projected disposable income for a 5-year period beginning on the date that the first payment is due under the plan will be applied to make payments under the plan.

(b) Subject to subsections (a) and (c) of this section, the plan may—

(1) designate a class or classes of unsecured claims, as provided in section 1122 of this title, but may not discriminate unfairly against any class so designated; however, such plan may treat claims for a consumer debt of the debtor if an individual is liable on such consumer debt with the debtor differently than other unsecured claims;

(2) modify the rights of holders of secured claims, other than a claim secured only by a security interest in real property that is the debtor's principal residence, or of holders of unsecured claims, or leave unaffected the rights of holders of any class of claims;

(3) provide for the curing or waiving of any default;

(4) provide for payments on any unsecured claim to be made concurrently with payments on any secured claim or any other unsecured claim;

(5) notwithstanding paragraph (2) of this subsection, provide for the curing of any default within a reasonable time and maintenance of payments while the case is pending on any unsecured claim or secured claim on which the last payment is due after the date on which the final payment under the plan is due;

(6) provide for the payment of all or any part of any claim allowed under section 1305 of this title;

(7) subject to section 365 of this title, provide for the assumption, rejection, or assignment of any executory contract or unexpired lease of the debtor not previously rejected under such section;

(8) provide for the payment of all or part of a claim against the debtor from property of the estate or property of the debtor;

(9) provide for the vesting of property of the estate, on confirmation of the plan or at a later time, in the debtor or in any other entity;

(10) provide for the payment of interest accruing after the date of the filing of the petition on unsecured claims that are nondischargeable under section 1328(a), except that such interest may be paid only to the extent that the debtor has disposable income available to pay such interest after making provision for full payment of all allowed claims; and

(11) include any other appropriate provision not inconsistent with this title.

(c) Notwithstanding subsection (b)(2) and applicable nonbankruptcy law—

(1) a default with respect to, or that gave rise to, a lien on the debtor's principal residence may be cured under paragraph (3) or (5) of subsection (b) until such residence is sold at a foreclosure sale that is conducted in accordance with applicable nonbankruptcy law; and

(2) in a case in which the last payment on the original payment schedule for a claim secured only by a security interest in real property that is the debtor's principal residence is due before the date on which the final payment under the plan is due, the plan may provide for the payment of the claim as modified pursuant to section 1325(a)(5) of this title.

(d)(1) If the current monthly income of the debtor and the debtor's spouse combined, when multiplied by 12, is not less than—

(A) in the case of a debtor in a household of 1 person, the median family income of the applicable State for 1 earner;

(B) in the case of a debtor in a household of 2, 3, or 4 individuals, the highest median family income of the applicable State for a family of the same number or fewer individuals; or

(C) in the case of a debtor in a household exceeding 4 individuals, the highest median family income of the applicable State for a family of 4 or fewer individuals, plus $825 per month for each individual in excess of 4,

the plan may not provide for payments over a period that is longer than 5 years.

(2) If the current monthly income of the debtor and the debtor's spouse combined, when multiplied by 12, is less than—

(A) in the case of a debtor in a household of 1 person, the median family income of the applicable State for 1 earner;

(B) in the case of a debtor in a household of 2, 3, or 4 individuals, the highest median family income of the applicable State for a family of the same number or fewer individuals; or

(C) in the case of a debtor in a household exceeding 4 individuals, the highest median family income of the applicable State for a family of 4 or fewer individuals, plus $825 per month for each individual in excess of 4,

the plan may not provide for payments over a period that is longer than 3 years, unless the court, for cause, approves a longer period, but the court may not approve a period that is longer than 5 years.

(e) Notwithstanding subsection (b)(2) of this section and sections 506(b) and 1325(a)(5) of this title, if it is proposed in a plan to cure a default, the amount necessary to cure the default, shall be determined in accordance with the underlying agreement and applicable nonbankruptcy law.

(f) A plan may not materially alter the terms of a loan described in section 362(b)(19) and any amounts required to repay such loan shall not constitute "disposable income" under section 1325.

§ 1323. Modification of Plan Before Confirmation

(a) The debtor may modify the plan at any time before confirmation, but may not modify the plan so that the plan as modified fails to meet the requirements of section 1322 of this title.

(b) After the debtor files a modification under this section, the plan as modified becomes the plan.

(c) Any holder of a secured claim that has accepted or rejected the plan is deemed to have accepted or rejected, as the case may be, the plan as modified, unless the modification provides for a change in the rights of such holder from what such rights were under the plan before modification, and such holder changes such holder's previous acceptance or rejection.

§ 1324. Confirmation Hearing

(a) Except as provided in subsection (b) and after notice, the court shall hold a hearing on confirmation of the plan. A party in interest may object to confirmation of the plan.

(b) The hearing on confirmation of the plan may be held not earlier than 20 days and not later than 45 days after the date of the meeting of creditors under section 341(a), unless the court determines that it would be in the best interests of the creditors and the estate to hold such hearing at an earlier date and there is no objection to such earlier date.

§ 1325. Confirmation of Plan

(a) Except as provided in subsection (b), the court shall confirm a plan if—

(1) The plan complies with the provisions of this chapter and with the other applicable provisions of this title;

(2) any fee, charge, or amount required under chapter 123 of title 28, or by the plan, to be paid before confirmation, has been paid;

(3) the plan has been proposed in good faith and not by any means forbidden by law;

(4) the value, as of the effective date of the plan, of property to be distributed under the plan on account of each allowed unsecured claim is not less than the amount that would be paid on such claim if the estate of the debtor were liquidated under chapter 7 of this title on such date;

(5) with respect to each allowed secured claim provided for by the plan—

(A) the holder of such claim has accepted the plan;

(B) (i) the plan provides that—

(I) the holder of such claim retain the lien securing such claim until the earlier of—

(aa) the payment of the underlying debt determined under nonbankruptcy law; or

(bb) discharge under section 1328; and

(II) if the case under this chapter is dismissed or converted without completion of the plan, such lien shall also be retained by such holder to the extent recognized by applicable nonbankruptcy law;

(ii) the value, as of the effective date of the plan, of property to be distributed under the plan on account of such claim is not less than the allowed amount of such claim; and

(iii) if—

(I) property to be distributed pursuant to this subsection is in the form of periodic payments, such payments shall be in equal monthly amounts; and

(II) the holder of the claim is secured by personal property, the amount of such payments shall not be less than an amount sufficient to provide to the holder of such claim adequate protection during the period of the plan; or

(C) the debtor surrenders the property securing such claim to such holder;

(6) the debtor will be able to make all payments under the plan and to comply with the plan;

(7) the action of the debtor in filing the petition was in good faith;

(8) the debtor has paid all amounts that are required to be paid under a domestic support obligation and that first become payable after the date of the filing of the petition if the debtor is required by a judicial or administrative order, or by statute, to pay such domestic support obligation; and

(9) the debtor has filed all applicable Federal, State, and local tax returns as required by section 1308.

For purposes of paragraph (5), section 506 shall not apply to a claim described in that paragraph if the creditor has a purchase money security interest securing the debt that is the subject of the claim, the debt was incurred within the 910-day period preceding the date of the filing of the petition, and the collateral for that debt consists of a motor vehicle (as defined in section 30102 of title 49) acquired for the personal use of the debtor, or if collateral for that debt consists of any other thing of value, if the debt was incurred during the 1-year period preceding that filing.

(b)(1) If the trustee or the holder of an allowed unsecured claim objects to the confirmation of the plan, then the court may not approve the plan unless, as of the effective date of the plan—

(A) the value of the property to be distributed under the plan on account of such claim is not less than the amount of such claim; or

(B) the plan provides that all of the debtor's projected disposable income to be received in the applicable commitment period beginning on the date that the first payment is due under the plan will be applied to make payments to unsecured creditors under the plan.

(2) For purposes of this subsection, the term "disposable income" means current monthly income received by the debtor (other than child support payments, foster care payments, or disability payments for a dependent child made in accordance with applicable nonbankruptcy law to the extent reasonably necessary to be expended for such child) less amounts reasonably necessary to be expended—

(A) (i) for the maintenance or support of the debtor or a dependent of the debtor, or for a domestic support obligation, that first becomes payable after the date the petition is filed; and

(ii) for charitable contributions (that meet the definition of "charitable contribution" under section 548(d)(3)) to a qualified religious or charitable entity or organization (as defined in section 548(d)(4)) in an amount not to exceed 15 percent of gross income of the debtor for the year in which the contributions are made; and

(B) if the debtor is engaged in business, for the payment of expenditures necessary for the continuation, preservation, and operation of such business.

(3) Amounts reasonably necessary to be expended under paragraph (2), other than subparagraph (A)(ii) of paragraph (2), shall be determined in accordance with subparagraphs (A) and (B) of section 707(b)(2), if the debtor has current monthly income, when multiplied by 12, greater than—

(A) in the case of a debtor in a household of 1 person, the median family income of the applicable State for 1 earner;

(B) in the case of a debtor in a household of 2, 3, or 4 individuals, the highest median family income of the applicable State for a family of the same number or fewer individuals; or

(C) in the case of a debtor in a household exceeding 4 individuals, the highest median family income of the applicable State for a family of 4 or fewer individuals, plus $825 per month for each individual in excess of 4.

(4) For purposes of this subsection, the "applicable commitment period"—

(A) subject to subparagraph (B), shall be—

(i) 3 years; or

(ii) not less than 5 years, if the current monthly income of the debtor and the debtor's spouse combined, when multiplied by 12, is not less than—

(I) in the case of a debtor in a household of 1 person, the median family income of the applicable State for 1 earner;

(II) in the case of a debtor in a household of 2, 3, or 4 individuals, the highest median family income of the applicable State for a family of the same number or fewer individuals; or

(III) in the case of a debtor in a household exceeding 4 individuals, the highest median family income of the applicable State for a family of 4 or fewer individuals, plus $825 per month for each individual in excess of 4; and

(B) may be less than 3 or 5 years, whichever is applicable under subparagraph (A), but only if the plan provides for payment in full of all allowed unsecured claims over a shorter period.

(c) After confirmation of a plan, the court may order any entity from whom the debtor receives income to pay all or any part of such income to the trustee.

§ 1326. Payments

(a)(1) Unless the court orders otherwise, the debtor shall commence making payments not later than 30 days after the date of the filing of the plan or the order for relief, whichever is earlier, in the amount—

(A) proposed by the plan to the trustee;

(B) scheduled in a lease of personal property directly to the lessor for that portion of the obligation that becomes due after the order for relief, reducing the payments under subparagraph (A) by the amount so paid and providing the trustee with evidence of such payment, including the amount and date of payment; and

(C) that provides adequate protection directly to a creditor holding an allowed claim secured by personal property to the extent the claim is attributable to the purchase of such property by the debtor for that portion of the obligation that becomes due after the order for relief, reducing the payments under subparagraph (A) by the amount so paid and providing the trustee with evidence of such payment, including the amount and date of payment.

(2) A payment made under paragraph (1)(A) shall be retained by the trustee until confirmation or denial of confirmation. If a plan is confirmed, the trustee shall distribute any such payment in accordance with the plan as soon as is practicable. If a plan is not confirmed, the trustee shall return any such payments not previously paid and not yet due and owing to creditors pursuant to paragraph (3) to the debtor, after deducting any unpaid claim allowed under section 503(b).

(3) Subject to section 363, the court may, upon notice and a hearing, modify, increase, or reduce the payments required under this subsection pending confirmation of a plan.

(4) Not later than 60 days after the date of filing of a case under this chapter, a debtor retaining possession of personal property subject to a lease or securing a claim attributable in whole or in part to the purchase price of such property shall provide the lessor or secured creditor reasonable evidence of the maintenance of any required insurance coverage with respect to the use or ownership of such property and continue to do so for so long as the debtor retains possession of such property.

(b) Before or at the time of each payment to creditors under the plan, there shall be paid—

(1) any unpaid claim of the kind specified in section 507(a)(2) of this title;

(2) if a standing trustee appointed under section 586(b) of title 28 is serving in the case, the percentage fee fixed for such standing trustee under section 586(e)(1)(B) of title 28; and

(3) if a chapter 7 trustee has been allowed compensation due to the conversion or dismissal of the debtor's prior case pursuant to section 707(b), and some portion of that compensation remains unpaid in a case converted to this chapter or in the case dismissed under section 707(b) and refiled under this chapter, the amount of any such unpaid compensation, which shall be paid monthly—

(A) by prorating such amount over the remaining duration of the plan; and

(B) by monthly payments not to exceed the greater of—

(i) $25; or

(ii) the amount payable to unsecured nonpriority creditors, as provided by the plan, multiplied by 5 percent, and the result divided by the number of months in the plan.

(c) Except as otherwise provided in the plan or in the order confirming the plan, the trustee shall make payments to creditors under the plan.

(d) Notwithstanding any other provision of this title—

(1) compensation referred to in subsection (b)(3) is payable and may be collected by the trustee under that paragraph, even if such amount has been discharged in a prior case under this title; and

(2) such compensation is payable in a case under this chapter only to the extent permitted by subsection (b)(3).

§ 1327. Effect of Confirmation

(a) The provisions of a confirmed plan bind the debtor and each creditor, whether or not the claim of such creditor is provided for by the plan, and whether or not such creditor has objected to, has accepted, or has rejected the plan.

(b) Except as otherwise provided in the plan or the order confirming the plan, the confirmation of a plan vests all of the property of the estate in the debtor.

(c) Except as otherwise provided in the plan or in the order confirming the plan, the property vesting in the debtor under subsection (b) of this section is free and clear of any claim or interest of any creditor provided for by the plan.

§ 1328. Discharge

(a) Subject to subsection (d), as soon as practicable after completion by the debtor of all payments under the plan, and in the case of a debtor who is required by a judicial or administrative order, or by statute, to pay a domestic support obligation, after such debtor certifies that all amounts payable under such order or such statute that are due on or before the date of the certification (including amounts due before the petition was filed, but only to the extent provided for by the plan) have been paid, unless the court approves a written waiver of discharge executed by the debtor after the order for relief under this chapter, the court shall grant the debtor a discharge of all debts provided for by the plan or disallowed under section 502 of this title, except any debt—

(1) provided for under section 1322(b)(5);

(2) of the kind specified in section 507(a)(8)(C) or in paragraph (1)(B), (1)(C), (2), (3), (4), (5), (8), or (9) of section 523(a);

(3) for restitution, or a criminal fine, included in a sentence on the debtor's conviction of a crime; or

(4) for restitution, or damages, awarded in a civil action against the debtor as a result of willful or malicious injury by the debtor that caused personal injury to an individual or the death of an individual.

(b) Subject to subsection (d), at any time after the confirmation of the plan and after notice and a hearing, the court may grant a discharge to a debtor that has not completed payments under the plan only if—

(1) the debtor's failure to complete such payments is due to circumstances for which the debtor should not justly be held accountable;

(2) the value, as of the effective date of the plan, of property actually distributed under the plan on account of each allowed unsecured claim is not less than the amount that would have been paid on such claim if the estate of the debtor had been liquidated under chapter 7 of this title on such date; and

(3) modification of the plan under section 1329 of this title is not practicable.

(c) A discharge granted under subsection (b) of this section discharges the debtor from all unsecured debts provided for by the plan or disallowed under section 502 of this title, except any debt—

(1) provided for under section 1322(b)(5) of this title; or

(2) of a kind specified in section 523(a) of this title.

(d) Notwithstanding any other provision of this section, a discharge granted under this section does not discharge the debtor from any debt based on an allowed claim filed under section 1305(a)(2) of this title if prior approval by the trustee of the debtor's incurring such debt was practicable and was not obtained.

(e) On request of a party in interest before one year after a discharge under this section is granted, and after notice and a hearing, the court may revoke such discharge only if—

(1) such discharge was obtained by the debtor through fraud; and

(2) the requesting party did not know of such fraud until after such discharge was granted.

(f) Notwithstanding subsections (a) and (b), the court shall not grant a discharge of all debts provided for in the plan or disallowed under section 502, if the debtor has received a discharge—

(1) in a case filed under chapter 7, 11, or 12 of this title during the 4-year period preceding the date of the order for relief under this chapter, or

(2) in a case filed under chapter 13 of this title during the 2-year period preceding the date of such order.

(g)(1) The court shall not grant a discharge under this section to a debtor unless after filing a petition the debtor has completed an instructional course concerning personal financial management described in section 111.

(2) Paragraph (1) shall not apply with respect to a debtor who is a person described in section 109(h)(4) or who resides in a district for which the United States trustee (or the bankruptcy administrator, if any) determines that the approved instructional courses are not adequate to service the additional individuals who would otherwise be required to complete such instructional course by reason of the requirements of paragraph (1).

(3) The United States trustee (or the bankruptcy administrator, if any) who makes a determination described in paragraph (2) shall review such determination not later than 1 year after the date of such determination, and not less frequently than annually thereafter.

(h) The court may not grant a discharge under this chapter unless the court after notice and a hearing held not more than 10 days before the date of the entry of the order granting the discharge finds that there is no reasonable cause to believe that—

(1) section 522(q)(1) may be applicable to the debtor; and

(2) there is pending any proceeding in which the debtor may be found guilty of a felony of the kind described in section 522(q)(1)(A) or liable for a debt of the kind described in section 522(q)(1)(B).

§ 1329. Modification of Plan After Confirmation

(a) At any time after confirmation of the plan but before the completion of payments under such plan, the plan may be modified, upon request of the debtor, the trustee, or the holder of an allowed unsecured claim, to—

(1) increase or reduce the amount of payments on claims of a particular class provided for by the plan;

(2) extend or reduce the time for such payments;

(3) alter the amount of the distribution to a creditor whose claim is provided for by the plan to the extent necessary to take account of any payment of such claim other than under the plan; or

(4) reduce amounts to be paid under the plan by the actual amount expended by the debtor to purchase health insurance for the debtor (and for any dependent of the debtor if such dependent does not otherwise have health insurance coverage) if the debtor documents the cost of such insurance and demonstrates that—

(A) such expenses are reasonable and necessary;

(B) (i) if the debtor previously paid for health insurance, the amount is not materially larger than the cost the debtor previously paid or the cost necessary to maintain the lapsed policy; or

(ii) if the debtor did not have health insurance, the amount is not materially larger than the reasonable cost that would be incurred by a debtor who purchases health insurance, who has similar income, expenses, age, and health status, and who lives in the same geographical location with the same number of dependents who do not otherwise have health insurance coverage; and

(C) the amount is not otherwise allowed for purposes of determining disposable income under section 1325(b) of this title;

and upon request of any party in interest, files proof that a health insurance policy was purchased.

(b)(1) Sections 1322(a), 1322(b), and 1323(c) of this title and the requirements of section 1325(a) of this title apply to any modification under subsection (a) of this section.

(2) The plan as modified becomes the plan unless, after notice and a hearing, such modification is disapproved.

(c) A plan modified under this section may not provide for payments over a period that expires after the applicable commitment period under section 1325(b)(1)(B) after the time that the first payment under the original confirmed plan was due, unless the court, for cause, approves a longer period, but the court may not approve a period that expires after five years after such time.

§ 1330. Revocation of an Order of Confirmation

(a) On request of a party in interest at any time within 180 days after the date of the entry of an order of confirmation under section 1325 of this title, and after notice and a hearing, the court may revoke such order if such order was procured by fraud.

(b) If the court revokes an order of confirmation under subsection (a) of this section, the court shall dispose of the case under section 1307 of this title, unless, within the time fixed by the court, the debtor proposes and the court confirms a modification of the plan under section 1329 of this title.

CHAPTER 15. ANCILLARY AND OTHER CROSS-BORDER CASES

§ 1501. Purpose and Scope of Application

(a) The purpose of this chapter is to incorporate the Model Law on Cross-Border Insolvency so as to provide effective mechanisms for dealing with cases of cross-border insolvency with the objectives of—

(1) cooperation between—

(A) courts of the United States, United States trustees, trustees, examiners, debtors, and debtors in possession; and

(B) the courts and other competent authorities of foreign countries involved in cross-border insolvency cases;

(2) greater legal certainty for trade and investment;

(3) fair and efficient administration of cross-border insolvencies that protects the interests of all creditors, and other interested entities, including the debtor;

(4) protection and maximization of the value of the debtor's assets; and

(5) facilitation of the rescue of financially troubled businesses, thereby protecting investment and preserving employment.

(b) This chapter applies where—

(1) assistance is sought in the United States by a foreign court or a foreign representative in connection with a foreign proceeding;

(2) assistance is sought in a foreign country in connection with a case under this title;

(3) a foreign proceeding and a case under this title with respect to the same debtor are pending concurrently; or

(4) creditors or other interested persons in a foreign country have an interest in requesting the commencement of, or participating in, a case or proceeding under this title.

(c) This chapter does not apply to—

(1) a proceeding concerning an entity, other than a foreign insurance company, identified by exclusion in section 109(b);

(2) an individual, or to an individual and such individual's spouse, who have debts within the limits specified in section 109(e) and who are citizens of the United States or aliens lawfully admitted for permanent residence in the United States; or

(3) an entity subject to a proceeding under the Securities Investor Protection Act of 1970, a stockbroker subject to subchapter III of chapter 7 of this title, or a commodity broker subject to subchapter IV of chapter 7 of this title.

(d) The court may not grant relief under this chapter with respect to any deposit, escrow, trust fund, or other security required or permitted under any applicable State insurance law or regulation for the benefit of claim holders in the United States.

SUBCHAPTER I—GENERAL PROVISIONS

Section

1502. Definitions
1503. International Obligations of the United States
1504. Commencement of Ancillary Case
1505. Authorization to Act in a Foreign Country
1506. Public Policy Exception
1507. Additional Assistance
1508. Interpretation

§ 1502. Definitions

For the purposes of this chapter, the term—

(1) "debtor" means an entity that is the subject of a foreign proceeding;

(2) "establishment" means any place of operations where the debtor carries out a nontransitory economic activity;

(3) "foreign court" means a judicial or other authority competent to control or supervise a foreign proceeding;

(4) "foreign main proceeding" means a foreign proceeding pending in the country where the debtor has the center of its main interests;

(5) "foreign nonmain proceeding" means a foreign proceeding, other than a foreign main proceeding, pending in a country where the debtor has an establishment;

(6) "trustee" includes a trustee, a debtor in possession in a case under any chapter of this title, or a debtor under chapter 9 of this title;

(7) "recognition" means the entry of an order granting recognition of a foreign main proceeding or foreign nonmain proceeding under this chapter; and

(8) "within the territorial jurisdiction of the United States", when used with reference to property of a debtor, refers to tangible property located within the territory of the United States and intangible property deemed under applicable nonbankruptcy law to be located within that territory, including any property subject to attachment or garnishment that may properly be seized or garnished by an action in a Federal or State court in the United States.

§ 1503. International Obligations of the United States

To the extent that this chapter conflicts with an obligation of the United States arising out of any treaty or other form of agreement to which it is a party with one or more other countries, the requirements of the treaty or agreement prevail.

§ 1504. Commencement of Ancillary Case

A case under this chapter is commenced by the filing of a petition for recognition of a foreign proceeding under section 1515.

§ 1505. Authorization to Act in a Foreign Country

A trustee or another entity (including an examiner) may be authorized by the court to act in a foreign country on behalf of an estate created under section 541. An entity authorized to act under this section may act in any way permitted by the applicable foreign law.

§ 1506. Public Policy Exception

Nothing in this chapter prevents the court from refusing to take an action governed by this chapter if the action would be manifestly contrary to the public policy of the United States.

§ 1507. Additional Assistance

(a) Subject to the specific limitations stated elsewhere in this chapter the court, if recognition is granted, may provide additional assistance to a foreign representative under this title or under other laws of the United States.

(b) In determining whether to provide additional assistance under this title or under other laws of the United States, the court shall consider whether such additional assistance, consistent with the principles of comity, will reasonably assure—

(1) just treatment of all holders of claims against or interests in the debtor's property;

(2) protection of claim holders in the United States against prejudice and inconvenience in the processing of claims in such foreign proceeding;

(3) prevention of preferential or fraudulent dispositions of property of the debtor;

(4) distribution of proceeds of the debtor's property substantially in accordance with the order prescribed by this title; and

(5) if appropriate, the provision of an opportunity for a fresh start for the individual that such foreign proceeding concerns.

§ 1508. Interpretation

In interpreting this chapter, the court shall consider its international origin, and the need to promote an application of this chapter that is consistent with the application of similar statutes adopted by foreign jurisdictions.

SUBCHAPTER II—ACCESS OF FOREIGN REPRESENTATIVES AND CREDITORS TO THE COURT

Section

1509. Right of Direct Access
1510. Limited Jurisdiction
1511. Commencement of Case under Section 301, 302, or 303
1512. Participation of a Foreign Representative in a Case under This Title
1513. Access of Foreign Creditors to a Case under This Title
1514. Notification to Foreign Creditors Concerning a Case under This Title

§ 1509. Right of Direct Access

(a) A foreign representative may commence a case under section 1504 by filing directly with the court a petition for recognition of a foreign proceeding under section 1515.

(b) If the court grants recognition under section 1517, and subject to any limitations that the court may impose consistent with the policy of this chapter—

(1) the foreign representative has the capacity to sue and be sued in a court in the United States;

(2) the foreign representative may apply directly to a court in the United States for appropriate relief in that court; and

(3) a court in the United States shall grant comity or cooperation to the foreign representative.

(c) A request for comity or cooperation by a foreign representative in a court in the United States other than the court which granted recognition shall be accompanied by a certified copy of an order granting recognition under section 1517.

(d) If the court denies recognition under this chapter, the court may issue any appropriate order necessary to prevent the foreign representative from obtaining comity or cooperation from courts in the United States.

(e) Whether or not the court grants recognition, and subject to sections 306 and 1510, a foreign representative is subject to applicable nonbankruptcy law.

(f) Notwithstanding any other provision of this section, the failure of a foreign representative to commence a case or to obtain recognition under this chapter does not affect any right the foreign representative may have to sue in a court in the United States to collect or recover a claim which is the property of the debtor.

§ 1510. Limited Jurisdiction

The sole fact that a foreign representative files a petition under section 1515 does not subject the foreign representative to the jurisdiction of any court in the United States for any other purpose.

§ 1511. Commencement of Case Under Section 301, 302, or 303

(a) Upon recognition, a foreign representative may commence—

(1) an involuntary case under section 303; or

(2) a voluntary case under section 301 or 302, if the foreign proceeding is a foreign main proceeding.

(b) The petition commencing a case under subsection (a) must be accompanied by a certified copy of an order granting recognition. The court where the petition for recognition has been filed must be advised of the foreign representative's intent to commence a case under subsection (a) prior to such commencement.

§ 1512. Participation of a Foreign Representative in a Case Under This Title

Upon recognition of a foreign proceeding, the foreign representative in the recognized proceeding is entitled to participate as a party in interest in a case regarding the debtor under this title.

§ 1513. Access of Foreign Creditors to a Case Under This Title

(a) Foreign creditors have the same rights regarding the commencement of, and participation in, a case under this title as domestic creditors.

(b)(1) Subsection (a) does not change or codify present law as to the priority of claims under section 507 or 726, except that the claim of a foreign creditor under those sections shall not be given a lower priority than that of general unsecured claims without priority solely because the holder of such claim is a foreign creditor.

(2) (A) Subsection (a) and paragraph (1) do not change or codify present law as to the allowability of foreign revenue claims or other foreign public law claims in a proceeding under this title.

(B) Allowance and priority as to a foreign tax claim or other foreign public law claim shall be governed by any applicable tax treaty of the United States, under the conditions and circumstances specified therein.

§ 1514. Notification to Foreign Creditors Concerning a Case Under This Title

(a) Whenever in a case under this title notice is to be given to creditors generally or to any class or category of creditors, such notice shall also be given to the known creditors generally, or to creditors in the notified class or category, that do not have addresses in the United States. The court may order that appropriate steps be taken with a view to notifying any creditor whose address is not yet known.

(b) Such notification to creditors with foreign addresses described in subsection (a) shall be given individually, unless the court considers that, under the circumstances, some other form of notification would be more appropriate. No letter or other formality is required.

(c) When a notification of commencement of a case is to be given to foreign creditors, such notification shall—

(1) indicate the time period for filing proofs of claim and specify the place for filing such proofs of claim;

(2) indicate whether secured creditors need to file proofs of claim; and

(3) contain any other information required to be included in such notification to creditors under this title and the orders of the court.

(d) Any rule of procedure or order of the court as to notice or the filing of a proof of claim shall provide such additional time to creditors with foreign addresses as is reasonable under the circumstances.

SUBCHAPTER III—RECOGNITION OF A FOREIGN PROCEEDING AND RELIEF

Section

1515. Application for Recognition
1516. Presumptions Concerning Recognition
1517. Order Granting Recognition
1518. Subsequent Information
1519. Relief That May Be Granted upon Filing Petition for Recognition
1520. Effects of Recognition of a Foreign Main Proceeding
1521. Relief That May Be Granted upon Recognition
1522. Protection of Creditors and Other Interested Persons
1523. Actions to Avoid Acts Detrimental to Creditors
1524. Intervention by a Foreign Representative

§ 1515. Application for Recognition

(a) A foreign representative applies to the court for recognition of a foreign proceeding in which the foreign representative has been appointed by filing a petition for recognition.

(b) A petition for recognition shall be accompanied by—

(1) a certified copy of the decision commencing such foreign proceeding and appointing the foreign representative;

(2) a certificate from the foreign court affirming the existence of such foreign proceeding and of the appointment of the foreign representative; or

(3) in the absence of evidence referred to in paragraphs (1) and (2), any other evidence acceptable to the court of the existence of such foreign proceeding and of the appointment of the foreign representative.

(c) A petition for recognition shall also be accompanied by a statement identifying all foreign proceedings with respect to the debtor that are known to the foreign representative.

(d) The documents referred to in paragraphs (1) and (2) of subsection (b) shall be translated into English. The court may require a translation into English of additional documents.

§ 1516. Presumptions Concerning Recognition

(a) If the decision or certificate referred to in section 1515(b) indicates that the foreign proceeding is a foreign proceeding and that the person or body is a foreign representative, the court is entitled to so presume.

(b) The court is entitled to presume that documents submitted in support of the petition for recognition are authentic, whether or not they have been legalized.

(c) In the absence of evidence to the contrary, the debtor's registered office, or habitual residence in the case of an individual, is presumed to be the center of the debtor's main interests.

§ 1517. Order Granting Recognition

(a) Subject to section 1506, after notice and a hearing, an order recognizing a foreign proceeding shall be entered if—

(1) such foreign proceeding for which recognition is sought is a foreign main proceeding or foreign nonmain proceeding within the meaning of section 1502;

(2) the foreign representative applying for recognition is a person or body; and

(3) the petition meets the requirements of section 1515.

(b) Such foreign proceeding shall be recognized—

(1) as a foreign main proceeding if it is pending in the country where the debtor has the center of its main interests; or

(2) as a foreign nonmain proceeding if the debtor has an establishment within the meaning of section 1502 in the foreign country where the proceeding is pending.

(c) A petition for recognition of a foreign proceeding shall be decided upon at the earliest possible time. Entry of an order recognizing a foreign proceeding constitutes recognition under this chapter.

(d) The provisions of this subchapter do not prevent modification or termination of recognition if it is shown that the grounds for granting it were fully or partially lacking or have ceased to exist, but in considering such action the court shall give due weight to possible prejudice to parties that have relied upon the order granting recognition. A case under this chapter may be closed in the manner prescribed under section 350.

§ 1518. Subsequent Information

From the time of filing the petition for recognition of a foreign proceeding, the foreign representative shall file with the court promptly a notice of change of status concerning—

(1) any substantial change in the status of such foreign proceeding or the status of the foreign representative's appointment; and

(2) any other foreign proceeding regarding the debtor that becomes known to the foreign representative.

§ 1519. Relief That May Be Granted upon Filing Petition for Recognition

(a) From the time of filing a petition for recognition until the court rules on the petition, the court may, at the request of the foreign representative, where relief is urgently needed to protect the assets of the debtor or the interests of the creditors, grant relief of a provisional nature, including—

(1) staying execution against the debtor's assets;

(2) entrusting the administration or realization of all or part of the debtor's assets located in the United States to the foreign representative or another person authorized by the court, including an examiner, in order to protect and preserve the value of assets that, by their nature or because of other circumstances, are perishable, susceptible to devaluation or otherwise in jeopardy; and

(3) any relief referred to in paragraph (3), (4), or (7) of section 1521(a).

(b) Unless extended under section 1521(a)(6), the relief granted under this section terminates when the petition for recognition is granted.

(c) It is a ground for denial of relief under this section that such relief would interfere with the administration of a foreign main proceeding.

(d) The court may not enjoin a police or regulatory act of a governmental unit, including a criminal action or proceeding, under this section.

(e) The standards, procedures, and limitations applicable to an injunction shall apply to relief under this section.

(f) The exercise of rights not subject to the stay arising under section 362(a) pursuant to paragraph (6), (7), (17), or (27) of section 362(b) or pursuant to section 362(o) shall not be stayed by any order of a court or administrative agency in any proceeding under this chapter.

§ 1520. Effects of Recognition of a Foreign Main Proceeding

(a) Upon recognition of a foreign proceeding that is a foreign main proceeding—

(1) sections 361 and 362 apply with respect to the debtor and the property of the debtor that is within the territorial jurisdiction of the United States;

(2) sections 363, 549, and 552 apply to a transfer of an interest of the debtor in property that is within the territorial jurisdiction of the United States to the same extent that the sections would apply to property of an estate;

(3) unless the court orders otherwise, the foreign representative may operate the debtor's business and may exercise the rights and powers of a trustee under and to the extent provided by sections 363 and 552; and

(4) section 552 applies to property of the debtor that is within the territorial jurisdiction of the United States.

(b) Subsection (a) does not affect the right to commence an individual action or proceeding in a foreign country to the extent necessary to preserve a claim against the debtor.

(c) Subsection (a) does not affect the right of a foreign representative or an entity to file a petition commencing a case under this title or the right of any party to file claims or take other proper actions in such a case.

§ 1521. Relief That May Be Granted upon Recognition

(a) Upon recognition of a foreign proceeding, whether main or nonmain, where necessary to effectuate the purpose of this chapter and to protect the assets of the debtor or the interests of the creditors, the court may, at the request of the foreign representative, grant any appropriate relief, including—

(1) staying the commencement or continuation of an individual action or proceeding concerning the debtor's assets, rights, obligations

or liabilities to the extent they have not been stayed under section 1520(a);

(2) staying execution against the debtor's assets to the extent it has not been stayed under section 1520(a);

(3) suspending the right to transfer, encumber or otherwise dispose of any assets of the debtor to the extent this right has not been suspended under section 1520(a);

(4) providing for the examination of witnesses, the taking of evidence or the delivery of information concerning the debtor's assets, affairs, rights, obligations or liabilities;

(5) entrusting the administration or realization of all or part of the debtor's assets within the territorial jurisdiction of the United States to the foreign representative or another person, including an examiner, authorized by the court;

(6) extending relief granted under section 1519(a); and

(7) granting any additional relief that may be available to a trustee, except for relief available under sections 522, 544, 545, 547, 548, 550, and 724(a).

(b) Upon recognition of a foreign proceeding, whether main or nonmain, the court may, at the request of the foreign representative, entrust the distribution of all or part of the debtor's assets located in the United States to the foreign representative or another person, including an examiner, authorized by the court, provided that the court is satisfied that the interests of creditors in the United States are sufficiently protected.

(c) In granting relief under this section to a representative of a foreign nonmain proceeding, the court must be satisfied that the relief relates to assets that, under the law of the United States, should be administered in the foreign nonmain proceeding or concerns information required in that proceeding.

(d) The court may not enjoin a police or regulatory act of a governmental unit, including a criminal action or proceeding, under this section.

(e) The standards, procedures, and limitations applicable to an injunction shall apply to relief under paragraphs (1), (2), (3), and (6) of subsection (a).

(f) The exercise of rights not subject to the stay arising under section 362(a) pursuant to paragraph (6), (7), (17), or (27) of section 362(b) or pursuant to section 362(o) shall not be stayed by any order of a court or administrative agency in any proceeding under this chapter.

§ 1522. Protection of Creditors and Other Interested Persons

(a) The court may grant relief under section 1519 or 1521, or may modify or terminate relief under subsection (c), only if the interests of the creditors and other interested entities, including the debtor, are sufficiently protected.

(b) The court may subject relief granted under section 1519 or 1521, or the operation of the debtor's business under section 1520(a)(3), to conditions it considers appropriate, including the giving of security or the filing of a bond.

(c) The court may, at the request of the foreign representative or an entity affected by relief granted under section 1519 or 1521, or at its own motion, modify or terminate such relief.

(d) Section 1104(d) shall apply to the appointment of an examiner under this chapter. Any examiner shall comply with the qualification requirements imposed on a trustee by section 322.

§ 1523. Actions to Avoid Acts Detrimental to Creditors

(a) Upon recognition of a foreign proceeding, the foreign representative has standing in a case concerning the debtor pending under another chapter of this title to initiate actions under sections 522, 544, 545, 547, 548, 550, 553, and 724(a).

(b) When a foreign proceeding is a foreign nonmain proceeding, the court must be satisfied that an action under subsection (a) relates to assets that, under United States law, should be administered in the foreign nonmain proceeding.

§ 1524. Intervention by a Foreign Representative

Upon recognition of a foreign proceeding, the foreign representative may intervene in any proceedings in a State or Federal court in the United States in which the debtor is a party.

SUBCHAPTER IV—COOPERATION WITH FOREIGN COURTS AND FOREIGN REPRESENTATIVES

Section

1525. Cooperation and Direct Communication Between the Court and Foreign Courts or Foreign Representatives
1526. Cooperation and Direct Communication Between the Trustee and Foreign Courts or Foreign Representatives
1527. Forms of Cooperation

§ 1525. Cooperation and Direct Communication Between the Court and Foreign Courts or Foreign Representatives

(a) Consistent with section 1501, the court shall cooperate to the maximum extent possible with a foreign court or a foreign representative, either directly or through the trustee.

(b) The court is entitled to communicate directly with, or to request information or assistance directly from, a foreign court or a foreign representative, subject to the rights of a party in interest to notice and participation.

§ 1526. Cooperation and Direct Communication Between the Trustee and Foreign Courts or Foreign Representatives

(a) Consistent with section 1501, the trustee or other person, including an examiner, authorized by the court, shall, subject to the supervision of the court, cooperate to the maximum extent possible with a foreign court or a foreign representative.

(b) The trustee or other person, including an examiner, authorized by the court is entitled, subject to the supervision of the court, to communicate directly with a foreign court or a foreign representative.

§ 1527. Forms of Cooperation

Cooperation referred to in sections 1525 and 1526 may be implemented by any appropriate means, including—

(1) appointment of a person or body, including an examiner, to act at the direction of the court;

(2) communication of information by any means considered appropriate by the court;

(3) coordination of the administration and supervision of the debtor's assets and affairs;

(4) approval or implementation of agreements concerning the coordination of proceedings; and

(5) coordination of concurrent proceedings regarding the same debtor.

SUBCHAPTER V—CONCURRENT PROCEEDINGS

Section

1528. Commencement of a Case under This Title after Recognition of a Foreign Main Proceeding
1529. Coordination of a Case under This Title and a Foreign Proceeding
1530. Coordination of More Than 1 Foreign Proceeding
1531. Presumption of Insolvency Based on Recognition of a Foreign Main Proceeding
1532. Rule of Payment in Concurrent Proceedings

§ 1528. Commencement of a Case Under This Title After Recognition of a Foreign Main Proceeding

After recognition of a foreign main proceeding, a case under another chapter of this title may be commenced only if the debtor has assets in the United States. The effects of such case shall be restricted to the assets of the debtor that are within the territorial jurisdiction of the United States and, to the extent necessary to implement cooperation and coordination under sections 1525, 1526, and 1527, to other assets of the debtor that are within the jurisdiction of the court under sections 541(a) of this title, and 1334(e) of title 28, to the extent that such other assets are not subject to the jurisdiction and control of a foreign proceeding that has been recognized under this chapter.

§ 1529. Coordination of a Case Under This Title and a Foreign Proceeding

If a foreign proceeding and a case under another chapter of this title are pending concurrently regarding the same debtor, the court shall seek cooperation and coordination under sections 1525, 1526, and 1527, and the following shall apply:

(1) If the case in the United States is pending at the time the petition for recognition of such foreign proceeding is filed—

(A) any relief granted under section 1519 or 1521 must be consistent with the relief granted in the case in the United States; and

(B) section 1520 does not apply even if such foreign proceeding is recognized as a foreign main proceeding.

(2) If a case in the United States under this title commences after recognition, or after the date of the filing of the petition for recognition, of such foreign proceeding—

(A) any relief in effect under section 1519 or 1521 shall be reviewed by the court and shall be modified or terminated if inconsistent with the case in the United States; and

(B) if such foreign proceeding is a foreign main proceeding, the stay and suspension referred to in section 1520(a) shall be modified or terminated if inconsistent with the relief granted in the case in the United States.

(3) In granting, extending, or modifying relief granted to a representative of a foreign nonmain proceeding, the court must be satisfied that the relief relates to assets that, under the laws of the United States, should be administered in the foreign nonmain proceeding or concerns information required in that proceeding.

(4) In achieving cooperation and coordination under sections 1528 and 1529, the court may grant any of the relief authorized under section 305.

§ 1530. Coordination of More Than 1 Foreign Proceeding

In matters referred to in section 1501, with respect to more than 1 foreign proceeding regarding the debtor, the court shall seek cooperation and coordination under sections 1525, 1526, and 1527, and the following shall apply:

(1) Any relief granted under section 1519 or 1521 to a representative of a foreign nonmain proceeding after recognition of a foreign main proceeding must be consistent with the foreign main proceeding.

(2) If a foreign main proceeding is recognized after recognition, or after the filing of a petition for recognition, of a foreign nonmain proceeding, any relief in effect under section 1519 or 1521 shall be reviewed by the court and shall be modified or terminated if inconsistent with the foreign main proceeding.

(3) If, after recognition of a foreign nonmain proceeding, another foreign nonmain proceeding is recognized, the court shall grant, modify, or terminate relief for the purpose of facilitating coordination of the proceedings.

§ 1531. Presumption of Insolvency Based on Recognition of a Foreign Main Proceeding

In the absence of evidence to the contrary, recognition of a foreign main proceeding is, for the purpose of commencing a proceeding under section 303, proof that the debtor is generally not paying its debts as such debts become due.

§ 1532. Rule of Payment in Concurrent Proceedings

Without prejudice to secured claims or rights in rem, a creditor who has received payment with respect to its claim in a foreign proceeding pursuant to a law relating to insolvency may not receive a payment for the same claim in a case under any other chapter of this title regarding the debtor, so long as the payment to other creditors of the same class is proportionately less than the payment the creditor has already received.

FEDERAL RULES OF BANKRUPTCY PROCEDURE

Rule

1015. Consolidation or Joint Administration of Cases Pending in Same Court
2002. Notices to Creditors, Equity Security Holders, Administrators in Foreign Proceedings, Persons Against Whom Provisional Relief is Sought in Ancillary and Other Cross-Border Cases, United States, and United States Trustee
2003. Meeting of Creditors or Equity Security Holders
2004. Examination
2014. Employment of Professional Persons
2016. Compensation for Services Rendered and Reimbursement of Expenses
2017. Examination of Debtor's Transactions with Debtor's Attorney
2019. Disclosure Regarding Creditors and Equity Security Holders in Chapter 9 and Chapter 11 Cases
3014. Election Under §1111(b) by Secured Creditor in Chapter 9 Municipality or Chapter 11 Reorganization Case
4001. Relief from Automatic Stay; Prohibiting or Conditioning the Use, Sale, or Lease of Property; Use of Cash Collateral; Obtaining Credit; Agreements
4005. Burden of Proof in Objecting to Discharge
4007. Determination of Dischargeability of a Debt
7001. Scope of Rules of Part VII
8002. Time for Filing Notice of Appeal
8007. Stay Pending Appeal; Bonds; Suspension of Proceedings
9014. Contested Matters
9029. Local Bankruptcy Rules; Procedure When There is No Controlling Law

Rule 1015. Consolidation or Joint Administration of Cases Pending in Same Court

(a) Cases Involving Same Debtor. If two or more petitions by, regarding, or against the same debtor are pending in the same court, the court may order consolidation of the cases.

(b) Cases Involving Two or More Related Debtors. If a joint petition or two or more petitions are pending in the same court by or against (1) spouses, or (2) a partnership and one or more of its general partners, or (3) two or more general partners, or (4) a debtor and an affiliate, the court may order a joint administration of the estates. Prior to entering an order the court shall give consideration to protecting creditors of different estates against potential conflicts of interest. An order directing joint administration of individual cases of spouses shall, if one spouse has elected the exemptions under §522(b)(2) of the Code and the other has elected the exemptions under §522(b)(3), fix a reasonable time within which either may amend the election so that both shall have elected the same exemptions. The order shall notify the debtors that unless they elect the same exemptions within the time fixed by the court, they will be deemed to have elected the exemptions provided by §522(b)(2).

(c) Expediting and Protective Orders. When an order for consolidation or joint administration of a joint case or two or more cases is entered pursuant to this rule, while protecting the rights of the parties under the Code, the court may enter orders as may tend to avoid unnecessary costs and delay.

Rule 2002. Notices to Creditors, Equity Security Holders, Administrators in Foreign Proceedings, Persons Against Whom Provisional Relief is Sought in Ancillary and Other Cross-Border Cases, United States, and United States Trustee

(a) Twenty-One-Day Notices to Parties in Interest. Except as provided in subdivisions (h), (i), (l), (p), and (q) of this rule, the clerk, or some other person as the court may direct, shall give the debtor, the trustee, all creditors and indenture trustees at least 21 days' notice by mail of:

(1) the meeting of creditors under §341 or §1104(b) of the Code, which notice, unless the court orders otherwise, shall include the debtor's employer identification number, social security number, and any other federal taxpayer identification number;

(2) a proposed use, sale, or lease of property of the estate other than in the ordinary course

of business, unless the court for cause shown shortens the time or directs another method of giving notice;

(3) the hearing on approval of a compromise or settlement of a controversy other than approval of an agreement pursuant to Rule 4001(d), unless the court for cause shown directs that notice not be sent;

(4) in a chapter 7 liquidation, a chapter 11 reorganization case, or a chapter 12 family farmer debt adjustment case, the hearing on the dismissal of the case or the conversion of the case to another chapter, unless the hearing is under §707(a)(3) or §707(b) or is on dismissal of the case for failure to pay the filing fee;

(5) the time fixed to accept or reject a proposed modification of a plan;

(6) a hearing on any entity's request for compensation or reimbursement of expenses if the request exceeds $1,000;

(7) the time fixed for filing proofs of claims pursuant to Rule 3003(c);

(8) the time fixed for filing objections and the hearing to consider confirmation of a chapter 12 plan; and

(9) the time fixed for filing objections to confirmation of a chapter 13 plan.

(b) Twenty-Eight-Day Notices to Parties in Interest. Except as provided in subdivision (l) of this rule, the clerk, or some other person as the court may direct, shall give the debtor, the trustee, all creditors and indenture trustees not less than 28 days' notice by mail of the time fixed (1) for filing objections and the hearing to consider approval of a disclosure statement or, under §1125(f), to make a final determination whether the plan provides adequate information so that a separate disclosure statement is not necessary; (2) for filing objections and the hearing to consider confirmation of a chapter 9 or chapter 11 plan; and (3) for the hearing to consider confirmation of a chapter 13 plan.

(c) Content of Notice.

(1) *Proposed Use, Sale, or Lease of Property*. Subject to Rule 6004, the notice of a proposed use, sale, or lease of property required by subdivision (a)(2) of this rule shall include the time and place of any public sale, the terms and conditions of any private sale and the time fixed for filing objections. The notice of a proposed use, sale, or lease of property, including real estate, is sufficient if it generally describes the property. The notice of a proposed sale or lease of personally identifiable information under §363(b)(1) of the Code shall state whether the sale is consistent with any policy prohibiting the transfer of the information.

(2) *Notice of Hearing on Compensation.* The notice of a hearing on an application for compensation or reimbursement of expenses required by subdivision (a)(6) of this rule shall identify the applicant and the amounts requested.

(3) *Notice of Hearing on Confirmation When Plan Provides for an Injunction.* If a plan provides for an injunction against conduct not otherwise enjoined under the Code, the notice required under Rule 2002(b)(2) shall:

(A) include in conspicuous language (bold, italic, or underlined text) a statement that the plan proposes an injunction;

(B) describe briefly the nature of the injunction; and

(C) identify the entities that would be subject to the injunction.

(d) Notice to Equity Security Holders. In a chapter 11 reorganization case, unless otherwise ordered by the court, the clerk, or some other person as the court may direct, shall in the manner and form directed by the court give notice to all equity security holders of (1) the order for relief; (2) any meeting of equity security holders held pursuant to §341 of the Code; (3) the hearing on the proposed sale of all or substantially all of the debtor's assets; (4) the hearing on the dismissal or conversion of a case to another chapter; (5) the time fixed for filing objections to and the hearing to consider approval of a disclosure statement; (6) the time fixed for filing objections to and the hearing to consider confirmation of a plan; and (7) the time fixed to accept or reject a proposed modification of a plan.

(e) Notice of No Dividend. In a chapter 7 liquidation case, if it appears from the schedules that there are no assets from which a dividend can be paid, the notice of the meeting of creditors may include a statement to that effect; that it is unnecessary to file claims; and that if sufficient assets become available for the payment of a dividend, further notice will be given for the filing of claims.

(f) Other Notices. Except as provided in subdivision (l) of this rule, the clerk, or some other person as the court may direct, shall give the debtor, all creditors, and indenture trustees notice by mail of:

(1) the order for relief;

(2) the dismissal or the conversion of the case to another chapter, or the suspension of proceedings under §305;

(3) the time allowed for filing claims pursuant to Rule 3002;

(4) the time fixed for filing a complaint objecting to the debtor's discharge pursuant to §727 of the Code as provided in Rule 4004;

(5) the time fixed for filing a complaint to determine the dischargeability of a debt pursuant to §523 of the Code as provided in Rule 4007;

(6) the waiver, denial, or revocation of a discharge as provided in Rule 4006;

(7) entry of an order confirming a chapter 9, 11, 12, or 13 plan;

(8) a summary of the trustee's final report in a chapter 7 case if the net proceeds realized exceed $1,500;

(9) a notice under Rule 5008 regarding the presumption of abuse;

(10) a statement under §704(b)(1) as to whether the debtor's case would be presumed to be an abuse under §707(b); and

(11) the time to request a delay in the entry of the discharge under §§1141(d)(5)(C), 1228(f), and 1328(h). Notice of the time fixed for accepting or rejecting a plan pursuant to Rule 3017(c) shall be given in accordance with Rule 3017(d).

(g) Addressing Notices.

(1) Notices required to be mailed under Rule 2002 to a creditor, indenture trustee, or equity security holder shall be addressed as such entity or an authorized agent has directed in its last request filed in the particular case. For the purposes of this subdivision—

(A) a proof of claim filed by a creditor or indenture trustee that designates a mailing address constitutes a filed request to mail notices to that address, unless a notice of no dividend has been given under Rule 2002(e) and a later notice of possible dividend under Rule 3002(c)(5) has not been given; and

(B) a proof of interest filed by an equity security holder that designates a mailing address constitutes a filed request to mail notices to that address.

(2) Except as provided in §342(f) of the Code, if a creditor or indenture trustee has not filed a request designating a mailing address under Rule 2002(g)(1) or Rule 5003(e), the notices shall be mailed to the address shown on the list of creditors or schedule of liabilities, whichever is filed later. If an equity security holder has not filed a request designating a mailing address under Rule 2002(g)(1) or Rule 5003(e), the notices shall be mailed to the address shown on the list of equity security holders.

(3) If a list or schedule filed under Rule 1007 includes the name and address of a legal representative of an infant or incompetent person, and a person other than that representative files a request or proof of claim designating a name and mailing address that differs from the name and address of the representative included in the list or schedule, unless the court orders otherwise, notices under Rule 2002 shall be mailed to the representative included in the list or schedules and to the name and address designated in the request or proof of claim.

(4) Notwithstanding Rule 2002(g)(1)–(3), an entity and a notice provider may agree that when the notice provider is directed by the court to give a notice, the notice provider shall give the notice to the entity in the manner agreed to and at the address or addresses the entity supplies to the notice provider. That address is conclusively presumed to be a proper address for the notice. The notice provider's failure to use the supplied address does not invalidate any notice that is otherwise effective under applicable law.

(5) A creditor may treat a notice as not having been brought to the creditor's attention under §342(g)(1) only if, prior to issuance of the notice, the creditor has filed a statement that designates the name and address of the person or organizational subdivision of the creditor responsible for receiving notices under the Code, and that describes the procedures established by the creditor to cause such notices to be delivered to the designated person or subdivision.

(h) Notices to Creditors Whose Claims are Filed.
(1) *Voluntary Case.* In a voluntary chapter 7 case, chapter 12 case, or chapter 13 case, after 70 days following the order for relief under that chapter or the date of the order converting the case to chapter 12 or chapter 13, the court may direct that all notices required by subdivision (a) of this rule be mailed only to:

- the debtor;
- the trustee;
- all indenture trustees;
- creditors that hold claims for which proofs of claim have been filed; and
- creditors, if any, that are still permitted to file claims because an extension was granted under Rule 3002(c)(1) or (c)2.

(2) *Involuntary Case.* In an involuntary chapter 7 case, after 90 days following the order for relief under that chapter, the court may direct that all notices required by subdivision (a) of this rule be mailed only to:

- the debtor;
- the trustee;
- all indenture trustees;
- creditors that hold claims for which proofs of claim have been filed; and
- creditors, if any, that are still permitted to file claims because an extension was granted under Rule 3002(c)(1) or (c)2.

(3) *Insufficient Assets.* In a case where notice of insufficient assets to pay a dividend has been given to creditors under subdivision (e) of this rule, after 90 days following the mailing of a notice of the time for filing claims under Rule 3002(c)(5), the court may direct that notices be mailed only to the entities specified in the preceding sentence.

(i) Notices to Committees. Copies of all notices required to be mailed pursuant to this rule shall be mailed to the committees elected under §705 or appointed under §1102 of the Code or to their authorized agents. Notwithstanding the foregoing subdivisions, the court may order that notices required by subdivision (a)(2), (3) and (6) of this rule be transmitted to the United States trustee and be mailed only to the committees elected under §705 or appointed under §1102 of the Code or to their authorized agents and to the creditors and equity security holders who serve on the trustee or debtor in possession and file a request that all notices be mailed to them. A committee appointed under §1114 shall receive copies of all notices required by subdivisions (a)(1), (a)(5), (b), (f)(2), and (f)(7), and such other notices as the court may direct.

(j) Notices to the United States. Copies of notices required to be mailed to all creditors under this rule shall be mailed (1) in a chapter 11 reorganization case, to the Securities and Exchange Commission at any place the Commission designates, if the Commission has filed either a notice of appearance in the case or a written request to receive notices; (2) in a commodity broker case, to the Commodity Futures Trading Commission at Washington, D.C.; (3) in a chapter 11 case, to the Internal Revenue Service at its address set out in the register maintained under Rule 5003(e) for the district in which the case is pending; (4) if the papers in the case disclose a debt to the United States other than for taxes, to the United States attorney for the district in which the case is pending and to the department, agency, or instrumentality of the United States through which the debtor became indebted; or (5) if the filed papers disclose a stock interest of the United States, to the Secretary of the Treasury at Washington, D.C.

(k) Notices to United States Trustee. Unless the case is a chapter 9 municipality case or unless the United States trustee requests otherwise, the clerk, or some other person as the court may direct, shall transmit to the United States trustee notice of the matters described in subdivisions (a)(2), (a)(3), (a)(4), (a)(8), (a)(9), (b), (f)(1), (f)(2), (f)(4), (f)(6), (f)(7), (f)(8), and (q) of this rule and notice of hearings on all applications for compensation or reimbursement of expenses. Notices to the United States trustee shall be transmitted within the time prescribed in subdivision (a) or (b) of this rule. The United States trustee shall also receive notice of any other matter if such notice is requested by the United States trustee or ordered by the court. Nothing in these rules requires the clerk or any other person to transmit to the United States trustee any notice, schedule, report, application or other document in a case under the Securities Investor Protection Act, 15 U.S.C. §78aaa et seq.

(l) Notice by Publication. The court may order notice by publication if it finds that notice by mail is impracticable or that it is desirable to supplement the notice.

(m) Orders Designating Matter of Notices. The court may from time to time enter orders designating the matters in respect to which, the entity to whom, and the form and manner in which notices shall be sent except as otherwise provided by these rules.

(n) Caption. The caption of every notice given under this rule shall comply with Rule 1005. The caption of every notice required to be given by the debtor to a creditor shall include the information required to be in the notice by §342(c) of the Code.

(o) Notice of Order for Relief in Consumer Case. In a voluntary case commenced by an individual debtor whose debts are primarily consumer debts, the clerk or some other person as the court may direct shall give the trustee and all creditors notice by mail of the order for relief within 21 days from the date thereof.

(p) Notice to a Creditor With a Foreign Address.

(1) If, at the request of the United States trustee or a party in interest, or on its own initiative, the court finds that a notice mailed within the time prescribed by these rules would not be sufficient to give a creditor with a foreign address to which notices under these rules are mailed reasonable notice under the circumstances, the court may order that the notice be supplemented with notice by other means or that the time prescribed for the notice by mail be enlarged.

(2) Unless the court for cause orders otherwise, a creditor with a foreign address to which notices under this rule are mailed shall be given at least 30 days' notice of the time fixed for filing a proof of claim under Rule 3002(c) or Rule 3003(c).

(3) Unless the court for cause orders otherwise, the mailing address of a creditor with a foreign address shall be determined under Rule 2002(g).

(q) Notice of Petition for Recognition of Foreign Proceeding and of Court's Intention to Communicate With Foreign Courts and Foreign Representatives.

(1) *Notice of Petition for Recognition.* After the filing of a petition for recognition of a foreign proceeding, the court shall promptly schedule and hold a hearing on the petition. The clerk, or some other person as the court may direct, shall forthwith give the debtor, all persons or bodies authorized to administer foreign proceedings of the debtor, all entities against whom provisional relief is being sought under §1519 of the Code, all parties to litigation pending in the United States in which the debtor is a party at the time of the filing of the petition, and such other entities as the court may direct, at least 21 days' notice by mail of the hearing. The notice shall state whether the petition seeks recognition as a foreign main proceeding or foreign nonmain proceeding and shall include the petition and any other document the court may require. If the court consolidates the hearing on the petition with the hearing on a request for provisional relief, the court may set a shorter notice period, with notice to the entities listed in this subdivision.

(2) *Notice of Court's Intention to Communicate with Foreign Courts and Foreign Representatives.* The clerk, or some other person as the court may direct, shall give the debtor, all persons or bodies authorized to administer foreign proceedings of the debtor, all entities against whom provisional relief is being sought under §1519 of the Code, all parties to litigation pending in the United States in which the debtor is a party at the time of the filing of the petition, and such other entities as the court may direct, notice by mail of the court's intention to communicate with a foreign court or foreign representative.

Rule 2003. Meeting of Creditors or Equity Security Holders

(a) Date and Place. Except as otherwise provided in §341(e) of the Code, in a chapter 7 liquidation or a chapter 11 reorganization case, the United States trustee shall call a meeting of creditors to be held no fewer than 21 and no more than 40 days after the order for relief. In a chapter 12 family farmer debt adjustment case, the United States trustee shall call a meeting of creditors to be held no fewer than 21 and no more than 35 days after the order for relief. In a chapter 13 individual's debt adjustment case, the United States trustee shall call a meeting of creditors to be held no fewer than 21 and no more than 50 days after the order for relief. If there is an appeal from or a motion to vacate the order for relief, or if there is a motion to dismiss the case, the United States trustee may set a later date for the meeting. The meeting may be held at a regular place for holding court or at any other place designated by the United States trustee within the district convenient for the parties in interest. If the United States trustee designates a place for the meeting which is not regularly staffed by the United States trustee or an assistant who may preside at the meeting, the meeting may be held not more than 60 days after the order for relief.

(b) Order of Meeting.

(1) *Meeting of Creditors.* The United States trustee shall preside at the meeting of creditors. The business of the meeting shall include the examination of the debtor under oath and, in a chapter 7 liquidation case, may include the election of a creditors' committee and, if the case is not under subchapter V of chapter 7, the election of a trustee. The presiding officer shall have the authority to administer oaths.

(2) *Meeting of Equity Security Holders.* If the United States trustee convenes a meeting of equity security holders pursuant to §341(b) of the Code, the United States trustee shall fix a date for the meeting and shall preside.

(3) *Right To Vote.* In a chapter 7 liquidation case, a creditor is entitled to vote at a meeting if, at or before the meeting, the creditor has filed a proof of claim or a writing setting forth facts evidencing a right to vote pursuant to §702(a) of the Code unless objection is made to the claim or the proof of claim is insufficient on its face. A creditor of a partnership may file a proof of claim or writing evidencing a right to vote for the trustee for the estate of the general partner notwithstanding that a trustee for the estate of the partnership has previously qualified. In the event of an objection to the amount or allowability of a claim for the purpose of voting, unless the court orders otherwise, the United States trustee shall tabulate the votes for each alternative presented by the dispute and, if resolution of such dispute is necessary to determine the result of the election, the tabulations for each alternative shall be reported to the court.

(c) Record of Meeting. Any examination under oath at the meeting of creditors held pursuant to §341(a) of the Code shall be recorded verbatim by the United States trustee using electronic sound recording equipment or other means of recording, and such record shall be preserved by the United States trustee and available for public access until two years after the conclusion of the meeting of creditors. Upon request of any entity, the United States trustee shall certify and provide a copy or transcript of such recording at the entity's expense.

(d) Report of Election and Resolution of Disputes in a Chapter 7 Case.

(1) *Report of Undisputed Election.* In a chapter 7 case, if the election of a trustee or a member of a creditors' committee is not disputed, the United States trustee shall promptly file a report of the election, including the name and address of the person or entity elected and a statement that the election is undisputed.

(2) *Disputed Election.* If the election is disputed, the United States trustee shall promptly file a report stating that the election is disputed, informing the court of the nature of the dispute, and listing the name and address of any candidate elected under any alternative presented by the dispute. No later than the date on which the report is filed, the United States trustee shall mail a copy of the report to any party in interest that has made a request to receive a copy of the report. Pending disposition by the court of a disputed election for trustee, the interim trustee shall continue in office. Unless a motion for the resolution of the dispute is filed no later than 14 days after the United States trustee files a report of a disputed election for trustee, the interim trustee shall serve as trustee in the case.

(e) Adjournment. The meeting may be adjourned from time to time by announcement at the meeting of the adjourned date and time. The presiding official shall promptly file a statement specifying the date and time to which the meeting is adjourned.

(f) Special Meetings. The United States trustee may call a special meeting of creditors on request of a party in interest or on the United States trustee's own initiative.

(g) Final Meeting. If the United States trustee calls a final meeting of creditors in a case in which the net proceeds realized exceed $1,500, the clerk shall mail a summary of the trustee's final account to the creditors with a notice of the meeting, together with a statement of the amount of the claims allowed. The trustee shall attend the final meeting and shall, if requested, report on the administration of the estate.

Rule 2004. Examination

(a) Examination on Motion. On motion of any party in interest, the court may order the examination of any entity.

(b) Scope of Examination. The examination of an entity under this rule or of the debtor under §343 of the Code may relate only to the acts, conduct, or property or to the liabilities and financial condition of the debtor, or to any matter which may affect the administration of the debtor's estate, or to the debtor's right to a discharge. In a family farmer's debt adjustment case under chapter 12, an individual's debt adjustment case under chapter 13, or a reorganization case under chapter 11 of the Code, other than for the reorganization of a railroad, the examination may also relate to the operation of any business and the desirability of its continuance, the source of any money or property acquired or to be acquired by the debtor for purposes of consummating a plan and the consideration given or offered therefor, and any other matter relevant to the case or to the formulation of a plan.

(c) Compelling Attendance and Production of Documents or Electronically Stored Information. The attendance of an entity for examination and for the production of documents or electronically stored information, whether the examination is to be conducted within or without the district in which the case is pending, may be compelled as provided in Rule 9016 for the attendance of a witness at a hearing or trial. As an officer of the court, an attorney may issue and sign a subpoena on behalf of the court where the case is pending if the attorney is admitted to practice in that court.

(d) Time and Place of Examination of Debtor. The court may for cause shown and on terms as it may impose order the debtor to be examined under this rule at any time or place it designates, whether within or without the district wherein the case is pending.

(e) Mileage. An entity other than a debtor shall not be required to attend as a witness unless lawful mileage and witness fee for one day's attendance shall be first tendered. If the debtor resides more than 100 miles from the place of examination when required to appear for an examination under this rule, the mileage allowed by law to a witness shall be tendered for any distance more than 100 miles from the debtor's residence at the date of the filing of the first petition commencing a case under the Code or the residence at the time the debtor is required to appear for the examination, whichever is the lesser.

Rule 2014. Employment of Professional Persons

(a) Application for and Order of Employment. An order approving the employment of attorneys, accountants, appraisers, auctioneers, agents, or other professionals pursuant to §327, §1103, or §1114 of the Code shall be made only on application of the trustee or committee. The application shall be filed and, unless the case is a chapter 9 municipality case, a copy of the application shall be transmitted by the applicant to the United States trustee. The application shall state the specific facts showing the necessity for the employment, the name of the person to be employed, the reasons for the selection, the professional services to be rendered, any proposed arrangement for compensation, and, to the best of the applicant's knowledge, all of the person's connections with the debtor, creditors, any other party in interest, their respective attorneys and accountants, the United States trustee, or any person employed in the office of the United States trustee. The application shall be accompanied by a verified statement of the person to be employed setting forth the person's connections with the debtor, creditors, any other party in interest, their respective attorneys and accountants, the United States trustee, or any person employed in the office of the United States trustee.

(b) Services Rendered by Member or Associate of Firm of Attorneys or Accountants. If, under the Code and this rule, a law partnership or corporation is employed as an attorney, or an accounting partnership or corporation is employed as an accountant, or if a named attorney or accountant is employed, any partner, member, or regular associate of the partnership, corporation, or individual may act as attorney or accountant so employed, without further order of the court.

Rule 2016. Compensation for Services Rendered and Reimbursement of Expenses

(a) Application for Compensation or Reimbursement. An entity seeking interim or final compensation for services, or reimbursement of necessary expenses, from the estate shall file an application setting forth a detailed statement of (1) the services rendered, time expended and expenses incurred, and (2) the amounts requested. An application for compensation shall include a statement as to what payments have theretofore been made or promised to the applicant for services rendered or to be rendered in any capacity whatsoever in connection with the case, the source of the compensation so paid or promised, whether any compensation previously received has been shared and whether an agreement or understanding exists between the applicant and any other entity for the sharing of compensation received or to be received for services rendered in or in connection with the case, and the particulars of any sharing of compensation or agreement or understanding therefor, except that details of any agreement by the applicant for the sharing of compensation as a member or regular associate of a firm of lawyers or accountants shall not be required. The requirements of this subdivision shall apply to an application for compensation for services rendered by an attorney or accountant even though the application is filed by a creditor or other entity. Unless the case is a chapter 9 municipality case, the applicant shall transmit to the United States trustee a copy of the application.

(b) Disclosure of Compensation Paid or Promised to Attorney for Debtor. Every attorney for a debtor, whether or not the attorney applies for compensation, shall file and transmit to the United States trustee within 14 days after the order for relief, or at another time as the court may direct, the statement required by §329 of the Code including whether the attorney has shared or agreed to share the compensation with any other entity. The statement shall include the particulars of any such sharing or agreement to share by the attorney, but the details of any agreement for the sharing of the compensation with a member or regular associate of the attorney's law firm shall not be required. A supplemental statement shall be filed and transmitted to the United States trustee within 14 days after any payment or agreement not previously disclosed.

(c) Disclosure of Compensation Paid or Promised to Bankruptcy Petition Preparer. Before a petition is filed, every bankruptcy petition preparer for a debtor shall deliver to the debtor, the declaration under penalty of perjury required by §110(h)(2). The declaration shall disclose any fee, and the source of any fee, received from or on behalf of the debtor within 12 months of the filing of the case and all unpaid fees charged to the debtor. The declaration shall also describe the services performed and documents prepared or caused to be prepared by the bankruptcy petition preparer. The declaration shall be filed with the petition. The petition preparer shall file a supplemental statement within 14 days after any payment or agreement not previously disclosed.

Rule 2017. Examination of Debtor's Transactions with Debtor's Attorney

(a) Payment or Transfer to Attorney Before Order for Relief. On motion by any party in interest or on the court's own initiative, the court after notice and a hearing may determine whether any payment of money or any transfer of property by the debtor, made directly or indirectly and in contemplation of the filing of a petition under the Code by or against the debtor or before entry of the order for relief in an involuntary case, to an attorney for services rendered or to be rendered is excessive.

(b) Payment or Transfer to Attorney After Order for Relief. On motion by the debtor, the United States trustee, or on the court's own initiative, the court after notice and a hearing may determine whether any payment of money or any transfer of property, or any agreement therefor, by the debtor to an attorney after entry of an order for relief in a case under the Code is excessive, whether the payment or transfer is made or is to be made directly or indirectly, if the payment, transfer, or agreement therefor is for services in any way related to the case.

Rule 2019. Disclosure Regarding Creditors and Equity Security Holders in Chapter 9 and Chapter 11 Cases

(a) Definitions. In this rule the following terms have the meanings indicated:

(1) "Disclosable economic interest" means any claim, interest, pledge, lien, option, participation, derivative instrument, or any other right or derivative right granting the holder an economic interest that is affected by the value, acquisition, or disposition of a claim or interest.

(2) "Represent" or "represents" means to take a position before the court or to solicit votes regarding the confirmation of a plan on behalf of another.

(b) Disclosure by Groups, Committees, and Entities.

(1) In a chapter 9 or 11 case, a verified statement setting forth the information specified in subdivision (c) of this rule shall be filed by every group or committee that consists of or represents, and every entity that represents, multiple creditors or equity security holders that are (A) acting in concert to advance their common interests, and (B) not composed entirely of affiliates or insiders of one another.

(2) Unless the court orders otherwise, an entity is not required to file the verified statement described in paragraph (1) of this subdivision solely because of its status as:

(A) an indenture trustee;

(B) an agent for one or more other entities under an agreement for the extension of credit;

(C) a class action representative; or

(D) a governmental unit that is not a person.

(c) Information Required. The verified statement shall include:

(1) the pertinent facts and circumstances concerning:

(A) with respect to a group or committee, other than a committee appointed under §1102 or §1114 of the Code, the formation of the group or committee, including the name of each entity at whose instance the group or committee was formed or for whom the group or committee has agreed to act; or

(B) with respect to an entity, the employment of the entity, including the name of each creditor or equity security holder at whose instance the employment was arranged;

(2) if not disclosed under subdivision (c)(1), with respect to an entity, and with respect to each member of a group or committee:

(A) name and address;

(B) the nature and amount of each disclosable economic interest held in relation to the debtor as of the date the entity was employed or the group or committee was formed; and

(C) with respect to each member of a group or committee that claims to represent any entity in addition to the members of the group or committee, other than a committee appointed under §1102 or §1114 of the Code, the date of acquisition by quarter and year of each disclosable economic interest, unless acquired more than one year before the petition was filed;

(3) if not disclosed under subdivision (c)(1) or (c)(2), with respect to each creditor or equity security holder represented by an entity, group, or committee, other than a committee appointed under §1102 or §1114 of the Code:

(A) name and address; and

(B) the nature and amount of each disclosable economic interest held in relation to the debtor as of the date of the statement; and

(4) a copy of the instrument, if any, authorizing the entity, group, or committee to act on behalf of creditors or equity security holders.

(d) Supplemental Statements. If any fact disclosed in its most recently filed statement has changed materially, an entity, group, or committee shall file a verified supplemental statement whenever it takes a position before the court or solicits votes on the confirmation of a plan. The supplemental statement shall set forth the material changes in the facts required by subdivision (c) to be disclosed.

(e) Determination of Failure to Comply; Sanctions.

(1) On motion of any party in interest, or on its own motion, the court may determine whether there has been a failure to comply with any provision of this rule.

(2) If the court finds such a failure to comply, it may:

(A) refuse to permit the entity, group, or committee to be heard or to intervene in the case;

(B) hold invalid any authority, acceptance, rejection, or objection given, procured, or received by the entity, group, or committee; or

(C) grant other appropriate relief.

Rule 3014. Election Under §1111(b) by Secured Creditor in Chapter 9 Municipality or Chapter 11 Reorganization Case

An election of application of §1111(b)(2) of the Code by a class of secured creditors in a chapter 9 or 11 case may be made at any time prior to the conclusion of the hearing on the disclosure statement or within such later time as the court may fix. If the disclosure statement is conditionally approved pursuant to Rule 3017.1, and a final hearing on the disclosure statement is not held, the election of application of §1111(b)(2) may be made not later than the date fixed pursuant to Rule 3017.1(a)(2) or another date the court may fix. In a case under subchapter V of chapter 11 in which § 1125 of the Code does not apply, the election may be made not later than a date the court may fix. The election shall be in writing and signed unless made at the hearing on the disclosure statement. The election, if made by the majorities required by §1111(b)(1)(A)(i), shall be binding on all members of the class with respect to the plan.

Rule 4001. Relief from Automatic Stay; Prohibiting or Conditioning the Use, Sale, or Lease of Property; Use of Cash Collateral; Obtaining Credit; Agreements

(a) Relief From Stay; Prohibiting or Conditioning the Use, Sale, or Lease of Property.

(1) *Motion.* A motion for relief from an automatic stay provided by the Code or a motion to prohibit or condition the use, sale, or lease of property pursuant to §363(e) shall be made in accordance with Rule 9014 and shall be served on any committee elected pursuant to §705 or appointed pursuant to §1102 of the Code or its authorized agent, or, if the case is a chapter 9municipality case or a chapter 11 reorganization case and no committee of unsecured creditors has been appointed pursuant to §1102, on the creditors included on the list filed pursuant to Rule 1007(d), and on such other entities as the court may direct.

(2) *Ex Parte Relief.* Relief from a stay under §362(a) or a request to prohibit or condition the use, sale, or lease of property pursuant to §363(e) may be granted without prior notice only if (A) it clearly appears from specific facts shown by affidavit or by a verified motion that immediate and irreparable injury, loss, or damage will result to the movant before the adverse party or the attorney for the adverse party can be heard in opposition, and (B) the movant's attorney certifies to the court in writing the efforts, if any, which have been made to give notice and the reasons why notice should not be required. The party obtaining relief under this subdivision and §362(f) or §363(e) shall immediately give oral notice thereof to the trustee or debtor in possession and to the debtor and forthwith mail or otherwise transmit to such adverse party or parties a copy of the order granting relief. On two days' notice to the party who obtained relief from the stay without notice or on shorter notice to that party as the court may prescribe, the adverse party may appear and move reinstatement of the stay or reconsideration of the order prohibiting or conditioning the use, sale, or lease of property. In that event, the court shall proceed expeditiously to hear and determine the motion.

(3) *Stay of Order.* An order granting a motion for relief from an automatic stay made in accordance with Rule 4001(a)(1) is stayed until the expiration of 14 days after the entry of the order, unless the court orders otherwise.

(b) Use of Cash Collateral.

(1) *Motion; Service.*

(A) *Motion.* A motion for authority to use cash collateral shall be made in accordance with Rule 9014 and shall be accompanied by a proposed form of order.

(B) *Contents.* The motion shall consist of or (if the motion is more than five pages in length) begin with a concise statement of the relief requested, not to exceed five pages, that lists or summarizes, and sets out the location within the relevant documents of, all material provisions, including:

(i) the name of each entity with an interest in the cash collateral;

(ii) the purposes for the use of the cash collateral;

(iii) the material terms, including duration, of the use of the cash collateral; and

(iv) any liens, cash payments, or other adequate protection that will be provided to each entity with an interest in the cash collateral or, if no additional adequate protection is proposed, an explanation of why each entity's interest is adequately protected.

(C) *Service.* The motion shall be served on: (1) any entity with an interest in the cash collateral; (2) any committee elected under §705 or appointed under §1102 of the Code, or its authorized agent, or, if the case is a chapter 9 municipality case or a chapter 11 reorganization case and no committee of unsecured creditors has been appointed under §1102, the creditors included on the list filed under Rule 1007(d); and (3) any other entity that the court directs.

(2) *Hearing*. The court may commence a final hearing on a motion for authorization to use cash collateral no earlier than 14 days after service of the motion. If the motion so requests, the court may conduct a preliminary hearing before such 14-day period expires, but the court may authorize the use of only that amount of cash collateral as is necessary to avoid immediate and irreparable harm to the estate pending a final hearing.

(3) *Notice*. Notice of hearing pursuant to this subdivision shall be given to the parties on whom service of the motion is required by paragraph (1) of this subdivision and to such other entities as the court may direct.

(c) Obtaining Credit.

(1) *Motion; Service.*

(A) *Motion*. A motion for authority to obtain credit shall be made in accordance with Rule 9014 and shall be accompanied by a copy of the credit agreement and a proposed form of order.

(B) *Contents*. The motion shall consist of or (if the motion is more than five pages in length) begin with a concise statement of the relief requested, not to exceed five pages, that lists or summarizes, and sets out the location within the relevant documents of, all material provisions of the proposed credit agreement and form of order, including interest rate, maturity, events of default, liens, borrowing limits, and borrowing conditions. If the proposed credit agreement or form of order includes any of the provisions listed below, the concise statement shall also: briefly list or summarize each one; identify its specific location in the proposed agreement and form of order; and identify any such provision that is proposed to remain in effect if interim approval is granted, but final relief is denied, as provided under Rule 4001(c)(2). In addition, the motion shall describe the nature and extent of each provision listed below:

(i) a grant of priority or a lien on property of the estate under §364(c) or (d);

(ii) the providing of adequate protection or priority for a claim that arose before the commencement of the case, including the granting of a lien on property of the estate to secure the claim, or the use of property of the estate or credit obtained under §364 to make cash payments on account of the claim;

(iii) a determination of the validity, enforceability, priority, or amount of a claim that arose before the commencement of the case, or of any lien securing the claim;

(iv) a waiver or modification of Code provisions or applicable rules relating to the automatic stay;

(v) a waiver or modification of any entity's authority or right to file a plan, seek an extension of time in which the debtor has the exclusive right to file a plan, request the use of cash collateral under §363(c), or request authority to obtain credit under §364;

(vi) the establishment of deadlines for filing a plan of reorganization, for approval of a disclosure statement, for a hearing on confirmation, or for entry of a confirmation order;

(vii) a waiver or modification of the applicability of nonbankruptcy law relating to the perfection of a lien on property of the estate, or on the foreclosure or other enforcement of the lien;

(viii) a release, waiver, or limitation on any claim or other cause of action belonging to the estate or the trustee, including any modification of the statute of limitations or other deadline to commence an action;

(ix) the indemnification of any entity;

(x) a release, waiver, or limitation of any right under §506(c); or

(xi) the granting of a lien on any claim or cause of action arising under §§544, 545, 547, 548, 549, 553(b), 723(a), or 724(a).

(C) *Service*. The motion shall be served on: (1) any committee elected under §705 or appointed under §1102 of the Code, or its authorized agent, or, if the case is a chapter 9 municipality case or a chapter 11 reorganization case and no committee of unsecured creditors has been appointed under §1102, on the creditors included on the list filed under Rule 1007(d); and (2) on any other entity that the court directs.

(2) *Hearing.* The court may commence a final hearing on a motion for authority to obtain credit no earlier than 14 days after service of the motion. If the motion so requests, the court may conduct a hearing before such 14-day period expires, but the court may authorize the obtaining of credit only to the extent necessary to avoid immediate and irreparable harm to the estate pending a final hearing.

(3) *Notice.* Notice of hearing pursuant to this subdivision shall be given to the parties on whom service of the motion is required by paragraph (1) of this subdivision and to such other entities as the court may direct.

(4) *Inapplicability in a Chapter 13 Case.* This subdivision (c) does not apply in a chapter 13 case.

(d) Agreement Relating to Relief From the Automatic Stay, Prohibiting or Conditioning the Use, Sale, or Lease of Property, Providing Adequate Protection, Use of Cash Collateral, and Obtaining Credit.

(1) *Motion; Service.*

(A) *Motion.* A motion for approval of any of the following shall be accompanied by a copy of the agreement and a proposed form of order:

(i) an agreement to provide adequate protection;

(ii) an agreement to prohibit or condition the use, sale, or lease of property;

(iii) an agreement to modify or terminate the stay provided for in §362;

(iv) an agreement to use cash collateral; or

(v) an agreement between the debtor and an entity that has a lien or interest in property of the estate pursuant to which the entity consents to the creation of a lien senior or equal to the entity's lien or interest in such property.

(B) *Contents.* The motion shall consist of or (if the motion is more than five pages in length) begin with a concise statement of the relief requested, not to exceed five pages, that lists or summarizes, and sets out the location within the relevant documents of, all material provisions of the agreement. In addition, the concise statement shall briefly list or summarize, and identify the specific location of, each provision in the proposed form of order, agreement, or other document of the type listed in subdivision (c)(1)(B). The motion shall also describe the nature and extent of each such provision.

(C) *Service.* The motion shall be served on: (1) any committee elected under §705 or appointed under §1102 of the Code, or its authorized agent, or, if the case is a chapter 9 municipality case or a chapter 11 reorganization case and no committee of unsecured creditors has been appointed under §1102, on the creditors included on the list filed under Rule 1007(d); and (2) on any other entity the court directs.

(2) *Objection.* Notice of the motion and the time within which objections may be filed and served on the debtor in possession or trustee shall be mailed to the parties on whom service is required by paragraph (1) of this subdivision and to such other entities as the court may direct. Unless the court fixes a different time, objections may be filed within 14 days of the mailing of the notice.

(3) *Disposition; Hearing.* If no objection is filed, the court may enter an order approving or disapproving the agreement without conducting a hearing. If an objection is filed or if the court determines a hearing is appropriate, the court shall hold a hearing on no less than seven days' notice to the objector, the movant, the parties on whom service is required by paragraph (1) of this subdivision and such other entities as the court may direct.

(4) *Agreement in Settlement of Motion.* The court may direct that the procedures prescribed in paragraphs (1), (2), and (3) of this subdivision shall not apply and the agreement may be approved without further notice if the court determines that a motion made pursuant to subdivisions (a), (b), or (c) of this rule was sufficient to afford reasonable notice of the material provisions of the agreement and opportunity for a hearing.

Rule 4005. Burden of Proof in Objecting to Discharge

At the trial on a complaint objecting to a discharge, the plaintiff has the burden of proving the objection.

Rule 4007. Determination of Dischargeability of a Debt

(a) Persons Entitled To File Complaint. A debtor or any creditor may file a complaint to obtain a determination of the dischargeability of any debt.

(b) Time for Commencing Proceeding Other Than Under §523(c) of the Code. A complaint other than under §523(c) may be filed at any time. A case may be reopened without payment of an additional filing fee for the purpose of filing a complaint to obtain a determination under this rule.

(c) Time for Filing Complaint Under §523(c) in a Chapter 7 Liquidation, Chapter 11 Reorganization, Chapter 12 Family Farmer's Debt Adjustment Case, or Chapter 13 Individual's Debt Adjustment Case; Notice of Time Fixed. Except as otherwise provided in subdivision (d), a complaint to determine the dischargeability of a debt under §523(c) shall be filed no later than 60 days after the first date set for the meeting of creditors under §341(a). The court shall give all creditors no less than 30 days' notice of the time so fixed in the manner provided in Rule 2002. On motion of a party in interest, after hearing on notice, the court may for cause extend the time fixed under this subdivision. The motion shall be filed before the time has expired.

(d) Time for Filing Complaint Under §523(a)(6) in a Chapter 13 Individual's Debt Adjustment Case; Notice of Time Fixed. On motion by a debtor for a discharge under §1328(b), the court shall enter an order fixing the time to file a complaint to determine the dischargeability of any debt under §523(a)(6) and shall give no less than 30 days' notice of the time fixed to all creditors in the manner provided in Rule 2002. On motion of any party in interest, after hearing on notice, the court may for cause extend the time fixed under this subdivision. The motion shall be filed before the time has expired.

(e) Applicability of Rules in Part VII. A proceeding commenced by a complaint filed under this rule is governed by Part VII of these rules.

Rule 7001. Scope of Rules of Part VII

An adversary proceeding is governed by the rules of this Part VII. The following are adversary proceedings:

(1) a proceeding to recover money or property, other than a proceeding to compel the debtor to deliver property to the trustee, or a proceeding under §554(b) or §725 of the Code, Rule 2017, or Rule 6002;

(2) a proceeding to determine the validity, priority, or extent of a lien or other interest in property, but not a proceeding under Rule 3012 or Rule 4003(d);

(3) a proceeding to obtain approval under §363(h) for the sale of both the interest of the estate and of a co-owner in property;

(4) a proceeding to object to or revoke a discharge, other than an objection to discharge under §§727(a)(8),[1] (a)(9), or 1328(f);

(5) a proceeding to revoke an order of confirmation of a chapter 11, chapter 12, or chapter 13 plan;

(6) a proceeding to determine the dischargeability of a debt;

(7) a proceeding to obtain an injunction or other equitable relief, except when a chapter 9, chapter 11, chapter 12, or chapter 13 plan provides for the relief;

(8) a proceeding to subordinate any allowed claim or interest, except when a chapter 9, chapter 11, chapter 12, or chapter 13 plan provides for subordination;

(9) a proceeding to obtain a declaratory judgment relating to any of the foregoing; or

(10) a proceeding to determine a claim or cause of action removed under 28 U.S.C. §1452

Rule 8002. Time for Filing Notice of Appeal

(a) In General.

(1) *Fourteen-Day Period.* Except as provided in subdivisions (b) and (c), a notice of appeal must be filed with the bankruptcy clerk within 14 days after entry of the judgment, order, or decree being appealed.

(2) *Filing Before the Entry of Judgment.* A notice of appeal filed after the bankruptcy court announces a decision or order—but before entry of the judgment, order, or decree—is treated as filed on the date of and after the entry.

(3) *Multiple Appeals.* If one party files a timely notice of appeal, any other party may file a notice of appeal within 14 days after the date when the first notice was filed, or within the time otherwise allowed by this rule, whichever period ends later.

(4) *Mistaken Filing in Another Court.* If a notice of appeal is mistakenly filed in a district court, BAP, or court of appeals, the clerk

of that court must state on the notice the date on which it was received and transmit it to the bankruptcy clerk. The notice of appeal is then considered filed in the bankruptcy court on the date so stated.

(5) *Entry Defined.*

(A) A judgment, order, or decree is entered for purposes of this Rule 8002(a):

(i) when it is entered in the docket under Rule 5003(a), or

(ii) if Rule 7058 applies and Rule 58(a) F.R.Civ.P. requires a separate document, when the judgment, order, or decree is entered in the docket under Rule 5003(a) and when the earlier of these events occurs:

- the judgment, order, or decree is set out in a separate document; or
- 150 days have run from entry of the judgment, order, or decree in the docket under Rule 5003(a).

(B) A failure to set out a judgment, order, or decree in a separate document when required by Rule 58(a) F.R.Civ.P. does not affect the validity of an appeal from that judgment, order, or decree.

(b) Effect of a Motion on the Time to Appeal.

(1) *In General.* If a party files in the bankruptcy court any of the following motions and does so within the time allowed by these rules, the time to file an appeal runs for all parties from the entry of the order disposing of the last such remaining motion:

(A) to amend or make additional findings under Rule 7052, whether or not granting the motion would alter the judgment;

(B) to alter or amend the judgment under Rule 9023;

(C) for a new trial under Rule 9023; or

(D) for relief under Rule 9024 if the motion is filed within 14 days after the judgment is entered

(2) *Filing an Appeal Before the Motion is Decided.* If a party files a notice of appeal after the court announces or enters a judgment, order, or decree—but before it disposes of any motion listed in subdivision (b)(1)—the notice becomes effective when the order disposing of the last such remaining motion is entered.

(3) *Appealing the Ruling on the Motion.* If a party intends to challenge an order disposing of any motion listed in subdivision (b)(1)—or the alteration or amendment of a judgment, order, or decree upon the motion—the party must file a notice of appeal or an amended notice of appeal. The notice or amended notice must comply with Rule 8003 or 8004 and be filed within the time prescribed by this rule, measured from the entry of the order disposing of the last such remaining motion.

(4) *No Additional Fee.* No additional fee is required to file an amended notice of appeal.

(c) Appeal by an Inmate Confined in an Institution.

(1) *In General.* If an institution has a system designed for legal mail, an inmate confined there must use that system to receive the benefit of this Rule 8002(c)(1). If an inmate files a notice of appeal from a judgment, order, or decree of a bankruptcy court, the notice is timely if it is deposited in the institution's internal mail system on or before the last day for filing and:

(A) it is accompanied by:

(i) a declaration in compliance with 28 U.S.C. § 1746—or a notarized statement—setting out the date of deposit and stating that first-class postage is being prepaid; or

(ii) evidence (such as a postmark or date stamp) showing that the notice was so deposited and that postage was prepaid; or

(B) the appellate court exercises its discretion to permit the later filing of a declaration or notarized statement that satisfies Rule 8002(c)(1)(A)(i).

(2) *Multiple Appeals.* If an inmate files under this subdivision the first notice of appeal, the 14-day period provided in subdivision (a)(3) for another party to file a notice of appeal runs from the date when the bankruptcy clerk dockets the first notice.

(d) Extending the Time to Appeal.

(1) *When the Time May be Extended.* Except as provided in subdivision (d)(2), the bankruptcy court may extend the time to file a notice of appeal upon a party's motion that is filed:

(A) within the time prescribed by this rule; or

(B) within 21 days after that time, if the party shows excusable neglect.

(2) *When the Time May Not be Extended.* The bankruptcy court may not extend the time to file a notice of appeal if the judgment, order, or decree appealed from:

(A) grants relief from an automatic stay under §362, 922, 1201, or 1301 of the Code;

(B) authorizes the sale or lease of property or the use of cash collateral under §363 of the Code;

(C) authorizes the obtaining of credit under §364 of the Code;

(D) authorizes the assumption or assignment of an executory contract or unexpired lease under §365 of the Code;

(E) approves a disclosure statement under §1125 of the Code; or

(F) confirms a plan under §943, 1129, 1225, or 1325 of the Code.

(3) *Time Limits on an Extension.* No extension of time may exceed 21 days after the time prescribed by this rule, or 14 days after the order granting the motion to extend time is entered, whichever is later.

Rule 8007. Stay Pending Appeal; Bonds; Suspension of Proceedings

(a) Initial Motion in the Bankruptcy Court.

(1) *In General.* Ordinarily, a party must move first in the bankruptcy court for the following relief:

(A) a stay of a judgment, order, or decree of the bankruptcy court pending appeal;

(B) the approval of a bond or other security provided to obtain a stay of judgment;

(C) an order suspending, modifying, restoring, or granting an injunction while an appeal is pending; or

(D) the suspension or continuation of proceedings in a case or other relief permitted by subdivision (e).

(2) *Time to File.* The motion may be made either before or after the notice of appeal is filed.

(b) Motion in the District Court, the BAP, or the Court of Appeals on Direct Appeal.

(1) *Request for Relief.* A motion for the relief specified in subdivision (a)(1)—or to vacate or modify a bankruptcy court's order granting such relief—may be made in the court where the appeal is pending.

(2) *Showing or Statement Required.* The motion must:

(A) show that moving first in the bankruptcy court would be impracticable; or

(B) if a motion was made in the bankruptcy court, either state that the court has not yet ruled on the motion, or state that the court has ruled and set out any reasons given for the ruling.

(3) *Additional Content.* The motion must also include:

(A) the reasons for granting the relief requested and the facts relied upon;

(B) affidavits or other sworn statements supporting facts subject to dispute; and

(C) relevant parts of the record.

(4) *Serving Notice.* The movant must give reasonable notice of the motion to all parties.

(c) Filing a Bond or Other Security. The district court, BAP, or court of appeals may condition relief on filing a bond or other security with the bankruptcy court.

(d) Bond or Other Security for a Trustee or the United States. The court may require a trustee to file a bond or other security when the trustee appeals. A bond or other security is not required when an appeal is taken by the United States, its officer, or its agency or by direction of any department of the federal government.

(e) Continuation of Proceedings in the Bankruptcy Court. Despite Rule 7062 and subject to the authority of the district court, BAP, or court of appeals, the bankruptcy court may:

(1) suspend or order the continuation of other proceedings in the case; or

(2) issue any other appropriate orders during the pendency of an appeal to protect the rights of all parties in interest.

Rule 9014. Contested Matters

(a) **Motion.** In a contested matter not otherwise governed by these rules, relief shall be requested by motion, and reasonable notice and opportunity for hearing shall be afforded the party against whom relief is sought. No response is required under this rule unless the court directs otherwise.

(b) Service. The motion shall be served in the manner provided for service of a summons and complaint by Rule 7004 and within the time determined under Rule 9006(d). Any written response to the motion shall be served within the time determined under Rule 9006(d). Any paper served after the motion shall be served in the manner provided by Rule 5(b) F.R.Civ.P.

(c) Application of Part VII Rules. Except as otherwise provided in this rule, and unless the court directs otherwise, the following rules shall apply: 7009, 7017, 7021, 7025, 7026, 7028–7037, 7041, 7042, 7052, 7054–7056, 7064, 7069, and 7071. The following subdivisions of Fed. R. Civ. P. 26, as incorporated by Rule 7026, shall not apply in a contested matter unless the court directs otherwise: 26(a)(1) (mandatory disclosure), 26(a)(2) (disclosures regarding expert testimony) and 26(a)(3) (additional pre-trial disclosure), and 26(f) (mandatory meeting before scheduling conference/discovery plan). An entity that desires to perpetuate testimony may proceed in the same manner as provided in Rule 7027 for the taking of a deposition before an adversary proceeding. The court may at any stage in a particular matter direct that one or more of the other rules in Part VII shall apply. The court shall give the parties notice of any order issued under this paragraph to afford them a reasonable opportunity to comply with the procedures prescribed by the order.

(d) Testimony of Witnesses. Testimony of witnesses with respect to disputed material factual issues shall be taken in the same manner as testimony in an adversary proceeding.

(e) Attendance of Witnesses. The court shall provide procedures that enable parties to ascertain at a reasonable time before any scheduled hearing whether the hearing will be an evidentiary hearing at which witnesses may testify.

Rule 9029. Local Bankruptcy Rules; Procedure When There is No Controlling Law

(a) Local Bankruptcy Rules.

(1) Each district court acting by a majority of its district judges may make and amend rules governing practice and procedure in all cases and proceedings within the district court's bankruptcy jurisdiction which are consistent with—but not duplicative of—Acts of Congress and these rules and which do not prohibit or limit the use of the Official Forms. Rule 83 F.R.Civ.P. governs the procedure for making local rules. A district court may authorize the bankruptcy judges of the district, subject to any limitation or condition it may prescribe and the requirements of 83 F.R.Civ.P., to make and amend rules of practice and procedure which are consistent with—but not duplicative of—Acts of Congress and these rules and which do not prohibit or limit the use of the Official Forms. Local rules shall conform to any uniform numbering system prescribed by the Judicial Conference of the United States.

(2) A local rule imposing a requirement of form shall not be enforced in a manner that causes a party to lose rights because of a nonwillful failure to comply with the requirement.

(b) Procedure When There is No Controlling Law. A judge may regulate practice in any manner consistent with federal law, these rules, Official Forms, and local rules of the district. No sanction or other disadvantage may be imposed for noncompliance with any requirement not in federal law, federal rules, Official Forms, or the local rules of the district unless the alleged violator has been furnished in the particular case with actual notice of the requirement.

TITLE 18—CRIMES AND CRIMINAL PROCEDURE

CHAPTER 9—BANKRUPTCY

Section
151. Definition
152. Concealment of Assets; False Oaths and Claims; Bribery
156. Knowing Disregard of Bankruptcy Law or Rule
157. Bankruptcy Fraud
158. Designation of United States Attorneys and Agents of the Federal Bureau of Investigation to Address Abusive Reaffirmations of Debt and Materially Fraudulent Statements in Bankruptcy Schedules

CHAPTER 203—ARREST AND COMMITMENT

Section
3057. Bankruptcy Investigations

CHAPTER 213—LIMITATIONS

Section
3284. Concealment of Bankrupt's Assets

CHAPTER 9— BANKRUPTCY

§ 151. Definition.

As used in this chapter, the term "debtor" means a debtor concerning whom a petition has been filed under title 11.

§ 152. Concealment of Assets; False Oaths and Claims; Bribery.

A person who—

(1) knowingly and fraudulently conceals from a custodian, trustee, marshal, or other officer of the court charged with the control or custody of property, or, in connection with a case under title 11, from creditors or the United States Trustee, any property belonging to the estate of a debtor;

(2) knowingly and fraudulently makes a false oath or account in or in relation to any case under title 11;

(3) knowingly and fraudulently makes a false declaration, certificate, verification, or statement under penalty of perjury as permitted under section 1746 of title 28, in or in relation to any case under title 11;

(4) knowingly and fraudulently presents any false claim for proof against the estate of a debtor, or uses any such claim in any case under title 11, in a personal capacity or as or through an agent, proxy, or attorney;

(5) knowingly and fraudulently receives any material amount of property from a debtor after the filing of a case under title 11, with intent to defeat the provisions of title 11;

(6) knowingly and fraudulently gives, offers, receives, or attempts to obtain any money or property, remuneration, compensation, reward, advantage, or promise thereof for acting or forbearing to act in any case under title 11;

(7) in a personal capacity or as an agent or officer of any person or corporation, in contemplation of a case under title 11 by or against the person or any other person or corporation, or with intent to defeat the provisions of title 11, knowingly and fraudulently transfers or conceals any of his property or the property of such other person or corporation;

(8) after the filing of a case under title 11 or in contemplation thereof, knowingly and fraudulently conceals, destroys, mutilates, falsifies, or makes a false entry in any recorded information (including books, documents, records, and papers) relating to the property or financial affairs of a debtor; or

(9) after the filing of a case under title 11, knowingly and fraudulently withholds from a custodian, trustee, marshal, or other officer of the court or a United States Trustee entitled to its possession, any recorded information (including books, documents, records, and

papers) relating to the property or financial affairs of a debtor,

shall be fined under this title, imprisoned not more than 5 years, or both.

§ 156. Knowing Disregard of Bankruptcy Law or Rule.

(a) Definitions.—In this section—

(1) the term "bankruptcy petition preparer" means a person, other than the debtor's attorney or an employee of such an attorney, who prepares for compensation a document for filing; and

(2) the term "document for filing" means a petition or any other document prepared for filing by a debtor in a United States bankruptcy court or a United States district court in connection with a case under title 11.

(b) Offense.—If a bankruptcy case or related proceeding is dismissed because of a knowing attempt by a bankruptcy petition preparer in any manner to disregard the requirements of title 11, United States Code, or the Federal Rules of Bankruptcy Procedure, the bankruptcy petition preparer shall be fined under this title, imprisoned not more than 1 year, or both.

§ 157. Bankruptcy Fraud.

A person who, having devised or intending to devise a scheme or artifice to defraud and for the purpose of executing or concealing such a scheme or artifice or attempting to do so—

(1) files a petition under title 11, including a fraudulent involuntary petition under section 303 of such title;

(2) files a document in a proceeding under title 11; or

(3) makes a false or fraudulent representation, claim, or promise concerning or in relation to a proceeding under title 11, at any time before or after the filing of the petition, or in relation to a proceeding falsely asserted to be pending under such title,

shall be fined under this title, imprisoned not more than 5 years, or both.

§ 158. Designation of United States Attorneys and Agents of the Federal Bureau of Investigation to Address Abusive Reaffirmations of Debt and Materially Fraudulent Statements in Bankruptcy Schedules.

(a) In General.—The Attorney General of the United States shall designate the individuals described in subsection (b) to have primary responsibility in carrying out enforcement activities in addressing violations of section 152 or 157 relating to abusive reaffirmations of debt. In addition to addressing the violations referred to in the preceding sentence, the individuals described under subsection (b) shall address violations of section 152 or 157 relating to materially fraudulent statements in bankruptcy schedules that are intentionally false or intentionally misleading.

(b) United States Attorneys and Agents of the Federal Bureau of Investigation.—The individuals referred to in subsection (a) are—

(1) the United States attorney for each judicial district of the United States; and

(2) an agent of the Federal Bureau of Investigation for each field office of the Federal Bureau of Investigation.

(c) Bankruptcy Investigations.—Each United States attorney designated under this section shall, in addition to any other responsibilities, have primary responsibility for carrying out the duties of a United States attorney under section 3057.

(d) Bankruptcy Procedures.—The bankruptcy courts shall establish procedures for referring any case that may contain a materially fraudulent statement in a bankruptcy schedule to the individuals designated under this section.

CHAPTER 203—ARREST AND COMMITMENT

§ 3057. Bankruptcy Investigations.

(a) Any judge, receiver, or trustee having reasonable grounds for believing that any violation under chapter 9 of this title or other laws of the United States relating to insolvent debtors, receiverships or reorganization plans has been committed, or that an investigation should be had in connection therewith, shall report to the appropriate United States attorney all the facts and circumstances of the case, the names of the witnesses and the offense or offenses believed to have been committed. Where one of such officers has made such report, the others need not do so.

(b) The United States attorney thereupon shall inquire into the facts and report thereon to the referee, and if it appears probable that any such offense has been committed, shall without delay, present the matter to the grand jury, unless upon inquiry and examination he decides that the ends of public justice do not require investigation or prosecution, in which case he shall report the facts to the Attorney General for his direction.

CHAPTER 213—LIMITATIONS

§ 3284. Concealment of Bankrupt's Assets.

The concealment of assets of a debtor in a case under title 11 shall be deemed to be a continuing offense until the debtor shall have been finally discharged or a discharge denied, and the period of limitations shall not begin to run until such final discharge or denial of discharge.

TITLE 28—JUDICIARY AND JUDICIAL PROCEDURE

PART I—ORGANIZATION OF COURTS

CHAPTER 6—BANKRUPTCY JUDGES

Section
151. Designation of Bankruptcy Courts
152. Appointment of Bankruptcy Judges
157. Procedures
158. Appeals
159. Bankruptcy Statistics

PART II—DEPARTMENT OF JUSTICE

CHAPTER 39—UNITED STATES TRUSTEES

Section
581. United States Trustees
586. Duties; Supervision by Attorney General
589b. Bankruptcy Data

PART III—COURT OFFICERS AND EMPLOYEES

CHAPTER 57—GENERAL PROVISIONS APPLICABLE TO COURT OFFICERS AND EMPLOYEES

Section
959. Trustees and Receivers Suable; Management; State Laws

PART IV—JURISDICTION AND VENUE

CHAPTER 85—DISTRICT COURTS; JURISDICTION

Section
1334. Bankruptcy Cases and Proceedings

CHAPTER 87—DISTRICT COURTS; VENUE

Section
1408. Venue of Cases under Title 11
1409. Venue of Proceedings Arising under Title 11 or Arising in or Related to Cases under Title 11
1410. Venue of Cases Ancillary to Foreign Proceedings
1411. Jury Trials
1412. Change of Venue

CHAPTER 89—DISTRICT COURTS; REMOVAL OF CASES FROM STATE COURTS

Section
1452. Removal of Claims Related to Bankruptcy Cases

CHAPTER 6—BANKRUPTCY JUDGES

§ 151. Designation of Bankruptcy Courts.

In each judicial district, the bankruptcy judges in regular active service shall constitute a unit of the district court to be known as the bankruptcy court for that district. Each bankruptcy judge, as a judicial officer of the district court, may exercise the authority conferred under this chapter with respect to any action, suit, or proceeding and may preside alone and hold a regular or special session of the court, except as otherwise provided by law or by rule or order of the district court.

§ 152. Appointment of Bankruptcy Judges.

(a) (1) Each bankruptcy judge to be appointed for a judicial district, as provided in paragraph (2), shall be appointed by the court of appeals of the United States for the circuit in which such district is located. Such appointments shall be made after considering the recommendations of the Judicial Conference submitted pursuant to subsection (b). Each bankruptcy judge shall be appointed for a term of fourteen years, subject to the provisions of subsection (e). However, upon the expiration of the term, a bankruptcy judge may, with the approval of the judicial council of the circuit, continue to perform the duties of the office until the earlier of the date which is 180 days after the expiration of the term or the date of the appointment of a successor. Bankruptcy judges shall serve as judicial officers of the United States district court established under Article III of the Constitution.

§ 157. Procedures.

(a) Each district court may provide that any or all cases under title 11 and any or all proceedings arising under title 11 or arising in or related to a case under title 11 shall be referred to the bankruptcy judges for the district.

(b) (1) Bankruptcy judges may hear and determine all cases under title 11 and all core proceedings arising under title 11, or arising in a case under title 11, referred under subsection (a) of this section, and may enter appropriate orders and judgments, subject to review under section 158 of this title.

(2) Core proceedings include, but are not limited to—

(A) matters concerning the administration of the estate;

(B) allowance or disallowance of claims against the estate or exemptions from property of the estate, and estimation of claims or interests for the purposes of confirming a plan under chapter 11, 12, or 13 of title 11 but not the liquidation or estimation of contingent or unliquidated personal injury tort or wrongful death claims against the estate for purposes of distribution in a case under title 11;

(C) counterclaims by the estate against persons filing claims against the estate;

(D) orders in respect to obtaining credit;

(E) orders to turn over property of the estate;

(F) proceedings to determine, avoid, or recover preferences;

(G) motions to terminate, annul, or modify the automatic stay;

(H) proceedings to determine, avoid, or recover fraudulent conveyances;

(I) determinations as to the dischargeability of particular debts;

(J) objections to discharges;

(K) determinations of the validity, extent, or priority of liens;

(L) confirmations of plans;

(M) orders approving the use or lease of property, including the use of cash collateral;

(N) orders approving the sale of property other than property resulting from claims brought by the estate against persons who have not filed claims against the estate;

(O) other proceedings affecting the liquidation of the assets of the estate or the adjustment of the debtor-creditor or the equity security holder relationship, except personal injury tort or wrongful death claims; and

(P) recognition of foreign proceedings and other matters under chapter 15 of title 11.

(3) The bankruptcy judge shall determine, on the judge's own motion or on timely motion of a party, whether a proceeding is a core proceeding under this subsection or is a proceeding that is otherwise related to a case under title 11. A determination that a proceeding is not a core proceeding shall not be made solely on the basis that its resolution may be affected by State law.

(4) Non-core proceedings under section 157(b)(2)(B) of title 28, United States Code, shall not be subject to the mandatory abstention provisions of section 1334(c)(2).

(5) The district court shall order that personal injury tort and wrongful death claims shall be tried in the district court in which the bankruptcy case is pending, or in the district court in the district in which the claim arose, as determined by the district court in which the bankruptcy case is pending.

(c) (1) A bankruptcy judge may hear a proceeding that is not a core proceeding but that is otherwise related to a case under title 11. In such proceeding, the bankruptcy judge shall submit proposed findings of fact and conclusions of law to the district court, and any final order or judgment shall be entered by the district judge after considering the bankruptcy judge's proposed findings and conclusions and after reviewing de novo those matters to which any party has timely and specifically objected.

(2) Notwithstanding the provisions of paragraph (1) of this subsection, the district court, with the consent of all the parties to the proceeding, may refer a proceeding related to a case under title 11 to a bankruptcy judge to hear and determine and to enter appropriate orders and judgments, subject to review under section 158 of this title.

(d) The district court may withdraw, in whole or in part, any case or proceeding referred under this section, on its own motion or on timely motion of any party, for cause shown. The district court shall, on timely motion of a party, so withdraw a proceeding if the court determines that resolution of the proceeding requires consideration of both title 11 and other laws of the United States regulating organizations or activities affecting interstate commerce.

(e) If the right to a jury trial applies in a proceeding that may be heard under this section by a bankruptcy judge, the bankruptcy judge may conduct the jury trial if specially designated to exercise such jurisdiction by the district court and with the express consent of all the parties.

§ 158. Appeals.

(a) The district courts of the United States shall have jurisdiction to hear appeals[1]

(1) from final judgments, orders, and decrees;

(2) from interlocutory orders and decrees issued under section 1121(d) of title 11 increasing or reducing the time periods referred to in section 1121 of such title; and

(3) with leave of the court, from other interlocutory orders and decrees;

and, with leave of the court, from interlocutory orders and decrees, of bankruptcy judges entered in cases and proceedings referred to the bankruptcy judges under section 157 of this title. An appeal under this subsection shall be taken only to the district court for the judicial district in which the bankruptcy judge is serving.

(b)(1) The judicial council of a circuit shall establish a bankruptcy appellate panel service composed of bankruptcy judges of the districts in the circuit who are appointed by the judicial council in accordance with paragraph (3), to hear and determine, with the consent of all the parties, appeals under subsection (a) unless the judicial council finds that—

(A) there are insufficient judicial resources available in the circuit; or

(B) establishment of such service would result in undue delay or increased cost to parties in cases under title 11.

Not later than 90 days after making the finding, the judicial council shall submit to the Judicial Conference of the United States a report containing the factual basis of such finding.

(2) (A) A judicial council may reconsider, at any time, the finding described in paragraph (1).

(B) On the request of a majority of the district judges in a circuit for which a bankruptcy appellate panel service is established under paragraph (1), made after the expiration of the 1-year period beginning on the date such service is established, the judicial council of the circuit shall determine whether a circumstance specified in subparagraph (A) or (B) of such paragraph exists.

(C) On its own motion, after the expiration of the 3-year period beginning on the date a bankruptcy appellate panel service is established under paragraph (1), the judicial council of the circuit may determine whether a circumstance specified in subparagraph (A) or (B) of such paragraph exists.

(D) If the judicial council finds that either of such circumstances exists, the judicial council may provide for the completion of the appeals then pending before such service and the orderly termination of such service.

(3) Bankruptcy judges appointed under paragraph (1) shall be appointed and may be reappointed under such paragraph.

(4) If authorized by the Judicial Conference of the United States, the judicial councils of 2 or more circuits may establish a joint bankruptcy appellate panel comprised of bankruptcy judges from the districts within the circuits for which such panel is established, to hear and determine, upon the consent of all the parties, appeals under subsection (a) of this section.

(5) An appeal to be heard under this subsection shall be heard by a panel of 3 members of the bankruptcy appellate panel service, except that a member of such service may not hear an appeal originating in the district for which

[1] So in original. Probably should be followed by a dash.

such member is appointed or designated under section 152 of this title.

(6) Appeals may not be heard under this subsection by a panel of the bankruptcy appellate panel service unless the district judges for the district in which the appeals occur, by majority vote, have authorized such service to hear and determine appeals originating in such district.

(c)(1) Subject to subsections (b) and (d)(2), each appeal under subsection (a) shall be heard by a 3-judge panel of the bankruptcy appellate panel service established under subsection (b)(1) unless—

(A) the appellant elects at the time of filing the appeal; or

(B) any other party elects, not later than 30 days after service of notice of the appeal;

to have such appeal heard by the district court.

(2) An appeal under subsections (a) and (b) of this section shall be taken in the same manner as appeals in civil proceedings generally are taken to the courts of appeals from the district courts and in the time provided by Rule 8002 of the Bankruptcy Rules.

(d) (1) The courts of appeals shall have jurisdiction of appeals from all final decisions, judgments, orders, and decrees entered under subsections (a) and (b) of this section.

(2)(A) The appropriate court of appeals shall have jurisdiction of appeals described in the first sentence of subsection (a) if the bankruptcy court, the district court, or the bankruptcy appellate panel involved, acting on its own motion or on the request of a party to the judgment, order, or decree described in such first sentence, or all the appellants and appellees (if any) acting jointly, certify that—

(i) the judgment, order, or decree involves a question of law as to which there is no controlling decision of the court of appeals for the circuit or of the Supreme Court of the United States, or involves a matter of public importance;

(ii) the judgment, order, or decree involves a question of law requiring resolution of conflicting decisions; or

(iii) an immediate appeal from the judgment, order, or decree may materially advance the progress of the case or proceeding in which the appeal is taken;

and if the court of appeals authorizes the direct appeal of the judgment, order, or decree.

(B) If the bankruptcy court, the district court, or the bankruptcy appellate panel—

(i) on its own motion or on the request of a party, determines that a circumstance specified in clause (i), (ii), or (iii) of subparagraph (A) exists; or

(ii) receives a request made by a majority of the appellants and a majority of appellees (if any) to make the certification described in subparagraph (A);

then the bankruptcy court, the district court, or the bankruptcy appellate panel shall make the certification described in subparagraph (A).

(C) The parties may supplement the certification with a short statement of the basis for the certification.

(D) An appeal under this paragraph does not stay any proceeding of the bankruptcy court, the district court, or the bankruptcy appellate panel from which the appeal is taken, unless the respective bankruptcy court, district court, or bankruptcy appellate panel, or the court of appeals in which the appeal in pending, issues a stay of such proceeding pending the appeal.

(E) Any request under subparagraph (B) for certification shall be made not later than 60 days after the entry of the judgment, order, or decree.

§ 159. Bankruptcy Statistics.

(a) The clerk of the district court, or the clerk of the bankruptcy court if one is certified pursuant to section 156(b) of this title, shall collect statistics regarding debtors who are individuals with primarily consumer debts seeking relief under chapters 7, 11, and 13 of title 11. Those statistics shall be in a standardized format prescribed by the Director of the Administrative Office of the United States Courts (referred to in this section as the "Director").

(b) The Director shall—

(1) compile the statistics referred to in subsection (a);

(2) make the statistics available to the public; and

(3) not later than July 1, 2008, and annually thereafter, prepare, and submit to Congress a report concerning the information collected

under subsection (a) that contains an analysis of the information.

(c) The compilation required under subsection (b) shall—

(1) be itemized, by chapter, with respect to title 11;

(2) be presented in the aggregate and for each district; and

(3) include information concerning—

(A) the total assets and total liabilities of the debtors described in subsection (a), and in each category of assets and liabilities, as reported in the schedules prescribed pursuant to section 2075 of this title and filed by debtors;

(B) the current monthly income, average income, and average expenses of debtors as reported on the schedules and statements that each such debtor files under sections 521 and 1322 of title 11;

(C) the aggregate amount of debt discharged in cases filed during the reporting period, determined as the difference between the total amount of debt and obligations of a debtor reported on the schedules and the amount of such debt reported in categories which are predominantly nondischargeable;

(D) the average period of time between the date of the filing of the petition and the closing of the case for cases closed during the reporting period;

(E) for cases closed during the reporting period—

(i) the number of cases in which a reaffirmation agreement was filed; and

(ii) (I) the total number of reaffirmation agreements filed;

(II) of those cases in which a reaffirmation agreement was filed, the number of cases in which the debtor was not represented by an attorney; and

(III) of those cases in which a reaffirmation agreement was filed, the number of cases in which the reaffirmation agreement was approved by the court;

(F) with respect to cases filed under chapter 13 of title 11, for the reporting period—

(i) (I) the number of cases in which a final order was entered determining the value of property securing a claim in an amount less than the amount of the claim; and

(II) the number of final orders entered determining the value of property securing a claim;

(ii) the number of cases dismissed, the number of cases dismissed for failure to make payments under the plan, the number of cases refiled after dismissal, and the number of cases in which the plan was completed, separately itemized with respect to the number of modifications made before completion of the plan, if any; and

(iii) the number of cases in which the debtor filed another case during the 6-year period preceding the filing;

(G) the number of cases in which creditors were fined for misconduct and any amount of punitive damages awarded by the court for creditor misconduct; and

(H) the number of cases in which sanctions under rule 9011 of the Federal Rules of Bankruptcy Procedure were imposed against debtor's attorney or damages awarded under such Rule.

CHAPTER 39—UNITED STATES TRUSTEES

§ 581. United States Trustees.

(a) The Attorney General shall appoint one United States trustee for each of the following regions composed of Federal judicial districts (without regard to section 451):

(1) The judicial districts established for the States of Maine, Massachusetts, New Hampshire, and Rhode Island.

(2) The judicial districts established for the States of Connecticut, New York, and Vermont.

(3) The judicial districts established for the States of Delaware, New Jersey, and Pennsylvania.

(4) The judicial districts established for the States of Maryland, North Carolina, South Carolina, Virginia, and West Virginia and for the District of Columbia.

(5) The judicial districts established for the States of Louisiana and Mississippi.

(6) The Northern District of Texas and the Eastern District of Texas.

(7) The Southern District of Texas and the Western District of Texas.

(8) The judicial districts established for the States of Kentucky and Tennessee.

(9) The judicial districts established for the States of Michigan and Ohio.

(10) The Central District of Illinois and the Southern District of Illinois; and the judicial districts established for the State of Indiana.

(11) The Northern District of Illinois; and the judicial districts established for the State of Wisconsin.

(12) The judicial districts established for the States of Minnesota, Iowa, North Dakota, and South Dakota.

(13) The judicial districts established for the States of Arkansas, Nebraska, and Missouri.

(14) The District of Arizona.

(15) The Southern District of California; and the judicial districts established for the State of Hawaii, and for Guam and the Commonwealth of the Northern Mariana Islands.

(16) The Central District of California.

(17) The Eastern District of California and the Northern District of California; and the judicial district established for the State of Nevada.

(18) The judicial districts established for the States of Alaska, Idaho (exclusive of Yellowstone National Park), Montana (exclusive of Yellowstone National Park), Oregon, and Washington.

(19) The judicial districts established for the States of Colorado, Utah, and Wyoming (including those portions of Yellowstone National Park situated in the States of Montana and Idaho).

(20) The judicial districts established for the States of Kansas, New Mexico, and Oklahoma.

(21) The judicial districts established for the States of Alabama, Florida, and Georgia and for the Commonwealth of Puerto Rico and the Virgin Islands of the United States.

(b) Each United States trustee shall be appointed for a term of five years. On the expiration of his term, a United States trustee shall continue to perform the duties of his office until his successor is appointed and qualifies.

(c) Each United States trustee is subject to removal by the Attorney General.

§ 586. Duties; Supervision by Attorney General.

(a) Each United States trustee, within the region for which such United States trustee is appointed, shall—

(1) establish, maintain, and supervise a panel of private trustees that are eligible and available to serve as trustees in cases under chapter 7 of title 11;

(2) serve as and perform the duties of a trustee in a case under title 11 when required under title 11 to serve as trustee in such a case;

(3) supervise the administration of cases and trustees in cases under chapter 7, 11 (including subchapter V of chapter 11), 12, 13, or 15 of title 11 by, whenever the United States trustee considers it to be appropriate—

(A)(i) reviewing, in accordance with procedural guidelines adopted by the Executive Office of the United States Trustee (which guidelines shall be applied uniformly by the United States trustee except when circumstances warrant different treatment), applications filed for compensation and reimbursement under section 330 of title 11; and

(ii) filing with the court comments with respect to such application and, if the United States Trustee considers it to be appropriate, objections to such application;

(B) monitoring plans and disclosure statements filed in cases under chapter 11 of title 11 and filing with the court, in connection with hearings under sections 1125 and 1128 of such title, comments with respect to such plans and disclosure statements;

(C) monitoring plans filed under chapters 12 and 13 of title 11 and filing with the court, in connection with hearings under sections 1224, 1229, 1324, and 1329 of such title, comments with respect to such plans;

(D) taking such action as the United States trustee deems to be appropriate to ensure that all reports, schedules, and fees required to be filed under title 11 and this title by the debtor are properly and timely filed;

(E) monitoring creditors' committees appointed under title 11;

(F) notifying the appropriate United States attorney of matters which relate to the occurrence of any action which may constitute a crime under the laws of the United States and, on the request of the United States attorney, assisting the United States attorney in carrying out prosecutions based on such action;

(G) monitoring the progress of cases under title 11 and taking such actions as the United States trustee deems to be appropriate to prevent undue delay in such progress;

(H) in small business cases (as defined in section 101 of title 11), performing the additional duties specified in title 11 pertaining to such cases; and

(I) monitoring applications filed under section 327 of title 11 and, whenever the United States trustee deems it to be appropriate, filing with the court comments with respect to the approval of such applications;

(4) deposit or invest under section 345 of title 11 money received as trustee in cases under title 11;

(5) perform the duties prescribed for the United States trustee under title 11 and this title, and such duties consistent with title 11 and this title as the Attorney General may prescribe;

(6) make such reports as the Attorney General directs, including the results of audits performed under section 603(a) of the Bankruptcy Abuse Prevention and Consumer Protection Act of 2005;

(7) in each of such small business cases—

(A) conduct an initial debtor interview as soon as practicable after the date of the order for relief but before the first meeting scheduled under section 341(a) of title 11, at which time the United States trustee shall—

(i) begin to investigate the debtor's viability;

(ii) inquire about the debtor's business plan;

(iii) explain the debtor's obligations to file monthly operating reports and other required reports;

(iv) attempt to develop an agreed scheduling order; and

(v) inform the debtor of other obligations;

(B) if determined to be appropriate and advisable, visit the appropriate business premises of the debtor, ascertain the state of the debtor's books and records, and verify that the debtor has filed its tax returns; and

(C) review and monitor diligently the debtor's activities, to determine as promptly as possible whether the debtor will be unable to confirm a plan; and

(8) in any case in which the United States trustee finds material grounds for any relief under section 1112 of title 11, apply promptly after making that finding to the court for relief.

(b) If the number of cases under subchapter V of chapter 11 or chapter 12 or 13 of title 11 commenced in a particular region so warrants, the United States trustee for such region may, subject to the approval of the Attorney General, appoint one or more individuals to serve as standing trustee, or designate one or more assistant United States trustees to serve in cases under such chapter. The United States trustee for such region shall supervise any such individual appointed as standing trustee in the performance of the duties of standing trustee.

(c) Each United States trustee shall be under the general supervision of the Attorney General, who shall provide general coordination and assistance to the United States trustees.

(d)(1) The Attorney General shall prescribe by rule qualifications for membership on the panels established by United States trustees under paragraph (a)(1) of this section, and qualifications for appointment under subsection (b) of this section to serve as standing trustee in cases under subchapter V of chapter 11 or chapter 12 or 13 of title 11. The Attorney General may not require that an individual be an attorney in order to qualify for appointment under subsection (b) of this section to serve as standing trustee in cases under subchapter V of chapter 11 or chapter 12 or 13 of title 11.

(2) A trustee whose appointment under subsection (a)(1) or under subsection (b) is terminated or who ceases to be assigned to cases filed under title 11, United States Code, may obtain judicial review of the final agency decision by commencing an action in the district court of the United States for the district for which the panel to which the trustee is appointed under subsection (a)(1), or in the district court of the United States for the district in which the trustee is appointed under subsection (b) resides, after first exhausting all available administrative remedies, which if the trustee so elects, shall also include an administrative

hearing on the record. Unless the trustee elects to have an administrative hearing on the record, the trustee shall be deemed to have exhausted all administrative remedies for purposes of this paragraph if the agency fails to make a final agency decision within 90 days after the trustee requests administrative remedies. The Attorney General shall prescribe procedures to implement this paragraph. The decision of the agency shall be affirmed by the district court unless it is unreasonable and without cause based on the administrative record before the agency.

(e)(1) The Attorney General, after consultation with a United States trustee that has appointed an individual under subsection (b) of this section to serve as standing trustee in cases under subchapter V of chapter 11 or chapter 12 or 13 of title 11, shall fix—

(A) a maximum annual compensation for such individual consisting of—

(i) an amount not to exceed the highest annual rate of basic pay in effect for level V of the Executive Schedule; and

(ii) the cash value of employment benefits comparable to the employment benefits provided by the United States to individuals who are employed by the United States at the same rate of basic pay to perform similar services during the same period of time; and

(B) a percentage fee not to exceed—

(i) in the case of a debtor who is not a family farmer, ten percent; or

(ii) in the case of a debtor who is a family farmer, the sum of—

(I) not to exceed ten percent of the payments made under the plan of such debtor, with respect to payments in an aggregate amount not to exceed $450,000; and

(II) three percent of payments made under the plan of such debtor, with respect to payments made after the aggregate amount of payments made under the plan exceeds $450,000;

based on such maximum annual compensation and the actual, necessary expenses incurred by such individual as standing trustee.

(2) Such individual shall collect such percentage fee from all payments received by such individual under plans in the cases under subchapter V of chapter 11 or chapter 12 or 13 of title 11 for which such individual serves as standing trustee. Such individual shall pay to the United States trustee, and the United States trustee shall deposit in the United States Trustee System Fund—

(A) any amount by which the actual compensation of such individual exceeds 5 per centum upon all payments received under plans in cases under chapter 12 or 13 of title 11 for which such individual serves as standing trustee; and

(B) any amount by which the percentage for all such cases exceeds—

(i) such individual's actual compensation for such cases, as adjusted under subparagraph (A) of paragraph (1); plus

(ii) the actual, necessary expenses incurred by such individual as standing trustee in such cases. Subject to the approval of the Attorney General, any or all of the interest earned from the deposit of payments under plans by such individual may be utilized to pay actual, necessary expenses without regard to the percentage limitation contained in subparagraph (d)(1)(B) of this section.

(3) After first exhausting all available administrative remedies, an individual appointed under subsection (b) may obtain judicial review of final agency action to deny a claim of actual, necessary expenses under this subsection by commencing an action in the district court of the United States for the district where the individual resides. The decision of the agency shall be affirmed by the district court unless it is unreasonable and without cause based upon the administrative record before the agency.

(4) The Attorney General shall prescribe procedures to implement this subsection.

(5) In the event that the services of the trustee in a case under subchapter V of chapter 11 of title 11 are terminated by dismissal or conversion of the case, or upon substantial consummation of a plan under section 1183(c)(1) of that title, the court shall award compensation to the trustee consistent with services performed by the trustee and the limits on the compensation of the trustee established pursuant to paragraph (1) of this subsection.

(f)(1) The United States trustee for each district is authorized to contract with auditors to perform audits in cases designated by the United States trustee, in accordance with the procedures established under section 603(a) of the Bankruptcy Abuse Prevention and Consumer Protection Act of 2005.

(2)(A) The report of each audit referred to in paragraph (1) shall be filed with the court and transmitted to the United States trustee. Each report shall clearly and conspicuously specify any material misstatement of income or expenditures or of assets identified by the person performing the audit. In any case in which a material misstatement of income or expenditures or of assets has been reported, the clerk of the district court (or the clerk of the bankruptcy court if one is certified under section 156(b) of this title) shall give notice of the misstatement to the creditors in the case.

(B) If a material misstatement of income or expenditures or of assets is reported, the United States trustee shall—

(i) report the material misstatement, if appropriate, to the United States Attorney pursuant to section 3057 of title 18; and

(ii) if advisable, take appropriate action, including but not limited to commencing an adversary proceeding to revoke the debtor's discharge pursuant to section 727(d) of title 11.

§ 589b. Bankruptcy Data.

(a) Rules.—The Attorney General shall, within a reasonable time after the effective date of this section, issue rules requiring uniform forms for (and from time to time thereafter to appropriately modify and approve)—

(1) final reports by trustees in cases under subchapter V of chapter 11 and chapters 7, 12, and 13 of title 11; and

(2) periodic reports by debtors in possession or trustees in cases under chapter 11 of title 11.

(b) Reports.—Each report referred to in subsection (a) shall be designed (and the requirements as to place and manner of filing shall be established) so as to facilitate compilation of data and maximum possible access of the public, both by physical inspection at one or more central filing locations, and by electronic access through the Internet or other appropriate media.

(c) Required Information.—The information required to be filed in the reports referred to in subsection (b) shall be that which is in the best interests of debtors and creditors, and in the public interest in reasonable and adequate information to evaluate the efficiency and practicality of the Federal bankruptcy system. In issuing rules proposing the forms referred to in subsection (a), the Attorney General shall strike the best achievable practical balance between—

(1) the reasonable needs of the public for information about the operational results of the Federal bankruptcy system;

(2) economy, simplicity, and lack of undue burden on persons with a duty to file reports; and

(3) appropriate privacy concerns and safeguards.

(d) Final Reports.—The uniform forms for final reports required under subsection (a) for use by trustees under subchapter V of chapter 11 and chapters 7, 12, and 13 of title 11 shall, in addition to such other matters as are required by law or as the Attorney General in the discretion of the Attorney General shall propose, include with respect to a case under such title—

(1) information about the length of time the case was pending;

(2) assets abandoned;

(3) assets exempted;

(4) receipts and disbursements of the estate;

(5) expenses of administration, including for use under section 707(b), actual costs of administering cases under chapter 13 of title 11;

(6) claims asserted;

(7) claims allowed; and

(8) distributions to claimants and claims discharged without payment,

in each case by appropriate category and, in cases under subchapter V of chapter 11 and chapters 12 and 13 of title 11, date of confirmation of the plan, each modification thereto, and defaults by the debtor in performance under the plan.

(e) Periodic Reports.—The uniform forms for periodic reports required under subsection (a) for use by trustees or debtors in possession under chapter 11 of title 11 shall, in addition to such other matters as are required by law or as the Attorney General in the discretion of the Attorney General shall propose, include —

(1) information about the industry classification, published by the Department of Commerce, for the businesses conducted by the debtor;

(2) length of time the case has been pending;

(3) number of full-time employees as of the date of the order for relief and at the end of each reporting period since the case was filed;

(4) cash receipts, cash disbursements and profitability of the debtor for the most recent period and cumulatively since the date of the order for relief;

(5) compliance with title 11, whether or not tax returns and tax payments since the date of the order for relief have been timely filed and made;

(6) all professional fees approved by the court in the case for the most recent period and cumulatively since the date of the order for relief (separately reported, for the professional fees incurred by or on behalf of the debtor, between those that would have been incurred absent a bankruptcy case and those not); and

(7) plans of reorganization filed and confirmed and, with respect thereto, by class, the recoveries of the holders, expressed in aggregate dollar values and, in the case of claims, as a percentage of total claims of the class allowed.

CHAPTER 57—GENERAL PROVISIONS APPLICABLE TO COURT OFFICERS AND EMPLOYEES

§ 959. Trustees and Receivers Suable; Management; State Laws.

(a) Trustees, receivers or managers of any property, including debtors in possession, may be sued, without leave of the court appointing them, with respect to any of their acts or transactions in carrying on business connected with such property. Such actions shall be subject to the general equity power of such court so far as the same may be necessary to the ends of justice, but this shall not deprive a litigant of his right to trial by jury.

(b) Except as provided in section 1166 of title 11, a trustee, receiver or manager appointed in any cause pending in any court of the United States, including a debtor in possession, shall manage and operate the property in his possession as such trustee, receiver or manager according to the requirements of the valid laws of the State in which such property is situated, in the same manner that the owner or possessor thereof would be bound to do if in possession thereof.

CHAPTER 85—DISTRICT COURTS; JURISDICTION

§ 1334. Bankruptcy Cases and Proceedings.

(a) Except as provided in subsection (b) of this section, the district courts shall have original and exclusive jurisdiction of all cases under title 11.

(b) Except as provided in subsection (e)(2), and notwithstanding any Act of Congress that confers exclusive jurisdiction on a court or courts other than the district courts, the district courts shall have original but not exclusive jurisdiction of all civil proceedings arising under title 11, or arising in or related to cases under title 11.

(c)(1) Except with respect to a case under chapter 15 of title 11, nothing in this section prevents a district court in the interest of justice, or in the interest of comity with State courts or respect for State law, from abstaining from hearing a particular proceeding arising under title 11 or arising in or related to a case under title 11.

(2) Upon timely motion of a party in a proceeding based upon a State law claim or State law cause of action, related to a case under title 11 but not arising under title 11 or arising in a case under title 11, with respect to which an action could not have been commenced in a court of the United States absent jurisdiction under this section, the district court shall abstain from hearing such proceeding if an action is commenced, and can be timely adjudicated, in a State forum of appropriate jurisdiction.

(d) Any decision to abstain or not to abstain made under subsection (c) (other than a decision not to abstain in a proceeding described in subsection (c)(2)) is not reviewable by appeal or otherwise by the court of appeals under section 158(d), 1291, or 1292 of this title or by the Supreme Court of the United States under section 1254 of this title. Subsection (c) and this subsection shall not be construed to limit the applicability of the stay provided for by section 362 of title 11, United States Code, as such section applies to an action affecting the property of the estate in bankruptcy.

(e) The district court in which a case under title 11 is commenced or is pending shall have exclusive jurisdiction—

(1) of all the property, wherever located, of the debtor as of the commencement of such case, and of property of the estate; and

(2) over all claims or causes of action that involve construction of section 327 of title 11, United States Code, or rules relating to disclosure requirements under section 327.

CHAPTER 87—DISTRICT COURTS; VENUE

§ 1408. Venue of Cases Under Title 11.

Except as provided in section 1410 of this title, a case under title 11 may be commenced in the district court for the district—

(1) in which the domicile, residence, principal place of business in the United States, or principal assets in the United States, of the person or entity that is the subject of such case have been located for the one hundred and eighty days immediately preceding such commencement, or for a longer portion of such one-hundred-and-eighty-day period than the domicile, residence, or principal place of business, in the United States, or principal assets in the United States, of such person were located in any other district; or

(2) in which there is pending a case under title 11 concerning such person's affiliate, general partner, or partnership.

§ 1409. Venue of Proceedings Arising Under Title 11 or Arising in or Related to Cases Under Title 11.

(a) Except as otherwise provided in subsections (b) and (d), a proceeding arising under title 11 or arising in or related to a case under title 11 may be commenced in the district court in which such case is pending.

(b) Except as provided in subsection (d) of this section, a trustee in a case under title 11 may commence a proceeding arising in or related to such case to recover a money judgment of or property worth less than $1,525 or a consumer debt of less than $22,700, or a debt (excluding a consumer debt) against a noninsider of less than $27,750, only in the district court for the district in which the defendant resides.

(c) Except as provided in subsection (b) of this section, a trustee in a case under title 11 may commence a proceeding arising in or related to such case as statutory successor to the debtor or creditors under section 541 or 544(b) of title 11 in the district court for the district where the State or Federal court sits in which, under applicable nonbankruptcy venue provisions, the debtor or creditors, as the case may be, may have commenced an action on which such proceeding is based if the case under title 11 had not been commenced.

(d) A trustee may commence a proceeding arising under title 11 or arising in or related to a case under title 11 based on a claim arising after the commencement of such case from the operation of the business of the debtor only in the district court for the district where a State or Federal court sits in which, under applicable nonbankruptcy venue provisions, an action on such claim may have been brought.

(e) A proceeding arising under title 11 or arising in or related to a case under title 11, based on a claim arising after the commencement of such case from the operation of the business of the debtor, may be commenced against the representative of the estate in such case in the district court for the district where the State or Federal court sits in which the party commencing such proceeding may, under applicable nonbankruptcy venue provisions, have brought an action on such claim, or in the district court in which such case is pending.

§ 1410. Venue of Cases Ancillary to Foreign Proceedings.

A case under chapter 15 of title 11 may be commenced in the district court of the United States for the district—

(1) in which the debtor has its principal place of business or principal assets in the United States;

(2) if the debtor does not have a place of business or assets in the United States, in which there is pending against the debtor an action or proceeding in a Federal or State court; or

(3) in a case other than those specified in paragraph (1) or (2), in which venue will be consistent with the interests of justice and the convenience of the parties, having regard to the relief sought by the foreign representative.

§ 1411. Jury Trials.

(a) Except as provided in subsection (b) of this section, this chapter and title 11 do not affect any right to trial by jury that an individual has under applicable nonbankruptcy law with regard to a personal injury or wrongful death tort claim.

(b) The district court may order the issues arising under section 303 of title 11 to be tried without a jury.

§ 1412. Change of Venue.

A district court may transfer a case or proceeding under title 11 to a district court for another district, in the interest of justice or for the convenience of the parties.

CHAPTER 89—DISTRICT COURTS; REMOVAL OF CASES FROM STATE COURTS

§ 1452. Removal of Claims Related to Bankruptcy Cases.

(a) A party may remove any claim or cause of action in a civil action other than a proceeding before the United States Tax Court or a civil action by a governmental unit to enforce such governmental unit's police or regulatory power, to the district court for the district where such civil action is pending, if such district court has jurisdiction of such claim or cause of action under section 1334 of this title.

(b) The court to which such claim or cause of action is removed may remand such claim or cause of action on any equitable ground. An order entered under this subsection remanding a claim or cause of action, or a decision to not remand, is not reviewable by appeal or otherwise by the court of appeals under section 158(d), 1291, or 1292 of this title or by the Supreme Court of the United States under section 1254 of this title.

FAIR DEBT COLLECTION PRACTICES ACT

Section

§ 801. Short Title
§ 802. Congressional Findings and Declaration of Purpose
§ 803. Definitions
§ 804. Acquisition of Location Information
§ 805. Communication in Connection with Debt Collection
§ 806. Harassment or Abuse
§ 807. False or Misleading Representations
§ 808. Unfair Practices
§ 809. Validation of Debts
§ 810. Multiple Debts
§ 811. Legal Actions by Debt Collectors
§ 812. Furnishing Certain Deceptive Forms
§ 813. Civil Liability
§ 814. Administrative Enforcement
§ 815. Reports to Congress by the Bureau; Views of Other Federal Agencies
§ 816. Relation to State Laws
§ 817. Exemption for State Regulation
§ 818. Exception for Certain Bad Check Enforcement Programs Operated by Private Entities
§ 819. Effective Date

As amended by Pub. L. 109-351, §§ 801-02, 120 Stat. 1966 (2006)

§ 801. Short Title (15 U.S.C. 1601 note).

This title may be cited as the "Fair Debt Collection Practices Act."

§ 802. Congressional Findings and Declaration of Purpose (15 U.S.C. 1692).

(a) There is abundant evidence of the use of abusive, deceptive, and unfair debt collection practices by many debt collectors. Abusive debt collection practices contribute to the number of personal bankruptcies, to marital instability, to the loss of jobs, and to invasions of individual privacy.

(b) Existing laws and procedures for redressing these injuries are inadequate to protect consumers.

(c) Means other than misrepresentation or other abusive debt collection practices are available for the effective collection of debts.

(d) Abusive debt collection practices are carried on to a substantial extent in interstate commerce and through means and instrumentalities of such commerce. Even where abusive debt collection practices are purely intrastate in character, they nevertheless directly affect interstate commerce.

(e) It is the purpose of this title to eliminate abusive debt collection practices by debt collectors, to insure that those debt collectors who refrain from using abusive debt collection practices are not competitively disadvantaged, and to promote consistent State action to protect consumers against debt collection abuses.

§ 803. Definitions (15 U.S.C. 1692a).

As used in this subchapter—

(1) The term "Bureau" means the Bureau of Consumer Financial Protection.

(2) The term "communication" means the conveying of information regarding a debt directly or indirectly to any person through any medium.

(3) The term "consumer" means any natural person obligated or allegedly obligated to pay any debt.

(4) The term "creditor" means any person who offers or extends credit creating a debt or to whom a debt is owed, but such term does not include any person to the extent that he receives an assignment or transfer of a debt in default solely for the purpose of facilitating collection of such debt for another.

(5) The term "debt" means any obligation or alleged obligation of a consumer to pay money arising out of a transaction in which the money, property, insurance, or services which are the subject of the transaction are primarily for personal, family, or household purposes, whether or not such obligation has been reduced to judgment.

(6) The term "debt collector" means any person who uses any instrumentality of interstate commerce or the mails in any business the principal purpose of which is the collection of any debts, or who regularly collects or attempts to collect, directly or indirectly, debts owed or due or asserted to be owed or due another. Notwithstanding the exclusion provided by clause (F) of the last sentence of this paragraph, the term includes any creditor who, in the process of collecting his own debts, uses any name other than his own which would indicate that a third person is collecting or attempting to collect such debts. For the purpose of section 1692f(6) of this title, such term also includes any person who uses any instrumentality of interstate commerce or the mails in any business the principal purpose of which is the enforcement of security interests. The term does not include—

(A) any officer or employee of a creditor while, in the name of the creditor, collecting debts for such creditor;

(B) any person while acting as a debt collector for another person, both of whom are related by common ownership or affiliated by corporate control, if the person acting as a debt collector does so only for persons to whom it is so related or affiliated and if the principal business of such person is not the collection of debts;

(C) any officer or employee of the United States or any State to the extent that collecting or attempting to collect any debt is in the performance of his official duties;

(D) any person while serving or attempting to serve legal process on any other person in connection with the judicial enforcement of any debt;

(E) any nonprofit organization which, at the request of consumers, performs bona fide consumer credit counseling and assists consumers in the liquidation of their debts by receiving payments from such consumers and distributing such amounts to creditors; and

(F) any person collecting or attempting to collect any debt owed or due or asserted to be owed or due another to the extent such activity (i) is incidental to a bona fide fiduciary obligation or a bona fide escrow arrangement; (ii) concerns a debt which was originated by such person; (iii) concerns a debt which was not in default at the time it was obtained by such person; or (iv) concerns a debt obtained by such person as a secured party in a commercial credit transaction involving the creditor.

(7) The term "location information" means a consumer's place of abode and his telephone number at such place, or his place of employment.

(8) The term "State" means any State, territory, or possession of the United States, the District of Columbia, the Commonwealth of Puerto Rico, or any political subdivision of any of the foregoing.

§ 804. Acquisition of Location Information (15 U.S.C. 1692b).

Any debt collector communicating with any person other than the consumer for the purpose of acquiring location information about the consumer shall—

(1) identify himself, state that he is confirming or correcting location information concerning the consumer, and, only if expressly requested, identify his employer;

(2) not state that such consumer owes any debt;

(3) not communicate with any such person more than once unless requested to do so by such person or unless the debt collector reasonably believes that the earlier response of such person is erroneous or incomplete and that such person now has correct or complete location information;

(4) not communicate by post card;

(5) not use any language or symbol on any envelope or in the contents of any communication effected by the mails or telegram that indicates that the debt collector is in the debt collection business or that the communication relates to the collection of a debt; and

(6) after the debt collector knows the consumer is represented by an attorney with regard to the subject debt and has knowledge of, or can readily ascertain, such attorney's name and address, not communicate with any person other than that attorney, unless the attorney fails to respond within a reasonable period of time to communication from the debt collector.

§ 805. Communication in Connection with Debt Collection (15 U.S.C. 1692c).

(a) Communication with the Consumer Generally. Without the prior consent of the consumer given directly to the debt collector or the express permission of a court of competent jurisdiction, a debt collector may not communicate with a consumer in connection with the collection of any debt—

(1) at any unusual time or place or a time or place known or which should be known to be inconvenient to the consumer. In the absence of knowledge of circumstances to the contrary, a debt collector shall assume that the convenient time for communicating with a consumer is after 8 o'clock antemeridian and before 9 o'clock postmeridian, local time at the consumer's location;

(2) if the debt collector knows the consumer is represented by an attorney with respect to such debt and has knowledge of, or can readily ascertain, such attorney's name and address, unless the attorney fails to respond within a reasonable period of time to a communication from the debt collector or unless the attorney consents to direct communication with the consumer; or

(3) at the consumer's place of employment if the debt collector knows or has reason to know that the consumer's employer prohibits the consumer from receiving such communication.

(b) Communication with Third Parties. Except as provided in section 1692b of this title, without the prior consent of the consumer given directly to the debt collector, or the express permission of a court of competent jurisdiction, or as reasonably necessary to effectuate a postjudgment judicial remedy, a debt collector may not communicate, in connection with the collection of any debt, with any person other than the consumer, his attorney, a consumer reporting agency if otherwise permitted by law, the creditor, the attorney of the creditor, or the attorney of the debt collector.

(c) Ceasing Communication. If a consumer notifies a debt collector in writing that the consumer refuses to pay a debt or that the consumer wishes the debt collector to cease further communication with the consumer, the debt collector shall not communicate further with the consumer with respect to such debt, except—

(1) to advise the consumer that the debt collector's further efforts are being terminated;

(2) to notify the consumer that the debt collector or creditor may invoke specified remedies which are ordinarily invoked by such debt collector or creditor; or

(3) where applicable, to notify the consumer that the debt collector or creditor intends to invoke a specified remedy.

If such notice from the consumer is made by mail, notification shall be complete upon receipt.

(d) "Consumer" Defined. For the purpose of this section, the term "consumer" includes the consumer's spouse, parent (if the consumer is a minor), guardian, executor, or administrator.

§ 806. Harassment or Abuse (15 U.S.C. 1692d).

A debt collector may not engage in any conduct the natural consequence of which is to harass, oppress, or abuse any person in connection with the collection of a debt. Without limiting the general application of the foregoing, the following conduct is a violation of this section:

(1) The use or threat of use of violence or other criminal means to harm the physical person, reputation, or property of any person.

(2) The use of obscene or profane language or language the natural consequence of which is to abuse the hearer or reader.

(3) The publication of a list of consumers who allegedly refuse to pay debts, except to a consumer reporting agency or to persons meeting the requirements of section 1681a(f) or 1681b(3) of this title.

(4) The advertisement for sale of any debt to coerce payment of the debt.

(5) Causing a telephone to ring or engaging any person in telephone conversation repeatedly or continuously with intent to annoy, abuse, or harass any person at the called number.

(6) Except as provided in section 1692b of this title, the placement of telephone calls without meaningful disclosure of the caller's identity.

§ 807. False or Misleading Representations (15 U.S.C. 1692e).

A debt collector may not use any false, deceptive, or misleading representation or means in connection with the collection of any debt. Without limiting the general application of the foregoing, the following conduct is a violation of this section:

(1) The false representation or implication that the debt collector is vouched for, bonded by, or affiliated with the United States or any State, including the use of any badge, uniform, or facsimile thereof.

(2) The false representation of—

(A) the character, amount, or legal status of any debt; or

(B) any services rendered or compensation which may be lawfully received by any debt collector for the collection of a debt.

(3) The false representation or implication that any individual is an attorney or that any communication is from an attorney.

(4) The representation or implication that nonpayment of any debt will result in the arrest or imprisonment of any person or the seizure, garnishment, attachment, or sale of any property or wages of any person unless such action is lawful and the debt collector or creditor intends to take such action.

(5) The threat to take any action that cannot legally be taken or that is not intended to be taken.

(6) The false representation or implication that a sale, referral, or other transfer of any interest in a debt shall cause the consumer to—

(A) lose any claim or defense to payment of the debt; or

(B) become subject to any practice prohibited by this subchapter.

(7) The false representation or implication that the consumer committed any crime or other conduct in order to disgrace the consumer.

(8) Communicating or threatening to communicate to any person credit information which is known or which should be known to be false, including the failure to communicate that a disputed debt is disputed.

(9) The use or distribution of any written communication which simulates or is falsely represented to be a document authorized, issued, or approved by any court, official, or agency of the United States or any State, or which creates a false impression as to its source, authorization, or approval.

(10) The use of any false representation or deceptive means to collect or attempt to collect any debt or to obtain information concerning a consumer.

(11) The failure to disclose in the initial written communication with the consumer and, in addition, if the initial communication with the consumer is oral, in that initial oral communication, that the debt collector is attempting to collect a debt and that any information obtained will be used for that purpose, and the failure to disclose in subsequent communications that the communication is from a debt collector, except that this paragraph shall not apply to a formal pleading made in connection with a legal action.

(12) The false representation or implication that accounts have been turned over to innocent purchasers for value.

(13) The false representation or implication that documents are legal process.

(14) The use of any business, company, or organization name other than the true name of the debt collector's business, company, or organization.

(15) The false representation or implication that documents are not legal process forms or do not require action by the consumer.

(16) The false representation or implication that a debt collector operates or is employed by a consumer reporting agency as defined by section 1681a(f) of this title.

§ 808. Unfair Practices (15 U.S.C. 1692f).

A debt collector may not use unfair or unconscionable means to collect or attempt to collect any debt. Without limiting the general application of the foregoing, the following conduct is a violation of this section:

(1) The collection of any amount (including any interest, fee, charge, or expense incidental to the principal obligation) unless such amount is expressly authorized by the agreement creating the debt or permitted by law.

(2) The acceptance by a debt collector from any person of a check or other payment instrument postdated by more than five days unless such person is notified in writing of the debt collector's intent to deposit such check or instrument not more than ten nor less than three business days prior to such deposit.

(3) The solicitation by a debt collector of any postdated check or other postdated payment instrument for the purpose of threatening or instituting criminal prosecution.

(4) Depositing or threatening to deposit any postdated check or other postdated payment instrument prior to the date on such check or instrument.

(5) Causing charges to be made to any person for communications by concealment of the true purpose of the communication. Such charges include, but are not limited to, collect telephone calls and telegram fees.

(6) Taking or threatening to take any nonjudicial action to effect dispossession or disablement of property if—

(A) there is no present right to possession of the property claimed as collateral through an enforceable security interest;

(B) there is no present intention to take possession of the property; or

(C) the property is exempt by law from such dispossession or disablement.

(7) Communicating with a consumer regarding a debt by post card.

(8) Using any language or symbol, other than the debt collector's address, on any envelope when communicating with a consumer by use of the mails or by telegram, except that a debt collector may use his business name if such name does not indicate that he is in the debt collection business.

§ 809. Validation of Debts (15 U.S.C. 1692g).

(a) Within five days after the initial communication with a consumer in connection with the collection of any debt, a debt collector shall, unless the following information is contained in the initial communication or the consumer has paid the debt, send the consumer a written notice containing—

(1) the amount of the debt;

(2) the name of the creditor to whom the debt is owed;

(3) a statement that unless the consumer, within thirty days after receipt of the notice, disputes the validity of the debt, or any portion thereof, the debt will be assumed to be valid by the debt collector;

(4) a statement that if the consumer notifies the debt collector in writing within the thirty-day period that the debt, or any portion thereof, is disputed, the debt collector will obtain verification of the debt or a copy of a judgment against the consumer and a copy of such verification or judgment will be mailed to the consumer by the debt collector; and

(5) a statement that, upon the consumer's written request within the thirty-day period, the debt collector will provide the consumer with the name and address of the original creditor, if different from the current creditor.

(b) If the consumer notifies the debt collector in writing within the thirty-day period described in subsection (a) of this section that the debt, or any portion thereof, is disputed, or that the consumer requests the name and address of the original creditor, the debt collector shall cease collection of the debt, or any disputed portion thereof, until the debt collector obtains verification of the debt or a copy of a judgment, or the name and address of the original creditor, and a copy of such verification or judgment, or name and address of the original creditor, is mailed to the consumer by the debt collector. Collection activities and communications that do not otherwise violate this subchapter may continue during the 30-day period referred to in subsection (a) of this section unless the consumer has notified the debt collector in writing that the debt, or any portion of the debt, is disputed or that the consumer requests the name and address of the original creditor. Any collection activities and communication during the 30-day period may not overshadow or be inconsistent with the disclosure of the consumer's right to dispute the debt or request the name and address of the original creditor.

(c) The failure of a consumer to dispute the validity of a debt under this section may not be construed by any court as an admission of liability by the consumer.

(d) A communication in the form of a formal pleading in a civil action shall not be treated as an initial communication for purposes of subsection (a).

(e) The sending or delivery of any form or notice which does not relate to the collection of a debt and is expressly required by the Internal Revenue Code of 1986, chapter 94 of this title [15 U.S.C.A. § 6801 et seq.], or any provision of Federal or State law relating to notice of data security breach or privacy, or any regulation prescribed under any such provision of law, shall not be treated as an initial communication in connection with debt collection for purposes of this section.

§ 810. Multiple Debts (15 U.S.C. 1692h).

If any consumer owes multiple debts and makes any single payment to any debt collector with respect to such debts, such debt collector may not apply such payment to any debt which is disputed by the consumer and, where applicable, shall apply such payment in accordance with the consumer's directions.

§ 811. Legal Actions by Debt Collectors (15 U.S.C. 1692i).

(a) Any debt collector who brings any legal action on a debt against any consumer shall—

(1) in the case of an action to enforce an interest in real property securing the consumer's obligation, bring such action only in a judicial district or similar legal entity in which such real property is located; or

(2) in the case of an action not described in paragraph (1), bring such action only in the judicial district or similar legal entity—

(A) in which such consumer signed the contract sued upon; or

(B) in which such consumer resides at the commencement of the action.

(b) Nothing in this subchapter shall be construed to authorize the bringing of legal actions by debt collectors.

§ 812. Furnishing Certain Deceptive Forms (15 U.S.C. 1692j).

(a) It is unlawful to design, compile, and furnish any form knowing that such form would be used to create the false belief in a consumer that a person other than the creditor of such consumer is participating in the collection of or in an attempt to collect a debt such consumer allegedly owes such creditor, when in fact such person is not so participating.

(b) Any person who violates this section shall be liable to the same extent and in the same manner as a debt collector is liable under section 1692k of this title for failure to comply with a provision of this subchapter.

§ 813. Civil Liability (15 U.S.C. 1692k).

(a) Except as otherwise provided by this section, any debt collector who fails to comply with any provision of this subchapter with respect to any person is liable to such person in an amount equal to the sum of—

(1) any actual damage sustained by such person as a result of such failure;

(2) (A) in the case of any action by an individual, such additional damages as the court may allow, but not exceeding $1,000; or

(B) in the case of a class action, (i) such amount for each named plaintiff as could be recovered under subparagraph (A), and (ii) such amount as the court may allow for all other class members, without regard to a minimum individual recovery, not to exceed the lesser of $500,000 or 1 per centum of the net worth of the debt collector; and

(3) in the case of any successful action to enforce the foregoing liability, the costs of the action, together with a reasonable attorney's fee as determined by the court. On a finding by the court that an action under this section was brought in bad faith and for the purpose of harassment, the court may award to the defendant attorney's fees reasonable in relation to the work expended and costs.

(b) In determining the amount of liability in any action under subsection (a) of this section, the court shall consider, among other relevant factors—

(1) in any individual action under subsection (a)(2)(A) of this section, the frequency and persistence of noncompliance by the debt collector, the nature of such noncompliance, and the extent to which such noncompliance was intentional; or

(2) in any class action under subsection (a)(2)(B) of this section, the frequency and persistence of noncompliance by the debt collector, the nature of such noncompliance, the resources of the debt collector, the number of persons adversely affected, and the extent to which the debt collector's noncompliance was intentional.

(c) A debt collector may not be held liable in any action brought under this subchapter if the debt collector shows by a preponderance of evidence that the violation was not intentional and resulted from a bona fide error notwithstanding the maintenance of procedures reasonably adapted to avoid any such error.

(d) An action to enforce any liability created by this subchapter may be brought in any appropriate United States district court without regard to the amount in controversy, or in any other court of competent jurisdiction, within one year from the date on which the violation occurs.

(e) No provision of this section imposing any liability shall apply to any act done or omitted in good faith in conformity with any advisory opinion of the Bureau, notwithstanding that after such act or omission has occurred, such opinion is amended, rescinded, or determined by judicial or other authority to be invalid for any reason.

§ 814. Administrative Enforcement (15 U.S.C. 1692l).

(a) Federal Trade Commission

The Federal Trade Commission shall be authorized to enforce compliance with this subchapter, except to the extent that enforcement of the requirements imposed under this subchapter is specifically committed to another Government agency under any of paragraphs (1) through (5) of subsection (b), subject to subtitle B of the Consumer Financial Protection Act of 2010. For purpose of the exercise by the Federal Trade Commission of its functions and powers under the Federal Trade Commission Act (15 U.S.C. 41 et seq.), a violation of this subchapter shall be deemed an unfair or deceptive act or practice in violation of that Act. All of the functions and powers of the Federal Trade Commission under the Federal Trade Commission Act are available to the Federal Trade Commission to enforce compliance by any person with this subchapter, irrespective of whether that person is engaged in commerce or meets any other jurisdictional tests under the Federal Trade Commission Act, including the power to enforce the provisions of this subchapter, in the same manner as if the violation had been a violation of a Federal Trade Commission trade regulation rule.

(b) Applicable provisions of law

Subject to subtitle B of the Consumer Financial Protection Act of 2010, compliance with any requirements imposed under this subchapter shall be enforced under—

(1) section 8 of the Federal Deposit Insurance Act, by the appropriate Federal banking agency, as defined in section 3(q) of the Federal Deposit Insurance Act (12 U.S.C. § 1813(q)), with respect to—

(A) national banks, Federal savings associations, and Federal branches and Federal agencies of foreign banks;

(B) member banks of the Federal Reserve System (other than national banks), branches and agencies of foreign banks (other than Federal branches, Federal agencies, and insured State branches of foreign banks), commercial lending companies owned or controlled by foreign banks, and organizations operating under section 25 or 25A of the Federal Reserve Act; and

(C) banks and State savings associations insured by the Federal Deposit Insurance Corporation (other than members of the Federal Reserve System), and insured State branches of foreign banks;

(2) the Federal Credit Union Act, by the Administrator of the National Credit Union Administration with respect to any Federal credit union;

(3) subtitle IV of Title 49, by the Secretary of Transportation, with respect to all carriers subject to the jurisdiction of the Surface Transportation Board;

(4) part A of subtitle VII of Title 49, by the Secretary of Transportation with respect to any air carrier or any foreign air carrier subject to that part;

(5) the Packers and Stockyards Act, 1921 (except as provided in section 406 of that Act), by the Secretary of Agriculture with respect to any activities subject to that Act; and

(6) subtitle E of the Consumer Financial Protection Act of 2010, by the Bureau, with respect to any person subject to this subchapter.

The terms used in paragraph (1) that are not defined in this subchapter or otherwise defined in section 3(s) of the Federal Deposit Insurance Act (12 U.S.C. 1813(s)) shall have the meaning given to them in section 1(b) of the International Banking Act of 1978 (12 U.S.C. 3101).

(c) For the purpose of the exercise by any agency referred to in subsection (b) of this section of its powers under any Act referred to in that subsection, a violation of any requirement imposed under this subchapter shall be deemed to be a violation of a requirement imposed under that Act. In addition to its powers under any provision of law specifically referred to in subsection (b) of this section, each of the agencies referred to in that subsection may exercise, for the purpose of enforcing compliance with any requirement imposed under this subchapter any other authority conferred on it by law, except as provided in subsection (d).

(d) Except as provided in section 1029(a) of the Consumer Financial Protection Act of 2010, the Bureau may prescribe rules with respect to the collection of debts by debt collectors, as defined in this subchapter.

§ 815. Reports to Congress by the Bureau; Views of Other Federal Agencies (15 U.S.C. 1692m).

(a) Not later than one year after the effective date of this subchapter and at one-year intervals thereafter, the Bureau shall make reports to the

Congress concerning the administration of its functions under this subchapter, including such recommendations as the Bureau deems necessary or appropriate. In addition, each report of the Bureau shall include its assessment of the extent to which compliance with this subchapter is being achieved and a summary of the enforcement actions taken by the Bureau under section 1692l of this title.

(b) In the exercise of its functions under this subchapter, the Bureau may obtain upon request the views of any other Federal agency which exercises enforcement functions under section 1692l of this title.

§ 816. Relation to State Laws (15 U.S.C. 1692n).

This subchapter does not annul, alter, or affect, or exempt any person subject to the provisions of this subchapter from complying with the laws of any State with respect to debt collection practices, except to the extent that those laws are inconsistent with any provision of this subchapter, and then only to the extent of the inconsistency. For purposes of this section, a State law is not inconsistent with this subchapter if the protection such law affords any consumer is greater than the protection provided by this subchapter.

§ 817. Exemption for State Regulation (15 U.S.C. 1692o).

The Bureau shall by regulation exempt from the requirements of this subchapter any class of debt collection practices within any State if the Bureau determines that under the law of that State that class of debt collection practices is subject to requirements substantially similar to those imposed by this subchapter, and that there is adequate provision for enforcement.

§ 818. Exception for Certain Bad Check Enforcement Programs Operated by Private Entities (15 U.S.C. 1692p).

(a) In general—

(1) Treatment of Certain Private Entities. Subject to paragraph (2), a private entity shall be excluded from the definition of a debt collector, pursuant to the exception provided in section 1692a(6) of this title, with respect to the operation by the entity of a program described in paragraph (2)(A) under a contract described in paragraph (2)(B).

(2) Conditions of Applicability. Paragraph (1) shall apply if—

(A) a State or district attorney establishes, within the jurisdiction of such State or district attorney and with respect to alleged bad check violations that do not involve a check described in subsection (b) of this section, a pretrial diversion program for alleged bad check offenders who agree to participate voluntarily in such program to avoid criminal prosecution;

(B) a private entity, that is subject to an administrative support services contract with a State or district attorney and operates under the direction, supervision, and control of such State or district attorney, operates the pretrial diversion program described in subparagraph (A); and

(C) in the course of performing duties delegated to it by a State or district attorney under the contract, the private entity referred to in subparagraph (B)—

(i) complies with the penal laws of the State;

(ii) conforms with the terms of the contract and directives of the State or district attorney;

(iii) does not exercise independent prosecutorial discretion;

(iv) contacts any alleged offender referred to in subparagraph (A) for purposes of participating in a program referred to in such paragraph—

(I) only as a result of any determination by the State or district attorney that probable cause of a bad check violation under State penal law exists, and that contact with the alleged offender for purposes of participation in the program is appropriate; and

(II) the alleged offender has failed to pay the bad check after demand for payment, pursuant to State law, is made for payment of the check amount;

(v) includes as part of an initial written communication with an alleged offender a clear and conspicuous statement that—

(I) the alleged offender may dispute the validity of any alleged bad check violation;

(II) where the alleged offender knows, or has reasonable cause to believe, that the alleged bad check violation is the result of theft or forgery of the check, identity theft, or other fraud that is not the result of the conduct of the alleged offender, the alleged offender may file a crime report with the appropriate law enforcement agency; and

(III) if the alleged offender notifies the private entity or the district attorney in writing, not later than 30 days after being contacted for the first time pursuant to clause (iv), that there is a dispute pursuant to this subsection, before further restitution efforts are pursued, the district attorney or an employee of the district attorney authorized to make such a determination makes a determination that there is probable cause to believe that a crime has been committed; and

(vi) charges only fees in connection with services under the contract that have been authorized by the contract with the State or district attorney.

(b) Certain checks excluded.—A check is described in this subsection if the check involves, or is subsequently found to involve—

(1) a postdated check presented in connection with a payday loan, or other similar transaction, where the payee of the check knew that the issuer had insufficient funds at the time the check was made, drawn, or delivered;

(2) a stop payment order where the issuer acted in good faith and with reasonable cause in stopping payment on the check;

(3) a check dishonored because of an adjustment to the issuer's account by the financial institution holding such account without providing notice to the person at the time the check was made, drawn, or delivered;

(4) a check for partial payment of a debt where the payee had previously accepted partial payment for such debt;

(5) a check issued by a person who was not competent, or was not of legal age, to enter into a legal contractual obligation at the time the check was made, drawn, or delivered; or

(6) a check issued to pay an obligation arising from a transaction that was illegal in the jurisdiction of the State or district attorney at the time the check was made, drawn, or delivered.

(c) Definitions.—For purposes of this section, the following definitions shall apply:

(1) State or District Attorney. — The term "State or district attorney" means the chief elected or appointed prosecuting attorney in a district, county (as defined in section 2 of title 1, United States Code), municipality, or comparable jurisdiction, including State attorneys general who act as chief elected or appointed prosecuting attorneys in a district, county (as so defined), municipality or comparable jurisdiction, who may be referred to by a variety of titles such as district attorneys, prosecuting attorneys, commonwealth's attorneys, solicitors, county attorneys, and state's attorneys, and who are responsible for the prosecution of State crimes and violations of jurisdiction-specific local ordinances.

(2) Check.— The term "check" has the same meaning as in section 5002(6) of Title 12.

(3) Bad Check Violation.—The term "bad check violation" means a violation of the applicable State criminal law relating to the writing of dishonored checks.

§ 819. Effective Date (15 U.S.C. 1692 note). This title takes effect upon the expiration of six months after the date of its enactment, but section 809 shall apply only with respect to debts for which the initial attempt to collect occurs after such effective date.

TITLE 26—FEDERAL TAX LIEN ACT

Section

§ 6321. Lien for Taxes
§ 6322. Period of Lien
§ 6323. Validity and Priority Against Certain Persons

§ 6321. Lien for Taxes.

If any person liable to pay any tax neglects or refuses to pay the same after demand, the amount (including any interest, additional amount, addition to tax, or assess-able penalty, together with any costs that may accrue in addition thereto) shall be a lien in favor of the United States upon all property and rights to property, whether real or personal, belonging to such person.

§ 6322. Period of Lien.

Unless another date is specifically fixed by law, the lien imposed by section 6321 shall arise at the time the assessment is made and shall continue until the liability for the amount so assessed (or a judgment against the taxpayer arising out of such liability) is satisfied or becomes unenforceable by reason of lapse of time.

§ 6323. Validity and Priority Against Certain Persons.

(a) Purchasers, holders of security interests, mechanic's lienors, and judgment lien creditors. The lien imposed by section 6321 shall not be valid as against any purchaser, holder of a security interest, mechanic's lienor, or judgment lien creditor until notice thereof which meets the requirements of subsection (f) has been filed by the Secretary.

(b) Protection for certain interests even though notice filed. Even though notice of a lien imposed by section 6321 has been filed, such lien shall not be valid—

(1) Securities. With respect to a security (as defined in subsection (h)(4))—

(A) as against a purchaser of such security who at the time of purchase did not have actual notice or knowledge of the existence of such lien; and

(B) as against a holder of a security interest in such security who, at the time such interest came into existence, did not have actual notice or knowledge of the existence of such lien.

(2) Motor vehicles. With respect to a motor vehicle (as defined in subsection (h)(3)), as against a purchaser of such motor vehicle, if—

(A) at the time of the purchase such purchaser did not have actual notice or knowledge of the existence of such lien, and

(B) before the purchaser obtains such notice or knowledge, he has acquired possession of such motor vehicle and has not thereafter relinquished possession of such motor vehicle to the seller or his agent.

(3) Personal property purchased at retail. With respect to tangible personal property purchased at retail, as against a purchaser in the ordinary course of the seller's trade or business, unless at the time of such purchase such purchaser intends such purchase to (or knows such purchase will) hinder, evade, or defeat the collection of any tax under this title.

(4) Personal property purchased in casual sale [See § 3.32 of *Rev. Proc. 2004-71 (26 USCS § 1* note) for provision that, for calendar year 2005, a federal tax lien is not valid against certain purchasers under this paragraph that purchased personal property in a casual sale for less than $1,200.]. With respect to household goods, personal effects, or other tangible personal property described in section 6334(a) purchased (not for resale) in a casual sale for less than $1,000, as against the purchaser, but only if such purchaser does not have actual notice or knowledge (A) of the existence of such lien, or (B) that this sale is one of a series of sales.

(5) Personal property subject to possessory lien. With respect to tangible personal property subject to a lien under local law securing the reasonable price of the repair or improvement of such property, as against a holder of such a lien, if such holder is, and has been, continuously

in possession of such property from the time such lien arose.

(6) Real property tax and special assessment liens. With respect to real property, as against a holder of a lien upon such property, if such lien is entitled under local law to priority over security interests in such property which are prior in time, and such lien secures payment of—

(A) a tax of general application levied by any taxing authority based upon the value of such property;

(B) a special assessment imposed directly upon such property by any taxing authority, if such assessment is imposed for the purpose of defraying the cost of any public improvement; or

(C) charges for utilities or public services furnished to such property by the United States, a State or political subdivision thereof, or an instrumentality of any one or more of the foregoing.

(7) Residential property subject to a mechanic's lien for certain repairs and improvements [Caution: See § 3.32 of *Rev. Proc. 2004-71 (26 USCS § 1* note) for provision that, for calendar year 2005, a federal tax lien is not valid against a mechanic's lienor under this paragraph that repaired or improved certain residential property if the contract price with the owner is not more than $6,020.]. With respect to real property subject to a lien for repair or improvement of a personal residence (containing not more than four dwelling units) occupied by the owner of such residence, as against a mechanic's lienor, but only if the contract price on the contract with the owner is not more than $5,000.

(8) Attorneys' liens. With respect to a judgment or other amount in settlement of a claim or of a cause of action, as against an attorney who, under local law, holds a lien upon or a contract enforcible against such judgment or amount, to the extent of his reasonable compensation for obtaining such judgment or procuring such settlement, except that this paragraph shall not apply to any judgment or amount in settlement of a claim or of a cause of action against the United States to the extent that the United States offsets such judgment or amount against any liability of the taxpayer to the United States.

(9) Certain insurance contracts. With respect to a life insurance, endowment, or annuity contract, as against the organization which is the insurer under such contract, at any time—

(A) before such organization had actual notice or knowledge of the existence of such lien;

(B) after such organization had such notice or knowledge, with respect to advances required to be made automatically to maintain such contract in force under an agreement entered into before such organization had such notice or knowledge; or

(C) after satisfaction of a levy pursuant to section 6332 (b), unless and until the Secretary delivers to such organization a notice, executed after the date of such satisfaction, of the existence of such lien.

(10) Deposit-secured loans. With respect to a savings deposit, share, or other account with an institution described in section 581 or 591, to the extent of any loan made by such institution without actual notice or knowledge of the existence of such lien, as against such institution, if such loan is secured by such account.

(c) Protection for certain commercial transactions financing agreements, etc.

(1) In general. To the extent provided in this subsection, even though notice of a lien imposed by section 6321 has been filed, such lien shall not be valid with respect to a security interest which came into existence after tax lien filing but which—

(A) is in qualified property covered by the terms of a written agreement entered into before tax lien filing and constituting—

(i) a commercial transactions financing agreement,

(ii) a real property construction or improvement financing agreement, or

(iii) an obligatory disbursement agreement, and

(B) is protected under local law against a judgment lien arising, as of the time of tax lien filing, out of an unsecured obligation.

(2) Commercial transactions financing agreement. For purposes of this subsection—

(A) Definition. The term "commercial transactions financing agreement" means an agreement (entered into by a person in the course of his trade or business)—

(i) to make loans to the taxpayer to be secured by commercial financing security acquired by the taxpayer in the ordinary course of his trade or business, or

(ii) to purchase commercial financing security (other than inventory) acquired by the taxpayer in the ordinary course of his trade or business;

but such an agreement shall be treated as coming within the term only to the extent that such loan or purchase is made before the 46th day after the date of tax lien filing or (if earlier) before the lender or purchaser had actual notice or knowledge of such tax lien filing.

(B) Limitation on qualified property. The term "qualified property", when used with respect to a commercial transactions financing agreement, includes only commercial financing security acquired by the taxpayer before the 46th day after the date of tax lien filing.

(C) Commercial financing security defined. The term "commercial financing security" means (i) paper of a kind ordinarily arising in commercial transactions, (ii) accounts receivable, (iii) mortgages on real property, and (iv) inventory.

(D) Purchaser treated as acquiring security interest. A person who satisfies subparagraph (A) by reason of clause (ii) thereof shall be treated as having acquired a security interest in commercial financing security

(3) Real property construction or improvement financing agreement. For purposes of this subsection—

(A) Definition. The term "real property construction or improvement financing agreement" means an agreement to make cash disbursements to finance—

(i) the construction or improvement of real property,

(ii) a contract to construct or improve real property, or

(iii) the raising or harvesting of a farm crop or the raising of livestock or other animals.

For purposes of clause (iii), the furnishing of goods and services shall be treated as the disbursement of cash.

(B) Limitation on qualified property. The term "qualified property", when used with respect to a real property construction or improvement financing agreement, includes only—

(i) in the case of subparagraph (A)(i), the real property with respect to which the construction or improvement has been or is to be made,

(ii) in the case of subparagraph (A)(ii), the proceeds of the contract described therein, and

(iii) in the case of subparagraph (A)(iii), property subject to the lien imposed by section 6321 at the time of tax lien filing and the crop or the livestock or other animals referred to in subparagraph (A)(iii).

(4) Obligatory disbursement agreement. For purposes of this subsection—

(A) Definition. The term "obligatory disbursement agreement" means an agreement (entered into by a person in the course of his trade or business) to make disbursements, but such an agreement shall be treated as coming within the term only to the extent of disbursements which are required to be made by reason of the intervention of the rights of a person other than the taxpayer.

(B) Limitation on qualified property. The term "qualified property", when used with respect to an obligatory disbursement agreement, means property subject to the lien imposed by section 6321 at the time of tax lien filing and (to the extent that the acquisition is directly traceable to the disbursements referred to in subparagraph (A)) property acquired by the taxpayer after tax lien filing.

(C) Special rules for surety agreements. Where the obligatory disbursement agreement is an agreement ensuring the performance of a contract between the taxpayer and another person—

(i) the term "qualified property" shall be treated as also including the proceeds of the contract the performance of which was ensured, and

(ii) if the contract the performance of which was ensured was a contract to construct or improve real property, to produce goods, or to furnish services, the term "qualified property" shall be treated as also including any tangible personal property used by the taxpayer in the performance of such ensured contract.

(d) 45-day period for making disbursements. Even though notice of a lien imposed by section 6321 has been filed, such lien shall not be valid with respect to a security interest which came into existence after tax lien filing by reason of disbursements made before the 46th day after the date of tax lien filing, or (if earlier) before the person making such disbursements had actual notice or knowledge of tax lien filing, but only if such security interest—

(1) is in property (A) subject, at the time of tax lien filing, to the lien imposed by section 6321, and (B) covered by the terms of a written agreement entered into before tax lien filing, and

(2) is protected under local law against a judgment lien arising, as of the time of tax lien filing, out of an unsecured obligation.

(e) Priority of interest and expenses. If the lien imposed by section 6321 is not valid as against a lien or security interest, the priority of such lien or security interest shall extend to—

(1) any interest or carrying charges upon the obligation secured,

(2) the reasonable charges and expenses of an indenture trustee or agent holding the security interest for the benefit of the holder of the security interest,

(3) the reasonable expenses, including reasonable compensation for attorneys, actually incurred in collecting or enforcing the obligation secured,

(4) the reasonable costs of insuring, preserving, or repairing the property to which the lien or security interest relates,

(5) the reasonable costs of insuring payment of the obligation secured, and

(6) amounts paid to satisfy any lien on the property to which the lien or security interest relates, but only if the lien so satisfied is entitled to priority over the lien imposed by section 6321, to the extent that, under local law, any such item has the same priority as the lien or security interest to which it relates.

(f) Place for filing notice; form.

(1) Place for filing. The notice referred to in subsection (a) shall be filed—

(A) Under State laws.

(i) Real property. In the case of real property, in one office within the State (or the county, or other governmental subdivision), as designated by the laws of such State, in which the property subject to the lien is situated; and

(ii) Personal property. In the case of personal property, whether tangible or intangible, in one office within the State (or the county, or other governmental subdivision), as designated by the laws of such State, in which the property subject to the lien is situated, except that State law merely conforming to or reenacting Federal law establishing a national filing system does not constitute a second office for filing as designated by the laws of such State; or

(B) With clerk of district court. In the office of the clerk of the United States district court for the judicial district in which the property subject to the lien is situated, whenever the State has not by law designated one office which meets the requirements of subparagraph (A); or

(C) With Recorder of Deeds of the District of Columbia. In the office of the Recorder of Deeds of the District of Columbia, if the property subject to the lien is situated in the District of Columbia.

(2) Situs of property subject to lien. For purposes of paragraphs (1) and (4), property shall be deemed to be situated—

(A) Real property. In the case of real property, at its physical location; or

(B) Personal property. In the case of personal property, whether tangible or intangible, at the residence of the taxpayer at the time the notice of lien is filed.

For purposes of paragraph (2)(B), the residence of a corporation or partnership shall be deemed to be the place at which the principal executive office of the business is located, and the residence of a taxpayer whose residence is without the United States shall be deemed to be in the District of Columbia.

(3) Form. The form and content of the notice referred to in subsection (a) shall be prescribed

by the Secretary. Such notice shall be valid notwithstanding any other provision of law regarding the form or content of a notice of lien.

(4) Indexing required with respect to certain real property. In the case of real property, if—

(A) under the laws of the State in which the real property is located, a deed is not valid as against a purchaser of the property who (at the time of purchase) does not have actual notice or knowledge of the existence of such deed unless the fact of filing of such deed has been entered and recorded in a public index at the place of filing in such a manner that a reasonable inspection of the index will reveal the existence of the deed, and

(B) there is maintained (at the applicable office under paragraph (1)) an adequate system for the public indexing of Federal tax liens,

then the notice of lien referred to in subsection (a) shall not be treated as meeting the filing requirements under paragraph (1) unless the fact of filing is entered and recorded in the index referred to in subparagraph (B) in such a manner that a reasonable inspection of the index will reveal the existence of the lien.

(5) National filing systems. The filing of a notice of lien shall be governed solely by this title and shall not be subject to any other Federal law establishing a place or places for the filing of liens or encumbrances under a national filing system.

(g) Refiling of notice. For purposes of this section —

(1) General rule. Unless notice of lien is refiled in the manner prescribed in paragraph (2) during the required refiling period, such notice of lien shall be treated as filed on the date on which it is filed (in accordance with subsection (f)) after the expiration of such refiling period.

(2) Place for filing. A notice of lien refiled during the required refiling period shall be effective only—

(A) if—

(i) such notice of lien is refiled in the office in which the prior notice of lien was filed, and

(ii) in the case of real property, the fact of refiling is entered and recorded in an index to the extent required by subsection (f)(4); and

(B) in any case in which, 90 days or more prior to the date of a refiling of notice of lien under subparagraph (A), the Secretary received written information (in the manner prescribed in regulations issued by the Secretary) concerning a change in the taxpayer's residence, if a notice of such lien is also filed in accordance with subsection (f) in the State in which such residence is located.

(3) Required refiling period. In the case of any notice of lien, the term "required refiling period" means—

(A) the one-year period ending 30 days after the expiration of 10 years after the date of the assessment of the tax, and

(B) the one-year period ending with the expiration of 10 years after the close of the preceding required refiling period for such notice of lien.

(4) Transitional rule. Notwithstanding paragraph (3), if the assessment of the tax was made before January 1, 1962, the first required refiling period shall be the calendar year 1967.

(h) Definitions. For purposes of this section and section 6324—

(1) Security interest. The term "security interest" means any interest in property acquired by contract for the purpose of securing payment or performance of an obligation or indemnifying against loss or liability. A security interest exists at any time

(A) if, at such time, the property is in existence and the interest has become protected under local law against a subsequent judgment lien arising out of an unsecured obligation, and

(B) to the extent that, at such time, the holder has parted with money or money's worth.

(2) Mechanic's lienor. The term "mechanic's lienor" means any person who under local law has a lien on real property (or on the proceeds of a contract relating to real property) for services, labor, or materials furnished in connection with the construction or improvement of such property. For purposes of the preceding sentence, a person has a lien on the earliest date such lien becomes valid under local law against

subsequent purchasers without actual notice, but not before he begins to furnish the services, labor, or materials.

(3) Motor vehicle. The term "motor vehicle" means a self-propelled vehicle which is registered for highway use under the laws of any State or foreign country.

(4) Security. The term "security" means any bond, debenture, note, or certificate or other evidence of indebtedness, issued by a corporation or a government or political subdivision thereof, with interest coupons or in registered form, share of stock, voting trust certificate, or any certificate of interest or participation in, certificate of deposit or receipt for, temporary or interim certificate for, or warrant or right to subscribe to or purchase, any of the foregoing; negotiable instrument; or money.

(5) Tax lien filing. The term "tax lien filing" means the filing of notice (referred to in subsection (a)) of the lien imposed by section 6321.

(6) Purchaser. The term "purchaser" means a person who, for adequate and full consideration in money or money's worth, acquires an interest (other than a lien or security interest) in property which is valid under local law against subsequent purchasers without actual notice. In applying the preceding sentence for purposes of subsection (a) of this section, and for purposes of section 6324—

(A) a lease of property,

(B) a written executory contract to purchase or lease property,

(C) an option to purchase or lease property or any interest therein, or

(D) an option to renew or extend a lease of property,

which is not a lien or security interest shall be treated as an interest in property.

(i) Special rules.

(1) Actual notice or knowledge. For purposes of this subchapter, an organization shall be deemed for purposes of a particular transaction to have actual notice or knowledge of any fact from the time such fact is brought to the attention of the individual conducting such transaction, and in any event from the time such fact would have been brought to such individual's attention if the organization had exercised due diligence. An organization exercises due diligence if it maintains reasonable routines for communicating significant information to the person conducting the transaction and there is reasonable compliance with the routine. Due diligence does not require an individual acting for the organization to communicate information unless such communication is part of his regular duties or unless he has reason to know of the transaction and that the transaction would be materially affected by the information.

(2) Subrogation. Where, under local law, one person is subrogated to the rights of another with respect to a lien or interest, such person shall be subrogated to such rights for purposes of any lien imposed by section 6321 or 6324.

(3) Forfeitures. For purposes of this subchapter, a forfeiture under local law of property seized by a law enforcement agency of a State, county, or other local governmental subdivision shall relate back to the time of seizure, except that this paragraph shall not apply to the extent that under local law the holder of an intervening claim or interest would have priority over the interest of the State, county, or other local governmental subdivision in the property.

(4) Cost-of-living adjustment. In the case of notices of liens imposed by section 6321 which are filed in any calendar year after 1998, each of the dollar amounts under paragraph (4) or (7) of subsection (b) shall be increased by an amount equal to—

(A) such dollar amount, multiplied by

(B) the cost-of-living adjustment determined under section 1(f)(3) for the calendar year, determined by substituting "calendar year 1996" for "calendar year 2016" in subparagraph (A)(ii) thereof.

If any amount as adjusted under the preceding sentence is not a multiple of $10, such amount shall be rounded to the nearest multiple of $10.

(j) Withdrawal of notice in certain circumstances.

(1) In general. The Secretary may withdraw a notice of a lien filed under this section and this chapter shall be applied as if the withdrawn notice had not been filed, if the Secretary determines that—

(A) the filing of such notice was premature or otherwise not in accordance with administrative procedures of the Secretary,

(B) the taxpayer has entered into an agreement under section 6159 to satisfy the tax liability for which the lien was imposed by means of installment payments, unless such agreement provides otherwise,

(C) the withdrawal of such notice will facilitate the collection of the tax liability, or

(D) with the consent of the taxpayer or the National Taxpayer Advocate, the withdrawal of such notice would be in the best interests of the taxpayer (as determined by the National Taxpayer Advocate) and the United States.

Any such withdrawal shall be made by filing notice at the same office as the withdrawn notice. A copy of such notice of withdrawal shall be provided to the taxpayer.

(2) Notice to credit agencies, etc. Upon written request by the taxpayer with respect to whom a notice of a lien was withdrawn under paragraph (1), the Secretary shall promptly make reasonable efforts to notify credit reporting agencies, and any financial institution or creditor whose name and address is specified in such request, of the withdrawal of such notice. Any such request shall be in such form as the Secretary may prescribe.